fix

Maryland

Miller & Levine
Biology
FOUNDATION EDITION

Kenneth R. Miller, Ph.D.
Professor of Biology, Brown University
Providence, Rhode Island

Joseph S. Levine, Ph.D.
Science Writer and Producer
Concord, Massachusetts

Boston, Massachusetts • Chandler, Arizona • Glenview, Illinois • Upper Saddle River, New Jersey

Print Components
Maryland Student Foundation Edition
Maryland Teacher's Foundation Edition
Study Workbook A
Study Workbook A, Teacher's Edition
Study Workbook B: Reading Foundations
Study Workbook B: Reading Foundations, Teacher's Edition
Laboratory Manual A
Laboratory Manual A, Teacher's Edition
Laboratory Manual B: Skill Foundations
Laboratory Manual B: Skill Foundations, Teacher's Edition
Probeware Lab Manual
Assessment Resources
Transparencies

Technology Components
Biology.com
Untamed Science® Video Series: BioAdventures DVD
Classroom Resources DVD-ROM
ExamView CD-ROM
Virtual BioLab DVD-ROM with Lab Manual

English Language Learners
Teacher's ELL Handbook
Multilingual Glossary

Additional Credits for Custom Pages:

MD3: T and B, Stew Milne. **MD3:** L, Courtesy of Grant Wiggins; R, Jen-Yi Wu. **MD9:** TL, Pete Oxford/Minden Pictures; MR, Piotr Naskrecki/Minden Pictures. **MD10:** Ed Rescheke/Peter Arnold, Inc. **MD11:** Andrew Syred/Photo Researchers, Inc. **MD12:** T, Colin Keates/DK Images; B, Colin Keates/Dorling Kindersley, Courtesy of the Natural History Museum, London. **MD13:** TR, Southhampton General Hospital/Science Photo Library/Photo Researchers, Inc.; B, Bkgrnd, Neil Lucas/npl/Minden Pictures; BL, Georgette Douwma/ Getty Images; ML, Peter Chadwick/DK Images; **MD14:** T, Ben Twist/istockphoto.com; B, Nature Picture Library/Alamy. **MD15:** L, Ingo Arndt , MINDEN PICTURES; R, Nigel J. Dennis; Gallo Images/CORBIS. **MD19:** Bkgd, L, SuperStock/age fotostock; Inset, L, OKRAD/iStockphoto; Bkgd, R, National Park Service; Inset, R, Edgewater Media/Shutterstock. **MD20:** Bkgd, L, George Grall/Getty Images; Inset, L, Andrew J. Martinez/Photo Researchers, Inc.; Bkgd, R, Michael Townsend/Getty Images; Inset, R, drsuth48 /Shutterstock. **MD21:** Bkgd, L, Dr. R. Wayne Tyndall/MD Dept. of Natural Resources; Inset, R, Merlin Tuttle/Photo Researchers, Inc.; Bkgd, R, Michael P. Gadomski/Photo Researchers, Inc.; Inset, R, Photo Researchers, Inc. **MD22:** Bkgd, L, David Trozzo/Alamy; Inset, L, mlorenz/Shutterstock; Bkgd, R, Michael P. Gadomski/Photo Researchers, Inc.; Inset, R, Ed Cesar/Photo Researchers, Inc. **MD23:** ©Jaap Hart/iStockphoto. **MD29:** ©Michael Bagley/iStockphoto. **MD33:** JeninVA/Shutterstock. **MD35:** Courtesy of Beng Chiak Tang. **MD36:** Stew Milne.

Taken from:

Biology: Foundation Edition
By Kenneth R. Miller, Ph.D. and Joseph S. Levine, Ph.D.
Copyright © 2010 by Pearson Education, Inc.
Published by Pearson Education, Inc.
Upper Saddle River, New Jersey, 07458

Biology: Maryland Edition
By Kenneth R. Miller, Ph.D. and Joseph S. Levine, Ph.D.
Copyright © 2011 by Pearson Education, Inc.
Published by Pearson Education, Inc.
Upper Saddle River, New Jersey, 07458

Front matter sections, *Ecosystem of Maryland & Maryland Voluntary State Curriculum for Biology* taken from:

Copyright © 2012 by Pearson Learning Solutions. All rights reserved.

Pearson Learning Solutions, 501 Boylston Street, Suite 900, Boston, MA 02116
A Pearson Education Company
www.pearsoned.com

Printed in the United States of America

1 2 3 4 5 6 7 8 9 10 V011 17 16 15 14 13 12

000200010271290549   CP

ISBN-13:   978-1-256-65611-1
ISBN-10:   1-256-65611-9

About the Authors

Kenneth R. Miller grew up in Rahway, New Jersey, attended the local public schools, and graduated from Rahway High School in 1966. Miller attended Brown University on a scholarship and graduated with honors. He was awarded a National Defense Education Act fellowship for graduate study, and earned his Ph.D. in Biology at the University of Colorado. Miller is professor of Biology at Brown University in Providence, Rhode Island, where he teaches courses in general biology and cell biology.

Miller's research specialty is the structure of biological membranes. He has published more than 70 research papers in journals such as *Cell, Nature,* and *Scientific American.* He has also written the popular trade books *Finding Darwin's God* and *Only a Theory.* He is a fellow of the American Association for the Advancement of Science.

Miller lives with his wife, Jody, on a small farm in Rehoboth, Massachusetts. He is the father of two daughters, one a wildlife biologist and the other a high-school history teacher. He swims competitively in the masters' swimming program and umpires high school and collegiate softball.

Joseph S. Levine was born in Mount Vernon, New York, where he attended public schools. He earned a B.S. in Biology at Tufts University, a master's degree from the Boston University Marine Program, and a Ph.D. at Harvard University. His research has been published in scientific journals ranging from *Science* to *Scientific American,* and in several academic books. He has taught introductory biology, ecology, marine biology, neurobiology, and coral reef biology at Boston College and in the Boston University Marine Program. He has also co-taught a field biology course for high-school teachers entitled "Rainforests and Reefs" at the Organization for Tropical Studies in Costa Rica.

After receiving a Macy Fellowship in Science Broadcast Journalism at WGBH-TV, Levine dedicated himself to improving public understanding of science. His popular scientific writing has appeared in five trade books and in magazines such as *Smithsonian, GEO,* and *Natural History.* He has produced science features for National Public Radio and has designed exhibit programs for state aquarium projects in Texas, New Jersey, and Florida. Since 1987, Levine has served as scientific advisor at WGBH, where he worked on NOVA programs including *Judgment Day,* and on projects including the OMNI-MAX films *Cocos: Island of Sharks* and *Coral Reef Adventure.* He also served as science editor for the PBS series *The Secret of Life* and *The Evolution Project.*

Levine and his family live in Concord, Massachusetts, a short distance from Thoreau's Walden Pond.

Build a Solid Foundation

The *Miller & Levine Biology: Foundation Edition* is a new type of program. It offers the same content as *Miller & Levine Biology* made more accessible with:

- **Embedded reading support**
- **Inquiry** activities that promote scientific thinking
- **Engaging visuals** that enhance instruction
- **Adapted ancillary support**
- **Digital instruction for the next-generation,** built for 21st Century learners

Reading Foundations

The Foundation Edition provides enhanced reading support with embedded reading strategies to make content more accessible.

Build Understanding provides suggestions on how to use graphic organizers as a framework for learning.

Build Vocabulary boxes highlight academic and scientific vocabulary from the chapter.

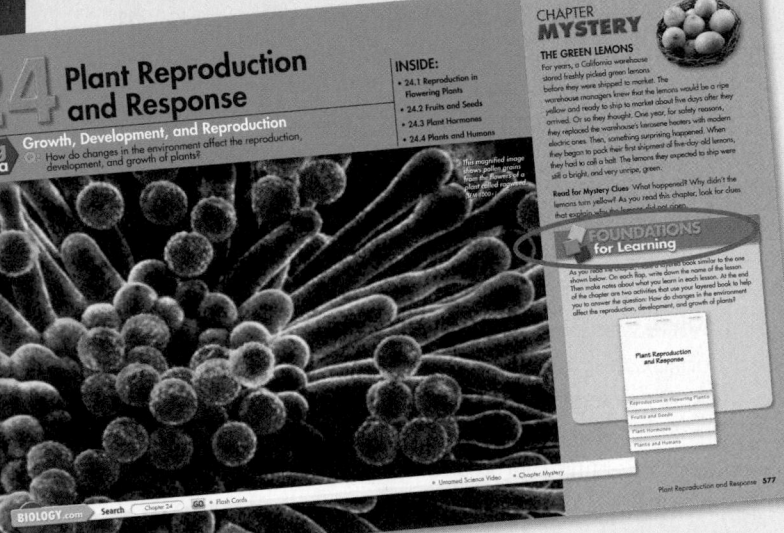

BUILD Understanding

Two-Column Table Make a two-column table. Write the heading *Male Gametophyte* in the heading of one column. Write the heading *Female Gametophyte* in the second column. As you read, take notes about each gametophyte.

In Your Workbook Go to your workbook to learn more about tables. Complete the table for Lesson 24.1.

BUILD Vocabulary

double fertilization
the process of fertilization in angiosperms, in which the first event produces the zygote, and the second event produces the endosperm within the seed

endosperm
the food-rich tissue that nourishes a seedling as it grows

PREFIXES
The prefix *endo-* comes from a Greek word that means "within." Endosperm is located within a seed.

BUILD Connections

GROWING PAINS
Lots of growth can mean lots of trouble—both in a town and in a cell.

Foundations for Learning are activities that feature manipulatives you can use to organize key concepts as you read a chapter.

Build Connections are chapter features that help you create a connection between Big Ideas, putting science in a real-world context tied to a clear and easy-to-follow graphic.

Visuals Enhance Instruction

Stunning instructional visuals throughout each chapter offer a unique way to see what science looks like.

Visual analogies offer a way to relate key concepts to things you may see in your daily life. Visual summaries tie together the key concepts in a clear and easy-to-follow graphic. The magazine-style Visual Guide to the Diversity of Life provides a unique way to explore Earth's major organisms with key characteristics, habitats, behaviors, and other important facts.

BUILD Connections

GROWING PAINS
Lots of growth can mean lots of trouble—both in a town and in a cell.

PASSERIFORMES: Passerines
Also called perching birds, this is by far the largest and most diverse group of birds, with about 5000 species. Most are songbirds. Examples: flycatchers, mockingbirds, cardinals, crows, chickadees, and finches.

Animals

Ferruginous Hawk

FALCONIDAE AND ACCIPITRIDAE:
Falcons, eagles, and hawks
These fierce predators, often called raptors, typically have powerful hooked bills, large wingspans, and sharp talons. Raptors have powerful flight muscles and keen eyesight, enabling them to see prey at a distance. Examples: Eurasian kestrel, golden eagle, Galápagos hawk

PICIDAE AND RAMPHASTIDAE:
Woodpeckers and toucans

Hooded Warbler

Scarlet Tanager

Blue Grosbeak

Student Support Ensures Success

Biology is not a "one-size-fits-all" subject. *Miller & Levine Biology: Foundation Edition* provides content in ways that fit your unique learning style. The *Foundation* program offers workbooks that are written at an accessible reading level and work hand-in-hand with the *Foundation* Student Edition to help provide extra support to ensure content mastery. The accompanying ELL handbook also provides support for ELL classrooms.

The *Foundation Edition* supports all students with 2 levels of resources.

Study Workbook B

The adapted Study Workbook for the *Miller & Levine Biology: Foundation Edition* will help you:

- preview a chapter
- work with the key vocabulary
- practice strategies for learning the content
- review for chapter and unit tests
- learn strategies for taking standardized tests

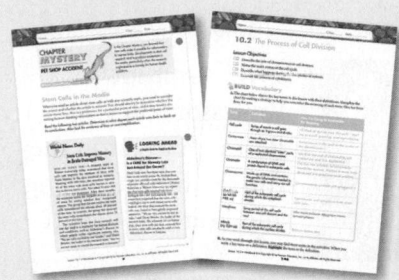

Lab Manual B

The adapted Lab Manual provides connections from the text to help you conduct lab experiments. You are encouraged to apply concepts, analyze data, and draw conclusions from lab activities. The *Extend Your Inquiry* feature encourages you to consider concepts outside of the step-by-step laboratory process.

Biology.com—Your Online Habitat for Learning

Featuring the latest in instructional technology, Biology.com is an engaging program that brings biology concepts to life. Visual, interactive, and differentiated components help reinforce content and provide a broad understanding of scientific concepts.

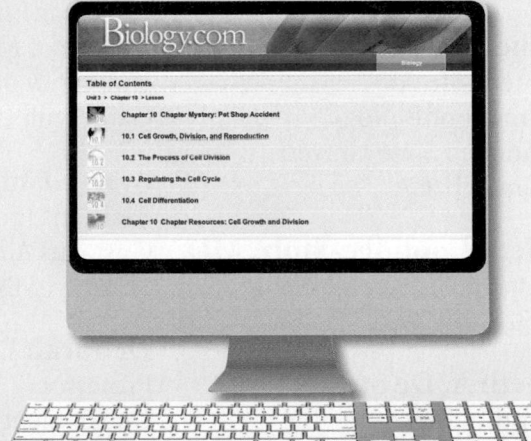

Biology.com offers:

For Students:

- Complete *Foundation* Student Edition with audio helps you read along online
- Interactive visuals, tutorials, and simulations help you build connections as concepts come alive online.
- Scaffolded self-assessment prepares you for content mastery and end–of–course testing.

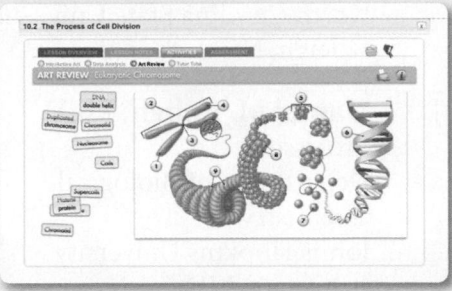

For Teachers:

- Lesson planner with leveled activities crafts lessons to support all levels of students.
- Lesson overview presentations help present the Big Ideas of each lesson
- Comprehensive, auto-graded assessment and remediation for different levels of students
- Editable worksheets that allow teachers to cater their lessons to your classroom's needs

  Search — Lesson 22.4 — GO • Art Review

Consultants/Reviewers

 **Grant Wiggins, Ed.D.** is a co-author of the *Understanding by Design Handbook.* His approach to instructional design provides teachers with a disciplined way of thinking about curriculum design, assessment, and instruction that moves teaching from covering content to ensuring understanding.

Big idea Big Ideas are one of the core components of the Understanding by Design approach in *Miller & Levine Biology: Foundation Edition.* Big Ideas, such as the Cellular Basis of Life, establish a conceptual framework for the program. Each chapter in the Student Edition provides opportunities to link back to the Big Ideas. Since Understanding by Design is by nature a teaching tool, additional applications of this philosophy can be found in the Teacher's Edition.

The Association for Supervision of Curriculum Development (ASCD), publisher of the "Understanding by Design Handbook" co-authored by Grant Wiggins and registered owner of the trademark "Understanding by Design", has not authorized, approved or sponsored this work and is in no way affiliated with Pearson or its products.

 **Jim Cummins** is Professor and Canada Research Chair in the Curriculum, Teaching and Learning department at the Ontario Institute for Studies in Education at the University of Toronto. His research focuses on literacy development in multilingual schools and the role of technology in promoting language and literacy development.

 Program materials for *Miller & Levine Biology: Foundation Edition* incorporate research-based essential principles using Dr. Cummins's Into/Through/Beyond structure. You will find ample support for ELL instruction in the Teacher's Edition, Teacher's ELL Handbook, Multilingual Glossary, and Spanish components offered with this program.

Content Reviewers

Lily Chen
Associate Professor
Department of Biology
San Francisco State University
San Francisco, CA

Elizabeth Coolidge-Stolz, MD
Medical/Life Science Writer/Editor
North Reading, MA

Elizabeth A. De Stasio, Ph.D.
Raymond H. Herzog
Professor of Science
Associate Professor of Biology
Lawrence University
Appleton, WI

Jennifer C. Drew, Ph.D.
Lecturer/Scientist
University of Florida
Kennedy Space Center, FL

Donna H. Duckworth, Ph.D.
Professor Emeritus
College of Medicine
University of Florida
Gainesville, FL

Alan Gishlick, Ph.D.
Assistant Professor
Gustavus Adolphus College
St. Peter, MN

Deborah L. Gumucio, Ph.D.
Professor
Department of Cell and
Developmental Biology
University of Michigan
Ann Arbor, MI

Janet Lanza, Ph.D.
Professor of Biology
University of Arkansas
at Little Rock
Little Rock, AR

Charles F. Lytle, Ph.D.
Professor of Zoology
North Carolina State University
Raleigh, NC

Martha Newsome, DDS
Adjunct Instructor of Biology
Cy-Fair College, Fairbanks Center
Houston, TX

Jan A. Pechenik, Ph.D.
Professor of Biology
Tufts University
Medford, MA

Imara Y. Perera, Ph.D.
Research Assistant, Professor
Department of Plant Biology
North Carolina State University
Raleigh, NC

Daniel M. Raben, Ph.D.
Professor
Department of Biological
Chemistry
Johns Hopkins University
Baltimore, MD

Megan Rokop, Ph.D.
Educational Outreach Program
Director
Broad Institute of MIT and
Harvard
Cambridge, MA

Gerald P. Sanders
Former Biology Instructor
Grossmont College
Julian, CA

Ronald Sass, Ph.D.
Professor Emeritus
Rice University
Houston, TX

Linda Silveira, Ph.D.
Professor
University of Redlands
Redlands, CA

Richard K. Stucky, Ph.D.
Curator of Paleontology and
Evolution
Denver Museum of Nature and
Science
Denver, CO

Robert Thornton, Ph.D.
Senior Lecturer Emeritus
Department of Plant Biology
College of Biological Sciences
University of California at Davis
Davis, CA

Edward J. Zalisko, Ph.D.
Professor of Biology
Blackburn College
Carlinville, IL

ESL Lecturer

**Nancy Vincent Montgomery,
Ed.D.**
Southern Methodist University
Dallas, TX

High-School Reviewers

Christine Bill
Sayreville War Memorial High
School
Parlin, NJ

Jean T. (Caye) Boone
Central Gwinnett High School
Lawrenceville, GA

Samuel J. Clifford, Ph.D.
Biology Teacher
Round Rock High School
Round Rock, TX

Jennifer Collins, M.A.
South County Secondary School
Lorton, VA

Roy Connor, M.S.
Science Department Head
Muncie Central High School
Muncie, IN

Norm Dahm, Jr.
Belleville East High School
Belleville, IL

Cora Nadine Dickson
Science Department Chair
Jersey Village High School
Cypress Fairbanks ISD
Houston, TX

Dennis M. Dudley
Science Department Chair/
Teacher
Shaler Area High School
Pittsburgh, PA

Mary K. Dulko
Sharon High School
Sharon, MA

Erica Everett, M.A.T., M.Ed.
Science Department Chair
Manchester-Essex Regional High
School
Manchester, MA

Heather M. Gannon
Elisabeth Ann Johnson High
School
Mt. Morris, MI

Virginia Glasscock
Science Teacher
California High School
Whittier, CA

Ruth Gleicher
Biology Teacher
Niles West High School
Skokie, IL

Lance Goodlock
Biology Teacher/Science
Department Chairperson
Sturgis High School
Sturgis, MI

W. Tony Heiting, Ph.D.
State Science Supervisor (retired)
Iowa Department of Education
Panora, IA

Patricia Anne Johnson, M.S.
Biology Teacher
Ridgewood High School
Ridgewood, NJ

Judith Decherd Jones, M.A.T.
NBCT AYA Science
East Chapel Hill High School
Chapel Hill, NC

Shellie Jones
Science Teacher
California High School
Whittier, CA

Michelle Lauria, M.A.T.
Biology Teacher
Hopkinton High School
Hopkinton, MA

Kimberly Lewis
Science Department Chair
Wellston High School
Wellston, OH

Consultants *(continued)*

Lenora Lewis
Teacher
Creekview High School
Canton, GA

JoAnn Lindell-Overton, M.Ed.
Supervisor of Secondary Science
Chesapeake Public Schools
Chesapeake, VA

Lender Luse
H.W. Byers High School
Holly Springs, MS

Molly J. Markey, Ph.D.
Science Teacher
Newton Country Day School of the Sacred Heart
Newton, MA

Rebecca McLelland-Crawley
Biological Sciences Teacher
Piscataway, NJ

Mark L. Mettert, M.S. Ed.
Science Department Chair
New Haven High School
New Haven, IN

Jane Parker
Lewisville High School North
Lewisville, TX

Ian Pearce
Educator
Austin, TX

Jim Peters
Science Resource Teacher
Carroll County Public Schools
Westminster, MD

Michelle Phillips, M.A.T.
Secondary Science: Education
Science Teacher
Jordan High School
Durham, NC

Randy E. Phillips
Science Teacher/Department Chair
Green Bay East High School
Green Bay, WI

Nancy Richey
Educator
Longmont, CO

Linda Roberson
Department Chairman
Jenks Freshman Academy
Jenks, OK

Sharon D. Spencer
Assistant Principal
Bronx Center for Science and Math
Bronx, NY

Stephen David Wright, M.S.
Biology Teacher
Montgomery County Public Schools
Columbia, MD

Alan W. Zimroth, M.S.
Science Teacher/Department Chairperson
Hialeah-Miami Lakes High School
Hialeah, FL

Contents

UNIT 1 — The Nature of Life   1–51

UNIT 2 — Ecology   53–156

BIOLOGY.com   • Go Digital. See what awaits you at Biology.com.

UNIT 3 Cells 157–257

⁴ Genetics 259–376

UNIT 5 Evolution   377–476

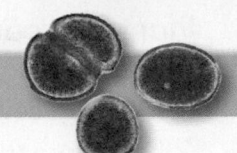

UNIT 7 Animals

UNIT 8 The Human Body — 711–858

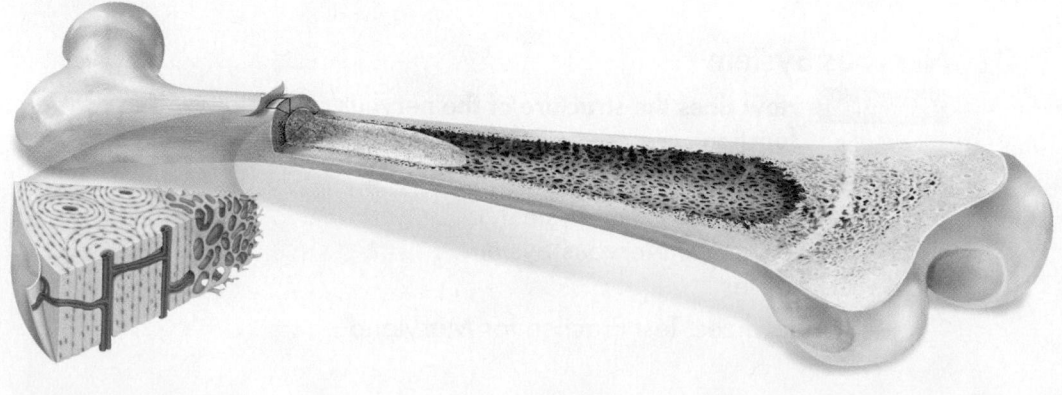

BIOLOGY.com ⟩ ● Go Digital. See what awaits you at Biology.com.

Labs and Activities

INQUIRY into Scientific Thinking

Labs and Activities (continued)

Design Your Own Lab

Forensics Lab

Real-World Lab

Skills Lab

BUILD Connections
with Visual Analogies

Ecosystems of Maryland

From the heights of the Allegheny Mountains, through the gently rolling Piedmont to the Coastal Plain, Maryland is full of life. The changing temperatures and plentiful rainfall have allowed many different kinds of organisms to coexist in a relatively small area. Throughout Maryland, differences in elevation, soil, flooding regime, and other factors support rich terrestrial and aquatic ecosystems. This book will help you understand the components of Maryland's ecosystems, and the interactions that occur within them. Why study biology? Because it's all around you!

Blue Crab

Estuaries and Coastal Waters

Chesapeake Bay is the largest estuary in the United States. Estuaries occur where bodies of fresh water meet the ocean. The constant supply of nutrients from land and the movement of changing ocean tides provide a wide range of conditions in which diverse communities can thrive. There's something for everyone! For example, in Chesapeake Bay many kinds of algae grow together, forming dense underwater algal beds. They provide vital food and habitat for many of the 70 or so species of fish, including shad and sturgeon, that spend at least a portion of their lives in Maryland's estuaries. With all of these fish around, it is not surprising that many different fish-eating birds such as brown pelicans, terns, and loons make Chesapeake Bay their home. Estuaries are also vital nurseries for animals such as American oysters, menhaden, and blue crab, which keep Maryland's coastal waters well stocked. Whales, sharks, tunas, jacks, and mackerel are only a few of the animals that enjoy the prey-rich waters off Maryland's coast.

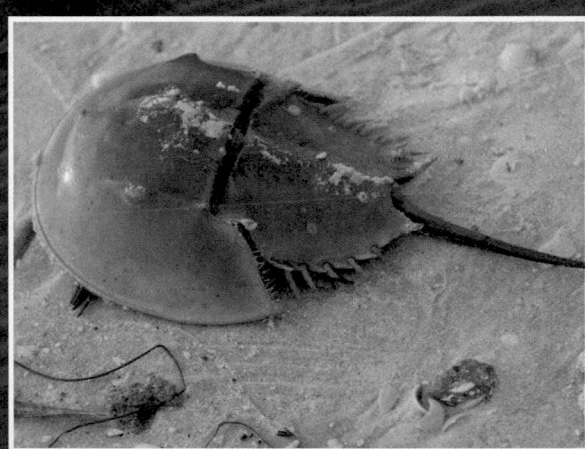

Horseshoe Crab

Coastal Dunes and Barrier Islands

Most of Maryland's coastal areas and barrier islands have sandy beaches. Winds and waves reshape these beaches by moving the sands from place to place. Behind the beaches are sand dunes, which are constantly resculpted by wind. Only a few types of plants, such as glassworts and some grasses, are able to grow on these windswept dunes. Further from the beach, however, the sand dunes are more stable, so taller and woodier plants and trees are able to grow. The beaches are home to many kinds of organisms, including large populations of migrating birds. On their way north to summer breeding grounds, sandpipers and plovers stop in to feast on horseshoe crab eggs. These birds rely on the energy-rich eggs, stolen from sandy nests, to fuel the rest of their journey north. They don't bother the adult horseshoe crabs though. This is perhaps because birds don't like the taste of the copper-based respiratory pigment, hemocyanin, found in adult horseshoe crabs. It is hemocyanin that makes the horseshoe crab's blood look blue when exposed to air.

American Eel

Rivers and Streams

Ninety-five percent of Maryland's numerous streams and rivers flow into Chesapeake Bay. Many streams flow through shady forests and are inhabited by insects and by fish such as trout and minnows. As the streams flow down to the coastal plains and join together forming rivers, the diversity of organisms increases greatly. The wider rivers are not as shaded. Sunlight enables algal growth, which provides important nutrients for the trout, perch, sunfish, and freshwater mussels that are common in these waters. Along the banks, mink, northern river otters, American beavers, muskrats, wood ducks, loons, grebes, and eastern snapping turtles make their homes. Another important inhabitant of these waters is the American eel. Once they are ready to breed, sometimes after 30 years, they will migrate far out into the middle of the Sargasso Sea in the Atlantic Ocean. Here, they will mate once, spawn, and die. The currents will carry the larvae back to the coast, from which the young eels will eventually make their long journey back to their home waters.

Great Egret

Wetlands

There are many kinds of wetlands. For example, *swamps* are forests of trees such as bald cypress, red maple, and black gum, which are flooded for at least part of the year. *Shrub wetlands* are similar to swamps, but have shorter trees and shrubs such as buttonbush and smooth alder. *Marshes* are flooded areas of grasses and plants such as arrow arum and wild rice. These and other wetlands are common throughout Maryland, from the Allegheny Mountains to the floodplains, and along the coast. Some organisms are specialized to live in a specific type of wetland. Others are generalists, able to live in many kinds of wetlands. Birds such as terns, ducks, geese, and herons thrive in marshes. Other birds, such as the great egret, are equally comfortable in swamps and shrub wetlands, where they live alongside mammals, including white-tailed deer, red fox, striped skunk, long-tailed weasel, mink, and northern river otter. The great egret builds bulky stick nests and feeds on small mammals, and sometimes birds, when it cannot spear a tasty fish.

Edwards' Hairstreak

Grasslands

Grasslands are treeless plains, which are maintained by periodic fires and large grazers that prevent trees and shrubs from settling in the area. However, blackjack and post oak trees are scattered throughout Maryland's few remaining grasslands. Serpentine grasslands are a rare type of grassland found in northern Maryland. They have nutrient-poor soils and high levels of magnesium, which are toxic to most plants. And yet, serpentine grasslands are home to 34 rare and endangered plant species that are specially adapted to the harsh conditions. True prairie grasses such as little bluestem, Indiangrass, and purple threeawn are common here. Birds such as short-eared owls and Northern bobwhites nest on the ground as white-tailed deer graze nearby. Edwards' Hairstreaks are butterflies that feed on milkweed in the grasslands and roost in post oak thickets as adults. Their larvae, however, live with Allegheny mound-builder ants. The ants protect the larvae from parasitic wasps. In return, the larvae become ant juice bars—secreting a clear fluid that the ants drink!

Eastern Red Bat

Loblolly Pine-Oak Forests

Loblolly pine-oak forests occur in a wide range of conditions. In dry areas, the trees may never reach their full height, leaving the canopy open and enabling shrubs such as blueberry, huckleberry, and mountain laurel to flourish here. In wetter areas, loblolly pine, southern red oak, white oak, and post oak provide shaded conditions ideal for an understory of American holly. Birds such as thrushes, warblers, and woodpeckers are abundant in the trees, which makes these areas great for birdwatching. If you are lucky, you might even catch a common gray fox watching you from a high tree limb. Gray foxes use their claws to climb trees for fruit and to avoid predators. They share the canopy with other mammals such as the Eastern red bat. Unlike many bats that roost in enclosed spaces, Eastern red bats roost on tree branches where they blend in with the leaves. These bats emerge from their roosts in the evenings to forage for insects. On the ground, coyotes, raccoons, and white-tailed deer live with many other mammals, amphibians, and reptiles.

Bobcat

Mesic Deciduous Forests

Mesic deciduous forests occur in moist, stable areas that allow many different kinds of hardwoods such as American beech, tulip poplars, oaks, and hickories to form the canopy. The understory features American hornbeam, white flowering dogwood, and pawpaw. In drier areas, where the soil tends to be relatively nutrient poor, American beech and a variety of oaks comprise the understory. Huckleberries and blueberries can form patches of dense growth here as well. Many of the animals found in mesic deciduous forests are common to the other kinds of forests, but the richer understory here provides more cover for a much larger variety of organisms. With so much prey, these forests attract a variety of predators such as coyotes and foxes. Bobcats also prowl these forests, stalking and ambushing rodents, reptiles, birds, and bats. They can even take down a white-tailed deer if the opportunity arises. So, you can't blame a New England cottontail rabbit for being nervous, especially at dusk and dawn, when bobcats are looking for a meal.

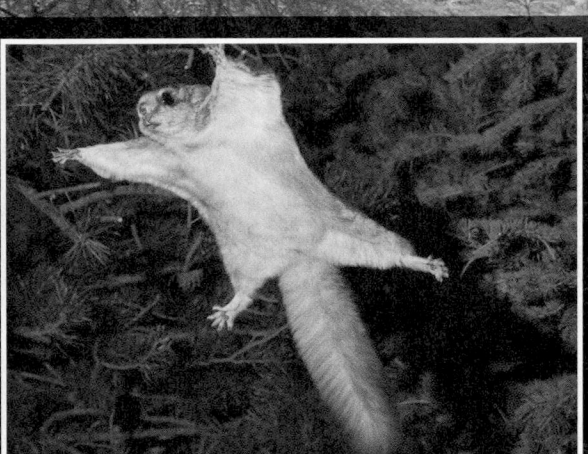

Flying Squirrel

Northern Conifer-Hardwood Forests

Northern conifer-hardwood forests are mainly found in the Allegheny Mountains, often bordering wetlands and streams. These forests vary in their conifer-to-hardwood composition. Conifer-rich forests have more eastern hemlock, red spruce, and white pine than mixed hardwoods. In mostly hardwood forests, sugar maple, yellow birch, and black cherry are more abundant than northern conifers. However, the midstory and understory are similar in both kinds of forest, and include striped maple, witch hazel, and frequent patches of great laurel. Many of the animals found here are also common in other forest types. However, there seems to be a greater diversity of birds, such as the barred owl, brown creeper, and hairy woodpecker, in these forests than in other types of forests. In addition to birds and bats, other animals also live high up in the trees. Northern flying squirrels can glide up to 45 meters to land on red spruce branches. They nest in woodpecker cavities, and are active mainly at night to avoid predators they might encounter on the forest floor.

Maryland Voluntary State Curriculum for Biology

The Maryland Voluntary State Curriculum (VSC) seeks to help students acquire the necessary scientific and technological knowledge and skills to become responsible, informed citizens in the global community of the 21st century.

How is the VSC for Biology organized?

The Voluntary State Curriculum for Biology includes two of Maryland's Core Learning Goals for Science:
- Goal 1 Skills and Processes
- Goal 3 Concepts of Biology

Each Core Learning Goal contains expectations and indicators for student learning and achievement. You will find references to these indicators on the pages of your textbook.

How is the VSC for Biology tested?

Starting with the graduating class of 2009, all Maryland students are required to pass either a High School Assessment (HSA) or equivalent exam in Biology to graduate. The Biology HSA contains both multiple-choice and short-answer questions based on the Core Learning Goals. Some indicators are not tested on the Biology HSA. These indicators are marked with an asterisk (*) on the following pages.

Maryland State House
Annapolis, Maryland

Science Core Learning Goals

Learning Goal 1: Skills and Processes

The student will demonstrate ways of thinking and acting inherent in the practice of science. The student will use the language and instruments of science to collect, organize, interpret, calculate, and communicate information.

Expectation 1.1 The student will demonstrate ways of thinking and acting inherent in the practice of science. The student will use the language and instruments of science to collect, organize, interpret, calculate, and communicate information.

SPI 1.1.1 The student will recognize that real problems have more than one solution and decisions to accept one solution over another are made on the basis of many issues.

SPI 1.1.2 The student will modify or affirm scientific ideas according to accumulated evidence.

SPI 1.1.3 The student will critique arguments that are based on faulty, misleading data or on the incomplete use of numbers.

SPI 1.1.4 The student will recognize data that are biased.

SPI 1.1.5 The student will explain factors that produce biased data.

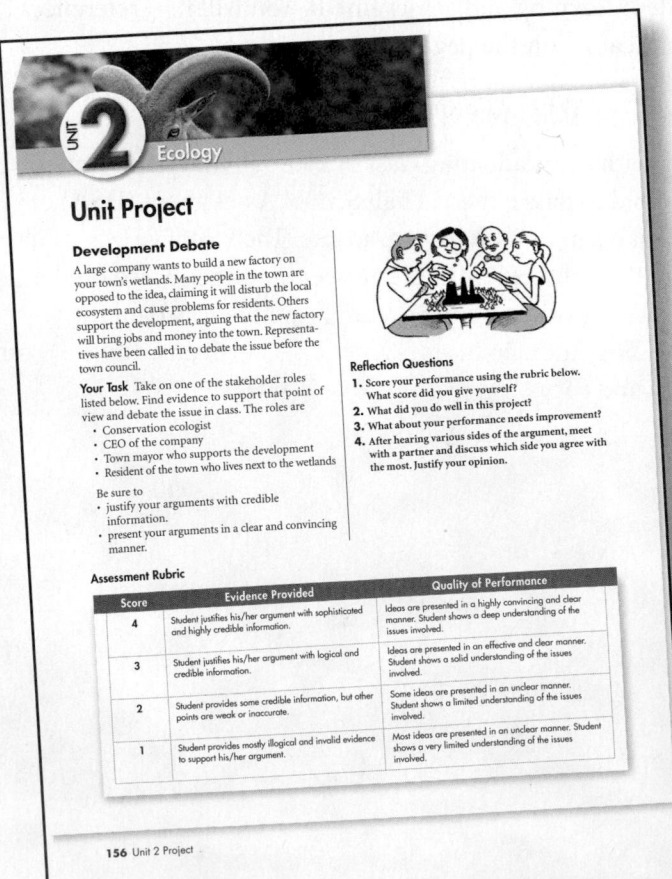

What It Means to You

Science is a human endeavor and, as such, it involves people interpreting data and making observations. You need to realize that bias can affect the judgments people make. You will have plenty of opportunity to investigate scientific questions yourself, as well as review others' work. You will need to be open to the possibility of bias.

Where You Will Learn It

Chapter 1 will introduce you to the nature of science. Chapter Labs will provide plenty of opportunities for you to work with real data.

SPI 1.2.1 The student will identify meaningful, answerable scientific questions.

SPI 1.2.2 The student will modify or affirm scientific ideas according to accumulated evidence.*

SPI 1.2.3 The student will formulate a working hypothesis.

SPI 1.2.4 The student will test a working hypothesis.*

SPI 1.2.5 The student will select appropriate instruments and materials to conduct an investigation.

SPI 1.2.6 The student will identify appropriate methods for conducting an investigation (independent and dependent variables, proper controls, repeat trials, appropriate sample size, etc.).

SPI 1.2.7 The student will use relationships discovered in the lab to explain phenomena observed outside the laboratory.

SPI 1.2.8 The student will defend the need for verifiable data.

What It Means to You

Science is often described as a way of knowing, addressing questions that deal with the natural world. Not all questions can be answered by science. Those that can have to be asked in a certain way— a way which enables them to be tested.

Where You Will Learn It

Chapter 1 introduces you to the methodology of science. The labs and activities in the *Miller & Levine Biology: Foundation Edition* program will give you plenty of opportunity to hone your inquiry skills.

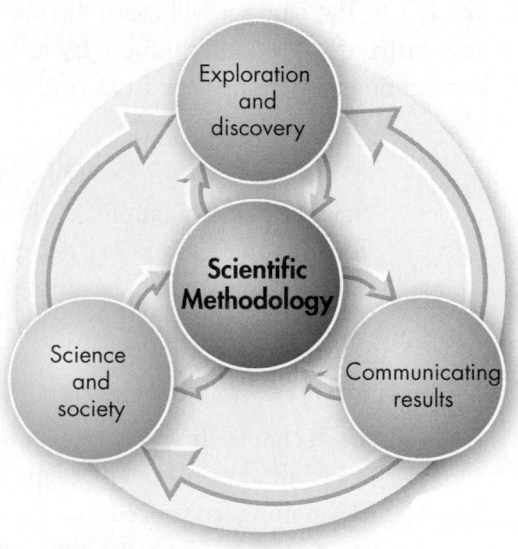

Adapted from *Understanding Science*, UC Berkeley, Museum of Paleontology

OBSERVING AND ASKING QUESTIONS

Location A

Location B

Researchers observed that marsh grass grows taller in some places than others. This observation led to a question: *Why do marsh grasses grow to different heights in different places?*

INFERRING AND HYPOTHESIZING

More nitrogen?

The researchers inferred that something limits grass growth in some places. It could be any environmental factor— temperature, sunlight, water, or nutrients. Based on their knowledge of salt marshes, they proposed a hypothesis: *Marsh grass growth is limited by available nitrogen.*

Science Learning Goal 1: Skills and Processes *(continued)*

Expectation 1.3 The student will carry out scientific investigations effectively and employ the instruments, systems of measurement, and materials of science appropriately.

SPI 1.3.1 The student will develop and demonstrate skills in using lab and field equipment to perform investigative techniques.*

SPI 1.3.2 The student will recognize safe laboratory procedures.

SPI 1.3.3 The student will demonstrate safe handling of the chemicals and materials of science.*

SPI 1.3.4 The student will learn the use of new instruments and equipment by following instructions in a manual or from oral direction.*

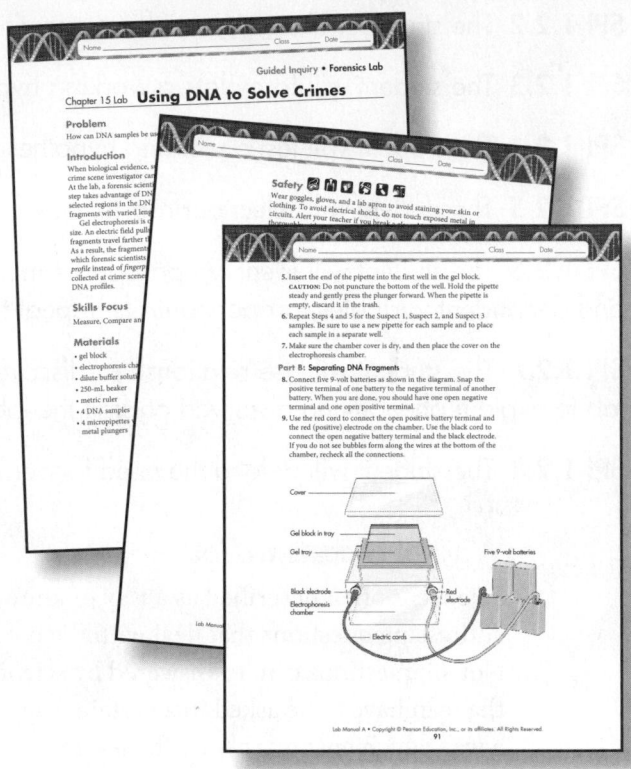

What It Means to You

Scientific investigations involve formulating hypotheses, designing experiments, making accurate measurements, and collecting data.

Where You Will Learn It

Each chapter in *Miller & Levine Biology: Foundation Edition* has a chapter lab that is introduced as a Prelab in your book. Design Your Own labs will give you practice formulating hypotheses and developing lab procedures. Real-World and Forensic labs will help guide you in answering questions of interest to scientists. Skills labs will help you practice working with measurements and various types of equipment and materials. All labs will guide you in how to carry out experiments safely.

DESIGNING CONTROLLED EXPERIMENTS

Control Group

No nitrogen added

Experimental Group

Nitrogen added

The researchers selected similar plots of marsh grass. All plots had similar plant density, soil type, input of freshwater, and height above average tide level. The plots were divided into control and experimental groups.

The researchers added nitrogen fertilizer (the independent variable) to the experimental plots. They then observed the growth of marsh grass (the dependent variable) in both experimental and control plots.

Expectation 1.4 The student will demonstrate that data analysis is a vital aspect of the process of scientific inquiry and communication.

SPI 1.4.1 The student will organize data appropriately using techniques such as tables, graphs, and webs. (for graphs axes labeled with appropriate quantities, appropriate units on axes, axes labeled with appropriate intervals, independent and dependent variables on correct axes, appropriate title)

SPI 1.4.2 The student will analyze data to make predictions, decisions, or draw conclusions.

SPI 1.4.3 The student will use experimental data from various investigators to validate results.

SPI 1.4.4 The student will determine the relationships between quantities and develop the mathematical model that describes these relationships.

SPI 1.4.5 The student will check graphs to determine that they do not misrepresent results.

SPI 1.4.6 The student will describe trends revealed by data.

SPI 1.4.7 The student will determine the sources of error that limit the accuracy or precision of experimental results.

SPI 1.4.8 The student will use models and computer simulations to extend his/her understanding of scientific concepts.*

SPI 1.4.9 The student will use analyzed data to confirm, modify, or reject a hypothesis.

What It Means to You

Scientists often rely on visual displays of data when analyzing and communicating results. Their ability to measure accurately is critical. They must also be aware of degrees of precision and limits to accuracy when evaluating their own work and that of others.

Where You Will Learn It

Miller & Levine Biology: Foundation Edition offers plenty of opportunities to work with data in many of the chapter labs.

COLLECTING AND ANALYZING DATA

The researchers sampled all the plots throughout the growing season. They measured growth rates and plant sizes, and analyzed the chemical composition of living leaves.

DRAWING CONCLUSIONS

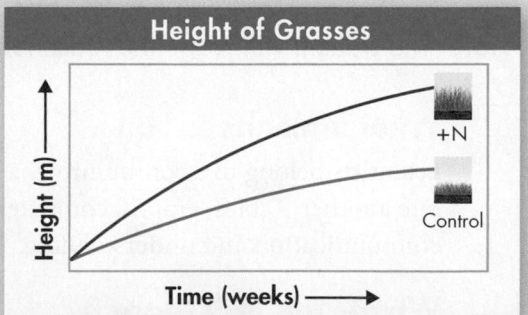

Data from all plots were compared and evaluated by statistical tests. Data analysis confirmed that marsh grasses in experimental plots with additional nitrogen did, in fact, grow taller and larger than controls. The hypothesis and its predictions were supported.

Science Learning Goal 1: Skills and Processes *(continued)*

Expectation 1.5 The student will use appropriate methods for communicating in writing and orally the processes and results of scientific investigation.

SPI 1.5.1 The student will demonstrate the ability to summarize data (measurements/observations).

SPI 1.5.2 The student will explain scientific concepts and processes through drawing, writing, and/or oral communication.

SPI 1.5.3 The student will use computers and/or graphing calculators to produce the visual materials (tables, graphs, and spreadsheets) that will be used for communicating results.*

SPI 1.5.4 The student will use tables, graphs, and displays to support arguments and claims in both written and oral communication.

SPI 1.5.5 The student will create and/or interpret graphics. (scale drawings, photographs, digital images, field of view, etc.)

SPI 1.5.6 The student will read a technical selection and interpret it appropriately.

SPI 1.5.7 The student will use, explain, and/or construct various classification systems.

SPI 1.5.8 The student will describe similarities and differences when explaining concepts and/or principles.

SPI 1.5.9 The student will communicate conclusions derived through a synthesis of ideas.

Expectation 1.6 The student will use mathematical processes.

SPI 1.6.1 The student will use ratio and proportion in appropriate situations to solve problems.

SPI 1.6.2 The student will use computers and/or graphing calculators to perform calculations for tables, graphs, or spreadsheets.

SPI 1.6.3 The student will express and/or compare small and large quantities using scientific notation and relative order of magnitude.

SPI 1.6.4 The student will manipulate quantities and/or numerical values in algebraic equations.

SPI 1.6.5 The student will judge the reasonableness of an answer.

What It Means to You

Scientists belong to a community that must share information. Scientists communicate with one another. Tables, graphs, computer models, and mathematics are critical aspects of scientific communication and understanding.

Where You Will Learn It

You will be asked to communicate your understanding and discoveries in the many of different activities offered throughout *Miller & Levine Biology: Foundation Edition*. You will also have many opportunities to work with mathematical processes.

Expectation 1.7 The student will show that connections exist both within the various fields of science and among science and other disciplines including mathematics, social studies, language arts, fine arts, and technology.

SPI 1.7.1 The student will apply the skills, processes and concepts of biology, chemistry, physics, or earth science to societal issues.

SPI 1.7.2 The student will identify and evaluate the impact of scientific ideas and/or advancements in technology on society.

SPI 1.7.3 The student will describe the role of science in the development of literature, art, and music.*

SPI 1.7.4 The student will recognize mathematics as an integral part of the scientific process.*

SPI 1.7.5 The student will investigate career possibilities in the various areas of science.*

SPI 1.7.6 The student will explain how development of scientific knowledge leads to the creation of new technology and how technological advances allow for additional scientific accomplishments.

What It Means to You

Science is everywhere, not just in what you study at school. It is integral to the technologies we use everyday, the decisions we make about how to interact with our environment and other living things. Science is even present in how we express ourselves artistically.

Where You Will Learn It

Chapter 1 covers different aspects of biological study, then in Chapter 2 you learn about its connection to chemistry. Throughout the book, you will see different ways biology connects to other sciences, as well as how biologists make use of mathematics.

Thomas Point Lighthouse, on the Chesapeake Bay, marks the dangerous Thomas Point Shoal. The shoal is a hazard to large ships

Science Core Learning Goals

Learning Goal 3: Concepts of Biology

The student will demonstrate ways of thinking and acting inherent in the practice of science. The student will use the language and instruments of science to collect, organize, interpret, calculate, and communicate information.

Expectation 3.1: Biochemistry The student will be able to explain the correlation between the structure and function of biologically important molecules and their relationship to cell processes.

CLG 3.1.1 Describe the unique characteristics of chemical substances and macromolecules utilized by living systems.

CLG 3.1.2 Discuss factors involved in the regulation of chemical activity as part of a homeostatic mechanism.

CLG 3.1.1 Compare the transfer and use of matter and energy in photosynthetic and nonphotosynthetic organisms.

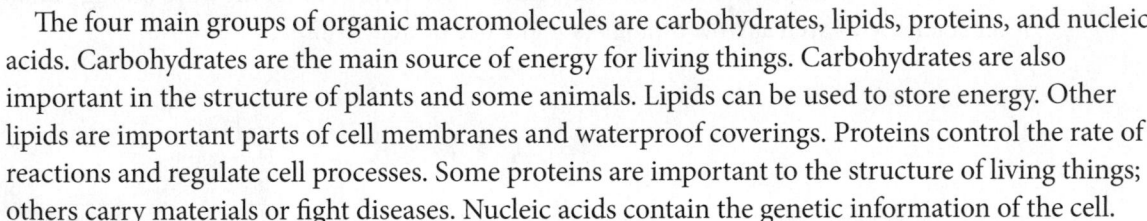

Heme group

Amino acids

What It Means to You

Four main groups of large carbon compounds, or organic macromolecules, are essential to the functions of all living things. These molecules are the building blocks of all cells. They form the different structures found in cells, such as the nucleus, cell membrane, cell wall, and mitochondria.

The four main groups of organic macromolecules are carbohydrates, lipids, proteins, and nucleic acids. Carbohydrates are the main source of energy for living things. Carbohydrates are also important in the structure of plants and some animals. Lipids can be used to store energy. Other lipids are important parts of cell membranes and waterproof coverings. Proteins control the rate of reactions and regulate cell processes. Some proteins are important to the structure of living things; others carry materials or fight diseases. Nucleic acids contain the genetic information of the cell.

The cells of an organism work together to maintain homeostasis, keeping cells, tissues, and organs functioning. The energy and material needed to support life is largely the result of photosynthesis, which removes carbon dioxide from the atmosphere, releasing oxygen into the atmosphere. Cellular respiration uses that oxygen to release energy from food and power the activity needed to keep an organism alive. Only plants and some algae are able to capture energy through photosynthesis. Living things use ATP to store and release energy.

Where You Will Learn It

This material is covered in Chapters 2, 7–9, with information on protein synthesis covered in Chapters 12 and 13. The behavior of organic molecules within different organisms is discussed in Chapters 20, 22, 23, 24, 25, 27, 28, 30, 31, 32, 33, and 34.

SAMPLE QUESTION

1. Which type of molecule is the main source of energy for living things?

    A. enzymes   B. proteins   C. nucleic acids   D. carbohydrates

CLG 3.2.1 Explain the processes and the function of related structures found in unicellular and multicellular organisms.

CLG 3.2.2 Conclude that cells exist within a narrow range of environmental conditions and changes to that environment, either naturally occurring or induced, may cause changes in the metabolic activity of the cell or organism.

What It Means to You

Cells are the basic units of structure and function in living things. Cellular structures and processes work together to keep the cell in equilibrium in response to changes in its environment. To carry out these processes, organisms must obtain and use energy. Cellular processes that transform energy include photosynthesis and respiration. Organisms obtain the energy they need from the breakdown of food molecules by cellular respiration and fermentation.

Cells exist within a narrow range of phyical conditions, such as temperature and pH, and must respond to changes in the environment to survive. Cells must also keep a proper balance of water and other materials. The cell membrane controls what materials enter and leave a cell. In passive transport, materials move across the cell membrane without using cellular energy. The active transport of materials across a membrane requires energy.

Where You Will Learn It

The physical environment of cells is covered in Chapter 2. Cellular structures and processes are covered in Chapters 7–10. Cell behavior and structure as it relates to different types of organisms is discussed in Chapters 20–35.

SAMPLE QUESTIONS

1. Some cells are able to carry out both cellular respiration and fermentation. Which environment would favor the release of energy by fermentation?
A. a high level of carbon dioxide
B. a low level of carbon dioxide
C. a high level of oxygen
D. a low level of oxygen

2. In osmosis, a substance that moves across a cell membrane tends to move
A. away from the area of equilibrium
B. away from the area where it is less concentrated.
C. away from the area where it is more concentrated.
D. toward the area where it is more concentrated.

3. During the development of a multicellular organism, many different types of cells can arise from a single cell. Which cellular process allows for this to occur?
A. differentiation
B. binary fission
C. fertilization
D. respiration

Science Learning Goal 3: Concepts of Biology *(continued)*

Expectation 3.3: Genetics The student will analyze how traits are inherited and passed on from one generation to another.

CLG 3.3.1 Demonstrate that the sorting and recombination of genes during sexual reproduction has an effect on variation in offspring.

CLG 3.3.2 Illustrate and explain how expressed traits are passed from parent to offspring.

CLG 3.3.3 Explain how a genetic trait is determined by the code in a DNA molecule.

CLG 3.3.4 Interpret how the effects of DNA alteration can be beneficial or harmful to the individual, society, and/or the environment.

What It Means to You

Sexual reproduction increases genetic diversity because the offspring receive genetic material from two parents. Meiosis, the process that produces sex cells, or gametes, further enables genetic diversity within the gamete of each parent as does any change, or mutation, to its DNA. DNA is the material that carries the genetic code of the cell and passes inherited traits from parents to offspring.

Molecules of DNA are made up of long, double strands of nucleotides. The genetic code is the order of nucleotides on the strands of DNA, which in turn determine the order in which amino acids will be put together to make proteins. The code for each amino acid is a specific set of three nucleotides called a codon. The genetic code and the environment in which an organism develops and grows determine the characteristics of that organism. You will learn about Mendel and how the laws of heredity can be used to predict the chances that an offspring will inherit certain traits. You will also learn how DNA can be manipulated and the issues that raises for science and society.

Where You Will Learn It

You will learn about genes, DNA, and genetic engineering in Chapters 11–15. You will learn about the molecular aspects of genetic variation and its affects on populations and the evolution of species in Chapters 17 and 19. You will also learn more about sexual reproduction in various types of organisms in Chapters 20, 21, 22, 24, 25, 28, and 34.

SAMPLE QUESTIONS

1. Meiosis begins with a single diploid cell and produces
   A. 2 diploid cells
   B. 2 haploid cells
   C. 4 diploid cells
   D. 4 haploid cells

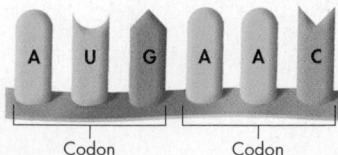
Codon   Codon

2. From which DNA template was the strand of mRNA above transcribed?
   A. TACTTG
   B. ATGAAC
   C. AUGAAC
   D. UACUUG

CLG 3.4.1 Explain how new traits may result from new combinations of existing genes or from mutations of genes in reproductive cells within a population.

CLG 3.4.2 Estimate degrees of relatedness among organisms or species.

What It Means to You

Modern scientists organize living things into groups based on evolutionary relationships. Evolution explains the great diversity of life on Earth and the ways that living things have changed over time. Since Darwin first proposed his theory of biological evolution, scientists have found an enormous body of evidence that supports this theory. This evidence includes the fossil record, the distribution of organisms around the world, the universal genetic code, and similarities in the structure and development of organisms.

Where You Will Learn It

Some of the cellular aspect of evolution are covered in Chapters 7 and 10 and in the context of genes in Chapter 12. The evolution chapters (Chapters 16–19) provide in-depth coverage, with some aspects also covered in the context of different types of organisms (Chapters 20–22, 25–29). See also the use of cladograms in the Visual Guide to the Diversity of Life found at the back of this book.

The wild ponies of Assateague Island in Maryland are owned and cared for by the U.S. Park Service. They are the only wild herd found grazing east of the Rocky Mountains.

SAMPLE QUESTIONS

1. Darwin based his development of his theory of evolution on many different observations. Which of the following did Darwin NOT observe?
A. geographic distribution of organisms   C. universal genetic code
B. fossils   D. artificial selection of domesticated animals

2. Which of the following provides evidence that living things have been evolving for millions of years?
A. fossil record   C. mutations
B. natural variation within a species   D. analogous structures

Science Learning Goal 3: Concepts of Biology (continued)

Expectation 3.5: Ecology The student will investigate the interdependence of diverse living organisms and their interactions with components of the biosphere.

CLG 3.5.1 Analyze the relationships between biotic diversity and abiotic factors in environments and the resulting influence on ecosystems.

CLG 3.5.2 Analyze the interrelationships and interdependencies among different organisms and explain how these relationships contribute to the stability of the ecosystem.

CLG 3.5.3 Investigate how natural and human-made changes in environmental conditions will affect individual organisms and the dynamics of populations.

CLG 3.5.4 Illustrate how all organisms are part of and depend on two major global food webs that are positively or negatively influenced by human activity and technology.

What It Means to You

Living organisms interact with living things (biotic factors) and nonliving things (abiotic factors) around them. Living things depend on one another and their environment to survive. You will learn how matter and energy move between organisms and their environment through the complex interactions of a food web. You will explore how living things are affected by changes in their environment. You will also examine ways that humans change the environment and the impact of those changes on ecosystems.

Where You Will Learn It

This material is covered in the ecology chapters (Chapters 3–6) as well as in the context of evolution (Chapters 16 and 19) and throughout the chapters describing different types of organisms (Chapters 20, 21, 23, 24, 26, 27, 28, 29, 31, and 35).

SAMPLE QUESTIONS

8. Which of the following describes how a population will likely grow when resources are limited?
   A. logistic growth
   B. exponential growth
   C. demographic transitional growth
   D. competitive growth

9. This diagram shows an aquatic food web. Which two carnivores compete for the Ross seal as a food source?
   A. crabeater seal and blue whale
   B. blue whale and leopard seal
   C. crabeater seal and krill
   D. killer whale and leopard seal

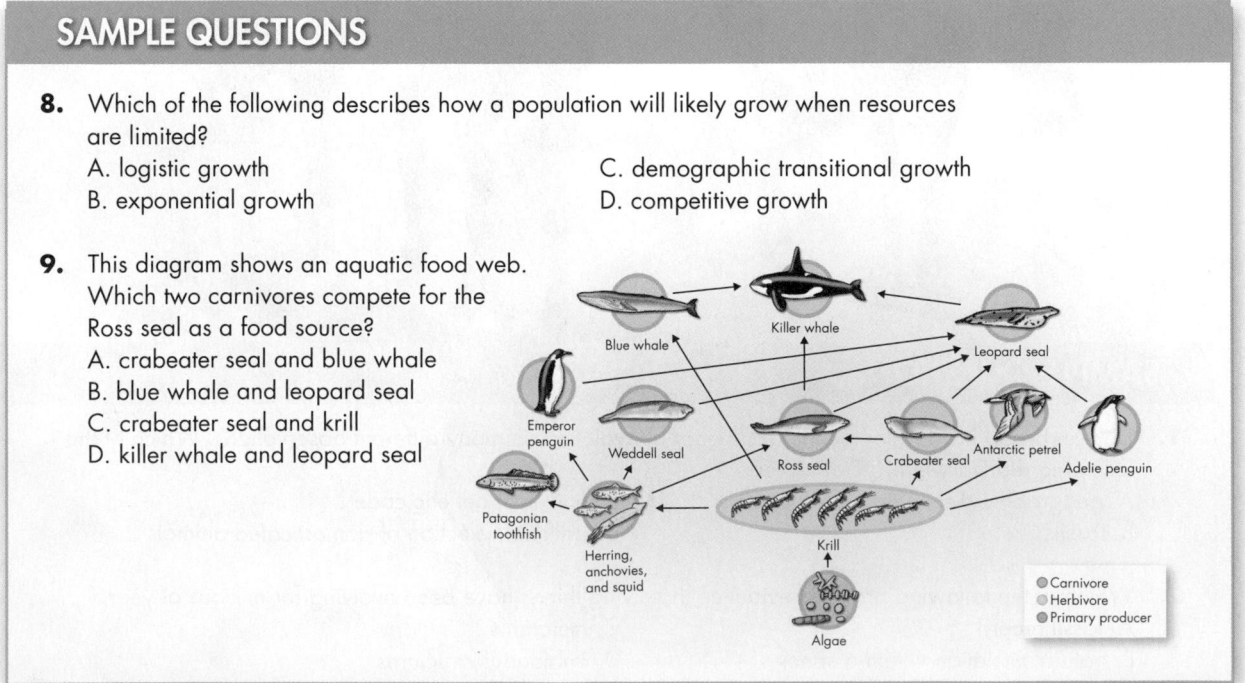

Dear Student:

Welcome to our world—the endlessly fascinating world of biology.

I can guess what some of you are thinking right now. "Fascinating? Yeah, right. Totally." Well, give us—and biology—a chance to show you that the study of the natural world really is more exciting, more fascinating, and more important to you personally than you've ever realized. In fact, biology is more important to our daily lives today than it has ever been.

Why? Three words: "We are one." This isn't meant in a "touchy-feely" or "New Age" way. "We" includes all forms of life on Earth. And "are one" means that all of us are tied together more tightly, in more different ways, than anyone imagined until recently.

Both our "hardware" (body structures) and our "software" (genetic instructions and biochemical processes that program body functions) are incredibly similar to those of all other living things. Genetic instructions in our bodies are written in the same universal code as instructions in bacteria and palm trees. As biologists "read" and study that code, they find astonishingly similar processes in all of us. That's why medical researchers can learn about human diseases that may strike you or your family by studying not only apes and pigs and mice, but even yeasts. We are one on the molecular level.

All organisms interact with one another and with the environment to weave our planet's web of life. Organisms make rain forests and coral reefs, prairies and swamps—and farms and cities. We interact, too, with the winds and ocean currents that tie our planet together. Human activity is changing local and global environments in ways that we still don't understand . . . and that affect our ability to produce food and protect ourselves from diseases. We are one ecologically with the rest of life on Earth.

All organisms evolve over time, adapting to their surroundings. If humans alter the environment, other organisms respond to that change. When we use antibiotics against bacteria, they develop resistance to our drugs. If we use pesticides against insects, they become immune to our poisons. We are one in our ability to evolve over time.

Those are the kinds of connections you will find in this book. Microscopic. Enormous. Amusing. Threatening. But always fascinating. That's why—no matter where you start off in your attitude about biology—we think you are in for some surprises!

Sincerely,

Joe Levine

Dear Student,

Biology is one of the subjects you're going to study this year, but I hope you'll realize from the very first pages of this book that biology is a lot more than just a "subject." Biology is what makes an eagle fly, a flower bloom, or a caterpillar turn into a butterfly. It's the study of ourselves—of how our bodies grow and change and respond to the outside world, and it's the study of our planet, a world transformed by the actions of living things. Of course, you might have known some of this already. But there's something more—you might call it a "secret" that makes biology unique.

That secret is that you've come along at just the right time. In all of human history, there has never been a moment like the present, a time when we stood so close to the threshold of answering the most fundamental questions about the nature of life. You belong to the first generation of students who can read the human genome almost as your parents might have read a book or a newspaper. You are the first students who will grow up in a world that has a chance to use that information for the benefit of humanity, and you are the very first to bear the burden of using that knowledge wisely.

If all of this seems like heavy stuff, it is. But there is another reason we wrote this book, and we hope that is not a secret at all. Science is fun! Biologists aren't a bunch of serious, grim-faced, middle-aged folks in lab coats who think of nothing but work. In fact, most of the people we know in science would tell you honestly, with broad grins on their faces, that they have the best jobs in the world. They would say there's nothing that compares to the excitement of doing scientific work, and that the beauty and variety of life make every day a new adventure.

We agree, and we hope that you'll keep something in mind as you begin the study of biology. You don't need a lab coat or a degree or a laboratory to be a scientist. What you do need is an inquiring mind, the patience to look at nature carefully, and the willingness to figure things out. We've filled this book with some of the latest and most important discoveries about living things, but we hope we've also filled it with something else: our wonder, our amazement, and our sheer delight in the variety of life itself. Come on in, and enjoy the journey!

Sincerely,

Ken Miller

The Nature of Life

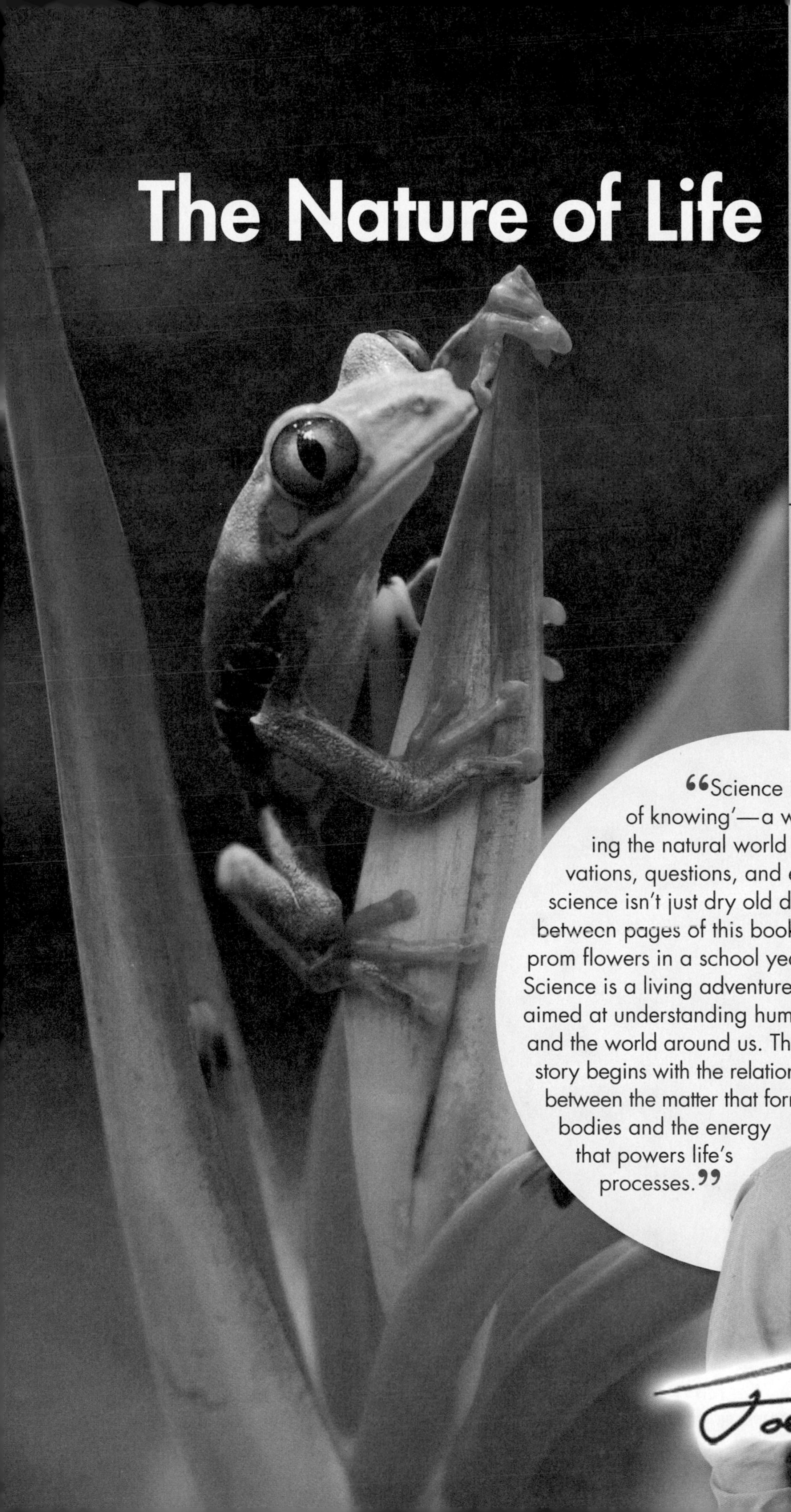

UNIT 1

Chapters

1 The Science of Biology

2 The Chemistry of Life

INTRODUCE the Big ideas

- **Science as a Way of Knowing**
- **Matter and Energy**

"Science is 'a way of knowing'—a way of explaining the natural world through observations, questions, and experiments. But science isn't just dry old data, pressed between pages of this book like prom flowers in a school yearbook. Science is a living adventure story, aimed at understanding humans and the world around us. That story begins with the relationship between the matter that forms our bodies and the energy that powers life's processes."

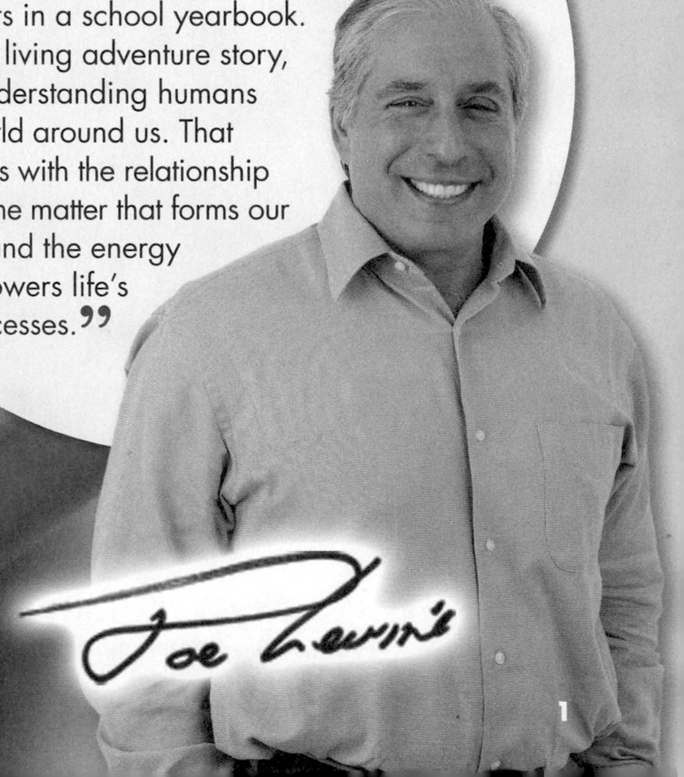

1

The Science of Biology

Big idea

Science as a Way of Knowing

Q: What role does science play in the study of life?

BIOLOGY.com ▸ Search ⟨ Chapter 1 ⟩ **GO** • Flash Cards

Paleontologists study ancient life. These students at the Academy of Natural Sciences in Philadelphia are working in the dinosaur lab. By using scientific skills such as observation and inference, scientists can learn how ancient animals lived.

CHAPTER MYSTERY

HEIGHT BY PRESCRIPTION

A doctor gives a shot of a powerful chemical to an eight-year-old boy named David. This boy is perfectly healthy. He shows no signs of being sick. The "problem" that he is being treated for is very common. He is short for his age.

The chemical David is being given is human growth hormone, or HGH. HGH, together with genes and diet, controls growth during childhood. Some people produce little or no HGH. These people are extremely short and may have other health problems. But David has a normal amount of HGH. He is short because his parents are both healthy, short people.

But if David isn't sick, why does his doctor prescribe HGH? Where does HGH come from? Is it safe? And what does its use in David's case say about science and society?

Read for Mystery Clues As you read this chapter, look for clues about the nature of science, the role of technology in our modern world, and the relationship between science and society. Then, solve the mystery.

FOUNDATIONS for Learning

All living things share certain characteristics. Biology is the study of these characteristics. Before you read the chapter, make an Inspired Shape Tree. Your tree should have a trunk and eight branches. Write "Characteristics of Living Things" on the trunk. Then, as you read Lesson 3, describe a different characteristic on each branch. At the end of the chapter are two activities that use your tree to help answer the question: What role does science play in the study of life?

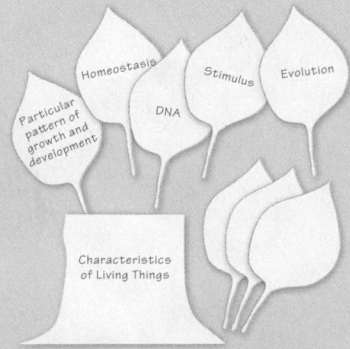

• Untamed Science Video • Chapter Mystery

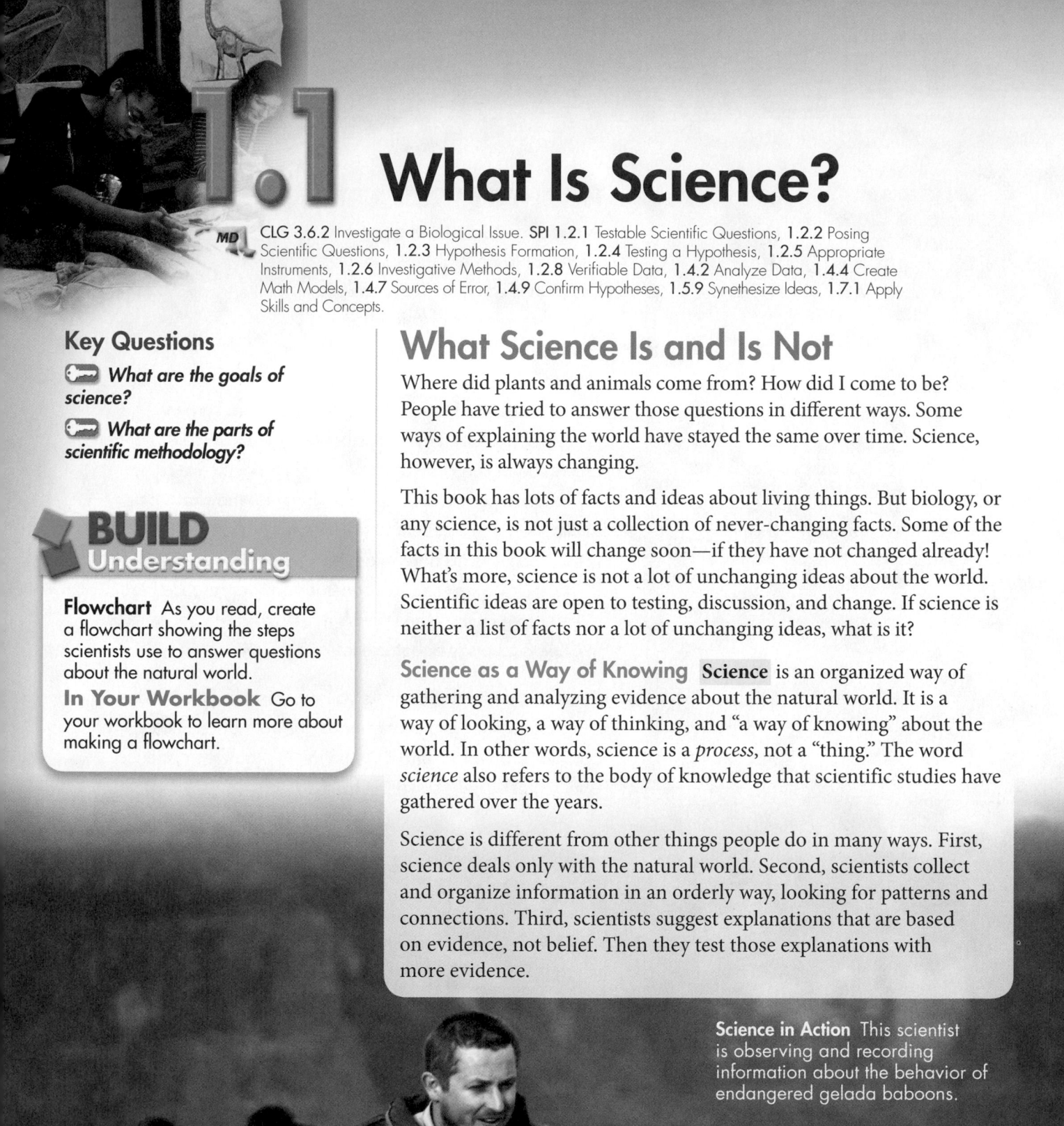

What Is Science?

MD CLG **3.6.2** Investigate a Biological Issue. SPI **1.2.1** Testable Scientific Questions, **1.2.2** Posing Scientific Questions, **1.2.3** Hypothesis Formation, **1.2.4** Testing a Hypothesis, **1.2.5** Appropriate Instruments, **1.2.6** Investigative Methods, **1.2.8** Verifiable Data, **1.4.2** Analyze Data, **1.4.4** Create Math Models, **1.4.7** Sources of Error, **1.4.9** Confirm Hypotheses, **1.5.9** Synethesize Ideas, **1.7.1** Apply Skills and Concepts.

Key Questions

🔑 *What are the goals of science?*

🔑 *What are the parts of scientific methodology?*

BUILD Understanding

Flowchart As you read, create a flowchart showing the steps scientists use to answer questions about the natural world.

In Your Workbook Go to your workbook to learn more about making a flowchart.

What Science Is and Is Not

Where did plants and animals come from? How did I come to be? People have tried to answer those questions in different ways. Some ways of explaining the world have stayed the same over time. Science, however, is always changing.

This book has lots of facts and ideas about living things. But biology, or any science, is not just a collection of never-changing facts. Some of the facts in this book will change soon—if they have not changed already! What's more, science is not a lot of unchanging ideas about the world. Scientific ideas are open to testing, discussion, and change. If science is neither a list of facts nor a lot of unchanging ideas, what is it?

Science as a Way of Knowing Science is an organized way of gathering and analyzing evidence about the natural world. It is a way of looking, a way of thinking, and "a way of knowing" about the world. In other words, science is a *process*, not a "thing." The word *science* also refers to the body of knowledge that scientific studies have gathered over the years.

Science is different from other things people do in many ways. First, science deals only with the natural world. Second, scientists collect and organize information in an orderly way, looking for patterns and connections. Third, scientists suggest explanations that are based on evidence, not belief. Then they test those explanations with more evidence.

Science in Action This scientist is observing and recording information about the behavior of endangered gelada baboons.

The Goals of Science From a scientific view, objects in the universe, and all interactions among those objects, are ruled by natural laws. One goal of science is to use an understanding of those laws to give natural explanations for events in the natural world. Science also aims to use those explanations to understand patterns in nature and to make useful predictions about natural events.

🔑 **Key Question** What are the goals of science?
The goals of science are to give explanations for natural events, to understand patterns, and to make predictions.

Science, Change, and Uncertainty Scientists know a lot about nature. Yet, much of nature remains a mystery because science never stands still. This constant change does not mean science has failed. It shows that science is always improving.

Science rarely "proves" anything in absolute terms. Scientists aim for the best understanding that can be found. Uncertainty is a part of science and is part of what makes science exciting!

Scientific Methodology

There isn't any single "scientific method." But there is a general style of investigation that can be called scientific methodology. The parts of scientific methodology are described below.

Observing and Asking Questions Scientific studies begin with **observation,** the act of noticing and describing what is happening in an orderly way. Observation leads to new questions.

Inferring and Forming a Hypothesis After asking questions, scientists use further observations to make inferences. An inference is an idea based on what is already known. Inference, along with imagination, can lead to a hypothesis. A **hypothesis** is a scientific explanation for a set of observations that can be tested.

BUILD Vocabulary

science
an organized way of gathering and analyzing evidence about the natural world

observation
a process of noticing and describing events or processes in a careful, orderly way

hypothesis
a possible explanation for a set of observations or a possible answer to a scientific question

📖 WORD ORIGINS
The word *science* comes from the Latin word *scientia*, which means "knowledge." Science represents knowledge that has been gathered over time.

Salt Marsh Experiment Scientists made observations about a salt marsh. Then they used scientific methodology to answer the questions that came from their observations.

Observing and Asking Questions

Location A

Location B

Scientists observed that marsh grass grows taller in some places than others. This observation led to a question: *Why do marsh grasses grow to different heights in different places?*

Inferring and Hypothesizing

More nitrogen?

The scientists inferred that something limits grass growth in some places. Temperature, sunlight, water, or nutrients could cause the difference. Based on their knowledge of salt marshes, they proposed a hypothesis: *Marsh grass growth is limited by available nitrogen.*

controlled experiment
an experiment in which only one variable is changed

control group
the group in an experiment that is exposed to the same conditions as the experimental group except for one independent variable

data
evidence; information gathered from observations

🔑 RELATED WORD FORMS

The word *data* is plural for *datum*. To help you remember that *data* is plural, you can think of data as being a lot of information and datum as just one piece of information.

Designing Controlled Experiments Testing a hypothesis often involves an experiment that keeps track of variables, or the things that can change. A few examples of variables include temperature, light, and time. Whenever possible, a hypothesis should be tested by an experiment in which only one variable is changed. All other variables should be kept unchanged, or controlled. An experiment in which only one variable is changed is called a **controlled experiment.**

▶ *Controlling Variables* Why are variables controlled? The reason is that if more than one variable is changed in an experiment, scientists cannot easily tell which variable caused the results. The variable that is changed is called the independent variable. The variable that is observed and that changes because of modifications to the independent variable is called the dependent variable.

▶ *Control and Experimental Groups* An experiment is usually divided into control and experimental groups. A **control group** is treated the same as the experimental group except for one independent variable. Scientists often repeat their experiments several times to see if they get the same results. This process is called replicating the experiment. So, scientists set up several sets of control and experimental groups, rather than just a single pair.

Collecting and Analyzing Data Scientists make detailed records of experimental observations by gathering information called **data.** There are two main kinds of data. Quantitative data are numbers found by counting or measuring. Qualitative data describe things that cannot be counted.

Designing Controlled Experiments

The scientists selected areas that had similar numbers of plants and similar soil type, water supply, and height above the water level. The areas were divided into control and experimental groups.

The scientists added nitrogen fertilizer (the independent variable) to the experimental groups. They then observed the growth of marsh grass (the dependent variable) in both experimental and control groups.

▶ **Research Tools** Scientists pick the right tools for collecting and analyzing data. The tools may be simple, such as metersticks and calculators, or they may be complex, such as computers or robots. Charts and graphs are also tools that help scientists organize data.

▶ **Sources of Error** Scientists must avoid errors in data collection and analysis. Errors may happen when using tools. Tools have limited accuracy or can be read incorrectly. Data analysis and decisions about sample size must be carried out carefully to avoid errors. Sometimes experimental and control groups are very large. Why? The reason is because there are always differences among subjects in the groups. The larger the sample size, the more sure scientists are about their data analysis.

Drawing Conclusions Scientists use data to support or refute the hypothesis, to change the hypothesis, or to draw a valid conclusion. Hypotheses are often not shown to be completely right or wrong by an experiment. Rather, the data may show that the scientists have the right idea but are wrong about a few things. In that case, scientists change the first hypothesis, make new predictions, and design new experiments.

Key Question What are the seven parts of scientific methodology?
Scientific methodology involves observing and asking questions, making inferences and forming hypotheses, doing controlled experiments, collecting and analyzing data, and drawing conclusions.

Collecting and Analyzing Data

The scientists sampled all the areas during the growing season. They measured growth rates and plant sizes, and analyzed the chemicals in the leaves.

Drawing Conclusions

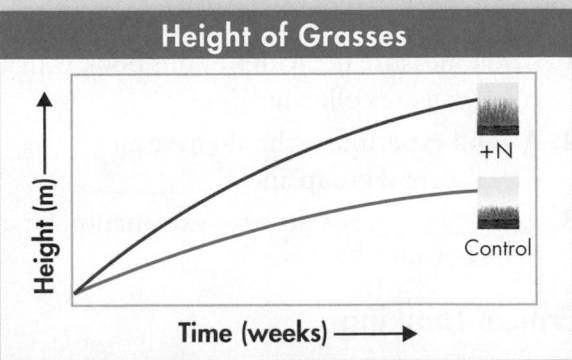

Data from all the areas were compared and evaluated. Data confirmed that marsh grasses with added nitrogen grow taller and larger than marsh grasses without added nitrogen. The hypothesis and its predictions were supported.

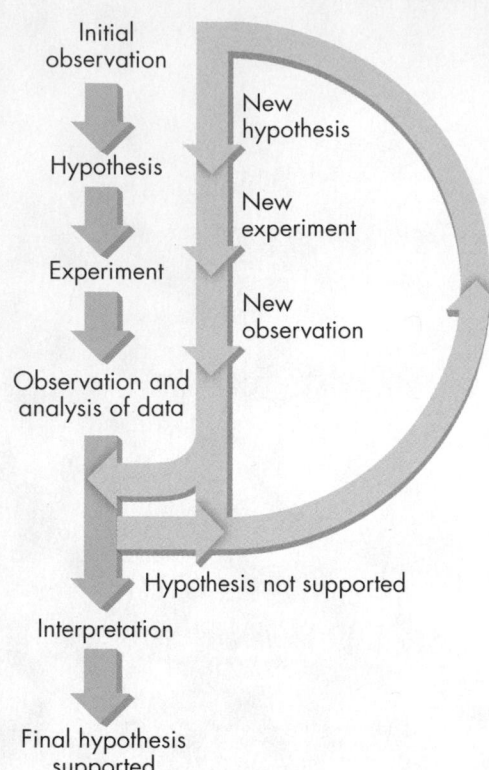

Initial observation

↓

Hypothesis

↓

Experiment

↓

Observation and analysis of data

↓

Interpretation

↓

Final hypothesis supported

New hypothesis

New experiment

New observation

Hypothesis not supported

Revising Hypotheses During an investigation, scientists may have to change their hypotheses and redo experiments several times.

When Experiments Are Not Possible It is not always possible to test a hypothesis with an experiment. In some cases, scientists come up with hypotheses that can be tested by observations. For example, scientists who study how animals behave might want to learn how animal groups act in the wild. Studying this kind of natural behavior means that the scientists must go into the wild and watch the animals without bothering them. When scientists analyze data from these observations, they may come up with hypotheses that can be tested in different ways.

Sometimes, ethics keeps scientists from doing certain kinds of experiments. Ethics are beliefs about what is wrong or right. Some experiments on people are not ethical to do. For example, suppose that some scientists think that a chemical causes cancer in people who breathe it in. The scientists cannot make people breathe the chemical to see if they are correct! Instead, the scientists search for people who have already breathed in the chemical. Then, the scientists study people who have not breathed in the chemical.

When experiments are not possible, scientists still try to control as many variables as possible. They might not use people in their study who have serious health problems or known genetic conditions. Medical scientists often study large groups of subjects so that genetic differences between people do not give results that may be misleading.

CHECK Understanding

Apply Vocabulary

Use the highlighted words from the lesson to complete each sentence correctly.

1. If you measure the width of this book with a ruler, you are collecting _____.

2. A good experiment should have an experimental group and a(n) _____.

3. A(n) _____ is a possible explanation for a set of observations.

Critical Thinking

4. Explain List the goals of science.

5. Explain Why are hypotheses so important to controlled experiments?

6. Write to Learn Answer the first clue of the mystery. Be sure your answer identifies the independent and dependent variables.

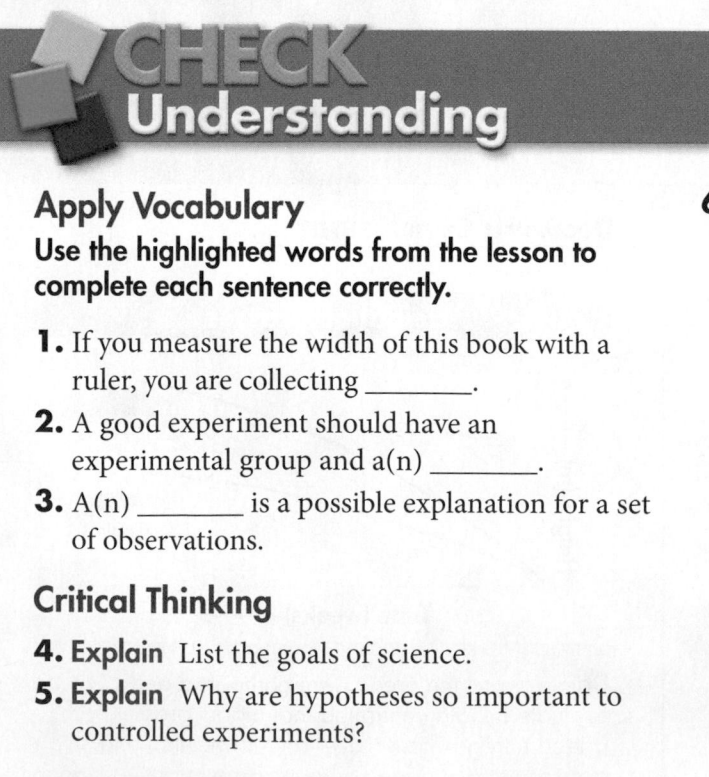

MYSTERY CLUE

Describe a controlled experiment that would test the hypothesis that extra HGH helps children grow taller. What ethical issues can you imagine in actually carrying out such a study? (**Hint:** See p. 6.)

MD CLG 3.6.1 Analyze Consequences. SPI 1.1.1 Problems and Solutions, 1.1.3 Critique Arguments, 1.1.4 Biased Data, 1.1.5 Producing Biased Data, 1.2.8 Verifiable Data, 1.7.1 Apply Skills and Concepts, 1.7.2 Evaluate Ideas, 1.7.6 Science and Technology.

Exploration and Discovery: Where Ideas Come From

Scientific methodology is the heart of science. But that "heart" is only part of the full "body" of science. The full body of science is shown in the Process of Science at the bottom of this page. Part of science is exploration and discovery. How do exploration and discovery start? They often begin with scientific attitudes, practical problems, and new technology.

Scientific Attitudes Good scientists share scientific attitudes that lead them to exploration and discovery.

▶ *Curiosity* Scientists are curious and ask questions about what they observe. Results from previous studies also raise curiosity and lead to new questions.

▶ *Skepticism* Scientists are skeptics, which means that they question existing ideas and hypotheses. They also do not believe ideas without evidence.

▶ *Open-Mindedness* Scientists must be open-minded. They must be willing to accept new ideas that they may not agree with.

▶ *Creativity* Scientists need to think creatively to design experiments that provide good data.

🔑 **Key Question** What scientific attitudes help make new ideas? **Curiosity, skepticism, open-mindedness, and creativity help scientists come up with new ideas.**

Practical Problems Sometimes, ideas for scientific investigations come from practical problems. For example, people want cars that do not cause air pollution. Practical problems lead to questions, hypotheses, and experiments.

Key Questions

🔑 What scientific attitudes help make new ideas?

🔑 Why is peer review important?

🔑 What is a scientific theory?

🔑 How are science and society related?

BUILD Understanding

Previewing Visuals Before you read, study the figure on the last page of this section. As you read, use the figure to describe the role that science plays in society.

In Your Workbook Go to your workbook to learn more about previewing visuals.

The Process of Science The arrows show that the different parts of science are connected in many ways. So, the process of science is flexible, unpredictable, and always changing.

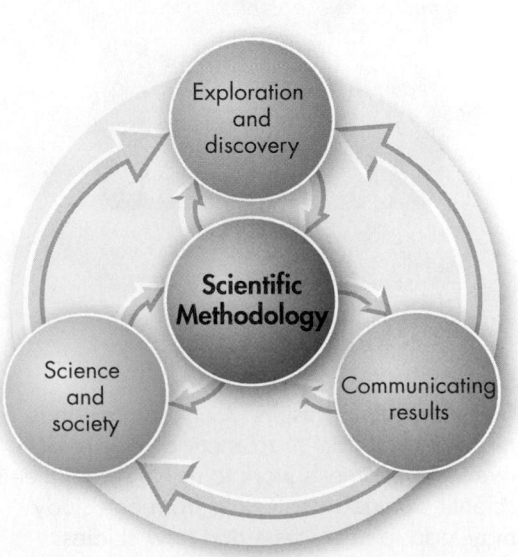

Exploration and Discovery Ideas in science can turn up in many ways—from curiosity to the need to solve a certain problem. Scientists often begin investigations by making observations, asking questions, talking to other scientists, and reading about other experiments.

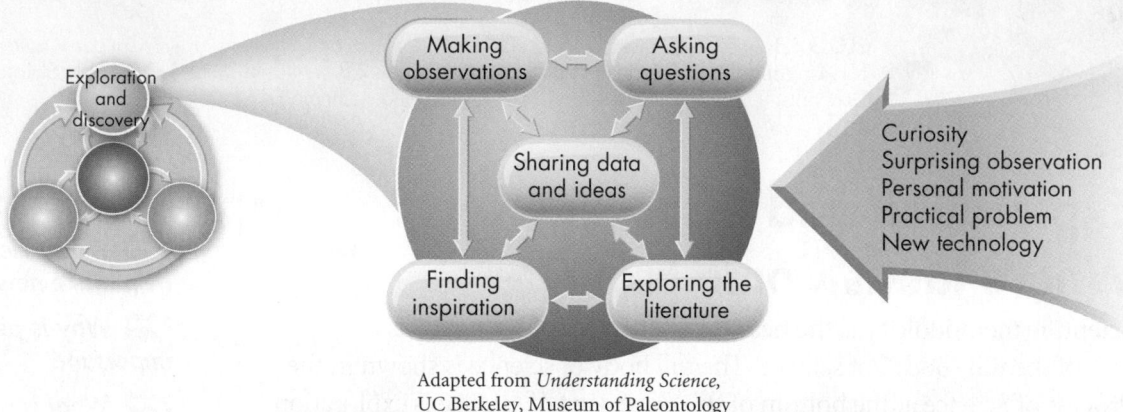

Adapted from *Understanding Science,*
UC Berkeley, Museum of Paleontology

The Role of Technology
Technology, science, and society are closely linked. Discoveries in science may lead to new technologies. Those technologies, in turn, enable scientists to ask new questions or to gather data in new ways. Technology can also have big impacts on daily life. For instance, it is now possible to make vitamins, antibiotics, and hormones that before were only available naturally.

Communicating Results: Reviewing and Sharing Ideas

Data collection and analysis can take a long time. Scientists may work on a single study for months or even years. Then, the scientists communicate results to other scientists.

Peer Review Scientists share their findings with other scientists by publishing papers that go through peer review. In peer review, papers are reviewed by other scientists. These reviewers read papers looking for mistakes and other problems. Peer review does not make sure that a piece of work is correct, but it does make sure that the work meets standards set by the scientific community. Publishing peer-reviewed papers in journals lets scientists share ideas and review each other's work.

Sharing Knowledge and New Ideas How do new findings fit into what is already known about science? Perhaps the findings lead to new questions. Each of those questions could lead to new hypotheses and new controlled experiments.

Key Question Why is peer review important?
Publishing peer-reviewed papers in journals lets scientists share ideas and review each other's work.

Adapted from *Understanding Science,*
UC Berkeley, Museum of Paleontology

Communicating Results Communication is an important part of science. Scientists look over one another's work to make sure it meets scientific standards. Results from one study may lead to new ideas and new studies.

Replicating Procedures

Scientists often repeat each other's experiments. They do this to make sure that the data and conclusions of the first scientist are correct. So, when scientists write papers to publish in journals, they must describe the procedures that they followed. The descriptions have to be good enough so that other scientists can repeat the first scientist's experiment.

❶ Working with a partner behind a screen, arrange ten blocks into an unusual structure.

❷ Write directions that others can use to build the same structure without seeing it.

❸ Exchange directions with another team.

❹ Build the other team's structure by following the directions.

❺ Compare each new structure to the original. Identify which parts of the directions were clear and correct, and which parts were hard to understand or follow.

Analyze and Conclude

1. Evaluate How could you have written better directions?

2. Infer Why is it important that scientists write procedures that can be repeated?

In Your Workbook Get more help for this activity in your workbook.

Scientific Theories

In science, a **theory** is a well-tested explanation that accounts for a lot of observations and hypotheses and that lets scientists make good predictions. For example, Charles Darwin's early observations and hypotheses about change over time grew for years before he collected them into a theory of evolution by natural selection. Today, this theory is a central idea in biology.

A useful theory that has been tested and supported in many ways may become the most accepted view among scientists. But no theory is thought to be absolute truth. Science is always changing. As new evidence is found, a theory may be changed or replaced by a more useful explanation.

Key Question What is a scientific theory?
A scientific theory is a well-tested explanation that accounts for a lot of observations and hypotheses and that lets scientists make good predictions.

theory
a well-tested explanation that unifies a broad range of observations and hypotheses, and enables scientists to make accurate predictions about new situations

bias
a particular preference or point of view that is personal, rather than scientific

✦ MULTIPLE MEANINGS

The word *theory* is used both in science and in everyday life. In everyday life, when you say, "I have a theory," you may mean, "I have a hunch." But in science, a theory is much stronger than a hunch—it is a well-tested explanation.

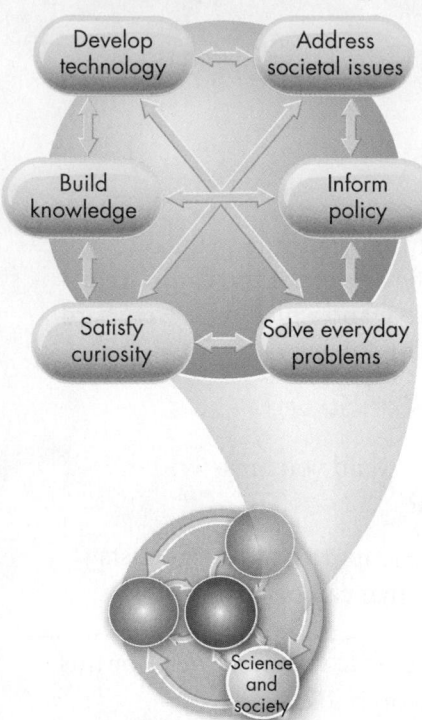

Adapted from *Understanding Science*, UC Berkeley, Museum of Paleontology

Develop technology ↔ Address societal issues

Build knowledge ↔ Inform policy

Satisfy curiosity ↔ Solve everyday problems

Science and society

Science and Society Science can help society or change how people in society do things. But society also affects science. Problems and questions in society may lead scientists to do new experiments.

Science and Society

Many important questions can only be answered with the help of scientific information. But very few of these questions can be answered by science alone. These questions involve the society in which we live. Using science involves understanding its limitations and how it fits into society.

Science, Ethics, and Morality When scientists explain "why" something happens, their explanation is about only nature. Science does not include ethical or moral views. Scientists can try to explain what life is. But science cannot answer questions about why life exists or what the meaning of life is.

Avoiding Bias How science is used in society can be affected by bias. A **bias** is a certain preference or point of view that is personal, rather than scientific. Examples of biases include personal taste and liking one thing over another.

Scientists try to avoid bias. But scientific data can be used in the wrong way by people who want to prove a certain point. However, if enough of us understand science, we can help make sure that science is used in only helpful, correct ways.

Understanding and Using Science As you read this book, don't think of it as an encyclopedia. Don't memorize the scientific facts and ideas. Instead, try to understand how scientists developed those ideas. Understanding science will help you make decisions that also fit with society's values.

🔑 **Key Question** How are science and society related? **Using science involves understanding its limitations and how it fits into society.**

✓CHECK Understanding

Apply Vocabulary
Use the highlighted words from the lesson to complete the sentence correctly.

1. A point of view that is personal rather than scientific is a _____.

2. Scientists can use a _____ to make good predictions.

Critical Thinking
3. Explain What does it mean to be skeptical? Why is skepticism a good quality in a scientist?

4. Explain Describe some of the limitations of science.

5. Write to Learn Write the answer to the second clue of the mystery.

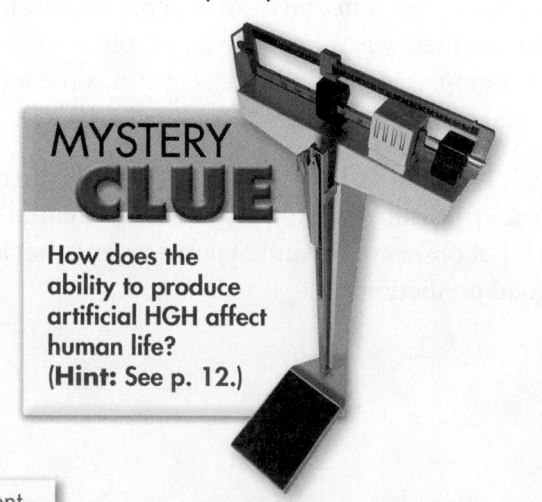

MYSTERY **CLUE**

How does the ability to produce artificial HGH affect human life? (Hint: See p. 12.)

BIOLOGY.com ⟩ Search [Lesson 1.2] [GO] • Lesson Assessment

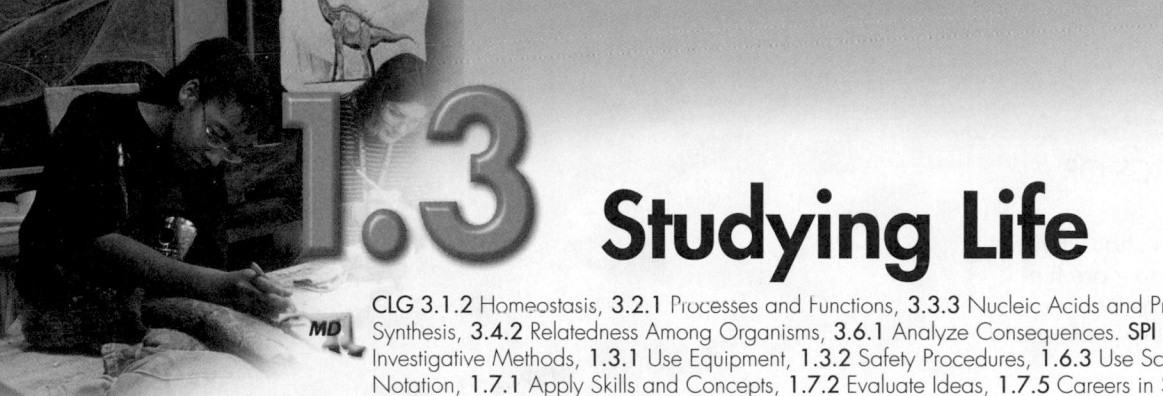

1.3 Studying Life

CLG **3.1.2** Homeostasis, **3.2.1** Processes and Functions, **3.3.3** Nucleic Acids and Protein Synthesis, **3.4.2** Relatedness Among Organisms, **3.6.1** Analyze Consequences. SPI **1.2.6** Investigative Methods, **1.3.1** Use Equipment, **1.3.2** Safety Procedures, **1.6.3** Use Scientific Notation, **1.7.1** Apply Skills and Concepts, **1.7.2** Evaluate Ideas, **1.7.5** Careers in Science.

Characteristics of Living Things

Think about news stories that you have seen or heard. Bird flu spreads around the world killing thousand of birds and threatening an epidemic. People who use illegal drugs get permanent brain damage. These and many other stories are about biology—the study of living things. (The Greek word *bios* means "life," and *-logy* means "study of.")

Biology is the study of life. But what is life? What is the difference between living things and nonliving matter? It is not as simple as you might think to describe what makes something alive. No single characteristic is enough to describe a living thing. Also, some nonliving things share one or more traits with living things. For example, automobiles and clouds (which are not alive) move around. However, mushrooms and trees (which are alive) stay in one spot.

Despite these difficulties, we can list characteristics that most living things have in common. Living things are made up of basic units called cells, are based on a universal genetic code, obtain and use materials and energy, grow and develop, reproduce, respond to their environment, maintain a stable internal environment, and change over time.

Key Question What characteristics do all living things share? **Living things are made up of basic units called cells, are based on a universal genetic code, obtain and use materials and energy, grow and develop, reproduce, respond to their environment, maintain a stable internal environment, and change over time.**

Key Questions

- What characteristics do all living things share?
- What are the big ideas of biology?
- How do different fields of biology differ in the way they study life?
- Why is the metric system important in science?

BUILD Understanding

Concept Map As you read, draw a concept map showing the big ideas in biology.

In Your Workbook Go to your workbook and finish the concept map for Lesson 1.3.

Is It Alive? The fish are clearly alive, but what about the colorful structure above them? Is it alive? Yes! It is an animal called elkhorn coral. Corals show all the characteristics of living things.

THE CHARACTERISTICS OF LIVING THINGS

Apple trees share certain characteristics with other living things. How are the apple tree and the grass growing below similar? How are they different?

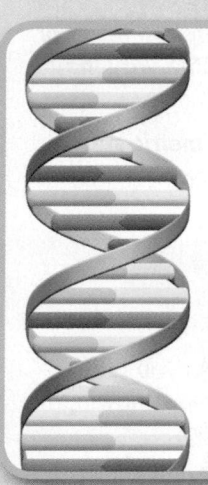

Living things are based on a universal genetic code. All organisms store the information they need to live, grow, and reproduce in a genetic code written in a molecule called **DNA.** That information is copied and passed from parent to offspring. With a few small differences, life's genetic code is almost the same in every living thing on Earth.

The information in an apple tree's DNA directs all of the tree's life processes.

Living things grow and develop. Every organism has a certain pattern of growth and development. During development, a single fertilized egg divides again and again. As these cells divide, they differentiate, which means they begin to look different from one another and to do different jobs.

An apple tree develops from a tiny seed.

Living things respond to their environment. Organisms notice and react to stimuli from their environment. A **stimulus** is a signal to which a living thing reacts.

Some plants can produce poisons to ward off caterpillars that feed on its leaves.

Living things reproduce. All living things make new similar living things. Most plants and animals engage in sexual reproduction. In sexual reproduction, cells from two parents come together to form the first cell of a new living thing. Other living things reproduce through asexual reproduction, in which a single living thing makes offspring exactly the same as itself.

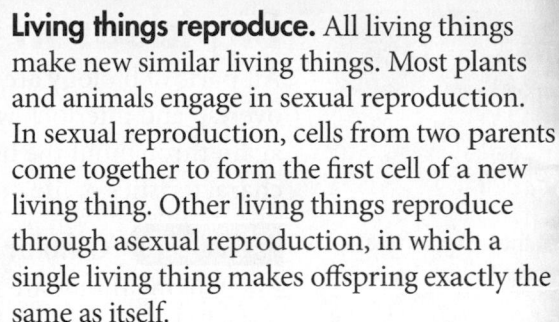

Flowers form as part of the apple tree's reproductive cycle.

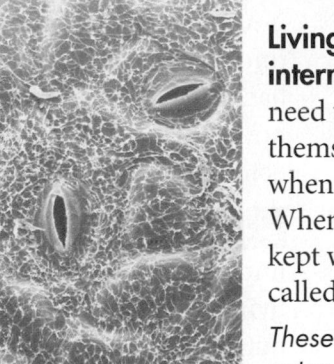

Living things maintain a stable internal environment. All living things need to keep conditions inside themselves as constant as possible, even when conditions outside of them change. When conditions inside organisms are kept within certain limits, this is called **homeostasis.**

These cells help leaves control gases that enter and leave the plant. SEM 1200×

Living things get and use material and energy. All living things must take in materials and energy to grow, develop, and reproduce. The chemical reactions through which a living thing builds up or breaks down materials are called **metabolism.**

Different metabolic reactions happen in leaves.

Taken as a group, living things evolve. Over generations, groups of living things evolve, or change over time. Evolutionary change links all forms of life to a common origin more than 3.5 billion years ago. Evidence of this shared history is found in all parts of living things and fossils, from body parts to proteins to information in DNA.

Signs of one of the first land plants are preserved in rock over 400 million years old.

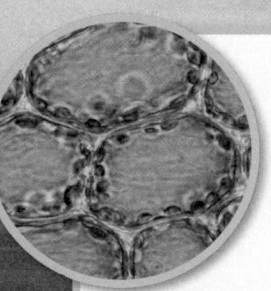

Living things are made up of cells. Living things are made up of one or more cells—the smallest units considered fully alive. Cells can grow, respond to their surroundings, and reproduce. Even though cells are small, they are complex and very organized.

One branch of a tree is made up of millions of cells. LM 250×

biology
the scientific study of life

DNA
the genetic material that organisms inherit from their parents

stimulus
a signal to which an organism responds

homeostasis
the relatively constant internal physical and chemical conditions that organisms maintain

metabolism
the combination of chemical reactions through which an organism builds up or breaks down materials

biosphere
the part of Earth in which life exists, including land, water, and air or atmosphere

PREFIXES

The prefix *homeo-* means "the same" or "similar." Homeostasis is how the body keeps conditions inside the same at all times.

Big Ideas in Biology

All parts of biology are tied together by big ideas. These big ideas overlap and interlock with one another. They will come up again and again throughout the book. Many of these big ideas overlap with the characteristics of life or the nature of science.

Big idea **Cellular Basis of Life** Living things are made of cells. Many living things are made up of only a single cell; they are called unicellular organisms. Plants and animals are multicellular. Cells in multicellular organisms display many different sizes, shapes, and functions.

Big idea **Information and Heredity** Living things carry information written in a universal genetic code in their DNA. The information coded in DNA forms an unbroken chain that stretches back roughly 3.5 billion years. Yet, the DNA inside your cells right now can affect your future, such as your risk of getting cancer and the color of your children's hair.

Big idea **Matter and Energy** Life needs matter that serves as nutrients to build body parts and energy that fuels the body. Some living things, such as plants, get energy from sunlight and take up nutrients from air, water, and soil. Other living things, including most animals, eat plants or other animals to get both nutrients and energy. The need for matter and energy ties all living things on Earth together into a living web of relationships.

Big idea **Growth, Development, and Reproduction** All living things reproduce, which means that they make more individuals. Offspring are almost always smaller than adults, so they grow and develop as they mature.

Big idea **Homeostasis** Living things keep a fairly stable internal environment. For most organisms, any problems with homeostasis may have serious or deadly consequences.

Big idea **Evolution** Evolutionary change ties all forms of life to a common beginning more than 3.5 billion years ago. Evolution is the central organizing idea of all biology.

Different But Similar This colorful bird is different from the plant it is sitting on. Yet, the two living things are similar on the molecular level. Unity and diversity of life is a big idea in biology.

Big idea Structure and Function Each major group of living things has evolved its own set of body parts. These parts make certain functions possible. Living things have evolved into different forms as species have adapted to life in different places.

Big idea Unity and Diversity of Life Although life comes in a huge variety of forms, all living things are similar at the molecular level. All living things are made up of a common set of molecules, have DNA, and use proteins to build their body parts and carry out their functions. Evolutionary theory explains both this unity of life and its diversity.

Big idea Interdependence in Nature All forms of life on Earth are connected into a **biosphere,** which means "living planet." Within the biosphere, living things are linked to one another and to the land, water, and air around them. Relationships between living things and where they live depend on the cycling of matter and the flow of energy.

Big idea Science as a Way of Knowing Science is not a list of facts. The job of science is to use observations, questions, and experiments to explain the natural world. Good scientific research finds rules and patterns that can explain and predict at least some events in nature.

Key Question What are the big ideas of biology?
Biology's big ideas are the cellular basis of life; information and heredity; matter and energy; growth, development, and reproduction; homeostasis; evolution; structure and function; unity and diversity of life; interdependence in nature; and science as a way of knowing.

Fields of Biology

Biology is made up of many overlapping fields that use different tools to study life from the level of molecules to the whole planet. Here's a peek into a few of the many branches of biology.

Global Ecology The world is affected by everything that living things do. Global ecological studies using satellites and huge computers are letting us learn about people's global impact, which affects all life on Earth.

Biotechnology This field is based on the ability to read, write, and edit the genetic code. We may soon learn to correct or replace genes that cause diseases. But biotechnology also raises a lot of ethical, legal, and social questions.

Building the Tree of Life Biologists have found about 1.8 million different kinds of living things. Scientists want to use computers to gather what is known about all organisms to put all living things into a single "Tree of All Life."

Biotechnology This plant biologist is analyzing genetically modified rice plants.

Evolution of Diseases An entomologist, a person who studies insects, and other researchers inspect mosquito traps in Florida. Mosquitoes can transmit diseases to people.

Genomics and Molecular Biology A molecular biologist is analyzing a DNA sequence.

Ecology and Evolution of Diseases Over time, viruses, bacteria, and other organisms that cause disease evolve so that they still infect people, even as we try to fight them. Understanding how germs change and react to their surroundings is important for keeping people healthy.

Genomics and Molecular Biology Scientists are looking at the DNA of many different living things. Scientists analyze the data with powerful computers to learn about growth, development, and the history of life on Earth.

Key Question How do different fields of biology differ in the way they study life?
Biology is made up of many overlapping fields that use different tools to study life from the level of molecules to the whole planet.

Performing Biological Investigations

Scientists use a common system of measurement and practice safety when doing studies.

Scientific Measurement Most scientists use the metric system when gathering data and doing experiments. The metric system is a system of measurement in which units are based on multiples of 10. A revised version of the metric system is called the International System of Units, or SI. The metric system is easy to use because it's based on multiples of 10.

Safety Scientists are trained to be safe when doing investigations. Whenever you work in your biology lab, you must follow safety rules, too. Careful preparation is the key to staying safe while doing activities. Before doing any activity, be sure you understand the safety rules. Also, read all the steps in the activity and make sure that you understand them.

The most important safety rule is to always follow your teacher's instructions. You are responsible for your own safety and that of your teacher and classmates. If you are handling live animals, you are responsible for their safety, too.

Key Question Why is the metric system important in science?
Most scientists use the metric system when collecting data and performing experiments.

Common Metric Units	
Length	**Mass**
1 meter (m) = 100 centimeters (cm) 1 meter = 1000 millimeters (mm) 1000 meters = 1 kilometer (km)	1 kilogram (kg) = 1000 grams (g) 1 gram = 1000 milligrams (mg) 1000 kilograms = 1 metric ton (t)
Volume	**Temperature**
1 liter (L) = 1000 milliliters (mL) 1 liter = 1000 cubic centimeters (cm³)	0°C = freezing point of water 100°C = boiling point of water

The Metric System Scientists usually use the metric system in their work. These penguins have been trained to hop onto the scale to be weighed.

✓CHECK Understanding

Apply Vocabulary
Use the highlighted words from the lesson to complete the sentence correctly.

1. All the information that an animal needs to live is stored in its _____.

2. The part of Earth where living things are found is called the _____.

3. All the reactions by which a living thing builds up and breaks down matter is its _____.

Critical Thinking
4. Applying Concepts Suppose you feel hungry, so you reach for an apple in a fruit bowl. How do stimuli both outside and inside of your body lead you to take the apple?

5. Relate Cause and Effect Suppose that two scientists are doing an experiment using dangerous chemicals. How might their safety be affected by not using a common measurement?

6. Write to Learn Write the answer to the third clue of the mystery.

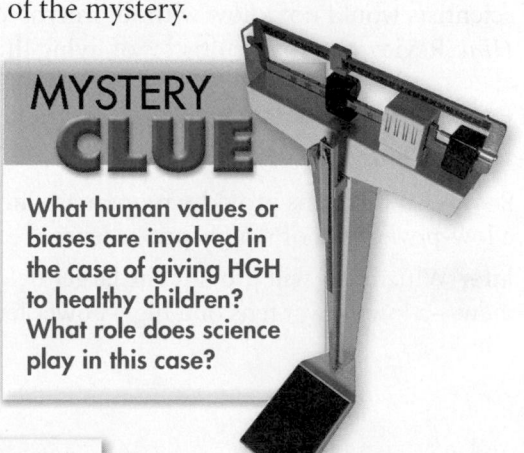

MYSTERY CLUE

What human values or biases are involved in the case of giving HGH to healthy children? What role does science play in this case?

BIOLOGY.com ⟩ Search (Lesson 1.3) **GO** • Lesson Assessment

 MD SPI **1.3.1** Use Equipment, **1.3.3** Safe Handling of Materials, **1.3.4** Learn New Scientific Equipment, **1.5.5** Create and Interpret Graphics, **1.6.1** Ratio and Proportion, **1.6.5** Judge Answers.

Pre-Lab: Using a Microscope to Estimate Size

Problem How can you use a microscope to estimate the size of an object?

Materials compound microscope, transparent 15-cm plastic ruler, prepared slide of plant root or stem, prepared slide of bacteria

Lab Manual Chapter 1 Lab

Skills Focus Observe, Measure, Calculate, Predict

Connect to the **Big idea** Science provides a way of knowing the world. The use of technology to gather data is a central part of modern science. In biology, the compound microscope is a vital tool. With a microscope, you can observe objects that are too tiny to see with the unaided eye. These objects include cells, which are the basis for all life.

In this lab, you will explore another important use of the microscope. You will use the microscope to estimate the size of cells.

Background Questions

a. Explain How did the invention of the microscope help scientists know the natural world?

b. Explain How can a microscope help a scientist use scientific methodology?

c. Infer List one important fact about life that scientists would not know without microscopes. *Hint:* Review the characteristics of living things.

Pre-Lab Questions

Preview the procedure in the lab manual.

1. Review Which lens provides more magnification— a low-power lens or a high-power lens?

2. Infer Which lens will provide the larger field of view—a low-power lens or a high-power lens?

3. Calculate Eight cells fit across a field of view of 160 μm. What is the width of each cell? **MATH**

4. Predict Which cell do you think will be larger, the plant cell or the bacterial cell? Give a reason for your answer.

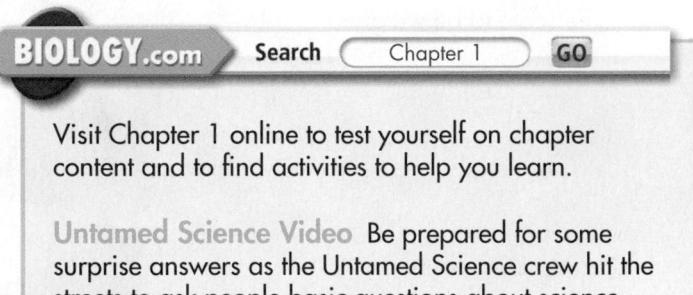

Visit Chapter 1 online to test yourself on chapter content and to find activities to help you learn.

Untamed Science Video Be prepared for some surprise answers as the Untamed Science crew hit the streets to ask people basic questions about science and biology.

Art in Motion Learn about the steps scientists use to solve problems. Change the variables, and watch what happens!

Art Review Review your understanding of the various steps of experimental processes.

InterActive Art Design your own experiment to test Redi's and Pasteur's spontaneous generation experiments.

1.1 What Is Science?

- The goals of science are to give natural explanations for natural events, to understand patterns, and to make predictions.

- Scientific methodology involves observing and asking questions, making inferences and forming hypotheses, doing controlled experiments, collecting and analyzing data, and drawing conclusions.

science (p. 4)
observation (p. 5)
hypothesis (p. 5)
controlled experiment (p. 6)
control group (p. 6)
data (p. 6)

1.2 Science in Context

- Curiosity, skepticism, open-mindedness, and creativity help scientists come up with new ideas.

- Publishing peer-reviewed papers in journals lets scientists share ideas and review each other's work.

- A scientific theory is a well-tested explanation that accounts for a lot of observations and hypotheses and that lets scientists make good predictions.

- Using science involves understanding its limitations and how it fits into society.

theory (p. 11)　　　bias (p. 12)

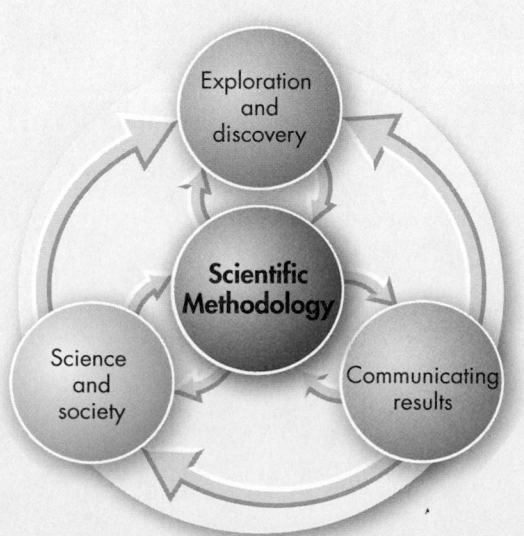

1.3 Studying Life

- Living things are made up of basic units called cells, are based on a universal genetic code, obtain and use materials and energy, grow and develop, reproduce, respond to their environment, maintain a stable internal environment, and change over time.

- Biology's big ideas are the cellular basis of life; information and heredity; matter and energy; growth, development, and reproduction; homeostasis; evolution; structure and function; unity and diversity of life; interdependence in nature; and science as a way of knowing.

- Biology is made up of many overlapping fields that use different tools to study life from the level of molecules to the whole planet.

- Most scientists use the metric system when collecting data and performing experiments.

biology (p. 13)
DNA (p. 14)
stimulus (p. 14)
homeostasis (p. 15)
metabolism (p. 15)
biosphere (p. 17)

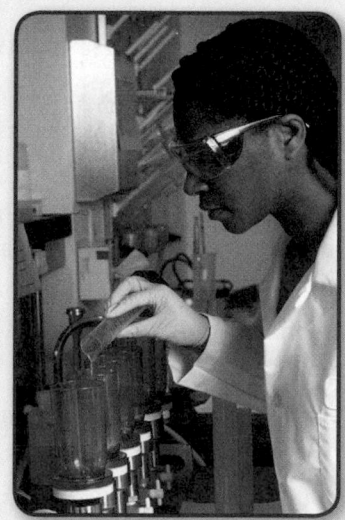

Science as a Way of Knowing

Write an answer to the question below.

Q: What role does science play in the study of life?

Constructed Response

Write an answer to each of the questions below. The answer to each question should be one or two paragraphs long. To help you begin, read the **Hints** below each of the questions.

1. **Why are questions so important in the scientific method?**

   Hint Scientific investigation begins with observation.

2. **Predict some problems that might happen if some scientists used SI units to measure objects and other scientists used inches.**

   Hint Scientists need to replicate each other's experiments.

   Hint The metric system is based on multiples of 10.

3. **Suppose that a classmate says that a wooden chair is alive. He says that the wood comes from a tree and that trees are alive. Explain why your classmate is right or wrong.**

   Hint If something does not have all the characteristics of living things, it is not alive.

Foundations for Learning Wrap-Up

Use the Inspired Shape Tree that you made when you started the chapter as a tool to help you learn the characteristics of living things.

Activity 1 Remove a branch from your Inspired Shape Tree. Write the characteristic on a sheet of paper. Then, write a brief description of what would happen to a tree if the tree did not have that characteristic. Continue until you have removed all the branches from your Inspired Shape Tree.

Activity 2 Remove the branches from your Inspired Shape Tree. Turn each branch over and write one or two words related to the characteristic on the front side of the branch. Mix up the branches. Have a partner read the words on one of the branches. Try to explain the characteristic of that branch. If your partner thinks that you explained the characteristic clearly, he or she will give you the branch to attach to your tree trunk. Continue until all the branches are picked. Take turns.

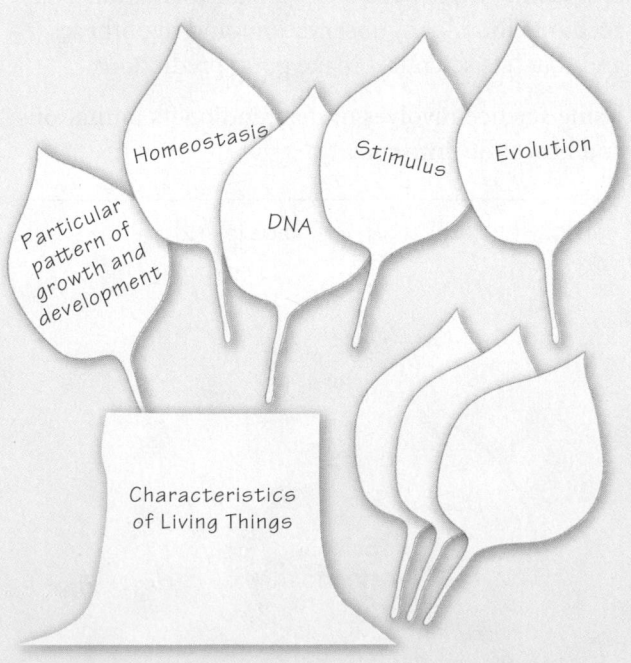

1.1 What Is Science?

Understand Key Concepts

1. Which of the following statements about a controlled experiment is true?
   a. All the variables must be kept the same.
   b. Only one variable is tested at a time.
   c. All hypotheses can be tested by setting up a controlled experiment.
   d. Controlled experiments cannot be performed on living things.

> **Test-Taking Tip**
>
> **Read All the Answer Choices** If you are not sure of the answer to a question, read all of the choices before picking one. Then begin to cross out incorrect answers. Read question 1 again. If all the variables are kept the same, the experiment would not show any changes in the dependent variable. So, **a** is not correct. Choices **c** and **d** are not correct. Some experiments cannot be tested with controlled experiments, and some controlled experiments can be done on living things. Therefore, **b** is the correct answer.

2. An inference is
   a. the same as an observation.
   b. a logical interpretation of an observation.
   c. a statement involving numbers.
   d. a way to avoid bias.

3. To be useful in science, a hypothesis must be
   a. measurable.   c. testable.
   b. observable.   d. correct.

Think Critically

4. **Apply Concepts** Suggest an experiment that would test the hypothesis that one food is better than another at speeding an animal's growth.

5. **Explain** Explain why you cannot draw a conclusion about the effect of one variable in an investigation when other key variables are not controlled.

1.2 Science in Context

Understand Key Concepts

6. A skeptical attitude in science
   a. prevents scientists from accepting new ideas.
   b. makes the acceptance of new ideas more likely.
   c. means a new idea will only be accepted if it is backed by evidence.
   d. is unimportant.

7. The purpose of peer review in science is to ensure that
   a. all scientific research is funded.
   b. the results of experiments are correct.
   c. all scientific results are published.
   d. published results meet standards set by the scientific community.

8. A scientific theory is
   a. the same as a hypothesis.
   b. a well-tested explanation that unifies a broad range of observations.
   c. the same as the conclusion of an experiment.
   d. the first step in a controlled experiment.

Think Critically

9. **Infer** How would having a scientific attitude help you in everyday activities—in trying to learn a new skill, for example?

10. **Apply Concepts** If you were one of the reviewers of a paper submitted for publication, what criteria would you use to determine whether or not the paper should be published?

1.3 Studying Life

Understand Key Concepts

11. The process in which two cells from different parents unite to produce the first cell of a new organism is called
    a. homeostasis.   c. asexual reproduction.
    b. development.   d. sexual reproduction.

Think Critically

12. Interpret Visuals Each of the following safety symbols might appear in a laboratory activity in this book. Describe what each symbol stands for. (**Hint:** Refer to Appendix B.)

1   2   3   4

Connecting Concepts

Use Science Graphs

The following graphs show the size of four different populations over a period of time. Use the graphs to answer questions 13–15.

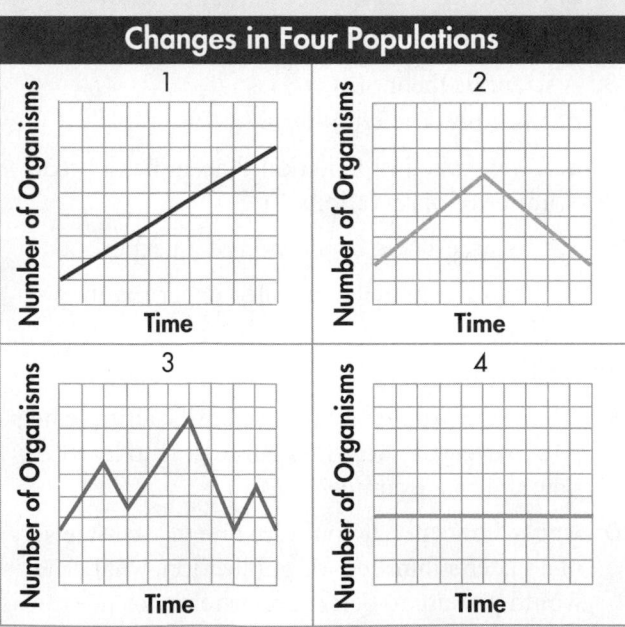

Changes in Four Populations

13. Analyze Data Write a sentence summarizing what each graph shows.

14. Interpret Graphs What information is missing from the graphs? (**Hint** Look at the *x* and *y* axes.)

15. Compare and Contrast Graphs of completely different events can look alike. Select one of the graphs and explain how the shape of the graph could apply to a different set of events.

solve the CHAPTER MYSTERY

HEIGHT BY PRESCRIPTION

Although scientific studies have not proved that HGH makes adults much taller, studies suggest that extra HGH may help some short kids grow taller sooner. David's doctor prescribed HGH so that David and his parents would not complain that HGH was not given as an option.

This situation is new. HGH used to be available only from cadavers, or dead bodies, and it was given only to people who had severe medical problems. Then, genetic engineering made it possible to make a lot of HGH—safe medicine for sick people.

Soon drug companies began trying to sell HGH to parents of healthy, short kids.

As David's case shows, science can change lives, but new scientific knowledge may raise more questions than they answer. Just because science makes something possible, does that mean it's right to do it? This question is difficult to answer. When thinking about how science should be applied, we must consider both its limitations and its context in society.

1. Relate Cause and Effect Search the Internet for the latest data on the use of HGH by healthy children.

2. Predict HGH was among the first products to come out of genetic engineering. Many more will follow. As products become available that could change other inherited traits, what challenges will society face?

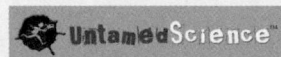 **Never Stop Exploring Your World.** Finding the solution to the HGH mystery is only the beginning. Take a video field trip with the ecogeeks of Untamed Science to see where this mystery leads.

Multiple Choice

1. To ensure that a scientific work is free of bias and meets standards set by the scientific community, a research group's work is peer reviewed by
   A other scientists.
   B the general public.
   C the researchers' friends.
   D lawmakers. SPI 1.1.1

2. The term for the chemical reactions in which organisms build up or break down materials is
   A biotechnology.
   B genetics.
   C metabolism.
   D genomics. CLG 3.4.2

3. Which of the following is NOT an attitude that scientists need?
   A bias
   B skepticism
   C creativity
   D open-mindedness SPI 1.1.1

4. A bird-watcher sees an unusual bird at a feeder. He takes careful notes on the bird's color, shape, and other physical features and then goes to a reference book to see if he can identify the species. What part of scientific thinking is most apparent in this situation?
   A observation
   B inference
   C hypothesis formation
   D controlled experimentation SPI 1.2.6

5. Unlike sexual reproduction, asexual reproduction involves
   A two cells. C one parent.
   B two parents. D one nonliving thing.
   CLG 3.2.1

6. One meter is equal to
   A 1000 millimeters.
   B 1 millimeter.
   C 10 kilometers.
   D 1 milliliter. SPI 1.6.3

Questions 7–8

Once a month, a pet owner recorded the mass of her puppy in a table. When the puppy was 3 months old, she started to feed it a "special puppy food" she saw advertised on TV.

Change in a Puppy's Mass Over Time		
Age (months)	Mass at Start of Month (kg)	Change in Mass per Month (kg)
2	5	–
3	8	+3
4	13	+5

7. According to the table, which statement is true?
   A The puppy's mass increased at the same rate for each month shown.
   B The puppy's mass was less than 5 kg at the start of the new diet.
   C The puppy gained 5 kg between age 3 and 4 months.
   D The puppy gained 13 kg as a result of the new diet. SPI 1.4.2

8. All of the following statements about the pet owner's study are true EXCEPT
   A The owner used the metric system.
   B The owner recorded data.
   C The owner could graph the data.
   D The owner conducted a controlled experiment. SPI 1.2.6

Open-Ended Response

9. Explain how a controlled experiment works.
   SPI 1.2.6

If You Have Trouble With . . .								
Question	1	2	3	4	5	6	7	8	9
See Lesson	1.2	1.3	1.2	1.1	1.3	1.3	1.1	1.1	1.1

2 The Chemistry of Life

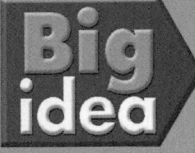

Big idea: Matter and Energy

Q: What are the basic chemical principles that affect living things?

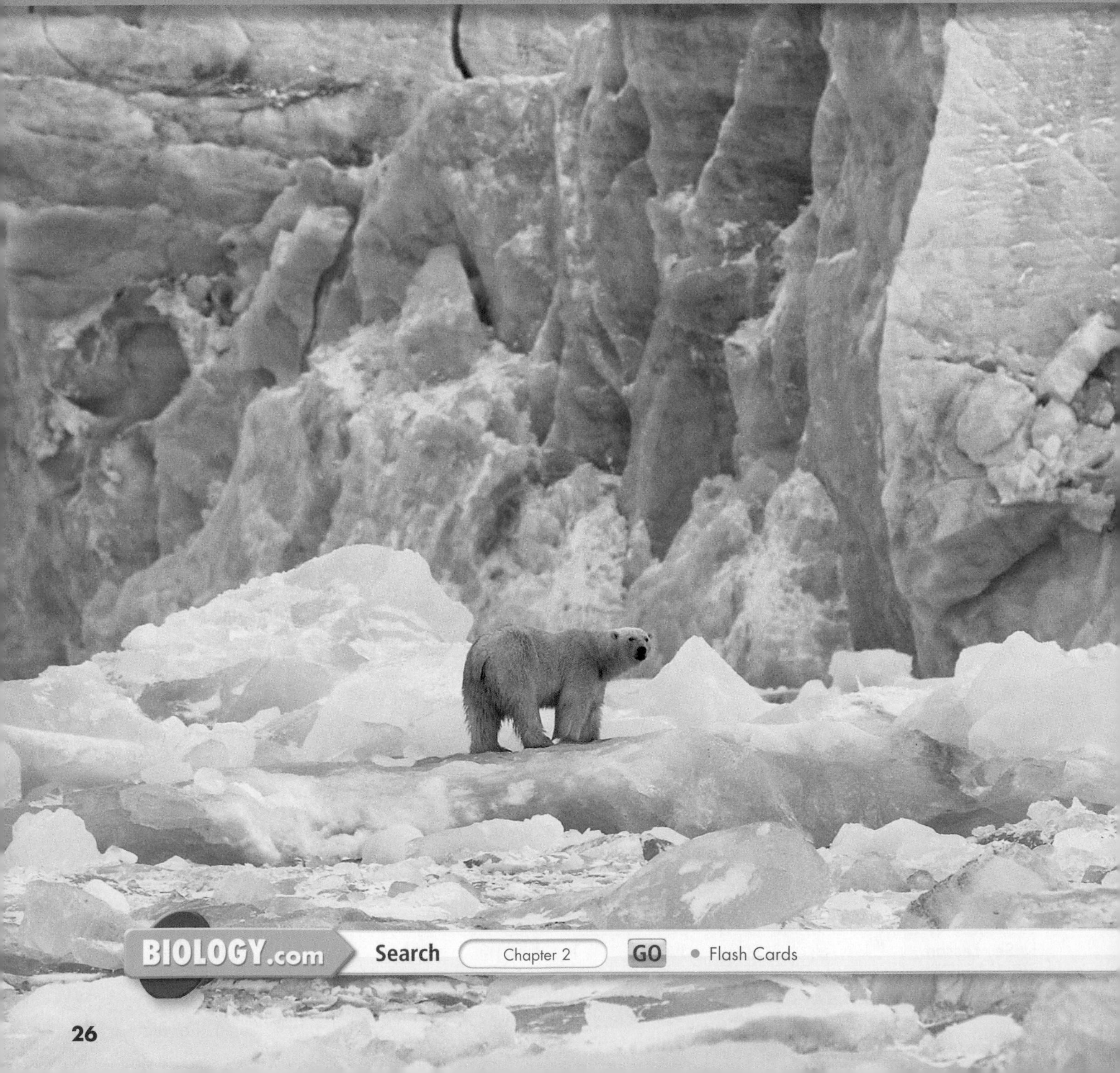

BIOLOGY.com Search Chapter 2 GO • Flash Cards

CHAPTER MYSTERY

THE GHOSTLY FISH

Most fish have red blood, just like other vertebrates. Red blood cells carry oxygen, a gas needed for life. The cell's red color comes from an oxygen-binding protein called hemoglobin (HEE muh gloh bin).

But some fish don't have red blood cells. Their blood is clear. Because they live in cold antarctic waters and look ghostly, they are called "ice fish." How do ice fish live without red blood cells?

Read for Mystery Clues As you read this chapter, look for clues to help you explain the ice fish's clear blood. Think about the chemistry that might be involved. Then, solve the mystery.

MD **MARYLAND VOLUNTARY STATE CURRICULUM**

Biology Indicators/Core Learning Goals (CLG) 3.1.1, 3.1.2, 3.1.3, 3.2.2. **Skills and Process Indicators (SPI)** 1.2.4, 1.3.1, 1.3.2, 1.3.3, 1.4.1, 1.4.6, 1.4.8, 1.4.9, 1.5.2, 1.5.8, 1.5.9, 1.6.3, 1.7.1. See lessons for details.

Polar bears live on the Svalbard islands of Norway. Living conditions on the islands are hard. The water is locked in ice. But some living things can still get the matter and energy that they need to survive.

FOUNDATIONS for Learning

Vocabulary words are important for learning the key ideas of this chapter. Before you read this chapter, make a vocabulary quiz sheet. Fold a sheet of paper into three equal parts lengthwise. As you read the chapter, write the vocabulary words in the first column. Write the definition for each word in the second column next to the word. Then, cut the third column to make tabs. The tabs will cover up the definitions. At the end of the chapter are two activities that use the vocabulary quiz sheet to answer the question: What are the basic chemical principles that affect living things?

Chapter 2	Definition	
Atom	The basic unit of matter.	
Electron	Negatively charged particle	
Element		
Isotope		
Compound		
Ionic Bond		
Covalent Bond		

• Untamed Science Video   • Chapter Mystery

2.1 The Nature of Matter

MD SPI 1.4.8 Use Models, 1.5.8 Compare.

Key Questions

🔑 **What three particles make up atoms?**

🔑 **How are all of the isotopes of an element similar?**

🔑 **How do compounds differ from the elements in them?**

🔑 **What are the main kinds of chemical bonds?**

BUILD Understanding

Previewing Visuals Before you read the chapter, study the carbon atom figure below. Learn where in an atom you can find protons, neutrons, and electrons.

In Your Workbook Go to your workbook for a way to preview visuals.

Atoms

Nearly 2500 years ago, the Greek philosopher Democritus asked a simple question: If you break a stick of chalk in half, are both parts still chalk? The answer, of course, is yes. What happens if you break it in half again and again? Can you keep breaking it without changing it into something else? Democritus thought that there had to be a limit, and he was right. He called the smallest piece the atom. The **atom** is the basic unit of matter. The study of chemistry begins with atoms.

Atoms are very small. Placed side by side, 100 million atoms would make a row only about as wide as your little finger! Although they are small, atoms are made up of even smaller particles called protons, neutrons, and electrons.

Protons and Neutrons Protons and neutrons have about the same mass. However, protons are positively charged particles (+) and neutrons carry no charge at all. Strong forces hold protons and neutrons together to form the nucleus. The **nucleus** is the center of the atom.

Electrons An **electron** is a negatively charged particle (–). An electron has only 1/1840 the mass of a proton. Electrons are always moving around the nucleus. They are attracted to the positively charged nucleus. But electrons stay outside the nucleus because of the energy of their motion. Atoms have equal numbers of electrons and protons. So, the positive and negative charges balance and atoms have no charge.

🔑 **Key Question** What three particles make up atoms?
Protons, neutrons, and electrons are the particles that make up atoms.

A Carbon Atom A carbon atom has 6 protons and 6 electrons, in addition to the neutrons in its nucleus. Like all atoms, it has no charge, since the number of protons and electrons is equal.

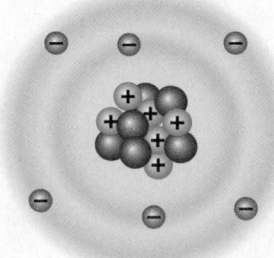

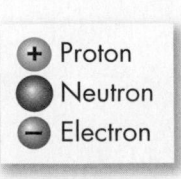

⊕ Proton
⬤ Neutron
⊖ Electron

Elements and Isotopes

An **element** is a pure substance that is made up of only one kind of atom. Each element has a one- or two-letter symbol. For example, the symbol for carbon is C, and the symbol for sodium is Na. The number of protons in the atom of an element is the element's atomic number. Carbon's atomic number is 6 because carbon atoms have 6 protons. Carbon atoms also have 6 electrons.

Isotopes Atoms of an element may have different numbers of neutrons. For example, all atoms of carbon have 6 protons, but each atom may have 6, 7, or 8 neutrons. Atoms of the same element that have different numbers of neutrons are **isotopes** (EYE suh tohps). The total number of protons and neutrons in an atom is the atom's mass number. Isotopes are named using their mass numbers. A carbon atom with 6 neutrons has a mass number of 12 and is called carbon-12. The table below shows the isotopes of carbon.

Radioactive Isotopes Some isotopes are radioactive, which means that the nucleus of the atom breaks down at a constant rate over time. When these isotopes break down, they give off energy or particles called radiation. Radiation can be dangerous, but radioactive isotopes have important uses.

Radioactive isotopes can help determine the ages of rocks and fossils. Radiation can help find and treat cancer and kill bacteria. Radioactive isotopes can also serve as labels or "tracers" to follow how substances move in organisms.

 **Key Question** How are all of the isotopes of an element similar?

Isotopes of an element all have the same number of protons.

Isotopes of Carbon

Isotope	Number of Protons	Number of Electrons	Number of Neutrons
Carbon–12 (nonradioactive)	6	6	6
Carbon–13 (nonradioactive)	6	6	7
Carbon–14 (radioactive)	6	6	8

Carbon Isotopes Isotopes of carbon have the same number of protons but different numbers of neutrons. Isotopes are named by their mass number, which is the total number of protons and neutrons. So, an isotope that has 6 protons and 6 neutrons is called carbon-12.

Chemical Compounds

Most elements are not found as single atoms. Instead, they are joined with other elements in compounds. A **compound** is a substance formed by the chemical combination of two or more elements in definite amounts. The number of each element in a compound can be shown by chemical formulas. For example, water has 2 atoms of hydrogen and 1 atom of oxygen. So, the chemical formula for water is H_2O.

The physical and chemical properties of a compound are different from the properties of the elements that make up the compound. For example, hydrogen and oxygen are gases at room temperature. But they can combine explosively to form liquid water.

🔑 **Key Question** How do compounds differ from the elements in them?
Compounds have chemical and physical properties that are different from the properties of the elements in them.

Chemical Bonds

The atoms in compounds are held together by chemical bonds. The two main kinds of chemical bonds are ionic and covalent bonds.

Ionic Bonds An **ionic bond** is formed when one or more electrons are moved, or transferred, from one atom to another. An atom that loses electrons becomes positively charged. An atom that gains electrons has a negative charge. These positively and negatively charged atoms are known as ions. Oppositely charged ions are attracted to each other.

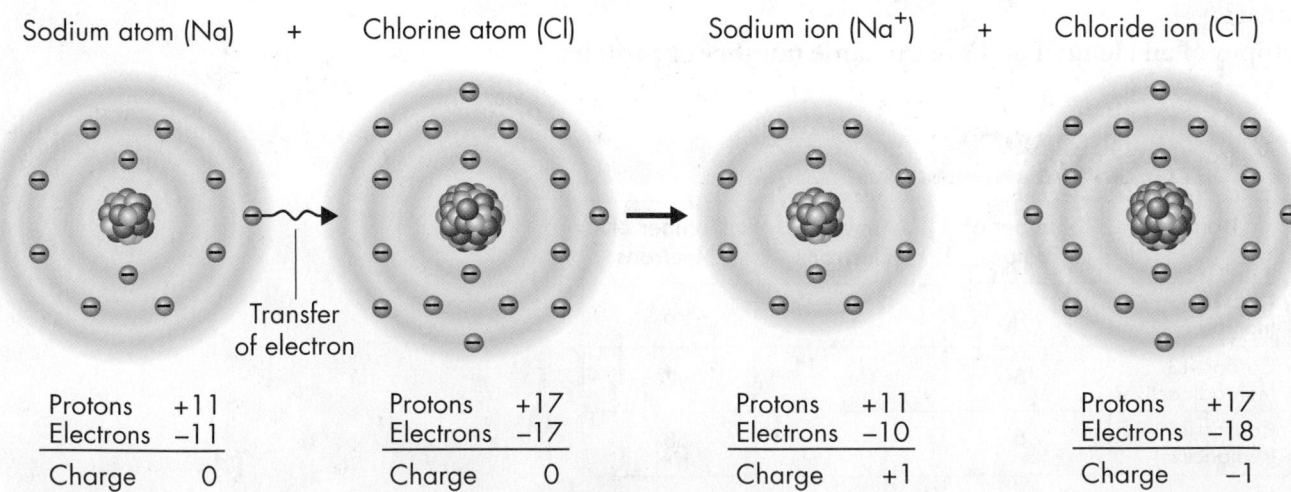

| Sodium atom (Na) | Chlorine atom (Cl) | Sodium ion (Na⁺) | Chloride ion (Cl⁻) |

Protons	+11	Protons	+17	Protons	+11	Protons	+17
Electrons	–11	Electrons	–17	Electrons	–10	Electrons	–18
Charge	0	Charge	0	Charge	+1	Charge	–1

Ionic Bonding Table salt is made up of sodium ions and chloride ions. A sodium ion (Na^+) forms when a sodium atom loses 1 electron. A chloride ion (Cl^-) forms when a chlorine atom gains 1 electron. These oppositely charged ions attract each other and form an ionic bond.

Covalent Bonds Sometimes electrons are shared by atoms instead of being moved from one atom to another. What does it mean to share electrons? It means that the electrons travel around the nuclei of both atoms, forming a **covalent bond.** There are different types of covalent bonds. When atoms share 2 electrons, the bond is a single covalent bond. If atoms share 4 electrons, then the bond is a double bond. Atoms can also share 6 electrons and form a triple bond.

The structure that results when atoms are joined together by covalent bonds is called a molecule. The **molecule** is the smallest unit of most compounds. The bonds in a water molecule are covalent bonds. Each hydrogen atom in a water molecule is joined to the oxygen atom by a single covalent bond. Oxygen can also form double bonds. For example, the oxygen molecules that you breathe are 2 oxygen atoms joined by a double bond.

🔑 **Key Question** What are the main kinds of chemical bonds?
The main kinds of chemical bonds are ionic bonds and covalent bonds.

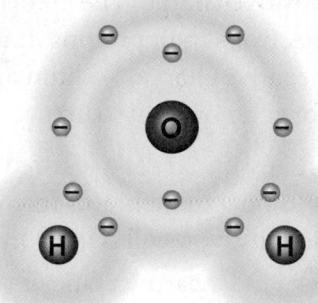

Covalent Bonding In a water molecule, each hydrogen atom shares 2 electrons with the oxygen atom. So, each hydrogen atom is joined to the oxygen atom by a covalent bond.

Water molecule (H_2O)

CHECK Understanding

Apply Vocabulary
Use the highlighted words from the lesson to complete each sentence correctly.

1. A(n) _____ is the basic unit of matter.

2. Sodium and chlorine form a(n) _____ when an electron moves from the sodium atom to the chlorine atom.

3. _____ are negatively charged and move around the nucleus of an atom.

Critical Thinking

4. Infer An atom of calcium has 20 protons. How many electrons does it have?

5. Compare and Contrast Compare carbon-12 and carbon-14 atoms. How are they the same, and how are they different?

6. Apply Concepts A potassium atom can easily lose 1 electron. What kind of bond will potassium form with chlorine?

7. Write to Learn Answer the first clue of the mystery. Write two or three sentences that include the words *atom* and *electron*.

MYSTERY CLUE

Fish do not break water molecules apart to get oxygen. Instead, they use oxygen gas that is dissolved in the water. How are the atoms in an oxygen molecule joined together? (**Hint:** See above.)

Model an Ionic Compound

Ionic bonds are formed when electrons transfer from one atom to another. Sodium chloride, or table salt, is an ionic compound. To form table salt, sodium "gives" an electron to chlorine. The sodium atom then has more protons than electrons. It is an ion with a positive charge. The chlorine atom has more electrons than protons. It is an ion with a negative charge. Sodium and chloride ions form an orderly structure called a crystal.

In Lesson 2.1, you learned about ionic bonds and how these bonds form in table salt. In this activity, you will build a model of table salt.

❶ Find a partner. One of you will make a model of a sodium atom, and the other will make a model of a chlorine atom.

❷ Use the table below to find the correct number of electrons in your atom. Use popcorn kernels to represent the electrons in your atom.

❸ Write the number of protons in your atom in the center of an index card and draw a circle around this number. This circle is the nucleus of your atom.

❹ Arrange the correct number of electrons (popcorn kernels) on the index card around the nucleus.

❺ Move your atom close to your partner's atom. Use the two atom models to form the ionic compound sodium chloride—table salt. (Form the ionic compound by moving an electron from one atom to the other.)

❻ In table salt, the closely packed sodium and chloride ions form an orderly structure called a crystal. Using your compound models, work in a small group to model a sodium chloride crystal.

Analyze and Conclude

1. Relate Cause and Effect Describe how the popcorn kernels (electrons) moved as you formed the ionic bond. What electrical charges resulted from the movement?

2. Use Models How did you arrange the ions in the crystal model? Why did you choose this arrangement?

In Your Workbook Go to your workbook for more help with this activity.

Isotope	Number of Protons	Number of Electrons	Number of Neutrons
Sodium-23	11	11	12
Chrorline-35	17	17	18

2.2 Properties of Water

MD CLG 3.1.1 Chemical Substances and Macromolecules, 3.1.2 Homeostasis, 3.1.3 Matter and Energy, 3.2.2 Changes in Metabolic Activity. SPI 1.5.8 Compare, 1.6.3 Use Scientific Notation.

The Water Molecule

Water is a compound found over most of Earth's surface. In fact, just finding liquid water on a planet tells scientists that there could be life on that planet. What properties of water make it so important?

A Polar Molecule Like other molecules, water (H_2O) is neutral. The positive charges on its 10 protons balance out the negative charges on its 10 electrons. But an oxygen atom has 8 protons whereas a hydrogen atom has only 1. So, the electrons in a water molecule are pulled more toward the oxygen atom. They spend more time near the oxygen atom than near the hydrogen atoms. The oxygen atom is found on one end of the water molecule and the hydrogen atoms are on the other. As a result, the oxygen end of the molecule has a slight negative charge and the hydrogen end has a slight positive charge.

A molecule in which the charges are unevenly spread out is said to be "polar." The charges on a polar molecule are written in parentheses, ($-$) or ($+$), to show that they are weaker than the charges on ions such as Na^+ and Cl^-.

Hydrogen Bonds Because of their partial positive and negative charges, polar molecules such as water can attract each other. The pull between a partially positive hydrogen atom on one molecule and a partially negative oxygen atom on another is an example of a hydrogen bond. Hydrogen bonds form between the hydrogen atoms and oxygen atoms of different water molecules. Because water is a polar molecule, it can form many hydrogen bonds. Hydrogen bonds are not as strong as covalent or ionic bonds. But the hydrogen bonds do give water some special properties.

Key Questions

🔑 **How does the structure of water lead to its special properties?**

🔑 **How does water's polarity affect its properties as a solvent?**

🔑 **Why is it important for cells to buffer solutions against rapid changes in pH?**

BUILD Understanding

Venn Diagram As you read, draw a Venn diagram to compare solutions and suspensions. The diagram should show similarities and differences between the two.

In Your Workbook Go to your workbook to learn more about making a Venn diagram. Complete the Venn diagram for Lesson 2.2.

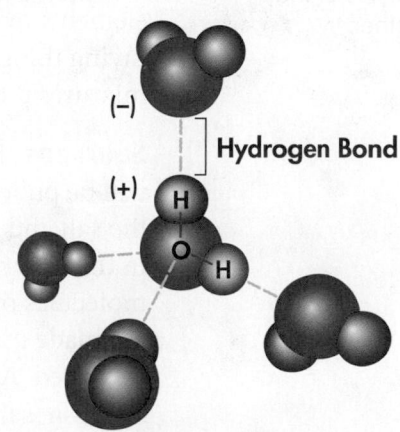

Hydrogen Bonding The molecules shown are water molecules. The red atoms are oxygen, and the blue atoms are hydrogen. The dashed lines show the hydrogen bonds that can form between water molecules.

Adhesion Adhesion between the molecules in the glass and the molecules in the water causes water to stick to the sides of this glass tube. The water climbs up the sides, and the water dips down in the middle. This curved water surface is called a meniscus.

BUILD
Vocabulary

cohesion
the attraction between molecules of the same substance

adhesion
the force of attraction between different kinds of molecules

solution
a type of mixture in which all the components are evenly distributed

suspension
a mixture of water and nondissolved material

acid
a compound that releases hydrogen ions (H^+) in solution; a solution with a pH of less than 7

base
a compound that releases hydroxide ions (OH^-) in solution; a solution with a pH of more than 7

buffer
a compound that prevents sharp, sudden changes in pH

🔧 PREFIXES

The prefix *co-* means "together." Cohesion pulls molecules of the same substance together.

▶ *Cohesion* Because a water molecule can have as many as four hydrogen bonds at the same time, water is very cohesive. **Cohesion** (koh HEE zhun) is an attraction between molecules of the same substance. Cohesion pulls water molecules together. It causes surface tension, which enables some insects to walk on water's surface.

▶ *Adhesion* On the other hand, **adhesion** (ad HEE zhun) is an attraction between molecules of different substances. Adhesion between water and glass makes the surface of water in a tube curve upward along the sides of the tube. Adhesion also makes water rise in a narrow tube. This effect is called capillary action. Capillary action helps draw water out of the roots of a plant and up into its stems and leaves.

▶ *Heat Capacity* Another special property of water is its high heat capacity. Heat capacity is the amount of heat energy needed to increase a substance's temperature. In order for the temperature of water to rise, the molecules must move faster. The hydrogen bonds make it hard for water molecules to move faster. This property allows large bodies of water like oceans and lakes to absorb large amounts of energy without large changes in temperature.

🗝 **Key Question** How does the structure of water lead to its special properties?
Water is polar, so it can form hydrogen bonds. These bonds give water special properties, including cohesion, adhesion, and a high heat capacity.

Solutions and Suspensions

Water is often found as part of a mixture. A mixture is made up of elements or compounds that are combined but not bonded together. Living things are partly made up of water mixtures. Two kinds of mixtures that are made with water are solutions and suspensions.

Solutions If you put table salt in water, the ions on the salt's surface will be pulled toward the polar water molecules. Ions break away from the salt and are surrounded by water molecules. The ions spread out in the water to make a solution. A **solution** is a mixture in which the molecules of the mixed substances are evenly spread out. Solutions are made up of one or more solutes in a solvent. A solute is what is dissolved. A solvent is what does the dissolving. So, in a saltwater solution, salt is the solute and water is the solvent. Because water is polar, it can dissolve ionic compounds and other polar molecules.

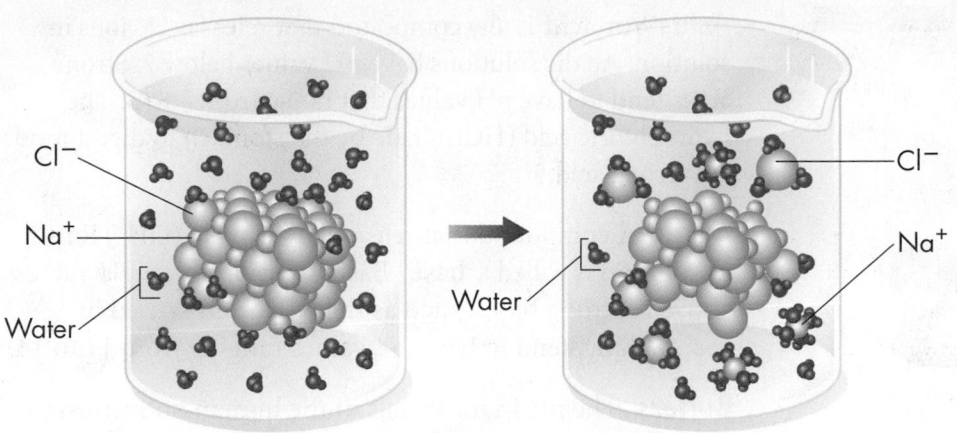

A Salt Solution An ionic compound, such as salt, dissolves in water. The water molecules surround the ions and pull them apart.

Suspensions Some things do not dissolve in water. But they may break into pieces so small that they do not settle out. Mixtures of water and nondissolved material that do not settle out are **suspensions.** Some important fluids in living things are both solutions and suspensions. Blood is mostly water. The water in the blood contains many dissolved compounds. But blood also has cells and other particles in suspension.

🔑 **Key Question** How does water's polarity affect its properties as a solvent?
Because water is polar, it can dissolve ionic compounds and other polar molecules.

Acids, Bases, and pH

Water molecules sometimes break apart to form ions. This reaction can be shown by a chemical equation. The double arrows show that the reaction can happen in either direction.

$$H_2O \rightleftharpoons H^+ + OH^-$$

$$\text{water} \rightleftharpoons \text{hydrogen ion} + \text{hydroxide ion}$$

The pH Scale Chemists use a measurement system called the pH scale to show the concentration of H^+ ions in solution. The pH scale ranges from 0 to 14. At a pH of 7, the concentration of H^+ ions and OH^- ions is equal. Pure water has a pH of 7. Solutions that have a pH below 7 are acidic. They have more H^+ ions than OH^- ions. The lower the pH is, the greater the acidity is. Solutions that have a pH above 7 are basic. They have more OH^- ions than H^+ ions. The higher the pH is, the more basic the solution is.

The pH Scale The concentration of H^+ ions determines whether a solution is acidic or basic.

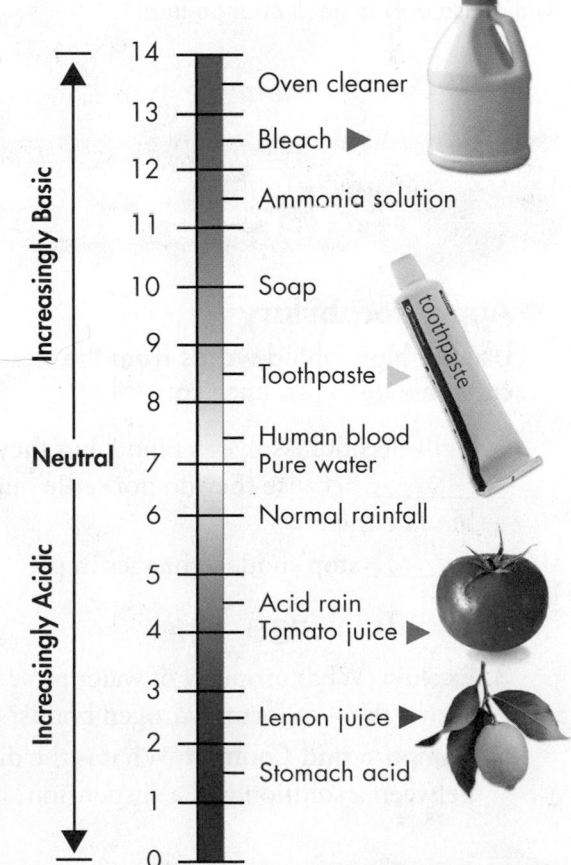

Increasingly Basic

Neutral

Increasingly Acidic

14	Oven cleaner
13	Bleach ▶
12	Ammonia solution
11	
10	Soap
9	
8	Toothpaste ▶
7	Human blood / Pure water
6	Normal rainfall
5	
4	Acid rain / Tomato juice ▶
3	
2	Lemon juice ▶
1	Stomach acid
0	

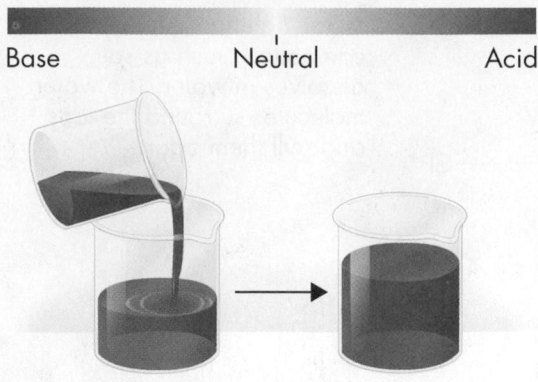

Base · Neutral · Acid

Unbuffered base + acid = acidic pH

Buffered base + acid = basic pH

Buffers Adding an acid to a solution without a buffer causes the pH of the solution to drop. But if the solution has a buffer, adding an acid will cause only a small change in pH.

Acids An **acid** is any compound that releases H⁺ ions in solution. Acidic solutions have pH values below 7. Strong acids tend to have pH values that range from 1 to 3. The hydrochloric acid (HCl) made by the stomach to digest food is a strong acid.

Bases A compound that releases hydroxide (OH⁻) ions in solution is called a **base.** Basic solutions have pH values above 7. Strong bases, such as the lye (NaOH) used in soapmaking, tend to have pH values ranging from 11 to 14.

Buffers The pH in most cells in the human body must stay between 6.5 and 7.5. If the pH is lower or higher, it will affect the chemical reactions that take place in cells. So, keeping pH from changing is an important part of homeostasis (hoh mee oh STAY sis). Homeostasis is the process of keeping a stable internal environment inside living things. One way to control pH is with buffers. **Buffers** are weak acids or bases that can react with strong acids or bases to stop sharp, sudden changes in pH. Blood has a normal pH of 7.4. Sudden changes in blood pH are usually stopped by buffers. Buffers play an important role in keeping homeostasis in living things.

🔑 **Key Question** Why is it important for cells to buffer solutions against rapid changes in pH?
Buffers play an important role in keeping homeostasis in living things.

CHECK Understanding

Apply Vocabulary
Use the highlighted words from the lesson to complete each sentence correctly.

1. Cells do not dissolve in blood, but they form a _____ because they do not settle out of the blood either.

2. _____ stop sudden changes in pH.

Critical Thinking

3. Explain What property of water molecules allows them to form hydrogen bonds?

4. Compare and Contrast What is the difference between a solution and a suspension?

5. Infer During exercise many chemical changes happen in the body, including a drop in blood pH, which can be very serious. How is the body able to deal with such changes?

6. Write to Learn Answer the second clue of the mystery.

MYSTERY CLUE

The ability of a gas to dissolve increases as temperatures decrease. How might the temperature of antarctic water affect the amount of dissolved oxygen available for ice fish? **(Hint:** See p. 34.)

2.3 Carbon Compounds

MD CLG 3.1.1 Chemical Substances and Macromolecules.

The Chemistry of Carbon

The chemistry of carbon is very important for living things. In fact, a whole branch of chemistry is set aside just to study carbon compounds. Why is carbon so interesting? There are two reasons. First, carbon atoms have four electrons available for bonding. These four electrons allow carbon atoms to form as many as four strong covalent bonds. Carbon can bond with many elements, including hydrogen, oxygen, phosphorus, sulfur, and nitrogen, to form the molecules of living things. Organisms are made up of molecules that consist of carbon and these other elements.

The second reason carbon compounds are so interesting is that carbon atoms can bond with each other. Bonding between carbon atoms gives carbon the ability to form chains that can be unlimited in length. These carbon-carbon bonds can be single, double, or triple covalent bonds. Chains of carbon atoms can even close up on themselves to form rings. Carbon can form millions of different large and complex structures. No other element comes close to matching carbon's ability to make so many different compounds.

Key Question What elements does carbon bond with to make up life's molecules? **Carbon bonds with hydrogen, oxygen, phosphorus, sulfur, and nitrogen to form life's molecules.**

Key Questions

What elements does carbon bond with to make up the molecules of living things?

What are the functions of each of the four groups of macromolecules?

BUILD Understanding

Compare/Contrast Table As you read, make a table that compares and contrasts the four groups of macromolecules.

In Your Workbook Go to your workbook to learn more about making a compare/contrast table. Fill out the compare/contrast table for Lesson 2.3.

Isooctane   Benzene   Butadiene   Acetylene   Methane

Carbon Structures Carbon can form single, double, or triple bonds with other carbon atoms. Each line between atoms in a molecular structure is one covalent bond. Carbon atoms can form straight chains, rings, or branched chains.

carbohydrate
a compound made up of carbon, hydrogen, and oxygen atoms; a type of nutrient that is the main source of energy for the body

lipid
a macromolecule made mostly from carbon and hydrogen atoms; includes fats, oils, and waxes

🔩 WORD ORIGINS _____

Carbohydrate is a combination of the prefix *carbo-*, which means "carbon," and the word *hydrate*, which means "water."

Macromolecules

Many of the carbon compounds in living cells are so large that they are known as macromolecules or "giant molecules." Macromolecules are made from thousands or even hundreds of thousands of smaller molecules. The smaller units, or monomers, join together to form polymers (PAHL uh murz). The monomers in a polymer may be the same, like links in a chain. Or, the monomers may be different, like different colored beads in a necklace.

Scientists sort the macromolecules found in living things into groups based on their chemical makeup. The four major groups of macromolecules found in living things are carbohydrates, lipids, nucleic acids, and proteins.

Carbohydrates Compounds made up of carbon, hydrogen, and oxygen atoms are called **carbohydrates.** There are usually twice as many hydrogen atoms as carbon or oxygen atoms in these molecules. Living things use carbohydrates as their main source of energy. Carbohydrates give plants, some animals, and other organisms structure. Sugars are carbohydrates. The breakdown of sugars, such as glucose, supplies energy for cell activities. Many living things store extra sugar as a carbohydrate called starch.

▶ *Simple Sugars* Single sugar molecules are called both monosaccharides (mahn oh SAK uh rydz) and simple sugars. Besides glucose, simple sugars include galactose, which is found in milk, and fructose, which is found in many fruits. Table sugar, sucrose, is made up of glucose and fructose. Since sucrose is made of two sugars it is called a disaccharide.

🗝 **Key Question** What are the functions of carbohydrates?
Carbohydrates provide energy and structural support for living things.

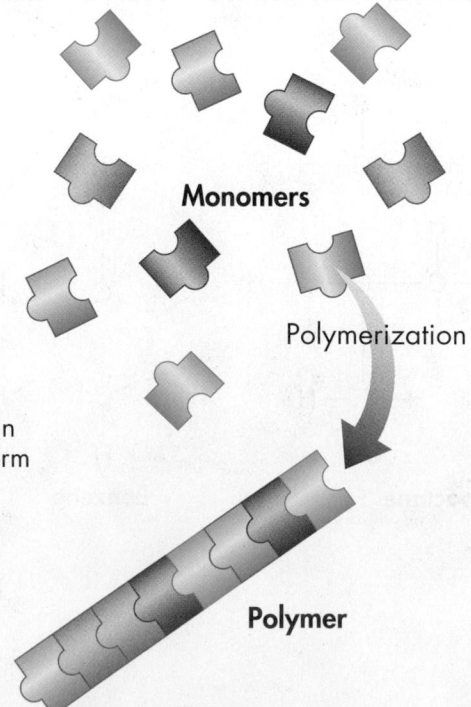

Monomers

Polymerization

Polymer

Polymerization Most macromolecules are formed by a process known as polymerization (pah lih mur ih ZAY shun). In this process, monomers join together to form polymers. Polymers can get very large.

Carbohydrates Sugars and starches are carbohydrates. Starches form when sugars join together in long chains.

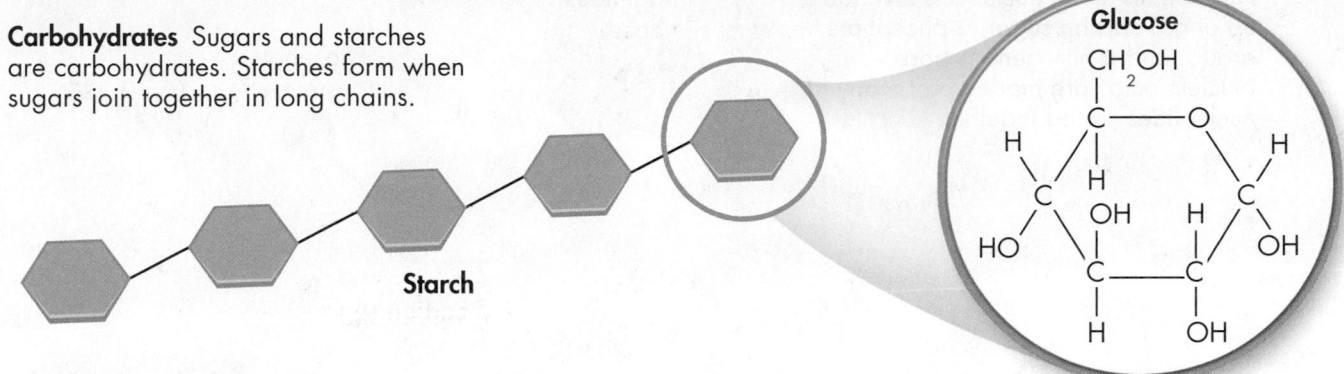

Starch

Glucose

▶ *Complex Carbohydrates* The large macromolecules formed when simple sugars join together are called complex carbohydrates. Many animals store extra sugar in a complex carbohydrate called glycogen. When the amount of glucose in your blood runs low, glycogen is broken down into glucose, which then goes into the blood. The glycogen stored in your muscles gives energy to muscles so that you can move.

Plants use a different complex carbohydrate, called starch, to store extra sugar. Plants also make another complex carbohydrate called cellulose. Cellulose gives plants their strength and rigidity. Cellulose is the major part of wood and paper, so you are looking at cellulose as you read these words!

Lipids Fats, oils, and waxes are common lipids. **Lipids** are macromolecules that generally do not dissolve in water and are made mostly of carbon and hydrogen atoms. Some lipids store energy. Others form biological membranes, and some produce waterproof coverings on cells and tissues.

Many lipids are formed when a glycerol molecule joins with compounds called fatty acids. If each carbon atom in a lipid's fatty acids is joined to other carbon atoms by only single bonds, the lipid is called saturated. This means that the fatty acid has the most hydrogen atoms it can have. If there is at least one carbon-carbon double bond in a fatty acid, the fatty acid is called unsaturated. You have probably seen the terms *saturated* and *unsaturated* on food labels. Lipids that have unsaturated fatty acids are liquid at room temperature. Olive oil is one such lipid.

🔑 **Key Question** What are the functions of lipids? **Lipids are used to store energy and are parts of membranes and waterproof coverings.**

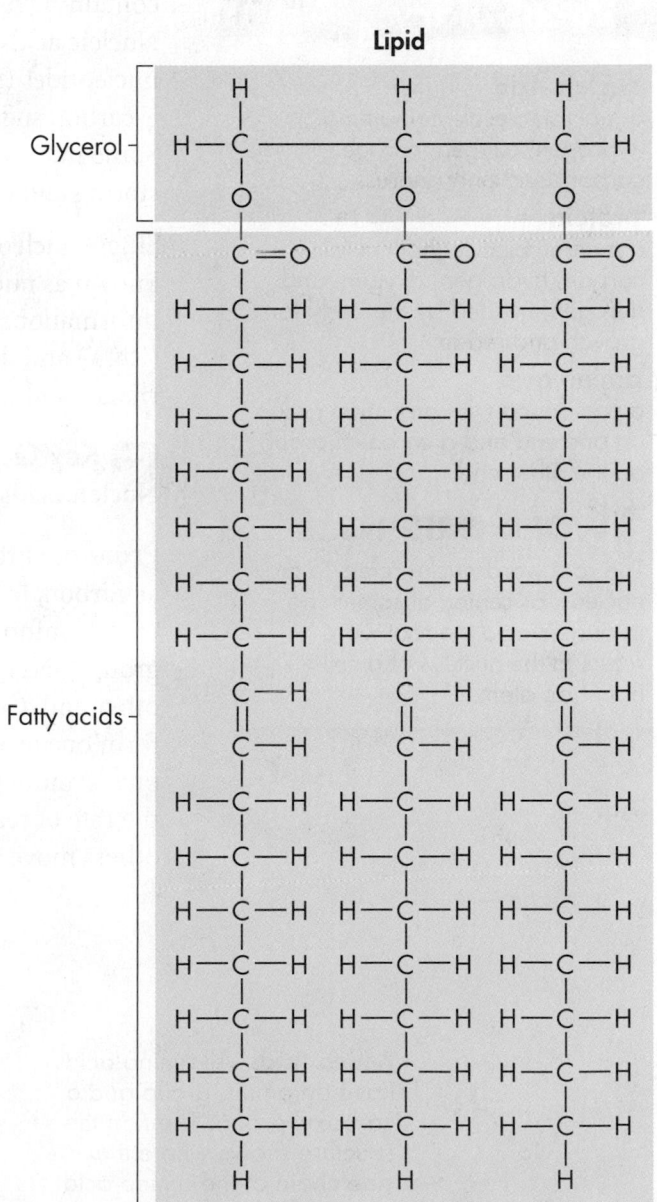

Lipid

Lipids Lipids are made up of a glycerol molecule and fatty acids.

Nucleotides Each nucleotide is made up of a 5-carbon sugar, a phosphate group, and a nitrogenous base. Nucleic acids are made up of many nucleotides joined together.

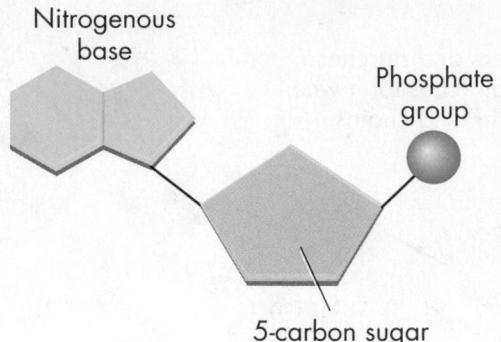

Nitrogenous base

Phosphate group

5-carbon sugar

BUILD
Vocabulary

nucleic acid
a macromolecule containing hydrogen, oxygen, nitrogen, carbon, and phosphorus

protein
a macromolecule that contains carbon, hydrogen, oxygen, and nitrogen; needed by the body for growth and repair

amino acid
a compound with an amino group on one end and a carboxyl group on the other end

✵ WORD ORIGINS

The root word *nucle-* refers to a nucleus, or center, of something. In *nucleic acid* the root word refers to the nucleus of a cell, not of an atom.

Nucleic Acids **Nucleic** (noo KLEE ik) **acids** are macromolecules containing hydrogen, oxygen, nitrogen, carbon, and phosphorus. Nucleic acids are polymers. They are made up of monomers called nucleotides (NOO klee oh tydz). Nucleotides have three parts: a 5-carbon sugar, a phosphate group ($-PO_4$), and a nitrogenous base. Some nucleotides, including adenosine triphosphate (ATP), help in storing and transferring energy.

Single nucleotides can be linked by covalent bonds into long chains known as nucleic acids. Nucleic acids store and transmit genetic information. There are two kinds of nucleic acids: ribonucleic acid (RNA) and deoxyribonucleic acid (DNA). RNA contains the sugar ribose, and DNA contains the sugar deoxyribose.

🔑 **Key Question** What are the functions of nucleic acids?
Nucleic acids store and transmit genetic information.

Proteins Proteins are macromolecules that contain nitrogen as well as carbon, hydrogen, and oxygen. **Proteins** are polymers of molecules called amino acids. **Amino acids** are compounds with an amino group ($-NH_2$) on one end and a carboxyl group ($-COOH$) on the other end. Covalent bonds called peptide bonds link amino acids to form one or more polypeptides. A protein is a molecule made from one or more polypeptides. Some proteins control cell processes and the rate of reactions. Others form important parts in cells, while still others move substances into or out of cells or help to fight disease.

Amino Acids All amino acids have an amino group and a carboxyl group. The *R* in the structure shows where the side chain of the amino acid goes. Different side chains have different properties.

General Structure of Amino Acids

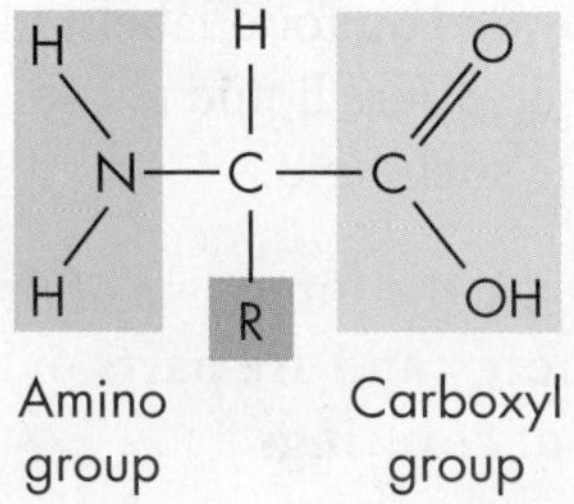

H
|
H—N—C—C=O
| |
H   R   OH

Amino group   Carboxyl group

▶ *Structure and Function* More than 20 different amino acids are found in nature. All amino acids are the same in the regions where they may be joined together by covalent bonds. This uniformity allows any amino acid to be joined to any other amino acid. Each amino acid has a different side chain called an R-group. The side chains have different properties. Some chains are acidic and some are basic. Some are polar, some are nonpolar, and some even contain large ring structures. Because the side chains are so different, proteins are diverse macromolecules.

▶ *Levels of Structure* Amino acids are joined in long chains according to instructions coded in DNA. Scientists describe proteins as having four levels of structure. A protein's primary structure is the order of its amino acids. Its secondary structure is the folding of the polypeptide chain. The third level of structure is the three-dimensional arrangement of a chain. Proteins that have more than one chain have a fourth level of structure. The fourth level describes how the different chains are placed next to each other. Hemoglobin, a protein in red blood cells that helps move oxygen in blood, has four levels of structure. The shape of a protein is kept by many forces, including ionic, covalent, and hydrogen bonds. The heme groups in the protein bind oxygen and also give hemoglobin its red color.

🗝 **Key Question** What are the functions of proteins? **Some proteins control cell processes and the rate of reactions. Others form important parts in cells, while still others move substances into or out of cells or help to fight disease.**

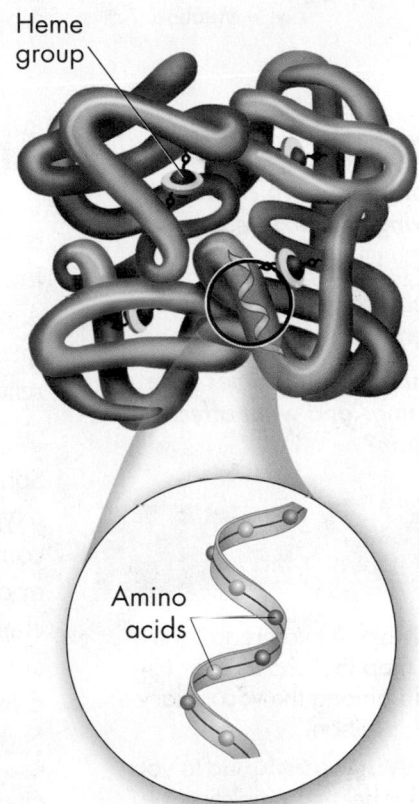

Heme group

Amino acids

Protein Structure Hemoglobin is a protein made up of four polypeptide chains. Near the center of each polypeptide is an iron-containing heme group. An oxygen molecule is bound by each heme group.

✓CHECK Understanding

Apply Vocabulary
Use the highlighted words from the lesson to complete each sentence correctly.

1. Fats, oils, and waxes do not dissolve in water and are kinds of macromolecules called _____.

2. _____ store genetic information.

3. Compounds made up of carbon, hydrogen, and oxygen that are the main source of energy for the body are called _____.

Critical Thinking

4. Relate Cause and Effect Why can carbon form so many different structures?

5. Explain How do living things use lipids?

6. Sequence What are the four levels of organization in a protein?

7. Write to Learn Make a chart that shows the monomers that make up three of the four kinds of macromolecules.

BIOLOGY.com ▶ Search (Lesson 2.3) GO • Lesson Assessment

2.4 Chemical Reactions and Enzymes

MD CLG 3.1.1 Chemical Substances and Macromolecules, 3.1.2 Homeostasis, 3.2.2 Changes in Metabolic Activity. SPI 1.5.2 Communicate Information, 1.5.8 Compare.

Key Questions

🔑 What happens to chemical bonds during chemical reactions?

🔑 How do energy changes affect whether a chemical reaction will happen?

🔑 What role do enzymes play in living things and what affects their function?

BUILD Understanding

Concept Map As you read, make a concept map that shows the relationship among the vocabulary words in this lesson.

In Your Workbook Go to your workbook for help in completing the concept map for Lesson 2.4.

Chemical Reactions

Living things are made up of chemical compounds. But chemistry is not just what life is made of—chemistry is also what life does. Everything that happens in living things is based on chemical reactions. A **chemical reaction** is a process that changes one set of chemicals into another. Chemical reactions also involve changes in energy. Some reactions release energy, and some use energy. This is also true for chemical reactions that happen in living things.

Some chemical reactions happen slowly, such as the reaction of iron and oxygen to form rust. Other reactions happen quickly. The elements or compounds that go into a chemical reaction are reactants. The elements or compounds that come out of a chemical reaction are products. During chemical reactions, some chemical bonds are broken and other bonds are formed. An important reaction in your bloodstream removes carbon dioxide from the body. That reaction is shown below.

🔑 **Key Question** What happens to chemical bonds during chemical reactions?
During chemical reactions, some bonds are broken and other bonds are formed.

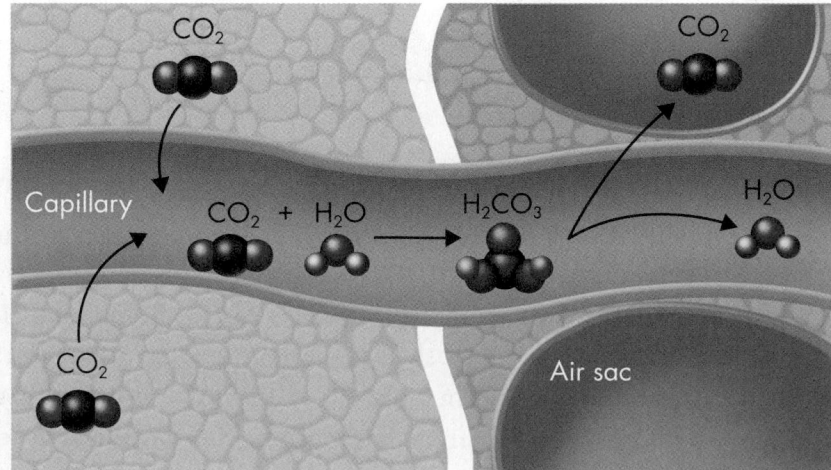

Body Tissues — Lungs

Reaction in the Bloodstream Carbon dioxide (CO_2) reacts with water (H_2O) to make carbonic acid (H_2CO_3). Your blood carries carbonic acid to your lungs. In your lungs, carbonic acid breaks apart to form water and carbon dioxide. You then breathe the carbon dioxide out.

Energy in Reactions

Energy is given off or taken in whenever chemical bonds are formed or broken. This means that chemical reactions involve changes in energy.

Energy Changes Energy changes are very important in determining whether a chemical reaction will happen. Chemical reactions that give off energy often happen on their own. Chemical reactions that take in energy will not happen without a source of energy. The burning of hydrogen gas gives off energy. Hydrogen reacts with oxygen to make water vapor.

$$2H_2 + O_2 \longrightarrow 2H_2O$$

If the hydrogen explodes, light and sound are given off in addition to the water vapor. The reverse reaction, in which water is changed into hydrogen and oxygen gas, requires so much energy that it doesn't happen by itself. In fact, the only way to reverse the reaction is to pass an electrical current through water to break the water down.

Energy Sources To stay alive, organisms need to carry out reactions that need added energy. Every living thing must have a source of energy to carry out these chemical reactions. Plants get that energy by trapping and storing the energy from sunlight in energy-rich compounds. Animals get their energy when they eat plants or other animals. Humans release energy needed to live when they break down the food they eat.

Activation Energy Chemical reactions that give off energy do not always happen on their own. If they did, the pages of this book might burst into flames! The cellulose in paper can burn and give off heat and light. However, paper burns only if you light it with a match, which gives enough energy to start the reaction. Chemists call the energy that is needed to get a reaction started **activation energy.** Energy is involved in all chemical reactions, whether the overall reaction gives off or takes in energy.

🔑 **Key Question** How do energy changes affect whether a chemical reaction will happen?
Chemical reactions that give off energy often happen on their own. Chemical reactions that take in energy will not happen without a source of energy.

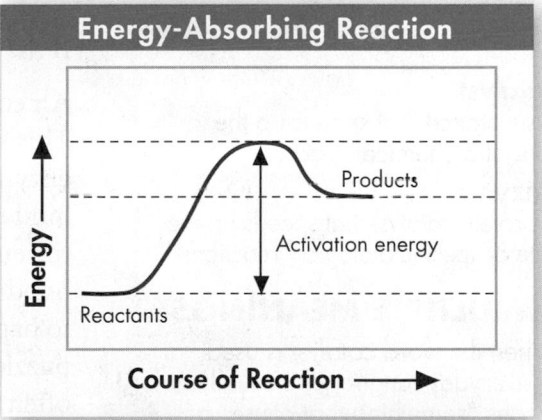

Energy-Absorbing Reaction

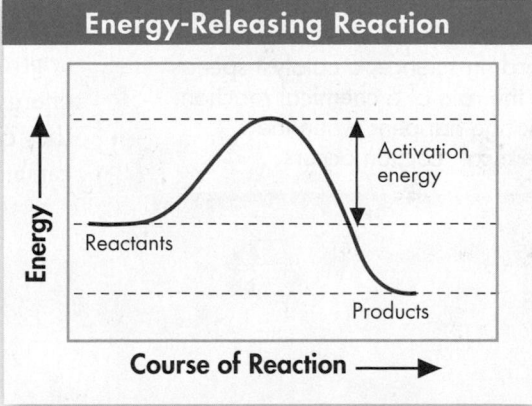

Energy-Releasing Reaction

Activation Energy The high point of each graph shows the energy needed for the reaction to happen. The difference between this needed energy and the energy of the reactants is the activation energy.

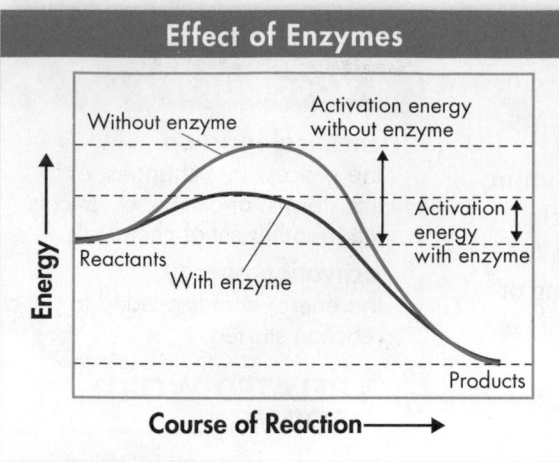

Effect of Enzymes

Without enzyme

Activation energy without enzyme

Energy

Reactants

With enzyme

Activation energy with enzyme

Products

Course of Reaction

Effect of Enzymes Adding an enzyme lowers the activation energy of reactions. The enzyme speeds up reactions.

Enzymes

Some chemical reactions that make life possible are too slow to make them practical for living tissue. These chemical reactions need the help of catalysts. A **catalyst** is a substance that speeds up the rate of a chemical reaction. Catalysts work by lowering a reaction's activation energy.

Nature's Catalysts Many reactions in living things need catalysts. **Enzymes** are proteins that act as catalysts in living things. Enzymes speed up chemical reactions that take place in cells. Each enzyme generally works on only one chemical reaction in the body. Like other catalysts, enzymes lower activation energies. This has a big effect on how quickly a reaction happens. An enzyme affects the speed of a reaction in your blood that joins carbon dioxide and water to make carbonic acid, as shown below.

$$CO_2 + H_2O \longrightarrow H_2CO_3$$

Left to itself, this reaction is very slow. It is so slow, in fact, that dangerous levels of carbon dioxide could build up in your body. But the enzyme carbonic anhydrase makes the reaction happen immediately so that carbon dioxide is removed quickly.

Enzymes and Substrates How do enzymes do their jobs? For a chemical reaction to take place, the reactants must hit each other with enough energy for existing bonds to break and for new bonds to form. If the reactants do not have enough energy, they will not react.

An enzyme has a site where reactants can be brought together to react. This site lowers the energy needed for a reaction. The reactants of enzyme-catalyzed reactions are known as substrates. The substrates bind to a site on the enzyme called the active site. At the active site, the enzyme changes a substrate slightly so that a specific chemical bond is weakened. This weakened bond allows a chemical reaction to happen quickly. The active site and the substrates fit together like puzzle pieces. The fit is so precise that the active site and substrates are often compared to a lock and key.

Controlling How Enzymes Work Enzymes have important roles in controlling chemical reactions, making materials that cells need, giving off energy, and sending information. Enzymes are catalysts for reactions, so they can be affected by many things. Temperature, pH, and other molecules can affect how enzymes work.

Many enzymes are affected by changes in temperature. Enzymes made by human cells usually work best at around 37° Celsius, or normal human body temperature. Enzymes also work best at certain pH values. For example, enzymes in the stomach work best in acidic solutions. Also, most enzymes are controlled by molecules that switch the enzymes "on" or "off" as needed.

🔑 **Key Question** What role do enzymes play in living things and what affects their function? **Enzymes speed up chemical reactions that take place in cells. Temperature, pH, and other molecules can affect how enzymes work.**

BUILD Connections

UNLOCKING ENZYMES
The red molecule is a substrate and the blue molecule is the enzyme that it fits into. The gap in the enzyme is the active site. The fit between the enzyme and the substrate is like the fit between a lock and key.

In Your Workbook Go to your workbook to explain why a lock and key is a good analogy for a substrate and an enzyme.

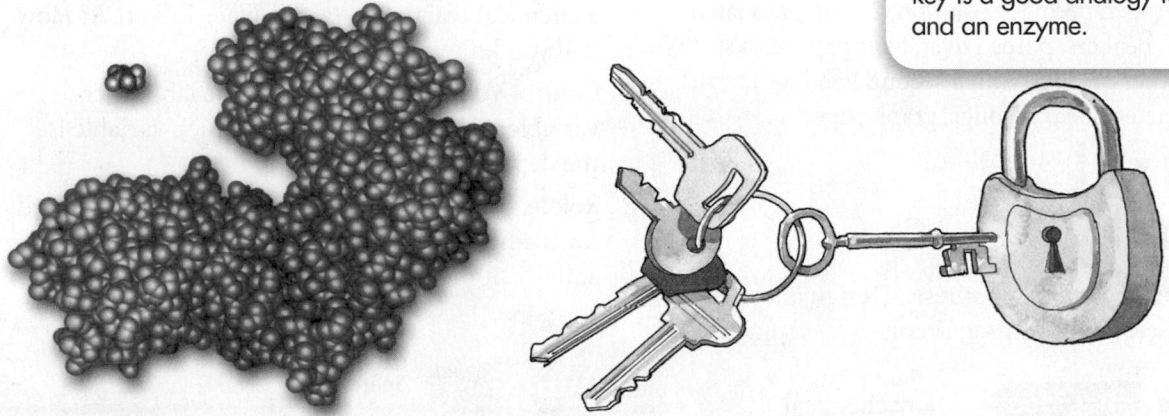

CHECK Understanding

Apply Vocabulary
Use the highlighted words from the lesson to complete each sentence correctly.

1. During a(n) _____, some chemical bonds are broken and others are formed.

2. A(n) _____ is a protein that speeds up reactions in living things.

Critical Thinking

3. Use Analogies A change in pH can change the shape of a protein. How might a change in pH affect the function of an enzyme? (**Hint:** Think about the lock and key analogy.)

4. Compare and Contrast Describe the difference between a reaction that often happens on its own and one that does not.

5. Explain Explain how enzymes work, including the role of the active site.

6. Review What happens to chemical bonds during chemical reactions?

7. Apply Concepts Why is the melting of ice not a chemical reaction?

8. Write to Learn Answer the third clue of the mystery. Consider how temperature might affect chemical reactions.

MYSTERY CLUE
The chemical reactions of living things happen more slowly at lower temperatures. How would very cold antarctic waters affect the ice fish's need for oxygen? (**Hint:** See above.)

Design Your Own Lab

MD CLG 3.1.1 Chemical Substances and Macromolecules, 3.2.2 Changes in Metabolic Activity, SPI 1.2.4 Testing a Hypothesis, 1.3.1 Use Equipment, 1.3.2 Safety Procedures, *(continued below)*

Pre-Lab: Temperature and Enzymes

Problem How does temperature affect the rate of an enzyme-catalyzed reaction?

Materials raw liver, forceps, petri dish, dropper pipette, 1% hydrogen peroxide solution, 25-mL graduated cylinder, 50-mL beakers, puréed liver, filter paper disks, paper towels, timer or clock with a second hand, water baths, thermometers, beaker tongs, graph paper

Lab Manual Chapter 2 Lab

Skills Focus Form a Hypothesis, Design an Experiment, Measure, Interpret Graphs

Connect to the Big idea Many chemical reactions in living organisms could not take place without enzymes. Enzymes catalyze the reactions that release energy from nutrients. They also catalyze the synthesis of the complex molecules that organisms need to grow and stay healthy. One factor that affects the action of enzymes is temperature. Think about why people store some foods in a refrigerator. The cold temperature limits the ability of enzymes to break down, or spoil, those foods.

Do high temperatures have the opposite effect on enzymes? Do they become more and more active as the temperature rises? In this lab, you will investigate the effect of temperature on an enzyme-catalyzed reaction.

Background Questions

a. Review Why do many reactions that occur in cells require enzymes? How do enzymes speed up chemical reactions?

b. Review Name three variables that can affect enzyme activity.

c. Use Analogies Use eggs and a frying pan on a stove as an analogy for reactants and an enzyme. Use the control knob on the stove burner as an analogy for how a variable can affect the action of an enzyme.

Pre-Lab Questions

Preview the procedure in the lab manual.

1. Relate Cause and Effect How will you know that a chemical reaction is taking place in Part A? How will you know in Part B?

2. Control Variables In Part B of the lab, which variable will you manipulate? Which variable is the dependent variable?

3. Relate Cause and Effect How is the time required for the filter-paper disk to float related to the activity of the enzyme?

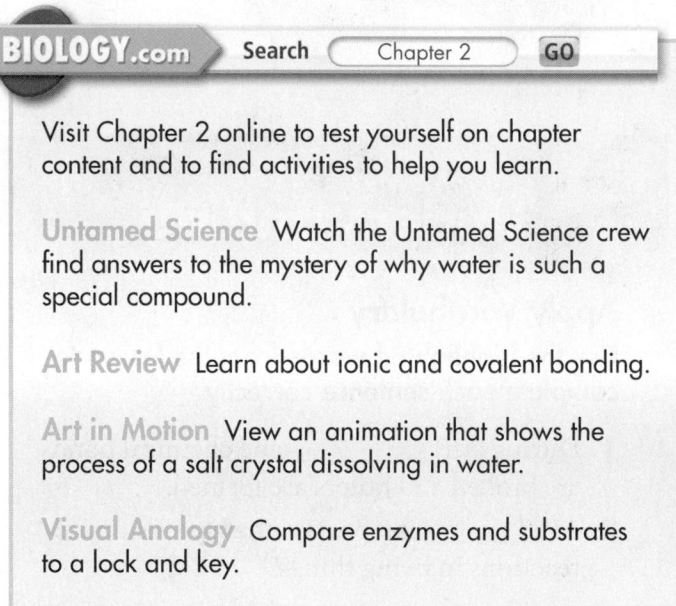

BIOLOGY.com Search ⟨ Chapter 2 ⟩ GO

Visit Chapter 2 online to test yourself on chapter content and to find activities to help you learn.

Untamed Science Watch the Untamed Science crew find answers to the mystery of why water is such a special compound.

Art Review Learn about ionic and covalent bonding.

Art in Motion View an animation that shows the process of a salt crystal dissolving in water.

Visual Analogy Compare enzymes and substrates to a lock and key.

MD 1.3.3 Safe Handling of Materials, 1.4.1 Organize Data, 1.4.4 Create Math Models, 1.4.6 Determine Trends, 1.4.9 Confirm Hypotheses, 1.5.9 Synthesize Ideas, 1.7.1 Apply Skills and Concepts.

2.1 The Nature of Matter

- The particles that make up atoms are protons, neutrons, and electrons.

- All isotopes of an element have the same number of protons and the same chemical properties.

- The physical and chemical properties of a compound are usually very different from those of the elements that make it up.

- The main kinds of chemical bonds are ionic bonds and covalent bonds.

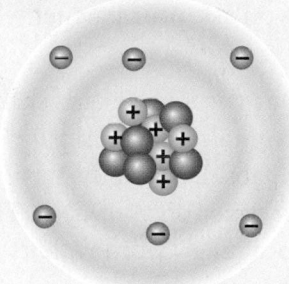

atom (p. 28)   compound (p. 30)
nucleus (p. 28)   ionic bond (p. 30)
electron (p. 28)   covalent bond (p. 31)
element (p. 29)   molecule (p. 31)
isotope (p. 29)

2.2 Properties of Water

- Water is a polar molecule. It is able to form many hydrogen bonds, which makes water cohesive and adhesive.

- Water's polar nature gives it the ability to dissolve both ionic compounds and other polar molecules.

- Buffers play an important role in maintaining homeostasis in organisms.

cohesion (p. 34)   acid (p. 36)
adhesion (p. 34)   base (p. 36)
solution (p. 34)   buffer (p. 36)
suspension (p. 35)

2.3 Carbon Compounds

- Carbon can bond with many elements, including hydrogen, oxygen, phosphorus, sulfur, and nitrogen, to form the molecules of life.

- Living things use carbohydrates as their main source of energy. Plants, some animals, and other living things also use carbohydrates for structural purposes.

- Lipids can be used to store energy. Some lipids are important parts of biological membranes and waterproof coverings.

- Nucleic acids store and transmit genetic information.

- Some proteins control cell processes and the rate of reactions. Others form important parts in cells, while still others move substances into or out of cells or help to fight disease.

carbohydrate (p. 38)   protein (p. 40)
lipid (p. 39)   amino acid (p. 40)
nucleic acid (p. 40)

2.4 Chemical Reactions and Enzymes

- During chemical reactions, some bonds are broken and other bonds are formed.

- Chemical reactions that give off energy often happen on their own. Chemical reactions that take in energy will not happen without a source of energy.

- Enzymes speed up chemical reactions that take place in cells.

- Temperature, pH, and other molecules can affect how enzymes work.

chemical reaction (p. 42)   catalyst (p. 44)
activation energy (p. 43)   enzyme (p. 44)

2 CHECK Understanding

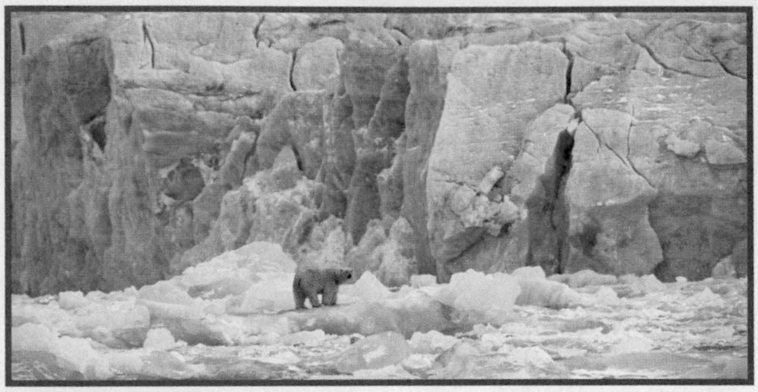

Assess the Big idea **Matter and Energy**

Write an answer to the question below.
Q: What are the basic chemical principles that affect living things?

Constructed Response

Write an answer to each of the questions below. The answer to each question should be one or two paragraphs long. To help you begin, read the **Hints** below each of the questions.

1. **How are chemical compounds related to the electrons in atoms?**

   Hint Chemical compounds are made when two or more elements are chemically joined.

   Hint Molecules of compounds are formed when atoms of elements form bonds with each other.

2. **How does the structure of a water molecule help water dissolve ionic compounds?**

   Hint The atoms in water are joined by covalent bonds.

   Hint The electrons in water are not evenly spread out.

3. **Explain which of the four groups of macromolecules are polymers and which are not.**

   Hint A polymer is a large compound made by the joining of many monomers.

Foundations for Learning Wrap-Up

Use the vocabulary quiz sheet that you made when you started the chapter as a tool to help you learn the important words from this chapter. Do Activity 1 before you do Activity 2.

Activity 1 Compare your quiz sheet with a partner's quiz sheet. If your partner's sheet has words that you do not have, add them to your own sheet. Fold the tabs over the definitions. Then, swap sheets with your partner and take turns quizzing each other on the definitions of the words. Open each word's matching tab as you ask your partner what the word means.

Activity 2 Cut your vocabulary quiz sheet so that the words and definitions are on separate slips of paper. Cut off the tabs. Discard the tabs. Mix up the remaining slips of paper on your desk. Then, work to match up each vocabulary word with its definition.

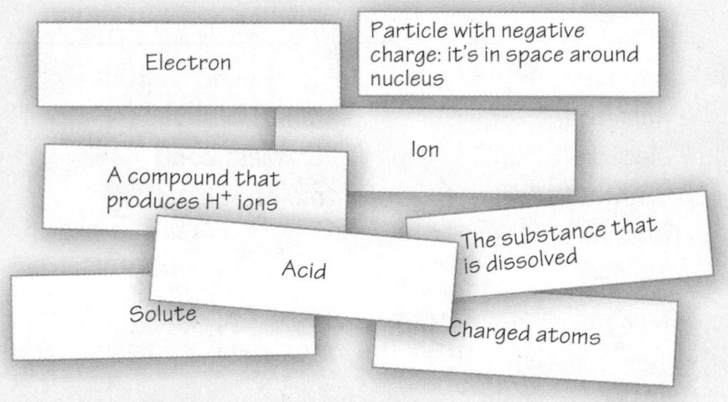

2.1 The Nature of Matter

Understand Key Concepts

1. The positively charged particle in an atom is a(n)
   a. electron.
   c. neutron.
   b. ion.
   d. proton.

2. Two or more atoms are joined in definite amounts in any
   a. compound.
   c. isotope.
   b. element.
   d. symbol.

3. A covalent bond is formed by the
   a. gaining of electrons.
   b. losing of electrons.
   c. sharing of electrons.
   d. transfer of electrons.

Test-Taking Tip

Choose Among Similar Answers The answers for question 3 all end with "of electrons," so those words will not matter when picking an answer. You have to look at only the first word of each answer. When you do, you should realize that "gaining" and "losing" are part of a "transfer" of electrons. So, answers **a**, **b**, and **d** are all related and cannot all be correct. So, answer **c** is the right answer.

Think Critically

4. **Compare and Contrast** Describe how ionic bonds and covalent bonds are similar and how they are different.

2.2 Properties of Water

Understand Key Concepts

5. When you mix salt and water together in a beaker, you cause them to form a
   a. compound.
   c. mixture.
   b. solution.
   d. suspension.

6. A compound that releases hydrogen ions (H^+) in solution is a(n)
   a. acid.
   c. polymer.
   b. base.
   d. salt.

Think Critically

7. **Explain** Explain the properties of cohesion and adhesion. Then, give an example of each property.

8. **Apply Concepts** A student mixes a spoonful of sugar in a glass of water. Explain what the student has made using the terms *solution*, *solute*, and *solvent*.

2.3 Carbon Compounds

Understand Key Concepts

9. Proteins are polymers formed from
   a. amino acids.
   b. lipids.
   c. nucleic acids.
   d. simple sugars.

10. Carbohydrates are made up of all of the following elements EXCEPT
    a. carbon.
    c. oxygen.
    b. hydrogen.
    d. sodium.

Think Critically

11. **Apply Concepts** Explain the relationship between monomers and polymers using complex carbohydrates as an example.

12. **Explain** Describe the structure of a lipid and explain how to tell if the lipid is saturated or unsaturated.

2.4 Chemical Reactions and Enzymes

Understand Key Concepts

13. In a chemical reaction, a reactant binds to an enzyme at a place known as the
    a. active site.
    c. product.
    b. catalyst.
    d. substrate.

14. An enzyme speeds up a reaction by

a. giving off energy.

b. taking in energy.

c. lowering the activation energy.

d. raising the activation energy.

Think Critically

15. Infer An enzyme made by the human body is put in a solution in a lab. The temperature of the solution is 20°C. How would this temperature affect how the enzyme works? Explain your answer.

16. Use Analogies Explain why a lock and key are used to describe the way an enzyme works.

Connecting Concepts

Use Science Graphics

The following graph shows the total amount of product from a chemical reaction performed at three different temperatures. The same enzyme was involved in each case. Use the graph to answer questions 17–19.

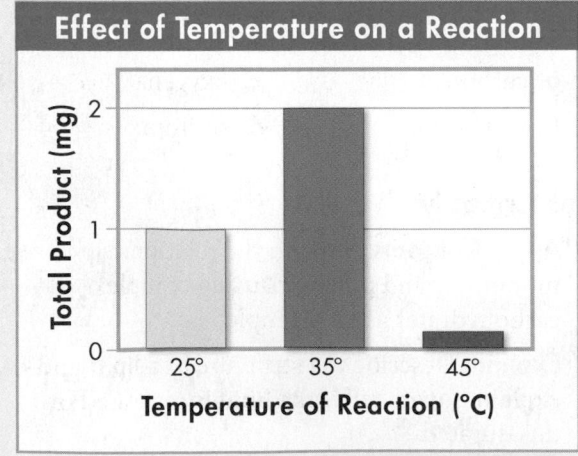

Effect of Temperature on a Reaction

17. Interpret Graphs At which temperature was the greatest amount of product formed?

18. Draw Conclusions Describe the results of each reaction. How can you explain these results?

19. Predict A student performs the same chemical reaction at 30°C. About how much product can she expect to get?

THE GHOSTLY FISH

The protein hemoglobin allows the blood of most fishes to carry nearly 50 times the oxygen it would without the protein. The ghostly white look of the antarctic ice fish comes from its clear blood—blood without hemoglobin. Ice fish can live without hemoglobin because of the properties of very cold water.

Oxygen dissolves in seawater, providing the oxygen that fishes need to live. Fishes take in dissolved oxygen directly through their gills, where it passes into their blood. More oxygen can dissolve in water when the water is cold. So, the icy cold antarctic waters have a lot of oxygen.

The large gills and scaleless skin of ice fish let them take in oxygen efficiently from the water. Compared to red-blooded fishes, ice fish have a higher blood volume, thinner blood, and larger hearts. Their blood can carry more dissolved oxygen. The large hearts can pump the thinner blood through the body faster. These and other physical features, along with the chemistry of oxygen in very cold water, enable ice fish to live where many other living things cannot.

1. Relate Cause and Effect Ice fish produce antifreeze proteins to keep their blood from freezing. Their body temperature stays below 0°C. How does low body temperature affect the blood's ability to carry dissolved oxygen?

2. Infer People living at high altitudes generally have more hemoglobin in their blood than people living at sea level. Why do you think this is so?

3. Predict If the antarctic oceans were to warm up, how might this affect ice fish?

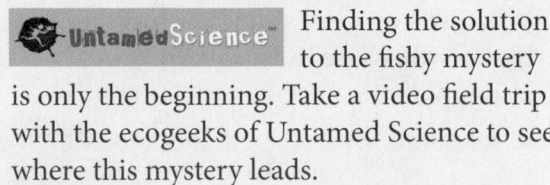 Finding the solution to the fishy mystery is only the beginning. Take a video field trip with the ecogeeks of Untamed Science to see where this mystery leads.

Standardized Test Practice for Maryland

Multiple Choice

1. The elements or compounds that enter into a chemical reaction are called
   A products.   C active sites.
   B catalysts.   D reactants.   CLG 3.1.2

2. Chemical bonds that involve the total transfer of electrons from one atom or group of atoms to another are called   CLG 3.1.1
   A covalent bonds.   C hydrogen bonds.
   B ionic bonds.   D oxygen bonds.

3. Which of the following is NOT a macromolecule found in living organisms?
   A protein   C sodium chloride
   B nucleic acid   D lipid   CLG 3.1.1

4. Which combination of particle and charge is correct?
   A proton: positively charged
   B electron: positively charged
   C neutron: negatively charged
   D electron: no charge   CLG 3.1.1

5. In which of the following ways do isotopes of the same element differ?
   A in number of neutrons only
   B in number of protons only
   C in numbers of neutrons and protons
   D in number of neutrons and in mass   CLG 3.1.1

6. Which of the following molecules is made up of glycerol and fatty acids?
   A sugars
   B starches
   C lipids
   D nucleic acids   CLG 3.1.1

7. Nucleotides consist of a phosphate group, a nitrogenous base, and a
   A fatty acid.
   B lipid.
   C 5-carbon sugar.
   D 6-carbon sugar.   CLG 3.1.1

Questions 8–9

The enzyme catalase speeds up the chemical reaction that changes hydrogen peroxide into oxygen and water. The amount of oxygen given off is an indication of the rate of the reaction.

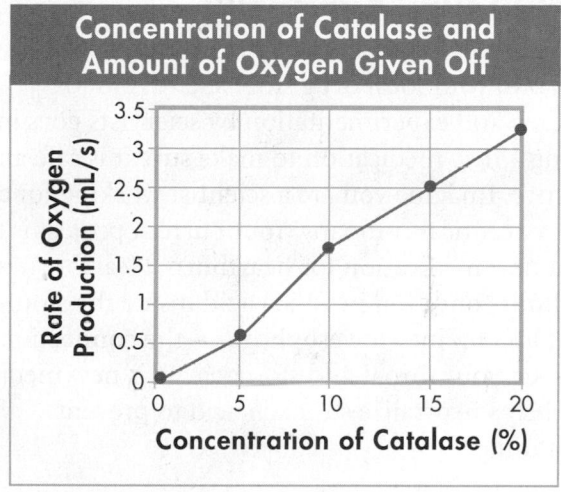

Concentration of Catalase and Amount of Oxygen Given Off

8. Based on the graph, what can you conclude about the relationship between enzyme concentration and reaction rate?
   A Reaction rate decreases with increasing enzyme concentration.
   B Reaction rate increases with decreasing enzyme concentration.
   C Reaction rate increases with increasing enzyme concentration.   SPI 1.4.6
   D The variables are indirectly proportional.

9. Which concentration of catalase will produce the fastest reaction rate?
   A 5%   C 15%
   B 10%   D 20%   SPI 1.4.2

Open-Ended Response

10. List some of the properties of water that make it such a unique substance.   CLG 3.1.1

If You Have Trouble With . . .

Question	1	2	3	4	5	6	7	8	9	10
See Lesson	2.4	2.1	2.3	2.1	2.1	2.3	2.3	2.4	2.4	2.2

Unit Project

Design the Experiment

Did you ever wonder how a medication goes from the lab to your local drug store shelf? A lot of research and experimentation by scientists goes into testing a new medication to make sure it is safe and effective. Imagine you are a scientist working for a pharmaceutical company. Your current project is to test a new medication for heartburn. Heartburn is a painful condition in which acid inside the stomach backs up into the esophagus—the connection between your throat and stomach. This new medication helps neutralize stomach acid to prevent irritation.

Your Task Design *three* possible experiments to test the safety and effectiveness of the new heartburn medication. Before you begin, think about how you will know if the medication actually neutralizes stomach acid. Once you've written your procedures, you will propose the experiments to your company's Executive Board for Research and Development.

For each experiment,
- identify clear independent and dependent variables.
- identify a control.
- form a hypothesis— predict the results you'd expect to find if the medication worked.
- write a specific procedure that tests your hypothesis.

Reflection Questions

1. Score your experimental designs using the rubric below. What score did you give yourself?
2. What did you do well in this project?
3. What about your designs needs improvement?
4. Are there any ethical dilemmas related to your experiments? Explain.

Assessment Rubric

Score	Scientific Content	Quality of Experiments
4	Correctly and extensively applies knowledge and understanding of unit concepts (i.e., pH scale) to experimental designs and predictions.	Experimental designs are clever and effectively test the hypotheses. Experimental conditions are carefully controlled and variables are correctly identified.
3	Applies relevant knowledge and understanding of unit concepts (i.e., pH scale) to experimental designs and predictions.	Experimental designs are logical and test the hypotheses. Experimental conditions are controlled and variables are correctly identified.
2	Applies relevant knowledge and understanding of unit concepts (i.e., pH scale) incompletely to experimental designs and predictions.	Experimental designs need some revisions—some parts are unclear or do not fully test the hypotheses. Variables and controls need corrections.
1	Does not correctly apply knowledge and understanding of unit concepts (i.e., pH scale) to experimental designs and predictions.	Experimental designs are unclear and do not test the hypotheses. Variables and controls listed are incorrect or absent.

Ecology

Chapters

INTRODUCE the
Big ideas

- Matter and Energy
- Interdependence in Nature

❝Earth is a living planet on which all forms of life are linked to one another, and to land, water, and air. Through those links, energy flows and matter cycles in patterns that support life, including human society. We know enough about these patterns to realize that they are changing, due to human activity, in ways that we don't understand. Our challenge is to study our impact on the biosphere and plan for a healthy future.❞

Joe Levine

3 The Biosphere

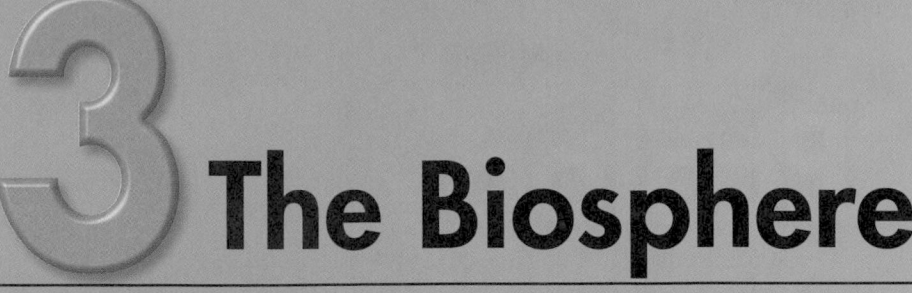

Big ideas > **Matter and Energy, Interdependence in Nature**
Q: How do Earth's living and nonliving parts interact
and affect the survival of organisms?

*Great White Egret
among some plants in
the Florida Everglades*

BIOLOGY.com > Search Chapter 3 GO • Flash Cards

MARYLAND VOLUNTARY STATE CURRICULUM

Biology Indicators/Core Learning Goals (CLG) 3.1.3, 3.2.2, 3.5.1, 3.5.2, 3.5.3, 3.5.4. **Skills and Processes Indicators (SPI)** 1.2.2, 1.2.6, 1.2.7, 1.3.1, 1.3.3, 1.4.2, 1.5.2, 1.5.5, 1.5.7, 1.5.8, 1.5.9, 1.6.1, 1.6.3, 1.7.1, 1.7.4. See lessons for details.

CHAPTER
MYSTERY

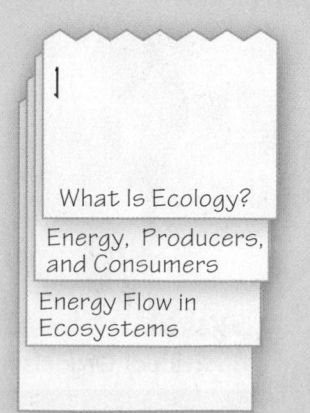

CHANGES IN THE BAY

Marine life in Rhode Island's Narragansett Bay is changing. One clue to those changes comes from fishing boat captains. These captains now boast about catching bluefish in November—a month after bluefish used to head south for winter. But catches of winter flounder are not as plentiful as they once were.

Other changes have also been observed in the bay. The annual spring increase in plant and animal growth is disappearing. Researchers working in the bay also report something puzzling. There are changes in the activities of bacteria living in mud on the bay floor.

What's going on? Farms, towns, and cities surround the bay. But direct human influence on the bay has not changed much lately. So why are there so many changes to the bay's plant and animal populations?

Read for Mystery Clues Could these changes be related to mud-dwelling bacteria? As you read the chapter, look for clues to help you understand the interactions of plants, animals, and bacteria in Narragansett Bay. Then, solve the mystery.

FOUNDATIONS for Learning

Make a layered book by stapling 4 sheets of paper together. Make sure that 2 to 3 cm at the bottom of each page is visible. Label the top page What Is Ecology? Label the remaining pages with the titles of Lessons 2, 3, and 4. Write the major headings from each lesson on the pages. When you finish reading a section, write a summary of the section in your layered book. Remember to use your vocabulary words in your summaries.

What Is Ecology?

Energy, Producers, and Consumers

Energy Flow in Ecosystems

● Untamed Science Video   ● Chapter Mystery

3.1 What Is Ecology?

MD · CLG 3.2.2 Changes in Metabolic Activity, 3.5.1 Factors Influencing Ecosystems, 3.5.2 Interdependence of Organisms in the Biosphere, 3.5.3 Population Dynamics, 3.5.4 Global Food Webs. SPI 1.2.2 Posing Scientific Questions, 1.2.6 Investigative Methods, 1.5.8 Compare, 1.7.1 Apply Skills and Concepts.

Key Questions

🔑 What is ecology?

🔑 What are biotic and abiotic factors?

🔑 What methods are used in ecological studies?

BUILD Understanding

Venn Diagram Make a Venn diagram that shows how the environment consists of biotic factors and abiotic factors. The diagram should also show how some components are truly a mixture of both. Use examples from the lesson.

In Your Workbook Go to your workbook for help completing the Venn diagram for Lesson 3.1.

Studying Our Living Planet

Science writer Lewis Thomas once wrote: "Viewed from the distance of the moon, the astonishing thing about the earth . . . is that it is alive." That sounds good. But what does it mean? In a scientific sense, how is Earth a "living planet"? And how do we study it?

Biologists use the term *biosphere* when they talk about life on a global scale. The **biosphere** consists of all life on Earth and all parts of the Earth where life exists. This includes land, water, and the atmosphere. The biosphere contains every organism, from underground bacteria to giant rain forest trees, even humans. It extends from about 8 kilometers above Earth's surface to as far as 11 kilometers below the surface of the ocean.

The Science of Ecology Organisms in the biosphere interact with each other. But they also interact with their surroundings, or environment. The study of these interactions is called **ecology.** Ecology is the scientific study of the interactions between organisms and their physical environment.

Organisms respond to each other and to their environments. Organisms also affect each other and change their environments. These interactions produce an ever-changing, or dynamic, biosphere.

Individual Organism

Levels of Organization The kinds of questions that ecologists ask about the living environment can vary. The questions depend on the level at which the ecologist works.

A **population** is a group of individuals that belong to the same species and live in the same area.

An assemblage of different populations that live together in a defined area is called a **community.**

Ecology and Economics Some people think that ecology doesn't really matter to people very much. But humans depend on ecological processes to produce many things we need, such as food and clean water. Food, water, and other things we need are often worth money. That's why ecology is linked to the field called economics. Economics is concerned with human interactions based on money or trade.

Levels of Organization Ecologists ask many questions about organisms and their environments. Some ecologists focus on the ecology of individual organisms. Others try to understand how interactions among organisms (including humans) influence our global environment. Ecological studies may focus on levels of organization that include those shown below.

🔑 **Key Question** What is ecology?
Ecology is the scientific study of interactions among organisms and between organisms and their physical environment.

Biotic and Abiotic Factors

Ecologists use the word *environment* to refer to all conditions, or factors, surrounding an organism. Environmental conditions include biotic factors and abiotic factors.

Biotic Factors A **biotic factor** is any living part of the environment. Biotic factors include animals, plants, mushrooms, and bacteria. For example, the insects that a bullfrog might eat are biotic factors. Another biotic factor relating to the bullfrog is the heron that might eat the bullfrog. Species that compete with the bullfrog for food or space are also biotic factors.

BUILD Vocabulary

biosphere
a part of Earth in which life exists, including land, water, and air, or atmosphere

ecology
the scientific study of interactions among organisms and between organisms and their environment

population
a group of individuals of the same species that live in the same area

community
a group of different populations that live together in a defined area

ecosystem
all the organisms that live in a place, together with their physical environment

biome
a group of ecosystems that share similar climates and typical organisms

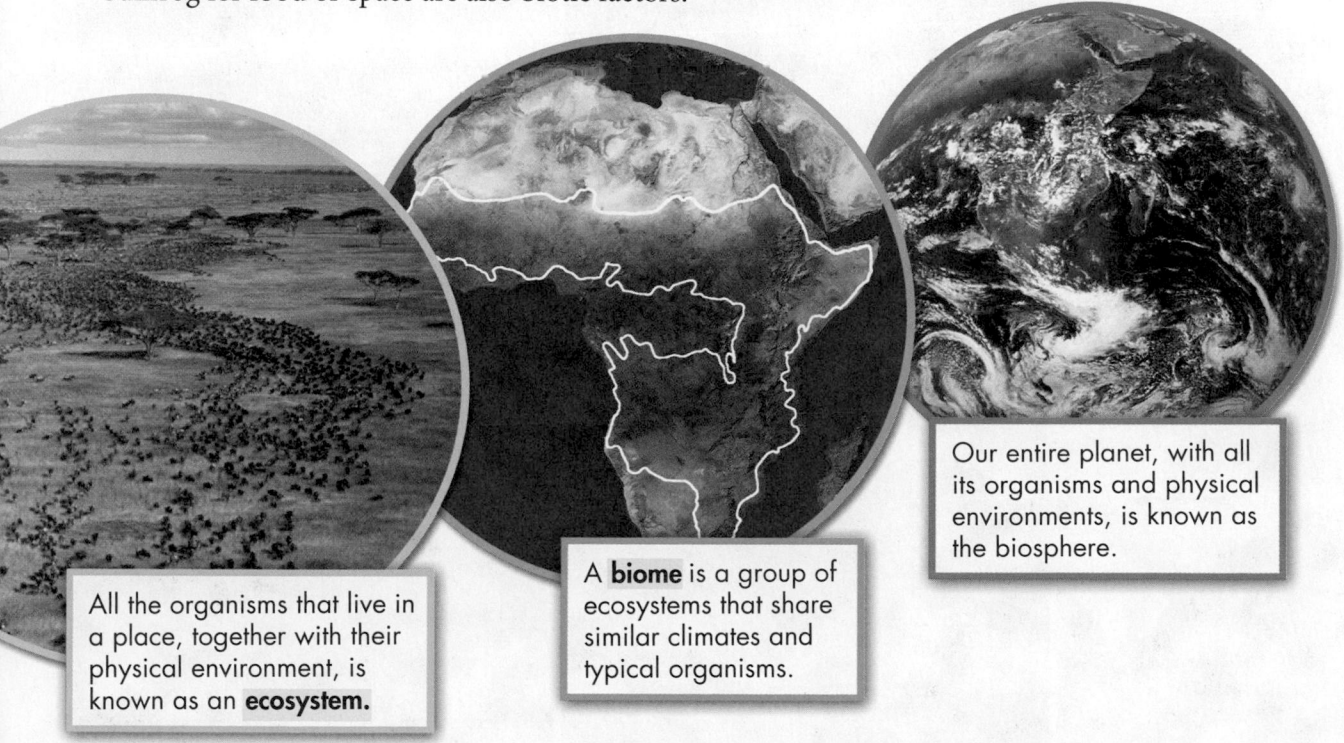

All the organisms that live in a place, together with their physical environment, is known as an **ecosystem.**

A **biome** is a group of ecosystems that share similar climates and typical organisms.

Our entire planet, with all its organisms and physical environments, is known as the biosphere.

BUILD Vocabulary

biotic factor
any living part of the environment with which an organism might interact

abiotic factor
a physical, or nonliving, factor that shapes an ecosystem

🔧 PREFIXES

The prefix *bio-* comes from the Greek word *bios*, which means "living tissue."

Abiotic Factors An **abiotic factor** is any nonliving part of the environment. Abiotic factors include things like sunlight, precipitation, and water currents. For example, a bullfrog might be affected by water availability, temperature, and humidity.

Biotic and Abiotic Factors Together The difference between biotic and abiotic factors is not always simple. Many physical factors can be strongly influenced by the activities of organisms. Remember the bullfrog? It lives in soft "muck" along the shores of ponds. This muck is a mix of biotic factors such as bacteria and abiotic factors such as sand. Trees and shrubs around the pond affect the amount of sunlight that reaches its shoreline. Plant roots determine how much soil is held in place and how much washes into the pond. This kind of dynamic mix of biotic and abiotic factors shapes every environment.

🔑 **Key Question** What are biotic and abiotic factors?
Biological influences on organisms are called biotic factors. Physical elements of an ecosystem are called abiotic factors.

Biotic and Abiotic Factors
This pond is affected by a combination of biotic and abiotic factors.

Biotic Factors | Environment (Biotic and Abiotic) | Abiotic Factors

Ecological Methods

Ecologists study many different parts of the biosphere and often use different research tools. But all ecologists use three scientific approaches to their work: observation, experimentation, and modeling.

Observation Observation is often the first step in asking ecological questions. Some observations are simple: Which species live here? Other observations are more complex: How does an animal protect its young from predators? These types of questions may form the first step in designing experiments and models.

Experimentation Experiments can be used to test hypotheses. Suppose an ecologist wants to see how growing plants react to different temperatures. He or she may set up an artificial environment in a greenhouse to test the plants' responses. Other experiments carefully alter conditions in selected parts of natural ecosystems.

Modeling Many ecological events occur over long periods of time or over large distances. These events are difficult to study directly. Ecologists make models to help them understand these events. These models are usually based on data collected through observation and experimentation. Then more observations are made to test predictions based on those models.

Ecology Field Work The three basic approaches to ecological research involve observing, experimenting, and modeling. This ecologist is measuring a Mediterranean tortoise.

🔑 **Key Question** What methods are used in ecological studies? **Modern ecologists use three methods in their work: observation, experimentation, and modeling.**

✓CHECK Understanding

Apply Vocabulary
Use the highlighted words from the lesson to complete each sentence correctly.

1. The _____ extends from about 8 kilometers above the Earth's surface to as far as 11 kilometers below ocean's surface.

2. The science that studies all the interactions between living and nonliving parts of an ecosystem is called _____.

3. A herd of wildebeests living on the Serengeti Plain would be classified as a _____ within an ecosystem.

Critical Thinking

4. **Explain** Is weather a biotic or abiotic factor? Explain your answer.

5. **Compare and Contrast** How are biotic and abiotic factors related? How are they different?

6. **Write to Learn** Answer the first clue of the mystery. Write a paragraph that explains why you think the three abiotic factors you chose are important.

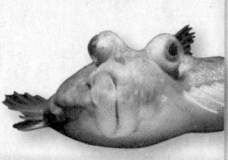

MYSTERY **CLUE**

What are three examples of abiotic factors that might affect life in the Narragansett Bay? **(Hint:** See p. 58.)

3.2 Energy, Producers, and Consumers

MD CLG 3.1.3 Matter and Energy, 3.5.2 Interdependence of Organisms in the Biosphere.
SPI 1.5.2 Communicate Information, 1.5.7 Classification Systems, 1.5.8 Compare.

Key Questions

🔑 What are primary producers?

🔑 How do consumers obtain energy and nutrients?

BUILD Understanding

Concept Map As you read, use the highlighted vocabulary words to create a concept map that organizes the information in the lesson.

In Your Workbook Go to your workbook for help in completing your concept map.

Primary Producers

Organisms need energy for growth, reproduction, and their own metabolic processes. Without energy, there are no life functions!

No organism can create energy—organisms can only use energy from other sources. Where does that energy come from? Sunlight is the ultimate energy source for most life on Earth. But some organisms get their energy from chemical energy that is stored in inorganic chemical compounds.

Only algae, certain bacteria, and plants can capture energy from sunlight or chemicals. This energy is converted into forms that living cells can use. Such organisms are called **autotrophs.** They use solar or chemical energy to produce "food" by making organic molecules from inorganic compounds. Organisms that eat autotrophs use the energy stored in the bonds of these molecules. That's why autotrophs are also called **primary producers.** Primary producers are the first producers of energy-rich compounds that other organisms need to survive. Primary producers are essential to the flow of energy through the biosphere.

Energy From the Sun The most common primary producers capture solar energy through photosynthesis. Photosynthesis captures light energy and uses it to power chemical reactions. These reactions convert carbon dioxide and water into oxygen and energy-rich carbohydrates. Photosynthesis adds oxygen to the atmosphere and removes carbon dioxide. Without photosynthesis, there would not be enough oxygen for you to breathe! Plants are the main photosynthetic producers on land. Algae fill that role in freshwater ecosystems and in the sunlit upper layers of the ocean. Photosynthetic bacteria are the important primary producers in tidal flats and salt marshes.

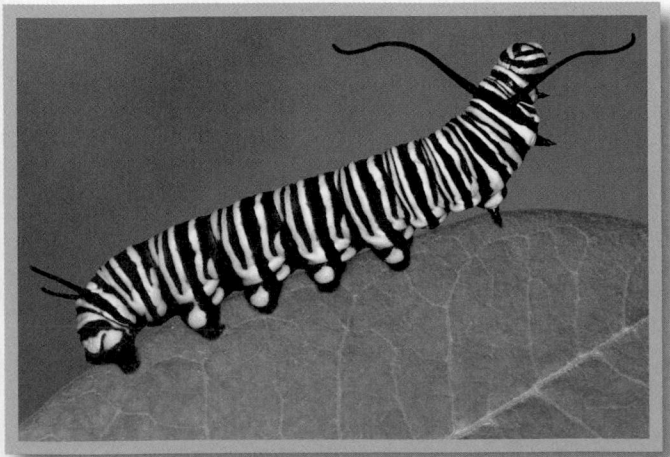

Primary Producers Plants get energy from sunlight and turn it into nutrients. These nutrients can be eaten and used for energy by animals such as this caterpillar.

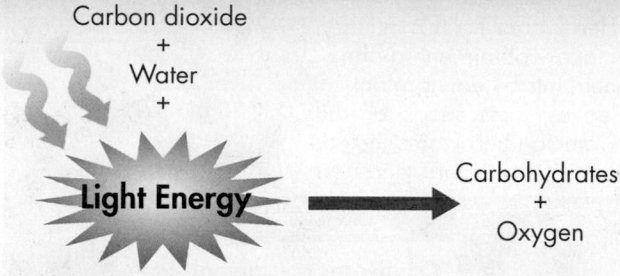

Carbon dioxide
+
Water
+
Light Energy ⟶ Carbohydrates
+
Oxygen

Photosynthesis

Photosynthesis
Plants use the energy from sunlight to carry out the process of photosynthesis. As a result, energy-rich carbohydrates are produced.

Life Without Light About 30 years ago, biologists found thriving ecosystems around deep-sea volcanic vents. Without light for photosynthesis, how did the primary producers capture energy? They used a process called chemosynthesis (kee moh SIN thuh sis) to harness energy from inorganic molecules. Chemosynthesis uses chemical energy to produce carbohydrates. Some chemosynthetic organisms live in hot springs while others live in tidal marshes.

🔑 **Key Question** What are primary producers?
Primary producers are the first producers of energy-rich compounds that are later used by other organisms.

Consumers

Animals, fungi, and many bacteria cannot capture energy directly from the environment. These organisms, called **heterotrophs** (HET uh roh trohfs), must get energy from other organisms by consuming them. So heterotrophs are also called **consumers.**

Types of Consumers Consumers are classified by the ways in which they acquire energy and nutrients. As you will see, the definition of *food* can vary quite a lot among different categories of consumers.

Beyond Consumer Categories The simple consumer categories often do not express how nature really works. For example, seeds and fruits are richer in nutrients and easier to digest than leaves. So herbivores that eat different plant parts need different types of digestive systems. Carnivores do not stay in their own categories, either. Hyenas are carnivores but will scavenge if they get a chance. This means it is important to understand how energy and nutrients move through ecosystems.

🔑 **Key Question** How do consumers obtain energy and nutrients?
Organisms that rely on other organisms for energy and nutrients are called consumers.

BUILD Vocabulary

autotroph
an organism that is able to capture energy from sunlight or chemicals and use it to produce its own food from inorganic compounds; also called a producer

primary producer
the first producer of energy-rich compounds that are later used by other organisms

heterotroph
an organism that obtains food by consuming other living things; also called a consumer

consumer
an organism that relies on other organisms for its energy and food supply; also called a heterotroph

⚑ PREFIXES

The prefix *auto-* means "by itself." The Greek word *trophikos* means "to feed." This means that an autotroph can be described as a "self feeder." It does not need to eat other organisms for food.

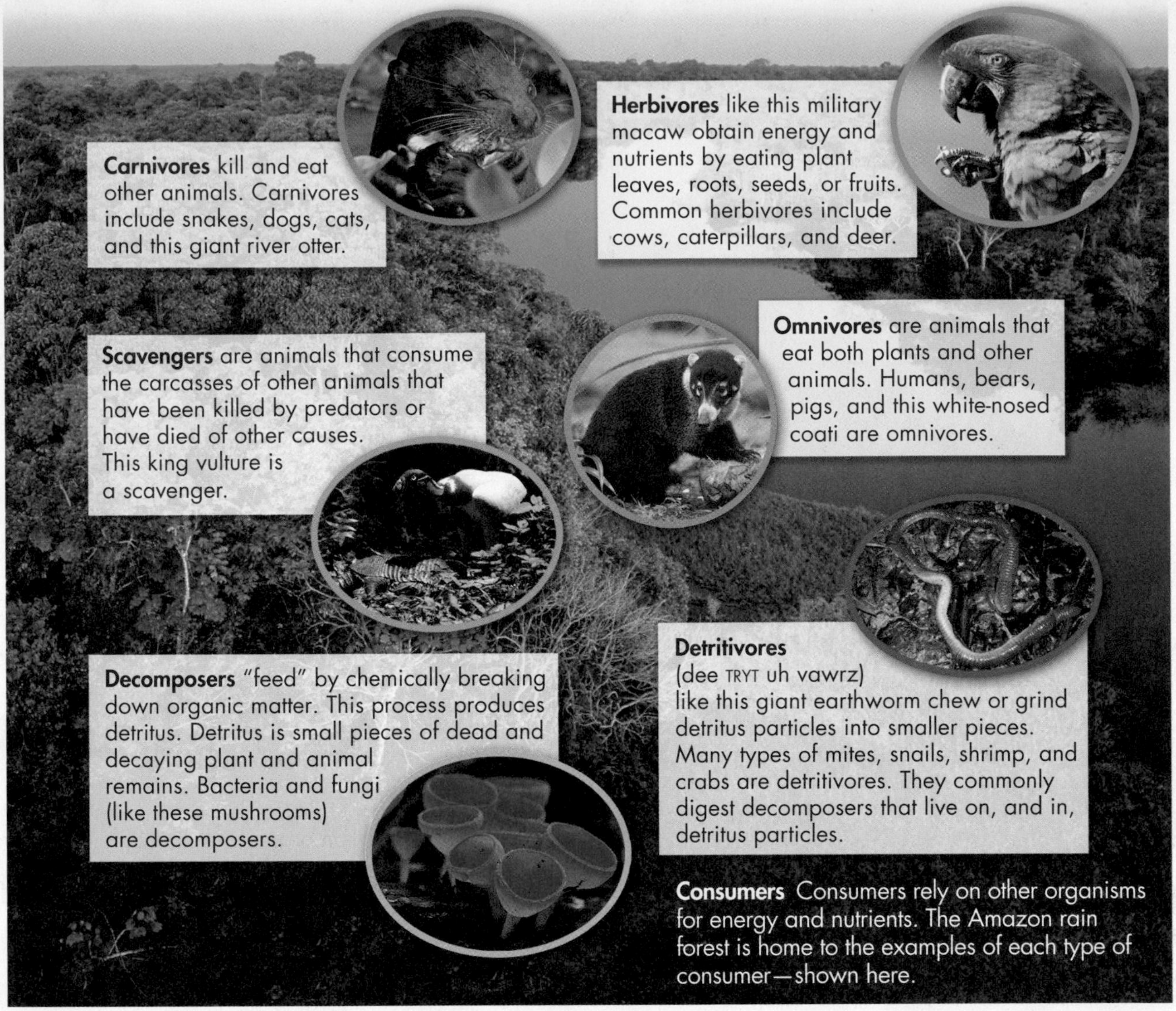
Carnivores kill and eat other animals. Carnivores include snakes, dogs, cats, and this giant river otter.
Herbivores like this military macaw obtain energy and nutrients by eating plant leaves, roots, seeds, or fruits. Common herbivores include cows, caterpillars, and deer.
Scavengers are animals that consume the carcasses of other animals that have been killed by predators or have died of other causes. This king vulture is a scavenger.
Omnivores are animals that eat both plants and other animals. Humans, bears, pigs, and this white-nosed coati are omnivores.
Decomposers "feed" by chemically breaking down organic matter. This process produces detritus. Detritus is small pieces of dead and decaying plant and animal remains. Bacteria and fungi (like these mushrooms) are decomposers.
Detritivores (dee TRYT uh vawrz) like this giant earthworm chew or grind detritus particles into smaller pieces. Many types of mites, snails, shrimp, and crabs are detritivores. They commonly digest decomposers that live on, and in, detritus particles.

Consumers Consumers rely on other organisms for energy and nutrients. The Amazon rain forest is home to the examples of each type of consumer—shown here.

CHECK Understanding

Apply Vocabulary

Use the highlighted words from the lesson to complete each sentence correctly.

1. Consumers are classified as ______ because they are unable to make their own food.

2. Autotrophs are also known as ______ because they are the first organisms to produce energy-rich compounds in an ecosystem.

Critical Thinking

3. Explain How do consumers obtain energy?

4. Compare and Contrast How are detritivores different from decomposers? Give an example of each.

5. Write to Learn Answer the second clue of the mystery. Write a paragraph explaining the relationship between detritivores and decomposers in an ecosystem.

MYSTERY CLUE

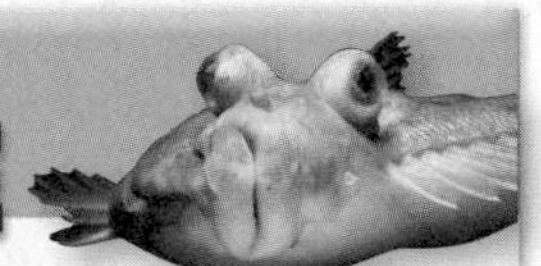

Bacteria are important members of the living community in Narragansett Bay. How do you think the bacterial communities on the floor of the bay might be linked to its producers and consumers? (Hint: See above.)

BIOLOGY.com Search Lesson 3.2 GO • Lesson Assessment • Art Review

3.3 Energy Flow in Ecosystems

MD CLG 3.1.3 Matter and Energy, 3.5.2 Interdependence of Organisms in the Biosphere, 3.5.4 Global Food Webs. SPI 1.5.5 Create and Interpret Graphics, 1.6.1 Ratio and Proportion, 1.6.3 Use Scientific Notation.

Food Chains and Food Webs

What happens to energy stored in body tissues when one organism eats another? It moves from the "eaten" to the "eater." In every ecosystem, primary producers and consumers are linked through feeding relationships. There are many different feeding relationships in an ecosystem. But energy flows through the ecosystem in a one-way stream, from primary producers to various consumers.

Food Chains You can think of energy as passing through an ecosystem in a series of steps. This series of steps is called a **food chain.** In a food chain, organisms transfer energy by eating and being eaten. Food chains can vary in length. Look at the aquatic food chain below. The primary producers are a mixture of floating algae (called phytoplankton) and attached algae. These primary producers may be eaten by small fishes, such as flagfish. Larger fishes, like the largemouth bass, eat the small fishes. The bass are preyed upon by large wading birds, such as the anhinga. In the end, the anhinga may be eaten by an alligator. Therefore there are four steps in this food chain. So the top carnivore is four steps removed from the primary producer.

Food Webs In most ecosystems, feeding relationships are much more complicated than a simple chain can describe. One reason for this is that many animals eat more than one kind of food. Take Africa's Serengeti Plain, for example. Herbivores such as zebras, gazelles, and buffaloes often graze upon several different species of grasses. Several predators such as lions, hyenas, and leopards, in turn, often prey upon those herbivores! Ecologists call this network of feeding interactions a **food web.**

Key Questions

🔑 **How does energy flow through ecosystems?**

🔑 **What do the three types of ecological pyramids illustrate?**

BUILD Understanding

Preview Visuals Before you read, look at the diagrams called Food Chains and Food Web in the Everglades. Note how the diagrams are similar and how they are different.

In Your Workbook Complete the chart in Lesson 3.3 by noting the similarities and differences between the two diagrams.

Food Chains Food chains show the one-way flow of energy in an ecosystem.

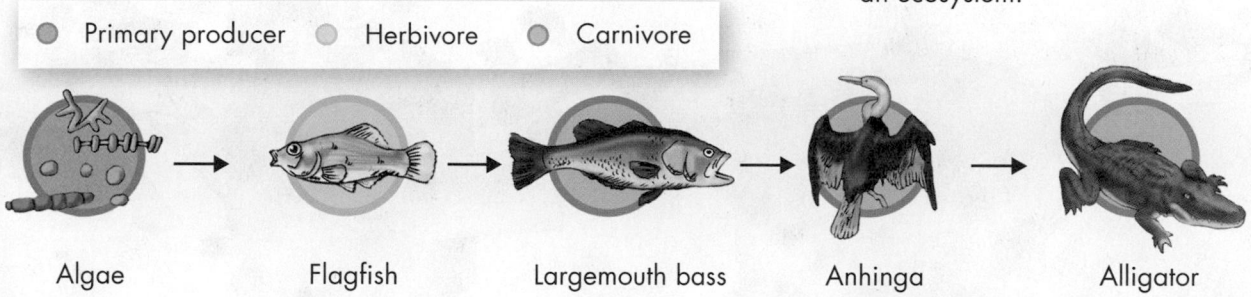

| ● Primary producer | ● Herbivore | ● Carnivore |

Algae → Flagfish → Largemouth bass → Anhinga → Alligator

BUILD Vocabulary

food chain
a series of steps in an ecosystem in which organisms transfer energy by eating and being eaten

food web
a network of complex interactions formed by the feeding relationships among the various organisms in an ecosystem

trophic level
each step in a food chain or food web

ecological pyramid
an illustration of the relative amounts of energy or matter contained within each trophic level in a given food chain or food web

🐾 ACADEMIC WORDS

An ecological pyramid looks more like a triangle than a pyramid. But ecologists call it a pyramid because it has layers that get smaller as you go toward the top—just like an Egyptian pyramid.

BUILD Connections

EARTH'S RECYCLING CENTER

Decomposers break down dead and decaying matter and release nutrients that can be reused by primary producers.

In Your Workbook How are decomposers like a recycling center? Go to your workbook to explain.

▶ *Food Chains Within Food Webs* The Everglades are a complex marshland ecosystem in southern Florida, with many overlapping feeding relationships. These relationships have been simplified —many species have been left out—and represented in the food web to the right. Many different paths can be taken from a primary producer to a predator. Each path is a food chain. So, a food web links together all of the food chains in an ecosystem. Now, you can begin to appreciate how complicated food webs are!

▶ *Decomposers and Detritivores in Food Webs* Decomposers and detritivores are as important in most food webs as other consumers are. Look again at the Everglades web. White-tailed deer, moorhens, raccoons, grass shrimp, crayfish, and flagfish feed at least partly on primary producers. But most producers die without being eaten, so decomposers convert that dead material to detritus. The detritus is eaten by detritivores, such as crayfish, grass shrimp, and worms. At the same time, the decomposition process releases nutrients that can be used by primary producers. Decomposers are nature's recyclers. Without decomposers, nutrients would remain locked in dead organisms.

Food Webs and Disturbance Relationships in food webs are not simple, so a disturbance can have dramatic effects. Look again at the food web. What might happen to the feeding relationships in it after a disturbance? Suppose an oil spill caused a major decrease in the number of decomposers. How might that affect the populations of detritivores? Would a change in those populations affect how pig frogs feed? How might a change in frog feeding behavior affect other species the frogs eat? As you can see, a decrease in decomposers would affect the whole web.

🔑 **Key Question** How does energy flow through ecosystems? **Energy flows through an ecosystem in a one-way stream, from primary producers to various consumers.**

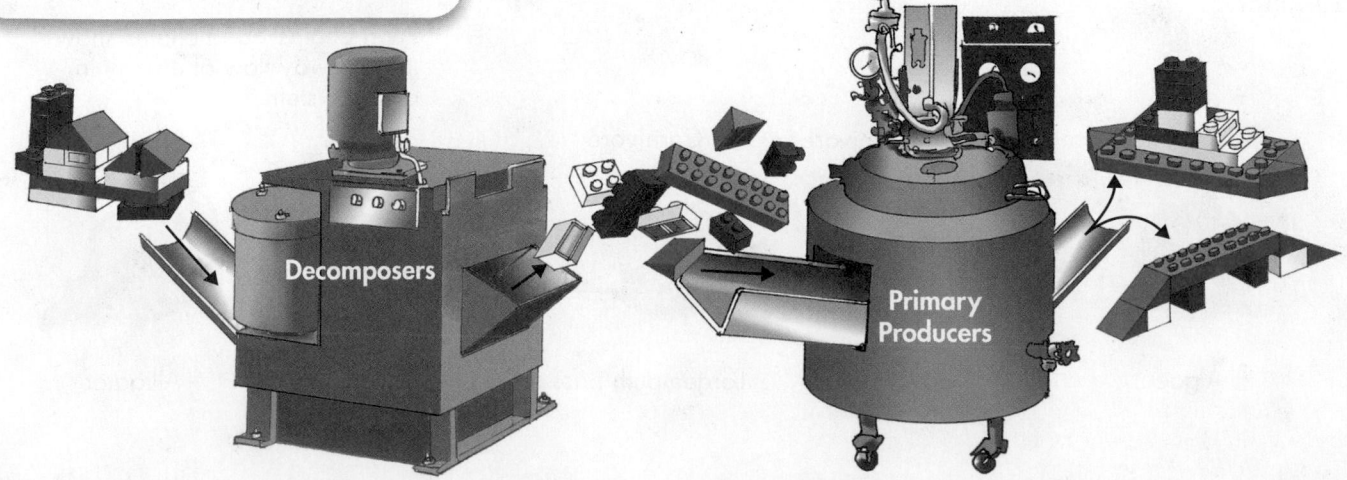

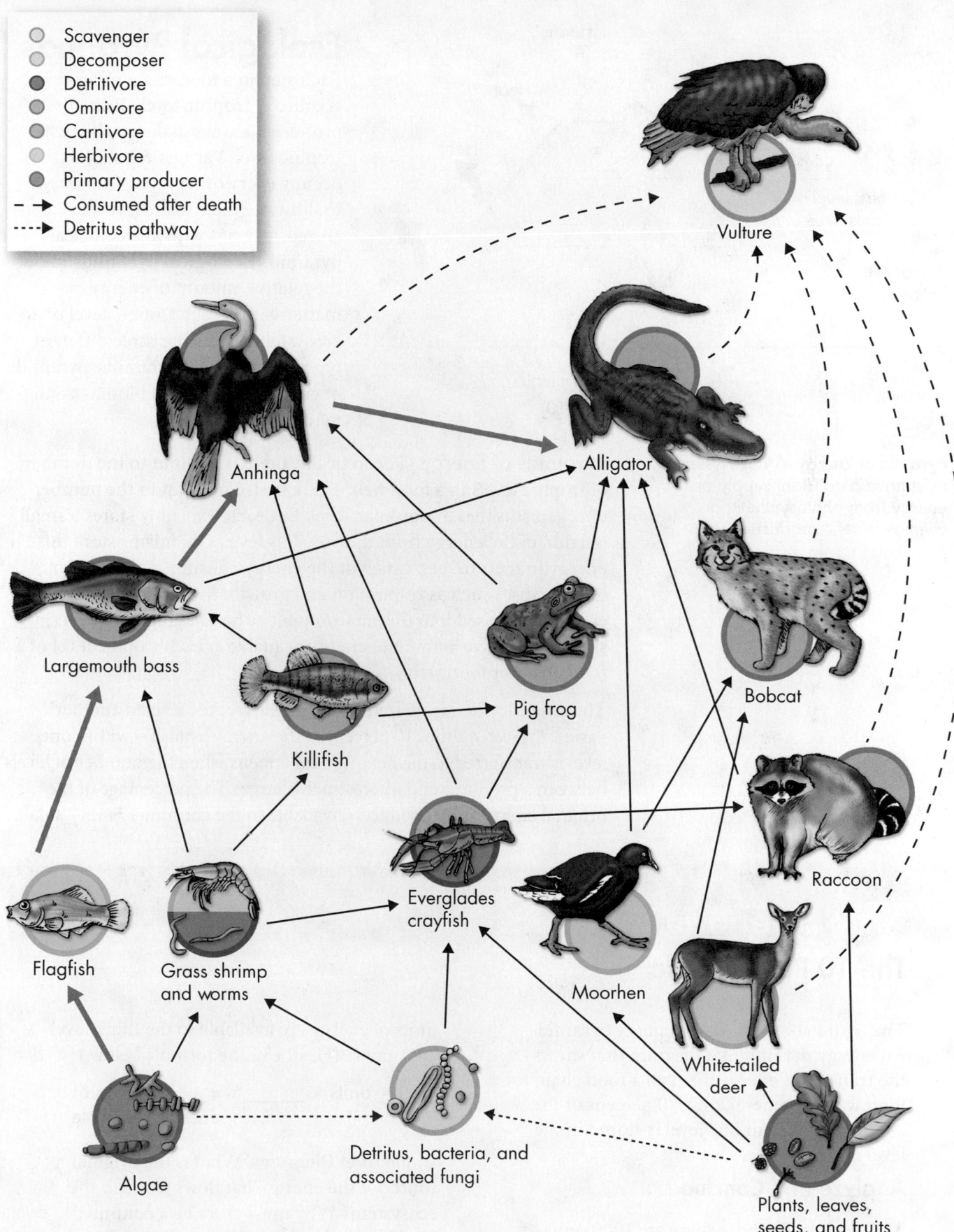

Food Web in the Everglades This illustration of a food web shows some of the feeding relationships within the Florida Everglades. The orange-highlighted aquatic food chain is one of many chains that make up this food web.

Legend:
- Scavenger
- Decomposer
- Detritivore
- Omnivore
- Carnivore
- Herbivore
- Primary producer
- – → Consumed after death
- ---→ Detritus pathway

Labels: Vulture, Anhinga, Alligator, Largemouth bass, Killifish, Pig frog, Bobcat, Raccoon, Flagfish, Grass shrimp and worms, Everglades crayfish, Moorhen, White-tailed deer, Algae, Detritus, bacteria, and associated fungi, Plants, leaves, seeds, and fruits

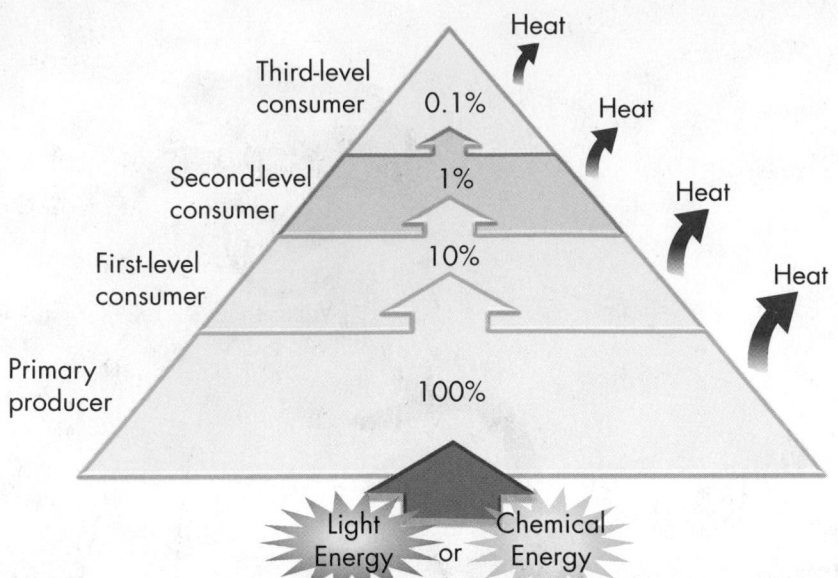

Heat

Third-level consumer — 0.1%

Heat

Second-level consumer — 1%

Heat

First-level consumer — 10%

Heat

Primary producer — 100%

Light Energy or Chemical Energy

Ecological Pyramids

Each step in a food chain or food web is called a **trophic level.** Primary producers always make up the first trophic level. Various consumers occupy every other level. One way to illustrate the trophic levels in an ecosystem is with an ecological pyramid. **Ecological pyramids** show the relative amount of energy or matter within each trophic level of an ecosystem. There are three different types of ecological pyramids: pyramids of energy, pyramids of biomass, and pyramids of numbers.

Pyramid of Energy An ecosystem must have a constant supply of energy from photosynthetic or chemosynthetic producers.

Pyramids of Energy Theoretically, there is no limit to the number of trophic levels in a food web. There is also no limit to the number of organisms that live on each level. But each level only stores a small portion of the energy from the previous level. Organisms store this energy in their tissues. Much of the energy consumed is spent on life processes such as respiration and growth. Most of the remaining energy is released into the environment as heat. Pyramids of energy show the relative amount of energy available at each trophic level of a food chain or food web.

The efficiency of energy transfer from one trophic level to another varies. Typically, about 10 percent of the energy available within one level is transferred to the next. What happens when the number of levels between a producer and a consumer is large? The percentage of the original energy from producers available to the consumer is very small.

INQUIRY into Scientific Thinking

GUIDED INQUIRY

The 10 Percent Rule

The figure above shows an energy pyramid. An energy pyramid is a diagram that shows the transfer of energy through a food chain or food web. In general, only 10 percent of the energy available in one level is stored in the level above.

Analyze and Conclude

1. Calculate Suppose there are 1000 units of energy available at the producer level of the energy pyramid. Approximately how many units of energy are available to the third-level consumer? (Hint: Use the formula below.)

_____ units × _____ % = _____ units of energy available

2. Interpret Diagrams What is the original source of the energy that flows through the ecosystem? Why must there be a continual supply of energy into the ecosystem?

In Your Workbook Get more help for this activity in your workbook.

Pyramids of Biomass and Numbers The total amount of living tissue within a trophic level is called its **biomass.** Biomass is usually measured in grams of organic matter per unit area. The amount of energy available to a trophic level helps determine the amount of biomass it can support. A pyramid of biomass illustrates the relative amount of living tissue available at each trophic level in an ecosystem.

Ecologists interested in the number of organisms at each trophic level use a pyramid of numbers. A pyramid of numbers shows the relative number of individual organisms at each trophic level in an ecosystem. Usually, the shapes of the pyramids of biomass and numbers are similar for an ecosystem. In this shape, the numbers of individuals on each level decrease from the level below it. The result might look something like the pyramid to the right.

In some cases, consumers are much smaller than the organisms they feed upon. For example, thousands of insects may graze on a single tree. Countless mosquitoes can feed off a few deer. Both the tree and deer have a lot of biomass, but they each represent only one organism. In such cases, the pyramid of numbers may be turned upside down, but the pyramid of biomass is right side up.

🔑 **Key Question** What do the three types of ecological pyramids illustrate? **A pyramid of energy shows the relative amounts of energy available at each trophic level of an ecosystem. A pyramid of biomass illustrates the relative amount of living organic matter available at each trophic level. A pyramid of numbers shows the relative number of organisms at each trophic level.**

Pyramids of Biomass and Numbers In most cases, pyramids of biomass and numbers follow the same general pattern. In the field modeled here, there are more individual primary producers than first-level consumers. And the primary producers collectively have more mass. With each step to a higher trophic level, biomass and numbers decrease.

CHECK Understanding

Apply Vocabulary

Use the highlighted words from the lesson to complete each sentence correctly.

1. A(n) _____ is a way of representing the feeding relationships within an ecosystem.

2. A step in a food chain or food web is called a _____.

Critical Thinking

3. Write to Learn Answer the mystery clue.

MYSTERY CLUE

Zooplankton in Narragansett Bay graze on floating algae. The zooplankton now graze more actively during the winter than ever before. How might this affect the annual late-winter "bloom" of algae?

3.4 Cycles of Matter

MD CLG 3.1.3 Matter and Energy, 3.5.1 Factors Influencing Ecosystems, 3.5.2 Interdependence of Organisms in the Biosphere, 3.5.3 Population Dynamics, 3.5.4 Global Food Webs. SPI 1.5.5 Create and Interpret Graphics, 1.5.8 Compare.

Key Questions

🔑 How does matter move through the biosphere?

🔑 How does water cycle through the biosphere?

🔑 What is the importance of the main nutrient cycles?

🔑 How does nutrient availability relate to the primary productivity of an ecosystem?

BUILD Understanding

Main Idea and Details Chart
Make a main idea and details chart using the green and blue headings in this lesson. Fill in the details as you read to help you organize the information.

In Your Workbook Go to your workbook to learn more about making a main idea and details chart. Complete the chart for Lesson 3.4.

Recycling in the Biosphere

Energy passes in one direction from one trophic level to the next. Eventually it escapes into the environment as heat along the way. Energy in the form of sunlight is constantly entering the biosphere. But Earth doesn't receive a steady supply of new matter from space. Instead, matter is recycled. Elements, such as oxygen, carbon, and hydrogen, pass from one organism to another and from one ecosystem to another. They also pass among parts of the biosphere through closed loops called **biogeochemical cycles.** The flow of energy powers these cycles. Cycles of matter involve *bio*logical processes, *geo*logical processes, and *chemical* processes. Human activity can also play an important role. Matter is transformed as it moves through these cycles. It is never created or destroyed—just changed. The processes involved in biogeochemical cycles can be classified in the following ways:

▶ *Biological Processes* Biological processes consist of any and all activities performed by living organisms. These processes include eating, breathing, "burning" food, and eliminating waste products.

▶ *Geological Processes* Geological processes include volcanic eruptions and the formation and breakdown of rock. They also include major movements of matter within and below the surface of the earth.

▶ *Chemical and Physical Processes* Chemical and physical processes include the formation of clouds and precipitation. They also include the flow of running water and the action of lightning.

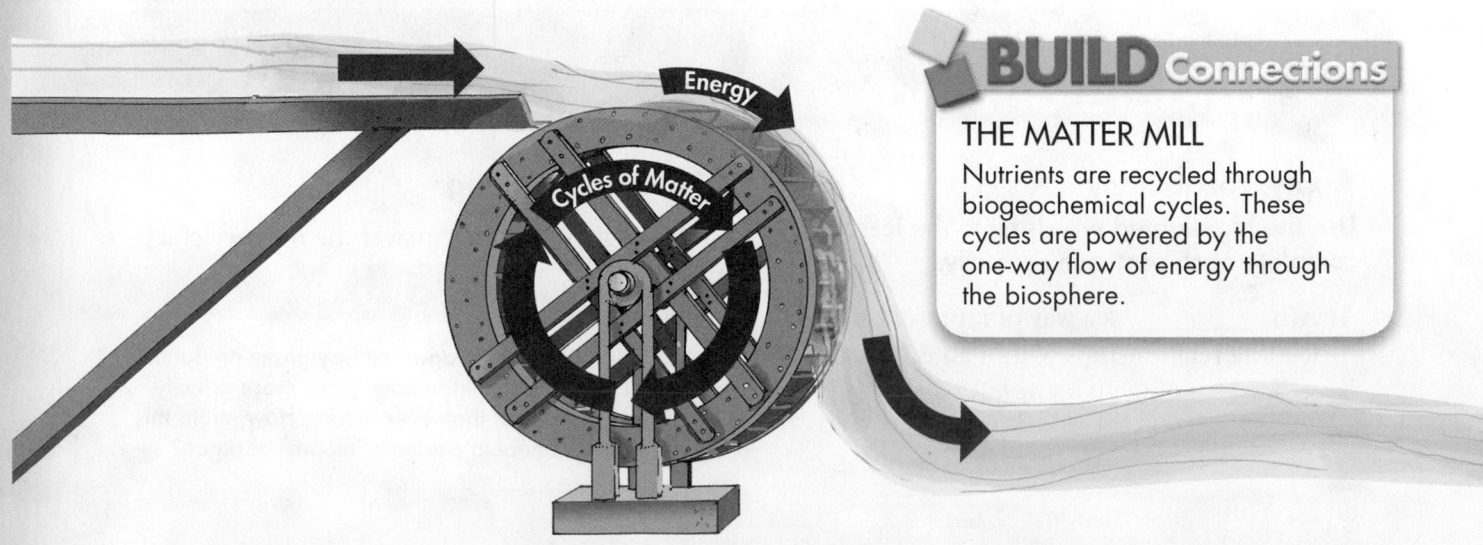

BUILD Connections

THE MATTER MILL

Nutrients are recycled through biogeochemical cycles. These cycles are powered by the one-way flow of energy through the biosphere.

▶ *Human Activity* Mining and burning fossil fuels, and burning forests, affect the cycles of matter. So does clearing land for building and farming. Manufacturing and using fertilizers also influence cycles of matter.

These cycles pass the same atoms and molecules around again and again. Just think—carbon atoms in your body may once have been part of the tail of a dinosaur!

🔑 **Key Question** How does matter move through the biosphere? **Matter is recycled within and between ecosystems.**

The Water Cycle

Water constantly moves between the oceans, the atmosphere, and land. It can be inside organisms or outside them. Water molecules usually enter the atmosphere by evaporating from bodies of water or from plant leaves. When it evaporates, water becomes a gas called water vapor.

Winds can transport water vapor over great distances. In cooling air, the vapor condenses into tiny droplets that form clouds. When the droplets become large enough, they fall to Earth's surface as precipitation. This can be in the form of rain, snow, sleet, or hail. Precipitation can become runoff, flowing along the surface of land into a river or stream. It can also be absorbed into the ground, becoming groundwater. Groundwater enters plants through their roots or flows into bodies of water. If it penetrates deeply into the ground, it becomes part of underground reservoirs. Water that re-enters the atmosphere through transpiration or evaporation begins the cycle again.

🔑 **Key Question** How does water cycle through the biosphere? **Water continuously moves between the oceans, the atmosphere, and land. Sometimes the water is outside living organisms and sometimes it is inside them.**

BUILD Vocabulary

biogeochemical cycle
a process in which elements, chemical compounds, and other forms of matter are passed from one organism to another and from one part of the biosphere to another

🔧 **ROOT WORDS**
The term *biogeochemical* is formed by combining the words *biological*, *geological*, and *chemical*.

The Water Cycle This diagram shows the main processes in the water cycle. Scientists estimate that it can take as long as 4000 years to complete one cycle.

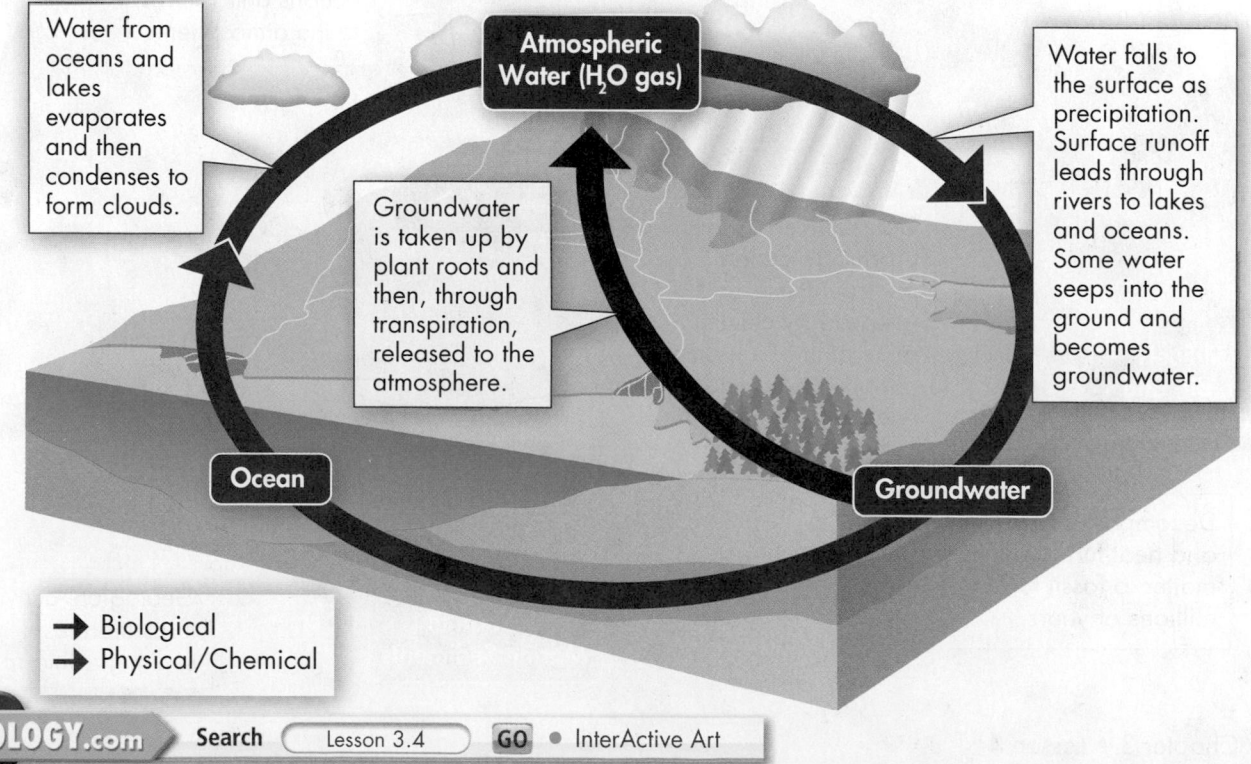

Water from oceans and lakes evaporates and then condenses to form clouds.

Atmospheric Water (H₂O gas)

Groundwater is taken up by plant roots and then, through transpiration, released to the atmosphere.

Water falls to the surface as precipitation. Surface runoff leads through rivers to lakes and oceans. Some water seeps into the ground and becomes groundwater.

Ocean

Groundwater

→ Biological
→ Physical/Chemical

Nutrient Cycles

Nutrients are chemical substances organisms need to build tissues and carry out life functions. Like water, they pass through organisms and the environment through biogeochemical cycles. The three most important cycles move carbon, nitrogen, and phosphorus through the biosphere.

The Carbon Cycle Carbon is a major component of all organic compounds, including carbohydrates, lipids, proteins, and nucleic acids. There are several major carbon reservoirs in the biosphere. For example, carbon is found in calcium carbonate ($CaCO_3$). This mineral is found in animal skeletons and several kinds of rocks. Carbon and oxygen form carbon dioxide gas (CO_2). CO_2 is an important component of the atmosphere and is also dissolved in oceans. Coal, oil, natural gas, and forests also are important carbon reservoirs.

The Carbon Cycle Carbon is found in several large reservoirs in the biosphere. In the atmosphere, it is found as carbon dioxide gas (CO_2); in the oceans, as dissolved carbon dioxide; on land, in organisms, rocks, and soil; and underground, as coal, petroleum, and calcium carbonate.

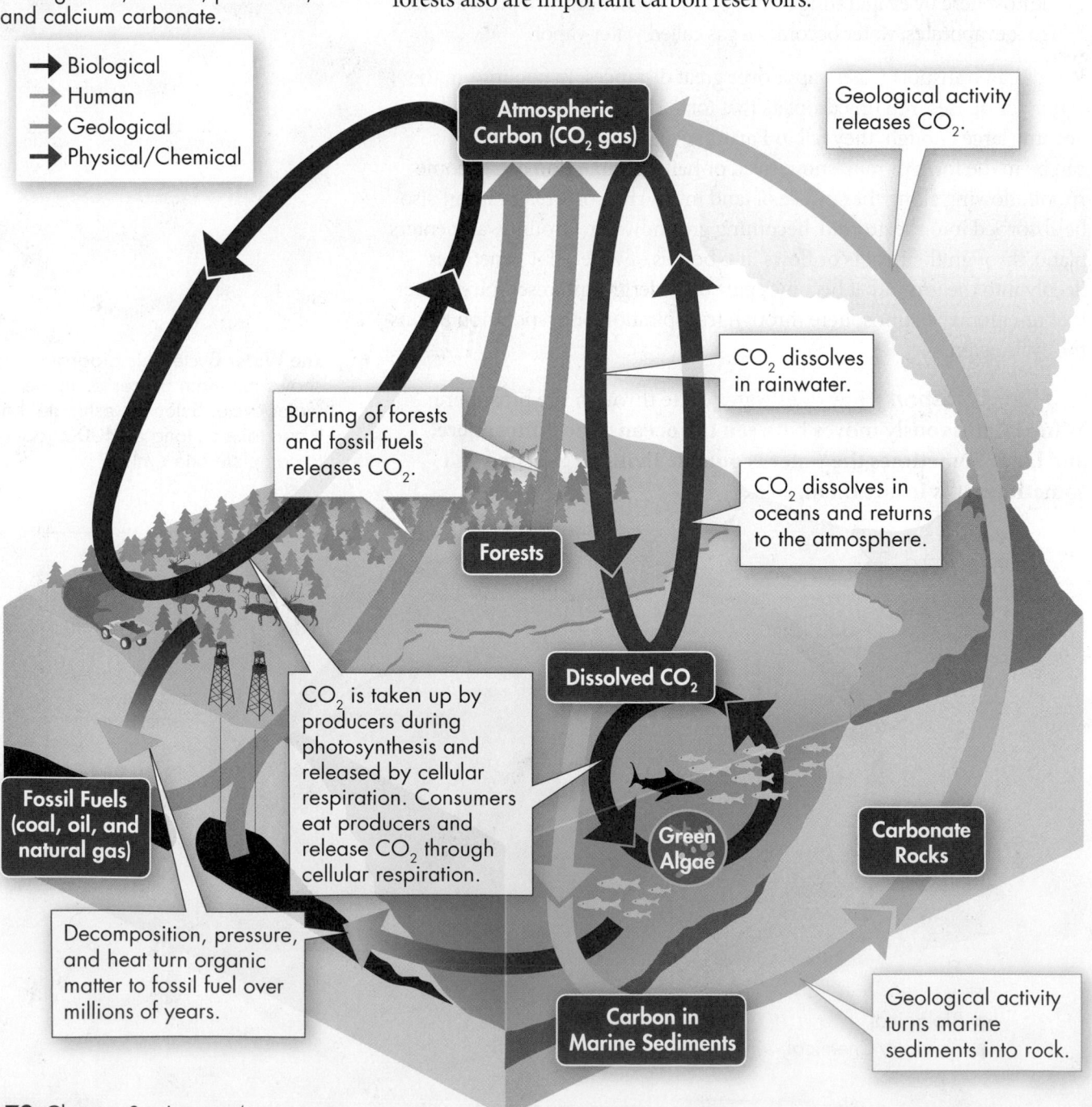

→ Biological
→ Human
→ Geological
→ Physical/Chemical

Atmospheric Carbon (CO_2 gas)

Geological activity releases CO_2.

CO_2 dissolves in rainwater.

Burning of forests and fossil fuels releases CO_2.

CO_2 dissolves in oceans and returns to the atmosphere.

Forests

Dissolved CO_2

CO_2 is taken up by producers during photosynthesis and released by cellular respiration. Consumers eat producers and release CO_2 through cellular respiration.

Green Algae

Fossil Fuels (coal, oil, and natural gas)

Carbonate Rocks

Decomposition, pressure, and heat turn organic matter to fossil fuel over millions of years.

Carbon in Marine Sediments

Geological activity turns marine sediments into rock.

The figure to the left shows the carbon cycle. Notice how carbon often moves between different parts of the cycle as carbon dioxide. Stored carbon is found in organic matter, fossil fuels, rocks, and the skeletons of organisms.

The Nitrogen Cycle All organisms need nitrogen to make amino acids and nucleic acids. Nitrogen exists as a gas (N_2) in the atmosphere. Nitrogen is found in soil in compounds such as ammonia (NH_3), and in nitrate (NO_3^-) and nitrite (NO_2^-) ions. These substances also exist in wastes and decomposing organic matter. Several forms of dissolved nitrogen can be found in the oceans and other large water bodies.

Nitrogen gas is the most common form of nitrogen on Earth. But only certain kinds of bacteria can use nitrogen gas directly. These bacteria use a process called **nitrogen fixation** to convert nitrogen gas to ammonia. Some of these bacteria live in the soil and on the roots of certain plants, such as peanuts and peas. Other kinds of bacteria convert ammonia into nitrates and nitrites. Primary producers use these compounds to make proteins and nucleic acids. Consumers eat producers and reuse the nitrogen to make their own proteins and nucleic acids. Decomposers release ammonia, nitrates, and nitrites from wastes and dead organisms. Producers can reuse these compounds. There are also some soil bacteria that convert nitrates to nitrogen gas. The process of converting nitrates to nitrogen gas is called **denitrification.** Denitrification provides the bacteria with energy. Humans also add nitrogen to the biosphere by manufacturing and using fertilizers. Runoff often carries excess fertilizer into surface water or groundwater.

BUILD
Vocabulary

nitrogen fixation
the process of converting nitrogen gas into nitrogen compounds that plants can absorb and use

denitrification
the process by which soil bacteria convert nitrates into nitrogen gas

ACADEMIC WORDS
The verb *accumulate* means "to collect or gather." Carbon accumulates, or collects, in the soil and in the oceans where it cycles among organisms or is turned into fossil fuels.

The Nitrogen Cycle The atmosphere is the largest reservoir of nitrogen in the biosphere. Nitrogen also cycles through the soil and through the tissues of living organisms.

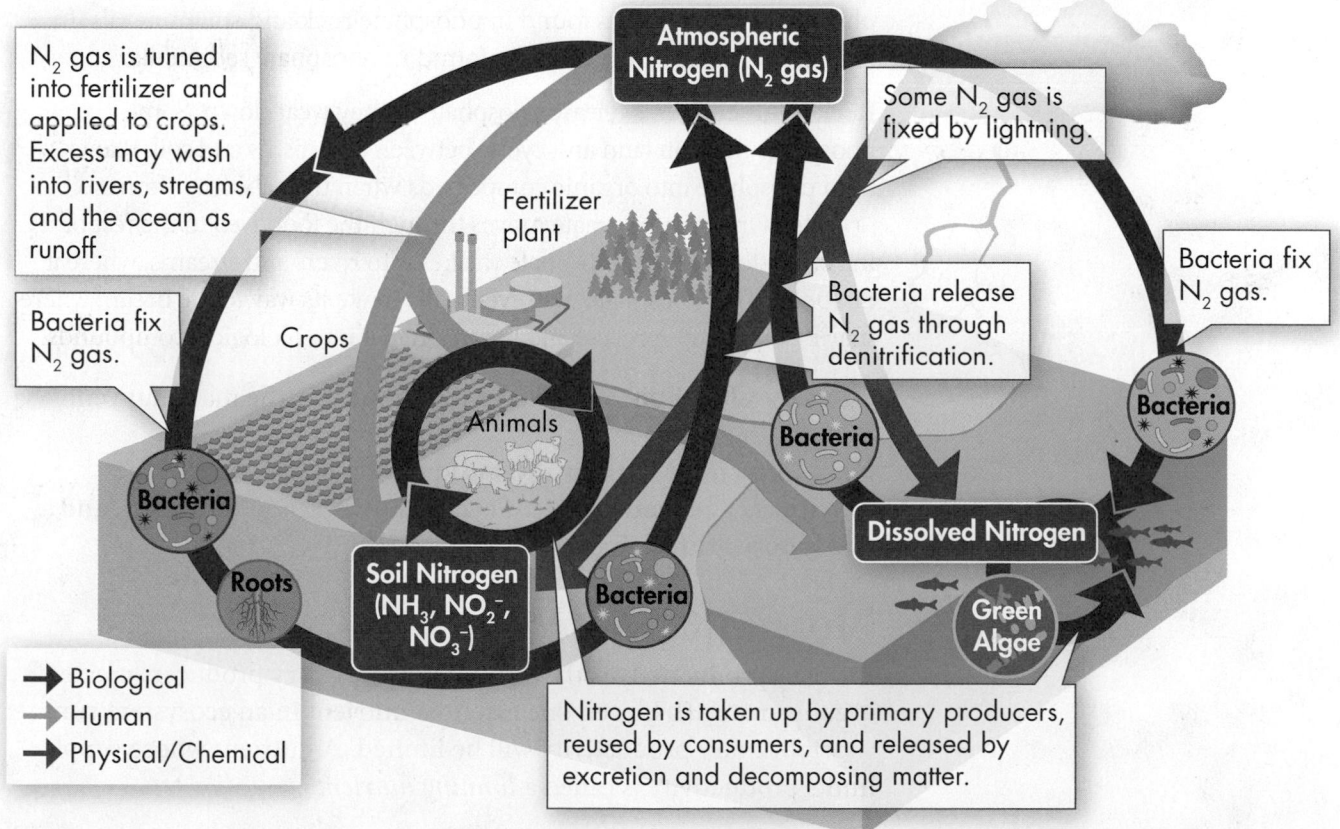

N_2 gas is turned into fertilizer and applied to crops. Excess may wash into rivers, streams, and the ocean as runoff.

Some N_2 gas is fixed by lightning.

Bacteria fix N_2 gas.

Bacteria fix N_2 gas.

Bacteria release N_2 gas through denitrification.

Atmospheric Nitrogen (N_2 gas)

Fertilizer plant

Crops

Animals

Bacteria

Bacteria

Bacteria

Bacteria

Dissolved Nitrogen

Roots

Soil Nitrogen (NH_3, NO_2^-, NO_3^-)

Green Algae

→ Biological
→ Human
→ Physical/Chemical

Nitrogen is taken up by primary producers, reused by consumers, and released by excretion and decomposing matter.

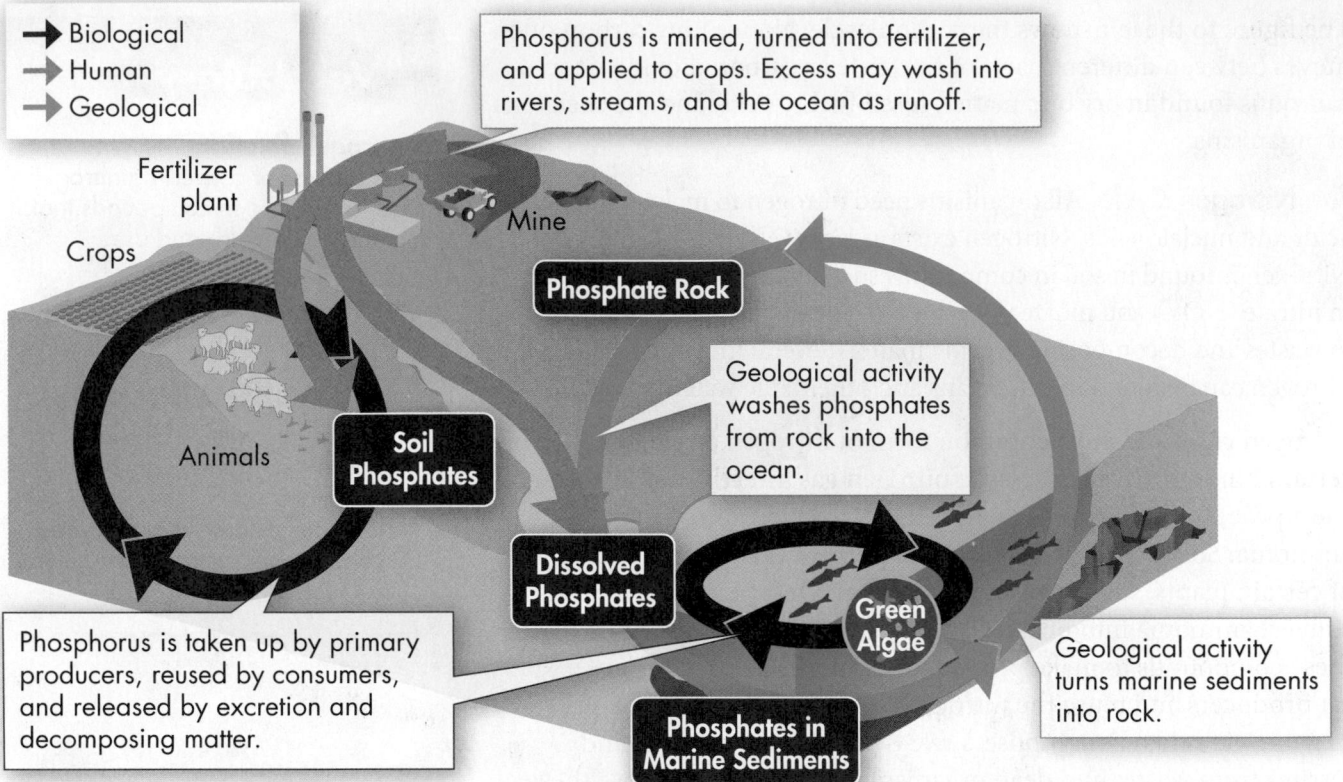

Biological
Human
Geological

Fertilizer plant

Crops

Mine

Phosphate Rock

Phosphorus is mined, turned into fertilizer, and applied to crops. Excess may wash into rivers, streams, and the ocean as runoff.

Geological activity washes phosphates from rock into the ocean.

Animals

Soil Phosphates

Dissolved Phosphates

Green Algae

Geological activity turns marine sediments into rock.

Phosphorus is taken up by primary producers, reused by consumers, and released by excretion and decomposing matter.

Phosphates in Marine Sediments

The Phosphorus Cycle Phosphorus in the biosphere cycles among the land, ocean, sediments, and living organisms. Unlike other nutrients, phosphorus is not found in significant quantities in the atmosphere.

The Phosphorus Cycle Phosphorus is essential to living organisms. It is an important part of molecules such as DNA and RNA. Although phosphorus is important biologically, it is not abundant in the biosphere. Phosphorus does not enter the atmosphere in large amounts. Phosphorus remains mostly on land and in the ocean as inorganic phosphate. On land it is found in phosphate rock and soil minerals. In the ocean, it may be dissolved or found in phosphate sediments.

Rocks and sediments release phosphate as they wear down. Some phosphate stays on land and cycles between organisms and soil. Plants bind phosphate into organic compounds when they absorb it from soil or water. Organic phosphate moves through the food web to the rest of the ecosystem. Other phosphate washes into rivers and streams, where it dissolves. This phosphate may eventually make its way to the ocean, where marine organisms process and incorporate it into biological compounds.

Key Question What is the importance of the main nutrient cycles?
Organisms need nutrients to build tissues and carry out life functions. The main nutrient cycles move carbon, nitrogen, and phosphorus through the biosphere.

Nutrient Limitation

Primary productivity is the rate at which primary producers create organic material. If even one essential nutrient in an ecosystem runs short, primary productivity will be limited. A nutrient whose supply limits productivity is called a *limiting nutrient*.

Nutrient Limitation in Soil On many farms, growth of crop plants is limited by a lack of one or more nutrients in the soil. That's why farmers use fertilizers! Most fertilizers contain large amounts of nitrogen, phosphorus, and potassium. These nutrients help plants grow better in poor soil. Micronutrients such as calcium, magnesium, sulfur, iron, and manganese are necessary in relatively small amounts. These elements are sometimes included in specialty fertilizers. Chemical fertilizers do not contain carbon. Plants get carbon from carbon dioxide during photosynthesis. All nutrient cycles work together like the gears in the figure to the right. If a nutrient runs short, the whole system slows down or even stops.

Nutrient Limitation in Aquatic Ecosystems The open oceans of the world are nutrient-poor compared to many land areas. In saltwater environments, nitrogen is typically the limiting nutrient. Phosphorus is typically the limiting nutrient in freshwater environments.

Sometimes an aquatic ecosystem receives a large input of a limiting nutrient. For instance, a heavy rain may cause runoff from heavily fertilized fields. The extra nutrients can cause a dramatic increase in the amount of algae and other primary producers. If there are not enough consumers to eat the algae, an algal bloom can occur. During an algal bloom, algae can cover the water's surface and disrupt the functioning of an ecosystem.

Key Question How does nutrient availability relate to the primary productivity of an ecosystem?
The availability of nutrients may limit primary productivity, even when sunlight and water are plentiful.

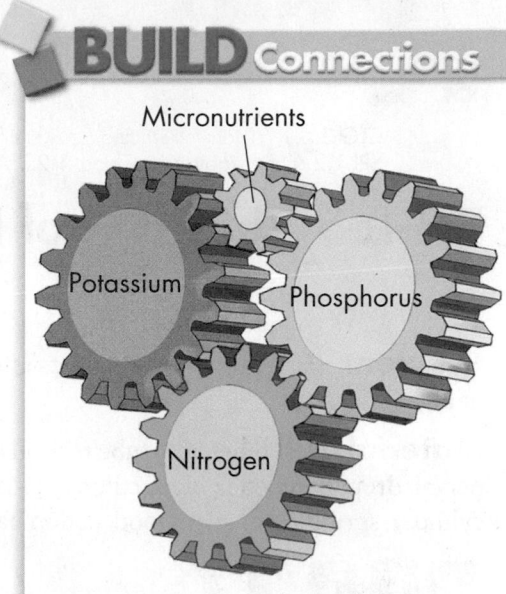

BUILD Connections

Micronutrients

Potassium

Phosphorus

Nitrogen

INTERLOCKING NUTRIENTS
The movement of each nutrient through ecosystems depends on the movement of all the others, because all are needed for living systems to function.

CHECK Understanding

Apply Vocabulary
Use the highlighted words from the lesson to complete each sentence correctly.

1. Bacteria convert nitrogen gas into ammonia using a process called _____.
2. Nutrients move between organisms, the atmosphere, the land, and the water in a series of processes called _____.

Critical Thinking

3. **Explain** How does the way that matter flows through an ecosystem differ from the way that energy flows?
4. **Relate Cause and Effect** A farmer plants a field of corn and fertilizes it with a low-nitrogen fertilizer.

The corn receives plenty of sunlight and water, but does not grow well. What might be preventing the corn from growing?

5. **Write to Learn** Answer the fourth clue to the mystery. Think about how nitrogen enters the water. Is the increase in nitrogen in the water caused by nitrogen fixation or denitrification?

MYSTERY CLUE

Recently, researchers discovered that levels of dissolved nitrogen in the bay have increased. Since human activity hasn't changed much, which organisms in the bay might be responsible? (**Hint:** See p. 71.)

 MD CLG 3.5.1 Factors Influencing Ecosystems, 3.5.2 Interdependence of Organisms in the Biosphere. SPI 1.2.6 Investigative Methods, 1.2.7 Apply Results, 1.3.1 Use Equipment, *(continued below)*

Pre-Lab: The Effect of Fertilizer on Algae

Problem How do excess nutrients affect the growth of algae?

Materials test tubes, test-tube rack, glass-marking pencil, dropper pipettes, algae culture, 25-mL graduated cylinder, spring water, plant food, cotton balls, grow light

Lab Manual Chapter 3 Lab

Skills Focus Predict, Compare and Contrast, Infer

Connect to the Big idea In a healthy ecosystem, nutrients cycle among primary producers, consumers, and decomposers. The growth of primary producers is limited by the availability of nutrients. Humans can intentionally increase the amount of nutrients in an ecosystem. For example, farmers may add fertilizer to the soil in which they grow crops. But the addition of nutrients to an ecosystem is not always planned. For example, runoff from soil that contains fertilizer may flow into coastal waters or freshwater ponds. In this lab, you will observe what happens when algae that live in those waters are provided with excess nutrients.

Background Questions

a. Review What is a limiting nutrient?

b. Explain Why do farmers use fertilizers?

c. Classify What role do algae play in freshwater ecosystems?

Pre-Lab Questions

Preview the procedure in the lab manual.

1. Design an Experiment What is the independent variable in this experiment?

2. Predict After four days, how will you be able to tell which test tube has more algae?

3. Control Variables Why will you grow *Chlorella* in spring water instead of pond water?

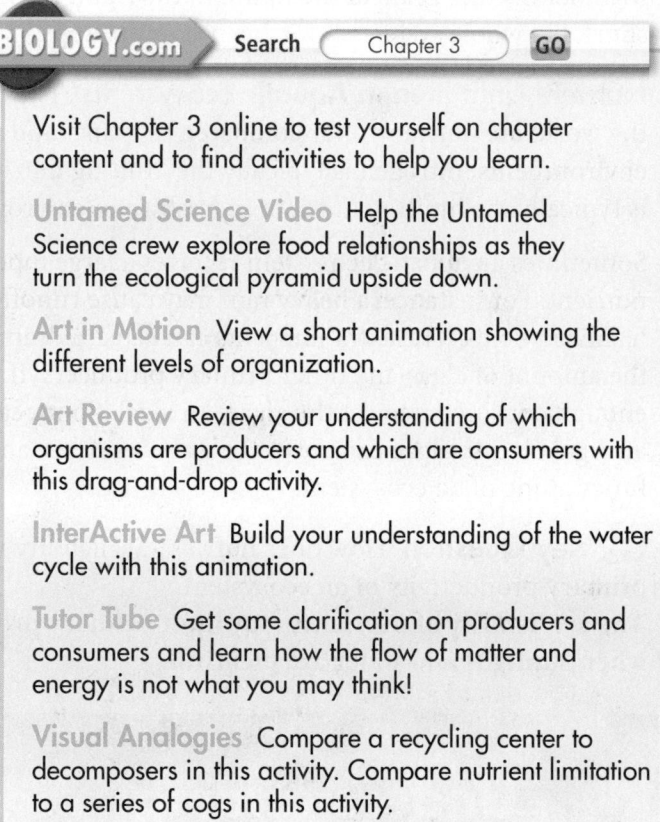

BIOLOGY.com Search [Chapter 3] GO

Visit Chapter 3 online to test yourself on chapter content and to find activities to help you learn.

Untamed Science Video Help the Untamed Science crew explore food relationships as they turn the ecological pyramid upside down.

Art in Motion View a short animation showing the different levels of organization.

Art Review Review your understanding of which organisms are producers and which are consumers with this drag-and-drop activity.

InterActive Art Build your understanding of the water cycle with this animation.

Tutor Tube Get some clarification on producers and consumers and learn how the flow of matter and energy is not what you may think!

Visual Analogies Compare a recycling center to decomposers in this activity. Compare nutrient limitation to a series of cogs in this activity.

 MD 1.3.3 Safe Handling of Materials, 1.5.9 Synthesize Ideas.

3.1 What Is Ecology?

- Ecology is the scientific study of interactions among organisms and between organisms and their physical environment.

- A biotic factor is any living part of the environment.

- An abiotic factor is any nonliving part of the environment.

- Modern ecologists use three methods in their work: observation, experimentation, and modeling.

biosphere (p. 56)   community (p. 56)
ecology (p. 56)   biotic factor (p. 57)
population (p. 56)   abiotic factor (p. 58)

3.2 Energy, Producers, and Consumers

- Primary producers are the first producers of energy-rich compounds that are later used by other organisms.

- Organisms that rely on the other organisms for energy and nutrients are called consumers.

autotroph (p. 60)   heterotroph (p. 61)
primary producer (p. 60)   consumer (p. 61)

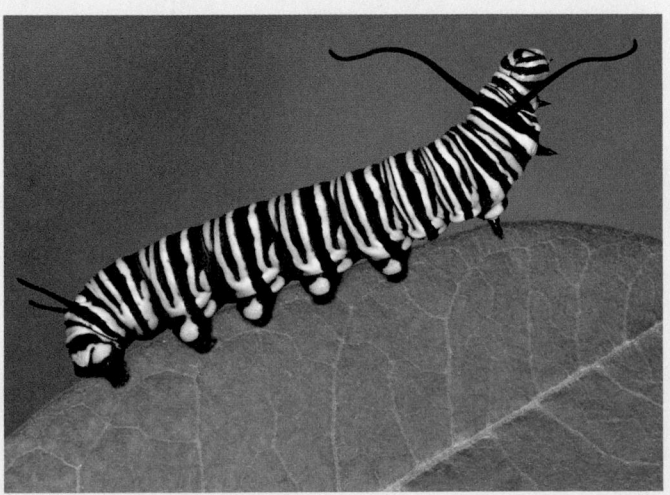

3.3 Energy Flow in Ecosystems

- Energy flows through an ecosystem in a one-way stream, from primary producers to various consumers.

- Pyramids of energy show the relative amount of energy available at each trophic level of an ecosystem. A pyramid of biomass illustrates the relative amount of living organic matter available at each trophic level. A pyramid of numbers shows the relative number of individual organisms at each trophic level.

food chain (p. 63)   ecological pyramid (p. 66)
food web (p. 63)   biomass (p. 67)
trophic level (p. 66)

3.4 Cycles of Matter

- Matter is recycled within and between ecosystems.

- Water continuously moves between the oceans, the atmosphere, and land. Sometimes the water is outside living organisms and sometimes it is inside them.

- Organisms need nutrients to build tissues and carry out life functions. The main nutrient cycles move carbon, nitrogen, and phosphorus through the biosphere.

- The availability of nutrients may limit primary productivity, even when sunlight and water are plentiful.

biogeochemical cycle (p. 68)
nitrogen fixation (p. 71)
denitrification (p. 71)

Assess the Big idea
Matter and Energy, Interdependence in Nature

Write an answer to the question below.

Q: How do Earth's living and nonliving parts interact and affect the survival of organisms?

Constructed Response

Write an answer to each of the numbered questions below. The answer to each question should be one or two paragraphs. To help you begin, read the **Hints** below the questions.

1. **Why does the amount of energy available at each trophic level limit the number of organisms it can support?**

   Hint Only 10 percent of the energy from a given trophic level is transferred to the next trophic level.

   Hint Most of the energy transferred to a trophic level is used for life processes.

2. **How does a wildfire affect the carbon cycle?**

   Hint Trees are a part of an ecosystem's biomass.

3. **Why is it important for farmers to fertilize land used for crops?**

   Hint Primary productivity is limited by the availability of nutrients.

   Hint Which nutrients are found in high concentrations in plant material?

Foundations for Learning Wrap-Up

The layered book you made as you read the chapter is a tool you can use to arrange your thoughts about the biosphere.

Activity 1 Working with a partner, take turns explaining the important concepts in each lesson using your layered book.

Activity 2 Working in small groups, create two fishbone maps like the one shown below. One map will represent Matter and Energy. The second map will focus on Interdependence in Nature. Fill in the maps with details from your layered book. Use the maps to answer the following questions:

- How do plants and animals interact to move matter and energy through the biosphere?

- How do the biogeochemical cycles interact to move matter and energy between land, water, and air?

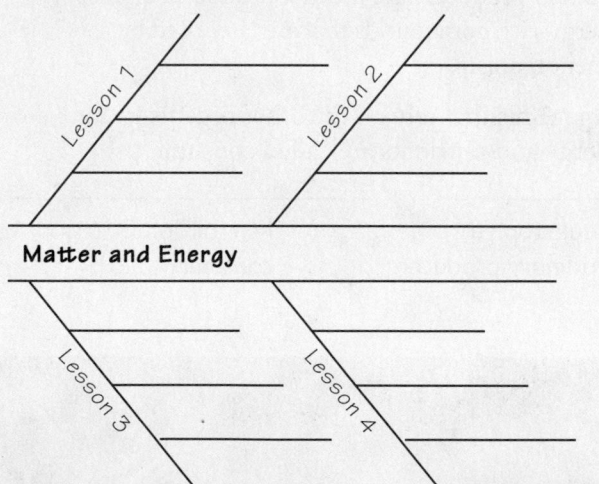

Understand Key Concepts

1. The term that ecologists use to indicate life on a global scale is
   - **a.** ecosystem.
   - **b.** biome.
   - **c.** biosphere.
   - **d.** ecology.

2. Which term describes a group of different species that live together in a defined area?
   - **a.** a population
   - **b.** a community
   - **c.** an ecosystem
   - **d.** a biosphere

Test-Taking Tip

Anticipate the Answer Think of your answer before looking at the answer choices. Then select the answer choice that comes closest to your own. In question 2, answer **b** is correct because a community is the only term that includes different species in a specific area.

Think Critically

3. **Pose Questions** You live near a pond that you have observed for years. One year you notice the water contains a massive overgrowth of green algae. What is a question you might have about this unusual growth?

3.2 Energy, Producers, and Consumers

Understand Key Concepts

4. Primary producers are organisms that
   - **a.** rely on other organisms for their energy and food supply.
   - **b.** consume plant and animal remains and other dead matter.
   - **c.** use energy from the environment to make complex organic molecules from inorganic molecules.
   - **d.** obtain energy by eating only plants.

5. Which of the following organisms is a decomposer?

a. **b.** **c.** **d.**

6. Which of the following describes how ALL consumers get their energy?
   - **a.** directly from the sun
   - **b.** from eating primary producers
   - **c.** from inorganic chemicals like hydrogen sulfide
   - **d.** from eating organisms that are living or were once living

Think Critically

7. **Classify** Classify each of the following as an herbivore, a carnivore, an omnivore, or a detritivore: earthworm, bear, cow, snail, snake, human.

3.3 Energy Flow in Ecosystems

Understand Key Concepts

8. The series of steps in which a large fish eats a small fish that has eaten algae is a
   - **a.** food web.
   - **b.** food chain.
   - **c.** pyramid of numbers.
   - **d.** pyramid of biomass.

9. The total amount of living tissue at each trophic level in an ecosystem can be shown in a(n)
   - **a.** energy pyramid.
   - **b.** pyramid of numbers.
   - **c.** biomass pyramid.
   - **d.** biogeochemical cycle.

10. What happens to energy in a trophic level that is not stored or used for life processes?

Think Critically

11. **Sequence** Describe a food chain of which you are a member. You may draw or use words to describe the chain.

3.4 Cycles of Matter

Understand Key Concepts

12. Nutrients move through an ecosystem in

    a. biogeochemical cycles.

    b. water cycles.

    c. energy pyramids.

    d. ecological pyramids.

13. List two ways in which water enters the atmosphere in the water cycle.

14. What is meant by "nutrient limitation"?

Think Critically

15. Infer Ecologists discovered that trout were dying in a stream that ran through some farmland. Nitrogen fertilizer had been used on the crops growing on this farmland. What do you think happened in the stream that caused the fish to die?

Connecting Concepts

Use Science Graphics

The graph below shows the effect of annual rainfall on the rate of primary productivity in an ecosystem. Use the graph to answer questions 16 and 17.

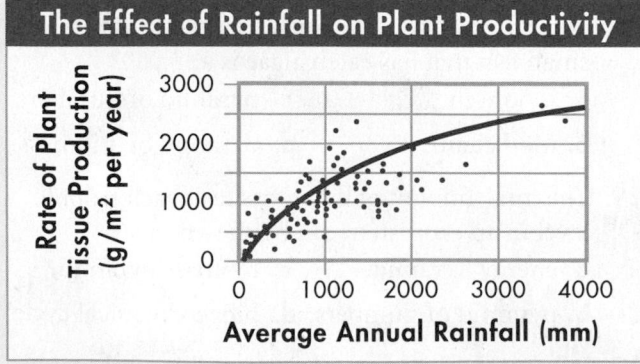

The Effect of Rainfall on Plant Productivity

Rate of Plant Tissue Production (g/m² per year) vs Average Annual Rainfall (mm)

16. Interpret Graphs What happens to productivity as rainfall increases?

17. Apply Concepts What factors other than water might affect primary productivity?

solve the CHAPTER MYSTERY

CHANGES IN THE BAY

One hypothesis suggests that rising water temperatures have caused most of the changes in Narragansett Bay. The bay's temperature has risen more than 1.5°C (3°F) since 1960. This warmth encourages bluefish to stay in the bay later in the fall. It also allows predatory warm-water shrimp to remain in the bay all winter. These shrimp feed on baby flounder. Warmer water also enables zooplankton to graze heavily on marine algae. This stops the late-winter algal bloom. The algal bloom used to provide organic carbon to the entire food web.

The result of these changes seems to be a shift in the activities of bacteria. The bacteria are responsible for transforming nitrogen. When the spring bloom provided organic carbon, bacteria denitrified the water. This released nitrogen into the atmosphere. Now, the bacterial community has changed and actually fixes nitrogen. This brings more of it into the water. No one knows how this will affect the long-term health of the bay and coastal waters.

1. Compare and Contrast In one paragraph, compare the way the bay used to be with the way the bay is now. Be sure to include changes in the food web and nitrogen cycle.

2. Infer Narragansett Bay harbors sea jellies that prefer warm water and have previously been present only in summer and early fall. These sea jellies eat fish eggs, fish larvae, and zooplankton. If the bay continues to warm, what do you think might happen to the population of sea jellies in the bay?

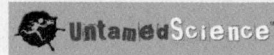 Finding out about Narragansett Bay is only the beginning. Take a video field trip with the ecogeeks of Untamed Science to see where this mystery leads.

Standardized Test Practice for Maryland

Multiple Choice

1. A group of individuals that belong to a single species and that live together in a defined area is termed a(n)
   A population.   C community.
   B ecosystem.   D biome.   CLG 3.5.1

2. Which of the following is NOT true about matter in the biosphere?
   A Matter is recycled in the biosphere.
   B Biogeochemical cycles transform and reuse molecules.
   C The total amount of matter decreases over time.
   D Water and nutrients pass between organisms and the environment.   CLG 3.1.3

3. Which is a source of energy for Earth's living things?
   A wind energy only
   B sunlight only
   C wind energy and sunlight
   D sunlight and chemical energy   CLG 3.1.3

4. Which of the following is a primary producer?
   A a producer, like algae
   B a carnivore, like a lion
   C an omnivore, like a human
   D a detritivore, like an earthworm   CLG 3.5.2

5. Human activities, such as the burning of fossil fuels, move carbon through the carbon cycle. Which other processes also participate in the carbon cycle?
   A biological processes only
   B geochemical processes only
   C chemical processes only
   D a combination of biological, geological, and chemical processes   CLG 3.1.3

6. What are the physical, or nonliving components of an ecosystem called?
   A abiotic factors
   B temperate conditions
   C biotic factors
   D antibiotic factors   CLG 3.5.1

Questions 7–8

The diagrams below represent the amount of biomass and the numbers of organisms in an ecosystem.

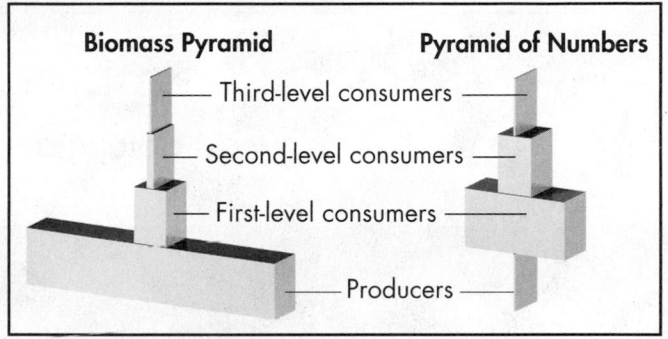

Biomass Pyramid   **Pyramid of Numbers**
— Third-level consumers —
— Second-level consumers —
— First-level consumers —
— Producers

7. What can you conclude about the ecosystem from the pyramid of numbers shown?
   A There are more first-level consumers than producers.
   B There are more third-level consumers than second-level consumers.
   C There are more producers than first-level consumers.
   D There are more second-level consumers than first-level consumers.   CLG 3.5.2

8. What can you conclude about the producers in the ecosystem based on the two pyramids shown?
   A The producers in the ecosystem are probably very small organisms.
   B There are no producers in the ecosystem.
   C The producers in the ecosystem are probably large organisms.
   D Decomposers in the ecosystem outnumber the producers in the ecosystem.   CLG 3.5.2

Open-Ended Response

9. What ultimately happens to the bulk of matter in any trophic level of a biomass pyramid—that is, the matter that does not get passed to the trophic level above?   CLG 3.5.2

If You Have Trouble With . . .

Question	1	2	3	4	5	6	7	8	9
See Lesson	3.1	3.4	3.2	3.2	3.4	3.1	3.3	3.3	3.3

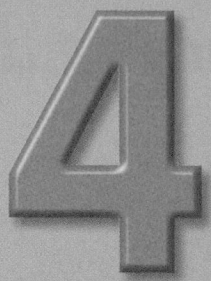

4 Ecosystems and Communities

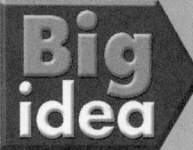

Big idea: Interdependence in Nature

Q: How do abiotic and biotic factors shape ecosystems?

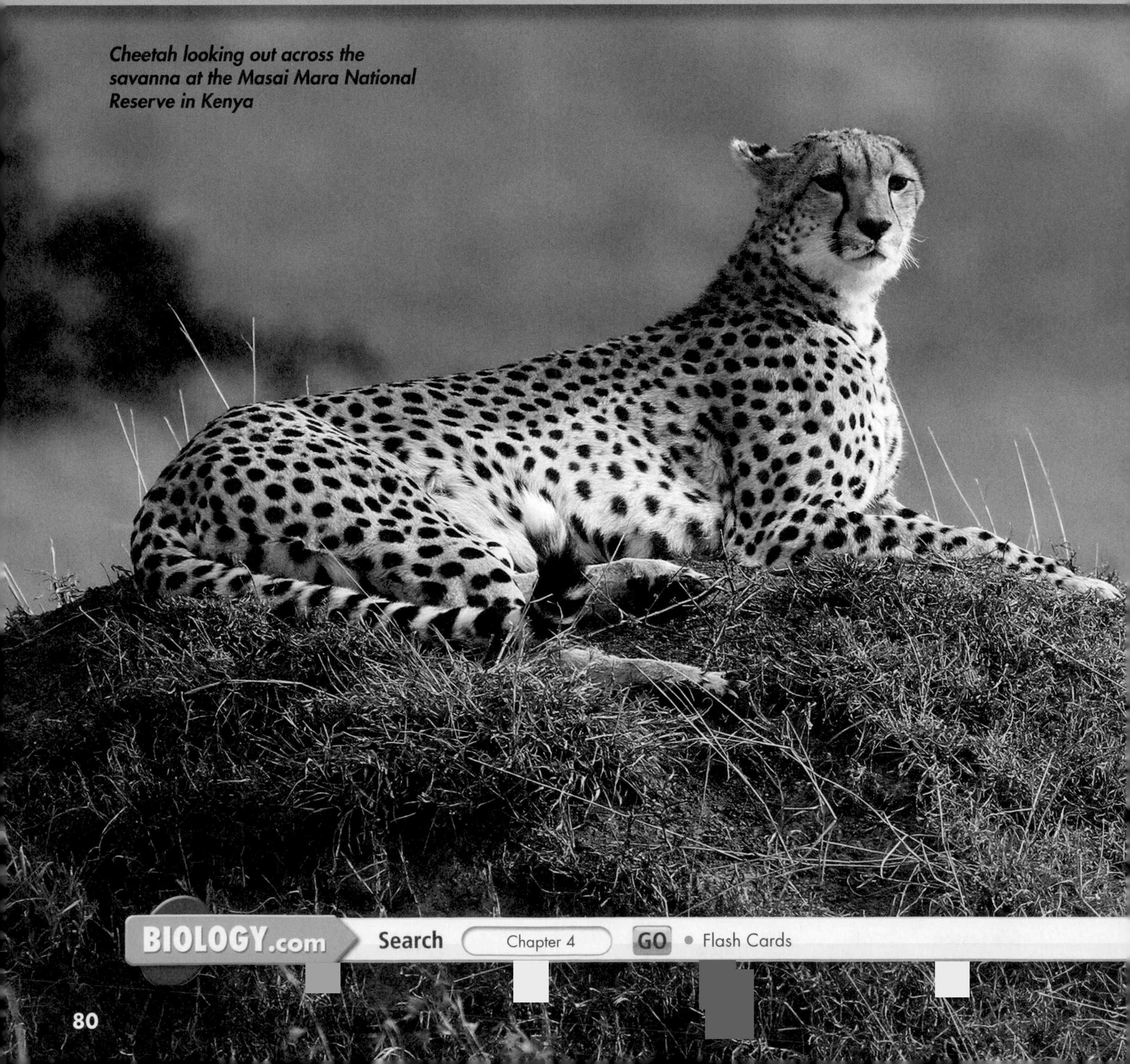

Cheetah looking out across the savanna at the Masai Mara National Reserve in Kenya

MARYLAND VOLUNTARY STATE CURRICULUM

Biology Indicators/Core Learning Goals (CLG) 3.1.3, 3.5.1, 3.5.2, 3.5.3, 3.5.4. **Skills and Processes Indicators (SPI)** 1.2.7, 1.4.1, 1.4.2, 1.4.6, 1.4.8, 1.5.2, 1.5.5, 1.5.7, 1.5.8, 1.5.9, 1.6.5. See lessons for details.

CHAPTER MYSTERY

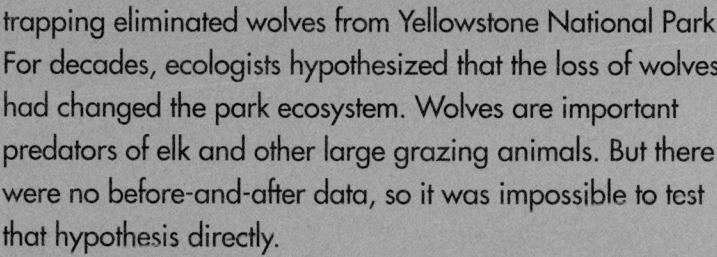

THE WOLF EFFECT

During the 1920s, hunting and trapping eliminated wolves from Yellowstone National Park. For decades, ecologists hypothesized that the loss of wolves had changed the park ecosystem. Wolves are important predators of elk and other large grazing animals. But there were no before-and-after data, so it was impossible to test that hypothesis directly.

Then, in the mid-1990s, wolves were reintroduced to Yellowstone. Researchers watched park ecosystems carefully. Soon, the number of elk in parts of the park began to fall just as predicted. But, unpredictably, forest and stream communities have changed, too. Could a "wolf effect" be affecting organisms in the park's woods and streams?

Read for Mystery Clues As you read this chapter, look for connections among Yellowstone's organisms and their environment. Then, solve the mystery.

FOUNDATIONS for Learning

Before you read the chapter, write each vocabulary word on an index card. As you read the chapter, write down the definition of each term on the back of the card in your own words. You can put the cards in categories to help you remember the definitions. Make a second set of cards containing the different types of ecosystems. At the end of the chapter are two activities that use the cards to answer the question: How do abiotic and biotic factors shape ecosystems?

Wetland	Canopy	Predation
Benthos	Taiga	Pioneer species
Estuary		

• Untamed Science Video   • Chapter Mystery

4.1 Climate

MD | CLG 3.5.1 Factors Influencing Ecosystems. SPI 1.4.1 Organize Data, 1.4.6 Analyze Trends, 1.5.8 Compare.

Key Questions

🔑 *What is climate?*

🔑 *What factors determine global climate?*

BUILD Understanding

Preview Visuals Before you read, look at the Climate Zones diagram. What does it tell you about how the heat from the sun affects Earth's climates?

In Your Workbook Go to your workbook for more help with previewing visuals.

BUILD Vocabulary

climate
the average year-to-year conditions of temperature and precipitation in an area over a long period of time

microclimate
environmental conditions within a small area that differ significantly from the climate of the surrounding area

greenhouse effect
the process in which certain gases (carbon dioxide, methane, and water vapor) trap sunlight energy in Earth's atmosphere as heat

🗝 PREFIXES

The prefix *hemi-* in *hemisphere* means "half." The Northern Hemisphere is the northern half of Earth.

Weather and Climate

When you think of climate, you might think of major storms like Hurricane Katrina or a drought in the southeastern states. But, big storms and seasonal droughts are better described as weather instead of climate. So, what is climate and how is it different from weather? How do climate and weather affect organisms and ecosystems?

Weather and climate both involve variations in temperature, precipitation, and other environmental factors. Weather is the day-to-day condition of Earth's atmosphere. Weather where you live may be clear and sunny one day but rainy and cold the next. **Climate** refers to average conditions over long periods of time. A region's climate is defined by year-after-year patterns of temperature and precipitation.

However, environmental conditions can vary over small distances, creating **microclimates.** For example, south-facing sides of trees and buildings in the Northern Hemisphere receive more sunlight. They are often warmer and drier than north-facing sides. These differences can be very important to many organisms.

🔑 **Key Question** What is climate?
A region's climate is defined by year-after-year patterns of temperature and precipitation.

Factors That Affect Climate

What causes differences in climate? Global climate is shaped by many factors, including solar energy trapped in the biosphere. Latitude and the transport of heat by winds and ocean currents also help shape global climate.

Solar Energy and the Greenhouse Effect The main force that shapes our climate is solar energy that arrives as sunlight and strikes Earth's surface. Some solar energy is reflected back into space, and some is absorbed and converted into heat. Some of that heat radiates back into space, and some is trapped in the biosphere. The balance between heat that stays in the biosphere and heat lost to space determines Earth's average temperature. This balance is largely controlled by the concentrations of carbon dioxide, methane, and water vapor in the atmosphere. These gases are called greenhouse gases.

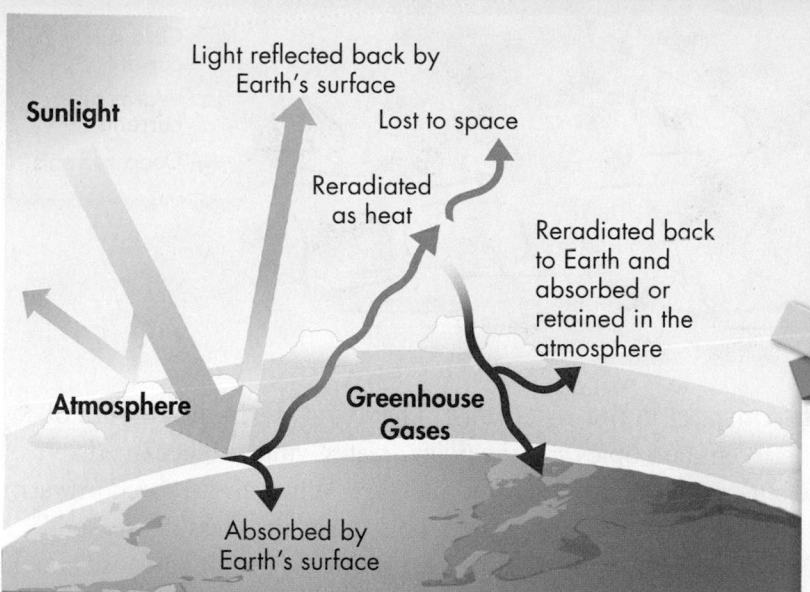

Light reflected back by
Earth's surface

Sunlight

Lost to space

Reradiated
as heat

Reradiated back
to Earth and
absorbed or
retained in the
atmosphere

Atmosphere

Greenhouse
Gases

Absorbed by
Earth's surface

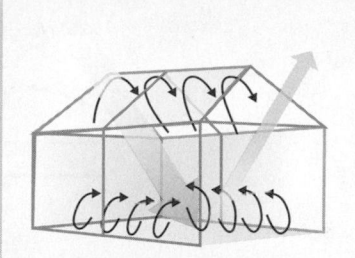

BUILD Connections

THE GREENHOUSE EFFECT
Greenhouse gases in the atmosphere allow solar radiation to enter the biosphere. But they slow down the radiation of Earth's heat back to space.

In Your Workbook Go to your workbook to explore the greenhouse analogy further.

Greenhouse gases act like the glass in a greenhouse. The glass allows visible light to enter but traps heat. This effect is called the **greenhouse effect.** If greenhouse gas concentrations rise, they trap more heat, warming Earth. If their concentrations fall, more heat escapes, cooling Earth. Without the greenhouse effect, Earth would be about 30° Celsius cooler than it is today.

Latitude and Solar Energy Near the equator, solar energy is intense because the sun is almost directly overhead at noon all year. But this same amount of solar energy is spread out over a much larger area near the poles than near the equator. This spreading is caused by the curvature of the Earth. So Earth's polar areas annually receive less intense solar energy, and therefore heat, from the sun. This difference in heat distribution creates three different climate zones: tropical, temperate, and polar.

The tropical zone (tropics) includes the areas near the equator. The tropical zone receives nearly direct sunlight all year. It is located between 23.5° north and 23.5° south latitudes. The two temperate zones are on either side of the tropical zone between 23.5° and 66.5° north and south latitudes. Beyond the temperate zones are the polar zones, between 66.5° and 90° north and south latitudes. Temperate and polar zones receive very different amounts of solar energy at different times of the year. This variation is because Earth's axis is tilted. The tilt causes solar radiation to strike the Earth at an angle. The angle varies from summer to winter as the Earth revolves around the sun. During winter in the temperate and polar zones, the sun is much lower in the sky. The days are also shorter, and solar energy is less intense.

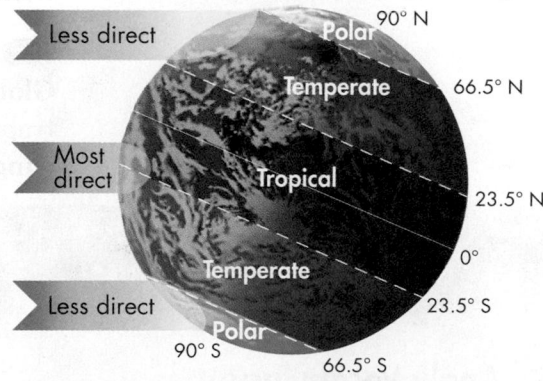

Less direct
Most direct
Less direct

Polar — 90° N
Temperate — 66.5° N
Tropical — 23.5° N
0°
Temperate
Polar — 23.5° S
90° S — 66.5° S

Climate Zones Earth's climate zones are produced by unequal distribution of the sun's heat on Earth's surface. Polar regions receive less solar energy per unit area than tropical regions. This means they receive less heat, too. The tilt of Earth's axis causes the distribution of sunlight to change over the course of the year.

Cold surface currents
Warm surface currents
Deep currents

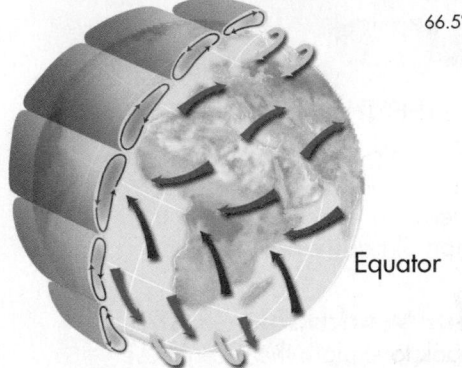

Equator

← Polar easterlies
← Westerlies
← Northeast trade winds
← Southeast trade winds

Winds and Currents Earth's winds (above left) and ocean currents (above right) interact to help produce climate patterns. The paths of winds and currents are the result of heating and cooling, Earth's rotation, and geographic features.

Heat Transport in the Biosphere The difference in the amount of heat between the tropics and the poles creates wind and ocean currents. These currents transport heat and moisture. When air is heated in warm areas such as the tropics, it expands. This warm air is less dense, so it rises. After it rises, it spreads north and south. As the air spreads, it cools and sinks. At the same time, chilled air at the poles sinks toward Earth's surface. It pushes air at the surface outward. This air warms as it travels over the surface, so it rises. These upward and downward movements of air create winds. Winds transport heat from regions of rising warmer air to regions of sinking cooler air. Earth's rotation causes winds to blow generally from west to east over the temperate zones. Winds blow from east to west over the tropics and the poles.

Similar patterns of heating and cooling occur in the oceans. Winds push surface water, causing ocean currents. These currents transport enormous amounts of heat. Air that passes over warm currents picks up moisture and heat. Air that passes over cool currents is cooled. In this way, surface currents affect the weather and climate of nearby landmasses. Deep ocean currents are caused by cold water near the poles sinking and flowing along the ocean floor. This water rises in warmer regions through a process called upwelling.

🔑 **Key Question** What factors determine global climate? **Global climate is shaped by many factors, including solar energy trapped in the biosphere. Latitude and the transport of heat by winds and ocean currents also shape global climate.**

CHECK Understanding

Apply Vocabulary
Use the highlighted words from the lesson to complete each sentence correctly.

1. The _____ is caused by gases in the atmosphere trapping heat, causing the Earth to warm.

2. A _____ develops when environmental conditions vary over small distances.

Critical Thinking

3. **Explain** How is climate different from weather?

4. **Quick Write** Research the average monthly high temperature (in °C) for Quito, Ecuador. Quito is a city on the equator. Plot the temperature data in a line graph. Describe the pattern shown.

4.2 Niches and Community Interactions

MD CLG **3.5.1** Factors Influencing Ecosystems, **3.5.2** Interdependence of Organisms in the Biosphere, **3.5.3** Population Dynamics, **3.5.4** Global Food Webs. SPI **1.5.5** Create and Interpret Graphics, **1.5.7** Classification Systems, **1.5.8** Compare.

The Niche

Different organisms live in different places. For example, one organism may live on a coral reef and another in the desert. What determines where an organism can live? Each species has a range of conditions under which it can grow and reproduce. These conditions help define where and how an organism lives.

Tolerance Every species has its own range of tolerance. Tolerance is the ability to survive and reproduce under a range of environmental conditions. When an environmental condition is outside of an organism's optimum range, the organism becomes stressed. It uses more energy to maintain homeostasis, and less for growth and reproduction. A species has an upper and lower limit of tolerance for every environmental factor. It cannot survive beyond those limits. A species' tolerance for environmental conditions helps determine its **habitat.** A habitat is the general place where an organism lives.

Defining the Niche Describing a species' habitat is important. But ecologists also study a species' ecological "job"—where and how it "makes a living." An organism's job is part of its **niche** (nitch). A niche describes what an organism does and how it interacts with the environment. A niche includes the way a species obtains **resources** to survive and reproduce. Resources include any necessity of life, such as water, nutrients, light, food, and space.

Key Question What is a niche?
A niche is the range of physical and biological conditions in which a species lives. It includes the way the species obtains what it needs to survive and reproduce.

Competition

Organisms often try to use a limited resource in the same place at the same time as other organisms. This process is called competition. Plant roots compete for water and nutrients in the soil. Animals compete for food, mates, and places to live and raise their young. Competition can occur among members of the same species (intraspecific competition) and between members of different species (interspecific competition).

Key Questions

🔑 **What is a niche?**

🔑 **How does competition shape communities?**

🔑 **How do predation and herbivory shape communities?**

🔑 **What are the three primary ways that organisms depend on each other?**

BUILD Understanding

Concept Map Use the highlighted vocabulary words to create a concept map that organizes the information in this lesson.

In Your Workbook Go to your workbook for help completing a concept map. Complete the concept map in Lesson 4.2.

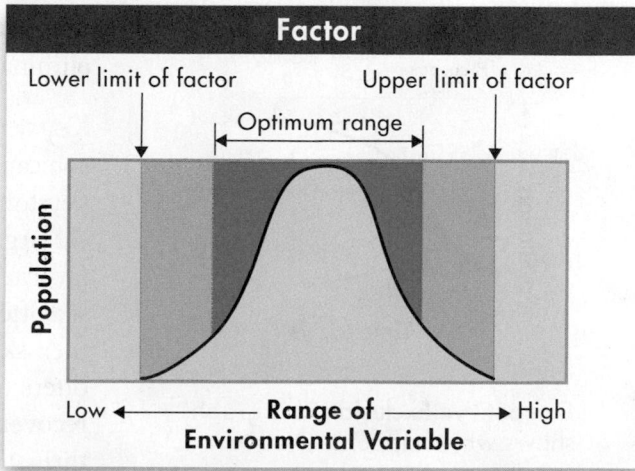

Tolerance A single environmental factor, such as sunlight or temperature, can affect population size. Organisms become more rare in zones of physiological stress (medium blue) and are absent from zones of intolerance (light blue).

habitat an area where an organism lives, including the biotic and abiotic factors that affect it

niche the full range of physical and biological conditions in which an organism lives and the way in which the organism uses those conditions

resource any necessity of life, such as water, nutrients, light, food, or space

predation an interaction in which one animal (the predator) captures and feeds on another animal (the prey)

herbivory an interaction in which one animal (the herbivore) feeds on producers (such as plants)

🔑 ROOT WORDS

The word *herb* means "a flowering plant without woody stems." When used as a root word, it usually refers to the leaves and flowers of plants. Animals that practice herbivory often prefer to eat leaves and flowers, but they may eat other plant parts as well.

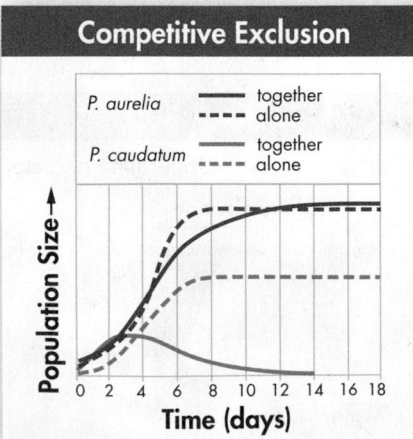

Competitive Exclusion

P. aurelia — together ---- alone
P. caudatum — together ---- alone

Population Size →

0 2 4 6 8 10 12 14 16 18
Time (days)

Competitive Exclusion This graph shows what happens when two species of paramecia compete for the same resources. In separate cultures, the two species easily survive. But in the same culture, one species outcompetes the other. The losing species dies off.

The Competitive Exclusion Principle No two species can occupy the same niche in the same habitat at the same time. This fact is an ecological rule called the competitive exclusion principle. Direct competition between different species for a limited resource almost always produces a winner and a loser. The losing species dies out.

Dividing Resources Species usually divide similar resources instead of competing for them. For example, three species of warblers can all live in the same trees and feed on insects. One species feeds on high branches. Another feeds on low branches. The third feeds in the middle. In this way, each species has its own niche.

🔑 Key Question How does competition shape communities? **Competition causes species to divide resources. It helps determine the number and kinds of species in a community. It also determines the niche each species occupies.**

Predation, Herbivory, and Keystone Species

What happens if a group of animals eats all the available food in the area? They will no longer have anything to eat! That's why predator-prey and herbivore-plant interactions are very important.

Predator-Prey Relationships **Predation** (pree DAY shun) is an interaction in which one animal (predator) captures and feeds on another animal (prey). Predators can affect the size of prey populations in a community. For example, owls are predators that help regulate the populations of mice and other small mammals.

Herbivore-Plant Relationships **Herbivory** is an interaction in which one animal (herbivore) feeds on producers (such as plants). Herbivores can affect the size and distribution of plant populations in a community. For example, dense populations of white-tailed deer are eliminating some plants from many places in the United States.

Keystone Species Sometimes a population change in a single species can cause dramatic changes in its community. This species is called a keystone species. Pacific sea otters are a keystone species. These otters eat large numbers of sea urchins. Sea urchins are herbivores. Their favorite food is kelp, giant algae that grow in the ocean. A century ago, sea otters were nearly eliminated by hunting. Sea urchin numbers then skyrocketed, and the urchins devoured the kelp. Once the sea otters were protected as an endangered species, the otter population recovered. The sea urchin populations dropped, and the kelp thrived again.

🔑 Key Question How do predation and herbivory shape communities? **Predators can affect where prey populations can survive. Herbivores can help determine where populations of certain plants can survive.**

Symbioses

Any relationship in which two species live closely together is called **symbiosis** (sim by OH sis). Biologists recognize three main classes of symbiotic relationships in nature: mutualism, parasitism, and commensalism.

Mutualism The sea anemone uses its sting to capture prey and to protect itself from predators. But clownfish are immune to anemone stings. They hide from predators in the anemone's deadly tentacles. When an anemone is attacked, the clownfish fiercely chase away the much larger fish. This relationship is an example of **mutualism,** because both animals benefit from the relationship.

Parasitism Ticks live on the bodies of mammals, feeding on their blood and skin. This is an example of **parasitism** (PAR uh sit iz um). In this relationship, an organism lives inside or on another organism and harms it. The parasite obtains all or part of its nutrients from the host organism. Parasites weaken but usually do not kill their host.

Commensalism Small marine animals called barnacles often attach themselves to a whale's skin. The barnacles have no effect on the whale. They benefit from the constant movement of water and food particles past the swimming whale. This is an example of **commensalism** (kuh MEN sul iz um). In this relationship, one organism benefits and the other is neither helped nor harmed.

Key Question What are the three primary ways that organisms depend on each other? **The three main classes of symbiotic relationships are mutualism, parasitism, and commensalism.**

BUILD Vocabulary

symbiosis
a relationship in which two species live closely together

mutualism
the symbiotic relationship in which both species benefit from the relationship

parasitism
the symbiotic relationship in which one organism lives on or inside another organism and harms it

commensalism
the symbiotic relationship in which one organisms benefits and the other is neither helped nor harmed

ROOT WORDS

The word *commensal* means "eating together at the same table." So organisms that practice commensalism could be said to be dinner companions.

CHECK Understanding

Apply Vocabulary
Use the highlighted words from the lesson to complete each sentence correctly.

1. A _____ is something that is essential for an organism's life.

2. A relationship in which the interaction between organisms is helpful to both is called _____.

Critical Thinking

3. Compare and Contrast What is the difference between a predator and a parasite?

4. Write to Learn Answer the first clue of the mystery.

MYSTERY CLUE

One of the favorite prey species of the wolves in Yellowstone is elk. How do you think this relationship could affect the ability of certain *plants* to grow in Yellowstone? (**Hint:** See p. 86.)

4.3 Succession

MD CLG 3.5.1 Factors Influencing Ecosystems, 3.5.2 Interdependence of Organisms in the Biosphere, 3.5.3 Population Dynamics. SPI 1.5.2 Communicate Information, 1.5.9 Synthesize Ideas.

Key Questions

🔑 How do communities change over time?

🔑 Do ecosystems return to "normal" following a disturbance?

BUILD Understanding

Compare/Contrast Table As you read, create a table comparing primary and secondary succession.

In Your Workbook Go to your workbook to learn more about creating a compare/contrast table.

Primary Succession Primary succession occurs on newly exposed surfaces. In Glacier Bay, Alaska, a retreating glacier exposed barren rock. Over the course of more than 100 years, a series of changes has led to the hemlock and spruce forest currently found in the area. Changes in this community will continue for centuries.

Primary and Secondary Succession

In 1883, an eruption blew the volcanic island of Krakatau in the Indian Ocean to pieces. A tiny barren island remained. By 1929, a forest with over 300 species covered the island. Today it is a mature rain forest. Krakatau is an example of **ecological succession.** Succession is a series of more-or-less predictable changes that occur in a community over time. As succession proceeds, the number of different species present typically increases.

Primary Succession Volcanic explosions and retreating glaciers can create new land or sterilize existing areas. Both events leave only exposed bare rock—no soil or plant life. Succession that begins in an area that has no existing community is called **primary succession.**

The first species to colonize barren areas are called **pioneer species.** One pioneer that grows on bare rock is lichen. Lichen is an example of mutualism between a fungus and an alga. Lichens fix atmospheric nitrogen into useful forms for other organisms. Over time, they break down rock and add organic material to form soil. Some grasses are also pioneer species.

Secondary Succession Existing communities are not always completely destroyed by disturbances. In these cases, **secondary succession** occurs. Secondary succession proceeds faster than primary succession. The soil remains, so new and surviving vegetation regrows rapidly.

Time

15 years   35 years   80 years   115+ years

Secondary succession often follows a wildfire, hurricane, or other natural disturbance. To us, these events are disasters, but many species are adapted to them. Forest fires kill some trees, but spare others—and may stimulate their seeds to germinate. Secondary succession can also follow human activities like logging and farming.

Why Succession Occurs Every organism changes the environment it lives in. In one model of succession, as one species alters its environment, other species find it easier to compete for resources and survive. Lichens add organic matter and form soil. Then mosses and other plants are able to colonize and grow. Organic matter accumulates and soon other species move in. Tree branches produce shade and cooler temperatures nearer the ground. Over time, more and more species can find suitable niches and survive.

⊶ Key Question How do communities change over time? **Ecosystems change over time, especially after disturbances. As some species die out, new species move in.**

Climax Communities

Ecologists used to think that succession in a given area always proceeded through the same stages. The end result was a specific and stable community called a climax community. But recent studies have shown that succession doesn't always follow the same path. Climax communities are not always uniform and stable.

Succession After Natural Disturbances Natural disturbances are common in many communities. Healthy coral reefs and tropical rain forests recover from storms. Healthy temperate forests and grasslands recover from wildfires. Sometimes succession in a healthy ecosystem reproduces the original climax community after a natural disturbance. But multiple disturbances take place at different times in some ecosystems. This causes climax communities that are not uniform. They look like patchwork quilts because different areas are in varying stages of succession. Some climax communities are disturbed so often that they can't really be called stable.

Secondary Succession Secondary succession occurs in disturbed areas where parts of previous ecosystems still remain. This series shows changes taking place in abandoned fields in the Carolinas. Over the last century, the fields have passed through several stages and matured into oak forests. Changes will continue for years to come.

Time

3 years   5 years   40+ years

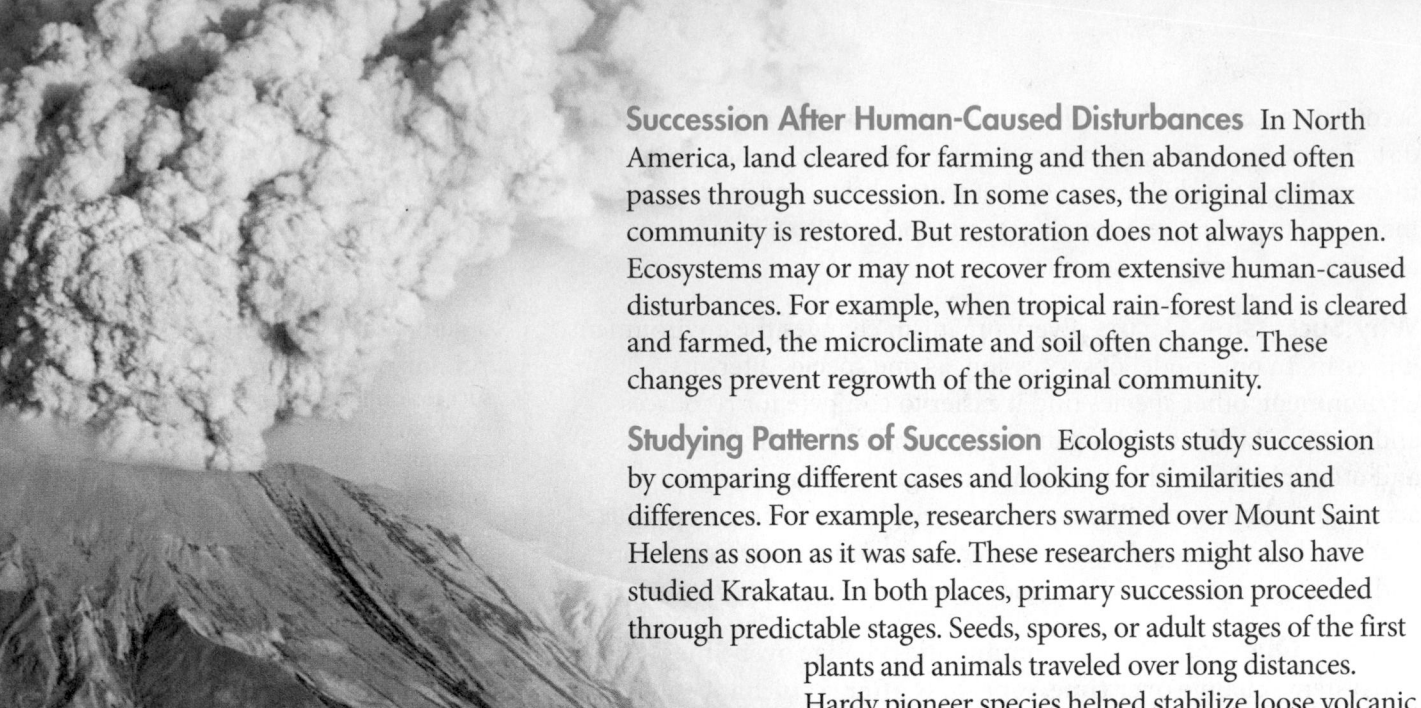

Succession After Human-Caused Disturbances In North America, land cleared for farming and then abandoned often passes through succession. In some cases, the original climax community is restored. But restoration does not always happen. Ecosystems may or may not recover from extensive human-caused disturbances. For example, when tropical rain-forest land is cleared and farmed, the microclimate and soil often change. These changes prevent regrowth of the original community.

Studying Patterns of Succession Ecologists study succession by comparing different cases and looking for similarities and differences. For example, researchers swarmed over Mount Saint Helens as soon as it was safe. These researchers might also have studied Krakatau. In both places, primary succession proceeded through predictable stages. Seeds, spores, or adult stages of the first plants and animals traveled over long distances. Hardy pioneer species helped stabilize loose volcanic debris, which allowed later plant species to take root.

Studies of Krakatau and Mount Saint Helens prove that early stages of primary succession are slow. Opportunity can play a large role in determining which species colonize at different times.

🔑 **Key Question** Do ecosystems return to "normal" following a disturbance?
In healthy ecosystems, secondary succession often reproduces the original climax community after a natural disturbance. But ecosystems may or may not recover from widespread disturbances caused by humans.

Studying Succession These Forest Service rangers are surveying plants and animals that have returned to Mount Saint Helens. The volcano erupted in 1980, leaving only barren land for miles.

CHECK Understanding

Apply Vocabulary
Use the highlighted words from the lesson to complete each sentence correctly.

1. The first species to colonize an area during ecological succession is called a _____.
2. Succession that begins after a wildfire is usually _____, because soil is already present.
3. Succession that begins after a volcanic eruption is usually _____, because it starts with bare rock.

Critical Thinking
4. **Explain** What is a climax community?
5. **Relate Cause and Effect** What kinds of conditions might prevent a community from returning to its predisturbance state?
6. **Quick Write** Look at the photo below. Write a paragraph explaining what sort of succession this is, and why.

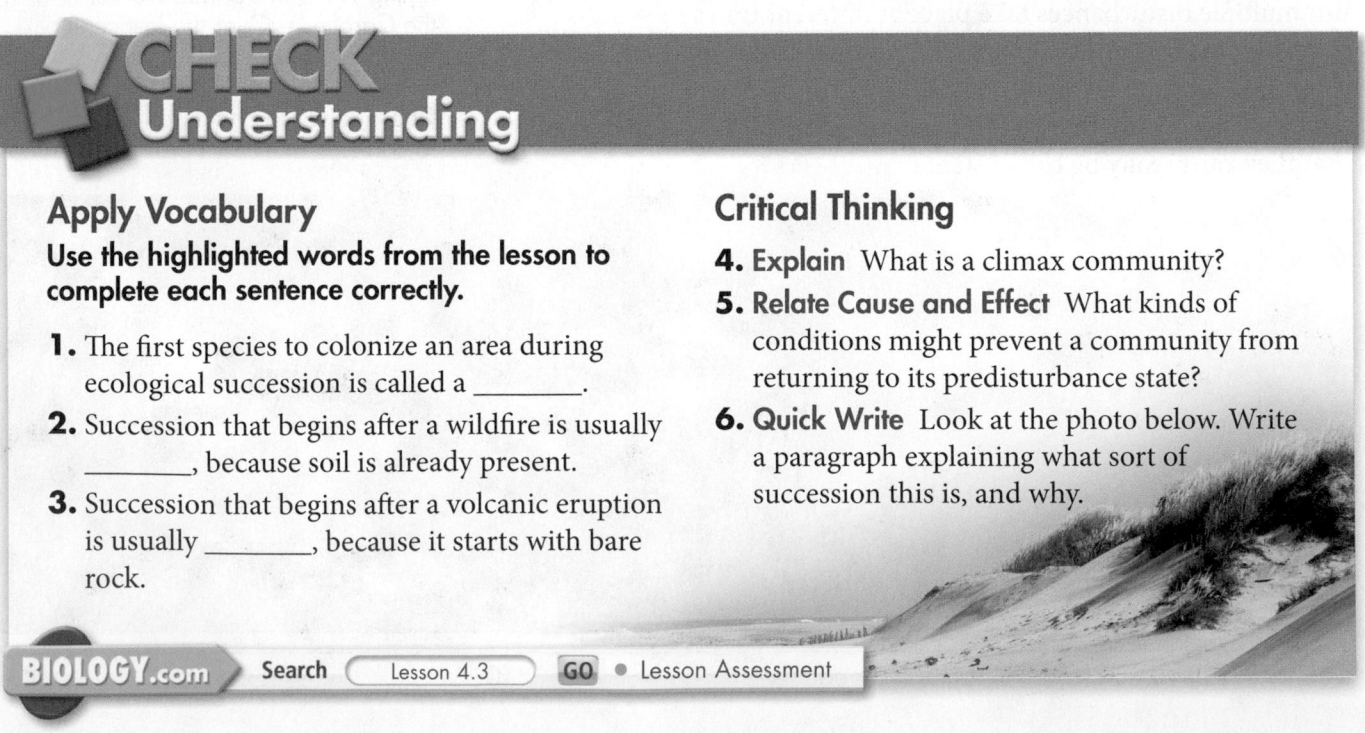

BIOLOGY.com Search (Lesson 4.3) [GO] • Lesson Assessment

4.4 Biomes

CLG 3.5.1 Factors Influencing Ecosystems, 3.5.2 Interdependence of Organisms in the Biosphere, 3.5.4 Global Food Webs. SPI 1.4.1 Organize Data, 1.4.2 Analyze Data, 1.4.6 Determine Trends, 1.5.7 Classification Systems, 1.5.8 Compare, 1.5.9 Synthesize Ideas.

The Major Biomes

Why are the characteristics of biological communities different from one place to another? You learned that latitude affects global climate. So does the heat transported by winds. But regions with similar latitudes and prevailing winds may have different climates and biological communities. Why? Because other factors can also influence climate. These factors include an area's nearness to an ocean or a mountain range.

Regional Climates Oregon, for example, borders the Pacific Ocean, which has cold currents flowing from north to south. Cold currents make the region cooler in summer than other places at the same latitude. Similarly, prevailing winds traveling west to east push moist air upward against the Cascade Mountains. The air expands and cools, causing the moisture to condense and form clouds. The clouds then drop rain or snow on western Oregon. But the air descends on the eastern side of the mountains, becoming warmer and drier. So, much less rain falls in east Oregon. West and east Oregon have very different regional climates. Therefore, the areas also have different plant and animal communities.

Key Questions

🔑 **What abiotic and biotic factors characterize biomes?**

🔑 **What areas are not easily classified into a major biome?**

BUILD Understanding

Preview Visuals Before you read, preview the biome map. Study the names of the biomes carefully.

In Your Workbook As you read, examine the photographs of the biomes. Complete the table in Lesson 4.4 by filling in the missing information.

Biomes This map shows the locations of the world's major biomes. Each biome has a characteristic climate and community of organisms.

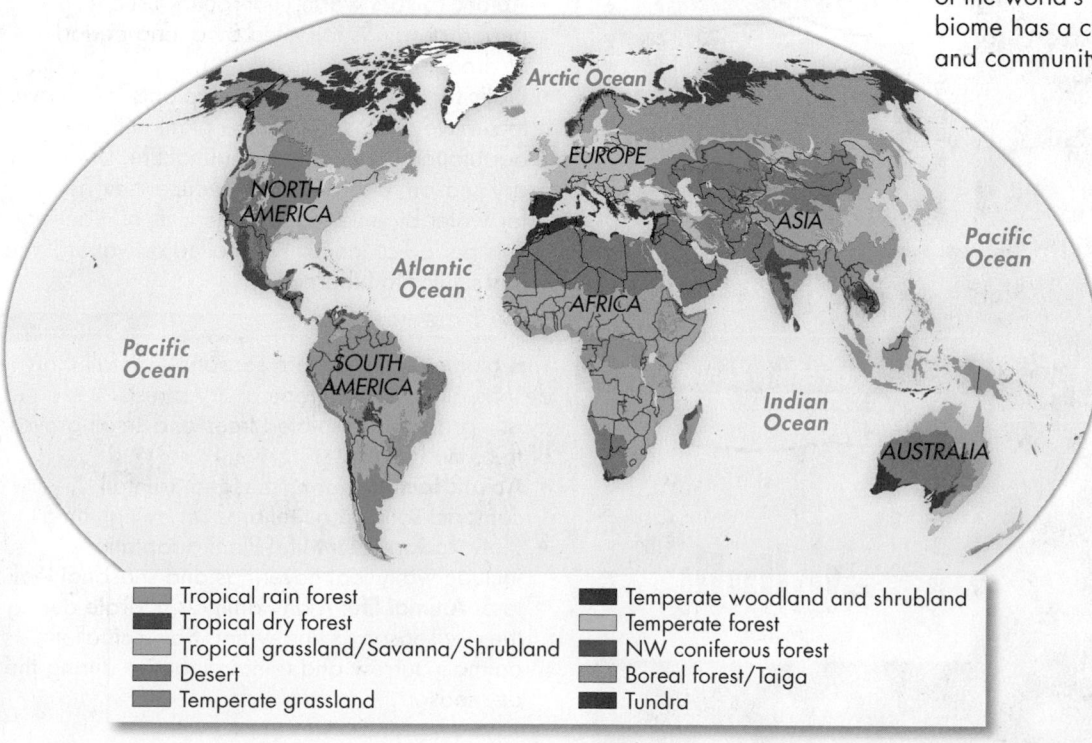

- Tropical rain forest
- Tropical dry forest
- Tropical grassland/Savanna/Shrubland
- Desert
- Temperate grassland
- Temperate woodland and shrubland
- Temperate forest
- NW coniferous forest
- Boreal forest/Taiga
- Tundra

Defining Biomes Earth's terrestrial ecosystems are classified into ten groups of regional climate communities called biomes. A biome is described by its abiotic factors, such as climate and soil type. Each biome has a seasonal pattern of temperature and precipitation. A biome is also described by its biotic factors, such as plant and animal life. Organisms in each biome have adaptations so they can live and reproduce in the environment. Plant and animal communities often vary even if they are in the same biome. Variations can be caused by differences in exposure, elevation, or local soil conditions. Human activity or community interactions may also change local conditions.

Key Question What abiotic and biotic factors characterize biomes? **Biomes are described in terms of abiotic factors like climate and soil type. They are also described by biotic factors like plant and animal life.**

TROPICAL RAIN FOREST

Belem, Brazil

Tropical rain forests have more species than all the other biomes combined. They get at least 2 meters of rain a year! Tall trees form a dense, leafy covering called a **canopy**. The canopy shades a layer of shorter trees and vines called the **understory**.
- **Abiotic factors** hot and wet year-round; thin, nutrient-poor soils subject to erosion
- **Biotic factors–Plant life:** Understory plants use large leaves to compete for limited light. **Animal life:** Animals are active all year. Many use camouflage to hide from predators.

TROPICAL DRY FOREST

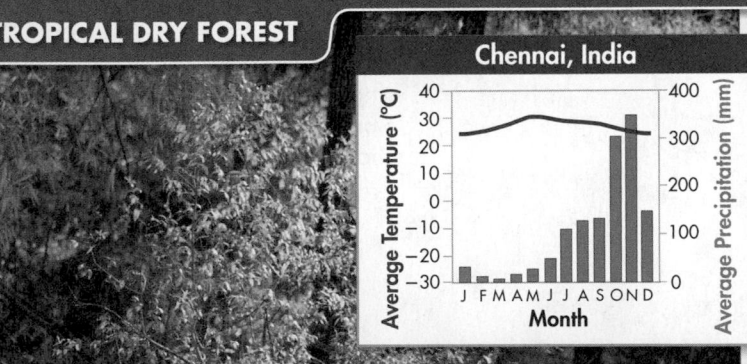

Chennai, India

Tropical dry forests grow in areas where rainy seasons alternate with dry seasons.
- **Abiotic factors** warm year-round; usually, a period of rain is followed by a long period of drought
- **Biotic factors–Plant life:** Some plants lose leaves to survive the dry season. A plant with this adaptation is *deciduous*. **Animal life:** During dry season, many animals reduce their need for water by entering long periods of inactivity. This period of inactivity is called estivation, and it is similar to hibernation.

TROPICAL GRASSLAND/ SAVANNA/SHRUBLAND

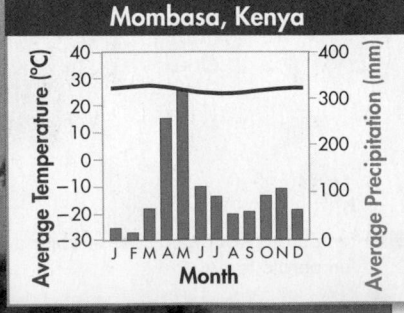

Mombasa, Kenya

This biome receives more seasonal rainfall than deserts but less than tropical dry forests. It is mostly grass, with isolated trees and small groves of trees and shrubs.
- **Abiotic factors** warm; seasonal rainfall; compact soils; frequent fires set by lightning
- **Biotic factors–Plant life:** Plant adaptations include waxy leaf coverings and seasonal leaf loss. **Animal life:** Many animals migrate during the dry season to find water. Some smaller animals burrow and remain inactive during the dry season.

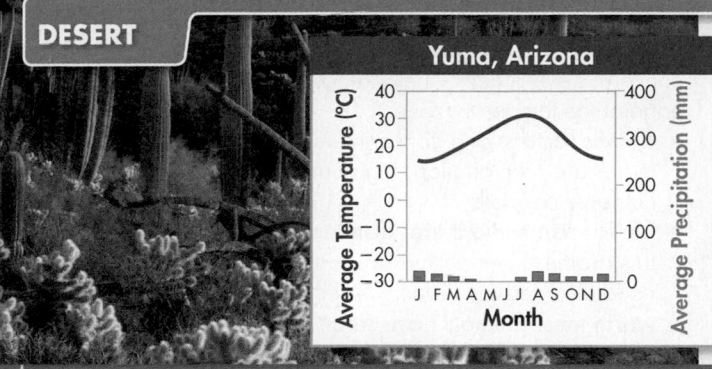

DESERT

Yuma, Arizona

Deserts have less than 25 centimeters of precipitation annually. Deserts vary greatly, depending on elevation and latitude. Many deserts undergo extreme daily temperature changes, alternating between hot and cold.
- **Abiotic factors** low precipitation; variable temperatures
- **Biotic factors—Plant life:** Many plants store water in their tissues. They also minimize leaf surface area to cut down on water loss. **Animal life:** Many desert animals get water from the food they eat. Many are active at night to avoid the hottest parts of the day.

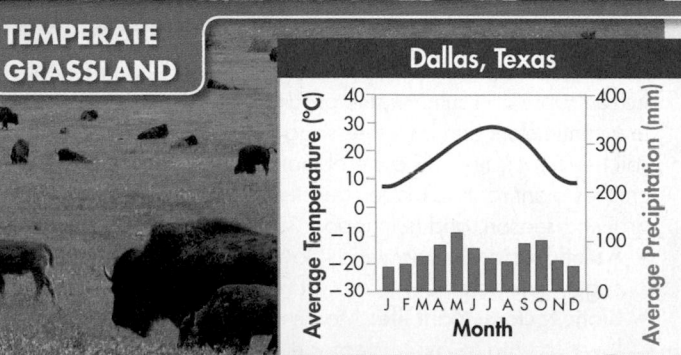

TEMPERATE GRASSLAND

Dallas, Texas

Plant communities are mostly grasses, which have been maintained by periodic fires and heavy grazing. Their soils are fertile and ideal for growing crops. For this reason, most have been converted for agriculture.
- **Abiotic factors** warm to hot summers; cold winters; moderate seasonal precipitation; occasional fires
- **Biotic factors—Plant life:** Grassland plants are resistant to grazing and fire. **Animal life:** Predation is a threat for smaller animals because of the open environment. Camouflage and burrowing are common adaptations.

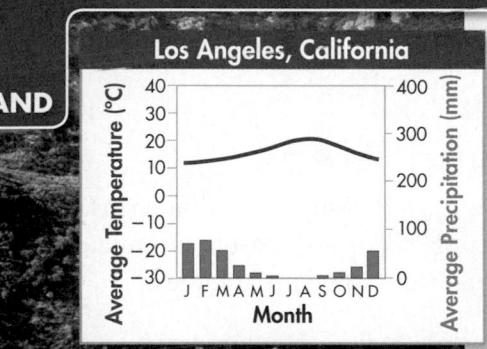

TEMPERATE WOODLAND AND SHRUBLAND

Los Angeles, California

Open woodlands have large areas of grasses and wildflowers mixed with oak and other trees. Fire is a constant threat because of dense, low, oily plants.
- **Abiotic factors** hot dry summers; cool moist winters; thin, nutrient-poor soils; periodic fires
- **Biotic factors—Plant life:** Plants in this biome have adapted to drought. They have tough waxy leaves that resist water loss. **Animal life:** Animals tend to be browsers that eat varied diets of grasses, leaves, shrubs, and other vegetation.

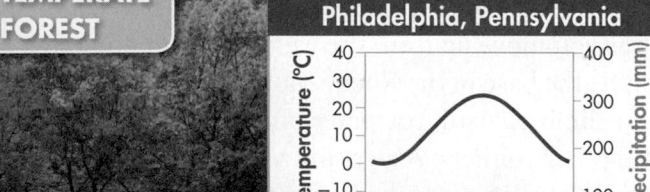

TEMPERATE FOREST

Philadelphia, Pennsylvania

Temperate forests are mostly made up of deciduous and evergreen coniferous (koh NIF ur us) trees. Soils are fertile, and are often rich in **humus.** Humus is a material formed from decaying leaves and other organic matter.
- **Abiotic factors** cold to moderate winters; warm summers; year-round precipitation; fertile soils
- **Biotic factors—Plant life:** Deciduous trees drop their leaves in autumn and go dormant in winter. **Animal life:** Animals must cope with changing weather. Bare trees leave animals exposed in winter.

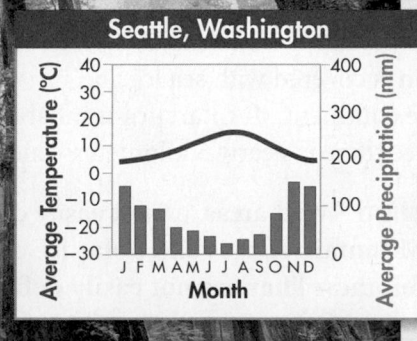

NORTHWESTERN CONIFEROUS FOREST

Seattle, Washington

The forest has a variety of conifers, flowering trees, and shrubs. Moss often covers tree trunks and the forest floor. This biome is sometimes called a "temperate rain forest" because of its lush vegetation.
- **Abiotic factors** mild temperatures; abundant precipitation in fall, winter, and spring; cool dry summers
- **Biotic factors—Plant life:** This biome is less diverse than a tropical rain forest. Ample water and nutrients support lush, dense plant growth. Trees here are among the world's tallest. **Animal life:** Camouflage helps insects and ground-dwelling mammals avoid predation.

Ecosystems and Communities **93**

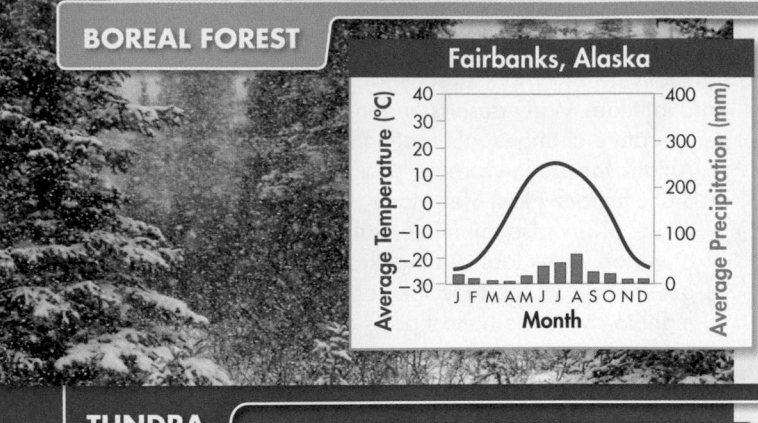

BOREAL FOREST

Fairbanks, Alaska

Graph: Average Temperature (°C) left axis: 40, 30, 20, 10, 0, −10, −20, −30. Average Precipitation (mm) right axis: 400, 300, 200, 100, 0. Month axis: J F M A M J J A S O N D

Boreal forests, or **taiga** (TY guh), are dense forests of coniferous evergreens. They are found along the northern edge of the temperate zone.
- **Abiotic factors** long cold winters; short mild summers; moderate precipitation; high humidity; acidic, nutrient-poor soils
- **Biotic factors–Plant life:** Conifers are well suited to this biome. Their shape sheds snow. Wax-covered, needlelike leaves reduce water loss. **Animal life:** To stay warm most animals have small limbs and ears, and fat or downy feathers for insulation.

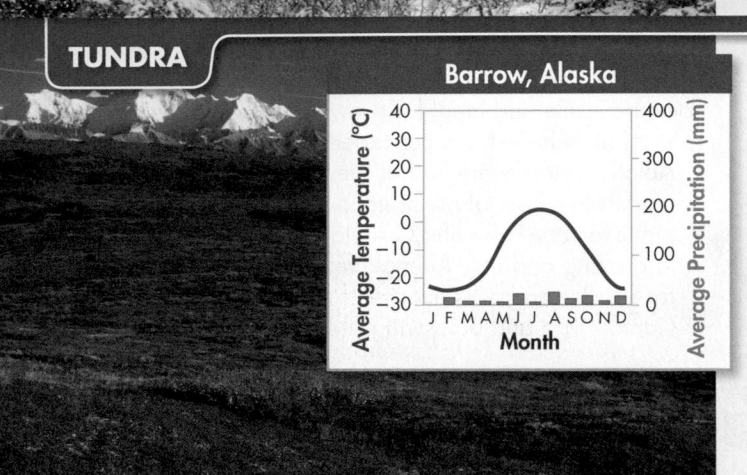

TUNDRA

Barrow, Alaska

Graph: Average Temperature (°C) left axis: 40, 30, 20, 10, 0, −10, −20, −30. Average Precipitation (mm) right axis: 400, 300, 200, 100, 0. Month axis: J F M A M J J A S O N D

The tundra is identified by **permafrost,** a layer of permanently frozen subsoil. In summer, the ground thaws to a depth of a few centimeters and becomes soggy. In winter, the top layer of soil freezes again. This cycle of thawing and freezing rips and crushes plant roots. Cold temperatures, high winds, a short growing season, and humus-poor soils also limit plant height.
- **Abiotic factors** strong winds; low precipitation; short and soggy summers; long, cold, dark winters; permafrost
- **Biotic factors–Plant life:** Mosses and other plants are low-growing to avoid damage from frequent strong winds. **Animal life:** Many animals migrate to avoid long harsh winters. Animals that live in the tundra year-round have adaptations such as natural antifreeze to limit heat loss.

BUILD Vocabulary

canopy a dense covering formed by the leafy tops of tall rain forest trees

understory the layer in a rain forest found underneath the canopy formed by shorter trees and vines

humus material formed from decaying leaves and other organic matter

taiga a biome with long cold winters and a few months of warm weather; dominated by coniferous evergreens; also called boreal forest

permafrost a layer of permanently frozen subsoil found in the tundra

✿ WORD ORIGINS

The word *taiga* is Russian for "dense evergreen forest." Gradually, it became the name of the biome where these Russian forests are found.

Other Land Areas

Some land areas are not easily defined in terms of a typical community of plants and animals. For this reason, mountain ranges and polar ice caps are not usually classified into biomes.

Mountain Ranges Mountain ranges exist on all continents and in many biomes. Conditions such as temperature and precipitation vary with elevation. Exposure to wind increases and soil types and organisms change as you move up from the valley to the mountain summit. For example, the base of the Rocky Mountains in Colorado is grassland. As you climb upward, you enter pine woodland, then a forest of spruce and other conifers. Aspen and willow trees grow in thickets along protected valley streambeds. Near the top, winds are strong and batter open fields of wildflowers. The stunted vegetation resembles tundra. Glaciers are often found at the peaks.

Polar Ice Caps Polar regions border the tundra and are cold year-round. There are few plants, but some algae grow on snow and ice. Animal life includes marine mammals, insects, and mites. In the north, the Arctic Ocean is covered with sea ice and inhabited by polar bears. In the south, the continent of Antarctica is inhabited by many species of penguins. The ice there is nearly 5 kilometers thick in places.

🔑 **Key Question** What areas are not easily classified into a major biome? **Mountain ranges and polar ice caps are not usually classified into biomes. They are not easily defined in terms of a typical community of plants and animals.**

INQUIRY into Scientific Thinking

Which Biome?

An ecologist collected climate data from two locations. The graph shows the monthly average temperatures in the two locations. The total yearly precipitation in Location A is 273 cm. In Location B, the total yearly precipitation is 11 cm.

Analyze and Conclude

1. Interpret Graphs What is the variable plotted on the horizontal (X) axis? What is the variable plotted on the vertical (Y) axis?

2. Interpret Graphs How would you describe the temperature over the course of the year in the two locations?

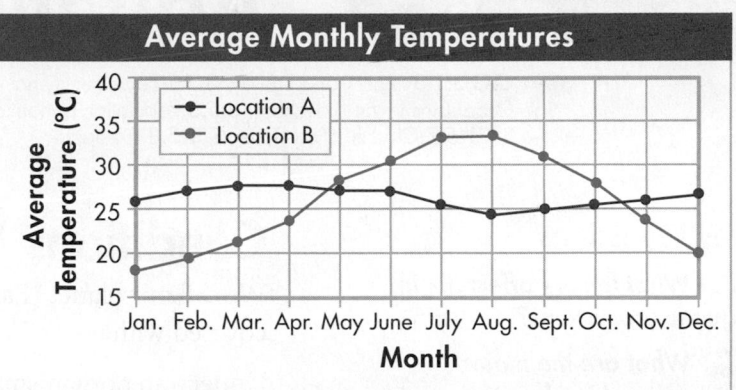

Average Monthly Temperatures

Location A
Location B

Average Temperature (°C)

Jan. Feb. Mar. Apr. May June July Aug. Sept. Oct. Nov. Dec.

Month

3. Draw Conclusions In which biome would you expect to find each location, given the precipitation and temperature data? Explain your answer.

In Your Workbook Go to your workbook for more help wth this activity.

CHECK Understanding

Apply Vocabulary

Use the highlighted words from the lesson to complete each sentence correctly.

1. The _____ in a tropical rain forest is made up of shorter trees and vines that live in the shade of the tallest trees.

2. The soils in temperate forests are often rich in _____, which is made up of decaying leaves and organic matter.

3. Dense coniferous forests and animals with small ears and limbs are characteristics of the _____ biome.

Critical Thinking

4. Explain How are biomes classified?

5. Write to Learn Answer the second clue of the mystery. Be sure to include the effect of microclimates in your answer.

MYSTERY CLUE

Yellowstone has high mountain slopes and valleys with streams. Moose and elk prefer to graze in the valleys instead of on the mountain slopes. How do you think their preference might affect Yellowstone's plant communities? **(Hint:** See p. 94.)

BIOLOGY.com Search (Lesson 4.4) **GO** • Lesson Assessment

4.5 Aquatic Ecosystems

MD CLG 3.1.3 Matter and Energy, 3.5.1 Factors Influencing Ecosystems, 3.5.2 Interdependence of Organisms in the Biosphere, 3.5.3 Population Dynamics, 3.5.4 Global Food Webs. SPI 1.5.7 Classification Systems, 1.5.8 Compare.

Key Questions

🔑 **What factors affect life in aquatic ecosystems?**

🔑 **What are the major categories of freshwater ecosystems?**

🔑 **Why are estuaries so important?**

🔑 **How do ecologists usually classify marine ecosystems?**

BUILD Understanding

Compare/Contrast Table As you read, note the similarities and differences between freshwater and marine ecosystems in a compare/contrast table.

In Your Workbook Go to Lesson 4.5 in your workbook to learn more about making a compare/contrast table.

The Photic Zone Sunlight penetrates only a limited distance into aquatic ecosystems. Whatever the depth, the photic zone is the only area in which photosynthesis can occur.

Conditions Underwater

We call our planet "Earth." But almost three fourths of Earth's surface is covered with water. What is life like underwater?

Underwater organisms are affected by a variety of environmental factors. These factors include the water depth, temperature, flow, and amount of dissolved nutrients. Runoff from land can affect some factors, so distance from shore also shapes marine communities.

Water Depth Sunlight only penetrates a short distance through water. This region is called the photic zone. It ranges from 200 meters deep (tropical seas) to less than a few meters (swamps). Photosynthetic algae called phytoplankton live here. They are eaten by tiny free-floating animals called zooplankton. Below the photic zone is the dark aphotic zone, where photosynthesis cannot occur.

Many aquatic organisms live on, or in, rocks and sediments on the bottoms of lakes, streams, and oceans. These organisms are called the **benthos,** and their habitat is the benthic zone. In shallow waters the benthos are in the photic zone. Algae and rooted aquatic plants grow here. In the aphotic zone, chemosynthetic autotrophs are the only primary producers.

Temperature and Currents Aquatic habitats are warmer near the equator and colder near the poles. Temperature in aquatic habitats also varies with depth. The deepest parts of lakes and oceans are often colder than surface waters. Currents can dramatically affect water temperature, too. They can carry water that is noticeably warmer or cooler than normal into a given area.

Nutrient Availability Aquatic organisms need certain substances to live, including oxygen, nitrogen, potassium, and phosphorus. The type and availability of these dissolved substances varies within and between bodies of water. This difference greatly affects the types of organisms that can survive there.

🔑 **Key Question** What factors affect life in aquatic ecosystems? **Aquatic organisms are affected primarily by the water's depth, temperature, flow, and amount of dissolved nutrients.**

Freshwater Ecosystems

Only 3 percent of Earth's surface water is fresh water. Freshwater ecosystems can be divided into three main categories: rivers and streams, lakes and ponds, and freshwater wetlands.

Rivers and Streams Rivers, streams, creeks, and brooks often originate from underground water sources in mountains or hills. Water has little plant life here. Downstream, sediments build up and plants establish themselves. Farther downstream, water may wander slowly through flat areas. Animals in many rivers and streams depend for food on plants and other animals that live along the banks.

Lakes and Ponds Food webs in lakes and ponds often are based on plankton and attached algae and plants. **Plankton** is a general term that includes both phytoplankton and zooplankton. Water typically flows in and out of lakes and ponds. It also circulates between the surface and the benthos during at least some seasons. This movement distributes heat, oxygen, and nutrients.

Freshwater Wetlands A **wetland** is an ecosystem in which water either covers the soil or is present at or near the surface for at least part of the year. Water may flow through wetlands or remain still. Wetlands are often nutrient-rich and highly productive, and they serve as breeding grounds for many organisms. Freshwater wetlands purify water by filtering pollutants. Wetlands help to prevent flooding by absorbing and slowly releasing water. Three main types of freshwater wetlands are freshwater bogs, freshwater marshes, and freshwater swamps. Saltwater wetlands are called estuaries.

🔑 **Key Question** What are the major categories of freshwater ecosystems?
Freshwater ecosystems can be divided into three main categories: rivers and streams, lakes and ponds, and freshwater wetlands.

Freshwater Ecosystems Freshwater ecosystems include streams, lakes, and freshwater wetlands (bogs, marshes, and swamps).

Freshwater Wetland: Bog | Freshwater Wetland: Marsh | Freshwater Wetland: Swamp | Stream | Lake

Estuaries

Estuaries (ES tyoo ehr ee) are wetlands that form where a river meets the sea. They contain a mixture of fresh water and salt water and are affected by ocean tides. Many are shallow, so enough sunlight reaches the benthos to power photosynthesis. Estuaries support an astonishing amount of biomass. They serve as breeding and nursery grounds for many important fish and shellfish species.

Salt marshes are temperate estuaries. Salt marshes have salt-tolerant grasses above the low-tide line and seagrasses below water. The Chesapeake Bay in Maryland is a salt marsh. Mangrove swamps, such as the Everglades, are tropical estuaries. They are identified by several species of salt-tolerant trees, called mangroves.

Key Question Why are estuaries so important?
Estuaries serve as breeding and nursery grounds for many ecologically and commercially important fish and shellfish species.

Estuaries Salt marshes and mangrove swamps are estuaries. These are areas where fresh water from rivers meets salt water.

Marine Ecosystems

Marine ecosystems usually occupy specific zones within the ocean, based on depth and distance from shore.

Intertidal Zone Organisms in the intertidal zones are subjected to regular and extreme changes in temperature. At high tide, they are submerged in seawater and often battered by waves and currents. At low tide, they are exposed to air and sunlight.

Coastal Ocean The coastal ocean extends from the low-tide mark to the outer edge of the continental shelf. The continental shelf is the relatively shallow border that surrounds the continents. Water here is brightly lit and often supplied with nutrients by freshwater runoff from land. This makes coastal oceans highly productive. Kelp forests and coral reefs are two exceptionally important coastal communities.

Open Ocean The open ocean begins at the edge of the continental shelf. It is divided into the photic zone and the aphotic zone.

▶ *The Open Ocean Photic Zone* The open ocean typically has low nutrient levels and supports only the smallest species of phytoplankton. Still, because of its enormous area, most photosynthesis on Earth occurs in the sunlit top 100 meters of the open ocean.

▶ *The Open Ocean Aphotic Zone* The permanently dark aphotic zone includes the deepest parts of the ocean. Its food webs are usually based on organisms that fall from the photic zone. Some food webs here are based on chemosynthetic primary producers.

Key Question How do ecologists usually classify marine ecosystems? **Ecologists divide the ocean into zones based on depth and distance from shore.**

Creature From the Deep This silver hatchetfish lives in the aphotic zone of the Gulf of Mexico.

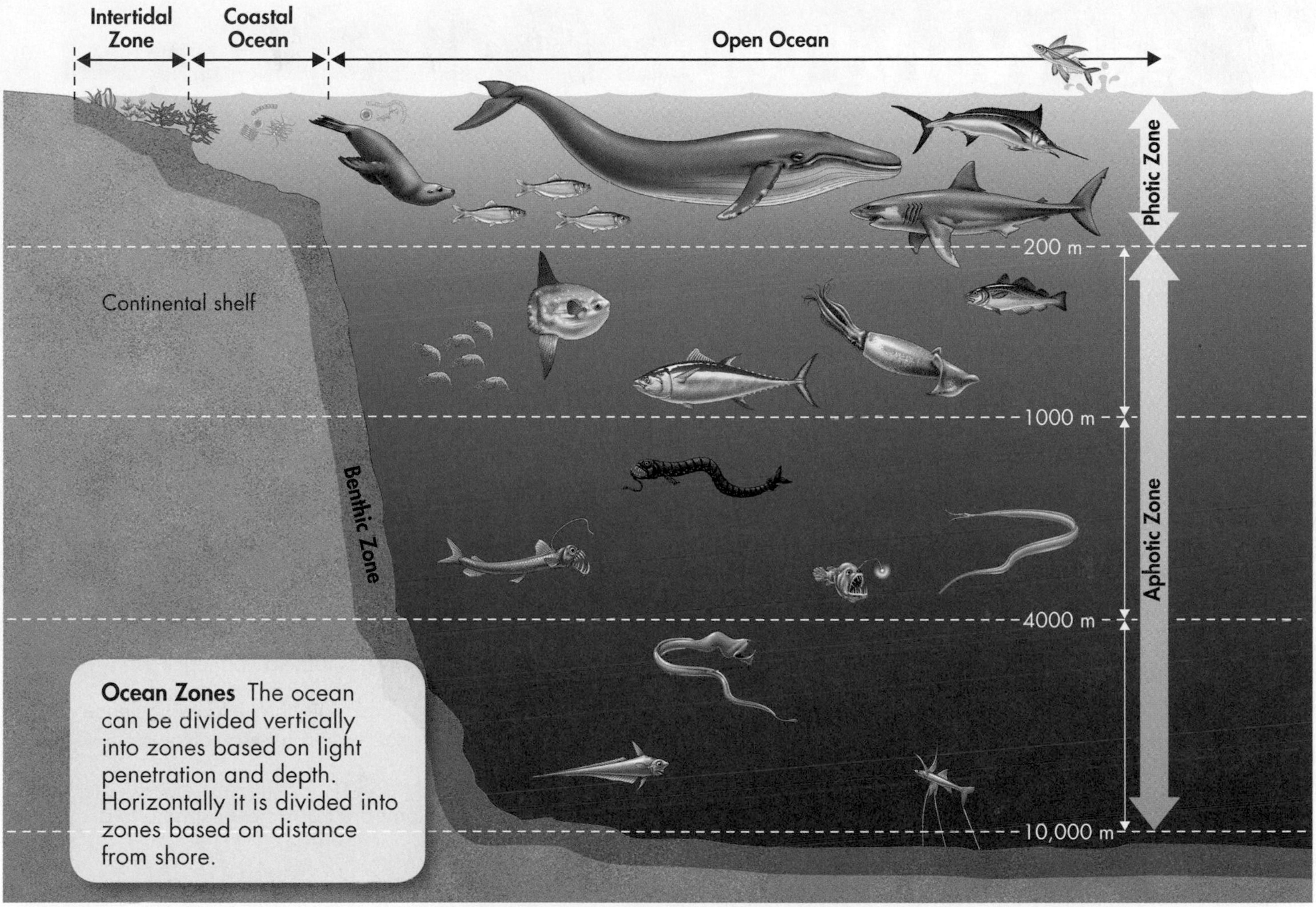

Intertidal Zone | Coastal Ocean | Open Ocean

Photic Zone

Continental shelf

Benthic Zone

200 m

1000 m

Aphotic Zone

4000 m

10,000 m

Ocean Zones The ocean can be divided vertically into zones based on light penetration and depth. Horizontally it is divided into zones based on distance from shore.

CHECK Understanding

Apply Vocabulary

Use the highlighted words from the lesson to complete each sentence correctly.

1. _____ is the group of organisms that is often at the base of food webs in open-water aquatic ecosystems.

2. Aquatic organisms that grow in the sediments at the bottom of a pond or lake are called the _____.

Critical Thinking

3. Explain What are the primary abiotic factors that affect life underwater?

4. Apply Concepts Why is it important to protect estuaries?

5. Write to Learn Answer the third clue to the mystery. Where do you think the streams in Yellowstone most likely originate?

MYSTERY CLUE

How might the presence or absence of plants along stream banks affect life in Yellowstone's streams? (**Hint:** See p. 97.)

BIOLOGY.com   Search (Lesson 4.5   **GO** ● Art Review   ● Lesson Assessment

 **R**eal-World Lab

OPEN-ENDED INQUIRY

 MD CLG 3.5.1 Factors Influencing Ecosystems. SPI 1.2.7 Apply Results, 1.4.8 Use Models, 1.5.5 Create and Interpret Graphics, 1.6.5 Judge Answers.

Pre-Lab: Abiotic Factors and Plant Selection

Problem How can you decide which plants will thrive in a garden?

Materials plant hardiness zone map, plant catalogs, graph paper, tape measure or metersticks

Lab Manual Chapter 4 Lab

Skills Focus Classify, Analyze Data, Use Models

Connect to the Big idea Why are white birch trees abundant in Minnesota, but not in the Florida Keys? Why do coconut palms grow in the Florida Keys, but not in Minnesota? Simply put, white birch trees could not tolerate the hot summers in the Keys and coconut palms could not tolerate the cold winters in Minnesota. A plant's habitat is determined by its range of tolerance for temperature and other abiotic factors. In other words, abiotic factors limit where a given plant can live.

In this lab, you will plan a garden for a specific location. You will select plants for the garden that can tolerate the abiotic factors in this location.

Background Questions

a. Review What is an abiotic factor? List three examples other than temperature.

b. Review What kinds of resources do plants need?

c. Relate Cause and Effect Give an example of an adaptation that helps a plant survive in a biome with low precipitation.

Pre-Lab Questions

Preview the procedure in the lab manual.

1. Predict How will knowing the plant hardiness zone for your area help you plan a garden?

2. Relate Cause and Effect What is the relationship between the last frost and the length of the growing season?

3. Infer A plant species grows well in one location in a small garden but does not grow as well in another location. Suggest one possible reason for this difference.

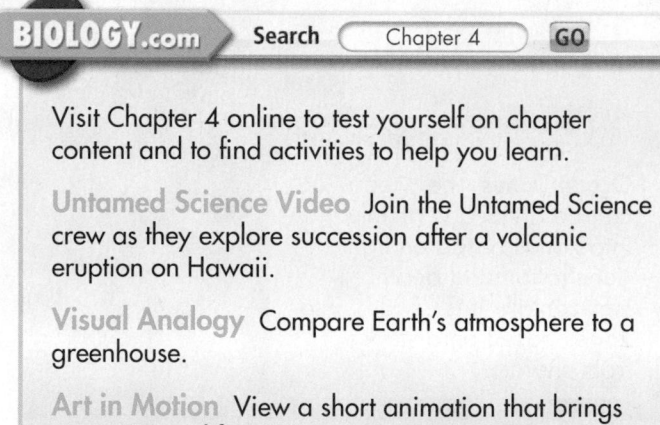

BIOLOGY.com Search [Chapter 4] GO

Visit Chapter 4 online to test yourself on chapter content and to find activities to help you learn.

Untamed Science Video Join the Untamed Science crew as they explore succession after a volcanic eruption on Hawaii.

Visual Analogy Compare Earth's atmosphere to a greenhouse.

Art in Motion View a short animation that brings succession to life.

Art Review Review your understanding of ocean zones with this drag-and-drop activity.

4.1 Climate

- A region's climate is defined by year-after-year patterns and averages of temperature and precipitation.

- Global climate is shaped by many factors, including the amount of solar energy that is trapped in the biosphere. The transport of heat by winds and ocean currents also shapes global climate.

climate (p. 82)   greenhouse effect (p. 83)
microclimate (p. 82)

4.2 Niches and Community Interactions

- A niche is the range of physical and biological conditions in which a species lives. It includes the way that a species obtains what it needs to survive and reproduce.

- Competition causes species to divide resources. It helps determine the number and kinds of species in a community. It also helps to shape the niche each species occupies.

- Predators and herbivores can affect the size of other populations in a community. Predators can affect where prey populations can survive. Herbivores can help determine where populations of certain plants can survive and grow.

- The three main classes of symbiotic relationships in nature are mutualism, parasitism, and commensalism.

habitat (p. 85)   symbiosis (p. 87)
niche (p. 85)   mutualism (p. 87)
resource (p. 85)   parasitism (p. 87)
predation (p. 86)   commensalism (p. 87)
herbivory (p. 86)

4.3 Succession

- Ecosystems change over time, especially after disturbances. As some species die out, new species move in.

- In healthy ecosystems, secondary succession often reproduces the original climax community after a natural disturbance. But ecosystems may or may not recover from widespread disturbances caused by humans.

ecological succession (p. 88)
primary succession (p. 88)
pioneer species (p. 88)
secondary succession (p. 88)

4.4 Biomes

- Biomes are described in terms of abiotic factors like climate and soil type. They are also described by biotic factors like plant and animal life.

- Mountain ranges and polar ice caps are not usually classified into biomes. They are not easily defined in terms of a typical community of plants and animals.

canopy (p. 92)   taiga (p. 94)
understory (p. 92)   permafrost (p. 94)
humus (p. 93)

4.5 Aquatic Ecosystems

- Aquatic organisms are affected primarily by the water's depth, temperature, flow, and amount of dissolved nutrients.

- Freshwater ecosystems can be divided into three main categories: rivers and streams, lakes and ponds, and freshwater wetlands.

- Estuaries serve as spawning and nursery grounds for many ecologically and commercially important fish and shellfish species.

- Ecologists divide the ocean into zones based on depth and distance from shore.

benthos (p. 96)   wetland (p. 97)
plankton (p. 97)   estuary (p. 98)

 Assess the **Big idea**

Interdependence in Nature

Write an answer to the question below.

Q: How do abiotic and biotic factors shape an ecosystem?

Constructed Response

Write an answer to each of the numbered questions below. The answer to each question should be one or two paragraphs. To help you begin, read the **Hints** below the questions.

1. **How do abiotic factors determine which organisms are involved in primary succession after a volcanic eruption?**

   Hint Volcanic eruptions deposit large amounts of volcanic rock and ash.

   Hint Volcanoes can be found in many different biomes.

2. **How does introducing an invasive species into an ecosystem demonstrate the competitive exclusion principle?**

   Hint Introduced species often have no predators or parasites in their new environments. How might this affect their competition with native species?

3. **What type of symbiosis occurs between a cow and the bacteria in its stomach?**

   Hint The bacteria can digest cellulose, but the cow cannot.

Foundations for Learning Wrap-Up

Use the index cards you prepared when you started the chapter as tools to organize your thoughts about ecosystems and communities.

Activity 1 Working with a partner, take turns picking vocabulary index cards at random. Identify each term as a biotic factor or an abiotic factor in an ecosystem and explain why it is biotic or abiotic.

Activity 2 Working in a small group, divide all the vocabulary and ecosystem cards into groups by lesson. Construct concept maps by arranging the cards on a table and explain how the terms are related.

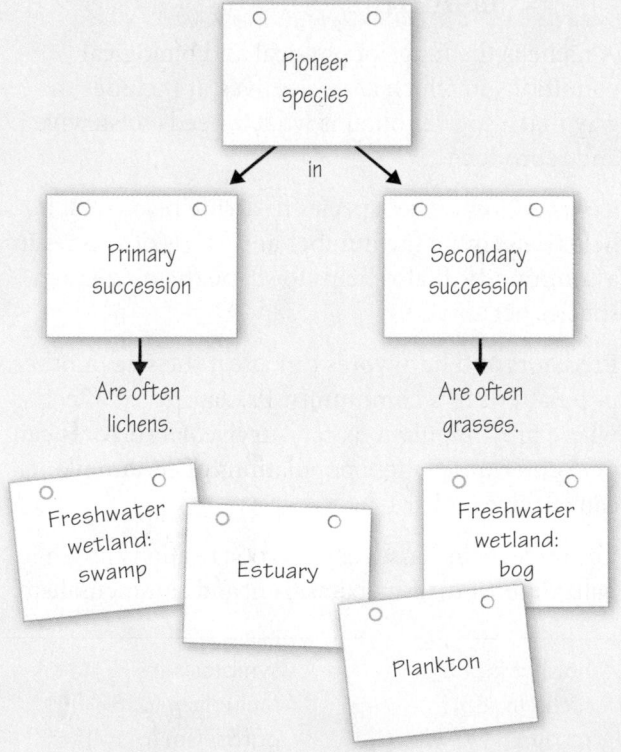

4.1 Climate

Understand Key Concepts

1. The average temperature in a certain valley is usually higher than that of the surrounding countryside. This means that the valley has its own
   a. weather.
   c. rainfall.
   b. climate.
   d. microclimate.

> **Test-Taking Tip**
>
> **Choose Among Similar Answers** Sometimes questions have answer choices that are similar to each other. It may help if you first define each of the answer choices. In question 2, answer choices **a,** **b,** and **d** are similar. The correct answer is **d** because microclimate refers to the conditions in a small area. A valley is a small area.

2. Distinguish between *weather* and *climate*.

Think Critically

3. **Apply Concepts** Based on the relative positions of the sun and Earth, explain why Earth has climate zones and seasons.

4.2 Niches and Community Interactions

Understand Key Concepts

4. The relationship between a tick and its host is an example of
   a. mutualism.
   c. commensalism.
   b. parasitism.
   d. succession.

5. What is the competitive exclusion principle?

Think Critically

6. **Compare and Contrast** How are predation and parasitism different?

4.3 Succession

Understand Key Concepts

7. Fires, hurricanes, and other natural disturbances can result in
   a. commensalism.
   c. parasitism.
   b. competition.
   d. succession.

8. The first organisms to repopulate an area affected by a volcanic eruption are called
   a. keystone species.
   c. primary producers.
   b. climax species.
   d. pioneer species.

9. Describe two major causes of ecological succession.

Think Critically

10. **Relate Cause and Effect** Why does secondary succession usually proceed faster than primary succession?

4.4 Biomes

Understand Key Concepts

11. Permafrost characterizes the biome called
    a. taiga.
    c. savanna.
    b. boreal forest.
    d. tundra.

12. Why are there generally few plants in a desert?

Think Critically

13. **Apply Concepts** Although the amount of precipitation is low, most parts of the tundra are very wet during the summer. How would you explain this apparent contradiction?

4 CHECK Understanding

4.5 Aquatic Ecosystems

Understanding Key Concepts

14. Kelp forests and coral reefs are types of communities found in which marine ecosystem?

a. intertidal zone

b. open ocean photic zone

c. coastal ocean

d. open ocean aphotic zone

15. How are salt marshes and mangrove swamps alike?

Think Critically

16. Infer The deep ocean lies within the aphotic zone and is very cold. What are some unique characteristics that might enable animals to live in the deep ocean?

Connecting Concepts

Use Science Graphics

The following table presents primary productivity (measured in grams of organic matter produced per year per square meter) for several ecosystems. Use the table below to answer questions 17 and 18.

Productivity of Aquatic and Land Ecosystems	
Ecosystem	**Average Primary Productivity**
Aquatic Ecosystems	
Coral reef	2500
Estuary	1800
Open ocean	125
Land Ecosystems	
Tropical rain forest	2200
Tropical savanna	900
Tundra	90

17. Interpret Tables According to the table, which ecosystem is most productive?

18. Infer The open ocean is among the least productive ecosystems per square meter. But most of Earth's photosynthesis takes place in its photic zone. How might the amount of water that covers Earth explain why these two facts can both be true?

solve the CHAPTER MYSTERY

THE WOLF EFFECT

Removing wolves from Yellowstone National Park contributed to an increase in the number of elk. These elk grazed so heavily that the seedlings and shoots of aspens, willows, and other trees could not grow. This was especially a problem along streams. Fewer trees meant beavers built fewer dams, which led to an increase in runoff and erosion. Aquatic food webs broke down, affecting birds, fish, and other animals. The recent reintroduction of wolves has caused a decrease in the overall elk population. The presence of wolves seems to have reduced elk grazing along certain streams. That may be in part because wolves are killing more elk. It may also be in part because elk have learned to stay away from places like stream banks and valleys. Wolves can attack them most easily in these areas.

In recent years, researchers have shown that streamside vegetation is exhibiting secondary succession. The aspen and willow trees are starting to grow back. There have been numerous other changes as well. Fewer elk mean more food for smaller animals. The increase in small prey, in turn, has brought diverse predators into the community. Carcasses abandoned by the wolves provide food for scavengers. In short, organisms from every trophic level have been affected by the Yellowstone wolves.

1. Predict The Yellowstone wolf and elk are linked through a predator-prey relationship. If a disease were to strike the elk population, how would this affect the wolves?

2. Apply Concepts Why might you consider the wolves to be a keystone species?

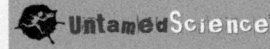 **Never Stop Exploring Your World.** The mystery of the Yellowstone wolves is just the beginning. Take a video field trip with the ecogeeks of Untamed Science to see where this mystery leads.

Multiple Choice

1. The factor that generally has the greatest effect on determining a region's climate is its
   A longitude.
   B abundant plant species.
   C distance from the equator.
   D closeness to a river.   CLG 3.5.1

2. All of the following are abiotic factors that affect global climate EXCEPT
   A latitude.   C solar energy.
   B longitude.   D ocean currents.
                                              CLG 3.5.1

3. The way an organism makes its living, including its interactions with biotic and abiotic factors of its environment, is called the organism's
   A habitat.   C lifestyle.
   B niche.   D biome.   CLG 3.5.2

4. If a newly introduced species fills a niche that is normally occupied by a native species, the two species compete. One of the species may die out as a result of
   A competitive exclusion.
   B predation.
   C commensalism.
   D mutualism.   CLG 3.5.2

5. Photosynthetic algae are MOST likely to be found in
   A the open-ocean benthic zone.
   B the aphotic zone.
   C the photic zone.
   D ocean trenches.   CLG 3.5.4

6. The water in an estuary is
   A salt water only.
   B poor in nutrients.
   C fresh water only.
   D a mixture of fresh water and salt water.
                                              CLG 3.5.4

7. In which biome do organisms have the greatest tolerance to dry conditions?
   A tundra   C tropical savanna
   B desert   D boreal forest
                                              CLG 3.5.4

Questions 8–9

Month-by-month climate data for the city of Lillehammer, Norway, is shown in the table below.

Climate Data for Lillehammer, Norway		
Month	Average Temperature (°C)	Average Precipitation (mm)
Jan.	−8.1	38.1
Feb.	−6.2	27.9
Mar.	−3.9	30.5
Apr.	3.3	35.6
May	8.9	45.7
June	13.9	63.5
July	16.4	81.3
Aug.	14.2	88.9
Sept.	9.5	58.4
Oct.	3.9	63.5
Nov.	−3.8	50.8
Dec.	−6.1	48.3

8. Which type of graph would be BEST suited to showing the precipitation data from the table?
   A bar graph   C pie chart
   B pictograph   D scatter plot   SPI 1.4.1

9. For a given set of data, the range is the difference between highest and lowest points. The average annual temperature range, in °C, for Lillehammer is approximately
   A −8.
   B 8.5.
   C 16.5.
   D 24.5.   SPI 1.4.2

Open-Ended Response

10. Why are lichens especially well adapted to play the role of pioneer organisms in an ecological succession?   CLG 3.5.2

If You Have Trouble With . . .

Question	1	2	3	4	5	6	7	8	9	10
See Lesson	4.1	4.1	4.2	4.2	4.5	4.5	4.4	4.1	4.1	4.3

5 Populations

BIOLOGY.com > Search (Chapter 5) GO • Flash Cards

Millions of red crabs live on Christmas Island in the Indian Ocean. Each year, all of the adult crabs move from forest to sea to breed.

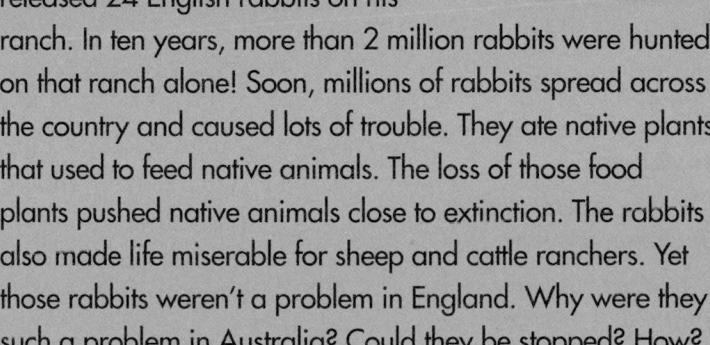

CHAPTER
MYSTERY

A PLAGUE OF RABBITS

In 1859, an Australian farmer released 24 English rabbits on his ranch. In ten years, more than 2 million rabbits were hunted on that ranch alone! Soon, millions of rabbits spread across the country and caused lots of trouble. They ate native plants that used to feed native animals. The loss of those food plants pushed native animals close to extinction. The rabbits also made life miserable for sheep and cattle ranchers. Yet those rabbits weren't a problem in England. Why were they such a problem in Australia? Could they be stopped? How?

Read for Mystery Clues As you read this chapter, look for clues to help you predict why this rabbit population grew so much. Think about factors that affect population growth. Then, solve the mystery at the end of the chapter.

FOUNDATIONS for Learning

Before you read this chapter, read the lesson titles and headings. Then, fold a piece of paper into three columns. In the first column, list what you know about populations. In the second column, write questions about what you want to learn. In the third column, you will write what you have learned. There are two activities at the end of the chapter that will require you to use your paper to answer the question: What factors contribute to changes in populations?

What Do I KNOW?	What Do I WANT to Know?	What Have I LEARNED?

5.1 How Populations Grow

MD CLG **3.5.1** Factors Influencing Ecosystems, **3.5.3** Population Dynamics, **3.5.4** Global Food Webs.
SPI **1.4.2** Analyze Data, **1.5.5** Create and Interpret Graphics, **1.7.1** Apply Skills and Concepts,
1.7.4 Recognize Mathematics.

Key Questions

 How do ecologists study populations?

 What factors affect population growth?

 What happens during exponential growth?

 What is logistic growth?

BUILD Understanding

Concept Map As you read, make a concept map that organizes the information in this lesson.

In Your Workbook Go to your workbook for help in completing the concept map. Complete the concept map for Lesson 5.1.

Describing Populations

About 60 years ago, a fish farmer in Florida tossed some hydrilla plants into a canal. These few plants, which were brought here from Asia, reproduced quickly. Today, hydrilla can be found across Florida and many other states. Because hydrilla grow so thickly, they kill other plants and animals. Why do hydrilla grow so quickly?

Ecologists try to answer such questions. Ecologists study a population's range, density, growth rate, and age structure.

Geographic Range A population's geographic range describes the spaces where it lives. Different populations can have very different ranges. For example, the range of a bacterial population may be tiny. But the population of cod in the western Atlantic Ocean ranges from Greenland to North Carolina.

Density and Distribution Population density is the number of individuals of a species per unit area. In a meadow, for example, you might find a dense population of grasses but a less dense population of spiders. Population distribution describes how the organisms are spread across their range. The distribution of a population may be random, uniform, or clumped.

Growth Rate A population's growth rate tells you if the population size is getting bigger, smaller, or staying the same. The population of hydrilla in Florida has a very high growth rate. Populations can also decrease in size. The cod population, which is decreasing, has a negative growth rate.

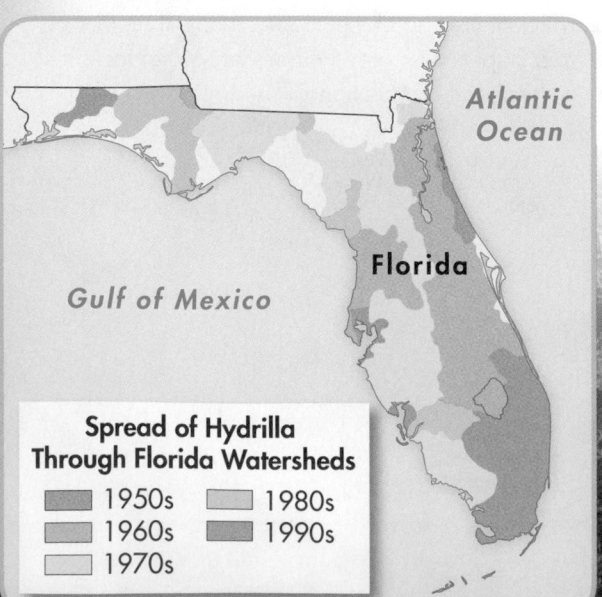

Spread of Hydrilla Through Florida Watersheds
- 1950s
- 1960s
- 1970s
- 1980s
- 1990s

Atlantic Ocean

Florida

Gulf of Mexico

Invasive Hydrilla Hydrilla has spread throughout most of Florida in just a few decades. Efforts to control the waterweed cost millions of dollars a year.

Age Structure The **age structure** of a population describes the number of males and females of each age in the population. Age structure is important because in animals only the females between certain ages can reproduce.

🔑 **Key Question** How do ecologists study populations? **Ecologists study a population's range, density, growth rate, and age structure.**

Population Growth

The size of a population changes based on how many individuals are added to it or removed from it. How are individuals added or removed?

Birthrate and Death Rate A population may grow if more individuals are born than die in any period of time. In this case, the birthrate is higher than the death rate. If the death rate is higher, the population may shrink. If these rates are about the same, the population may stay the same size.

Immigration and Emigration When individuals move into a population's range, the process is called **immigration** (im uh GRAY shun). When individuals move out of the range, it is called **emigration** (em uh GRAY shun). If immigration rates are higher than emigration rates, the population will grow.

🔑 **Key Question** What factors affect population growth? **Population growth is affected by birthrate and death rate. It can also be affected by immigration and emigration.**

Exponential Growth

Imagine that a population has all the food and space it needs. It also has protection from predators and disease. Imagine also that its waste products are all removed. Under these conditions, the population will grow.

Organisms That Reproduce Rapidly Imagine a single bacterium that divides to form two cells every 20 minutes. Those two cells divide to form four cells. Those four cells divide again. So, after three 20-minute periods, there are $2 \times 2 \times 2$, or 8 cells, which can also be written using an exponent: 2^3 cells.

This situation is called exponential (eks poh NEN shul) growth. In **exponential growth,** the larger a population gets, the more quickly it grows. When you graph the growth, the graph is in the shape of a J.

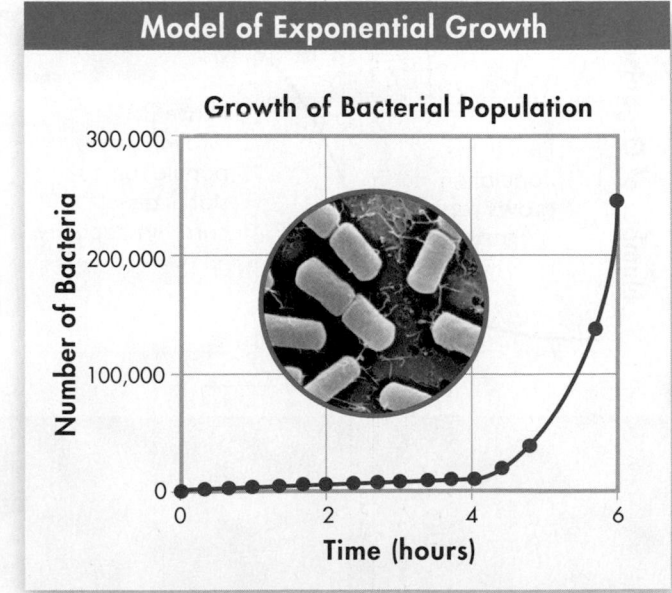

Model of Exponential Growth

Growth of Bacterial Population

Exponential Growth When there are plenty of resources and few predators or diseases, populations will grow exponentially. This graph shows the characteristic J-shaped curve of exponential growth.

Organisms in New Environments Does exponential growth ever happen in nature? Yes! That's what happened with hydrilla, and with many other species that humans have introduced into new habitats. When a species is moved into a new habitat, its population often grows exponentially for a time. But think about this situation for a minute. Can this growth continue without stopping?

🔑 **Key Question** What happens during exponential growth? **In exponential growth, the larger a population gets, the more quickly it grows.**

Logistic Growth

Exponential growth presents us with a puzzle. Obviously, bacteria and hydrilla don't cover the planet. This means that populations in the real world don't grow exponentially for very long. Sooner or later, population growth slows down. But why?

Phases of Growth To begin to answer this question, let's see what happens when a few individuals are brought into a new area. Usually the population will go through three phases. You have read a bit about the first phase—exponential growth. In the next phases, the growth slows and eventually stops.

▶ *Phase 1: Exponential Growth* After a short time, the population begins to grow exponentially. There is plenty of food. There is plenty of space. The death rate is low. The birthrate is high. The rate of growth increases more and more quickly.

▶ *Phase 2: Growth Slows Down* In most populations, exponential growth does not last very long. At some point, the growth must slow down. The population keeps growing, but it does not grow as quickly.

▶ *Phase 3: Growth Stops* At some point, the growth rate drops to zero. The population size stays about the same.

Logistic Growth Population growth slows down as resources become limited. This graph shows the characteristic S-shaped curve of logistic growth.

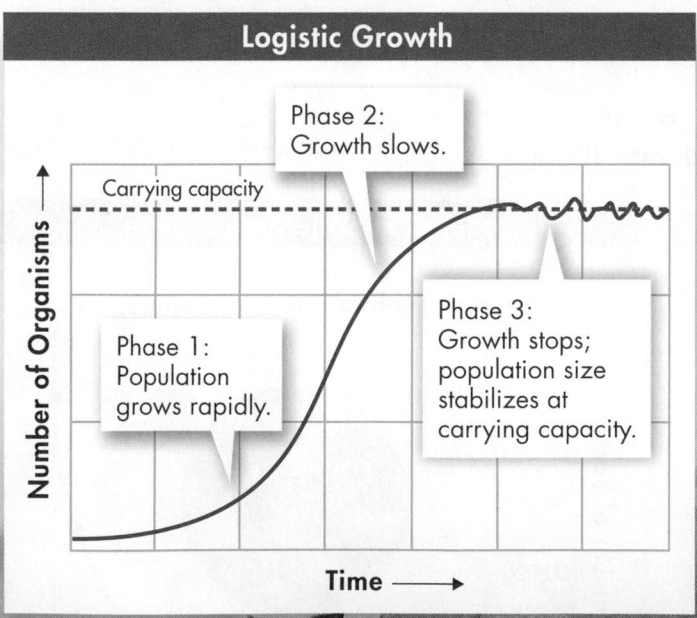

Logistic Growth

Phase 2: Growth slows.

Carrying capacity

Number of Organisms

Phase 1: Population grows rapidly.

Phase 3: Growth stops; population size stabilizes at carrying capacity.

Time

The Logistic Growth Curve When a population's growth slows down and stops, it is called **logistic growth.** A logistic growth curve is shaped like an S.

What kinds of changes in a population cause logistic growth? A population grows when the number of organisms added to the population is more than the number of organisms that leave the population. Population growth may slow for several reasons. Growth may slow because the birthrate slows. Growth may slow because the death rate increases. Immigration and emigration can also affect growth rates. If immigration decreases or emigration increases, growth will slow.

Carrying Capacity In the third phase of logistic growth, the population stops growing. Population growth stops when the birthrate and death rate are the same and when immigration equals emigration. Look again at the logistic growth curve. There is a broken, horizontal line in the graph where the population size stays about the same. This population size is the largest number of individuals an area can support. The largest number of individuals that an area can support is called the **carrying capacity.** The population size may go up or down somewhat. However, the size stays very near the carrying capacity.

Key Question What is logistic growth?
Logistic growth happens when the growth of a population begins as exponential growth and then slows and stops.

BUILD Vocabulary

logistic growth
a growth pattern in which a population's growth rate slows or stops, following a period of exponential growth

carrying capacity
the largest number of individuals of a population that a given environment can support

RELATED WORD FORMS
The word *logistics* means the way someone handles the resources of a project or event. The adjective *logistic* is used in this sense to describe growth that can be supported by the available resources.

CHECK Understanding

Apply Understanding
Use the highlighted words from the lesson to complete each sentence correctly.

1. _____ sometimes happens when a new kind of organism is introduced in an area.

2. The number of males and females of each age group in a certain population is called the _____.

3. The number of organisms an area can support over a long period of time is called the _____.

Critical Thinking

4. Relate Cause and Effect More dandelion seedlings develop in a lawn than dandelion plants are pulled. What is likely to happen to the lawn's dandelion population?

5. Explain Describe logistic growth.

6. Apply Concepts A few European gypsy moths were accidentally released from a laboratory near Boston. Describe what might have happened to the population over the next several years.

7. Write to Learn Answer the first clue of the mystery. Think about the different phases of population growth.

MYSTERY **CLUE**

What kind of growth is the rabbit population in Australia demonstrating? Why does that cause problems? (**Hint:** See p. 110.)

5.2 Limits to Growth

MD CLG **3.5.1** Factors Influencing Ecosystems, **3.5.2** Interdependence of Organisms in the Biosphere, **3.5.3** Population Dynamics, **3.5.4** Global Food Webs. SPI **1.4.1** Organize Data, **1.4.2** Analyze Data, **1.4.6** Determine Trends, **1.7.2** Evaluate Ideas.

Key Questions

🔑 What factors determine carrying capacity?

🔑 What limiting factors depend on population density?

🔑 What limiting factors do not usually depend on population density?

BUILD Understanding

Preview Before you read this lesson, write down the headings and look at the figures. As you read, write the main idea under each heading.

In Your Workbook Go to your workbook for help previewing the lesson.

Limiting Factors

Now that you have seen *how* populations tend to grow in nature, you can explore *why* they grow as they do. What factors cause the growth to slow down? What determines the carrying capacity of an environment for a species?

Think about the hydrilla discussed in Lesson 5.1. In Asia, the population reached its carrying capacity. Then, it stopped growing. In the United States, hydrilla just keeps growing. The same thing happened when a few nonnative gypsy moths were accidentally released near Boston. Within a few years, these plant-eating pests had spread across the northeastern United States. Gypsy moths and hydrilla do not seem to have a carrying capacity. What is happening?

A **limiting factor** is any factor that controls the size of a population. The number of predators in an area may be a limiting factor. How much food is available may be a limiting factor. Limiting factors keep most natural populations from growing out of control. Limiting factors determine the carrying capacity of an environment for a species.

Some factors depend on the density of the population. They depend on how many individuals live in one place. Other factors affect a population no matter how many individuals live in an area.

🔑 **Key Question** What factors determine carrying capacity? **Limiting factors determine the carrying capacity of a population.**

Density-Dependent Limiting Factors

Some limiting factors affect populations most when the individuals live close together. These limiting factors depend on the population density and are called **density-dependent limiting factors.** There are several different kinds of density-dependent limiting factors.

Population Size

can be limited by

- Competition
- Predation
- Parasitism and disease
- Unusual weather
- Natural disaster

Limiting Factors Many factors can limit population growth. Some of these factors depend on population density. Others do not.

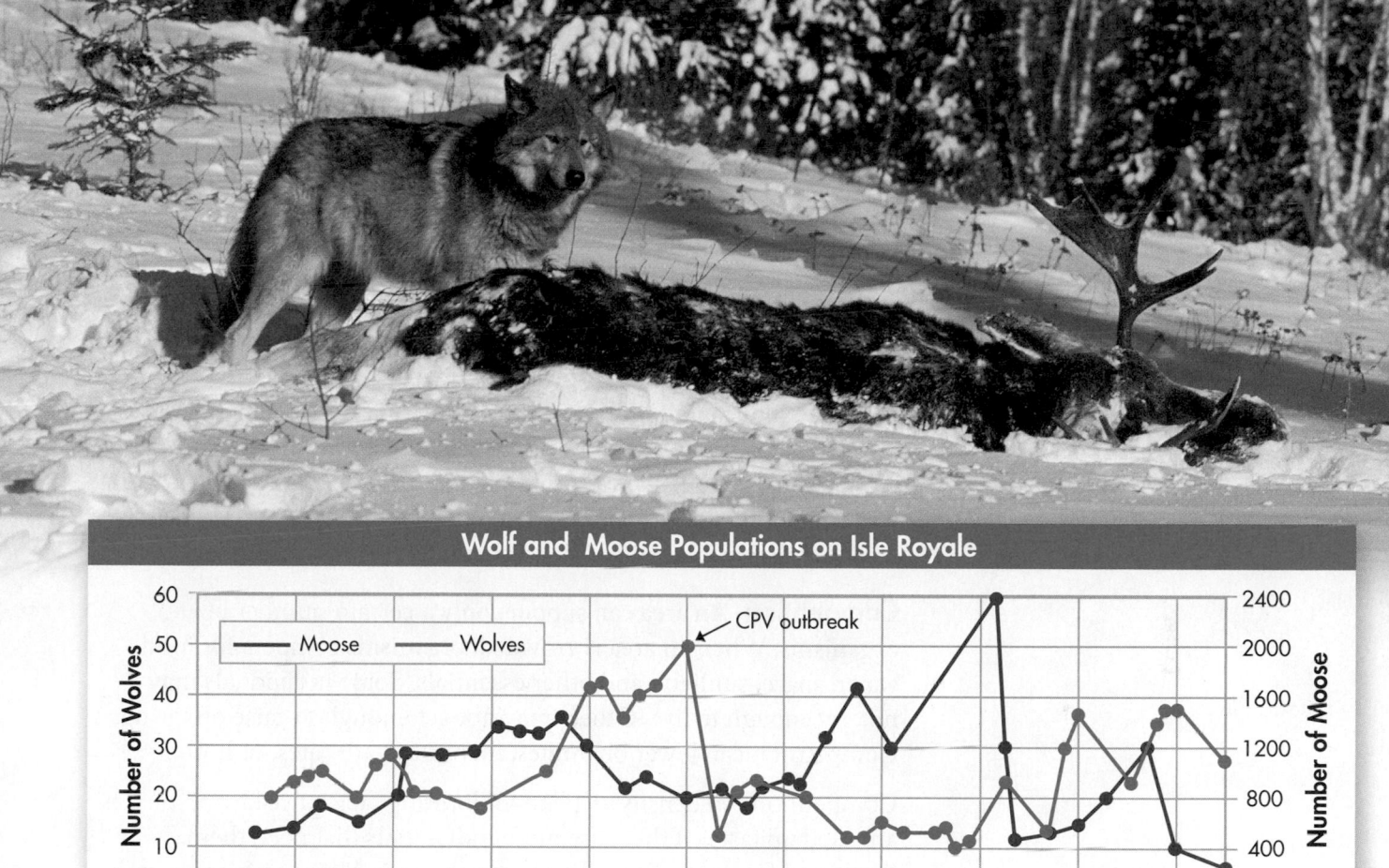

Wolf and Moose Populations on Isle Royale

Moose and Wolf Populations on Isle Royale Moose and wolves on Isle Royale affect each other's population growth. In this case, the moose population was also affected by changes in food supply. The wolf population was also impacted by a virus (CPV) in 1980.

Predators One important density-dependent factor is the relationship between predators and prey. The populations of moose and wolves on Isle Royale in Lake Superior are one example. When the moose population is high, wolves catch them easily. So the wolf population then grows. More wolves mean that more moose are killed than are born. The moose population falls. With fewer moose, the wolves starve. The wolf population falls. Eventually, the moose population rises again, and the cycle repeats.

People can also limit population sizes. In New England, people are predators of codfish. People catch more and more fish each year. The cod population has gotten much smaller. If people killed fewer cod, the population could rise again. Scientists are studying the cod population. They want to learn how many fish can be caught each year without risking the entire population.

BUILD Vocabulary

limiting factor
a factor that causes the growth of a population to decrease

density-dependent limiting factor
a limiting factor that depends on population size

ACADEMIC WORDS

You learned that the word *factor* is a feature that contributes to an event or result. A limiting factor, however, is a feature that contributes to a change in population growth.

Parasites The ticks on this hedgehog are parasites. They can spread diseases to the hedgehog.

Herbivores From the plant's point of view, herbivores are predators. So it makes sense that the populations of herbivores and plants go up and down over time. Moose on Isle Royale eat balsam fir. When there are a lot of moose living in parts of Isle Royale, the fir population falls. Then, the moose begin to starve. As the moose population drops, the fir population goes back up.

Parasites and Disease Parasites and organisms that cause disease feed on their hosts. This feeding weakens the host and can cause disease or death. When hosts live close together, the hosts come into contact with each other more often. Therefore, diseases and parasites spread more easily from one host to the next. The wolf population on Isle Royale dropped quickly around 1980. This decline was due to a viral disease that spread quickly through the large, dense wolf population. Only three females and ten males survived.

Competition An area can support only a certain number of organisms. When an area is crowded, organisms compete for food, water, space, sunlight, and other essentials. Some individuals may not get enough to live. Others may not get enough to raise offspring. Competition can lower birthrates, increase death rates, or both.

Competition is a density-dependent limiting factor because resources are used up faster if there are more individuals that need them. Space and food are often related to each other. Many grazing animals compete for territories. They use the territories to graze and raise offspring. If they do not have a territory, then they cannot find a mate and produce offspring.

Overcrowding In some populations, overcrowding causes fighting. Too much fighting may lead to stress. Stress can make it harder for the body to fight sickness. In some cases, stress can even cause females to kill their offspring. So, stress from overcrowding can lower birthrates, raise death rates, and increase rates of emigration.

🔑 **Key Question** What limiting factors depend on population density?
Competition depends on population density. Predators, herbivores, parasites, and diseases affect crowded populations more. Stress can also affect a dense population.

Density-Independent Limiting Factors

Some limiting factors do not depend on how many individuals live close together. These factors affect all populations in almost the same ways and are called **density-independent limiting factors.** Bad weather, such as a hurricane or drought, is a density-independent limiting factor. Natural disasters, such as wildfires, do not depend on density either. Large storms can sometimes kill most of a population. For example, insects may be washed away by a heavy rain.

True Density Independence? It is sometimes difficult to say that a factor is truly density independent. On Isle Royale, the moose population grew quickly after the wolf population dropped. Then, a very cold winter came. Snow covered the plants the moose ate. Many moose died. If there had been fewer moose, they may have found enough food. In this case, two factors worked together to limit the population.

Controlling Introduced Species People have tried many things to control hydrilla in the United States. Density-independent limiting factors have not solved the problem. Using chemicals and machines to kill or remove the hydrilla have worked only temporarily. So far, the best plan of control seems to be the introduction of sterilized grass carp fish to eat the plants.

🔑 **Key Question** What limiting factors do not usually depend on population density?
Unusual weather and natural disasters can act as density-independent limiting factors.

Effects of a Severe Drought on a Population During a drought, dead fish lie rotting on the banks of the Paraná de Manaquiri River in Brazil.

CHECK Understanding

Use the highlighted words from the lesson to complete each sentence correctly.

1. A flood is an example of a _____ because it usually affects all populations in the same way.
2. Limiting factors that affect large, dense populations more than small, scattered populations are called _____.

Critical Thinking

3. **Apply Concepts** How do limiting factors affect the growth of populations?
4. **Relate Cause and Effect** What is the relationship between competition and population size?

5. **Apply Concepts** Arctic foxes eat lemmings. What is likely to happen to the lemming population if the arctic fox population were to increase quickly?
6. **Write to Learn** Answer the second clue of the mystery. Think about factors that might be different in England than in Australia.

MYSTERY CLUE

What factors do you think could limit the size of a rabbit population? (Hint: See p. 114.)

BIOLOGY.com ▸ Search ⟨ Lesson 5.2 ⟩ **GO** • Lesson Assessment

How Does Competition Affect Growth?

Individuals who live near each other compete for what they need. There is usually only so much food, water, space, and sunlight to go around. The individuals who get enough of these resources live longer, healthier lives. They tend to produce more offspring. Individuals who do not get enough may not survive. Some individuals may get enough food or water to survive but not enough to raise offspring. In this way, competition can affect the size of a population.

Competition is a density-dependent limiting factor. Resources are used up more quickly by large, dense populations. Small, scattered populations do not use as many resources. In these populations, competition is not usually a limiting factor.

In Lesson 5.2, you learned about competition and other limiting factors. In this activity, you will explore how competition affects the growth of bean sprouts.

❶ Label two paper cups 3 and 15. Prepare the two cups by completing the following steps:

- Make five or six small holes in the bottom of each cup.
- Fill each cup two-thirds full with potting soil.
- Plant 3 bean seeds in cup 3.
- Plant 15 bean seeds in cup 15.

❷ Water both cups so that the soil is moist but not wet.

❸ Put the cups in a location that gets bright, indirect light. Water the cups equally as needed.

❹ Count the seedlings every other day for two weeks. Draw a chart like the one below to record your data. (You planted your seeds on Day 0.)

Analyze and Conclude

1. Observe What differences did you observe between the two cups?

In Your Workbook Get more help for this activity in your workbook.

	Day 2	Day 4	Day 6	Day 8	Day 10	Day 12	Day 14
Date							
Cup 3							
Cup 15							

5.3 Human Population Growth

MD CLG 3.5.3 Population Dynamics. SPI 1.4.5 Check Graphs, 1.4.6 Determine Trends, 1.5.5 Create and Interpret Graphics, 1.6.3 Use Scientific Notation, 1.7.1 Apply Skills and Concepts, 1.7.2 Evaluate Ideas, 1.7.4 Recognize Mathematics.

Historical Overview

For most of human history, the human population grew slowly. Food was hard to find. The death rate was high because of predators and disease. Today, four human babies are born every second. The human population could reach 9 billion in your lifetime. What changes have made it possible for the human population to grow so quickly?

Exponential Human Population Growth As life became easier, the human population began to grow more rapidly. During the Industrial Revolution in the 1800s, people learned how to ship goods around the world. Food supplies became more reliable. Healthcare and medicine improved. People learned more about sanitation and nutrition. Because of all these improvements, death rates dropped. But the birthrate stayed very high. This combination of lower death rates and high birthrates led to exponential growth of the human population.

World Population Growth Slows The human population growth rate was highest around 1962–1963. The population is still growing very rapidly. However, the rate of growth is slowing.

It took 123 years for the population to go from 1 billion in 1804 to 2 billion in 1927. It took only 33 years to reach 3 billion. The time it took to add another billion people continued to decrease until 1999. Since then, the growth rate has slowed. What has been happening to slow human growth?

Key Question How has the size of the human population changed over time? **For a long time, the population grew slowly. In the 1800s, the population began to grow exponentially.**

Key Questions

🔑 **How has the size of the human population changed over time?**

🔑 **Why do population growth rates differ among countries?**

BUILD Understanding

Preview Visuals Before you read, preview the graphs throughout the lesson. Make a list of questions about the graphs. Then, as you read, write down the answers to your questions.

In Your Workbook Go to your workbook to review the graphs.

Human Population Growth Over Time For a long time, the human population grew very slowly. Technological advances lowered death rates. Then, the global population began to increase much more quickly.

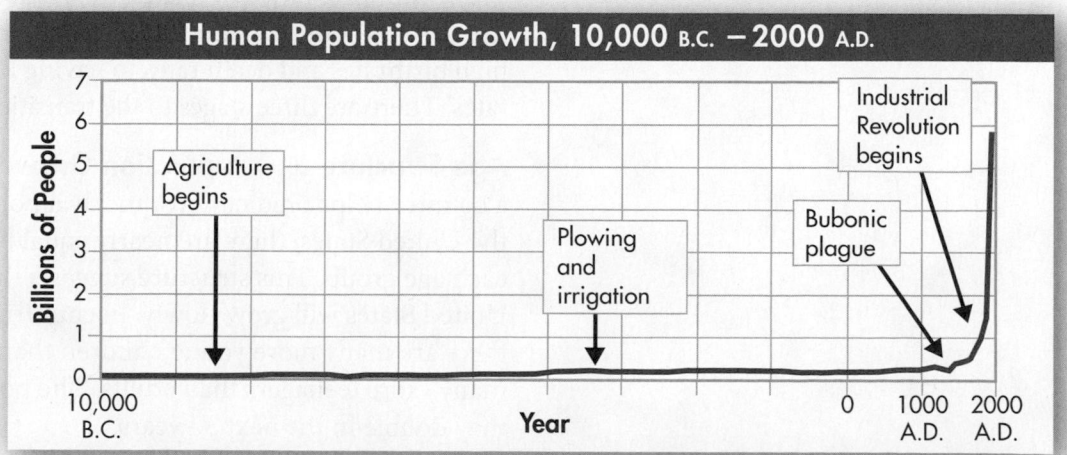

Human Population Growth, 10,000 B.C. – 2000 A.D.

Billions of People / Year

Agriculture begins
Plowing and irrigation
Industrial Revolution begins
Bubonic plague

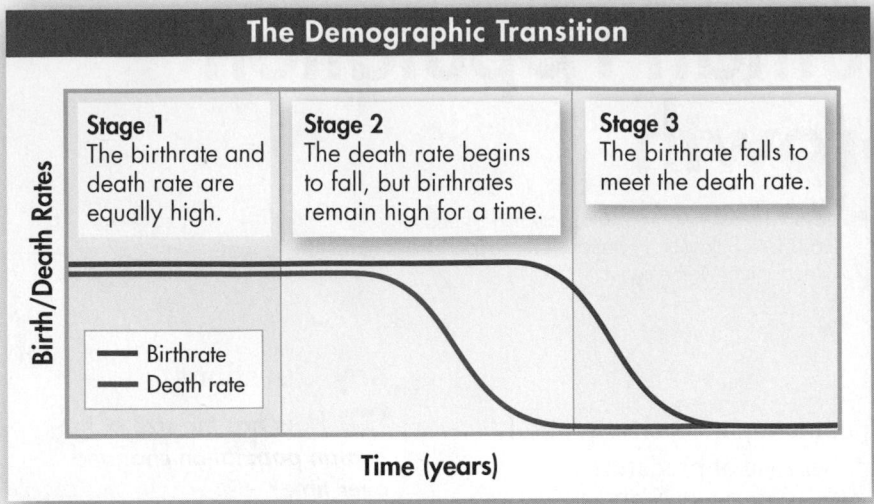

The Demographic Transition

Stage 1
The birthrate and death rate are equally high.

Stage 2
The death rate begins to fall, but birthrates remain high for a time.

Stage 3
The birthrate falls to meet the death rate.

Birth/Death Rates

— Birthrate
— Death rate

Time (years)

The Demographic Transition
Stage 1: Birthrates and death rates are high for most of history.
Stage 2: Advances in nutrition, sanitation, and medicine lower death rates. Birthrates remain high. There are many more births than deaths. The population increases exponentially.
Stage 3: As living standards rise, families have fewer children and the birthrate falls. Population growth slows. The demographic transition is complete when the birthrate meets the death rate.

Patterns of Human Population Growth

The world population growth rate has slowed a lot recently. In some countries, however, the growth rate is still high. In fact, most of the world's population growth is happening in only ten countries. India and China are leading the growth.

Scientists have identified several things that affect population growth. The scientific study of human populations is called **demography** (duh MAH gruh fee). Demography looks at characteristics of human populations. It tries to explain how those populations will change over time. Scientists study birthrates, death rates, and the age structure of a population. They use this information to explain why some countries have high growth rates and some countries grow more slowly.

The Demographic Transition For a long time, human societies had very high birthrates and death rates. Then, death rates dropped and birthrates remained high. Over the past century, birthrates in the United States, Japan, and much of Europe also fell. The growth rates in these countries slowed dramatically. These countries have completed the demographic transition. In the **demographic transition,** a population changes from having high birthrates and death rates to having low birthrates and death rates. There are three stages to the transition, as shown above.

Age Structure and Population Growth The age structure in a country helps predict how quickly a population will grow. In the United States, there are nearly equal numbers of people in each age group. This structure suggests that the population of the United States will grow slowly. In countries such as Guatemala, there are many more young children than teenagers. There are many more teenagers than adults. The population of Guatemala may double in the next 30 years.

Future Population Growth People who study demography look at many factors to predict how the human population will grow. Age structure is one important factor. They also study how diseases affect death rates. Right now, AIDS is causing very high death rates in Africa and parts of Asia.

The world population may reach 9 billion people by the year 2050. Will the human population level out to a logistic growth curve? Countries growing rapidly right now would need to complete the demographic transition.

It is expected that the world population will grow more slowly over the next 50 years than it did over the last 50 years. The growth rate will probably still be higher than zero in 2050. If so, our population will continue to grow. In the next chapter, you will learn about the effect of human population growth on the biosphere.

Key Question Why do population growth rates differ among countries?
Birthrates, death rates, and age structure are different in different countries. These differences cause some countries to have high growth rates and others to have low growth rates.

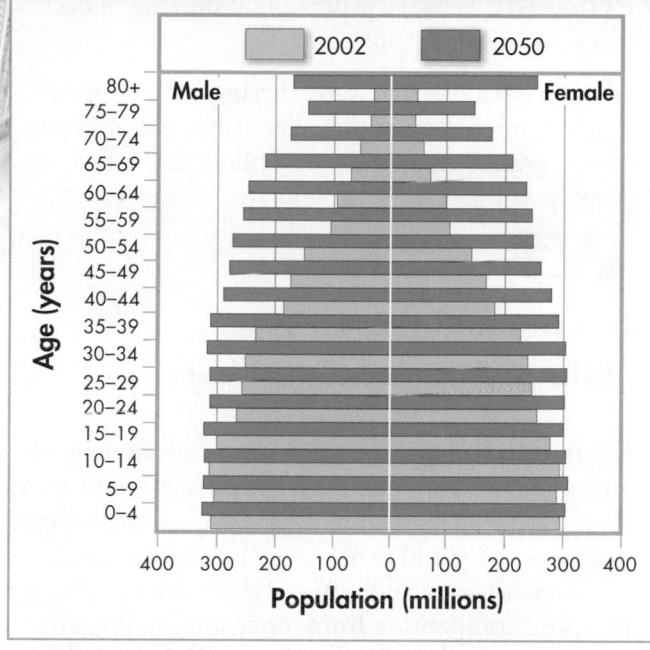

Age Structure of World Population

A Growing Population The information for this graph was taken from the U.S. Census Bureau, International Database. The graph shows the projected age structure of the world population in 2050. The photo above shows a housing complex in Hong Kong, China. Each apartment building is home to thousands of people.

CHECK Understanding

Apply Vocabulary
Use the highlighted terms from the lesson to complete each sentence correctly.

1. People who study _____ look at characteristics, such as age structure, death rate, and birthrate to predict how human populations will change.

2. In the third stage of the _____, the birthrate and death rate are equal.

Critical Thinking

3. **Apply Concepts** If every married couple in a country were to decide to have only one child, what would happen to the country's population growth?

4. **Relate Cause and Effect** The human population grew very slowly for most of human history. In about 1800, the population began growing exponentially. What factors contributed to this growth pattern?

5. **Write to Learn** In one or two paragraphs, describe the three stages of demographic transition. Explain how the population growth rate changes at each stage.

 CLG 3.5.1 Factors Influencing Ecosystems, **3.5.3** Population Dynamics. **SPI 1.2.2** Posing Scientific Questions, **1.3.1** Use Equipment, **1.3.3** Safe Handling of Materials, *(continued below)*

Pre-Lab: The Growth Cycle of Yeast

Problem What type of population growth occurs in a yeast culture?

Materials yeast culture, stirring rod, dropper pipettes, microscope slides, coverslips, microscope, 10-mL graduated cylinder, test tubes, test-tube rack, graph paper

Lab Manual Chapter 5 Lab

Skills Measure, Calculate, Interpret Graphs

Connect to the **Big idea** Populations depend on, and are limited by, their environments. A population can grow when its members have the resources they need to survive and reproduce. Factors that can limit those resources include natural disasters, such as forest fires, and competition from other species. Predation and disease are also limiting factors for populations.

In nature, populations often experience cycles of growth and decline. In this lab, you will investigate whether such a cycle occurs in yeast populations.

Background Questions

a. Review What is the carrying capacity of a population?

b. Sequence Briefly describe the three phases of logistic growth.

c. Relate Cause and Effect Describe two different ways that a population might achieve a growth rate of zero.

d. Classify After two weeks of hot and sunny days with very little rain, the blades of grass in a backyard began to wither and die. Were any of the factors that caused the decline of the grass population dependent on density? Explain.

Pre-Lab Questions

Preview the procedure in the lab manual.

1. Infer Why was grape juice used to prepare the yeast cultures instead of plain water?

2. Calculate Suppose you have to do one dilution of your culture before you are able to count the yeast cells. If you count 21 yeast cells in the diluted sample, how many yeast cells were in the same area of the undiluted sample?

3. Predict What do you think will happen to a yeast population between Day 3 and Day 7? Give reasons for your answer.

BIOLOGY.com Search (Chapter 5) GO

Visit Chapter 5 online to test yourself on chapter content and to find activities to help you learn.

Untamed Science Join the Untamed Science crew as they learn the latest techniques for counting populations.

Art in Motion View a short animation that brings age-structure diagrams to life.

Art Review Review your understanding of limiting factors with this drag-and-drop activity.

InterActive Art Manipulate factors such as starting population size, birthrate, and death rate to see how they would impact moose and wolf populations over time.

 1.4.1 Organize Data, **1.4.6** Determine Trends.

5.1 How Populations Grow

- Ecologists study a population's range, density, growth rate, and age structure.

- Population growth is affected by birthrate and death rate. It can also be affected by immigration and emigration.

- In exponential growth, the population grows more and more quickly.

- Logistic growth happens when the growth of a population slows and then stops.

---

age structure (p. 109)
immigration (p. 109)
emigration (p. 109)
exponential growth (p. 109)
logistic growth (p. 111)
carrying capacity (p. 111)

5.2 Limits to Growth

- Limiting factors determine the carrying capacity of a population.

- Competition depends on population density. Predators, herbivores, parasites, and diseases affect crowded populations more than small, scattered populations. Stress can also affect a dense population.

- Unusual weather and natural disasters can act as density-independent limiting factors.

---

limiting factor (p. 112)
density-dependent limiting factor (p. 112)
density-independent limiting factor (p. 114)

5.3 Human Population Growth

- For a long time, the population grew slowly. In the 1800s, the population began to grow exponentially.

- Birthrates and death rates are different in different countries. The age structures are different. Countries with high birthrates and low death rates are growing quickly. The United States, Japan, and much of Europe have completed the demographic transition, and their growth rates have slowed.

---

demography (p. 118)
demographic transition (p. 118)

Assess the Big idea ▶ Interdependence in Nature

Write an answer to the question below.

Q: What factors contribute to changes in populations?

Constructed Response

Write an answer to each of the questions below. The answer to each question should be one or two paragraphs long. To help you begin, read the **Hints** below each of the questions.

1. **Why should people be cautious about introducing organisms into new environments?**

   Hint When organisms are introduced into new environments, they may not face natural predators.

   Hint A limiting factor is a factor that controls the growth of a population.

2. **Natural populations do not grow exponentially for very long. Why not?**

   Hint In exponential growth, the larger a population gets, the faster it grows.

   Hint Carrying capacity is the maximum number of organisms of a species an area can support.

Foundations for Learning Wrap-Up

Use the folded paper chart you made before reading the chapter as a tool to help you organize your thoughts about populations.

Activity 1 On your own, reread the questions you asked at the beginning of the chapter. Write the answers to these questions in the third section of your page, under the heading, What Have I Learned?

Activity 2 Trade charts with a partner. Compare your questions and answers. If one of you had any difficulty answering the questions, find the answers together. Also, double-check the information you each wrote in the first and third columns. Is everything correct? If not, work together to correct your charts.

What Do I KNOW?
- A population is a group of one kind of organism living in the same area.
- Some populations grow. Some populations get smaller.

What Do I WANT to Know?
- Why do some populations get bigger and others get smaller?
- How do different populations in the same area affect each other?

What Have I LEARNED?
- •
- •

5.1 How Populations Grow

Understanding Key Concepts

1. The space taken up by a population is known as its
   - **a.** growth rate.
   - **b.** geographic range.
   - **c.** age structure.
   - **d.** population density.

2. The graph below represents
   - **a.** carrying capacity.
   - **b.** exponential growth.
   - **c.** logistic growth.
   - **d.** age structure.

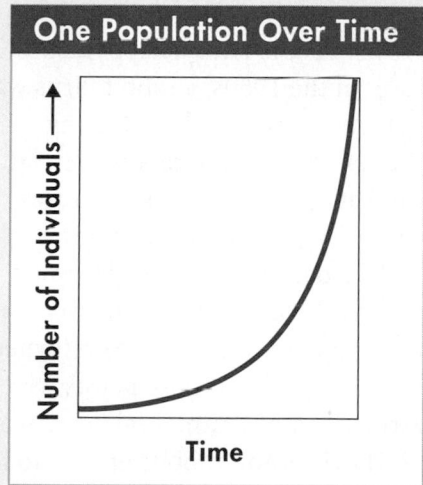

One Population Over Time

Number of Individuals →

Time

Test-Taking Tip

Interpret Visuals Look carefully at visuals. In the graph in question 2, the number of individuals is increasing very quickly over time. The growth rate is increasing over time as well. The graph of logistic growth is shaped like the letter S. The graph of exponential growth is shaped like the letter J. So, answer **c** is not correct. Answer **b** is the correct answer.

3. The largest population size that can survive in a given area is called
   - **a.** logistic growth.
   - **b.** carrying capacity.
   - **c.** exponential growth.
   - **d.** population density.

4. What is the difference between immigration and emigration?

Think Critically

5. **Use Analogies** How is the carrying capacity of a road like the carrying capacity of an ecosystem?

5.2 Limits to Growth

6. A limiting factor that depends on the population size is called a
   - **a.** density-dependent limiting factor.
   - **b.** density-independent limiting factor.
   - **c.** predator-prey relationship.
   - **d.** parasitic relationship.

7. Which of the following is a density-independent limiting factor?
   - **a.** predators
   - **b.** unusual weather
   - **c.** competition
   - **d.** overcrowding

8. Describe how the populations of moose and wolves on Isle Royale affect each other. How does an increase in the population of one affect the population of the other?

9. Why are parasites considered a density-dependent limiting factor?

Think Critically

10. **Predict** What would happen to a population of predators if there were a sudden increase in food for the prey? Explain your answer.

5.3 Human Population Growth

11. What is the scientific study of human populations called?
   - **a.** immigration
   - **b.** emigration
   - **c.** demographic transition
   - **d.** demography

12. What is the last stage of the demographic transition?
   - **a.** The birthrate and death rate are both very high.
   - **b.** The death rate is low, and the birthrate is very high.
   - **c.** The birthrate and death rate are both low.
   - **d.** The birthrate is low, and the death rate is very high.

13. Describe the general trend of human population growth over time.

Think Critically

14. Compare and Contrast One small town is made up mainly of senior citizens. How would you expect this town's population to change over the next several years? Compare this growth to that of a small town that is made up mostly of newly married couples in their twenties.

Connecting Concepts

Use Science Graphics

The following data come from the United Nations Department of Economic and Social Affairs, Population Division. The table shows when the world population reached 1 billion and when it reached or will reach each additional billion. Use the data table to answer questions 15 and 16.

World Population Milestones		
Population (billion)	Year	Time Interval (years)
1	1804	—
2	1927	123
3	1960	33
4	1974	14
5	1987	13
6	1999	12
7	2012	13
8	2027	15
8.9	2050	23

15. Observe When did the world population reach 1 billion people? When did it reach 6 billion?

16. Interpret Tables Describe the trend in population growth since the 1-billion-people mark.

solve the CHAPTER MYSTERY

A PLAGUE OF RABBITS

Before the farmer let those 24 rabbits go in 1859, Australia had no wild rabbits. So the rabbits had very few predators, parasites, and diseases. Rabbits reproduce quickly. The population jumped from 24 to millions in less than ten years. Large rabbit populations cause a lot of damage.

Australians have tried many things to manage the population. They have tried fencing and poisoning. They have tried to ruin burrows. People have used parasites and disease. In the 1950s, a rabbit virus was deliberately introduced. It killed many rabbits. But eventually, the rabbit populations rose again. Later, a new virus that causes rabbit hemorrhagic disease (RHD) was introduced. Rabbit populations dropped again. In several places, the results were dramatic. Native trees and shrubs returned. It had been thought that these plants were locally extinct! Native animals also recovered. But the RHD virus and rabbits appear to have reached a new balance. Rabbit populations are rising again.

1. Predict Wildcats and foxes were also introduced to Australia. These predators have come to depend on rabbits as prey. How do you think wildcats and foxes would be affected by a large drop in the rabbit population?

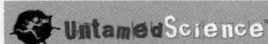 **Never Stop Exploring Your World.** Finding the solution to the rabbit population mystery is only the beginning. Take a video field trip with the ecogeeks of Untamed Science to see where this mystery leads.

Standardized Test Practice for Maryland

Multiple Choice

1. The movement of individuals into an area is called
   A immigration.
   B emigration.
   C population growth rate.
   D population density. _CLG 3.5.3_

2. All other things being equal, the size of a population will decrease if
   A birthrate exceeds the death rate.
   B immigration rate exceeds emigration rate.
   C death rate exceeds birthrate.
   D birthrate equals death rate. _CLG 3.5.3_

3. Which of the following is NOT an example of a density-dependent limiting factor?
   A natural disaster   C competition
   B predator   D disease _CLG 3.5.3_

4. A population like that of the United States with an age structure of roughly equal numbers in each of the age groups can be predicted to
   A grow rapidly over a 30-year-period and then stabilize.
   B grow little for a generation and then grow rapidly.
   C fall slowly and steadily over many decades.
   D show slow and steady growth for some time into the future. _CLG 3.5.3_

5. In the presence of unlimited resources and in the absence of disease and predation, what would probably happen to a bacterial population?
   A logistic growth   C endangerment
   B exponential growth   D extinction _CLG 3.5.3_

6. Which of the following statements best describes human population growth?
   A The growth rate has remained constant over time.
   B Growth continues to increase at the same rate.
   C Growth has been exponential in the last few hundred years.
   D Birthrate equals death rate. _CLG 3.5.3_

7. Which of the following refers to when a population's birthrate equals its death rate?
   A limiting factor
   B carrying capacity
   C exponential growth
   D population density _CLG 3.5.3_

Questions 8–9

Use the graph below to answer the following questions.

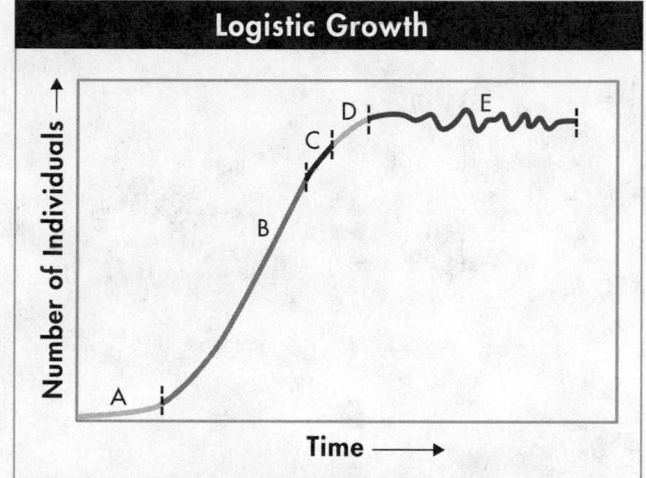

8. Which time interval(s) in the graph shows exponential growth?
   A D and E   C C and D
   B A and B   D E only _SPI 1.4.2_

9. Which time interval(s) in the graph depicts the effects of limiting factors on the population?
   A A only   C C, D, and E
   B A and B   D C and D _SPI 1.4.2_

Open-Ended Response

10. When a nonnative species is imported into a new ecosystem, the population sometimes runs wild. Explain why this might be the case. _CLG 3.5.3_

If You Have Trouble With . . .

Question	1	2	3	4	5	6	7	8	9	10
See Lesson	5.1	5.1	5.2	5.3	5.1	5.3	5.1	5.1	5.2	5.2

6 Humans in the Biosphere

Big idea > Interdependence in Nature

Q: How have human activities shaped local and global ecology?

This image was taken from space. The lights are obvious. The brightest spots are the most developed. But they may not be the most populated spots. There are more than 6.5 billion people on Earth. Development is just one way humans have affected the biosphere.

BIOLOGY.com > Search | Chapter 6 | GO • Flash Cards

MD **MARYLAND VOLUNTARY STATE CURRICULUM**

Biology Indicators/Core Learning Goals (CLG) 3.1.2, 3.1.3, 3.4.1, 3.5.1, 3.5.2, 3.5.3, 3.5.4, 3.6.1, 3.6.2. **Skills and Processes Indicators (SPI)** 1.1.1, 1.2.2, 1.2.5, 1.2.6, 1.3.1, 1.3.3, 1.4.1, 1.4.2, 1.4.6, 1.4.9, 1.5.2, 1.5.7, 1.5.9, 1.6.1, 1.7.1, 1.7.2, 1.7.6. See lessons for details.

CHAPTER
MYSTERY

MOVING THE *MOAI*

Easter Island is a tiny island off the coast of Chile. The original islanders came from Polynesia. They called themselves Rapa Nui. They carved hundreds of huge stone statues called *moai* (MOH eye). Each statue weighs between 10 and 14 tons. About 800 years ago, the Rapa Nui moved the huge stones from quarries to places all around the island. Nearly all theories about this process suggest that strong, large logs were needed to move the *moai*. Yet, by the time Europeans landed on the island in 1722, there was no sign of any trees large enough to provide such logs. What had happened?

Read for Mystery Clues As you read this chapter, look for clues about the interactions of the Rapa Nui with their island environment. Then solve the mystery at the end of the chapter.

FOUNDATIONS
for Learning

Before you read this chapter, make a mini book. Fold two pieces of notebook paper in half and then in half again in the other direction. Staple along the longer folded edge. This edge will be the spine of your book. Cut the folds along the folded edge. You should now have sixteen pages. Write the title of the chapter on the front cover of your mini book and each of the key questions within the chapter at the top of its own page. As you read the chapter, answer each key question in your own words. Use the remaining pages for additional notes.

6.1 A Changing Landscape

MD CLG 3.5.1 Factors Influencing Ecosystems, 3.5.2 Interdependence of Organisms in the Biosphere, 3.5.3 Population Dynamics, 3.5.4 Global Food Webs. SPI 1.1.1 Problems and Solutions, 1.6.1 Ratio and Proportion, 1.7.1 Apply Skills and Concepts, 1.7.2 Evaluate Ideas.

Key Questions

🔑 How do our daily activities affect the environment?

🔑 What is the relationship between resource use and sustainable development?

BUILD Understanding

Lesson Preview Before you read this lesson, write down the headings and look at the figures. Write one or two sentences about what topics you think will be covered. As you read, write the main idea under each heading.

In Your Workbook Go to your workbook to identify the main ideas of this lesson.

The Effect of Human Activity

People from Polynesia began to settle in Hawaii around 1600 years ago. These island people had customs that protected the natural resources. They did not catch fish during spawning season. If they cut down a coconut tree, they planted two trees to replace it. These settlers changed their environment. But they managed their islands carefully. Local ecosystems provided enough fresh water, fertile soil, fish, and other needs to support the population.

Europeans began moving to Hawaii in the late 1700s. These new settlers didn't understand the limits of island ecosystems. They imported many plants and animals. They cleared forests to plant crops. They covered land with housing and tourist developments. What happened?

Living on Island Earth Humans, like all living things, depend on Earth's life-support systems. We also change the environment when we obtain food, get rid of wastes, and build homes. These changes are most obvious on islands, such as Hawaii. Because islands are small, they have limited resources. If local ecosystems cannot supply food and other basic needs, they must be brought in from far away. That's the situation in Hawaii today. Fresh water is getting scarce. Food must be brought in from thousands of miles away.

On large continents, there used to be plenty of space, food, and water. So most of us don't think of land, food, or water as limited resources. But human activity has now used or changed half of all land not covered by ice and snow. As our population reaches 7 billion, we may be getting close to Earth's carrying capacity. Earth begins to feel like a very large island. Humans affect the biosphere of Earth through agriculture, development, and industry.

The Lesson of Hawaii The picture on the left is of Kalalau Valley on Kauai. It looks almost untouched by humans. The picture on the right is of Waikiki Beach on Oahu. Human development is very visible.

Agriculture Agriculture has been vital to human history. Once people could grow a dependable supply of food, they could gather together and live in towns and cities. Living in these large groups encouraged the growth of civilization.

Farmers have been able to double the world's food production over the last 50 years. One way they did this is through monoculture. **Monoculture** is the practice of clearing a lot of land to plant a single crop year after year. Farmers use machines to efficiently sow, tend, and harvest the crops. This is how farmers have supplied food for nearly 7 billion people. But monoculture can pollute soil and water. Also, running farm machinery and producing fertilizer both use a lot of fossil fuels.

Development In modern times, small settlements grew into crowded cities. Suburbs then grew out from those cities. All those dense human communities produce lots of wastes. If wastes are not treated properly, they can pollute the land, air, and water resources. Also, spreading development uses up farmland and divides natural habitats into fragments.

Industrial Growth The Industrial Revolution of the 1800s changed human society. Industry and science have led to many modern conveniences. We have comfortable homes and clothing and many electrical devices for work and play. It takes a lot of energy to produce and power these modern conveniences. We get most of this energy by burning fossil fuels—coal, oil, and natural gas. Also, industries have often gotten rid of wastes by dumping them into the air, water, and soil. All these activities can harm the environment.

Key Question How do our daily activities affect the environment?
People affect the environment through agriculture, development, and industrial growth. These activities affect the quality of Earth's natural resources, including soil, water, and the atmosphere.

Monoculture Soybean fields dominate this landscape.

Reduce, Reuse, Recycle

Each person on Earth affects the biosphere. The garbage you throw out each day is one way you affect the biosphere. In this activity, you will find out how much you throw away in one day.

❶ Get three containers to hold your trash for one day. Label the containers Reuse, Recycle, and Trash.

❷ Throughout the day, collect your dry garbage.

❸ Sort the garbage into the three containers. Items that cannot be reused or recycled will go into the Trash container. Be sure to wash your hands when you are done.

Analyze and Conclude

1. Analyze Data Compare the amount of garbage in each of your containers. About what percentage of the total did you put into each container?

2. Predict What do you think happens to the things you throw out? Think of at least three ways that garbage can impact living things.

3. Evaluate List three ways you can reduce the amount of trash you throw out each day.

In Your Workbook Get more help for this activity in your workbook.

Sustainable Development

Ecosystem Services Hennepin and Hopper Lakes is a wetland in Illinois. It was drained for farming in 1900. The smaller image shows how the area looked when it was farmland. In 2003, the area was restored. The larger image shows how it looks now.

We depend on healthy ecosystems to provide natural resources such as clean air and water. We usually take clean air and water for granted. But if the environment cannot provide them, our cities and towns must spend money to provide them. For example, drinking water is often filtered by wetlands. Water then flows through streams and rivers and is stored in lakes. But if the water sources or wetlands are polluted or damaged, water quality may fall. When this happens, cities and towns must build and run expensive water treatment plants to provide safe drinking water.

Renewable and Nonrenewable Resources There are two main types of natural resources. A **renewable resource** can be made or replaced by a healthy ecosystem. A single southern white pine is a renewable resource. A new tree can grow in place of an old tree that dies or is cut down. But some resources are nonrenewable. A **nonrenewable resource** cannot be replaced in a reasonable amount of time. Fossil fuels are nonrenewable resources. They take millions of years to form. When we use up the fossil fuels that are already here, they are basically gone forever.

Sustainable Resource Use We can learn to use natural resources to meet our needs without causing long-term environmental damage. Using resources this way is called sustainable development. Sustainable development should cause no long-term harm to the soil, water, and climate. It should use as little energy and materials as possible. It must be able to withstand droughts, floods, and heat waves or cold snaps. Sustainable development must also work well enough to help people improve their standard of living.

🔑 **Key Question** What is the relationship between resource use and sustainable development?
Sustainable development uses natural resources to meet human needs without causing long-term damage to the environment.

BUILD Vocabulary

renewable resource
a resource that can be produced or replaced by healthy ecosystem functions

nonrenewable resource
a resource that cannot be replenished by natural processes within a reasonable amount of time

🔖 RELATED WORD FORMS

The word *renew* is used to mean "to extend the checkout time for a library book" and "to begin again." These uses are related to renewable resources and nonrenewable resources. Renewable resources can be used over and over again. Nonrenewable resources cannot.

CHECK Understanding

Apply Vocabulary
Use the highlighted words from the lesson to complete each sentence correctly.

1. When farmers plant the same crop in a field year after year, they are practicing _____.
2. Coal, oil, and natural gas are examples of _____ because they cannot be replaced in a reasonable amount of time.

Critical Thinking

3. **Relate Cause and Effect** How might practices that allow farmers to grow more crops affect a developing nation's population? How might the practices affect the nation's environmental health?
4. **Compare and Contrast** Explain why energy from the sun is a renewable resource but energy from oil is a nonrenewable resource.

5. **Apply Concepts** Imagine that a large shopping center is being built near your school. Until now, the land was basically untouched. There was a clump of trees and a large grassy field. How might the shopping center affect your local ecosystem?
6. **Write to Learn** Answer the first clue of the mystery. Keep in mind what can happen when an organism is introduced to a new environment.

MYSTERY CLUE

Easter Island's first colonists brought with them banana trees, taro root, and chickens. They may also have brought small mammals, such as rats. What impact might these new organisms have had on the island's ecosystems? (**Hint:** See p. 128.)

6.2 Using Resources Wisely

MD · CLG **3.5.1** Factors Influencing Ecosystems, **3.5.2** Interdependence of Organisms in the Biosphere, **3.5.3** Population Dynamics, **3.5.4** Global Food Webs, **3.6.1** Analyze Consequences. SPI **1.1.1** Problems and Solutions, **1.4.2** Analyze Data, **1.4.6** Determine Trends, **1.5.9** Synthesize Ideas, **1.7.1** Apply Skills and Concepts, **1.7.2** Evaluate Ideas.

Key Questions

🔑 **Why is soil important, and how do we protect it?**

🔑 **What are the primary sources of water pollution?**

🔑 **What are the major forms of air pollution?**

BUILD Understanding

Concept Map As you read, make a concept map to organize the information in this lesson.

In Your Workbook Go to your workbook for help completing the concept map.

Soil Resources

Our economy is built on the use of natural resources. We cannot just stop using land for farming. Yet, we need to protect the health of ecosystems that supply us with renewable resources. How can we get what we need from local and global environments in a sustainable way?

You may not think of soil as a resource. Yet, many things you need depend on healthy soil. Food production depends on crops. Paper comes from trees. All these plants we rely on need healthy soil.

The mineral- and nutrient-rich portion of the soil is called topsoil. Good topsoil absorbs and holds the water that plants need but also allows some water to drain. It is rich in nutrients but low in salts. Topsoil can be renewable if it is managed well. Good topsoil is produced by many years of interactions between soil and plants. These processes take a long time to form good topsoil. But topsoil can be damaged or lost quickly. For example, large areas across the Great Plains in the United States were poorly farmed for years. Then, a very bad drought hit in the 1930s. The combination of bad farming and drought eroded topsoil. Crops failed. The area became like a desert. People began to call the Plains the "dust bowl." Thousands of people lost their homes and their jobs.

Soil Erosion The dust bowl was caused, in part, by the way the prairie was used as farmland. Soil erosion happens when wind or water take soil away. Soil erosion is often worse if land is plowed and left bare between plantings. Plant roots hold soil in place. If plants are taken out of the soil, then the soil is easily washed away. Sometimes, farming, overgrazing, and very little rain can turn farmland into desert. This is what happened in the Great Plains in the 1930s. The process is called **desertification.** About 40 percent of Earth's land is thought to be at risk for desertification.

The Dust Bowl A ranch in Boise City, Idaho, is about to be hit by a cloud of dry soil on April 15, 1935.

The loss of forests, called **deforestation,** can also harm soils. Unfortunately, more than half of the world's old-growth forests have already been lost. Old-growth forests are forests that have never been cut. Deforestation can lead to severe soil erosion. Soils and microclimates can change so much that trees cannot grow there again. For example, topsoil in tropical rain forests is usually thin and not very fertile. The soil is often useful for only a few years after the forest is cut down.

Soil Use and Sustainability Soil is most likely to erode when it is completely bare. Leaving stems and roots in the soil between plantings can help hold soil in place. Also, different plants use different nutrients from the soil. When farmers plant different crops at different times of the year or in different years, it is called crop rotation. Crop rotation can help stop erosion and the loss of nutrients.

Another way to limit soil erosion is by contour plowing. Contour plowing is the practice of planting crops across the slope of the land instead of down the slope. This method reduces water runoff and erosion.

What are options for sustainable forestry? Cutting down only some of the mature trees within a forest can allow growth of younger trees without damaging the whole forest or its soil. Tree farms can also protect soil and make the trees themselves a renewable resource.

Key Question Why is soil important, and how do we protect it?
Soil allows plants, including crops, to grow. Farming practices such as crop rotation and leaving stems and roots in the soil between plantings can help protect soil from erosion and a loss of nutrients. Cutting only some mature trees and using tree farms can also protect soil.

Freshwater Resources

Fresh water is usually considered a renewable resource. However, some sources of fresh water are not renewable. The Ogallala aquifer runs under eight states from South Dakota to Texas. It took more than a million years to fill. Today, more water is being pumped out than is returning through rain. The aquifer is likely to run dry in 20 to 40 years.

In many parts of the world, the amount of fresh water is limited. Only 3 percent of the water on Earth is fresh water. We must be careful to protect the ecosystems that collect and purify fresh water.

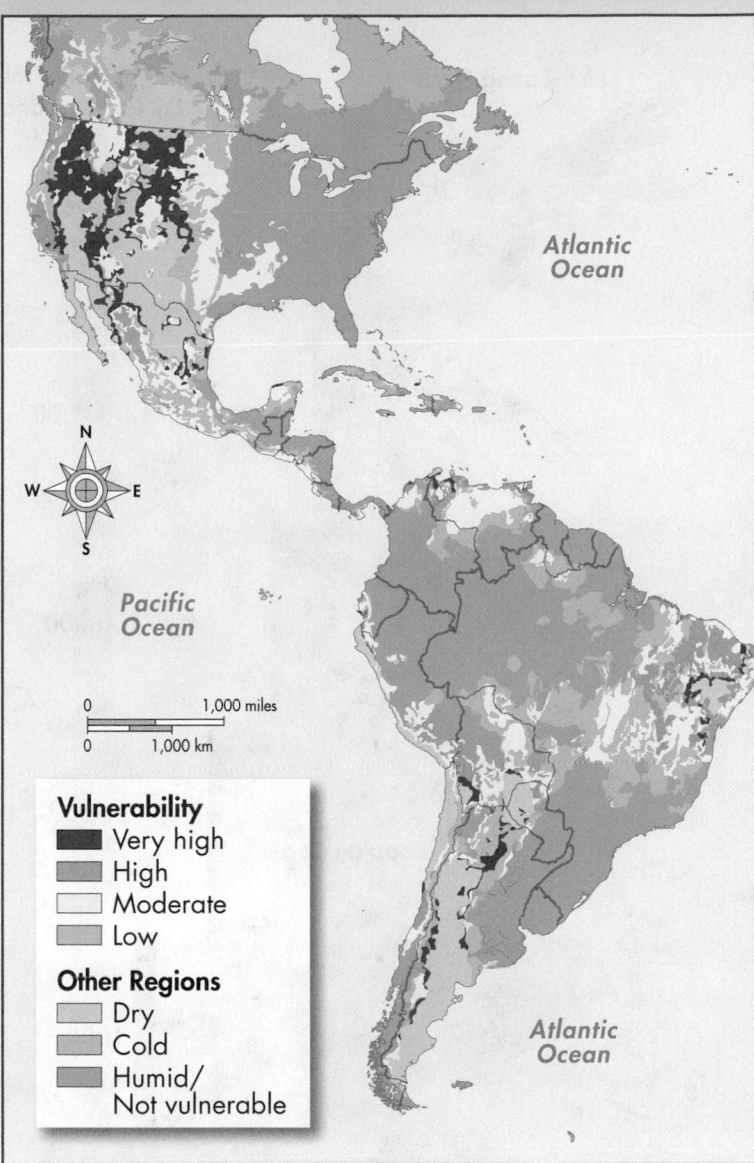

Vulnerability
- Very high
- High
- Moderate
- Low

Other Regions
- Dry
- Cold
- Humid/ Not vulnerable

Desertification Risk The U.S. Department of Agriculture identifies the risk of desertification. The risk is based on soil type and climate.

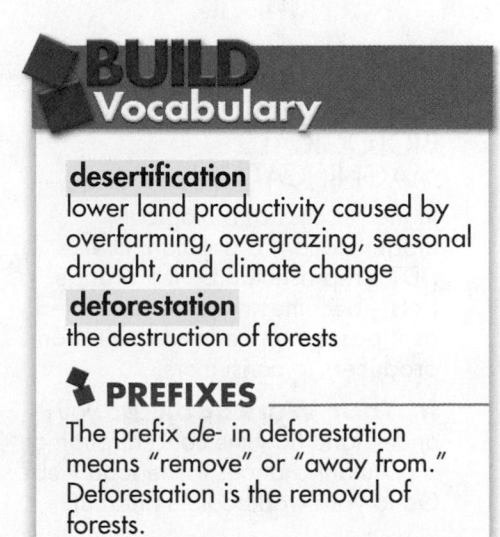

BUILD Vocabulary

desertification
lower land productivity caused by overfarming, overgrazing, seasonal drought, and climate change

deforestation
the destruction of forests

PREFIXES

The prefix *de-* in deforestation means "remove" or "away from." Deforestation is the removal of forests.

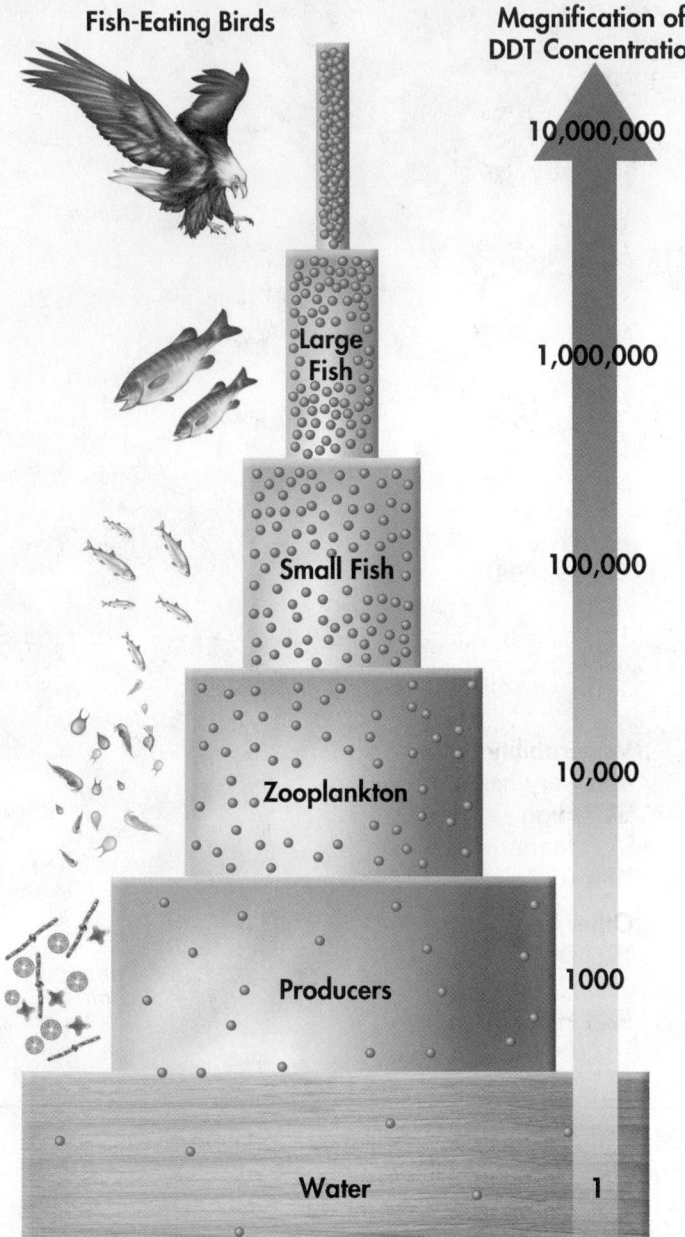

Fish-Eating Birds

Magnification of DDT Concentration

10,000,000

1,000,000

Large Fish

100,000

Small Fish

10,000

Zooplankton

1000

Producers

Water 1

Water Pollution Freshwater sources can be affected by different kinds of pollution. A pollutant is any harmful material that can enter land, water, or air. When a pollutant enters water supplies from one spot, the source is called a point source. A factory or an oil spill are examples of point sources. When pollutants enter from many smaller sources, the sources are called nonpoint sources. Grease and oil washed off of roads are from nonpoint sources. Chemicals released into the air by factories and cars are also nonpoint sources.

▶ *Industrial and Agricultural Chemicals*
Sometimes, a pollutant remains in the ecosystem for a long time. PCBs are a group of chemicals that were used in industry until the 1970s. These chemicals can still be found in parts of the Great Lakes and some coastal areas. Heavy metals like lead and mercury are also industrial pollutants.

Monoculture has increased the use of pesticides and insecticides. These chemicals can enter the water supply. Pesticides can be very dangerous pollutants. For example, DDT is a cheap, long-lasting type of pesticide that controls agricultural pests and mosquitoes. But when DDT gets into rivers and lakes, it can have serious effects.

These effects are caused by a process called **biological magnification.** Biological magnification begins when a pollutant is picked up by a primary producer, such as plants or algae. If the pollutant is not broken down, it stays in the plant tissues. Then, herbivores eat the plants. If the herbivores do not break down the pollutant, it gets concentrated in their tissues. When carnivores eat the herbivores, the compound is concentrated even more. Pollutant concentration keeps getting higher as the pollutant gets passed along the food chain. In the highest trophic levels, a pollutant may reach 10 million times its original concentration in the water.

High concentrations of pollutants can cause serious problems for wildlife and humans. High DDT concentrations in pelicans, falcons, and eagles caused these birds to lay eggs with thin, fragile shells. These eggs often didn't hatch, so the populations of these birds dropped.

BUILD Connections

BIOLOGICAL MAGNIFICATION

In the process of biological magnification, a pollutant like DDT—represented by the orange dots—becomes more concentrated as it passes up the food chain from producers to consumers.

In Your Workbook Do you understand how the concentration of a pollutant changes in the food web? Go to your workbook to find out.

▶ *Sewage* Have you ever stopped to think what happens after you flush your toilet? After you flush, the wastes become sewage. Sewage carries a lot of nitrogen and phosphorus. Healthy ecosystems can deal with some amount of these nutrients. However, large amounts of sewage can cause many bacteria and algae to grow. These organisms use up the water's oxygen. This depletion of the oxygen causes places called "dead zones." Other organisms are not likely to survive in dead zones. Sewage also carries tiny organisms that can spread disease.

Water Quality and Sustainability One way to make sure we have enough water is to protect ecosystems involved in the water cycle. For example, plants and forests around a water supply help to absorb excess nutrients and filter out pollutants. We must protect the land containing these plants. The land whose groundwater, streams, and rivers drain into the same body of water is called a watershed. In order to clean up a body of water, you must protect the whole watershed.

Cutting pollution rates can improve the water quality in a watershed. Sewage treatment can help prevent dead zones. In place of chemicals, farmers can sometimes use predators and parasites to keep insect populations small. Farmers may also use less-poisonous sprays and crop rotation.

Using less water is also important. One way to use less water in agriculture is to water the crops by drip irrigation. In drip irrigation, water is given directly to the roots of the plants that need it.

🔑 **Key Question** What are the primary sources of water pollution? **The primary sources of water pollution are industrial and agricultural chemicals, residential sewage, and nonpoint sources.**

Drip Irrigation One way to protect water supplies is to use less water. These cabbages are supplied water directly through drip irrigation. Tiny holes in water hoses allow farmers to deliver water only where it is needed.

BUILD Vocabulary

biological magnification the increasing concentration of a harmful substance in organisms at higher trophic levels in a food chain or food web

🗝 RELATED WORD FORMS _____

To magnify means "to increase the apparent or actual size of an object." In this context, the noun *magnification* refers to the increased concentration of a pollutant in organisms that are at higher levels of the food chain.

Atmospheric Resources

The atmosphere has a direct effect on health. The atmosphere gives us the oxygen we need to breathe. The upper atmosphere contains a form of oxygen called ozone. Ozone protects us from the sun's ultraviolet radiation. The atmosphere also contains other gases such as carbon dioxide, methane, and water vapor. These gases are called greenhouse gases. Greenhouse gases help keep the Earth's temperature stable.

The atmosphere cannot be "used up." So, it is not important to call it renewable or nonrenewable. Instead, it is important to understand what human activities do to it.

Air Pollution Many things, including the burning of fossil fuels, can cause air pollution. Some forms of air pollution are smog, acid rain, greenhouse gases, and particulates. When air is not clean, it can be hard to breathe. People who suffer from asthma and allergies will notice this effect the most. Certain types of air pollution can also cause global climate change.

▶ *Smog* If you have been to a large city, then you have probably seen smog. Smog is a gray-brown haze in the air. It is formed by chemical reactions among air pollutants. These reactions form ozone. High in the atmosphere, ozone protects life on Earth. Near ground level, ozone is dangerous, especially to people with difficulty breathing. In the 2008 Summer Olympics, many athletes were concerned about the level of smog in the air.

▶ *Acid Rain* Burning fossil fuels releases chemicals that combine with water vapor in the air to form acids. When the acids fall as rain, it is called acid rain. In some areas, acid rain damages leaves and changes the chemistry of soil and surface water. It can release toxic elements from soil, allowing them to move through the biosphere.

▶ *Greenhouse Gases* When we burn forests and fossil fuels, we release carbon dioxide into the atmosphere. Many kinds of farming release methane into the air. Natural concentrations of these greenhouse gases in the atmosphere control Earth's temperature. But by raising greenhouse gas concentrations, human activity plays a role in causing global warming and climate change.

▶ *Particulates* Particulates are tiny pieces of ash and dust. These are released by some industrial processes and by some diesel engines. Very small particulates can cause serious health problems when they enter the lungs.

Smog The 2008 Summer Olympics were held in Beijing, China. For many weeks before the games, factories were closed and fewer cars were allowed on the streets. Yet Beijing remained under a blanket of dense smog.

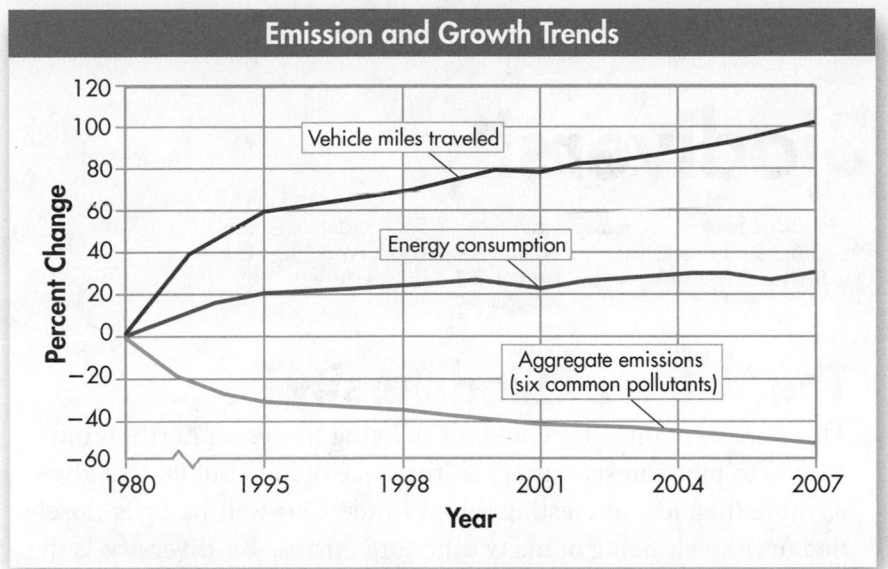

Emission and Growth Trends

Percent Change (y-axis): 120, 100, 80, 60, 40, 20, 0, −20, −40, −60

Vehicle miles traveled

Energy consumption

Aggregate emissions (six common pollutants)

Year (x-axis): 1980, 1995, 1998, 2001, 2004, 2007

Air Pollution Trends This graph summarizes findings of the United States Environmental Protection Agency (EPA). It shows the total percent change from 1980–2007 for energy consumption, vehicle mileage, and the combined concentration of six common pollutants—carbon monoxide, lead, nitrogen oxides, organic compounds, particulates, and sulfur dioxide.

Air Quality and Sustainability It is hard to clean up the air. Air doesn't stay in one place and doesn't "belong" to anyone. But many countries have made rules about car and truck emissions. These efforts are improving the air quality around the world. At one time, all gasoline had the metal lead in it. Car and truck exhaust carried lead into the air. Lead from the air washed onto land and into rivers and streams. The United States banned lead in gasoline in 1996. Now the lead levels in soils, rivers, and streams are much lower than they used to be.

Key Question What are the major forms of air pollution? **Common forms of air pollution include smog, acid rain, greenhouse gases, and particulates.**

CHECK Understanding

Apply Vocabulary
Use the highlighted words from the lesson to complete each sentence correctly.

1. When a forest is cleared so that farmers can plant crops, the process is called _____.

2. Pollutant concentrations may be much higher in consumers than in producers because of _____.

Critical Thinking

3. **Explain** Why is it important to protect soil resources?

4. **Apply Concepts** How can sewage affect a water source?

5. **Interpret Graphs** Look at the "Emission and Growth Trends" graph above. Describe the trends in emissions since 1980. Is this trend expected based on the rest of the data shown in the graph? Explain your answer.

6. **Write to Learn** Answer the second clue of the mystery. Before you answer, reread the introduction to the chapter mystery.

MYSTERY CLUE

Forests of palm trees with strong, tall trunks and edible seeds once covered most of Easter Island. Why would the islanders have cut down these forests? What effect would deforestation have had? (**Hint:** See page 133.)

Biodiversity

MD CLG **3.4.1** Evolutionary Change, **3.5.1** Factors Influencing Ecosystems, **3.5.2** Interdependence of Organisms in the Biosphere, **3.5.3** Population Dynamics, **3.5.4** Global Food Webs, **3.6.1** Analyze Consequences. SPI **1.1.1** Problems and Solutions, **1.7.1** Apply Skills and Concepts, **1.7.2** Evaluate Ideas.

Key Questions

🔑 **Why is biodiversity important?**

🔑 **What are the most significant threats to biodiversity?**

🔑 **How do we preserve biodiversity?**

BUILD Understanding

T-Chart As you read the lesson, make a T-chart. In the left column, write the headings in the lesson. In the right column, write the main ideas from each heading.

In Your Workbook Go to your workbook to learn more about T-charts.

BUILD Vocabulary

biodiversity
the total of the variety of organisms in the biosphere; also called biological diversity

🖋 ACADEMIC WORDS

Variety and *variation* are nouns that refer to the differences among a group of things. Biodiversity is the total of all the different kinds of organisms, ecosystems, and genetic information in the biosphere.

The Value of Biodiversity

There are so many different kinds of living things on Earth. From deserts to pine forests, variety is "the spice of life." But variety gives us more than just interesting things to see. Our well-being is closely tied to the well-being of many other organisms. **Biodiversity** is the total of all the genetically based variation in all organisms in the biosphere. What are the different types of biodiversity? What is the value of biodiversity to society?

Types of Biodiversity There are three levels of biodiversity: ecosystem diversity, species diversity, and genetic diversity. Ecosystem diversity means the many different kinds of ecosystems that exist in the biosphere. Many different habitats, communities, and ecological processes are important to biodiversity. Species diversity is the number of different species in the biosphere or in a particular place. Biologists have studied and named more than 1.8 million species. They think that there are at least 30 million that no one has discovered yet. Single-celled organisms make up most of the diversity. But new species of multicellular organisms, like the snake below, are also being found.

Genetic diversity can mean all the different forms of genetic information carried by one species or by all organisms on Earth. In many ways, genetic diversity is the most basic kind of biodiversity. Genetic diversity is also the hardest kind to see and appreciate. If a population loses genetic diversity, it is less likely to be able to survive changes in its environment.

A New Species This tiny snake is native to the island of Barbados. It is one of many species that has been discovered recently. Photos of the snake were released in 2008.

Valuing Biodiversity Biodiversity is one of Earth's greatest natural resources. Biodiversity is very important in medicine and agriculture. Healthy and diverse ecosystems are important for soil, water, and air quality. Because you can't touch, taste, or smell biodiversity, it is easy to forget its value. But when biodiversity is lost, the biosphere and humanity may face serious consequences.

▶ *Biodiversity and Medicine* Many medicines are based on substances in wild species. Aspirin and penicillin were first made using wild species. The chemicals in wild species are used to treat depression and cancer. These chemicals are put together based on directions found in genes. When we lose biodiversity, we lose genetic information that may have been useful in medicine.

▶ *Biodiversity and Agriculture* Genetic diversity is also important in agriculture. Most crop plants have wild relatives. These wild plants may carry genes for such important features as disease resistance and pest resistance. If we lose the wild plants, we may lose those genes.

▶ *Biodiversity and Healthy Ecosystems* The number and variety of species in an ecosystem can affect the ecosystem's health. The loss of species may make an ecosystem less valuable to people. Sometimes changes in the population of a single species can change the whole ecosystem. Such important species are often called keystone species. Also, healthy and diverse ecosystems are important for soil, water, and air quality.

🔑 **Key Question** Why is biodiversity important? **Biodiversity is important in medicine and agriculture. Also, healthy and diverse ecosystems are important for soil, water, and air quality.**

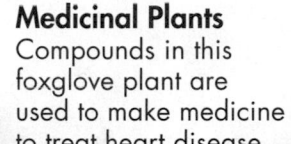

Medicinal Plants Compounds in this foxglove plant are used to make medicine to treat heart disease.

Potato Diversity The genetic diversity of wild potatoes in South America can be seen in the colorful varieties shown here. The International Potato Center in Peru houses a "library" of more than 4500 tuber varieties.

Keystone Species The sea otter is a keystone species. Sea otters eat sea urchins. Sea urchins eat kelp. When the otter population falls, the sea urchin population goes up. When the sea urchin population goes up, the kelp population drops.

Threats to Biodiversity

Species have been changing and dying out since life began. In fact, scientists think that over 99 percent of the species that have ever lived are now extinct. So extinction is not new. But human activity today is causing the greatest wave of extinctions since the dinosaurs died off. Scientists compare this loss of biodiversity to destroying a library before its books are read.

People reduce biodiversity by changing habitats, hunting, and introducing species into new places. Pollution and climate change also lower biodiversity.

Altered Habitats Often, people change a natural habitat into farmland or land for housing. When this happens, the number of species living nearby will go down. Some species may even become extinct. A species can be at risk even if a habitat is not completely destroyed. Development often breaks a habitat into smaller pieces. This process is called **habitat fragmentation.** This fragmentation leaves little habitat "islands." Competition for food, space, and other resources is very high. Some organisms are forced to leave. Others do not survive.

Hunting and the Demand for Wildlife Products People can push species to extinction by hunting them. In the 1800s, hunting wiped out the Carolina parakeet and the passenger pigeon. Endangered species in the United States are now protected from hunting. But hunting still threatens rare animals in Africa, South America, and Southeast Asia. Some animals are hunted for meat. Others are hunted for their hides or skins. Sometimes, animals are hunted to be sold as pets. Habitat fragmentation is very hard on hunted animals. Fragmentation leaves the hunted animals with fewer hiding places.

Habitat Fragmentation Housing developments in Florida have formed the pattern of forest "islands" shown here. Habitat fragmentation limits biodiversity and the potential size of populations.

Introduced Species In Chapter 5, you read about rabbits in Australia and about hydrilla plants in Florida. When a species is put into a new environment, its population can grow very quickly. The new species may out-compete native plants and animals. When this happens, the new species is called invasive.

Pollution Many pollutants can also lower biodiversity. For example, DDT prevents birds from laying healthy eggs. In the United States, many bird populations decreased because of DDT. Acid rain can hurt plants and animals on land and in the water. The increased carbon dioxide in the air is dissolving in oceans. The dissolved carbon dioxide makes the oceans more acidic. This increased acidity threatens the biodiversity on coral reefs and in other ocean ecosystems.

Climate Change A change in climate can be a major threat to biodiversity. Species are adapted to their environment. A species may survive only within a certain temperature range. Species also need a certain amount of rain. If temperatures or rainfall change, organisms may need to move to survive. Species in fragmented habitats are even more affected by climate change. If global temperatures rise as much as many researchers predict, many species will become extinct.

🔑 **Key Question** What are the most significant threats to biodiversity?
Biodiversity is threatened by changing habitats, hunting, and introduced species. Pollution and climate change also threaten biodiversity.

Conserving Biodiversity

What can we do to protect biodiversity? Should we focus on one species? Should we try to save an entire ecosystem? We need to do both. We also need to consider human needs and interests.

Protecting Individual Species The Association of Zoos and Aquariums (AZA) tries to protect organisms, one species at a time. A key part of their plans is a captive breeding program. Members of the AZA choose and manage mating pairs. They are trying to increase genetic diversity. The goal is to return the organisms to the wild. The AZA is currently trying to protect more than 180 species. The giant panda is one of these species.

Preserving Habitats and Ecosystems Scientists are not only trying to save individual species. Now, they have begun to focus on protecting entire ecosystems. This can help many species at once. Governments and conservation groups work to set aside land for parks and reserves. The United States has national parks, forests, and other protected areas.

Saving an Individual Species A number of efforts are being made to save the giant panda. These efforts include captive breeding and reintroduction programs. Here, a specialist from China holds one of twin pandas born at a zoo in Madrid, Spain.

Ecotourism A tourist gets an elephant-size kiss from one of the rescued elephants at Thailand's Elephant Nature Park. This kind of park helps protect biodiversity and brings tourist dollars to the area.

Biologists face the challenge of finding the best areas to protect. They have identified ecological hot spots to make sure conservation efforts happen in places where they are most needed. An ecological hot spot is a place where many species and habitats are in immediate danger of extinction. Biologists hope that identifying these spots will help them focus on the right places.

Considering Local Interests In order to protect biodiversity, people need to change their habits. Sometimes, they even need to change their jobs. In these cases, it is helpful to give money or other rewards in support for the changes. In the United States, the government has given tax breaks to people who buy hybrid cars or who put solar panels on their houses. In Africa, Central America, and Southeast Asia, countries have set aside land for parks and nature reserves.

Industries are also encouraged to change their habits. For example, companies may be rewarded for releasing less carbon into the environment. These examples show that conservation efforts work best when they are based on scientific information and when they benefit the affected community.

Key Question How do we preserve biodiversity?
To preserve biodiversity, we need to protect individual species as well as whole ecosystems. We also need to keep human interests and needs in mind.

CHECK Understanding

Apply Vocabulary
Use the highlighted words from the lesson to complete each sentence correctly.

1. The number of different species in the biosphere or in a particular place is one level of _____.

2. The process of _____ often leaves small "islands" of space for animals and plants to live between more developed land.

Critical Thinking

3. **Apply Concepts** How are people helped by biodiversity?

4. **Relate Cause and Effect** What usually happens to the size and diversity of populations after development causes habitat fragmentation?

5. **Explain** Why is it important to consider local interests when finding ways to protect local ecosystems?

6. **Write to Learn** Answer the third clue in the mystery. In your answer, use the terms *introduced species* and *compete*.

MYSTERY CLUE

Almost all of the coconut shells on Easter Island show signs of having been gnawed on by rats, which are not native to the Island. Coconuts hold the seeds of the coconut palm tree. How do you think the rats affected the coconut palm population? (**Hint:** See p. 141.)

BIOLOGY.com ⟩ Search ⟨ Lesson 6.3 ⟩ **GO** • Lesson Assessment

CLG **3.5.1** Factors Influencing Ecosystems, **3.5.3** Population Dynamics, **3.5.4** Global Food Webs, **3.6.1** Analyze Consequences, **3.6.2** Investigate a Biological Issue. SPI **1.1.1** Problems and Solutions, **1.4.2** Analyze Data, **1.4.6** Determine Trends, **1.5.2** Communicate Information, **1.7.1** Apply Skills and Concepts, **1.7.2** Evaluate Ideas, **1.7.6** Science and Technology.

Ecological Footprints

Every year, the United States Environmental Protection Agency (EPA) gives out up to ten Environmental Youth Awards. These awards are given to students with ideas that protect the environment in ways that meet the needs of local people. One winner encouraged people who fish to stop using lead weights. These weights put lead in the water. The lead can make the plants and animals that live in or drink the water sick. Another group of winners found ways to reduce waste at their school. Their program saved the school more than a million dollars. This kind of leadership will help us find a new direction for the future.

What is our impact on the biosphere? Think about the kind and amount of resources each of us uses. Ecologists use a concept called the ecological footprint. The **ecological footprint** describes the total area of the land and water ecosystems that provide the resources that each person uses. Ecological footprints include resources such as energy, food, water, and shelter. They also include the resources needed to absorb wastes such as sewage and greenhouse gases. An ecological footprint can be used to determine the carrying capacity for humans.

Footprint Limitations Ecologists talk about the ecological footprint of individuals, of countries, and of the world's population. It is difficult, if not impossible, to calculate an exact footprint. The idea is very new. There is not yet a standard way of measuring footprint size. Also, footprints give only a "snapshot" of the resources used at a particular point in time.

Key Questions

🔑 **How does the average ecological footprint in America compare to the world's average?**

🔑 **How can ecology guide us toward a sustainable future?**

BUILD Understanding

Compare/Contrast Table As you read, make a table comparing the challenges associated with the ozone layer, fisheries, and global climate. Note the problem observed, the causes identified, and the solutions implemented.

In Your Workbook Go to your workbook for help completing the compare/contrast table for Lesson 6.4.

BUILD Connections

ECOLOGICAL FOOTPRINTS

The food you eat, the miles you travel, and the electricity you use all contribute to your—and the population's—ecological footprint.

In Your Workbook Do you understand the analogy of the ecological footprint? Go to your workbook for extra practice.

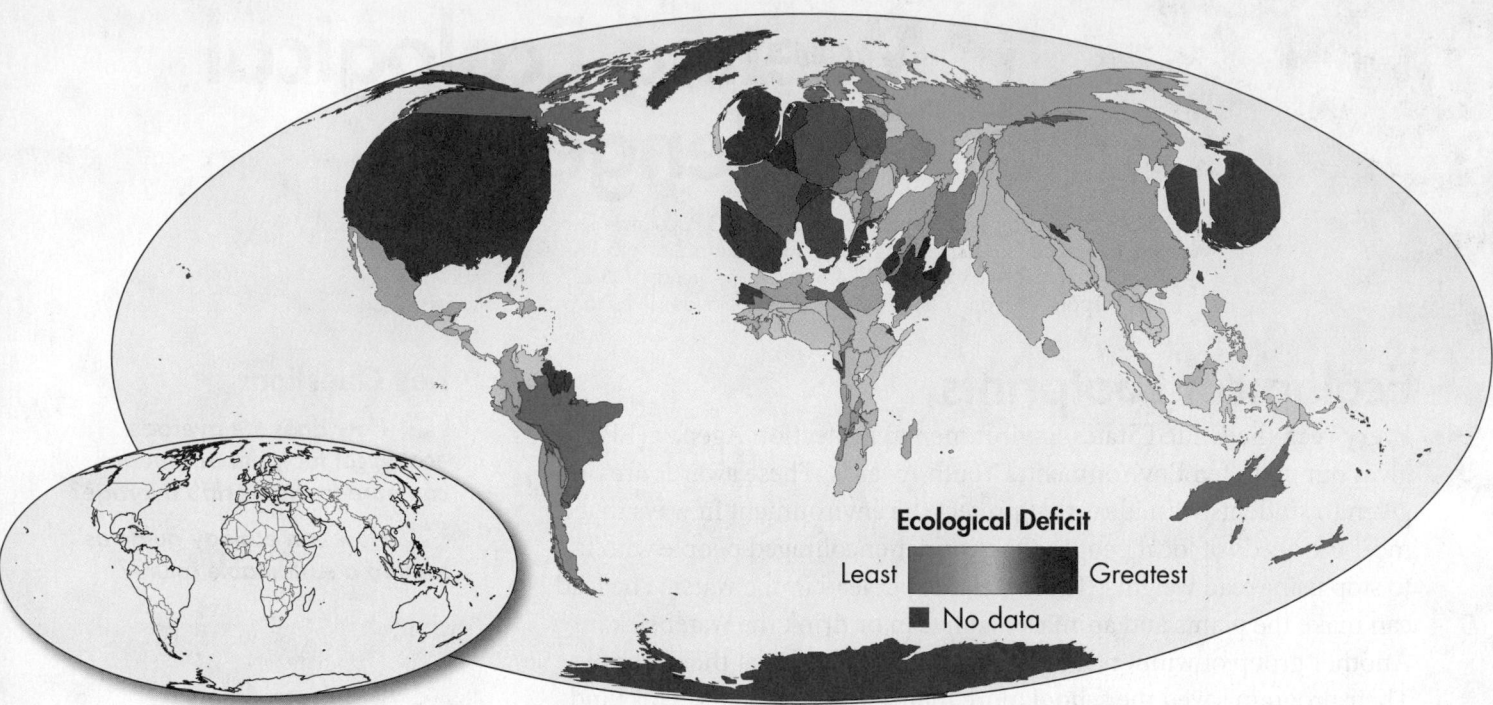

Ecological Deficit

Least   Greatest

■ No data

Relative Footprint This world map shows each country in proportion to its ecological footprint. The average American has an ecological footprint more than four times the world's average. By contrast, the average person in the African nation of Zambia has a footprint a little over one fourth the global average. Compare each country's footprint size on the color map to its actual size on the smaller map.

Comparing Footprints Calculating an exact footprint is almost impossible. However, this idea can be very useful when comparing different populations. For example, each person in the United States uses more than four times as many resources as the worldwide average. On average, each person in the United States uses almost twice as many resources as someone in England. To calculate the ecological footprint of an entire country, researchers first calculate the footprint of an average citizen. Then they multiply that footprint by the population of the country.

🔑 Key Question How does the average ecological footprint in America compare to the world's average?
The average American has an ecological footprint of more than four times the global average.

Ecology in Action

Our ecological footprints are very important to the future of the biosphere. Global population growth and technology are also important. We often hear more stories about ecological challenges than ecological successes. But good ecological research can make a difference. Ecologists follow three basic steps: (1) recognize the problem; (2) find the cause; (3) change behavior. Following these steps can lead us to a sustainable future.

🔑 Key Question How can ecology guide us toward a sustainable future?
By (1) recognizing the problem, (2) determining the cause, and (3) changing our behavior, we can make a difference.

Case Study #1: Atmospheric Ozone

Near the ground, ozone is a pollutant. However, ozone forms an important layer high in the atmosphere. This layer is called the **ozone layer.** The ozone layer absorbs the ultraviolet (UV) rays from the sun. UV can cause sunburn and skin cancer. It also damages eyes and lowers resistance to disease. In extreme cases, UV can damage plants and algae. By absorbing UV light, the ozone layer is like a global suncreen.

The following is an ecological success story. Over four decades, society has recognized a problem, identified its cause, and cooperated internationally to address the global problem.

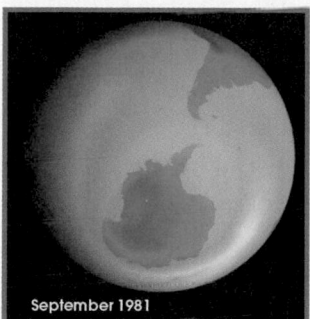 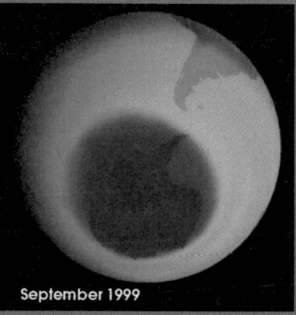

September 1981   September 1999

The Disappearing Ozone

CFC-Containing Refrigerators

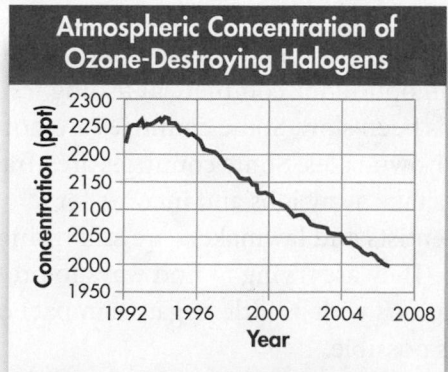

The Decline of CFCs

❶ **Recognizing a Problem: "Hole" in the Ozone Layer** In the 1970s, scientists realized that the ozone concentration over Antarctica was dropping during the winter. The area was called an ozone hole. Of course, there was not a real hole in the atmosphere. There was less ozone. For several years, the ozone hole was getting bigger each year.

❷ **Researching the Cause: CFCs** In 1974, research showed that gases called chlorofluorocarbons (CFCs) could hurt the ozone layer. CFCs had been used in spray cans, refrigerators, and air conditioners. They were also used to make plastic foams.

❸ **Changing Behavior: Regulation of CFCs** Once the research was accepted by scientists, the rest was up to governments. There was a big response. Following the recommendations of ozone researchers, 191 countries agreed to ban most uses of CFCs. CFCs can stay in the atmosphere for a hundred years. So, the effects of CFCs on the ozone layer are still visible. But current data suggest that the ozone hole will "close" in the next fifty years.

Case Study #2: North Atlantic Fisheries

In 1950, fishermen around the world caught about 19 million tons of seafood. In 1997, fishermen caught more than 90 million tons. People thought that the fish supply was an endless, renewable resource. However, commercial fish populations are now dropping dramatically. This problem is one that society is still working on.

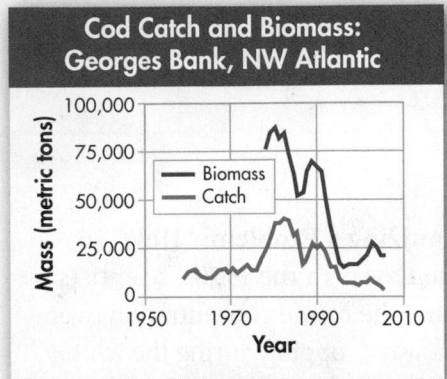

Cod Catch and Biomass: Georges Bank, NW Atlantic

The Decline of Cod As the mass of the cod populations dropped, the catch also decreased.

Overfishing

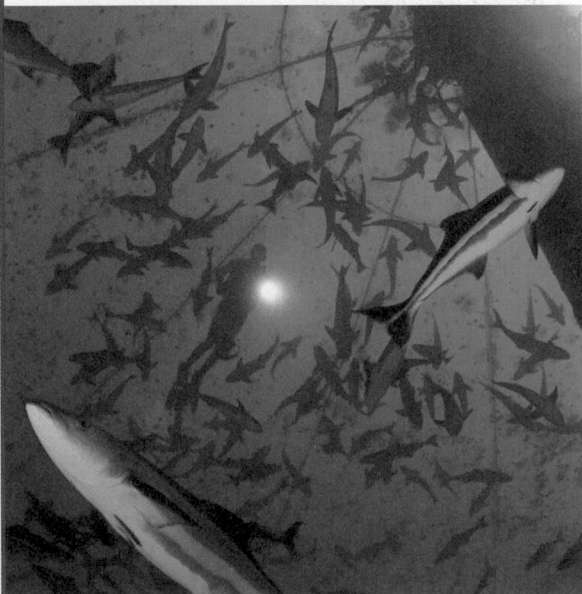

Aquaculture

❶ **Recognizing a Problem: More Work, Fewer Fish** The amount of cod caught rises and falls each year. Sometimes, these differences are because of natural differences in ocean ecosystems. Often, however, low fish catches happen when boats start taking too many fish. From the 1950s to the 1970s, fishermen began using larger boats and more high-tech equipment to find fish. At first, the fishermen caught more fish. Then the catches began falling again. The mass of cod in the ocean has decreased significantly since the 1980s. Fishermen cannot catch what isn't there.

❷ **Researching the Cause: Overfishing** Ecologists gathered data including age structure and growth rates. Fish populations were getting smaller. By the 1990s, the cod populations had dropped so low that researchers were afraid the fish might disappear forever. It became clear that more fish were being caught than were being born.

❸ **Changing Behavior: Regulation of Fisheries** The United States has set up rules for commercial fishing. These rules state how many fish of what size can be caught. Certain places have been closed to fishing until populations rise again. Other places are closed during breeding seasons. These rules are helping some populations but not all. Aquaculture, the farming of aquatic animals, can also help. It offers an option for commercial fishing.

Progress has been slow. Some countries are not setting up their own rules. Some countries are afraid that these rules take away jobs and income for fishermen. Scientists and lawmakers are still trying to find a solution. They are trying to find ways to protect the fish populations with as little negative impact on the industry as possible.

Case Study #3: Climate Change

Global climate is affected by the cycles of matter and everything that humans do. This includes cutting and burning forests, manufacturing, driving cars, and making electricity. The Intergovernmental Panel On Climate Change (IPCC) began in 1988. Its goal is to provide the best scientific information on climate change. The 2007 report from the IPCC gives the most reliable current information on climate change.

❶ Recognizing the Problem: Global Warming The IPCC report states that global temperatures are rising. This rise in average temperature is called global warming. The report also covers climate change. Temperature, rain, and other factors can change because of global warming. Scientists studied physical and biological evidence of climate change.

● **Physical Evidence** Earth's temperatures are getting warmer, sea ice is melting, and sea levels arc rising. Eleven of the twelve years between 1995 and 2006 were among the warmest years ever recorded. People began recording temperatures in 1850. Earth's average global temperature rose by 0.74°C between 1906 and 2005. The largest changes are taking place in and near the Arctic Circle. Alaska's average temperature rose 2.4°C in fifty years. Sea level has risen 1.8 mm each year since 1961. This rise is being caused by warmer water expanding and by melting glaciers, ice caps and polar sheets.

A Warming Earth

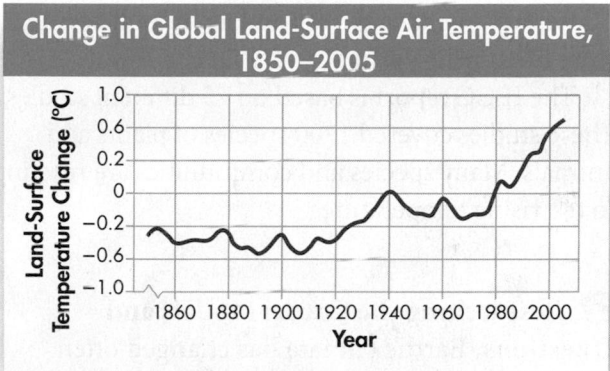

Change in Global Land-Surface Air Temperature, 1850–2005

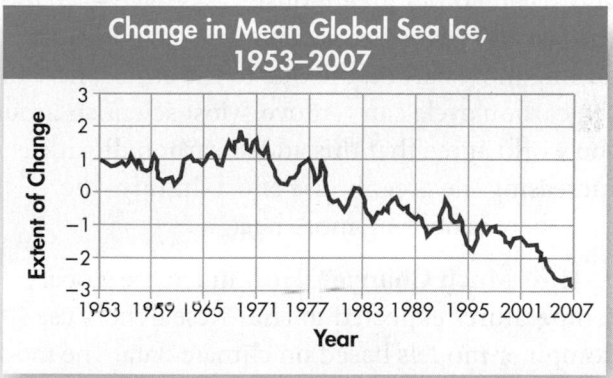

Change in Mean Global Sea Ice, 1953–2007

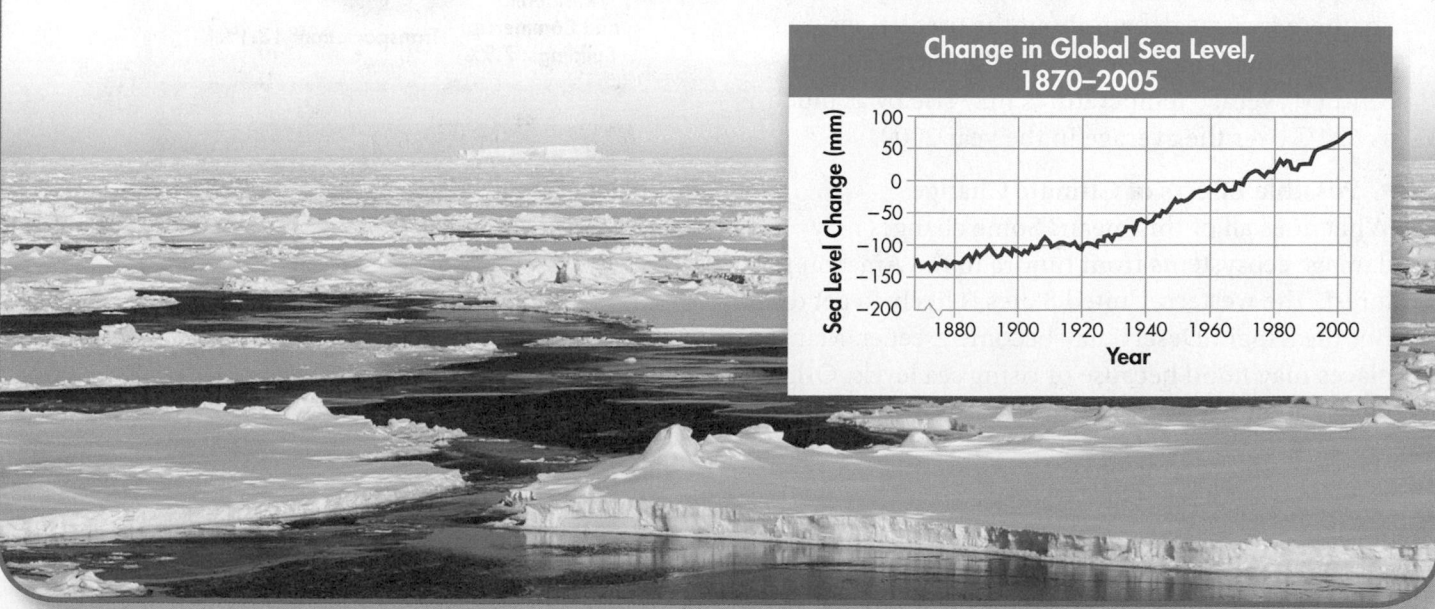

Change in Global Sea Level, 1870–2005

- **Biological Evidence** Small changes in climate that people barely notice can be important to other organisms. Temperature, humidity, and rain affect where an organism can live. If temperatures rise, organisms need to move to cooler places. They may move away from the equator or higher up a mountainside. Plant flowering and animal breeding are also affected by rising temperatures. These organisms may respond as though spring were beginning earlier.

The IPCC report is based on 75 different studies. These studies covered 1700 species of plants and animals. Many species and communities are reacting to the rising temperatures.

Biological Evidence
This yellow-bellied marmot is coming out of hibernation over a month earlier than it used to.

❷ **Researching the Cause: Models and Questions** Earth's climate has changed often during its history. Concentrations of carbon dioxide and several other greenhouse gases have risen over the last 200 years. People and their activities are adding more carbon dioxide to the atmosphere than the carbon cycle can remove. Most scientists around the world agree that this added carbon dioxide is increasing the greenhouse effect. In turn, the biosphere is holding more heat.

- **How Much Change?** How much are global temperatures expected to rise? Researchers use computer models based on climate data. The models are complex, and they make many assumptions. So, there is some debate about the predictions. Several models suggest that, by the end of this century, average temperatures may rise by as much as 6.4°C over the average in the year 2000.

- **Possible Effects of Climate Change** What does all of this mean? Some changes may damage ecosystems from tundra to the Amazon rain forest. The western United States is likely to get drier. But the Sahara Desert may become greener. Many places may flood because of rising sea levels. Other places in North America may face more droughts.

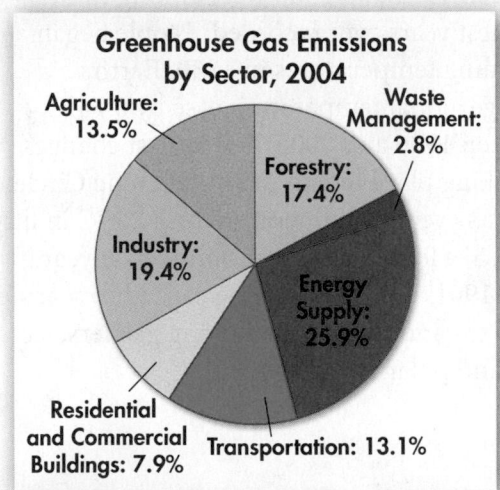

Greenhouse Gas Emissions by Sector, 2004

Agriculture: 13.5%
Waste Management: 2.8%
Forestry: 17.4%
Industry: 19.4%
Energy Supply: 25.9%
Residential and Commercial Buildings: 7.9%
Transportation: 13.1%

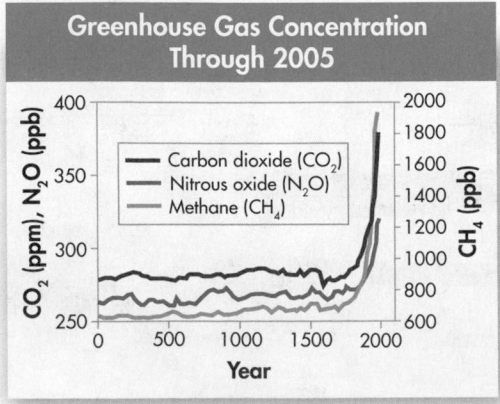

Greenhouse Gas Concentration Through 2005

Carbon dioxide (CO_2)
Nitrous oxide (N_2O)
Methane (CH_4)

3 **Changing Behavior: The Challenges Ahead** You have read how research has led to changes that are protecting the ozone layer and helping to bring back fish populations. Global climate change presents many challenges. The changes in behavior will need to be major. The changes will affect economies and many other fields besides biology. Some changes will depend on new technology for renewable energy and more efficient energy use.

Nations around the world have begun to work out agreements to protect the atmosphere and the climate. As the world and our nation work through these challenges, remember that the world is our island of life. Hopefully, there will come a day when we reach the common goal of preserving the quality of life on Earth.

Little Changes, Big Results We have begun to see electric cars, recycled products, and green buildings in response to the need for more efficient energy use.

✓CHECK Understanding

Apply Vocabulary
Use the highlighted words from the lesson to complete each sentence correctly.

1. All of the energy you use, food you eat, and garbage you throw out contribute to your _____.

2. Beginning in the 1970s, scientists began to realize that the _____ over Antarctica was getting thinner.

Critical Thinking

3. Apply Concepts How is the concept of the ecological footprint limited? When is the concept most useful?

4. Sequence Describe the three steps ecologists can use to lead us toward a sustainable future.

5. Write to Learn Look back at the A Warming Earth graphs on page 147. Describe what these graphs tell us about global climate change.

BIOLOGY.com Search (Lesson 6.4) **GO** • Lesson Assessment

Design Your Own Lab

OPEN-ENDED INQUIRY

MD CLG **3.1.2** Homeostasis, **3.1.3** Matter and Energy. SPI **1.2.2** Posing Scientific Questions, **1.2.5** Select Materials, **1.2.6** Investigative Methods, **1.3.1** Use Equipment, *(continued below)*

Pre-Lab: Acid Rain and Seeds

Problem How does acid rain affect seed germination?

Materials large test tubes, test-tube rack, glass-marking pencil, 25-mL graduated cylinder, solutions of vinegar and water, pH paper, dried beans, paper towels, zip-close plastic bags, stick-on labels, hand lens, graph paper

Lab Manual Chapter 6 Lab

Skills Focus Design an Experiment, Organize Data, Measure, Graph

Connect to the Big idea Every organism alters its environment in some way. Elephants uproot trees, prairie dogs dig tunnels, and corals build reefs. But no other organism has as much impact on the global environment as humans. One of the ways that humans affect global ecology is by burning fossil fuels. The burning produces carbon dioxide, which can accumulate in the atmosphere and cause climate change. Other products react with water to form nitric and sulfuric acids. Rain that contains these acids can damage many things, including stone statues and growing plants. In this lab, you will investigate the effect of acid rain on seeds.

Background Questions

a. Review What does a pH scale measure?

b. Review Which solution is more acidic, one with a pH of 4.0 or one with a pH of 5.0, and why?

c. Explain Use the water cycle to trace the path from acids in water vapor to plants.

Pre-Lab Questions

Preview the procedure in the lab manual.

1. Compare and Contrast How are the solutions you will use in this experiment similar? How are they different?

2. Using Models What do the solutions represent?

3. Infer How will you know that a seed has germinated?

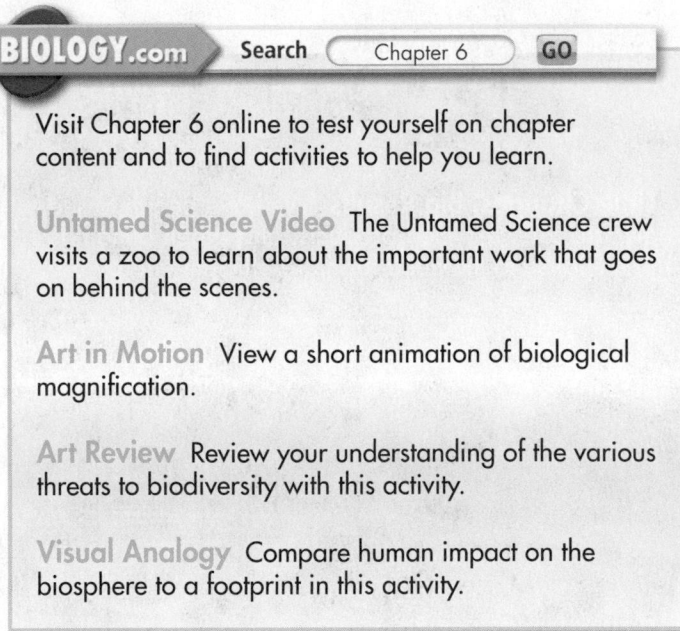

BIOLOGY.com   Search   Chapter 6   GO

Visit Chapter 6 online to test yourself on chapter content and to find activities to help you learn.

Untamed Science Video The Untamed Science crew visits a zoo to learn about the important work that goes on behind the scenes.

Art in Motion View a short animation of biological magnification.

Art Review Review your understanding of the various threats to biodiversity with this activity.

Visual Analogy Compare human impact on the biosphere to a footprint in this activity.

 MD **1.3.3** Safe Handling of Materials, **1.4.1** Organize Data, **1.4.9** Confirm Hypotheses, **1.7.1** Apply Skills and Concepts.

6 CHAPTER Summary

6.1 A Changing Landscape

- People affect the environment through agriculture, development, and industrial growth.

- Sustainable development uses natural resources to meet human needs without causing long-term damage to the environment.

monoculture (p. 129)
renewable resource (p. 131)
nonrenewable resource (p. 131)

6.2 Using Resources Wisely

- Soil allows plants, including crops, to grow. Farming practices such as crop rotation and leaving stems and roots in the soil between plantings can help protect soil from erosion and a loss of nutrients. Cutting only some mature trees and using tree farms can also protect soil.

- The primary sources of water pollution are industrial and agricultural chemicals, residential sewage, and nonpoint sources.

- Common forms of air pollution include smog, acid rain, greenhouse gases, and particulates.

desertification (p. 132)
deforestation (p. 133)
biological magnification (p. 134)

6.3 Biodiversity

- Biodiversity is important in medicine and agriculture. Also, healthy and diverse ecosystems are important for soil, water, and air quality.

- Biodiversity is threatened by changing habitats, hunting, and introduced species. Pollution and climate change also threaten biodiversity.

- To preserve biodiversity, we need to protect whole ecosystems as well as individual species. We also need to figure out how to preserve the environment while helping people improve their standard of living.

biodiversity (p. 138)
habitat fragmentation (p. 140)

6.4 Meeting Ecological Challenges

- The average American has an ecological footprint of more than four times the global average.

- By (1) recognizing a problem in the environment, (2) determining the cause, and (3) changing our behavior, we can move toward a sustainable future.

ecological footprint (p. 143)
ozone layer (p. 145)

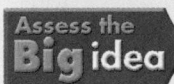 Big idea
Interdependence in Nature

Write an answer to the question below.

Q: How have human activities shaped local and global ecology?

Constructed Response

Write an answer to each of the questions below. The answer to each question should be one or two paragraphs long. To help you begin, read the **Hints** below each of the questions.

1. **Why does the concentration of pollutants, such as DDT, increase in higher levels of a food chain?**

   Hint When DDT is consumed by an organism, the body does not break it down.

   Hint Primary producers can pick up a pollutant directly from the environment.

2. **Describe the relationship between agriculture and soil quality.**

   Hint Soil erosion happens when wind or water takes soil away.

   Hint Topsoil is the mineral- and nutrient-rich portion of soil.

   Hint Topsoil can be a renewable resource, but it can be lost or damaged quickly.

Foundations for Learning Wrap-Up

Use the mini book you created before reading the chapter as a tool to help you organize your thoughts about humans in the biosphere.

Activity 1 Working with a partner, review your answers to the key questions. Did you both answer the questions correctly and completely? If not, work together to make any corrections.

Activity 2 Working in a small group, use your mini books to prepare a lecture on how human activities have shaped ecosystems. In your lecture, mention how your own activities shape local and global ecology. Present one idea about what you could do as a school to reduce your ecological footprint.

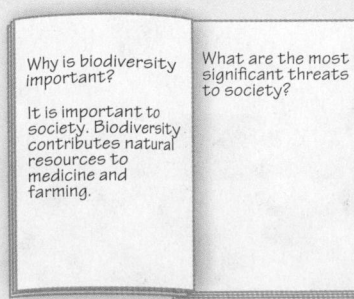

Why is biodiversity important?

It is important to society. Biodiversity contributes natural resources to medicine and farming.

What are the most significant threats to society?

6.1 A Changing Landscape

Understand Key Concepts

1. A resource that can be replenished or replaced is called
   a. common.
   c. nonrenewable.
   b. renewable.
   d. recycled.

2. The concept of using natural resources to meet the needs of humans without causing long-term environmental damage is called
   a. monoculture.
   b. sustainable development.
   c. recycling.
   d. resource renewal.

Test-Taking Tip

Read All of the Answer Choices Take the time to read all of the answer choices carefully. Question 2 asks for the word or phrase that is defined in the question. Decide whether you know the definitions of the answer choices. Once you define all of the answer choices, you'll find that **b** is the correct answer. Sustainable development is the use of natural resources in an environmentally conscious way.

3. Describe how Hawaiian settlers negatively affected the islands after the 1700s.

4. Explain how Earth is like an island.

Think Critically

5. **Compare and Contrast** How are renewable resources and nonrenewable resources alike? How are they different?

6.2 Using Resources Wisely

6. The loss of topsoil through the action of water or wind is called
   a. acid rain.
   c. desertification.
   b. erosion.
   d. monoculture.

7. Look closely at the image of the food web shown below. In which organism would the concentration of a pesticide probably be highest?
   a. hawk
   c. frog
   b. rabbit
   d. grasses

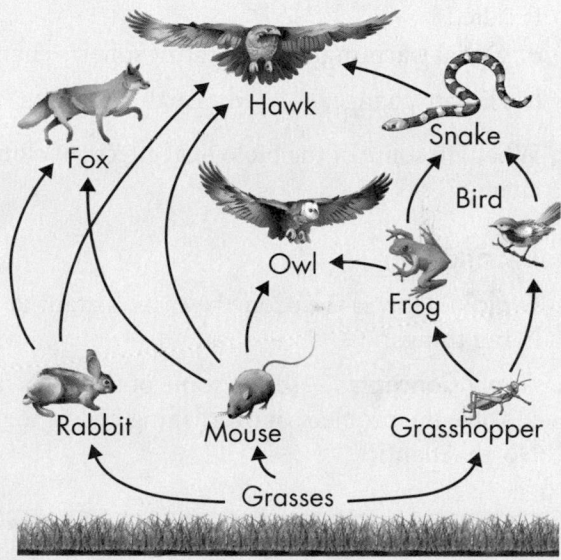

8. How can forests be managed in a sustainable way?

9. What are some of the common sources of water pollution?

Think Critically

10. **Relate Cause and Effect** How does the use of fossil fuels negatively impact Earth's atmosphere?

6.3 Biodiversity

11. Which of the following is NOT a term for one of the three levels of biodiversity?
    a. species diversity
    c. genetic diversity
    b. population diversity
    d. ecosystem diversity

12. A place where many species and habitats are in immediate danger of extinction is called a(n)
    a. altered habitat.
    c. ecological hot spot.
    b. habitat fragment.
    d. dead zone.

13. What are the major threats to biodiversity?

Think Critically

14. **Compare and Contrast** Explain the difference between species diversity and ecosystem diversity.

6.4 Meeting Ecological Challenges

Understand Key Concepts

15. The increase in the average temperature on Earth is called

   a. global warming.   **c.** atmospheric change.

   b. climate change.   **d.** Earth warming.

16. What are some of the biological effects of climate change?

Think Critically

17. Explain How is the ozone layer important to living things?

18. Apply Concepts Describe some of the steps taken to solve the problem of overfishing cod in the North Atlantic.

Connecting Concepts

Use Science Graphics

The graph shows the amount of bluefin tuna caught by the United States in the Atlantic Ocean between 2002 and 2006. Use the graphics to answer questions 19 and 20.

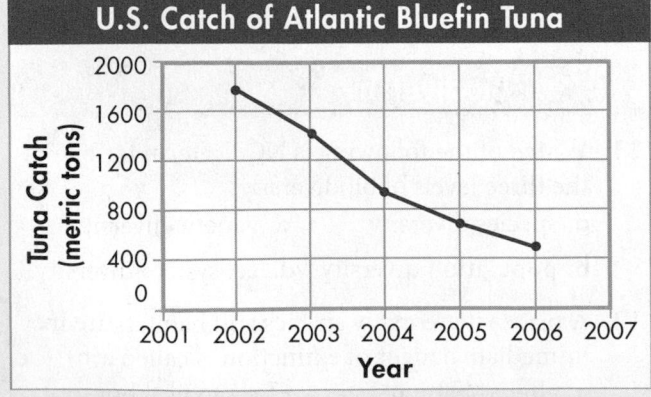

U.S. Catch of Atlantic Bluefin Tuna

(y-axis: Tuna Catch (metric tons); x-axis: Year)

19. Predict What trend would you expect to see in the annual catch from 2006 to 2007?

20. Propose a Solution What recommendations would you make to help the bluefin tuna population recover in the next decade or two?

---

solve the CHAPTER MYSTERY

MOVING THE *MOAI*

Easter Island did not have as much biodiversity as the Hawaiian Islands. This made it less resistant to ecological damage. The Rapa Nui cut palm trees for agriculture and for wood to make fishing canoes. They also used large logs from palm trees to move *moai*. They cleared fields and did not protect the soil from erosion. Healthy topsoil washed away.

The Rapa Nui brought rats to the island. Rat populations grew exponentially. Hordes of hungry rats killed young palm trees. They ate coconuts and their seeds.

The combination of human activities and introduced species destroyed almost all of Easter Island's forests. Because of deforestation and the difficult climate, the island has been able to house very few people ever since.

1. Relate Cause and Effect Easter Island is about half the size of Long Island, New York. How did its small size affect the outcome of deforestation and the introduction of rats?

2. Compare and Contrast Gather information about the geography, climate, and biological diversity on the Hawaiian Islands and on Easter Island. How do you think the differences made the islands respond differently to human settlement?

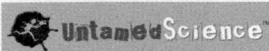 **Never Stop Exploring Your World.** The mystery of Easter Island is just the beginning. Take a video field trip with the ecogeeks of Untamed Science to see where this mystery leads.

Multiple Choice

1. Which of the following statements about renewable resources is TRUE?
   A They are found only in tropical climates.
   B They can never be depleted.
   C They are replaceable by natural means.
   D They never regenerate.   CLG 3.5.3

2. Which of the following is a nonrenewable resource?
   A wind   C coal
   B fresh water   D topsoil   CLG 3.5.3

3. Which of the following is NOT a direct effect of deforestation?
   A decreased productivity of the ecosystem
   B soil erosion
   C biological magnification
   D habitat destruction   CLG 3.5.3

4. The total variation in all organisms in the biosphere is called
   A biodiversity.
   B species diversity.
   C ecosystem diversity.
   D genetic diversity.   CLG 3.5.2

5. Ozone is made up of
   A hydrogen.   C nitrogen.
   B oxygen.   D chlorine.   CLG 3.5.3

6. Ozone depletion in the atmosphere has been caused by
   A monoculture.
   B CFCs.
   C suburban sprawl.
   D soil erosion.   CLG 3.5.3

7. In a food chain, concentrations of harmful substances may increase in higher levels in the food chain in a process known as
   A biological magnification.
   B genetic drift.
   C biological succession.
   D pesticide resistance.   CLG 3.5.4

Questions 8–9

Fire ants first arrived in the United States in 1918, probably on a ship traveling from South America to Alabama. The maps below show the geographic location of the U.S. fire ant population in 1953 and 2001.

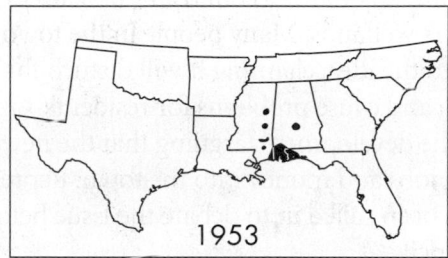
1953

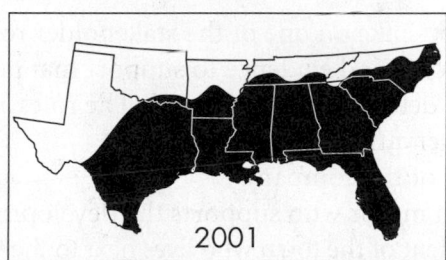
2001

8. Which of the following statements about fire ants in the United States is TRUE?
   A They reproduce slowly.
   B They are a native species of the United States.
   C They are an introduced species.
   D They do not compete with other ant species.   SPI 1.5.5

9. By 2010, fire ants are MOST likely to
   A have spread to a larger area.
   B have reached their carrying capacity.
   C die out.
   D return to South America.   SPI 1.4.2

Open-Ended Response

10. Describe how ecologists use the ecological footprint concept.   CLG 3.5.4

If You Have Trouble With . . .

Question	1	2	3	4	5	6	7	8	9	10
See Lesson	6.1	6.2	6.2	6.3	6.2	6.4	6.2	6.3	6.3	6.4

Unit Project

Development Debate

A large company wants to build a new factory on your town's wetlands. Many people in the town are opposed to the idea, claiming it will disturb the local ecosystem and cause problems for residents. Others support the development, arguing that the new factory will bring jobs and money into the town. Representatives have been called in to debate the issue before the town council.

Your Task Take on one of the stakeholder roles listed below. Find evidence to support that point of view and debate the issue in class. The roles are

- Conservation ecologist
- CEO of the company
- Town mayor who supports the development
- Resident of the town who lives next to the wetlands

Be sure to
- justify your arguments with credible information.
- present your arguments in a clear and convincing manner.

Reflection Questions

1. **Score your performance using the rubric below. What score did you give yourself?**
2. **What did you do well in this project?**
3. **What about your performance needs improvement?**
4. **After hearing various sides of the argument, meet with a partner and discuss which side you agree with the most. Justify your opinion.**

Assessment Rubric

Score	Evidence Provided	Quality of Performance
4	Student justifies his/her argument with sophisticated and highly credible information.	Ideas are presented in a highly convincing and clear manner. Student shows a deep understanding of the issues involved.
3	Student justifies his/her argument with logical and credible information.	Ideas are presented in an effective and clear manner. Student shows a solid understanding of the issues involved.
2	Student provides some credible information, but other points are weak or inaccurate.	Some ideas are presented in an unclear manner. Student shows a limited understanding of the issues involved.
1	Student provides mostly illogical and invalid evidence to support his/her argument.	Most ideas are presented in an unclear manner. Student shows a very limited understanding of the issues involved.

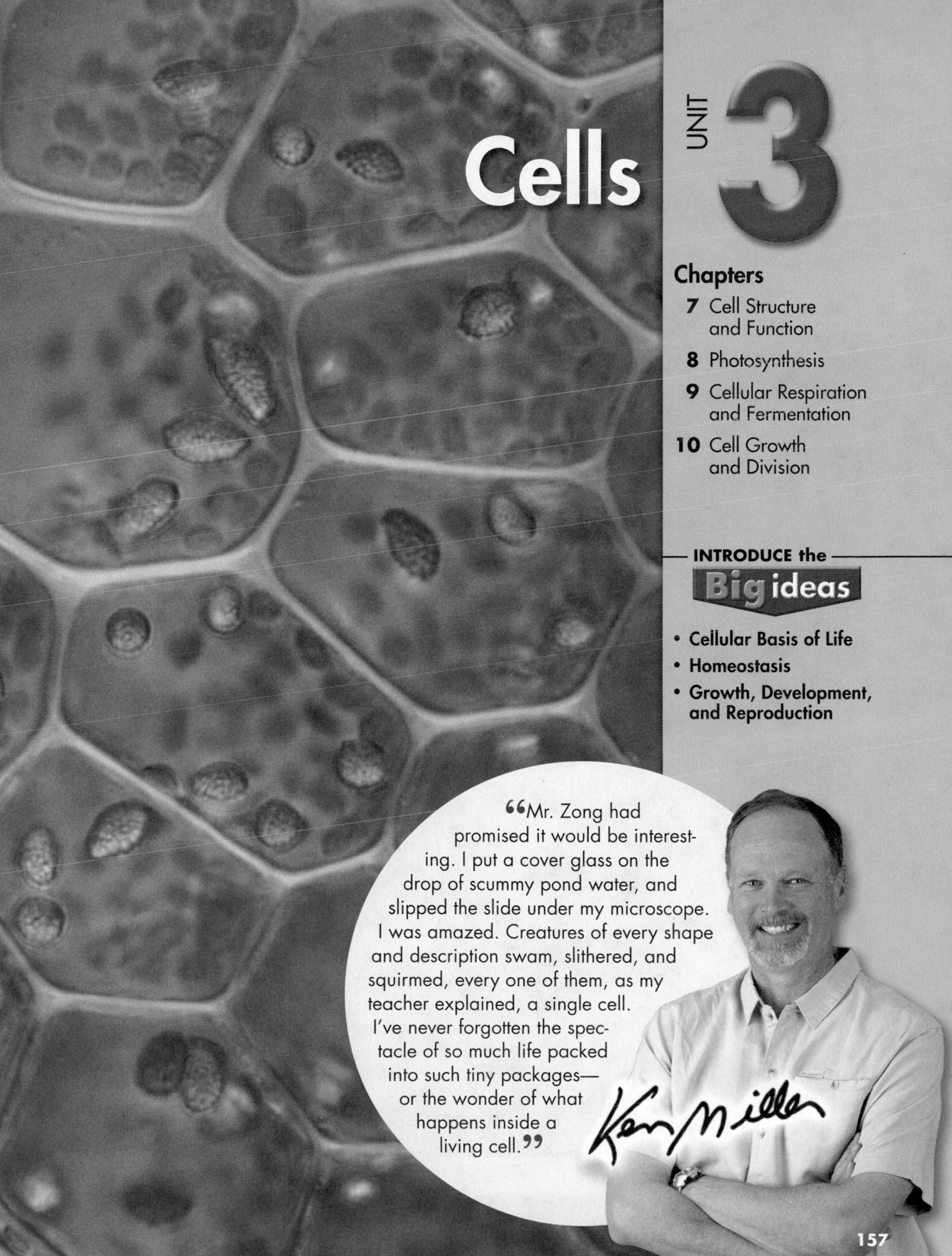

Cells

INTRODUCE the Big ideas

- **Cellular Basis of Life**
- **Homeostasis**
- **Growth, Development, and Reproduction**

"Mr. Zong had promised it would be interesting. I put a cover glass on the drop of scummy pond water, and slipped the slide under my microscope. I was amazed. Creatures of every shape and description swam, slithered, and squirmed, every one of them, as my teacher explained, a single cell. I've never forgotten the spectacle of so much life packed into such tiny packages— or the wonder of what happens inside a living cell."

Ken Miller

157

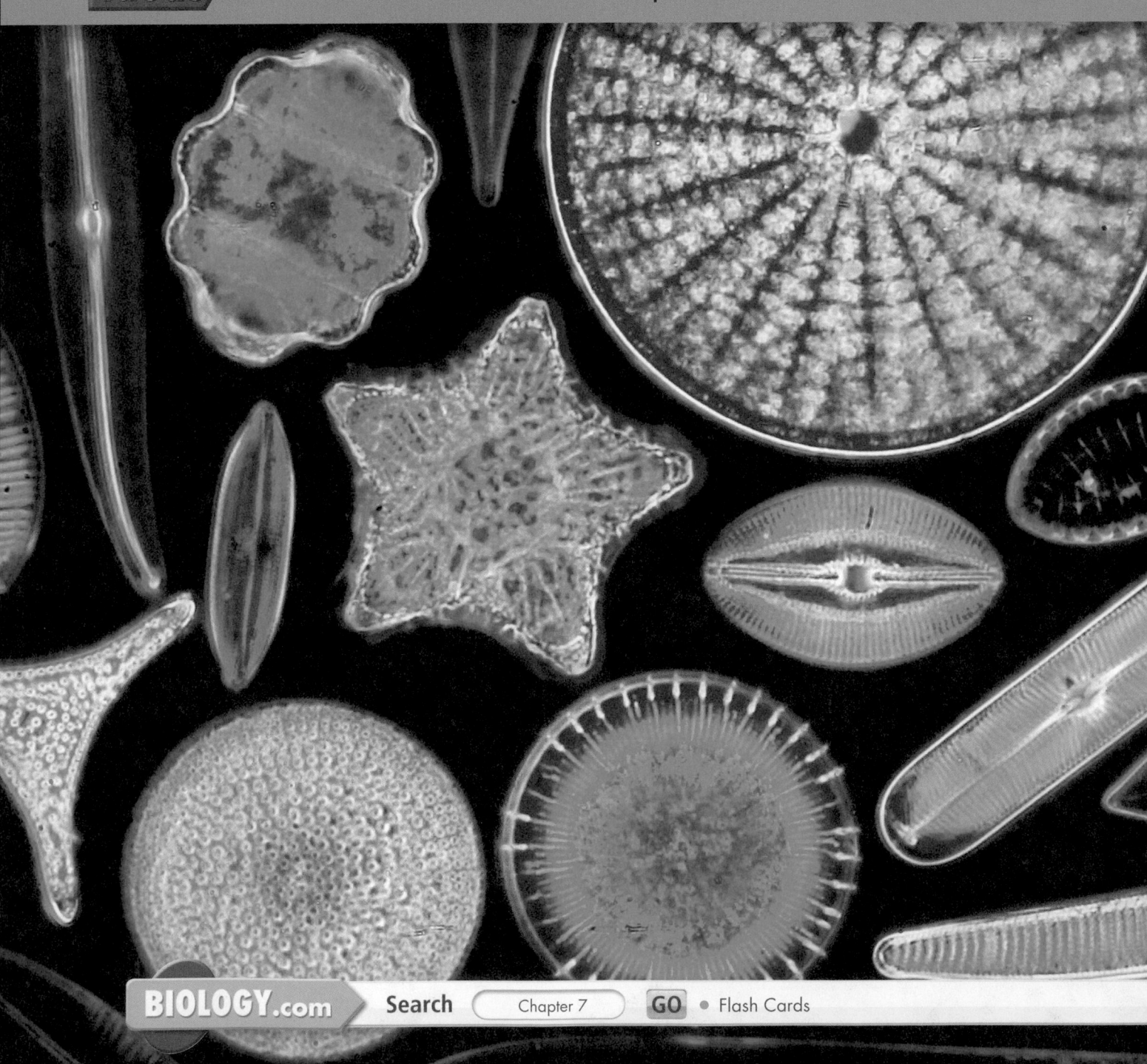

BIOLOGY.com > Search (Chapter 7) GO • Flash Cards

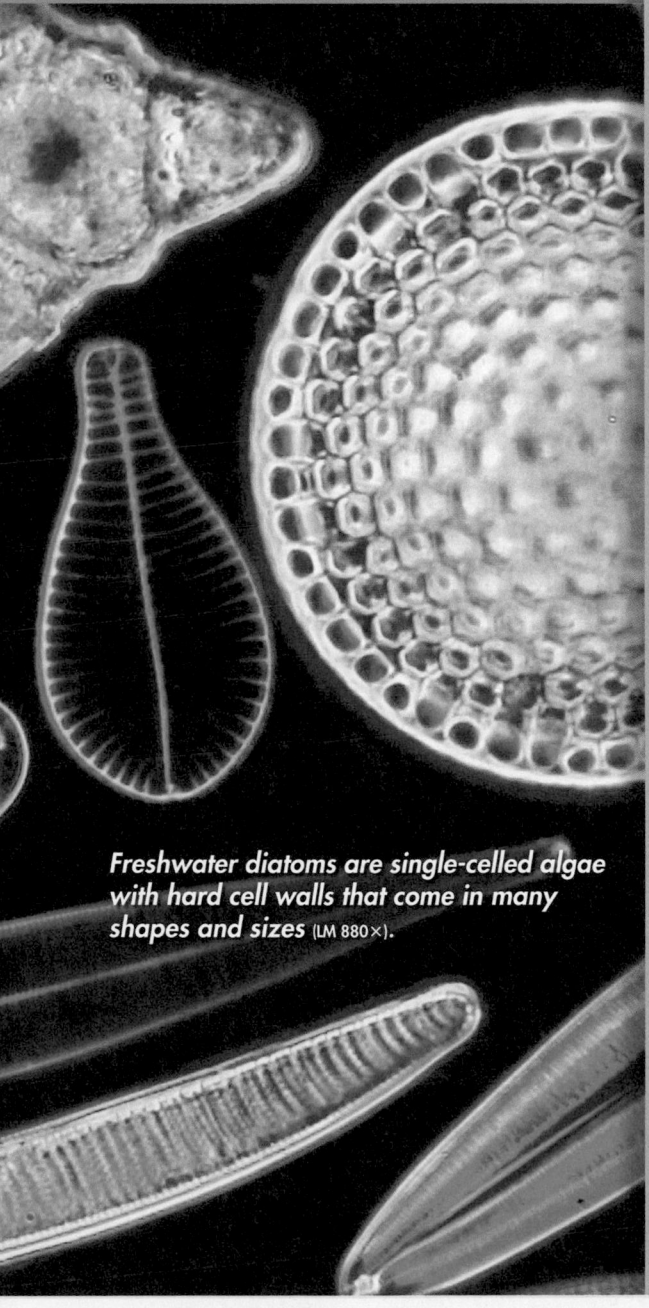

*Freshwater diatoms are single-celled algae
with hard cell walls that come in many
shapes and sizes* (LM 880×).

CHAPTER
MYSTERY

DEATH BY . . . WATER?

Michelle was healthy and 25 years old when
she ran in her first marathon. The hot and
humid weather made everyone sweat a lot,
so Michelle drank water whenever she could.
Slowly, she began to feel weak and confused.
At the end of the run, Michelle staggered
into a medical tent. Her head hurt and she
felt nauseous. After telling a volunteer how she felt, she
collapsed onto the floor. Thinking she was dehydrated,
the volunteer gave Michelle even more water. But,
Michelle felt worse and worse. They rushed her to the
hospital, where she had a seizure and fell into a coma.
Why did giving Michelle water make her condition
worse?

Read for Mystery Clues As you read this chapter, look
for clues to help you predict how water made Michelle
sick. Then, solve the mystery at the end of the chapter.

FOUNDATIONS
for Learning

Just as you have special body structures that let you do different
things, cells have special parts that help keep them alive. Before
you read the chapter, get 15 index cards and punch holes in
them as shown below. As you read each lesson, write on the
cards the name of each cell part. Draw a picture of the cell part
and briefly describe what it does. At the end of the chapter are
two activities that use the cards. They will help you answer the
question: How are cell structures adapted to their functions?

Nucleus

• Untamed Science Video • Chapter Mystery

7.1 Life Is Cellular

MD CLG **3.2.1** Processes and Functions, **3.4.2** Relatedness Among Organisms.
SPI **1.3.1** Use Equipment, **1.5.7** Classification Systems, **1.5.8** Compare, **1.7.6** Science and Technology.

Key Questions

🔑 *What is the cell theory?*

🔑 *How do microscopes work?*

🔑 *How are prokaryotic and eukaryotic cells different?*

BUILD Understanding

Concept Map Make a concept map to organize information about cells. As you read, fill in the circles to show the most important parts of the concept and how they are connected.

In Your Workbook Go to your workbook to learn more about how to use a concept map. Complete the concept map activity for Lesson 7.1.

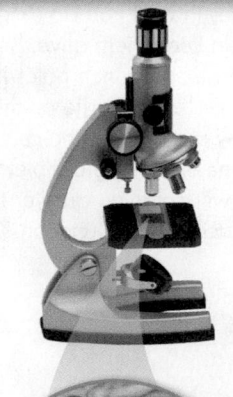

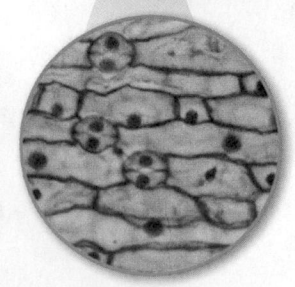

Cell Stains This onion leaf skin has been stained to show the shapes of the cells and some of their parts.

LM 35×

The Discovery of the Cell

There is an old saying that goes "Seeing is believing." A great example of this concept is the discovery of the cell. You cannot see cells with your eyes alone. Without tools to make cells visible, for centuries, scientists did not even know that there were cells. The microscope changed all of this.

Early Microscopes In the late 1500s, eyeglass makers in Europe found that they could use several glass lenses together to make very small things easy to see. Before long, they had built the first true microscopes from these lenses.

In 1665, Robert Hooke used a microscope to look at thin slices of cork from plants. The cork seemed to be made of many tiny, empty boxes. Hooke called these boxes "cells." Today we know that **cells,** which are the basic units of life, are not empty boxes. In fact, they are full of working parts, each with its own job. Cells are the smallest living unit of any organism. Around the same time that Hooke looked at cork, Anton van Leeuwenhoek looked at water. To his amazement, the microscope allowed him to see a world of tiny living things that seemed to be everywhere. He even found living bacterial cells in his own mouth.

The Cell Theory Scientists made many discoveries about cells in the next 200 years. These discoveries are summarized in the **cell theory,** a fundamental concept of biology. The cell theory states:

- All living things are made up of cells.
- Cells are the basic units of structure and function in living things.
- New cells come from existing cells.

🔑 **Key Question** What is the cell theory?
The cell theory states that all living things are made up of cells, that cells are the basic units of structure and function in living things, and that new cells come from existing cells.

Exploring the Cell

A microscope gives you a larger view of something very small, such as a cell. Light microscopes use glass lenses to focus light and magnify the object. Electron microscopes produce even higher magnifications by using electrons instead of light.

Light Microscopes and Cell Stains The type of microscope that you are probably most familiar with is a compound light microscope. A light microscope lets light pass through an object. Its two lenses focus the light to form an image. Some of the light scatters as it passes through the lenses. Because of this scattering of light, light microscopes can make clear images of objects only to a magnification of about 1000 times. Most living cells are nearly clear like glass. This makes it very hard to see what is inside them. So scientists use stains or dyes to show the different structures inside cells.

Electron Microscopes To study very small things, such as a DNA molecule, scientists use electron microscopes. Instead of focusing light, electron microscopes focus beams of electrons using magnetic fields. Electron microscopes can show things that are 1 billionth of a meter in size.

There are two major types of electron microscopes: transmission and scanning. Transmission electron microscopes send beams of electrons through thin slices of cells and tissues. In scanning electron microscopes, a beam of electrons is scanned over the surface of an object to give a three-dimensional image of the object's surface. Electron microscopes can be used only to look at cells and tissues that are no longer living. They make pictures that are black and white. Scientists often use computers to add "false colors" that make some structures stand out. False colors can be added to images from electron microscopes and light microscopes.

Key Question How do microscopes work?
Most microscopes use lenses to magnify the image of an object by focusing light or electrons.

Images From Microscopes Images of yeast cells from a light microscope (LM 500×), transmission electron microscope (TEM 4375×), and a scanning electron microscope (SEM 3750×)

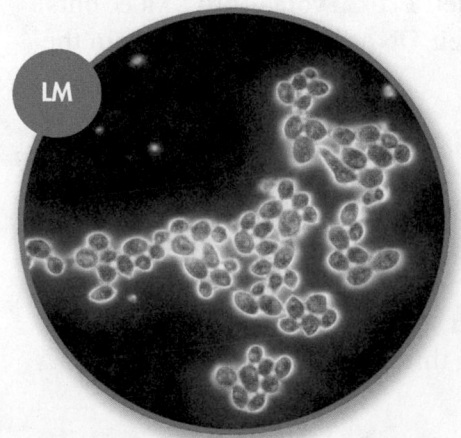

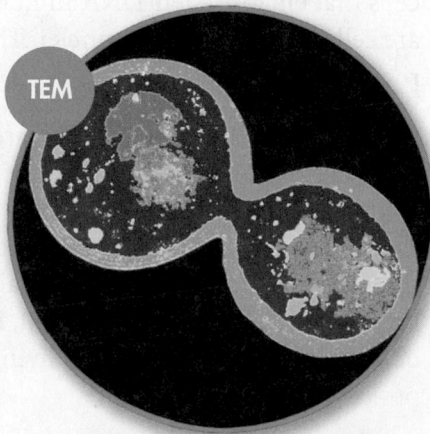

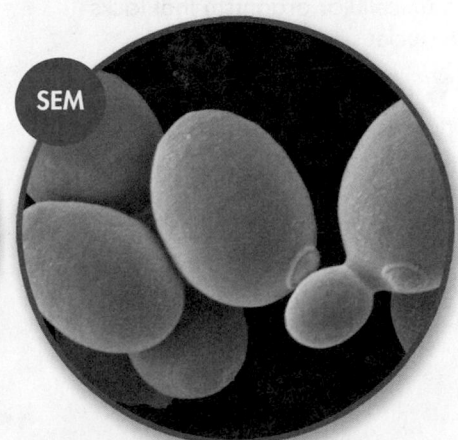

What Is a Cell?

All living things are made up of cells. Cells are not usually visible without a microscope. In this activity, you will use a light microscope to observe several cells.

❶ Obtain a slide of a plant leaf or a slice of a plant stem.

• Look at the slide using a microscope.

• Sketch one or more cells.

• Describe the shape of the cells and how the different parts of a cell look.

❷ Repeat step 1 with slides of nerve cells, bacteria, and paramecia.

❸ Compare the cells.

• List what they have in common.

• List some of their differences.

Analyze and Conclude

Classify Classify the cells you studied into two or more groups. Explain what characteristics you used to put each cell in its group.

In Your Workbook Go to your workbook for more help with this activity.

BUILD
Vocabulary

nucleus
a structure that contains the cell's genetic material in the form of DNA

eukaryote
an organism whose cells contain a nucleus

prokaryote
a unicellular organism that lacks a nucleus

✎ WORD ORIGINS

The word *prokaryote* comes from the Greek word *karyon*, meaning "kernel," or nucleus. The prefix *pro-* means "before." Prokaryotic cells first came about before any cells had nuclei.

Prokaryotes and Eukaryotes

Cells come in many different shapes and sizes. Even though they are different, at some point in their lives all cells have DNA. DNA is the molecule that carries genetic information. Also, all cells are surrounded by a thin, flexible barrier called a cell membrane.

There are two main kinds of cells. One kind has a nucleus, and the other does not. The **nucleus** (plural: nuclei) holds the cell's DNA. There are two membranes around the nucleus. The nucleus also controls many of the cell's activities. **Eukaryotes** (yoo KAR ee ohts) are cells that enclose their DNA in nuclei. **Prokaryotes** (pro KAR ee ohts) are cells that do not have nuclei. Their DNA is not separated from the rest of the cell.

Prokaryotes Prokaryotic cells are generally smaller and simpler than eukaryotic cells. The DNA of prokaryotic cells is not held inside a nucleus. Instead, the DNA floats freely in the cell. Even though they are simpler than eukaryotes, prokaryotes do all the activities that living things must do to be called "alive." They grow, reproduce, respond to the environment, and, in some cases, glide along surfaces or swim through liquids. The living things that we call bacteria are prokaryotes.

Eukaryotes Eukaryotic cells are generally larger and more complex than prokaryotic cells. Most eukaryotic cells have dozens of structures and membranes inside them. Many of these structures have special jobs. In eukaryotic cells, the nucleus separates the DNA from the rest of the cell. Eukaryotes can be very different from one another. Some, like the ones commonly called "protists," live as single cells. Others make up large organisms with many cells—plants, animals, and fungi.

Key Question How are prokaryotic and eukaryotic cells different? **Prokaryotic cells do not have a nucleus. In eukaryotic cells, the nucleus separates the DNA from the rest of the cell.**

Cell Types Eukaryotic cells (including plant and animal cells) are usually more complex than prokaryotic cells.

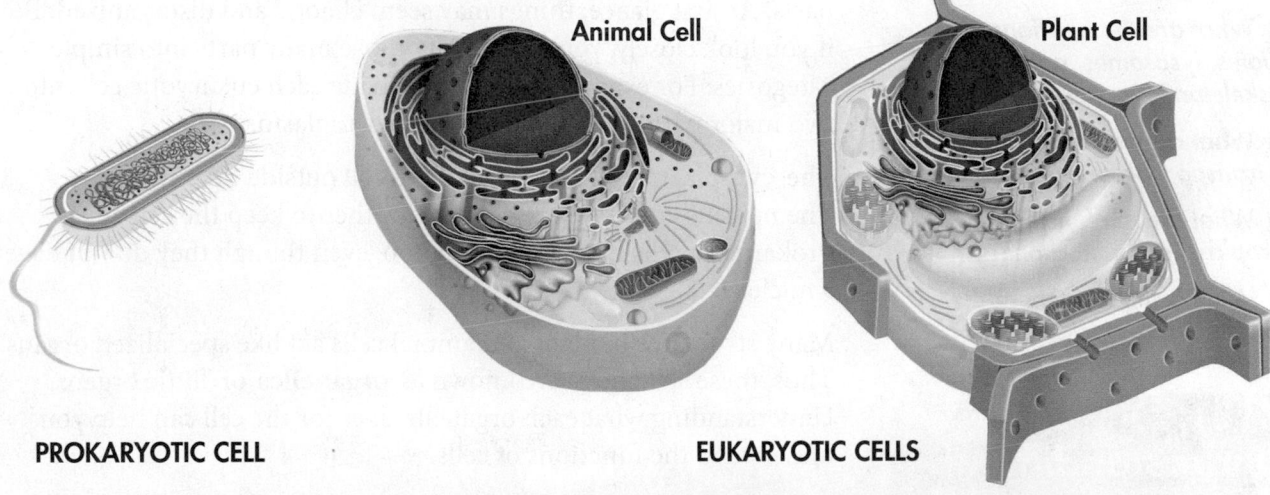

Animal Cell

Plant Cell

PROKARYOTIC CELL

EUKARYOTIC CELLS

✓CHECK Understanding

Apply Vocabulary
Use the highlighted words from the lesson to complete each sentence correctly.

1. _____ are the basic units of all living things.

2. According to the _____, all living things are made of cells.

3. Cells whose DNA is held in a nucleus are _____.

Critical Thinking

4. Apply Concepts Bacteria cells are living in a test tube. What does the cell theory tell you about where these cells came from?

5. Infer A picture from a microscope is black and white and shows only the surface features of the cell. What type of microscope most likely made this picture?

6. Compare and Contrast How are prokaryotes and eukaryotes alike? What is the main difference between them?

7. Write to Learn Answer the first clue of the mystery.

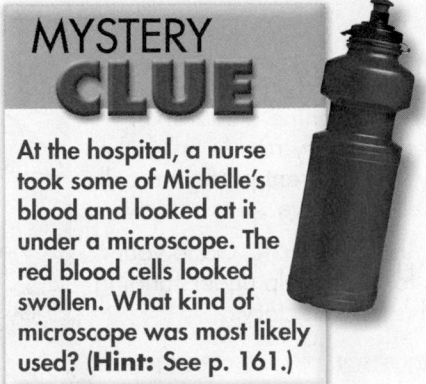

MYSTERY CLUE

At the hospital, a nurse took some of Michelle's blood and looked at it under a microscope. The red blood cells looked swollen. What kind of microscope was most likely used? (**Hint:** See p. 161.)

7.2 Cell Structure

MD CLG 3.1.1 Chemical Substances and Macromolecules, 3.1.3 Matter and Energy, 3.2.1 Processes and Functions, 3.3.3 Nucleic Acids and Protein Synthesis, 3.4.2 Relatedness Among Organisms. SPI 1.4.8 Use Models, 1.5.7 Classification Systems, 1.5.8 Compare.

Key Questions

🔑 What is the role of the cell nucleus?

🔑 What are the functions of vacuoles, lysosomes, and the cytoskeleton?

🔑 What organelles help make and transport proteins?

🔑 What are the functions of chloroplasts and mitochondria?

🔑 What is the function of the cell membrane?

BUILD Understanding

Venn Diagram Create a Venn diagram that shows how prokaryotes and eukaryotes are the same and different.

In Your Workbook Go to your workbook to learn more about making a Venn diagram. Complete the Venn diagram for Lesson 7.2.

Cell Organization

Like a factory, a eukaryotic cell is a busy place with many different parts. At first glance, things may seem chaotic and disorganized. But if you look closely, you can classify those many parts into simpler categories. For example, it's easy to divide each eukaryotic cell into two major parts: the nucleus and the cytoplasm.

The **cytoplasm** is the portion of the cell outside the nucleus. The nucleus and cytoplasm work together to keep the cell alive. Prokaryotic cells have cytoplasm, too, even though they do not have a nucleus.

Many structures in plant and animal cells act like specialized organs. Thus, these structures are known as **organelles** or "little organs." Understanding what each organelle does for the cell can help you understand the functions of cells.

The Cell as a Factory In some ways, a eukaryotic cell is much like a factory. The different organelles of the cell are like the specialized machines, trained workers, and assembly lines of the factory. And, like workers at factories, cells follow instructions and make products. In this chapter, you will read about many ways that the parts of a cell are like the parts of a factory.

BUILD Connections

THE CELL AS A FACTORY

Each different machine and worker helps make a factory run. In much the same way, the different parts in a cell help the cell to survive.

In Your Workbook Go to your workbook for more help understanding how a cell is like a factory.

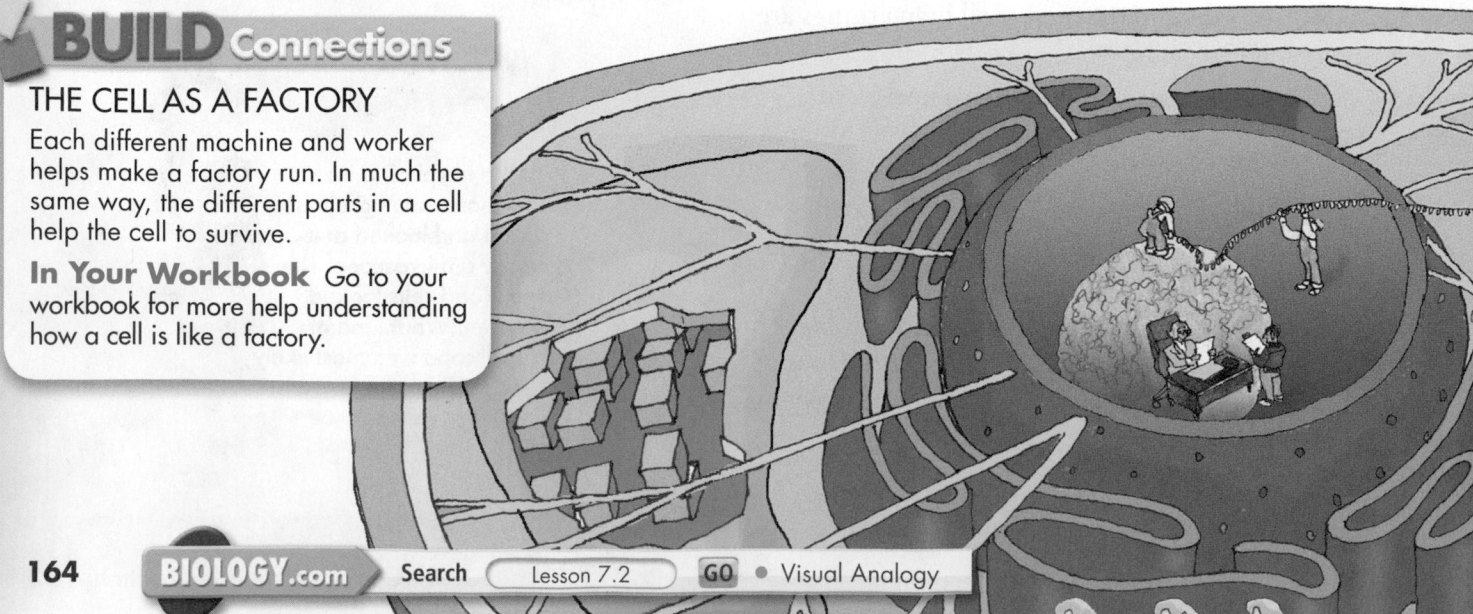

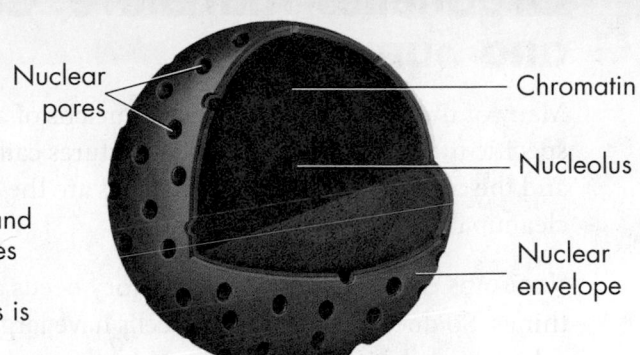

Nuclear pores

Chromatin

Nucleolus

Nuclear envelope

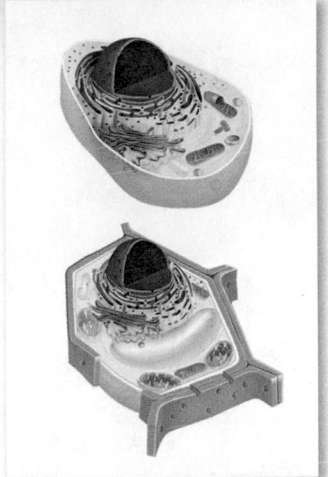

The Nucleus

The nucleus holds DNA and controls most of what goes on in the cell. The small, dense area in the nucleus is the nucleolus.

The Nucleus In the same way that the main office controls a large factory, the nucleus is the control center of the cell. The nucleus holds nearly all of the cell's DNA. DNA contains the coded directions for making proteins and other important molecules. Prokaryotic cells do not have a nucleus, but they have DNA that codes the same kinds of directions.

The nucleus is surrounded by a nuclear envelope made up of two membranes. The nuclear envelope is dotted with thousands of holes. These holes allow material to move into and out of the nucleus. Messages, directions, and blueprints move in and out of a factory's main office. In a similar way, proteins, RNA, and other molecules move through the holes in the nuclear envelope to and from the rest of the cell.

Most nuclei also have a small dense spot known as the nucleolus (noo KLEE uh lus). The nucleolus is where ribosomes are first put together. Ribosomes are used by the cell to build proteins.

Key Question What is the role of the cell nucleus?
The nucleus holds nearly all of the cell's DNA, which has the coded directions for making proteins and other important molecules.

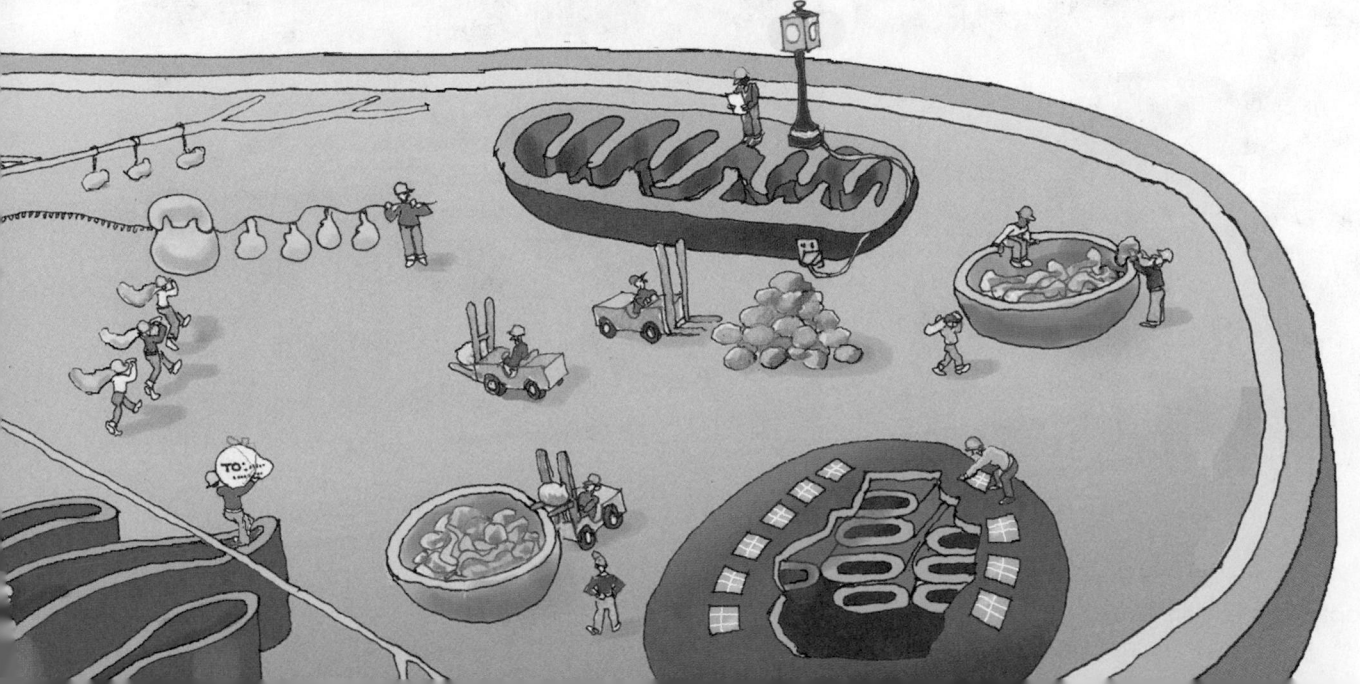

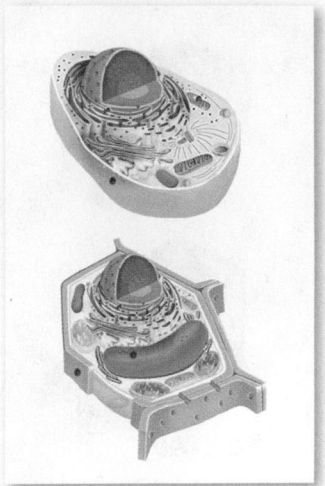

Organelles That Store, Clean Up, and Support

Many of the organelles outside the nucleus of a eukaryotic cell have specific functions. They include structures called vacuoles, lysosomes, and the cytoskeleton. These organelles are the cell's storage space, cleanup crew, and support structure.

Vacuoles and Vesicles Every factory needs a place to store things. So does every cell. Many cells have large, membrane sacs called **vacuoles** (VAK yoo ohlz). Vacuoles store materials like water, salts, proteins, and sugars. In many plant cells, there is a single, large central vacuole filled with liquid. The pressure of this large vacuole makes the cell firm and lets the plant hold up heavy parts, such as leaves and flowers.

Vacuoles are also found in some single-celled organisms and in some animals. A paramecium has an organelle called a contractile vacuole. By contracting over and over, this vacuole pumps extra water out of the cell.

Nearly all eukaryotic cells have much smaller membrane sacs called vesicles. Vesicles store and move materials between organelles as well as to and from the outside of the cell.

Lysosomes Even the neatest, cleanest factory needs a cleanup crew. That's where lysosomes (LY suh sohmz) come in. **Lysosomes** are small organelles filled with enzymes that break down lipids, sugars, and proteins into smaller molecules. These smaller molecules can be used by the rest of the cell. Lysosomes also help break down organelles that are no longer useful. They carry out the important job of removing "junk" that might otherwise pile up in the cell. Many human diseases are linked to lysosomes that stop working correctly. Animal cells have lysosomes, and a few special kinds of plant cells also have them.

Vacuoles The central vacuole of plant cells stores salts, proteins, and sugars. A paramecium's contractile vacuole keeps the water levels just right by pumping water out.

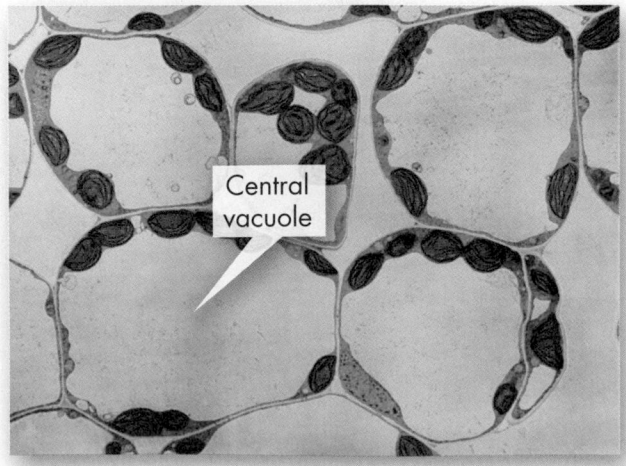

Central vacuole

TEM 7000×

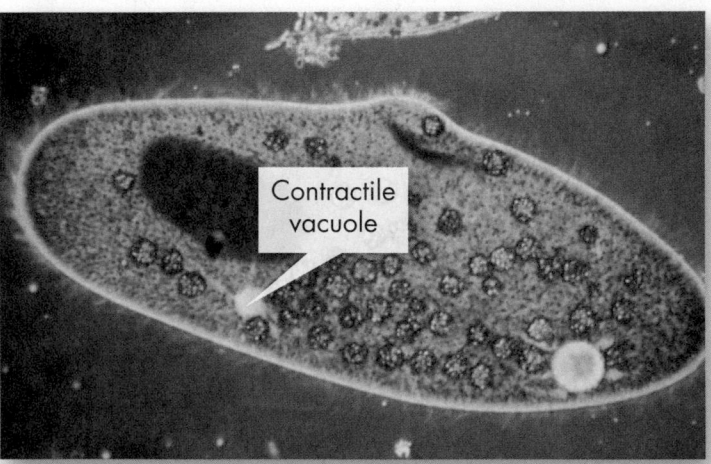

Contractile vacuole

LM 500×

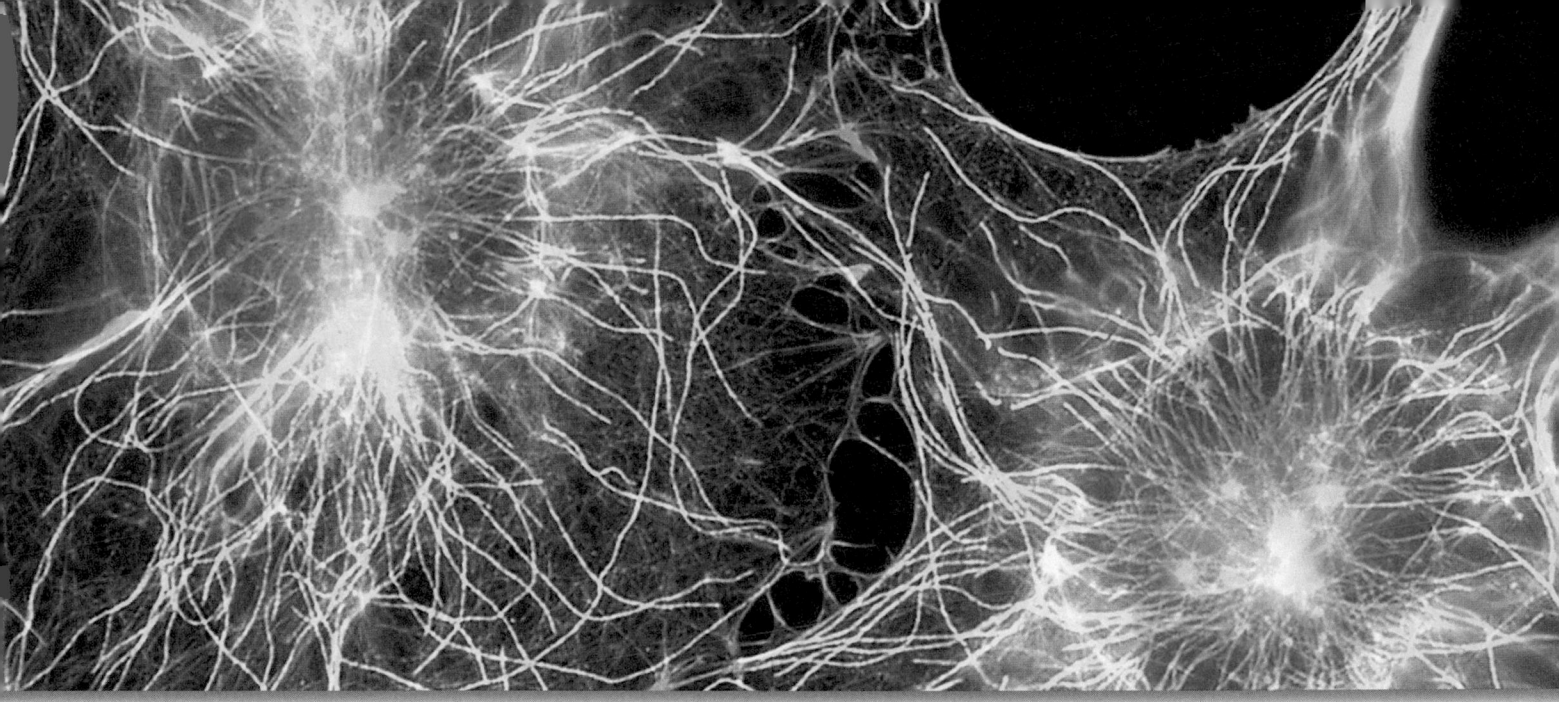

LM 1175×

The Cytoskeleton A factory building has strong beams and columns that hold up its walls and roof. Eukaryotic cells get their shape from a web of proteins known as the **cytoskeleton.** Some parts of the cytoskeleton help move materials between different parts of the cell. These parts are much like conveyor belts in a factory. Some cells use parts of the cytoskeleton to help them move. The cytoskeleton includes two types of protein filaments called microfilaments and microtubules.

▶ *Microfilaments* Microfilaments are threadlike structures made up of a protein called actin. In some cells they form an internal flexible web. This web supports the cell. Microfilaments also help some cells move. Microfilaments are built, taken apart, and then built again in different parts of the cell, allowing amoebas and other cells to crawl along surfaces.

▶ *Microtubules* Microtubules are like thin, hollow pipes. They are made up of proteins known as tubulins. Microtubules help the cell keep its shape. They are also found in hairlike organelles called cilia and flagella that help some cells swim. Cilia and flagella whip back and forth, pushing cells along or moving fluids along the surfaces of cells.

Microtubules are also important in cell division. They form a structure known as the mitotic spindle. This structure helps to separate the different sets of DNA that each daughter cell will get. In animal cells, organelles called centrioles (SEN tree ohlz) are also formed from tubulins. Centrioles are found near the nucleus and help organize cell division. Plant cells do not have centrioles.

🔑 **Key Question** What are the functions of vacuoles, lysosomes, and the cytoskeleton?
Vacuoles store materials. Lysosomes break down large molecules and old organelles. The cytoskeleton helps the cell keep its shape and move.

Cytoskeleton The cytoskeleton supports and gives shape to the cell. Dyes have been used to color different parts of the cell in this picture. Microfilaments are pale purple, microtubules are yellow, and nuclei are green.

BUILD Vocabulary

vacuole
the cell organelle that stores materials such as water, salts, proteins, and carbohydrates

lysosome
the cell organelle that breaks down lipids, carbohydrates, and proteins into small molecules that can be used by the rest of the cell

cytoskeleton
the network of protein filaments in a eukaryotic cell that gives the cell its shape and internal organization and is involved in movement

🖋 WORD ORIGINS

The prefix *lys-* comes from the Greek word *lysis*, which refers to "loosening" or "dissolving." The suffix *-some* comes from the Greek word *soma*, which means "body." A lysosome is a small body in the cell that dissolves, or breaks up, wastes in the cell.

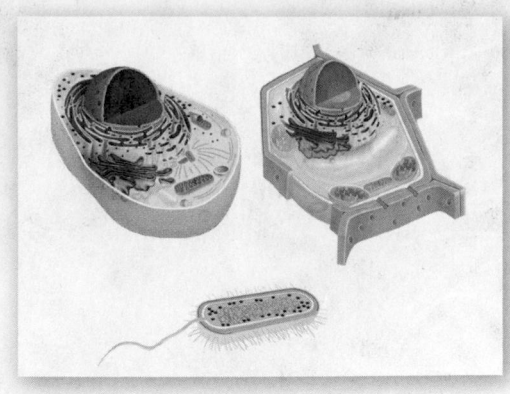

Organelles That Build Proteins

Living things are always working, building new molecules all the time, especially proteins. Proteins help carry out chemical reactions and make up important parts of the cell. Because proteins are so important, a big part of the cell is used for making them and moving them around.

Ribosomes Proteins are made on ribosomes. **Ribosomes** are small units of RNA and protein found in the cytoplasm of all cells. Ribosomes make proteins by following coded directions that come from DNA. Each ribosome is like a factory worker that makes proteins on orders that come from its DNA "boss." Many ribosomes are free in the cytoplasm. Others are attached to the endoplasmic reticulum.

Endoplasmic Reticulum The **endoplasmic reticulum** (en doh PLAZ mik rih TIK yuh lum), or ER, is a membrane system where lipid parts of the cell membrane are put together. Proteins and other materials that are shipped from the cell are also put together on the ER. There are two types of ER: rough and smooth.

▶ *Rough ER* Proteins are made on the rough endoplasmic reticulum, or rough ER. It is called "rough" because the ribosomes on its surface make it bumpy. Newly made proteins leave these ribosomes and enter the rough ER. Enzymes inside the rough ER make changes to some of the proteins. Some proteins made on the rough ER will leave the cell. Others are membrane proteins and proteins that go to lysosomes and other specialized locations inside the cell.

BUILD Connections

MAKING PROTEINS

Together, ribosomes, the endoplasmic reticulum, and the Golgi apparatus make, package, and ship proteins.

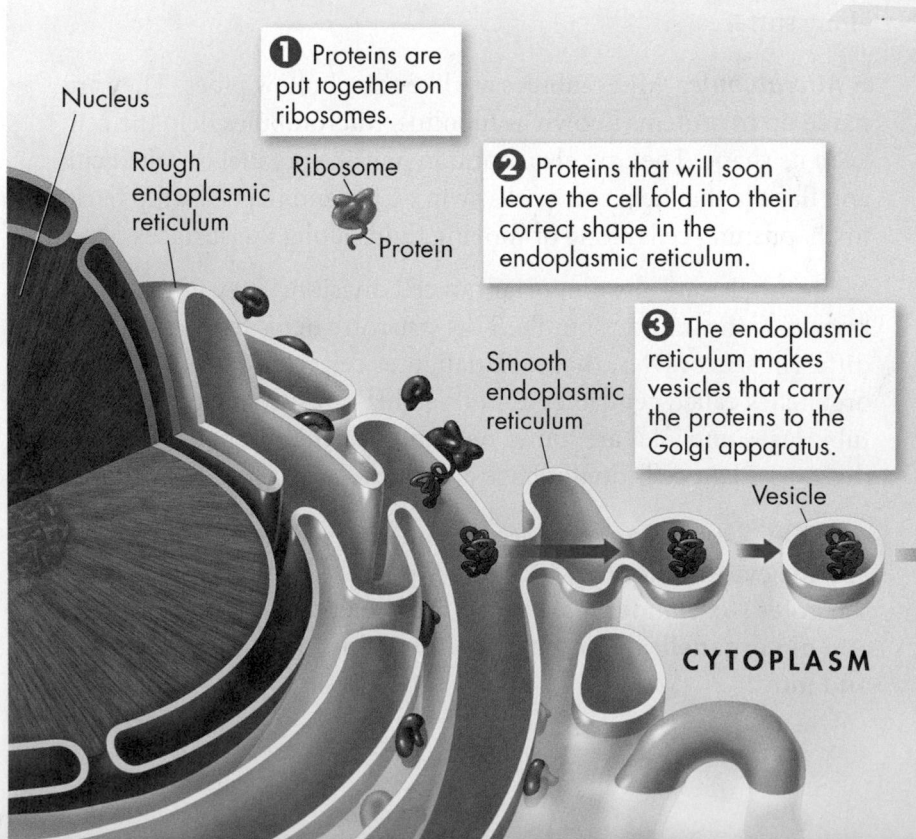

Nucleus

Rough endoplasmic reticulum

Ribosome

Protein

Smooth endoplasmic reticulum

❶ Proteins are put together on ribosomes.

❷ Proteins that will soon leave the cell fold into their correct shape in the endoplasmic reticulum.

❸ The endoplasmic reticulum makes vesicles that carry the proteins to the Golgi apparatus.

Vesicle

CYTOPLASM

► *Smooth ER* The other part of the ER is known as smooth endoplasmic reticulum, or smooth ER. It is called "smooth" because there are no ribosomes on its surface. In many cells, the smooth ER has groups of enzymes that do special tasks. They make membrane lipids and get rid of toxins, such as drugs. Liver cells, which play a key part in getting rid of drugs, often have large amounts of smooth ER.

Golgi Apparatus In eukaryotic cells, proteins made on the rough ER move next into an organelle called the **Golgi apparatus.** This organelle looks like a stack of flat membrane sacs. It is like the "shipping station" of the cell. Proteins have molecular "address tags" that point out where they need to go. The ER "reads" these tags and bundles the proteins into tiny vesicles. The vesicles bud from the ER and carry the proteins to the Golgi apparatus. The Golgi apparatus changes, sorts, and packages proteins and other materials from the ER. Some of them are stored in the cell, while others are sent outside the cell.

🔑 **Key Question** What organelles help make and transport proteins?
Proteins are put together on ribosomes in the cytoplasm and on the rough ER. The Golgi apparatus changes, sorts, and packages proteins and other materials for "shipment."

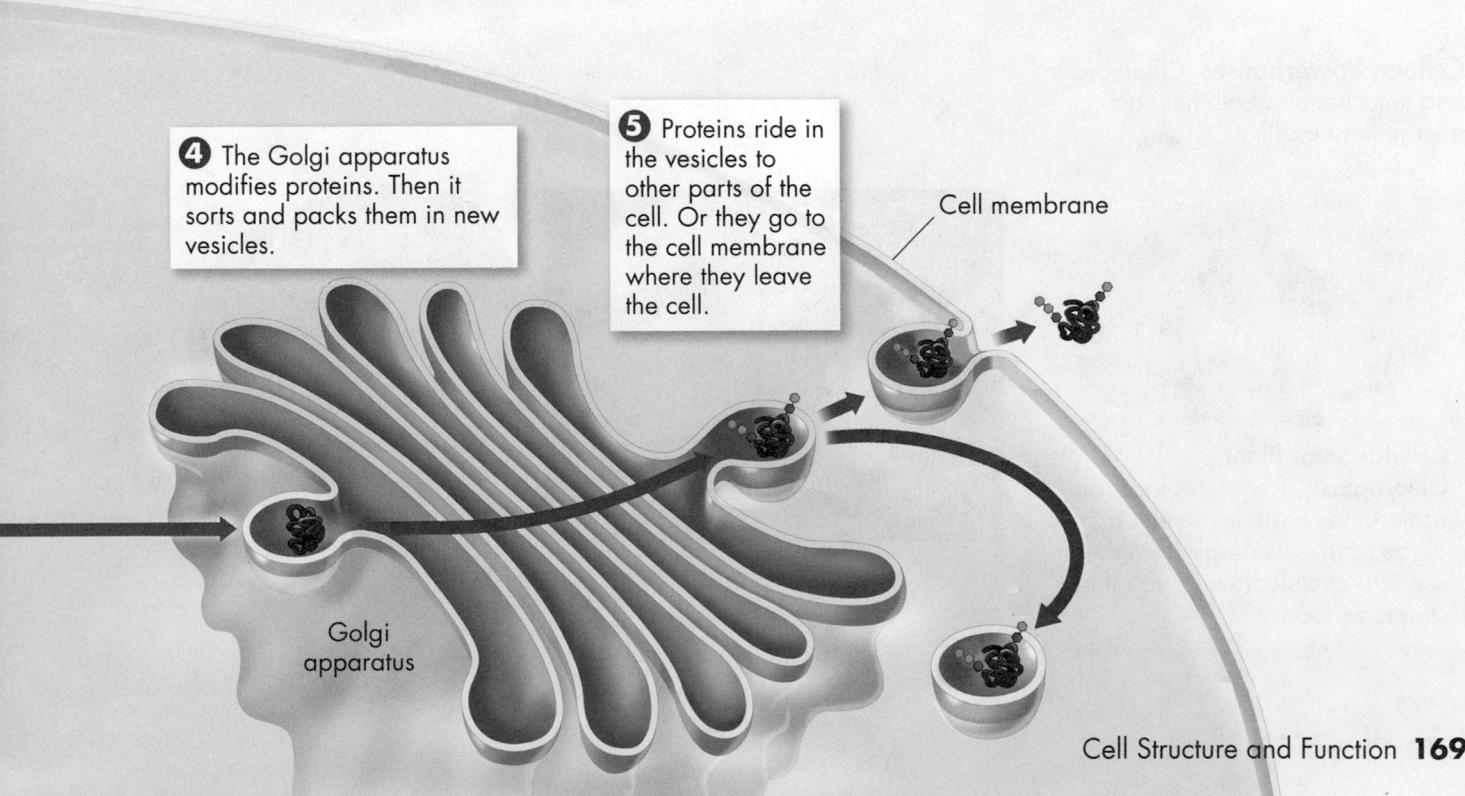

4 The Golgi apparatus modifies proteins. Then it sorts and packs them in new vesicles.

5 Proteins ride in the vesicles to other parts of the cell. Or they go to the cell membrane where they leave the cell.

Cell membrane

Golgi apparatus

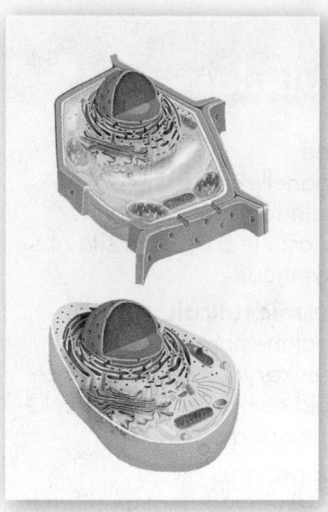

Organelles That Capture and Release Energy

All living things need a source of energy. Factories are connected to the local power company, but how do cells get energy? Most cells are powered by food molecules that are built using energy from the sun.

Chloroplasts Plants and some other living things have chloroplasts (KLAWR uh plasts). **Chloroplasts** are like solar power plants. They take the energy from sunlight and change it into energy stored in food. This process is called photosynthesis (foh toh SIN thuh sis). Two membranes surround chloroplasts. Inside the chloroplasts are large stacks of other membranes. These hold the green pigment chlorophyll.

Mitochondria Nearly all eukaryotic cells, including plant cells, have mitochondria (myt oh KAHN dree uh; singular: mitochondrion). **Mitochondria** are the power plants of the cell. Mitochondria change the chemical energy stored in food into compounds that are easier for the cell to use. Like chloroplasts, mitochondria are surrounded by two membranes—an outer membrane and an inner membrane. The inner membrane is much larger than the outer one. It is folded up inside the organelle.

Chloroplasts and mitochondria have their own genetic information in the form of small DNA molecules.

Key Question What are the functions of chloroplasts and mitochondria?
Chloroplasts take the energy from sunlight and change it into food in a process called photosynthesis. Mitochondria change the chemical energy stored in food into compounds that are easier for the cell to use.

Cellular Powerhouses Chloroplasts and mitochondria both help get energy for the cell.

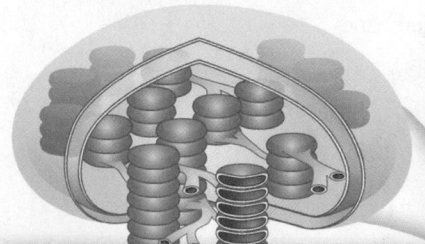

Cellular Solar Plants
Chloroplasts, found in plants and some other organisms such as algae, convert energy from the sun into chemical energy that is stored as food.

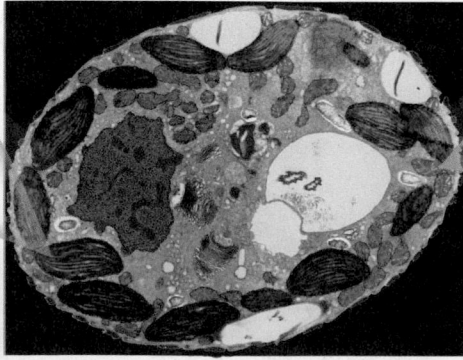

TEM 4500×

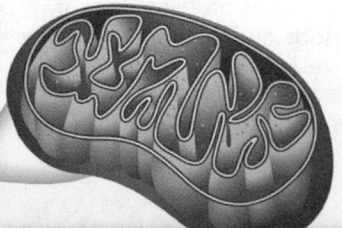

Cellular Power Plants
Mitochondria convert chemical energy stored in food into a form that can be used easily by the cell.

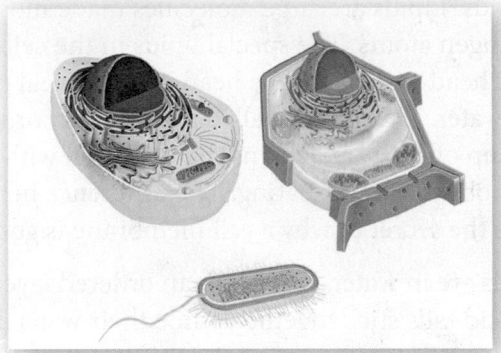

Cellular Boundaries

A working factory needs walls and a roof to protect it from the weather outside. The roof and walls also keep the factory's products safe until they are ready to be shipped out. Cells have similar needs, and they meet them in a similar way. All cells are surrounded by a barrier known as the cell membrane. Many cells also have a stiff layer around the membrane known as a cell wall.

Cell Walls The main job of the cell wall is to support, shape, and protect the cell. Most prokaryotes and many eukaryotes, such as plant cells, have cell walls. Animal cells do not have cell walls. Cell walls lie outside the cell membrane. Most cell walls can let water, oxygen, carbon dioxide, and other materials pass through easily. Cell walls give plants the strength they need to stand up straight. In trees and other large plants, nearly all of the tissue we call wood is made up of cell walls. In fact, the cellulose fiber used to make paper, including the pages of this book, comes from these cell walls.

BUILD Vocabulary

chloroplast
an organelle found in cells of plants and some other organisms that captures the energy from sunlight and converts it into chemical energy

mitochondrion
a cell organelle that converts the chemical energy stored in food into compounds that are more convenient for the cell to use

lipid bilayer
a flexible double-layered sheet that makes up the cell membrane and forms a barrier between the cell and its surroundings

❦ WORD ORIGINS

The Greek root *chloro-* means "green." The root *-plast* means "shape." Chloroplasts are the green-colored, round shapes in the cells of leaves.

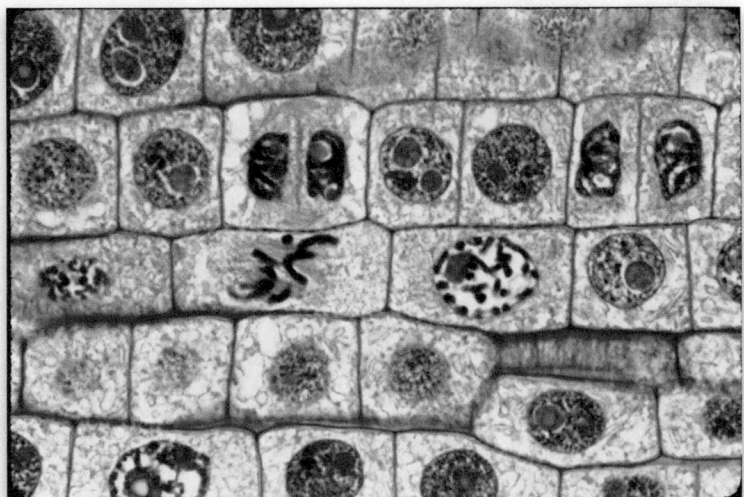

Cell Walls Rigid cell walls give these onion cells their shape (LM 700×).

Cell Membranes All cells have cell membranes. They are made up of a double-layered sheet called a **lipid bilayer.** The lipid bilayer makes membranes flexible and lets them form a strong barrier between the cell and its surroundings. The cell membrane controls what enters and leaves the cell. It also protects and supports the cell.

▶ **Lipids** As you can tell from the name, each layer of the lipid bilayer is made up of lipids. Lipids are large molecules made mostly from carbon and hydrogen atoms. The special lipids in the cell membrane have two parts: a head and a tail. The head is a chemical group that mixes well with water. The head is called hydrophilic, or water-loving. The tail is made up of fatty acid chains that mix well with oil. The tail is called hydrophobic, or water-hating. The difference between these heads and tails is the secret to why a cell membrane is good at its job.

When these lipids are in water, they form an ordered layer. Their oil-loving fatty acid tails stick together, while their water-loving heads mix with the water. When two of these layers come together, they are like a sandwich. The water-loving parts of the lipids form the outside layer. The oily parts of the lipids stick together to form the inner layer. A lipid bilayer is the result. As you can see in the picture below, the head groups of lipids in a bilayer are on the outside and inside of the cell. The fatty acid tails form an oily layer inside the membrane that keeps water out.

Cell Membrane The cell membrane keeps track of the movement of materials in and out of the cell. Cell membranes are made up of a lipid bilayer that has proteins and sugars set into it.

TEM 3000×

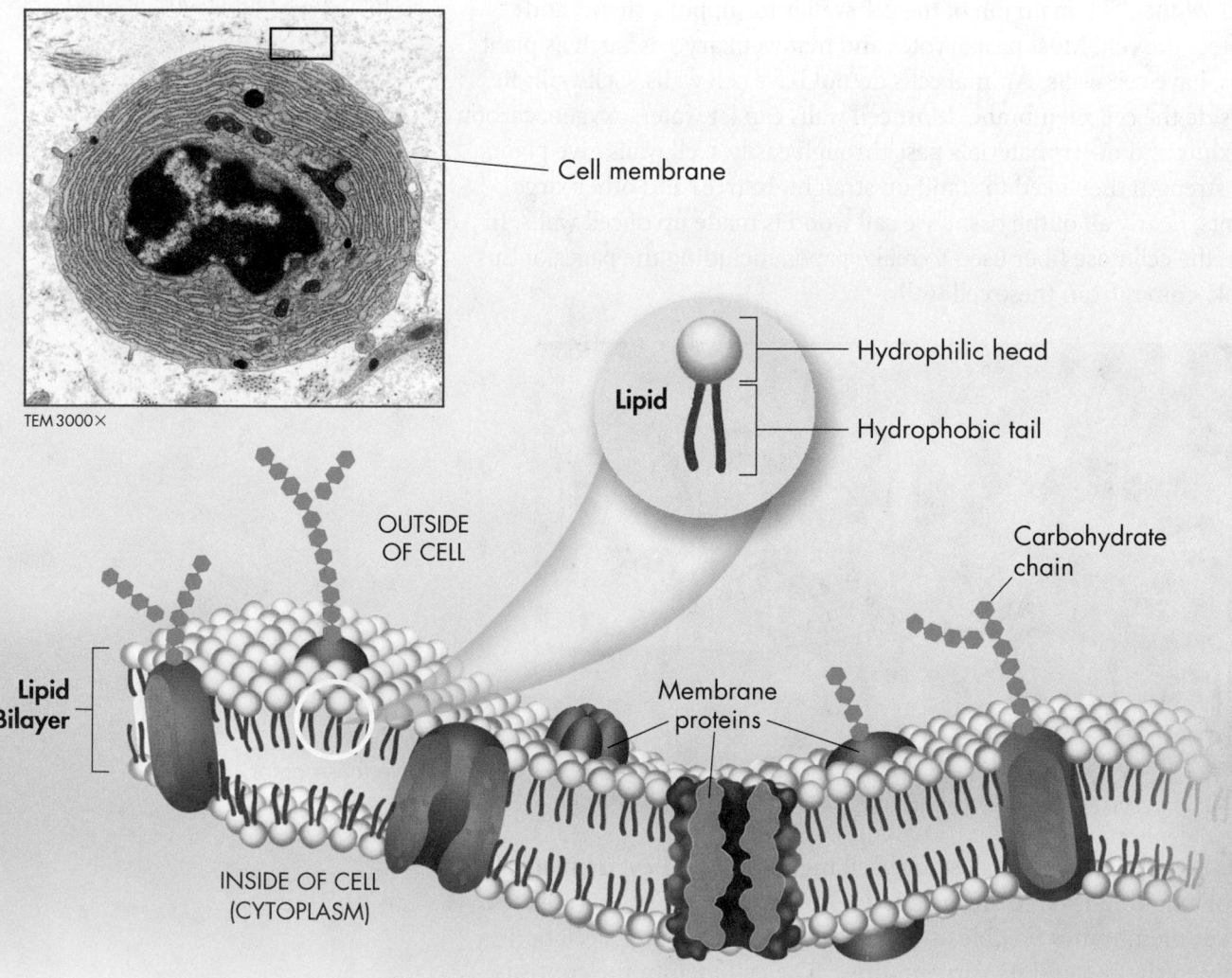

Cell membrane

Lipid — Hydrophilic head

— Hydrophobic tail

OUTSIDE OF CELL

Carbohydrate chain

Lipid Bilayer

Membrane proteins

INSIDE OF CELL (CYTOPLASM)

▶ **How Membranes Work** The lipid bilayers of most cell membranes contain many different proteins. Some of the proteins form channels and pumps that help to move material across the cell membrane. Sugar molecules are attached to many of these proteins. They act like name cards that help cells tell each other what they are doing. Other proteins attach directly to the cytoskeleton. They help the cell react to its surroundings by using the membranes to help the cell move or change shape.

As you know, some things are allowed to enter and leave a factory, and some are not. The same is true for living cells. Although many substances can cross cell membranes, some are too large to cross the lipid bilayer. Others have too much charge to pass through it. If a substance is able to cross a membrane, the membrane is said to be permeable to it. A membrane is not permeable to substances that cannot pass across it. Most cell membranes are selectively permeable, which means that some substances can pass across them and others cannot.

🔑 **Key Question** What is the function of the cell membrane? **The cell membrane keeps track of what enters and leaves the cell and also protects and supports the cell.**

CHECK Understanding

Apply Vocabulary

Use the highlighted words from the lesson to complete each sentence correctly.

1. A large sac that stores water, salts, and other materials for the cell is called a _____.

2. _____ are filled with enzymes that can break down substances in cells to be used later.

3. Microtubules and microfilaments make up the _____, which helps the cell hold its shape.

4. The _____ makes up the cell membrane, which acts as a flexible protective boundary for the cell.

Critical Thinking

5. **Review** What are the two major parts of a eukaryotic cell?

6. **Use Analogies** How is the role of the nucleus in a cell similar to the role of the captain on a sports team?

7. **Apply Concepts** How do contractile vacuoles help maintain water balance in a paramecium?

8. **Sequence** Describe the steps in making, packaging, and exporting a protein from a cell.

9. **Review** What is the function of mitochondria?

10. **Write to Learn** In your own words, explain how lipid molecules are arranged in the cell membrane. In your answer, use the words *bilayer*, *hydrophilic*, and *hydrophobic*.

BIOLOGY.com ▶ Search ⟨ Lesson 7.2 ⟩ GO • Lesson Assessment

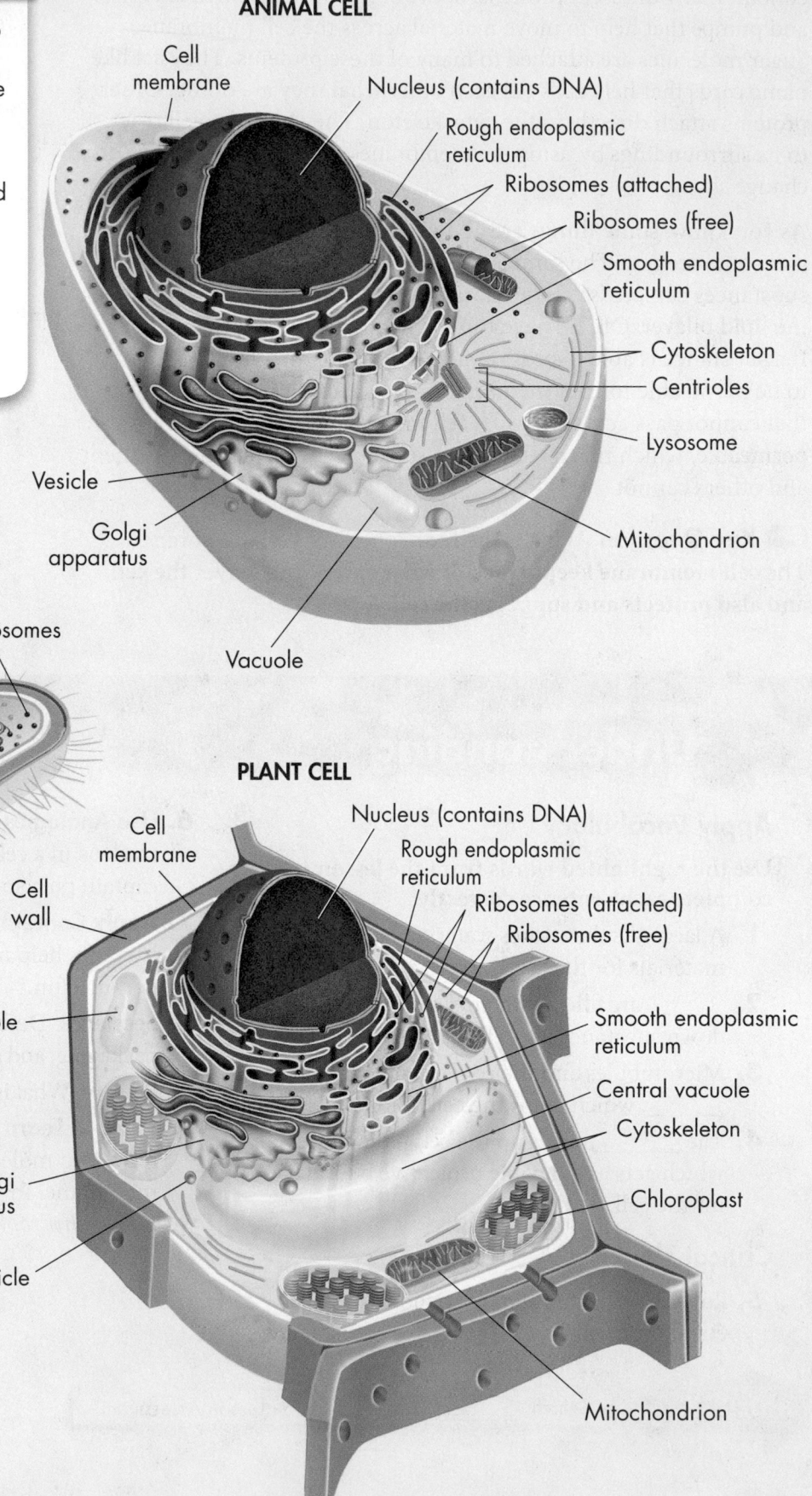

BUILD Connections

COMPARING TYPICAL CELLS

Eukaryotic cells have many different kinds of organelles. Some of these organelles are also found in prokaryotic cells. The table on the facing page compares prokaryotic cells, animal cells, and plant cells.

In Your Workbook Do you know the differences between animal cells, plant cells, and prokaryotic cells? Go to your workbook to test yourself.

ANIMAL CELL

Cell membrane

Nucleus (contains DNA)

Rough endoplasmic reticulum

Ribosomes (attached)

Ribosomes (free)

Smooth endoplasmic reticulum

Cytoskeleton

Centrioles

Lysosome

Mitochondrion

Vesicle

Golgi apparatus

Vacuole

PROKARYOTIC CELL

DNA

Ribosomes

Cell membrane

Cell wall

PLANT CELL

Cell membrane

Cell wall

Nucleus (contains DNA)

Rough endoplasmic reticulum

Ribosomes (attached)

Ribosomes (free)

Vacuole

Smooth endoplasmic reticulum

Central vacuole

Cytoskeleton

Chloroplast

Golgi apparatus

Vesicle

Mitochondrion

	Structure	Function	Prokaryote	Eukaryote: Animal	Plant
Cellular Control Center	Nucleus	Contains DNA	*Prokaryote DNA is found in cytoplasm.*	✓	✓
Organelles That Store, Clean Up, and Support	Vacuoles and vesicles	Store materials		✓	✓
	Lysosomes	Break down and recycle macromolecules		✓	✓ (rare)
	Cytoskeleton	Maintains cell shape; moves cell parts; helps cells move	*Prokaryotic cells have protein filaments similar to actin and tubulin.*	✓	✓
	Centrioles	Organize cell division		✓	
Organelles That Build Proteins	Ribosomes	Synthesize proteins	✓	✓	✓
	Endoplasmic reticulum	Assembles proteins and lipids		✓	✓
	Golgi apparatus	Modifies, sorts, and packages proteins and lipids for storage or transport out of the cell		✓	✓
Organelles That Capture and Release Energy	Chloroplasts	Convert solar energy to chemical energy stored in food	*In some prokaryotic cells, photosynthesis occurs in association with internal photosynthetic membranes.*		✓
	Mitochondria	Convert chemical energy in food to usable compounds	*Prokaryotes carry out these reactions in the cytoplasm rather than in specialized organelles.*	✓	✓
Cellular Boundaries	Cell wall	Shapes, supports, and protects the cell	✓		✓
	Cell membrane	Regulates materials entering and leaving cell; protects and supports cell	✓	✓	✓

7.3 Cell Transport

MD CLG 3.1.1 Chemical Substances and Macromolecules, 3.1.2 Homeostasis, 3.1.3 Matter and Energy, 3.2.1 Processes and Functions, 3.2.2 Changes in Metabolic Activity. SPI 1.5.8 Compare.

Key Questions

🔑 **What is passive transport?**

🔑 **What is active transport?**

BUILD Understanding

Compare/Contrast Table As you read, create a compare/contrast table for passive and active transport.

In Your Workbook Go to your workbook for help making the compare/contrast table.

Diffusion Diffusion is the process by which molecules of a substance move from an area of higher concentration (where they are closer together) to an area of lower concentration (where they are more spread out).

Passive Transport

Nearly every nation tries to control the things that move across its borders. A cell has a border, too. And the cell needs to control what crosses its border. The cell's border is the cell membrane.

One of the most important jobs of the cell membrane is to keep up the right balance between the liquid in the cell and the liquid around the cell. It does so by keeping track of the movement of molecules across the membrane.

Diffusion Cytoplasm contains many different substances dissolved in water. These substances move in this solution, run into each other, and spread out randomly. They tend to move from an area where there are more of them to an area where there are fewer of them. Think about when you add sugar to tea. The sugar molecules will move away from their original positions and move throughout the hot liquid. The process by which particles move from an area of high concentration (close together) to an area of lower concentration (spread apart) is known as **diffusion** (dih FYOO zhun).

Suppose there is more of a substance on one side of a cell membrane than on the other. If the substance can cross the membrane, its particles will diffuse toward the area of lower concentration. The particles will keep moving to the other side until the sides are even. Once there are equal numbers on both sides, the particles will move from both sides at equal rates.

Diffusion does not need energy from the cell. The movement of materials across the cell membrane without using cellular energy is called passive transport.

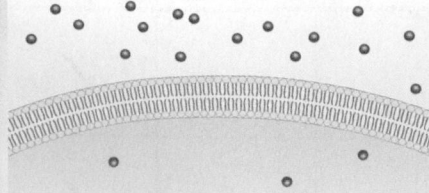

There are more particles on one side of the membrane than on the other. Particles are always moving across the membrane in both directions.

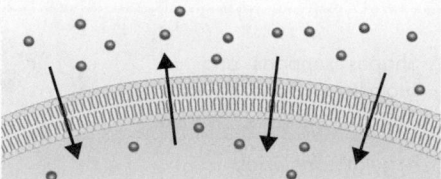

Diffusion causes particles to move in one direction at a faster rate. They move from the side of the membrane with the higher concentration to the side with the lower concentration.

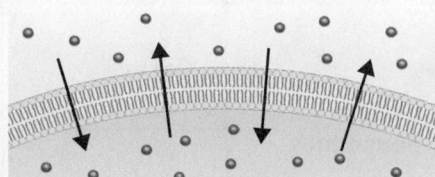

Once both sides are even, particles keep moving across the membrane in both directions at the same rate. There is no net change in concentration.

Facilitated Diffusion Remember that cell membranes are built around lipid bilayers. The lipids let small, uncharged molecules pass most easily. But many charged ions, such as Cl⁻, and large molecules, such as the sugar glucose, seem to pass right through cell membranes much more quickly than they should. It's almost as if they have a shortcut.

In fact, they do. Proteins in the cell membrane act as carriers, or channels. They make it easy for certain molecules to cross. For example, red blood cells have proteins that let glucose pass through them in either direction. This process, in which molecules that cannot diffuse across the membrane alone instead pass through protein channels, is known as **facilitated diffusion.** This action does not use energy. Facilitated diffusion is a form of passive transport.

Osmosis Most cell membranes are selectively permeable. That term means they allow some things to cross, but not others. Water is a good example. The movement of water across a selectively permeable membrane is called **osmosis.** Water molecules do not mix well with lipid bilayers. So water has a hard time passing across some cell membranes. However, many cells have water channel proteins, known as aquaporins (ak wuh PAWR inz) in their membranes. These channels let water pass right through. In osmosis, as in all diffusion, molecules move from higher concentrations to lower concentrations—lower concentrations of water.

▶ *How Osmosis Works* Look at the picture of the U-shaped tube below. The barrier at the bottom of the tube will let water through in both directions. It will not let sugar pass. To start, there are more sugar molecules on the right side of the barrier than on the left. Even though water molecules move in both directions, they move at a greater rate toward the side with the concentrated sugar solution. Water will tend to move across the barrier until the sugar molecules on both sides are evenly spaced.

A Water Channel Protein
Water can pass into and out of the cell through aquaporins in the cell membrane.

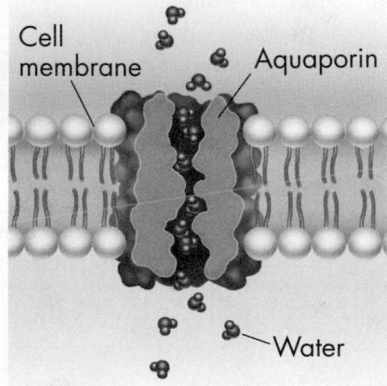

Cell membrane   Aquaporin

Water

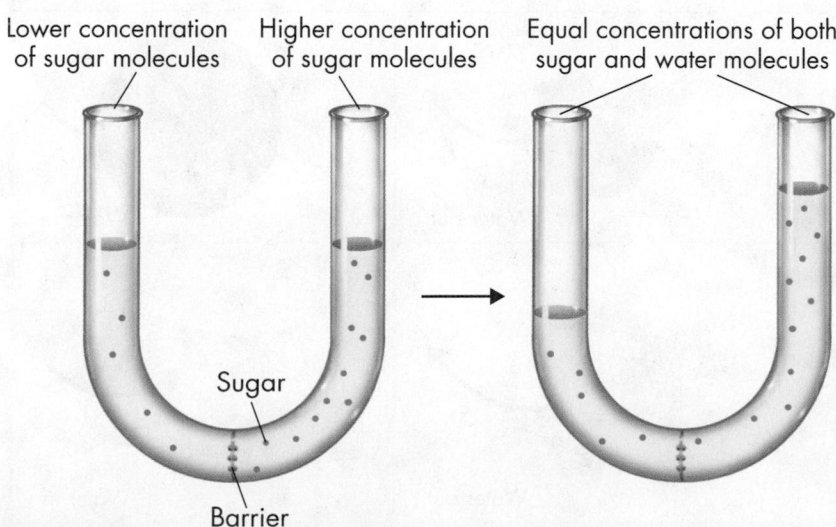

Lower concentration of sugar molecules   Higher concentration of sugar molecules   Equal concentrations of both sugar and water molecules

Sugar

Barrier

Osmosis In a laboratory experiment, water can move through a barrier that will not let sugar pass through it. Water molecules move from one side to the other until the sugar is evenly spaced. In the end, there will be more solution on one side of the barrier than on the other.

osmotic pressure
the pressure that must be applied to prevent osmotic movement across a selectively permeable membrane

✒ ACADEMIC WORDS

The word *pressure* means "force applied over an area." Water pressure is caused by the force of water molecules hitting the sides of their container. Osmotic pressure is caused by the difference in the forces of water molecules hitting either side of the cell membrane.

Osmotic Pressure Osmotic pressure inside an animal cell causes the cell to swell and burst. In plant cells, osmotic pressure inside the central vacuole pushes the cell's insides against the cell wall.

▶ *Osmotic Pressure* Sometimes cell membranes have solutions that are the same on both sides. Sometimes the solutions are different. When the solutions inside and outside of the cell are the same, the solutions are said to be isotonic. Isotonic means "same strength" and refers to the concentration of the dissolved particles, not the water. When the solution outside of the cell has a higher concentration than the inside solution, the outside solution is hypertonic. This word means "above strength." When the solution outside of the cell has a lower concentration, it is hypotonic, or "below strength."

Sometimes there are differences in concentration of salts, sugars, proteins, and other dissolved molecules on one side of the cell membrane. These differences produce a force known as **osmotic pressure,** which can cause the movement of water out of or into a cell through osmosis. Osmotic pressure can cause an animal cell in a hypertonic solution to shrink as water moves out. An animal cell in a hypotonic solution will swell as water moves into it. Eventually, the cell may burst like an overinflated balloon. In plant cells, osmotic pressure can cause changes in the size of the central vacuole. A shrunken central vacuole does not give the same support to the cell as a full one. This loss of support is why plants wilt when they do not get enough water.

🗝 Key Question What is passive transport?
The movement of materials across the cell membrane without using energy is called passive transport.

The Effects of Osmosis on Cells

	Isotonic: The concentration is the same inside and outside the cell. Water molecules move at the same rate in both directions.	Hypertonic: The outside solution has a higher concentration than the solution inside the cell. Movement of water molecules out of the cell causes it to shrink.	Hypotonic: The outside solution has a lower concentration than the solution inside the cell. Movement of water molecules into the cell causes it to swell.
Solution			
Animal Cell	Water in and out	Water out	Water in
Plant Cell	Water in and out	Water out	Water in

Protein Pumps
Chemical energy is used to pump ions across the cell membrane. Protein pumps grab ions on one side of the membrane, change shape, and let go of them on the other.

Endocytosis
The membrane forms a pocket around a particle outside the cell. The pocket pinches closed on the inside of the cell, forming a vesicle. The vesicle breaks loose, bringing the particle into the cell.

Exocytosis
A vesicle inside the cell carries a particle to the cell membrane. The membrane of the vesicle sticks to and becomes part of the cell membrane. The particle is forced out of the cell.

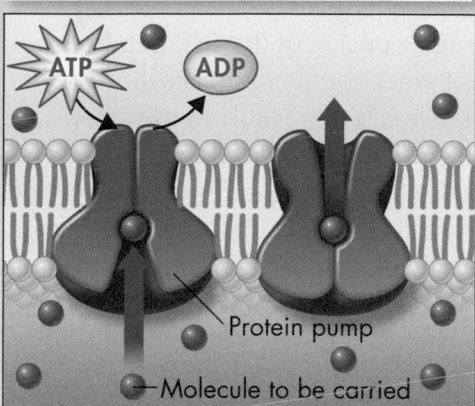

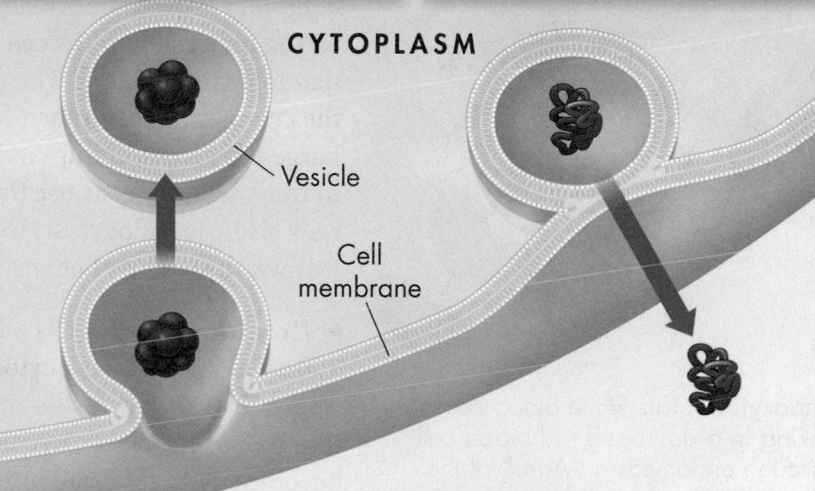

CYTOPLASM

Vesicle

Cell membrane

Protein pump

Molecule to be carried

BUILD Connections

ACTIVE TRANSPORT
Energy from the cell is needed to move particles from an area of lower concentration to an area of higher concentration.

In Your Workbook Do you understand the three kinds of active transport? Go to your workbook for more practice.

Active Transport

Diffusion allows particles to move from the side of the membrane where they are crowded to the side where they are not so crowded. But what happens when the cell needs to move even more particles to the side that is already more concentrated? This takes energy. Active transport is the movement of particles across the cell membrane using energy. The major kinds of active transport are shown in the picture above. Small molecules or ions move across a cell membrane through the work of protein pumps found in the membrane. Larger molecules and big clumps of material can also be moved across the cell membrane by processes known as endocytosis and exocytosis.

Moving Molecules Small molecules and ions are carried across membranes by proteins that act like pumps. Many cells use protein pumps to move calcium, potassium, and sodium ions across cell membranes. Changes in protein shape seem to be an important part of the pumping process. Chemical energy causes a change in the shape of the protein, so the protein binds the substance on one side of the membrane, then lets it go on the other side. A lot of the energy used by cells in their daily activities goes toward keeping active transport working. Using energy lets cells move substances to concentrated areas, even when diffusion might tend to move these substances in the opposite direction.

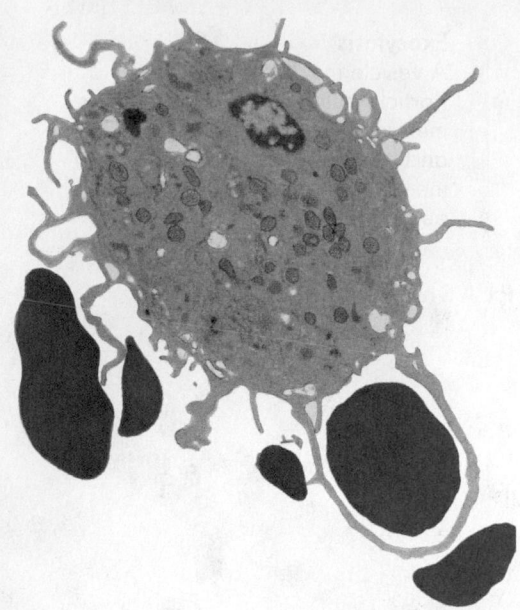

Endocytosis This white blood cell is taking in a damaged red blood cell through endocytosis. "Arms" of the white blood cell's cell membrane have completely surrounded the red blood cell (TEM 5300×).

Moving Larger Particles Larger molecules and even solid clumps of material cannot pass through protein pumps. They must be moved from one side of the membrane to the other through vesicles. Two types of active transport that use vesicles to move larger particles are endocytosis and exocytosis.

▶ *Endocytosis* Endocytosis (en doh sy TOH sis) is the process of taking material into the cell through a pocket of the cell membrane that folds into the cell. The pocket pinches off and breaks loose from the cell membrane. It then forms a vesicle or vacuole in the cytoplasm. Large molecules, clumps of food, and even whole cells can be taken up in this way. Amoebas use this method for taking in food. White blood cells also use endocytosis to "eat" damaged cells. Taking in material in this way uses a lot of energy. It is a form of active transport.

▶ *Exocytosis* Many cells release large amounts of material through a process known as exocytosis (ek soh sy TOH sis). Exocytosis is the opposite of endocytosis—materials leave the cell instead of coming into it. During exocytosis, the membrane of a vesicle sticks to and becomes part of the cell membrane. As the membranes fuse, the contents of the vesicle are forced out of the cell. Cells use exocytosis to get rid of wastes and to give off chemical signals.

🔑 **Key Question** What is active transport?
The movement of materials from an area of lower concentration to an area of higher concentration is known as active transport. Active transport requires energy.

CHECK Understanding

Apply Vocabulary
Use the highlighted words from the lesson to complete each sentence correctly.

1. Diffusion of particles through protein channels is called _____.

2. Osmosis produces a force known as _____.

Critical Thinking

3. Compare and Contrast How is endocytosis similar to exocytosis? How are they different?

4. Apply Concepts What would happen to the cells of a saltwater plant if the plant were placed in fresh water?

5. Write to Learn Answer the second clue of the mystery.

MYSTERY CLUE

As Michelle ran, she sweated. Sweating made her lose salts from her bloodstream. As she drank more water, the concentration of salts and minerals in her bloodstream got lower. How do you think these things made Michelle's problem worse? (**Hint:** See p. 176.)

 BIOLOGY.com ▸ Search (Lesson 7.3) GO • Lesson Assessment

7.4 Homeostasis and Cells

MD | CLG 3.1.2 Homeostasis, 3.2.1 Processes and Functions. SPI 1.5.9 Synthesize Ideas.

The Cell as an Organism

It is sometimes hard to remember that all living things have certain characteristics in common. All living things are made of cells. They all have the same kinds of organelles. But, clearly, living things are not all the same.

Sometimes, a single cell is the whole organism. In fact, there are many more single-celled organisms on Earth than there are organisms with many cells. Just like other living things, single-celled organisms must maintain **homeostasis**—relatively constant internal physical and chemical conditions. To stay in this state single-celled organisms grow, respond to the environment, change food or sunlight into useful energy, and reproduce.

Single-celled organisms include both prokaryotes and eukaryotes. Prokaryotes, especially bacteria, are very adaptable. They live almost everywhere—in the soil, on leaves, in the ocean, in the air, and even within the human body. Many eukaryotes also spend their lives as single cells. Some types of algae are single cells found in oceans, lakes, and streams around the world. Yeasts, or unicellular fungi, have an important job breaking down nutrients, making them available for other living things.

Key Question How do individual cells maintain homeostasis?
To maintain homeostasis, unicellular organisms grow, respond to the environment, change food or sunlight into useful energy, and reproduce.

Single-Celled Life Single-celled organisms, like this freshwater protozoan, must be able to carry out all of the functions necessary for life (SEM 600×).

Key Questions

How do individual cells maintain homeostasis?

How do the cells of multicellular organisms work together to maintain homeostasis?

BUILD Understanding

Preview Visuals Before you read, look at the Levels of Organization image at the top of the next page. Then write two questions you have about the figure. As you read, write answers to your questions.

In Your Workbook Go to your workbook for help answering your questions. Complete the preview visuals activity for Lesson 7.4.

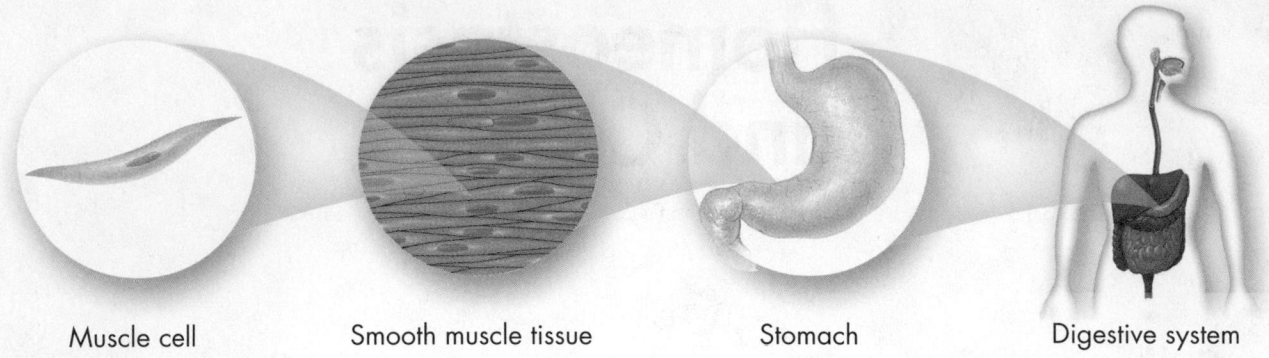

Muscle cell   Smooth muscle tissue   Stomach   Digestive system

Levels of Organization From simplest to most complex, the levels of organization in a many-celled organism are cells, tissues, organs, and organ systems.

Multicellular Life

The cells of human beings and other many-celled organisms do not live on their own. They need other cells to survive. Like the members of a winning baseball team, they must work together. In baseball, each player plays a different position. To play the game well, players communicate with one another, sending and receiving signals. Cells in a many-celled organism work the same way. They become specialized for certain jobs. They communicate with one another to maintain homeostasis.

Cell Specialization The cells of a many-celled organism are specialized. Different kinds of cells have different jobs. Some cells are specialized for movement. Others must react to the environment. Still others must make substances that the organism needs. No matter what its job, each specialized cell helps the organism maintain homeostasis. For example, cells that line the air passages in your lungs have cilia (SIL ee uh). These hairlike parts sweep dust away to keep your lungs clean. These specialized cells are packed with mitochondria that make the chemical energy that powers their cilia.

Levels of Organization The specialized cells of many-celled organisms are organized into tissues. A **tissue** is a group of similar cells that that work together to do a particular job. Many tasks in the body are too complicated to be carried out by just one kind of tissue. In these cases, groups of tissues work together as an **organ.** For example, each muscle in your body is an organ. Within a muscle, however, there are nervous tissues and connective tissues. Each kind of tissue has a special job that helps the organ do its job. A group of organs that work together to do a job is called an **organ system.** For example, the stomach, pancreas, and intestines work together as the digestive system to break down food and take up nutrients.

Cellular Communication Cells in a large organism use chemical signals to communicate. These chemical signals are passed from one cell to another. They can speed up or slow down the activities of the cells that receive them. They can even cause a cell to change what it is doing in an instant.

In order to communicate, certain cells form connections, or cellular junctions, to neighboring cells. Some of these junctions hold cells together firmly. Others allow small molecules carrying chemical messages or signals to pass from one cell to the next. To "understand" one of these chemical signals, a cell must have a receptor that sticks to the chemical signal. Some receptors are on the cell membrane. Other kinds of receptors are inside the cytoplasm.

The chemical signals sent by different kinds of cells can cause important changes in cells and tissues. For example, the signal that causes heart muscle cells to contract begins in a place known as the pacemaker. Ions carry the signal from cell to cell through a special connection known as a gap junction. This junction can cause the millions of heart muscle cells to contract as one in a single heartbeat.

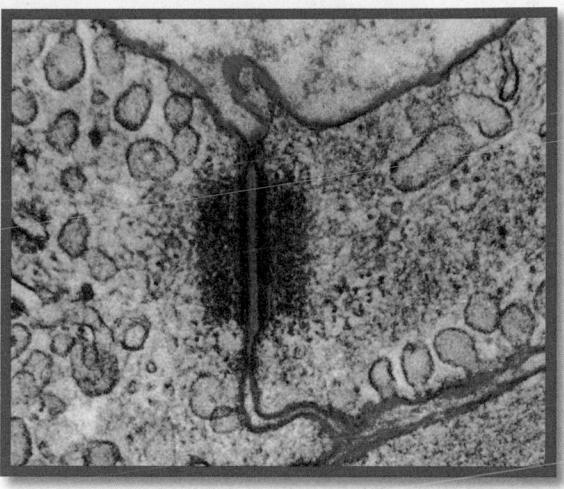

Cellular Junctions Some junctions, like the one seen in brown in this micrograph of capillary cells in the gas bladder of a toadfish, hold cells together in tight formations (TEM 21,600×).

🔑 **Key Question** How do the cells of multicellular organisms work together to maintain homeostasis?
The cells of many-celled organisms have specialized jobs and communicate with one another to maintain homeostasis.

CHECK Understanding

Apply Vocabulary
Use the highlighted words from the lesson to complete each sentence correctly.

1. _____ is the relatively constant internal physical and chemical conditions of a cell or organism.

2. Many similar specialized cells working together make up a(n) _____.

3. Many organs make up a(n) _____.

Critical Thinking

4. **Review** What is homeostasis?

5. **Explain** What do unicellular organisms do to maintain homeostasis?

6. **Predict** Using what you know about the ways muscles move, predict which organelles would be most common in muscle cells.

7. **Apply Concepts** The contractile vacuole is an organelle found in some single-celled organisms. Contractile vacuoles pump out fresh water that builds up in the cell from osmosis. How is this activity an example of the way the cell maintains homeostasis?

8. **Sequence** List the different levels of organization in many-celled organisms from most complex to least complex.

9. **Write to Learn** Write a paragraph that explains how cells in a many-celled organism are like teammates on a sports team.

 CLG 3.1.2 Homeostasis, 3.2.1 Processes and Functions. SPI 1.3.1 Use Equipment, 1.3.3 Safe Handling of Materials, 1.4.8 Use Models, 1.5.8 Compare, 1.5.9 Synthesize Ideas.

Pre-Lab: Detecting Diffusion

Problem How can you determine whether solutes are diffusing across a membrane?

Materials 400-mL beaker, 25-mL graduated cylinder, 1% starch solution, plastic sandwich bag, twist tie, iodine solution, forceps

Lab Manual Chapter 7 Lab

Skills Focus Use Models, Analyze Data, Infer

Connect to the Big idea The cell membrane forms a thin flexible barrier between a cell and its surroundings. The cell membrane controls what enters the cell and what leaves the cell. Diffusion is the process responsible for much of the movement across a cell membrane. During diffusion, solutes move from an area of high concentration to an area of lower concentration. When water is the molecule that is diffusing, the process is called osmosis. Proteins embedded in the membrane can facilitate the diffusion of many particles, including water. In this lab, you will model the diffusion of small molecules.

Background Questions

a. Review What does it mean to say that a membrane is selectively permeable?

b. Explain Does the movement of molecules stop when the concentration of a solute is equal on both sides of a membrane? Explain.

c. Compare and Contrast What is the main difference between passive transport and active transport?

Pre-Lab Questions

Preview the procedure in the lab manual.

1. Draw Conclusions How will you know whether starch has diffused across the membrane?

2. Draw Conclusions How will you know whether iodine has diffused across the membrane?

3. Use Analogies How is a window screen similar to a cell membrane?

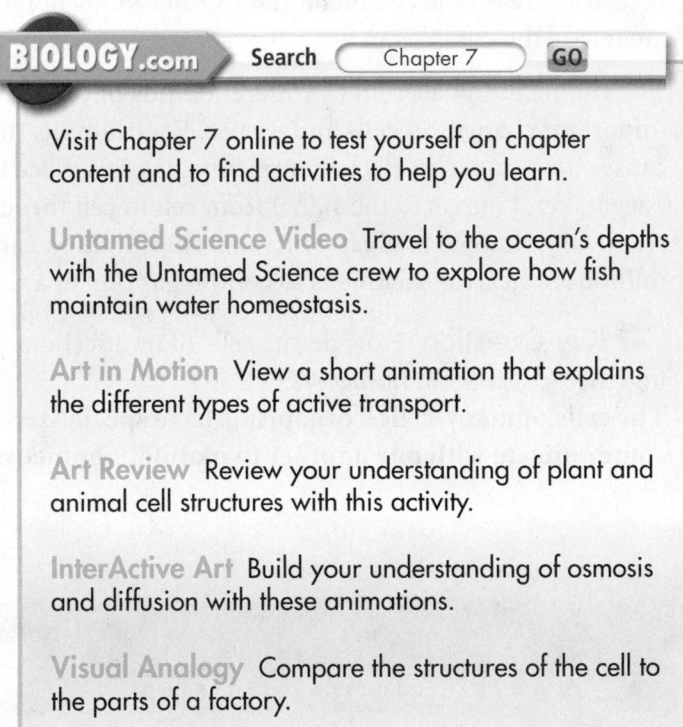

BIOLOGY.com   Search   ⌐ Chapter 7 ¬   GO

Visit Chapter 7 online to test yourself on chapter content and to find activities to help you learn.

Untamed Science Video Travel to the ocean's depths with the Untamed Science crew to explore how fish maintain water homeostasis.

Art in Motion View a short animation that explains the different types of active transport.

Art Review Review your understanding of plant and animal cell structures with this activity.

InterActive Art Build your understanding of osmosis and diffusion with these animations.

Visual Analogy Compare the structures of the cell to the parts of a factory.

Tutor Tube Hear suggestions from the tutor for help in remembering cell structures.

7 CHAPTER Summary

7.1 Life Is Cellular

- The cell theory states that (1) all living things are made up of cells, (2) cells are the basic units of structure and function in living things, and (3) new cells come from existing cells.

- Most microscopes use lenses to magnify the image of an object by focusing light or electrons.

- Prokaryotic cells do not have a nucleus. In eukaryotic cells, the nucleus holds the cell's genetic material.

cell (p. 160)   eukaryote (p. 162)
cell theory (p. 160)   prokaryote (p. 162)
nucleus (p. 162)

7.2 Cell Structure

- The nucleus holds nearly all of the cell's DNA.

- Vacuoles store water, salts, proteins, and sugars. Lysosomes break down old organelles and large molecules so that they can be used by the cell. The cytoskeleton helps the cell move and keep its shape.

- Proteins are put together on ribosomes.

- Proteins that will leave the cell and many kinds of membrane proteins are made on the rough ER. The Golgi apparatus then changes, sorts, and packages proteins for storage in the cell or for leaving the cell.

- Chloroplasts take the energy from sunlight and change it into chemical energy stored in food in a process called photosynthesis. Mitochondria change the chemical energy of food into compounds that are easier for the cell to use.

- The cell membrane keeps track of what enters and leaves the cell. It also protects and supports the cell.

cytoplasm (p. 164)   endoplasmic
organelle (p. 164)   reticulum (p. 168)
vacuole (p. 166)   Golgi apparatus (p. 169)
lysosome (p. 166)   chloroplast (p. 170)
cytoskeleton (p. 167)   mitochondrion (p. 170)
ribosome (p. 168)   lipid bilayer (p. 171)

7.3 Cell Transport

- Passive transport is the movement of materials across the cell membrane without using energy. Diffusion, facilitated diffusion, and osmosis are kinds of passive transport.

- Active transport uses energy. It is the movement of materials from an area of lower concentration to an area of higher concentration. Protein pumps, endocytosis, and exocytosis are kinds of active transport.

diffusion (p. 176)
facilitated diffusion (p. 177)
osmosis (p. 177)
osmotic pressure (p. 178)

7.4 Homeostasis and Cells

- To maintain homeostasis, single-celled organisms grow, respond to the environment, get and use energy, and reproduce.

- The cells of living things that have many cells become specialized for particular jobs. These cells must communicate with one another to maintain homeostasis.

homeostasis (p. 181)
tissue (p. 182)
organ (p. 182)
organ system (p. 182)

Assess the Big idea
Cellular Basis of Life, Homeostasis

Write an answer to the question below.

Q: How are cell structures adapted to their functions?

Constructed Response

Write an answer to each of the questions below. The answer to each question should be one or two paragraphs long. To help you begin, read the **Hints** below each of the questions.

1. **Infer** Prokaryotic cells have some structures in common with plant cells and some structures in common with animal cells. Which two types of cells are MOST likely more closely related to one another? Explain your reasoning.

   Hint Prokaryotic cells have cell walls, and some can carry out photosynthesis like plant cells can. However, they do not have a nucleus.

   Hint Plant and animal cells have organelles that are enclosed by membranes, which prokaryotic cells do not have.

2. **Analyze Concepts** What happens to lipids when they are dropped into water? How does this action explain the structure of cell membranes?

   Hint Lipids have a head that mixes well with water and a tail that mixes well with oil.

   Hint Cell membranes are made up of lipid bilayers.

Foundations for Learning Wrap-Up

Use the index cards you prepared when you started the chapter as a tool to help you organize what you learned about the structure and function of cell parts.

Activity 1 Recall that different kinds of cells can have different cell parts. Sort the cards into four piles. The first pile should be cell parts that all cells have. The second pile should be cell parts that only animal cells have. The third pile should be cell parts that only plant cells and animal cells have. The fourth pile should be cell parts that only plant cells and bacteria cells (prokaryotes) have. Label the bottom right-hand corner of each card with the letters *A*, *P*, and *B* (animal, plant, and bacteria) accordingly to show which type of cell has each cell part.

Activity 2 Using metal or plastic rings and a piece of cardboard, combine your cards into a flip chart as shown below. Work with a partner to write a lesson on cell parts that uses the flip chart to explain important concepts from the chapter. Then use the flip chart to present your lesson to a classmate.

7.1 Life Is Cellular

Understand Key Concepts

1. In many cells, the structure that controls the cell's activities is the
   a. cell membrane.   c. nucleolus.
   b. organelle.   d. nucleus.

2. Cells can be very different in size, shape, and the types of organelles they have. However, at some point all cells have DNA and
   a. a cell wall.   c. mitochondria
   b. a cell membrane. d. a nucleus.

> **Test-Taking Tip**
>
> **Watch for Qualifiers** When you are answering a question, watch out for words such as *all*, *none*, *always*, and *not*. In question 2, notice the word *all*. This question is asking what part ALL cells have in common. You know animal cells do not have a cell wall and prokaryotes do not have a nucleus or organelles. Mitochondria are organelles. All cells must have a cell membrane. The correct answer is b.

3. What three statements make up the cell theory?

Think Critically

4. **Infer** How did the invention of the microscope help scientists come up with the cell theory?

7.2 Cell Structure

Understand Key Concepts

5. In eukaryotic cells, the cell's genetic information is found in the
   a. ribosomes.   c. nucleus.
   b. lysosomes.   d. cell membrane.

6. The organelles that break down lipids, sugars, and proteins into small molecules that can be used by the cell are called
   a. vacuoles.   c. ribosomes.
   b. lysosomes.   d. microfilaments.

7. Cell membranes are made up of
   a. lipid bilayers.   c. carbohydrates.
   b. mitochondria.   d. ribosomes.

8. What is the function of a ribosome?

Think Critically

9. **Infer** The pancreas is an organ found in many animals. It makes enzymes that are used by other parts of the digestive system. Enzymes are proteins that help speed up reactions in the body. Which type of cell structure(s) might produce those enzymes? Explain your answer.

10. **Classify** For each of the following, tell whether the structure is found only in eukaryotes or in both eukaryotes and prokaryotes: cell membrane, mitochondria, ribosome, Golgi apparatus, nucleus, cytoplasm, and DNA.

7.3 Cell Transport

Understand Key Concepts

11. The movement of water molecules across a membrane that does not let all materials pass through it is known as
    a. exocytosis.   c. endocytosis.
    b. pumping.   d. osmosis.

12. Can other substances besides water undergo osmosis? Explain.

Think Critically

13. **Apply Concepts** What would happen to a sample of your red blood cells if they were placed in a hypotonic solution? Explain.

7 CHECK Understanding

7.4 Homeostasis and Cells

Understand Key Concepts

14. Which of the following is true of ALL single-celled organisms?
  a. They are all prokaryotes.
  b. They are all bacteria.
  c. They all reproduce.
  d. They all have a nucleus.

Think Critically

15. Infer Would you expect skin cells to contain more or less mitochondria than muscle cells? Explain your answer.

16. Infer Artificial pacemakers are devices that help keep heart muscle cells contracting at a steady rate. If a person needs an artificial pacemaker, what does that mean about his or her heart cells' ability to send and receive signals?

Connecting Concepts

Use Science Graphics

Use the data table to answer questions 17 and 18.

Cell Sizes	
Cell	**Approximate Diameter**
Escherichia coli (bacterium)	0.5–0.8 μm
Human erythrocyte (red blood cell)	6–8 μm
Human ovum (egg cell)	100 μm
Saccharomyces cerevisiae (yeast)	5–10 μm
Streptococcus pneumoniae (bacterium)	0.5–1.3 μm

17. Classify Tell whether each of the cells listed is prokaryotic or eukaryotic.

18. Infer *Chlamydomonas reinhardtii* is a single-celled organism with an approximate diameter of 10 μm. Based on the information given here, do you think it is a prokaryote or a eukaryote? Explain your answer.

solve the CHAPTER MYSTERY

DEATH BY...WATER?

During the race, Michelle drank plenty of water. However, she didn't replace the salts she lost in her sweat. As a result, her blood became hypotonic. Osmotic pressure led the cells in her brain (and throughout her body) to swell.

As Michelle's blood became less concentrated, cells in her brain sent chemical signals to her kidneys to stop removing salts from her bloodstream. However, she continued to sweat. Sweating caused her to continue to lose salt through her skin.

By the end of the race, Michelle had lost a lot of salt and minerals. She had taken in so much water that homeostasis had broken down. Her cells were damaged by osmotic pressure that was unbalanced.

When Michelle went to the hospital, the doctors found that she had hyponatremia, or water intoxication. Left untreated, this condition can lead to death.

1. Relate Cause and Effect When a person sweats, water and salts are lost from the body. Michelle drank water but did not replace salts. How did this affect her cells?

2. Infer Imagine that Michelle drank both water and sports drinks containing the salts she lost. Do you think she would have felt better or worse? Explain.

3. Infer Do you think that hyponatremia happens because of osmosis or active transport? Explain your reasoning.

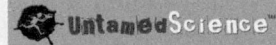 **Never Stop Exploring Your World.** Michelle's mysterious illness is just the beginning. Take a video field trip with the ecogeeks of Untamed Science to see where the mystery leads.

Standardized Test Practice for Maryland

Multiple Choice

1. Animal cells have all of the following EXCEPT
   A mitochondria.
   B chloroplasts.
   C a nucleus.
   D a cell membrane. CLG 3.4.2

2. The nucleus includes all of the following structures EXCEPT
   A cytoplasm.   C DNA.
   B a nuclear envelope.   D a nucleolus. CLG 3.2.1

3. The human brain is an example of a(n)
   A cell.
   B tissue.
   C organ.
   D organ system. CLG 3.2.1

4. Which cell structures are sometimes found attached to the endoplasmic reticulum?
   A chloroplasts
   B nuclei
   C mitochondria
   D ribosomes CLG 3.2.1

5. Which process always involves the movement of materials from inside the cell to outside the cell?
   A diffusion
   B exocytosis
   C endocytosis
   D osmosis CLG 3.2.1

6. Which of the following is an example of active transport?
   A facilitated diffusion
   B osmosis
   C diffusion
   D endocytosis CLG 3.2.1

7. The difference between prokaryotic and eukaryotic cells involves the presence of
   A a nucleus.
   B genetic material in the form of DNA.
   C chloroplasts.
   D a cell membrane. CLG 3.4.2

Questions 8 and 9

In an experiment, scientists placed plant cells in solutions that had different concentrations of the sugar sucrose. Then the scientists measured the rate at which the cells absorbed sucrose from the solution. The results are shown in the graph below.

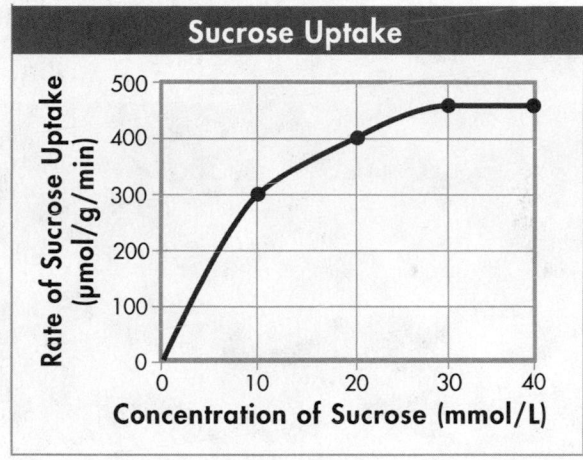

8. The graph shows that overall, sucrose
   A cannot be absorbed by plant cells.
   B uptake increased as concentration increased.
   C uptake decreased as concentration increased.
   D uptake stayed the same as concentration increased. SPI 1.4.2

9. Based on the graph, the rate of sucrose uptake
   A increased at a constant rate from 0 to 30 mmol/L.
   B decreased at varying rates from 0 to 30 mmol/L.
   C was less at 25 mmol/L than at 5 mmol/L.
   D was constant between 30 and 40 mmol/L. SPI 1.4.2

Open-Ended Response

10. What would you expect to happen if you placed a typical cell in fresh water? CLG 3.2.2

If You Have Trouble With . . .

Question	1	2	3	4	5	6	7	8	9	10
See Lesson	7.2	7.2	7.4	7.2	7.3	7.3	7.1	7.3	7.3	7.3

8 Photosynthesis

Cellular Basis of Life

Q: How do plants and other organisms capture energy from the sun?

Leaf cells from Canadian pondweed (Elodea canadensis) (LM 2430×)

BIOLOGY.com > Search [Chapter 8] **GO** • Chapter Mystery

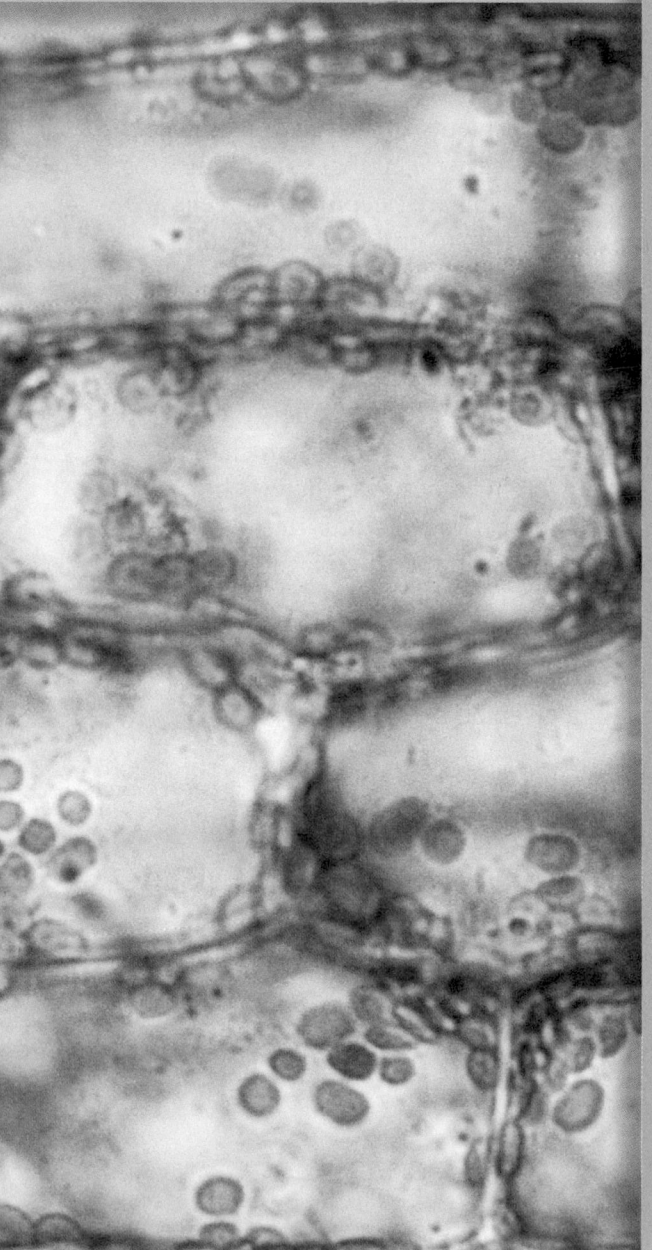

CHAPTER
MYSTERY

OUT OF THIN AIR?

When a tiny seed grows into a huge tree, where does all the extra mass come from? More than 300 years ago, a Flemish doctor named Jan van Helmont decided to find out. He chose a young willow tree that weighed just 2 kilograms. He planted it in a pot with 90 kilograms of dry soil and placed it in bright sunlight. He watered the plant as needed. Five years later, he took the tree from the pot and weighed it. It weighed about 77 kilograms. Where did the extra 75 kilograms come from? Did it come from the soil, the water—or right out of thin air?

Read for Mystery Clues As you read this chapter, look for clues to help you discover where the willow tree's extra mass came from. Then, solve the mystery at the end of the chapter.

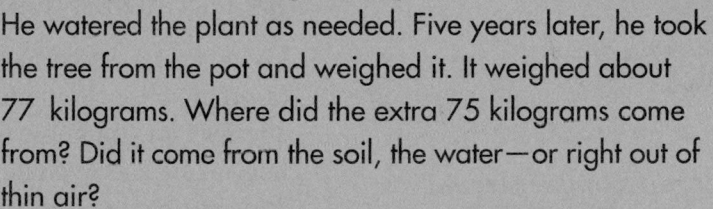

FOUNDATIONS
for Learning

Plant cells use light energy to make useful chemicals. These reactions take place in special parts of the cell. Before you read the chapter, label index cards with the words *water*, *carbon dioxide*, *oxygen*, *sugars*, and *light*. Label one sheet of paper as shown. At the end of the chapter are two activities that use the cards and sheets of paper to help answer the question: How do plants and other organisms capture energy from the sun?

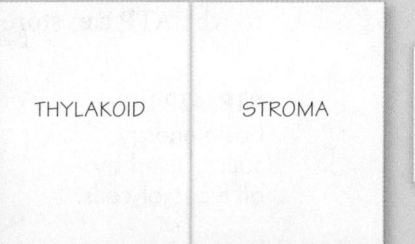

THYLAKOID   STROMA

Sugars

- Untamed Science Video   • Flash Cards

8.1 Energy and Life

MD CLG 3.1.3 Matter and Energy, 3.2.1 Processes and Functions. SPI 1.5.2 Communicate Information.

Key Questions

🔑 Why is ATP useful to cells?

🔑 What happens during photosynthesis?

BUILD Understanding

Compare/Contrast Table As you read, create a table that compares autotrophs and heterotrophs. Think about how they get energy. Include in your table a few examples of each type of living thing.

In Your Workbook Go to your workbook to learn more about making a compare/contrast table. Complete the compare/contrast table for Lesson 8.1.

Chemical Energy

Energy is the ability to do work. Nearly everything you do takes energy. Lights, radios, and computers all use electrical energy to run. When you toast marshmallows on a campfire, you are using heat energy to warm the food. A car runs on fuel—the chemical energy in gasoline. All these things need energy to work.

Living things need energy, too. It takes plenty of energy to play soccer or other sports. Sometimes it is not as easy to tell that something uses energy. Did you know that even when you are sleeping, your cells are busy using energy? They are using energy to build new molecules and get rid of wastes. Without the ability to get and use energy, cells would die.

Energy Changes Form Light, heat, and electricity are just three forms of energy. Chemical energy is another form of energy. Chemical energy is the energy stored in chemical bonds. Energy can change from one form to another. When you light a candle, the wax burns. Chemical bonds between carbon and hydrogen atoms in the wax are broken. New bonds form between these atoms and oxygen from the air. What you get are new molecules of carbon dioxide and water. The bonds in the new molecules store less energy than before. The extra chemical energy that came from the old bonds changes form. The extra energy becomes the heat and light given off by the candle's flame.

ATP Living things use chemical energy. One of the most important chemicals that cells use to store and give off energy is called **adenosine triphosphate** (uh DEN uh seen try FAHS fayt). It's known as **ATP** for short. ATP is made up of adenine, a sugar called ribose, and three phosphate groups. The phosphate groups are the key to why ATP can store and release energy.

ATP ATP is the basic energy source used by all types of cells.

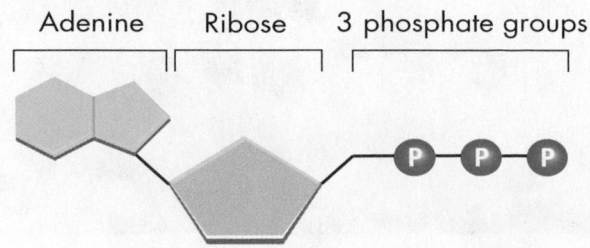

Adenine | Ribose | 3 phosphate groups

Storing Energy Adenosine diphosphate (ADP) is similar to ATP. However, ADP has only two phosphate groups instead of three. This difference is the key to how living things store energy. When a cell has extra energy, it can store small amounts of it by adding a phosphate group to ADP molecules, which turns ADP to ATP.

Releasing Energy Cells can give off the energy stored in ATP by breaking the chemical bonds between the second and third phosphate groups. A cell can add or subtract these phosphate groups whenever it needs to store or use energy.

Key Question Why is ATP useful to cells?
ATP can easily release and store energy by breaking and re-forming the bonds between its phosphate groups.

Using Chemical Energy Cells use ATP in many ways. For example, cells use it to power active transport. ATP provides the energy needed to move material into and out of many cells. ATP also helps proteins in muscles to slide closer together. This motion makes muscles flex. Cells that crawl, twist, and swim depend on ATP as well. Energy from ATP powers many other important events, such as the making of proteins and responses to chemical signals outside of the cell.

Short-Term Storage ATP is so useful that you might think cells would be packed with it. In fact, most cells have only a small amount—enough to last for a few seconds of activity. The reason is that ATP is great for giving off a small amount of energy very quickly. But, it is not good for storing large amounts for a long time. The sugar glucose is much better for energy storage. A single glucose molecule stores more than 90 times the energy of a molecule of ATP. So, it makes sense for cells to store energy in the form of glucose. Cells can then use the stored glucose to make ATP and ADP as needed.

ATP Comes From Food

Once cells use up their supply of ATP, they must somehow make more of it. So, where do living things get the energy they use to make ATP? The simple answer is that it comes from the chemical compounds that we call food. But, different living things get their food from different sources.

BUILD Vocabulary

adenosine triphosphate (ATP)
one of the principal chemical compounds that living things use to store and release energy

PREFIXES
The prefix *di-* means "two" and the prefix *tri-* means "three." A molecule of adenosine *tri*phosphate (ATP) has three phosphate groups, while adenosine *di*phosphate (ADP) has only two.

BUILD Connections

MOLECULAR BATTERY

When a phosphate group is added to an ADP molecule, it makes ATP. ADP has some energy, but not as much as ATP. ADP is like a partially charged battery. It can be fully charged by adding a phosphate group.

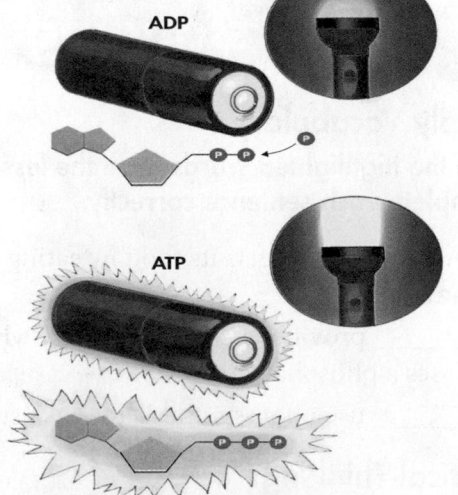

ADP

ATP

In Your Workbook Go to your workbook to learn more about how an ATP molecule stores energy.

heterotroph
a living thing that gets food by consuming, or eating, other living things

autotroph
a living thing that can capture energy from sunlight or chemicals to make its own food

photosynthesis
the process by which plants and other autotrophs use light energy to convert water and carbon dioxide into oxygen and high-energy carbohydrates such as sugars and starches

WORD ROOTS
Photosynthesis comes from the Greek words *photo*, meaning "light," and *synthesis*, meaning "putting together." Thus, *photosynthesis* means "using light to put something together."

Heterotrophs Eat Food Living things that get food by eating other living things are known as **heterotrophs.** Some heterotrophs get their food by eating plants, such as grasses. Others, such as the cheetah shown at right, get food by eating other animals. Still other heterotrophs—mushrooms, for example—get food by breaking down the tissues of dead things.

Autotrophs Make Food The energy in nearly all food molecules first came from the sun. Plants, algae, and some bacteria can use light energy from the sun to make their own food. Living things that make their own food are called **autotrophs.** All life on Earth depends on autotrophs to get energy from sunlight and store it in the molecules that make up food. The process by which autotrophs use the energy of sunlight to produce high-energy carbohydrates—sugars and starches—that can be used as food is known as **photosynthesis.**

Key Question What happens during photosynthesis?
During photosynthesis, plants change the energy of sunlight into chemical energy stored in the bonds of carbohydrates.

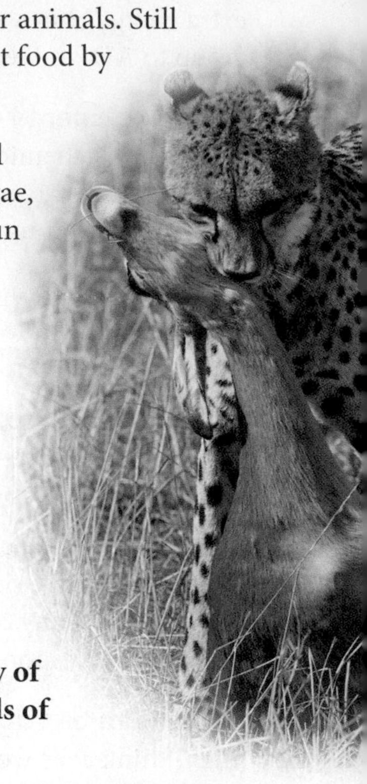

Autotrophs and Heterotrophs
Grass uses sunlight to make food. Cheetahs, in turn, get their energy by eating organisms who eat the grass.

CHECK Understanding

Apply Vocabulary
Use the highlighted words from the lesson to complete each sentence correctly.

1. An animal that gets its food by eating other animals is a(n) _____.
2. _____ provides a cell with energy when it loses a phosphate group.
3. _____ use photosynthesis to make sugars.

Critical Thinking

4. **Explain** Why are decomposers, such as mushrooms, heterotrophs and not autotrophs?

5. **Write to Learn** Answer the first clue of the mystery. In your answer explain how autotrophs get food and how that might lead to an increase in mass.

MYSTERY CLUE

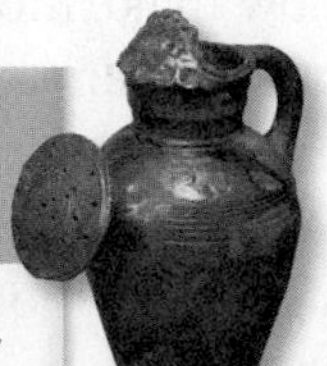

Like all plants, the willow tree van Helmont planted was an autotroph. How might its ability to use the sun's energy to make food help it gain mass? (**Hint:** See p. 193.)

8.2 Photosynthesis: An Overview

MD CLG 3.1.3 Matter and Energy, 3.2.1 Processes and Functions. SPI 1.3.1 Use Equipment, 1.5.2 Communicate Information.

Chlorophyll and Chloroplasts

Our lives, and the lives of nearly every living thing on Earth, depend on the sun and photosynthesis. For photosynthesis to take place, autotrophs must capture light energy from the sun.

Light Energy from the sun travels to Earth in the form of light. Sunlight, which our eyes see as "white" light, is actually a mixture of different wavelengths. Many of these wavelengths are visible to our eyes. Our eyes see the different wavelengths of visible light as different colors: shades of red, orange, yellow, green, blue, indigo, and violet.

Pigments Plants gather the sun's energy with light-absorbing molecules called pigments. The most important pigment in plants is chlorophyll (KLAWR uh fil). Out of all the different colors of light, the chlorophyll found in plants absorbs blue-violet light and red light the best. Chlorophyll does not absorb green light very well. Leaves look green because they reflect green light.

🔑 **Key Question** What role do pigments play in the process of photosynthesis?
Living things that carry out photosynthesis use pigments to get energy from sunlight.

Chloroplasts In plants, photosynthesis takes place inside organelles called chloroplasts. These organelles hold many flat, bag-shaped membranes called **thylakoids** (THY luh koydz). Thylakoids are connected to one another and arranged in stacks. These stacks are called grana. Chlorophyll and other pigments are found in these thylakoid membranes. The liquid-filled space around the thylakoids is known as the **stroma.** The picture below shows what makes up a chloroplast.

Key Questions

🔑 **What role do pigments play in the process of photosynthesis?**

🔑 **What are electron carrier molecules?**

🔑 **What are the reactants and products of photosynthesis?**

BUILD Understanding

KWL Chart Make a chart with three columns labeled What I **K**now, What I **W**ant to Know, and What I **L**earned. Before you read the lesson, fill in the first two columns. Complete the last column as you read the lesson.

In Your Workbook Go to your workbook to learn more about making a KWL chart. Complete the KWL chart for Lesson 8.2.

The Chloroplast In plants, photosynthesis takes place inside chloroplasts.

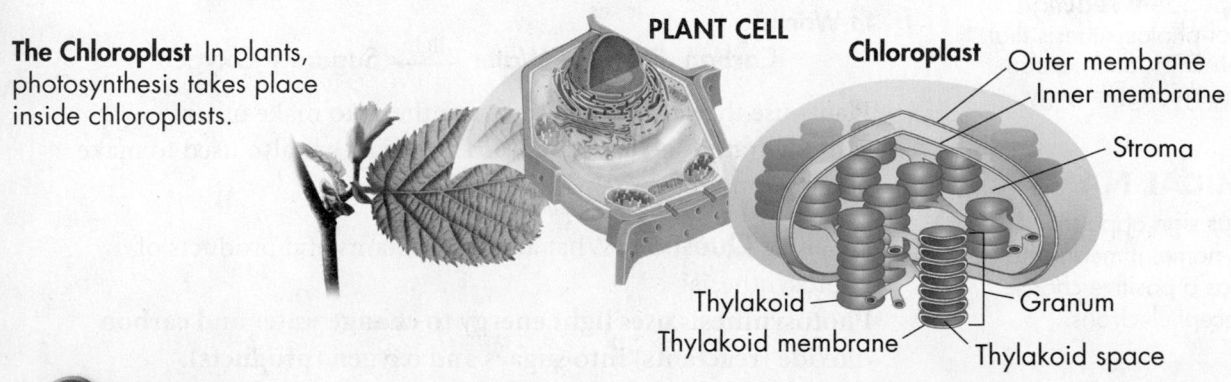

PLANT CELL

Chloroplast
— Outer membrane
— Inner membrane
— Stroma
Thylakoid —
Thylakoid membrane —
— Granum
— Thylakoid space

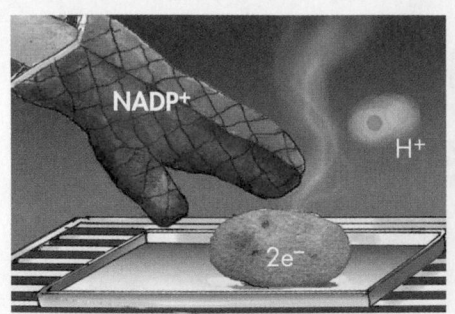

High-Energy Electrons

Light is a form of energy. Anything that absorbs light takes in energy. When chlorophyll takes in light, much of that energy is moved directly to electrons in the chlorophyll. The energy levels of the electrons go up. A stream of these high-energy electrons is what makes photosynthesis work.

These high-energy electrons cannot keep their energy for long on their own. They need a special carrier. Plant cells use molecules to carry high-energy electrons from chlorophyll to other places. One of these carrier molecules is **NADP⁺** (nicotinamide adenine dinucleotide phosphate). It accepts and holds two high-energy electrons, along with a hydrogen ion (H⁺). This process changes NADP⁺ into NADPH. The NADPH carries the electrons to other parts of the cell. There, the electrons and their energy can be used to help build useful molecules, such as sugars.

🔑 **Key Question** What are electron carrier molecules?
Electron carrier molecules are compounds that can transfer a pair of high-energy electrons, along with most of their energy, to another molecule.

A Summary of Photosynthesis

Photosynthesis has many steps. It usually has 6-carbon sugars ($C_6H_{12}O_6$) as the final product. All of the steps of photosynthesis can be summed up in the following equation:

In Symbols:
$$6CO_2 + 6H_2O \xrightarrow{\text{light}} C_6H_{12}O_6 + 6O_2$$

In Words:
$$\text{Carbon dioxide} + \text{Water} \xrightarrow{\text{light}} \text{Sugars} + \text{Oxygen}$$

Plants use the sugars from photosynthesis to make other carbohydrates, such as starches. The sugars are also used to make other compounds, such as proteins and lipids.

🔑 **Key Question** What are the reactants and products of photosynthesis?
Photosynthesis uses light energy to change water and carbon dioxide (reactants) into sugars and oxygen (products).

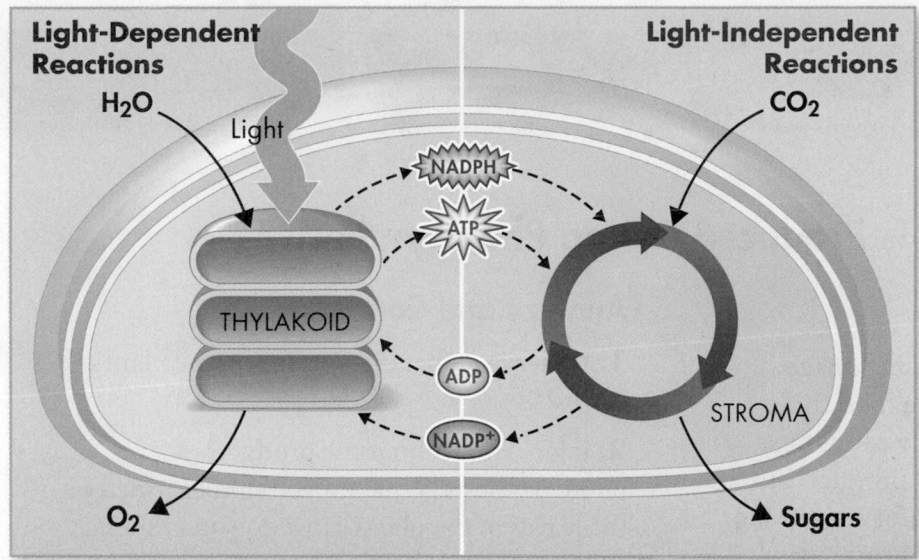

The Stages of Photosynthesis There are two stages of photosynthesis: light-dependent reactions and light-independent reactions.

Light-Dependent Reactions The equation for photosynthesis looks simple, but that is because it does not show all of the smaller steps. In fact, there are two sets of reactions. The first set is the **light-dependent reactions.** They take place in the thylakoids. These reactions need light and light-absorbing pigments to take place. They use energy from sunlight and electrons and hydrogen ions from water to make high-energy ATP and NADPH. Oxygen gas, the oxygen we breathe every day, is also released.

Light-Independent Reactions The second set of reactions in photosynthesis is called the **light-independent reactions.** In this set, plants use the ATP and NADPH made in the light-dependent reactions. They make high-energy sugars out of carbon dioxide from the air. Light-independent reactions do not need light. They take place in the stroma.

✓CHECK Understanding

Apply Vocabulary
Use the highlighted words from the lesson to complete each sentence correctly.

1. The set of reactions that takes place in the stroma are called the _____.
2. The light-dependent reactions need _____, a carrier molecule that is able to accept high-energy electrons and a hydrogen ion.

Critical Thinking

3. Describe the overall process of photosynthesis. Include the reactants and the products.

4. **Write to Learn** Answer the second clue of the mystery. Think about the things that plants need for photosynthesis. Which of these things might cause the plant to gain mass?

MYSTERY CLUE

Van Helmont concluded that water must have supplied the extra mass gained by the tree. In fact, he had only half of the answer. What photosynthesis reactant was he missing in his conclusion? (**Hint:** See p. 196.)

BIOLOGY.com Search (Lesson 8.2) GO • Lesson Assessment

What Waste Product Is Produced During Photosynthesis?

What is a waste product? It is like garbage in your kitchen. You may eat the food that comes out of a jar, but your body cannot use the jar. The empty jar is a waste product. But you might be able to use the jar for something else, like storing leftover soup. During many reactions, cells make waste products as well as needed products. Sometimes these waste products cannot be used by the cell at all. At other times, the waste product is used in another part of the cell or by other cells. In this activity, you will study photosynthesis in a water plant called *Elodea*. You will see one product of photosynthesis. You will decide if it is a waste product for this plant.

① Fill a clear, plastic cup halfway with sodium bicarbonate solution. This solution has carbon dioxide in it.

② **a.** Place a piece of plant in a test tube. Make sure that the cut part of the plant is at the bottom.

  b. Add sodium bicarbonate solution. **CAUTION:** *Be careful with glass.*

③ **a.** Hold your finger over the open end of the test tube.

  b. Turn the test tube over. Lower it to the bottom of the cup. Make sure no air is inside the test tube.

④ Place the cup in bright light.

⑤ Wait 20 minutes.

⑥ Look closely at the leaves. Write down what you see.

Analyze and Conclude

1. Observe What did you see on the plant's leaves?

2. Infer Think about the products of photosynthesis. What do you think formed on the leaves of the plant? How do you know?

3. Draw Conclusions Do you think that the product that formed on the leaves is a waste product? Explain.

4. Infer Think about the reactants of photosynthesis. What do you think happened to the carbon dioxide in the sodium bicarbonate solution?

5. Apply Concepts Which plant organelle carries out photosynthesis? How can you tell that this plant's cells have that organelle?

In Your Workbook Get more help for this activity in your workbook.

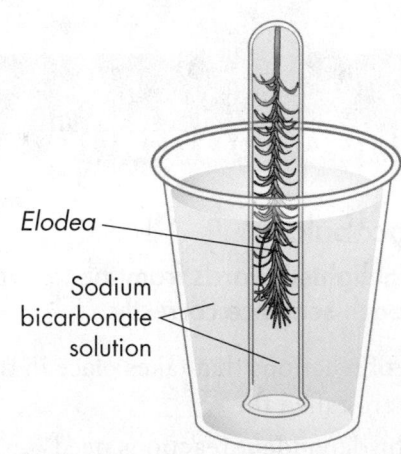

Elodea

Sodium bicarbonate solution

8.3 The Process of Photosynthesis

MD CLG 3.1.3 Matter and Energy, 3.2.1 Processes and Functions, 3.2.2 Changes in Metabolic Activity, 3.5.1 Factors Influencing Ecosystems. SPI 1.5.5 Create and Interpret Graphics, 1.5.8 Compare.

The Light-Dependent Reactions: Making ATP and NADPH

Remember that the steps of photosynthesis are divided into two sets. They are the light-dependent reactions and the light-independent reactions. The light-dependent reactions cannot take place in the dark. They are the reason that plants need light.

The light-dependent reactions take place in the thylakoids of chloroplasts. These baglike membranes hold groups of chlorophyll and proteins known as **photosystems.** Photosystems take in sunlight and use it to add energy to electrons. These electrons are passed to a set of carriers in the thylakoid membrane. There are two photosystems, and they are named in order of their discovery—not in the order that they do their work.

Photosystem II The pigments of photosystem II absorb light energy and release high-energy electrons. These electrons then get passed down the **electron transport chain.** This chain is a group of carrier proteins. They use energy from the electrons to pump H^+ ions inside the thylakoid.

As light shines on chlorophyll, more and more electrons enter the electron transport chain. Chlorophyll gets new electrons when enzymes break up water molecules (H_2O). As plants take electrons from water, oxygen and hydrogen are left behind. The oxygen goes into the air that we breathe. The hydrogen becomes ions that are left inside the thylakoid.

ATP Formation In photosystem II, hydrogen ions build up inside the thylakoid. Some of these ions come from water breaking up. Others come from the electron transport chain. The building up of H^+ ions inside the thylakoid makes the outside of the thylakoid more negatively charged than the inside. This difference in charge and number of H^+ ions on either side of the membrane is what powers the making of ATP.

H^+ ions cannot cross the membrane directly. Instead, they pass through a protein called ATP synthase that is like a revolving door in the membrane. The buildup of H^+ ions on one side causes them to pass through ATP synthase and force it to turn. As it turns, it adds a phosphate group to ADP to make ATP.

Key Questions

🔑 *What happens during the light-dependent reactions?*

🔑 *What happens during the light-independent reactions?*

🔑 *What factors affect photosynthesis?*

BUILD Understanding

Flowchart As you read, create a flowchart that clearly shows the steps of the light-dependent reactions.

In Your Workbook Go to your workbook to learn more about making a flowchart. Complete the flowchart for Lesson 8.3.

Photosystem I The electrons from photosystem II lost energy when they pumped ions across the membrane. In photosystem I, light gives them energy again. Then, they go through another electron transport chain. Here, they are used to make NADP$^+$ into NADPH, which goes on to the next set of reactions.

Summary of Light-Dependent Reactions The light-dependent reactions give off oxygen gas. They also make ATP and NADPH. These compounds are important for the cell. They provide the energy needed to build sugars in the light-independent reactions.

Key Question What happens during the light-dependent reactions?
The light-dependent reactions use water and energy from sunlight to make oxygen and change ADP and NADP$^+$ into the energy carriers ATP and NADPH.

Light-Dependent Reactions
The light-dependent reactions of photosynthesis take place in the thylakoids of the chloroplast. They use energy from sunlight to produce ATP, NADPH, and oxygen.

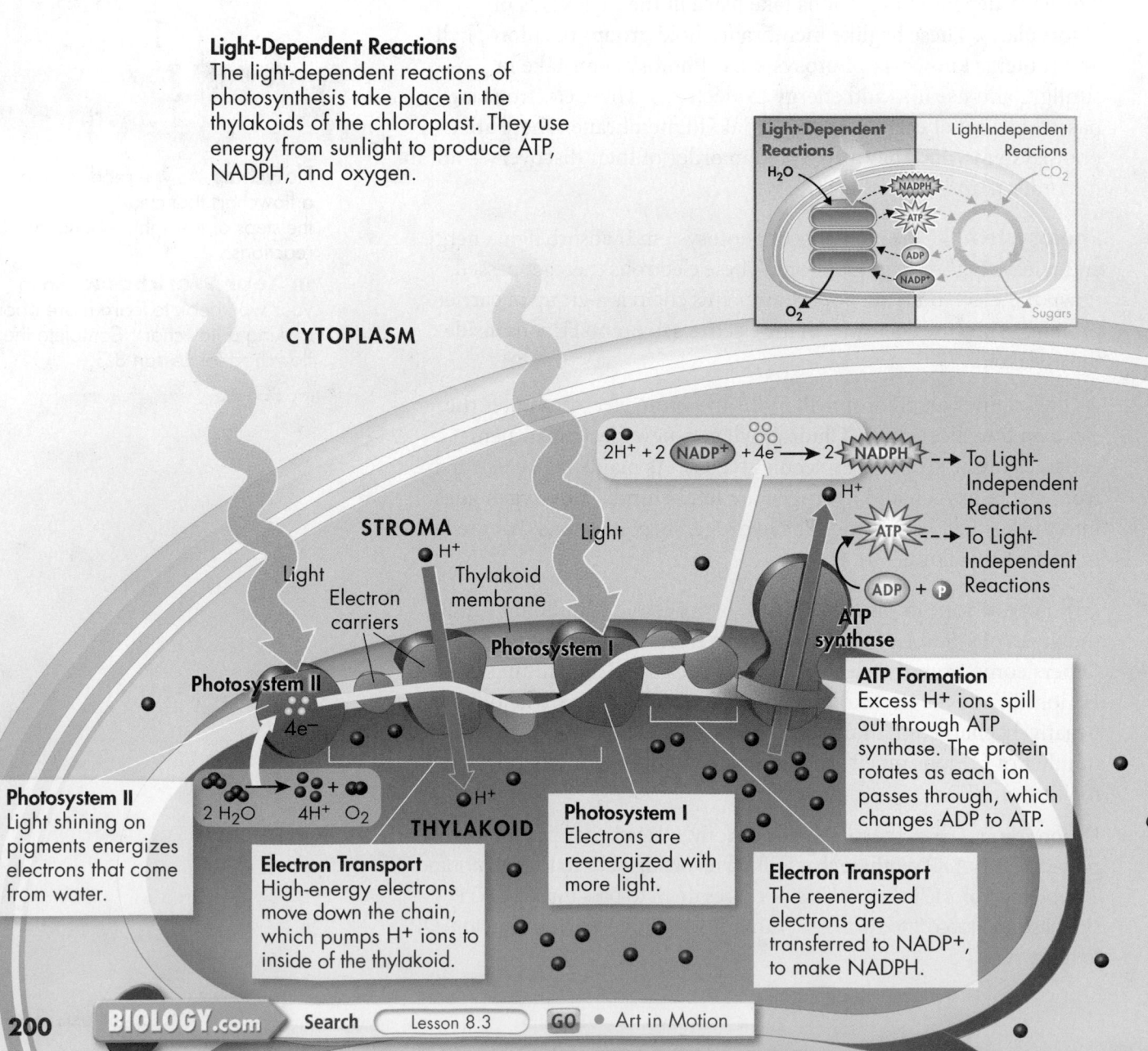

CYTOPLASM

STROMA

$2H^+ + 2$ NADP$^+$ $+ 4e^- \longrightarrow 2$ NADPH $\dashrightarrow$ To Light-Independent Reactions

ATP $\dashrightarrow$ To Light-Independent Reactions

ADP $+$ P

ATP synthase

ATP Formation
Excess H$^+$ ions spill out through ATP synthase. The protein rotates as each ion passes through, which changes ADP to ATP.

Light

H$^+$
Thylakoid membrane
Electron carriers

Photosystem I

Photosystem II

4e$^-$

Photosystem II
Light shining on pigments energizes electrons that come from water.

$2 H_2O \longrightarrow 4H^+ + O_2$

H$^+$

THYLAKOID

Electron Transport
High-energy electrons move down the chain, which pumps H$^+$ ions to inside of the thylakoid.

Photosystem I
Electrons are reenergized with more light.

Electron Transport
The reenergized electrons are transferred to NADP$^+$, to make NADPH.

Seeing Green The color green of most plants is caused by the reflection of green light by the pigment chlorophyll.

Light-Independent Reactions: Making Sugars

The ATP and NADPH made by the light-dependent reactions store a lot of chemical energy. However, they are not very stable. They last only a few minutes. During the light-independent reactions—also called the Calvin cycle—plants build high-energy sugars. These sugars are stable, so they can store energy for a long time. The Calvin cycle is named after the American scientist Melvin Calvin.

Carbon Dioxide Enters the Cycle One of the reactants of the Calvin cycle is carbon dioxide. It comes from the air around a plant. An enzyme joins carbon dioxide molecules with molecules that are already in the cell. Then, one chemical step at a time, the cycle produces energy-rich carbohydrates. These steps use energy from ATP and NADPH.

Sugar Production With each turn of the cycle, a few energy-rich carbohydrate molecules leave the cycle. This is the step that makes the Calvin cycle important. These molecules become the building blocks that the plant cell uses to make sugars, lipids, amino acids, and other compounds. The plant will use these compounds as the food and building materials it needs to grow.

The rest of the higher-energy molecules stay in the cycle. Enzymes use ATP to change them to molecules that will join with new carbon dioxide molecules. Then, the cycle begins again.

Summary of Light-Independent Reactions The Calvin cycle uses compounds made in the light-dependent reactions and carbon dioxide from the air to make sugars. The plant uses the sugars to meet its energy needs and to build molecules needed for growth. When other living things eat plants, they, too, get the energy they need.

Key Question What happens during the light-independent reactions?
During the light-independent reactions, ATP and NADPH are used to make high-energy sugars.

BUILD Vocabulary

photosystem
the light-collecting units of the chloroplast

electron transport chain
a series of proteins in which high-energy electrons are used to change ADP to ATP

WORD ROOTS
The Greek word *photo* means "light." A photosystem is a system of pigment molecules that collects energy from light.

The End Results The two parts of photosynthesis work together. The light-dependent reactions change the energy of sunlight into chemical energy. The light-independent reactions use that energy to make sugars from carbon dioxide and water. Both plants and animals use the sugars and oxygen from photosynthesis to live and grow.

Factors Affecting Photosynthesis

Temperature, Light, and Water Photosynthesis can speed up or slow down depending on several factors. Temperature is one factor that can affect the rate of photosynthesis. Photosynthesis enzymes work best between 0°C and 35°C. Light intensity is another factor. Very bright light speeds up photosynthesis. Water levels also affect the rate of photosynthesis.

Key Question What factors affect photosynthesis?
Three important factors that affect photosynthesis are temperature, light intensity, and the availability of water.

Light-Independent Reactions The light-independent reactions of photosynthesis take place in the stroma. They use ATP and NADPH from the light-dependent reactions to make high-energy sugars.

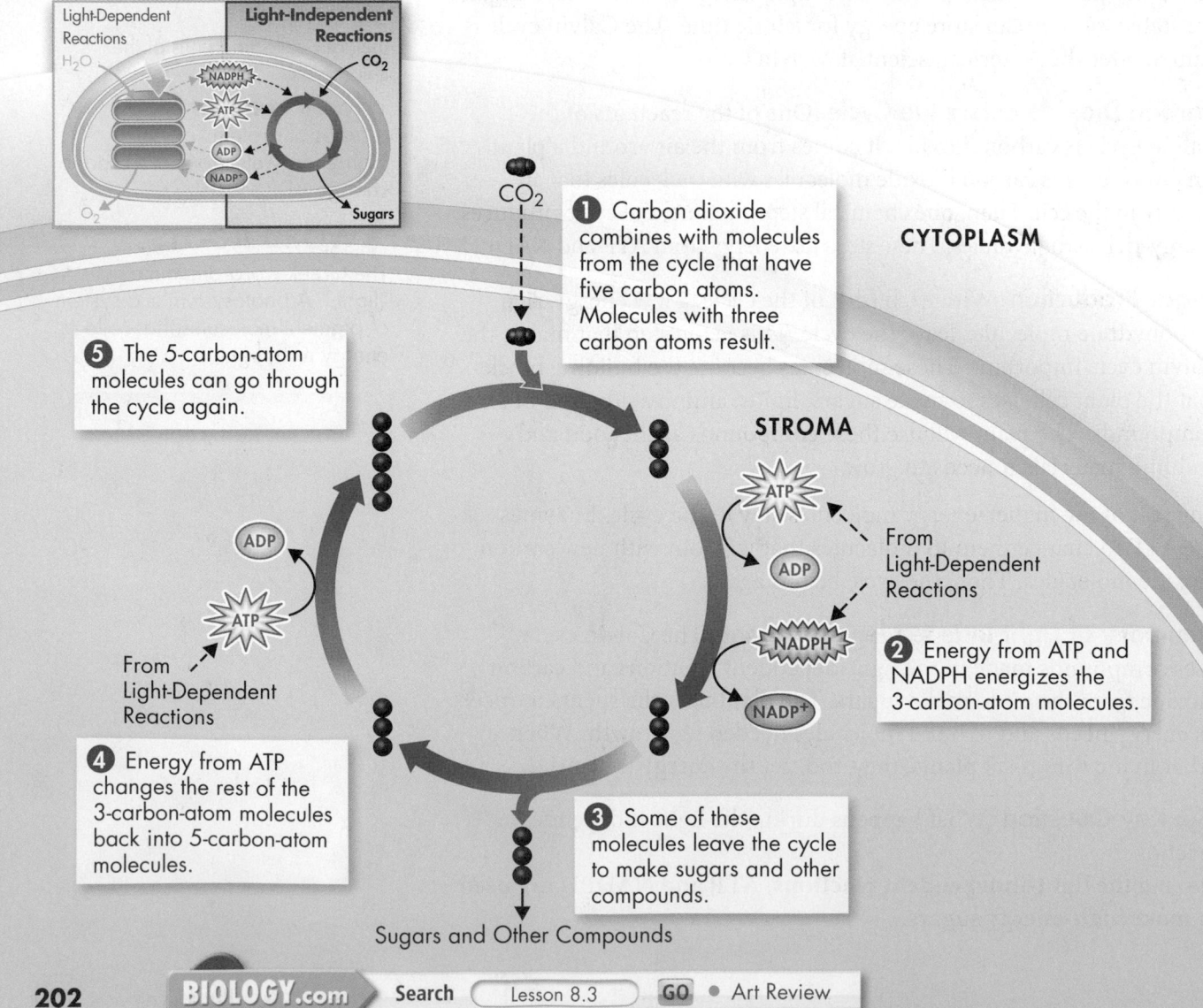

Light-Dependent Reactions
H_2O
Light-Independent Reactions
NADPH
ATP
ADP
NADP⁺
CO_2
Sugars
O_2

CO_2

1 Carbon dioxide combines with molecules from the cycle that have five carbon atoms. Molecules with three carbon atoms result.

CYTOPLASM

5 The 5-carbon-atom molecules can go through the cycle again.

STROMA

ATP
ADP
From Light-Dependent Reactions
NADPH
NADP⁺

2 Energy from ATP and NADPH energizes the 3-carbon-atom molecules.

ADP
ATP
From Light-Dependent Reactions

4 Energy from ATP changes the rest of the 3-carbon-atom molecules back into 5-carbon-atom molecules.

3 Some of these molecules leave the cycle to make sugars and other compounds.

Sugars and Other Compounds

Photosynthesis in Extreme Conditions Plants lose water through the tiny openings in their leaves that let in carbon dioxide. When it is hot, most plants close these openings to keep from drying out. But, doing so means less carbon dioxide enters, which slows photosynthesis. Some plants that live in dry, sunny areas have special ways to save water and still carry out photosynthesis.

C4 Plants C4 plants have a special chemical pathway that gets carbon into the Calvin cycle even when there is not much carbon dioxide available. The pathway uses extra ATP but lets the plants carry out photosynthesis when it is hot. Corn and sugar cane are examples of C4 plants.

CAM Plants CAM plants save water by taking air into their leaves only at night. In the dark, carbon dioxide is used to make acids. During the day, these acids are turned back into carbon dioxide for photosynthesis. Some examples of CAM plants are pineapple trees, many desert cacti, and ice plants.

CAM Plants Plants like this ice plant can survive in dry places. The leaves let in carbon dioxide only at night, minimizing water loss.

CHECK Understanding

Apply Vocabulary
Use the highlighted words from the lesson to complete each sentence correctly.

1. Energy produced by the _____ is used to pump hydrogen ions from the stroma to the inside of the thylakoid.

2. A _____ is a cluster of pigments and proteins that allows plants to absorb light energy and transfer it to electrons.

Critical Thinking

3. **Sequence** Put the following events of the light-dependent reactions in the order in which they occur: photosystem I, photosystem II, making NADPH, and pumping hydrogen ions into the inside of the thylakoid.

4. **Compare and Contrast** List at least three differences between the light-dependent and light-independent reactions of photosynthesis.

5. **Write to Learn** Answer the third clue of the mystery. How would labeling carbon atoms in carbon dioxide tell apart the products of photosynthesis?

MYSTERY CLUE

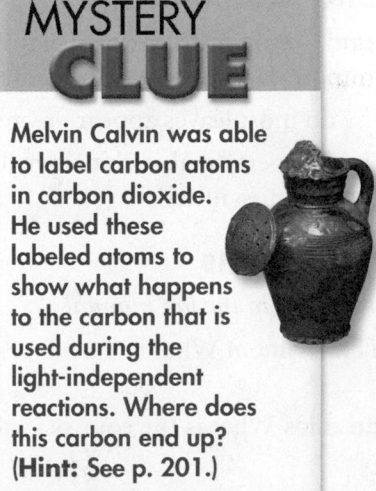

Melvin Calvin was able to label carbon atoms in carbon dioxide. He used these labeled atoms to show what happens to the carbon that is used during the light-independent reactions. Where does this carbon end up? (**Hint:** See p. 201.)

Skills Lab

GUIDED INQUIRY

MD CLG 3.1.3 Matter and Energy. SPI 1.2.6 Investigative Methods, 1.3.1 Use Equipment, 1.3.3 Safe Handling of Materials, 1.5.2 Communicate Information, 1.5.9 Synthesize Ideas.

Pre-Lab: Plant Pigments and Photosynthesis

Problem Do red leaves have the same pigments as green leaves?

Materials paper clips, one-hole rubber stoppers, chromatography paper strips, metric ruler, green and red leaves, coin, sheet of paper, large test tubes, test-tube rack, glass-marking pencil, 10-mL graduated cylinder, isopropyl alcohol, colored pencils

Lab Manual Chapter 8 Lab

Skills Focus Predict, Analyze Data, Draw Conclusions

Connect to the Big idea Almost all life on Earth depends, directly or indirectly, on energy from sunlight. Photosynthesis is the process in which light energy is captured and converted to chemical energy. Many reactions are required for this conversion, which takes place in the chloroplasts of plant cells. Some of the reactions depend on light and some do not. Plant pigments play a major role in the light-dependent reactions. In this lab, you will use chromatography to compare the pigments in red leaves with those in green leaves.

Background Questions

a. Compare and Contrast What do all plant pigments have in common? How are they different?

b. Review Why do most leaves appear green?

c. Review What property makes chlorophyll so important for photosynthesis?

Pre-Lab Questions

Preview the procedure in the lab manual.

1. Design an Experiment What is the purpose of this lab?

2. Control Variables What is the control in this lab?

3. Design an Experiment Why must the pigment line be at least 2 cm from the bottom of the paper?

4. Predict Will red leaves contain the same amount of chlorophyll as green leaves? Why or why not?

BIOLOGY.com > Search (Chapter 8) GO

Visit Chapter 8 online to test yourself on chapter content and to find activities to help you learn.

Untamed Science Video Journey to Panama with the Untamed Science crew to discover how CO_2 affects plant growth.

Data Analysis Look at pigment color data in the ocean to find out how marine algae photosynthesize in the blue light available underwater.

Tutor Tube Learn how to sort out the products and reactants in both the light-dependent and light-independent reactions.

Art Review Focus on the thylakoid membrane to review your knowledge of the light-dependent reactions.

InterActive Art Bring the components of photosynthesis together to run an animation.

Art in Motion Watch the steps of the light-dependent reactions in motion at the molecular level.

Visual Analogies Compare ATP production to a charged battery. See how the electron transport chain is like passing a hot potato.

8.1 Energy and Life

- ATP can easily release and store energy by breaking and re-forming the bonds between its phosphate groups.

- This ability makes ATP very useful as a basic energy source for all cells.

- During photosynthesis, plants change the energy of sunlight into chemical energy stored in the bonds of carbohydrates.

adenosine triphosphate (ATP) (p. 192)
heterotroph (p. 194)
autotroph (p. 194)
photosynthesis (p. 194)

8.2 Photosynthesis: An Overview

- Living things that carry out photosynthesis use pigments to get energy from sunlight.

- An electron carrier is a compound that can transfer a pair of high-energy electrons, along with most of their energy, to another molecule.

- Photosynthesis uses light energy to change water and carbon dioxide (reactants) into sugars and oxygen (products).

thylakoid (p. 195)   light-dependent
stroma (p. 195)   reactions (p. 197)
NADP$^+$ (p. 196)   light-independent
                                        reactions (p. 197)

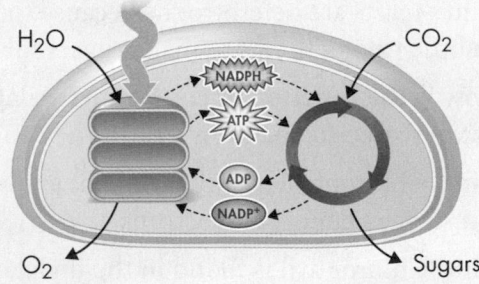

8.3 The Process of Photosynthesis

- The light-dependent reactions use energy from sunlight to make oxygen and change ADP and NADP$^+$ into the energy carriers ATP and NADPH.

- During the light-independent reactions, ATP and NADPH are used to make high-energy sugars.

- Three important factors that affect photosynthesis are temperature, light intensity, and the availability of water.

photosystem (p. 199)
electron transport chain (p. 199)

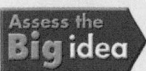

Assess the Big idea: Cellular Basis of Life

Write an answer to the question below.

Q: How do plants and other organisms capture energy from the sun?

Constructed Response

Write an answer to each of the questions below. The answer to each question should be one or two paragraphs. To help you begin, read the **Hints** below the questions.

1. **Yeasts are single-celled fungi that feed off of sugars in their environment. How do yeasts depend on other living things for survival?**

   Hint Many yeasts get their food from plants that produce sugars in fruits and saps.

   Hint Yeasts are heterotrophs because they rely on other living things to make sugars for them.

2. **How is the function of chlorophyll related to its very specific location within the cell?**

   Hint Chlorophyll absorbs sunlight and transfers its energy to electrons.

   Hint Chlorophyll is found in the thylakoid, where many steps of photosynthesis take place.

3. **The light-independent reactions are sometimes called the "dark reactions" to tell them apart from the light-dependent reactions. Do the steps of the light-independent reactions ever depend on light? Explain.**

   Hint The photosystems need light to energize electrons. These electrons are used to make ATP and NADPH.

   Hint NADPH and ATP are needed to carry out the light-independent reactions.

Foundations for Learning Wrap-Up

Use the index cards and notebook page you prepared when you started the chapter as a tool to help you organize your thoughts about photosynthesis.

Activity 1 Working with a partner, use the index cards and notebook page to create a diagram to show the two stages of photosynthesis. Then, use the index cards to create a chemical equation that summarizes photosynthesis.

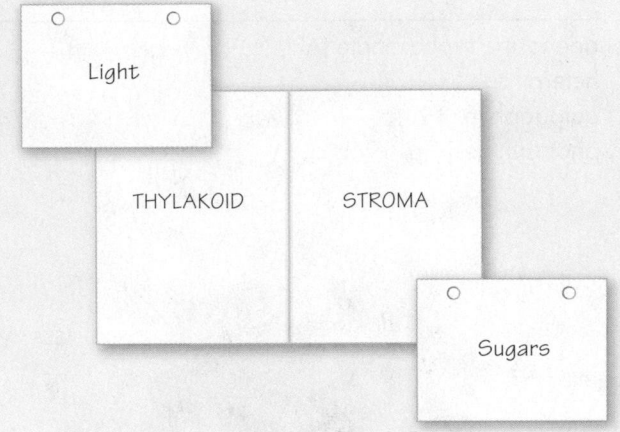

Activity 2 With your partner, label four more index cards with NADPH, ATP, ADP, and NADP$^+$. Using your diagram from Activity 1, add the cards to the diagram in the correct positions to complete the stages of photosynthesis. Draw arrows to show the movement of the molecules between the stages.

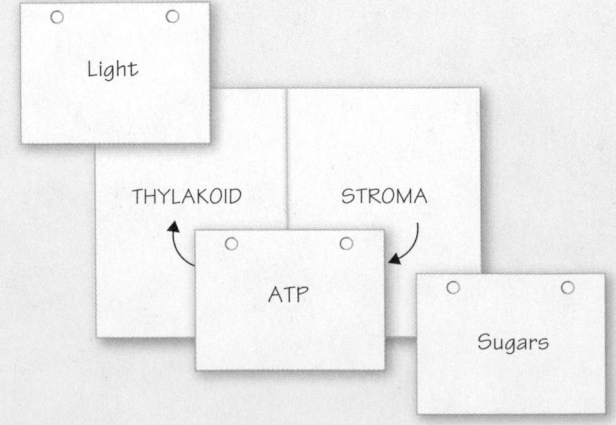

8.1 Energy and Life

Understand Key Concepts

1. Which of the following are autotrophs?
   a. deer　　**c.** leopards
   b. grasses　　**d.** mushrooms

Test-Taking Tip

Eliminate Incorrect Answers Read all of the answer choices carefully. Even if you are not sure of the correct answer, you may be able to cross out one or two of the answer choices that are incorrect. In question 1, answers **a** and **c** are incorrect because they are animals, and animals are heterotrophs. So, you can eliminate these answer choices.

2. Where do plants get the energy they need to carry out photosynthesis?
   a. air　　**c.** sunlight
   b. soil　　**d.** water
3. How does a molecule of ATP compare to a molecule of glucose in terms of the amount of energy stored?

Think Critically

4. **Relate Cause and Effect** How might the disappearance of all autotrophs on Earth affect other living things? Explain.

8.2 Photosynthesis: An Overview

Understand Key Concepts

5. In addition to light and chlorophyll, photosynthesis requires
   a. carbon dioxide and sugars.
   b. carbon dioxide and water.
   c. oxygen and sugars.
   d. oxygen and water.
6. What is the function of $NADP^+$?
   a. It absorbs light.
   b. It is an electron carrier.
   c. It is a light-reflecting pigment.
   d. It acts as long-term energy storage.
7. Some plants have leaves that are bright red. How do red leaves differ from green leaves in the types of light they absorb and reflect?

Think Critically

8. **Predict** Why would a plant grow better in white light than in green light? Explain your answer.

8.3 The Process of Photosynthesis

Understand Key Concepts

9. What drives the formation of ATP by ATP synthase?
   a. buildup of H^+ ions
   b. burning oxygen
   c. light absorption
   d. splitting carbon dioxide
10. Which substance from the light-dependent reactions of photosynthesis is a source of energy for the light-independent reactions?
    a. ADP　　**c.** NADPH
    b. H_2O　　**d.** pyruvic acid
11. The light-independent reactions of photosynthesis are also known as the
    a. ATP cycle.　　**c.** carbon cycle.
    b. Calvin cycle.　　**d.** sugar cycle.
12. Identify the chloroplast parts labeled A, B, and C. In which part(s) do the light-dependent reactions take place? In which part(s) do the light-independent reactions take place?

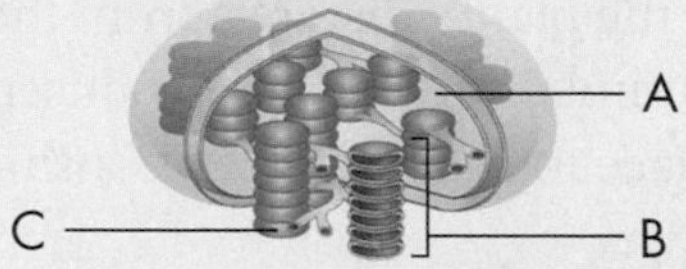

13. Discuss three factors that affect the rate at which photosynthesis takes place. Which steps of photosynthesis are affected by these factors?

Think Critically

14. Predict Suppose you water a potted plant and place it by a window in a clear, airtight jar. Predict how the rate of photosynthesis might be affected over the next few days. What might happen if the plant were left there for several weeks?

15. Form a Hypothesis Many of the sun's rays may be blocked by dust or clouds formed by volcanic eruptions or pollution. What are some possible short-term and long-term effects of this on plants in an area? On other forms of life?

Connecting Concepts

Use Science Graphics

A water plant placed under bright light gives off bubbles of oxygen. The table below contains the results of an experiment in which the distance from the light to the plant was varied. Use the data table to answer questions 16–18.

Oxygen Production	
Distance From Light (cm)	Bubbles Produced per Minute
10	39
20	22
30	8
40	5

16. Graph Use the data in the table to make a line graph.

17. Interpret Graphics Describe the trend in the data. How many bubbles would you predict if the light was moved to 50 cm away? Explain.

18. Draw Conclusions What relationship exists between the plant's distance from the light and the number of bubbles produced? What is taking place to cause this relationship? Explain your answer.

solve the CHAPTER MYSTERY

OUT OF THIN AIR?

Most plants grow out of the soil, so you might think that soil adds to plant mass. But, at the end of Jan van Helmont's experiment with the willow tree, he discovered that the mass of the soil was about the same—even though the tree had gained nearly 75 kilograms. Van Helmont decided that the mass must have come from water, because water was the only thing he had added. The tree grew parts that did contain atoms like those found in water, but what van Helmont didn't know was that the new parts also contained carbon. We now know that most of that carbon comes from carbon dioxide in air. Thus, mass comes from two sources: carbon dioxide and water. What form does the added mass take? Think about the origin of the word carbohydrate, from *carbo-*, meaning "carbon," and *hydrate*, meaning "to combine with water," and you have your answer.

1. Infer Although soil does not add much to plant mass, how might it help plants grow?

2. Infer Imagine that a scientist measures the exact mass of carbon dioxide and water that entered a plant and the exact mass of the sugars produced. Would these masses be identical? Why or why not?

3. Apply Concepts What do plants do with all of the sugars they make through photosynthesis? (*Hint:* Plant cells have mitochondria in addition to chloroplasts. What do mitochondria do?)

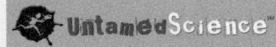 Finding the solution to the mystery is only the beginning. Take a video field trip with the ecogeeks of Untamed Science to see where the mystery leads.

Multiple Choice

1. Autotrophs differ from heterotrophs because they
   A use oxygen to burn food.
   B do not require oxygen to live.
   C make carbon dioxide as a product of using food.
   D make their own food from carbon dioxide and water. CLG 3.1.3

2. The principal pigment in plants is
   A chlorophyll.   C ATP.
   B oxygen.   D NADPH.   CLG 3.2.1

3. Which of the following is NOT produced in the light-dependent reactions of photosynthesis?
   A NADPH
   B sugars
   C hydrogen ions
   D ATP   CLG 3.1.3

4. Which of the following correctly summarizes photosynthesis?
   A $H_2O + CO_2 \xrightarrow{light} sugars + O_2$
   B $sugars + O_2 \xrightarrow{light} H_2O + CO_2$
   C $H_2O + O_2 \xrightarrow{light} sugars + CO_2$
   D $sugars + CO_2 \xrightarrow{light} H_2O + O_2$ CLG 3.1.3

5. The color of light that is LEAST useful to a plant during photosynthesis is
   A red.
   B blue.
   C green.
   D violet.   CLG 3.1.3

6. The first step in photosynthesis is the
   A synthesis of water.
   B production of sugars.
   C breakdown of carbon dioxide.
   D absorption of light energy.   CLG 3.1.3

7. In a typical plant, all of the following factors are necessary for photosynthesis EXCEPT
   A chlorophyll.   C oxygen.
   B light.   D water.   CLG 3.1.3

Questions 8–10

A scientist mashes up spinach leaves to make a liquid, or extract, that has lots of pigment in it. She places a drop of the liquid at one end of a strip of paper towel. After the liquid dries, she hangs the paper in a test tube containing alcohol so that only the tip of the paper is in the alcohol. As the alcohol is absorbed and moves up the paper, the different pigments separate as shown below.

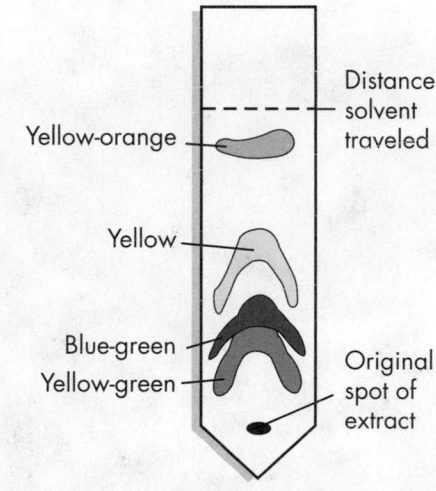

8. Which pigment traveled the shortest distance?
   A yellow-orange   C blue-green
   B yellow   D yellow-green   SPI 1.5.5

9. Which of the following is a valid conclusion that can be drawn from this information?
   A Spinach leaves use only chlorophyll during photosynthesis.
   B Spinach leaves contain several pigments.
   C Spinach leaves contain more orange pigment than yellow pigment.
   D Spinach leaves are yellow-orange rather than green.   SPI 1.4.2

10. In which organelle would MOST of these pigments be found?
    A vacuoles   C mitochondria
    B centrioles   D chloroplasts   CLG 3.2.1

Open-Ended Response

11. Describe how high-energy electrons are ultimately responsible for driving the reactions of photosynthesis.   CLG 3.1.3

If You Have Trouble With . . .

Question	1	2	3	4	5	6	7	8	9	10	11
See Lesson	8.1	8.2	8.2	8.2	8.2	8.3	8.3	8.2	8.2	8.2	8.3

9 Cellular Respiration and Fermentation

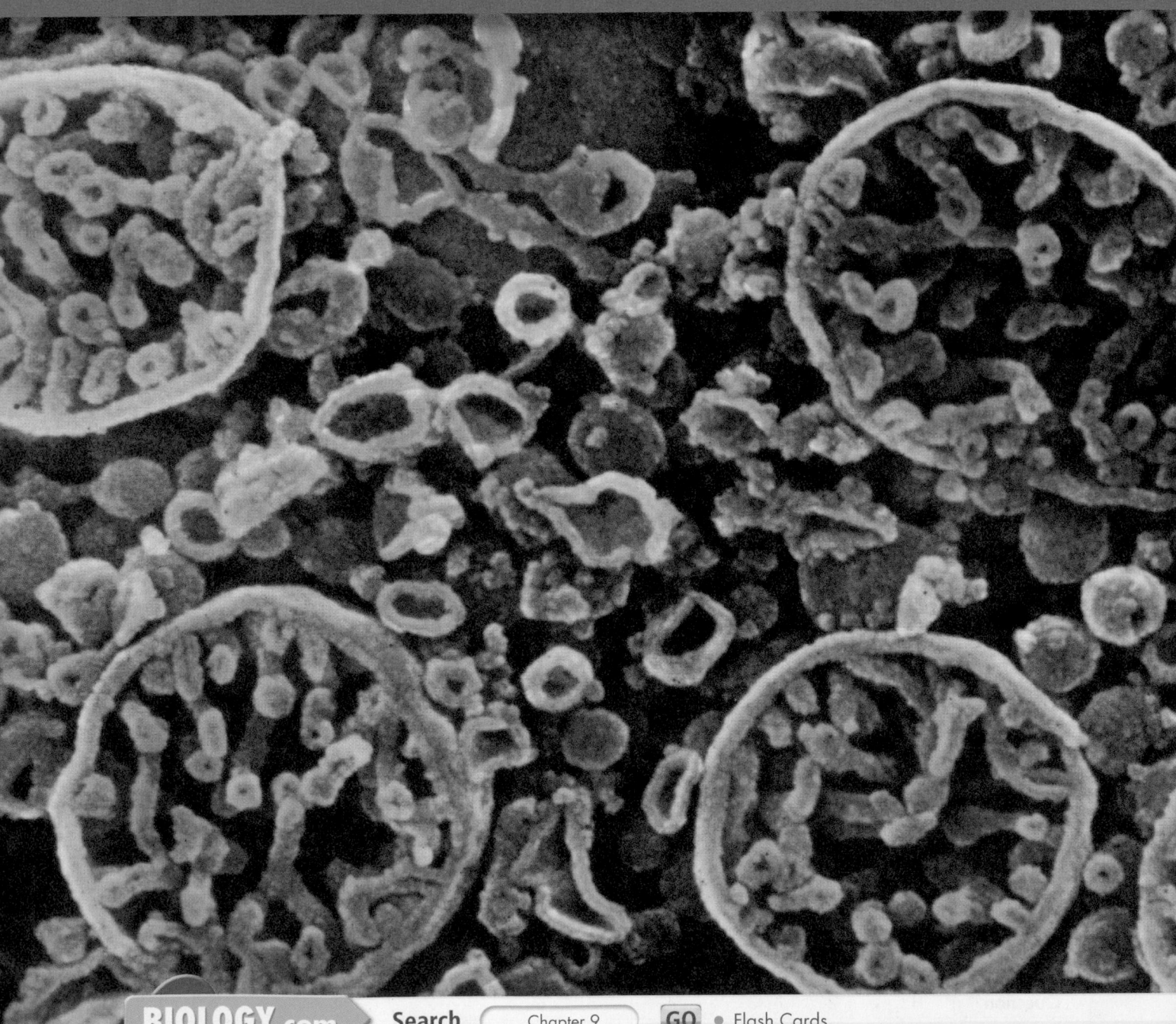

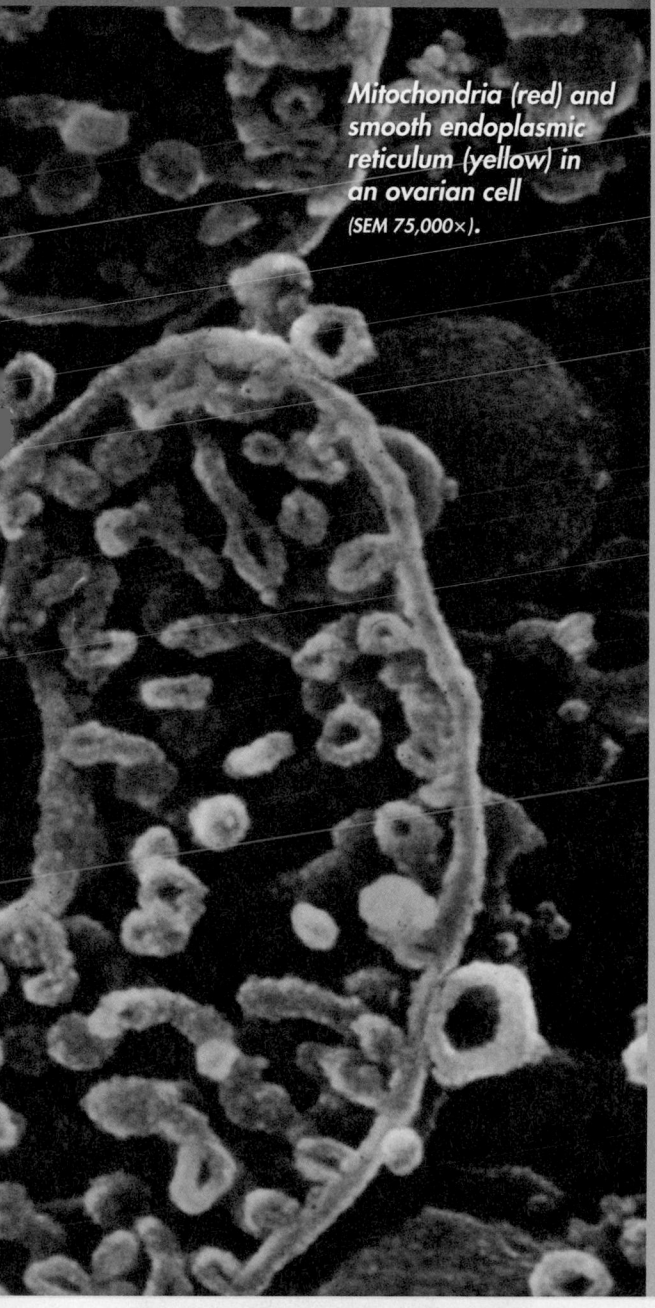

MARYLAND VOLUNTARY STATE CURRICULUM

Biology Indicators/Core Learning Goals (CLG) 3.1.1, 3.1.2, 3.1.3, 3.2.1, 3.2.2. **Skills and Processes Indicators (SPI)** 1.2.7, 1.3.1, 1.3.3, 1.4.1, 1.4.2, 1.5.3, 1.5.4, 1.5.5, 1.5.7, 1.5.8, 1.6.2. See lessons for details.

Mitochondria (red) and smooth endoplasmic reticulum (yellow) in an ovarian cell (SEM 75,000×).

CHAPTER MYSTERY

DIVING WITHOUT A BREATH

You know what it is like to feel out of breath. Just a few minutes of hard exercise can have some people huffing and puffing for air. But what if you couldn't get air? What if you were asked to hold your breath and exercise? Before too long, you'd run out of oxygen and pass out. You would not be able to get enough oxygen. It may seem like a bad idea to hold your breath while exercising, but there are animals that do it all the time—whales. Because whales are air-breathing mammals, they still need to come to the surface for air. But after a breath, some whales can dive underwater for as long as 45 minutes! How is that possible? Diving takes a lot of energy. How do whales stay active for so long on only one breath?

Read for Mystery Clues As you read this chapter, look for clues to help you discover how whales can stay underwater so long. Then, solve the mystery at the end of the chapter.

FOUNDATIONS for Learning

Cells need chemical energy to stay alive. Special parts of the cell help them get this energy. Before you read the chapter, label six index cards with the words *water, pyruvic acid, carbon dioxide, oxygen, energy,* and *glucose.* Label one sheet of paper with the words *cytoplasm* and *mitochondrion.* At the end of the chapter are two activities that use the cards and sheet of paper. They will help you answer the question: How do organisms obtain energy?

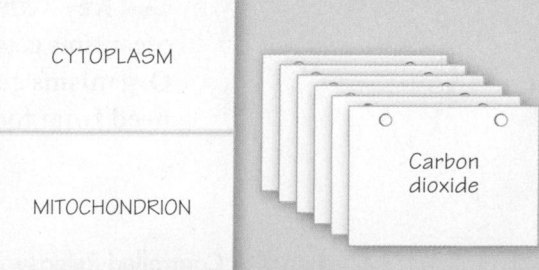

CYTOPLASM

MITOCHONDRION

Carbon dioxide

9.1 Cellular Respiration: An Overview

MD CLG 3.1.1 Chemical Substances and Macromolecules, 3.1.2 Homeostasis, 3.1.3 Matter and Energy, 3.2.1 Processes and Functions, 3.2.2 Changes in Metabolic Activity. SPI 1.4.2 Analyze Data, 1.5.7 Classification Systems, 1.5.8 Compare.

Key Questions

🔑 **Where do organisms get energy?**

🔑 **What is cellular respiration?**

🔑 **What is the relationship between photosynthesis and cellular respiration?**

BUILD Understanding

Preview Visuals Before you read, study The Stages of Cellular Respiration figure. Make a list of questions that you have about the figure. As you read, write down the answers to the questions.

In Your Workbook Go to your workbook to learn more about Previewing Visuals. Complete the Previewing Visuals activity for Lesson 9.1.

Chemical Energy and Food

How do you feel when you are hungry? Do you feel sluggish, dizzy, or a little weak? That weakness comes from a lack of the food you need for energy. But what does food have to do with energy?

Food gives living things the energy they need to grow. Some living things, such as plants, are autotrophs (AW toh trohfs). They make their own food through photosynthesis. Other living things are heterotrophs (HET ur oh trohfs). They have to eat other living things for food. For all living things, food molecules store chemical energy. Living things release that energy when they break those food molecules down.

Energy in food can be measured in units called calories. A calorie is the amount of energy needed to raise the temperature of 1 gram of water 1 degree Celsius. The Calorie you see on food labels is actually a kilocalorie, or 1000 calories. The amount of energy in different kinds of food varies. This is because of differences in the way the atoms in food molecules are bonded together. For example, 1 gram of the sugar glucose gives off 3811 calories of energy when it is burned. But, 1 gram of the fat found in beef gives off 8893 calories of energy when it is burned.

Cells break down food molecules over time, getting a little bit of chemical energy at key steps. This chemical energy helps cells use the energy in foods to make compounds such as ATP. ATP and other useful energy compounds directly power the activities of the cell.

🔑 **Key Question** Where do organisms get energy? **Organisms get the energy they need from food.**

A Controlled Release The energy stored in food is released slowly. If the energy were given off all at once, most of it would be lost as light and heat. That is what happens when a marshmallow catches fire.

You Are What You Eat

Different types of food can store very different amounts of energy. Most foods have a mix of proteins, carbohydrates, and fats. One gram of protein or a carbohydrate such as glucose has about 4 Calories. One gram of fat, though, has about 9 Calories. The table to the right shows what is found in one serving of some common foods.

Composition of Some Common Foods			
Food	Protein (g)	Carbohydrate (g)	Fat (g)
Apple, 1 medium	0	22	0
Bacon, 2 slices	5	0	6
Chocolate, 1 bar	3	23	13
Eggs, 2 whole	12	0	9
2% milk, 1 cup	8	12	5
Potato chips, 15 chips	2	14	10
Skinless roasted turkey, 3 slices	11	3	1

1. Interpret Data The food from the table that has the most protein is _____. The food that has the most carbohydrates is _____. The food that has the most fat is _____.

2. Calculate

a. How many Calories total are there in 2 slices of bacon?

b. How many Calories total are there in 3 slices of roasted turkey?

c. What is the difference in total Calories between these two foods? Why is there a difference?

3. Calculate Walking uses around 5 Calories per minute. At that rate, how many minutes would you have to walk to burn the Calories in one chocolate bar? Use the equations below to help you with your calculations.

____ Calories from protein
+ ____ Calories from carbohydrates
+ ____ Calories from fat
= ____ Total Calories in a chocolate bar

$$\frac{\_\_\_\_ \text{ Total Calories}}{5 \text{ Calories/minute}} = \_\_\_\_ \text{ minutes}$$

In Your Workbook Get more help for this activity in your workbook.

Overview of Cellular Respiration

Living things can get energy from food through cellular respiration. **Cellular respiration** is the process that releases energy from food, such as the simple sugar glucose, when there is oxygen present. Cellular respiration gives off carbon dioxide, water, and energy. The process can be summarized like this:

$$6O_2 + C_6H_{12}O_6 \longrightarrow 6CO_2 + 6H_2O + \text{Energy}$$

But cellular respiration does not take place in just one step. If it did, all of the energy from sugar would be given off at once. Most of it would be lost in the form of light and heat. A living cell has to release the chemical energy in food molecules a little bit at a time. The cell uses that energy to make ATP.

Key Question What is cellular respiration?
Cellular respiration is the process that releases energy from food when oxygen is present.

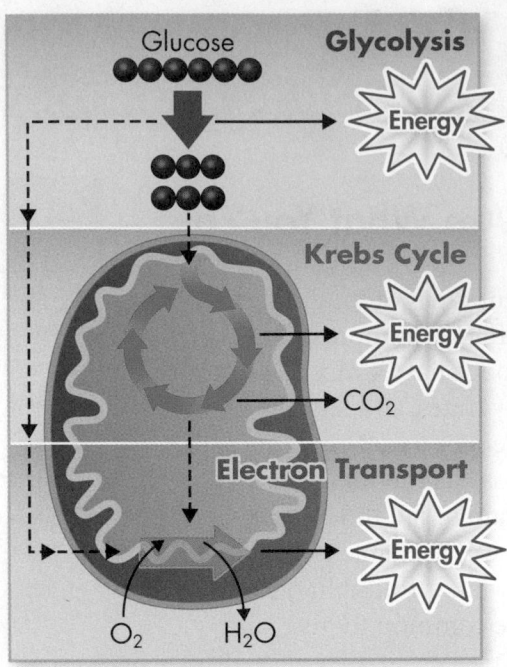

The Stages of Cellular Respiration
There are three stages to cellular respiration: glycolysis, the Krebs cycle, and the electron transport chain.

Three Main Stages Cellular respiration gets energy from food in three stages. These stages are glycolysis, the Krebs cycle, and the electron transport chain. When looking at these stages, it is helpful to use an example. We will use the sugar glucose. Glucose enters the first stage, known as glycolysis (gly KAHL ih sis). Only a small amount of energy is used to make ATP during this stage. The rest is still locked in the bonds of a molecule called pyruvic (py ROO vik) acid. Pyruvic acid enters the second stage, the Krebs cycle, where a little more energy is given off. Most of the energy from cellular respiration comes from the last stage, the electron transport chain. This stage uses oxygen and reactants from the other two stages to finish the job.

Oxygen and Energy You get oxygen from the air you breathe. Oxygen is used at the end of the electron transport chain. Any time a cell needs more energy, it needs more oxygen, too. That is why you breathe hard when you exercise. You use up energy and need more oxygen, which means taking more breaths.

Chemical pathways that need oxygen are called **aerobic,** which means "in air." The Krebs cycle and electron transport chain are both aerobic. Even though the Krebs cycle does not directly need oxygen, it cannot run without the electron transport chain, which does need oxygen. Glycolysis, however, does not need oxygen. It does not depend on an aerobic process, either. Glycolysis is **anaerobic,** which means "without air."

Mitochondria (myt oh KAHN dree uh) are the organelles most important in cellular respiration. Glycolysis actually takes place in the cytoplasm of a cell, but the Krebs cycle and electron transport chain take place inside the mitochondria. If oxygen is not present, another anaerobic path, known as fermentation, keeps glycolysis running. You will learn more about fermentation later in this chapter.

Comparing Photosynthesis and Cellular Respiration

If nearly all living things break down food through cellular respiration, why doesn't Earth run out of oxygen? Where does all of the carbon dioxide go? Where do the cells get food molecules from? Cellular respiration is balanced by photosynthesis. The energy from each process flows in opposite directions. The equations for photosynthesis and cellular respiration are the reverse of each other. Photosynthesis removes carbon dioxide from the air. Cellular respiration puts it back. Photosynthesis gives off oxygen and makes sugars. Cellular respiration uses that oxygen to get energy from sugars. Cellular respiration takes place in nearly all life: plants, animals, fungi, protists, and most bacteria. Photosynthesis, on the other hand, takes place only in plants, algae, and some bacteria.

🔑 **Key Question** What is the relationship between photosynthesis and cellular respiration?
Photosynthesis produces food molecules and removes carbon dioxide from the air, and cellular respiration puts it back. Photosynthesis gives off oxygen, and cellular respiration uses that oxygen to release energy from food.

Light energy

PHOTOSYNTHESIS

$C_6H_{12}O_6 + 6O_2$

ATP, Heat energy

$6H_2O + 6CO_2$

CELLULAR RESPIRATION

Opposite Processes Photosynthesis and cellular respiration can be thought of as opposite processes.

CHECK Understanding

Apply Vocabulary
Use the highlighted words from the lesson to complete each sentence correctly.

1. A process that needs oxygen to take place is called _____.

2. Glycolysis is _____ because it can happen when there is no oxygen.

Critical Thinking

3. Infer Do plant cells carry out cellular respiration? What organelle do they have that helps you know the answer?

4. Compare and Contrast How are the equations for cellular respiration and photosynthesis similar? How are they different?

5. Apply Concepts Aerobics is a kind of exercise that involves rhythmic movement and stretching, usually to music. What does the name *aerobics* tell you about this kind of exercise?

6. Write to Learn Answer the first clue of the mystery. Think about the difference between aerobic and anaerobic processes.

MYSTERY CLUE

If whales stay underwater for 45 minutes or more, do you think they mostly use aerobic or anaerobic processes? (**Hint:** See p. 214.)

The Process of Cellular Respiration

MD CLG 3.1.1 Chemical Substances and Macromolecules, 3.1.3 Matter and Energy, 3.2.1 Processes and Functions, 3.2.2 Changes in Metabolic Activity. SPI 1.5.5 Create and Interpret Graphics, 1.5.8 Compare.

Key Questions

🔑 **What happens during the process of glycolysis?**

🔑 **What happens during the Krebs cycle?**

🔑 **How does the electron transport chain use high-energy electrons from glycolysis and the Krebs cycle?**

🔑 **How much ATP does cellular respiration generate?**

BUILD Understanding

Compare/Contrast Table As you read, make a compare/contrast table for glycolysis, the Krebs cycle, and the electron transport chain. In your table, show where each step takes place, what reactants it uses, what products it makes, and how many molecules of ATP are made.

In Your Workbook Go to your workbook to learn more about making a compare/contrast table. Complete the compare/contrast table for Lesson 9.2.

Breaking Down Sugars Animals get sugars from food. Sugars such as glucose are then broken down by cells through the process of glycolysis.

Glycolysis

Food burns. In fact, flour is so flammable that is has caused many explosions. Because of this, you should never store flour above a stove. But how do living things get the energy they need from food without starting a fire?

Living things use a series of reactions and steps to get energy from food molecules. The first set of reactions in cellular respiration is known as **glycolysis.** In one of the reactions of glycolysis, a 6-carbon sugar made from glucose is split into two. The final step produces two molecules of pyruvic acid. Pyruvic acid has 3 carbons. Energy is given off as the bonds in glucose are broken and formed again between different atoms.

Making ATP Glycolysis gives off energy. But the cell needs to put in a little energy to get things going. At the beginning, 2 ATP molecules are used up. Glycolysis makes 4 ATP molecules. This gives the cell a net gain of 2 ATP molecules for each molecule of glucose that enters glycolysis.

Making NADH One of the steps of glycolysis passes 4 electrons to an electron carrier. This carrier is called **NAD⁺,** or nicotinamide adenine dinucleotide. Like NADP⁺ in photosynthesis, each NAD⁺ molecule can pick up a hydrogen ion and carry a pair of high-energy electrons. The new molecule is known as NADH. It holds the electrons until they can be moved to other molecules. Later on, when there is oxygen present, these high-energy electrons can be used to make even more ATP.

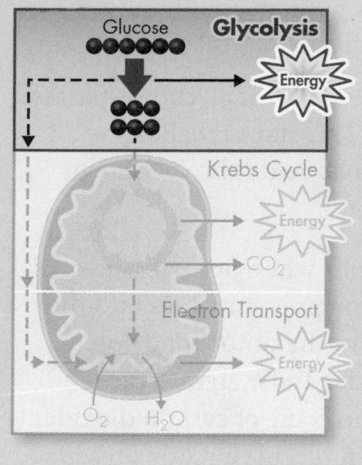

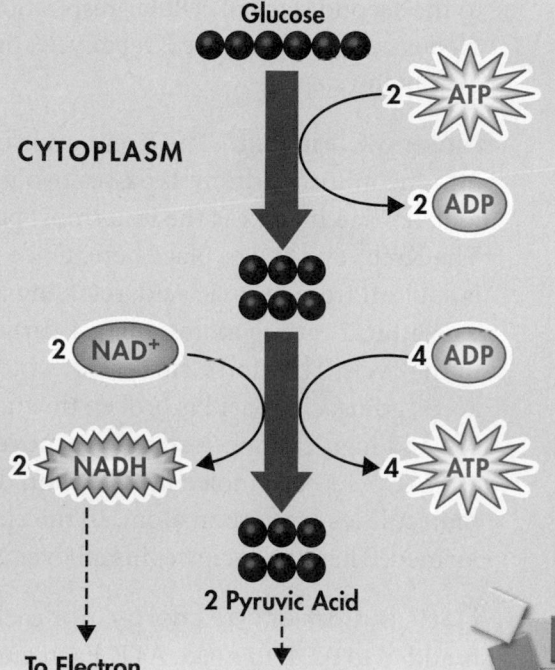

Glucose

CYTOPLASM

2 ATP

2 ADP

Splitting glucose to make 2 smaller molecules takes 2 molecules of ATP.

NAD⁺ picks up 4 high-energy electrons from a glycolysis reaction. This step makes 2 NADH.

2 NAD⁺

4 ADP

The last steps make 4 molecules of ATP, which means a net gain of 2 ATP.

2 NADH

4 ATP

2 Pyruvic Acid

To Electron Transport Chain

To Krebs Cycle

Why Glycolysis Is Useful During glycolysis, 4 ATP molecules are made from 4 ADP molecules. Given that 2 ATP molecules are used to start the process, there is a net gain of just 2 ATP molecules. Even though the energy given off by glycolysis is small, the process is so fast that cells can make thousands of ATP molecules in just a few milliseconds. The speed of glycolysis can be a big plus when the cell suddenly needs a lot of energy.

Besides speed, another useful thing about glycolysis is that it does not need oxygen. This means that glycolysis can quickly get chemical energy to cells when there is not any oxygen present. When oxygen is present, however, the pyruvic acid and NADH made during glycolysis become the materials needed for the other stages of cellular respiration.

🔑 **Key Question** What happens during the process of glycolysis? **During glycolysis, 1 molecule of glucose, which has 6 carbon atoms, is changed into 2 molecules of pyruvic acid, which each have 3 carbon atoms.**

BUILD Connections

Glycolysis Glycolysis is the first stage of cellular respiration. During glycolysis, glucose is broken down into 2 molecules of pyruvic acid. ATP and NADH are also made.

BUILD Vocabulary

glycolysis
The first set of reactions in cellular respiration in which a molecule of glucose is broken into two molecules of pyruvic acid

NAD⁺
nicotinamide adenine dinucleotide: an electron carrier involved in glycolysis

🕯 **WORD ORIGINS**

The Greek word *glukus* means "sweet." The Latin word *lysis* means to "loosen." The term *glycolysis* thus means "loosening" or "breaking glucose."

Krebs cycle
The second stage of cellular respiration in which pyruvic acid is broken down into carbon dioxide in a series of energy-extracting reactions.

matrix
the innermost compartment of the mitochondrion

WORD ORIGINS

The Krebs cycle was named after the British biologist Hans Krebs, who won the Nobel Prize in 1953 for its discovery.

The Krebs Cycle

When there is oxygen present, pyruvic acid made in glycolysis passes to the second stage of cellular respiration. This stage is called the **Krebs cycle.** During the Krebs cycle, pyruvic acid is broken down over many steps.

Making Citric Acid The Krebs cycle begins when pyruvic acid goes into the mitochondrion. It passes two membranes and goes into the matrix. The **matrix** is the innermost part of the mitochondrion. The Krebs cycle takes place here. Once inside the matrix, 1 carbon is split off from pyruvic acid, releasing a molecule of carbon dioxide. The other 2 carbon atoms join a 4-carbon molecule already present in the cycle. They form citric acid, which has 6 carbons. As the cycle keeps going, citric acid is broken down. More carbon dioxide is given off, and high-energy electrons are moved to energy carriers, such as NAD^+. As each molecule of carbon dioxide leaves, the citric acid molecule loses a carbon atom. In the end a 4-carbon molecule is formed. Then the cycle begins all over again.

Electron Carriers as Energy For each turn of the cycle, a phosphate is added to ADP to make ATP. Each glucose molecule causes two complete turns of the Krebs cycle. So, for each molecule of glucose, the cycle makes two more ATP molecules. When we add these to the two made in glycolysis, so far we have gained just 4 ATP molecules. That doesn't sound like much. However, most of the chemical energy released in the cycle goes to produce high-energy electrons. These are passed to the electron carriers NAD^+ and FAD. This changes them into NADH and $FADH_2$.

What happens to the carbon dioxide, ATP, and electron carriers produced in the Krebs cycle? Carbon dioxide is not useful to the cell. It is expelled every time you breathe out. The ATP molecules are very useful. They are immediately available as energy for cellular activities. When oxygen is present, the electron carrier molecules are used make huge amounts of ATP.

Key Question What happens during the Krebs cycle?
During the Krebs cycle, pyruvic acid is broken down into carbon dioxide in a series of steps that releases chemical energy.

Outer membrane

Intermembrane space

Inner membrane

Matrix

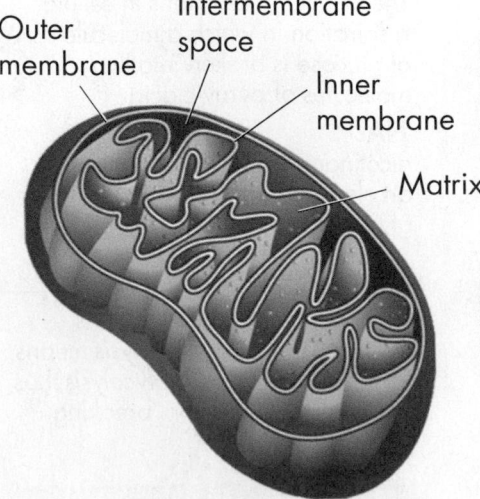

Mitochondrion The Krebs cycle takes place within the matrix, or the innermost space, of the mitochondrion.

Mitochondrion

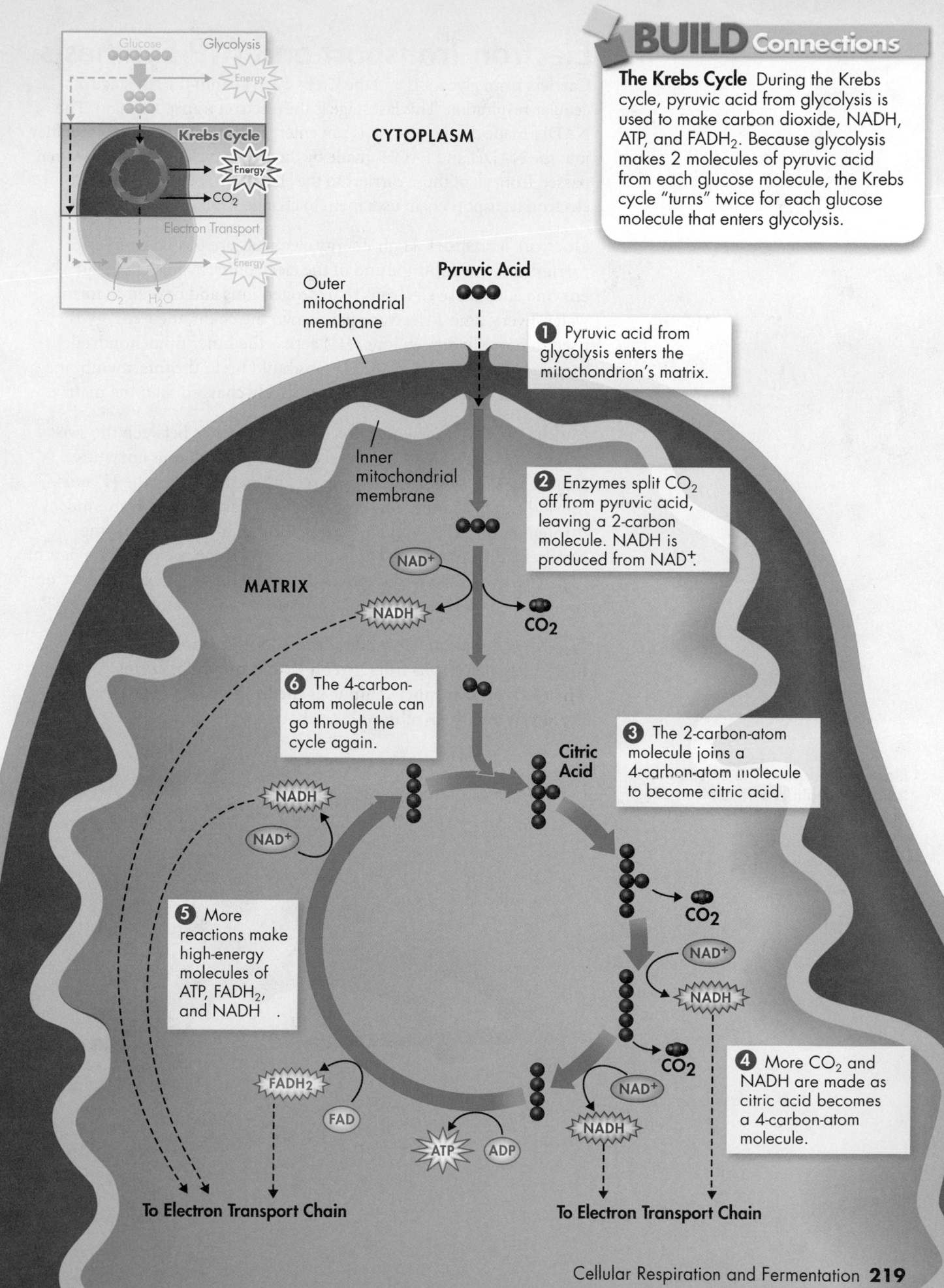

BUILD Connections

The Krebs Cycle During the Krebs cycle, pyruvic acid from glycolysis is used to make carbon dioxide, NADH, ATP, and $FADH_2$. Because glycolysis makes 2 molecules of pyruvic acid from each glucose molecule, the Krebs cycle "turns" twice for each glucose molecule that enters glycolysis.

Glucose   Glycolysis
Energy
Krebs Cycle
Energy
CO_2
Electron Transport
Energy
O_2 H_2O

Outer mitochondrial membrane

Pyruvic Acid

❶ Pyruvic acid from glycolysis enters the mitochondrion's matrix.

Inner mitochondrial membrane

❷ Enzymes split CO_2 off from pyruvic acid, leaving a 2-carbon molecule. NADH is produced from NAD^+.

MATRIX

NAD^+

NADH

CO_2

❻ The 4-carbon-atom molecule can go through the cycle again.

Citric Acid

❸ The 2-carbon-atom molecule joins a 4-carbon-atom molecule to become citric acid.

NADH

NAD^+

CO_2

NAD^+

NADH

❺ More reactions make high-energy molecules of ATP, $FADH_2$, and NADH .

CO_2

❹ More CO_2 and NADH are made as citric acid becomes a 4-carbon-atom molecule.

NAD^+

NADH

$FADH_2$

FAD

ATP   ADP

To Electron Transport Chain

To Electron Transport Chain

Cellular Respiration and Fermentation **219**

Electron Transport and ATP Synthesis

Carriers from glycolysis and the Krebs cycle go into the last stage of cellular respiration. This last stage is the electron transport chain. The NADH made during glycolysis can enter the mitochondrion. There, they join the NADH and $FADH_2$ made by the Krebs cycle. Electrons are then passed from all of those carriers to the electron transport chain. The electron transport chain uses them to change ADP into ATP.

Electron Transport High-energy electrons are passed from one carrier to the next. At the end of the electron transport chain, an enzyme adds these electrons to hydrogen ions and oxygen to form water. Every time 2 electrons pass down the chain, their energy is used to move hydrogen ions (H^+) across the inner mitochondrial membrane. As this happens, H^+ ions build up in the intermembrane space. That space becomes more positively charged than the matrix.

Making ATP The cell uses this charge difference between the two spaces to make ATP. As in photosynthesis, the cell uses enzymes known as ATP synthases. The charge difference makes the H^+ ions move through channels in these enzymes. Each time a H^+ ion moves through it, the ATP synthase turns. With each turn, the enzyme attaches a phosphate to ADP to produce ATP. On average, each pair of high-energy electrons that moves down the full length of the electron transport chain gives off enough energy to make 3 molecules of ATP.

Key Question How does the electron transport chain use high-energy electrons from glycolysis and the Krebs cycle?
The electron transport chain uses the high-energy electrons from glycolysis and the Krebs cycle to change ADP into ATP.

Electron Transport The electron transport chain provides most of the energy that athletes use during cellular respiration.

The Electron Transport Chain and ATP Synthesis The electron transport chain uses high-energy electrons carried by NADH and FADH$_2$ to change ADP into ATP.

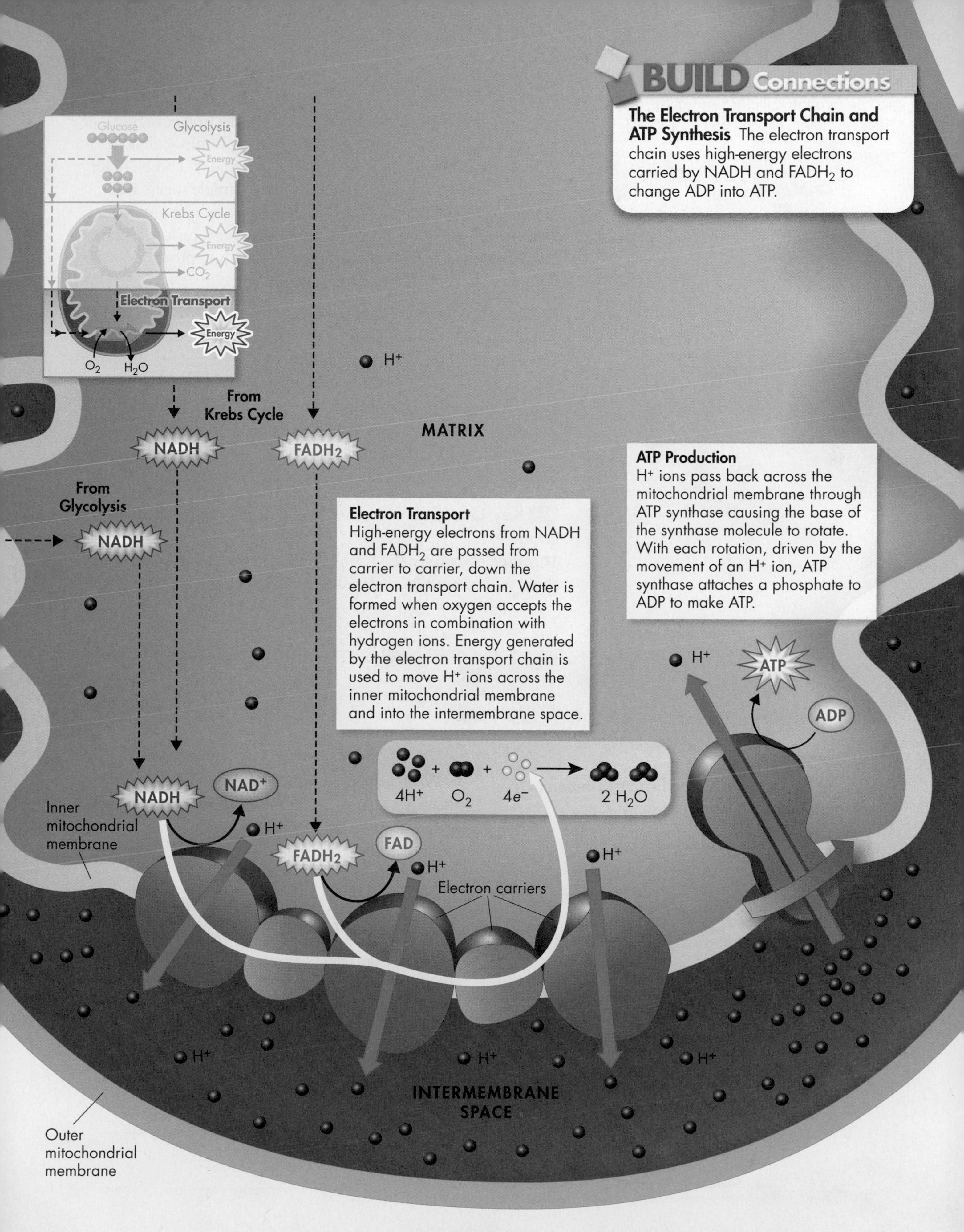

Glucose Glycolysis
Energy

Krebs Cycle
Energy
CO$_2$

Electron Transport
Energy
O$_2$ H$_2$O

H$^+$

From Krebs Cycle

NADH   FADH$_2$

MATRIX

From Glycolysis

NADH

ATP Production
H$^+$ ions pass back across the mitochondrial membrane through ATP synthase causing the base of the synthase molecule to rotate. With each rotation, driven by the movement of an H$^+$ ion, ATP synthase attaches a phosphate to ADP to make ATP.

Electron Transport
High-energy electrons from NADH and FADH$_2$ are passed from carrier to carrier, down the electron transport chain. Water is formed when oxygen accepts the electrons in combination with hydrogen ions. Energy generated by the electron transport chain is used to move H$^+$ ions across the inner mitochondrial membrane and into the intermembrane space.

H$^+$

ATP

ADP

$4H^+ + O_2 + 4e^- \rightarrow 2 H_2O$

Inner mitochondrial membrane

NADH   NAD$^+$

H$^+$

FADH$_2$ FAD

H$^+$

H$^+$

Electron carriers

H$^+$ H$^+$ H$^+$ H$^+$

INTERMEMBRANE SPACE

Outer mitochondrial membrane

Energy Totals Breaking down glucose through cellular respiration makes 36 molecules of ATP.

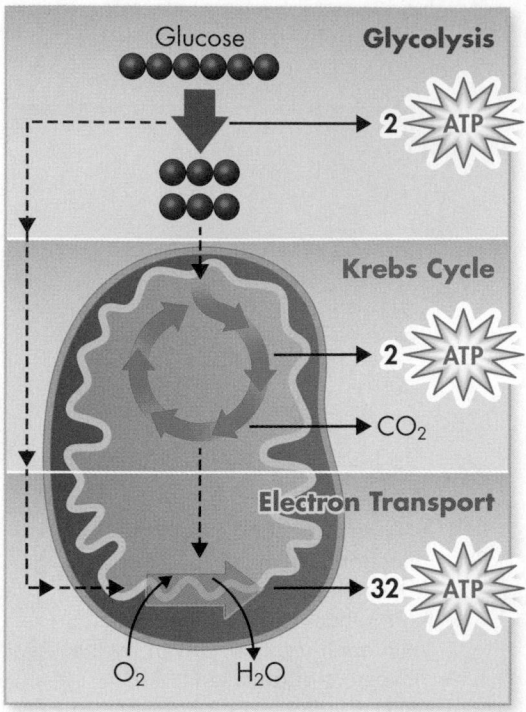

Glucose   **Glycolysis**

2 ATP

Krebs Cycle

2 ATP

CO$_2$

Electron Transport

32 ATP

O$_2$ H$_2$O

The Totals

Together, glycolysis, the Krebs cycle, and the electron transport chain make about 36 molecules of ATP per molecule of glucose. We eat more than just glucose, of course, but that's no problem for the cell. Complex sugars are broken down to simple sugars such as glucose. Lipids and proteins can be broken down into molecules that enter the Krebs cycle or glycolysis. Like a furnace, a cell can use more than one type of reactant, not just glucose, to produce energy. Both the cell and the furnace release heat.

How good is cellular respiration at capturing chemical energy? Those 36 ATP molecules represent about 36 percent of the total energy of glucose. That might not seem like much, but it means that the cell is actually better at using food than a car's engine is at burning gasoline! Just as the fuel in a car, the rest of the energy of glucose is given off as heat. This extra heat is one of the reasons your body feels warmer after exercise, and why your body temperature stays the same day and night.

Key Question How much ATP does cellular respiration generate?
Together, glycolysis, the Krebs cycle, and the electron transport chain make about 36 molecules of ATP per molecule of glucose.

CHECK Understanding

Apply Vocabulary
Use the highlighted words from the lesson to complete each sentence correctly.

1. Glucose is first split during _____.

2. _____ is an electron carrier that is used during glycolysis and the Krebs cycle.

3. During the _____, pyruvic acid is broken down into carbon dioxide.

4. The Krebs cycle takes place in the _____.

Critical Thinking

5. Compare and Contrast How is the function of NAD$^+$ similar to that of NADP$^+$?

6. Infer Why do you often breathe faster during heavy exercise? How is this related to oxygen and cellular respiration?

7. Use Analogies How is the cell like a furnace?

8. Write to Learn Answer the second clue of the mystery. In your answer, describe how whales and humans differ in their ability to stand CO$_2$ buildup in blood.

MYSTERY CLUE

When we are underwater, our bodies react to a buildup of CO$_2$ in the blood. This buildup makes us want to go to the surface and gasp for breath. The average human can hold his or her breath for only about a minute. Whales stay underwater for much longer. What does this suggest about a whale's ability to stand CO$_2$? **(Hint: See p. 218.)**

9.3 Fermentation

MD CLG 3.1.2 Homeostasis, 3.1.3 Matter and Energy, 3.2.1 Processes and Functions, 3.2.2 Changes in Metabolic Activity. SPI 1.5.8 Compare.

Fermentation

How do your cells get energy when you use up oxygen so quickly that you cannot get more oxygen fast enough? And what about organisms that live in places where there isn't oxygen? How do their cells get energy from food?

Glycolysis can make ATP quickly and it does not need oxygen. However, in just a few seconds, glycolysis fills all of the cell's NAD^+ molecules with electrons. Without oxygen, the electron transport chain does not run, so there is nowhere for the NADH molecules to leave their electrons. So, NADH doesn't get converted back to NAD^+. Without NAD^+, the cell cannot keep glycolysis going. That's where fermentation comes in. When oxygen is not present, glycolysis is followed by **fermentation.** During fermentation, cells change NADH to NAD^+ by passing the electrons back to pyruvic acid. The NAD^+ can then fuel glycolysis again. The cells can make ATP again. Fermentation is an aerobic process and takes place in the cytoplasm. Sometimes glycolysis and fermentation are called anaerobic respiration. There are two different kinds—alcoholic fermentation and lactic acid fermentation.

Alcoholic Fermentation Yeasts and a few other microorganisms use alcoholic fermentation. A summary of alcoholic fermentation after glycolysis is as follows:

$$\text{Pyruvic acid} + \text{NADH} \longrightarrow \text{Alcohol} + CO_2 + NAD^+$$

Humans use alcoholic fermentation to make alcoholic beverages. It is also what causes bread dough to rise. When yeast cells in the dough run out of oxygen, the dough begins to give off tiny bubbles of carbon dioxide. These bubbles form the air spaces you see in a slice of bread. The small amount of alcohol made in the dough evaporates when the bread is baked.

Key Questions

🔑 How do organisms generate energy when oxygen is not available?

🔑 How does the body produce ATP during different stages of exercise?

BUILD Understanding

Venn Diagram As you read, create a Venn diagram that compares alcoholic fermentation and lactic acid fermentation.

In Your Workbook Go to your workbook to learn more about making a Venn diagram. Complete the Venn diagram for Lesson 9.3.

fermentation
the process by which cells release
energy in the absence of oxygen

**RELATED WORD
FORMS**

The noun *fermentation* and the verb
ferment are related word forms.
Dough that is beginning to ferment
is just starting to undergo the
process of fermentation.

Lactic Acid Fermentation Most living things carry out fermentation
by changing pyruvic acid into lactic acid. Unlike alcoholic
fermentation, lactic acid fermentation does not give off carbon
dioxide. Like alcoholic fermentation, lactic acid fermentation makes
NAD^+ so that glycolysis can continue. Lactic acid fermentation after
glycolysis can be written as:

$$\text{Pyruvic acid} + \text{NADH} \longrightarrow \text{Lactic acid} + \text{NAD}^+$$

Bacteria that use lactic acid fermentation are used to make many
kinds of foods. Examples are cheese, yogurt, buttermilk, and sour
cream. The acid is part of why these foods have a sour taste. Many
kinds of pickles, sauerkraut, and kimchi are also made using lactic
acid fermentation.

People also use lactic acid fermentation. Many of the cells in our
body are able to make ATP by lactic acid fermentation when they
are without oxygen for a few seconds. Muscle cells use this kind of
fermentation when they need a lot of ATP for quick bursts of activity.

Lactic acid builds up in muscles after a burst of activity. The only way
to get rid of lactic acid is in a chemical pathway that uses extra oxygen.
This is why exercise can leave you huffing and puffing.

Key Question How do organisms generate energy when
oxygen is not available?
**In the absence of oxygen, fermentation releases energy from food
molecules by making ATP.**

Fermentation In alcoholic
fermentation, pyruvic acid from
glycolysis is changed into alcohol
and carbon dioxide. In lactic
acid fermentation, pyruvic acid
from glycolysis is changed into
lactic acid.

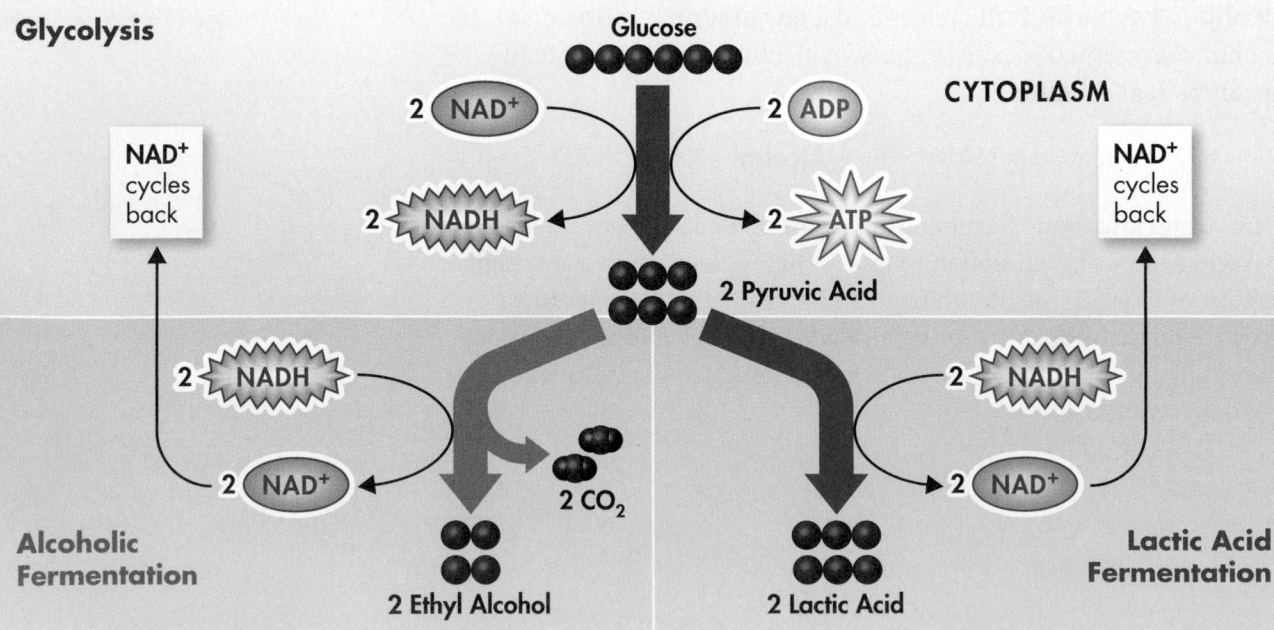

Glycolysis

Glucose

2 NAD$^+$ 2 ADP   **CYTOPLASM**

NAD$^+$
cycles
back

2 NADH   2 ATP

NAD$^+$
cycles
back

2 Pyruvic Acid

2 NADH   2 NADH

2 NAD$^+$ 2 CO$_2$ 2 NAD$^+$

**Alcoholic
Fermentation**

**Lactic Acid
Fermentation**

2 Ethyl Alcohol   2 Lactic Acid

Energy and Exercise

Think about the last time you ran a race. At each stage of the race your body used different paths to get energy. You have three main sources of ATP: ATP already in muscles, ATP made by lactic acid fermentation, and ATP made by cellular respiration. At the beginning of a race, the body uses all three sources. However, stored ATP and lactic acid fermentation can give energy only for a short time.

Quick Energy Cells usually have only a little ATP stored up from cellular respiration. At the very beginning of a race, the muscles have only enough for a few seconds of activity. Usually by the 50-meter mark, that store of ATP is nearly gone. Then, the muscle cells make their ATP by lactic acid fermentation, which gives enough ATP to last about 90 seconds, or about 200 or 300 meters.

Long-Term Energy For exercise longer than about 90 seconds, cellular respiration is the only way to keep making ATP. Your body stores energy in muscle in the form of the carbohydrate glycogen. These stores are usually enough to last for 15 or 20 minutes of activity. After that, your body begins to break down other stored molecules, including fats, for energy.

Energy and Exercise During a race, runners rely on the energy supplied by ATP to make it to the finish line.

🔑 **Key Question** How does the body produce ATP during different stages of exercise?
For quick bursts of energy, the body uses ATP already in muscles and ATP from lactic acid fermentation. For exercise longer than 90 seconds, the body uses cellular respiration.

CHECK Understanding

Apply Vocabulary
Use the highlighted words from the lesson to complete the following sentence correctly.

1. When there is no oxygen present, the cell uses _____ to make ATP.

Critical Thinking

2. Compare and Contrast What reactants and products do the two types of fermentation have in common?

3. Apply Why do runners breathe heavily after a sprint race?

4. Sequence List the body's sources of energy in the order in which they are used during a long-distance race.

5. Infer Why might aerobic exercise help someone lose weight?

6. Write to Learn Answer the third clue of the mystery. In your answer explain what whales do with lactic acid from fermentation.

MYSTERY CLUE

Whales use lactic acid fermentation to get much of their energy during a deep dive. If they can't breathe in to get oxygen, what do they do with all of the lactic acid made by fermentation? (**Hint:** See p. 224.)

# Real-World Lab

MD CLG 3.1.3 Matter and Energy. SPI 1.2.7 Apply Results, 1.3.1 Use Equipment, 1.3.3 Safe Handling of Materials, 1.4.1 Organize Data, 1.5.3 Use Computers to Produce *(continued below)*

Pre-Lab: Comparing Fermentation Rates of Sugars

Problem How does the type of sugar affect the rate of fermentation?

Materials probe interface, gas pressure probe, hot plate, 400-mL beaker, thermometer, ring stand, test-tube clamp, medium test tube, test-tube rack, sugar solution, yeast suspension, pipettes, vegetable oil, 1-hole rubber stopper, plastic tubing with lock fitting

Lab Manual Chapter 9 Lab

Skills Focus Predict, Measure, Analyze Data, Infer

Connect to the Big idea In most cells, the pathways that release energy from food start with the conversion of glucose to pyruvic acid. This process does not require oxygen. When oxygen is present, however, pyruvic acid can react to form a compound that is used in the second stage of cellular respiration. When oxygen is not present, the pyruvic acid can be used in an anaerobic pathway. This alternate pathway from glucose to ATP is called fermentation. In this lab, you will use yeast to ferment sugars and compare the rates of fermentation.

Background Questions

a. Review What is the importance of the NAD^+ that is produced during the fermentation of pyruvic acid?

b. Review What other products are produced besides NAD^+ when yeast ferment sugar?

c. Compare and Contrast How are simple sugars different from disaccharides? (If needed, review Lesson 2.3 in your textbook.)

d. Use Analogies What do fermentation and a detour that drivers must use when roads are closed have in common?

Pre-Lab Questions

Preview the procedure in the lab manual.

1. Infer What is the purpose of adding a layer of vegetable oil above the sugar and yeast mixture?

2. Relate Cause and Effect How will the rate of fermentation affect the gas pressure in a test tube?

3. Predict Which of the sugars do you think will have the highest rate of fermentation, and why?

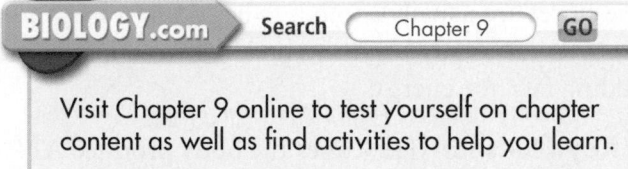

Visit Chapter 9 online to test yourself on chapter content as well as find activities to help you learn.

Untamed Science Video Go underwater with the Untamed Science crew to discover why marine mammals can stay submerged for such a long time.

Tutor Tube Improve your understanding of respiration by working "backward" from a breath of oxygen.

Art Review Review the components of electron transport and ATP synthesis.

InterActive Art See glycolysis and the Krebs cycle in action.

Art in Motion See how matter and energy cycle between photosynthesis and respiration.

 Data Tables, 1.5.4 Use Tables to Communicate Information, 1.5.8 Compare, 1.6.2 Use Computers to Perform Calculations.

9.1 Cellular Respiration: An Overview

- Living things get the energy they need from food.

- Cellular respiration is the process that releases energy from food when oxygen is present.

- Photosynthesis produces food molecules. Photosynthesis takes carbon dioxide from the air. Cellular respiration puts it back. Photosynthesis puts oxygen into the air. Cellular respiration uses that oxygen to get energy from food.

---

cellular respiration (p. 213)
aerobic (p. 214)
anaerobic (p. 214)

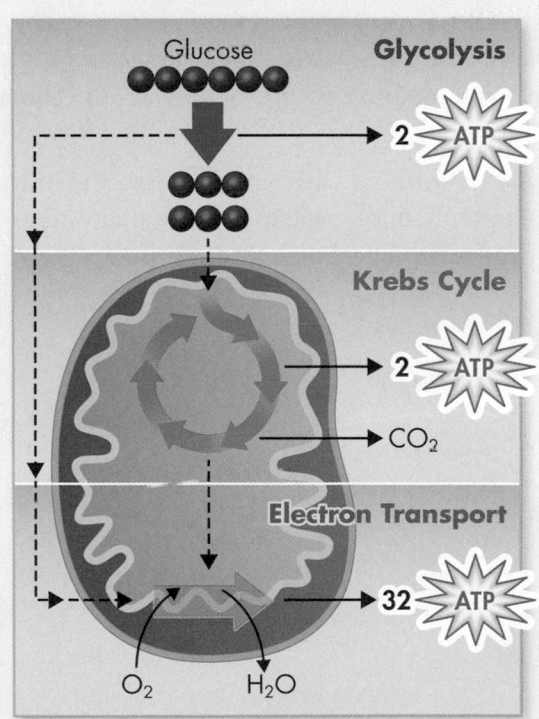

9.2 The Process of Cellular Respiration

- During glycolysis, 1 molecule of glucose, a 6-carbon compound, is changed into 2 molecules of pyruvic acid, a 3-carbon compound.

- During the Krebs cycle, pyruvic acid is broken down into carbon dioxide.

- The electron transport chain uses the high-energy electrons from glycolysis and the Krebs cycle to change ADP into ATP.

- Together, glycolysis, the Krebs cycle, and the electron transport chain make about 36 molecules of ATP per molecule of glucose.

---

glycolysis (p. 216)   Krebs cycle (p. 218)
NAD^+ (p. 216)   matrix (p. 223)

9.3 Fermentation

- When there is no oxygen, fermentation releases energy from food molecules by making ATP.

- For short, quick bursts of energy, the body uses ATP already in muscles and ATP made by lactic acid fermentation.

- For exercise longer than about 90 seconds, cellular respiration is the only way to continue making ATP.

---

fermentation (p. 223)

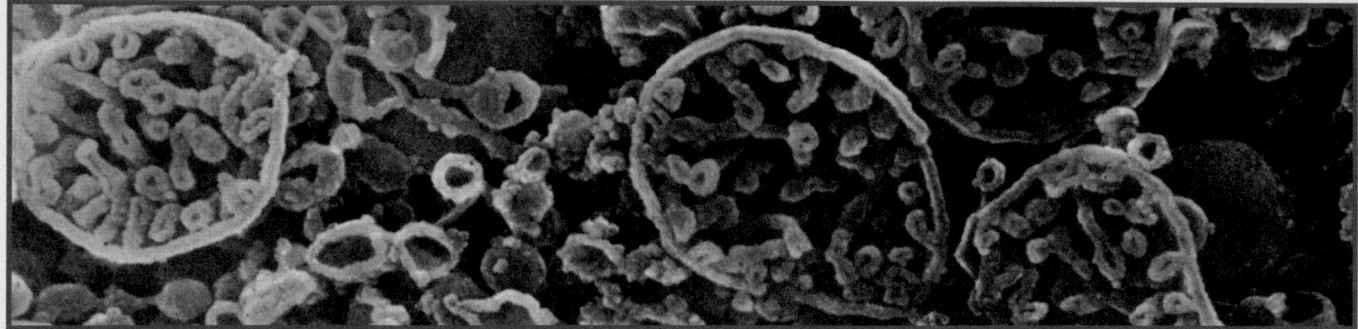

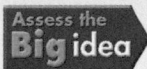 **Cellular Basis of Life**

Write an answer to the question below.
Q: How do organisms obtain energy?

Constructed Response

Write an answer to each of the questions below.
The answer to each question should be one or two
paragraphs. To help you begin, read the **Hints** below
the questions.

1. **Carbon dioxide is a waste product of
   cellular respiration. Plants carry out both
   photosynthesis and cellular respiration. Why
   is it wrong to say that carbon dioxide is a
   waste product in plants?**

   Hint Photosynthesis and cellular respiration are
   opposite processes.

   Hint The reactants for photosynthesis are
   carbon dioxide and water.

2. **When you run a race, you usually have a burst
   of energy at the beginning. But, that burst of
   energy soon fades, and you eventually settle
   down to a steady pace. How do the different
   pathways that the body takes to get energy
   explain how different parts of a race feel?**

   Hint Muscle cells get energy from three
   different sources during a race.

   Hint Stored ATP and lactic acid fermentation
   can give energy only for a short time.

3. **Some kinds of bread are lighter and more airy
   than others. How might rising and baking
   temperature affect how dense bread is?**

Hint Enzymes in cellular process often work
faster at higher temperatures.

Hint The air bubbles in bread are caused by
fermentation.

Foundations for Learning Wrap-Up

Use the index cards and notebook pages you
prepared when you started the chapter as a tool
to help you organize your thoughts about cellular
respiration.

Activity 1 Working with a partner, use the index
cards and notebook page to create a diagram to show
the three stages of cellular respiration.

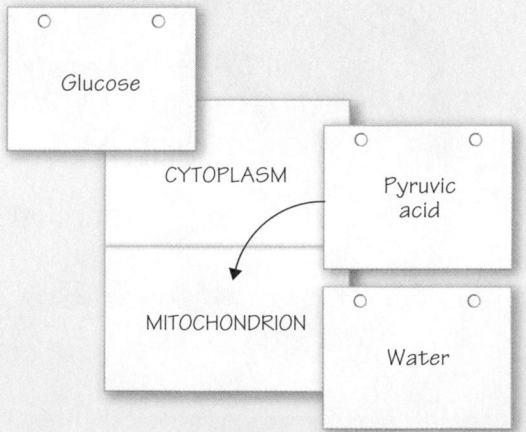

Activity 2 Working with a partner, label six more
index cards with the chemical symbols for each
word on the index cards from Activity 1. Then label
three more index cards with +, +, and →. Now use
the index cards to create a chemical equation that
summarizes cellular respiration.

9.1 Cellular Respiration: An Overview

Understand Key Concepts

1. Cells use the energy stored in food to make
   a. ADP.
   c. glucose.
   b. ATP.
   d. water.

2. The process that gets energy from food when oxygen is present is
   a. ATP synthase.
   c. photosynthesis.
   b. cellular respiration.
   d. synthesis.

3. The first step in getting energy in the cell by breaking down glucose is known as
   a. the Krebs cycle.
   c. fermentation.
   b. electron transport.
   d. glycolysis.

> **Test-Taking Tip**
>
> **Watch For Key Words** Read questions carefully for key words such as *first, most,* or *last.* Question 3 asks for the "*first* step in getting energy in the cell by breaking down glucose." Answers **a**, **b**, and **c** are all steps in getting energy. But, **d** is the first step. So **d** glycolysis, is the correct answer.

4. What does it mean if a process is *anaerobic?* Which part of cellular respiration is anaerobic?

Think Critically

5. **Compare and Contrast** Why are cellular respiration and photosynthesis considered opposite reactions?

9.2 The Process of Cellular Respiration

Understand Key Concepts

6. The net gain of energy from glycolysis is
   a. 8 ADP molecules.
   b. 4 ATP molecules.
   c. 3 pyruvic acid molecules.
   d. 2 ATP molecules.

7. The Krebs cycle takes place within the
   a. chloroplast.
   c. mitochondrion.
   b. cytoplasm.
   d. nucleus.

8. The electron transport chain uses the high-energy electrons from the Krebs cycle to
   a. make glucose.
   b. convert glucose to pyruvic acid.
   c. convert pyruvic acid to citric acid.
   d. move H^+ ions across the inner mitochondrial membrane.

9. What powers the making of ATP by ATP synthase?
   a. the splitting of glycogen
   b. the spinning of the mitochondrion
   c. the movement of ions across the membrane
   d. the movement of electrons through membrane channels

10. What happens to high-energy electrons made during the Krebs cycle?

Think Critically

11. **Compare and Contrast** How is the function of NAD^+ in cellular respiration similar to that of $NADP^+$ in photosynthesis?

12. **Use Models** Draw and label a mitochondrion surrounded by cytoplasm. Show where glycolysis, the Krebs cycle, and the electron transport chain take place in a eukaryotic cell.

9.3 Fermentation

Understand Key Concepts

13. Because fermentation takes place without oxygen, it is said to be
    a. aerobic.
    c. cyclic.
    b. anaerobic.
    d. oxygen-rich.

14. The process carried out by yeast that causes bread dough to rise is

   a. alcoholic fermentation.

   b. cellular respiration.

   c. lactic acid fermentation.

   d. mitosis.

15. Which of the following is a product of alcoholic fermentation?

   a. carbon dioxide   **c.** oxygen

   b. lactic acid   **d.** pyruvic acid

Think Critically

16. Predict Often, regular exercise causes the number of mitochondria in muscle cells to go up. How might that situation help someone do better at activities that use up a lot of energy?

Connecting the Concepts

Use Science Graphics

Use the nutritional information to answer questions 17 and 18.

Nutrition Facts

Serving Size   1 cup
Servings Per Container   About 2

Amount Per Serving

Calories 250	Calories from Fat 108

	% Daily Value*
Total Fat 12g	18%
Saturated Fat 3g	15%
Trans Fat 3g	
Total Carbohydrate 31g	10%
Dietary Fiber 0g	0%
Sugars 5g	
Protein "?"	

17. Apply Concepts On average, how many Calories are there in 1 gram of a lipid, carbohydrate, and protein? Why the differences?

18. Calculate How many grams of protein must there be in this food in order to account for the number of Calories per serving shown in the label?

DIVING WITHOUT A BREATH

To be able to stay underwater for 45-minutes at a time, whales use many different tricks. For example, whale blood can handle the large amount of CO_2 that is made during the Krebs cycle. This lets whales stay underwater for a long time without making them feel a need to go to the surface. The Krebs cycle and electron transport need oxygen. And once the oxygen is used—and it's used quickly!—whale muscles use lactic acid fermentation to get energy. In humans, lactic acid causes the pH of the blood to drop. If the blood gets too acidic, a dangerous state called acidosis can take place. Whale muscles can handle a lot of lactic acid. The lactic acid stays in the muscles without causing acidosis. When whales come up after a long dive, they breathe in oxygen, which clears away the lactic acid buildup.

1. Relate Cause and Effect Why must whales have blood that can hold a lot of CO_2?

2. Predict Myoglobin is a molecule that stores oxygen in muscles. Would you expect to find more or less myoglobin on average in the muscle cells of whales than in the muscle cells of humans? Explain.

3. Infer How might being able to dive into very deep water be an advantage for whales?

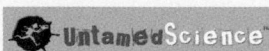 **Never Stop Exploring Your World.** Finding the solution to the mystery is only the beginning. Take a video field trip with the ecogeeks of Untamed Science to see where the mystery leads.

Standardized Test Practice for Maryland

Multiple Choice

1. What raw materials are needed for cellular respiration?
   - **A** glucose and carbon dioxide
   - **B** glucose and oxygen
   - **C** carbon dioxide and oxygen
   - **D** oxygen and lactic acid

   CLG 3.1.3

2. During the Krebs cycle
   - **A** hydrogen ions and oxygen form water.
   - **B** the cell gives off a small amount of energy through fermentation.
   - **C** each glucose molecule is broken down into 2 molecules of pyruvic acid.
   - **D** pyruvic acid is broken down into carbon dioxide over many steps.

   CLG 3.1.3

3. Which substance is needed to begin glycolysis?
   - **A** ATP
   - **B** NADP
   - **C** pyruvic acid
   - **D** carbon dioxide

   CLG 3.1.3

4. In eukaryotic cells, MOST of cellular respiration takes place in the
   - **A** nuclei.
   - **B** cytoplasm.
   - **C** mitochondria.
   - **D** cell walls.

   CLG 3.2.1

5. Which substance is broken down during glycolysis?
   - **A** carbon
   - **B** NAD^+
   - **C** glucose
   - **D** pyruvic acid

   CLG 3.1.3

6. The human body can use all of the following as energy sources EXCEPT
   - **A** ATP in muscles.
   - **B** glycolysis.
   - **C** lactic acid fermentation.
   - **D** alcoholic fermentation.

   CLG 3.1.3

7. During cellular respiration, which of the following are given off?
   - **A** CO_2 and O_2
   - **B** H_2O and O_2
   - **C** O_2 and H_2O
   - **D** CO_2 and H_2O

   CLG 3.1.3

8. Which of the following is an aerobic process?
   - **A** the Krebs cycle
   - **B** glycolysis
   - **C** alcoholic fermentation
   - **D** lactic acid fermentation

   CLG 3.1.3

Questions 9 and 10

The graph below shows the rate of alcoholic fermentation for yeast at different temperatures.

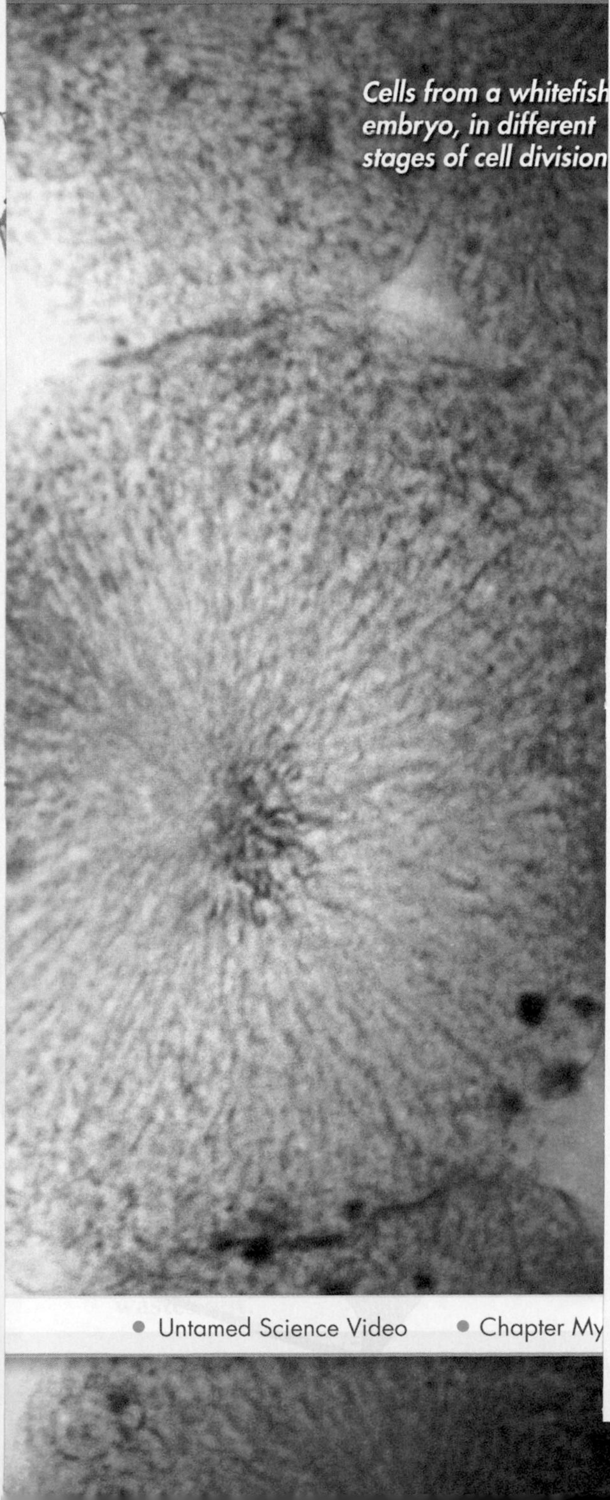

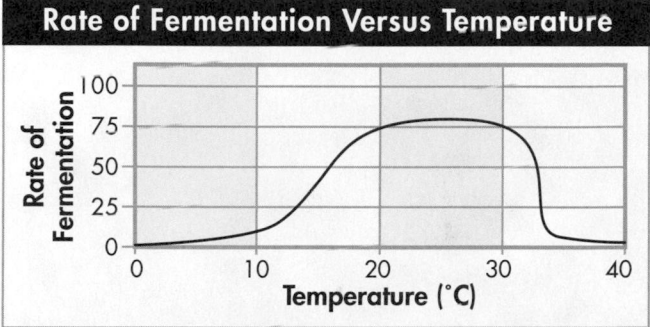

Rate of Fermentation Versus Temperature

9. According to the graph, what is the relationship between the rate of fermentation and temperature?
   - **A** The rate of fermentation continually increases as temperature increases.
   - **B** The rate of fermentation continually decreases as temperature increases.
   - **C** The rate of fermentation increases with temperature at first, then it rapidly decreases.
   - **D** The rate of fermentation decreases with temperature at first, then it rapidly increases.

   SPI 1.4.4

10. Which statement could explain the data shown in the graph?
    - **A** The molecules that carry out fermentation perform best at temperatures above 30°C.
    - **B** The yeast begins releasing carbon dioxide at 30°C.
    - **C** The yeast cannot survive above 30°C.
    - **D** The molecules that carry out fermentation perform best at temperatures below 10°C.

    SPI 1.4.2

Open-Ended Response

11. Explain how a sprinter gets energy during a 30-second race. Is the process aerobic or anaerobic? Compare it to a long-distance runner getting energy during a 5-kilometer race. CLG 3.2.2

If You Have Trouble With . . .

Question	1	2	3	4	5	6	7	8	9	10	11
See Lesson	9.1	9.2	9.2	9.1	9.2	9.3	9.1	9.1	9.3	9.3	9.3

MARYLAND VOLUNTARY STATE CURRICULUM

Biology Indicators/Core Learning Goals (CLG) 3.1.2, 3.2.1, 3.2.2, 3.3.1, 3.4.1, 3.4.2. **Skills and Processes Indicators (SPI** 1.2.4, 1.2.6, 1.3.1, 1.3.3, 1.4.8, 1.4.9, 1.5.2, 1.5.5, 1.5.8, 1.5.9, 1.6.1, 1.6.4, 1.7.1, 1.7.2, 1.7.6. See lessons for details.

Cells from a whitefish embryo, in different stages of cell division

- Untamed Science Video
- Chapter My

BIOLOGY.com Searc

BUILD
Vocabulary

cell division
a process by which a cell divides into two new daughter cells

asexual reproduction
a process by which a single parent reproduces by itself

sexual reproduction
a process by which two cells from different parents fuse, or join together, to produce the first cell of a new organism

PREFIXES

The prefix *a-* in *asexual* means "without." *Asexual reproduction* is reproduction without the fusion of cells.

Cell Division and Reproduction

Before it becomes too large, a growing cell divides. The two new cells are referred to as "daughter" cells. The process by which a cell divides into two cells is called **cell division.**

During the process of cell division, a cell makes a copy of its DNA. Each daughter cell gets its own copy. This copying solves the problem of information overload. Cell division also decreases a cell's volume, which allows for a better exchange of materials in and out of the cell. Cell division can also result in reproduction. Reproduction is the process by which organisms produce offspring—new organisms.

Asexual Reproduction For an organism made up of just one cell, cell division may be the only form of reproduction it needs. All the organism has to do is to copy its DNA and then divide. Reproduction by a single parent is called **asexual reproduction.** Offspring of asexual reproduction have the same genetic information as their parent.

Many multicellular organisms reproduce asexually. Hydras are small animals that live in ponds. They reproduce asexually by budding. As cells divide, the bud grows. The bud eventually separates from the parent. A budding hydra is shown below.

Sexual Reproduction Another way for an organism to reproduce is by **sexual reproduction.** Sexual reproduction results from the joining of two cells. Each cell comes from a different parent. Offspring of sexual reproduction have genetic information from both parents. Most animals and plants reproduce sexually. Some single-celled organisms also reproduce sexually. This type of reproduction happens when two cells come together and share DNA.

Asexual Reproduction Cell division leads to reproduction in single-celled organisms and some multicellular organisms.

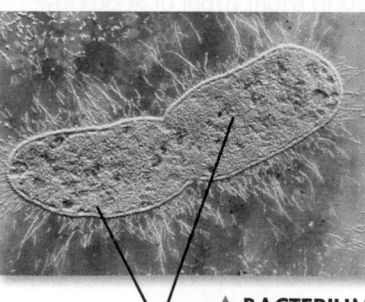

▲ **BACTERIUM**

Daughter cells form and then separate into two bacteria.

Buds can break off and live separated from the parent.

HYDRA

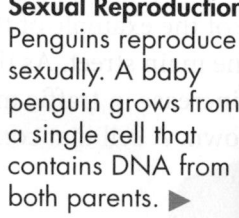

Sexual Reproduction Penguins reproduce sexually. A baby penguin grows from a single cell that contains DNA from both parents. ▶

Advantages Each method of reproduction has advantages. The main advantages of asexual reproduction are that it is quick and that it produces genetically identical offspring. An organism that is well suited for its environment can reproduce very quickly. The result is a large number of equally well-suited offspring. Asexual reproduction is one reason bacteria are able to grow so quickly when they find themselves in ideal conditions.

The main advantage of sexual reproduction is that offspring are genetically different from their parents. Sexual reproduction lets species "try out" new combinations of genetic information from one generation to the next. If the environment changes rapidly, some members of a species may be able to adjust to those changes.

Disadvantages Each method of reproduction also has disadvantages. In asexual reproduction, the lack of genetic diversity can be a disadvantage. Asexually reproducing organisms may not have needed characteristics if their environment changes rapidly. Sexual reproduction is generally slower than asexual reproduction, since it takes two parents instead of one to produce offspring.

Key Question How do asexual and sexual reproduction compare?
Asexual reproduction involves one parent—offspring have the same genetic material as the parent. Sexual reproduction involves two parents—offspring inherit genetic material from both parents.

BUILD Understanding

Venn Diagram Use a Venn diagram to compare and contrast asexual and sexual reproduction.

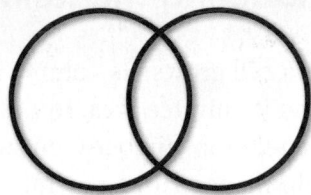

In Your Workbook Go to your workbook to learn more about making a Venn diagram. Complete the Venn diagram started for you.

CHECK Understanding

Apply Vocabulary
Use the highlighted words from the lesson to complete each sentence correctly.

1. For a growing cell, _____ solves the problems of overloading DNA and not being able to get enough materials in or out.

2. Offspring produced by _____ have a mix of DNA from two parents.

3. Cell division in a single-celled organism is a form of _____.

Critical Thinking

4. Compare and Contrast How does DNA in offspring produced by asexual reproduction compare to DNA in offspring produced by sexual reproduction?

5. Apply Concepts Describe advantages and disadvantages of asexual reproduction. Describe advantages and disadvantages of sexual reproduction.

6. Write to Learn Answer the first clue of the mystery. Write a paragraph that includes the terms *DNA* and *cell division*.

MYSTERY CLUE

As the salamander's wound heals, its body cells are dividing to repair the damage. How is this type of cell division similar to asexual reproduction? (**Hint:** See p. 236.)

Modeling the Relationship Between Surface Area and Volume

As a cell grows, its volume increases faster than its surface area. In Lesson 10.1, you saw the relationship between surface area and volume described as a ratio. A ratio is simply a comparison of two numbers. A ratio can be written as a fraction. The table shows how the ratios for 1-cm and 3-cm cubes are calculated.

Look at the calculations for a 3-cm cube.

- First, you calculate the surface area. The formula for the surface area of a cube is

  (length × width) × 6 sides
  (3 cm × 3 cm) × 6 = 54 cm^2

- Next, calculate the volume. The formula for the volume of a cube is

  length × width × height
  3 cm × 3 cm × 3 cm = 27 cm^3

- Finally, determine the ratio of surface area to volume. Write the ratio as a fraction.

  $$\frac{54}{27} = \frac{2}{1}$$

Notice that the fraction 54/27 has been simplified to 2/1. The ratio can also be written as 2 : 1, which is read as "2 to 1."

Analyze and Conclude

1. Predict How would the ratio for a 2-cm cube compare to cubes of 1 cm and 3 cm?

2. Calculate Use the formulas in the table to calculate the ratio of surface area to volume for a 2-cm cube. How accurate was your prediction?

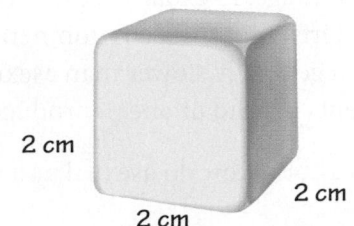

2 cm

2 cm

2 cm

| SA = 2 cm × 2 cm × 6 = _____ cm^2 |
| V = 2 cm × 2 cm × 2 cm = _____ cm^3 |
| Ratio = _____ : _____ |

In Your Workbook Get more help for this activity in your workbook.

Ratio of Surface Area to Volume in Cells		
Cell Size	1 cm 1 cm 1 cm	3 cm 3 cm 3 cm
Surface Area (length × width) × 6 sides	1 cm × 1 cm × 6 = 6 cm^2	3 cm × 3 cm × 6 = 54 cm^2
Volume length × width × height	1 cm × 1 cm × 1 cm = 1 cm^3	3 cm × 3 cm × 3 cm = 27 cm^3
Ratio of Surface Area to Volume	6/1 = 6 : 1	54/27 = 2 : 1

The Process of Cell Division

MD CLG 3.2.1 Processes and Functions, 3.4.2 Relatedness Among Organisms. SPI 1.5.5 Create and Interpret Graphics, 1.5.8 Compare, 1.5.9 Synthesize Ideas.

Chromosomes

Cells carry genetic information in DNA molecules. Even small cells like the bacterium *E. coli* are packed with DNA. In fact, the total length of the DNA molecule in *E. coli* is almost 1000 times the length of the cell. Clearly, that DNA has to be folded into the cell very carefully. Cells do this by packaging each molecule of DNA into a structure called a **chromosome.** Chromosomes make it possible to separate DNA precisely during cell division.

Prokaryotic Chromosomes Prokaryotic cells, such as *E. coli*, do not have a nucleus. The DNA molecules of prokaryotic cells are found in the cytoplasm. Usually, the genetic material is contained in a single, circle-shaped chromosome.

Eukaryotic Chromosomes The DNA molecules of eukaryotic cells are found in the cell nucleus. You are a eukaryote, as are all other animals and all plants. Eukaryotic cells have much more DNA than prokaryotes. And they package it into many chromosomes. The cells in your body have 46 chromosomes.

The chromosomes in eukaryotic cells form a close relationship with special proteins called histones. This combination of chromosomes and proteins is called **chromatin** (KROH muh tin). As a cell gets ready to divide, chromatin condenses, and individual chromosomes become visible inside the cell.

🔑 **Key Question** What is the job of chromosomes in cell division?
Chromosomes make it possible to separate DNA precisely during cell division.

Key Questions

🔑 *What is the job of chromosomes in cell division?*

🔑 *What are the main events of the cell cycle?*

🔑 *What events occur during each phase of mitosis?*

🔑 *How do daughter cells split apart after mitosis?*

BUILD Understanding

Two-Column Chart Use a two-column chart to take notes on the cell cycle. List the phases of the cell cycle in the first column. Describe the phases in the second column. Draw pictures to help you remember.

In Your Workbook Refer to your workbook for suggestions about how to use a two-column chart to organize your notes.

DNA molecule
Replicated chromosome
Histone proteins

Eukaryotic Chromosome
Histone proteins help to keep long molecules of DNA organized in eukaryotic cells. Before a cell divides, DNA molecules form into tighter and tighter coils that take the form of a chromosome.

chromosome
a threadlike structure that contains the genetic information that is passed from one generation of cells to the next

chromatin
a substance found in eukaryotic chromosomes that consists of DNA tightly coiled around histones

cell cycle
a series of events a cell goes through as it grows and divides

🕯 **WORD ORIGINS**

The words *cycle* and *circle* share the same root, *kyklos*, a Greek word meaning "wheel." Cycles are often drawn as circles because they are a series of events that repeat—or go around again and again.

The Cell Cycle

Cells go through a series of events as they grow and then divide. Altogether, these events are called the **cell cycle.** During the cell cycle, a cell grows, prepares for division by making a copy of its DNA, and then divides to form two daughter cells. Each daughter cell then begins the cycle again.

Before any cell divides, it must copy, or replicate, its DNA. What this means, of course, is that the cell must make, or synthesize, new strands of DNA so that each cell receives a complete set of genetic information.

The Prokaryotic Cell Cycle The prokaryotic cell cycle includes cell growth, DNA replication, and cell division. Cell division can happen quickly under good conditions. Most prokaryotic cells replicate, or copy, their DNA once they have grown to a certain size. When DNA replication is complete, or almost complete, the cell begins to divide. The process of cell division in prokaryotes is a form of asexual reproduction called binary fission.

After the chromosome is replicated, the two DNA molecules attach to different parts of the cell membrane. A group of fibers form between the molecules. As the fibers tighten, the cell is pinched across its center. The tightening fibers divide the cytoplasm and separate the cell into two cells. Binary fission results in two cells with the same genetic material.

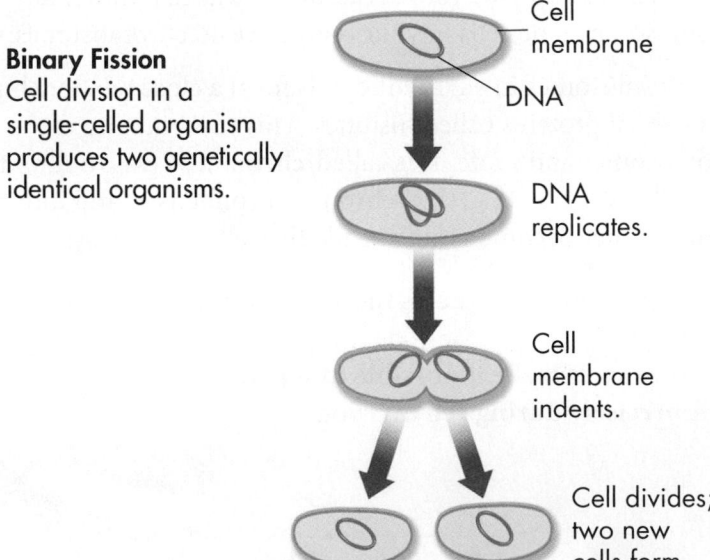

Binary Fission
Cell division in a single-celled organism produces two genetically identical organisms.

Cell membrane

DNA

DNA replicates.

Cell membrane indents.

Cell divides; two new cells form.

The Eukaryotic Cell Cycle The eukaryotic cell cycle has four parts or phases: G_1, S, G_2, and M. The period of growth between cell divisions is referred to as **interphase.** It includes G_1, S, and G_2. A cell prepares to divide during the fourth phase M. At the end of M phase, the cell divides into two daughter cells. The cycle begins again. Refer to the figure below as you read the description of each phase of the eukaryotic cell cycle.

▶ ***G_1 Phase: Cell Growth*** A cell does most of its growing during the G_1 phase. It increases in size and produces new proteins and organelles. The G in G_1 and G_2 stands for "gap." However, both G phases are periods of growth and activity.

▶ ***S Phase: DNA Replication*** The G_1 phase is followed by the S phase. The S stands for "synthesis." During the S phase, new DNA is synthesized when chromosomes are replicated.

▶ ***G_2 Phase: Preparing for Cell Division*** When DNA replication is complete, a cell enters the G_2 phase. During this phase, many of the organelles and molecules needed for cell division are produced. At the end of the G_2 phase, a cell is ready to begin the process of cell division.

▶ ***M Phase: Cell Division*** The M in M phase stands for **mitosis** (my TOH sis). Mitosis is the first stage of the M phase, a series of events that lead to the division of the cell nucleus. **Cytokinesis** (sy toh kin NEE sis) is the second stage. It ends with the division of the cytoplasm. At the end of the M phase, two new daughter cells begin the cycle again.

🔑 **Key Question** What are the main events of the cell cycle?
During the cell cycle, a cell grows, prepares for division, and divides to form two daughter cells. The eukaryotic cell cycle has two parts: interphase and cell division.

Eukaryotic Cell Cycle
The length of the yellow arrow indicates that eukaryotic cells spend most of their time in interphase. Cell division happens quickly.

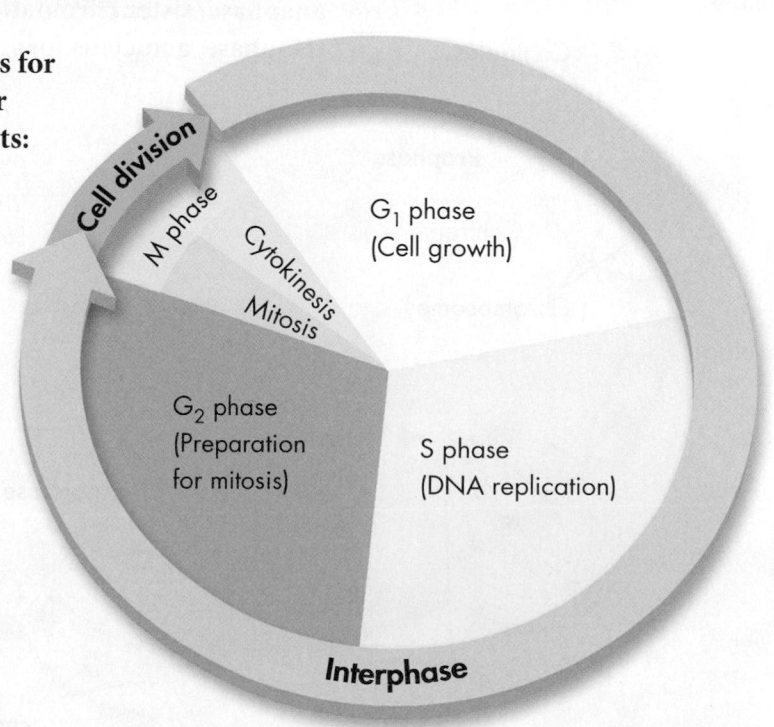

Cell division · M phase · Cytokinesis · Mitosis · G_1 phase (Cell growth) · G_2 phase (Preparation for mitosis) · S phase (DNA replication) · Interphase

Mitosis

Mitosis is divided into four phases: prophase, metaphase, anaphase, and telophase. Refer to the figure below as you read about the phases of mitosis.

Prophase Prophase is the first phase of mitosis. The replicated chromosomes become visible as DNA starts to condense. Each strand of DNA in a doubled chromosome is called a **chromatid.** The sister chromatids are joined at an area called the **centromere.** The nuclear envelope breaks down, and a spindle begins to form. A pair of structures called centrioles help to organize the spindle fibers.

Metaphase The second phase of mitosis is metaphase. The chromosomes line up at the center of the cell. Spindle fibers connect the centromere of each chromosome to the spindle.

Anaphase Anaphase is the third phase of mitosis. The centromeres split, and the sister chromatids separate. A complete set of chromosomes move to opposite sides of the cell.

Telophase The fourth and final phase is telophase. The chromosomes spread out into a tangle of chromatin. A nuclear envelope reforms around each group of chromosomes. The spindle begins to break apart. Mitosis is complete, but cell division still has one more step to go.

🔑 **Key Question** What events occur during each phase of mitosis? **During prophase, chromosomes become visible as DNA condenses and the nucleus breaks down. During metaphase, chromosomes line up across the center of the cell, attached to the spindle. During anaphase, sister chromatids separate and move apart. During telophase, a nucleus forms around each set of chromosomes.**

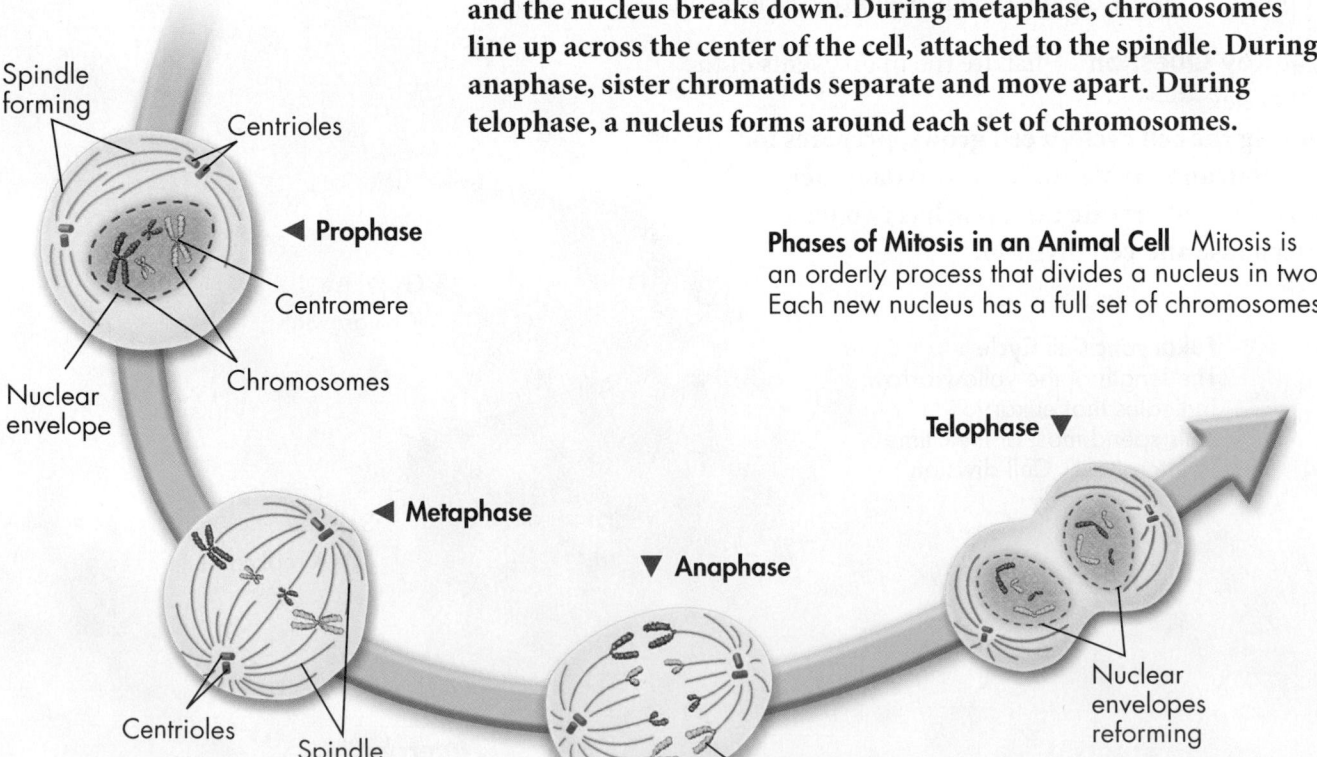

Spindle forming

Centrioles

◄ **Prophase**

Centromere

Chromosomes

Nuclear envelope

Centrioles

Spindle

◄ **Metaphase**

▼ **Anaphase**

Individual chromosomes

Telophase ▼

Nuclear envelopes reforming

Phases of Mitosis in an Animal Cell Mitosis is an orderly process that divides a nucleus in two. Each new nucleus has a full set of chromosomes.

Cytokinesis

Mitosis produces two nuclei, each with a complete set of chromosomes. All that is left to complete the M phase is the division of the cytoplasm. Cytokinesis completes cell division by splitting one cell into two daughter cells. The process is different in animal and plant cells.

Cytokinesis
The division of the cytoplasm occurs differently in animal cells and plant cells.

Cytokinesis in Animal Cells In animal cells, the cell membrane is pulled toward the center of the cell. Eventually the cytoplasm is divided into two nearly equal parts. Each part contains its own nucleus and organelles.

Cytokinesis in Plant Cells In plant cells the cell membrane is attached to a stiff cell wall. It is not flexible enough to pinch in. Instead a cell plate forms between the two nuclei. The cell plate develops into cell membranes that separate the two daughter cells. Next, a cell wall forms between the two new membranes. Each part contains its own nucleus and organelles.

Key Question How do daughter cells split apart after mitosis? **Cytokinesis divides the cytoplasm, splitting one cell into two. In animal cells, the cell membrane pinches in. In plant cells, a cell plate forms.**

The membrane draws inward.

Animal Cell

A cell plate forms.

Plant Cell

✓CHECK Understanding

Apply Vocabulary

Use the highlighted words from the lesson to complete each sentence correctly.

1. In prokaryotes, most cells have a single _____ that contains all the genetic material.

2. In eukaryotes, DNA and proteins combine to form _____.

3. The cell cycle of a eukaryote is divided into two stages: _____ and cell division.

4. In a eukaryotic cell, the chromosomes divide and separate during _____.

Critical Thinking

5. **Sequence** Draw a flowchart that follows a chromosome through a complete eukaryotic cell cycle.

6. **Compare and Contrast** How is cytokinesis in animals and plant cells alike and different?

7. **Write to Learn** Answer the second clue of the mystery. Think about what happens when you cut your finger. How quickly does your body repair the skin? What does that suggest?

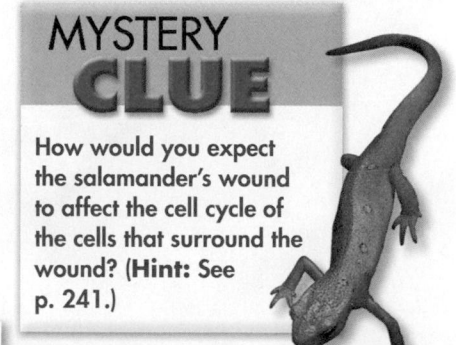

MYSTERY CLUE

How would you expect the salamander's wound to affect the cell cycle of the cells that surround the wound? (**Hint:** See p. 241.)

THE CELL CYCLE

The phases of mitosis and cytokinesis are shown here as part of the the cell cycle. These stages are typical of eukaryotic cells.

In Your Workbook Can you recognize all the phases of the cell cycle in a group of plant cells? Go to your workbook to find out.

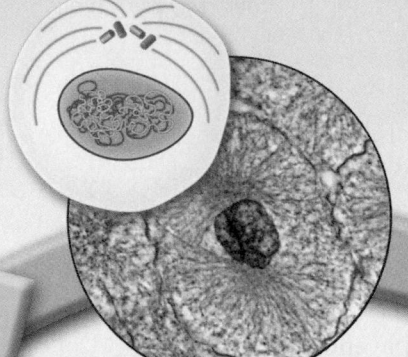

Interphase ▲
The cell grows and replicates its DNA and centrioles.

Prophase ▶
The chromatin condenses into chromosomes. The centrioles separate, and a spindle begins to form. The nuclear envelope breaks down.

◀ Cytokinesis
The cytoplasm pinches in half. Each daughter cell has an identical set of duplicate chromosomes.

Metaphase ▼
The chromosomes line up across the center of the cell. Each chromosome is connected to spindle fibers at its centromere.

▼ Telophase
The chromosomes gather at opposite ends of the cell and lose their distinct shapes. Two new nuclear envelopes will form.

Anaphase ▼
The sister chromatids separate into individual chromosomes and are moved apart.

10.3 Regulating the Cell Cycle

MD | CLG 3.2.1 Processes and Functions, 3.2.2 Changes in Metabolic Activity. SPI 1.7.2 Evaluate Ideas.

Controls on Cell Division

The cell cycle is a process cells go through as they grow and divide. In multicellular organisms, the cell cycle is carefully controlled. In your body, for example, skin cells grow and divide quickly. However, most of the cells in your muscles and nerves do not grow and divide. How do cells know when to divide?

Some cells respond to outside signals. For example, cells grown in a small culture dish will stop growing and dividing when they touch other cells. What happens when cells are removed from the dish? The remaining cells begin to grow and divide again. They stop again when they come in contact with other cells.

Something like this happens in your body when you cut your skin or break a bone. The cells at the edges of the injury begin to divide quickly. These new cells allow the injury to heal. When the healing process is almost done, the rate of cell division slows down. The cell cycle returns to normal.

Key Questions

🔑 **How is the cell cycle regulated?**

🔑 **How do cancer cells differ from other cells?**

BUILD Understanding

Concept Map Make a concept map to organize the information in the lesson. Start with the heading "Regulating the Cell Cycle." Then add the smaller green headings.

In Your Workbook Go to your workbook for help in completing the concept map.

New bone cells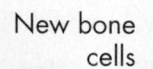

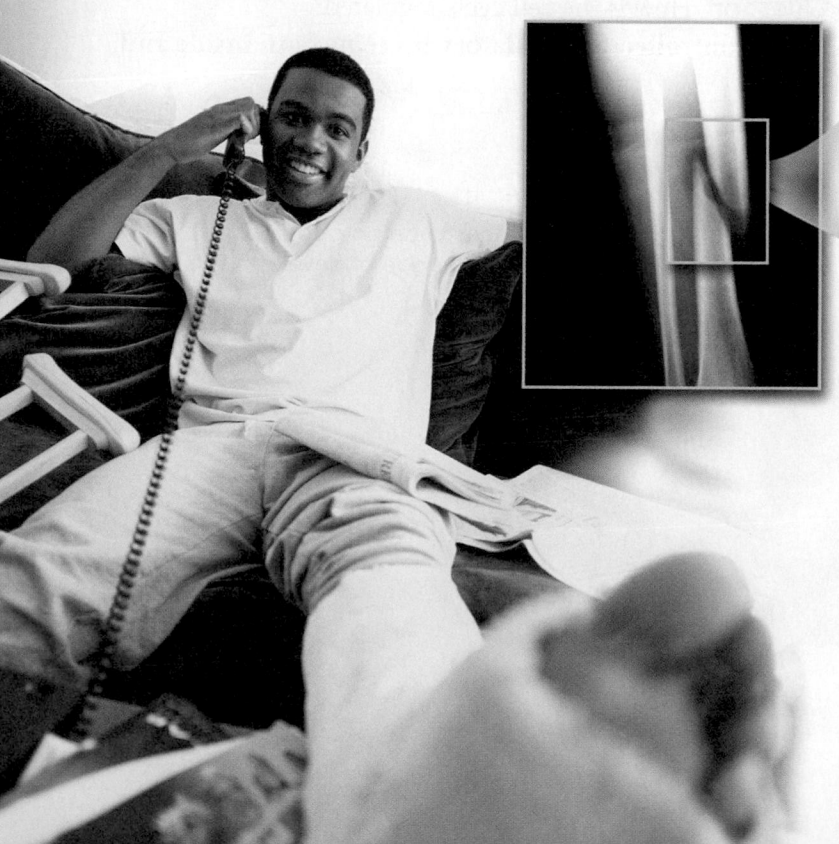

Cell Growth and Healing A broken bone affects the cell cycle. Cells in the injured area receive a signal to grow and divide quickly. This quick growth heals the break.

growth factor
an external regulatory protein that
stimulates the growth and division
of cells

apoptosis
a process in which a cell is
programmed to die

cancer
a disorder in which some of the
body's own cells lose the ability to
control growth

ACADEMIC WORDS

In the term *growth factor*, the
word *factor* means "something
that contributes to a result or
a process." Growth factors
contribute to many processes,
including the healing of broken
bones.

Regulatory Proteins For many years, biologists searched for the signals that controlled the cell cycle. They have found many different proteins that regulate, or control, the cell cycle.

▶ *External Regulators* Proteins that respond to events outside the cell are called external regulators. External regulators can cause the cell cycle to speed up or slow down. **Growth factors** are important external regulators. Growth-factor proteins control the cell cycle when you have an injury, such as a broken bone. They are also involved in controlling the cell cycle during the development of an embryo.

▶ *Internal Regulators* Proteins that respond to events inside the cell are called internal regulators. Internal regulators control the stages of the cell cycle. For example, internal regulators make sure that chromosomes have been replicated before mitosis starts. One important group of regulatory proteins are called cyclins. Cyclins regulate the timing of the cell cycle in eukaryotic cells.

Apoptosis Your body is producing new cells every day. Your body is also removing cells every day. Some cells die by accident because of damage or injury. Other cells, such as skin cells, are "programmed" to die. The process that brings an end to the cell cycle is called **apoptosis** (AYP up TOH sis). During apoptosis, a cell goes through a series of steps that lead to its death.

Apoptosis shapes the structure of tissues and organs in plants and animals. For example, look at the photos of a mouse foot below. Compare the shape of the embryonic foot to the adult foot. Cells between the mouse's toes are programmed to die during tissue development. The cells that remain form into toes.

Key Question How is the cell cycle regulated?
The cell cycle is controlled by regulatory proteins both inside and outside the cell.

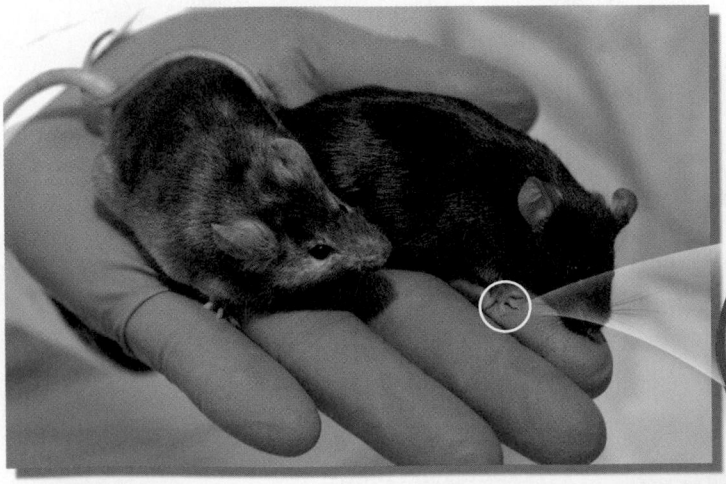

Apoptosis The cells between a mouse's toes undergo apoptosis during a late stage of development.

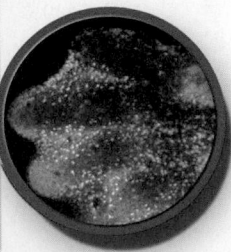

◀ Embryonic foot
(TEM 50X)

Cancer: Uncontrolled Cell Growth

Cancer is a disorder that shows what happens when cell growth is not controlled. Cancer develops when the body loses the ability to control growth in some of its cells. Cancer cells divide without control because they do not respond to the signals that regulate the cell cycle.

Cancerous Tumors Cancer cells form into a mass of cells called a tumor. The cancer cells can spread to nearby tissues and to other parts of the body. As cancer cells grow and divide, they use more and more of the nutrients needed by healthy cells. They can also prevent organs and tissues from functioning normally. Not all tumors are cancerous.

What Causes Cancer? Cancers are caused by damage to a cell's DNA. The damage, or defect, occurs in that part of the genetic material that regulates cell growth and division. Some of these defects are caused by tobacco smoking, radiation exposure, and viral infection.

Treatments for Cancer If a tumor is found early, doctors can often remove it with surgery. Skin cancer can usually be treated this way. In addition, beams of radiation can kill cancer cells. Doctors can also treat cancer with chemical compounds that kill or slow the growth of cancer cells. This treatment is called chemotherapy.

Key Question How do cancer cells differ from other cells?
Cancer cells do not respond to the signals that regulate the growth of most cells. As a result, cells divide uncontrollably.

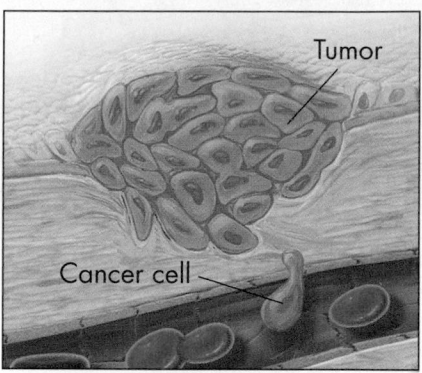

Cell Growth and Cancer Cancer starts when a cell begins to divide without control. A tumor forms. Cancer cells are dangerous because they can get into the bloodstream. From there, they can spread throughout the body.

CHECK Understanding

Use the highlighted words from the lesson to complete each sentence correctly.

1. _____ is a normal process that causes a cell to die.
2. Abnormal cells that do not die but continue to grow and divide cause _____.
3. External regulatory proteins that increase the rate of cell division during an organism's development are called _____.

Critical Thinking

4. **Infer** Why is cancer considered a disease of the cell cycle?
5. **Apply Concepts** How would the pattern of apoptosis differ in a duck's webbed foot compared to the pattern of apoptosis in a mouse's foot?
6. **Explain** What are cyclins? What do cyclins do?

7. **Write to Learn** Answer the third clue of the mystery. The image of the broken bone on the first page of this lesson will help you answer the question.

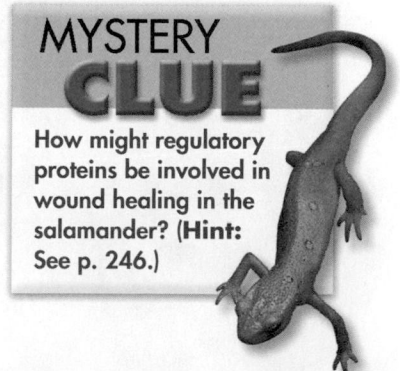

MYSTERY CLUE

How might regulatory proteins be involved in wound healing in the salamander? (**Hint:** See p. 246.)

10.4 Cell Differentiation

MD · CLG **3.1.2** Homeostasis, **3.2.1** Processes and Functions, **3.6.1** Analyze Consequences.
SPI **1.5.2** Communicate Information, **1.7.1** Apply Skills and Concepts, **1.7.2** Evaluate Ideas,
1.7.6 Science and Technology.

Key Questions

🔑 *How do cells become specialized for different functions?*

🔑 *What are stem cells?*

🔑 *What are some possible benefits and issues associated with stem cell research?*

BUILD Understanding

Compare/Contrast Table
Certain types of cells have the ability to differentiate. Use a table to write what you learn about these cells.

In Your Workbook Go to your workbook to see how to organize your compare/contrast table.

From One Cell to Many

Each of us started life as just one cell—a single fertilized egg. So did your pet dog or cat. The fertilized egg goes through an early stage of development called an **embryo.** As it grows, the embryo develops and changes. During the development process, the embryo's cells become different from one another. They differentiate.

What Is Differentiation? Cells become specialized through the process of **differentiation.** Your body has more than 200 different cell types. Notice that the word *differentiate* contains the word *different.* A differentiated cell has become different from the original cell that produced it.

What Is a Specialized Cell? Differentiated cells are specialized to perform certain jobs. In a plant, for example, some cells carry out photosynthesis. Other plant cells store sugars. Other plant cells create pathways for moving materials up and down. In your body, differentiated cells carry out certain jobs that keep you alive.

🔑 **Key Question** How do cells become specialized for different functions?
During the development of an organism, cells differentiate into many types of cells.

Specialized Plant Cells A buttercup plant is made up of cells that are specialized to carry out specific functions.

Cells that store sugar

Cells that transport materials

Cells that carry out photosynthesis

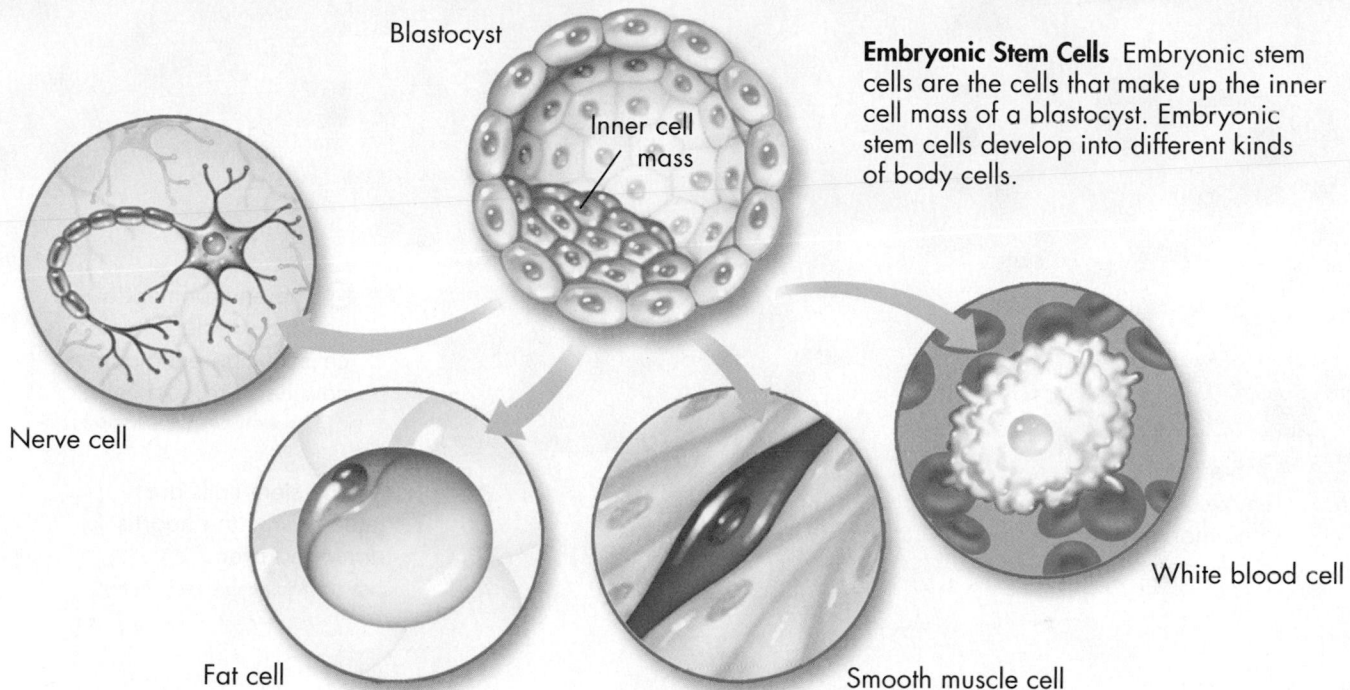

Blastocyst

Inner cell mass

Embryonic Stem Cells Embryonic stem cells are the cells that make up the inner cell mass of a blastocyst. Embryonic stem cells develop into different kinds of body cells.

Nerve cell

Fat cell

Smooth muscle cell

White blood cell

Stem Cells and Development

A fertilized egg divides over and over to form new cells. The fertilized egg and the cells produced by the first few divisions are totipotent. **Totipotent** (toh TIP uh tunt) cells can differentiate into any type of cell.

Human Development Early in development, a human embryo forms into a blastocyst. A blastocyst is a hollow ball of cells with a group of cells inside called the inner cell mass. The outer cells form tissues that attach the embryo to its mother. The inner cell mass becomes the embryo itself.

The cells of the inner cell mass are pluripotent. **Pluripotent** (plu RIP uh tunt) cells can develop into all the types of cells in the body. However, pluripotent cells cannot form the tissues that surround the embryo. Therefore, the cells of the inner cell mass are not totipotent.

Stem Cells Differentiated, specialized cells develop from unspecialized cells known as **stem cells.** Researchers are very interested in stem cells, because stem cells can develop into other types of cells.

▶ *Embryonic Stem Cells* The pluripotent cells that make up the early embryo are called embryonic stem cells. They will eventually produce all of the cells in the body. Scientists have experimented with stem cells grown in the laboratory. For example, scientists have been able to get mouse embryonic stem cells to develop into nerve cells, muscle cells, and even into sperm and egg cells.

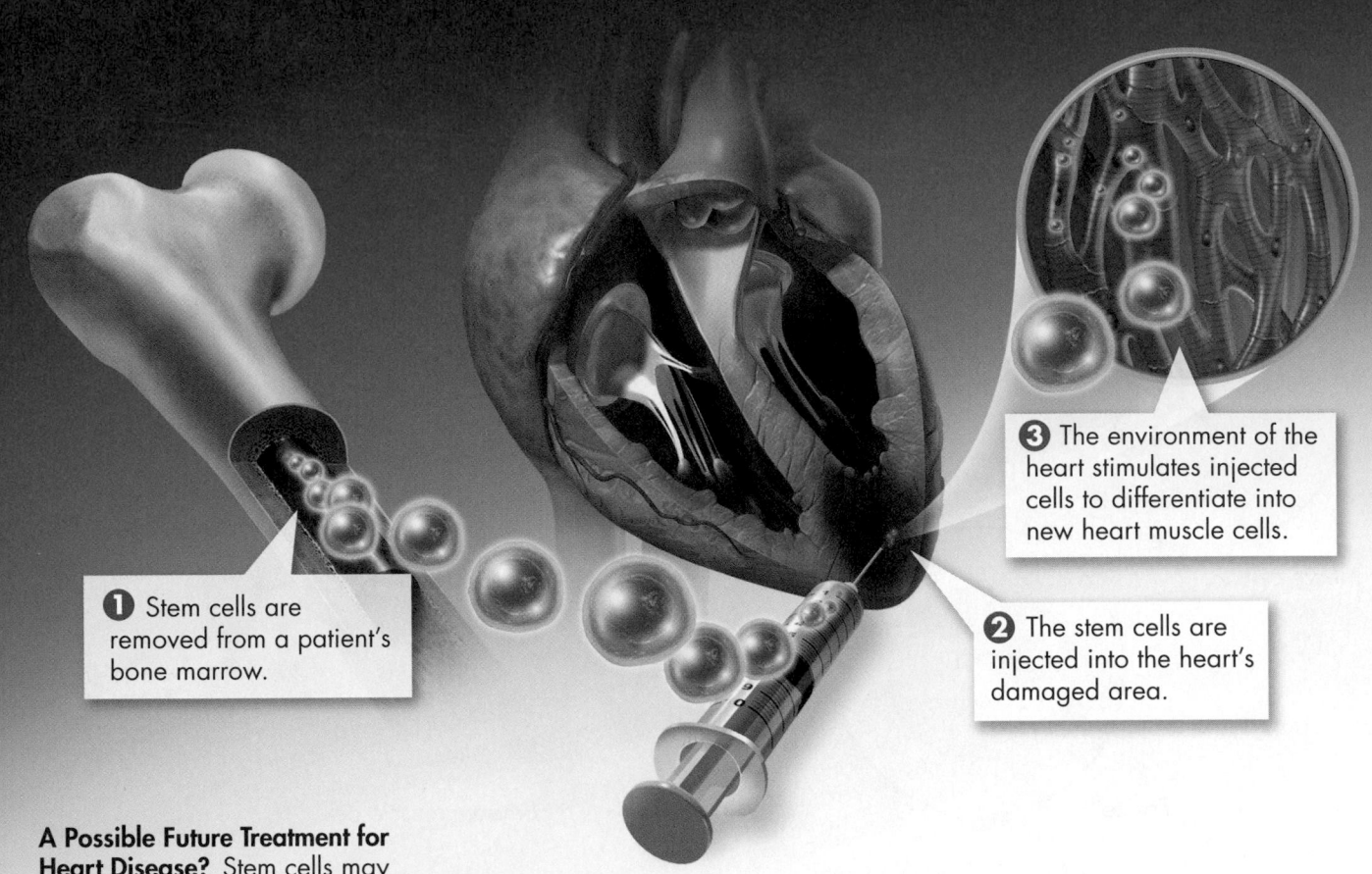

3 The environment of the heart stimulates injected cells to differentiate into new heart muscle cells.

1 Stem cells are removed from a patient's bone marrow.

2 The stem cells are injected into the heart's damaged area.

A Possible Future Treatment for Heart Disease? Stem cells may someday be used to reverse the damage caused by a heart attack. The diagram shows one method that scientists are investigating.

▶ *Adult Stem Cells* Adult organisms also contain some types of stem cells. For example, adult stem cells produce new skin and blood cells. Skin cells and blood cells only live a short time. Therefore, they need to be replaced all the time.

Adult stem cells are called **multipotent** (mul TIP uh tunt) cells. Multipotent means that they can produce many, but not all, types of differentiated cells. For example, adult stem cells in the bone marrow can develop into several types of blood cells.

🔑 **Key Question** What are stem cells?
Stem cells are the unspecialized cells from which differentiated cells develop.

Frontiers in Stem Cell Research

Scientists want to learn how stem cells keep the ability to differentiate into so many different types of cells. Scientists would also like to know why some cells in adults stay multipotent, but other cells lose their ability to differentiate.

Possible Benefits Research on stem cells is important. That is because scientists hope that stem cells might improve human health. Someday, stem cells might be used to fix cells that have been damaged. For example, stem cells might be used to repair heart-attack damage.

Ethical Issues Stem cell research may someday help humans. However, people disagree about whether certain kinds of stem cell research is right or wrong.

To obtain embryonic stem cells, scientists must usually destroy the embryo. Some people believe embryos should have the same protections as any person. These people object to research involving embryonic stem cells. Other people support research with embryonic stem cells. They believe it can improve and save human lives.

Scientists may be able to use technology to address some objections to embryonic stem cell research. For example, scientists hope to find a way to remove a few embryonic stem cells without damaging the embryo. In addition, scientists have been able to make adult stem cells act like pluripotent embryonic stem cells.

Key Question What are some possible benefits and issues associated with stem cell research?
Stem cells offer the possible benefit of using undifferentiated cells to repair or replace badly damaged cells and tissues. Human embryonic stem cell research is controversial because it involves issues of life and death.

CHECK Understanding

Apply Vocabulary

Use the highlighted words from the lesson to complete each sentence correctly.

1. A fertilized egg is a _____ cell, since all the different tissues of the body, including those that surround the embryo, develop from it.

2. The process in which cells become specialized to do different jobs is called _____.

3. Early in development, a human _____ forms into a hollow ball of cells called a blastocyst.

4. Specialized body cells develop from embryonic _____ cells.

5. Cells that are _____, such as those that produce skin and blood cells, can develop into some, but not all, types of specialized cells.

Critical Thinking

6. Interpret Visuals Look again at the picture called Embryonic Stem Cells. In your own words, describe what the picture shows.

7. Compare and Contrast How are totipotent and pluripotent cells alike? How are they different?

8. Explain Explain the potential benefits of stem cell research and the problems associated with this research.

9. Write to Learn Answer the fourth clue of the mystery. In your answer, explain how undifferentiated cells might be useful to the adult salamander.

MYSTERY CLUE

Some adult salamander cells never completely differentiate. What ability do these cells retain? (**Hint:** See p. 249.)

BIOLOGY.com Search (Lesson 10.4) **GO** • Lesson Assessment

Design Your Own Lab

CLG 3.2.1 Processes and Functions. SPI 1.2.4 Testing a Hypothesis, 1.2.6 Investigative Methods 1.3.1 Use Equipment, 1.3.3 Safe Handling of Materials, (continued below)

Pre-Lab: Regeneration in Planaria

Problem How potent are the stem cells in planaria?

Materials fresh water or spring water, planarians, petri dishes, glass-marking pencil, forceps, scalpel, dissecting microscope, glass microscope slide, lens paper, pipette, small paintbrush, clear ruler

Lab Manual Chapter 10 Lab

Skills Focus Form a Hypothesis, Design an Experiment, Draw Conclusions

Connect to the Big idea All cells come from existing cells. When most cells in a multicellular organism divide, they produce cells just like themselves. However, some cells can differentiate to form different types of cells. These cells enable an organism to repair tissue after an injury or in some cases to regenerate body parts. In this lab, you will investigate the ability of planarians to regenerate body parts.

Background Questions

a. Compare and Contrast What is the difference between totipotent stem cells and multipotent stem cells?

b. Apply Concepts What type of stem cell enables your body to produce cells, such as skin and blood cells that are constantly replaced by the body?

c. Apply Concepts What type of stem cell enables a salamander to regenerate its tail?

d. Compare and Contrast In what way is regeneration of a body part similar to asexual reproduction? In what way is it different?

Pre-Lab Questions

Preview the procedure in the lab manual.

1. Draw Conclusions Suppose a cut planarian regenerates completely. What would you conclude about its stem cells? Suppose the regeneration is incomplete. What would you conclude?

2. Control Variables In this lab, you will use an uncut planarian as a control. Explain why you need this control.

3. Infer Two planarians are cut at different locations. Regeneration occurs in one planarian, but not in the other. Based on these results, what might you infer about stem cells in planarians?

 BIOLOGY.com Search (Chapter 10) GO

Visit Chapter 10 online to test yourself on chapter content and to find activities to help you learn.

Untamed Science Video Journey with the Untamed Science crew to a research facility in Sweden to learn why scientists are studying regeneration in brittle stars.

Visual Analogy Compare a growing cell to a growing city to understand limits on cell size.

Tutor Tube Confused about chromosome terminology? Tune in to Tutor Tube to unravel the vocabulary of chromatin.

Art Review Test your knowledge of the structure of a eukaryotic chromosome.

InterActive Art See the phases of mitosis in action.

Art in Motion See what happens when cancerous cells invade normal tissue.

1.4.9 Confirm Hypotheses, 1.5.9 Synthesize Ideas.

10 CHAPTER Summary

10.1 Cell Growth, Division, and Reproduction

- Cells grow only so big before they divide. The larger a cell becomes, the more demands the cell places on its DNA. Also, a larger cell has more difficulty in moving enough nutrients in and wastes out.

- Organisms produced by asexual reproduction are genetically the same as the single cell that produced them.

- Organisms produced by sexual reproduction grow from a single cell that contains genetic information from two parents.

cell division (p. 236)
asexual reproduction (p. 236)
sexual reproduction (p. 236)

10.2 The Process of Cell Division

- Chromosomes are made up of DNA that carries a cell's genetic information.

- The eukaryotic cell cycle includes interphase, mitosis, and cytokinesis.

- Mitosis is divided into four phases in which replicated chromosomes and a cell's nucleus divide equally. In prophase, the chromosomes condense and the nucleus breaks down. In metaphase, the chromosomes line up at the center of the cell. In anaphase, sister chromatids separate. In telophase, a nucleus reforms around each set of separated chromosomes.

- Cytokinesis completes the process of cell division. It splits one cell into two.

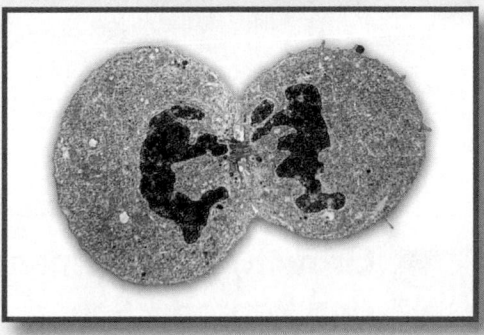

chromosome (p. 239)   mitosis (p. 241)
chromatin (p. 239)   cytokinesis (p. 241)
cell cycle (p. 240)   chromatid (p. 242)
interphase (p. 241)   centromere (p. 242)

10.3 Regulating the Cell Cycle

- Internal and external regulatory proteins help control a cell's growth and division.

- Apoptosis removes old or unneeded cells from an organism.

- Cancer cells do not respond to the signals that tell most cells to stop growing.

growth factors (p. 246)   cancer (p. 247)
apoptosis (p .246)

10.4 Cell Differentiation

- During the development of an organism, cells differentiate into many types of cells.

- Stem cells have the ability to differentiate into other types of cells.

- Stem cell research may offer many medical benefits, but it also raises ethical concerns.

embryo (p. 248)   pluripotent (p. 249)
differentiation (p. 248)   stem cells (p. 249)
totipotent (p. 249)   multipotent (p. 250)

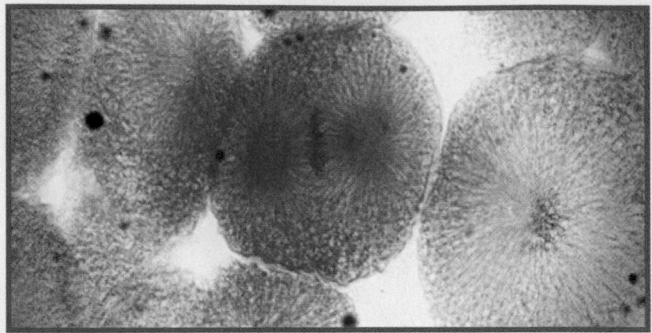

Growth, Development, and Reproduction

Assess the Big idea

Write an answer to the question below.

Q: How does a cell produce a new cell?

Constructed Response

Write an answer to each of the numbered questions below. The answer to each question should be one or two paragraphs. To help you begin, read the **Hints** below the questions.

1. **How does cell growth affect the ability of a cell to exchange materials with its environment?**

   Hint The exchange of materials is important to cells. Materials must come into a cell. Materials must go out of a cell.

   Hint As a cell grows, the relationship of its surface area to its volume changes.

2. **What are the main events of interphase?**

   Hint There are the three phases that make up interphase. List the phases in the order that they happen.

   Hint Look at the diagram called Eukaryotic Cell Cycle.

3. **In the future, how might stem cells be important for dealing with human health problems?**

   Hint Stem cells do things that most other cells cannot do.

Foundations for Learning Wrap-Up

Use the index cards you prepared when you started the chapter as a tool to help you organize your thoughts about cell growth and division.

Activity 1 Working with a partner, choose five index cards at random. Explain how each word is related to the other. If the words are not related, explain why. Take turn choosing cards.

Activity 2 Working in a small group, choose a group of cards whose terms are related. Construct a concept map by placing the cards on a table and describing how the words are connected. Make sure you use each of the cards at least once.

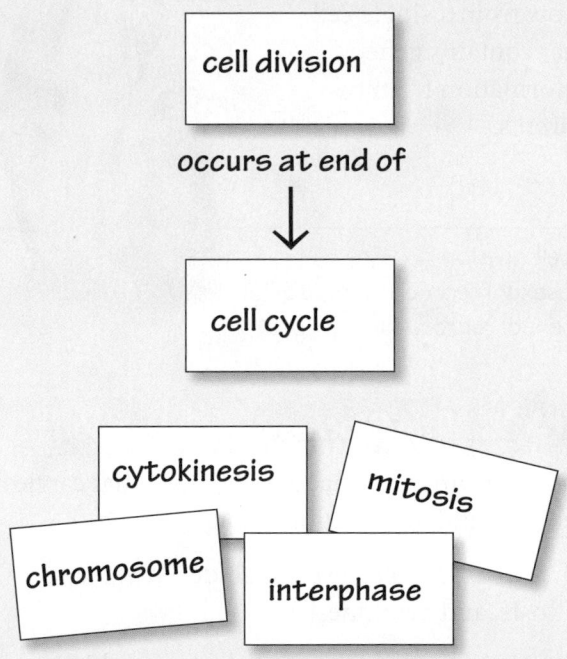

You may want to add a card for each phase of mitosis.

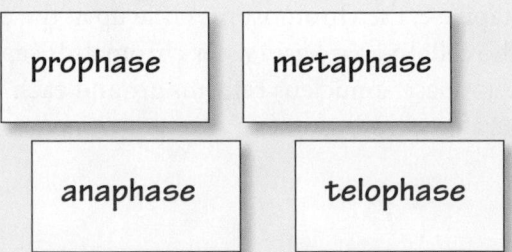

10.1 Cell Growth, Division, and Reproduction

Understand Key Concepts

1. A cell is limited in size by access to the genetic information contained in its
   a. cytoplasm.
   b. cell membrane.
   c. DNA.
   d. organelles.

Test-Taking Tip

Anticipate the Answer Think of your own answer before looking at the answer choices. Select the answer choice that comes closest to your own answer. In question 1, answer **c** is correct because genetic information is contained in DNA. All the other answers refer to cell parts. They are intended to distract you from the right answer.

2. Which material is it important for a cell to remove?
   a. water
   b. waste
   c. food
   d. oxygen

3. Identify one way in which asexual and sexual reproduction are alike and one way in which they are different.

Think Critically

4. **Relate Cause and Effect** In a rapidly changing environment, which organisms have an advantage—those that reproduce asexually or those that reproduce sexually? Explain.

10.2 The Process of Cell Division

Understand Key Concepts

5. For a cell to divide successfully, it must first
   a. form a new cell plate or cell membrane.
   b. divide its cytoplasm and organelles.
   c. increase its number of chromosomes.
   d. copy its genetic information.

6. The cell cycle in a eukaryotic cell is divided into
   a. prophase, anaphase, and telophase.
   b. interphase, metaphase, and cytokinesis
   c. interphase, mitosis, and cytokinesis.
   d. interphase, anaphase, and telophase.

7. What happens to a chromosome during cell division?

8. Identify the four phases of mitosis and give a brief description of what happens in each phase.

Think Critically

9. **Compare and Contrast** How does cell division in prokaryotes differ from cell division in eukaryotes?

10.3 Regulating the Cell Cycle

Understand Key Concepts

10. The timing in the cell cycle in eukaryotic cells is believed to be controlled by a group of closely related proteins known as
    a. chromatids.
    b. cyclins.
    c. centromeres.
    d. centrioles.

11. What type of regulatory proteins are activated when you break a bone?
    a. cyclins
    b. internal regulators
    c. bone cells
    d. growth factors

12. What effect do cancer cells have on the healthy cells that surround them?

13. What role does apoptosis play in a tadpole whose tail shrinks as it develops into a frog?

Think Critically

14. **Compare and Contrast** How are cancer cells different from other cells? How are they alike?

10.4 Cell Differentiation

Understand Key Concepts

15. Which type of cell can differentiate into any kind of cell?
- **a.** totipotent
- **b.** pluripotent
- **c.** multipotent
- **d.** differentiated

16. An organism at an early stage of development is
- **a.** a stem cell.
- **b.** a chromosome.
- **c.** a cytokinesis.
- **d.** an embryo.

17. What is cell differentiation? How is it important to an organism's development?

18. Describe how scientists may help ease the ethical concerns about stem cell research.

Think Critically

19. Relate Cause and Effect Suppose researchers discover how to make skin stem cells pluripotent. How might this affect treatments for heart attack patients?

Connecting Concepts

Use Science Graphics

Use the data table to answer the questions 20 and 21.

Life Spans of Various Human Cells		
Cell Type	**Life Span**	**Cell Division**
Red blood cells	<120 days	Cannot divide
Cardiac (heart) muscle	Long-lived	Cannot divide
Smooth muscle	Long-lived	Can divide
Neuron (nerve cell)	Long-lived	Most do not divide

20. Compare and Contrast Where would you expect to find active stem cells, in the bone where blood cells are produced or in the heart? Explain your thinking.

21. Infer Suppose cancer cells were added to the table. What would probably be written in the "Cell Division" column? Explain.

---

solve the CHAPTER MYSTERY

PET SHOP ACCIDENT

Julia checked the hurt salamander each day. About a month after the accident, Julia realized that a new leg was going to replace the lost one! Salamanders are one of a few vertebrates that can regenerate, or grow, a complete limb.

Look at the pictures that show how a new leg develops. Then answer the questions.

Week 1: Dedifferentiation
Cells in the wounded area dedifferentiate. This means they are unable to differentiate. Cells can no longer perform their specialized jobs.

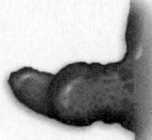

Week 3: Forming a web of cells
The dedifferentiated cells move to the wounded area. There they form a tangled web of growing, undifferentiated cells.

Week 5: Redifferentiation
The web of cells redifferentiate, again becoming differentiated. These new cells produce the new leg. The leg will continue to grow until it is full size.

1. Relate Cause and Effect Cells in the salamander's leg first had to dedifferentiate. Why was this a key part of growing a new leg?

2. Classify What type of stem cells do you think the tangled web of cells contain?

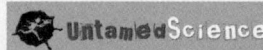 **Never Stop Exploring Your World.** Finding the solution to the pet shop mystery is only the beginning. Take a video field trip with the ecogeeks of Untamed Science to see where the mystery leads.

Standardized Test Practice for Maryland

Multiple Choice

1. Which statement is true regarding a cell's surface area-to-volume ratio?
   A As the size of a cell increases, its volume decreases.
   B As the size of a cell decreases, its volume increases.
   C Larger cells will have a greater surface area-to-volume ratio.
   D Smaller cells will have a greater surface area-to-volume ratio. CLG 3.2.1

2. Which of the following is *not* an advantage of asexual reproduction?
   A simple and efficient
   B produces large number of offspring quickly
   C increases genetic diversity
   D requires one parent CLG 3.2.1

3. At the beginning of cell division, a chromosome consists of two
   A centromeres.
   B centrioles.
   C chromatids.
   D spindles. CLG 3.2.1

4. What regulates the timing of the cell cycle in eukaryotes?
   A chromosomes
   B cyclins
   C nutrients
   D DNA and RNA CLG 3.2.1

5. The period between cell divisions is called
   A interphase.
   B prophase.
   C G_3 phase.
   D cytokinesis. CLG 3.2.1

6. Which of the following is true about totipotent cells?
   A Totipotent cells develop in the inner cell mass.
   B Totipotent cells are differentiated cells.
   C Totipotent cells can differentiate into any type of cell and tissue.
   D Adult stem cells are totipotent cells. CLG 3.2.1

7. A cell enters anaphase before all of its chromosomes have attached to the spindle. This may indicate that the cell is not responding to
   A internal regulators.
   B cyclins.
   C growth factors.
   D apoptosis. CLG 3.2.1

Questions 8–10

The spindle fibers of a dividing cell were labeled with a fluorescent dye. At the beginning of anaphase, a laser beam was used to stop the dye from glowing on one side of the cell, thereby marking the fibers, as shown in the second diagram. The laser did not inhibit the normal function of the fibers.

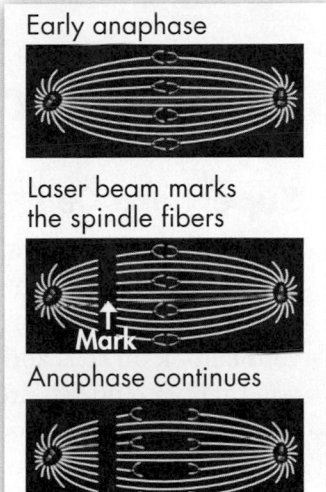
Early anaphase

Laser beam marks the spindle fibers

Mark

Anaphase continues

8. This experiment tests a hypothesis about
   A how chromosomes migrate during cell division.
   B how fluorescent dyes work in the cell.
   C the effect of lasers on cells.
   D why cells divide. SPI 1.2.3

9. The diagram shows that the spindle fibers
   A shorten on the chromosome side of the mark.
   B lengthen on the chromosome side of the mark.
   C shorten on the centriole side of the mark.
   D lengthen on the centriole side of the mark. SPI 1.5.5

10. A valid conclusion that can be drawn from this experiment is that the spindle fibers break down
    A at the centrioles.
    B in the presence of dye.
    C when marked by lasers.
    D when they are attached by chromosomes. SPI 1.4.2

Open-Ended Response

11. Explain why careful regulation of the cell cycle is important to multicellular organisms. CLG 3.2.1

If You Have Trouble With . . .

Question	1	2	3	4	5	6	7	8	9	10	11
See Lesson	10.1	10.1	10.2	10.3	10.2	10.4	10.3	10.2	10.2	10.2	10.3

Unit Project

Superhero Cell

Do you like reading comics? Have you ever designed a comic book of your own? Here's your chance! A high school teacher has contacted you asking for a comic book on cells and cell processes. She has told you that her students are just about to start studying cells and need a good introduction to the topic. You've been tasked with developing the story line and visuals that will provide the students with a basic understanding of cell structure and function. Remember that sometimes a picture can be worth a thousand words—so be creative!

Your Task Write a comic book about a "superhero cell" for an audience of high school students.

Be sure to
- incorporate important concepts and details about the structure and function of various organelles and cell processes.
- provide insight into the ways cells work and interact with their environment.
- be entertaining and creative.

Reflection Questions

1. Score your project using the rubric below. What score did you give yourself?
2. What did you do well on this project?
3. What about your project needs improvement?
4. Exchange your comic book with a classmate and have him/her read it. What did your partner like about your comic book? What did he/she think could use improvement?

Assessment Rubric

Score	Scientific Content	Quality of Comic Book
4	The comic book includes accurate details about the structures and functions of several organelles and cell processes. It provides exceptional insight into how a cell works and interacts with its environment.	The comic book is thoughtfully and creatively written and illustrated.
3	The comic book includes mostly accurate details about the structure and functions of organelles and cell processes. It provides good insight into how a cell works and interacts with its environment.	The comic book is well written and includes some creativity. Illustrations are clear.
2	The comic book includes a few details about the structure and functions of organelles and cell processes, with some inaccuracies. It provides some insight into how a cell works and interacts with its environment.	The comic book needs some edits and could use more creativity. Some parts of the story line and illustrations are difficult to follow.
1	The comic book includes vague and inaccurate information about the structure and functions of organelles and cell processes. It provides little insight into how a cell works and interacts with its environment.	The comic book needs significant edits and includes very little creativity. Story line and illustrations are unclear.

Genetics

INTRODUCE the Big ideas

- **Information and Heredity**
- **Cellular Basis of Life**
- **Science as a Way of Knowing**

"Do you look more like mom or dad? I once ran my daughter's DNA on a fingerprinting gel. It didn't settle whether she had her mother's eyes or mine, but half of the bands on that gel were identical to mine, and half, of course, to her mom's. It made me think just how remarkable human genetics really is. Our genes may come from our parents, but each of us gets a fresh shuffle and a brand-new deal of those genetic cards as we start our lives."

Ken Miller

11 Introduction to Genetics

Big idea

Information and Heredity

Q: How does biological information pass from one generation to another?

Labrador retrievers may be black, brown, or yellow.
Each puppy in a litter can have a different color
based on the genes it inherits.

BIOLOGY.com > Search   Chapter 11   GO • Flash Cards

MD **MARYLAND VOLUNTARY**
STATE CURRICULUM

**Biology Indicators/Core Learning
Goals (CLG)** 3.2.1, 3.3.1, 3.3.2. **Skills
and Processes Indicators (SPI)** 1.1.2,
1.4.1, 1.4.2, 1.4.3, 1.4.8, 1.5.2, 1.5.5,
1.5.8, 1.5.9, 1.6.1, 1.7.4. See lessons
for details.

GREEN PARAKEETS

Susan's birthday was coming up. Parakeets make great
pets, so Susan's parents wanted to give two birds to her
as a birthday present. At the pet store, they chose two
healthy green parakeets—one male and one female.
They knew that green was Susan's favorite color.

Susan was happy about her birthday present. She
fed the birds and kept their cage clean. A few weeks
later, Susan found three small eggs in the birds' nest.
When the eggs hatched, Susan was amazed. None
of the chicks was green! One chick was white, one
was blue, and one was yellow. Why weren't any of
them green? What had happened to the green color
of the birds' parents?

Read for Mystery Clues As you read this chapter, look
for clues to help you figure out why the parakeet chicks
were colored differently than their parents. Then solve
the mystery at the end of the chapter.

FOUNDATIONS
for Learning

Before you read the chapter, write each vocabulary word on
the open side of the Undercover Vocabulary Tool. As you read
the chapter, fill in the definitions. You can use different color
highlighters to show the different categories. At the end of
the chapter are two activities that use the tool to help answer
the question: How does information in cells pass from one
generation to another?

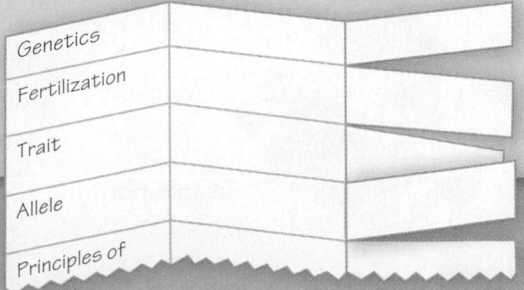

Genetics
Fertilization
Trait
Allele
Principles of

• Untamed Science Video   • Chapter Mystery

The Work of Gregor Mendel

MD CLG 3.3.1 Sexual Reproduction and Variation, 3.3.2 Inherited Traits. SPI 1.1.2 Scientific Ideas, 1.4.3 Use Data, 1.5.8 Compare.

Key Questions

🔑 *Where does an organism get its unique characteristics?*

🔑 *How are different forms of a gene passed to offspring?*

BUILD Understanding

Two-Column Chart Before you read, draw a line down the center of a piece of paper. On the left side, write the main ideas in this lesson. On the right side, note the details and examples that support each of those ideas.

In Your Workbook Go to your workbook to learn more about making a two-column chart for Lesson 11.1.

Pea Flower

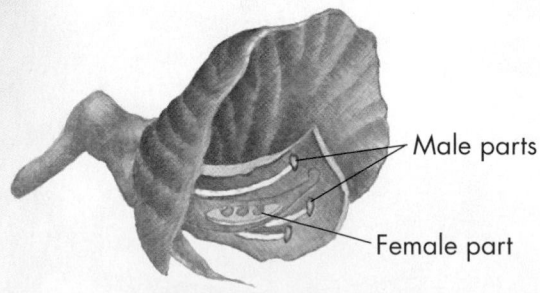

Male parts

Female part

Flower Parts Flowers have male parts and female parts. During fertilization, pollen is transferred from the male parts to the female parts.

The Experiments of Gregor Mendel

Every living thing has a set of characteristics inherited from its parent or parents. The scientific study of this biological inheritance is **genetics.** Genetics is the key to understanding what makes each organism unique.

The modern science of genetics was started by a monk named Gregor Mendel. Mendel was in charge of the garden in the monastery where he lived. In this garden, he did work that changed biology forever.

Mendel used ordinary garden peas in his studies. He used peas partly because peas are small and easy to grow. A single pea plant can make hundreds of offspring. Also, pea plants grow quickly and have many traits that are easy to see.

The Role of Fertilization When Mendel started his experiments, he knew that the male part of each flower makes pollen. Pollen contains the plant's male reproductive cells, called sperm. Mendel also knew that the female part of each flower makes reproductive cells called eggs. During sexual reproduction, male and female reproductive cells join in a process known as **fertilization** to make a new cell. In peas, this new cell develops into a tiny embryo wrapped inside a seed.

The male and female reproductive cells of pea plants are in every pea flower. Since pea flowers have both kinds of cells, a pea flower normally pollinates itself. A plant grown from a seed made by self-pollination has just one parent, because both reproductive cells came from the same plant.

True-Breeding Plants Mendel's monastery garden had several stocks of pea plants. These plants were "true-breeding." True-breeding plants are self-pollinating. They make offspring identical to themselves. The traits in each generation are the same. A **trait** is a specific characteristic, such as seed color or plant height, of an individual. A trait may vary from one individual to another. For example, one stock of Mendel's seeds made only tall plants. Another stock made only short ones. One stock made only green seeds. Another stock made only yellow seeds.

Crossbreeding Mendel wanted to learn more about how traits are passed from parent to offspring. So, he used pollen from one stock of plants to fertilize the female parts of flowers from other stocks of plants. This process is called cross pollination and produces a plant that has different parents.

Mendel studied seven different traits of pea plants. Each of the traits had two contrasting forms. Seed color is one example of a trait Mendel studied. The seeds were either green or yellow. Mendel wanted to see what would happen if he made a plant from two parents that had different traits. The offspring of crosses between parents with different traits are called hybrids.

Two Conclusions When a yellow-seed plant was crossed with a green-seed plant, all the offspring produced yellow seeds. It seemed that the green trait had disappeared. The same thing happened with each of the other traits. Mendel drew two conclusions from this.

▶ *Passing Traits to Offspring* First, Mendel found that an individual's characteristics are controlled by factors that are passed from parent to offspring. Today, scientists call these factors **genes** (jeenz). Each of the traits Mendel studied was controlled by a single gene that existed in two different forms. Each form of the gene controlled one form of a trait. For example, the gene for plant height came in one form that made tall plants and another form that made short plants. The different forms of the same gene are called **alleles** (uh LEELZ).

▶ *Dominant and Recessive Alleles* Mendel's second conclusion explains why some of the traits seemed to disappear in the offspring. This conclusion is called the **principle of dominance.** This principle states that some alleles are dominant and others are recessive (ree SESS iv). An organism with at least one dominant allele for a form of a trait will show that form of the trait. An organism with a recessive allele for a form of a trait will show that form only when the dominant allele for the trait is not there. In Mendel's experiments, the allele for tall plants was dominant, and the allele for short plants was recessive. Similarly, the allele for yellow seeds was dominant over the recessive allele for green seeds.

Key Question Where does an organism get its unique characteristics?
An individual's unique characteristics are determined by factors that are passed from parent to offspring.

Mendel's F₁ Crosses This table shows three of the characteristics Mendel studied.

Mendel's F₁ Crosses on Pea Plants			
	Seed Shape	**Seed Color**	**Seed Coat**
P	Round X Wrinkled	Yellow X Green	Gray X White
F₁	↓ Round	↓ Yellow	↓ Gray

segregation
the separation of alleles

gametes
sex cells

📝 WORD ORIGINS _____

Like the word *segment*, the word *segregate* comes from the Latin root word *segmentum*, which means "a piece cut off."

Segregation

When doing genetic crosses, we call each original pair of plants the P, or parental, generation. Their offspring are called the F_1 generation. Mendel had a question about his F_1 generation of pea plants. Had the recessive alleles simply disappeared, or were they still in the new plants? To find out, he had all seven kinds of F_1 hybrids self-pollinate. The offspring of an F_1 cross are called the F_2 generation. So, Mendel crossed the F_1 generation with itself to make the F_2 offspring.

Recessive Traits Reappear Mendel found that the traits controlled by the recessive alleles reappeared in the second generation. About one fourth of the F_2 plants showed the trait controlled by the recessive allele. Why did the recessive alleles seem to disappear in the F_1 generation and then reappear in the F_2 generation?

Explaining the F_1 Cross Mendel figured out that only the dominant alleles determined the traits of the F_1 generation. However, the trait controlled by the recessive allele did show up in some of the F_2 second generation of plants. So, Mendel realized that the allele for shortness had separated from the allele for tallness. When did this separation, or **segregation,** of alleles happen?

Mendel thought that the alleles for tallness and shortness in the F_1 plants must have segregated from each other during the formation of the gametes. **Gametes** (GAM eetz) are the sperm and egg cells that combine during fertilization.

Making Gametes Was Mendel right? Let's assume that the tall F_1 plants inherited two alleles controlling their height. They inherited an allele for tallness from their tall parent and an allele for shortness from their short parent. Because the allele for tallness is dominant, all the F_1 plants are tall. When each parent makes gametes, the alleles for each gene segregate from one another. Therefore, each gamete carries only one allele for each gene. So, each F_1 plant makes two kinds of gametes. Some have the tall allele, and some have the short allele.

P   Tall   X   Short

F_1 Tall   X   Tall

F_2 Tall   Tall   Tall   Short

Results of the F_1 Cross Recessive traits reappeared in the second generation when the first generation of plants were allowed to self-pollinate.

Look at the segregation diagram to see how alleles separate during gamete formation and then pair up again in the F_2 generation. A capital letter shows a dominant allele. A lowercase letter shows a recessive allele. Now we can see why the recessive trait for height, *t*, reappeared in Mendel's F_2 generation. Each F_1 plant in Mendel's cross made two kinds of gametes. Some had the allele for tallness, and some had the allele for shortness. Whenever a gamete that carried the *t* allele paired with another gamete that carried the *t* allele to make an F_2 plant, that F_2 plant was short. Every time a gamete carrying the *T* allele paired with another gamete carrying either the *T* or *t* allele, they made a tall plant. In other words, the F_2 generation had new combinations of alleles.

🗝️ **Key Question** How are different forms of a gene passed to offspring?
When gametes are made, the alleles for each trait separate from each other. That way each gamete carries only one allele from each gene.

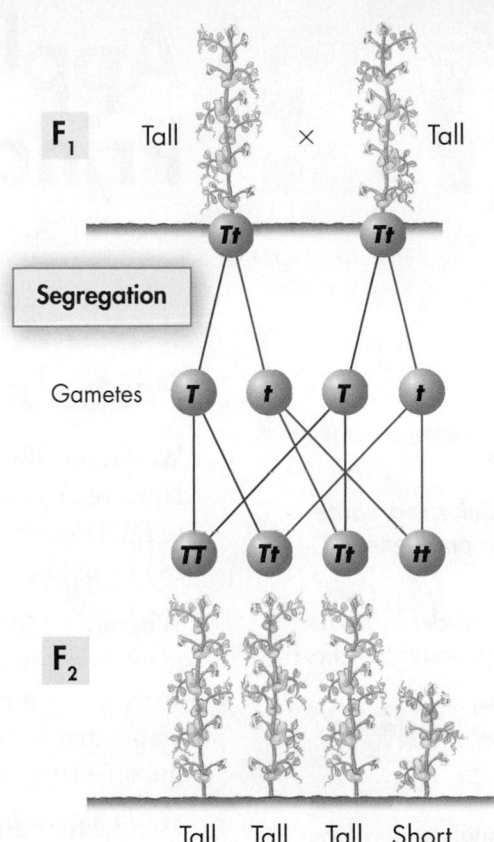

When gametes are made, the two alleles of each gene separate so that each gamete carries only a single copy of each gene. Each F_1 plant makes two types of gametes: those with an allele for tallness and those with an allele for shortness.

✓CHECK Understanding

Apply Vocabulary
Use the highlighted words from the lesson to complete each sentence.

1. The inherited factors that determine traits are called _____.

2. _____ is the process of male and female gametes joining.

Critical Thinking

3. Compare and Contrast How are dominant and recessive alleles alike and different?

4. Write to Learn Answer the first clue of the mystery. Write a paragraph that includes the terms *gene*, *allele*, and *trait*.

MYSTERY CLUE

Parakeets come in four colors: white, green, blue, and yellow. How many alleles might there be for feather color? (**Hint:** See p. 263.)

11.2 Applying Mendel's Principles

MD CLG 3.3.2 Inherited Traits. SPI 1.4.1 Organize Data, 1.4.2 Analyze Data, 1.6.1 Ratio and Proportion, 1.7.4 Recognize Mathematics.

Key Questions

🔑 How can we use probability to predict traits?

🔑 How do alleles segregate when more than one gene is involved?

🔑 What did Mendel contribute to what we know about genetics?

BUILD Understanding

Previewing Visuals Before you read, look at one of the figures in the lesson. Try to understand the purpose of that figure. As you read, compare your original impression to what you learn about the figure in the text. After you read, revise your statement if it was incorrect. Write a new statement if needed.

In Your Workbook Go to your workbook to learn more about previewing visuals. Complete the preview statement for Lesson 11.2.

Probability and Punnett Squares

We cannot always know exactly how a genetic cross will turn out. However, by carefully studying what happens in a cross, Mendel began to figure out how genetic information is inherited. This information can be used to find the possible outcomes of a genetic cross.

Whenever Mendel performed a cross with pea plants, he carefully identified and counted the offspring. So he had plenty of data to analyze. He noticed trends. For example, whenever he crossed two plants that were hybrids for stem height (*Tt*), about three fourths of the offspring were tall and about one fourth were short.

Mendel figured out that the principles of probability could be used to explain these results of his genetic crosses. **Probability** (prah buh BILL uh tee) is the likelihood that a particular event will happen. For example, think about flipping a coin. There are only two possible outcomes of a coin flip. The coin can land either heads up or tails up. The chance, or probability, of either outcome is the same. So, the probability that a single coin flip will land heads up is 1 chance in 2. This can be described as a probability of 1/2, or 50 percent.

If you flip a coin three times in a row, what is the probability that it will land heads up every time? Each coin flip is a separate event, with a 1/2 probability of the coin landing heads up. So, the probability of flipping three heads in a row is:

$$1/2 \times 1/2 \times 1/2 = 1/8$$

As you can see, you have 1 chance in 8 of flipping heads three times in a row. Remember: Past coin flips do not affect future coin flips. You may have just flipped 3 heads in a row. Those flips do not change the probability of the next flip. The probability for that flip is still 1/2.

Using Segregation to Predict Outcomes The same type of probability used to predict coin flips can also be used to help understand the outcomes of genetic crosses.

Probability When you flip a coin, the chance that the coin will land heads up is 1/2, or 50 percent.

When alleles segregate to form gametes, there are only two possible outcomes, just like when you flip a coin. Since a pea plant has two alleles for every gene, the probability that a gamete will get either allele is 1/2. If two pea plants that have one of each kind of allele (*Tt*) are crossed, what is the probability that an offspring plant will be short? Remember that to be short, a plant needs two *t* alleles. The chance of a gamete getting either allele is 1/2. Two gametes are in each cross. So, the probability of both gametes creating a *tt* plant is $1/2 \times 1/2 = 1/4$.

Organisms with the same characteristics can have different combinations of alleles. For example, the tall pea plants could be either *TT* or *Tt*. If an organism has two identical alleles of a gene, then the organism is **homozygous** (hoh moh ZY gus). The tall (*TT*) plants are homozygous because they have two identical alleles (*TT*) for a gene. The short plants are also homozygous because they have two identical alleles (*tt*) for a gene. If an organism has two different alleles for the same gene, then the organism is **heterozygous** (het ur oh ZY gus). The parents in this cross are heterozygous because they have two different alleles (*Tt*) for that gene.

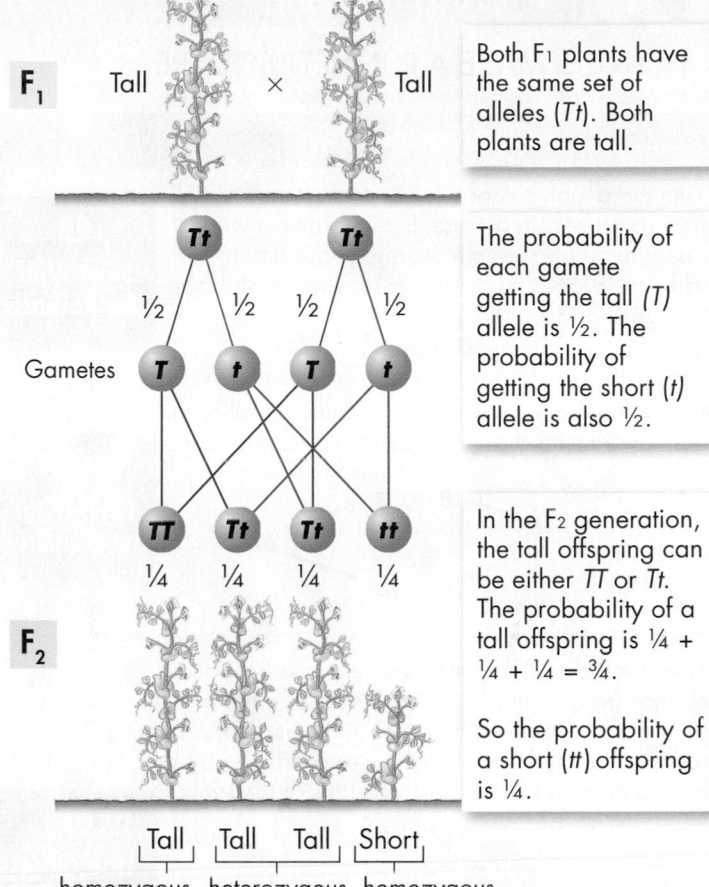

Both F₁ plants have the same set of alleles (*Tt*). Both plants are tall.

The probability of each gamete getting the tall (*T*) allele is ½. The probability of getting the short (*t*) allele is also ½.

In the F₂ generation, the tall offspring can be either *TT* or *Tt*. The probability of a tall offspring is ¼ + ¼ + ¼ = ¾.

So the probability of a short (*tt*) offspring is ¼.

Tall   Tall   Tall   Short

homozygous   heterozygous   homozygous

Genotype and Phenotype How many different combinations of the alleles *t* and *T* are possible? Three. The options are *Tt*, *TT*, and *tt*. How many different forms of the plant are possible? Two. The options are tall and short. Plants with the combinations *TT* and *Tt* are tall. Plants with the combination *tt* are short. Mendel noticed that all of the tall pea plants had the same **phenotype** (FEE nuh typ), or physical traits. They did not, however, have the same **genotype** (JEE nuh typ), or genetic makeup.

Using Punnett Squares One of the best ways to predict the outcome of a genetic cross is by drawing a simple diagram known as a Punnett square. Making a Punnett square is easy. You begin with a square. Then write all of the alleles that could be in the gametes from one parent along the top of the square. Then, write all possible alleles in the gametes from the other parent along the left side. Next, write every possible combination of alleles into the boxes inside the square. The next page shows instructions for making a Punnett square.

🔑 **Key Question** How can we use probability to predict traits?
Punnett squares use probability to predict combinations of alleles in a genetic cross.

One-Factor Cross

① Start With the Parents

Write the genotypes of the two organisms that will serve as parents in a cross. In this example we will cross a male and female osprey, or fish hawk, that are heterozygous for large beaks. They each have genotypes of *Bb*.

Bb and Bb

② Figure Out the Gametes

Determine what alleles would be found in all of the possible gametes that each parent could produce.

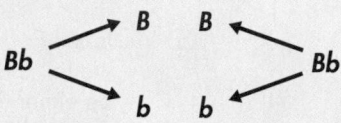

③ Line Them Up

Draw a table with enough squares for each pair of gametes from each parent. In this case, each parent can make two different types of gametes, *B* and *b*. Enter the genotypes of the gametes produced by both parents on the top and left sides of the table.

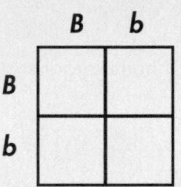

④ Write Out the New Genotypes

Fill in the table by combining the gametes' genotypes.

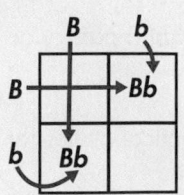 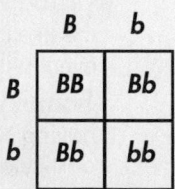

⑤ Figure Out the Results

Determine the genotype and phenotype of each offspring. Calculate the percentage of each. In this example, ¾ of the chicks will have large beaks, but only ½ will be heterozygous for this trait *(Bb)*.

	B	b
B	BB	Bb
b	Bb	bb

Two-Factor Cross

In this example we will cross two pea plants that are heterozygous for size (tall and short alleles) and pod color (green and yellow alleles). The genotypes of the two parents are *TtGg* and *TtGg*.

TtGg and TtGg

Determine what alleles would be found in all of the possible gametes that each parent could produce.

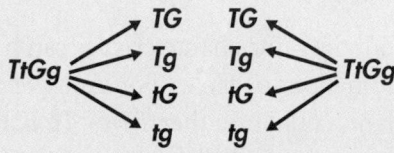

In this case, each parent can make 4 different types of gametes, so the table needs to be 4 rows by 4 columns, or 16 squares.

	TG	tG	Tg	tg
TG				
tG				
Tg				
tg				

Fill in the table by combining the gametes' genotypes.

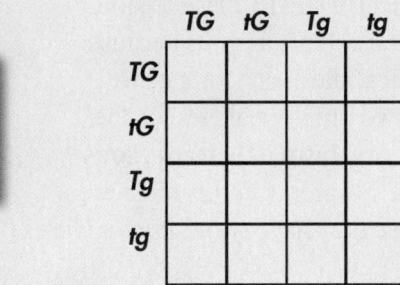

	TG	tG	Tg	tg
TG	TTGG	TtGG	TTGg	TtGg
tG	TtGG	ttGG	TtGg	ttGg
Tg	TTGg	TtGg	TTgg	Ttgg
tg	TtGg	ttGg	Ttgg	ttgg

In this example, the color of the squares represents pod color. Alleles written in black indicate short plants, while alleles written in red indicate tall plants.

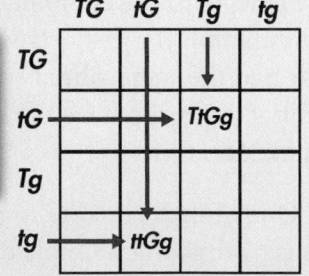

	TG	tG	Tg	tg
TG	TTGG	TtGG	TTGg	TtGg
tG	TtGG	ttGG	TtGg	ttGg
Tg	TTGg	TtGg	TTgg	Ttgg
tg	TtGg	ttGg	Ttgg	ttgg

Independent Assortment

Mendel wondered if alleles for one trait affected the alleles for another trait. For example, does the gene that determines the shape of a seed have anything to do with the gene for seed color? To find out, Mendel set up a cross that enabled him to study two different genes at the same time.

Getting the Seeds To get the seeds he needed, Mendel crossed true-breeding plants that made only round yellow peas with plants that produced only wrinkled green peas. The round yellow peas had the genotype *RRYY*. The wrinkled green peas had the genotype *rryy*. All of the F_1 offspring from this cross had round yellow peas with the genotype *RrYy*. This result showed that the alleles for yellow and round peas are dominant.

Showing Independent Assortment In the second part of this experiment, Mendel crossed two of these new *RrYy* plants from the F_1 generation to make the F_2 generation offspring. Remember that each plant was formed by the fusion of a gamete carrying the dominant *RY* alleles with another gamete carrying the recessive *ry* alleles. In Mendel's experiment, the F_2 plants made 556 seeds. Mendel sorted the seeds by trait. He noticed that 315 of the seeds were round and yellow, just like one parent. He saw that 32 seeds were wrinkled and green, just like the other parent. However, he also saw that 209 seeds had other combinations of phenotypes. Those included round and green peas and wrinkled and yellow peas. Those peas had to have allele combinations that were not found in either parent. This outcome showed that the alleles for seed shape segregated independently of those for seed color. Or to put it another way, genes that segregate independently do not influence each other's inheritance.

Mendel had discovered the principle of independent assortment. The principle of **independent assortment** states that genes for different traits can segregate independently when gametes are made. Independent assortment helps explain the many genetic variations we see in all living things.

🔑 Key Question How do alleles segregate when more than one gene is involved?
Genes for different traits segregate independently.

Two-Factor Cross: F_1

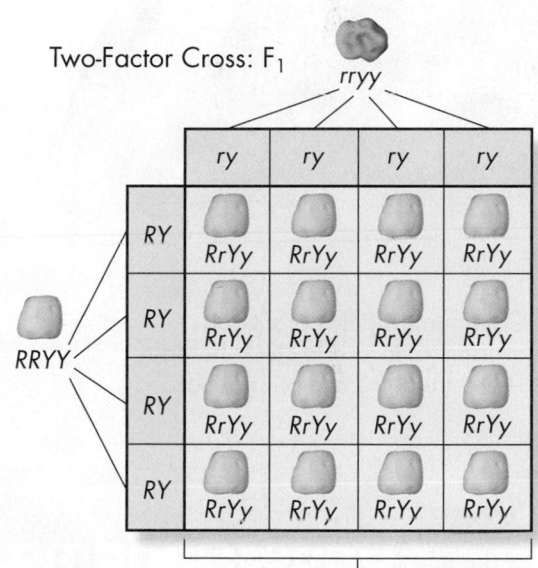

	ry	ry	ry	ry
RY	RrYy	RrYy	RrYy	RrYy
RY	RrYy	RrYy	RrYy	RrYy
RY	RrYy	RrYy	RrYy	RrYy
RY	RrYy	RrYy	RrYy	RrYy

F_1 Generation

Two-Factor Cross: F_2

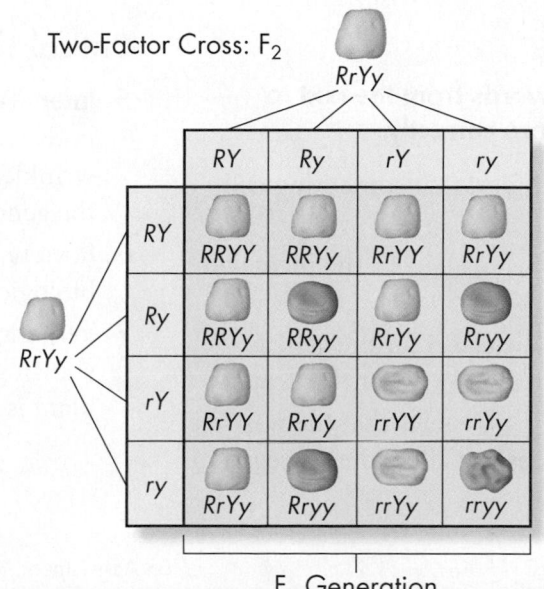

	RY	Ry	rY	ry
RY	RRYY	RRYy	RrYY	RrYy
Ry	RRYy	RRyy	RrYy	Rryy
rY	RrYY	RrYy	rrYY	rrYy
ry	RrYy	Rryy	rrYy	rryy

F_2 Generation

A Summary of Mendel's Principles

Today, Mendel's principles are the foundation of the modern science of genetics. These principles are below.

- Biological characteristics are inherited through units called genes. Genes are passed from parents to offspring.

- Sometimes there are two or more forms (alleles) of a gene for a single trait. Some forms of a gene may be dominant and others may be recessive.

- In most sexually reproducing organisms, each adult has two copies of each gene. Organisms get one copy from each parent. These alleles segregate from each other when gametes are made.

- Alleles for different genes usually segregate independently of each other.

Pea plants are not the only organisms used to study genetics. At the beginning of the 1900s, the American geneticist Thomas Hunt Morgan began to test Mendel's theories using fruit flies. The fruit fly is a good subject for genetic studies because it quickly produces hundreds of offspring. Using the fruit fly, Morgan and others tested all of Mendel's principles. The principles worked as well in fruit flies as they did in peas.

Key Question What did Mendel contribute to what we know about genetics? **Mendel's principles of heredity form the basis of modern genetics.**

Common fruit flies are good organisms to use to study heredity. These fruit flies are on a lemon.

CHECK Understanding

Apply Vocabulary
Use the highlighted words from the text to complete each sentence correctly.

1. _____ is the likelihood that something will happen.
2. If a pea plant has the _____ *Tt*, the plant will be tall.
3. If a rabbit has the alleles *BB* for the gene for fur color, the rabbit is _____ for that trait.
4. The principle of _____ states that the way one allele segregates does not affect the segregation of other alleles.

Critical Thinking

5. **Infer** Two pea plants with smooth seed pods are crossed. Some of the offspring have wrinkled seed pods. What can you infer about the genotypes of both parents?
6. **Review** What did Mendel conclude determines biological inheritance?
7. **Write to Learn** Make a Punnett square showing a cross between two pea plants. One plant is tall *Tt*, and the other is tall *TT*.

BIOLOGY.com   Search   Lesson 11.2   GO • Lesson Assessment

11.3 Other Patterns of Inheritance

MD CLG 3.3.2 Inherited Traits. SPI 1.4.2 Analyze Data, 1.5.2 Communicate Information.

Beyond Dominant and Recessive Alleles

We now know that heredity is a bit more complicated than Mendel thought. For example, most genes have more than two alleles. Also, many traits are controlled by more than one gene. Geneticists need to understand these other patterns of inheritance. That way, they can predict how complex traits will be inherited.

Codominance Sometimes neither allele is dominant over the other. If alleles have **codominance**, the phenotypes made by both alleles show up at the same time. For example, in certain kinds of chickens, the allele for black feathers is codominant with the allele for white feathers. Heterozygous chickens are speckled with black and white feathers. Because of codominant alleles, the black and white colors both appear. Many human genes also show codominance.

Incomplete Dominance The cross between two four o'clock plants shows a common exception to Mendel's principles. Some alleles are neither dominant or recessive. Cases where one allele is not completely dominant are called **incomplete dominance.** In incomplete dominance, the heterozygous phenotype lies somewhere between the two homozygous phenotypes. Four o'clock plants are an example of this. A cross between red-flowered (*RR*) and white-flowered (*WW*) plants results in offspring with pink flowers (*RW*).

BUILD Understanding

Finding Main Ideas Before you read the lesson, create a list of all the lesson's green and blue headings in order. Leave space under each heading for notes. As you read, write the main idea of each paragraph under the heading above it.

In Your Workbook Your workbook has a table for recording main ideas and details.

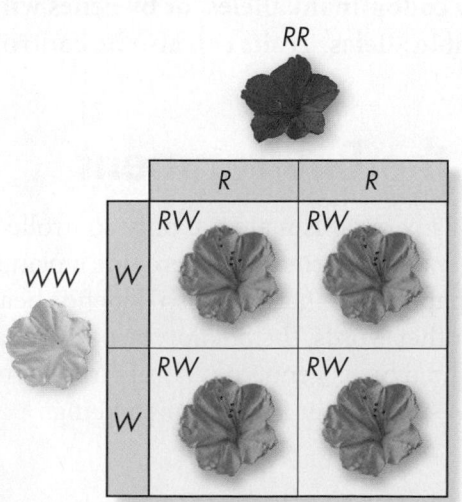

RR

WW

Incomplete Dominance
In four o'clock plants, the alleles for red and white flowers show incomplete dominance. Heterozygous (*RW*) plants have pink flowers.

codominance
a situation in which the phenotypes produced by both alleles are completely expressed

incomplete dominance
a situation in which one allele is not completely dominant over another allele

multiple alleles
a gene that has more than two alleles

polygenic traits
a trait controlled by two or more genes

🍫 PREFIXES _____

The prefix *co-* means *jointly* or *together*. Books written by coauthors are written by two people who share credit equally. Codominant alleles contribute equally to the phenotype of a trait.

Multiple Alleles So far, our examples have described genes for which there are only two alleles. In nature, such genes are not common. Many genes exist in several different forms. A gene with more than two alleles is said to have **multiple alleles.** An individual, of course, usually has only two copies of each gene. Within a population, however, there are many different alleles. Two individuals having two different alleles each could together have four different alleles for the same gene.

One of the best examples of multiple alleles is coat color in rabbits. A rabbit's coat color is controlled by one gene that has four possible alleles. The four known alleles display a pattern of simple dominance that can produce four coat colors. Many other genes have multiple alleles, including the human genes for blood type.

Polygenic Traits Many traits are controlled by several genes at work at the same time. Traits controlled by two or more genes are said to be **polygenic traits** (pahl ih JEN ik traytz). Polygenic means "many genes." For example, at least three genes are involved in making the reddish-brown pigment in the eyes of fruit flies. Different combinations of alleles for these three genes produce very different eye colors. Polygenic traits often show a wide range of phenotypes. The wide range of skin color in humans comes about partly because more than four different genes are likely to control this trait.

Be sure that you don't confuse polygenic traits with traits determined by one gene with multiple alleles. In multiple alleles, many different alleles exist for a gene in a population. However, an individual organism only has a single pair of these alleles. In polygenic traits, each individual organism has many different gene pairs that all work together on one trait.

🔑 Key Question What are some exceptions to Mendel's principles?
Traits can be controlled by incomplete dominant alleles. They can be controlled by codominant alleles, or by genes with more than two possible alleles. Traits can also be controlled by several genes.

Genes and the Environment

The characteristics of any organism are not only controlled by the genes that organism inherits. Genes provide a plan for development. What happens to that plan also depends heavily on the environment. In other words, the phenotype of an organism is only partly determined by its genotype. This is true no matter what the organism is—plant, fruit fly, or human being.

Consider the western white butterfly, *Pontia occidentalis*. It is found throughout western North America. People had noted for years that western whites hatching in the summer had different color patterns on their wings than those hatching in the spring. Scientific studies showed the reason. Butterflies hatching in the shorter days of springtime had greater levels of pigment in their wings. More pigment makes the markings of the springtime butterflies appear darker. In other words, the environment in which the butterflies develop affects how genes make pigments for the wings.

🔑 **Key Question** Does the environment have a role in how genes determine traits? **Environmental conditions can change gene expression and influence genetically controlled traits.**

Summer Buckeye Butterfly   Autumn Buckeye Butterfly

Temperature and Wing Color Buckeye butterflies also have different coloring depending on when they hatch. Summer butterflies are lighter than autumn butterflies.

✓CHECK Understanding

Use the highlighted words from the text to complete each sentence correctly.

1. When neither allele is dominant over the other, and both phenotypes are fully expressed, the alleles are said to be _____.

2. In _____, both alleles of a gene are expressed and the phenotype is a blend of the phenotypes of both alleles.

3. In _____, several genes control the phenotype.

Critical Thinking

4. **Review** Describe two inheritance patterns besides simple dominance.

5. **Apply** How could you test to see if soil temperature was responsible for a variation in flower color?

6. **Write to Learn** Answer the third clue by writing a paragraph about how polygenic traits are different from the kinds of traits Mendel observed.

MYSTERY CLUE

Green feathers don't actually have green pigments. Rather, they contain a mixture of blue and yellow pigments. Could feather color be controlled by more than one gene? (**Hint:** See p. 272.)

BIOLOGY.com ⟩ Search ⟨ Lesson 11.3 ⟩ GO ● Lesson Assessment

Human Blood Types

Red blood cells have protein markers on them. These antigens can cause a reaction if a person receives the wrong blood type during a blood transfusion. Human blood type A carries an A antigen, type B has a B antigen, and type AB has both antigens. Type O carries neither antigen. The gene for these antigens has three alleles: A, B, and O. A and B are dominant over O. When A and B appear together, they are codominant.

For a transfusion to succeed, it must not put a new antigen into the body of the person getting the blood. So, a person with type A blood may get type O. However, a person with type O may not get type A blood.

Another gene controls a second type of antigen, known as Rh factor. Rh⁺ individuals carry this protein. People with Rh⁻ do not carry it. The pie graph of the U.S. population shows the percentage of each blood type.

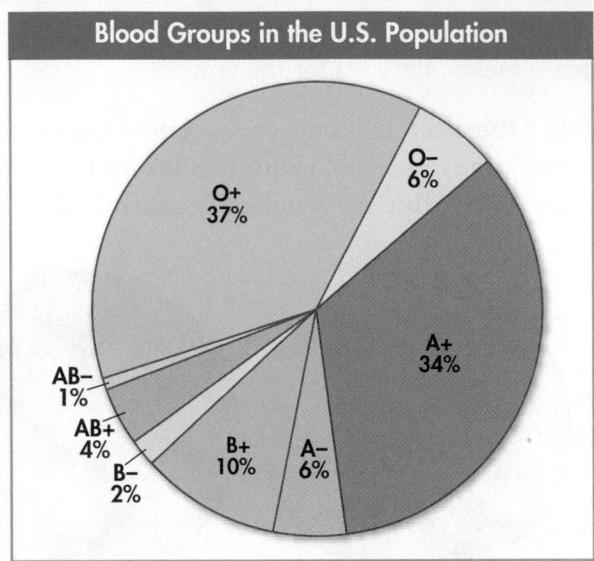

Blood Groups in the U.S. Population

O+ 37%
O− 6%
A+ 34%
A− 6%
B+ 10%
B− 2%
AB+ 4%
AB− 1%

Analyze and Conclude

1. Interpret Graphs Which blood type makes up the greatest percentage of the U.S. population?

2. Calculate What percentage of the U.S. population has Rh⁺ blood?

3. Predict Alleles are either dominant or recessive. The allele for type O is recessive to the alleles for types A and B. The allele for Rh⁺ is dominant over the allele for Rh⁻.

- Could a person with O⁺ blood have two parents with O⁻ blood? Explain.

- Could a person with O⁺ blood have a daughter with AB⁺ blood? Explain your answers.

4. Infer A person with type A, B, or AB blood may receive a transfusion of type O. However, a person with type O may not get types A or AB blood. A person with Rh⁺ blood can get Rh⁻ blood, but a person with Rh⁻ blood cannot get Rh⁺ blood.

Use the graph to answer the questions that follow.

- Which blood type can be donated to the largest percentage of individuals? Explain your answer.

- Which type can be donated to the smallest percentage of people? Explain your answer.

11.4 Meiosis

MD CLG 3.2.1 Processes and Functions, 3.3.1 Sexual Reproduction and Variation, 3.3.2 Inherited Traits. SPI 1.5.5 Create and Interpret Graphics, 1.5.8 Compare.

Chromosome Number

What happens in cells to make sure they pass on the correct number of genes? To understand how the number of genes is controlled, we need to learn what happens to chromosomes when gametes are made. Chromosomes are strands of DNA and protein inside the cell nucleus, and they are the carriers of genes. Genes are located in specific places on chromosomes.

Diploid Cells Think about the fruit flies that Morgan used. A body cell in an adult fruit fly has eight chromosomes. Four of the chromosomes come from its male parent, and four come from its female parent. These two sets of chromosomes are **homologous** (hoh MAHL uh gus), because each of the four chromosomes from the male parent has a similar chromosome from the female parent. A cell that has both sets of homologous chromosomes is said to be **diploid,** meaning "two sets." The diploid cells of most adult organisms have two complete sets of chromosomes and so two complete sets of genes. The diploid number of chromosomes can be shown using the symbol 2N. So, for fruit flies, the diploid number is 8, which can be written as 2N = 8.

Key Question How many sets of genes are found in most adult organisms?
The diploid cells of most adult organisms contain two complete sets of inherited chromosomes and so two complete sets of genes.

Haploid Cells Some cells have only a single set of genes on a single set of chromosomes. These cells are **haploid,** meaning "one set." The gametes of sexually reproducing organisms, such as fruit flies and peas, are haploid. For fruit fly gametes, the haploid number is 4. This amount can be written as N = 4.

Key Questions

🔑 **How many sets of genes are found in most adult organisms?**

🔑 **What happens during each phase of meiosis?**

🔑 **How is meiosis different from mitosis?**

🔑 **How can two alleles from different genes be inherited together?**

BUILD Understanding

Compare/Contrast Table
Before you read, make a compare/contrast table to show the differences between mitosis and meiosis. As you read, complete the table.

In Your Workbook Refer to your workbook for suggestions about how to use a compare/contrast table.

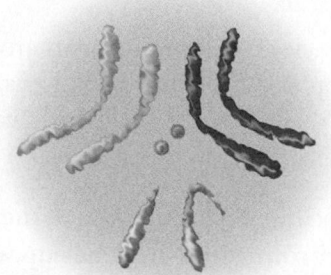

Fruit Fly Chromosomes These chromosomes are from a fruit fly. Each of the fruit fly's body cells is diploid, containing eight chromosomes.

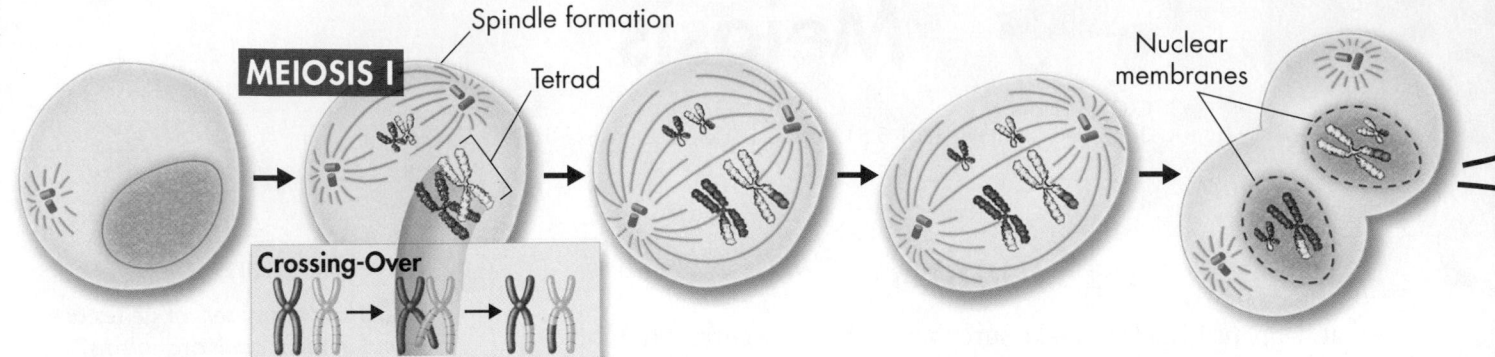

Spindle formation

MEIOSIS I

Tetrad

Crossing-Over

Nuclear membranes

Interphase
Cells undergo a round of DNA replication, forming duplicate chromosomes.

Prophase I
Each chromosome pairs with its corresponding homologous chromosome to form a tetrad.

Metaphase I
Spindle fibers attach to the chromosomes.

Anaphase I
The fibers pull the homologous chromosomes to opposite ends of the cell.

Telophase I and Cytokinesis
Nuclear membranes form. The cell separates into two cells.

Meiosis During meiosis, the number of chromosomes per cell is cut in half through the separation of the homologous chromosomes. The result of meiosis is 4 haploid cells that are genetically different from one another and from the original cell.

Phases of Meiosis

How are haploid cells made? Haploid cell are made by meiosis. **Meiosis** (my OH sis) is a process in which the number of chromosomes per cell is cut in half through the separation of homologous chromosomes in a diploid cell. Meiosis involves two rounds of cell division, called meiosis I and meiosis II. Let's see how meiosis takes place in a cell that has a diploid number of 4 ($2N = 4$).

Meiosis I Just before meiosis I, each chromosome is copied, or replicated. As in mitosis, each replicated chromosome is made of two identical chromatids joined at the center.

▶ *Prophase I* In prophase of meiosis I, each copied chromosome matches up with its homologous chromosome. This pairing makes a structure called a tetrad, which has four chromatids. As the tetrads form, they undergo a process called **crossing-over.** Chromatids from homologous chromosomes cross over one another, as shown in the art. Then, alleles from the crossed sections are exchanged. Crossing-over produces new combinations of alleles on each chromatid.

▶ *Metaphase I and Anaphase I* A spindle forms and attaches to each chromosome in the tetrad. The homologous chromosomes separate in anaphase I.

▶ *Telophase I and Cytokinesis* A nuclear membrane forms around each cluster of chromosomes in telophase I. During cytokinesis, the cell splits and two new haploid cells are made. The set of alleles in each cell is different from the set in the other cell.

🔑 **Key Question** What happens during each phase of meiosis I? **During prophase I, each copied chromosome matches up with its homologous chromosome. Crossing-over increases the allele combinations on chromatids.**

BUILD
Vocabulary

homologous
the term used to refer to chromosomes in which one set comes from the male parent and one set comes from the female parent

diploid
the term used to refer to a cell that contains two sets of homologous chromosomes

haploid
the term used to refer to a cell that contains only a single set of genes

🖊 **WORD ORIGINS**

The word *diploid* comes from the Greek root *di-*, which means "double" or "twice."

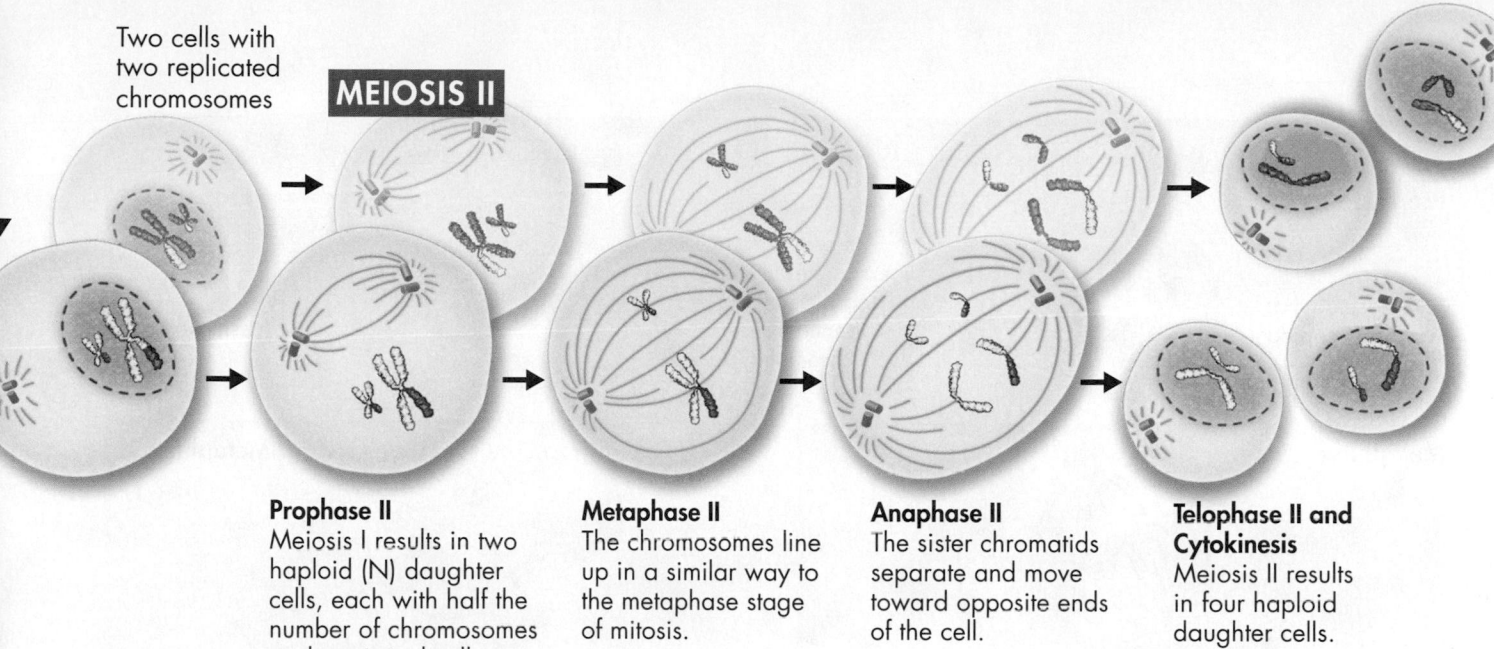

Two cells with two replicated chromosomes

MEIOSIS II

Prophase II
Meiosis I results in two haploid (N) daughter cells, each with half the number of chromosomes as the original cell.

Metaphase II
The chromosomes line up in a similar way to the metaphase stage of mitosis.

Anaphase II
The sister chromatids separate and move toward opposite ends of the cell.

Telophase II and Cytokinesis
Meiosis II results in four haploid daughter cells.

In metaphase I, the spindle fibers form. In anaphase I, the chromosomes separate. Then, in telophase, a nuclear membrane forms around the chromosomes. During cytokinesis, the cell splits, and two new cells are made.

Meiosis II The two cells get ready to divide once more. The chromosomes do not replicate before this division.

▶ *Prophase II* As the cells enter prophase II, their chromosomes become visible. Each prophase chromosome consists of two identical sister chromatids.

▶ *Metaphase II, Anaphase II, Telophase II, and Cytokinesis* During metaphase II, the chromosomes line up in the middle of the cell. As the cell enters anaphase II, the paired chromatids separate. When anaphase II is complete, the separated chromosomes cluster at opposite ends of the cell. In telophase II, the nuclear membrane forms around each cluster of chromosomes. In the example shown here, each of the four daughter cells produced in meiosis II receives two chromosomes. The four daughter cells now contain the haploid number (N)—two chromosomes each.

🔑 **Key Question** What happens during each phase of meiosis II? **As the cells enter prophase II, their chromosomes become visible. During metaphase II, the chromosomes line up in the middle of the cell. In the second anaphase, the chromatids separate. In the second telophase and cytokinesis, four new haploid cells are formed.**

Gametes to Zygotes The haploid cells made by meiosis II are gametes, which are important to heredity. Gametes, such as eggs and sperm, join in fertilization to form a **zygote** (ZY goht), which has new combinations of alleles. The zygote undergoes cell division by mitosis and grows into an organism.

BUILD Vocabulary

meiosis
the process in which the number of chromosomes per cell is cut in half through the separation of homologous chromosomes in a diploid cell

crossing-over
the process in which homologous chromosomes exchange portions of their chromatids during meiosis

zygote
a fertilized egg

🖋 **WORD ORIGINS**

The word *meiosis* comes from a Greek word that means "to lessen or reduce." Because of meiosis, gametes have a reduced number of chromosomes.

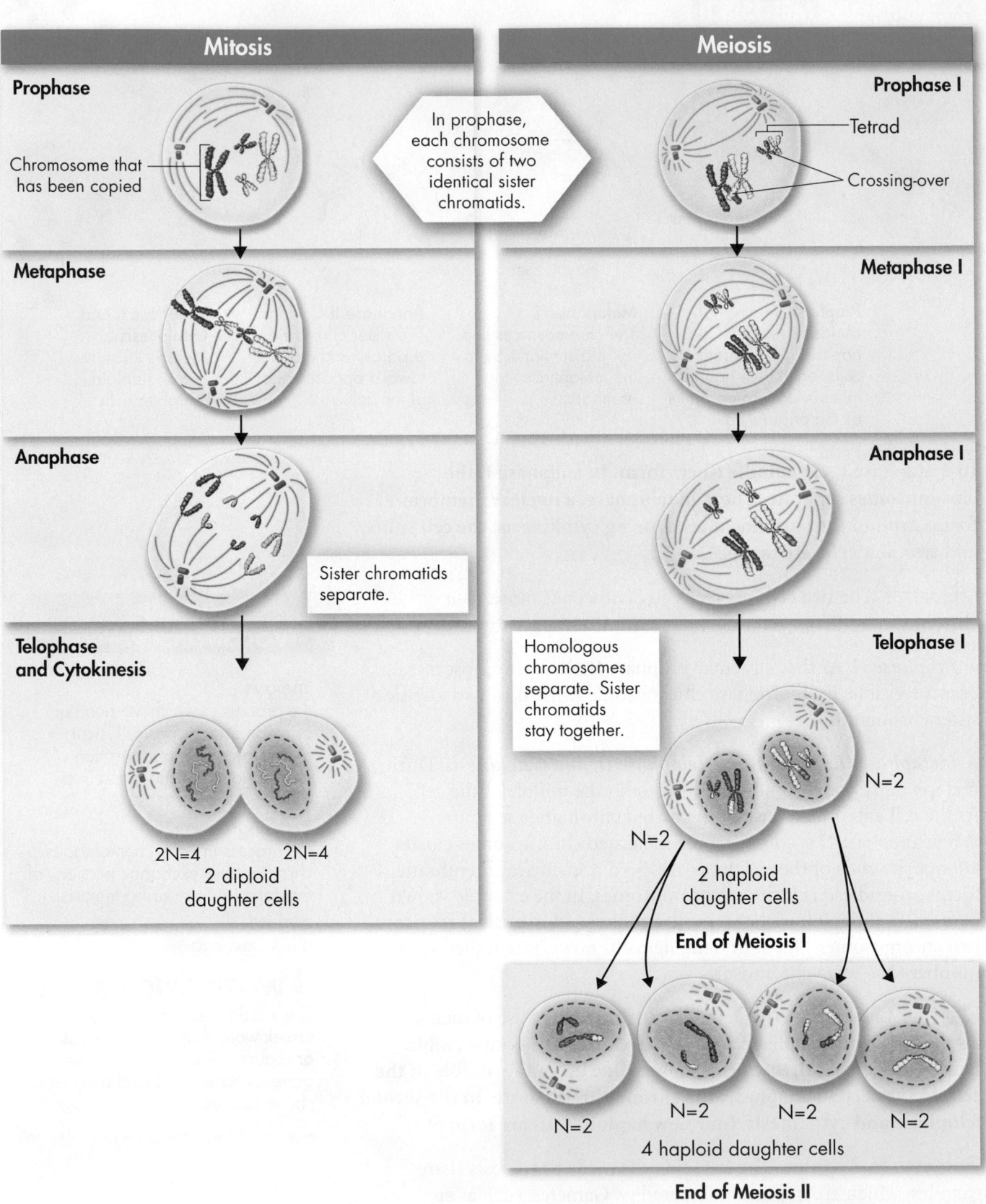

Mitosis

Prophase

Chromosome that has been copied

Metaphase

Anaphase

Sister chromatids separate.

Telophase and Cytokinesis

2N=4   2N=4
2 diploid daughter cells

In prophase, each chromosome consists of two identical sister chromatids.

Meiosis

Prophase I

Tetrad

Crossing-over

Metaphase I

Anaphase I

Telophase I

Homologous chromosomes separate. Sister chromatids stay together.

N=2

N=2

2 haploid daughter cells

End of Meiosis I

N=2   N=2   N=2   N=2
4 haploid daughter cells

End of Meiosis II

Comparing Meiosis and Mitosis

Even though mitosis and meiosis both involve chromosomes and cell division, they are very different. Mitosis can be a form of asexual reproduction. Meiosis is an early step in sexual reproduction. Review the table to compare the two processes.

🔑 **Key Question** How is meiosis different from mitosis? **Mitosis can be a form of asexual reproduction. It does not change the number of chromosomes. It makes two identical diploid cells. Meiosis is a step in sexual reproduction. It cuts the chromosome number in half. It makes four genetically different haploid cells.**

Gene Linkage and Gene Maps

Genes that are on the same chromosome are usually inherited together because they are linked and do not assort independently during meiosis. Thomas Hunt Morgan's research on fruit flies helped show gene linkage. Morgan used a fly with reddish-orange eyes and miniature wings in a series of test crosses. The genes for those two traits were almost always inherited together.

Linked genes are not always inherited together. When crossing-over happens during meiosis, linked genes can be separated. The farther apart genes are on a chromosome, the more likely crossing-over will separate them. This trend means that the rate of crossing-over can be used to locate and even to map genes on a chromosome.

🔑 **Key Question** How can two alleles from different genes be inherited together? **Alleles of different genes tend to be inherited together when those genes are on the same chromosome.**

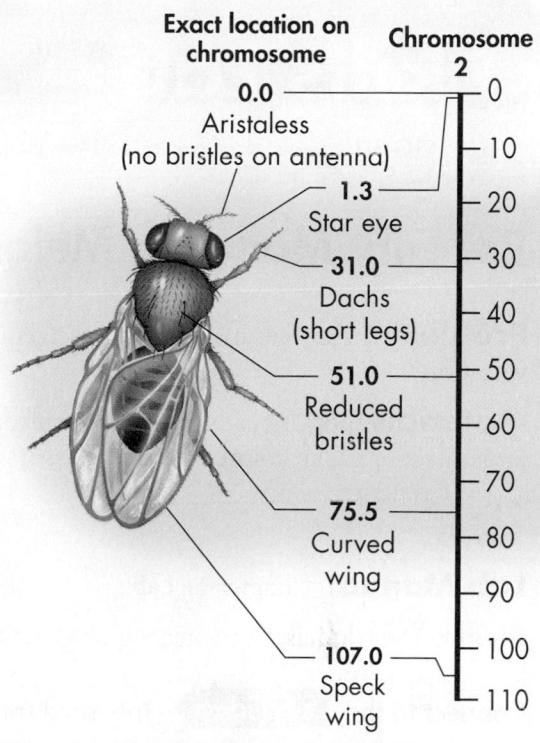

Exact location on chromosome	Chromosome 2
0.0 — Aristaless (no bristles on antenna)	0
	10
1.3 Star eye	20
31.0 Dachs (short legs)	30
	40
51.0 Reduced bristles	50
	60
	70
75.5 Curved wing	80
	90
107.0 Speck wing	100
	110

Gene Map Chromosomes are made of many genes linked together. Gene maps show how far apart these genes are from each other.

✓CHECK Understanding

Apply Vocabulary
Use the highlighted words from the text to complete each sentence correctly.

1. A cell that contains two sets of homologous chromosomes is _____.

2. A _____ is formed when an egg is fertilized by sperm.

Critical Thinking

3. Summarize What happens in meiosis I and II?

4. Write to Learn Answer the mystery clue.

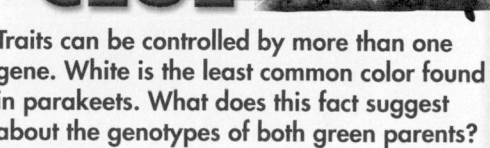

MYSTERY CLUE

Traits can be controlled by more than one gene. White is the least common color found in parakeets. What does this fact suggest about the genotypes of both green parents? (**Hint:** See p. 271.)

MD CLG 3.3.1 Sexual Reproduction and Variation, 3.3.2 Inherited Traits. SPI 1.4.8 Use Models, 1.5.9 Synthesize Ideas.

Pre-Lab: Modeling Meiosis

Problem How does meiosis increase genetic variation?

Materials pop-it beads, magnetic centromeres, large sheet of paper, colored pencils, scissors

Lab Manual Chapter 11 Lab

Skills Use Models, Sequence, Draw Conclusions

Connect to the Big idea Inherited traits are passed from parents to offspring in the form of genes. Offspring produced by sexual reproduction receive one set of genes from each parent when the reproductive cells, or gametes, combine. Meiosis is the process by which gametes are produced. During meiosis, new combinations of genes form when genes cross over from one homologous chromosome to the other. Also, the sorting of chromatids among gametes is random. Both crossing-over and sorting lead to greater diversity in the genes of a population.

In this lab, you will model the steps of meiosis and track what happens to alleles as they move from diploid cells to haploid gametes.

Background Questions

a. Review What are alleles?

b. Sequence What happens during prophase I of meiosis? What happens during metaphase I? What happens during anaphase I?

c. Compare and Contrast In what ways does meiosis differ from mitosis?

Pre-Lab Questions

Preview the procedure in the lab manual.

1. **Control Variables** Why must you use the same number of beads when you construct the second chromosome in Step 1?

2. **Infer** Why is the longer chromosome pair used to model crossing-over?

3. **Calculate** A diploid cell has two pairs of homologous chromosomes. How many different combinations of chromosomes could there be in the gametes? **MATH**

BIOLOGY.com Search ⟨ Chapter 11 ⟩ GO

Visit Chapter 11 online to test yourself on chapter content and to find activities to help you learn.

Untamed Science Video Travel back in time with the Untamed Science explorers as they prove Mendel was no pea brain!

Art in Motion View a short animation that brings the process of meiosis to life.

Art Review Review your understanding of multiple alleles, incomplete dominance, and other exceptions to Mendel's principles.

InterActive Art Build your understanding of Punnett squares with this animation.

Data Analysis Investigate the connection between crossing-over and gene location.

Tutor Tube Hear suggestions from the tutor for help remembering what happens to chromosomes during meiosis.

11 CHAPTER Summary

11.1 The Work of Gregor Mendel

- An individual's unique characteristics are determined by factors that are passed from parent to offspring.

- When gametes are made, the alleles for each trait separate from each other. That way each gamete carries only one allele from each gene.

genetics (p. 262)	principle of
fertilization (p. 262)	dominance (p. 263)
trait (p. 262)	segregation (p. 264)
gene (p. 263)	gamete (p. 264)
allele (p. 263)	

11.2 Applying Mendel's Principles

- Punnett squares use probability to predict combinations of alleles in a genetic cross.

- Genes for different traits segregate independently.

- Mendel's principles of heredity form the basis of modern genetics.

probability (p. 266)	genotype (p. 267)
homozygous (p. 267)	independent
heterozygous (p. 267)	assortment (p. 269)
phenotype (p. 267)	

11.3 Other Patterns of Inheritance

- Traits can be controlled by incomplete dominant alleles, codominant alleles, more than two possible alleles, and several genes.

- Environmental conditions can affect gene expression and influence genetically determined traits.

codominance (p. 271)	multiple alleles (p. 272)
incomplete	polygenic trait (p. 272)
dominance (p. 271)	

11.4 Meiosis

- The diploid cells of most adult organisms contain two complete sets of inherited chromosomes and so two complete sets of genes.

- Meiosis is a process of cell division that results in gametes that have half the number of chromosomes that other body cells have. In prophase I, copied chromosomes pair with their matching homologous chromosomes. At metaphase I, paired chromosomes line up across the center of the cell. In anaphase I, chromosome pairs move toward opposite ends of the cell. In telophase I, a nuclear membrane forms around each cluster of chromosomes. Cytokinesis then forms two new cells. As the cells enter prophase II, their chromosomes become visible. The final four phases of meiosis II result in four haploid daughter cells.

- Meiosis results in four genetically different haploid cells. Mitosis results in two genetically identical diploid cells.

- Alleles of different genes tend to be inherited together when those genes are on the same chromosome.

homologous (p. 275)	meiosis (p. 276)
diploid (p. 275)	crossing-over (p. 276)
haploid (p. 275)	zygote (p. 277)

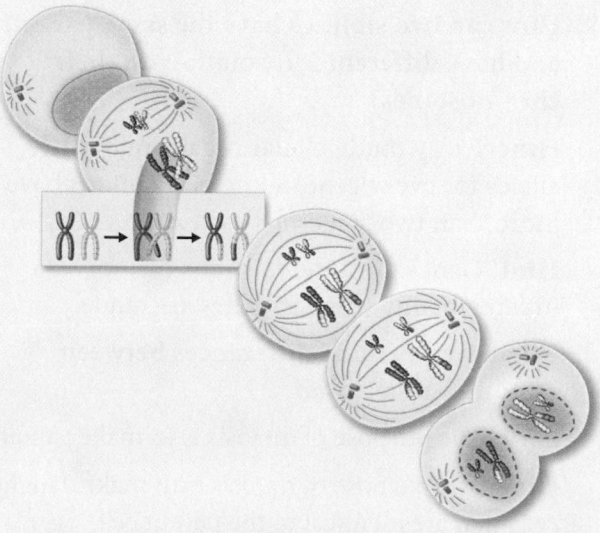

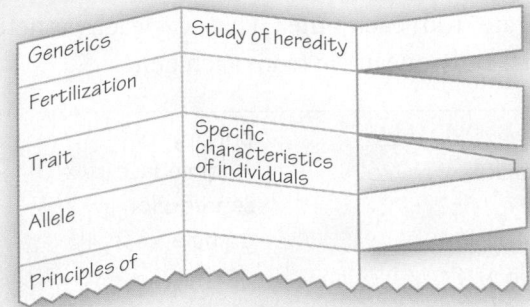

Foundations for Learning Wrap-Up

Use the undercover vocabulary tool you made as you read the chapter to help you review the material on heredity and meiosis.

Assess the Big idea **Information and Heredity**

Write an answer to the question below.

Q: How does biological information pass from one generation to another?

Constructed Response

Write an answer to each of the numbered questions below. The answer to each numbered question should be one or two paragraphs long. To help you begin, read the **Hints** below each of the questions.

1. **What did Mendel discover about biological characteristics?**

   Hint Mendel crossed pea plants and studied offspring.

   Hint Mendel learned that the traits of the parents affected the traits of the offspring.

2. **How can two siblings have the same parents and have different information on their chromosomes?**

   Hint Every multicellular organism has two alleles for every gene. Some populations have more than two alleles for each gene.

   Hint Genes for different traits can sort independently when gametes are made.

3. **What are the main differences between meiosis and mitosis?**

   Hint The purpose of meiosis is to make gametes.

   Hint The purpose of mitosis is to make daughter cells that are identical to the parent cell.

Activity 1 Form groups of three. Have one person read a definition from the terms on the undercover vocabulary tool. Have the other two students try to identify the terms associated with the definitions. Take turns reading the definitions.

Activity 2 Use scissors to carefully cut the definitions and terms from your undercover vocabulary tool. When all the terms and definitions are on separate pieces of paper, mix them up. Try to match the terms and the definitions.

11.1 The Work of Gregor Mendel

Understand Key Concepts

1. Different forms of a gene are called
   a. hybrids.
   c. alleles.
   b. dominant factors.
   d. recessive factors.

Test-Taking Tip

Use Time Wisely Before you start your test, look at the kinds of questions being asked. Usually, multiple-choice questions take less time to answer than critical-thinking questions. Be sure not to spend so much time on multiple-choice questions that you won't have time to answer the essay questions.

Think Critically

2. **Infer** Suppose Mendel crossed two pea plants and got both tall and short offspring. What could have been the genotypes of the two original plants? What genotype could *not* have been present?

11.2 Applying Mendel's Principles

Understand Key Concepts

3. Organisms that have two identical alleles for a particular trait are said to be
   a. hybrid.
   c. homozygous.
   b. heterozygous.
   d. dominant.

4. A Punnett square is used to determine the
   a. probable outcome of a cross.
   b. actual outcome of a cross.
   c. result of incomplete dominance.
   d. result of meiosis.

5. The physical characteristics of an organism are called its
   a. genetics.
   c. phenotype.
   b. heredity.
   d. genotype.

6. List the four basic principles of genetics that Mendel discovered in his experiments. Briefly describe each of these principles.

Think Critically

7. **Apply Concepts** In guinea pigs, the allele for a rough coat (*R*) is dominant over the allele for a smooth coat (*r*). A heterozygous guinea pig (*Rr*) and a homozygous recessive guinea pig (*rr*) have a total of nine offspring. Is it possible for all the offspring to have smooth coats? Explain your answer.

11.3 Other Patterns of Inheritance

Understand Key Concepts

8. A situation in which a gene has more than two alleles is known as
   a. complete dominance.
   b. codominance.
   c. polygenic dominance.
   d. multiple alleles.

9. Are an organism's characteristics determined only by its genes? Explain your answer.

Think Critically

10. **Interpret Visuals** Genes that control hair or feather color in some animals are expressed differently in the winter than in the summer. How might such a difference be beneficial to the ptarmigan shown here?

11.4 Meiosis

11. Unlike mitosis, meiosis in male mammals results in the formation of

   a. one haploid gamete.

   b. three diploid gametes.

   c. four diploid gametes.

   d. four haploid gametes.

Think Critically

12. Compare and Contrast Make a table that compares and contrasts meiosis and mitosis.

Connecting Concepts

Use Science Graphics

In pea plants, the coat, or covering, of the seed is either smooth or wrinkled. Suppose a researcher has two plants—one that makes smooth seeds and another that makes wrinkled seeds. The researcher crosses the wrinkled-seed plants and the smooth-seed plants, obtaining the following data. Use the data to answer questions 13 and 14.

13. Infer Mendel knew that the allele for smooth (R) seeds was dominant over the allele for wrinkled (r) seeds. If this cross was $Rr \times rr$, what numbers would fill the middle column?

Results of Seed Experiment		
Phenotype	**Number of Plants in the F₁ Generation**	
	Expected	**Observed**
Smooth seeds		60
Wrinkled seeds		72

14. Analyze Data Are the observed numbers consistent with the hypothesis that the cross is $Rr \times rr$? Explain your answer.

solve the CHAPTER MYSTERY

GREEN PARAKEETS

After talking to the owner of the pet store, Susan realized she had a rare gift. White parakeets are very uncommon. The pet shop owner told Susan that two genes control feather color. A dominant Y allele results in a yellow pigment. The dominant B allele controls melanin production.

- If the genotype contains a capital Y (either YY or Yy) and a capital B, the offspring will be green.

- If the genotype contains a capital Y (either YY or Yy) and two lowercase b's, the offspring will be yellow.

- If the genotype contains two lowercase y's, and a capital B, the offspring will be blue.

- If the genotype contains two lowercase y's and two lowercase b's, the offspring will be white. The Punnett square below shows the possible genotypes for the cross that produced Susan's baby parakeets. Copy this Punnett square onto a piece of paper. Use it to answer the questions that follow.

?	?	?	?	?
?	BBYY	BBYy	BbYY	BbYy
?	BBYy	BByy	BbYy	Bbyy
?	BbYY	BbYy	bbYY	bbYy
?	BbYy	Bbyy	bbYy	bbyy

1. Use Models Write "blue" in the squares that represent a blue parakeet. Write "yellow" in the squares that represent a yellow parakeet. Write "green" in the squares that represent a green parakeet.

2. Use Models Write "white" in the square that represents a white parakeet.

3. Apply Concepts What are the genotypes of the parents in this cross?

Multiple Choice

1. What happens to the chromosome number during meiosis?
A It doubles.
B It stays the same.
C It halves.
D It becomes diploid. CLG 3.3.1

2. Which ratio did Mendel find in his F_2 generation?
A 3 : 1
B 1 : 3 : 1
C 1 : 2
D 3 : 4 CLG 3.3.2

3. During which phase of meiosis is the chromosome number reduced?
A anaphase I
B metaphase I
C telophase I
D telophase II CLG 3.3.1

4. Two pink-flowering plants are crossed. The offspring flower as follows: 25% red, 25% white, and 50% pink. What pattern of inheritance does flower color in these flowers follow?
A dominance
B multiple alleles
C incomplete dominance
D polygenic traits CLG 3.3.2

5. The physical characteristics of an organism are its
A heredity.
B genotype.
C genetics.
D phenotype. CLG 3.3.2

6. Alleles for the same trait are separated from each other during the process of
A cytokinesis.
B meiosis I.
C meiosis II.
D metaphase II. CLG 3.3.1

7. Which of the following is NOT one of Gregor Mendel's principles?
A The alleles for different genes usually segregate independently.
B Some forms of a gene may be dominant.
C The inheritance of characteristics is determined by factors (genes).
D Crossing-over occurs during meiosis. CLG 3.3.2

Questions 8–10

The Punnett square below shows a cross between two pea plants each with round seeds.

	?	?
R	RR	Rr
R	RR	Rr

8. The unknown genotype is
A Rr.
B rR.
C rr.
D RR. SPI 1.4.2

9. Which statement is true about the cross in the Punnett square?
A Both parents are heterozygous for the trait.
B Both parents are homozygous for the trait.
C One parent is heterozygous and the other is homozygous for the trait.
D The trait is controlled by codominant alleles. SPI 1.4.1

10. What percentage of the offspring of this cross will produce round seeds?
A 0%
B 25%
C 50%
D 100% CLG 3.3.1

If You Have Trouble With . . .

Question	1	2	3	4	5	6	7	8	9	10
See Lesson	11.4	11.1	11.4	11.3	11.4	11.4	11.2	11.2	11.2	11.2

12 DNA

Big ideas Information and Heredity, Cellular Basis of Life

Q: What is the structure of DNA, and how does it function in genetic inheritance?

Genes are made of DNA. This sculpture at the University of California at Berkeley models the structure of DNA.

CHAPTER MYSTERY

UV LIGHT

"Put on your sunscreen!" You can hear people say this at beaches on a sunny day. Why do people say it? Sunlight can harm the skin. The most dangerous part of sunlight is the part we can't see: the ultraviolet (UV) rays of the electromagnetic spectrum. Overexposure to UV light harms skin cells. It can also cause a deadly form of skin cancer that kills nearly 10,000 Americans each year. Why is UV light so dangerous? How can these particular wavelengths of light harm our cells to the point of causing cell death and cancer?

Read for Mystery Clues As you read this chapter, look for clues to help you solve the question of why UV light is so harmful to skin cells. Then, solve the mystery.

FOUNDATIONS for Learning

The main ideas from the chapter can be found as the answers to the Key Questions. They are the building blocks of the Big Ideas. Before you read the chapter, go through and use the answers to the Key Questions to make Connected Ideas cards. Write only one idea per card. Use several cards to cover all the ideas in long answers. As you read through the chapter, make additional cards that describe important discoveries and the steps of processes you learn. At the end of the chapter are two activities that use the cards to help answer the question: What is the structure of DNA, and how does it function in genetic inheritance?

By studying bacterial transformation, Avery and other scientists discovered that DNA stores and passes genetic information from one generation of bacteria to the next.

Hershey and Chase's experiment with bacteriophages confirmed Avery's results, convincing many scientists that DNA was the genetic material found in genes.

The double-helix model explains Chargaff's rule of base pairing and how the two strands of DNA are held together.

When the cell divides, ...

• Untamed Science Video • Chapter Mystery

Identifying the Substance of Genes

MD | CLG 3.1.1 Chemical Substances and Macromolecules, 3.3.3 Nucleic Acids and Protein Synthesis, 3.3.4 DNA Alteration. SPI 1.1.2 Scientific Ideas, 1.5.2 Communicate Information, 1.5.7 Classification Systems.

Key Questions

🔑 *What clues did bacterial transformation give about the gene?*

🔑 *What role did bacterial viruses play in identifying genetic material?*

🔑 *What is the role of DNA in heredity?*

BUILD Understanding

Flowchart As you read this section, make a flowchart that shows how scientists came to understand the molecule known as DNA.

In Your Workbook Go to your workbook to learn more about making a flowchart. Complete the flowchart for Lesson 12.1.

BUILD Vocabulary

transformation
a process in which one strain of bacteria is changed by a gene or genes from another strain of bacteria

bacteriophage
a kind of virus that infects bacteria

🗝 SUFFIXES

The suffix *-phage* comes from the Greek word *phagien*, which means "to eat." Bacteriophages do not actually eat bacteria, but they can harm or kill them.

Bacterial Transformation

How do genes work? You need to know what genes are made of to answer that question. The first scientist to help figure this out was Frederick Griffith. He found two similar types (or strains) of bacteria in mice. One of the strains (S strain) caused pneumonia. Pneumonia is a deadly lung disease. The other strain (R strain) was harmless. Griffith wondered why the S strain was deadly but the R strain was harmless.

Griffith's Experiments When Griffith injected mice with disease-causing bacteria, the mice developed pneumonia and died. When he injected mice with harmless bacteria, the mice stayed healthy. Griffith thought the S strain might make a toxin that made mice sick. So, he heated some of the S cells to kill them. Then he injected the heat-killed S cells into mice. The mice survived. This suggested that the pneumonia was not caused by a toxin.

Next Griffith mixed heat-killed S cells with R cells. He injected the mixture into mice. Griffith was surprised because the mice got sick with pneumonia. He found live disease-causing bacteria in some of the dead mice. How did this happen if he had injected dead S cells?

Transformation The heat-killed bacteria had made the harmless bacteria deadly. Griffith wondered if a particular molecule from the deadly strain had changed the harmless R cells into S cells. He called this process **transformation.** If he was right, this molecule was passed along to the transformed bacteria. Identifying the molecule could be the key to understanding heredity.

The Molecular Cause of Transformation What molecule causes transformation? In 1944, a team led by Oswald Avery tried to find out. They thought knowing this molecule would allow them to know what made up genes. Avery and his team took a mixture of molecules out of heat-killed bacteria. They treated this mixture to destroy proteins, lipids, carbohydrates, and RNA, one at a time. Every time, transformation still occurred. But then they tried one more experiment in which they destroyed the DNA. This time, transformation did not happen. They concluded that DNA was the transforming molecule.

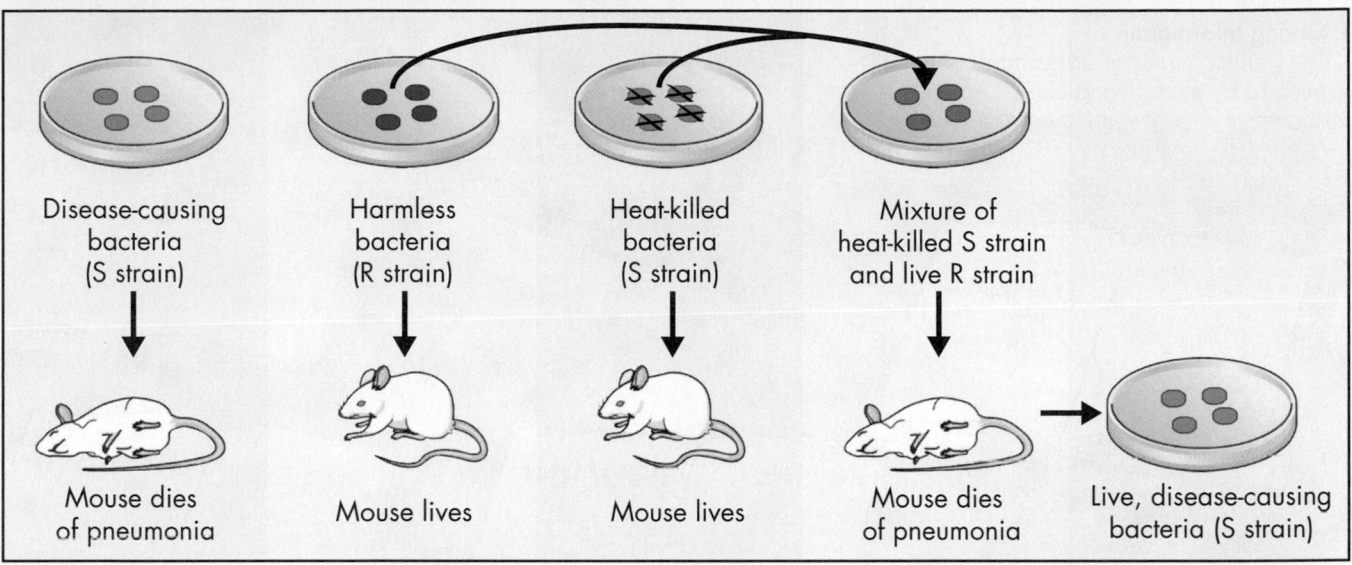

Disease-causing bacteria (S strain) → Mouse dies of pneumonia

Harmless bacteria (R strain) → Mouse lives

Heat-killed bacteria (S strain) → Mouse lives

Mixture of heat-killed S strain and live R strain → Mouse dies of pneumonia → Live, disease-causing bacteria (S strain)

🔑 **Key Question** What clues did bacterial transformation give about the gene? **Avery and other scientists discovered that DNA stores and passes genetic information from one generation of bacteria to the next.**

Bacterial Viruses

Other scientists tried to confirm Avery's discovery. In 1952, Alfred Hershey and Martha Chase used viruses to study DNA. Viruses are tiny, nonliving particles that can infect living cells.

Bacteriophage A **bacteriophage** is a kind of virus that infects bacterial cells. A bacteriophage sticks to the surface of the cell and injects its genetic information into it. The viral genes make many new bacteriophages, which destroy the bacterium. When the cell splits open, hundreds of new viruses burst out.

The Hershey-Chase Experiment Hershey and Chase used a bacteriophage that had a DNA core and a protein coat. They wanted to find out which part of the virus—the protein coat or the DNA core—entered bacterial cells. They made different parts of these viruses radioactive using two different tags. They used radioactive ^{35}S to tag the protein coats. They used radioactive ^{32}P to tag the DNA. Then, they infected bacterial cells with the viruses. After infection, Hershey and Chase separated the bacteria from the viruses. What they found was that the bacteria had received ^{32}P from the DNA but not ^{35}S from the coat. This finding confirmed that DNA is the molecule of heredity.

🔑 **Key Question** What role did bacterial viruses play in identifying genetic material?
Hershey and Chase's experiment with bacteriophages confirmed Avery's results, convincing many scientists that DNA was the genetic material found in genes.

Griffith's Experiments Griffith injected mice with four different samples of bacteria. Disease-causing bacteria that had been heat-killed did not kill the mice. Harmless bacteria did not kill the mice. But when the two strains were mixed together, the mice died. Griffith concluded that genetic information could be passed from one bacterial strain to another.

T4 Bacteriophage

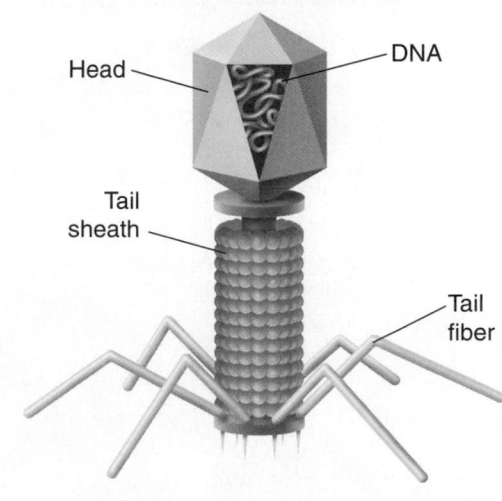

Head

DNA

Tail sheath

Tail fiber

Storing Information
The genetic material stores information needed by every living cell.

HOW TO BE A CELL
bestseller
How to Be a Cell

ION TRANSPORT

RESPIRATION

MOVEMENT

CELL GROWTH

BUILD Connections

THE MAIN FUNCTIONS OF DNA

Like DNA, the book in this diagram contains coded instructions for a cell to carry out important biological processes. The book, like DNA, can also be copied and passed along to the next generation. These three tasks— storing, copying, and passing on information—are also the three main functions of DNA.

The Role of DNA

After scientists learned that genes were made of DNA, they had another question. How could DNA do all the things that genes were known to do? The DNA that makes up genes must be capable of storing, copying, and passing on the genetic information in a cell. These three functions are similar to the way you might share an important book.

Storing Information The main job of DNA is to store information. The genes that make a flower purple must carry the information needed to make purple pigment. Genes for blood type and eye color must have the information needed for their jobs, as well. Other genes have to do even more. Genes control patterns of development. The instructions that cause a single cell to develop into an oak tree, a goldfish, or a dog must be written into the DNA of each of these organisms.

Copying Information A cell must make a complete copy of every one of its genes before the cell divides. After the experiments of Avery, Hershey, and Chase, scientists wanted to know how DNA is copied. The answer to this puzzle had to wait until the scientists could figure out the structure of DNA. Within a few weeks of learning DNA's structure, scientists suggested a way DNA could be copied. You will learn about this mechanism later in the chapter.

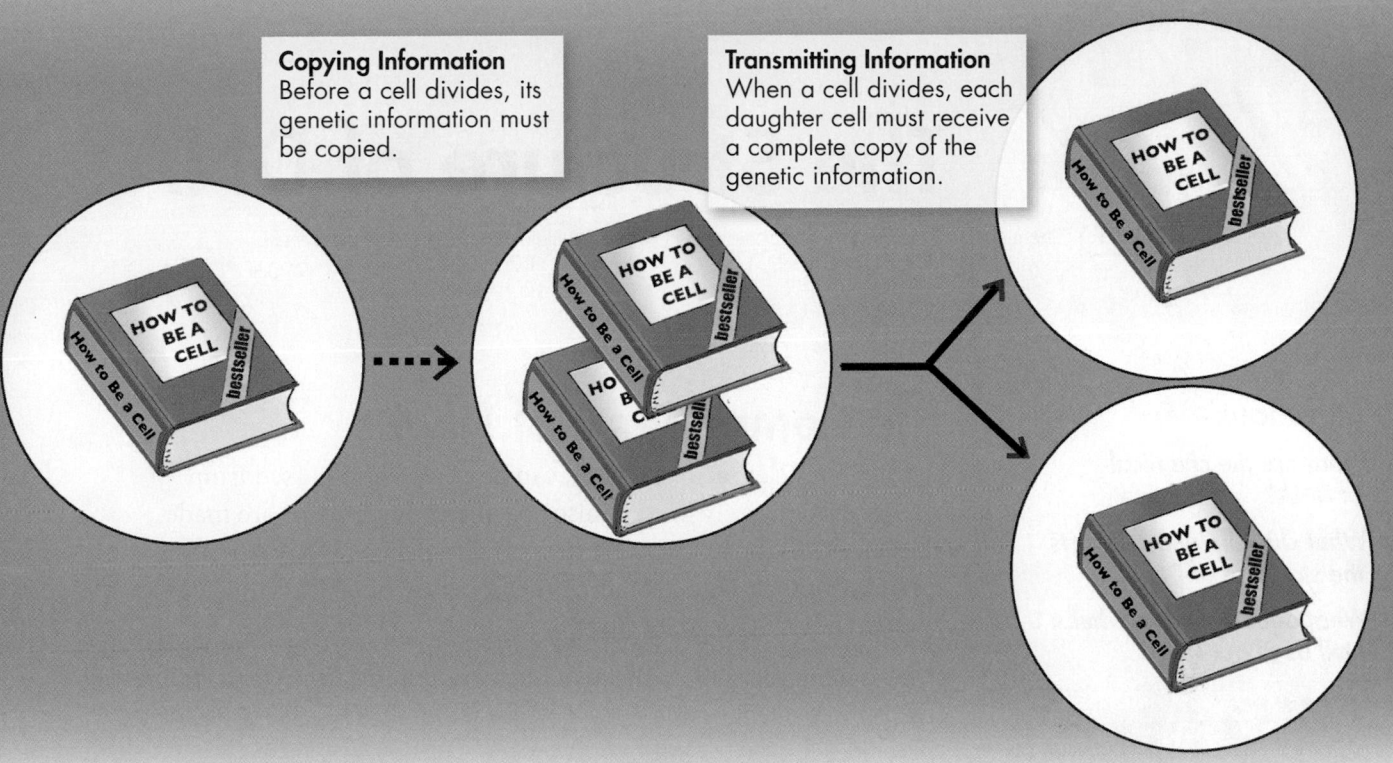

Copying Information
Before a cell divides, its genetic information must be copied.

Transmitting Information
When a cell divides, each daughter cell must receive a complete copy of the genetic information.

Transmitting Information Mendel's work showed that genes are passed down from parents to offspring. Therefore, DNA molecules must be carefully sorted and passed along when cells divide. Such careful sorting is especially important when reproductive cells are made in meiosis. Remember, the chromosomes of eukaryotic cells contain genes made of DNA. The loss of any DNA during meiosis might mean a loss of valuable genetic information that offspring might need to survive.

Key Question What is the role of DNA in heredity?
The DNA that makes up genes must be capable of storing, copying, and passing on the genetic information in a cell.

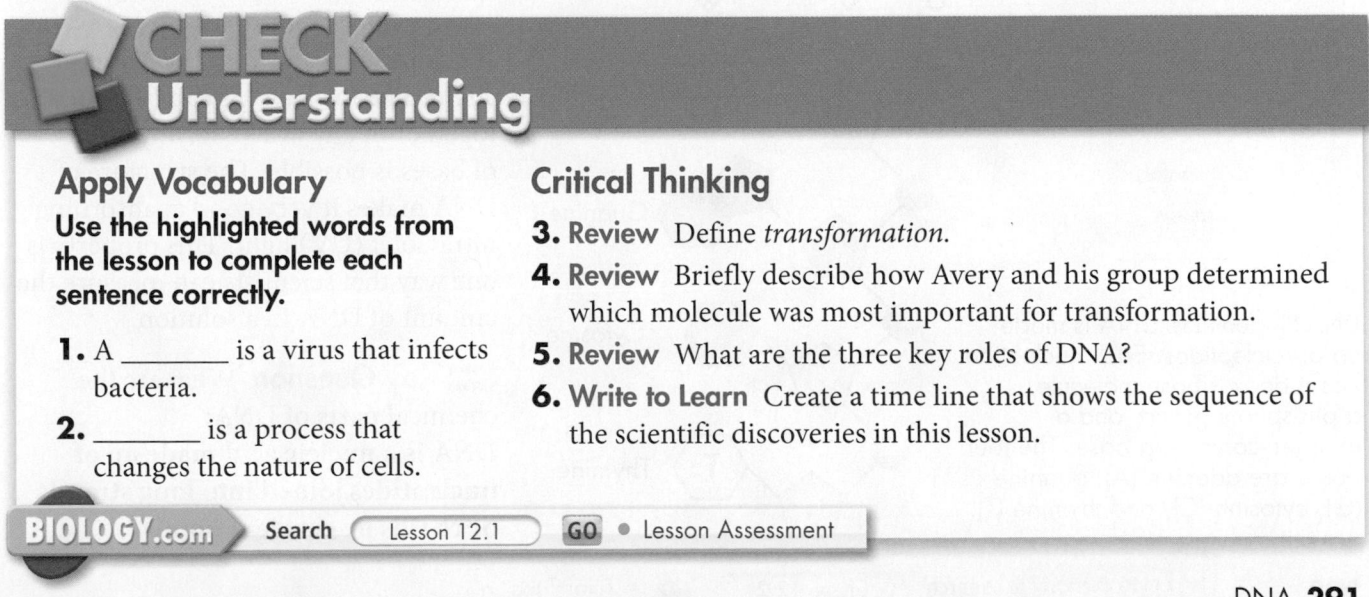

CHECK Understanding

Apply Vocabulary
Use the highlighted words from the lesson to complete each sentence correctly.

1. A _____ is a virus that infects bacteria.

2. _____ is a process that changes the nature of cells.

Critical Thinking

3. Review Define *transformation*.

4. Review Briefly describe how Avery and his group determined which molecule was most important for transformation.

5. Review What are the three key roles of DNA?

6. Write to Learn Create a time line that shows the sequence of the scientific discoveries in this lesson.

BIOLOGY.com 〉 Search (Lesson 12.1) **GO** ● Lesson Assessment

12.2 The Structure of DNA

MD | CLG **3.1.1** Chemical Substances and Macromolecules, **3.3.3** Nucleic Acids and Protein Synthesis.
SPI **1.1.2** Scientific Ideas, **1.4.8** Use Models, **1.5.9** Synthesize Ideas, **1.7.6** Science and Technology.

Key Questions

🔑 **What are the chemical parts of DNA?**

🔑 **What clues helped scientists solve the structure of DNA?**

🔑 **What does the double-helix model tell us about DNA?**

BUILD Understanding

T-Chart Make a T-chart with all the green and blue headings in the left column. As you read, find the key ideas for each heading. Write down a few key words from each main idea in the right column.

In Your Workbook Go to your workbook to learn more about T-charts. Finish the chart for Lesson 12.2.

The Components of DNA

Deoxyribonucleic acid, or DNA, can be copied and passed from one generation to the next. It also specifies how proteins are made. These features make DNA a very special molecule. DNA also has a special structure. Understanding the structure of DNA is the key to understanding how genes work.

DNA is a nucleic acid made up of nucleotides joined into long strands or chains by covalent bonds. Let's look at each of these parts more closely.

Nucleic Acids and Nucleotides Nucleic acids are long molecules found in cell nuclei. Like other big molecules, nucleic acids are made up of smaller subunits, or parts. These parts are linked together to form long chains. Nucleotides are the building blocks of nucleic acids. These nucleotides are made up of three basic parts: a 5-carbon sugar called deoxyribose, a phosphate group, and a nitrogenous base.

Nitrogenous Bases and Covalent Bonds Nitrogenous bases are bases that have nitrogen in them. DNA has four kinds of nitrogenous bases: adenine (AD uh neen) guanine (GWAH neen), cytosine (SY tuh zeen), and thymine (THY meen). Biologists often refer to the nucleotides in DNA by the first letters of their base names: A, G, C, and T. The nucleotides in a strand of DNA are joined by covalent bonds formed between the sugar of one nucleotide and the phosphate group of the next. The nitrogenous bases stick out sideways from the nucleotide chain. The nucleotides can be joined together in any order. So, any order of bases is possible. The structure of DNA makes it very good at absorbing ultraviolet (UV) light. This property is one way that scientists can measure the amount of DNA in a solution.

🔑 **Key Question** What are the chemical parts of DNA?
DNA is a nucleic acid made up of nucleotides joined into long strands or chains by covalent bonds.

DNA Nucleotides DNA is made up of nucleotides. Each nucleotide has a deoxyribose molecule, a phosphate group, and a nitrogen-containing base. The four bases are adenine (A), guanine (G), cytosine (C), and thymine (T).

Phosphate Group   *Deoxyribose*   *Base*

A — Adenine
G — Guanine
C — Cytosine
T — Thymine

Rosalind Franklin made X-ray diffraction pictures that helped determine the structure of DNA.

Erwin Chargaff

Franklin's X-ray diffraction photograph, May 1952

Solving the Structure of DNA

Knowing that DNA is made from long chains of nucleotides was only the beginning of understanding the structure of this molecule. The next step was to figure out how those chains are arranged.

Chargaff's Rule Erwin Chargaff had discovered years earlier that the percentages of adenine [A] and thymine [T] bases are almost equal in any sample of DNA. The same thing is true for guanine [G] and cytosine [C]. The observation that [A] = [T] and [G] = [C] became known as "Chargaff's rule." DNA samples from organisms as different as bacteria and humans obeyed this rule. However, no one knew why they did.

Franklin's X-Rays In the early 1950s, Rosalind Franklin began to study DNA. She used a technique called X-ray diffraction to get information about the structure of the DNA molecule. Her X-ray pictures showed that the strands in DNA are twisted around each other. This shape is known as a helix. She also showed that DNA is made of two strands. Other clues suggested that the nitrogenous bases are near the center of the DNA molecule.

The Work of Watson and Crick Meanwhile, James Watson and Francis Crick were also trying to understand the structure of DNA. They tried to build models of DNA out of cardboard and wire. Nothing worked. The pieces did not fit. Then, in 1953, Watson saw a copy of Franklin's X-ray picture. Immediately, he realized that it was the missing piece of the puzzle. Watson rushed back to tell Crick about the picture, and a few weeks later they had solved the structure of DNA.

Key Question What clues helped scientists solve the structure of DNA? **The clues in Franklin's X-ray pattern allowed Watson and Crick to build a model that explained the specific structure and properties of DNA.**

Clues to the Structure of DNA Erwin Chargaff and Rosalind Franklin both helped solve the puzzle of the structure of DNA.

A computer model of DNA

James Watson, at left, and Francis Crick with their model of a DNA molecule in 1953

Crick's original sketch of DNA

A Double Helix Watson and Crick determined that DNA has the structure of a double helix.

The Double-Helix Model

DNA is a double helix. A double helix looks like a twisted ladder. In the double-helix model of DNA, the two strands twist around each other like spiral staircases. Watson and Crick realized that the double helix explained Franklin's X-ray pattern. The shape also explains many of the most important properties of DNA. The double-helix model explains the reasons behind Chargaff's rule. It also explains how the two strands of DNA are held together. This model can even tell us how DNA carries genetic information.

Antiparallel Strands One of the surprising discoveries of the double-helix model is that the two strands of DNA run in opposite directions. As biochemists say, these strands are "antiparallel." Because of this arrangement, the nitrogenous bases on both strands meet at the center of the molecule. The structure also allows each strand of the double helix to carry a sequence of nucleotides. These bases are arranged almost like letters in a four-letter alphabet.

Hydrogen Bonding At first, Watson and Crick could not explain what forces held the two strands of DNA's double helix together. Then, they discovered that hydrogen bonds could form between certain nitrogenous bases. Hydrogen bonds are fairly weak forces. These bonds have just enough force to hold the two strands of DNA together.

Why would a molecule as important as DNA be held together by weak bonds? Well, if the two strands of the helix were held together by strong bonds, it might not be possible to pull them apart. As we will see, DNA's strands have to be able to separate easily to function.

Base Pairing Watson and Crick's DNA model showed that hydrogen bonds could hold the bases together along the center of the molecule. However, these bonds would form only between certain base pairs. Adenine paired with thymine, and guanine paired with cytosine. This nearly perfect fit between A–T and G–C nucleotides is known as **base pairing.**

Once they discovered the fit between bases, Watson and Crick realized that base pairing explained Chargaff's rule. It gave a reason why [A] = [T] and [G] = [C]. For every adenine in a double-stranded DNA molecule, there has to be one thymine. For each guanine, there is one cytosine. Their model explained Chargaff's observations. It also accounted for Rosalind Franklin's findings. At last, Watson and Crick were confident that they had come to the right conclusion.

🔑 **Key Question** What does the double-helix model tell us about DNA?
The double-helix model explains Chargaff's rule of base pairing and how the two strands of DNA are held together.

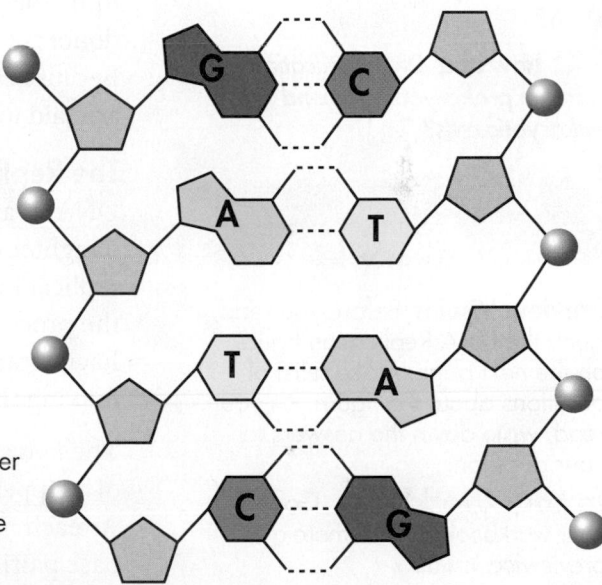

Base Pairing The two strands of DNA are held together by hydrogen bonds. The bonds here are represented by the dashes between the nitrogenous bases adenine and thymine, and between guanine and cytosine.

✓ CHECK Understanding

Apply Vocabulary

1. The principle of _____ states that bonds in DNA can form only between adenine and thymine and between guanine and cytosine.

Critical Thinking

2. **Review** List the chemical components of DNA.

3. **Relate Cause and Effect** Why are hydrogen bonds so important to the structure of DNA?

4. **Review** Describe the discoveries that led to the modeling of DNA.

5. **Review** Describe Watson and Crick's model of the DNA molecule.

6. **Write to Learn** Answer the first mystery clue.

MYSTERY CLUE

The energy from UV light can excite electrons in a substance. The excited electrons can cause chemical changes. What chemical changes might occur in the nitrogenous bases of DNA? (Hint: See p. 294.)

DNA Replication

MD | CLG 3.1.1 Chemical Substances and Macromolecules, 3.2.1 Processes and Functions, 3.3.3 Nucleic Acids and Protein Synthesis. SPI 1.4.8 Use Models, 1.5.8 Compare.

Key Questions

🗝 **What role does DNA polymerase play in copying DNA?**

🗝 **How does DNA replication differ in prokaryotic cells and eukaryotic cells?**

BUILD
Understanding

Preview Visuals Before you read, study the DNA Replication figure on the next page. Make a list of questions about the figure. As you read, write down the answers to your questions.

In Your Workbook Go to your workbook to learn more about previewing visuals.

BUILD
Vocabulary

replication
the process of copying DNA prior to cell division

🏷 USE SUFFIXES

The suffix *-tion* means "process of." A replica is a copy. So, replication is the process of making a copy.

Copying the Code

When Watson and Crick discovered the structure of DNA, they immediately recognized something important. Each strand of the double helix has all the information needed to make the other strand. Because each strand can be used to make the other strand, the strands are said to be complementary.

The Replication Process Before a cell divides, it makes a copy of its DNA in a process called **replication.** Replication makes sure that each daughter cell has the same complete set of DNA molecules. During replication, the DNA molecule first separates into two strands. Then, the process makes two new strands following the rules of base pairing. Each strand of the double helix of DNA is a template, or model, for making the new strand.

The two strands of the double helix separate, the same way two sides of a zipper come apart. This separation makes two replication forks. As each new strand forms, new bases are added following the rules of base pairing. Adenine (A) is always paired with thymine (T). Guanine (G) is always paired to cytosine (C). For example, a strand that has the base sequence TACGTT makes a strand with the base sequence ATGCAA. The end result is two DNA molecules. Each is identical to the other and to the original DNA molecule.

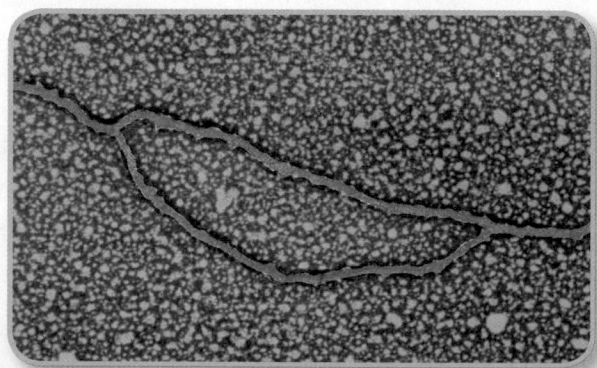

TEM 60,000×

Replication Forks The DNA molecule comes apart the way the two sides of a zipper come apart. The result is two areas called replication forks, where the DNA molecule can be copied. This micrograph shows a pair of replication forks in human DNA.

The Role of Enzymes DNA replication is carried out by special proteins called enzymes. These enzymes pull apart a molecule of DNA. They break the hydrogen bonds between base pairs. Then, they unwind the two strands. Each strand then serves as a template for making a new strand. The main enzyme involved in DNA replication is called **DNA polymerase** (PAHL ih mur ayz). DNA polymerase is an enzyme that joins individual nucleotides to make a new strand of DNA. DNA polymerase produces the sugar-phosphate bonds that join nucleotides together to form the new strands. DNA polymerase also checks each new DNA strand, so that each molecule is a close copy of the original.

🔑 **Key Question** What role does DNA polymerase play in copying DNA?
DNA polymerase is an enzyme that joins individual nucleotides to produce a new strand of DNA.

Telomeres The tips of chromosomes are known as **telomeres.** DNA in these regions is hard to replicate. Cells use a special enzyme called telomerase to fix this problem. Telomerase makes it less likely that genes will be damaged or lost during replication of rapidly dividing cells. Telomerase is often switched off in normal adult cells. But, in cancer cells, telomerase may be switched on. This may be one of the reasons why cancer cells are able to grow and divide rapidly.

DNA Replication During DNA replication, the DNA molecule makes two new complementary strands. Each strand of the double helix serves as a template for the new strand.

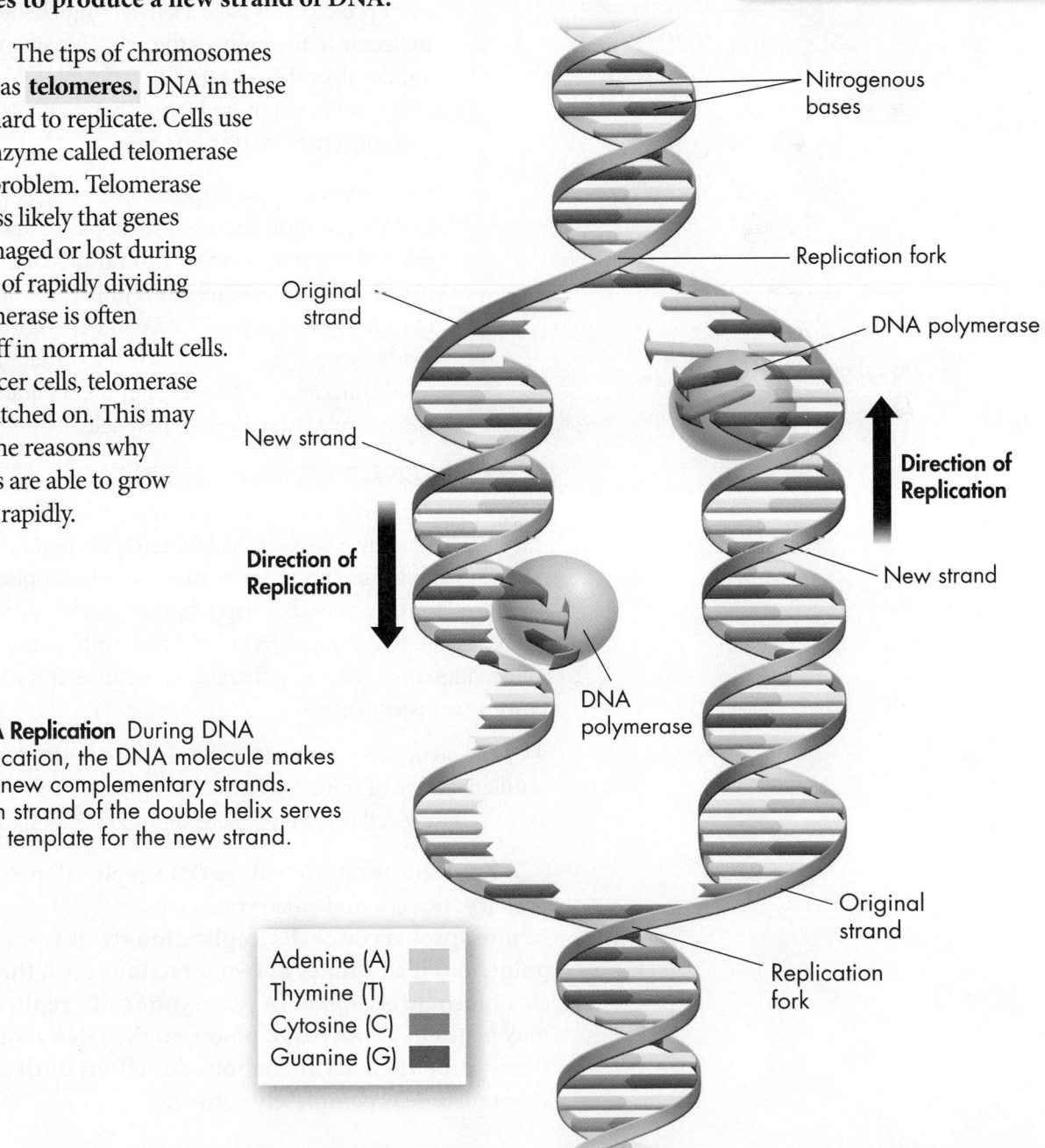

Nitrogenous bases

Replication fork

Original strand

DNA polymerase

New strand

Direction of Replication

Direction of Replication

New strand

DNA polymerase

Original strand

Replication fork

Adenine (A)
Thymine (T)
Cytosine (C)
Guanine (G)

DNA **297**

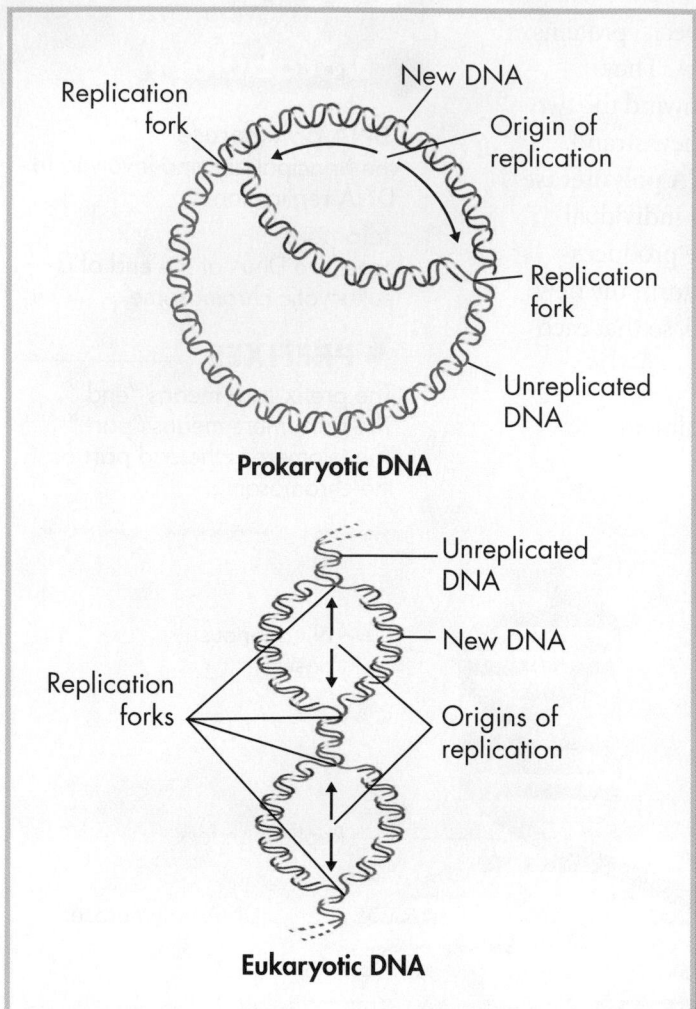

Prokaryotic DNA

Replication fork

New DNA

Origin of replication

Replication fork

Unreplicated DNA

Unreplicated DNA

New DNA

Replication forks

Origins of replication

Eukaryotic DNA

Differences in DNA Replication Replication in most prokaryotic cells (top) begins at one point and goes in two directions until the entire DNA ring is copied. In eukaryotic cells (bottom), replication happens at many starting points on chromosomes. Replication ends when all the chromosomes are copied.

Replication in Living Cells

Where is DNA found inside a cell? The cells of most prokaryotes have a single, ring-shaped DNA molecule in the body of the cell. This ring contains almost all of the cell's genetic information. Eukaryotic cells have much more DNA. Their DNA is found in chromosomes in the nucleus.

Prokaryotic DNA Replication In most prokaryotes, DNA replication starts when special proteins bind to one starting point on the chromosome. Replication usually goes in two directions until the whole chromosome is copied. Often, the two chromosomes made by replication are attached to different points inside the cell membrane. They are separated when the cell splits to make two new cells.

Eukaryotic DNA Replication Eukaryotic chromosomes are bigger than those of prokaryotes. In eukaryotic cells, replication may begin at many places on the DNA. Replication moves in both directions. Proteins check to make sure the copies are accurate. However, mistakes happen, and then the order of the bases in DNA changes. When the base order changes, the information on a gene may change. Sometimes this can have serious consequences.

As you learned in Chapter 10, the chromosomes stay together until anaphase of mitosis. Then, the chromosomes separate, and each new cell has a complete set of genes coded in DNA.

🔑 **Key Question** How does DNA replication differ in prokaryotic cells and eukaryotic cells?
In most prokaryotic cells, replication starts from a single point, and it continues in two directions until the whole chromosome is copied. In eukaryotic cells, replication may begin in hundreds of places on the DNA molecule. Replication then occurs in both directions until each chromosome is completely copied.

INQUIRY into Scientific Thinking

Modeling DNA Replication

1. Cut out small squares of blue and gray paper to represent phosphate and sugar molecules.
2. Cut out small strips of purple, green, red, and yellow paper to represent the four nitrogenous bases.
3. Build a set of five nucleotides using your paper strips and tape.
4. Using your nucleotides, tape together a single strand of DNA. For example you could make a pattern of bases that reads, "ATTGC."
5. Exchange your paper strand with a partner's strand.
6. Model DNA replication by creating a strand that is complementary to your partner's original strand.

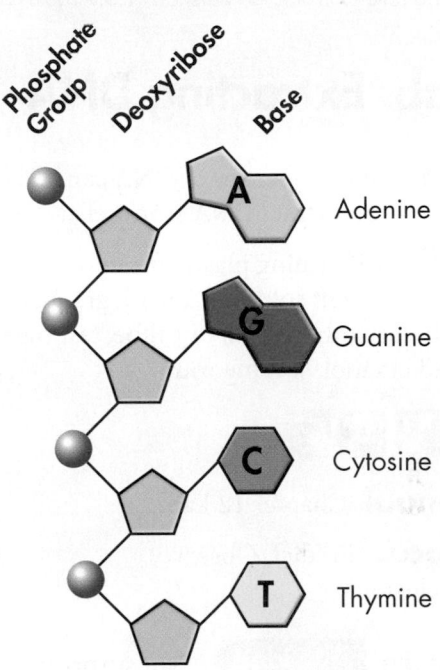

Phosphate Group
Deoxyribose
Base
A
Adenine
G
Guanine
C
Cytosine
T
Thymine

Analyze and Conclude

1. Use Models When you taped the nucleotides together, what enzyme were you modeling?

2. Analyze How does your model follow Chargaff's rule?

3. Evaluate How does your model differ from real DNA?

In Your Workbook Get more help for this activity in your workbook.

CHECK Understanding

Apply Vocabulary

Use the highlighted words from the lesson to complete the sentence correctly.

1. _______ are the tips of chromosomes.

2. _______ is the primary enzyme used in DNA replication.

Critical Thinking

3. Review How is DNA replicated?

4. Apply Concepts What is the role of DNA polymerase in DNA replication?

5. Compare and Contrast How is replication in eukaryotic cells different from replication in prokaryotic cells?

6. Write to Learn Answer the mystery clue.

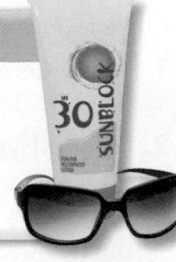

MYSTERY CLUE

UV light can cause chemical changes in bases. How might these chemical changes in bases affect the process of DNA replication? (Hint: See p. 297.)

30
SUNBLOCK

BIOLOGY.com Search Lesson 12.3 GO • Lesson Asessment • Art Review

 CLG 3.1.1 Chemical Substances and Macromolecules. SPI 1.3.1 Use Equipment, 1.3.3 Safe Handling of Materials, 1.5.9 Synthesize Ideas.

Pre-Lab: Extracting DNA

Problem What properties of DNA can you observe when you extract DNA from cells?

Materials self-sealing plastic freezer bag, ripe strawberry, detergent solution, 25-mL graduated cylinder, cheesecloth, funnel, test tube, test tube rack, chilled ethanol, stirring rod

Lab Manual Chapter 12 Lab

Skills Focus Predict, Observe, Draw Conclusions

Connect to the **Big idea** Not surprisingly, the molecules that store genetic information are long molecules. If the DNA from a human cell were unfolded, the double helix structure would be about one meter long. Yet, most of a cell's DNA can be folded and tightly packed inside the cell's tiny nucleus. How can scientists remove DNA from the nucleus so that it can be studied and analyzed? In this lab, you will learn that extracting DNA from living tissue is not as difficult as you might think.

Background Questions

a. Review Describe the structure of a DNA molecule.

b. Review What type of bond holds the strands of DNA together?

c. Apply Concepts How does the strength of those bonds affect how DNA functions?

Pre-Lab Questions

Preview the procedure in the lab manual.

1. Apply Concepts Why do strawberry cells need DNA?

2. Form a Hypothesis If you observe a cell nucleus under a compound microscope, you will not see a molecule of DNA. Why will you be able to see the DNA you extract?

3. Predict Use what you know about DNA to predict some of the physical properties of DNA.

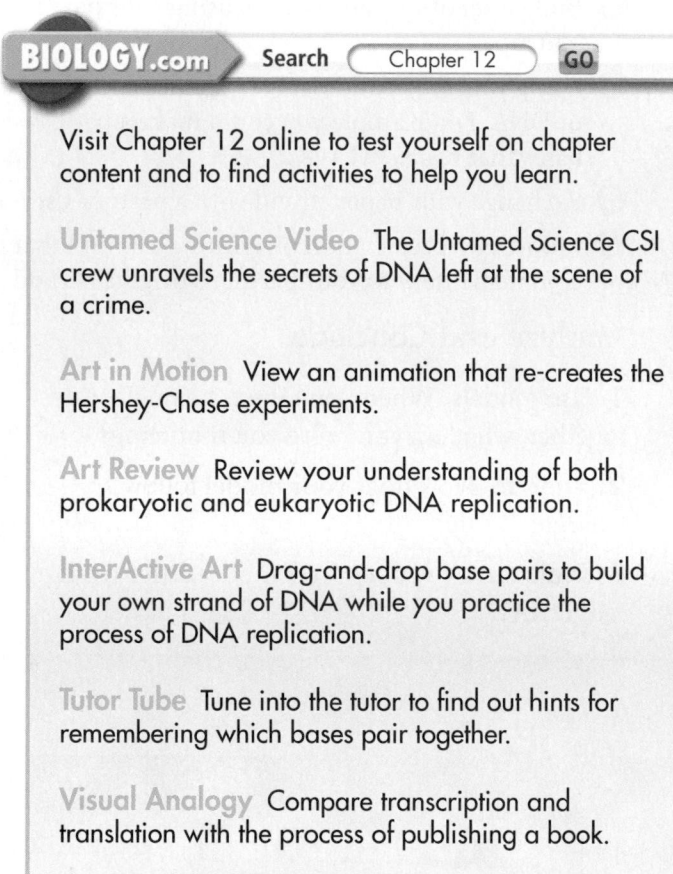

BIOLOGY.com Search Chapter 12 **GO**

Visit Chapter 12 online to test yourself on chapter content and to find activities to help you learn.

Untamed Science Video The Untamed Science CSI crew unravels the secrets of DNA left at the scene of a crime.

Art in Motion View an animation that re-creates the Hershey-Chase experiments.

Art Review Review your understanding of both prokaryotic and eukaryotic DNA replication.

InterActive Art Drag-and-drop base pairs to build your own strand of DNA while you practice the process of DNA replication.

Tutor Tube Tune into the tutor to find out hints for remembering which bases pair together.

Visual Analogy Compare transcription and translation with the process of publishing a book.

12.1 Identifying the Substance of Genes

- By studying bacterial transformation, Avery and other scientists discovered that DNA stores and passes genetic information from one generation of bacteria to the next.

- Hershey and Chase's experiment with bacteriophages confirmed Avery's results, convincing many scientists that DNA was the genetic material found in genes.

- The DNA that makes up genes must be capable of storing, copying, and transmitting the genetic information in a cell.

transformation (p. 288)
bacteriophage (p. 289)

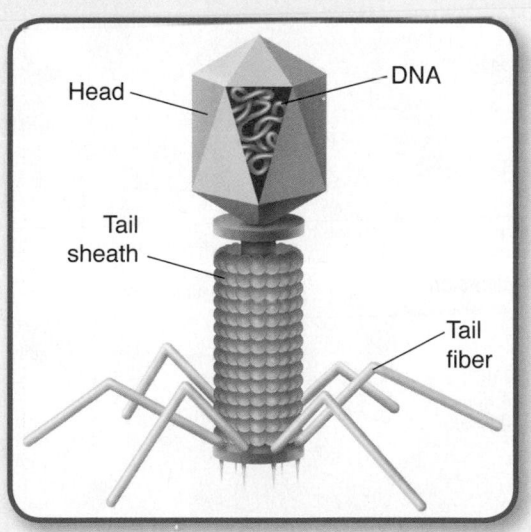

Head — DNA
Tail sheath
Tail fiber

12.2 The Structure of DNA

- DNA is a nucleic acid made up of nucleotides joined into long strands or chains by covalent bonds.

- The clues in Franklin's X-ray pattern allowed Watson and Crick to build a model that explained the specific structure and properties of DNA.

- The double-helix model explains the reasons behind Chargaff's rule and how the two strands of DNA are held together.

base pairing (p. 295)

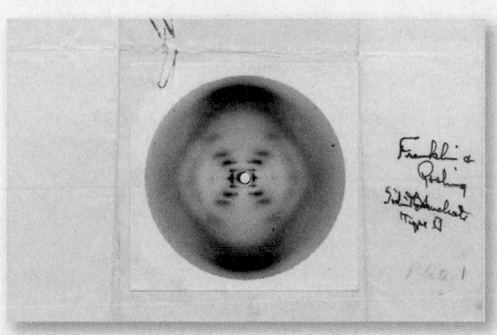

12.3 DNA Replication

- DNA polymerase is an enzyme that joins individual nucleotides to produce a new strand of DNA.

- In most prokaryotic cells, replication starts from a single point, and it continues in two directions until the entire chromosome is copied.

- In eukaryotic cells, replication may begin in hundreds of places on the DNA molecule. Replication then moves in both directions until each chromosome is completely copied.

replication (p. 296)
DNA polymerase (p. 297)
telomere (p. 297)

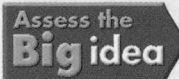 **Information and Heredity, Cellular Basis of Life**

Write an answer to the question below.

Q: What is the structure of DNA, and how does it function in genetic inheritance?

Constructed Response

Write an answer to each of the questions below. The answer to each question should be one or two paragraphs. To help you begin, read the **Hints** below the questions.

1. **How did Hershey and Chase confirm that genetic material was a nucleic acid?**

   Hint Bacteriophages are viruses that infect bacteria.

   Hint Viruses have a protein coat around a nucleic acid core.

2. **How did Chargaff's rule help Watson and Crick determine the structure of DNA?**

   Hint Adenine always pairs with thymine, and cytosine always pairs with guanine.

3. **If a change happens in the genetic code in the gamete of a eukaryotic parent, will offspring have that change, too?**

   Hint Changes in the genetic code can sometimes be copied when the DNA is copied.

Foundations for Learning Wrap-Up

Use the Connected Ideas cards you made as you read the chapter to help you organize your thoughts about DNA structure and replication.

Activity 1 Combine your cards with the cards of a partner. Using as many cards you can, make a time line of the history of the discoveries that led to understanding the structure of DNA.

Activity 2 With a partner, make cards to complete the two chains of connected ideas shown below. One chain shows the process of DNA replication in eukaryotes. The other chain shows the process of DNA replication in prokaryotes.

Prokaryotic Replication

A protein binds to one starting point.

Replication goes in two directions until the entire chromosome is copied.

Each ring binds to a place on the cell membrane.

When the cell divides, ...

Eukaryotic Replication

Replication begins at many places along the DNA chains.

Replication goes in both directions until the whole molecule is copied.

Proteins check for accuracy.

During anaphase, the chromatids ...

12.1 Identifying the Substance of Genes

Understand Key Concepts

1. The process by which one strain of bacterium is apparently changed into another strain is called
   a. transcription.
   c. duplication.
   b. transformation.
   d. replication.

Test-Taking Tip

Use Root Words As you read the answers, look for root words to help you choose the correct answer. The root words for the answers in question 1 are *transcrip*, *transform*, *duplica*, and *replica*. Remember that *transform* means "to change." Now read the question again. The question asks which process <u>changed</u> one strain of bacterium. You know that transformation means change, so **b** is the correct answer.

2. Bacteriophages are
   a. a form of bacteria.
   c. coils of DNA.
   b. enzymes.
   d. viruses.

3. Before DNA could be shown to be the genetic material in cells, scientists had to show that it could
   a. tolerate high temperatures.
   b. carry and make copies of information.
   c. be modified in response to environmental conditions.
   d. be broken down into small subunits.

4. Briefly describe the conclusion that could be drawn from the experiments of Frederick Griffith.

Think Critically

5. **Evaluate** Avery and his team identified DNA as the molecule that caused transformation. How did they control variables in their experiment to make sure that only DNA caused the change?

12.2 The Structure of DNA

Understand Key Concepts

6. A nucleotide does NOT contain a
   a. 5-carbon sugar.
   c. nitrogen base.
   b. protein.
   d. phosphate group.

7. According to Chargaff's rule of base pairing, which of the following is true about DNA?
   a. A = T, and C = G
   c. A = G, and T = C
   b. A = C, and T = G
   d. A = T = C = G

8. The bonds that hold the two strands of DNA together come from
   a. the attraction of phosphate groups for each other.
   b. strong bonds between nitrogenous bases and the sugar-phosphate backbone.
   c. hydrogen bonds between nitrogenous bases.
   d. carbon-to-carbon bonds in the sugar portion of the nucleotides.

9. Describe the parts and structure of a DNA nucleotide.

Think Critically

10. **Infer** Adenine and guanine are longer than thymine and cytosine. What would happen to the parallel strands if adenine were paired with guanine?

12.3 DNA Replication

Understand Key Concepts

11. The diagram below shows the process of DNA
    a. replication.
    c. transformation.
    b. digestion.
    d. transpiration.

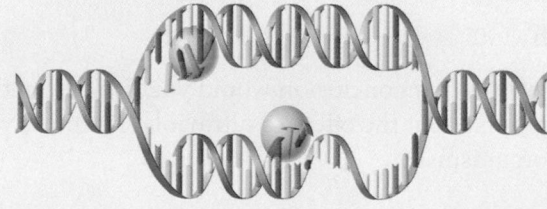

12. What is meant by the term *base pairing*?

13. Explain the process of replication. When a DNA molecule is replicated, how do the new molecules compare to the original molecule?

Think Critically

14. Use Analogies How is photocopying a page similar to DNA replication? Think of the original materials, the copying process, and the final products. Explain how the two processes are alike. Identify major differences.

Connecting Concepts

Use Science Graphics

A scientist studied the effect of exposing DNA to various wavelengths of ultraviolet light. The scientist determined the number of copying errors made after exposure to ultraviolet rays. The graph shows the results. Use the graph to answer questions 15 and 16.

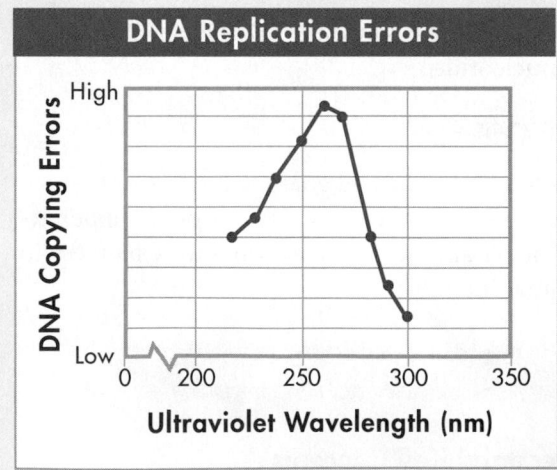

DNA Replication Errors

15. Interpret Graphs The most damaging effects of ultraviolet light on DNA replication occur closest to which wavelength?

a. 200   **c.** 300

b. 250   **d.** 350

16. Infer What conclusion would you draw from the graph about the effect of ultraviolet light on living organisms?

solve the CHAPTER MYSTERY

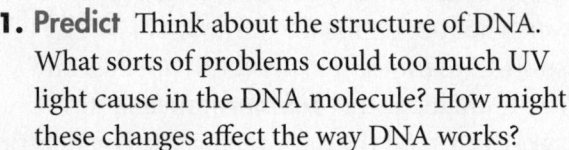

UV LIGHT

Nucleotides are small parts that are linked together to make the larger DNA molecule. The three parts of each nucleotide include a nitrogenous base—adenine, cytosine, guanine, or thymine (A, C, G, or T). The energy of ultraviolet light can cause chemical changes between the nitrogenous bases in DNA.

1. Predict Think about the structure of DNA. What sorts of problems could too much UV light cause in the DNA molecule? How might these changes affect the way DNA works?

2. Relate Cause and Effect Analyze the effects that UV light might have on skin cells. Why is UV light so dangerous? Why is the skin particularly vulnerable to it?

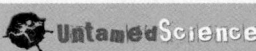 **Never Stop Exploring Your World.** Finding the connection between UV light and DNA is only the beginning. Take a video field trip with the ecogeeks of Untamed Science to see where the mystery leads.

Standardized Test Practice for Maryland

Multiple Choice

1. During replication, which sequence of nucleotides would bond with the DNA sequence TATGA?
   A TATGA   C CACTA
   B ATACT   D AGTAT   CLG 3.1.1

2. The scientist(s) responsible for the discovery of bacterial transformation is (are)
   A Watson and Crick.   C Griffith.
   B Avery.   D Franklin.   CLG 3.1.1

3. Which of the following does NOT describe the structure of DNA?
   A double helix
   B long chain of nucleotides
   C contains adenine-guanine pairs
   D sugar-phosphate backbone   CLG 3.1.1

4. What did Hershey and Chase's work show?
   A Genes are probably made of DNA.
   B Genes are probably made of protein.
   C Viruses contain DNA but not protein.
   D Bacteria contain DNA but not protein.
       CLG 3.1.1

5. The two "backbones" of the DNA molecule consist of
   A adenines and sugars.
   B phosphates and sugars.
   C adenines and thymines.
   D thymines and sugars.   CLG 3.1.1

6. When prokaryotic cells copy their DNA, replication begins at
   A one point on the DNA molecule.
   B two points on opposite ends of the DNA molecule.
   C dozens to hundreds of points along the molecule.
   D opposite ends of the molecule.   CLG 3.1.1

7. Compared to eukaryotic cells, prokaryotic cells contain
   A much more DNA.
   B much less DNA.
   C twice as much DNA.
   D the same amount of DNA.   CLG 3.1.1

Questions 8 and 9

Under ideal conditions, a single bacterial cell can reproduce every 20 minutes. The graph shows how the total number of cells under ideal conditions can change over time.

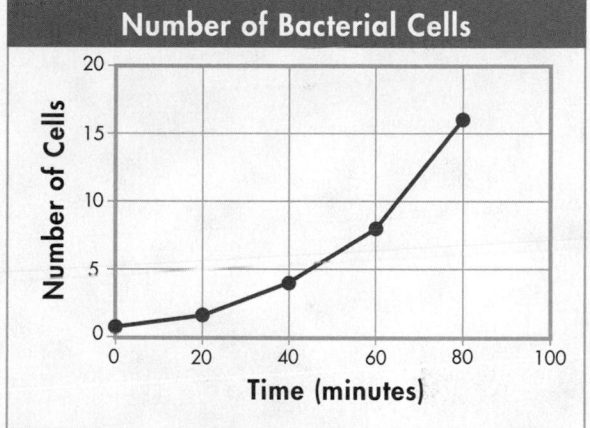

Number of Bacterial Cells

8. How many cells are present after 80 minutes?
   A 1   C 16
   B 2   D 32   SPI 1.4.2

9. If the DNA of this bacterium is 4 million base pairs in length, how many total molecules of A, T, C, and G are required for replication to be successful?
   A 2 million   C 8 million
   B 4 million   D 32 million   CLG 3.1.1

Open-Ended Response

10. Describe how eukaryotic cells are able to keep such large amounts of DNA in the small volume of the cell nucleus. (**Hint** Review the structure of a chromosome in Chapter 10.)   CLG 3.1.1

If You Have Trouble With . . .

Question	1	2	3	4	5	6	7	8	9	10
See Lesson	12.3	12.1	12.2	12.1	12.2	12.3	12.3	12.3	12.3	12.3

13 RNA and Protein Synthesis

Big idea

Information and Heredity

Q: How does information flow from DNA to RNA to direct the synthesis of proteins?

MD MARYLAND VOLUNTARY
STATE CURRICULUM

**Biology Indicators/Core Learning Goals
(CLG)** 3.1.1, 3.2.1, 3.2.2, 3.3.3, 3.3.4,
3.4.1, 3.4.2. **Skills and Processes
Indicators (SPI)** 1.2.2, 1.2.3, 1.2.4, 1.4.2,
1.4.8, 1.5.8, 1.5.9, 1.7.6. See lessons
for details.

*These two Bengal tigers both
have abnormal coloring due
to genetic mutations. Typical
Bengal tigers have dark
orange fur with black stripes.*

CHAPTER
MYSTERY

MOUSE-EYED FLY

It was not a science fiction movie. The
animal in the lab was real. It had two
forward-looking eyes. It also had eyes
on its knees and eyes on its hind legs. It
even had eyes in the back of its head! Yet,
as strange as it looked, this animal was not
a monster. It was simply a fruit fly with eyes
in very strange places. These eyes looked like
the fly's normal compound eyes. However, a mouse gene
transplanted into the fly's DNA had made them. How could
a mouse gene make extra eyes in a fly?

Read for Mystery Clues This gene normally controls the
growth of eyes in mice. As you read, look for clues to
explain how it could cause a fly to grow eyes in unusual
places. Then, solve the mystery.

FOUNDATIONS
for Learning

Create an Important Facts Envelope by drawing and cutting out
the shape below. Fold the flaps in order, taping flap 3 to flaps
1 and 2. As you read the chapter, record important facts on
slips of paper and put them in the envelope. Facts can include
key terms and drawings of processes. The facts and terms can
be organized into themes, such as "Mutations." At the end of
the chapter are two activities that use the facts to help answer
the question: How does information flow from DNA to RNA to
direct the synthesis of proteins?

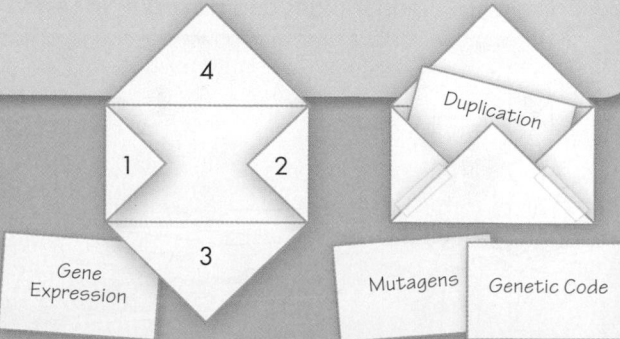

13.1 RNA

MD CLG 3.1.1 Chemical Substances and Macromolecules, 3.3.3 Nucleic Acids and Protein Synthesis. SPI 1.5.8 Compare.

Key Questions

🔑 *How does RNA differ from DNA?*

🔑 *How does the cell make RNA?*

BUILD Understanding

Preview Visuals Before you read, preview the Transcribing DNA Into RNA figure on the last page of this lesson. Write a prediction of how you think a cell makes RNA. Then, as you read, take notes on how a cell makes RNA. After you read, compare your notes to your prediction.

In Your Workbook Go to your workbook and complete the prediction chart in Lesson 13.1.

BUILD Connections

MASTER PLANS AND BLUEPRINTS

The roles of DNA and RNA molecules are like the two types of plans used by builders. DNA is like the master plan used by builders. RNA is like a cheap, disposable copy of that plan.

In Your Workbook Explore how DNA and RNA act like a cell's master plans and blueprints in Lesson 13.1.

The Role of RNA

We know that DNA is the genetic material. We also know that its sequence of nucleotides carries our genetic code. But DNA cannot put genes into action by itself. Ribonucleic acid, or **RNA,** is also needed. RNA, like DNA, is a nucleic acid made of a long chain of nucleotides.

Genes are made of instructions coded into DNA that tell cells how to build proteins. The first step in decoding these instructions is to copy part of the base sequence from DNA into RNA. RNA then uses these instructions to direct the making of proteins. Proteins help to determine an organism's characteristics.

Comparing DNA and RNA There are three important differences between RNA and DNA:

- The sugar in RNA is ribose, not deoxyribose.
- RNA is usually single-stranded, not double-stranded.
- RNA has uracil in place of thymine.

These chemical differences make it easy for enzymes in the cell to tell DNA and RNA apart. You can compare the different roles played by DNA and RNA molecules in the making of proteins to the two types of plans builders use. A master plan has all the information needed to make a building. That plan is valuable. So, builders use only copies of the plan, called blueprints, on the building site. The cell's "master plan" is its DNA, which it uses to prepare RNA "blueprints" for protein synthesis.

Key Question How does RNA differ from DNA?
There are three main differences between RNA and DNA. The sugar in RNA is ribose instead of deoxyribose. RNA is usually single-stranded and not double-stranded. RNA contains uracil in place of thymine.

Functions of RNA Think of an RNA molecule as a disposable copy of a piece of DNA. It is a working copy of a single gene. RNA has many jobs. But most RNA molecules just make proteins. This process is called protein synthesis. RNA controls how amino acids are made into proteins. There are three main kinds of RNA: messenger RNA, ribosomal RNA, and transfer RNA.

▶ *Messenger RNA* Most genes have instructions for assembling amino acids into proteins. **Messenger RNA** (mRNA) molecules carry copies of this information to ribosomes within the cell.

▶ *Ribosomal RNA* Proteins are put together on ribosomes. Ribosomes are small organelles made of two parts, or subunits. These subunits have several **ribosomal RNA** (rRNA) molecules and up to 80 different proteins.

▶ *Transfer RNA* A third kind of RNA molecule carries amino acids to the ribosome. This kind of RNA molecule is known as **transfer RNA** (tRNA).

RNA Synthesis

To understand how genes work, we need to learn how cells make RNA using the information found in DNA.

Transcription Most of the work of making RNA takes place during **transcription.** In transcription, RNA molecules are produced that are complementary to the DNA sequences in genes. The order of the RNA bases complements the base sequences of the DNA. In eukaryotes, RNA is made in the cell's nucleus. Then it moves to the cytoplasm to help make proteins.

Transcription requires an enzyme known as *RNA polymerase.* This enzyme is like DNA polymerase and binds to DNA during transcription. It pulls the DNA strands apart. One strand is used as a pattern to make a complementary strand of RNA. Hundreds or even thousands of RNA copies can be made from a single gene.

Key Question How does the cell make RNA?
In transcription, segments of DNA act as templates, or patterns, to make complementary RNA molecules.

Messenger RNA
Carries instructions for making proteins from nucleus to ribosomes in the cytoplasm.

Ribosome

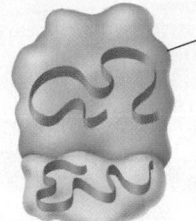

Ribosomal RNA
Forms an important part of both subunits of the ribosome.

Amino acid

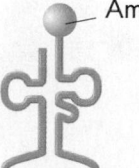

Transfer RNA
Carries amino acids to the ribosome and matches them to the coded mRNA message.

Types of RNA The three main types of RNA are messenger RNA, ribosomal RNA, and transfer RNA.

BUILD Vocabulary

ribonucleic acid (RNA)
a single-stranded nucleic acid that contains the sugar ribose

messenger RNA
a type of RNA that carries copies of instructions for the assembly of amino acids into proteins from DNA to the rest of the cell

ribosomal RNA
a type of RNA that combines with proteins to form ribosomes

transfer RNA
a type of RNA that carries each amino acid to a ribosome during protein synthesis

transcription
the synthesis of an RNA molecule from a DNA template, or pattern

Transcribing DNA Into RNA

During transcription, the enzyme RNA polymerase uses one strand of DNA as a template to put together nucleotides to make a strand of RNA.

Promoters How does RNA polymerase know where to start and stop making a strand of RNA? The enzyme binds only to promoters, regions of DNA that have specific base sequences. Promoters are signals in the DNA that show RNA polymerase exactly where to begin making RNA. Other signals in DNA cause transcription to stop when a new RNA molecule is finished.

RNA Editing Many RNA molecules are edited before they are ready to be used. Bits and pieces called introns are cut out and discarded from these RNAs. The remaining pieces, called exons, are then spliced back together.

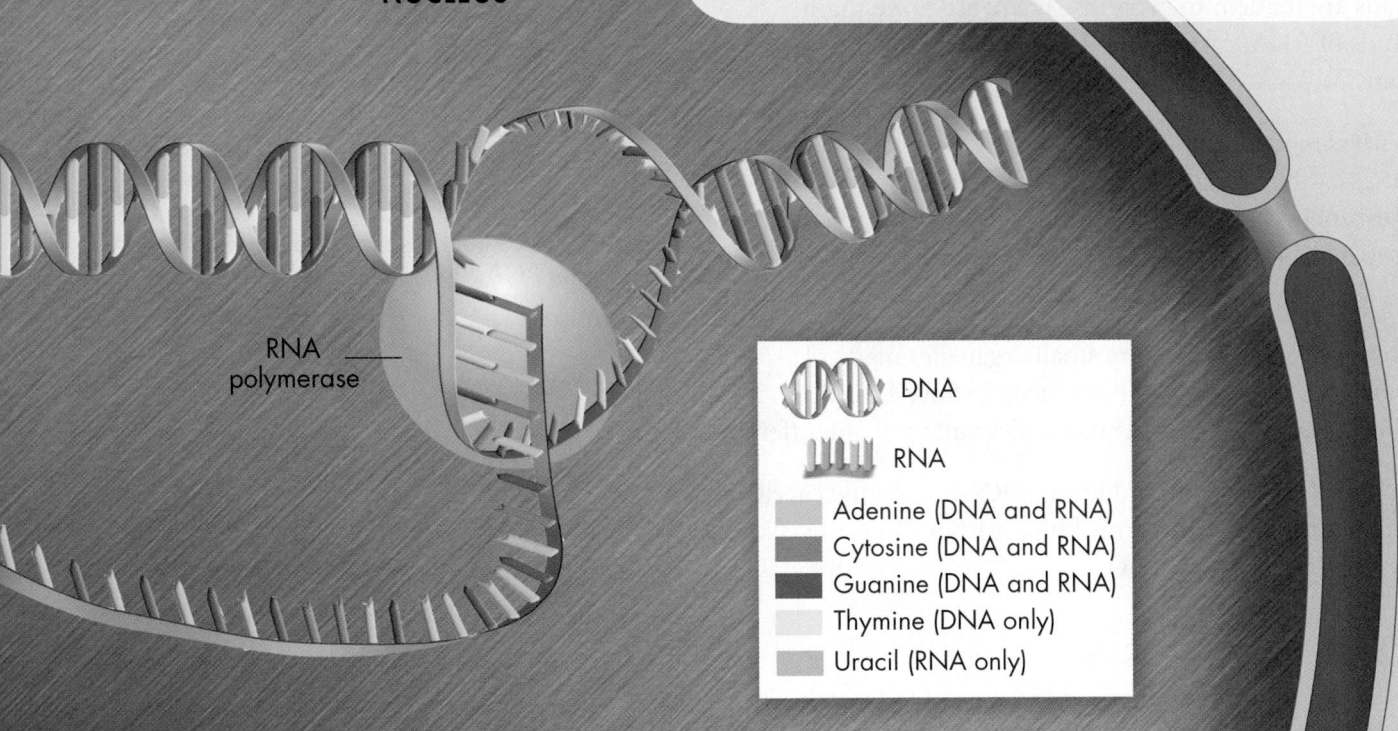

NUCLEUS

RNA polymerase

	DNA
	RNA
	Adenine (DNA and RNA)
	Cytosine (DNA and RNA)
	Guanine (DNA and RNA)
	Thymine (DNA only)
	Uracil (RNA only)

CHECK Understanding

Apply Vocabulary

Use the highlighted words from the lesson to complete each sentence correctly.

1. _____ carries amino acids.

2. _____ combines with up to 80 proteins to form an important organelle in the cytoplasm.

3. The information from DNA is transcribed into _____ and then carried out of the nucleus.

Critical Thinking

4. **Explain** Describe three main differences between RNA and DNA.

5. **Predict** What do you think would happen if introns were not removed from RNA?

6. **Write to Learn** Using the terms *RNA polymerase* and *transcription*, describe how RNA gets made.

BIOLOGY.com ▸ Search (Lesson 13.1) **GO** • Lesson Assessment • Art in Motion

13.2 Ribosomes and Protein Synthesis

MD | CLG 3.1.1 Chemical Substances and Macromolecules, 3.2.1 Processes and Functions, 3.3.3 Nucleic Acids and Protein Synthesis, 3.4.2 Relatedness Among Organisms. SPI 1.4.8 Use Models, 1.5.5 Create and Interpret Graphics, 1.7.6 Science and Technology.

The Genetic Code

The DNA bases in genes are like a code. You have to know the code to understand what the bases mean.

Remember that the first step in decoding genetic messages is using transcription to make RNA from a sequence of DNA bases. This RNA holds a code for making proteins. Proteins are made of long chains of amino acids called **polypeptides.** Up to 20 different amino acids are found in polypeptides.

The shape and function of a protein are determined by its amino acids and their sequence. How is the order of RNA bases related to the sequence of amino acids? RNA contains four different bases: adenine (A), cytosine (C), guanine (G), and uracil (U). These bases are like the letters of a language. We call this language the **genetic code.** Each word in the genetic code is three "letters," or three bases. Each three-base set is called a **codon.** A codon specifies one amino acid.

How to Read Codons There are four different bases in RNA. These four bases mean there are 64 possible three-base codons in the genetic code. Most amino acids can be specified by more than one codon. For example, six different codons—UUA, UUG, CUU, CUC, CUA, and CUG—specify the amino acid leucine.

Start and Stop Codons
Special codons tell the cell where to start and stop translating RNA. The codon AUG acts as the "start" codon for protein synthesis. After the start codon, mRNA is read three bases at a time.

Reading Codons The circular table shows the amino acid that corresponds to each of the 64 codons.

Key Questions

🔑 What is the genetic code, and how is it read?

🔑 What role does the ribosome play in assembling proteins?

🔑 What is the "central dogma" of molecular biology?

BUILD Understanding

Two-Column Chart In the left column of a two-column chart, write the section headings. In the right column, list the main ideas.

In Your Workbook Go to your workbook and complete the chart for Lesson 13.2.

❶ To decode the codon CAC, find the first letter in the set of bases at the center of the circle.

❷ Find the second letter of the codon A, in the "C" quarter of the next ring.

❸ Find the third letter, C, in the next ring, in the "C-A" grouping.

❹ Read the name of the amino acid in that sector—in this case histidine.

BUILD Vocabulary

polypeptide
a long chain of amino acids that makes proteins

genetic code
a collection of codons of mRNA, each of which directs the incorporation of a particular amino acid into a protein during protein synthesis

codon
a group of three nucleotide bases in mRNA that specify a particular amino acid to be incorporated into a protein

🔧 ROOT WORDS

The word *codon* was created by adding the suffix *-on* to the word *code*. Other scientific terms, such as *electron*, were formed in a similar way.

Translation continues until one of three different "stop" codons is reached. Then, translation stops and the polypeptide is complete.

🔑 **Key Question** What is the genetic code, and how is it read? **The genetic code is a code for making proteins. The genetic code is read three "letters" at a time. Each "word" is three bases long and corresponds to a single amino acid.**

Translation

The sequence of nucleotide bases in each mRNA strand is a set of instructions. The instructions give the order in which amino acids should be joined to make a polypeptide. Once a polypeptide is made, it folds into its final shape or joins with other polypeptides. Once it folds or joins with other polypeptides, it becomes a working protein.

To put together a complex toy, you need instructions. Once you read them, you can put the parts together. In the cell, the ribosome reads the instructions and puts together proteins. Ribosomes use the sequence of codons in mRNA to assemble amino acids into polypeptide chains. The decoding of an mRNA message into a protein is a process called **translation.**

Steps in Translation Transcription produces the mRNA molecules that are used in protein synthesis, or translation. In eukaroytes, transcription occurs in the cell's nucleus. After transcription, mRNA leaves the nucleus, and translation takes place in the cytoplasm. The figure below shows this process.

Translation The cell uses information from messenger RNA to make proteins during translation.

Messenger RNA
Messenger RNA is transcribed in the nucleus and then enters the cytoplasm.

Ⓐ Transfer RNA
Translation begins at AUG, the start codon. Each transfer RNA has an anticodon whose bases are complementary to the bases of a codon on the mRNA strand. The ribosome positions the start codon to attract its anticodon, which is part of the tRNA that binds methionine. The ribosome also binds the next codon and its anticodon.

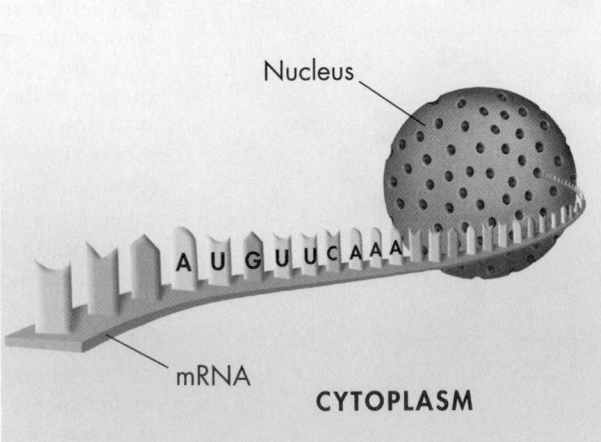

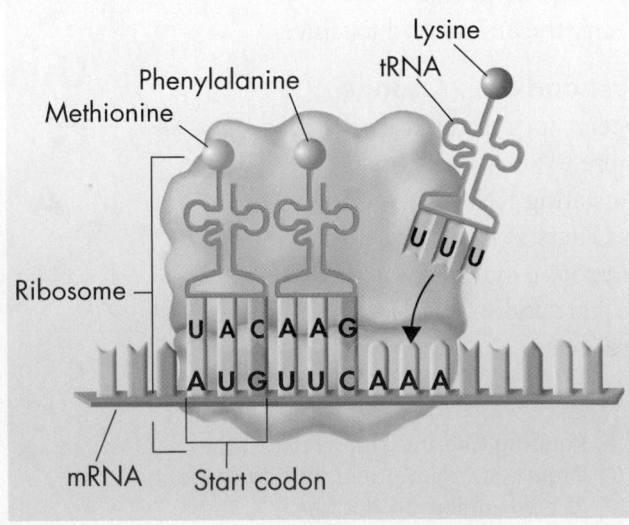

A *Transfer RNA* Translation begins when a ribosome attaches to an mRNA molecule in the cytoplasm. As each codon passes through the ribosome, tRNAs bring the correct amino acids into the ribosome. One at a time, the ribosome then attaches these amino acids to the growing polypeptide chain.

Each tRNA molecule carries just one kind of amino acid. Each tRNA molecule also has three unpaired bases. This set of bases is called the **anticodon.** Each tRNA anticodon is complementary to one mRNA codon.

The anticodon of the tRNA molecule for methionine is UAC. It will pair with the methionine codon, AUG. The ribosome has a second binding site for a tRNA molecule for the next codon. Notice that the second codon in the figure is UUC. A tRNA molecule with an AAG anticodon will bind to this codon. This tRNA molecule brings the amino acid phenylalanine into the ribosome.

B *Joining Amino Acids* Next, the ribosome helps make a peptide bond between the first and second amino acids. At the same time, the bond holding the first tRNA molecule to its amino acid is broken. That tRNA moves into an exit site, from which it leaves the ribosome. The ribosome moves to the next codon. Another tRNA then carries in the amino acid specified by that codon.

BUILD Vocabulary

translation
a process by which the sequence of bases of an mRNA is converted into the sequence of amino acids of a protein

anticodon
a group of three bases on a tRNA molecule that are complementary to the three bases of a codon of mRNA

PREFIXES

The prefix *anti-* is Latin for "against." When added to science terms, it can mean "opposite." An anticodon, then, has the opposite, or complementary, base sequence of its matching codon.

B **The Polypeptide "Assembly Line"**
The ribosome joins the two amino acids—methionine and phenylalanine—and breaks the bond between methionine and its tRNA. The tRNA floats away from the ribosome, allowing the ribosome to bind another tRNA. The ribosome moves along the mRNA, from right to left, binding new tRNA molecules and amino acids.

C **Completing the Polypeptide**
The process continues until the ribosome reaches one of the three stop codons. Once the polypeptide is complete, it and the mRNA are released from the ribosome.

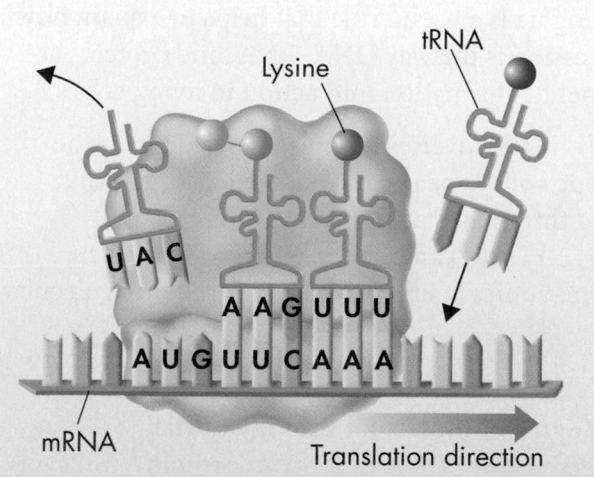

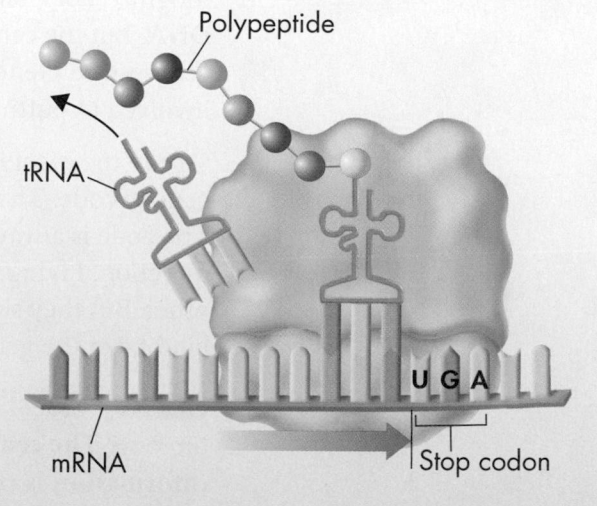

C *The Chain Grows* The polypeptide chain grows until the ribosome reaches a "stop" codon on the mRNA. Then, the ribosome releases both the newly formed polypeptide and the mRNA molecule. The process of translation is complete.

🔑 **Key Question** What role does the ribosome play in assembling proteins?
Ribosomes use the sequence of codons in mRNA to assemble amino acids into polypeptide chains.

The Roles of tRNA and rRNA in Translation All three kinds of RNA are put to work in the ribosome during translation. The mRNA molecule carries the coded message that directs the process. The tRNA molecules bring the correct amino acid for each codon on the mRNA. The rRNA and many proteins make up the ribosomes.

The Molecular Basis for Heredity

Gregor Mendel might have been surprised to learn that genes have instructions for putting proteins together. He might have asked what proteins have to do with traits of pea plants.

The answer is that proteins have everything to do with such traits. Remember that many proteins are enzymes. Enzymes help speed up and regulate chemical reactions. A gene that codes for an enzyme to make pigment controls flower color. Another gene makes proteins that control tissue growth in a leaf. Basically, proteins are tiny tools. Each one is designed to build or run a part of a living cell.

Once scientists learned that genes were made of DNA, other discoveries soon followed. Soon, a new scientific field called molecular biology had formed. Molecular biology tries to explain living organisms by studying them at the molecular level. It uses molecules like DNA and RNA as tools to understand living things. One of the earliest findings is now called the field's "central dogma," or basic rule. The central dogma states that information is transferred from DNA to RNA to protein. In real life, there are many exceptions to this "dogma." For example, some viruses pass information from RNA to DNA. But the central dogma is a useful rule that helps to explain how genes work. Gene expression is the way DNA, RNA, and proteins are involved in putting genetic information into action in living cells.

One of the most interesting discoveries of molecular biology is the genetic code. The genetic code is nearly universal to all organisms. The code is always read three bases at a time and in the same direction. Living things on Earth can be very different from each other. But they show great unity at life's most basic level, the molecular biology of the gene.

🔑 **Key Question** What is the "central dogma" of molecular biology? **The central dogma of molecular biology is that information is transferred from DNA to RNA to protein.**

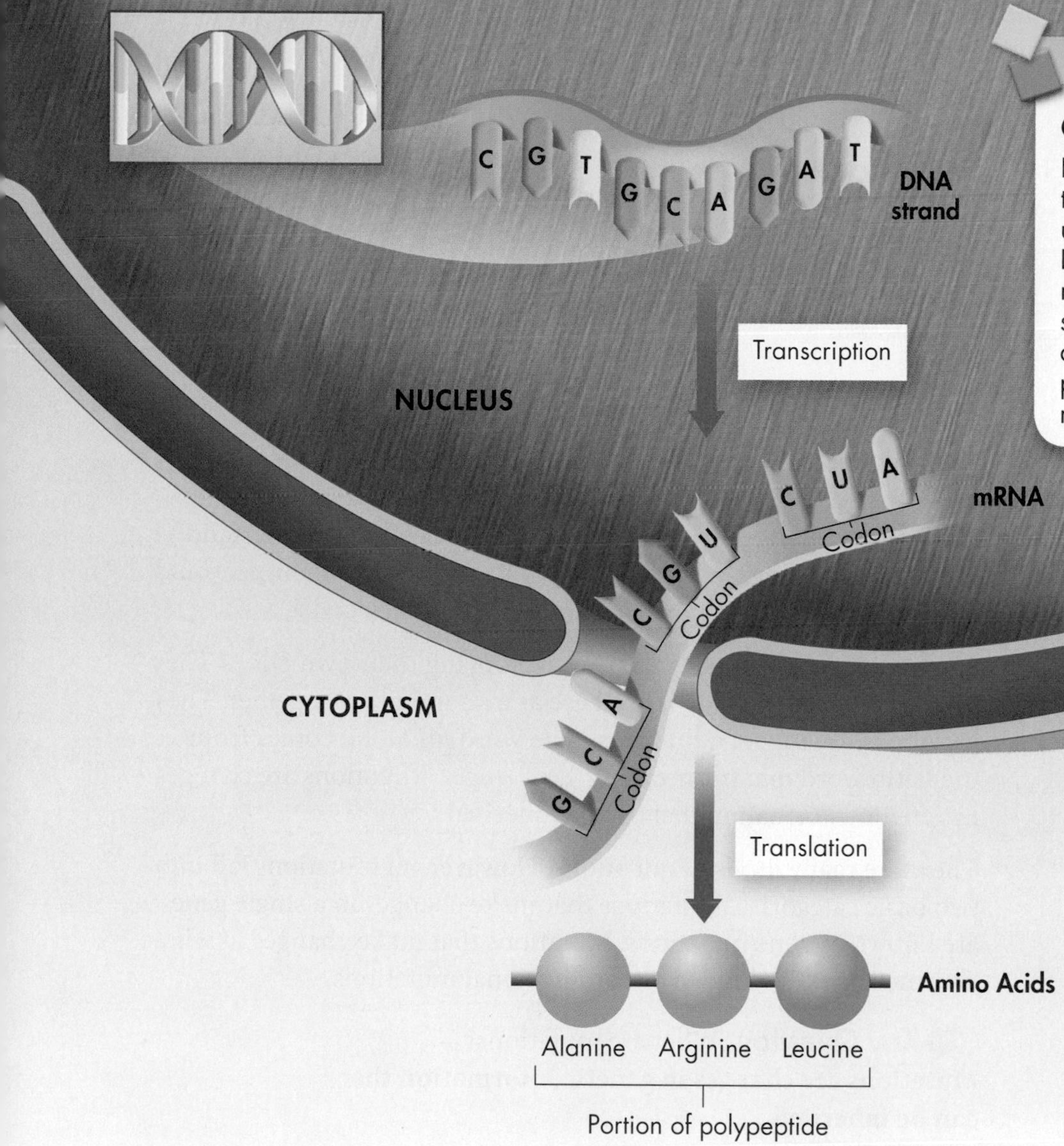

C G T G C A G A T **DNA strand**

GENE EXPRESSION

DNA carries information for the traits of an organism. The cell uses the sequence of bases in DNA as a template for making mRNA. The codons of mRNA spell out the sequence of amino acids in a protein. Those proteins play a key role in making an organism's traits.

NUCLEUS

Transcription

C U A
Codon **mRNA**

C G U
Codon

G C A
Codon

CYTOPLASM

Translation

Amino Acids

Alanine   Arginine   Leucine

Portion of polypeptide

CHECK Understanding

Apply Vocabulary

Use the highlighted words from the lesson to complete the sentence correctly.

1. A(n) _____ is a group of three bases on a tRNA molecule that are complementary to the three bases of a codon of mRNA.

Critical Thinking

2. Apply Concepts Using the Reading Codons circular table, identify the amino acids specified by codons UGG, AGG, and UGC.

3. Explain What does the term *gene expression* mean?

4. Explain How does a cell interpret the genetic code?

5. Write to Learn Answer the first clue for the chapter mystery. Include the term *codon* in your answer.

MYSTERY CLUE

What features of the genetic code make it possible for a mouse's gene to work inside the cells of a fly? (**Hint:** See p. 314.)

13.3 Mutations

MD CLG 3.1.1 Chemical Substances and Macromolecules, 3.2.1 Processes and Functions, 3.2.2 Changes in Metabolic Activity, 3.3.3 Nucleic Acids and Protein Synthesis, 3.3.4 DNA Alteration, 3.4.1 Evolutionary Change. SPI 1.4.8 Use Models, 1.5.5 Create and Interpret Graphics, 1.7.2 Evaluate Ideas

Key Questions

🔑 **What are mutations?**

🔑 **How do mutations affect genes?**

BUILD Understanding

Preview Visuals Before you read the lesson, look at the Point Mutations and Chromosomal Mutations figures. As you read, note the changes produced by various gene and chromosomal mutations.

In Your Workbook
Complete the chart in Lesson 13.3 of your workbook.

Types of Mutations

The order of bases in DNA is like the letters of a coded message. What would happen if a few of those letters changed and, so, accidentally changed the message? Could the cell still understand the code's meaning? What effects do you think those changes would have on genes and the polypeptides for which they code?

Sometimes cells do make mistakes in copying their own DNA. They insert the wrong base or skip a base as a strand is put together. These variations are called **mutations.** The word *mutation* comes from the Latin word *mutare*, meaning "to change." Mutations are changes in genetic information that can be inherited.

There are many kinds of mutations. However, all mutations fall into two basic categories. Mutations that make changes in a single gene are known as gene mutations. Mutations that make changes in whole chromosomes are known as chromosomal mutations.

🔑 **Key Question** What are mutations?
Mutations are changes in genetic information that can be inherited.

The shape of this flower is caused by a mutation that affects the growing areas of the flower tissue.

A genetic condition called leucism leaves this lion without pigments in its hair, skin, and eyes.

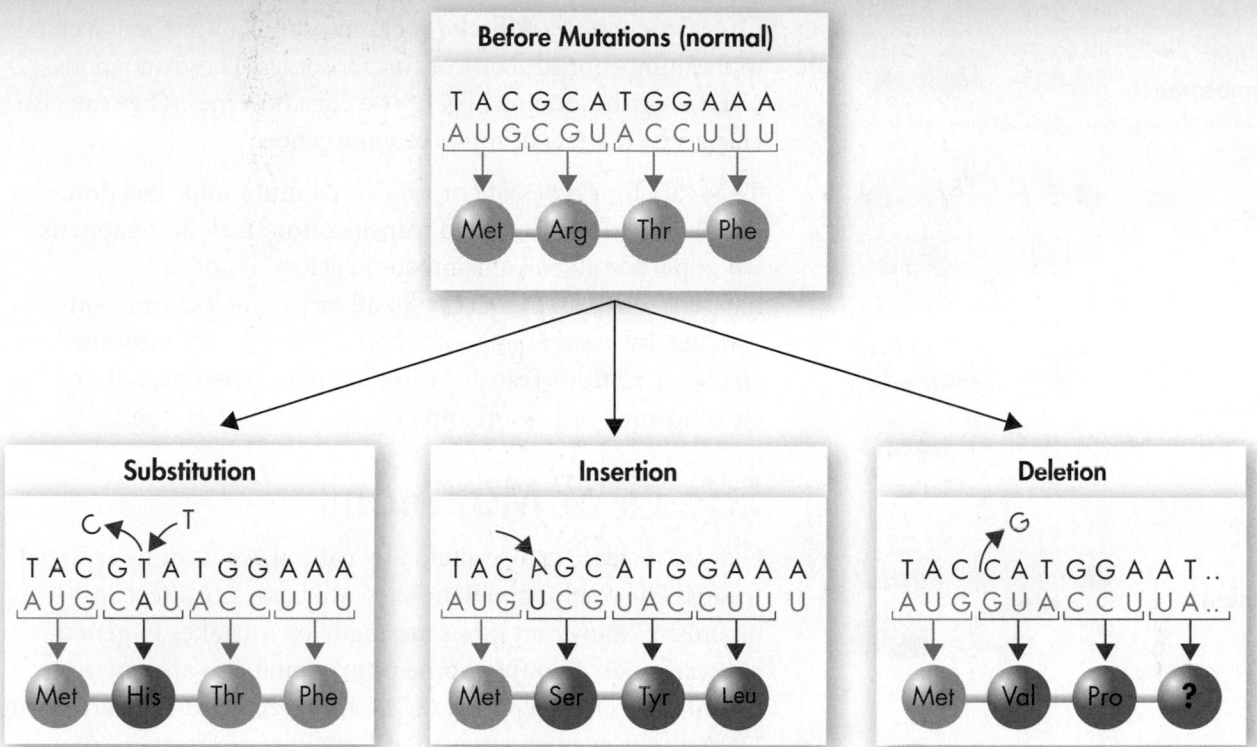

Gene Mutations Gene mutations that involve changes in one or a few nucleotides are known as **point mutations.** They happen at a single point in the DNA sequence. Point mutations include substitutions, insertions, and deletions, and they usually happen during replication. If a gene in one cell is changed, the change can be passed on during cell division. Every daughter cell will have the mutation. The figure above shows how point mutations occur.

▶ *Substitutions* In a substitution, one base is changed to a different base. Substitutions usually affect a single amino acid. Sometimes they have no effect at all. For example, a mutation might change one codon of mRNA from CCC to CCA. The codon would still call for the amino acid proline. But changing CCC to ACC would replace proline with the amino acid threonine.

▶ *Insertions and Deletions* Insertions and deletions are point mutations. An insertion adds a new base to the DNA sequence. A deletion removes a base from the DNA sequence. The effects of these changes can be dramatic. Remember that the genetic code is read three bases at a time. Reading the bases three at a time happens even if a nucleotide is added or taken away. After a change, the sets shift in every codon that comes after the mutation.

Insertions and deletions are also called **frameshift mutations** because they shift the "reading frame" of the genetic code. A shift in the reading frame can change every amino acid that follows the mutation. This change can alter a protein so much that it cannot do its job.

Point Mutations These diagrams show how changes in just one nucleotide can change the order of amino acids in proteins.

mutation
a change in the genetic material of a cell

point mutation
a gene mutation in which a single base pair in DNA has been changed

frameshift mutation
a mutation that shifts the "reading frame" of the genetic message by inserting or deleting a nucleotide

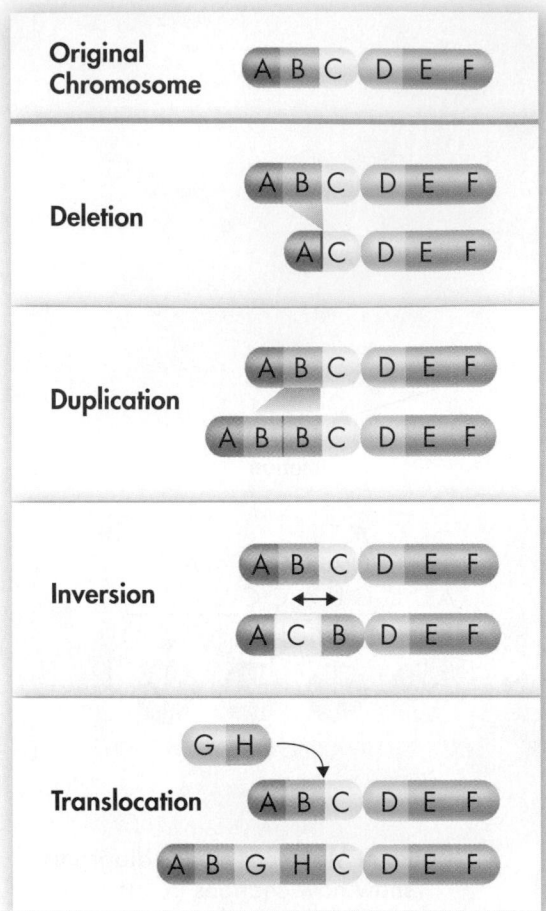

Original Chromosome	A B C D E F
Deletion	A B C D E F / A C D E F
Duplication	A B C D E F / A B B C D E F
Inversion	A B C D E F ↔ A C B D E F
Translocation	G H → A B C D E F / A B G H C D E F

Chromosomal Mutations Four types of mutations cause changes in whole chromosomes. The four types of chromosomal mutations are deletion, duplication, inversion, and translocation.

Chromosomal Mutations A chromosomal mutation is a change in the number or structure of chromosomes. These mutations can change the location of genes on chromosomes. They can also change the number of copies of some genes.

There are four types of chromosomal mutations: deletion, duplication, inversion, and translocation. Deletion happens when part or all of a chromosome is lost. Duplication happens when an extra copy of all or part of a chromosome is made. Inversion happens when parts of a chromosome change direction. Translocation happens when part of one chromosome breaks off and attaches to another one.

Effects of Mutations

Genetic material can be altered by natural events or by artificial means. The resulting mutations may or may not affect an organism. Many mutations are made by mistakes in genetic processes. For example, some point mutations are caused by mistakes in DNA replication. An incorrect base is inserted into DNA about once in every 10 million bases. However, small changes in genes can build up over time.

Mutagens Some mutations are caused by mutagens. **Mutagens** are chemical or physical agents in the environment. Chemical mutagens include some pesticides, tobacco smoke, and pollutants. Physical mutagens include X-rays and ultraviolet light. These mutagens can cause mutations at high rates. Sometimes the cell can repair the DNA. But when the cell cannot fix the DNA, the sequence changes become permanent.

Harmful and Helpful Mutations Mutations can help or harm organisms. However, most mutations have little or no effect on genes. So, there is little or no effect on the function of the proteins they make. In any case, mutations are important. Without mutations, there would be no genetic variation. Without genetic variation, species could not evolve.

Effects of a Point Mutation
Sickle cell disease affects the shape of red blood cells. The round cells in the image are normal red blood cells. The crescent and star-shaped cells are sickled cells. (SEM 1700×)

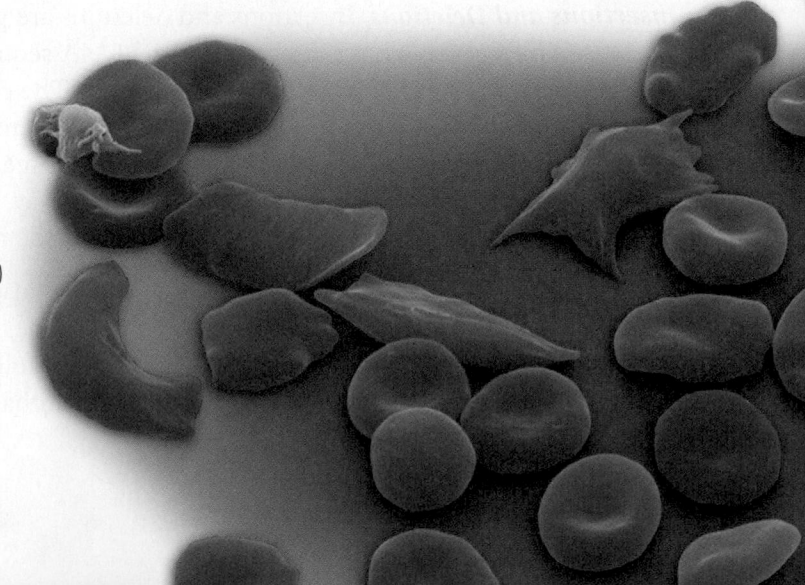

▶ *Harmful Effects* Some of the most harmful mutations make big changes in protein shape or gene activity. The proteins made by these mutations can get in the way of biological activities. For example, some cancers are caused by mutations. Sickle cell anemia is caused by a point mutation in one of the polypeptides of hemoglobin. Hemoglobin is the oxygen-carrying protein in red blood cells. The mutant protein causes red blood cells to change shape, giving them a sickle-like appearance. These sickled cells interfere with blood flow and cause severe problems in the bloodstream.

▶ *Helpful Effects* Some of the changes made by mutations can help an organism or species. These mutations make genes with functions that are useful to organisms in different environments. Mutations have made many African mosquitoes resistant to the chemicals once used to kill them. This resistance may be bad news for people. However, it is very helpful to the insects. Beneficial mutations happen in people, too. For example, one mutation makes bones stronger. Another mutation increases resistance to HIV, the virus that causes AIDS.

Plant and animal breeders often make use of "good" mutations. For example, sometimes a full set of chromosomes does not separate during meiosis. The gametes made may produce triploid (3N) or tetraploid (4N) organisms. The condition in which an organism has extra sets of chromosomes is called **polyploidy.** Polyploid plants are often larger and stronger than diploid plants.

Polyploid Plants The fruit of the Tahiti lime is seedless because of polyploidy. Changes to the ploidy number of citrus plants can affect the size and strength of the trees, the quality of the fruit, and the number of seeds in their fruit.

🔑 **Key Question** How do mutations affect genes? **The effects of mutations on genes vary widely. Some have little or no effect, and some produce beneficial variations. Some negatively disrupt gene function.**

CHECK Understanding

Apply Vocabulary
Use the highlighted words from the lesson to complete each sentence correctly.

1. A gene mutation in which a single base pair in DNA has been changed is a _____.
2. A mutation that shifts the "reading frame" of the genetic message by inserting or deleting a nucleotide is a _____.
3. A chemical that causes a mutation is called a _____.

Critical Thinking

4. **Explain** Describe the two main types of mutations.
5. **Apply Concepts** How do mutations affect living things?
6. **Write to Learn** Write the following DNA sequence GCTAATCGGCTA. Below this sequence, show how the sequence might look after a substitution mutation. Repeat this for a deletion mutation and an insertion mutation.

BIOLOGY.com ▶ Search (Lesson 13.3) **GO** • Lesson Assessment

13.4 Gene Regulation and Expression

MD CLG 3.1.1 Chemical Substances and Macromolecules, 3.3.3 Nucleic Acids and Protein Synthesis.
SPI 1.4.2 Analyze Data, 1.5.8 Compare, 1.5.9 Synthesize Ideas, 1.7.6 Science and Technology.

Key Questions

🔑 How are prokaryotic genes regulated?

🔑 How are genes regulated in eukaryotic cells?

🔑 What controls the development of cells and tissues in multicellular organisms?

BUILD Understanding

Concept Map As you read, create a concept map from the major headings of the lesson. Then identify the important ideas in each section to complete your map.

In Your Workbook Complete the concept map in Lesson 13.4.

Prokaryotic Gene Regulation

Think of a library filled with how-to books. Would you ever need to use all of those books at the same time? Of course not. If you wanted to know how to fix a leaky faucet, you'd find a book on plumbing. But, you would ignore the one on carpentry. Now picture a tiny bacterium like *E. coli,* which contains more than 4000 genes. These genes code for proteins that do everything from building cell walls to breaking down food. Do you think that *E. coli* uses every gene in its genetic library at the same time?

Most bacteria transcribe only the genes they need at any one time. For example, some genes produce enzymes used to digest certain types of food molecules. If these food molecules are not present, there is no need for these enzymes. As you might expect, bacteria turn these genes off when they are not needed. By controlling gene expression in this way, bacteria respond to change.

How do bacteria control genes? DNA-binding proteins in prokaryotes regulate genes by controlling transcription. Some of these proteins help switch genes on. Others turn genes off. How does an organism know when to turn a gene on or off? One way bacteria control making proteins is through operons. An **operon** is a group of genes that are regulated together. The genes in an operon have related jobs. *E. coli* provides a clear example of how this works. *E. coli* has 4288 genes that code for proteins. Three of these genes must be turned on together before the bacterium can use the sugar lactose as a food. Since these genes are operated together, they are called the *lac* operon.

Small Cell, Many Genes
This *E. coli* bacterium has more than 4000 genes. It was treated with an enzyme, which caused its DNA to spill out.

TEM 27,000×

The *Lac* Operon Why must *E. coli* be able to turn the *lac* genes on and off? Lactose is made up of two simple sugars, galactose and glucose. To use lactose for food, the bacterium must first move lactose across its cell membrane. Then it has to break the bond between glucose and galactose. These jobs are done by proteins coded for by the genes of the *lac* operon. The bacterium must transcribe these genes and make the proteins if lactose is its only food source. If grown on another food source, the bacterium does not need these proteins.

Remarkably, the bacterium almost seems to "know" when the proteins from these genes are needed. When lactose is not around, the *lac* genes are turned off by proteins. These proteins bind to DNA, blocking transcription.

Promoters and Operators On one side of the operon's three genes are two control regions. The first is a promoter (P). This is a site where RNA polymerase can bind to begin transcription. The other region is called the **operator** (O). The O site is where a DNA-binding protein known as the *lac* repressor can bind to DNA.

▶ *The **Lac** Repressor Blocks Transcription* When the *lac* repressor binds to the O region, RNA polymerase cannot reach the *lac* genes. RNA polymerase must bind to P to start transcription. So, the binding of the repressor protein switches the operon "off." It prevents the transcription of genes.

▶ *Lactose Turns the Operon "On"* If the repressor protein is always around, how can the *lac* genes ever be switched on? Besides its DNA binding site, the *lac* repressor protein has a binding site for lactose, too. When lactose is in the growth medium, it moves into the cell. It attaches to the *lac* repressor, changing the shape of the repressor protein. The change in shape causes the protein to fall off the operator. Now the repressor is no longer bound to the O site. RNA polymerase binds to the promoter and transcribes the genes of the operon. This transcription of the operon genes means that whenever lactose is present, the operon is automatically switched on.

Key Question How are prokaryotic genes regulated?
DNA-binding proteins in prokaryotes regulate genes by controlling transcription.

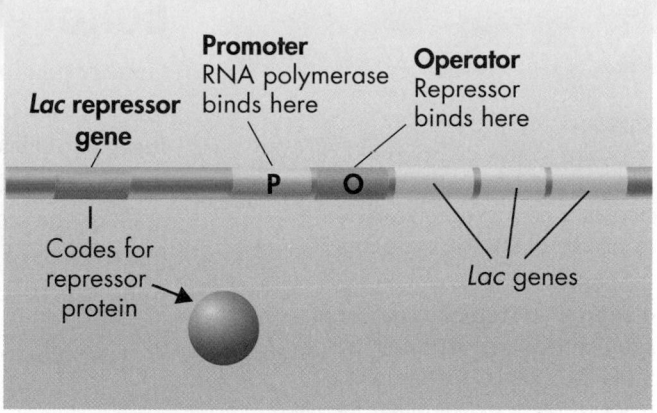

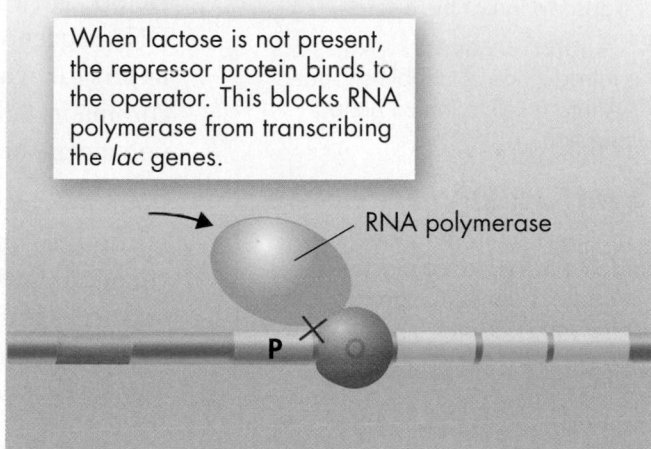

When lactose is not present, the repressor protein binds to the operator. This blocks RNA polymerase from transcribing the *lac* genes.

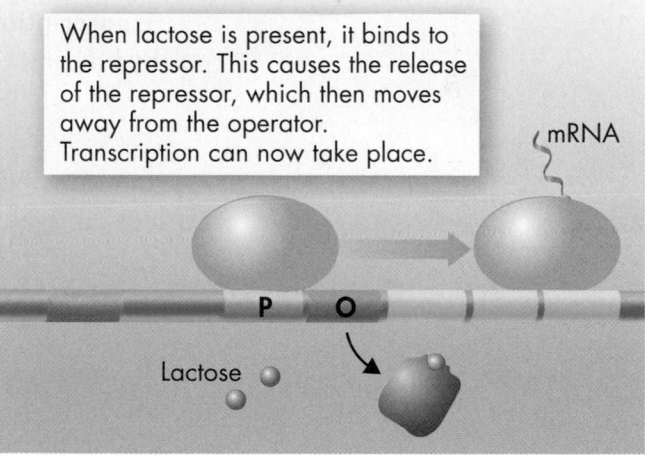

When lactose is present, it binds to the repressor. This causes the release of the repressor, which then moves away from the operator. Transcription can now take place.

Gene Expression in Prokaryotes The *lac* genes in *E. coli* are turned off by repressors. They are turned on in the presence of lactose.

operon
in prokaryotes, a group of adjacent genes that share a common operator and promoter and are transcribed into a single mRNA

operator
a short DNA region, adjacent to the promoter of a prokaryotic operon, that binds repressor proteins responsible for controlling the rate of transcription of the operon

RNA interference
the introduction of double-stranded RNA into a cell to inhibit gene expression

🖋 **MULTIPLE MEANINGS**

A machine operator controls a complicated piece of machinery. Similarly, a genetic operator controls transcription.

Eukaryotic Gene Regulation

Gene regulation in eukaryotes is much like gene regulation in prokaryotes, but there are differences. Most genes are controlled individually and use more complicated systems to control transcription. One important control is a piece of DNA called the TATA box. It is about 25 or 30 base pairs long and has the sequence TATATA or TATAAA. This region is usually found just in front of a gene. It binds a protein that helps move RNA polymerase into place to begin its job.

Transcription Factors Gene expression in eukaryotic cells is regulated in many ways. One way is to control transcription by using transcription factors. These proteins control gene expression by binding to regulatory DNA sequences, such as the TATA box. For example, some transcription factors can make transcription easier by opening up tightly packed chromatin. Several transcription factors usually have to bind before RNA polymerase binds to the promoter region.

Promoters have many binding sites for transcription factors. Certain factors turn on many genes at once. Factors may be controlled by chemical signals such as steroid hormones. These chemical messengers enter cells and bind to receptor proteins. These "receptor complexes" then act as transcription factors that bind to DNA. This binding allows a single chemical signal to turn on many genes.

🔑 **Key Question** How are genes regulated in eukaryotic cells? **Transcription factors control the expression of eukaryotic genes by binding DNA sequences in regulatory regions.**

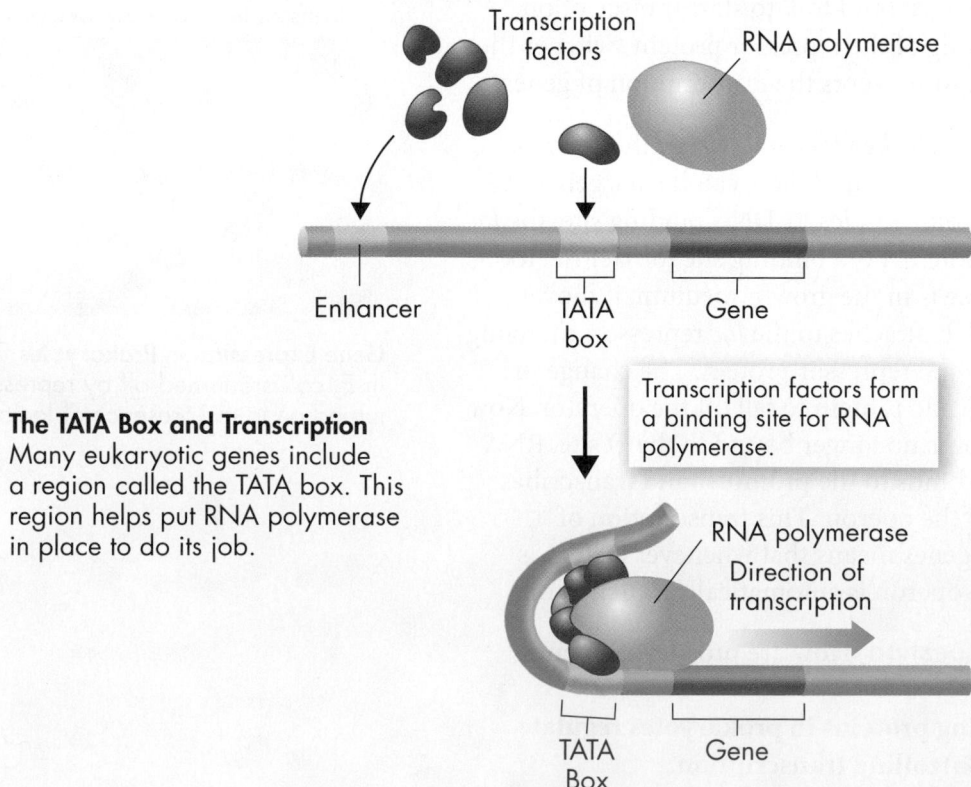

The TATA Box and Transcription
Many eukaryotic genes include a region called the TATA box. This region helps put RNA polymerase in place to do its job.

Transcription factors / RNA polymerase

Enhancer / TATA box / Gene

Transcription factors form a binding site for RNA polymerase.

RNA polymerase
Direction of transcription

TATA Box / Gene

Cell Specialization Why is gene regulation in eukaryotes more complicated than in prokaryotes? Every eukaryotic cell nucleus has all the genes of the body. But not all cells use every gene. This ability to selectively use genes means that nerve cells will not make enzymes that are only needed in the liver. Complex gene regulation is what makes specialization possible.

RNA Interference Other kinds of RNA are in the cell besides the major groups of RNA. Very small RNA molecules play a large role in regulating gene expression. They do so by interfering with mRNA.

After they are made by transcription, these small RNA molecules fold into double-stranded loops. An enzyme called the "Dicer" enzyme cuts, or dices, these double-stranded loops into microRNA (miRNA). Each miRNA molecule is about 20 base pairs in length. The two strands of the loops then separate. Next, one of the miRNA pieces attaches to a group of proteins. This forms what is known as a silencing complex. This complex binds to and destroys any mRNA containing the complementary sequence to the miRNA. The miRNA sticks to mRNA molecules and stops them from passing on their protein-making instructions. Using a silencing complex to block gene expression is called **RNA interference** (RNAi).

The Promise of RNAi Technology The discovery of RNAi has made it possible for researchers to switch genes on and off. They do this by inserting double-stranded RNA into cells. This technology is a powerful way to study gene expression in the laboratory. RNAi technology may also provide a way for medical scientists to turn off genes from viruses and cancer cells. So, RNAi may provide new ways to treat, and maybe even cure, diseases.

Genetic Control of Development

Controlling gene expression helps shape the way a multicellular organism develops. Each kind of specialized cell in an adult begins from the same fertilized egg cell. Different sets of genes are turned on and off as the embryo develops. Gene regulation helps cells change so that every cell can do a job. This kind of cell change and development is called cell differentiation.

Blocking Gene Expression MicroRNAs attach to mRNA molecules and stop them from passing on their protein-making instructions.

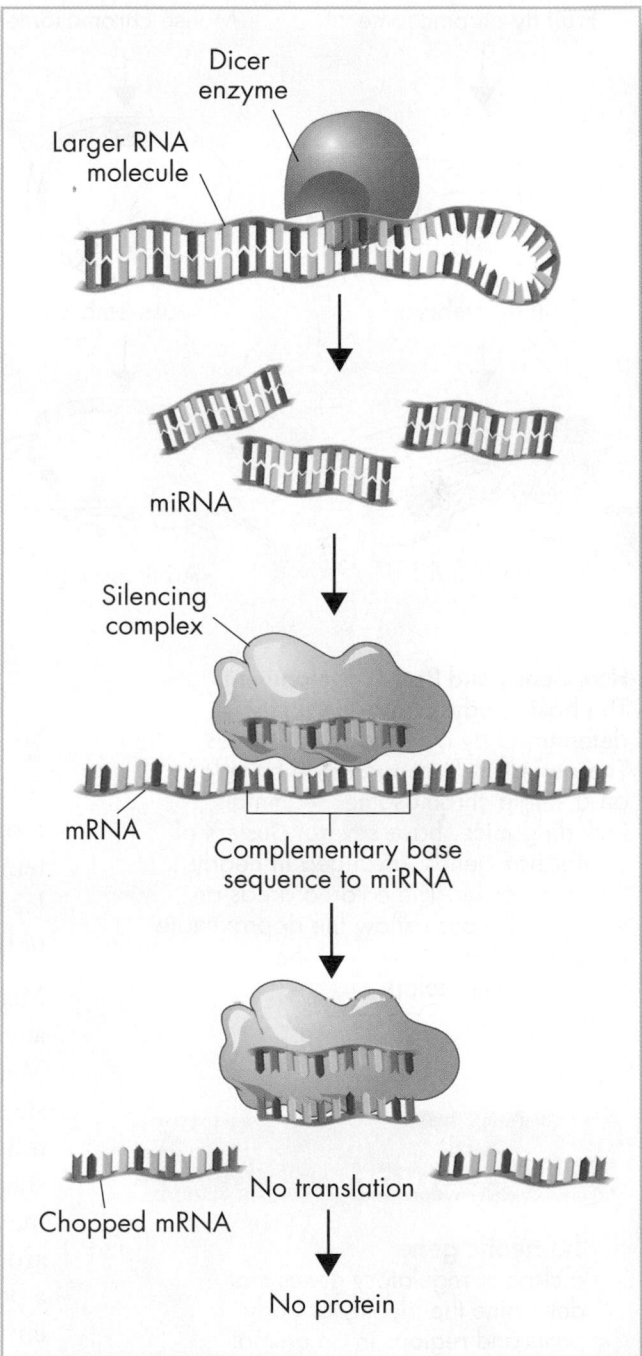

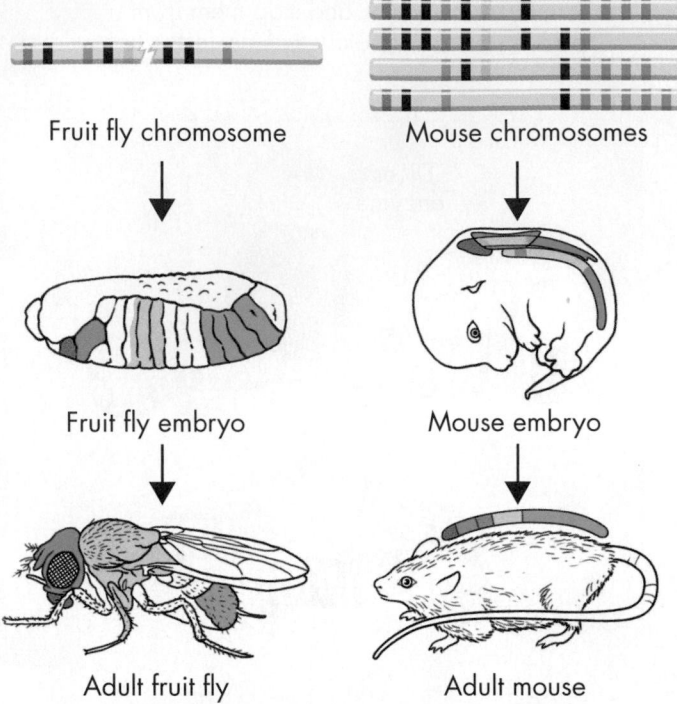

Fruit fly chromosome

Mouse chromosomes

Fruit fly embryo

Mouse embryo

Adult fruit fly

Adult mouse

Hox Genes and Body Development
The basic body plan of a fruit fly is determined by a series of hox genes. The genes are arranged side by side on a single chromosome. Mammals, including mice, have several clusters of similar hox genes, arranged in nearly the same order. The colored areas on the fly and mouse show the approximate areas affected by genes of the corresponding colors.

Homeotic Genes In many animals, a set of master control genes regulates organs that develop in specific parts of the body. These genes are known as **homeotic genes,** and they control the identity of different body parts.

Homeobox and Hox genes All homeotic genes share a similar DNA sequence, called the homeobox sequence. Homeobox genes code for transcription factors that turn on other genes. These genes are important in cell differentiation. They control features such as the presence of wings or legs.

Flies have a group of homeobox genes known as Hox genes. These Hox genes are located side by side in a single group. They determine the identities of each part of a fly's body. A Hox gene mutation can change which organs develop in certain parts of the body. Other animals, including humans, also have Hox genes. The genes always tell cells how to differentiate. So, nearly all animals share the same basic tools for building the different parts of the body.

Environmental Influences

An organism's environment plays a role in cell differentiation, too. In all kinds of organisms, environmental factors like temperature can change gene expression. One example is the *lac* operon in *E. coli*. It is switched on only when lactose is the only food source in the bacteria's environment.

Metamorphosis is another example of how organisms can alter gene expression in response to environmental changes. Metamorphosis involves a series of changes from one life stage to another. It is usually regulated by factors inside and outside of the body. As organisms move through their life stages, their cells differentiate to make new organs. Tadpoles may speed up their metamorphosis based on the conditions around them. This more rapid metamorphosis may happen if a pond is drying up quickly or if food is becoming scarce. The environmental changes are translated into hormonal changes. The hormones act to regulate gene expression, which controls the speed of metamorphosis. Temperature and population size can also affect the speed of metamorphosis.

Key Question What controls the development of cells and tissues in multicellular organisms?
Master control genes are like switches that trigger particular patterns of development and differentiation in cells and tissues.

The Discovery of RNA Interference

In 1998, Andrew Fire and Craig Mello performed an experiment that helped explain how RNA interference happens. They used RNA from a large gene called unc-22, which codes for a protein found in muscle cells. They made short pieces of mRNA that matched with two parts of the gene. Then they injected the mRNA into egg cells of the worm *C. elegans*. Some of their results are shown in the table.

Injections of mRNA into *C. elegans* Eggs		
Portion of Gene Used to Produce mRNA	Strand Injected	Result in Adult Worm
Unc-22 (exon 21–22)	Sense	Normal
	Antisense	Normal
	Sense + Antisense	Twitching
Unc-22 (exon 27)	Sense	Normal
	Antisense	Normal
	Sense + Antisense	Twitching

1. Interpret Data Which strand caused adult worms to twitch?

a. single-stranded mRNA (the "sense" strand)

b. its complementary strand ("antisense")

c. double-stranded RNA ("sense + antisense")

2. Infer Twitching happens when muscle cells cannot control their contractions. What does this suggest about the unc-22 protein in some of the worms?

3. Predict The scientists made their mRNA fragments from exons. Do you think their experiment would have worked if the fragments were made from introns? Explain your answer.

In Your Workbook Get more help for this activity in your workbook.

CHECK Understanding

Apply Vocabulary
Use the highlighted word from the lesson to complete the sentence correctly.

1. _____ are a class of regulatory genes that determine the identity of body parts and regions in an animal embryo.

Critical Thinking

2. Review How is the *lac* operon regulated?

3. Explain What is a promoter?

4. Review Describe how most eukaryotic genes are controlled.

5. Compare and Contrast How is gene regulation in prokaryotes and eukaryotes similar? How is it different?

6. Write to Learn Answer the third mystery clue.

MYSTERY CLUE
What do you think controls the growth and development of eyes in flies and mice? (Hint: See p. 324.)

Skills Lab

MD CLG 3.1.1 Chemical Substances and Macromolecules. SPI 1.4.8 Use Models.

Pre-Lab: From DNA to Protein Synthesis

Problem What are the steps involved in making a protein?

Lab Manual Chapter 13 Lab

Skills Focus Use Models, Sequence

Connect to the **Big idea** One of the most important tasks in a cell is the assembly of proteins from amino acids. This task always begins on ribosomes that are located throughout a cell's cytoplasm. The directions for the assembly of proteins are stored in DNA molecules. The information is carried to the ribosomes by a form of RNA called messenger RNA, or mRNA. In this lab, you will model the transcription of DNA and the translation of mRNA.

Background Questions

a. Review Is the following sequence from a DNA or mRNA molecule? How can you tell?

CUAAUGCCCUAGGGCACU

b. Compare and Contrast How are transcription and translation similar? How are they different?

c. Sequence List the following molecules in the order in which they take part in protein synthesis: amino acid, DNA, mRNA, tRNA.

Pre-Lab Questions

Preview the procedure in the lab manual.

1. Sequence Describe briefly the process you will use to decode the messages.

2. Compare and Contrast What role do stop codons play in protein synthesis? What are they used for in the coded messages?

3. Predict Which six letters will not appear in the coded messages? Give a reason for your answer.

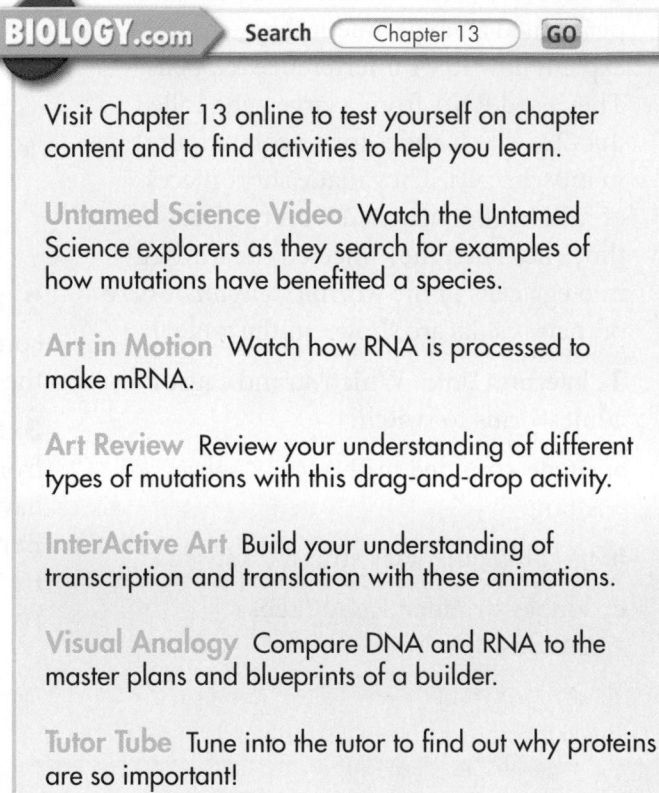

Visit Chapter 13 online to test yourself on chapter content and to find activities to help you learn.

Untamed Science Video Watch the Untamed Science explorers as they search for examples of how mutations have benefitted a species.

Art in Motion Watch how RNA is processed to make mRNA.

Art Review Review your understanding of different types of mutations with this drag-and-drop activity.

InterActive Art Build your understanding of transcription and translation with these animations.

Visual Analogy Compare DNA and RNA to the master plans and blueprints of a builder.

Tutor Tube Tune into the tutor to find out why proteins are so important!

13 CHAPTER Summary

13.1 RNA

- There are three main differences between RNA and DNA. The sugar in RNA is ribose instead of deoxyribose. RNA is generally single-stranded and not double-stranded. RNA contains uracil in place of thymine.

- RNA is made through a process called transcription. In transcription, stretches of DNA serve as templates to make complementary RNA molecules.

RNA (p. 308)
messenger RNA (p. 309)
ribosomal RNA (p. 309)
transfer RNA (p. 309)
transcription (p. 309)

13.2 Ribosomes and Protein Synthesis

- The genetic code is a code for making proteins. The genetic code is read three "letters" at a time. Each "word" is three bases long and corresponds to a single amino acid.

- Ribosomes use the sequence of codons in mRNA to put together amino acids into polypeptide chains. Long, functional polypeptide chains are proteins.

- The central dogma of molecular biology is that information is passed from DNA to RNA to protein. This means that the code used to make DNA, RNA, and proteins is almost universal among organisms.

polypeptide (p. 311)
genetic code (p. 311)
codon (p. 311)
translation (p. 312)
anticodon (p. 313)

13.3 Mutations

- Mutations are changes in genetic information that can be inherited. These changes in the genetic code can affect individuals. If the change is passed to offspring, it can affect whole species.

- The effects of mutations on genes vary widely. Some have little or no effect. Some make beneficial variations that are passed on to offspring. Some negatively disrupt gene function and harm the organism.

mutation (p. 316)
point mutation (p. 317)
frameshift mutation (p. 317)
mutagen (p. 318)
polyploidy (p. 319)

13.4 Gene Regulation and Expression

- DNA-binding proteins in prokaryotes regulate genes by controlling transcription.

- Transcription factors control the expression of eukaryotic genes by binding DNA sequences in regulatory regions.

- Master control genes are like switches that turn on and off development and differentiation in cells. The environment also can turn gene expression on or off.

operon (p. 320)
operator (p. 321)
RNA interference (p. 323)
homeotic gene (p. 324)

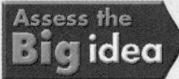 ## Information and Heredity

Write and answer the question below.

Q: How does information flow from DNA to RNA to direct the synthesis of proteins?

Constructed Response

Write an answer to each of the questions below. The answer to each question should be one or two paragraphs. To help you begin, read the **Hints** below the questions.

1. **Why does controlling an organism's proteins control its characteristics?**

   Hint Proteins help your body processes function.

   Hint Many of the body's parts are made of protein.

2. **How might a point mutation in a gene affect proteins?**

   Hint Genes are transcribed into mRNA.

   Hint mRNA is translated into protein using tRNA and rRNA.

3. **Why is a TATA box necessary for a eukaryotic gene to be expressed properly?**

   Hint A TATA box is usually found just before a gene.

   Hint A TATA box binds transcription factor proteins that help position RNA polymerase.

Foundations for Learning Wrap-Up

Activity 1 Working with a partner, figure out which important facts you both chose to record. Examine which facts one partner recorded that the other did not record. Each partner can explain the importance of his or her unmatched facts.

Activity 2 In groups of three, use the material in your Important Facts Envelopes to create information collages. (Be sure each person's initials are on the back of each fact.) Then, spread the facts out on a table, and put the facts in groups, such as "Translation," "Transcription," "or "Prokaryotes." Explain why each fact belongs in a particular group.

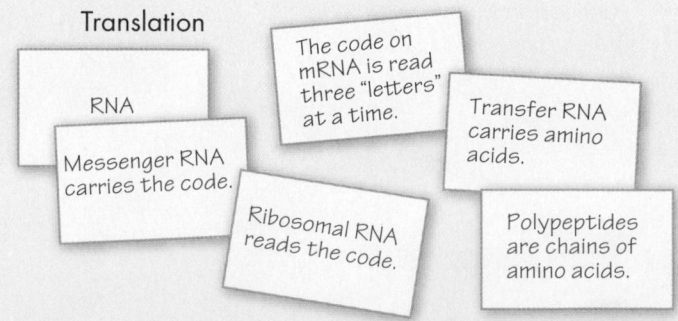

Translation

RNA

Messenger RNA carries the code.

The code on mRNA is read three "letters" at a time.

Ribosomal RNA reads the code.

Transfer RNA carries amino acids.

Polypeptides are chains of amino acids.

13.1 RNA

Understand Key Concepts

1. Which of the following describes RNA?
   a. RNA is usually double-stranded and contains the base thymine.
   b. RNA is usually single-stranded and contains the base uracil.
   c. RNA is longer than DNA and uses five bases to encode information.
   d. RNA is made in the nucleus of eukaryotic cells and stays there to carry out its functions.

2. The process by which the genetic code of DNA is copied into a strand of RNA is called
   a. translation.
   c. transformation.
   b. transcription.
   d. replication.

3. How does the enzyme that makes RNA know where to start transcribing the DNA?

Think Critically

4. **Apply Concepts** Suppose you start with the DNA strand ACCGTCAC. What would a messenger RNA strand transcribed from this DNA strand look like?

Test-Taking Tip

Use Scratch Paper Question 4 asks you to write the messenger RNA sequence that would be transcribed from the DNA sequence ACCGTCAC. Write the DNA sequence on scratch paper. Write the letters that represent the RNA bases directly underneath the DNA letters:

ACCGTCAC

UGGCAGUG

Once you have the right sequence, transfer it to your answer sheet.

13.2 Ribosomes and Protein Synthesis

Understand Key Concepts

5. In messenger RNA, each codon calls for a particular
   a. nucleotide.
   c. amino acid.
   b. enzyme.
   d. promoter.

6. The process of making proteins on the ribosome based on instructions from messenger RNA is called
   a. transcription.
   c. translation.
   b. transformation.
   d. molecular biology.

7. What is a codon?

8. How do anticodons work?

Think Critically

9. **Applying Concepts** A code on a DNA molecule for a specific amino acid is CTA. What would the messenger RNA codon be? What would the transfer RNA anticodon be?

13.3 Mutations

Understand Key Concepts

10. Changes in DNA sequences that affect genetic information are known as
    a. replications.
    c. transformations.
    b. mutations.
    d. translations.

11. A substance that can cause a change in the DNA code of an organism is called a
    a. toxin.
    c. nitrogenous base.
    b. mutagen.
    d. nucleotide.

12. Name and give examples of two major types of mutations.

13. How does a deletion mutation differ from a substitution mutation?

Think Critically

14. **Analyze** Can mutations have a positive effect? Explain your answer.

13.4 Gene Regulation and Expression

Understand Key Concepts

15. An expressed gene
   a. functions as a promoter.
   b. is transcribed into RNA.
   c. codes for just one amino acid.
   d. is made of mRNA.

16. Blocking gene expression in eukaryotes with microRNA strands is called RNA
   a. transcription.   **c.** interference.
   b. translation.   **d.** digestion.

17. How is gene expression controlled in prokaryotes?

18. What is a homeobox gene?

Think Critically

19. Explain How is cell differentiation controlled?

Connecting Concepts

Use Science Graphics

Use the data table to answer questions 20 and 21.

Codon Translation	
Amino Acid	**mRNA Codons**
Alanine (Ala)	GCA, GCG, GCU, GCC
Valine (Val)	GUA, GUG, GUU, GUC
Leucine (Leu)	CUA, CUG, CUU, CUC, UUA, UUG

20. Relate Cause and Effect The table shows mRNA codons for three amino acids. Suppose a substitution mutation occurred at the third nucleotide position of the codons for alanine. What would happen to the resulting protein?

21. Infer The three amino acids shown in the table have very similar—but not identical—properties. What substitution mutations could cause one of these amino acids to be switched for another? What might be the result?

solve the CHAPTER MYSTERY

MOUSE-EYED FLY

Years ago scientists discovered a fly gene they called eyeless. Mutations that turn off this gene cause flies to develop without eyes. Scientists later discovered a mouse gene, called *Pax6*, that was similar to eyeless. Transplanting an activated *Pax6* gene into a fruit fly causes eyes to grow in odd places. These eye growths happen even though mouse eyes and fly eyes are very different.

How can the *Pax6* gene perform the same role in animals that are so different? It probably began very early in the history of life. Then eyes were just patches of light-sensitive cells. They were found on the skin of the common ancestors of all animals. Master control genes like *Pax6* kept working as those organisms evolved and diversified. But their functions changed. All animals, including insects, worms, sea urchins, and humans, share many genes like *Pax6*.

1. Explain How are fly eyes and mouse eyes similar? How are they different?

2. Infer The *Pax6* and eyeless genes do not code for parts of the actual eye. These genes code for transcription factors. Think about the effect of *Pax6* when it is inserted into a fly. Why does it make sense that *Pax6* is a transcription factor?

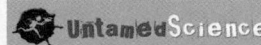 **Never Stop Exploring Your World.** Finding the solution to the mouse-eyed fly is only the beginning. Take a video field trip with the ecogeeks of Untamed Science to see where this mystery leads.

MD Standardized Test Practice for Maryland

Multiple Choice

1. How does RNA differ from DNA?
- **A** RNA contains uracil and deoxyribose.
- **B** RNA contains ribose and thymine.
- **C** RNA contains uracil and ribose.
- **D** RNA contains adenine and ribose.   CLG 3.1.1

2. How would the DNA sequence GCTATA be transcribed to mRNA?
- **A** GCUAUA
- **B** CGATAT
- **C** CGAUAU
- **D** GCUTUT   CLG 3.3.3

Questions 3–4

Use the chart below to answer the questions.

		Second Base in Code Word				
		A	**G**	**U**	**C**	
A		Lys	Arg	Ile	Thr	A
		Lys	Arg	Met	Thr	G
		Asn	Ser	Ile	Thr	U
		Asn	Ser	Ile	Thr	C
G		Glu	Gly	Val	Ala	A
		Glu	Gly	Val	Ala	G
		Asp	Gly	Val	Ala	U
		Asp	Gly	Val	Ala	C
U		"Stop"	"Stop"	Leu	Ser	A
		"Stop"	Trp	Leu	Ser	G
		Tyr	Cys	Phe	Ser	U
		Tyr	Cys	Phe	Ser	C
C		Gln	Arg	Leu	Pro	A
		Gln	Arg	Leu	Pro	G
		His	Arg	Leu	Pro	U
		His	Arg	Leu	Pro	C

(First Base in Code Word — left axis; Third Base in Code Word — right axis)

3. Which of the following codons signifies the end of translation?
- **A** CAA
- **B** UGA
- **C** AUC
- **D** CCA   CLG 3.3.3

4. Which of the chains of amino acids corresponds to the nucleotide sequence UCAAGCGUA?
- **A** glu-cys-pro
- **B** glu-asp-"stop"
- **C** thr-arg-met
- **D** ser-ser-val   CLG 3.3.3

5. In eukaryotes, functional messenger RNA molecules are made from
- **A** exons spliced together after introns are removed.
- **B** introns spliced together after exons are removed.
- **C** exons spliced together with introns.
- **D** long pieces of RNA shortened by the Dicer enzyme.   CLG 3.3.3

6. Promoters are
- **A** genes that code for individual proteins.
- **B** proteins that bind with DNA and prevent transcription.
- **C** DNA sequences near operons that regulate transcription.
- **D** small molecules that bind with repressor proteins.   CLG 3.3.3

Questions 7–8

Use the diagrams below to answer the questions.

Normal Chromosome: M N O P Q R S

Mutant 1: M P O N Q R S

Mutant 2: M N N O P Q R S

7. Mutant 1 is a(n)
- **A** deletion.
- **B** translocation.
- **C** inversion.
- **D** duplication.   SPI 1.5.5

8. Mutant 2 is a(n)
- **A** deletion.
- **B** translocation.
- **C** inversion.
- **D** duplication.   SPI 1.5.5

Open-Ended Response

9. What is the function of the *lac* repressor system in *E. coli*?   CLG 3.3.3

If You Have Trouble With . . .

Question	1	2	3	4	5	6	7	8	9
See Lesson	13.1	13.1	13.2	13.2	13.1	13.1	13.3	13.3	13.4

14.1 Human Chromosomes

MD CLG 3.3.1 Sexual Reproduction and Variation, 3.3.2 Inherited Traits. SPI 1.4.1 Organize Data, 1.4.8 Use Models, 1.5.2 Communicate Information, 1.5.9 Synthesize Ideas, 1.6.1 Ratio and Proportion, 1.6.5 Judge Answers.

Key Questions

🔑 What is a karyotype?

🔑 What patterns of inheritance do human traits follow?

🔑 How can pedigrees be used to analyze human inheritance?

BUILD Understanding

Spider Map Before you read, create a spider map of the major headings in the lesson. As you read, look for the main ideas and supporting details in each lesson.

In Your Workbook Go to your workbook for help creating spider maps. Complete the spider map in Lesson 14.1.

Karyotypes

What makes us human? We could try looking inside the cell with a microscope for the answer. But human cells look similar to cells from any other animal. To find what makes us human, we have to look deeper into the cell. That means we must look at the human **genome.** A genome is the full set of genetic information that an organism carries in its DNA. Remember that genes are on chromosomes. Chromosomes are bundles of DNA and protein found in the nuclei of eukaryotic cells.

To see human chromosomes clearly, cell biologists take pictures of cells during mitosis. The chromosomes are condensed and can be seen clearly at this time. Scientists then cut out the chromosomes from the photographs. They arrange the chromosome images into a picture known as a **karyotype** (KAR ee uh typ). A karyotype shows the complete diploid set of chromosomes. They are lined up together in pairs and arranged from largest to smallest. A typical human cell has 46 chromosomes, arranged in 23 pairs.

🔑 **Key Question** What is a karyotype?
A karyotype shows the complete diploid set of chromosomes. They are grouped in pairs and arranged from largest to smallest.

Sex Chromosomes Two of the 46 chromosomes in the human genome are known as **sex chromosomes** because they determine an individual's sex. Females have two copies of the X chromosome. Males have one X chromosome and one Y chromosome. All egg cells carry a single X chromosome. Half of all sperm cells carry an X chromosome and half carry a Y chromosome. The X chromosome has more than 1200 genes. The Y chromosome is smaller, and has about 140 genes.

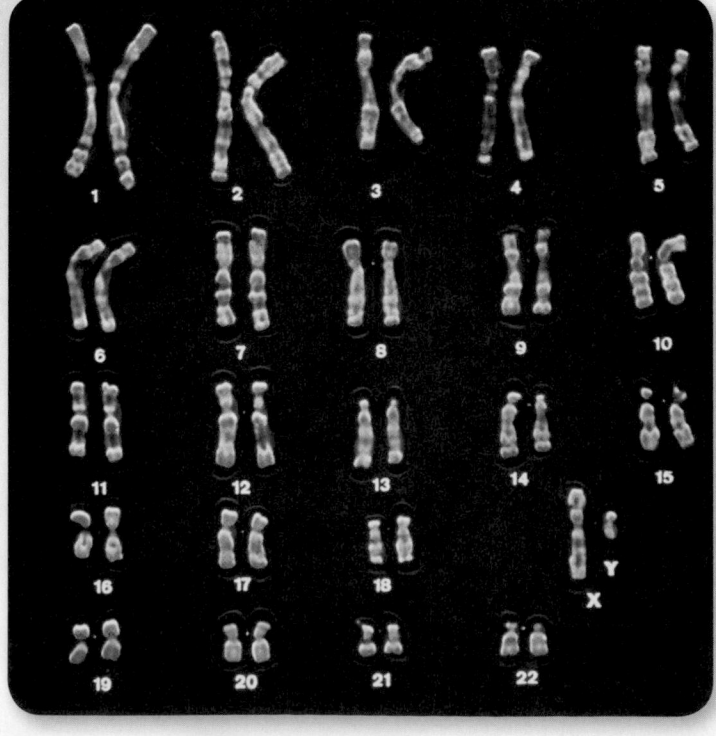

A Human Karyotype The nucleus of a human body cell has 23 pairs of chromosomes. These chromosomes have been cut out of a photograph and arranged to make a karyotype.

Autosomal Chromosomes The whole human genome has 46 chromosomes. There are 2 sex chromosomes. The other 44 are autosomal chromosomes, or *autosomes*. Most of the genetic information in the cell is on the autosomes.

Transmission of Human Traits

Scientists have learned many things about human genetics in recent years by studying DNA. Human genes, like the genes of other organisms, follow Mendelian patterns of inheritance.

Dominant and Recessive Alleles Many human traits follow a pattern of simple dominance. For example, a gene known as MC1R helps determine skin and hair color. A person with red hair usually has two recessive alleles for this gene. Dominant alleles for the MC1R gene help produce darker hair colors.

Codominant and Multiple Alleles Some alleles for human genes are codominant. One example is the ABO blood group, the set of alleles that determines your blood type. There are three alleles: I^A, I^B, and i. Alleles I^A and I^B are codominant. They make protein markers called antigens on the surface of red blood cells. People with alleles I^A and I^B make both A and B antigens, so they are blood type AB. The i allele is recessive. People with alleles I^AI^A or I^Ai make only the A antigen. They have blood type A. Those with I^BI^B or I^Bi alleles are type B. Those with two i alleles (ii) make no antigen. They have blood type O.

🔑 **Key Question** What patterns of inheritance do human traits follow?

Many human traits follow a pattern of simple dominance. The alleles for many human genes are codominant.

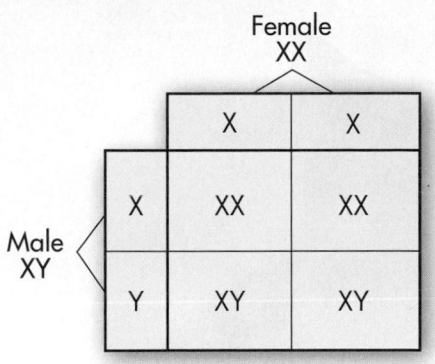

Sex Ratios Human egg cells have one X chromosome. Sperm cells have either one X chromosome or one Y chromosome. Half the offspring will be male. Half will be female.

Blood Groups

Phenotype (Blood Type)	Genotype	Antigen on Red Blood Cell	Safe Transfusions To	Safe Transfusions From
A	I^AI^A or I^Ai	A	A, AB	A, O
B	I^BI^B or I^Bi	B	B, AB	B, O
AB	I^AI^B	A and B	AB	A, B, AB, O
O	ii	None	A, B, AB, O	O

Human Blood Groups This table shows the relationship between genotype and phenotype for the ABO blood groups. It also shows which blood types can safely be transfused into people with other blood types.

X-Chromosome Inactivation
Female calico cats are tricolored, meaning they have three colors. The spot color on their fur is controlled by a gene on the X chromosome. Spots can be either orange or black. Their color depends on which X chromosome is turned off in that patch of skin.

Sex-Linked Inheritance The genes located on X and Y chromosomes show a pattern of inheritance called sex-linkage. A **sex-linked gene** is a gene on a sex chromosome. Only males have the genes on the Y chromosome. Since only males have a Y chromosome, boys inherit it from their father. The X chromosome comes from their mother. The fact that males have only one X chromosome can cause genetic problems.

For example, humans have three genes for color vision on their X chromosome. A defective allele for any of these genes results in colorblindness. A male's only copy of each allele is on his X chromosome. If he has one of these defective alleles, he will be unable to tell certain colors apart. Females have two X chromosomes, so they have two alleles for each of the color-vision genes. Since the defective alleles are recessive, in a female both copies of the recessive allele must be present to produce colorblindness. Because of this, colorblindness and other sex-linked recessive disorders show up much more often in males than in females.

Key Question What patterns of inheritance do human traits follow? **Because the X and Y chromosomes determine sex, the genes located on them show a pattern of inheritance called sex-linkage.**

X-Chromosome Inactivation One X chromosome is enough for cells in males. But what about cells in females? A cell only needs one X chromosome to function normally. Female cells adjust to having two X chromosomes by randomly inactivating genes on one of them. The inactive chromosome makes a dense area in the nucleus called a Barr body.

X-chromosome inactivation also occurs in other female mammals. For example, cats have a gene that controls the color of coat spots on their X chromosome. One X chromosome may have an allele for orange spots. The other may have an allele for black spots. Different X chromosomes are inactivated in various parts of a female's skin. This causes a mixture of orange and black spots in her fur. Male cats have just one X chromosome, so their spots are only one color.

Human Pedigrees

You can use Mendel's basic laws of genetics to find out if a trait is dominant or recessive. These same laws help you find out if the gene for that trait is autosomal or sex-linked. You can use a chart called a **pedigree** to show the pattern of inheritance for a trait. A pedigree shows the presence or absence of a trait according to the relationships between parents, siblings, and offspring.

The pedigree on the next page shows how one human trait passes through three generations of a family. At the top of the chart is a grandfather who had the white forelock trait. Two of his three children inherited the trait. Three grandchildren have the trait, but two do not.

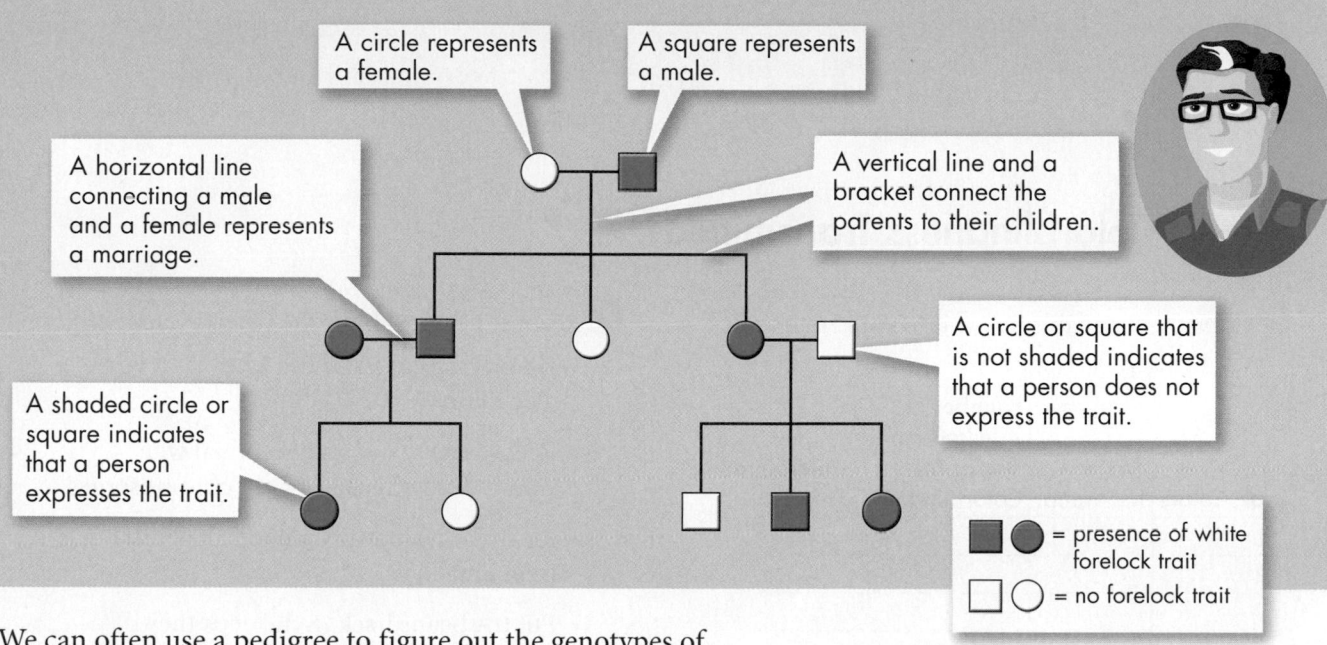

A circle represents a female.

A square represents a male.

A horizontal line connecting a male and a female represents a marriage.

A vertical line and a bracket connect the parents to their children.

A circle or square that is not shaded indicates that a person does not express the trait.

A shaded circle or square indicates that a person expresses the trait.

■ ● = presence of white forelock trait
□ ○ = no forelock trait

We can often use a pedigree to figure out the genotypes of family members. In the pedigree above, the allele for the white forelock trait is dominant. So, someone without the trait must have two recessive alleles. The grandfather at the top of the chart has this trait. So do two of his children. But the third child does not have a white forelock. So, the grandfather must be heterozygous for this trait.

Pedigree Example This diagram shows what the symbols in a pedigree represent.

🔑 **Key Question** How can pedigrees be used to analyze human inheritance? **The information learned from pedigrees helps determine the nature of genes and alleles associated with inherited human traits.**

CHECK Understanding

Apply Vocabulary

Use the highlighted words from the lesson to complete each sentence correctly.

1. A _____ contains all the instructions that are needed to build an organism.

2. An organism's paired chromosomes arranged in order from largest to smallest is called a _____.

Critical Thinking

3. Explain What does a pedigree show?

4. Predict Suppose a woman with type O blood and a man with type AB blood have children. What are the children's possible genotypes?

5. Write to Learn Answer the first clue of the mystery.

MYSTERY CLUE

Two sickle cell alleles are needed to produce sickle cell disease. Males and females develop sickle cell disease in equal frequencies. What do these statements suggest about the location of the gene responsible for the disorder? (**Hint:** See p. 336.)

How Is Colorblindness Transmitted?

❶ Copy the data table below into your notebook.

Trial	Colors	Sex of Individual	Number of X-linked Alleles for Colorblindness	Colorblind? (Yes/No)
1				
2				
3				
4				
5				
6				
7				
8				
9				
10				

❷ Label one plastic cup Mother and a second plastic cup Father.

❸ The white beans represent X chromosomes.

• Use a black marker to make a dot on each of 2 white beans. The dot represents the X-linked allele for colorblindness.

• Place 1 marked bean into each plastic cup.

❹ Place 1 more white bean into the cup labeled Mother.

❺ Red beans represent Y chromosomes. Place 1 red bean into the cup labeled Father.

❻ Close your eyes and pick one bean from each cup. This represents how each parent contributes a sex chromosome to a fertilized egg.

❼ Record the data about the beans you picked.

• Record the colors of the 2 beans in your data table.

• Record the sex of an individual who would carry this pair of sex chromosomes.

• Record how many X-linked alleles the individual has.

• Put the beans back in the cups they came from.

• Determine whether the individual would have colorblindness.

❽ Repeat steps 6 and 7 for a total of 10 pairs of beans.

Analyze and Conclude

1. Relate Cause and Effect How do human sex chromosomes keep the numbers of males and females roughly equal?

2. Calculate Calculate the class totals for each data column.

a. How many females were colorblind?

Number of colorblind females = _____

Percentage of females who were colorblind = _____

b. How many males were colorblind?

Number of colorblind males = _____

Percentage of males who were colorblind = _____

3. Use Models Does your model accurately represent how colorblindness is transmitted in a population? Explain. (*Hint:* See p. 336.)

In Your Workbook Get more help for this activity in your workbook.

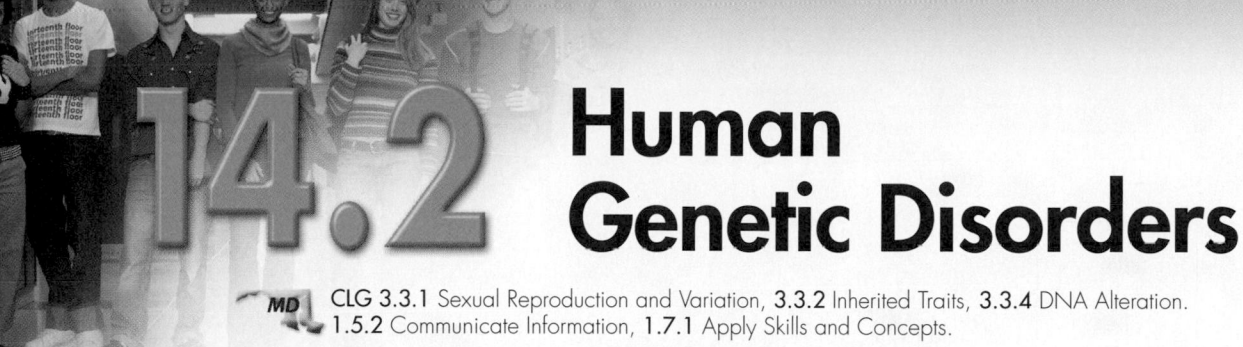

14.2 Human Genetic Disorders

MD CLG 3.3.1 Sexual Reproduction and Variation, 3.3.2 Inherited Traits, 3.3.4 DNA Alteration. 1.5.2 Communicate Information, 1.7.1 Apply Skills and Concepts.

From Molecule to Phenotype

Have you ever heard the expression "It runs in the family"? Family and friends may have said that about your smile or the shape of your ears. But what could this mean when they talk about genetic diseases and disorders? What is a genetic disorder?

We know that genes are made of DNA. We also know that they interact with the environment to make an individual's characteristics, or phenotype. The link between molecule and trait is often that simple and direct. Genotype and phenotype are directly connected, since changes in a gene's DNA sequence can change proteins. Changes in the proteins cells make may directly affect one's phenotype. In other words, there is a molecular basis for genetic disorders.

Disorders Caused by Individual Genes Thousands of genetic disorders are caused by changes in individual genes. These changes often affect specific proteins that do important jobs.

▶ *Sickle-Cell Disease* This disorder is caused by a flawed allele for a polypeptide in hemoglobin. Hemoglobin is the oxygen-carrying protein in red blood cells. The polypeptide made from the flawed allele makes hemoglobin molecules stick together at times. The attached molecules make long fibers that force the cells to be shaped like a sickle. This shape gives the disorder its name. Normal red blood cells are flexible. They can squeeze through tiny capillaries—the narrowest blood vessels in the body. Sickle-shaped cells are more rigid and tend to get stuck in the capillaries. If the blood stops moving through the capillaries, then damage to cells, tissues, and even organs can happen.

▶ *Huntington's Disease* Huntington's disease is caused by a dominant allele for a protein found in brain cells. The allele for this disease has a long string of bases. In the string, the codon CAG repeats over and over again, more than 40 times. CAG codes for the amino acid glutamine. No one knows for sure why this long string of glutamine causes the disease. People who have Huntington's disease suffer from decreasing mental abilities and uncontrollable movements. The symptoms usually do not appear until middle age. The greater the number of CAG codon repeats, the earlier the disease appears, and the more severe its symptoms are.

Key Questions

🔑 *How do small changes in DNA molecules affect human traits?*

🔑 *What are the effects of errors in meiosis?*

BUILD Understanding

Two-Column Chart Before you read, make a two-column chart. In the first column, write three questions you have about genetic disorders. As you read, fill in answers to your questions in the second column.

In Your Workbook Go to your workbook to learn more about making a two-column chart. Complete the chart in Lesson 14.2.

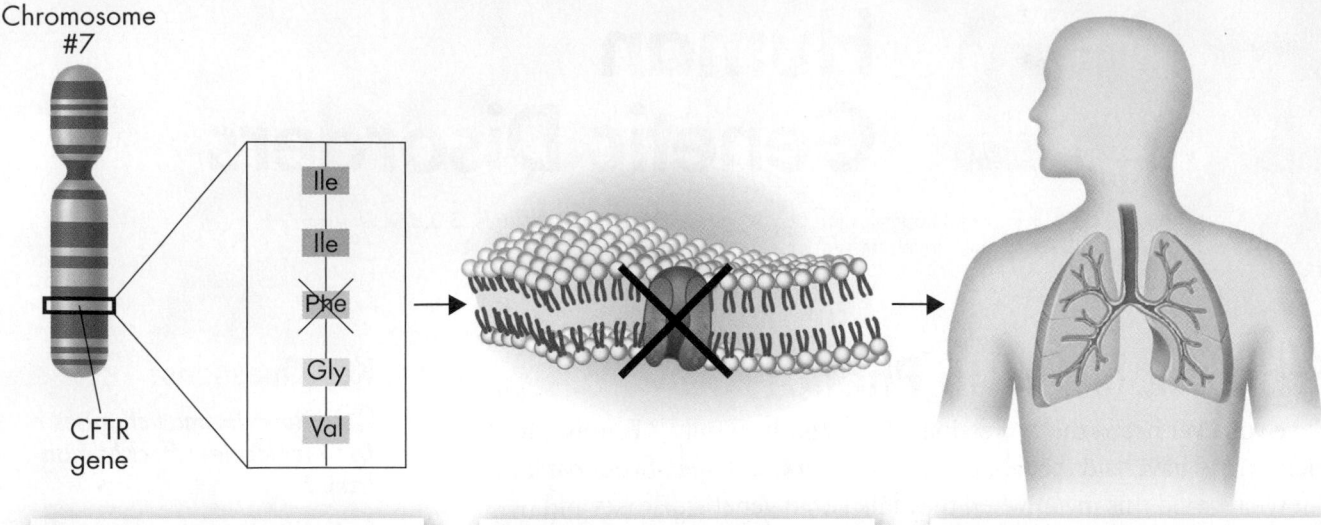

Chromosome #7

CFTR gene

Ile
Ile
Phe
Gly
Val

❶ The most common allele that causes cystic fibrosis is missing 3 DNA bases. So the amino acid phenylalanine is missing from the CFTR protein.

❷ Normal CFTR is a chloride ion channel in cell membranes. Abnormal CFTR cannot transport ions aross the cell membrane.

❸ The cells in the person's airways cannot transport chloride ions. So the airways become clogged with a thick mucus.

Mutations Cause Cystic Fibrosis
CF is usually caused by the deletion of three bases in the DNA of a single gene. So, the body does not make normal CFTR. CTFR is a protein needed to transport chloride ions.

▶ *Cystic Fibrosis* Known as CF for short, cystic fibrosis is usually caused by the deletion of three bases in one gene. This gene codes for a protein called CFTR. The loss of these bases removes one amino acid from CFTR. This causes the protein to fold incorrectly, so the protein cannot do its job.

The CF allele is recessive, so two copies of the defective allele are needed to cause the disorder. People with one normal copy of the CF allele are unaffected by CF. Children with CF have trouble digesting food. They also make thick, heavy mucus that blocks their lungs and airways.

🗝 **Key Question** How do small changes in DNA molecules affect human traits?
Changes in a gene's DNA sequence can change proteins by altering their amino acid sequences. This may directly affect a person's phenotype.

Genetic Advantages Diseases such as sickle cell disease and CF are still common in human populations. Why are the alleles for these diseases still around if they can kill those who have them? Sometimes having just one recessive allele can be an advantage.

A parasite that lives in red blood cells causes a disease called malaria. But the parasite cannot live in sickled blood cells. People with one copy of the sickle cell allele are resistant to the parasite. This resistance gives them a big advantage against malaria.

More than 1000 years ago, terrible epidemics of typhoid fever spread through cities in Europe. Typhoid is caused by a bacterium that enters the body through cells in the digestive system. The protein made by the CF allele helps block this bacterium from entering the cells. People with a single CF allele were less likely to die from typhoid.

Chromosomal Disorders

Meiosis usually works perfectly. Each human gamete, or sex cell, gets exactly 23 chromosomes. But occasionally something goes wrong. The most common error in meiosis occurs when homologous chromosomes do not separate. This mistake is called nondisjunction. **Nondisjunction** means "not coming apart."

If nondisjunction happens during meiosis, gametes can end up with the wrong number of chromosomes. This can lead to disorders. For example, if two copies of an autosomal chromosome fail to separate during meiosis, an individual may be born with three copies of that chromosome. This condition is called a trisomy. Down syndrome is trisomy of chromosome number 21. People with Down syndrome often have mental retardation and other birth defects.

Nondisjunction of sex chromosomes also causes problems. A female who inherits only one X chromosome usually has Turner's syndrome. Her sex organs do not develop at puberty, so she cannot have offspring. A male with an extra X chromosome has Klinefelter's syndrome. The extra chromosome interferes with meiosis, so the male usually cannot reproduce. There is no evidence of someone being born without any X chromosomes. So the genes on this chromosome are necessary for an embryo to survive and develop.

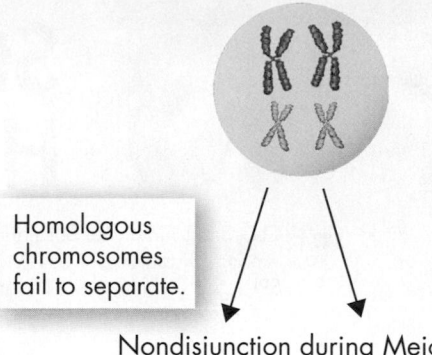

Homologous chromosomes fail to separate.

Nondisjunction during Meiosis I

Meiosis II

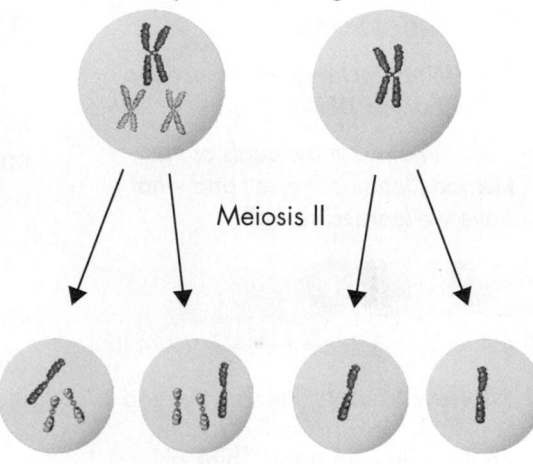

Nondisjunction This failure of meiosis causes gametes to have an abnormal number of chromosomes.

🔑 **Key Question** What are the effects of errors in meiosis? **If nondisjunction occurs during meiosis, gametes may receive an abnormal number of chromosomes. This change can lead to a disorder of chromosome numbers.**

✓CHECK Understanding

Apply Vocabulary
Use the highlighted words from the lesson to complete the sentence correctly.

1. When homologous chromosomes do not separate properly during meiosis, it is called _____.

Critical Thinking
2. Explain How can a small change in a person's DNA cause a genetic disorder?

3. Apply Concepts How does nondisjunction cause chromosomal disorders?

4. Write to Learn Answer the second clue in the mystery. Think about how proteins are made.

MYSTERY CLUE

Sickle cell disease occurs because a single amino acid is different. This difference causes a change in one of the hemoglobin proteins. What could produce this change? (**Hint:** See p. 340.)

14.3 Studying the Human Genome

MD CLG 3.1.1 Chemical Substances and Macromolecules, 3.3.4 DNA Alteration, 3.4.2 Relatedness Among Organisms, 3.6.1 Analyze Consequences, 3.6.2 Investigate a Biological Issue. SPI 1.5.2 Communicate Information, 1.7.1 Apply Skills and Concepts, 1.7.2 Evaluate Ideas, 1.7.4 Recognize Mathematics, 1.7.6 Science and Technology.

Key Questions

🔑 **What techniques are used to study human DNA?**

🔑 **What were the goals of the Human Genome Project, and what have we learned so far?**

BUILD Understanding

Preview Visuals Before you read Lesson 3, look at the illustrations on the following page. Think of three questions you have about the illustrations.

In Your Workbook Write your questions in the chart in Lesson 14.3. As you read, write the answers to your questions.

BUILD Vocabulary

restriction enzyme
an enzyme that cuts DNA at a sequence of nucleotides

gel electrophoresis
a procedure used to analyze DNA fragments by placing a mixture of DNA fragments at one end of a porous gel and applying an electrical voltage to the gel

🖋 WORD ORIGINS

The root word *phoresis* is from the Greek *phorein*, which means "to carry." In electrophoresis, an electric current carries suspended particles through a medium.

Manipulating DNA

Only a few decades ago, computers were big machines found only in laboratories or universities. Today, many people carry small, powerful computers to school and work. Decades ago, the human genome was unknown. Now, we can see our entire genome on the Internet. How long will it be before having a copy of your own genome is as common as carrying a cell phone?

Since discovering the genetic code, biologists have dreamed of reading the human genome. For a long time, it seemed impossible because working with molecules as large as DNA is difficult. Then scientists discovered tools to cut, separate, and replicate DNA. Now they can read the base sequences in DNA from any cell.

Cutting DNA To study DNA, scientists first cut it into smaller pieces using bacterial enzymes called **restriction enzymes.** Restriction enzymes cut a DNA molecule into exact pieces called restriction fragments. Different enzymes cut DNA in different places, and into pieces of different sizes.

Separating DNA After DNA is cut, scientists use a technique called **gel electrophoresis** to separate and analyze the fragments of DNA. A mixture of DNA fragments is put at one end of a gel. An electric current makes the DNA move toward one end of the gel. Smaller DNA fragments move faster and farther than large ones. The result is a pattern of bands on the gel. The pattern is based on the size of the DNA fragments.

Reading DNA After the DNA fragments have been separated, researchers read, or sequence, the DNA. Single-stranded DNA fragments are put in a test tube with DNA polymerase. Then the bases, A, T, G, and C, are added. DNA polymerase uses the bases to make many new DNA strands. Some of the bases are labeled with a chemical dye. When a dye-labeled base is added to a new DNA strand, the synthesis of that strand stops. When all the synthesis is done, the result is a series of color-coded DNA strands. The strands are different lengths. Researchers can then separate these strands by size on a gel. The order of colored bands on the gel tells the exact sequence of bases in the DNA.

🔑 **Key Question** What techniques are used to study human DNA? **Scientists use tools that cut, separate, and then replicate DNA base by base. Now they can read the base sequences in DNA from any cell.**

BUILD Connections

HOW SCIENTISTS MANIPULATE DNA

Scientists use tools to cut, separate, replicate, and sequence DNA. Knowing the sequence of DNA allows us to study specific genes.

Cutting DNA

A restriction enzyme is like a key that fits only one lock. The *Eco*RI restriction enzyme can only recognize the base sequence GAATTC. It cuts each strand of DNA between the G and A bases. This cut leaves single-stranded overhangs with the sequence AATT. The overhangs are called "sticky ends." The ends can bond, or "stick," to a DNA fragment with the complementary base sequence.

Separating DNA

Gel electrophoresis is used to separate DNA fragments. The fragments are first cut by restriction enzymes. Then, the fragments are put into wells on a gel. The gel is like a slice of gelatin. An electric voltage moves the shorter fragments faster than the longer fragments. Within an hour or two, the fragments all separate. Fragments of the same size show up as a band on the gel.

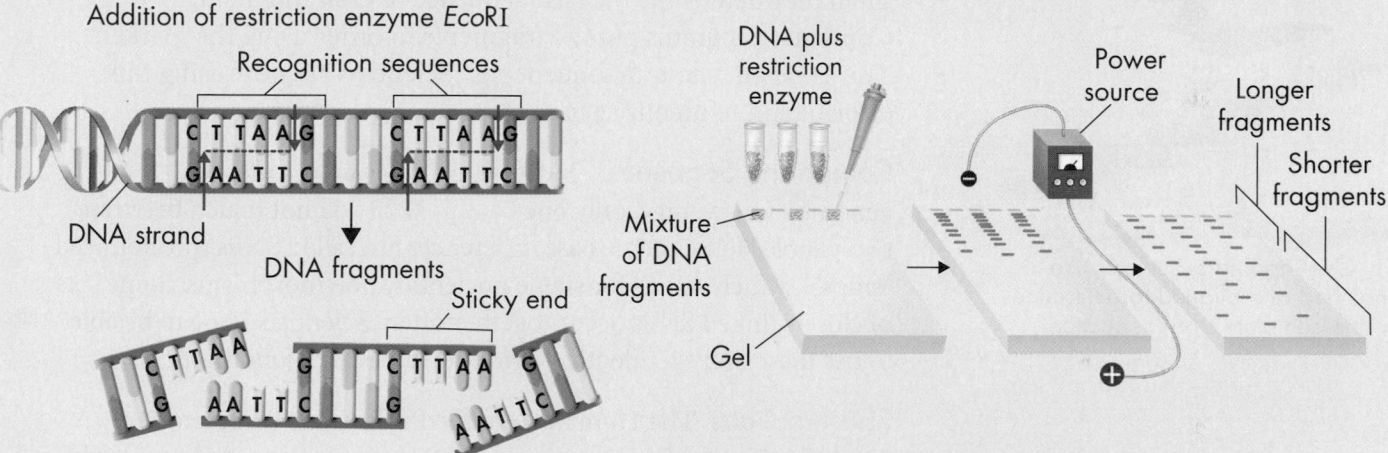

Addition of restriction enzyme *Eco*RI

Reading DNA

Some dye-labeled bases are mixed in with the regular bases added to make the new DNA. Each time a labeled base is added to the strand, DNA replication for that strand stops. Each kind of base is labeled with a different color. This labeling results in color-coded DNA fragments of different lengths. Gel electrophoresis is used to separate the fragments. Then scientists can "read" the DNA sequence from the gel.

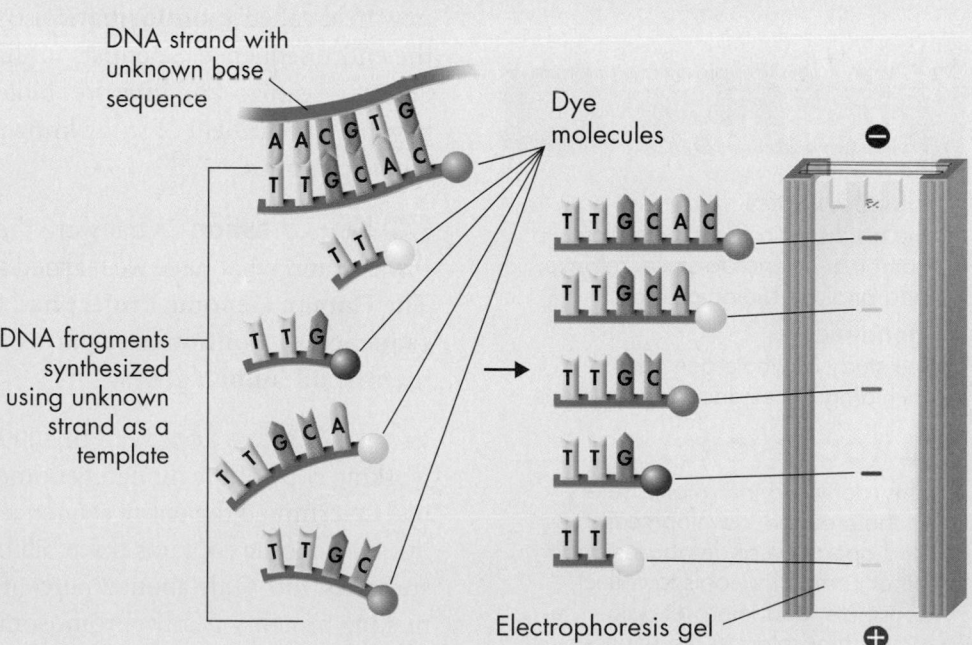

Base sequence as "read" from the order of the bands on the gel from bottom to top: **T G C A C**

This method rapidly sorts DNA fragments by using overlapping base sequences.

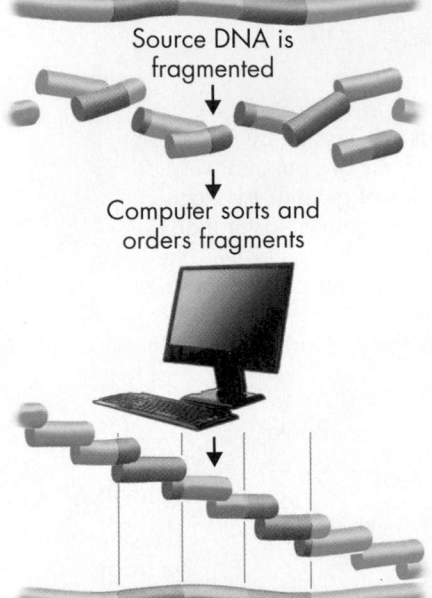

Source DNA is fragmented

Computer sorts and orders fragments

Overlapping sequences are matched and aligned to determine the complete DNA sequence.

BUILD Vocabulary

bioinformatics
the application of mathematics and computer science to store, retrieve, and analyze biological data

genomics
the study of whole genomes, including genes and their functions

⚡ ROOT WORDS

The root word *informatics* refers to the creation, development, and operation of databases and other computing tools to collect, organize, and interpret data. The prefix *bio-* refers to life sciences. In bioinformatics, life science data are collected in databases.

The Human Genome Project

In 1990, the United States and other countries began the 13-year Human Genome Project. The project had two main goals. One goal was to sequence all 3 billion base pairs of human DNA. The other was to identify all human genes. DNA sequencing was at the center of the Human Genome Project. How do scientists handle a sequencing project that big? First, they break up the whole genome into smaller pieces. Next, they determine the base sequences in regions of a DNA strand that are far apart. These regions act as markers, like mile markers on a long highway. Using the markers, researchers can find and return to specific places in the DNA.

Sequencing and Identifying Genes Once researchers have marked the DNA strands, they cut them into random fragments. Then they determine the base sequence of each fragment. Computer programs put the fragments in order using the markers. This is called "shotgun sequencing." Scientists are now using this information to identify genes.

Comparing Sequences Most people have almost identical genomes. On average, only one base in 1200 will not match between two people. These single base differences are called SNPs (pronounced "snips"), which stands for single nucleotide polymorphisms. Some sets of closely linked SNPs occur together often. Scientists hope to be able to use these SNPs to identify various diseases and conditions.

Sharing Data The Human Genome Project was completed in 2003. Copies of the human genome DNA sequence are now available on the Internet. One of the key research areas of the project was a new field called **bioinformatics.** By 2003, scientist had determined the entire sequence. Scientists in this field use computer tools to collect, organize, and interpret biological data. Bioinformatics also began a similar field of study known as **genomics**—the study of whole genomes.

🔑 **Key Question** What were the goals of the Human Genome Project, and what have we learned so far?
The Human Genome Project had two main goals. One was to sequence all 3 billion base pairs of human DNA. The other was to identify all human genes.

What We Have Learned In 2000, scientists announced that a working copy of the human genome was complete. By 2003, scientists had determined the entire sequence. Scientists had learned that the human genome contains three billion nucleotide bases. They found surprises, too. Only about 2 percent of our genome has codes for making proteins. Many chromosomes have large areas with very few genes. The scientists discovered that much of our genome is made up of genetic code from viruses. The project also identified genes linked to many diseases and disorders. Finally, the project found three million locations where single base pairs are different in humans.

Key Question What were the goals of the Human Genome Project, and what have we learned so far?

The Human Genome Project pinpointed genes. It matched some sequences in those genes with many diseases and disorders. It also identified about three million places where single-base DNA differences occur in humans.

New Questions The scientists in this project knew that their data could cause ethical, legal, and social problems. The problem areas include privacy, fairness in the use of and access to the data, and medical issues. In May 2008, the Genetic Information Nondiscrimination Act was passed into law. The act makes sure that U.S. companies cannot discriminate on the basis of information they learn from genetic tests.

What's Next There is much more to learn about the human genome. The 1000 Genomes Project began in 2008. It studies the genomes of 1000 people and builds a careful list of human variation. Data from the project will be used in studies of development and disease. The information may hold the key to successful research on new drugs. It may also lead to therapies to save human lives and keep people healthy.

Announcements
The first details of the human genome appeared in two well-known scientific journals in February 2001, *Science* and *Nature* (shown here).

CHECK Understanding

Apply Vocabulary
Use the highlighted terms from the lesson to complete each term correctly.

1. A scientist can use a _____ to cut a strand of DNA at a specific place.

2. _____ is the process that uses electrical current to separate DNA fragments by size.

3. _____ is a field of study that grew out of bioinformatics and includes the study of genes and their functions.

Critical Thinking
4. Explain What is the Human Genome Project?

5. Apply Concepts How might the Human Genome Project be used to benefit humankind?

6. Write to Learn Answer the third clue to the chapter mystery. How many bases are involved in the mutation?

MYSTERY CLUE

Scientists used SNPs to locate the sickle cell allele in genes that code for hemoglobin proteins. What does this tell you about the sickle cell mutation? (**Hint:** See p. 344.)

BIOLOGY.com Search (Lesson 14.3) **GO** • Lesson Assessment

Forensics Lab

MD CLG 3.3.2 Inherited Traits. SPI 1.4.2 Analyze Data, 1.4.3 Use Data, 1.5.9 Synthesize Ideas.

Pre-Lab: Using DNA to Identify Human Remains

Problem How can pedigrees help scientists identify human remains?

Lab Manual Chapter 14 Lab

Skills Focus Analyze Data, Draw Conclusions

Connect to the Big idea The nucleus is not the only location in a cell where DNA can be found. DNA is also found in the mitochondria of cells. This mitochondrial DNA, or mtDNA, exists as small loops, rather than long strands. Unlike nuclear DNA, mtDNA is inherited only from the mother. Thus, except for mutations, the sequence of nucleotides in mtDNA remains constant over many generations.

Less than one percent of a cell's DNA is mtDNA, but in that percentage are many copies of the small mtDNA molecules. So when forensic scientists cannot collect a suitable sample of nuclear DNA, they look for mtDNA. Usable mtDNA can often be found even after a body decays or is burned. In this lab, you will explore how mtDNA was used to help confirm the identity of bones that scientists thought belonged to members of the Romanov family.

The Romanovs ruled Russia for 300 years until the Bolshevik Revolution of 1918 resulted in the execution of Tsar Nicholas II and his family.

3. Infer If two people have the same mtDNA, what can you infer about their biological relationship?

BIOLOGY.com Search (Chapter 14) GO

Visit Chapter 14 online to test yourself on chapter content and to find activities to help you learn.

Untamed Science Video The Untamed Science crew identifies the chromosomes that carry genes for colorblindness.

Art in Motion View a short animation that explains nondisjunction.

Art Review Review your understanding of karyotypes with this drag-and-drop activity.

InterActive Art Learn all about pedigrees and how to make them with this animation.

Tutor Tube Why do traits sometimes "skip a generation"? Tune in to the tutor to find out.

Background Questions

a. Review What is a pedigree?

b. Explain In a pedigree, what does a circle represent? What does a square represent?

c. Infer How do you know that mtDNA isn't sorted and recombined during meiosis?

Pre-Lab Questions

Preview the procedure in the lab manual.

1. Infer The tsar and tsarina had five children. Did all seven family members have the same mtDNA? Give a reason for your answer.

2. Predict To confirm that bones belonged to the tsar's children, which living relative would be more useful—a relative of the tsar or a relative of the tsarina? Why?

14.1 Human Chromosomes

- A karyotype shows the complete diploid set of chromosomes. They are grouped in pairs and arranged from largest to smallest.

- Many human traits follow a pattern of simple dominance. The alleles for other human genes are codominant.

- Because the X and Y chromosomes determine sex, the genes located on them show a pattern of inheritance called sex-linkage.

- The information learned from pedigrees helps determine the nature of genes and alleles associated with inherited human traits.

genome (p. 334)
karyotype (p. 334)
sex chromosome (p. 334)
sex-linked gene (p. 336)
pedigree (p. 336)

14.2 Human Genetic Disorders

- Changes in a gene's DNA sequence can change proteins by altering their amino acid sequences. This change may directly affect a person's phenotype.

- If nondisjunction happens during meiosis, gametes may receive an abnormal number of chromosomes. This change can lead to a disorder of chromosome numbers.

nondisjunction (p. 341)

14.3 Studying the Human Genome

- Scientists use tools that cut, separate, and then replicate DNA base by base. Now they can read the base sequences in DNA from any cell.

- The Human Genome Project had two main goals. One was to sequence all 3 billion base pairs of human DNA. The other was to identify all human genes.

- The Human Genome Project pinpointed genes. It matched some sequences in those genes with many diseases and disorders. It also identified about 3 million locations where single-base DNA differences occur in humans.

restriction enzyme (p. 342)
gel electrophoresis (p. 342)
bioinformatics (p. 344)
genomics (p. 344)

Assess the Big idea ▸ Information and Heredity

Write an answer to the question below.

Q: How can we use genetics to study human inheritance?

Constructed Response

Write an answer to each of the questions below. The answer to each question should be one or two paragraphs. To help you begin, read the **Hints** below the questions.

1. **How are sex-linked traits inherited?**

   Hint Females have two copies of the alleles on the X chromosome.

   Hint Sex-linked traits are controlled by alleles on the X chromosome.

2. **How can a substitution mutation in a gene affect the ability of a cell to function properly?**

   Hint A substitution mutation replaces one DNA base with another base in a codon.

   Hint A change in a DNA base may change the amino acid coded for by the codon.

3. **Describe the tools and processes scientists use to manipulate DNA.**

   Hint Restriction enzymes cut DNA into short fragments at known locations.

   Hint Gel electrophoresis separates DNA fragments by their size.

Foundations for Learning Wrap-Up

Use the layered books you made as you read this chapter as tools to study and review the concepts of the chapter.

Activity 1 Exchange a layered book you made with a partner who made a similar book. Read the books aloud to each other and compare them. Add notes to each book, and correct any errors you find.

Activity 2 Look through your layered books and find one about the Human Genome Project or genetic disorders. With a partner, make notes on the book about either social or ethical problems that came up because of the Human Genome Project. Or make notes about a genetic advantage of having one of the genetic disorders.

Disorders Caused by Individual Genes

- protein folds badly, cell membranes cannot let Cl⁻ ions pass
- patients have thick mucus in lungs

Genetic Advantage:
- People with one CF allele did not get typhoid.

Cystic Fibrosis

Huntington's Disease

14.1 Human Chromosomes

Understand Key Concepts

1. A normal human diploid zygote contains
   a. 23 chromosomes.
   c. 44 chromosomes.
   b. 46 chromosomes.
   d. XXY chromosomes.

2. A chart that traces the inheritance of a trait in a family is called a(n)
   a. pedigree.
   c. genome.
   b. karyotype.
   d. autosome.

3. An example of a trait that is determined by multiple alleles is
   a. cystic fibrosis.
   c. Down syndrome.
   b. ABO blood groups.
   d. colorblindness.

4. Could a person with blood type alleles I^A and I^B have blood type A? Explain your answer (refer to the table on page 335).

Think Critically

5. **Predict** If a male is born colorblind, what do we know about his mother?

14.2 Human Genetic Disorders

Understand Key Concepts

6. A mutation involving a change in a single DNA base pair
   a. will definitely result in a genetic disease.
   b. will have no effect on the organism's phenotype.
   c. will produce a positive change.
   d. may have an effect on the organism's phenotype.

7. Cystic fibrosis is caused by
   a. nondisjunction of an autosome.
   b. a small change of three base pairs in DNA.
   c. nondisjunction of a sex chromosome.
   d. deletion of an entire gene from a chromosome.

8. What is a chromosomal disorder?

9. Analyze the human karyotype below. Which chromosomal disorder does it show?

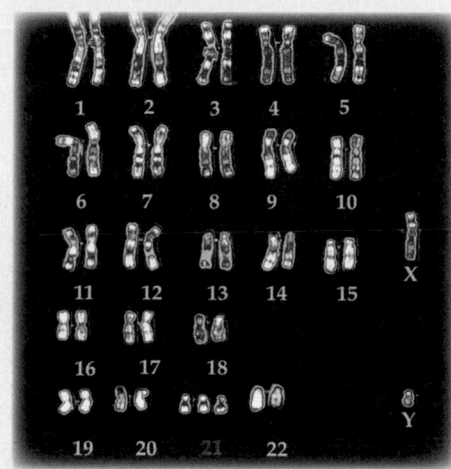

Think Critically

10. **Infer** Can a genetic counselor use a karyotype to identify a carrier of cystic fibrosis? Explain your answer.

14.3 Studying the Human Genome

Understand Key Concepts

11. The human genome consists of approximately how many DNA base pairs?
    a. 30,000
    c. 300,000,000
    b. 3,000,000
    d. 3,000,000,000

12. If you sequence short pieces of DNA and then use a computer to find overlapping sequences that map to a much longer DNA fragment, you are using
    a. genomics.
    b. hapmaps.
    c. shotgun sequencing.
    d. "sticky ends."

13. Cutting DNA into small pieces that can be sequenced is done by
   a. restriction enzymes.   **c.** gel electrophoresis.
   b. DNA polymerase.   **d.** RNA polymerase.

Test-Taking Tip

Choose Among Similar Answers Sometimes eliminating a known incorrect answer only helps a little. In question 13, we can eliminate **c** because it does not involve a cutting process. We also know that cutting is done with enzymes. But we still have three enzymes as possible answers. The names of the enzymes give us clues. We eliminate **d** because it refers to RNA. Since we know that polymerases build strands of DNA, this means that the only possible correct answer is **a.**

14. Describe the tools and processes that scientists use to manipulate human DNA.

Think Critically

15. Explain What is bioinformatics?

Connecting Concepts

Use Science Graphics

Use the data table to answer questions 16–17.

Chromosomes and Phenotypes		
Sex Chromosomes	Fruit Fly Phenotype	Human Phenotype
XX	Female	Female
XY	Male	Male
X	Male	Female
XXY	Female	Male

16. Interpret Tables Which organism requires a Y chromosome for maleness?

17. Predict Do you think the genes on the Y chromosome are necessary for survival? Explain your answer.

solve the CHAPTER MYSTERY

THE CROOKED CELL

Ava looked into her family's medical history. She found out that Uncle Eli's mother (Ava's grandmother) also had sickle cell disease. However, Uncle Eli's father did not. One of Ava's uncle's four children also had the disease. But Ava's father, who is Eli's only sibling, does not have sickle cell disease. Ava's mother does not have sickle cell disease, either. Ava's two siblings also show no signs of the disease.

1. Apply Concepts Does sickle cell disease follow a simple dominance pattern of heredity? Give evidence from the chapter and its clues to support your answer.

2. Draw Conclusions Think about your answer to question 1. What can you conclude about the inheritance of sickle cell disease in Ava's family? What might be Ava's chances of being a carrier of the sickle cell trait?

3. Classify What kind of medical test could Ava request that would help determine whether or not she has the sickle cell trait? Explain your answer.

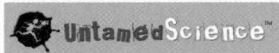 **Never Stop Exploring Your World.** Finding out about Ava's risk of sickle cell disease is only the beginning. Take a video field trip with the ecogeeks of Untamed Science to see where the mystery leads.

Multiple Choice

1. Which of the following disorders can be observed in a human karyotype?
   A colorblindness
   B trisomy 21
   C cystic fibrosis
   D sickle cell disease   CLG 3.3.4

2. Which of the following disorders is a direct result of nondisjunction?
   A sickle cell disease   C Huntington's disease
   B Turner's syndrome   D cystic fibrosis
                                            CLG 3.3.4

3. A woman is homozygous for A blood type. A man has AB blood type. What is the probability that the couple's child will have type B blood?
   A 0%   C 75%
   B 50%   D 100%   CLG 3.3.2

4. Cystic fibrosis is a genetic disorder caused by a
   A single base substitution in the gene for hemoglobin.
   B deletion of an amino acid from a chloride channel protein.
   C defective gene found on the X chromosome.
   D trisomy of chromosome 21.   CLG 3.3.4

5. The technique used to separate DNA strands of different lengths is
   A gel electrophoresis.
   B shotgun sequencing.
   C restriction enzyme digestion.
   D bioinformatics.   CLG 3.3.4

6. The study of whole genomes, including genes and their functions, is called
   A bioinformatics.
   B information science.
   C life science.
   D genomics.   CLG 3.3.1

7. DNA can be cut into shorter sequences by proteins known as
   A haplotypes.
   B polymerases.
   C restriction enzymes.
   D restriction fragments.   CLG 3.3.4

Questions 8–9

A student traced the recurrence of a widow's peak hairline in her family. Based on her interviews and observations, she drew the pedigree shown below.

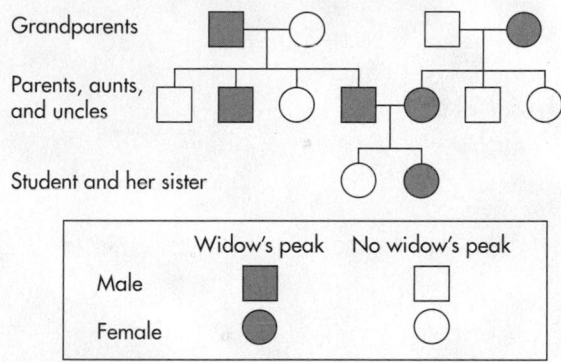

8. Which pattern of inheritance is consistent with the pedigree?
   A sex-linked inheritance
   B complete dominance
   C codominance
   D multiple alleles   SPI 1.5.5

9. What are the probable genotypes of the student's parents?
   A Mother—Ww; Father—ww
   B Mother—ww; Father—ww
   C Mother—WW; Father—Ww
   D Mother—Ww; Father—Ww   CLG 3.3.2

Open-Ended Response

10. Explain how the allele for sickle cell disease, which is a harmful allele when a person is homozygous, can be beneficial when a person is heterozygous.
                                       CLG 3.3.4

If You Have Trouble With . . .									
Question	1	2	3	4	5	6	7	8	9	10
See Lesson	14.1	14.2	14.1	14.2	14.3	14.3	14.3	14.1	14.1	14.2

Bacterial Mutations Mutations are changes in DNA that parents can pass to offspring. Mutations often happen on their own. However, breeders can also make mutations happen using radiation and chemicals. Many mutations hurt or kill the organism. Some do not. With luck and patience, breeders can grow mutants that have new, helpful characteristics. This way of making mutants has been very useful with bacteria. Because they are small, millions of bacteria can be treated with radiation or chemicals at the same time. Since so many bacteria are treated, the chances of making a useful mutant are good. This technique has let scientists develop hundreds of useful kinds of bacteria. For example, scientists are working to make bacteria that can clean up radioactive substances and metal pollution.

Polyploid Plants Drugs that keep chromosomes from separating during meiosis have been very useful in plant breeding. These drugs can make cells that have many times the normal number of chromosomes. Plants grown from these cells are called polyploid because they have many sets of chromosomes. Polyploidy is rare in animals. Plants, however, are much more likely than animals to survive with extra sets of chromosomes. Polyploidy can quickly make new kinds of plants that are larger and stronger than their diploid relatives. Scientists have made some important crop plants, including bananas and many varieties of citrus fruits, in this way.

Polyploid Crops			
Plant	Probable Ancestral Haploid Number	Chromosome Number	Ploidy Level
Domestic oat	7	42	6N
Peanut	10	40	4N
Sugar cane	10	80	8N
Banana	11	22, 33	2N, 3N
Cotton	13	52	4N

Ploidy Numbers Polyploid plants are often larger than other plants. So, farmers grow many polyploid varieties of crops on purpose. This table shows some polyploid crops.

Key Question How do people increase genetic variation?
Breeders can increase the genetic variation in a population by introducing mutations, which are the ultimate source of biological diversity.

CHECK Understanding

Apply Vocabulary
Use the highlighted words from the lesson to complete each sentence correctly.

1. _____ is the process of crossing two individuals that are not genetically alike.

Critical Thinking

2. **Explain** How can breeders introduce mutations?

3. **Review** What is the relationship between genetic variation and mutations?

4. **Apply Concepts** Suppose you are a geneticist trying to develop a sunflower with red petals and a short stem. As you compare the sunflowers you have on hand, what genetic variations would you look for?

5. **Write to Learn** Answer the following question in two or three sentences: How is selective breeding a kind of biotechnology?

15.2 Recombinant DNA

MD CLG **3.3.2** Inherited Traits, **3.3.3** Nucleic Acids and Protein Synthesis, **3.3.4** DNA Alteration, **3.4.2** Relatedness Among Organisms. SPI **1.7.2** Evaluate Ideas, **1.7.6** Science and Technology.

Copying DNA

Suppose you have an electronic game you want to change. If the game depends on a coded program in a computer microchip, you'd need to get the existing program out of the microchip. Then, you'd have to read the program and change it to your new program code. Finally, you would put the changed code back into the microchip. Believe it or not, this is very similar to genetic engineering.

How do you change an organism? Until recently, plant and animal breeders had to work with variations that already existed in nature. Now, scientists can transfer genes for particular traits from one organism to another. How does this gene transfer happen? Scientists first take DNA from cells. The DNA is then cut into pieces using restriction enzymes. Restriction enzymes cut DNA at specific base sequences. From a large DNA molecule, these enzymes may produce hundreds or even thousands of pieces. These pieces can then be separated by size.

If we were to cut DNA from the human genome, we might end up with millions of pieces of DNA. How do we find the DNA of a single gene among millions of pieces? It is kind of like finding a needle in a haystack. There is a huge pile of hay and one needle. Actually, you can find a needle in a haystack. You can toss the hay in front of a powerful magnet until something sticks. The hay won't stick, but a needle made of iron or steel will. Believe it or not, this method is similar to the way scientists find specific genes.

Finding Genes Douglas Prasher, a biologist, wanted to find a specific gene in a jellyfish. The gene codes for a molecule called green fluorescent protein, or GFP. This natural protein in the jellyfish absorbs energy from light and makes parts of the jellyfish glow.

To find the gene, Prasher studied the amino acid sequence of part of the GFP protein. Then, he figured out which mRNA sequence would make that protein. That mRNA sequence told him the DNA sequence of the gene. By making a piece of RNA that would match that DNA sequence, Prasher made the DNA "magnet" to find the GFP gene.

Fluorescent Gene The Pacific Ocean jellyfish gives off a bluish glow. A protein in the jellyfish absorbs the blue light and makes green fluorescence. This protein, called GFP, is now used in genetic engineering.

Key Questions

🔑 How do scientists copy the DNA of living organisms?

🔑 How is recombinant DNA used?

🔑 How can genes from one organism be inserted into another organism?

BUILD Understanding

Preview Visuals Before you read, preview the PCR Method figure. Write down any questions you have about the figure. As you read, find answers to your questions.

In Your Workbook Go to your workbook for help with previewing visuals.

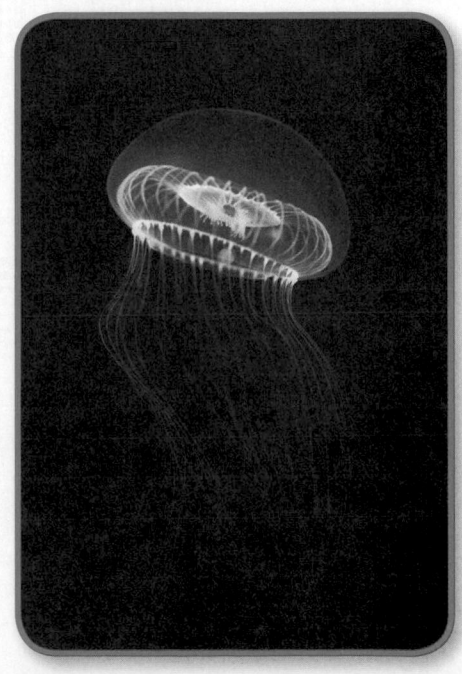

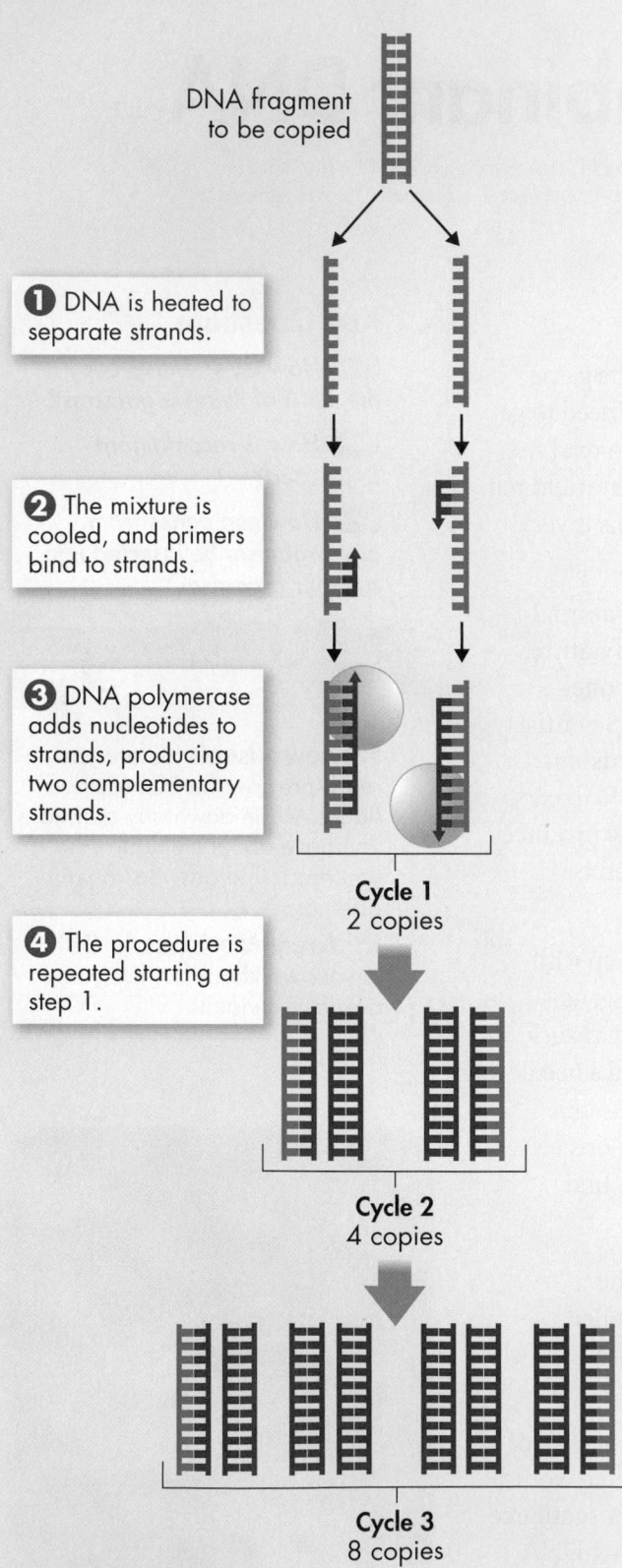

DNA fragment
to be copied

1 DNA is heated to separate strands.

2 The mixture is cooled, and primers bind to strands.

3 DNA polymerase adds nucleotides to strands, producing two complementary strands.

Cycle 1
2 copies

4 The procedure is repeated starting at step 1.

Cycle 2
4 copies

Cycle 3
8 copies

The PCR Method Polymerase chain reaction is used to make multiple copies of a gene. This method is useful even when only tiny amounts of DNA are available.

Polymerase Chain Reaction Once they find a gene, biologists often need to make many copies of it. To do this, biologists use a technique known as **polymerase chain reaction (PCR).** At one end of the original piece of DNA, a biologist adds a short piece of DNA that complements a portion of the sequence. At the other end, the biologist adds another short piece of complementary DNA. These short pieces are known as primers because they prepare, or prime, a place for DNA polymerase to start working.

The first step in using the PCR method to copy a gene is to use heat to separate the strands of a piece of DNA. Then, as the DNA cools, primers bind to the single strands. Next, DNA polymerase starts copying the DNA between the primers. These copies become templates used to make even more copies of the gene. In this way, just a few dozen cycles of copying the DNA can make billions of copies of a gene.

🔑 **Key Question** How do scientists copy the DNA of living organisms?
The first step in using the polymerase chain reaction method to copy a gene is to heat a piece of DNA, which separates its two strands. Then, as the DNA cools, primers bind to the single strands. Next, DNA polymerase starts copying the region between the primers. These copies can serve as templates to make more copies.

Changing DNA

Do you remember reading about Griffith's experiments on bacterial transformation? During transformation, a cell takes in DNA from outside the cell. Then that added DNA becomes part of the cell's own genome. Today, biologists know that Griffith's mixture of heat-killed bacteria had pieces of DNA in it. When he mixed those pieces of DNA with live bacteria, a few bacteria took up the DNA. Those bacteria cells changed. Griffith could do this only with DNA taken from other bacteria.

Combining DNA Fragments Today, scientists can make the DNA for any gene whose sequence they know. They can then put those genes into living cells. Changing genes for a practical purpose is called genetic engineering. How do scientists do this?

First, they build a DNA sequence with the gene or genes they want to put into a cell. Machines known as DNA synthesizers can make short pieces of DNA. These pieces made in a lab can then be joined to natural pieces of DNA using enzymes such as DNA ligase (LY gays). These enzymes join DNA molecules together. These same enzymes make it possible to take a gene from one organism and attach it to the DNA of another organism. DNA molecules made this way are called **recombinant DNA.** This technology works because any pair of complementary DNA sequences is likely to bond. They will bond even if each sequence comes from a different organism. Recombinant-DNA technology makes it possible to change the genetic makeup of living organisms. By working with DNA in this way, scientists can study how genes are put together and how they work.

Key Question How is recombinant DNA used?
Recombinant-DNA technology—joining together DNA from two or more sources—makes it possible to change the genetic composition of living organisms.

Plasmids and Genetic Markers Scientists working with recombinant DNA soon learned a few useful tricks. In addition to their own chromosomes, some bacteria have small circular DNA molecules called **plasmids.** One reason plasmids are useful is that they have their own replication "start" signals. That way, when the cell copies its own DNA, it copies the plasmid, too.

Plasmids are often used in recombinant DNA studies. Scientists insert a desired piece of DNA into a plasmid. Then they use transformation to add the recombinant plasmid to bacteria. The bacteria will then copy the new DNA along with the rest of the cell's genome.

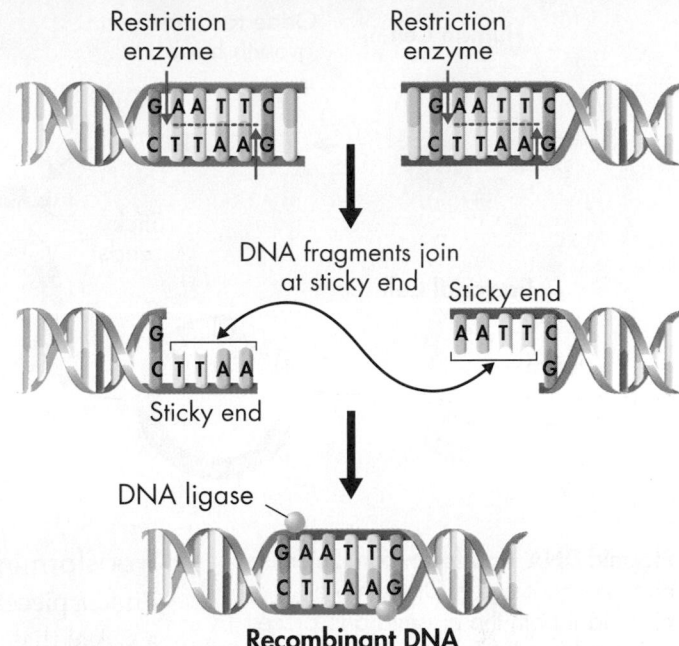

Joining DNA Pieces Together Recombinant DNA molecules are made up of DNA from different sources. Restriction enzymes cut DNA at specific sequences, making "sticky ends." Sticky ends are single-stranded bases of DNA at the end of a piece of DNA. DNA ligase allows two single-stranded pieces that are complementary to each other to stick together.

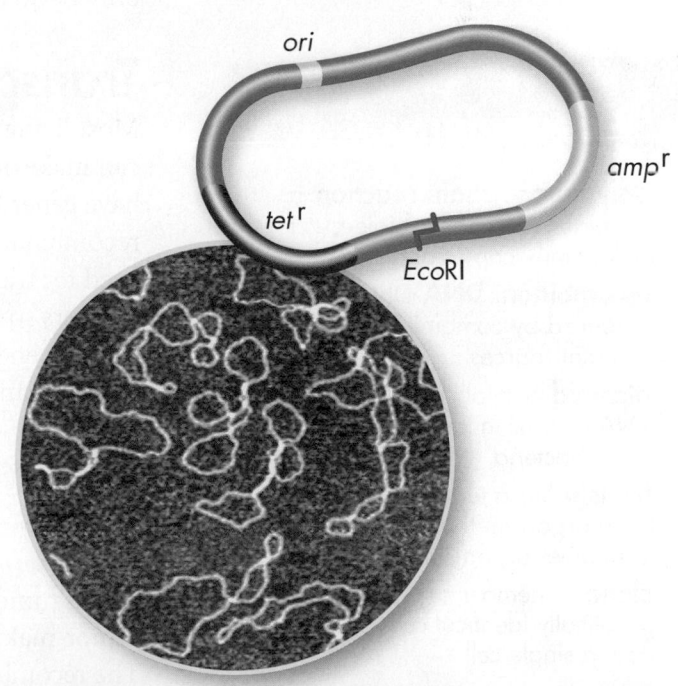

TEM 75,000×

A Plasmid Map Plasmids used for genetic engineering have a start signal, called the origin of replication (*ori*). They have a restriction enzyme cutting site, such as *Eco*R1. They also have genetic markers, like the antibiotic resistance genes *tet*^{r} and *amp*^{r} shown here.

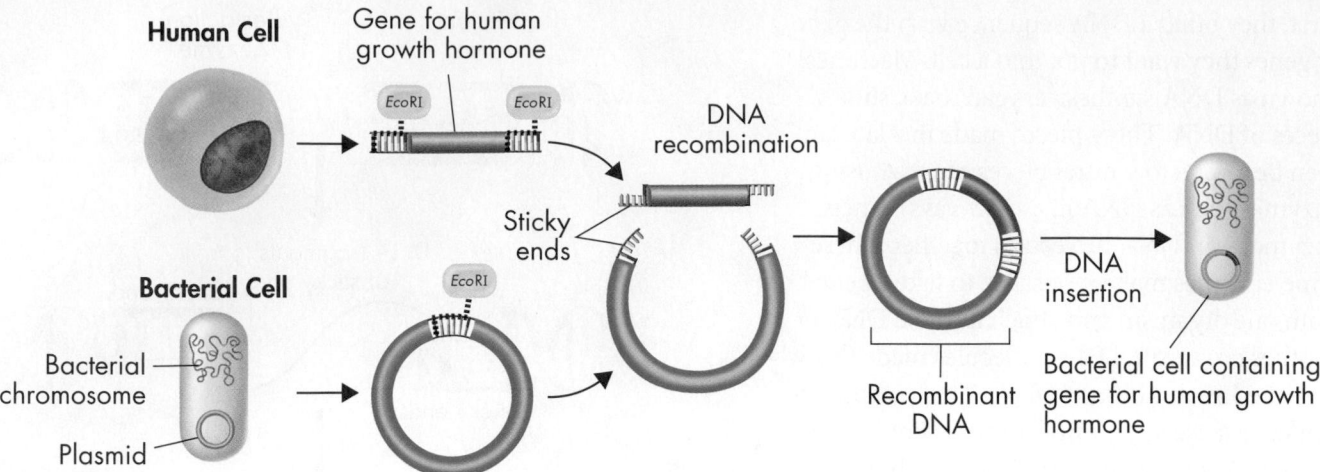

Human Cell — Gene for human growth hormone — *EcoRI* — *EcoRI*

DNA recombination

Sticky ends

Bacterial Cell

Bacterial chromosome

Plasmid — *EcoRI*

DNA insertion

Recombinant DNA

Bacterial cell containing gene for human growth hormone

Plasmid DNA Transformation Scientists can insert a piece of DNA into a plasmid if both the plasmid and piece of DNA have been cut by the same restriction enzyme. In this example, the gene for human growth hormone is added to a bacterial cell. First a human gene is inserted into bacterial DNA. Then the new combination of genes is put back into a bacterial cell. The cell then copies the recombinant DNA over and over again.

Transforming Bacteria How do scientists transform bacteria? First, a piece of DNA is joined to a plasmid. The plasmid DNA has a signal that starts replication. The plasmid also has one or more genetic markers. A genetic marker allows a scientist to identify which bacteria carry the plasmid. An example of a genetic marker is a gene for resistance to a specific antibiotic. This gene keeps the bacteria alive in the presence of that antibiotic. Researchers mix recombinant plasmids with bacteria. Only about one cell in a million may take up the plasmids, but that's more than enough. After transformation, the bacteria are treated with the antibiotic. Only those few cells that have been transformed survive, because only they carry the antibiotic-resistance gene.

Transgenic Organisms

Most living things share the same genetic code. So, scientists can make organisms that are transgenic. **Transgenic** organisms have genes from other organisms. They can be made by putting recombinant DNA into the genome of a host. The DNA molecules used for transformation of plant and animal cells have genetic markers so scientists can tell which cells have been transformed. Genetic engineers can make transgenic plants, animals, and microorganisms. By studying the traits of a genetically changed organism, scientists can learn about the function of the transferred gene. These studies helped us learn much more about genes.

Transgenic Plants Many plant cells can be transformed using *Agrobacterium*. This bacterium inserts a small DNA plasmid that makes tumors in a plant's cells. Scientists can turn off the plasmid's tumor-making gene and replace it with a piece of recombinant DNA. The recombinant plasmid can then be used to transform plant cells.

Transgenic Animals Scientists can transform animal cells, too. The egg cells of many animals are large enough that DNA can be injected into the nucleus. Once the DNA is in the nucleus, enzymes help insert the new DNA into the chromosomes of the host cell.

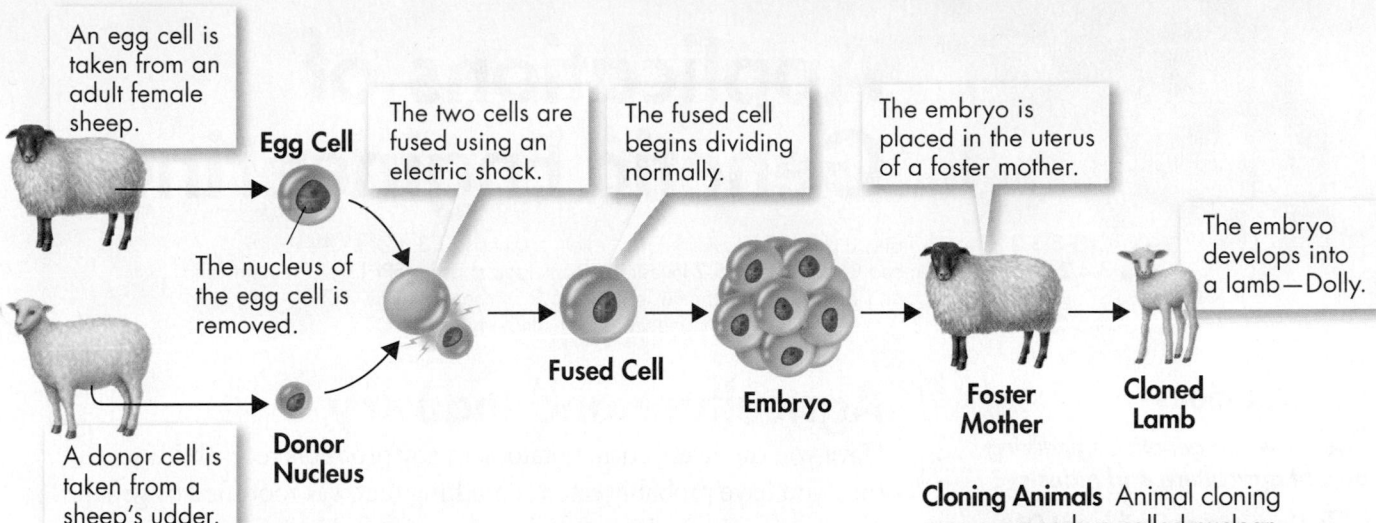

An egg cell is taken from an adult female sheep.

Egg Cell

The nucleus of the egg cell is removed.

A donor cell is taken from a sheep's udder.

Donor Nucleus

The two cells are fused using an electric shock.

The fused cell begins dividing normally.

Fused Cell

Embryo

The embryo is placed in the uterus of a foster mother.

Foster Mother

Cloned Lamb

The embryo develops into a lamb—Dolly.

Cloning Animals Animal cloning uses a procedure called nuclear transplantation. The process combines an egg cell with a donor nucleus to make an embryo.

DNA molecules can also be made with two ends that can recombine with specific sequences in the host chromosome. Once they do, the host gene found between those two sequences is replaced with a new gene. This kind of gene replacement has helped scientists figure out the roles of genes in many organisms.

Key Question How can genes from one organism be inserted into another organism? **Transgenic organisms can be produced by the insertion of recombinant DNA into the genome of a host organism.**

Cloning A **clone** is a member of a group of genetically identical cells made from a single cell. Cloning uses a single cell from an adult organism to grow a new individual. That individual, then, is genetically identical to the organism from which the cell was taken.

Cloned colonies of bacteria and other microorganisms are easy to grow. Multicellular organisms, such as animals, are harder to grow. In 1997, Scottish scientist Ian Wilmut announced that he had made a sheep, called Dolly, by cloning. The figure above shows the process.

CHECK Understanding

Apply Vocabulary
Use the highlighted words from the lesson to complete each sentence correctly.

1. _____ are small rings of DNA found in bacteria and yeast.

Critical Thinking

2. Infer Why would a scientist want to know the sequence of a DNA molecule?

3. Explain How do scientists use recombinant DNA?

4. Write to Learn Answer the first mystery clue.

MYSTERY CLUE

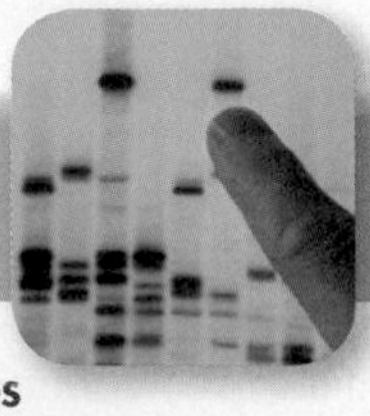

How could restriction enzymes be used to analyze the DNA evidence found on the suspect? (**Hint:** See page 357.)

15.3 Applications of Genetic Engineering

MD CLG 3.3.2 Inherited Traits, 3.3.3 Nucleic Acids and Protein Synthesis, 3.3.4 DNA Alteration, 3.4.2 Relatedness Among Organisms, 3.6.2 Investigate a Biological Issue. SPI 1.1.1 Problems and Solutions, 1.4.2 Analyze Data, 1.4.6 Determine Trends, 1.5.9 Synthesize Ideas, 1.7.1 Apply Skills and Concepts, 1.7.2 Evaluate Ideas, 1.7.6 Science and Technology.

Key Questions

🔑 How can genetic engineering benefit agriculture and industry?

🔑 How can recombinant-DNA technology improve human health?

🔑 How is DNA used to identify individuals?

BUILD Understanding

Main Idea and Details Chart
Taking notes is a way to organize the information you read. One way to take notes is to make a main idea and details chart while you read. Include details or evidence that supports each important idea.

In Your Workbook
Go to your workbook for more about using a main idea and details chart to organize information.

Agriculture and Industry

Have you eaten any corn, potatoes, or soy products recently? If so, then you have probably eaten something that was modified by genetic engineering. Everything we eat and much of what we wear come from living organisms. Researchers have used genetic engineering to try to improve the products we get from plants and animals.

GM Crops Since 1996, genetically modified (GM) plants have become an important part of our food supply. One type of modification has already been very useful to agriculture. It uses bacterial genes that make a protein called Bt toxin. This toxin is harmless to humans and most other animals. However, it kills the insects that eat it. So, plants with the Bt gene do not have to be sprayed with pesticides. They make more food per acre than unmodified plants, too. Scientists are also adding other traits to crops. Some are making plants that are resistant to viruses. Others are making crops that are slower to rot and spoil.

GM Animals Transgenic animals are also becoming more important to our food supply. For example, many dairy farms now raise cows that have been injected with hormones made by recombinant-DNA techniques. The hormones help the cows make more milk. Pigs can be genetically modified so they make leaner meat and cleaner wastes. Using growth-hormone genes, scientists have made transgenic salmon that grow much more quickly than wild salmon. This makes the fish easier to farm.

🔑 **Key Question** How can genetic engineering benefit agriculture and industry? **Ideally, genetic modification could lead to better, less expensive, and more nutritious food as well as less harmful manufacturing processes.**

Antibacterial Goat Milk
Scientists are working to add a gene for a natural antibiotic to the DNA of goats. Milk from these goats may help prevent infections in young children who drink it.

Genetically Modified Crops in the United States

U.S. farmers have started using many GM crops. Soybeans, cotton, and corn have been modified to tolerate herbicides and resist insect damage. The graph at the right shows the extent to which these crops were adopted between 1996 and 2007. The modified traits shown here include herbicide tolerance (HT) and insect resistance (Bt).

❶ **Analyze Data** Which two crops were most widely and rapidly adopted?

❷ **Draw Conclusions** Why do you think the levels of adoption fell at certain points over the period?

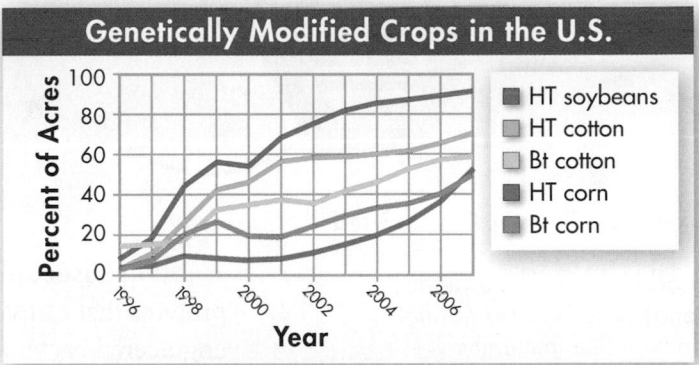

Genetically Modified Crops in the U.S.

- HT soybeans
- HT cotton
- Bt cotton
- HT corn
- Bt corn

❸ **Explain** Why can't the line showing the adoption of modified soybeans continue to grow past the 100 percent mark of the graph?

❹ **Infer** What would happen to herbicide-tolerant plants when farmers sprayed herbicide on the crops to kill weeds growing near them?

In Your Workbook Get more help for this activity in your workbook.

Health and Medicine

In a way, biotechnology has always been a part of medicine. Early physicians used substances from plants and animals to cure their patients. In the twentieth century, the use of vaccinations saved countless lives. Today, recombinant-DNA technology is the source of some of the most important and exciting advances in the prevention and treatment of disease.

Preventing Disease One interesting development in transgenic technology is golden rice. This rice contains increased amounts of provitamin A. A lack of provitamin A causes infant blindness and other problems. There is hope that provitamin A-rich golden rice will help prevent these problems. Some scientists are making transgenic plants and animals that make human antibodies to fight disease. Several laboratories have made transgenic sheep and pigs that make important human proteins in their milk. Many of these proteins can be taken from the milk and used as medicines in people.

Medical Research Transgenic animals are often used as test subjects in medical research. They can sometimes model human diseases caused by defective genes. Scientists can study a disease and then use the models to test new drugs that may help treat the disease.

Vitamin-Rich Rice Golden rice is a GM plant that has high levels of provitamin A. Two genes engineered into the rice genome help the grains produce and accumulate provitamin A.

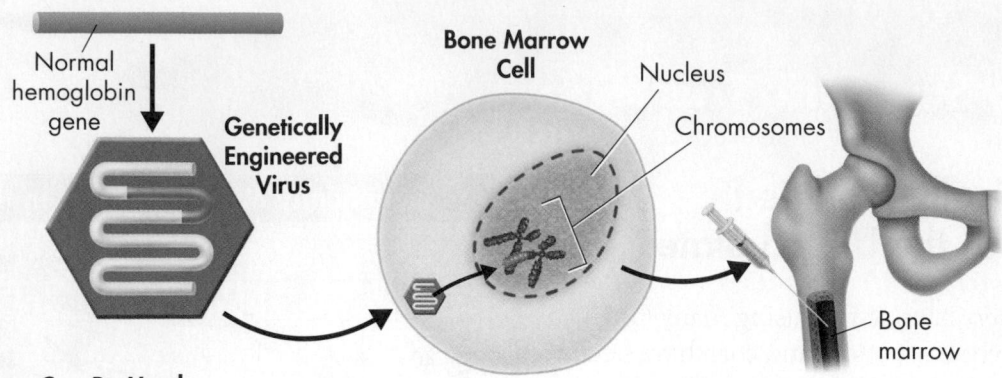

Normal hemoglobin gene

Genetically Engineered Virus

Bone Marrow Cell

Nucleus

Chromosomes

Bone marrow

How Gene Therapy Can Be Used
Gene therapy uses normal genes to add to or replace defective genes or to boost a normal function like immunity.

Treating Disease Recombinant DNA can be used to make important proteins that can save human lives. Products now made in genetically engineered bacteria include insulin to treat diabetes, blood-clotting factors for hemophiliacs, and human growth hormone.

Scientists are now trying to learn how to fix faulty genes in people. **Gene therapy** is the process of changing a gene to treat a disease or disorder. In gene therapy, a missing or faulty gene is replaced with a normal, working gene. This process lets the body make the protein or enzyme it needs. How are genes added to human cells? First, scientists make a virus that cannot reproduce and hurt people. Then they put DNA that has the working gene into their modified virus. Next, they infect the patient's cells with the virus carrying the gene. With luck, the virus will insert the healthy gene into the cells that need it and correct the problem.

Genetic Testing Suppose a couple wants to have children. Could they find out if they are carrying an allele for a genetic disorder? Genetic tests are now available for diagnosing hundreds of different disorders. For example, the CF allele has slightly different DNA sequences than the normal allele. So, genetic tests use a piece of DNA that is complementary to a defective allele to find that allele. Other genetic tests search for changes in cutting sites of restriction enzymes.

Examining Active Genes By studying which genes are active in cells, scientists can learn how cells work. Active genes make mRNA. So, scientists use a test to see what kinds of mRNA are in different kinds of cells. DNA microarray technology lets scientists learn the activity levels of thousands of genes at once. A **DNA microarray** is a glass slide to which spots of sequenced, single-stranded DNA have been tightly attached. Scientists then get mRNA from a cell they want to study. They make and label single-stranded DNA from the mRNA. Then, they add their labeled DNA to the wells of the array. They can tell which of the genes of the cell are active because the wells with those genes will also have labeled DNA.

🔑 **Key Question** How can recombinant-DNA technology improve human health?
Today recombinant-DNA technology is the source of some of the most important and exciting advances in the prevention and treatment of disease.

❶ Chromosomes contain many regions with repeated DNA sequences that do not code for proteins. These vary from person to person. Here, one sample has 12 repeats between genes A and B, while the second sample has 9 repeats between the same genes.

❷ Restriction enzymes are used to cut the DNA into fragments containing genes and repeats. Note that the repeat fragments from these two samples are of different lengths.

❸ The restriction fragments are separated according to size using gel electrophoresis. The DNA fragments containing repeats are then labeled using radioactive probes. This labeling produces a series of bands—the DNA fingerprint.

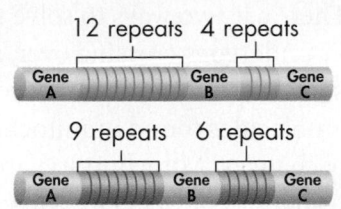

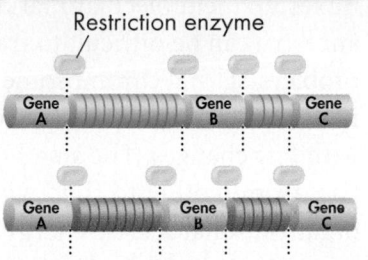

Restriction enzyme

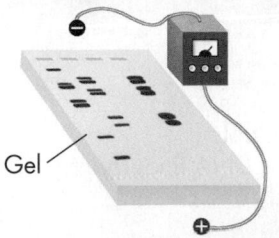

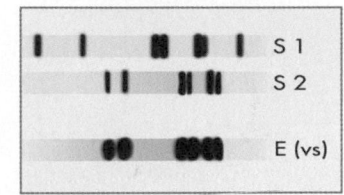

Gel

DNA fingerprint

Personal Identification

The human genome is so complex that no individual has DNA exactly like another individual. Identical twins are the only exception. Molecular biology has used this fact to make a powerful tool called DNA fingerprinting that is used to identify individuals. **DNA fingerprinting** analyzes pieces of DNA that may have little or no function in a cell. However, these pieces, called restriction fragments, vary widely from one person to another. How do scientists make a DNA fingerprint? DNA samples can be taken from blood or any other tissue. Then, restriction enzymes cut the DNA into pieces. Next, gel electrophoresis separates the pieces by size. A DNA probe finds the fragments that have highly variable regions. This is shown as a series of DNA bands on the gel. If enough enzymes and probes are used, the pattern of bands from one person is unlike anyone else's pattern of bands.

Forensic Science DNA fingerprinting has been used in the United States since the late 1980s. It has been of great help in **forensics**—the scientific study of crime scene evidence. DNA fingerprinting has helped solve crimes, convict criminals, and even overturn guilty verdicts. To date DNA evidence has saved more than 110 persons who were sentenced to death for crimes they didn't commit.

DNA forensics is used in wildlife conservation as well. African elephants are a highly vulnerable species. Poachers kill the animals illegally for their valuable tusks. To stop the ivory trade, African officials now use DNA fingerprinting to identify the herds from which the ivory has been taken.

Identifying Individuals
DNA fingerprinting is useful in solving crimes. The diagram shows how scientists match DNA evidence from a crime scene with two possible suspects.

Identifying Individuals
The pattern on this DNA fingerprint can belong to only one person.

Establishing Relationships How can we figure out who is the biological father of a child? DNA fingerprinting makes it easy to find alleles carried by the child that do not match those of the mother. Any such alleles must come from the child's biological father. The alleles will show up in the father's DNA fingerprint.

When genes are passed from parent to child, genetic recombination mixes up the molecular markers used for DNA fingerprinting. So, ancestry can be difficult to trace. There are two ways to solve this problem. The Y chromosome never undergoes crossing over, and only males carry it. So, Y chromosomes pass directly from father to son with few changes. The small DNA molecules found in mitochondria pass from mother to child with few changes. Mitochondria are organelles that release energy from sugar to power cells. They also carry DNA. It rarely changes. The DNA in mitochondria is passed from mother to child in the cytoplasm of the egg cell. These genetic markers can be used to trace ancestry over many generations.

Because mitochondrial DNA (mtDNA) is passed directly from mother to child, your mtDNA is the same as your mother's mtDNA, which is the same as her mother's mtDNA. This means that if two people have an exact match in their mtDNA, then there is a very good chance that they share a common maternal ancestor. Y-chromosome analysis has been used in the same way and has helped researchers settle longstanding historical questions.

Key Question How is DNA used to identify individuals?
DNA fingerprinting analyzes sections of DNA that may have little or no function but that vary widely from one individual to another.

CHECK Understanding

Apply Vocabulary
Use the highlighted words from the lesson to complete each sentence correctly.

1. An absent or faulty gene is replaced by a normal working gene using _____.

2. The study of blood or other crime scene evidence is _____.

Critical Thinking

3. Apply Concepts What is golden rice, and how has it helped people?

4. Explain What are the steps in DNA fingerprinting?

5. Write to Learn Write a paragraph that answers the chapter mystery clue.

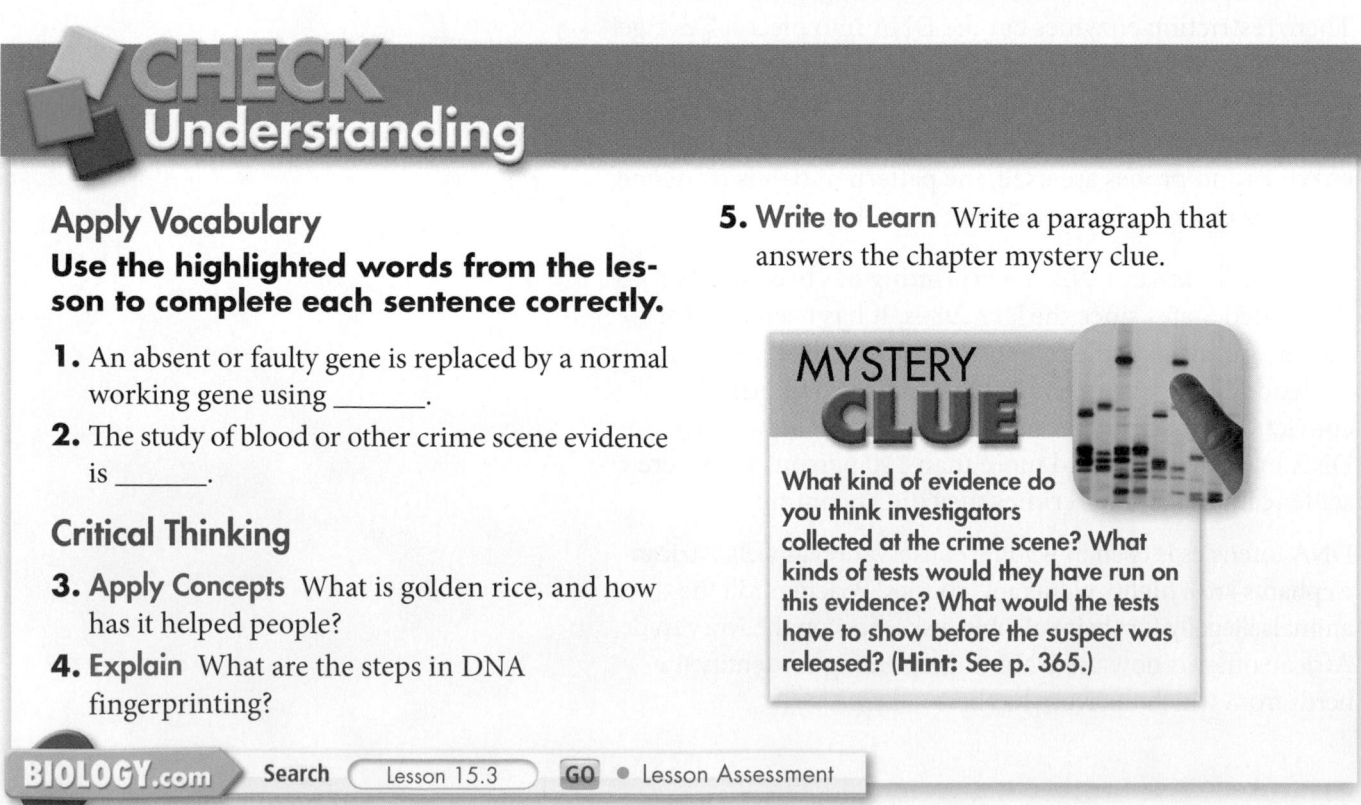

MYSTERY CLUE

What kind of evidence do you think investigators collected at the crime scene? What kinds of tests would they have run on this evidence? What would the tests have to show before the suspect was released? (Hint: See p. 365.)

BIOLOGY.com ⟩ Search (Lesson 15.3) **GO** • Lesson Assessment

15.4 Ethics and Impacts of Biotechnology

MD CLG **3.3.4** DNA Alteration, **3.4.2** Relatedness Among Organisms, **3.6.1** Analyze Consequences, **3.6.2** Investigate a Biological Issue. SPI **1.1.1** Problems and Solutions, **1.5.9** Synthesize Ideas, **1.7.1** Apply Skills and Concepts, **1.7.2** Evaluate Ideas, **1.7.6** Science and Technology.

Profits and Privacy

Who owns your genes? Could someone else use the information in your genes? When biotechnology and drug companies develop GM plants and animals, they protect their discoveries and innovations with patents. A patent is a legal tool that gives an individual or company the exclusive right to profit from its innovations for a number of years.

Patenting Life When you think about patents, you might think about an inventor protecting a new machine. However, molecules and DNA sequences can be patented, too. One fifth of the known genes in the human genome have been patented. Even laboratory techniques like PCR have been patented.

The ability to patent is meant to encourage new discovery. After all, patent holders have a good chance of making money. Sometimes, though, patent holders demand high fees that block other scientists from doing their research.

Now think about the information held in your own genome. Do you have exclusive rights to your DNA? Should you, like patent holders, be able to keep your genetic information confidential? When it comes to your own DNA, how much privacy are you entitled to?

🔑 **Key Question** What privacy issues does biotechnology raise? **Do you have exclusive rights to your DNA? Should you, like patent holders, be able to keep your genetic information confidential?**

Genetic Ownership People who serve in the U.S. armed forces give a DNA sample when they begin serving. Those DNA samples are used, if needed, to identify the remains of people who die in the line of duty. But what if the government wants to use a person's DNA sample for other tests? What if health-insurance companies want to refuse coverage to people who have a gene that makes them more likely to get an illness? The U.S. Congress debated these issues. The Genetic Information Nondiscrimination Act was signed into law in 2008. This act protects Americans against discrimination based on their genetic information.

Unknown Identities The Tomb of the Unknowns in Arlington National Cemetery holds the remains of unknown American soldiers. DNA testing now helps identify the remains of all U.S. military personnel who die in the line of duty.

Key Questions

🔑 *What privacy issues does biotechnology raise?*

🔑 *Are GM foods safe?*

🔑 *Should genetic modifications to humans and other organisms be closely regulated?*

BUILD Understanding

Two-Column Table As you read the lesson, think about the ethical issues involved in genetic engineering. Write the positives in a column titled Pros. Write the negatives in a column titled Cons.

In Your Workbook Go to your workbook to learn more about using a two-column table.

Safety of Transgenics

GM crops are controversial. People argue about the safety of using them. Are the foods from GM crops the same as those prepared from traditionally bred crops?

Pros of GM Foods The companies making seeds for GM crops would say that GM plants are better and safer than other crops. Farmers choose them because they have higher yields. They use less land and energy and help lower costs. They are insect resistant. So, they need fewer chemicals and help reduce pollution. Careful studies have not supported concerns about their safety. These studies seem to show that GM foods are safe to eat.

Cons of GM Foods Critics point out that no studies have tested whether long-term use of these foods might cause danger. Some worry that the insect resistance in GM plants may also hurt helpful insects. Herbicide-resistant plants allow farmers to use more weed killers, increasing pollution. Company patents on costly GM seeds may put small or poor farmers out of business.

In the United States, federal regulations treat GM foods and non-GM foods the same. So, GM foods do not have to face extra safety tests before entering the U.S. market. No additional labeling is required to identify a product as genetically modified unless its ingredients are very different from its non-GM counterpart. Some states, however, have introduced state legislation to require the labeling of GM foods. This would give consumers a choice.

Key Question Are GM foods safe? **Careful studies of such foods have provided no scientific support for concerns about their safety, and it does seem that foods made from GM plants are safe to eat. Even if GM food itself presents no hazards, there are many serious concerns about the unintended consequences that a shift to GM farming and ranching may have on agriculture.**

Labeling Foods
Some people want GM foods labeled so consumers can decide whether or not to use GM products.

Ethics of the New Biology

You've seen how easy it is to move genes from one organism to another. For example, the GFP gene can be taken from a jellyfish and spliced onto genes coding for important cellular proteins. This ability has led to significant new discoveries about how cells function.

The same GFP technology was used to make fluorescent zebra fish. Experiments moving the GFP gene have taught scientists much about cells and proteins. But, just because we have the technology to change an organism's characteristics, should we?

It would be great if genetic engineering led to cures for genetic diseases. However, should biologists try to make people taller or change their sex or looks? What will happen to the human species when we can design our bodies or those of our children? What will happen if biologists want to clone human beings? In a democratic nation, everyone is responsible for making sure that the tools science has given us are used wisely. This means that you need to be ready to help decide what should and should not be done with the human genome.

Key Question Should genetic modifications to humans and other organisms be closely regulated?
The issue: Just because we have the technology to modify an organism's characteristics, are we justified in doing so?

Gaining More Understanding
These fluorescent zebra fish were originally bred to help scientists find environmental pollutants. Today, the techniques used to produce such fish are widely used in research. Fluorescent labels are helping researchers to understand cancer and other diseases.

CHECK Understanding

Critical Thinking

1. **Apply Concepts** How could biotechnology affect your privacy?
2. **Explain** What are genetically modified foods?
3. **Form an Opinion** Should a vegetarian be concerned about eating a GM plant that contains DNA from a pig gene? Support your answer with details from the text.
4. **Explain** What are the main concerns about genetic engineering discussed in this chapter?

5. **Write to Learn** Answer the question in the mystery clue below.

MYSTERY CLUE

What privacy considerations, if any, should investigators have taken into account when obtaining the DNA evidence? (**Hint:** See p. 367.)

BIOLOGY.com ⟩ Search ⟨ Lesson 15.4 ⟩ GO • Lesson Assessment

MD SPI **1.3.1** Use Equipment, **1.3.3** Safe Handling of Materials, **1.4.2** Analyze Data, **1.5.2** Communicate Information, **1.5.9** Synthesize Ideas.

Pre-Lab: Using DNA to Solve Crimes

Problem How can DNA samples be used to connect a suspect to a crime scene?

Materials gel block, electrophoresis chamber, buffer solution, 250-mL beaker, metric ruler, DNA samples, micropipettes, 9-volt batteries, electric cords, staining tray, DNA stain, 100-mL graduated cylinder, clock or timer

Lab Manual Chapter 15 Lab

Skills Focus Measure, Compare and Contrast, Draw Conclusions

Connect to the Big idea Scientists who worked on the Human Genome Project had to develop methods for sequencing and identifying genes. Those methods have since been used for many other applications. For example, genetically altered bacteria are used to produce large amounts of life-saving drugs. Another example is the use of DNA evidence to solve crimes. In this lab, you will prepare and compare DNA "fingerprints," or profiles.

Background Questions

a. Review What characteristic of the human genome makes DNA a powerful tool for solving crimes?

b. Review What do the segments of DNA that are used to make DNA profiles have in common?

c. Apply Concepts When forensic scientists want to determine whether two DNA samples come from the same person, they analyze more than one section of DNA. Why would the results be less reliable if the scientists compared only one section of DNA?

Pre-Lab Questions

Preview the procedure in the lab manual.

1. Control Variables Why must you use a new pipette to load each DNA sample?

2. Relate Cause and Effect Why will the DNA samples separate into bands as they move through the gel?

3. Infer Why is purple tracking dye added to the DNA samples?

BIOLOGY.com   Search   (Chapter 15)   **GO**

Visit Chapter 15 online to test yourself on chapter content and to find activities to help you learn.

Untamed Science Video Pigeon breeding helps the Untamed Science crew unravel the mysteries of genetic engineering.

Art in Motion View a short animation that brings bacterial transformation to life.

Art Review Review your understanding of DNA fingerprinting with this drag-and-drop activity.

InterActive Art Build your understanding of key chapter concepts with these animations.

15.1 Selective Breeding

- Humans use selective breeding, which takes advantage of naturally occurring genetic variation, to pass wanted traits on to the next generation of organisms.

- Breeders can increase the genetic variation in a population by introducing mutations, which are the ultimate source of biological diversity.

selective breeding (p. 354) inbreeding (p. 355)
hybridization (p. 355) biotechnology (p. 355)

15.2 Recombinant DNA

- The first step in using the polymerase chain reaction method to copy a gene is to heat a piece of DNA, which separates its two strands. Then, as the DNA cools, primers bind to the single strands. Next, DNA polymerase starts copying the region between the primers. These copies can serve as templates to make still more copies.

- Recombinant-DNA technology is the joining together of DNA from two or more sources. This technology makes it possible to change the genetic makeup of living organisms.

- Transgenic organisms can be produced by the insertion of recombinant DNA into the genome of a host organism.

polymerase chain reaction (p. 358)
recombinant DNA (p. 359)
plasmid (p. 359)
transgenic (p. 360)
clone (p. 361)

15.3 Applications of Genetic Engineering

- Ideally, genetic modification could lead to better, less expensive, and more nutritious food as well as to less harmful manufacturing processes.

- Recombinant-DNA technology is advancing the prevention and treatment of disease.

- DNA fingerprinting analyzes sections of DNA that may have little or no function within the cell. However, these sections vary widely from one individual to another.

gene therapy (p. 364)
DNA microarray (p. 364)
DNA fingerprinting (p. 365)
forensics (p. 365)

15.4 Ethics and Impacts of Biotechnology

- Should you, like patent holders, be able to keep your genetic information confidential?

- Careful studies of GM foods have provided no scientific support for concerns about their safety.

- There are many concerns about unintended consequences that a shift to GM farming and ranching may have on agriculture.

- Just because we have the technology to modify an organism's characteristics, are we justified in doing so?

Assess the Big idea > Science as a Way of Knowing

Write an answer to the question below.

Q: How and why do scientists manipulate DNA in living cells?

Constructed Response

Write an answer to each of the questions below. The answer to each question should be one or two paragraphs long. To help you begin, read the **Hints** below each of the questions.

1. **How do breeders produce genetic variations that are not found in nature?**

   Hint Some treatments can cause mutations.

   Hint Some treatments can change the numbers of chromosomes in an organism.

2. **Describe what happens during a polymerase chain reaction.**

   Hint A polymerase chain reaction makes many copies of a gene.

   Hint Each new copy made can serve as a template to make more genes.

3. **Your friend suggests that genetic engineering makes it possible for biologists to produce an organism with any combination of characteristics—an animal with the body of a frog and the wings of a bat, for example. Do you think this is a reasonable statement? Explain your answer.**

   Hint All organisms share the same genetic code.

   Hint Organisms have millions of genes.

Foundations for Learning Wrap-Up

Use the cubes you made as you read the chapter. The cubes will help you review what you have learned about genetic engineering.

Activity 1 Working with a partner, take turns rolling one of the cubes. Read the word on top of the cube. Say the definition of the word. Your partner will tell you if you are correct. If you don't know the definition, you lose your turn. Continue until you have defined all the words at least once. The first player to get all the definitions correct is the winner.

Activity 2 Working with a partner, use both cubes. Take turns rolling both cubes. Tell how the words from the tops of the cubes are related. For example, for the cubes below, you could say, "Scientists use *plasmids* to make *transgenic* plants."

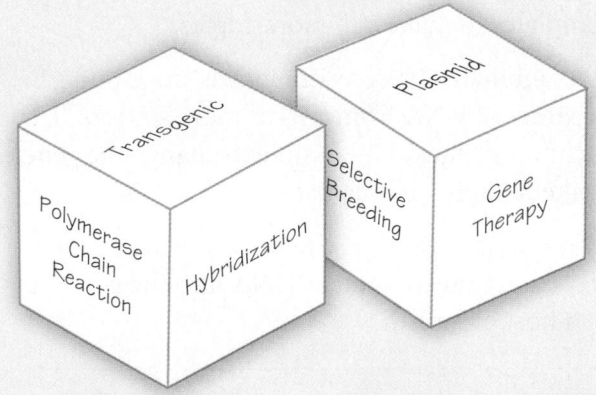

15.1 Selective Breeding

Understand Key Concepts

1. Crossing individuals with different traits to bring together their best characteristics is called
   a. domestication.
   b. inbreeding.
   c. hybridization.
   d. polyploidy.

2. Crossing individuals with similar characteristics so that those characteristics will appear in their offspring is called
   a. inbreeding.
   b. hybridization.
   c. recombination.
   d. polyploidy.

3. Taking advantage of naturally occurring variations in organisms to pass wanted traits on to future generations is called
   a. selective breeding.
   b. forensics.
   c. gene therapy.
   d. mutation.

4. What is polyploidy? When is this condition useful?

Think Critically

5. **Compare and Contrast** Hybridization and inbreeding are important methods used in selective breeding. How are the methods similar? How are they different?

Test-Taking Tip

Use Graphic Organizers Sometimes a question, such as question 5, asks you to compare and contrast two processes. Before you begin writing your answer, organize your ideas with a Venn diagram. Label one circle Hybridization. Label the other Inbreeding. Where the circles overlap, write Both.

15.2 Recombinant DNA

Understand Key Concepts

6. Organisms that have genes from other organisms are called
   a. transgenic.   c. donors.
   b. mutagenic.   d. clones.

7. A member of a population of genetically identical cells produced from a single cell is a
   a. clone.   c. mutant.
   b. plasmid.   d. sequence.

8. How does a transgenic plant differ from a hybrid plant?

Think Critically

9. **Apply Concepts** Describe one or more advantages of producing insulin and other proteins through genetic engineering.

15.3 Applications of Genetic Engineering

Understand Key Concepts

10. Which of the following characteristics is often genetically engineered into crop plants?
    a. improved flavor
    b. resistance to herbicides
    c. different colors
    d. thicker stems

Think Critically

11. **Infer** Suppose a human's bone marrow was removed, changed genetically, and returned to his body. Would the change be passed on to the patient's children? Explain your answer.

15.4 Ethics and Impacts of Biotechnology

Understand Key Concepts

12. The right to profit from a new genetic technology is protected by

   a. getting a copyright for the method.

   b. discovering a new gene.

   c. obtaining a patent.

   d. publishing its description in a journal.

13. Which of the following is most likely to be used in a court case to determine who the father of a particular child is?

   a. microarray analysis **c.** gene therapy

   b. DNA fingerprinting **d.** genetic engineering

Think Critically

14. Explain What is one argument used by critics of genetically modified foods?

Connecting Concepts

Use Science Graphics

Use the table below to answer question 15.

DNA Restriction Enzymes	
Enzyme	**Recognition Sequence**
*Bgl*III	A↓G A T C T T C T A G↑A
*Eco*RI	G↓A A T T C C T T A A↑G
*Hind*III	A↓A G C T T T T C G A↑A

15. Apply Concepts Copy the following DNA sequence and write its complementary strand ATGAGATCTACGGAATTCTCAAGCTTCGA ATCG. Where will each restriction enzyme in the table cut the DNA strand?

solve the CHAPTER MYSTERY

A CASE OF MISTAKEN IDENTITY

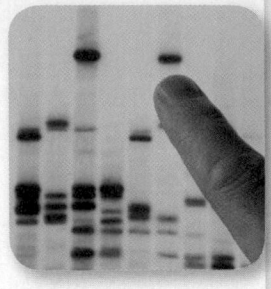

The first suspect was lucky: Twenty years earlier, it would have been an open-and-shut case. But by 1998, DNA fingerprinting was widely available. After the police took the suspect into custody, forensic scientists tested the DNA in the bloodstains on his shirt. Within a few hours, they knew they had the wrong suspect. Before long, the police caught the real attacker, who was then tried in a court and convicted of the crime.

1. Infer How did the investigators determine that the person they took into custody was not a suspect?

2. Apply Concepts Red blood cells don't have a nucleus; white blood cells do. Did the DNA evidence from the bloodstains come from the red blood cells, the white blood cells, or both? Explain your answer.

3. Predict What if the initial suspect was related to the victim? Would that have changed the result? Why or why not?

4. Predict What if this crime happened before DNA fingerprinting was discovered? What do you think the police would have done after they took in the first suspect?

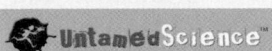 **Never Stop Exploring Your World.** Finding the solution to the case of mistaken identity is only the beginning. Take a video field trip with the ecogeeks of Untamed Science to see where the mystery leads.

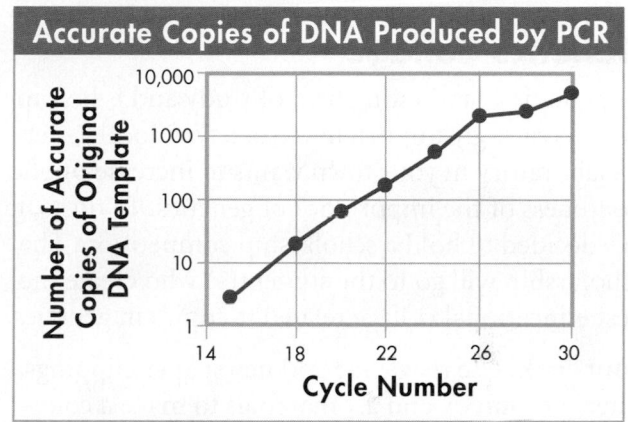
Multiple Choice

1. Polyploidy may produce new types of organisms that are larger and stronger than their diploid relatives in
   A animals.   C bacteria.
   B plants.   D fungi.   CLG 3.3.4

2. Which of the following characteristics does NOT apply to a plasmid?
   A made of DNA   C has circular loops
   B found in bacterial cells   D found in animal cells
   CLG 3.3.4

3. To separate DNA fragments from one another, scientists use
   A polymerase chain reaction.
   B DNA microarrays.
   C gel electrophoresis.
   D restriction enzymes.   CLG 3.3.4

4. Recombinant DNA technology involves
   A cutting DNA into nucleotides.
   B selective breeding.
   C joining DNA from two or more sources.
   D producing a cloned organism.   CLG 3.3.4

5. The activity of thousands of genes at one time can be followed using
   A polymerase chain reaction.
   B plasmid transformation.
   C restriction enzymes.
   D DNA microarrays.   CLG 3.3.4

6. Genetically engineered crop plants can benefit farmers by
   A increasing crop yield.
   B introducing chemicals into the environment.
   C increasing an animal's resistance to antibiotics.
   D changing the genomes of other crop plants.
   CLG 3.3.4

7. Genetic markers allow scientists to
   A clone animals.
   B separate strands of DNA.
   C make antibiotics.
   D identify transformed cells.   CLG 3.3.4

Questions 8–9

The graph below shows the number of accurate copies of DNA produced by polymerase chain reaction.

Accurate Copies of DNA Produced by PCR

8. What can you conclude about cycles 18 through 26?
   A PCR produced accurate copies of template DNA at an exponential rate.
   B The amount of DNA produced by PCR doubled with each cycle.
   C The DNA copies produced by PCR were not accurate copies of the original DNA template.
   D The rate at which PCR produced accurate copies of template DNA fell in later cycles.
   SPI 1.4.2

9. Based on the graph, which of the following might have happened between cycles 26 and 28?
   A PCR stopped producing accurate copies of the template.
   B The rate of reaction slowed.
   C All of the template DNA was used up.
   D A mutation occurred.   SPI 1.4.2

Open-Ended Response

10. Why are bacteria able to make human proteins when a human gene is inserted in them with a plasmid?   CLG 3.3.4

If You Have Trouble With . . .

Question	1	2	3	4	5	6	7	8	9	10
See Lesson	15.1	15.2	15.2	15.2	15.3	15.4	15.2	15.2	15.2	15.3

Unit Project

Genetics Collage

Genetics is a fascinating field of study and is becoming increasingly important to society. A local genetics laboratory in your town wants to increase public awareness of the importance of genetics. To do so, it has decided to hold a scholarship competition. The scholarship will go to the student(s) who create the best educational collage related to topics in genetics.

Your Task Use magazine and newspaper clippings, Internet sources, and art materials to make a colorful collage. The images should relate to three central questions.

1) Why is DNA important to a cell?
2) Why is DNA important to you, as a human being?
3) Why is DNA important to society as a whole?

Be sure to
- communicate answers to the above questions in the images, words, and phrases you choose.
- carefully design your collage so that it is clear and organized.

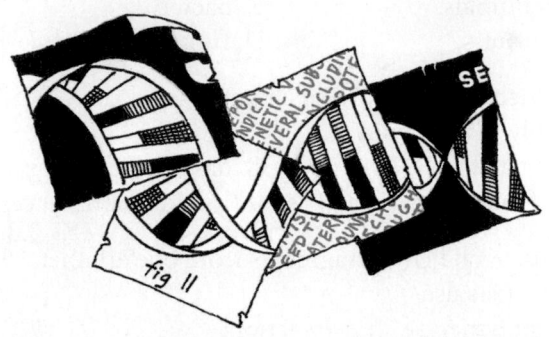

fig II

Reflection Questions

1. Score your collage using the rubric below. What score did you give yourself?
2. What did you do well in this project?
3. What about your collage needs improvement?
4. What could a person who didn't know much about DNA learn from your collage?

Assessment Rubric

Score	Scientific Content	Quality of Collage
4	Collage includes many important and thoughtful images related to the three central questions. Student demonstrates a deep understanding of genetics topics.	The collage is clear, organized, and creative.
3	Collage includes important images related to the three central questions. Student demonstrates an adequate understanding of genetics topics.	The collage is well designed and organized.
2	Collage is missing some important ideas and/or includes several insignificant ideas. Student demonstrates a limited level of understanding of genetics topics.	The collage could be better designed and organized.
1	Collage is missing several important ideas. Student demonstrates significant misunderstandings.	The collage is unclear and lacks a solid design.

Evolution

Chapters

INTRODUCE the
Big ideas

- **Evolution**
- **Unity and Diversity of Life**

"Darwin's theory of evolution by natural selection is often called 'the most important scientific idea that anyone has ever had.' Evolutionary theory provides the best scientific explanation for the unity and diversity of life. It unites all living things in a single tree of life and reminds us that humans are part of nature. As researchers explore evolutionary mysteries, they continue to marvel at Darwin's genius and his grand vision of the natural world."

377

16 Darwin's Theory of Evolution

Big idea **Evolution**
Q: What is natural selection?

CHAPTER
MYSTERY

SUCH DIFFERENT HONEYCREEPERS

Imagine walking in the misty rain forest on an island in Hawaii. This is home for birds found nowhere else on Earth. A red and black bird flies to a nearby branch. The bird is an 'i'iwi. It uses its long, curved beak to get the nectar from the flowers of a tree.

The 'i'iwi is one of a number of species of Hawaiian honeycreepers. The different species eat different foods. Some eat nectar. Others eat insects, seeds, or fruit. Many honeycreepers eat only the seeds or nectar of plants that are unique to Hawaii.

How did all these birds get to Hawaii? How did they come to eat such specialized foods?

Read for Mystery Clues As you read this chapter, look for clues that help explain the number and diversity of Hawaiian honeycreepers. Then, solve the mystery at the end of the chapter.

FOUNDATIONS for Learning

Cut a stiff piece of paper so it is square. Fold the square diagonally to make a triangle. Fold that triangle again to make a smaller triangle. Open the paper. You will see an X. Color in one quarter; you will not write on this part of the paper. Three triangular sections now remain. Label each with one of these topics: Struggle for Existence, Variation and Adaptation, and Survival of the Fittest. As you read, take notes about each of these topics on the back of the correct triangle. At the end of the chapter are two activities that will use your notes to help answer the question: What is natural selection?

16.1 Darwin's Voyage of Discovery

MD CLG **3.4.1** Evolutionary Change, **3.4.2** Relatedness Among Organisms, **3.5.1** Factors Influencing Ecosystems. SPI **1.5.1** Summarize Data, **1.5.2** Communicate Information.

Key Questions

🔑 **What was Charles Darwin's contribution to science?**

🔑 **What three patterns of biodiversity did Darwin note?**

BUILD Understanding

Preview Visuals Before you read, look at the map of Darwin's trip on the next page. Describe the path that the ship took around the world.

In Your Workbook Go to your workbook to learn about previewing visuals.

BUILD Vocabulary

evolution
change over time; the process by which modern organisms have descended from ancient organisms

🔖 **RELATED WORD FORMS**

The noun *evolution* is related to the verb *evolve*, which means "to change over time."

Darwin's Big Journey

If you had met young Charles Darwin, you would not have guessed that he would grow up to be a famous scientist. As a boy, Darwin was not a top student. He would rather watch birds or read for pleasure than study. Yet he would go on to develop one of the most important scientific theories of all time.

Darwin's Time Charles Darwin was a naturalist and scientist from England. He grew up in the early 1800s, a time when the scientific view of the world was changing. Geologists were learning that the world was very, very old. They also suggested that the world we see today is constantly changing. Biologists were saying that life on Earth had also changed. The process of change over time is called **evolution.**

Sailing Around the World While still a young man, Darwin was invited to sail around the world on a ship called the *Beagle.* The captain and his crew would be mapping the coast of South America during the five-year journey. Darwin planned to collect plant and animal specimens along the way. At the time, no one knew how important the trip would be. Darwin's observations during the journey would lead to his theory of evolution.

Darwin's Work Darwin's theory explains how modern organisms evolved over millions of years. It also tells how modern organisms came from shared, or *common*, ancestors. But Darwin's work does more than explain life's history. Evolution reminds us that life is always changing. An understanding of evolution helps us to explain and find ways to overcome many challenges we face today. These challenges include drug-resistant bacteria and deadly new viruses.

🔑 **Key Question** What was Charles Darwin's contribution to science?
Darwin developed a theory of evolution that explains how modern organisms evolved over long periods of time from common ancestors.

Observations Aboard the *Beagle*

The time Darwin spent studying birds and collecting bugs prepared him for his long trip around the world. On his trip, he studied and took notes about the amazing new plants and animals he saw. Darwin was surprised by the many different kinds of organisms he found. In just one day, he collected 68 species of beetles in the South American forest.

Darwin wanted to do more than just collect bugs and birds. He wanted to make sense of what he found. As he traveled, he noticed three patterns of biological diversity:

❶ Species vary around the world.

❷ Species vary locally.

❸ Species vary over time.

Species Vary Around the World Darwin visited habitats in South America, Australia, and Africa. In the grasslands of South America, he found large, flightless birds called rheas. Rheas look and act a lot like ostriches. Yet ostriches live only in Africa. Rheas live only in South America. In Australia's grasslands, Darwin found another flightless bird called the emu. He wondered why there were no large, flightless birds living in the grasslands of the northern parts of the world.

Darwin also noticed habitats in Australia that were ideal for rabbits. Why did no rabbits live there? And why were there no kangaroos in England? What did these patterns of distribution mean?

Key Question What did Darwin notice about biodiversity around the world? **Places around the world that had similar habitats often had different animals that were ecologically similar.**

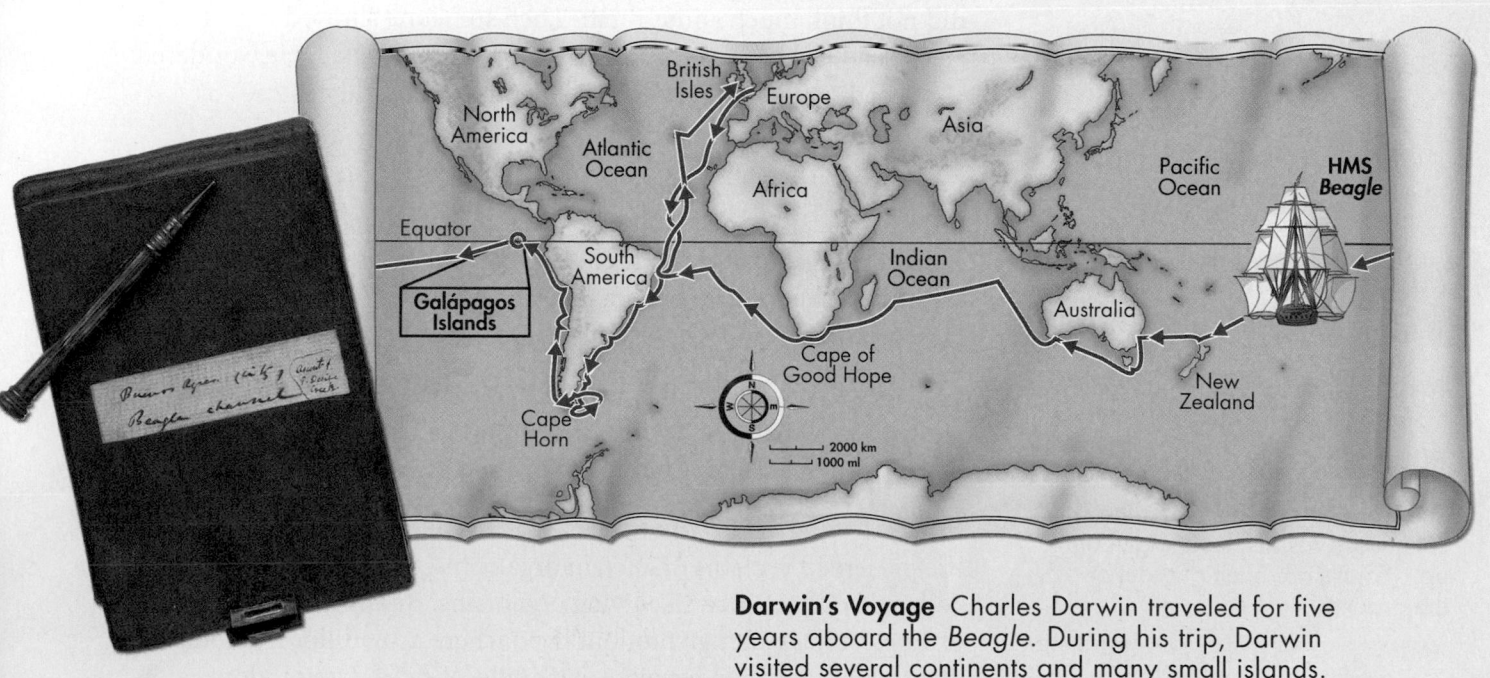

Darwin's Voyage Charles Darwin traveled for five years aboard the *Beagle*. During his trip, Darwin visited several continents and many small islands.

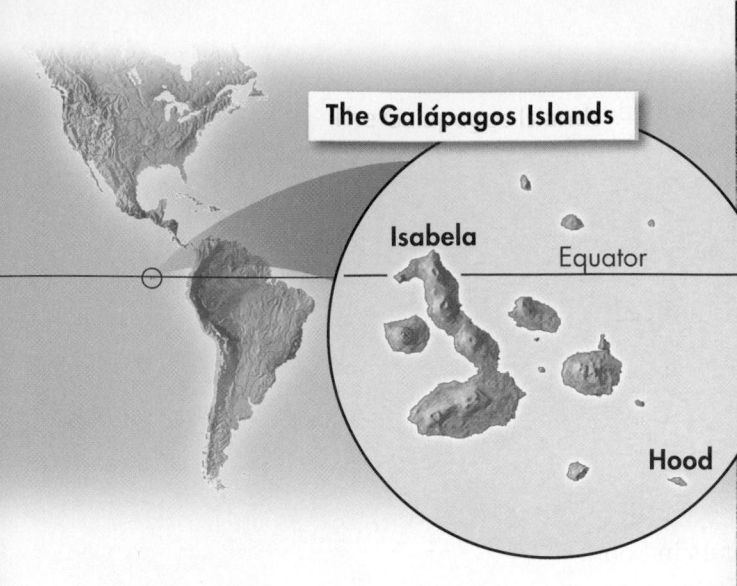

The Galápagos Islands

Isabela

Equator

Hood

Tortoise Diversity The tortoises of the Galápagos Islands have shells with different shapes. The shapes are related to the environment on the island where the tortoise lives.

Isabela Island Tortoise
Tortoises from Isabela Island have dome-shaped shells and short necks. Vegetation on this island is abundant and close to the ground.

Hood Island Tortoise
The shells of Hood Island tortoises are curved and open around their long necks and legs. This helps them to reach the island's sparse, high vegetation.

Species Vary Locally Darwin was puzzled over patterns he saw on a local level, too. For example, there were two kinds of rheas living in South America. One lived in the grasslands of Argentina. A different-looking rhea lived in the colder environment further south. Could their differences be related to their different environments?

The Galápagos Islands off the west coast of South America were also full of puzzles. The islands were small and close to each other, but often had different environments. Darwin noticed differences in the large land turtles called tortoises that lived on the islands. At first he did not think much about them. Then someone showed him that each island had its own type of tortoise with a unique shell. He wondered about the connection between environment and the features of an organism.

Darwin also noticed several kinds of small brown birds on the different Galápagos islands. The birds' beaks looked so different from each other that Darwin thought they were unrelated. Darwin sent samples of the birds to experts in England. Later he would learn how closely related—and important—these little birds were.

🔑 **Key Question** What did Darwin notice about biodiversity within a local area? **Darwin noticed that different, related species often lived in different habitats within a local area.**

Species Vary Over Time Darwin also collected fossils. **Fossils** are the preserved remains of ancient organisms. Some fossils Darwin collected did not look like living organisms. But others did. For example, the extinct glyptodont lived where armadillos live today. The glyptodont looked like a giant armadillo. Why did glyptodonts and armadillos look alike? Why did glyptodonts disappear?

Related Organisms? Ancient glyptodonts were similar to armadillos that live today, but far bigger. The art shows the size of an armadillo and a glyptodont. Darwin wondered if the ancient glyptodont was related to the modern armadillo.

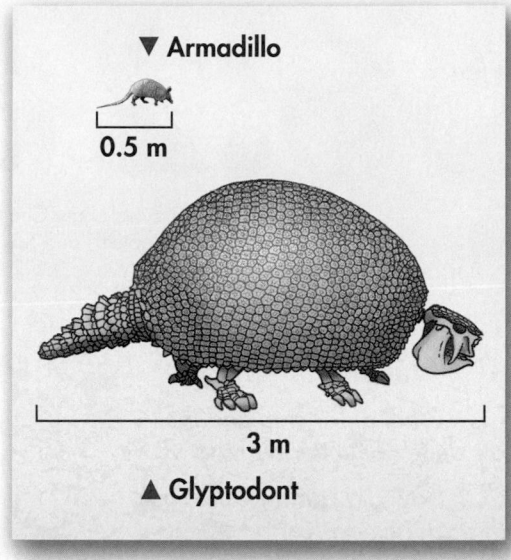

▼ Armadillo

0.5 m

3 m

▲ Glyptodont

Key Question What did Darwin notice when he compared some fossils to living species? **Darwin noticed that some fossils of extinct animals were similar to living species.**

Solving the Puzzle On the long trip home, Darwin thought about the patterns he had seen. The little brown birds he had collected were already causing excitement back home. Experts had found that they were all finches! These finches were similar to a species of finch that lives in South America. Darwin began to wonder if different Galápagos species might have evolved from ancestors in South America. The evidence he gathered on his trip suggested that species change over time by some natural process.

✓CHECK Understanding

Apply Vocabulary
Use the highlighted words from the lesson to complete each sentence correctly.

1. On his journey, Darwin collected _____, the preserved remains of ancient organisms.

2. The process of change over time is called _____.

Critical Thinking

3. Review What did Darwin's theory of biological evolution explain?

4. Relate Cause and Effect What ideas were changing in the scientific community at the time that Darwin traveled on the *Beagle*? How might these new ideas have influenced Darwin?

5. Review What three kinds of variations among organisms did Darwin observe during the voyage of the *Beagle*?

6. Infer Darwin found fossils of many organisms that did not resemble any living species. How might this finding have affected his understanding of life's diversity?

7. Write to Learn Answer the question in the mystery clue below. Remember that honeycreepers eat different kinds of foods. How might the sources of food differ from island to island?

MYSTERY CLUE

Like the small brown birds on the Galápagos, Hawaiian honeycreepers live on islands with different environments. How might these differences have affected honeycreeper evolution? (**Hint:** See p. 382.)

BIOLOGY.com Search Lesson 16.1 GO • Lesson Assessment

16.2 Ideas That Shaped Darwin's Thinking

MD CLG **3.4.1** Evolutionary Change, **3.4.2** Relatedness Among Organisms, **3.5.3** Population Dynamics. SPI **1.1.1** Problems and Solutions, **1.1.2** Scientific Ideas, **1.2.2** Posing Scientific Questions, **1.4.2** Analyze Data, **1.5.2** Communicate Information, **1.6.1** Ratio and Proportion, **1.6.4** Equations, **1.7.1** Apply Skills and Concepts.

Key Questions

🔑 **What did Hutton and Lyell conclude about Earth's history?**

🔑 **How did Lamarck propose that species evolve?**

🔑 **What was Malthus's view of population growth?**

🔑 **How is inherited variation used in artificial selection?**

BUILD Understanding

Main Idea and Details Chart As you read a lesson, you can organize the information in a main idea and details chart. Write all the green headings in the Main Idea column. Then write details about each main idea in the Supporting Details column.

In Your Workbook Go to your workbook to learn more about main idea and details charts.

An Ancient, Changing Earth

Like all scientists, Darwin developed his ideas by building on the work of others. Darwin worked in an exciting time of discovery. Naturalists were finding connections between animals and their environments.

In Darwin's time, many people believed that Earth was only a few thousand years old. They also believed that Earth had not changed much in that time. But scientists were beginning to find evidence that supported different ideas about Earth's history. These ideas were part of the new science of geology. Two of the best-known geologists were James Hutton and Charles Lyell. The ideas of both these geologists influenced Darwin's thinking.

Hutton and Geological Change Hutton described how geological processes shape the land. He suggested that great forces under Earth's surface push mountains upward. These same mountains are then worn down by wind and rain. Most of the processes Hutton described are very, very slow. To make the formations he observed, Earth would have to be much older than a few thousand years. Hutton introduced a concept called *deep time* to explain his ideas. Deep time is the idea that Earth's history is so long that it is difficult to imagine.

Ancient Rocks These rock layers in the Grand Canyon were laid down over millions of years. The river then slowly carved out the canyon over many more years.

Lyell's *Principles of Geology* Lyell argued that the laws of nature do not change over time. He concluded that geological processes in the past worked like the geological processes of today. Ancient volcanoes released lava, just as volcanoes do now. Rivers in the past cut deep canyons, just as rivers do today. Over time, these processes formed the modern landscape. Such changes would take millions of years.

🔑 **Key Question** What did Hutton and Lyell conclude about Earth's history? **Hutton and Lyell concluded that Earth is extremely old. Also, the processes that changed Earth in the past are the same processes that operate in the present.**

Lamarck's Evolutionary Hypotheses

Darwin was not the first scientist to say that species evolve over time. But earlier scientists disagreed on *how* evolution happened. The French scientist Jean-Baptiste Lamarck was one of the first scientists to hypothesize how evolution works. Lamarck suggested two ideas.

Lamarck's Ideas Lamarck proposed that all organisms are born with a desire to become better. He hypothesized that organisms could change their bodies so that they worked better in their environment. Lamarck also thought that organisms could change their bodies by using them in new ways. For example, consider a bird that walks in water looking for food. Long legs would be very useful to that bird. According to Lamarck's ideas, the bird's legs could become longer by stretching each day. Traits that change during the life of an organism are called *acquired characteristics*.

Lamarck also thought that acquired characteristics could be passed on to offspring. This idea is called the *inheritance of acquired traits*. Thus, over a few generations, the legs of a wading bird would get longer and longer.

Evaluating Lamarck's Hypotheses Today scientists know that most of Lamarck's ideas were wrong. Animals do not have a desire to become better. Evolution is not a process that makes animals more "perfect" over time. Scientists also know that there is no inheritance of acquired traits. Acquired characteristics cannot be passed on to offspring.

But Lamarck's work did help Darwin in several ways. Lamarck made a connection between an organism's body and its environment. He was one of the first scientists to suggest that organisms can change over time. He also tried to explain evolution using natural processes. Even though he was incorrect, Lamarck helped other biologists, including Darwin, form their ideas.

🔑 **Key Question** How did Lamarck propose that species evolve? **Lamarck suggested that individual organisms could change during their lifetimes by using or not using parts of their bodies. He also suggested that individuals could pass these changes on to their offspring.**

Acquired Characteristics? This long-legged water bird is a black-winged stilt. According to Lamarck, its long legs were the result of the bird's effort to stretch its legs so that it could wade in deep water.

Population Growth

The ideas of Thomas Malthus also helped Darwin. Malthus was an English economist who noticed that people were being born faster than people were dying. This led to overcrowding. Malthus thought that overcrowding led to conditions that would slow down population growth. These conditions included war, disease, and starvation.

Darwin saw that Malthus's ideas were true for all organisms. A maple tree can produce thousands of seeds every year. An oyster can lay millions of eggs. If all the offspring of a single species survived, that species would soon cover the world. Of course, this doesn't happen. Most offspring die. Only a few survive. Darwin thought it was important that only a few individuals survive to reproduce. It could be a key part of evolution. He wondered which individuals survive. Why did they survive?

Key Question What was Malthus's view of population growth? **Malthus reasoned that if the human population were to grow without control, then there would not be enough space and food for everyone to live.**

Overcrowding in London This drawing from the 1800s shows the crowded conditions in London when Darwin lived.

INQUIRY into Scientific Thinking

Variation in Peppers

As Darwin noted, most organisms produce more offspring than can survive in the environment. This may seem like a waste, but it does make evolutionary sense. Having many offspring makes it more likely that some will survive to reproduce. And more offspring means a wider variety of traits. This makes it is more likely that some traits will be helpful if the environment changes.

In this lab you will examine variations in the colors of peppers and the number of seeds produced.

❶ Get a green, yellow, red, or purple bell pepper.

❷ Slice open the pepper and count the number of seeds.

❸ Compare your data with the data of other students who have peppers of a different color.

Pepper Color	Number of Seeds

Analyze and Conclude

1. Calculate Use the equation below to find the average number of seeds for all of the peppers.

$$\text{Average number of seeds} = \frac{\text{total number of seeds}}{\text{total number of peppers}}$$

2. Calculate Determine the difference from the average for each of the peppers in your group.

3. Infer What other traits could you measure that might affect the success of the pepper plants?

In Your Workbook Get more help for this activity in your workbook.

Artificial Selection Darwin used artificial selection in breeding fancy pigeons at his home outside London.

Artificial Selection

Darwin also studied the work of farmers who bred plants and animals. Breeders knew that some trees produced larger fruits than other trees. Some cows produced more milk than others. Breeders selected only the plants and animals with the best traits for breeding. These traits were passed on to their offspring. Over time, selective breeding could form trees with even bigger fruit, or cows that gave even more milk. Nature provided the variation. Humans selected the traits they found useful. Darwin called this process **artificial selection.**

Darwin had no idea how heredity worked. He did know that variation occurs in wild species as well as farm species. Darwin saw how important this variation was to the process of evolution. He now had all the information he needed to explain evolution. When published, his theory would change the way people understood the living world.

🔑 **Key Question** How is inherited variation used in artificial selection? **In artificial selection, nature provides the variation, and humans select the traits they find useful.**

CHECK Understanding

Apply Vocabulary
Use the highlighted words from the lesson to complete each sentence correctly.

1. Breeders use _____ to produce better crops and livestock.

Critical Thinking

2. Explain How did Hutton and Lyell help to shape Darwin's thinking?

3. Apply Concepts What parts of Lamarck's theory of evolution were incorrect?

4. Explain How does artificial selection work?

5. Write to Learn Imagine that you are Darwin and you have just read Malthus's ideas about population. Write down Malthus's key ideas. Next to these ideas, write how they might apply to evolution.

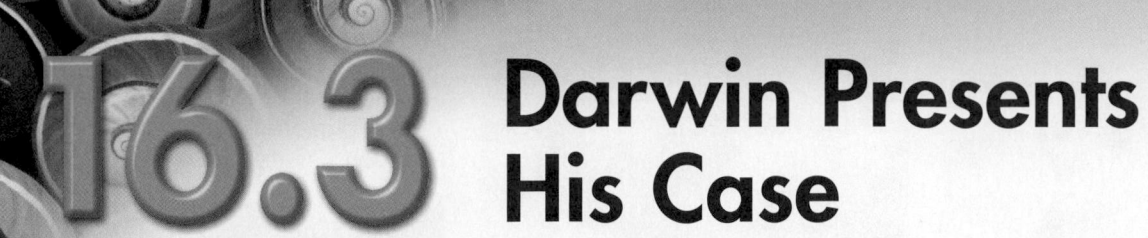

16.3 Darwin Presents His Case

MD CLG 3.3.2 Inherited Traits, 3.4.1 Evolutionary Change, 3.4.2 Relatedness Among Organisms, 3.5.2 Interdependence of Organisms in the Biosphere. SPI 1.5.2 Communicate Information.

Key Questions

🔑 Under what conditions does natural selection occur?

🔑 How does Darwin's theory explain the connection between living and extinct species?

BUILD Understanding

Preview Visuals Before you read this lesson, look at the pictures of grasshoppers on page 390. Read the information in the figure. Then write three questions you have about it. As you read, answer your questions.

In Your Workbook Go to your workbook to learn more about previewing visuals.

Evolution by Natural Selection

Soon after reading Malthus and thinking about artificial selection, Darwin worked out his theory of natural selection. Most of his scientific friends thought his ideas were brilliant. But Darwin did not feel ready to publish. He did not want to be attacked for his ideas, as Lamarck had been. Darwin did not share his theory with the public for 20 years. He spent this time collecting more information to support his theory.

In 1858, Darwin read the unpublished work of another scientist, Alfred Russel Wallace. Darwin was shocked to find that Wallace's thoughts on evolution were almost the same as his own! If Darwin did not act quickly, Wallace would be given credit for describing natural selection. The next year, Darwin published his first book on evolution. It was called *On the Origin of Species*.

The Struggle for Existence In his book, Darwin combined his own thoughts with ideas from Malthus and Lamarck. Like Malthus, Darwin saw that organisms produce more offspring than can survive. Members of a population must compete for food, water, living space, and other things needed to live. Those that do not get enough will not survive to reproduce. Darwin called this *the struggle for existence*.

Variation and Adaptation Darwin knew that members of a population have variation in traits. Many of these traits, called *heritable traits*, can be passed on to offspring. Darwin hypothesized that some heritable traits make survival easier. Any heritable trait that helps an organism survive in its environment is called an **adaptation.** Adaptations can be body parts, such as sharp claws or strong wings. Adaptations can also be behaviors, such as avoiding predators.

Survival of the Fittest Like Lamarck, Darwin saw how the body of each organism works well in its environment. Darwin knew that differences in adaptations affect fitness. **Fitness** describes how well an organism can survive and reproduce in its environment.

Some individuals have adaptations that make survival and reproduction easier. These individuals have high fitness. Individuals without these adaptations are more likely to die, and have less chance to produce offspring. These individuals have low fitness. This difference in success is called *survival of the fittest*.

ADAPTATIONS
Adaptations take many forms.

A scorpionfish's coloring is an example of camouflage— an adaptation that allows an organism to blend into its background and avoid predation.

Adaptations can be forms of behavior. Here, a crane is displaying defensive behavior in an effort to scare off the fox.

Mimicry is an adaptation in which an organism copies a more dangerous organism. The scarlet king snake is harmless, but it looks like, or mimics, the poisonous eastern coral snake, so predators avoid it, too.

Scarlet king snake

Eastern coral snake

Natural Selection Darwin named his method of evolution *natural selection*. In **natural selection,** organisms with traits that are the best match to their environment survive and leave more offspring. In some ways, natural selection is like artificial selection. In both forms of selection, only some individuals reproduce. In artificial selection, the breeder selects which individuals reproduce. In natural selection, the environment determines which individuals survive and reproduce.

Natural selection happens whenever certain conditions exist. First, more individuals are born than can survive. Second, there is heritable variation in the population. Third, some individuals have traits that make them more likely to survive and reproduce.

Populations continue to evolve as they become better adapted to their environment. Populations are also likely to change if the environment changes. Traits that were well suited to the old environment may not work as well in the new environment. New adaptations may evolve.

Key Question When does natural selection occur?
Natural selection occurs when more individuals are born than can survive (the struggle for existence), there is heritable variation (variation and adaptation), and individuals have different fitness rates (survival of the fittest).

adaptation a heritable characteristic that increases an organism's ability to survive and reproduce in an environment

fitness how well an organism can survive and reproduce in its environment

natural selection the process by which organisms that are most suited to their environment survive and reproduce most successfully; also called survival of the fittest

RELATED WORD FORMS

The verb *inherit* and the adjective *heritable* are related word forms. A trait that can be *inherited,* or passed on to offspring, is said to be *heritable.*

NATURAL SELECTION

This population of grasshoppers changes over time because of natural selection.

❶ The Struggle for Existence

Organisms produce more offspring than can survive. Grasshoppers can lay more than 200 eggs at a time. Only a few of these offspring survive to reproduce.

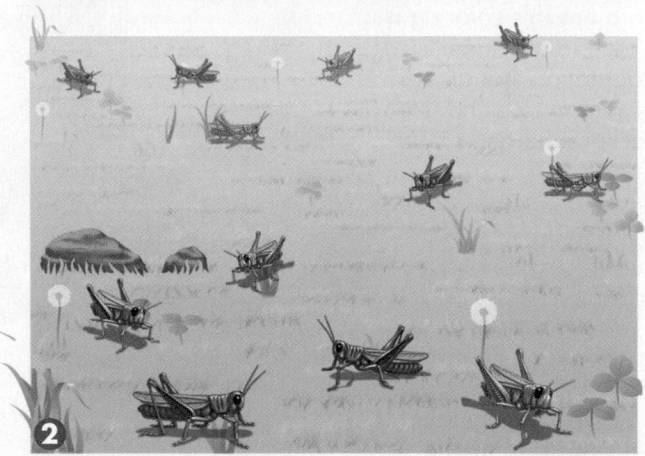

❷ Variation and Adaptation

There is variation in nature. Some variations that are inherited are adaptations. Adaptations increase the chance that an individual will survive and reproduce. In this population, body color is inherited—some grasshoppers are green and some are yellow. Green coloring is an adaptation that allows grasshoppers to blend into their environment.

❸ Survival of the Fittest

The color green serves as a form of camouflage. It is harder for predators to see green grasshoppers than yellow grasshoppers. Therefore, green grasshoppers have higher fitness than yellow grasshoppers. In this environment, more green grasshoppers are able to survive and reproduce than yellow grasshoppers.

❹ Natural Selection

Over time, green grasshoppers become more common than yellow grasshoppers. This is because
(1) more grasshoppers are born than can survive,
(2) individuals vary in color, and color is a heritable trait,
(3) green individuals have a higher fitness in this environment.

Common Descent

According to Darwin's theory, individuals that are well adapted to their environment survive and reproduce. Every organism alive today descended from parents who survived and reproduced. Those parents descended from their parents. This line of organisms continues back through time to the very earliest life forms.

In a similar way, Darwin proposed that species living today are descended from older species that survived and reproduced. Over time, those older species evolved into new species in a process he called *descent with modification*. Modification means "change." It can take thousands or even millions of years for new species to evolve. This length of time—deep time—was an idea Darwin borrowed from Hutton and Lyell. Deep time gave enough time for natural selection to work. Darwin pointed to the fossil record as evidence of descent with modification.

Darwin used the idea that species change over time to explain the great variety of life on Earth. Darwin drew the first evolutionary tree to show how organisms share ancient ancestors. This idea is called *common descent*. A single "tree of life" links all living things. If you look back in time far enough, all organisms are related.

Key Question How does common descent explain the connection between living and extinct species? **According to the principle of common descent, all species—living and extinct—are descended from ancient common ancestors.**

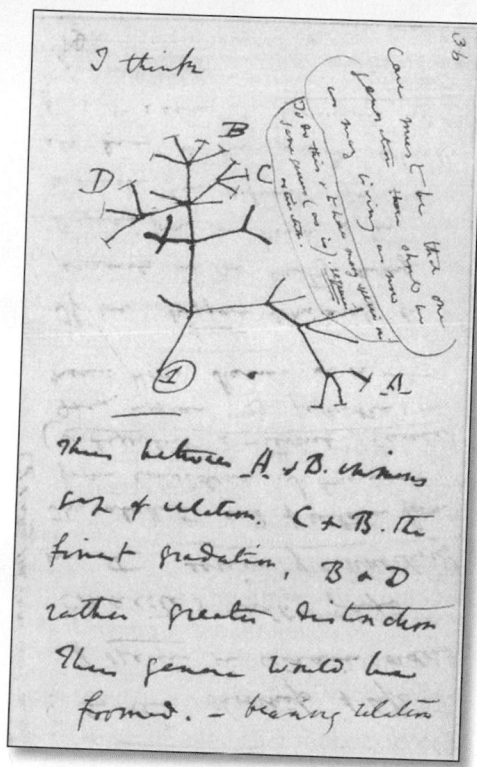

Descent With Modification This is a page from one of Darwin's notebooks. It shows the first evolutionary tree ever drawn. Note that Darwin wrote "I think" just above the tree.

CHECK Understanding

Apply Vocabulary
Use the highlighted words from the lesson to complete each sentence correctly.

1. Organisms with high _____ are more likely to survive and reproduce.

2. Sharp teeth and claws are _____ that help tigers capture their prey.

3. The traits that are most helpful for survival in an environment become more common through the process of _____.

Critical Thinking

4. **Apply Concepts** What do evolutionary trees show? What does a tree of life imply about all species living and extinct?

5. **Relate Cause and Effect** Briefly describe the process that causes a population to change by natural selection. Use the words *overproduction*, *variation*, *adaptation*, and *survival of the fittest*.

6. **Write to Learn** Answer the question in the mystery clue below.

MYSTERY CLUE

How might natural selection explain the history of the Hawaiian honeycreepers? (**Hint:** See p. 389.)

 BIOLOGY.com ▸ Search (Lesson 16.3) **GO** • Lesson Assessment

16.4 Evidence of Evolution

MD CLG **3.1.1** Chemical Substances and Macromolecules, **3.2.1** Functions and Processes, **3.3.3** Nucleic Acids and Protein Synthesis, **3.4.1** Evolutionary Change, **3.4.2** Relatedness Among Organisms, **3.5.2** Interdependence of Organisms in the Biosphere. SPI **1.1.1** Problems and Solutions, **1.1.2** Scientific Ideas, **1.2.1** Testable Scientific Questions, **1.2.3** Hypothesis Formation, **1.4.2** Analyze Data, **1.5.7** Classification Systems, **1.5.8** Compare, **1.7.6** Science and Technology.

Key Questions

🔑 *How does the geographic distribution of species today relate to their evolutionary history?*

🔑 *What do homologous structures and similarities in embryonic development suggest about the process of evolutionary change?*

🔑 *How do fossils help to show the descent of modern species from ancient ancestors?*

🔑 *How can molecular biology be used to trace the process of evolution?*

🔑 *What does recent research on the Galápagos finches show about natural selection?*

BUILD Understanding

Concept Map Make a concept map that shows the kinds of evidence that support the theory of evolution.

In Your Workbook Go to your workbook to learn more about making a concept map. Complete the concept map for Lesson 16.4.

Biogeography

When Darwin published *On the Origin of Species* in 1859, scientists were not able to test all of his ideas. But since then, scientists have discovered a great deal of evidence. This evidence comes from many different sciences—biogeography, anatomy, geology, chemistry, genetics, and even molecular biology. Amazingly, evidence from all of these areas supports Darwin's basic ideas about evolution.

Darwin used the science of biogeography to support his theory. **Biogeography** is the study of where organisms live and where their ancestors lived in the past. Darwin noted two important patterns: (1) Closely related organisms that live in different environments often show great differences. (2) Distantly related organisms that live in similar environments are often similar.

Closely Related but Different Darwin used biogeography to explain his observations in the Galápagos. He hypothesized that birds on the islands were descended from birds in South America. Natural selection in different environments had led to differences among the closely related populations.

Distantly Related but Similar Darwin compared plants and animals living in similar environments around the world. For example, he found ground-dwelling birds in the grasslands of Europe, Australia, and Africa. These organisms looked alike, but were not closely related. Because they lived in similar habitats, natural selection had led to similar adaptations.

🔑 **Key Question** How does the geographic distribution of species today relate to their evolutionary history?
Patterns linking adaptations to environments around the world provide evidence for natural selection.

Comparing Body Structure and Embryos

In Darwin's time, researchers had discovered that many different animals have similar structures. For example, the front legs of amphibians, birds, and reptiles all have the same basic bones! Darwin suggested that animals with similar structures are related. Their structures are inherited from a common ancestor.

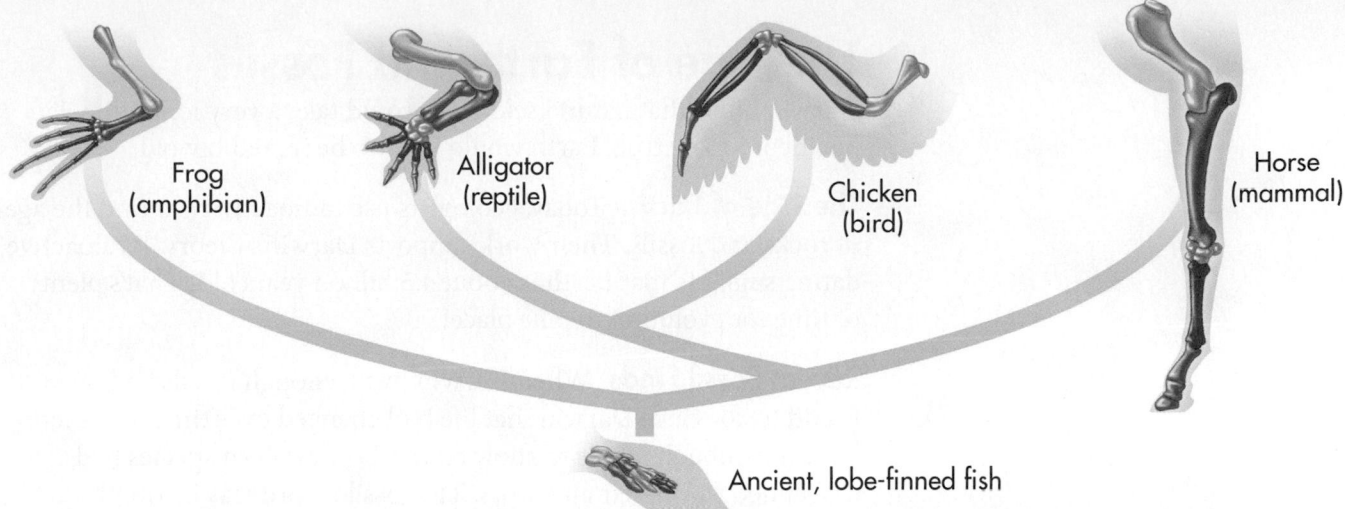

Frog
(amphibian)

Alligator
(reptile)

Chicken
(bird)

Horse
(mammal)

Ancient, lobe-finned fish

Homologous Structures Structures that are shared by related species and that have been inherited from a common ancestor are called **homologous structures.** These structures often show modifications, or differences. The more alike homologous structures are, the more closely related the organisms. Bird limbs are more like reptile limbs than mammal limbs. This means that birds and reptiles are more closely related than birds and mammals. Homologous structures do not always work the same way. A bird's wing and horse's leg are homologous, even though they work differently.

🔑 **Key Question** What do homologous structures suggest about the process of evolutionary change? **Evolutionary theory explains that homologous structures adapted to different purposes are the result of descent with modification from a common ancestor.**

Analogous Structures Sometimes body parts share a common function but are not structurally related. These structures are called **analogous structures.** The wings of bees, bats, and birds are analogous. Analogous structures do not show common descent.

Vestigial Structures Some homologous structures do not have important functions. **Vestigial structures** are inherited structures that have lost much of their original function. Vestigial structures may show evolutionary relationships. For example, the hipbones of dolphins are vestigial structures. They link dolphins to ancestors that used hipbones as they walked on land.

Embryology The early stages of many animals with backbones look very similar. You may look nothing like a chicken now. But your embryonic cells grew in similar patterns. These patterns of growth produced homologous tissues and organs. These similarities are evidence of common descent.

🔑 **Key Question** What do similarities in embryonic development suggest about the process of evolutionary change? **Similar patterns of embryo development provide evidence that organisms have descended from a common ancestor.**

Homologous Limb Bones
The limb bones of seemingly unrelated animals have the same basic structures. Matching colors allow you to compare homologous structures. The limbs evolved from an ancient fish, their common ancestor.

BUILD Vocabulary

biogeography
the study of past and present distribution of organisms

homologous structures
structures that are similar in different species of common ancestry

analogous structures
structures that are similar in function but not structure; they do not suggest common ancestry

vestigial structure
a structure that is reduced in size and has little or no function

🖊 **WORD ORIGINS**

The word *homologous* comes from the Greek word *homos*, which means "same." Homologous structures may not look exactly the same, but they share certain characteristics and a common ancestor.

The Age of Earth and Fossils

Darwin knew that natural selection would take a very long time. For his theory to be true, Earth would have to be incredibly old.

The Age of Earth. Today, geologists use radioactivity to find the age of rocks and fossils. Their work supports Darwin's theory. Radioactive dating suggests that Earth is about 4.5 billion years old. That's plenty of time for evolution to take place!

Recent Fossil Finds When Darwin lived, enough fossils had been found to convince Darwin that life had changed over time. But there were not enough fossils to show clearly how modern species had descended from their ancestors. The fossil record was incomplete.

Today, hundreds of new fossil discoveries show clearly how many modern species have evolved from older species. Scientists have found fossils of animals that were "in between" dinosaurs and birds. Other fossils link fishes to land animals. New finds even connect land animals to whales. The fossil record is still incomplete. But new discoveries continue to support Darwin's theory.

🔑 **Key Question** How do fossils help to show the descent of modern species from ancient ancestors? **Many recently discovered fossils form series that trace the evolution of modern species from extinct ancestors.**

BUILD Connections

EVIDENCE FROM FOSSILS

Recently, scientists have discovered more than 20 fossils that show how whales evolved from ancestors that walked on land. The drawings of the ancient animals are based on fossil evidence.

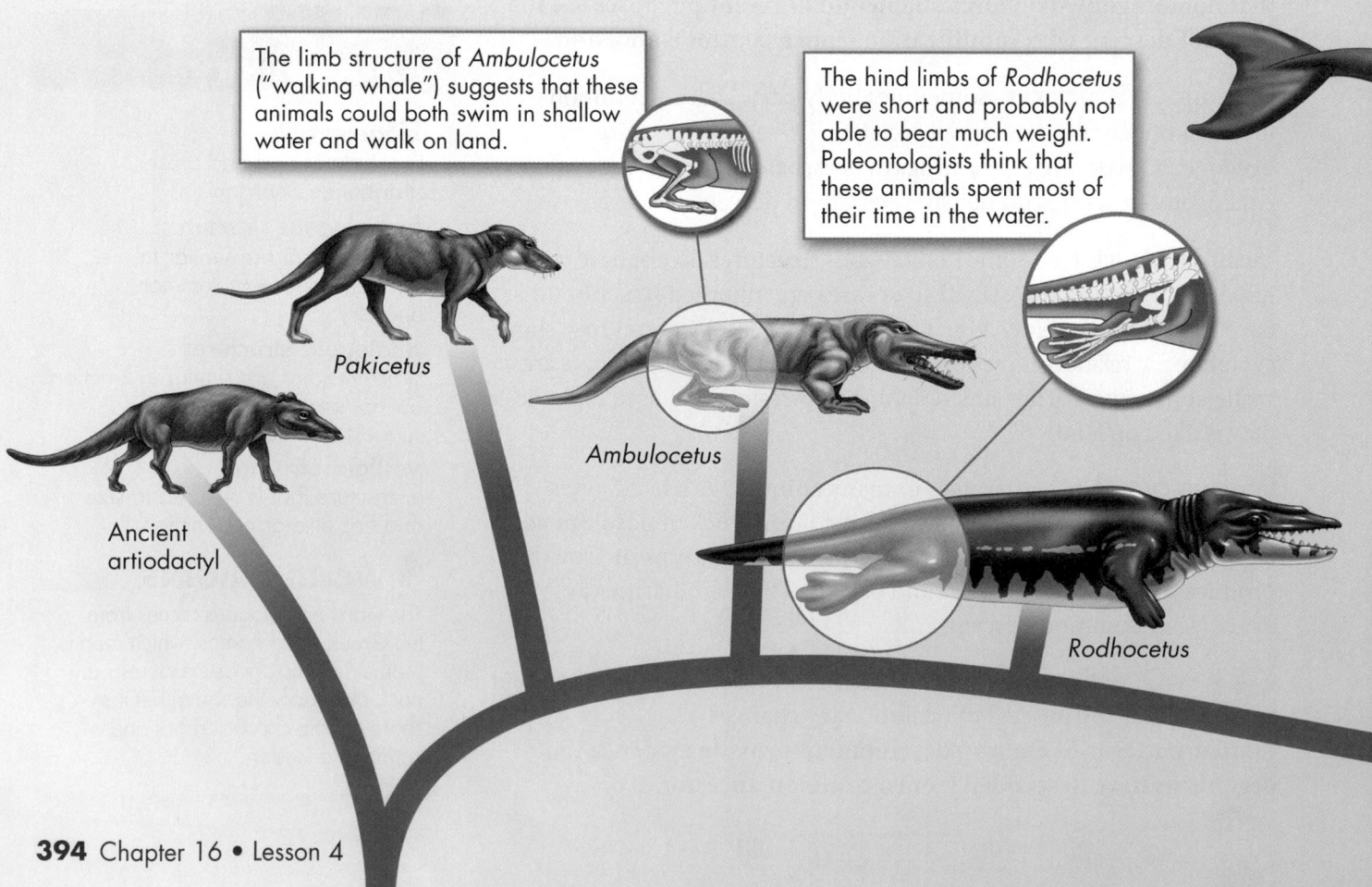

The limb structure of *Ambulocetus* ("walking whale") suggests that these animals could both swim in shallow water and walk on land.

The hind limbs of *Rodhocetus* were short and probably not able to bear much weight. Paleontologists think that these animals spent most of their time in the water.

Pakicetus

Ancient artiodactyl

Ambulocetus

Rodhocetus

Genetics and Molecular Biology

Darwin did not understand how heredity worked. Since his time, biologists have learned a great deal about heredity. Darwin would be glad to know that modern genetics strongly supports evolution.

Common Genetic Code All living cells use DNA and RNA to make proteins and to pass on genetic information. The code is nearly the same for all living things—bacteria, yeasts, plants, fungi, and animals. The shared genetic code is powerful evidence that all organisms evolved from a common ancestor that used this code.

Homologous Molecules Biologists have found many homologous molecules. For example, the protein cytochrome *c* is important in cellular respiration. Versions of this protein are found in almost all living things. Homologous proteins and genes are evidence of common descent.

Key Question How can molecular biology be used to trace the process of evolution? **The universal genetic code and homologous molecules provide molecular evidence of evolution.**

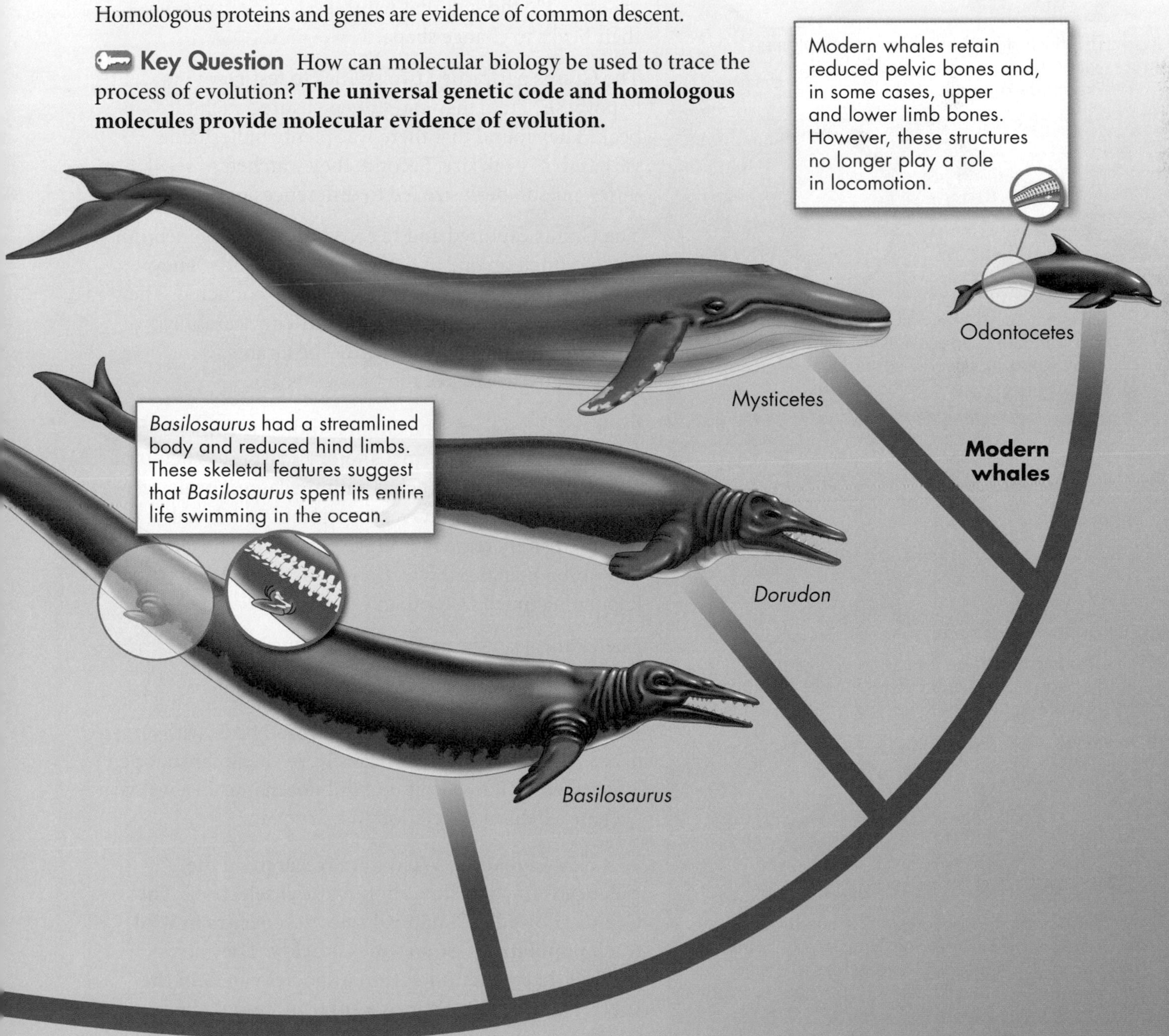

Modern whales retain reduced pelvic bones and, in some cases, upper and lower limb bones. However, these structures no longer play a role in locomotion.

Odontocetes

Mysticetes

Modern whales

Basilosaurus had a streamlined body and reduced hind limbs. These skeletal features suggest that *Basilosaurus* spent its entire life swimming in the ocean.

Dorudon

Basilosaurus

FINCH BEAK TOOLS

Finch beaks can be compared to different tools. The different beaks allow each species of finch to pick up and eat a different kind of food.

Tree Finches

Platyspiza

This finch strips bark from woody plants with a beak that grips and holds tightly, like a pair of pliers.

Certhidea

This finch feeds on small, exposed insects that it picks off plant surfaces. Its thin, straight, narrow beak works like needle-nose pliers or forceps to firmly grasp small objects at the tip.

Ground Finches

Pinaroloxias

This finch feeds on insects, fruit, and nectar. Its beak works like a curved, needle-nose pliers that are good at probing and grasping at the tip.

Geospiza

This finch feeds on large, thick seeds with a beak that is thick, strong, and sharp. This beak works like heavy-duty wire cutters to apply strong pressure and cutting force near its base.

Testing Natural Selection

The best way to gather evidence about evolution is to observe natural selection in action. Some scientists have designed laboratory experiments using bacteria that let them test ideas about natural selection. Others have carried out experiments with guppies. These studies support Darwin's ideas. But the best way to test ideas about natural selection is to observe it in the wild. Peter and Rosemary Grant did just that. They studied finches on the Galápagos Islands.

A Testable Hypothesis Darwin hypothesized that all the Galápagos finches had descended from a common ancestor. He thought that natural selection had caused their beaks to change shape.

The Grants performed two studies to test Darwin's hypothesis. First, they carefully measured each bird's beak. They found that there was plenty of heritable variation in beak size. Second, they watched to see if differences in beak size led to differences in fitness.

The Grants captured and released nearly every medium ground finch on one of the Galápagos Islands. They recorded which birds were alive and reproducing. They also recorded which birds had died. They carefully measured the beak of each bird. The Grants found variation in the sizes of the finches' beaks.

Natural Selection The Grants studied the finches for many years, during normal and dry seasons. When food was hard to find, the finches with the largest beaks were most likely to survive. Over a period of just decades, they observed an increase in average beak size. The Grants had observed natural selection in the wild. And it was happening much faster than expected!

The Grants also showed that variations help a species survive when the environment changes. In dry years, there were not enough small seeds for all of the finches. Competition among the finches favored birds with larger beaks. Finches with larger beaks were able to break open larger seeds. Thus, a trait that did not matter in a wet year became a helpful adaptation in a dry year.

Key Question What does research on the Galápagos finches show about natural selection? **The Grants showed that natural selection occurs in wild finch populations, sometimes quickly. They also showed that variation within a species can help the species adapt to and survive environmental changes.**

Survival of the Fittest and Beak Size
The Grants studied finches on the Galápagos Islands. This graph shows the survival of a population of ground finches. It shows that birds with larger beaks survived at a higher rate than birds with smaller beaks.

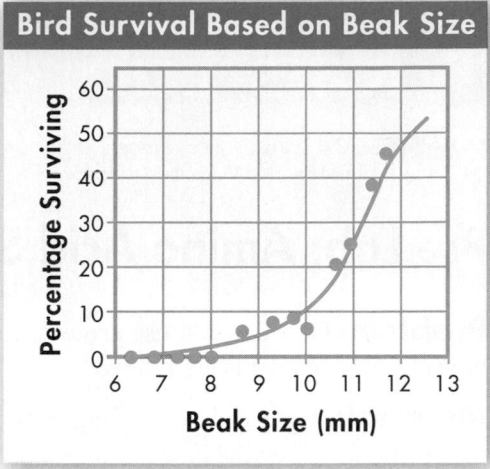

Bird Survival Based on Beak Size

Evaluating Evolutionary Theory Like any scientific theory, evolutionary theory is constantly reviewed with each new bit of information. New studies, tools, and techniques have continued to support most of Darwin's hypotheses. Today, evolution is important in all branches of biology, from ecology to medicine.

Many important questions about evolution are still being studied: Exactly how did life begin? How do new species arise? Why do some species become extinct? Biologists often disagree about answers to these questions. But biologists agree that evolution *is* happening. To biologists, evolution is the key to understanding the natural world.

CHECK Understanding

Apply Vocabulary
Use the highlighted words from the lesson to complete each sentence correctly.

1. Body parts of unrelated organisms that serve the same function are examples of _____.
2. Body parts in related organisms that are structurally similar are examples of _____.
3. Inherited structures that have lost much of their original function are called _____.

Critical Thinking

4. **Explain** What is biogeography?
5. **Compare and Contrast** What is the difference between homologous and analogous structures? Which are more important to evolutionary biologists? Why?
6. **Apply Concepts** How do recent fossil finds help to support evolution?

7. **Review** How do modern genetics and molecular biology support the theory of evolution?
8. **Draw Conclusions** How do the data collected by the Grants show that variation is important to the survival of a species?
9. **Write to Learn** Answer the question in the mystery clue below. The Hawaiian islands have different environments. Some islands are very wet. Others are much drier. How might these environments affect the natural selection of honeycreepers?

MYSTERY CLUE

How can biogeography be used to explain why some species of honeycreepers are found only on the Hawaiian Islands? (**Hint:** See p. 392.)

MD CLG 3.4.2 Relatedness Among Organisms. SPI 1.4.1 Organize Data, 1.5.2 Communicate Information, 1.5.9 Synthesize Ideas.

Pre Lab: Amino Acid Sequences: Indicators of Evolution

Problem How can you use proteins to determine how closely organisms are related?

Materials light-colored highlighting pen, graph paper

Lab Manual Chapter 16 Lab

Skills Focus Analyze Data, Graph, Draw Conclusions

Connect to the **Big idea** For years, scientists who studied evolution had to rely on only visible differences among organisms. Then a new source of evidence emerged. Biochemists were able to unravel the sequences of bases in DNA and amino acids in proteins. Scientists are able to use this data to confirm relationships based on anatomy. They also use the data to show that some species that appear very different are in fact more closely related than had been thought.

Biologists can compare the sequences of amino acids in a protein for two species. In general, when the total number of differences is small, the species are closely related. When the total number of differences is large, the species are more distantly related.

In this lab, you will compare amino acid sequences for one protein and analyze the results of a similar comparison for another protein. You will use both sets of data to predict relatedness among organisms.

Background Questions

a. Review What are homologous molecules?

b. Explain Why might scientists use molecules instead of anatomy to figure out how closely rabbits and fruit flies are related?

c. Relate Cause and Effect Amino acid sequences in the proteins of two species are similar. What can you conclude about the DNA in those species, and why?

Pre-Lab Questions

Preview the procedure in the lab manual.

1. Predict Based only on their anatomy, rank gorillas, bears, chimpanzees, and mice from most recent common ancestor with humans to least recent.

2. Use Analogies You tell a story to a second person who tells it to a third person, and so on. As the story is retold, changes are introduced. Over time, the number of changes increases. How is this process an analogy for what happens to DNA over time?

3. Infer Hemoglobin from two species is compared. On the long protein chains, there are three locations where the amino acids are different. Where would you place the common ancestor of the two species on the "tree of life," and why?

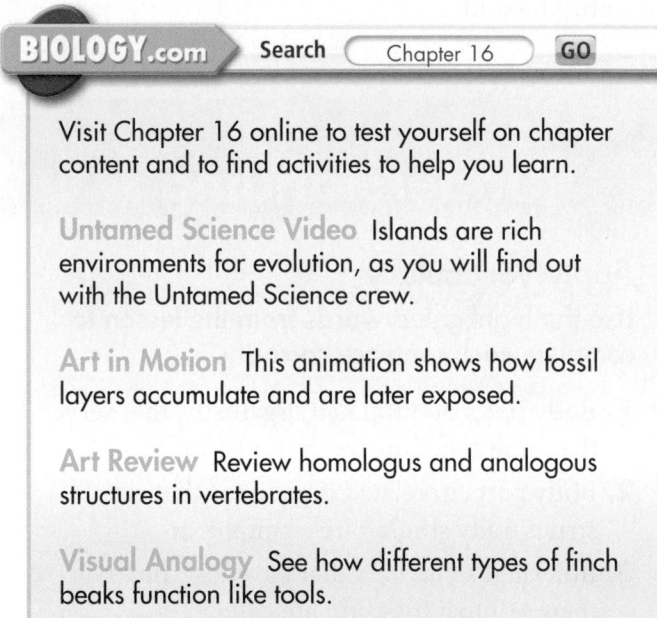

BIOLOGY.com Search [Chapter 16] **GO**

Visit Chapter 16 online to test yourself on chapter content and to find activities to help you learn.

Untamed Science Video Islands are rich environments for evolution, as you will find out with the Untamed Science crew.

Art in Motion This animation shows how fossil layers accumulate and are later exposed.

Art Review Review homologus and analogous structures in vertebrates.

Visual Analogy See how different types of finch beaks function like tools.

Data Analysis Collect population data for several generations of grasshoppers and then analyze how the population changed due to natural selection.

16 CHAPTER Summary

16.1 Darwin's Voyage of Discovery

- Darwin developed a theory of evolution that explains how organisms evolved over long periods of time from common ancestors.

- Darwin noticed that (1) different places around the world that had similar habitats often had different species that were ecologically similar; (2) different, related species often lived in different habitats within a local area; and (3) some fossils of extinct animals were similar to living species.

evolution (p. 380)
fossil (p. 382)

16.2 Ideas That Shaped Darwin's Thinking

- Hutton and Lyell concluded that Earth is extremely old. Also, the processes that changed Earth in the past are the same processes that operate in the present.

- Lamarck suggested that individual organisms could change during their lifetime by using or not using different parts of their bodies. He also suggested that individuals could pass these acquired traits on to their offspring. This would cause species to change over time.

- Malthus reasoned that if the human population were to grow without control, there would not be enough space and food for everyone to live.

- In artificial selection, nature provides the variation of traits. Humans select the traits they find useful.

artificial selection (p. 387)

16.3 Darwin Presents His Case

- Natural selection occurs whenever more individuals are born than can survive, there is heritable variation, and some individuals have higher fitness than others.

- The principle of common descent says that all species are descended from ancient common ancestors. This is true of living and extinct species.

adaptation (p. 388)
fitness (p. 388)
natural selection (p. 389)

16.4 Evidence of Evolution

- Patterns linking adaptations to environments around the world provide evidence for natural selection.

- Many recently discovered fossils form series that trace the evolution of modern species from extinct ancestors.

- Homologous structures and patterns of embryo development provide evidence that species have descended, with modification, from a common ancestor.

- Many recently discovered fossils form series that trace the evolution of modern species from extinct ancestors.

- The universal genetic code and homologous molecules provide molecular evidence of common descent.

- The Grants observed natural selection occurring in a wild finch population. They also showed that variation within a species can help the species adapt to and survive environmental changes.

biogeography (p. 392)
homologous structure (p. 393)
analogous structure (p. 393)
vestigial structure (p. 393)

Assess the Big idea Evolution

Write an answer to the question below.
Q: What is natural selection?

Constructed Response

Write an answer to each of the numbered questions below. The answer to each numbered question should be one or two paragraphs. To help you begin, read **Hints** below the questions.

1. **How was Darwin's theory of evolution influenced by the work of other scientists?**

   Hint Geologists such as Hutton and Lyell developed the concept of deep time.

   Hint Thomas Malthus described conditions that affect human populations. These conditions can also affect other organisms.

2. **How would Darwin explain the evolution of the long legs of the bird in the picture on page 385? How would his explanation differ from that of Lamarck?**

   Hint Read the caption to review some of Lamarck's ideas.

3. **Look back at the art of the natural selection of grasshoppers on page 390. Explain how conditions could change so that yellow grasshoppers are better adapted to their environment than green grasshoppers. What would happen to the relative numbers of green and yellow grasshoppers in the population?**

   Hint The word *camouflage* refers to a way of hiding in an environment. In your answer, explain how camouflage can be an adaptation.

Foundations for Learning Wrap-Up

You can use the notes you took about the steps of natural selection as a tool for review. First, you will make your sheet of paper into a pyramid. To do this, cut to the center along a fold next to the colored triangle. (Do not cut all the way through.) Now you have two flaps. Tape the flap with writing over the colored flap, so the two flaps make one side. You now have a three-sided pyramid.

Activity 1 Turn each side of your pyramid into a question. For example, "What is the struggle for existence?" Write the answer on a separate sheet of paper. Then look inside your pyramid to check your answer. Make any corrections or additions that are needed on your answer sheet. Then move on to the next question.

Activity 2 Work with a partner. Quiz each other on the stages of natural selection. Begin with a population of green grasshoppers that live in a habitat with green grass. Use the sides of your pyramid as clues. For example, you could ask, "How does the struggle for existence affect the grasshoppers?" If you cannot answer a question, check inside the pyramid.

Then take turns suggesting other kinds organisms that live in other environments. For example, you might describe the process of natural selection on a population of orange and pink fish that live on a coral reef. Be creative!

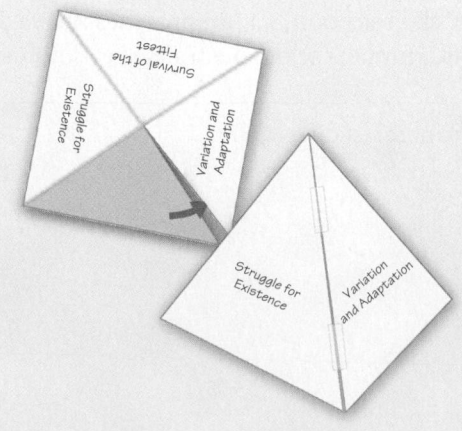

16.1 Darwin's Voyage of Discovery

Understand Key Concepts

1. Who observed variations in the characteristics of plants and animals on the Galápagos Islands?
   a. James Hutton
   c. Charles Lyell
   b. Thomas Malthus
   d. Charles Darwin

> **Test-Taking Tip**
>
> **Read Carefully!** Sometimes the difference between the correct answer and an incorrect answer is a single word. In question 1, you might be tempted to answer **c,** because Charles Lyell is similar to Charles Darwin. Try to think of the answer before you read the choices, then carefully read each choice.

2. In different parts of the world, Darwin found unrelated species that looked alike because
   a. the species lived in different environments.
   b. the species lived in similar environments.
   c. the species were closely related.
   d. the species once lived in the same place.

3. What connection did Darwin make between the Galápagos tortoises and their environments?

Think Critically

4. **Relate Cause and Effect** Why was Darwin's trip on the *Beagle* so important to his development of the theory of natural selection?

16.2 Ideas That Shaped Darwin's Thinking

Understand Key Concepts

5. Which of the following ideas proposed by Lamarck was later found to be incorrect?
   a. Acquired characteristics can be inherited.
   b. All species are descended from other species.
   c. Living things change over time.
   d. There is a relationship between an organism and its environment.

6. Which of the following would an animal breeder use to increase the amount of milk given by his herd of cows?
   a. overproduction
   b. genetic isolation
   c. acquired characteristics
   d. artificial selection

7. According to Malthus, what factors limit human population growth?

Think Critically

8. **Relate Cause and Effect** Lamarck made a very significant contribution to science, even though his explanation of evolution was wrong. Explain how Lamarck helped other scientists.

9. **Infer** Could artificial selection happen without inherited variation? Explain your answer.

16.3 Darwin Presents His Case

Understand Key Concepts

10. An inherited characteristic that increases an organism's ability to survive and reproduce in its environment is called a(n)
    a. vestigial structure.
    b. adaptation.
    c. homologous structure.
    d. variation.

11. What do evolutionary trees show?
    a. all life depends on trees
    b. all life is changing due to natural selection
    c. all living species are descended from earlier ancestors.
    d. all life evolves to the point of perfection

12. What is fitness, in evolutionary terms?

Think Critically

13. **Infer** Many species of birds build nests in which they lay eggs and care for their young. How does this behavior relate to reproductive fitness?

16.4 Evidence of Evolution

Understand Key Concepts

14. Series of related fossils are important evidence of evolution because they show
  a. how organisms changed over time.
  b. how animals behaved in their environments.
  c. how the embryos of organisms develop.
  d. molecular homologies.

15. The wing of a bird that cannot fly is an example of a(n)
  a. analogous structure.
  b. homologous structure.
  c. vestigial structure.
  d. molecular structure.

16. How does DNA provide evidence for common descent?

Think Critically

17. Evaluate Darwin hypothesized that natural selection led to the different beak shapes in the Galapagos finches. Describe how the Grants tested this hypothesis. Did their data support Darwin's hypothesis?

Connecting Concepts

Use Science Graphics
Use the illustration below to answer question 18.

18. Infer Based on what you can see, are the brown mice or white mice better adapted to their environment? Explain why.

solve the CHAPTER MYSTERY

SUCH DIFFERENT HONEYCREEPERS

Hawaiian honeycreepers like the i'iwi have a lot in common with the Galápagos finches. Like the finches, the honeycreepers are small birds found nowhere else on Earth. They live on islands far from the mainland. And like the finches, the 20 known species of honeycreepers are closely related to each other.

This suggests that the honeycreepers are all descended, with modification, from a recent common ancestor. Honeycreepers are recent in evolutionary terms. Biologists think the ancestor first arrived on the islands between 3 and 4 million years ago.

Many of the honeycreepers have specialized diets. Their adaptations allow them to use different food sources on the different islands. Today, habitat loss is making it harder for the honeycreepers to survive. Some species have already become extinct since humans settled on the islands.

1. Infer Imagine a small group of birds landed on one of the Hawaiian islands millions of years ago. This small population then reproduced. Do you think all of the descendants would have stayed on that one island? Explain your answer.

2. Infer Do you think that environmental conditions are the same everywhere on all of the Hawaiian Islands? How might the environment have affected the evolution of honeycreepers?

3. Form a Hypothesis Explain how the different species of honeycreepers in Hawaii today might have evolved from one ancestral species.

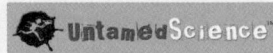 **Never Stop Exploring Your World.** Finding the solution to the honeycreeper mystery is only the beginning. Take a video field trip to Hawaii with the ecogeeks of Untamed Science to see where the mystery leads.

MD Standardized Test Practice for Maryland

Multiple Choice

1. Which scientist formulated the theory of evolution through natural selection?
   A Charles Darwin   C James Hutton
   B Thomas Malthus   D Jean-Baptiste Lamarck
   CLG 3.4.1

2. Lamarck's ideas about evolution were wrong because he proposed that
   A species change over time.
   B species descended from other species.
   C acquired characteristics can be inherited.
   D species are adapted to their environments.
   CLG 3.4.1

3. Lyell's *Principles of Geology* influenced Darwin because it explained how
   A organisms change over time.
   B adaptations occur.
   C Earth must be very old.
   D the Galápagos Islands formed.   CLG 3.4.1

4. A farmer's use of the best livestock for breeding is an example of
   A natural selection.   C extinction.
   B artificial selection.   D adaptation.   CLG 3.4.1

5. The ability of an individual organism to survive and reproduce in its natural environment is called
   A natural selection.
   B evolution.
   C descent with modification.
   D fitness.   CLG 3.4.1

6. Which of the following is an important concept in Darwin's theory of evolution by natural selection?
   A descent with modification
   B homologous molecules
   C processes that change the surface of Earth
   D the tendency toward perfection   CLG 3.4.1

7. Which of the following provides evidence for evolution?
   A fossil record
   B homologous structures of living organisms
   C geographical distribution of living things
   D all of the above   CLG 3.4.2

8. DNA and RNA provide evidence of evolution because
   A all organisms have nearly identical DNA and RNA.
   B no two organisms have exactly the same DNA.
   C each RNA codon specifies just one amino acid.
   D in most organisms, the same codons specify the same amino acids.   CLG 3.3.3

9. A bird's wings are homologous to a(n)
   A fish's tailfin.   C dog's front legs.
   B alligator's claws.   D mosquito's wings.
   CLG 3.2.1

Questions 10 and 11

The birds shown below are two of the species of finches Darwin found on the Galápagos Islands.

Woodpecker Finch   Large Ground Finch

10. What process produced the two different types of beaks shown?
    A artificial selection
    B natural selection
    C geographical distribution
    D disuse of the beak   CLG 3.4.1

11. The large ground finch obtains food by cracking seeds. Its short, strong beak is an example of
    A the struggle for existence.
    B the tendency toward perfection.
    C an adaptation.
    D a vestigial organ.   CLG 3.4.1

Open-Ended Response

12. Compare and contrast the processes of artificial selection and natural selection.   CLG 3.4.1

If You Have Trouble With . . .

Question	1	2	3	4	5	6	7	8	9	10	11	12
See Lesson	16.1	16.2	16.2	16.2	16.3	16.3	16.4	16.4	16.4	16.3	16.3	16.3

17 Evolution of Populations

Evolution

Q: How can populations evolve to form new species?

At first glance, these two butterflies look exactly the same. But if you look closely, you can see that the patterns on their wings are slightly different. Variations among members of a population make evolution possible. Sometimes evolution leads to new species.

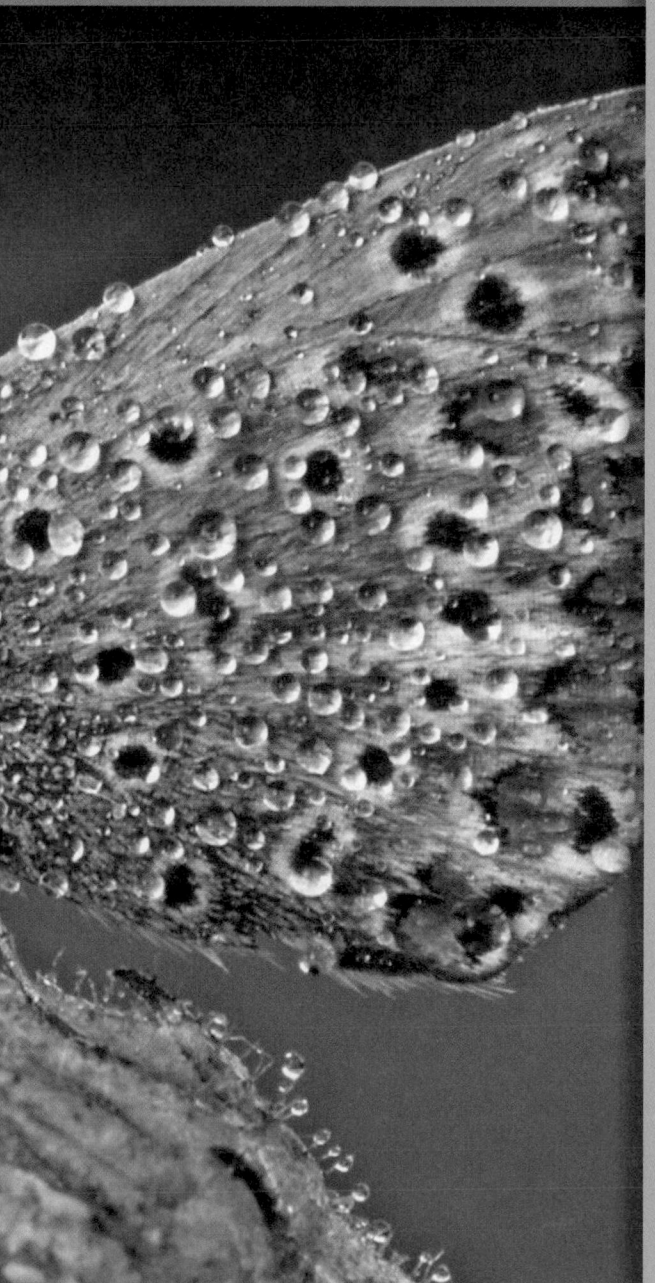

MD. **MARYLAND VOLUNTARY STATE CURRICULUM**

Biology Indicators/Core Learning Goals (CLG) 3.3.1, 3.3.2, 3.3.4, 3.4.1, 3.4.2, 3.5.1, 3.5.2. **Skills and Processes Indicators (SPI)** 1.4.2, 1.4.8, 1.5.8, 1.5.9, 1.6.1, 1.6.4, 1.7.4. See lessons for details.

CHAPTER
MYSTERY

KILLER DISEASE

In 1918, a new disease began to kill millions of people. Around the world, more than 40 million people died. What caused this terrible disease? It was an influenza virus. This virus was a strain of "the flu" that you can catch again and again. Every year different strains of these viruses appear and cause the flu.

How did this one virus become so deadly? Could such a deadly flu ever happen again? Scientists are searching for the answers to these questions. They are still very worried about the influenza virus, and the chance of another deadly disease. That is why they are watching the "bird flu" so closely.

Read for Mystery Clues As you read this chapter, look for clues that explain how new types of influenza virus appear. How is evolution involved? Then, solve the mystery at the end of the chapter.

FOUNDATIONS
for Learning

Fold a piece of paper into three equal sections. Then lay the paper out flat. At the top of the page, write "Sources of Genetic Variation," At the top of the middle section, write "Natural Selection." At the top of the bottom section, write "Isolation." As you read, make notes or drawings that relate to each heading. These notes will help you answer the question: How can populations evolve to form new species?

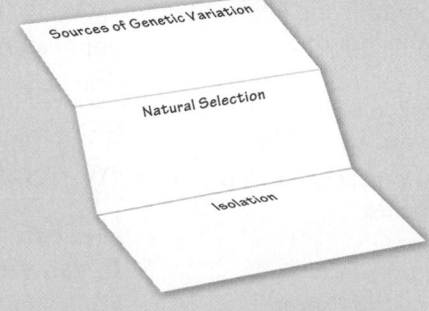

- Untamed Science Video - Chapter Mystery

17.1 Genes and Variation

MD CLG 3.3.1 Sexual Reproduction and Variation, 3.3.2 Inherited Traits, 3.3.4 DNA Alteration, 3.4.1 Evolutionary Change. SPI 1.4.2 Analyze Data, 1.5.8 Compare.

Key Questions

🔑 **How is evolution defined in genetic terms?**

🔑 **What are the sources of genetic variation?**

🔑 **What determines the number of phenotypes for a given trait?**

BUILD Understanding

Concept Map As you read, construct a concept map to describe the sources of genetic variation.

In Your Workbook Go to your workbook to learn more about making a concept map.

BUILD Vocabulary

gene pool all the genes, including all the different alleles for each gene, that are present in a population at any one time

allele frequency the number of times that an allele occurs in a gene pool, compared to the total number of alleles in that pool for the same gene

single-gene trait a trait controlled by one gene that has two alleles

polygenic trait a trait controlled by two or more genes

🖋 PREFIXES

The prefix *poly-* means "several or many." *Polygenic* means "many genes."

Genetics Joins Evolutionary Theory

When Darwin developed his theory of evolution, he did not know how heredity worked. He did not know the source of variation in a population. Mendel's studies were published while Darwin was alive. But no one understood the importance of Mendel's work. Mendel's work was rediscovered around 1900. When scientists combined Mendel's work with Darwin's theory, they could understand how traits were inherited. Today, evolution can be described in terms of genetics.

Genotype and Phenotype in Evolution Most plants and animals have two sets of genes—one set from each parent. These genes come in different forms, called alleles. The set of alleles found in an organism is called its genotype. An organism's genotype and its environment determine its phenotype. Phenotype is an organism's appearance and other characteristics, or traits.

Natural selection acts on phenotypes. It does not act directly on genes. In any population, some individuals have phenotypes (or traits) that are a better fit for their environment. Those individuals have higher fitness. In genetic terms, higher fitness means that they have more offspring and pass on more of their genes to the next generation.

Gene Pools A population is a group of individuals that mate and produce offspring. A **gene pool** contains all the alleles of all the genes in a population. In a gene pool, some alleles are common. Others are rare. **Allele frequency** is the number of times an allele occurs in a gene pool, compared to the total number of alleles for the same gene in that pool. Allele frequency is a percentage. The diagram on the next page shows the allele frequencies for fur color in a population of mice. In this population, the frequency of the dominant allele *B* (black) is 40 percent. The frequency of the recessive allele *b* (brown) is 60 percent.

If the frequency of an allele changes over time, the population is evolving. Only populations evolve, not individuals.

🔑 **Key Question** How is evolution defined in genetic terms? **In genetic terms, evolution involves a change in the frequency of alleles in a population over time.**

Sources of Genetic Variation

The members of a population differ from each other. Genetics explains the source of these variations.

Mutations A mutation is a genetic change. Most mutations are neutral and have little effect on fitness. Some mutations lower fitness by making survival and reproduction more difficult. Others increase fitness by making survival and reproduction easier. To play a role in evolution, a mutation must be passed from one generation to the next. The only mutations that can be passed on are those that are carried in egg or sperm cells.

Sexual Reproduction During sexual reproduction, the genes from two parents combine in new ways. This process can produce millions of different gene combinations. Crossing-over also mixes genes. Crossing-over happens during meiosis when chromosome pairs trade pieces of DNA.

Sexual reproduction creates new genotypes. But it does not change the frequency of alleles in the whole population. Sexual reproduction is like shuffling a deck of cards. You get new combinations of cards. But the deck always has the same number of kings and queens.

Lateral Gene Transfer Some single-celled organisms can pass genes from one individual to another. For example, many bacteria trade genes on plasmids. The passing of genes to an organism that is not an offspring is called lateral gene transfer. Lateral gene transfer is important in the evolution of single-celled organisms.

🔑 **Key Question** What are the sources of genetic variation? **Three sources of genetic variation are mutations, genetic recombination during sexual reproduction, and lateral gene transfer.**

Genetic Variation Genetic variation can produce differences in appearance, such as the different colors of the kernels on these ears of corn. Other kinds of genetic variation, such as resistance to disease, cannot be seen.

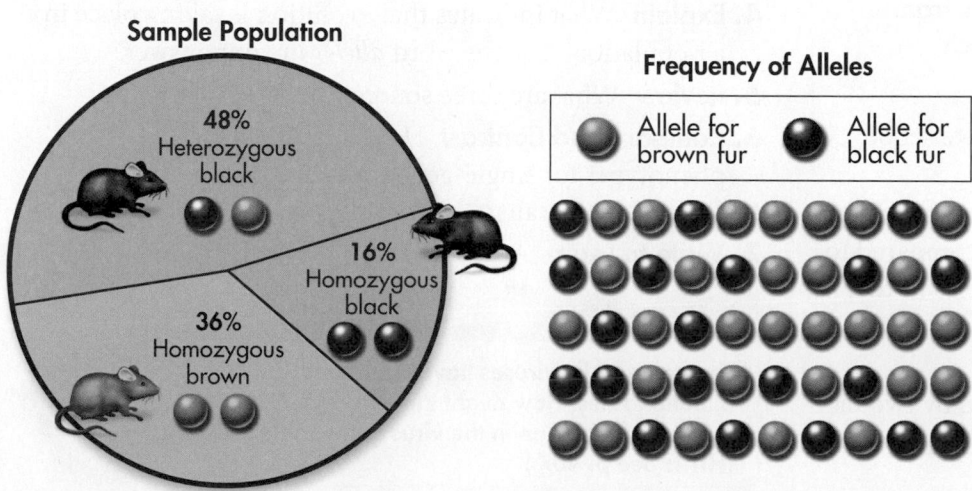

Sample Population

48% Heterozygous black

16% Homozygous black

36% Homozygous brown

Frequency of Alleles

Allele for brown fur   Allele for black fur

Alleles in a Population To determine whether a population is evolving, scientists study its allele frequencies. This diagram shows allele frequencies for fur color in a mouse population.

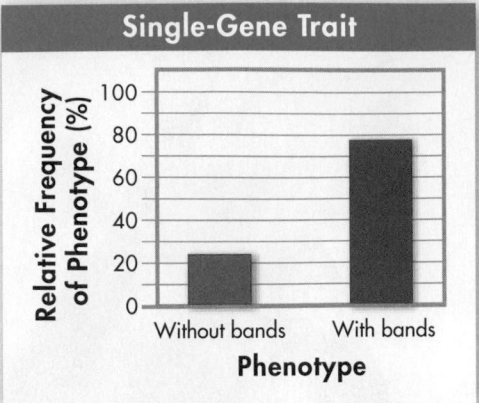

Single-Gene Trait

Relative Frequency of Phenotype (%)

Phenotype
Without bands   With bands

Two Phenotypes A single gene controls whether or not a snail's shell has bands.

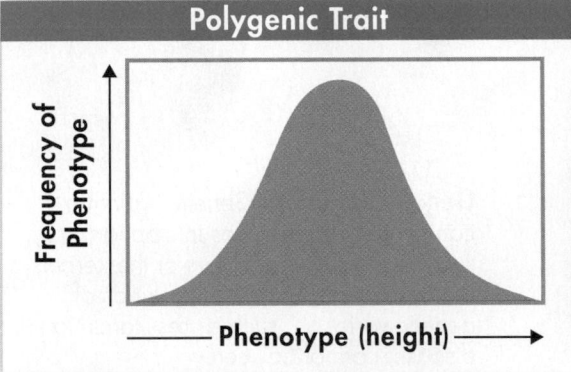

Polygenic Trait

Frequency of Phenotype

Phenotype (height)

A Range of Phenotypes Human height is controlled by several genes. Most individuals are of average height, so the graph's curve is highest in the middle.

Single-Gene and Polygenic Traits

Genes control phenotype in different ways. In some cases, a single gene controls a trait. In other cases, several genes work together to control a trait.

Single Gene Traits A trait controlled by just one gene is called a **single-gene trait.** Single-gene traits may have just two or three phenotypes. For example, in one type of snail, a single gene controls stripes on the shell. The gene has two alleles, one for striped shells and one for plain shells. There are only two possible phenotypes: with or without stripes.

Polygenic Traits A trait that is controlled by two or more genes is a **polygenic trait.** Polygenic traits can have many possible genotypes and phenotypes. In other words, there is a wide range of phenotypes for polygenic traits.

One example of a polygenic trait in humans is height. Individuals can be very tall, very short, or any height in between. You can measure the height of the members of your own class. Most students will be of average height. A graph of your data might be similar to the one shown at left. The shape of this graph is like the curve of a bell. A bell curve is typical for polygenic traits.

🔑 **Key Question** What determines the number of phenotypes for a given trait?
The number of phenotypes for a trait depends on how many genes control the trait.

CHECK Understanding

Apply Vocabulary
Use the highlighted words from the lesson to complete each sentence correctly.

1. A _____ is the complete set of genes in a population.

2. The number of times that an allele occurs in a gene pool, compared to the total number of alleles in that pool for the same gene is called _____.

3. A trait that is controlled by two or more genes is called a _____ trait.

Critical Thinking

4. **Explain** What indicates that evolution is taking place in a population? Use the word *alleles* in your answer.

5. **Review** What are three sources of genetic variation?

6. **Compare and Contrast** How does the range of phenotypes for single-gene traits differ from the range for polygenic traits?

7. **Write to Learn** Answer the mystery clue below.

MYSTERY CLUE

The genes of flu viruses have very high mutation rates. How might this affect the amount of variation in the virus gene pool? (Hint: See p. 407.)

Evolution as Genetic Change in Populations

MD CLG 3.3.2 Inherited Traits, 3.3.4 DNA Alteration, 3.4.1 Evolutionary Change. SPI 1.4.2 Analyze Data, 1.4.8 Use Models, 1.5.8 Compare, 1.6.1 Ratio and Proportion, 1.6.4 Equations, 1.7.4 Recognize Mathematics.

How Natural Selection Works

The word *fitness* can describe how healthy you are. But in evolution, *fitness* has a different meaning. *Fitness* describes individuals that have traits that help them survive and reproduce. Their traits are favored by natural selection. Individuals with high fitness have more offspring and pass on more of their genes. The alleles that produce these traits become more common in the population. This is the process of evolution.

Natural Selection on Single-Gene Traits In single-gene traits, natural selection can lead to changes in allele frequencies. When natural selection favors one trait over another, the allele for the favored trait becomes more common over time.

Imagine a population of brown lizards. A single gene that controls color mutates to form two new alleles: red and black. What happens to lizards with these new alleles? Red lizards are easier to see. They often get eaten before they can reproduce. For that reason, the red allele will probably not become common. Black lizards can warm up in the sun more quickly than brown lizards. The warmer black lizards can run from predators more quickly than brown lizards. Therefore, the frequency of the black allele is likely to increase. Over time, black lizards will become more common.

🔑 **Key Question** How does natural selection affect single-gene traits? **Natural selection on single-gene traits can lead to changes in allele frequencies. This leads to changes in phenotype frequencies.**

Key Questions

🔑 **How does natural selection affect single-gene and polygenic traits?**

🔑 **What is genetic drift?**

🔑 **What five conditions can disturb genetic equilibrium?**

BUILD Understanding

Preview Visuals Before you read, look at the chart below. What trend does the chart seem to show? How is it related to evolution?

In Your Workbook Go to your workbook to learn more about previewing visuals. Complete the previewing visuals chart for Lesson 17.2.

Selection on a Single-Gene Trait

Natural selection on a single-gene trait can cause changes in allele frequencies. Populations evolve as the frequency of alleles change, as seen in the lizards here.

Effect of Color Mutations on Lizard Survival

Initial Population	Generation 10	Generation 20	Generation 30
80%	80%	70%	40%
10%	0%	0%	0%
10%	20%	30%	60%

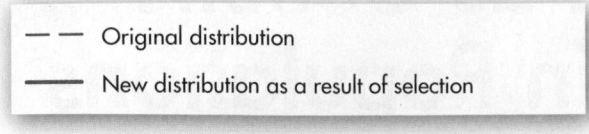
- - - Original distribution
——— New distribution as a result of selection

Directional Selection

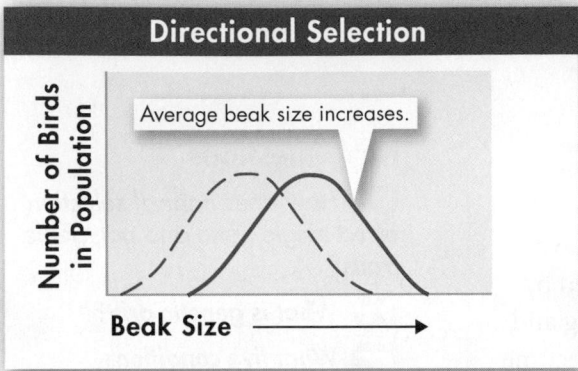

Number of Birds in Population

Average beak size increases.

Beak Size ——————→

Stabilizing Selection

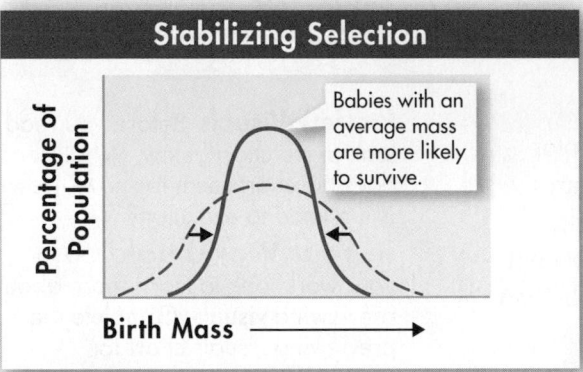

Percentage of Population

Babies with an average mass are more likely to survive.

Birth Mass ——————→

Disruptive Selection

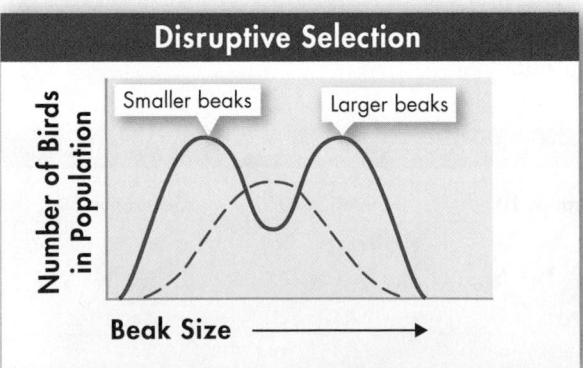

Number of Birds in Population

Smaller beaks   Larger beaks

Beak Size ——————→

Selection on Polygenic Traits Natural selection on polygenic traits has one of three patterns. These patterns are directional selection, stabilizing selection, or disruptive selection.

Natural Selection on Polygenic Traits Traits that are controlled by more than one gene produce a range of phenotypes. This range can often be shown by a bell curve. Natural selection can act on polygenic traits in one of three ways: directional selection, stabilizing selection, or disruptive selection.

▶ *Directional Selection* Sometimes natural selection favors organisms at one end of the bell curve. When individuals at one end of the curve have higher fitness than the others, **directional selection** takes place.

Imagine a population of birds that live on an island. The island has many large seeds with thick shells, but few small seeds. Birds with bigger beaks would have more to eat than birds with smaller beaks. Birds with bigger beaks would live longer and have more offspring. Over time, the average size of beaks would get bigger. Natural selection would move in one direction—toward larger beaks.

▶ *Stabilizing Selection* Sometimes natural selection favors the average individuals. When individuals near the center of the bell curve have the highest fitness, **stabilizing selection** takes place. Stabilizing selection shifts the ends of the curve closer to the middle.

Human babies are affected by stabilizing selection. Very small babies are usually less healthy and less likely to survive. Very large babies may have trouble being born. In this example, the fitness of the extremes is lower than that of the average.

▶ *Disruptive Selection* Sometimes the most extreme traits are most likely to survive and reproduce. The average types have a harder time surviving and reproducing. This situation is called **disruptive selection.** Disruptive selection can eventually create two distinct phenotypes. These phenotypes are shown by a curve with two peaks.

Suppose a population of birds lives on an island where medium-size seeds are rare. Most seeds are either large or small. Birds with very small or very large beaks would be more likely to survive. The population might split into two groups: one with smaller beaks and one with larger beaks.

🔑 **Key Question** How does natural selection affect polygenic traits? **Natural selection on polygenic traits can affect the relative fitness of phenotypes. Natural selection produces one of three types of selection: directional selection, stabilizing selection, or disruptive selection.**

Genetic Drift

Natural selection is not the only cause of evolutionary change. In small populations, chance events can cause evolution. A random change in the frequency of the alleles in a gene pool is called **genetic drift.** Genetic drift may be caused by the bottleneck effect or the founder effect.

Genetic Bottlenecks Sometimes, a disaster can kill off most of a population. For example, a flood or disease may leave only a few individuals alive. The small group of survivors might have a set of alleles that is very different from the lost population. When this small population grows, its gene pool will be different from the original population. A change in allele frequency following a dramatic loss of population is called the **bottleneck effect.** The bottleneck effect can greatly reduce the genetic diversity in a population.

The Founder Effect Genetic drift can also happen when a few individuals move into a new habitat. The small group may have a set of alleles that is different from the main population. The **founder effect** is a change in allele frequency that results from a small group starting a new population.

The hundreds of species of fruit flies on the different Hawaiian islands demonstrate the founder effect. All of these species came from a single species of fruit fly in South America. Each Hawaiian species has allele frequencies that differ from the original species.

⚷ Key Question What is genetic drift? **Genetic drift is the change in allele frequency that happens in small populations due to random events.**

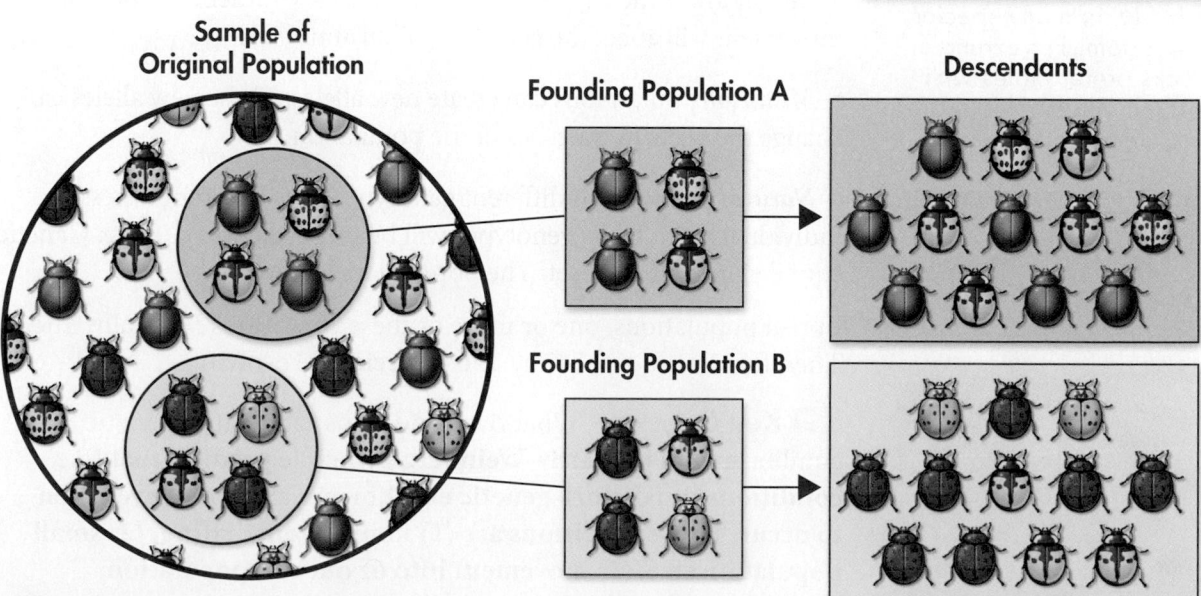

Founder Effect When a small group starts a new population, the descendants can differ from the original population. In the art, a diverse population gives rise to two very different populations.

Choosing a Mate In many species, mating is not random. For example, female peacocks prefer mates with big, colorful tail feathers. This is an example of sexual selection.

Evolution Versus Genetic Equilibrium

To understand how populations evolve, it helps to imagine a population that does *not* evolve. If a population is not evolving, the allele frequencies in the gene pool do not change. This condition is called **genetic equilibrium.**

Sexual Reproduction and Allele Frequency In sexual reproduction, genes are shuffled. This produces many new gene combinations. But meiosis and fertilization do not change the allele frequencies in the total population. Therefore, sexual reproduction alone does not affect genetic equilibrium.

The Hardy-Weinberg Principle The **Hardy-Weinberg principle** states that allele frequencies in a population will stay in genetic equilibrium unless something causes them to change. This principle predicts that five conditions can upset genetic equilibrium and cause a population to evolve.

▶ *Nonrandom Mating* In genetic equilibrium, individuals must mate with other individuals at random. But in many species, individuals choose mates that have particular traits, such as size or color. When individuals pick mates with certain heritable traits, the process is called **sexual selection.** If mates are selected for a particular trait, the frequency of that trait will increase.

▶ *Small Population* Genetic drift usually does not affect a large population. But it can affect small populations greatly. Therefore, evolution takes place more easily in a small population.

▶ *Movement Into or Out of the Population* Individuals that join a population may add new alleles to the gene pool. Individuals that leave can lower the frequency of certain alleles. Either direction of movement will affect the genetic equilibrium.

▶ *Mutations* Mutations can create new alleles. These new alleles can change the allele frequencies of the population.

▶ *Natural Selection* If different genotypes have different fitness, individuals with those genotypes will be more likely to survive. Genetic equilibrium will be upset. The population will evolve.

In real populations, one or more of these conditions is usually true. Therefore, most of the time, most species are evolving.

🗝 **Key Question** What five conditions can disturb genetic equilibrium? **The Hardy-Weinberg principle predicts that five conditions can disturb genetic equilibrium and cause evolution to occur. These conditions are (1) nonrandom mating, (2) small population size, (3) movement into or out of a population, (4) mutations, and (5) natural selection.**

Allele Frequency

The Hardy-Weinberg principle can be used to predict the frequencies of genotypes in a population that is not evolving. This equation can be used to predict the percentages of the possible genotypes in a population:

$$p^2 + 2pq + q^2 = 1, \text{ where}$$

p and q stand for two alleles of the same gene; p^2 and q^2 stand for the homozygous genotypes; pq stands for the heterozygous genotype.

Sample Problem

A population has two alleles for a gene: A (dominant) and a (recessive). In one generation, the frequency of allele A is 60% and the frequency of allele a is 40%. What will be the frequencies of each genotype in the next generation?

1. From genetics, you know that a cross of these two alleles can produce three genotypes: *AA, Aa,* and *aa.* In the equation, allele A will be p, and allele a will be q.

$$
\begin{array}{ccccccc}
p^2 & + & 2pq & + & q^2 & = & 1 \\
AA & + & 2Aa & + & aa & = & 1, \text{ or } \mathbf{100\%}
\end{array}
$$

2. Substitute the known frequencies for alleles A and a.

$A = 60\%$, or **0.60** $a = 40\%$, or **0.40**

$A^2 = 36\%$, or **0.36** $a^2 = 16\%$, or **0.16**

$2Aa = 2\ (0.60 \times 0.40) = 2\ (0.24) = 0.48$, or **48%**

The next generation will have these frequencies: 36% *AA;* 48% *Aa;* 16% *aa.* If the population does not show these frequencies, evolution is taking place.

Practice Problems

Some members of a human population have a genetic condition. The condition is controlled by two alleles, S (dominant) and s (recessive). The condition affects only individuals that are homozygous for the recessive allele (*ss*). Heterozygous individuals (*Ss*) do not have the condition. The s allele is found in 6% of the population.

1. Calculate What percentage of the population carries the S allele? (**Hint:** $p + q = 100\%$)

2. Calculate What are the frequencies of the *SS, Ss,* and *ss* genotypes?

3. Calculate In a population of 10,000 people, how many people would have the condition?

CHECK
Understanding

Apply Vocabulary
Use the highlighted words from the lesson to complete each sentence correctly.

1. The change in allele frequency after a dramatic drop in the size of a population is called the _____.

2. The change in allele frequency caused by the migration of a small group is called the _____.

3. The _____ identifies conditions necessary for gene frequencies in a population to remain constant.

Critical Thinking

4. Relate Cause and Effect How does natural selection affect a single-gene trait?

5. Compare and Contrast Compare directional selection and disruptive selection.

6. Relate Cause and Effect What is genetic equilibrium? What five conditions are necessary to maintain genetic equilibrium?

7. Write to Learn Answer the mystery clue below.

MYSTERY CLUE

Normally, your immune system can kill invading viruses. What would happen if a flu virus had a mutation that your immune system could not fight? (**Hint:** See p. 409.)

The Process of Speciation

MD CLG 3.4.1 Evolutionary Change, 3.4.2 Relatedness Among Organisms, 3.5.2 Interdependence of Organisms in the Biosphere.

Key Questions

🔑 **What types of isolation lead to the formation of new species?**

🔑 **What is the current hypothesis about Galápagos finch speciation?**

BUILD Understanding

Compare/Contrast Table In a compare/contrast table, describe the three mechanisms of reproductive isolation.

In Your Workbook Go to your workbook to learn more about using compare/contrast tables. Complete the compare/contrast table for Lesson 17.3.

BUILD Vocabulary

species
a population whose members can breed and produce fertile offspring

speciation
the formation of a new species

reproductive isolation
the separation of a species or population so that members can no longer interbreed

geographic isolation
a form of reproductive isolation in which two populations are separated by geographic barriers such as rivers, mountains, or bodies of water

Isolating Mechanisms

Biologists define a **species** as a population whose members can breed and produce fertile offspring. How does one species become two? If members of a population can no longer mate, a new species may evolve. The formation of a new species is called **speciation.**

Breeding connects the gene pool of a species. If a species is split into two parts, genetic changes in one part of the gene pool cannot spread to the other. When two populations can no longer mate and produce offspring, **reproductive isolation** has occurred. Geography, behavior, and time can separate populations from each other.

Geographic Isolation When populations are separated by a barrier, such as a river, mountain, or ocean, **geographic isolation** can occur. For example, the Abert's and Kaibab squirrels once belonged to the same population. About 10,000 years ago, a small population became isolated north of the Grand Canyon. Since then, genetic drift and natural selection have led to two different-looking populations.

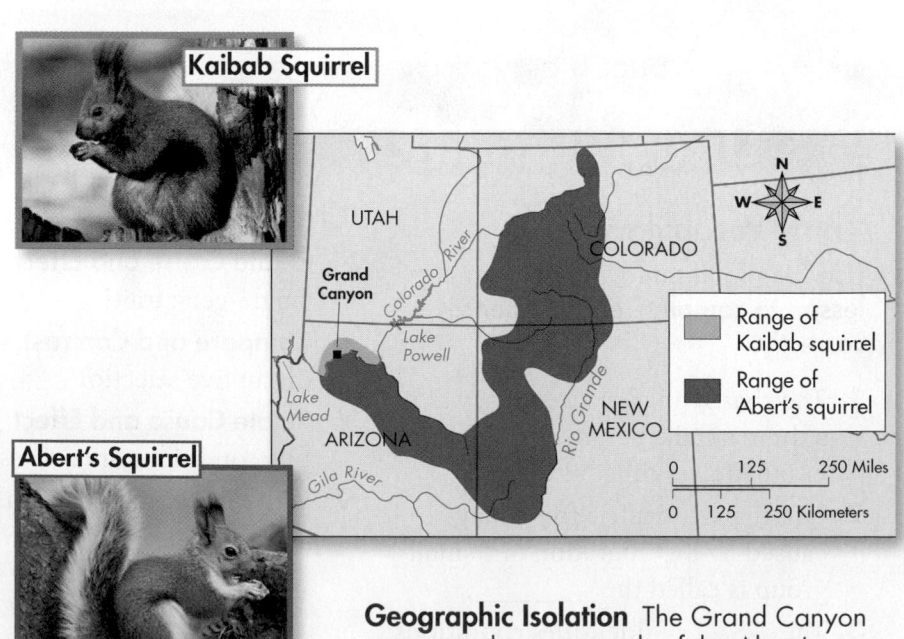

Kaibab Squirrel

Abert's Squirrel

Range of Kaibab squirrel
Range of Abert's squirrel

Geographic Isolation The Grand Canyon separates the gene pools of the Abert's squirrel and the Kaibab squirrel. The two populations are still the same species, but they have evolved striking differences.

Behavioral Isolation If two interbreeding populations develop different behaviors, such as different mating dances, then **behavioral isolation** can happen. Two nearly identical species of birds—eastern meadowlarks and western meadowlarks—share the same habitat. These two species do not interbreed because their mating songs are different.

Temporal Isolation A third isolating mechanism is temporal isolation. **Temporal isolation** happens when populations that live in the same habitat reproduce at different times.

🗝 **Key Question** What types of isolation lead to new species? **New species can arise from behavioral isolation, geographic isolation, and temporal isolation.**

Speciation in Darwin's Finches

Since Darwin, many scientists have studied the Galápagos finches. The Grants showed that under the right conditions, natural selection can happen quickly. This knowledge makes the Galápagos finches a good choice for describing how speciation might work in real life.

Speciation probably began when a small number of finches founded a new population. This population was geographically isolated from the main population. Over time, the gene pool changed. According to the currently accepted hypothesis, isolation, competition, and natural selection formed new species that could no longer interbreed.

Founders Arrive Many years ago, a few finches from South America arrived on one of the islands. Maybe they were blown there by a storm. The small group survived and reproduced. Because of the founder effect, the allele frequencies of this new population were different from the original population.

Geographic Isolation These finches do not usually fly over open water, so the population was geographically isolated. The founder effect, geographic isolation, and natural selection led to the evolution of a new species of finch. Eventually some of these finches moved to a new island, where the process was repeated.

Changes in Gene Pools The environment on the second island may have had different plants with larger seeds. Directional selection would have favored birds with larger beaks. Over time, a population with larger beaks evolved.

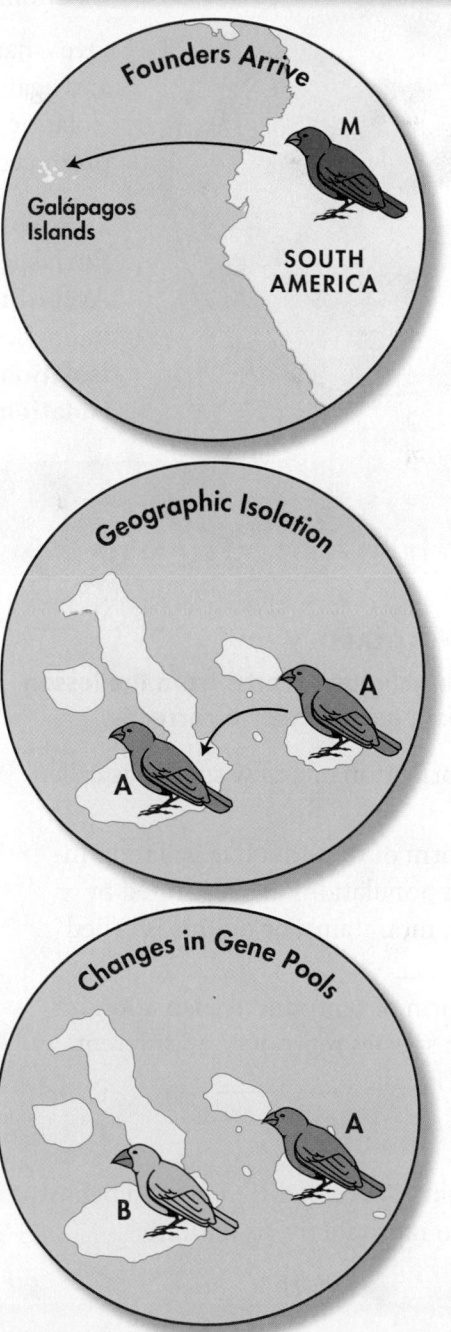

Behavioral Isolation

Behavioral Isolation Imagine that a few birds from the second island cross back to the first island. Will the two populations interbreed? Probably not. Finches choose mates carefully. They like mates that look like themselves. A small-beaked bird will not breed with a large-beaked bird. Even though they share the same habitat, the two populations are now isolated by behavior. They have become two different species.

Competition and More Evolution The two new species live together and compete for seeds. During the dry season, it is difficult to find enough seeds to eat. Individuals with very small beaks have greater success than birds with average-size beaks. Small-beaked birds can specialize in eating very small seeds that birds with average-size beaks cannot eat. Over time the differences lead to reproductive isolation. A third species evolves.

Competition and Continued Evolution

Over many years, this process could have repeated itself again and again on the different islands. The combination of geographic isolation, behavioral isolation, and natural selection could have produced the 13 different finch species found in the Galápagos today.

🔑 **Key Question** What is the current hypothesis about Galápagos finch speciation?
According to this hypothesis, speciation in Galápagos finches happened by the founding of a new population, geographic isolation, changes in the new population's gene pool, behavioral isolation, and ecological competition.

CHECK Understanding

Apply Vocabulary
Use the highlighted words from the lesson to complete each sentence correctly.

1. The formation of a new species is called _____.

2. The form of reproductive isolation in which populations are separated by rivers, mountains, or oceans is called _____.

3. The form of reproductive isolation in which species reproduce at different times is called _____.

Critical Thinking

4. Explain How can differences in behavior lead to reproductive isolation?

5. Sequence Scientists hypothesize that a series of events lead to the evolution of different species of finches on the Galápagos islands. List the following events in the correct order: behaviors prevent the birds from interbreeding; changes in gene pool; geographic isolation; a small group of birds arrives from South America.

6. Write to Learn Answer the question in the mystery clue below. Use the word *gene pool* in your answer.

MYSTERY CLUE

A population of viruses inside an animal is isolated from other virus populations. How might this isolation affect virus evolution? (**Hint:** See p. 414.)

17.4 Molecular Evolution

MD CLG **3.3.1** Sexual Reproduction and Variation, **3.4.1** Evolutionary Change, **3.4.2** Relatedness Among Organisms. **SPI 1.5.9** Synthesize Ideas.

Molecular Clocks

A genome is the complete set of genes found in an organism. Each gcnome has many genes. For example, your body has about 25,000 working genes! Scientists often study genomes to learn how organisms have evolved. By comparing the genes of different organisms, scientists can test different hypotheses. Some hypotheses suggest how closely organisms are related. Other hypotheses suggest how long ago evolutionary lines split apart. One way to test these hypotheses is by using DNA as a molecular clock. A **molecular clock** uses mutation rates in DNA to estimate how long ago two organisms shared a common ancestor.

Ticking Mutations Some kinds of mutations happen at a steady rate, like seconds ticking on a clock. As time passes, more and more mutations happen. Some mutations help or hurt the survival of an organism. Because these mutations are affected by natural selection, they cannot be used as "molecular ticks." But many mutations do not affect an organisms's fitness. Such mutations are said to be *neutral*. Neutral mutations change DNA without affecting an organism's fitness.

Neutral mutations can collect in the DNA of different species at about the same rate. Scientists can compare the number of neutral mutations in specific sequences of DNA from different organisms. The more differences there are, the more mutations have happened. By counting mutations, researchers can estimate how long it has been since the two organisms shared a common ancestor.

Key Questions

🔑 *What are molecular clocks?*

🔑 *Where do new genes come from?*

🔑 *How may Hox genes be involved in evolutionary change?*

BUILD Understanding

Flowchart A flowchart is a way to show the steps in a process. As you read about gene duplication, make a flowchart that shows how duplicate genes evolve.

In Your Workbook Go to your workbook to learn more about making a flowchart. Complete the flowchart for Lesson 17.4.

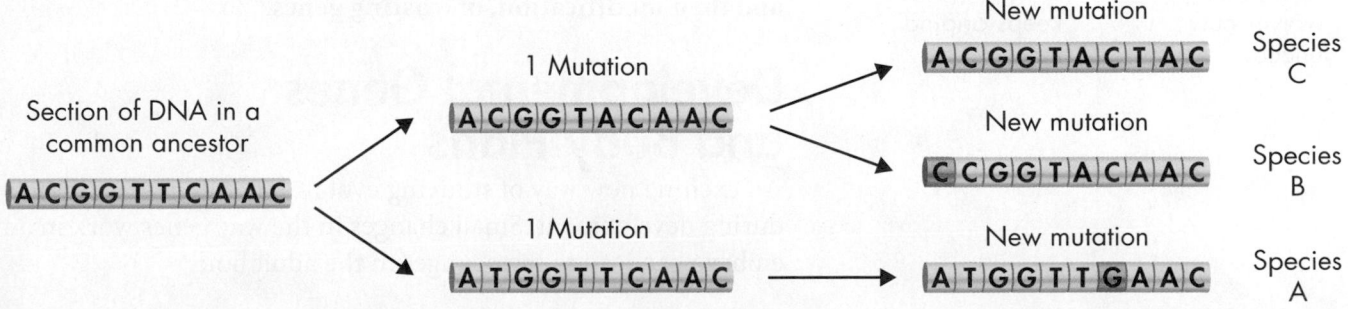

Molecular Clock By comparing DNA sequences, biologists can estimate how closely related species are. Two species that have only a few different mutations shared an ancestor recently. Species that have many different mutations shared an ancestor long ago.

Gene Duplication
In this diagram, a gene is first duplicated. Then one of the two genes mutates.

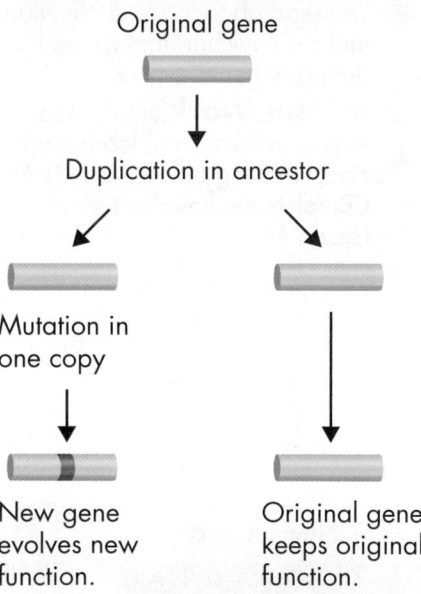

Original gene

Duplication in ancestor

Mutation in one copy

New gene evolves new function.

Original gene keeps original function.

Rate of Mutation Not all genes mutate at the same rate. You can think of a gene that mutates quickly as the second hand on a clock. These genes are useful for measuring evolution that happens over a short time. Other genes mutate more slowly. Such genes are used to measure evolution that takes place over a much longer time.

Key Question What are molecular clocks?
Molecular clocks are pieces of DNA that mutate at a known rate. Scientists use molecular clocks to estimate how much time has passed since two species shared a common ancestor.

Gene Duplication

Humans have about 25,000 working genes. Where did all these genes come from? Modern genes probably evolved from a much smaller number of genes in the earliest forms of life.

Copying Genes One way that the number of genes grew so large was by the duplication, or copying, of existing genes. Duplication can happen during meiosis as chromosome pairs exchange DNA. Sometimes one chromosome ends up with extra DNA during the exchange.

Duplicate Genes Evolve Sometimes a duplicated gene mutates. The mutation changes the way the gene works. The mutated copy of the gene performs a new role. The original gene continues to perform its old role.

Gene Families Several copies of a gene can form a group of related genes that is called a gene family. Genes in a family usually make slightly different proteins that carry out similar roles. For example, one gene family makes several kinds of oxygen-carrying proteins. This gene family evolved from just one original gene.

Key Question Where do new genes come from?
One way that new genes evolve is through the duplication, and then modification, of existing genes.

Developmental Genes and Body Plans

An exciting new way of studying evolution looks at gene activity during development. Small changes in the way genes work in an embryo can lead to big changes in the adult body.

Hox Genes and Evolution Hox genes are a group of genes that play an important role in animal development. Hox genes determine which parts of the embryo develop arms, legs, or wings. Hox genes also control the size and shape of the adult body parts.

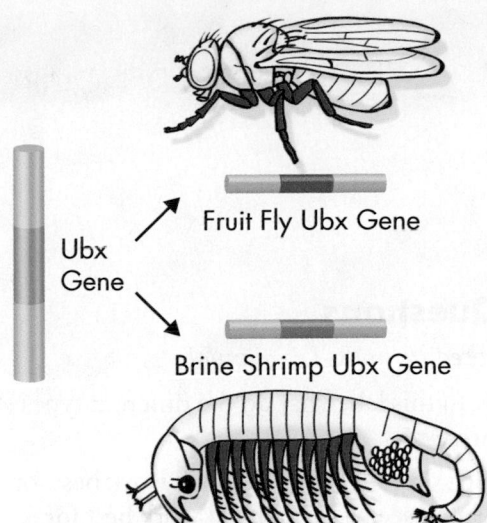

Ubx Gene

Fruit Fly Ubx Gene

Brine Shrimp Ubx Gene

Changes in a Hox Gene
Fruits flies and brine shrimp share a common ancestor. The Hox gene called Ubx directs the development of legs in both animals. Millions of years ago, mutations on Ubx caused fruit flies to have six legs and brine shrimp to have many legs.

Shrimp and insects share an ancient common ancestor. This ancestor had dozens of legs. Shrimp still have many legs, but insects have only six. What happened to those other legs? A single mutation in a Hox gene turns off the growth of some pairs of legs. Thus, a change in one Hox gene can cause a major difference between two groups of animals.

Timing Is Everything The growth of an embryo is carefully controlled by genes. Growth starts and stops at exact times. Small changes in starting and stopping times can make a big difference in the final organism. For example, small changes in timing can make the difference between long, slender fingers and short, stubby toes.

🔑 **Key Question** How may Hox genes be involved in evolutionary change? **Even small changes in Hox genes can produce large changes in adult animals.**

✓CHECK Understanding

Apply Vocabulary
Use the highlighted words from the lesson to complete each sentence correctly.

1. When scientists use the rates of mutation in DNA to estimate how long two species have been evolving separately, they are using a _____ .

Critical Thinking

2. Relate Cause and Effect How can crossing-over result in gene duplication?

3. Relate Cause and Effect How can a duplicate gene become a new gene with a different function?

4. Review What is the function of Hox genes?

5. Relate Cause and Effect Why have small changes in Hox genes had such a great effect on the evolution of animal diversity?

6. Write to Learn How does time affect the number of differences in the genes of two species with a common ancestor?

BIOLOGY.com   Search   Lesson 17.4   GO   • Lesson Assessment

MD **CLG 3.5.1** Factors Influencing Ecosystems. **SPI 1.4.2** Analyze Data, **1.4.8** Use Models, **1.5.9** Synthesize Ideas, **1.6.4** Equations.

Pre-Lab: Competing for Resources

Problem How can competition lead to speciation?

Materials assorted tools, large and small seeds, large and small paper plates, timer or clock with second hand

Lab Manual Chapter 17 Lab

Skills Focus Use Models, Predict, Apply Concepts

Connect to the **Big idea** Speciation is not easy to see in nature. Usually, new phenotypes take years to emerge or become common enough to be noticed. Also, new phenotypes can be difficult to track in a complex environment. For scientists who want to study speciation, islands can provide an ideal environment.

Peter and Rosemary Grant spent years studying finches on the Galápagos Islands. They measured and recorded the traits and diets of hundreds of birds. During a year with a severe drought, the Grants were able to observe natural selection in action as food became scarce. In this lab you will model variation in bird beaks and diet to demonstrate the impact of competition on survival and speciation.

Background Questions

a. Review What is speciation?

b. Relate Cause and Effect How did geographic isolation lead to speciation among the Galápagos finches?

c. Compare and Contrast How does an adaptation differ from other inherited traits?

Pre-Lab Questions

Preview the procedure in the lab manual.

1. Use Models In this lab, what do the different types of tools represent?

2. Predict Which tools do you think will work best for picking up small seeds? Which will work best for picking up large seeds?

3. Design an Experiment Why will the time you have to collect seeds be limited?

 **BIOLOGY**.com   Search   (Chapter 17)   GO

Visit Chapter 17 online to test yourself on chapter content and to find activities to help you learn.

Untamed Science Video Climb the cliffs of Hawaii with the Untamed Science crew to discover how geographic isolation can result in a new species.

Art Review Review your understanding of alleles and allele frequencies in a population.

Art in Motion Watch how different types of selection change the types of individuals that comprise a population.

Tutor Tube Learn more about the mechanisms of speciation from the tutor.

17.1 Genes and Variation

- Evolution is change in the frequency of alleles in a population over time.

- Three sources of genetic variation are mutations, genetic recombination during sexual reproduction, and lateral gene transfer.

- The number of phenotypes produced for a trait depends on how many genes control the trait.

gene pool (p. 406)
allele frequency (p. 406)
single-gene trait (p. 408)
polygenic trait (p. 408)

17.2 Evolution as Genetic Change in Populations

- Natural selection on single-gene traits can lead to changes in allele frequencies. This can lead to changes in phenotype frequencies.

- Natural selection on polygenic traits can affect the relative fitness of phenotypes. This selective pressure can cause one of three types of selection: directional selection, stabilizing selection, and disruptive selection.

- Genetic drift may occur in small populations. By chance, individuals that carry one allele may leave more offspring than other individuals leave. Over time, a series of chance events can cause an allele to become more or less common in a population.

- The Hardy-Weinberg principle predicts that five conditions can cause evolution to take place: (1) nonrandom mating, (2) small population size, (3) movement into or out of the population, (4) mutations, and (5) natural selection.

directional selection (p. 410)
stabilizing selection (p. 410)
disruptive selection (p. 410)
genetic drift (p. 411)
bottleneck effect (p. 411)
founder effect (p. 411)
genetic equilibrium (p. 412)
Hardy-Weinberg principle (p. 412)
sexual selection (p. 412)

Competition and Continued Evolution

17.3 The Process of Speciation

- When populations become reproductively isolated, they can evolve into separate species. Reproductive isolation can develop in a variety of ways. These include behavioral isolation, geographic isolation, and temporal isolation.

- Speciation in Galápagos finches most likely occurred by: founding of a new population, geographic isolation, changes in the population's gene pool, behavioral isolation, and ecological competition.

species (p. 414)
speciation (p. 414)
reproductive isolation (p. 414)
geographic isolation (p. 414)
behavioral isolation (p. 415)
temporal isolation (p. 415)

17.4 Molecular Evolution

- A molecular clock uses mutation rates in DNA to estimate the time that two species have been evolving separately.

- One way that new genes evolve is through the duplication, and then modification, of existing genes.

- Small changes in Hox gene activity during development can produce large changes in adult animals.

molecular clock (p. 417)

 **Evolution**

Write an answer to the question below.

Q: How can populations evolve to form new species?

Constructed Response

Write an answer to each of the numbered questions below. The answer to each numbered question should be one or two paragraphs long. To help get ideas, read the **Hints** below the questions.

1. **Why is genetic variation in a population necessary for natural selection to take place? Use the words *fitness* and *phenotype* in your answer.**

   Hint The fitness of an organism depends upon the conditions of its environment.

2. **How does population size affect evolution?**

   Hint The Hardy-Weinberg principle describes the conditions under which a population will *not* evolve.

3. **On the Galápagos Islands, there is a species of finch that eats only fruit. Describe a process by which this species may have evolved from a species that eats many kinds of foods.**

   Hint Refer to the art on pages 415 and 416.

Foundations for Learning Wrap-Up

When you have finished taking notes, fold the paper into a triangle with the notes on the outside. Tape the ends together to make a table tent, as shown below.

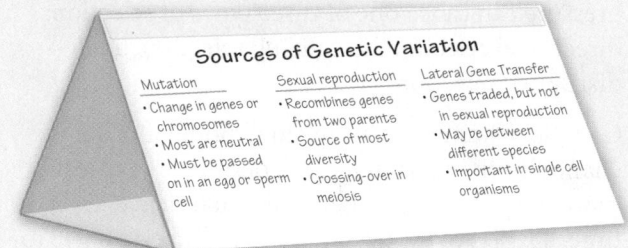

Activity 1 Work with a partner to review each of the main topics. Ask a partner to pick a side of your table tent—Sources of Genetic Variation, Natural Selection, or Isolation. Have your partner form a question or two about each topic, such as "What are three sources of genetic diversity?" While you answer, your partner will watch your table tent to be sure you have answered correctly and completely. When you have answered all three sides, change roles.

Activity 2 Use your table tent to explain how a new species of birds may have arisen on an island. Begin with the side labeled Sources of Genetic Variation. You may also refer to the art about the speciation in Darwin's finches in Lesson 17.3.

17.1 Genes and Variation

Understand Key Concepts

1. The combined genetic information of a population forms a
   - a. genotype.
   - c. phenotype.
   - b. gene pool.
   - d. bottleneck.

Test-Taking Tip

Read Before You Choose Read all the choices before you pick your answer. Sometimes a choice can be partly correct, but there is a better choice later in the list. In question 1, you might be tempted to answer **a**, because a genotype is a set of genes. But genotypes refer to individuals, not populations. So **b**, gene pool, is the best choice.

2. Mutations that improve an individual's ability to survive and reproduce are
   - a. harmful.
   - c. helpful.
   - b. neutral.
   - d. chromosomal.

3. Identify two ways that sexual reproduction is a source of genetic variation.

Think Critically

4. **Compare and Contrast** Compare the effects of two mutations: a mutation in a body cell and a mutation in an egg cell. Which mutation could affect evolution? Why?

17.2 Evolution as Genetic Change in Populations

Understand Key Concepts

5. In a population, short individuals have a greater fitness than average-size or tall individuals. This difference in fitness could lead to
   - a. directional selection.
   - b. stabilizing selection.
   - c. disruptive selection.
   - d. artificial selection.

6. A change in the allele frequency of a small population that is caused by chance is known as
   - a. a gene pool.
   - b. the Hardy-Weinberg principle.
   - c. variation.
   - d. genetic drift.

7. What is *fitness* in genetic terms?

8. How does meiosis in sexual reproduction affect the frequency of alleles in a population?

Think Critically

9. **Apply Concepts** Why is genetic drift most common in small populations?

10. **Infer** Genetic equilibrium is rare in most populations. Why do you think this is the case?

17.3 The Process of Speciation

Understand Key Concepts

11. When two populations no longer interbreed, what is the result?
    - a. genetic equilibrium
    - b. reproductive isolation
    - c. stabilizing selection
    - d. artificial selection

12. Two populations of turtles nest on an island. One of the species nests in June. The other species nests in August. These two species are separated by
    - a. temporal isolation.
    - b. geographical isolation.
    - c. genetic isolation.
    - d. behavioral isolation.

13. Why is variation important to the survival of a species when the environment changes?

Think Critically

14. **Relate Cause and Effect** Before a population splits into two different species, there must usually be reproductive isolation. Explain why this is so.

17.4 Molecular Evolution

Understand Key Concepts

15. Hox genes are important to evolution because
  a. they mutate often.
  b. they are only found in egg and sperm cells.
  c. they are immune to natural selection.
  d. they have a large effect on the traits of an organism.

16. What are scientists counting when using a molecular clock?
  a. mutations
  b. genes
  c. gene families
  d. chromosomes

17. What are neutral mutations?

18. Why do molecular clocks use mutations that have no effect on phenotype?

Think Critically

19. Sequence Describe how duplicate genes can lead to the creation of new genes.

Connecting Concepts

Use Science Graphics

Use the data table to answer questions 20 and 21.

Frequency of Alleles		
Year	Frequency of Allele *B*	Frequency of Allele *b*
1910	0.81	0.19
1930	0.49	0.51
1950	0.25	0.75
1970	0.10	0.90

20. Interpret Tables Describe the trend shown by the data in the table.

21. Form a Hypothesis What might account for the trend shown by the data?

solve the CHAPTER MYSTERY

KILLER DISEASE

The genes of flu viruses mutate often. Also, different strains of flu can swap genes. These mutations and the ability to gene swap gives the viruses plenty of genetic diversity.

Natural selection acts on viruses in the environment of your own body! Viruses have proteins on their surfaces that make them targets for your immune system. Viruses with proteins that your body recognizes will be destroyed. These viruses have low fitness. Viruses that your body can't recognize have a higher fitness.

Viruses evolve new proteins often. This makes them harder for your immune system to recognize. That's when you get sick. That's also why you can have the flu one winter, and then get another strain the next winter.

Rarely, flu virus evolution produces a very new protein. Your immune system is unable to recognize or fight these new proteins. Such flu viruses can be deadly, as was the influenza virus of 1918. If a strain like that appeared today, it would kill many people.

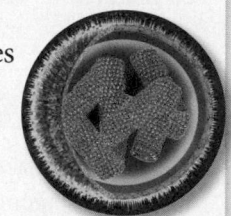

Influenza Virus

1. Infer Vaccines help prepare your body for an infection. Doctors recommend that people receive a new vaccine for the flu every year. People do not need to receive a new vaccine for measles every year. What does this suggest about a difference between the measles virus and flu viruses?

2. Apply Concepts Can you think of other issues in public health that relate directly to evolution?

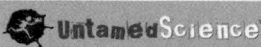 **Never Stop Exploring Your World.** Finding the solution to the epidemic mystery is only the beginning. Take a video field trip with the ecogeeks of Untamed Science to see where the mystery leads.

Multiple Choice

1. Which of the following conditions is MOST likely to result in changes in allele frequencies in a population?
   A random mating
   B small population size
   C no migrations into or out of a population
   D absence of natural selection   CLG 3.4.1

2. Mutations and the genetic recombination that occurs during sexual reproduction are both sources of
   A genetic variation.   C genetic equilibrium.
   B stabilizing selection.   D genetic drift.
   CLG 3.3.1

3. In a population of lizards, the smallest and largest lizards are more easily preyed upon than medium-size lizards. What kind of natural selection is MOST likely to occur in this situation?
   A genetic drift
   B sexual selection
   C stabilizing selection
   D directional selection   CLG 3.4.1

4. Populations of antibiotic-resistant bacteria are the result of the process of
   A natural selection.   C genetic drift.
   B temporal isolation.   D artificial selection.
   CLG 3.4.1

5. If species A and B have very similar genes and proteins, what is probably true?
   A Species A and B share a relatively recent common ancestor.
   B Species A evolved independently of species B for a long period.
   C Species A is younger than species B.
   D Species A is older than species B.   CLG 3.4.2

6. When two species reproduce at different times, the situation is called
   A genetic drift.
   B temporal selection.
   C temporal isolation.
   D lateral gene transfer.   CLG 3.4.1

7. The length of time that two species have been evolving separately can be estimated using
   A genetic drift.   C a molecular clock.
   B gene duplication.   D Hox genes.   CLG 3.4.2

Questions 8–9

The graphs below show the changes in crab color at one beach.

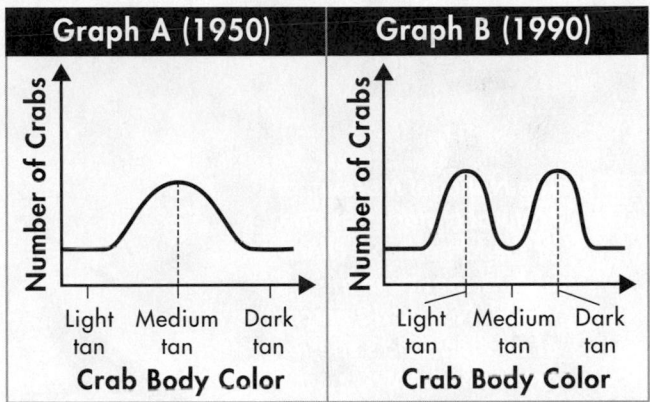

8. What process occurred over the 40-year period?
   A artificial selection
   B directional selection
   C stabilizing selection
   D disruptive selection   SPI 1.4.2

9. Which of the following is MOST likely to have caused the change in the distribution?
   A A new predator arrived that preferred dark-tan crabs.
   B A new predator arrived that preferred light-tan crabs.
   C A change in beach color made medium-tan crabs the least visible to predators.
   D A change in beach color made medium-tan crabs the most visible to predators.   SPI 1.4.2

Open-Ended Response

10. How does evolution change the relative frequency of alleles in a gene pool? Why does this happen?
    CLG 3.4.1

If You Have Trouble With . . .

Question	1	2	3	4	5	6	7	8	9	10
See Lesson	17.3	17.1	17.2	17.2	17.4	17.3	17.4	17.2	17.2	17.1

18 Classification

Big idea **Unity and Diversity of Life**
Q: What is the goal of biologists who classify living things?

The National Museum of Natural History has one of the largest collections of bird species in the world. Nearly 80 percent of all the world's species are found here.

MYSTERY

GRIN AND BEAR IT

If you just looked at polar bears and brown bears, you would probably think that they were different species. Polar bears are much larger than brown bears. Their paws let them swim and walk on snow and ice. Their white fur hides them in the snow. In contrast, brown bears are brown. And their paws are not as big.

Polar bears and brown bears look very different. They also act differently. Do those differences mean that they are different species? Remember the definition of a species: "a group of similar organisms that can breed and produce fertile offspring." Polar bears and brown bears *can* interbreed and produce fertile offspring. This should make them the same species. Are they?

Read for Mystery Clues As you read this chapter, look for clues to help you decide if polar bears and brown bears are separate species. Then, solve the mystery at the end of the chapter.

MD **MARYLAND VOLUNTARY STATE CURRICULUM**

Biology Indicators/Core Learning Goals **(CLG)** 3.4.1, 3.4.2. **Skills and Processes Indicators (SPI)** 1.1.1, 1.1.2, 1.2.6, 1.2.7, 1.4.1, 1.4.2, 1.5.2, 1.5.5, 1.5.7, 1.5.8, 1.5.9. See lessons for details.

FOUNDATIONS for Learning

To understand biological classification, you will need to learn a few new words. Write the following words on index cards: *Domain, Kingdom, Phylum, Class, Order, Family, Genus,* and *Species.*

Domain	Phylum	Kingdom	Family
Species	Class	Order	Genus

As you read the chapter, write the definition for each word on the back of the card. Also, write down examples of the terms. You will use these cards for two activities at the end of the chapter. They will help you answer the question: What is the goal of biologists who classify living things?

• Untamed Science Video   • Chapter Mystery

18.1 Finding Order in Diversity

MD CLG 3.4.2 Relatedness Among Organisms. SPI 1.1.1 Problems and Solutions, 1.4.1 Organize Data, 1.5.5 Create and Interpret Graphics, 1.5.7 Classification Systems.

Key Questions

🔑 What are the goals of binomial nomenclature and systematics?

🔑 How did Linnaeus group species into larger taxa?

BUILD Understanding

Preview Visuals Before you read, look at the diagram From Species to Kingdom on p. 431. Notice all the levels of classification. As you read about each level, look at the diagram again.

In Your Workbook Go to your workbook to learn more about previewing visuals.

Binomial Nomenclature The scientific name of the polar bear is *Ursus maritimus*, which means "marine bear."

Assigning Scientific Names

The first step in studying the diversity of life is to describe and name each species. For names to be useful, everyone must use the same name for each species.

People in different places often use different words to describe the same organism. Using common names can cause problems. For example, the words *cougar*, *puma*, *panther*, and *mountain lion* are all common names for the same animal. Sometimes, people use the same name for different organisms. For example, in the United Kingdom, a *buzzard* is a kind of hawk. In the United States, a *buzzard* is a vulture. And of course, a person who does not speak English would not use any of these names!

By the 1700s, scientists knew that it was too confusing to call organisms by their common names. They agreed to use a Latin or Greek name for each species. At first, this did not help much. The early names were very long and complicated. The name for a tree might be "Oak with deeply divided leaves that have no hairs on their undersides and no teeth around their edges." Also, scientists used different characteristics to describe species.

Binomial Nomenclature In the 1730s, a Swedish scientist named Carolus Linnaeus developed a two-word naming system called **binomial nomenclature.** In binomial nomenclature, each species is assigned a scientific name that has two words. Scientific names are written in italics. The first word begins with a capital letter. The second word is lowercase.

The scientific name for the polar bear is *Ursus maritimus*. The first part of the name—*Ursus*—is the genus to which the organism belongs. A **genus** (plural: genera, JEHN er uh) is a group of closely related species. The genus *Ursus* contains five other species of bears, including *Ursus arctos*, the brown bear.

The second part of a scientific name is unique to each species. This part of the name often describes an important trait or the organism's habitat. The word *maritimus* comes from the Latin word for "sea." Polar bears live on ice that floats in the sea.

🔑 **Key Question** What is the goal of binomial nomenclature?
In binomial nomenclature, each species is given a two-part scientific name.

USING A DICHOTOMOUS KEY

A dichotomous key is used to identify organisms. The key is made up of a series of statements about visible traits. Each statement can be considered a question that can be answered yes or no. The answers lead you to new statements until you have identified your organism. Use the key to identify the leaf shown here. Note the clues to help you at each step.

Step	Leaf Characteristics	Tree
1a	Compound leaf (leaves divided into leaflets) . . . go to Step 2	
1b	Simple leaf (leaf not divided into leaflets) . . . go to Step 4	
2a	Leaflets all attached at a central point	Buckeye▶ 
2b	Leaflets attached at several points . . . go to Step 3	
3a	Leaflets tapered with pointed tips	 ◀Pecan
3b	Leaflets oval with rounded tips	Locust▶ 
4a	Veins branched out from one central point . . . go to Step 5	
4b	Veins branched off main vein in middle of the leaf . . . go to Step 6	
5a	Heart-shaped leaf	Redbud▶ 
5b	Star-shaped leaf	 ◀Sweet gum
6a	Leaf with jagged edges	Birch
6b	Leaf with smooth edges	Magnolia▶ 

> Because your leaf is a simple leaf, you skip ahead to Step 4.

> Continue reading the statements until you determine the identity of your leaf.

> Because your leaf has jagged edges, you determine that it's from a birch tree.

Carolus Linnaeus

Classifying Species Into Larger Groups In addition to naming organisms, biologists organize, or classify, species into larger groups. The science of naming and grouping organisms is called **systematics** (sis tuh MAT iks). In systematics, biologists try to place organisms into groups that have biological meaning. Organisms in a group should be more similar to one another than they are to organisms in other groups. Biologists call these groups *taxa* (singular: taxon).

You may not know it, but you use classification systems all the time. For example, you may talk about "teachers" or "pets." You also refer to smaller groups, such as "biology teachers" or "dogs." When you do this, you are using names for groups that many people understand.

🗝 **Key Question** What is the goal of systematics?
The goal of systematics is to organize living things into groups that have biological meaning.

The Linnaean Classification System

Linnaeus developed the system of binomial nomenclature. He also developed a classification system for organizing species into larger groups. Linnaeus classified species according to physical similarities and differences.

Linnaeus's original classification system had four levels, or ranks. Over time, his system grew to include seven levels: species, genus, family, order, class, phylum, and kingdom. As you read about these levels, look at the diagram of the classification of the Bactrian camel shown on the next page. The scientific name of the camel that has two humps is *Camelus bactrianus*. (Bactria was an ancient country in Asia.)

▶ *Species* A species is a group of individuals that can interbreed and produce fertile offspring.

▶ *Genus* As its name tells you, the Bactrian camel belongs to the genus *Camelus*. The genus *Camelus* also includes the dromedary camel, *Camelus dromedaries*, which has only one hump.

▶ *Family* Llamas belong to the genus *Lama*. Because camels and llamas share many traits, they are classified in the same family. A **family** is a group that includes genera that share similar traits. The family that includes *Camelus* and *Lama* is Camelidae.

▶ *Order* Closely related families are grouped together in the next larger rank—an **order.** Camels and llamas (Camelidae) are grouped with several other families, including the deer family and the cattle family. Together they form the order Artiodactyla. This order includes hoofed animals that have an even number of toes.

▶ *Class* Similar orders are grouped together into the next larger rank, called a **class.** The order Artiodactyla is placed with other mammals in the class Mammalia.

▶ *Phylum* Classes are grouped into a **phylum.** The class Mammalia is grouped with birds, reptiles, amphibians, and fishes into the phylum Chordata. All of the members of this phylum have a nerve cord along their back.

▶ *Kingdom* The largest of Linnaeus's taxonomic groups is called the **kingdom.** The Bactrian camel is placed in the kingdom Animalia. Kingdom Animalia includes all animals.

🔑 **Key Question** How did Linnaeus group species into larger taxa? **Over time, Linnaeus's original classification system grew to include seven levels: species, genus, family, order, class, phylum, and kingdom.**

From Species to Kingdom The diagram shows how a Bactrian camel, *Camelus bactrianus*, is grouped within each level of classification. Only a few organisms are shown for the levels that are larger than genus.

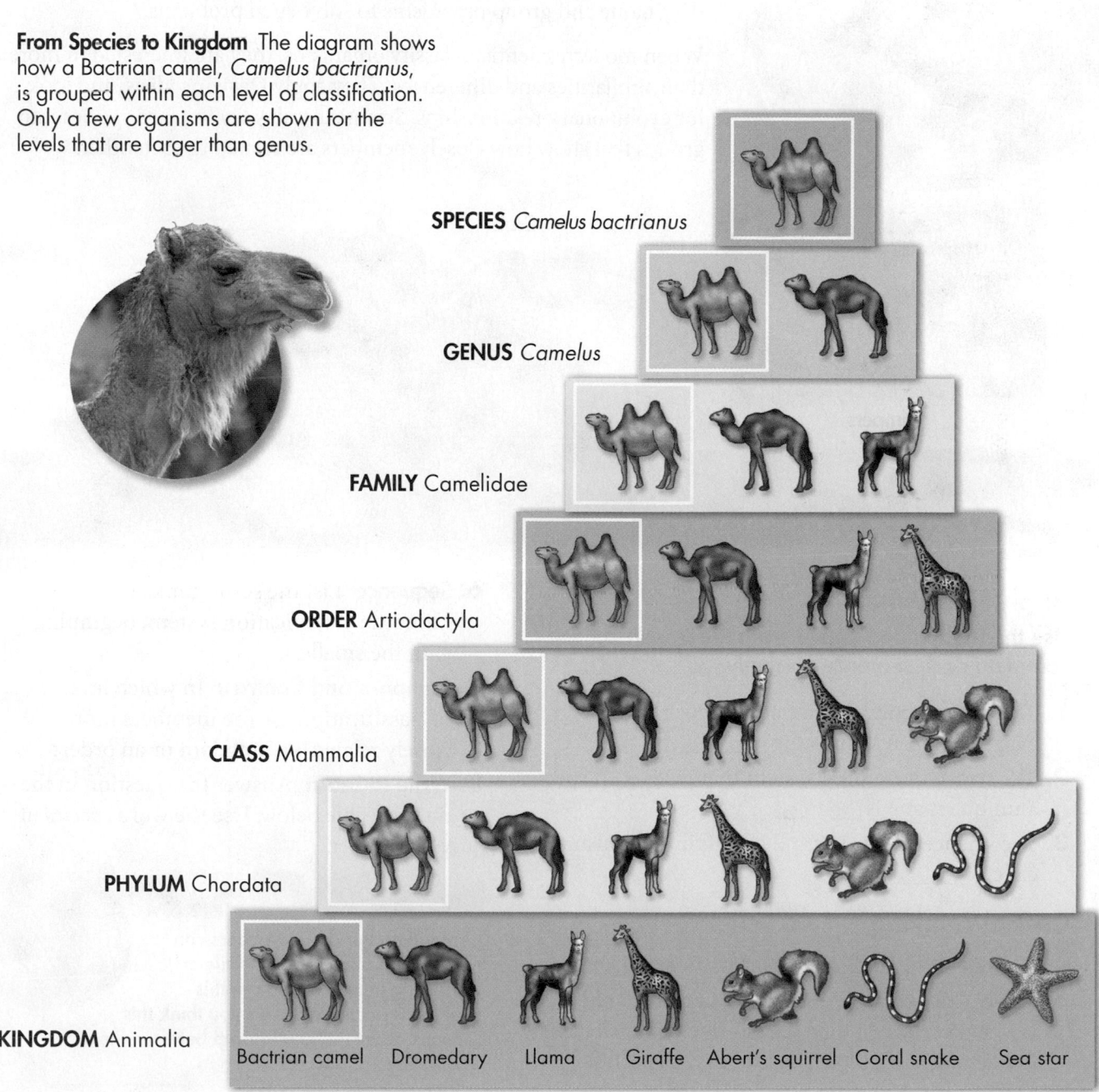

SPECIES *Camelus bactrianus*

GENUS *Camelus*

FAMILY Camelidae

ORDER Artiodactyla

CLASS Mammalia

PHYLUM Chordata

KINGDOM Animalia

Bactrian camel　Dromedary　Llama　Giraffe　Abert's squirrel　Coral snake　Sea star

Looks Can Be Deceiving

Classifying organisms based on traits that are easy to see can lead to problems. Barnacles and limpets look very similar, yet they are not closely related. Barnacles and crabs do not look alike, yet they *are* closely related.

Barnacles

Limpets

Problems With Traditional Classification

Individual species tend to define themselves by choosing with whom to mate. Thus, there is a "natural" definition of a species. But higher ranks, such as genus and family, are defined by biologists.

Linnaeus grouped organisms into larger taxa based on similarities and differences that could be seen. Linneaus chose his characteristics carefully. For this reason, many of his groups are still used in modern classification. But it is not always obvious which traits should be used to define a group. For example, would you call a dolphin a fish, because it looks like a fish? Or would you call it a mammal, because it is warmblooded and produces milk? Scientists have changed the way they name and group organisms to solve such problems.

When modern scientists classify organisms, they are interested in more than similarities and differences. They apply Darwin's ideas, and look for evolutionary relationships. Scientists today try to place species into groups that show how closely members are related to each other.

Crab

✓CHECK Understanding

Apply Vocabulary

Use the highlighted words from the lesson to complete each sentence correctly.

1. The largest group in Linnaeus's seven-level classification system is the _____.

2. The two-part naming system that gives each species a unique name is _____.

3. The science of naming and classifying organisms is called _____.

Critical Thinking

4. **Explain** Why do biologists classify organisms?

5. **Apply Concepts** The scientific name of a red maple is *Acer rubrum*. Which part of this name identifies the genus? Which part describes the species?

6. **Sequence** List the seven ranks in the Linnaean classification system, beginning with the smallest.

7. **Compare and Contrast** In which level of classification are the members more closely related—a kingdom or an order?

8. **Write to Learn** Answer the question in the mystery clue below. Use the word *species* in your answer.

MYSTERY CLUE

Polar bears and brown bears can interbreed and produce fertile offspring in zoos. In nature this rarely happens. What do you think this means about the relationship between them? (Hint: See p. 430.)

Modern Evolutionary Classification

MD CLG 3.4.1 Evolutionary Change, 3.4.2 Relatedness Among Organisms. SPI 1.4.2 Analyze Data, 1.5.5 Create and Interpret Graphics, 1.5.7 Classification Systems, 1.5.8 Compare.

Evolutionary Classification

Linnaeus began classifying organisms more than one hundred years before Darwin published his ideas about a "tree of life." Darwin's ideas suggested a new way to classify organisms. Biologists today use evolutionary relationships to place species into larger groups, or taxons.

Common Ancestors Evolutionary classification groups species into larger taxa, in which all members are descended from a common ancestor. All members of any group should be more closely related to each other than to members of any other group. The larger the taxon, the farther back in time all of its members shared a common ancestor. The study of how living and extinct organisms are related is called phylogeny (fy LAHJ uh nee).

Clades Evolutionary classification puts organisms into groups called clades. A **clade** is a group of species that includes a single common ancestor and all of its descendants. A clade includes both living and extinct organisms. Clades must be monophyletic (mahn oh fy LET ik). A **monophyletic group** includes a single common ancestor and *all* of its descendants. Monophyletic groups cannot include any organisms that are *not* descended from the common ancestor.

Some taxa that were defined before evolutionary classification are monophyletic. But others are not. These groups have a common ancestor but do not include all of its descendants. Class Reptilia (reptiles) is not monophyletic. So in evolutionary classification, reptiles are not a true group.

🔑 **Key Question** What is the goal of evolutionary classification? **The goal of evolutionary classification is to group species into larger categories that show lines of evolutionary descent, rather than overall similarities and differences.**

Cladograms

In evolutionary classification, biologists compare carefully selected traits. They use these traits to determine the order in which groups of organisms branched off from a common ancestor. This information is used to link clades together in a cladogram. A **cladogram** is a drawing that shows relationships among species and larger taxa by showing how evolutionary lines branched off a common ancestor.

Key Questions

🔑 **What is the goal of evolutionary classification?**

🔑 **What is a cladogram?**

🔑 **How are DNA sequences used in classification?**

BUILD Understanding

T-Chart As you read a lesson, you can organize the information in a T-chart. Write all the key questions on the left side of the chart. Answer each question on the right side of the chart.

In Your Workbook Go to your workbook to learn more about T-charts.

BUILD Vocabulary

clade an evolutionary branch of a cladogram that includes a single ancestor and all its descendants

monophyletic group a group that consists of a single ancestral species and all its descendants and excludes any organisms that are not descended from that common ancestor

cladogram a diagram showing patterns of shared characteristics among species

derived character a trait that arose in the most recent common ancestor of an evolutionary line and was passed on to its descendants

Building a Cladogram A cladogram shows the relationships among different evolutionary lines.

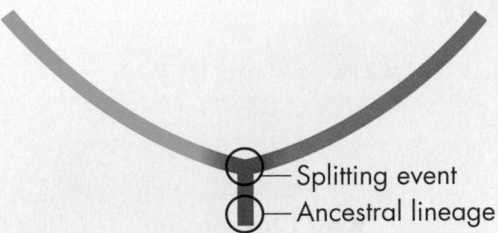

1 Cladograms are diagrams showing how evolutionary lines, or lineages, split from each other over time. This diagram shows a single ancestral lineage splitting into two. The point of splitting is called a "node" in the cladogram.

- Splitting event
- Ancestral lineage

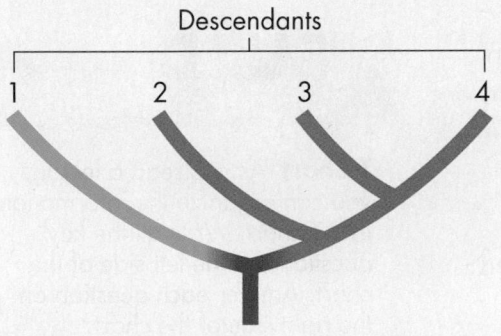

Descendants

1   2   3   4

2 How recently lineages share a common ancestor reflects how closely the lineages are related to one another. Here, lineages 3 and 4 are each more closely related to each other than either of them is to any other lineage.

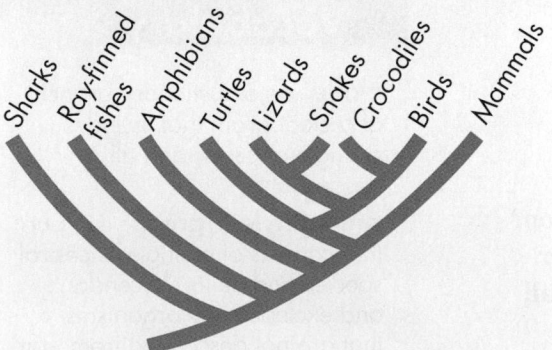

Sharks Ray-finned fishes Amphibians Turtles Lizards Snakes Crocodiles Birds Mammals

3 This cladogram shows the evolutionary relationships among vertebrates, animals with backbones.

Building Cladograms Look at the cladograms on the left. Each cladogram looks like a tree with branches. The bottom, or "root," shows the common ancestor of all the organisms in the cladogram. The point where each branch splits off is called a *node*. Each node represents a speciation event. In speciation, one species splits into two new species. A node shows the last point at which the two new lines shared a common ancestor.

In a cladogram, the pattern of the branches shows how closely organisms are related. Look at cladogram 2. Notice that lines 3 and 4 share a common ancestor more recently than either does with line 2. Therefore, lines 3 and 4 are more closely related to each other than either is to line 2.

🔑 **Key Question** What is a cladogram?
A cladogram links groups of organisms by showing how evolutionary lines branched off from common ancestors.

Derived Characters Biologists focus on particular characteristics, or traits, to put organisms into clades. A **derived character** is a trait that arose in the most recent common ancestor of a group and was passed on to its descendants. For example, having four limbs is a derived character in clade Tetrapoda. The common ancestor of all tetrapods had four limbs. Hair is a derived character for the clade Mammalia. All mammals have hair. But having four limbs is not a derived character for mammals. If it were, only mammals would have that trait.

Lost Traits Sometimes descendents lose a derived character. For example, snakes are reptiles, members of the clade Tetrapoda. But snakes do not have four limbs. During the process of evolution, snakes lost their legs.

Biologists must be careful about using the *absence* of a trait in classification. Distantly related groups can sometimes lose the same trait. For example, both whales and snakes have lost their legs. But whales and snakes are not very closely related. Snakes are more closely related to other reptiles than to whales.

Interpreting Cladograms The cladogram on the next page shows the evolutionary line of the cat family. At the lower left is the common ancestor of all animals with four legs. The position of the nodes shows the order in which different groups branched off. First, amphibians branched off from the line leading to clade Amniota. (Amniota includes reptiles and mammals.) Next, reptiles branched off from the line leading to the clade Mammalia, and so on. Notice that smaller clades fit within larger clades. For example, clade Amniota is part of clade Tetrapoda.

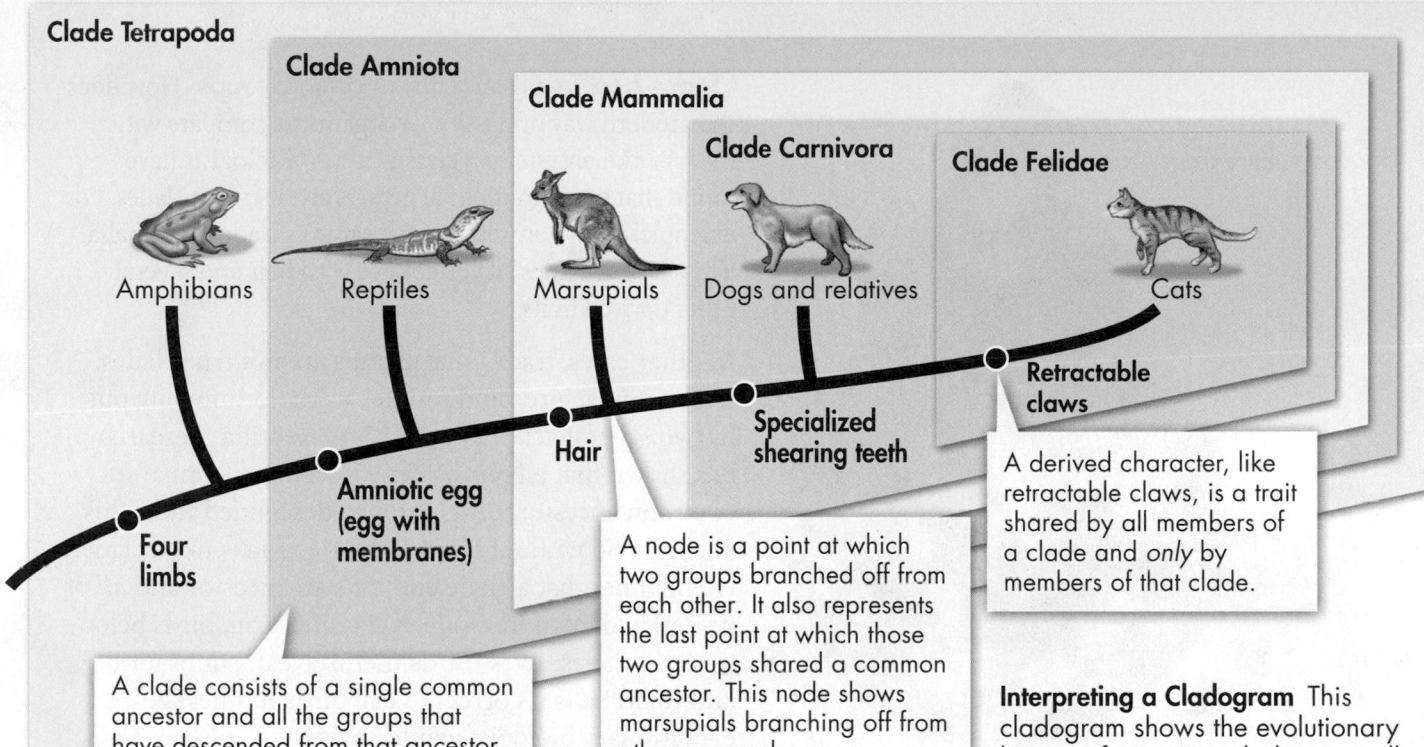

Clade Tetrapoda

Clade Amniota

Clade Mammalia

Clade Carnivora

Clade Felidae

Amphibians

Reptiles

Marsupials

Dogs and relatives

Cats

Retractable claws

Hair

Specialized shearing teeth

Amniotic egg (egg with membranes)

Four limbs

A clade consists of a single common ancestor and all the groups that have descended from that ancestor.

A node is a point at which two groups branched off from each other. It also represents the last point at which those two groups shared a common ancestor. This node shows marsupials branching off from other mammals.

A derived character, like retractable claws, is a trait shared by all members of a clade and *only* by members of that clade.

Interpreting a Cladogram This cladogram shows the evolutionary history of cats. In a cladogram, all organisms in a clade share a set of derived characters. Notice that smaller clades are nested within larger clades.

Derived characters are listed along the main trunk. Each trait is a derived character for all the organisms to the right. For example, marsupials, dogs, and cats all have hair. On the cladogram, they are to the right of the common ancestor that had hair. The last derived character on the cladogram is retractable claws. Members of the cat family can retract, or pull back, their claws. Members of the dog family do not have this trait.

INQUIRY into Scientific Thinking

Constructing a Cladogram

❶ Find the list of organisms in the table at right. Then look at the list of derived characters. The more characters that two organisms share, the more closely related they are.

❷ Find the organism in the table that is *least* closely related to the others. That organism will be the first organism on your cladogram.

❸ Use the information in the table to complete your cladogram. Put each organism on a separate branch.

❹ Write the derived characters along the main trunk.

In Your Workbook Go to your workbook for more help with cladograms.

Derived Characters in Organisms

Organism	Derived Character		
	Backbone	Legs	Hair
Earthworm	Absent	Absent	Absent
Trout	Present	Absent	Absent
Lizard	Present	Present	Absent
Human	Present	Present	Present

Analyze and Conclude

1. Interpret Tables What trait separates the earthworm from the other animals?

2. Classify Do you have enough information to decide where to put a frog on your cladogram? Explain your answer.

3. Draw Conclusions Does your cladogram indicate that lizards and humans share a more recent common ancestor than either does with an earthworm? Explain your answer.

Hooded vulture from Africa

American vulture

DNA and Classification
Scientists today compare DNA to help classify organisms. Vultures from Africa and American vultures were once grouped together in the falcon family. DNA analysis has shown that American vultures are more closely related to storks than to African vultures.

Stork

Clades and Traditional Taxonomic Groups How does the modern way of classifying organisms compare with the traditional system of classification? Biologists have found that many traditional groups are also true clades. For example, class Mammalia is the same as clade Mammalia. This clade includes all vertebrates with hair and several other derived traits.

In other cases, traditional groups are not true clades. For example, birds and reptiles were traditionally put in two separate classes—Aves and Reptilia. Research has shown that all reptiles are descended from a common ancestor. Birds are also descended from this ancestor. So without birds, class Reptilia is not a clade. (Remember that a clade contains an ancestor and *all* of its descendants.) In modern classification, birds belong to three clades: Aves (birds themselves), Dinosauria, and Reptilia. Is it correct to call birds reptiles? An evolutionary biologist would say yes!

DNA in Classification

Most of the examples of evolutionary classification you have read about are based on physical traits such as fur, bones, and teeth. The goal of modern systematics is to understand the relationships of *all* life on Earth. If two organisms do not share any obvious features, how can you tell if they are related?

Genes as Derived Characters Remember that all species inherit genes on strands of DNA. Very different organisms often share a number of homologous genes. The similarities and differences in these homologous genes can tell how closely related organisms are. Because genes mutate at a steady rate, they can be used as molecular clocks. The more similar the genes in two organisms are, the more recently they shared a common ancestor. In these comparisons, genes and mutations are used as derived characters.

New Techniques Redraw Old Trees Information from DNA is helping to make evolutionary trees more accurate. For example, look at the three birds on the left. The hooded vulture from Africa looks like the American vulture in the middle. Both vultures were once classified in the same clade. But by studying their DNA, researchers have learned that American vultures are more closely related to storks than to African vultures.

Raccoons Red pandas Giant pandas Bears

Common Ancestor

Classification of Pandas Biologists once classified the red panda and giant panda together. Recently, DNA studies have shown that the giant panda shares a more recent common ancestor with bears than with red pandas or raccoons.

Evidence from DNA has also helped biologists classify pandas. Giant pandas and red pandas share many traits. For example, both pandas have bones in the wrist that work like a human thumb. But studies of DNA show that giant pandas share more recent ancestors with bears than with raccoons. So giant pandas are now classified with bears in the family Ursidae. Red pandas are placed in a clade that also includes raccoons, seals, and weasels.

🔑 **Key Question** How are DNA sequences used in classification? **In general, the more derived genetic characters that two species share, the more recently they shared a common ancestor. This information also tells how closely they are related.**

CHECK Understanding

Apply Vocabulary
Use the highlighted words from the lesson to complete each sentence correctly.

1. _____ are groups of species that include a single common ancestor and all descendants of that ancestor.

2. A _____ is a diagram that shows the evolutionary relationships among clades.

3. A trait that evolved in a recent common ancestor and was passed on to the descendants of that ancestor is called a _____.

Critical Thinking
4. Explain How does evolutionary classification differ from traditional classification?

5. Apply Concepts What do the locations of derived characters on a cladogram show?

6. Relate Cause and Effect Explain how DNA analysis changed the classification of giant pandas.

7. Write to Learn Answer the question in the mystery clue below.

MYSTERY CLUE

When DNA is compared, some brown bears are more closely related to polar bears than they are to other brown bears. What do you think this means for the classification of polar bears? (**Hint:** See p. 436.)

BIOLOGY.com   Search   (Lesson 18.2)   GO • Lesson Assessment

CLG 3.4.2 Relatedness Among Organisms. SPI 1.1.1 Problems and Solutions, 1.1.2 Scientific Ideas, 1.5.7 Classification Systems.

Key Questions

🔑 What are the six kingdoms of life as they are now identified?

🔑 What does the tree of life show?

BUILD Understanding

Concept Map As you read, construct a concept map describing the characteristics of the three domains.

In Your Workbook Go to your workbook to learn about making a concept map.

BUILD Vocabulary

domain a larger, more inclusive taxonomic category than a kingdom

Bacteria the domain of unicellular prokaryotes that have cell walls containing peptidoglycan

Archaea the domain of unicellular prokaryotes that have cell walls that do not contain peptidoglycan

🖋 WORD ORIGINS

The domain Archaea and kingdom Archaebacteria come from the Greek word *arkhaios*, which means "ancient or primitive." Archaea live in harsh environments that may resemble early, or primitive, conditions on Earth.

Changing Ideas About Kingdoms

Since the time of Linnaeus, biologists have worked to improve the system of classification. Classification today is based on the most recent discoveries and reflects evolutionary relationships. As scientists learn more and more about living and extinct organisms, the classification system will continue to change.

Linnaeus's original system had only two kingdoms: plants and animals. Animals were organisms that moved and used food for energy. Plants included everything that was not an animal. Over the years, classification at the level of the kingdom has changed greatly.

Five Kingdoms In the late 1800s, researchers discovered that single-celled organisms were very different from plants and animals. A third kingdom, called Protista, was created to contain all microorganisms. Later, biologists gave yeasts, molds, and mushrooms their own kingdom: Fungi. When biologists realized how different bacteria were from other organisms, they added a fifth kingdom: Monera. (Bacteria are prokaryotes, or organisms that lack a nucleus and other organelles.) The research and discoveries that expanded the classification system from two to five kingdoms took more than 200 years.

Six Kingdoms More recently, biologists studying bacteria reached a surprising conclusion. Kingdom Monera contained two very different kinds of bacteria. So the bacteria were divided into two new kingdoms: Eubacteria and Archaebacteria. These two new kingdoms give us the six kingdoms used in modern classification.

🔑 **Key Question** What are the six kingdoms of life as they are now identified?
The six-kingdom classification system includes the kingdoms Eubacteria, Archaebacteria, Protista, Fungi, Plantae, and Animalia.

Three Domains Genetic studies show that the two groups of bacteria are very different from each other. The bacteria are also very different from all the other organisms, or eukaryotes. To reflect these differences, biologists have added a new level of classification—the domain. A **domain** is larger and includes more than a kingdom.

Classification of Living Things

DOMAIN	Bacteria	Archaea	Eukarya			
KINGDOM	Eubacteria	Archaebacteria	"Protista"	Fungi	Plantae	Animalia
CELL TYPE	Prokaryote	Prokaryote	Eukaryote	Eukaryote	Eukaryote	Eukaryote
CELL STRUCTURES	Cell walls with peptidoglycan	Cell walls without peptidoglycan	Cell walls of cellulose in some; some have chloroplasts	Cell walls of chitin	Cell walls of cellulose; chloroplasts	No cell walls or chloroplasts
NUMBER OF CELLS	Unicellular	Unicellular	Most unicellular; some colonial; some multicellular	Most multicellular; some unicellular	Most multicellular: some green algae unicellular	Multicellular
MODE OF NUTRITION	Autotroph or heterotroph	Autotroph or heterotroph	Autotroph or heterotroph	Heterotroph	Autotroph	Heterotroph
EXAMPLES	*Streptococcus, Escherichia coli*	Methanogens, halophiles	*Amoeba, Paramecium,* slime molds, giant kelp	Mushrooms, yeasts	Mosses, ferns, flowering plants	Sponges, worms, insects, fishes, mammals

Three Domains Today organisms are grouped into three domains and six kingdoms. This table shows the key characteristics used to classify organisms into these major taxonomic groups.

There are three domains. Domain **Bacteria** contains the organisms in kingdom Eubacteria. Domain **Archaea** contains the organisms in kingdom Archaebacteria. Domain Eukarya contains the kingdoms Fungi, Plantae, and Animalia, and "Protista." Why are there quotation marks around the word "Protista"? Scientists have found that the members of the old kingdom Protista do not form a monophyletic group. The many kinds of unicellular eukaryotes do not have a single common ancestor. Therefore, "Protista" is not a true clade.

The Tree of All Life

Evolutionary classification is a rapidly changing science. It has a difficult goal—to show all life on a single evolutionary tree. Evolutionary biologists often change the way that organisms are grouped. They also change the names of groups. Cladograms show hypotheses about the relationships among groups. These hypotheses change as more evidence becomes available.

Domain Bacteria Members of the domain Bacteria are single-celled prokaryotes. They do not have a nucleus. They have thick cell walls that contain a substance called peptidoglycan. Bacteria are a very diverse group. Some live in the soil. Some make their own food by photosynthesis. And some are parasites that cause deadly diseases.

SEM 13,000×

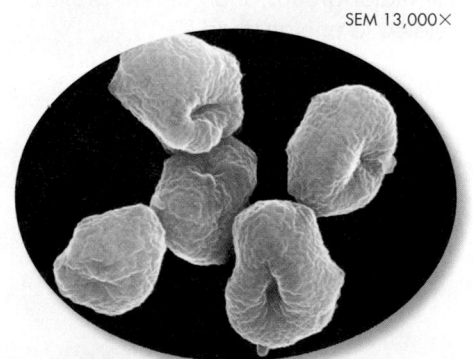

Sulfolobus This member of the domain Archaea lives in hot springs. It thrives in acidic environments that have large amounts of sulfur.

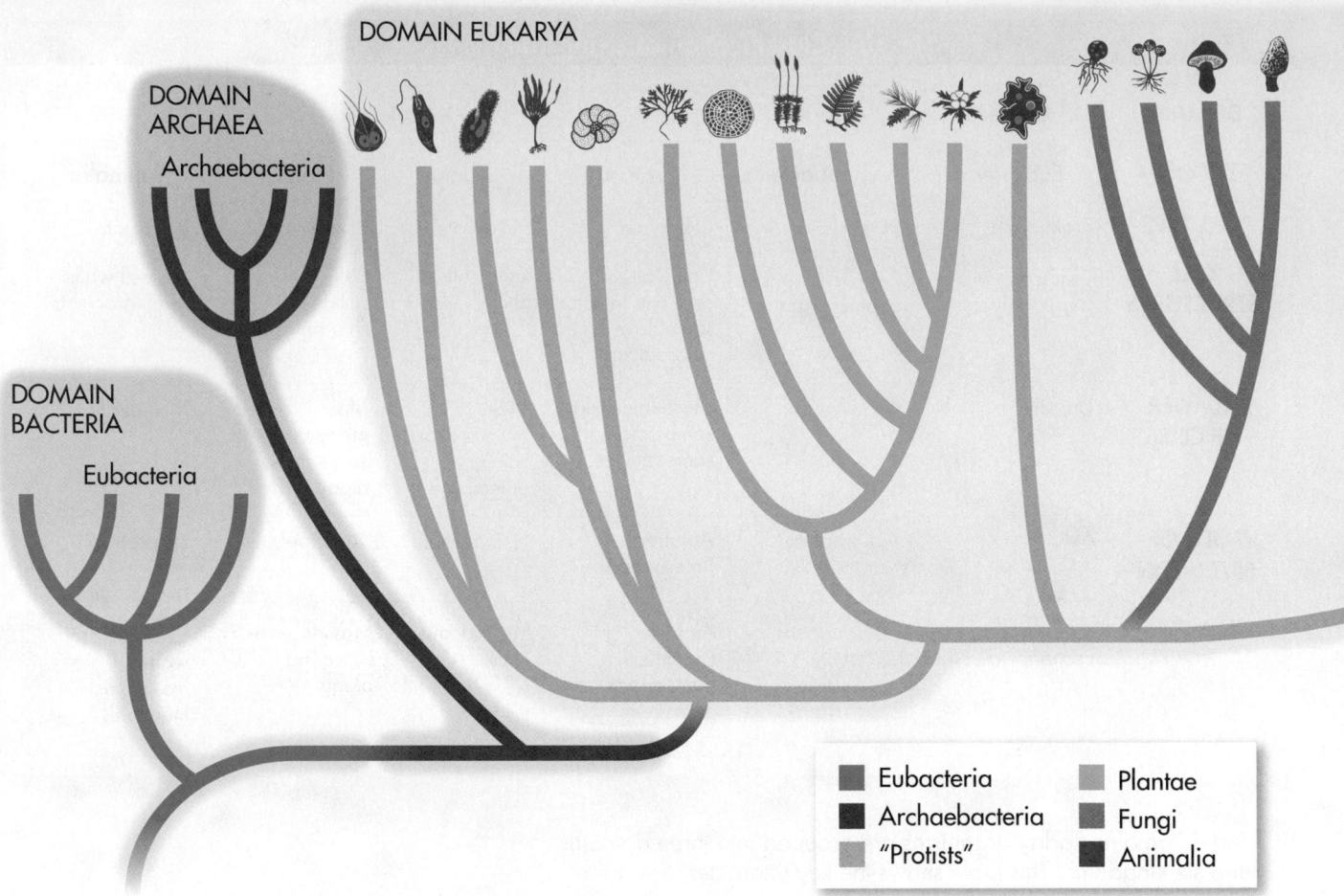

DOMAIN EUKARYA

DOMAIN ARCHAEA
Archaebacteria

DOMAIN BACTERIA
Eubacteria

■ Eubacteria	■ Plantae
■ Archaebacteria	■ Fungi
■ "Protists"	■ Animalia

Tree of Life The tree of life shows the most recent hypothesis about how the major groups of organisms are related to one another.

Domain Archaea Members of the domain Archaea are also single-celled prokaryotes. They have unusual cell membranes. Their cell walls do not have peptidoglycan. These bacteria live in some of the most extreme environments on Earth. Some live in hot springs. Others live in very salty water. Still others live only in places that have no oxygen.

Domain Eukarya The domain **Eukarya** contains all of the organisms that have a nucleus. It includes four major groups from the six-kingdom system: "Protista," Fungi, Plantae, and Animalia.

▶ **"Protists"** In the cladogram above, notice that kingdom "Protista" is spread out over several different branches. This kingdom is not monophyletic, so many members are not closely related. Recent studies of these organisms have divided them into at least five clades. Each of these clades is more closely related to other groups than to other "protists." Most "protists" are single-celled organisms, but the brown algae are multicellular. Some "protists" are photosynthetic. Others are heterotrophic.

▶ **Fungi** Members of the kingdom Fungi are heterotrophs that have cell walls containing chitin. Most fungi feed on dead organisms. Fungi release enzymes that digest food outside of their body. The body of the fungus then absorbs the digested food. Most fungi, such as mushrooms, are multicellular. Some, such as yeasts, are single-celled.

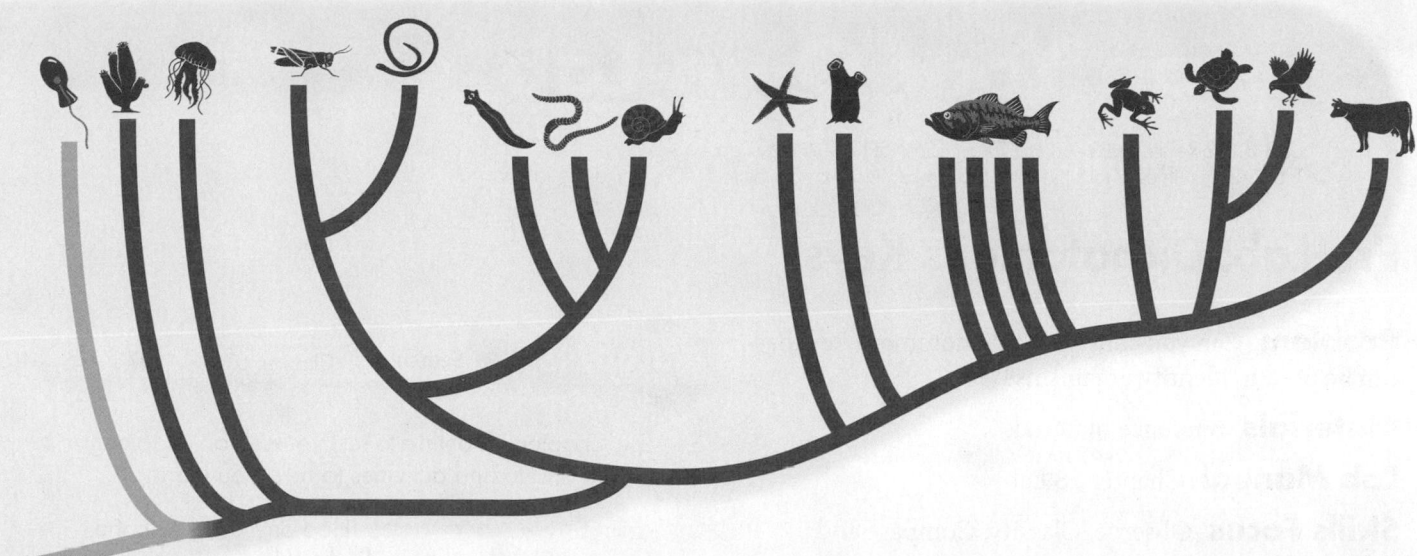

▶ *Plantae* Members of the kingdom Plantae make their own food by photosynthesis. They also have cell walls that contain cellulose. Most are multicellular. Green algae, once considered to be protists, are now classified as plants. Many green algae are single-celled organisms.

▶ *Animalia* Members of kingdom Animalia are multicellular and do not have cell walls. Animals are heterotrophic. To get energy, they feed on other organisms or the remains of other organisms. Most animals can move from place to place, at least in part of their life cycle.

Key Question What does the tree of life show?
The tree of life shows current hypotheses about the evolutionary relationships among the groups within the three domains of life.

CHECK Understanding

Apply Vocabulary
Use the highlighted words from the lesson to complete each sentence correctly.

1. The three _____ are very large groups that help to organize the six kingdoms.

2. The domain _____ includes protists, fungi, plants, and animals.

3. The domain _____ includes bacteria that live in very harsh environments.

Critical Thinking

4. Review What are the six kingdoms of life as they are now identified?

5. Classify Which kingdoms include prokaryotes? Which kingdoms include eukaryotes?

6. Relate Cause and Effect Why did biologists add the level of "domain"?

7. Write to Learn Do you think the tree of life cladogram will always stay the same as it appears in your book? Explain your answer.

BIOLOGY.com ▷ Search (Lesson 18.3) GO ● Lesson Assessment

Design Your Own Lab

MD CLG 3.4.2 Relatedness Among Organisms. SPI 1.2.6 Investigative Methods, 1.2.7 Apply Results, 1.5.2 Communicate Information, 1.5.7 Classification Systems, 1.5.9 Synthesize Ideas.

Pre-Lab: Dichotomous Keys

Problem Can you construct a dichotomous key that can be used to identify organisms?

Materials reference materials

Lab Manual Chapter 18 Lab

Skills Focus Observe, Classify, Compare and Contrast, Sequence

Connect to the Big idea Given the enormous variety of life on Earth, not even experts can identify every organism they observe. Experts and amateurs use dichotomous keys to identify organisms. These keys are based on the appearance of organisms. A key is a series of paired statements. Readers select the statement that best describes an organism at each step until the organism is identified and named. In this lab, you will practice using a dichotomous key. Then you will construct your own key for a group of organisms.

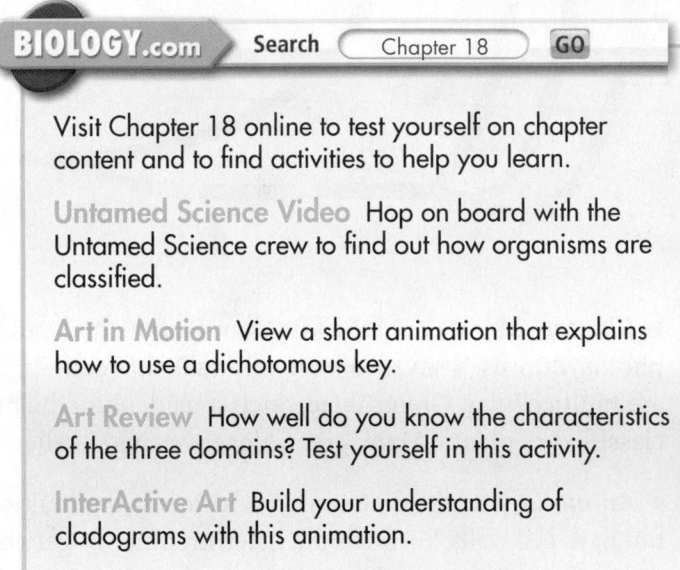

BIOLOGY.com   Search   Chapter 18   GO

Visit Chapter 18 online to test yourself on chapter content and to find activities to help you learn.

Untamed Science Video Hop on board with the Untamed Science crew to find out how organisms are classified.

Art in Motion View a short animation that explains how to use a dichotomous key.

Art Review How well do you know the characteristics of the three domains? Test yourself in this activity.

InterActive Art Build your understanding of cladograms with this animation.

Background Questions

a. Review Why do biologists prefer to identify an organism by its scientific name?

b. Compare and Contrast How is the way modern biologists group species into larger categories different from the system that Linnaeus used?

c. Review How many choices does a dichotomous key provide at each step?

Pre-Lab Questions

Preview the procedure in the lab manual.

1. Observe Name three different physical traits that are used in the shark dichotomous key.

2. Apply Concepts After you make a list of physical traits that you can use in your dichotomous key, how will you decide which trait to pick for the first step?

18 CHAPTER Summary

18.1 Finding Order in Diversity

- In binomial nomenclature, each species is given a two-part scientific name.

- The goal of systematics is to organize living things into groups that have biological meaning.

- Over time, Linnaeus's original classification system was expanded to include seven levels: species, genus, family, order, class, phylum, and kingdom.

binomial nomenclature (p. 428)
genus (p. 428)
systematics (p. 430)
family (p. 430)
order (p. 430)
class (p. 430)
phylum (p. 431)
kingdom (p. 431)

18.2 Modern Evolutionary Classification

- The goal of evolutionary classification is to group species into larger categories that reflect lines of evolutionary descent, rather than overall similarities and differences.

- A cladogram links groups of organisms by showing how evolutionary lines branched off from common ancestors over time.

- In general, the more derived genetic characters that two species share, the more recently they shared a common ancestor. This information also tells how closely two species are related.

clade (p. 433)
monophyletic group (p. 433)
cladogram (p. 433)
derived character (p. 434)

18.3 Building the Tree of Life

- The six-kingdom system of classification includes the kingdoms Eubacteria, Archaebacteria, Protista, Fungi, Plantae, and Animalia.

- The tree of life shows current hypotheses about evolutionary relationships among the groups within the three domains of life.

domain (p. 438)
Bacteria (p. 439)
Archaea (p. 439)
Eukarya (p. 440)

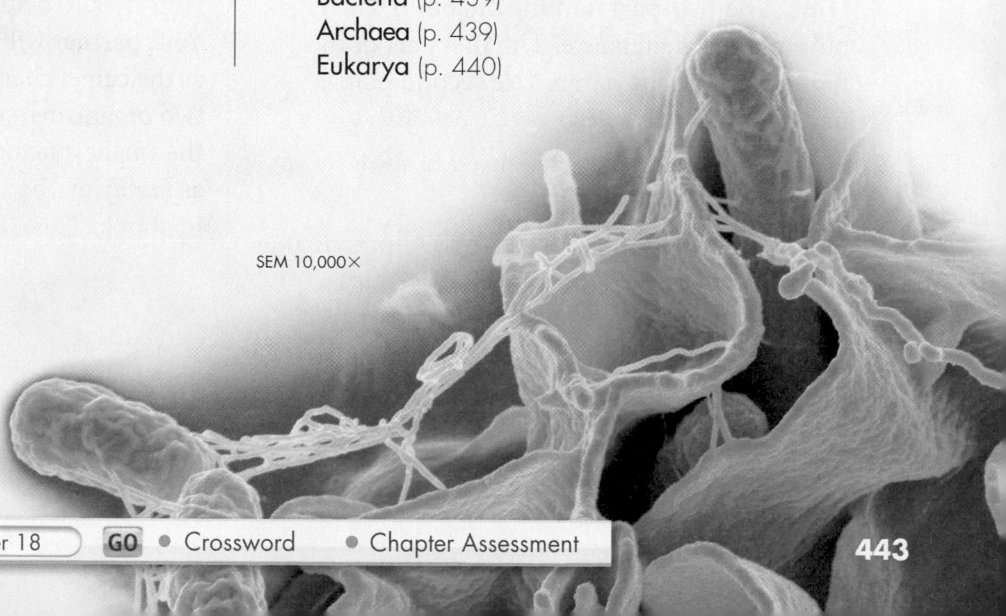

SEM 10,000×

Assess the Big idea — Unity and Diversity of Life

Write an answer to the question below.

Q: What is the goal of biologists who classify living things?

Constructed Response

Write an answer to each of the numbered questions below. The answer to each numbered question should be one or two paragraphs long. To help you begin, read the **Hints** below the questions.

1. **Why do biologists give each species its own two-part name?**

   Hint The two-part naming system is called binomial nomenclature. The first part of the name is the genus name. The second part is unique to each species.

2. **How are derived characters used to show evolutionary relationships?**

   Hint A cladogram is a visual way of organizing and presenting evolutionary relationships among a group of organisms.

3. **Is the kingdom Protista a true clade? Explain your answer.**

   Hint Look at the tree of life. Where are the protists located?

Foundations for Learning Wrap-Up

Use the index cards that you made at the beginning of the chapter as a tool for review.

Activity 1 Shuffle the cards until they are no longer in order. Then lay the cards on your desk and arrange them in order, from the largest group to the smallest. Repeat this activity until it becomes easy.

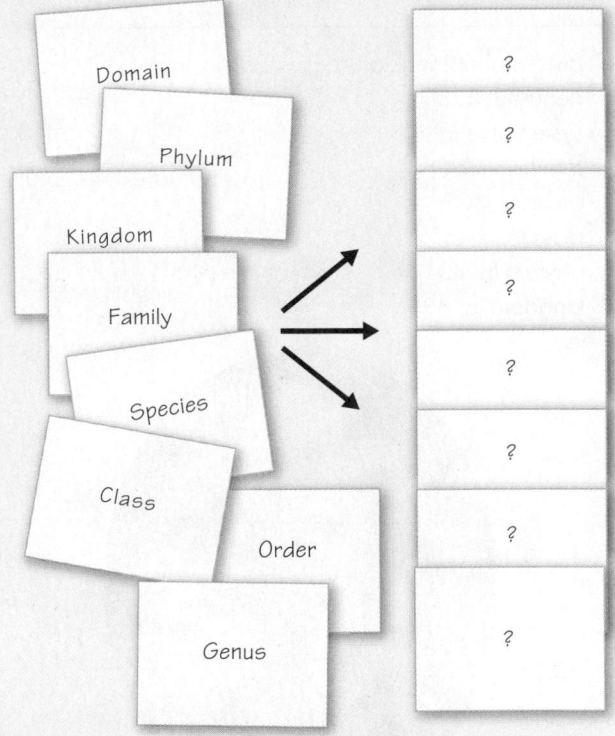

Activity 2 Work with a partner. Lay your cards on your desk to help you with the following activity. Your partner will use examples in the textbook, such as the camel chart on page 431. He or she will name two organisms, such as *camel* and *squirrel*. Name the smallest taxon that both animals belong to, such as *family* or *kingdom*. Check your answers in the textbook. Then, switch roles with your partner.

18.1 Finding Order in Diversity

Understand Key Concepts

1. By looking at its name, you know that *Rhizopus nigricans* must be
   a. a plant.
   b. an animal.
   c. in the genus *nigricans*.
   d. in the genus *Rhizopus*.

2. A useful classification system does NOT
   a. show relationships.
   b. reveal evolutionary trends.
   c. use different names for the same organism.
   d. change the taxon of an organism based on new data.

> **Test-Taking Tip**
>
> **Watch for Qualifiers** When reading a question, watch out for the words NOT, EXCEPT, ALL, and ONLY. These words can change a correct answer into an incorrect answer. For example, the word NOT appears in question 2 above. Without this word, choices **a, b,** and **d** could all be correct, since they all describe a useful classification system. The word NOT is a signal to look for the one exception. The correct answer is **c,** because a useful classification system does NOT use different names for the same organism.

3. In Linnaeus's system of classification, orders are grouped together into
   a. genera. c. families.
   b. species. d. classes.

4. The largest and most inclusive rank in the Linnaean classification system is the
   a. kingdom. c. phylum.
   b. order. d. domain.

5. What features of binomial nomenclature make it useful for scientists around the world?

Think Critically

6. **Classify** Venn diagrams can be used to show groups within groups. The Venn diagram below shows four groups as circles—A, B, C, and D. Each shape is a taxonomic level. Shapes that overlap share common members. Shapes that do not overlap do not share members. Use these levels to label the shapes in the diagram: *kingdom Animalia, phylum Chordata, class Insecta,* and *class Mammalia.* Give reasons for your labels. (**Hint:** See the diagram on p. 431.)

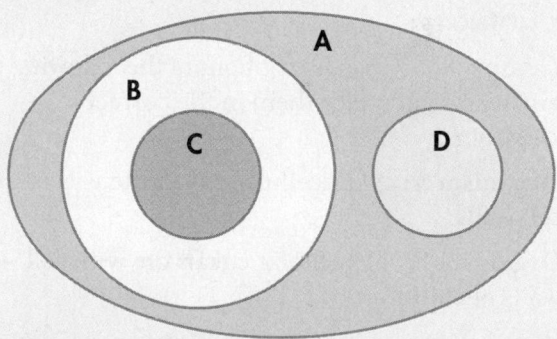

18.2 Modern Evolutionary Classification

Understand Key Concepts

7. A specific trait that is used to construct a cladogram is called a
   a. taxon. c. clade.
   b. structural feature. d. derived character.

8. A branch of a cladogram that consists of a single common ancestor and all its descendants is called
   a. cladistics. c. a clade.
   b. a kingdom. d. a class.

9. What does each node in a cladogram represent?

Think Critically

10. **Apply Concepts** Hair is a derived character for clade Mammalia. Having four limbs is not a derived character for this clade. Explain why this is so. For which clade is four limbs a derived character?

18.3 Building the Tree of Life

Understand Key Concepts

11. Which of the following kingdoms contains ONLY heterotrophs?
   a. Protista
   b. Fungi
   c. Plantae
   d. Eubacteria

12. What characteristics are used to place an organism in the domain Bacteria?

Think Critically

13. Classify Study the descriptions of the following organisms and place them in the correct kingdoms.

   Organism A: Multicellular eukaryote without cell walls.

   Organism B: Unicellular eukaryote with cell walls of chitin.

Connecting Concepts

Use Science Graphs

The cladogram below shows the relationships among three imaginary groups of organisms—groups A, B, and C. Use the cladogram to answer questions 14–16.

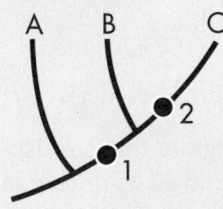

14. Interpret Visuals Which groups share derived character 1?

15. Apply Concepts What does the node, or fork, between characters 1 and 2 represent?

16. Infer Which group split off from the other groups first?

solve the CHAPTER MYSTERY

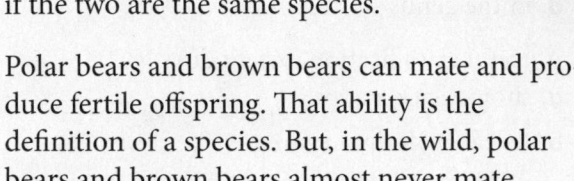

GRIN AND BEAR IT

Most biologists classify the polar bear, *Ursus maritimus*, as a separate species from the brown bear, *Ursus arctos*. The teeth, body shape, metabolism, and behavior of polar bears are very different from those of brown bears. But some researchers now wonder if the two are the same species.

Polar bears and brown bears can mate and produce fertile offspring. That ability is the definition of a species. But, in the wild, polar bears and brown bears almost never mate.

DNA analysis makes the question harder to answer, not easier. Different populations of brown bears have different genetic makeups. Some populations of brown bears have DNA that is different from that of polar bears. Other brown bears have DNA that is more similar to polar bears than to other brown bears. It may be that polar bears are not a separate species after all. It may also be that brown bears by themselves do not form a single clade.

1. Classify List the evidence that supports classifying polar bears and brown bears as two separate species. Then list the evidence that shows that polar bears and brown bears belong to the same species.

2. Infer What evidence exists that different populations of brown bears belong to different clades?

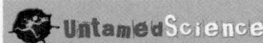 **Never Stop Exploring Your World.** Solving the mystery of scientific classification is only the beginning. Take a video field trip with the ecogeeks of Untamed Science to see where the mystery leads.

Standardized Test Practice for Maryland

Multiple Choice

1. Which of the following is NOT a characteristic of Linnaeus's system for naming organisms?
   A two-part name
   B multipart name describing several traits
   C name that identifies the organism's genus
   D name that includes the organism's species identifier
   SPI 1.5.7

2. In which of the following are the taxa in correct order?
   A phylum, kingdom, species
   B genus, order, family
   C kingdom, phylum, class
   D order, class, family
   SPI 1.5.7

3. In the six-kingdom system of classification, which kingdoms contain unicellular organisms?
   A Eubacteria only
   B Eubacteria and "Protista" only
   C Archaebacteria only
   D Eubacteria, Archaebacteria, Plantae, and "Protista"
   SPI 1.5.7

4. If species A and B have very similar genes, which of the following statements is probably true?
   A Species A and B shared a relatively recent common ancestor.
   B Species A evolved independently of species B for a long period.
   C Species B is older than species A.
   D Species A is older than species B.
   CLG 3 4.2

5. The taxon called Eukarya is a(n)
   A order.   C kingdom.
   B phylum.   D domain.
   SPI 1.5.7

6. Bacteria are classified into
   A two domains.
   B three domains.
   C three species.
   D three kingdoms.
   SPI 1.5.7

Questions 7–9

The cladogram below shows the evolutionary relationships among four groups of plants. Use the cladogram to answer questions 7–9.

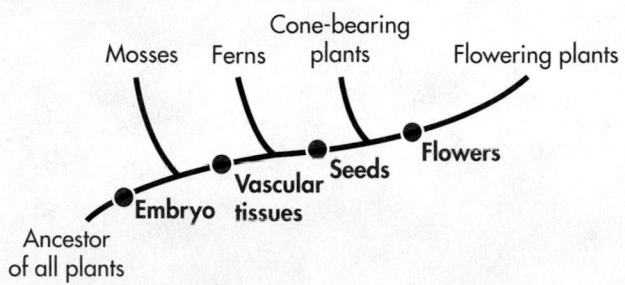

7. Which of the following groups, by themselves, do NOT form a clade?
   A cone-bearing plants and flowering plants
   B ferns, cone-bearing plants, and flowering plants
   C mosses and ferns
   D mosses, ferns, cone-bearing plants, and flowering plants
   SPI 1.5.5

8. Which of the following groups share the most recent common ancestor?
   A cone-bearing plants and flowering plants
   B mosses and ferns
   C mosses and cone-bearing plants
   D ferns and flowering plants
   SPI 1.5.5

9. Which derived character appeared first during the course of the plants' evolution?
   A seeds
   B flowers
   C embryo
   D vascular tissues
   SPI 1.5.5

Open-Ended Response

10. Why have biologists changed many of Linnaeus's original classifications of organisms?
    SPI 1.1.2

If You Have Trouble With . . .

Question	1	2	3	4	5	6	7	8	9	10
See Lesson	18.1	18.1	18.3	18.2	18.3	18.3	18.2	18.2	18.2	18.2

19 History of Life

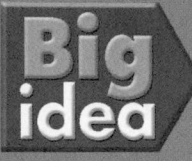

Big idea: Evolution

Q: How do fossils help biologists understand the history of life on Earth?

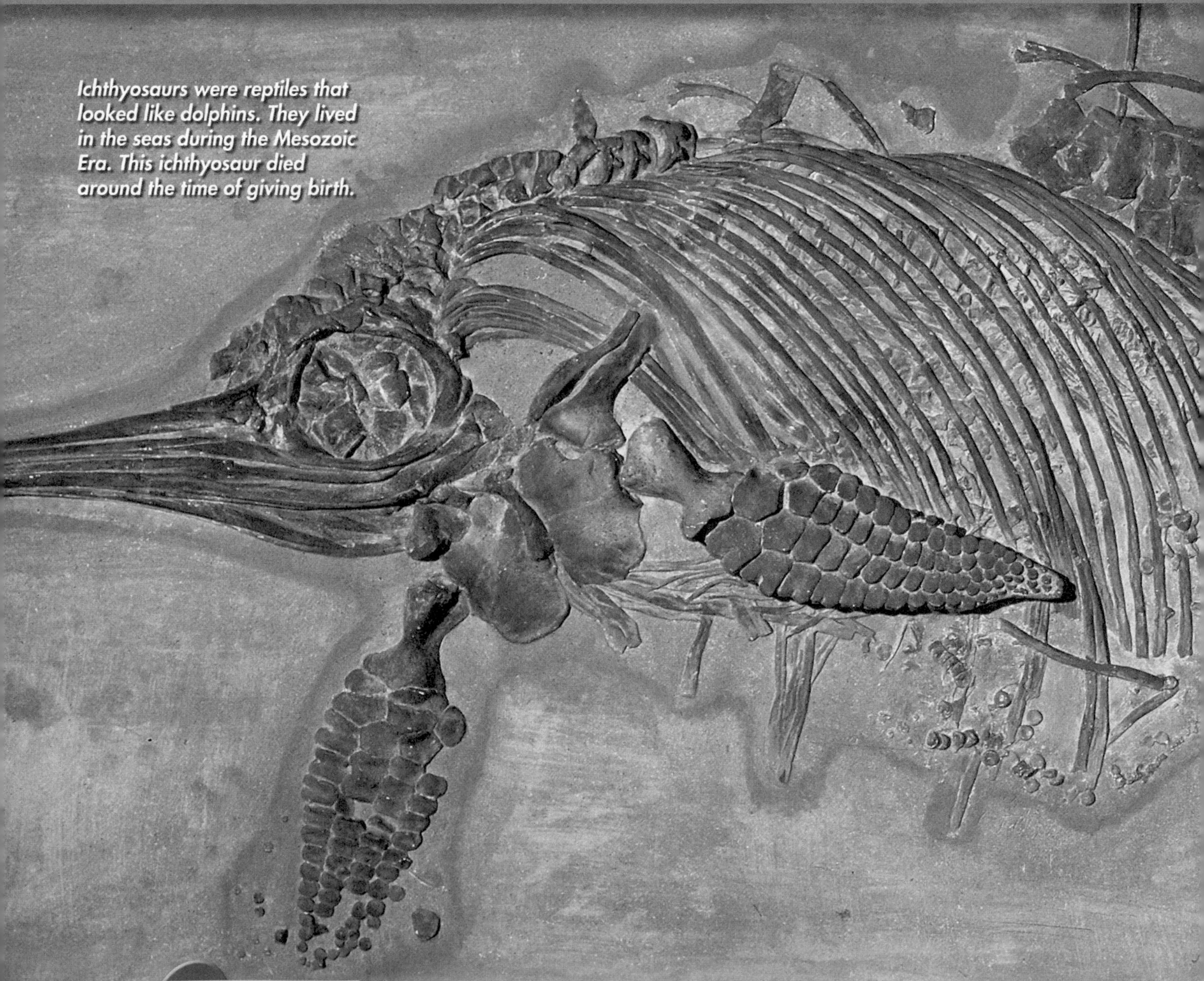

Ichthyosaurs were reptiles that looked like dolphins. They lived in the seas during the Mesozoic Era. This ichthyosaur died around the time of giving birth.

BIOLOGY.com Search Chapter 19 GO • Flash Cards

MARYLAND VOLUNTARY STATE CURRICULUM

Biology Indicators/Core Learning Goals (CLG) 3.1.1, 3.2.1, 3.3.1, 3.4.1, 3.4.2, 3.5.2, 3.5.3. **Skills and Processes Indicators (SPI)** 1.1.1, 1.4.1, 1.4.2, 1.4.8, 1.5.2, 1.5.5, 1.5.7, 1.5.8, 1.5.9, 1.7.6. See lessons for details.

CHAPTER
MYSTERY

MURDER IN THE PERMIAN

About 250 million years ago, life on Earth nearly came to an end. This time is known as the Permian extinction, because it happened at the end of the Permian Period. The Permian extinction may be the greatest murder mystery in the history of the world. Whatever happened back then killed about 96 percent of marine species and 70 percent of terrestrial vertebrate species.

Scientists once thought that this extinction happened over a long period. But new fossils suggest that it took no more than 200,000 years. In geology, that is a short amount of time.

Read for Mystery Clues As you read this chapter, look for clues to help you decide what could have killed so much of life on Earth. Then, solve the mystery at the end of the chapter.

FOUNDATIONS
for Learning

As you read the chapter, you will learn about key events in the history of life. To help remember these events, you will make folded tabs for 12 key events. Start with two sheets of notebook paper. Fold the sheets in half lengthwise. Cut each sheet into six pieces to make 12 folded tabs, as shown below. As you read, make notes about the key events on the inside of each tab. Be sure to include the time when each event took place. At the end of the chapter are two activities that use the folded tabs to help answer the question:
How do fossils help biologists understand the history of life on Earth?

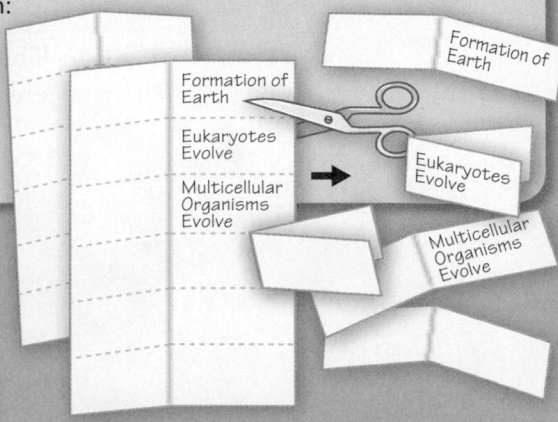

19.1 The Fossil Record

MD CLG 3.4.2 Relatedness Among Organisms, 3.5.2 Interdependence of Organisms in the Biosphere, 3.5.3 Population Dynamics. SPI 1.4.1 Organize Data, 1.4.2 Analyze Data, 1.4.8 Use Models, 1.5.5 Create and Interpret Graphics, 1.5.7 Classification Systems, 1.5.8 Compare, 1.7.6 Science and Technology.

Key Questions

🔑 What do fossils reveal about ancient life?

🔑 How do we date events in Earth's history?

🔑 How was the geologic time scale established, and what are its major divisions?

🔑 How have our planet's environment and living things interacted to shape the history of life on Earth?

BUILD Understanding

Main Ideas and Details Chart
One way to take notes is to make a main ideas and details chart. In the left column, write down the main idea. In the right column, write down details that support the main idea.

In Your Workbook Go to your workbook to learn more about making a main idea and details chart. Complete the chart for Lesson 19.1.

Fossils and Ancient Life

Fossils are one of the most important sources of information about ancient life. All fossils together make up the history of life on Earth called the *fossil record*. The scientists who study fossils are called **paleontologists** (pay lee un TAHL uh jists).

Types of Fossils Many fossils are the preserved remains of organisms. Usually, only hard parts of organisms, such as shell, teeth, bone, or wood, are preserved. (Soft body parts usually rot or are eaten before they can be preserved.) Fossils can be as large as a whole animal. Others are as tiny as bacteria or pollen grains. Many fossils are just pieces of an organism—a few teeth or bits of bone. Some fossils are called *trace* fossils. Trace fossils are signs of activity, such as footprints, burrows, or even droppings.

What Fossils Show Only a tiny percentage of ancient organisms became fossils. Although incomplete, the fossil record holds enough information to teach us a great deal about ancient life. Without fossils, we would know almost nothing about extinct species. An **extinct** species has no living members.

Fossils can show how an organism lived or what it ate. By comparing fossils to living organisms, paleontologists can trace the evolution of a body part or a whole species. Bone structure and footprints can show how an animal moved. Fossils from plants, such as leaves and pollen, can tell whether an area was a swamp or a forest. When plant and animal fossils are found together, paleontologists can learn about ancient ecosystems.

🔑 **Key Question** What do fossils reveal about ancient life?
The fossil record shows the structure of ancient organisms, their environment, and the way in which they lived.

Fossil Fish Like this 50-million-year-old fossil of a fish, most fossils form from the hard parts of organisms.

Dating Earth's History

To understand the fossil record, we need a time scale to tell what happened when. To find the age of rocks and fossils, scientists use relative dating and radiometric dating.

Sedimentary Rocks Fossils are usually found in sedimentary rock. Most sedimentary rocks form when sediments settle to the bottom of a body of water. Sediments are tiny particles, such as sand and clay. Over time, more and more layers of sediment build up. The weight of the many layers and chemical reactions turn the sediments into rock. As sediments build up, they bury dead organisms that have settled to the bottom. The remains of these organisms may become fossils.

Relative Dating When sedimentary rocks form, new layers are laid on top of older rocks. The layers on the bottom are usually older than the layers above them. Therefore, fossils in lower layers are usually older than fossils in upper layers. Scientists use the position of the layers to find the relative age of fossils. **Relative dating** places rock layers and their fossils in order according to time. Relative dating does not tell the age of a fossil in years.

To find the relative age of rock layers and their fossils, scientists use **index fossils.** Index fossils help scientists identify rocks and fossils of the same age that are found in different places. An index fossil must be easy to recognize. It should be found in only a few rock layers. (That would mean that it lived for only a short time.) But the layers that hold the index fossil must be found in many places.

BUILD Vocabulary

paleontologist a scientist who studies fossils

extinct the word used to describe a species that has died out and has no living members

relative dating a method of determining the age of a fossil by comparing its placement with that of fossils in other rock layers

index fossil a distinctive fossil that is used to establish and compare the relative ages of rock layers and the fossils they contain

WORD ORIGINS

The word *paleontologist* comes from the Greek word *palaios*, meaning "ancient." A paleontologist studies the remains of ancient life.

Index Fossils Each of these fossils is an index fossil. If the same index fossil is found in two different rock layers, the rock layers are probably about the same age. Use the index fossils to find which layers are missing from each location. Layers may be missing because they were never laid down or because they were worn away.

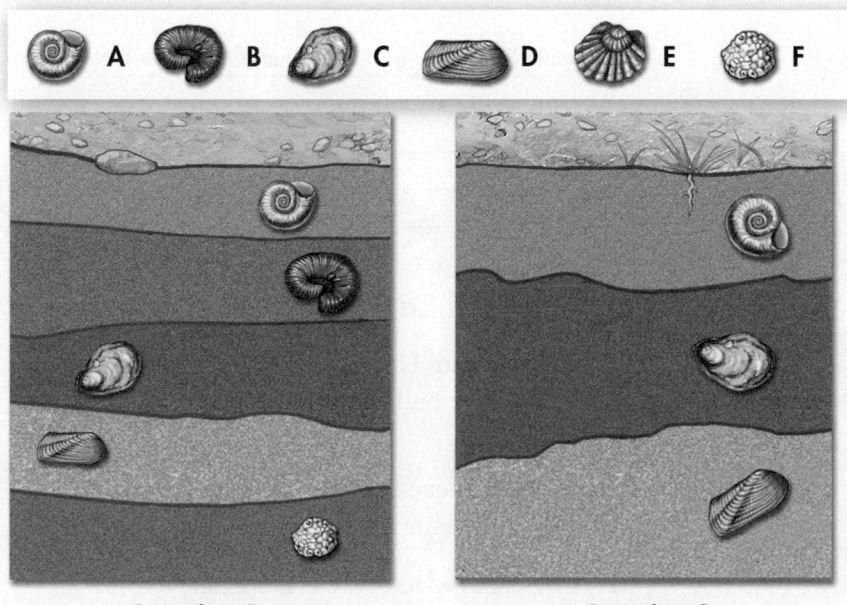

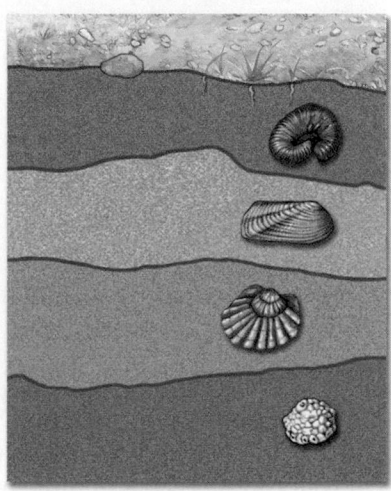

Location 1   **Location 2**   **Location 3**

Radiometric Dating In **radiometric dating,** scientists use radioactive isotopes to find the age of rocks and fossils. These isotopes decay, or break down, into nonradioactive isotopes at a steady rate. A **half-life** is the time it takes for half of the radioactive atoms in a sample to decay. After one half-life, half of the radioactive atoms have decayed. Radiometric dating gives the *absolute age*, or age in years.

Different radioactive isotopes decay at different rates, so they have different half-lives. Carbon-14 has a half-life of 5730 years. It is useful for finding the age of organisms that lived in the recent past—the last 60,000 years. Because carbon-14 is found in living organisms, it can be used to date fossils directly.

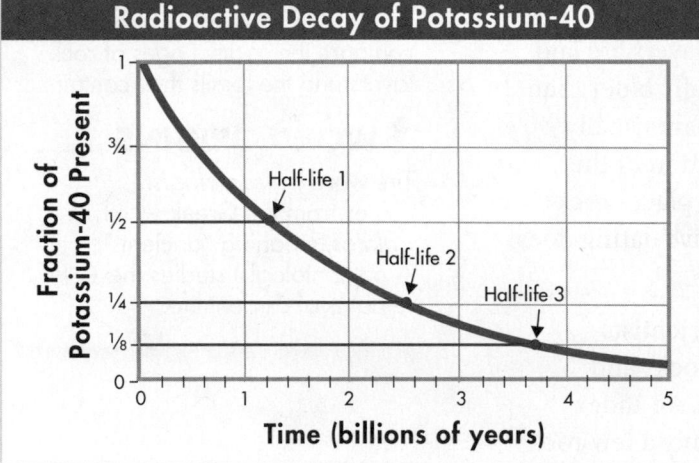

Radioactive Decay of Potassium-40

Time (billions of years)

Radioactive Decay A half-life is the time it takes for half of the radioactive atoms in a sample to decay. The half-life of potassium-40 is 1.26 billion years.

Isotopes with longer half-lives are used to date older fossils. Isotopes used for dating very old fossils include potassium-40 (half-life: 1.26 billion years), uranium-238 (half-life: 4.5 billion years), and rubidium-87 (half-life: 48.8 billion years). These isotopes are found in rocks, but not in fossils. To date an older fossil, researchers first find the age of the rocks in which the fossil is found. They then use this information to infer the age of the fossil itself.

Key Question How do we date events in Earth's history? **Relative dating can be used to determine whether a fossil is older or younger than other fossils. Radiometric dating uses the proportion of radioactive to nonradioactive isotopes to find the absolute age of a sample.**

INQUIRY into Scientific Thinking

Modeling Half-Life

❶ Make a data table like the one to the right.

❷ Take a sheet of paper, and cut out 100 1-cm squares. Write an *X* on one side of each square. Put all the squares in a cup.

❸ Mix the squares in the cup. Then spill them out.

❹ Remove all the squares that have the *X* showing. These represent radioactive isotopes that have decayed into different isotopes.

❺ Repeat steps 3 and 4 until there are five or fewer squares left.

❻ Make a graph of your results. Put the number of spills on the *x*-axis. Put the number of squares left after each spill on the *y*-axis.

Spill Number	Number of Squares Left
1	
2	
3	
4	
5	

Analyze and Conclude

1. Analyze Data How many spills did you need to remove half the squares? To remove three fourths?

2. Calculate If each spill represents 100 years, what is the half-life of the squares?

In Your Workbook Get more help for this activity in your workbook.

Geologic Time Scale

	Eon	Era	Period	Time (millions of years ago)
	Phanerozoic	Cenozoic	Quaternary	2–present
			Neogene	23–2
			Paleogene	66–23
		Mesozoic	Cretaceous	146–66
			Jurassic	200–146
			Triassic	251–200
		Paleozoic	Permian	299–251
			Carboniferous	359–299
			Devonian	416–359
			Silurian	444–416
			Ordovician	488–444
			Cambrian	542–488
Pre-cambrian Time	Protero-zoic			2500–542
	Archean			4000–2500
	Hadean			About 4600–4000

Geologic Time Scale The basic divisions of the geologic time scale are eons, eras, and periods. About 90 percent of Earth's history took place before the Cambrian Period.

Geologic Time Scale

Geologists and paleontologists have made a time line of Earth's history called the **geologic time scale.** The most recent version is shown above.

Establishing the Time Scale At first, scientists studied rock layers and index fossils to place them in order according to their relative ages. Then scientists noticed major changes in the fossil record between certain rock layers. Geologists used the boundaries between these layers to mark the end of one time division and the beginning of another. Years later, radiometric dating was used to find the ages of each of the layers. The geologic time scale is always being tested and corrected.

Key Question How was the geologic time scale established, and what are its major divisions? **The geologic time scale is based on both relative and absolute dating. The major divisions of the time scale are eons, eras, and periods.**

BUILD Vocabulary

radiometric dating a method for determining the age of a sample by comparing the amount of radioactive atoms to the nonradioactive atoms of the same element

half-life the length of time required for half of the radioactive atoms in a sample to decay

geologic time scale the time line used to represent Earth's history

PREFIXES

The prefix *radio-* means "radiation" or "radiant energy." In radiometric dating, scientists measure the amount of radiation given off by a sample.

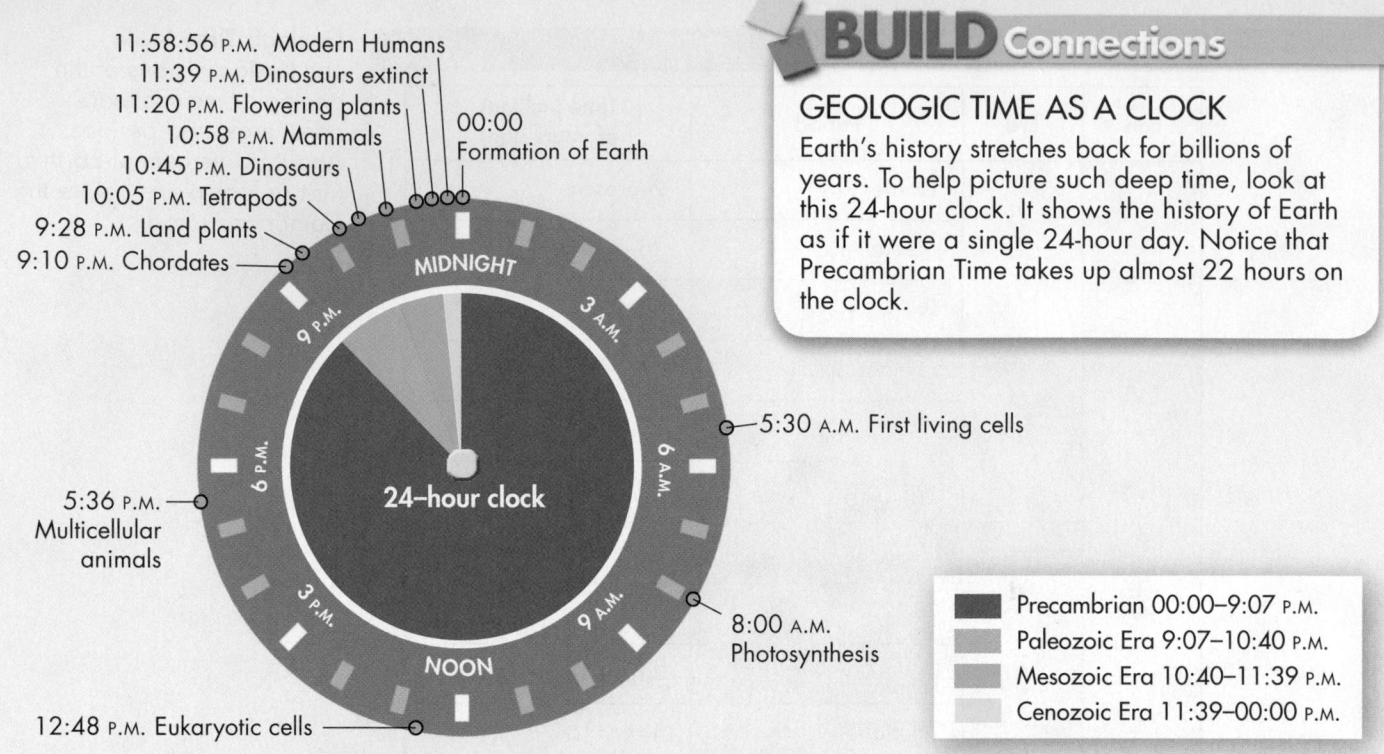

11:58:56 P.M. Modern Humans
11:39 P.M. Dinosaurs extinct
11:20 P.M. Flowering plants
10:58 P.M. Mammals
10:45 P.M. Dinosaurs
10:05 P.M. Tetrapods
9:28 P.M. Land plants
9:10 P.M. Chordates

00:00
Formation of Earth

MIDNIGHT

24–hour clock

5:36 P.M.
Multicellular
animals

5:30 A.M. First living cells

8:00 A.M.
Photosynthesis

NOON

12:48 P.M. Eukaryotic cells

Precambrian 00:00–9:07 P.M.
Paleozoic Era 9:07–10:40 P.M.
Mesozoic Era 10:40–11:39 P.M.
Cenozoic Era 11:39–00:00 P.M.

Divisions of the Geologic Time Scale Divisions of geologic time have different lengths. For example, the Cambrian Period lasted 54 million years. The Cretaceous Period lasted 80 million years. Eons are the largest divisions of time. Eons are divided into **eras.** Eras are further divided into **periods.** Periods range in length from hundreds of millions of years to just 2 million years.

Life on a Changing Planet

In our planet's long history, its physical environment has undergone many changes. These changes have greatly affected life on Earth.

The Physical Environment Some of the factors that have changed the physical environment are plate tectonics, changing climates, and collisions with objects from space.

▶ *Geological Forces* Geologic forces can form mountain ranges and move continents. The theory of **plate tectonics** states that Earth's surface is divided into huge plates. These plates move very slowly. Over long periods of time, their movement has pushed continents together, then pulled them apart again. The movement of the plates causes earthquakes and volcanoes.

The movement of the continents has affected the distribution of organisms. For example, Africa and South America are now separated by the Atlantic Ocean. But fossils of a reptile called *Mesosaurus* have been found on both Africa and South America. These fossils are evidence that these two continents were once joined together.

BUILD Vocabulary

era a major division of geologic time; usually divided into two or more periods

period a division of geologic time into which eras are subdivided

plate tectonics the theory that explains the slow movement of solid continental plates over Earth's mantle

🖋 **WORD ORIGINS**
The word *tectonics* from the Greek *tekton*, which means "builder." Plate tectonics is the theory that explains the movement of continents, formation of volcanoes, and mountain building.

▶ **Changing Climate** Earth's climate has changed greatly over the history of life. Many of these changes were caused by small shifts in temperature. For example, during the great ice ages, temperatures were only about 5°C cooler than they are now. These small changes had a big effect on living things.

▶ **Comets and Asteroids** Evidence shows that large objects from space have crashed into Earth several times. These collisions threw large amounts of dust into the air. This dust would have blocked enough sunlight to cause global cooling and other kinds of climate change. Such events could have caused organisms around the world to go extinct.

Biological Forces Living organisms also play a major role in shaping the environment. Earth's early oceans held very little oxygen. The first photosynthetic organisms began using carbon dioxide and giving off oxygen. Since then, our planet has never been the same! As levels of carbon dioxide dropped, the climate cooled.

Even today, organisms shape the landscape as they build soil from rock and sand. Plants, animals, fungi, and microorganisms are part of the cycles of carbon, nitrogen, and oxygen. Earth is indeed a living planet!

🔑 **Key Question** How have our planet's environment and living things interacted to shape the history of life on Earth? **Geological forces, changing climates, and collisions with comets and asteroids have changed the habitats of living organisms. The actions of living organisms have also changed conditions in the land, water, and atmosphere of Earth.**

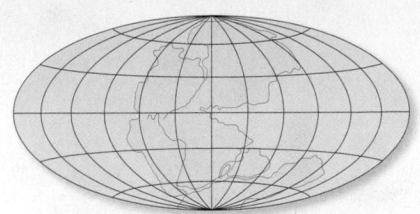

End of Permian Period At the end of the Permian Period, Earth's continents collided to form one giant landmass called Pangaea.

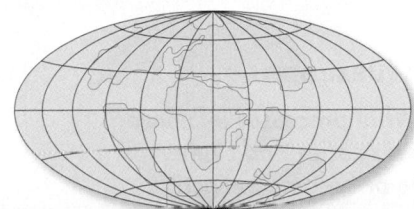

End of Cretaceous Period By the end of the Cretaceous Period, the continents as we know them began to drift apart.

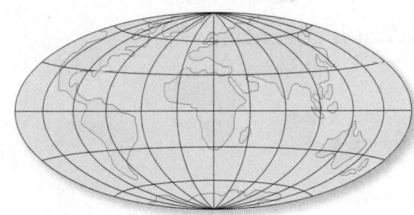

Present Day

The Changing Face of Earth Over the last 225 million years, the movement of the continents has changed Earth dramatically.

CHECK Understanding

Apply Vocabulary
Use the highlighted words from the lesson to complete each sentence correctly.

1. In _____, rock layers and their fossils are placed in order according to time.
2. Fossils that are used to determine the relative ages of rock layers are called _____.
3. The _____ of a radioactive element is the amount of time it takes for one half of the atoms in a sample to decay.

Critical Thinking

4. **Explain** What can a paleontologist learn from fossils?

5. **Review** What are the two ways in which geologists determine the age of fossils?
6. **Explain** How are eras and periods related?
7. **Relate Cause and Effect** Describe two ways that plate tectonics has affected life on Earth.
8. **Write to Learn** Answer the first clue in the mystery.

MYSTERY CLUE

Paleontologists discovered dramatic changes in the fossil record at the end of the Permian Period. What methods do you think they used to date that change at 251 million years ago? (**Hint:** See p. 452.)

Patterns and Processes of Evolution

MD | CLG 3.4.1 Evolutionary Change, 3.4.2 Relatedness Among Organisms. SPI 1.4.8 Use Models, 1.5.5 Create and Interpret Graphics, 1.5.7 Classification Systems, 1.5.8 Compare.

Key Questions

🔑 What processes influence whether species and clades survive or become extinct?

🔑 How fast does evolution take place?

🔑 What are two patterns of macroevolution?

🔑 What is coevolution?

BUILD Understanding

Concept Map Make a concept map that includes the patterns of macroevolution shown in this lesson.

In Your Workbook Go to your workbook to learn more about making concept maps. Complete the concept map for Lesson 19.2.

Speciation and Extinction

The fossil record shows a parade of organisms that evolved, survived for a time, and then disappeared. More than 99 percent of all the species that ever lived are now extinct. How have so many different groups evolved? Why are so many extinct?

The study of Earth's history leaves no doubt that life has changed over time. Many changes took place within species. Others took place in larger groups and over longer periods of time. Major changes in structure, behavior, and ecology are **macroevolutionary patterns.** The ways that new species form and others become extinct are macroevolutionary patterns. The extinction of the dinosaurs is a macroevolutionary pattern. So is the increase in the number of flowering plants.

Macroevolution and Cladistics Paleontologists study fossils to learn about the history of life. Part of their work is classifying fossils. As with living species, cladistics is used to classify fossil species. Paleontologists use shared derived characteristics to place fossils in clades. Paleontologists put some fossils into clades that contain only extinct organisms. They classify others in clades with organisms that are alive today.

Cladograms often show that a fossil species is related to a living species. Usually this does not mean that the fossil was the direct ancestor of the living species. For example, the cladogram on the facing page shows many dinosaurs that descended from a line of common ancestors. These dinosaurs were not the direct ancestors of modern birds.

Adaptation and Extinction Throughout the history of life, organisms have lived in changing environments. When conditions change, the process of evolution allows some species to adapt. These species thrive in the new environment. Other species do not adapt. Eventually, those species become extinct.

The rate of speciation and extinction varies from clade to clade. Some clades contain many species that have survived for long periods of time. Other clades have only a few species, which soon become extinct.

Why are some clades more successful than others? Part of the answer to this question is species diversity. Variation among species in a clade is like the variation among individuals in a species. Both are "raw material" for evolution.

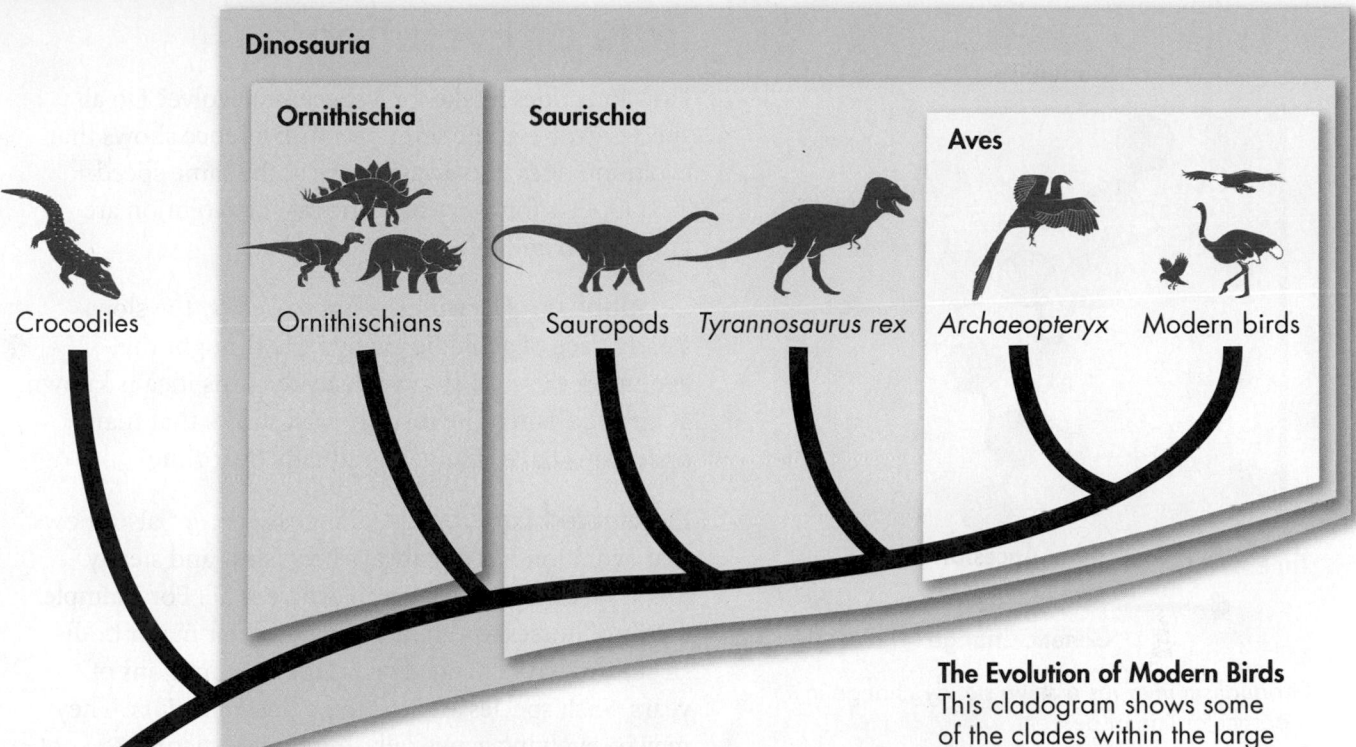

Dinosauria

Ornithischia

Saurischia

Aves

Crocodiles

Ornithischians

Sauropods

Tyrannosaurus rex

Archaeopteryx

Modern birds

The Evolution of Modern Birds
This cladogram shows some of the clades within the large clade Reptilia. Notice that clade Dinosauria is represented today by modern birds.

Genetic variation increases the chance that a species will survive in a changing environment. In the same way, the diversity of species in a clade increases the chance that a clade will survive. If new species evolve more quickly than species become extinct, a clade will survive. If extinctions happen faster than speciation, a clade will die out.

Clade Reptilia is a highly successful clade. It includes living organisms such as snakes, lizards, and turtles. It also includes dinosaurs, which lived for tens of millions of years. Most species in clade Dinosauria are now extinct. But clade Dinosauria also included some species that adapted to new conditions. Descendants of those species are still alive today. We call them birds.

Patterns of Extinction Some species become extinct because of the slow and steady process of natural selection. This "everyday" extinction is called **background extinction.** Other species go extinct in a relatively short period. This process is called **mass extinction.** In a mass extinction, entire ecosystems vanish. Some mass extinctions may have been caused by a single event, such as the large asteroid that hit Earth at the end of the Cretaceous period. Other mass extinctions were probably due to several causes working together, such as volcanic eruptions, changing climates, and changing sea levels.

 **Key Question** What processes influence whether species and clades survive or become extinct? **If the rate of speciation in a clade is equal to or greater than the rate of extinction, the clade will survive. If the rate of extinction is greater than the rate of speciation, the clade will become extinct.**

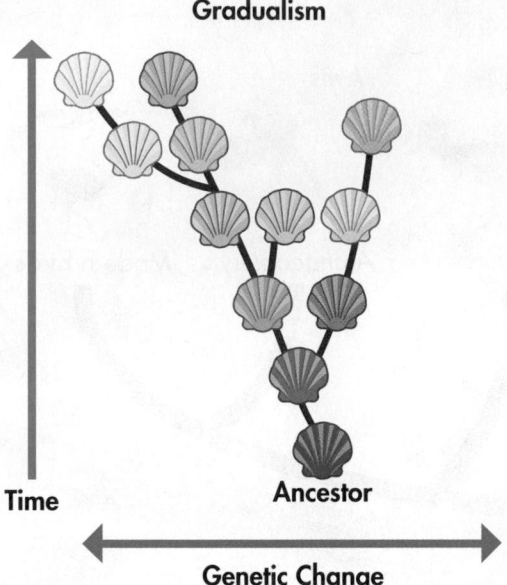

Gradualism

Time

Ancestor

Genetic Change

Gradualism involves a slow, steady change in a particular line of descent.

Punctuated Equilibrium

Time

Ancestor

Genetic Change

Punctuated equilibrium involves stable periods interrupted by rapid changes.

Models of Evolution Biologists have two different ways of looking at and thinking about the rate of evolution: gradualism and punctuated equilibrium. These simplified drawings compare the two patterns.

Rate of Evolution

How long does it take for a species to evolve? Do all species evolve at the same speed? Evidence shows that evolution does not always move at the same speed. Two models for describing the rate of evolution are gradualism and punctuated equilibrium.

Gradualism Darwin was impressed by the slow, steady pace of geologic change. He thought that evolution was also slow and steady. This idea is known as **gradualism.** The fossil record shows that many organisms have changed gradually over time.

Punctuated Equilibrium The fossil record also shows that evolution has not always been slow and steady. Some species do not seem to evolve at all. For example, fossils of horseshoe crabs show that their major body structures have changed very little over millions of years. Such species are said to be in *equilibrium*. They may be evolving genetically, but their structures do not change much.

Fossils of other organisms show periods of stability and rapid change. Equilibrium that is interrupted by periods of rapid change is **punctuated equilibrium.** Some biologists suggest that most new species are produced during these periods of rapid change. (But remember that evolution takes place according to the geologic time scale. To a geologist, "rapid change" may mean thousands of years!)

Rapid Change After Equilibrium Small, isolated populations can evolve rapidly. This rapid evolution is possible because genetic changes spread more quickly among fewer individuals. Rapid evolution may also happen when a small group moves to a new environment. That is what happened with the Galápagos finches.

Mass extinctions can lead to rapid evolution. After a mass extinction, there are fewer competing species. As a result, more "jobs" are available for new species. The fossil record shows that after a mass extinction, the groups that survive evolve rapidly. Biodiversity is eventually restored.

Key Question How fast does evolution take place? **Evidence shows that evolution has moved at different rates for different organisms at different times over the long history of life on Earth.**

Adaptive Radiation and Convergent Evolution

Two important patterns of macroevolution are adaptive radiation and convergent evolution. Darwin noticed both of these patterns as he traveled on the *Beagle*.

Adaptive Radiation Fossils show that a single species can evolve into a clade with many species. All of these species have variations on the original ancestor's body plan. The new species may fill different ecological niches. **Adaptive radiation** is the process by which a single species or small group of species evolves into several different forms that live in different ways. Sometimes, this process can happen relatively quickly. Adaptive radiation can happen when species move to a new environment or after a mass extinction. It can also happen when a new adaptation lets a species live in an environment that had not been used before.

▶ *Adaptive Radiations in the Fossil Record* Dinosaurs lived for about 150 million years during the Mesozoic. They arose from several adaptive radiations of reptiles. Fossils show that when dinosaurs were at their greatest diversity, mammals were small and not very diverse. After most of the dinosaurs became extinct, an adaptive radiation of mammals began. That radiation led to the great diversity of mammals of the Cenozoic Era.

▶ *Modern Adaptive Radiation* Two examples of adaptive radiation are the Galápagos finches and Hawaiian honeycreepers. Their stories are similar: A single species evolved into many different species. Both finches and honeycreepers evolved different beaks and behaviors that let them eat different kinds of food.

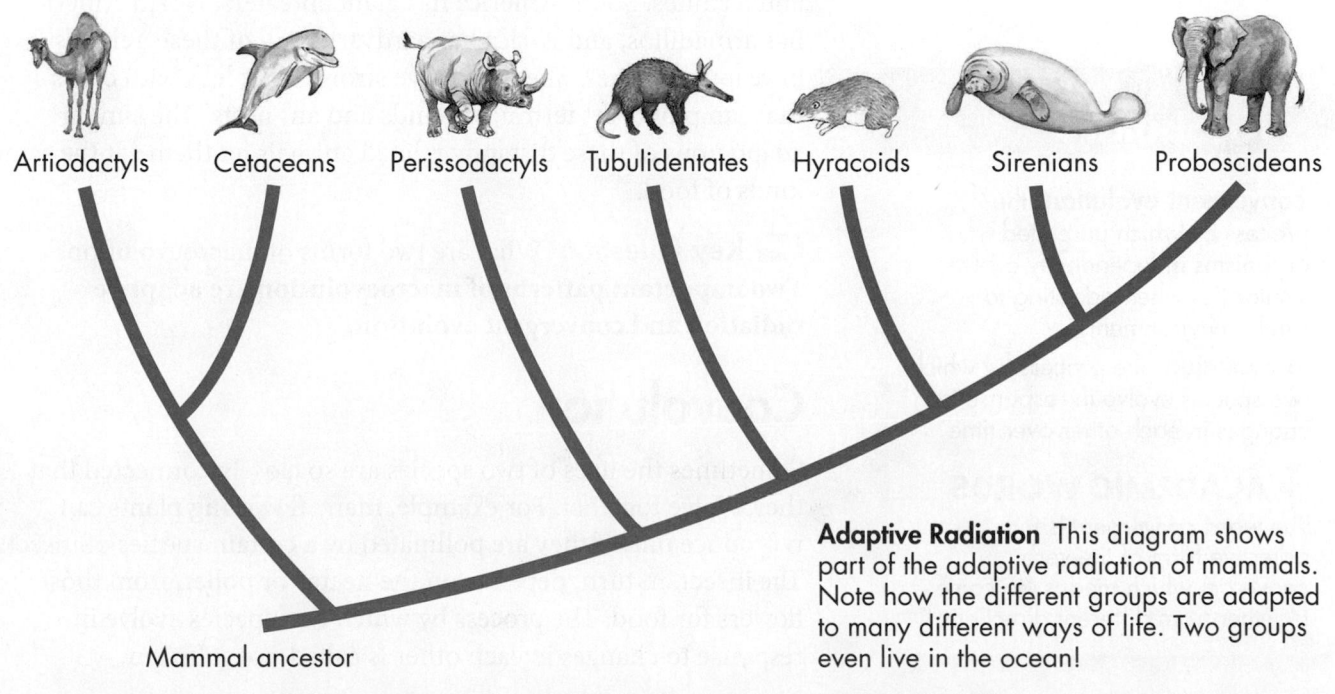

Artiodactyls   Cetaceans   Perissodactyls   Tubulidentates   Hyracoids   Sirenians   Proboscideans

Mammal ancestor

Adaptive Radiation This diagram shows part of the adaptive radiation of mammals. Note how the different groups are adapted to many different ways of life. Two groups even live in the ocean!

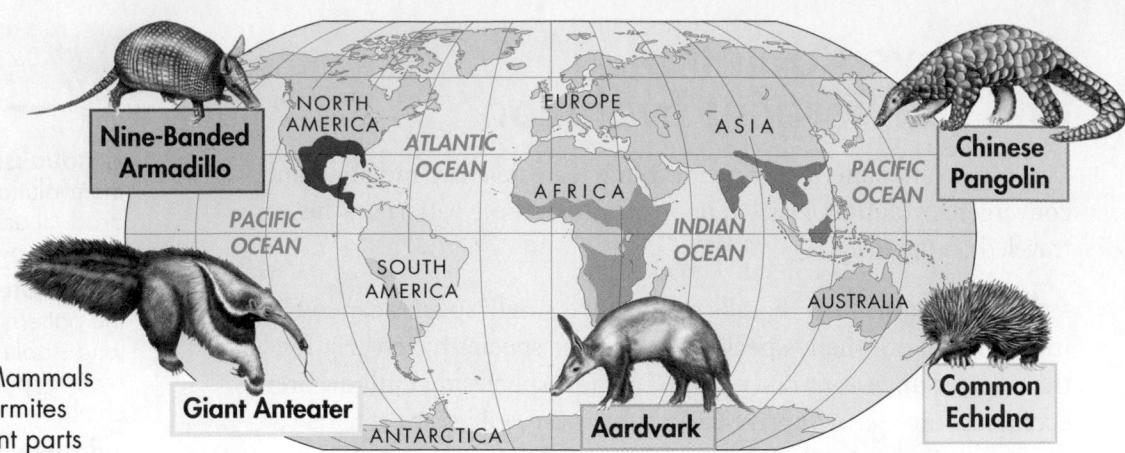

Convergent Evolution Mammals that feed on ants and termites are found in five different parts of the world. These species are unrelated. But they all have powerful front claws, a long hairless snout, and a tongue covered with sticky saliva. These adaptations are very useful for hunting and eating insects.

Nine-Banded Armadillo

Chinese Pangolin

Giant Anteater

Aardvark

Common Echidna

Convergent Evolution Sometimes, organisms in different places evolve in similar environments. These organisms start out with different structures. But they face similar selection pressures. In such cases, natural selection may cause different body structures to evolve in ways that let them carry out similar functions. Over time, the different organisms become more and more alike. This process is called convergent evolution. In **convergent evolution,** natural selection forms similar structures and characteristics in organisms that are not closely related.

During the voyage of the *Beagle,* Darwin noticed similarities among large grassland birds on different continents. Although they look alike, emus, rheas, and ostriches are not closely related. All three of these birds have long, strong legs let them run swiftly through tall grasses. These three flightless birds are an example of convergent evolution.

The different kinds of anteaters also show convergent evolution. Most continents have mammals that specialize in eating ants and termites. South America has giant anteaters, North America has armadillos, and Africa has aardvarks. All of these animals have long tongues. They also have strong front legs with claws that can pull apart termite mounds and ant nests. The similar adaptations of these distantly related animals let them eat the same kinds of food.

🔑 **Key Question** What are two forms of macroevolution? **Two important patterns of macroevolution are adaptive radiation and convergent evolution.**

Coevolution

Sometimes the lives of two species are so closely connected that they evolve together. For example, many flowering plants can reproduce only if they are pollinated by a certain species of insect. The insect, in turn, depends on the nectar or pollen from those flowers for food. The process by which two species evolve in response to changes in each other is called **coevolution.**

Flowers and Pollinators Coevolution of flowers and pollinators is common and can lead to unusual results. For example, Darwin discovered a flower with a long structure called a spur. The spur was 40 centimeters long. At the bottom of the spur was a supply of nectar. Nectar in flowers usually attracts pollinators. But what pollinator could reach down such a long tube? Darwin predicted that the plant must be pollinated by an insect with mouth parts that could reach to the bottom of the spur. About 40 years later, scientists discovered a moth with a 40-centimeter-long feeding tube. This moth matched Darwin's prediction!

Plants and Herbivorous Insects Coevolution also takes place between plants and the insects that eat them. Insects have been eating flowering plants ever since both groups evolved. In some cases, plants have evolved poisons to protect themselves from being eaten. But insects have evolved in response to the poisons. Natural selection has favored any individuals that are resistant to the poisons.

Milkweed plants are poisonous to many insects. But the caterpillars of monarch butterflies are able to eat their leaves. In fact, the monarch caterpillars store the milkweed poisons in their bodies. The poisons help protect the monarchs from predators!

🔑 **Key Question** What is coevolution? **The relationship between two organisms may become so specific that neither organism can survive without the other. Thus, an evolutionary change in one organism is usually followed by a change in the other organism.**

Coevolution Milkweed plants produce poisons that protect them from being eaten. But monarch butterflies have coevolved with the milkweed plants. Their caterpillars can eat milkweed leaves without harm. In fact, monarchs store the milkweed poisons in their own bodies. This poison protects the monarchs against *their* predators!

✓CHECK Understanding

Apply Vocabulary
Use the highlighted words from the lesson to complete each sentence correctly.

1. An event during which many species become extinct over a short period of time is a _____.

2. The slow, steady "everyday" rate of extinction that has happened throughout the history of life is called _____.

3. The process by which two species evolve in response to changes in each other over time is called _____.

Critical Thinking

4. Review How does variation within a clade affect the clade's chance of surviving environmental change?

5. Compare and Contrast Explain how punctuated equilibrium is different from gradualism.

6. Review What is adaptive radiation?

7. Apply Concepts Describe an example of coevolution.

8. Write to Learn Answer the second clue of the mystery. Use the words *cellular respiration* in your answer.

MYSTERY CLUE

Evidence indicates that before the Permian extinction, the oceans lost most of their oxygen. What effect do you think the loss of oxygen had on most organisms? (**Hint:** See p. 457.)

BIOLOGY.com ▸ Search ⟨ Lesson 19.2 ⟩ GO • Lesson Assessment

Earth's Early History

MD CLG 3.1.1 Chemical Substances and Macromolecules, 3.2.1 Processes and Functions, 3.3.1 Sexual Reproduction and Variation, 3.4.1 Evolutionary Change, 3.4.2 Relatedness Among Organisms. SPI 1.1.1 Problems and Solutions, 1.5.7 Classification Systems, 1.5.9 Synthesize Ideas.

Key Questions

🔑 **What do scientists hypothesize about early Earth and the origin of life?**

🔑 **What do scientists hypothesize about the origins of DNA and RNA?**

🔑 **What theory explains the origin of eukaryotic cells?**

🔑 **What is the evolutionary significance of sexual reproduction?**

BUILD Understanding

Flowchart Construct a flowchart that shows what scientists hypothesize about early Earth. Show the major steps from the origin of Earth to the appearance of eukaryotic cells.

In Your Workbook Go to your workbook to learn about making a flowchart. Complete the flowchart for lesson 19.3.

Early Earth Violent volcanic eruptions helped shape Earth's early history.

The Mysteries of Life's Origins

How did life on Earth begin? What were the earliest forms of life? Scientists are working hard to answer these questions. As new evidence comes to light, hypotheses about early life are likely to change.

Evidence suggests that Earth formed from pieces of rock and dust. One or more huge objects crashed into the young Earth, causing it to melt. For millions of years, volcanoes erupted. Comets and asteroids crashed into the surface. About 4.2 billion years ago, Earth cooled enough for solid rocks to form. Rain fell, and oceans formed.

The Early Atmosphere The early atmosphere held little or no oxygen. It was mostly carbon dioxide, water vapor, and nitrogen. It also had smaller amounts of carbon monoxide, hydrogen sulfide, and hydrogen cyanide. A few deep breaths would have killed you! These gases probably made the sky orange. Dissolved iron probably made the oceans brown. This was the Earth on which life began.

🔑 **Key Question** What do scientists hypothesize about early Earth? **Earth's early atmosphere was mainly carbon dioxide, water vapor, and nitrogen, with lesser amounts of carbon monoxide, hydrogen sulfide, and hydrogen cyanide. It contained little or no oxygen.**

The First Organic Molecules Could organic molecules have formed on early Earth? In 1953, Stanley Miller and Harold Urey did an experiment to answer that question. They built a system of tubes and containers filled with water vapor, methane, ammonia, and hydrogen. They thought that this mixture of gases was like that of Earth's early atmosphere. To represent lightning, they hit the gases with sparks of electricity. After a week, they had made 12 amino acids. Amino acids are the building blocks of proteins!

We now know that Miller and Urey were wrong about the mixture of gases in the early atmosphere. But new experiments based on more current ideas have also made organic compounds. In 1995, Miller repeated the experiment with a more accurate mix of gases. This time, he made cytosine and uracil, two bases found in RNA.

🔑 **Key Question** What do scientists hypothesize about the origin of life? **Miller and Urey's experiment suggested how mixtures of the organic compounds necessary for life could have arisen from simpler compounds in the atmosphere of early Earth.**

Formation of Microspheres The compounds made by the Miller-Urey experiments are a long way from living cells. How could living cells develop from this "stew" of organic compounds? The leap from nonlife to life is the greatest gap in scientific hypotheses about the history of life.

Large organic compounds sometimes form tiny bubbles called *microspheres*. Microspheres might have played a role in the evolution of cells. Like cells, they have selectively permeable membranes that allow water to pass through. Microspheres also have a simple means of storing and releasing energy. Several hypotheses suggest that microspheres may have developed the characteristics of living cells as early as 3.8 billion years ago.

Evolution of RNA and DNA Another unanswered question is the origin of RNA and DNA. Remember that cells are controlled by information stored in DNA. The information on DNA is transcribed onto RNA, which is used to form proteins. How could such a complex system evolve? The key to the answer may be RNA. Modern RNA is involved in many of life's reactions. The "RNA world" hypothesis suggests that RNA existed before DNA. The RNA-based system could then have evolved into the more complex DNA-based system.

Key Question What do scientists hypothesize about the origins of DNA and RNA?
The "RNA world" hypothesis proposes that RNA existed by itself before DNA. From this simple RNA-based system, several steps could have led to DNA-directed protein synthesis.

❷ A mixture of methane, ammonia, and hydrogen is added to the water vapor.

❸ The circulating gases are bombarded by sparks of electricity.

Condensation chamber

❹ Cold water cools the chamber, causing droplets to form.

❶ Water is heated, and water vapor forms.

❺ After a week, liquid is collected and contains amino acids and other organic compounds.

Miller-Urey Experiment Miller and Urey modeled conditions on ancient Earth. They produced amino acids by passing sparks through a mixture of gases.

Origin of RNA and DNA One hypothesis about the origin of life suggests that RNA evolved before DNA. Scientists have not yet demonstrated the later stages of this process in a laboratory setting.

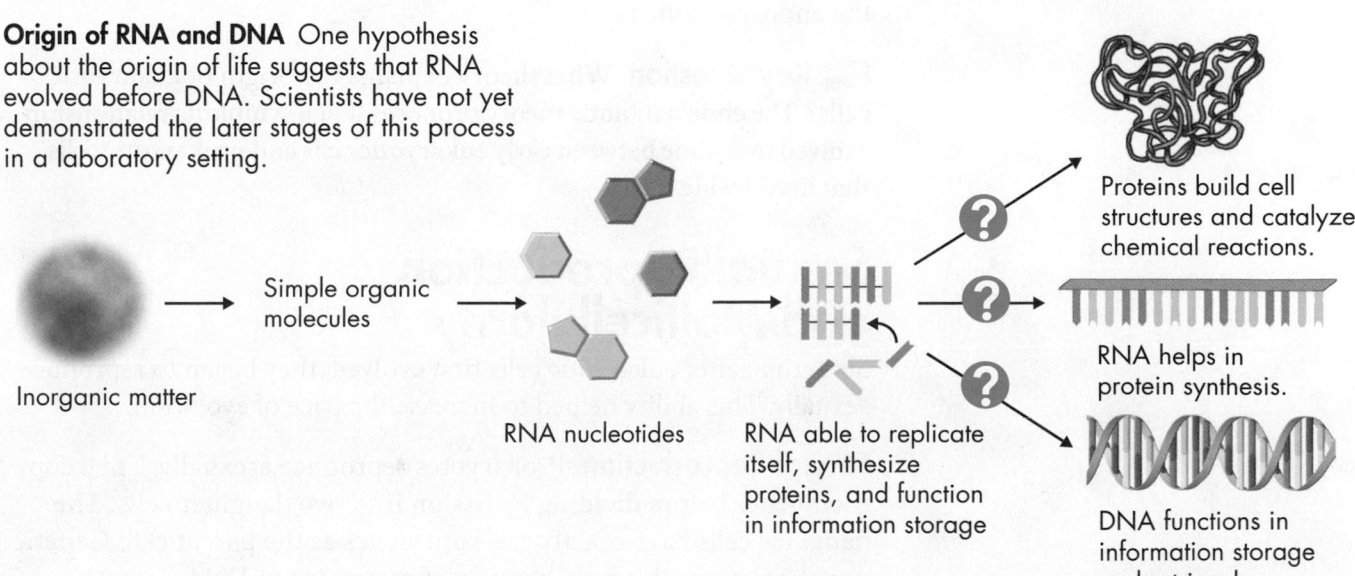

Inorganic matter → Simple organic molecules → RNA nucleotides → RNA able to replicate itself, synthesize proteins, and function in information storage

Proteins build cell structures and catalyze chemical reactions.

RNA helps in protein synthesis.

DNA functions in information storage and retrieval.

endosymbiotic theory
the theory that proposes that
eukaryotic cells formed from a
symbiotic relationship among
several different prokaryotic cells

PREFIXES

The prefix *endo-* in *endosymbiotic
theory* means "within." The
endosymbiotic theory involves a
symbiotic relationship between
eukaryotic cells and the bacteria
within them.

Production of Free Oxygen The oldest fossils are found in rocks that are more than 3.5 billion years old. These prokaryotic cells evolved without oxygen. (Remember that the early atmosphere had very little oxygen.) Later, photosynthetic bacteria became common. By 2.2 billion years ago, photosynthetic cells were giving off great amounts of oxygen. This oxygen changed the atmosphere. In a few hundred million years, the amount of oxygen reached today's levels. For early life, this new gas was a deadly poison! It caused many early life forms to die out. Other organisms evolved ways to protect themselves from oxygen. Many organisms evolved the ability to use oxygen for respiration.

Origin of Eukaryotic Cells

One of the most important events in the history of life was the evolution of eukaryotic cells. How did these complex cells evolve from their prokaryotic ancestors?

Endosymbiotic Theory About 2.2 billion years ago, some kinds of prokaryotes began to evolve features found in eukaryotes. According to the **endosymbiotic theory,** prokaryotes became part of those early eukaryotes. At first, prokaryotic "guests" lived inside the eukaryotes. Over time, the "guests" became a part of their hosts. The "guests" became the mitochondria and chloroplasts of modern eukaryotic cells. Mitochondria evolved from bacteria that helped their hosts use oxygen. Chloroplasts evolved from photosynthetic bacteria that made food for their host cells.

Modern Evidence In 1963, the American biologist Lynn Margulis found that the DNA of chloroplasts and mitochondria was like the DNA of bacteria. She also noted that the ribosomes of these organelles are very similar to those of bacteria. Finally, these organelles divide by fission, just like bacteria. The similarities between mitochondria, chloroplasts, and bacteria provide strong support for the endosymbiotic theory.

Key Question What theory explains the origin of eukaryotic cells? **The endosymbiotic theory proposes that a symbiotic relationship evolved over time between early eukaryotic cells and prokaryotic cells that lived inside them.**

Sexual Reproduction and Multicellularity

Sometime after eukaryotic cells first evolved, they began to reproduce sexually. This ability helped to increase the pace of evolution.

Sexual Reproduction Prokaryotes reproduce asexually. They copy their genes before dividing by fission into two daughter cells. The daughter cells have exactly the same genes as the parent cell. Genetic variation is possible only because of mutations in DNA.

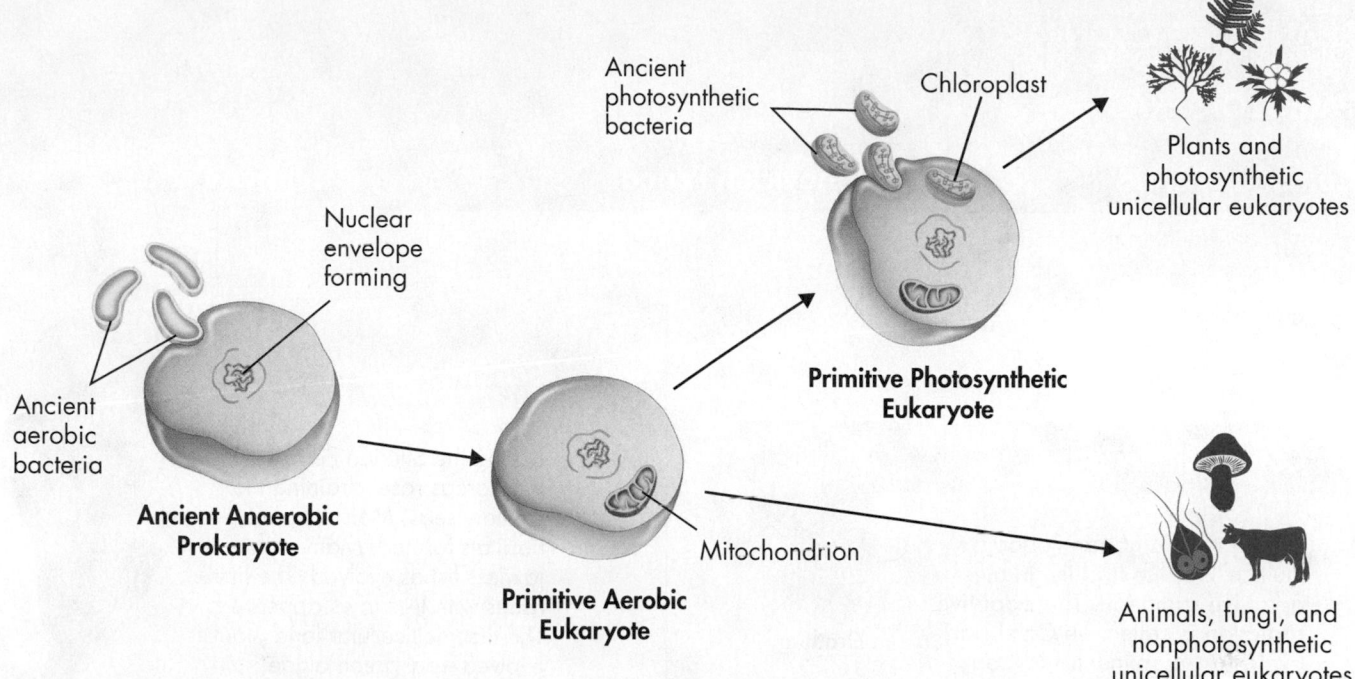

Ancient photosynthetic bacteria

Chloroplast

Plants and photosynthetic unicellular eukaryotes

Nuclear envelope forming

Primitive Photosynthetic Eukaryote

Ancient aerobic bacteria

Ancient Anaerobic Prokaryote

Mitochondrion

Primitive Aerobic Eukaryote

Animals, fungi, and nonphotosynthetic unicellular eukaryotes

When eukaryotes reproduce sexually, the offspring receive genes from two parents. Meiosis and fertilization increase genetic variation through new gene combinations. Genetic variation is the raw material for natural selection. More variation means a population can evolve more quickly. Genetic variation helps populations adapt to new conditions.

Multicellularity Multicellular organisms evolved a few hundred million years after the evolution of sexual reproduction. Early multicellular organisms underwent a series of adaptive radiations. The result was a great diversity of organisms.

Key Question What is the evolutionary significance of sexual reproduction? **The development of sexual reproduction sped up evolutionary change because it increased genetic variation.**

Endosymbiotic Theory
The endosymbiotic theory states that eukaryotic cells evolved from a relationship formed with bacteria. Ancient bacteria may have entered primitive eukaryotic cells and remained there as organelles.

Apply Vocabulary
Use the highlighted word from the lesson to complete the sentence correctly.

1. The _____ states that mitochondria and chloroplasts evolved from symbiotic bacteria living inside eukaryotes.

Critical Thinking
2. Apply Concepts What evidence supports the endosymbiotic theory?

3. Review Describe Earth's early atmosphere.

4. Relate Cause and Effect Why is the development of sexual reproduction so important in the history of life?

5. Sequence Put the following events in the order in which they occurred: *sexual reproduction, development of eukaryotic cells, free oxygen in atmosphere,* and *development of photosynthesis.*

6. Write to Learn Write a paragraph that describes the experiment conducted by Miller and Urey. What was their hypothesis? What was their procedure? What conclusion could they draw from their results?

| Cambrian Period | Ordovician Period | Silurian Period |

Silurian Period

During the Silurian Period, land areas rose, draining the shallow seas. Moist tropical habitats formed. Many different jawless fishes evolved. The first fishes with true jaws appeared. The first multicellular land plants evolved from green algae. Arthropods become the first animals to live on land.

▲ Sea Lily Fossil

Cambrian Period

During the Cambrian Period, multicellular life had its greatest adaptive radiation. This adaptive radiation is called the Cambrian Explosion. Continents moved in ways that created shallow seas over much of Earth. Many organisms in the seas evolved hard shells and outer skeletons. The first jawless fishes appeared. The Cambrian ended with a mass extinction. Nearly one third of all animal groups died.

▲ Elrathia

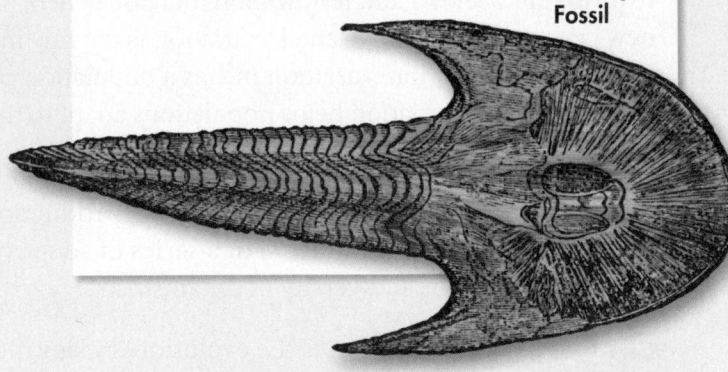

▲ Cephalaspis (raylike jawless fish)

▼ Stenaster (early sea star)

Pleurocystes (early echinoderms) ▼

Ordovician Period

Oceans flooded large parts of the land, making more shallow seas. Groups that had survived the Cambrian extinction evolved rapidly. Adaptive radiations led to great diversity in the major animal phyla. Invertebrates were the most common animals in the seas. Early vertebrates evolved bony coverings.

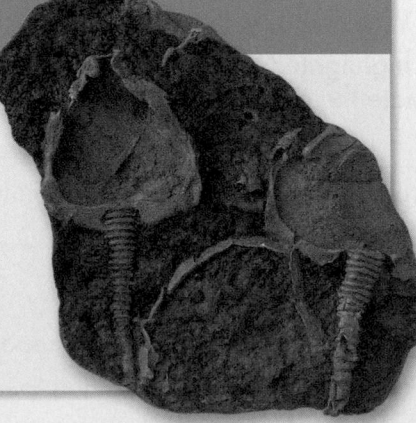

Devonian Period

During the Devonian Period, invertebrates and vertebrates thrived in the seas. Fishes evolved jaws, bony skeletons, and scales. Sharks began their adaptive radiation. Certain groups of fishes evolved leglike fins; some of these evolved into the first amphibians. Some land plants, such as ferns, adapted to drier areas. Insects began their adaptive radiation on land.

◀ **Fossil Fern From Carboniferous Period**

Permian Period

During the Permian Period, the diversity of invertebrates, vertebrates, and plants on land increased. Reptiles experienced their first adaptive radiation. This produced the ancestors of modern reptiles, dinosaurs, and mammals. The Permian Period ended with the biggest mass extinction of all time. More than 50 percent of animal families on land disappeared. More than 95 percent of species in the oceans became extinct.

▲ **Crinoid**

Early Amphibian ▼

Carboniferous Period

During the Carboniferous Period, mountains pushed upward. Mountain building formed a wide range of habitats, from swampy lowlands to drier uplands. Giant ferns, club mosses, and horsetails formed huge swampy forests. Amphibians, insects, and plants had major adaptive radiations. Winged insects evolved into many forms, including huge dragonflies and cockroaches. For early plants, insects were predators. For early vertebrates, insects were food. The first reptiles evolved from ancient amphibians.

Triassic Period	Jurassic Period	Cretaceous Period

Triassic Period

During the Triassic Period, fishes, insects, reptiles, and cone-bearing plants that survived the Permian extinction evolved rapidly. The first dinosaurs evolved. During the late Triassic, the earliest mammals evolved. These mammals were about the size of a mouse.

▲ **Living Horsetail**　　▲ **Horsetail Fossil**

Cretaceous Period

During the Cretaceous Period, dinosaurs like *Tyrannosaurus rex* roamed ▲ *T. rex* **Skeleton** the land. Flying reptiles and birds flew in the sky. Turtles, crocodiles, and other reptiles swam with fishes and invertebrates in the seas. Leafy trees, shrubs, and flowering plants evolved and experienced adaptive radiations. The Cretaceous ended with another mass extinction. More than half of all plant and animal groups were wiped out. All dinosaurs except the ancestors of modern birds became extinct.

Jurassic Period

During the Jurassic Period, dinosaurs became the most diverse group of animals on land. They "ruled" for about 150 million years. Different types of dinosaurs lived at different times. One line of dinosaurs evolved feathers and led to modern birds. *Archaeopteryx*, the first feathered fossil to be discovered, evolved during this time.

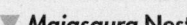

◄ **Pterodactyl Fossil**

▼ *Maiasaura* **Nest**

CENOZOIC ERA

| Paleogene Period | Neogene Period | Quaternary Period |

Paleogene Period

During the Paleogene Period, climates changed from warm and moist to cool and dry. Flowering plants, grasses, and insects thrived. In drier areas, open woods and grasslands replaced forests. After the extinction of the dinosaurs, mammals underwent a major adaptive radiation. Ancestors of cattle, deer, and sheep evolved and spread across the grasslands. In the oceans, the first whales evolved.

▲ Early Mammal

Neogene Period

During the Neogene Period, crashing continents pushed up modern mountain ranges. In North America, the Rockies, Cascades, and Sierra Nevada formed. Ice and snow built up at higher elevations and in the Arctic. Falling sea levels and moving continents created connections between North and South America, and between Africa, Europe, and Asia. These connections allowed land animals to move between continents. As climates became cooler and drier, grasslands increased. Grazing animals evolved digestive systems that allowed them to digest the grasses.

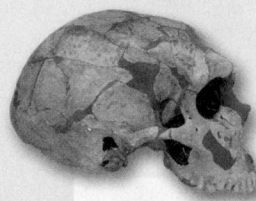

◀ Neanderthal Skull

Quaternary Period

During the Quaternary Period, Earth cooled. In a series of ice ages, glaciers moved over parts of Europe and North America. So much water was frozen in glaciers that sea levels fell by more than 100 meters. Then, about 20,000 years ago, the climate began to warm. Glaciers slowly melted, and sea levels rose. In the oceans, algae, coral, mollusks, fishes, and mammals thrived. Insects and birds shared the skies. On land, mammals, including bats, cats, dogs, cattle, and mammoths, became common. Between 6 and 7 million years ago, one group of mammals began an adaptive radiation that led to the ancestors and relatives of modern humans.

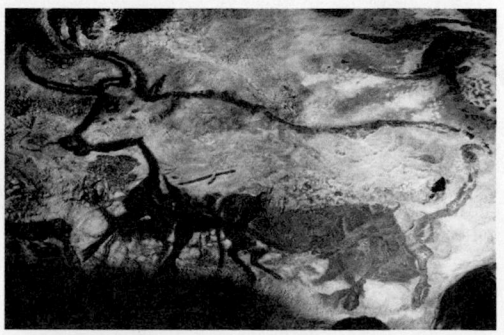

▲ Cave Painting

MD CLG 3.4.2 Relatedness Among Organisms. SPI 1.5.2 Communicate Information, 1.5.7 Classification Systems, 1.5.9 Synthesize Ideas.

Pre-Lab: Using Index Fossils

Problem How can fossils be used to determine the relative ages of rock layers?

Materials scissors

Lab Manual Chapter 19 Lab

Skills Focus Interpret Visuals, Sequence, Draw Conclusions

Connect to the **Big idea** When detectives work on a case, they may look for items with a time stamp, such as parking tickets and credit card slips. Such items can help detectives piece together a sequence of events. Events related to a crime usually occur within a relatively short period of time. In contrast, the events that paleontologists study will have occurred over millions of years. Placing these events in their proper order can be challenging. The clues that a paleontologist uses to sequence events in the history of life are fossils buried in rock layers. In this lab, you will use fossils to place rock layers in order from oldest to youngest.

Background Questions

a. Review What is a fossil? What are the characteristics of a good index fossil?

b. Explain What characteristic of radioactive decay allows scientists to assign specific ages to rock layers?

c. Classify How do fossils help geologists decide where one division of geologic time should end and another division begin?

Pre-Lab Questions

Preview the procedure in the lab manual.

1. Organize Data After you cut out the drawings of the rock layers, how will you begin the process of sorting the layers by age?

2. Infer *Desmatosuchus* was a crocodile relative that lived only during the Triassic Period. Horsetails are plants that first appeared in the Triassic Period and still exist. Which of these organisms would be more useful as an index fossil for the Triassic Period? Why?

3. Use Analogies Luke found a box of photos labeled 1970–1995. Each photo shows his entire extended family. No dates appear on the photos. Luke knows that his grandmother died in 1985 and his uncle was born in 1975. Luke's sister was born in 1990. How can Luke use this information to sort the photos into four batches? How are Luke's relatives similar to index fossils?

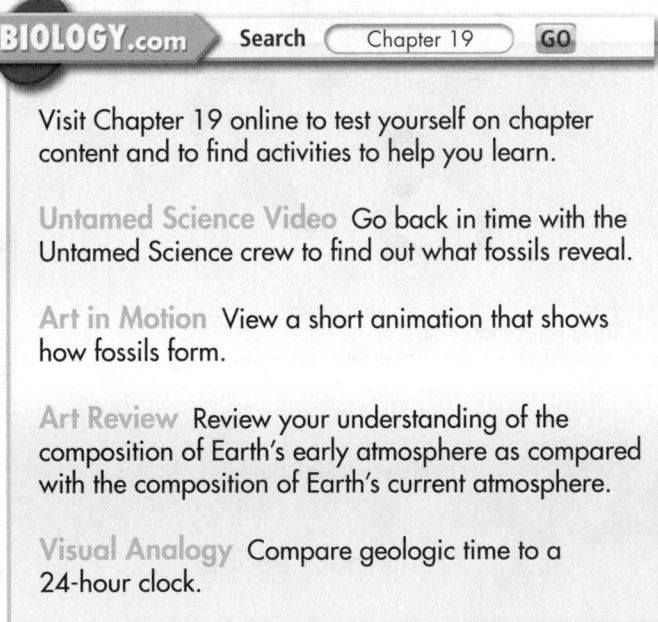

BIOLOGY.com Search ⟨ Chapter 19 ⟩ GO

Visit Chapter 19 online to test yourself on chapter content and to find activities to help you learn.

Untamed Science Video Go back in time with the Untamed Science crew to find out what fossils reveal.

Art in Motion View a short animation that shows how fossils form.

Art Review Review your understanding of the composition of Earth's early atmosphere as compared with the composition of Earth's current atmosphere.

Visual Analogy Compare geologic time to a 24-hour clock.

19.1 The Fossil Record

- From the fossil record, paleontologists learn about the structure of ancient organisms, their environment, and the way in which they lived.

- Relative dating allows paleontologists to determine whether a fossil is older or younger than other fossils. Radiometric dating uses the proportion of radioactive to nonradioactive isotopes to calculate the absolute age of a sample.

- The geologic time scale is based on both relative and absolute dating. The major divisions of the geologic time scale are eons, eras, and periods.

- Throughout Earth's history, geological forces, changing climates, and collisions with objects from space have changed the habitats of living organisms. Over time, the actions of living organisms have also changed conditions in the land, water, and atmosphere of Earth.

paleontologist (p. 450)
extinct (p. 450)
relative dating (p. 451)
index fossil (p. 451)
radiometric dating (p. 452)
half-life (p. 452)
geologic time scale (p. 453)
era (p. 454)
period (p. 454)
plate tectonics (p. 454)

19.2 Patterns and Processes of Evolution

- If the rate of speciation in a clade is equal to or greater than the rate of extinction, the clade will survive. If the rate of extinction in a clade is greater than the rate of speciation, the clade will become extinct.

- Evidence shows that evolution has moved at different rates for different organisms at different times over the long history of life on Earth.

- Two important patterns of macroevolution are adaptive radiation and convergent evolution.

- Adaptive radiation is the process by which a single species or a small group of species evolves quickly into several different species that live in different ways.

- Convergent evolution is the process by which unrelated organisms evolve into similar forms.

- The relationship between two organisms that are coevolving often becomes so specific that neither organism can survive without the other. Thus, an evolutionary change in one organism is usually followed by a change in the other organism.

macroevolutionary patterns (p. 456)
background extinction (p. 457)
mass extinction (p. 457)
gradualism (p. 458)
punctuated equilibrium (p. 458)
adaptive radiation (p. 459)
convergent evolution (p. 460)
coevolution (p. 460)

19.3 Earth's Early History

- Earth's early atmosphere contained little or no oxygen. It was mostly carbon dioxide, water vapor, and nitrogen, with lesser amounts of carbon monoxide, hydrogen sulfide, and hydrogen cyanide.

- Miller and Urey's experiment suggested how mixtures of the organic compounds necessary for life could have arisen from simpler compounds found in the atmosphere of early Earth.

- The "RNA world" hypothesis proposes that RNA existed by itself before DNA. From this simple RNA-based system, several steps could have led to DNA-directed protein synthesis.

- The endosymbiotic theory proposes that a symbiotic relationship evolved over time between early eukaryotic cells and the prokaryotic cells within them.

- The development of sexual reproduction sped up evolutionary change because sexual reproduction increases genetic variation.

endosymbiotic theory (p. 464)

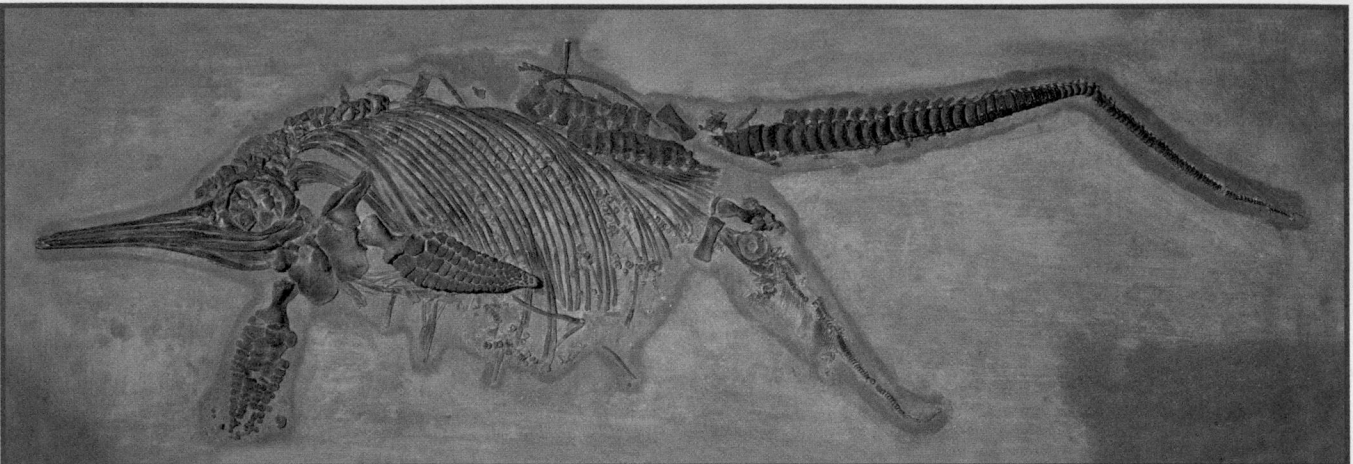

 **Evolution**

Write an answer to the question below.
Q: How do fossils help biologists understand the history of life on Earth?

Constructed Response

Write an answer to each of the numbered questions below. The answer to each numbered question should be one or two paragraphs long. To help you begin, read the **Hints** below the questions.

1. **Why doesn't the fossil record always show a progression of changing fossils for the evolution of each species?**

   Hint Fossils can only form under the right conditions.

   Hint Use the terms *equilibrium* and *punctuated equilibrium* in your answer.

2. **What role have mass extinctions played in the history of life?**

   Hint Think of what happened to the mammals after most of the dinosaurs became extinct.

3. **How does the formation of sedimentary rock give paleontologists information about the sequence in which life forms appeared on Earth?**

   Hint To help plan your answer, review the art of index fossils on page 451.

Foundations for Learning Wrap-Up

Use the tabs that you made at the beginning of the chapter as a tool for review.

Activity 1 Lay your folded tabs on your desk, with the titles on top. Mix them so they are out of order. Then arrange them in order like the fossils in layers of rock, with the oldest events on the bottom. Repeat this activity until it becomes easy.

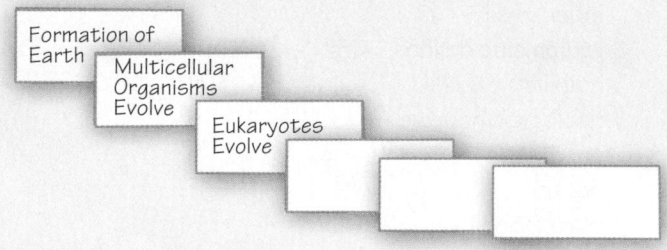

Activity 2 Work with a partner to make a time line out of your tabs. Cut a piece of string so it is 10 meters long. Fasten the string to a sturdy object at eye level. Attach the other end to an object or wall so that the string is level and tight. Hang the "Formation of Earth" tab at one end of the string. Then arrange all the tabs in order according to time.

Next, use the geologic time scale to place each event in the correct place on your string. Each meter of length stands for 400 million years. Each centimeter stands for 4 million years. Use the information from your textbook to help date each event. Your tabs will be very crowded at the end of the string!

19.1 The Fossil Record

Understand Key Concepts

1. Scientists who specialize in the study of fossils are called
   a. biologists.
   b. zoologists.
   c. geologists.
   d. paleontologists.

Test-Taking Tip

Read Answers Carefully! In multiple choice questions, you might be tempted to answer the first response that seems correct. In question 1, you might answer **a** or **c**. But "**d.** paleontologists" is the best choice. Try to think of the answer before you read the choices. Then read each choice.

2. According to the theory of plate tectonics,
   a. Earth's climate has changed many times.
   b. Earth's continents move very slowly.
   c. evolution occurs at different rates.
   d. giant asteroids crashed into Earth in the past.

3. An isotope that can be used to determine the age of recent fossils is
   a. carbon-14.
   b. potassium-40.
   c. rubidium-87.
   d. uranium-238.

4. How have the activities of organisms affected Earth's environment?

Think Critically

5. **Relate Cause and Effect** Why have so few organisms become fossils?

6. **Calculate** The half-life of carbon-14 is 5730 years. What is the age of a fossil containing ¼ the amount of carbon-14 found in living organisms? Explain your calculation.

19.2 Patterns and Processes of Evolution

Understand Key Concepts

7. The process that produces similar structures in unrelated groups of organisms is
   a. adaptive radiation.
   b. coevolution.
   c. convergent evolution.
   d. macroevolution.

8. Cladograms that are based on the fossil record always show
   a. only organisms that are direct ancestors of the others.
   b. relationships based on shared derived characters.
   c. that clades contain only extinct species.
   d. relative ages of organisms in the clade.

9. Explain the process of adaptive radiation, and give an example.

Think Critically

10. **Compare and Contrast** How is mass extinction different from background extinction?

11. **Infer** What do you think would have happened to the evolution of flowering plants if there had been no pollinators present?

19.3 Earth's Early History

Understand Key Concepts

12. Earth's early atmosphere contained little or no
    a. water vapor.   c. nitrogen.
    b. carbon dioxide.   d. oxygen.

13. In their experiment that modeled conditions on early Earth, Miller and Urey used electric sparks to
    a. simulate temperature.
    b. simulate sunlight.
    c. simulate lightning.
    d. simulate atmospheric gases.

14. How are microspheres similar to living cells?

15. How did the addition of oxygen to Earth's atmosphere affect the evolution of life?

Think Critically

16. **Use Models** In the Miller-Urey experiment, what did the water and gases represent? What part of Miller and Urey's set-up represents rain?

17. **Relate Cause and Effect** How do you think that the eukaryotic cells that took in the ancestors of mitochondria and chloroplasts benefited from the relationship?

Connecting Concepts

Use Science Graphs

The diagram shows rock layers in two different places. Use the diagram to answer questions 18–20.

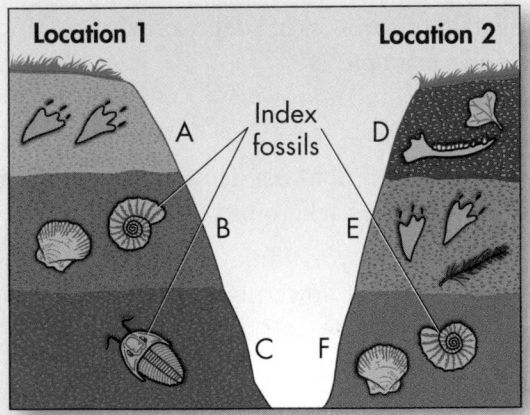

18. **Interpret Visuals** Which fossils are probably older, those in layer A or those in layer C? How do you know?

19. **Infer** Which rock layer in location 2 is probably about the same age as layer B in location 1? How do you know?

20. **Apply Concepts** What are the characteristics of a useful index fossil?

solve the CHAPTER MYSTERY

MURDER IN THE PERMIAN

Solving a mystery that is 250 million years old is not easy! Scientists have been working to solve this puzzle for years, and they are still working on it. Recently, scientists have studied the chemistry of Permian rocks and changes in the fossil record. These scientists have concluded that huge, long-lasting volcanic eruptions in Siberia released enormous amounts of carbon dioxide. This carbon dioxide caused massive changes in global climate. Was this the cause of the mass extinction?

Other researchers found that during the Permian, oxygen levels dropped to roughly half of what they are today. Huge parts of the oceans lost all oxygen. On land, there would have been very little oxygen. Mystery solved?

Finally, there is evidence that an asteroid hit Earth! Such a collision would throw so much dust into the air that global climates would have changed. To this day, paleontologists are testing different hypotheses to explain what caused the mass extinction. These hypotheses are constantly changing. In fact, they have probably changed again since this book was written!

1. **Compare and Contrast** How do current hypotheses about the Permian extinction compare with the main theory about the Cretaceous extinction?

2. **Form a Hypothesis** From the information in this book, suggest an explanation for the Permian mass extinction.

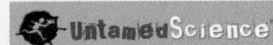 **Never Stop Exploring Your World.** Solving the mystery of the mass extinction is only the beginning. Take a video field trip with the ecogeeks of Untamed Science to see where the mystery leads.

Standardized Test Practice for Maryland

Multiple Choice

1. Index fossils are from species that lived
   A in a small area for a short time.
   B in a small area for a long time.
   C over a large area for a short time.
   D over a large area for a long time.   CLG 3.4.2

2. What happens if the rate of extinction in a clade is greater than the rate of speciation?
   A The clade will eventually become extinct.
   B The clade will continue to exist.
   C The species in the clade will become more varied.
   D The number of species in the clade will stay the same.   CLG 3.4.1

3. Which of the following is evidence for the endosymbiotic theory?
   A Mitochondria and chloroplasts contain DNA similar to bacterial DNA.
   B Mitochondria and chloroplasts have similar functions in the cell.
   C Mitochondria and chloroplasts have no DNA of their own.
   D Mitochondria and chloroplasts can live when removed from the eukaryotic cell.   CLG 3.2.1

4. Potassium-40 is useful for dating very old fossils because
   A it has a very long half-life.
   B it has a very short half-life.
   C most organisms contain more potassium than carbon.
   D it is found only in certain rock layers.   CLG 3.4.2

5. The movement of continents has played a significant role in evolution because
   A continents move rapidly and some organisms cannot adjust.
   B without the movement of continents, there would be no water on Earth.
   C the movement of continents has caused environments to change.
   D all mass extinctions are the result of continental drift.   CLG 3.4.1

Questions 6 and 7

The graph shows the decay of radioactive isotope atoms. Use the information in the graph to answer the questions that follow.

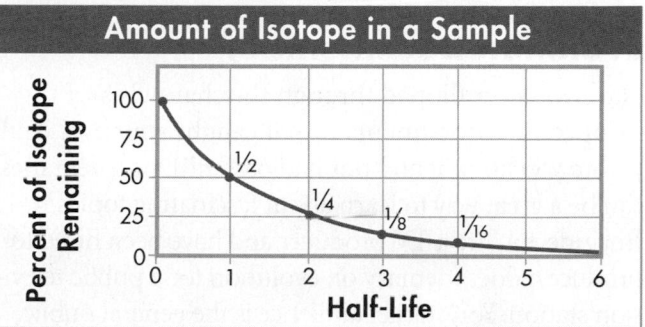

6. The half-life of thorium-230 is 75,000 years. How long will it take for $\frac{7}{8}$ of the original amount of thorium-230 in a sample to decay?
   A 75,000 years
   B 225,000 years
   C 25,000 years
   D 150,000 years   SPI 1.4.2

7. The half-life of potassium-40 is about 1.3 billion years. After four half-lives have passed, how much of the original sample will be left?
   A $\frac{1}{16}$
   B $\frac{1}{16} \times 1300$ million grams
   C $\frac{1}{4}$
   D $\frac{1}{4} \times 1300$ million grams   SPI 1.4.2

Open-Ended Response

8. How does the process by which sedimentary rock forms allow scientists to determine the relative ages of fossils?   CLG 3.4.2

If You Have Trouble With . . .

Question	1	2	3	4	5	6	7	8
See Lesson	19.1	19.2	19.3	19.1	19.1	19.1	19.1	19.1

Unit Project

Evolution Documentary

Have you ever flipped through the channels and stopped on a documentary that caught your eye? And before you knew it an hour had passed? Documentaries can be a great way to learn about fascinating topics. Imagine you are a TV producer and have been hired to produce a documentary on evolution for a public television station. Your target audience is the general public.

Your Task Write a script for a 5–10 minute segment of an evolution documentary and present it to your class.

Be sure to
- discuss evidence for evolution by bringing in specific examples.
- present the information clearly and in an engaging manner.
- explain why the misconceptions listed below are *not* true:
  1) Evolution causes organisms to improve—life has gotten better over time.
  2) Evolution is not observable or testable.
  3) Gaps in the fossil record disprove evolution.
  4) Natural selection involves organisms "trying" to adapt.
  5) Natural selection is the only way that populations can change over time.

Reflection Questions

1. Score your documentary using the rubric below. What score did you give yourself?
2. What did you do well in this project?
3. What needs improvement?
4. What do you think a member of the general public would learn from your documentary?

Assessment Rubric

Score	Scientific Content	Quality of Documentary Script
4	Documentary provides accurate evidence for evolution and clearly corrects several misconceptions.	Information is presented in a clear, organized, and engaging manner.
3	Documentary provides some accurate evidence for evolution and attempts to correct misconceptions.	Information is presented in a clear and organized manner, but it could be more engaging.
2	Documentary provides little evidence for evolution and does not correct misconceptions well.	Information could be presented in a clearer manner. The script needs editing.
1	Documentary does not provide evidence for evolution and does not attempt to correct misconceptions.	Information is presented in a disorganized and confusing manner. The script needs a lot of editing.

From Microorganisms to Plants

INTRODUCE the Big ideas

- **Unity and Diversity of Life**
- **Structure and Function**
- **Growth, Development, and Reproduction**
- **Cellular Basis of Life**
- **Interdependence in Nature**

"In sports, a most valuable player, or MVP, is the person most responsible for a team's success. Which organisms are the MVPs of life? Certainly not us—we could disappear from this planet, and other forms of life would go on just fine. The real stars of life on Earth, its MVPs, are its microorganisms, fungi, and plants. We almost never notice these superstars, unless we look very closely, but without them our lives would be impossible."

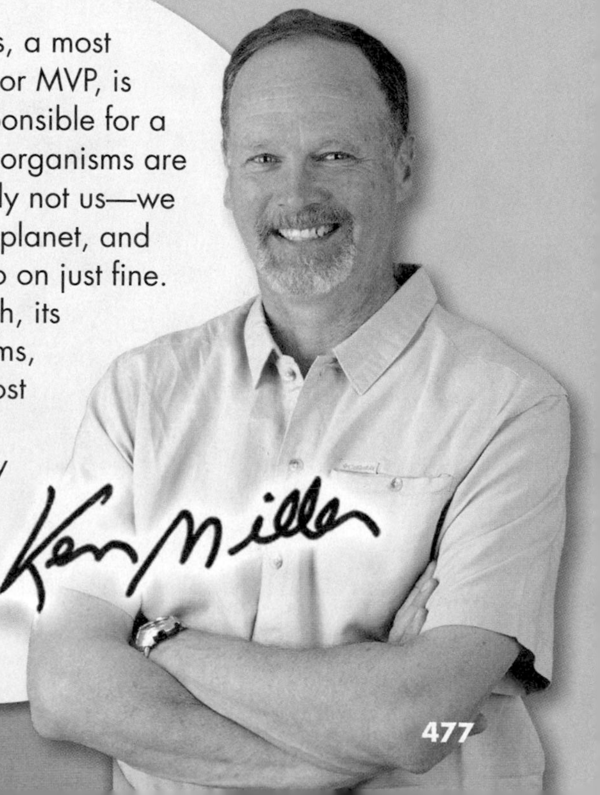

Ken Miller

20 Viruses and Prokaryotes

Big idea ▶ **Cellular Basis of Life**
Q: Are all microbes that make us sick made of living cells?

A scientist looks at colonies of E. coli bacteria on a petri dish.

BIOLOGY.com ▶ Search [Chapter 20] [GO] • Flash Cards

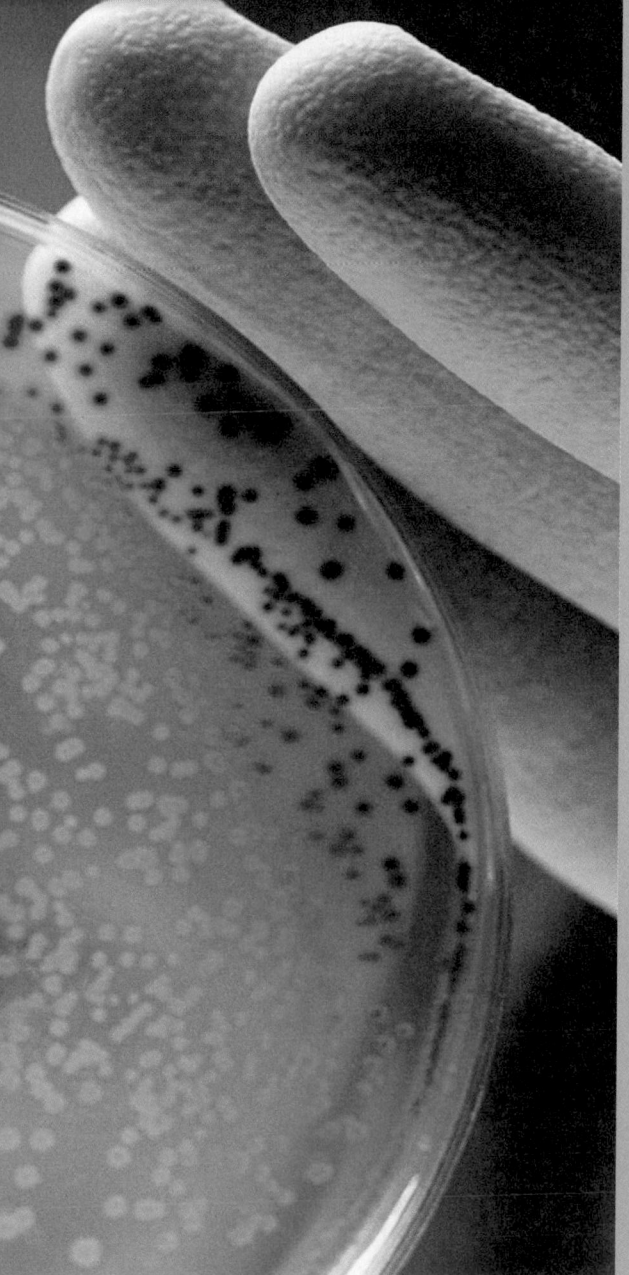

CHAPTER
MYSTERY

THE MAD COWS

In 1986, something strange began
to happen to cattle in Great Britain.
Without warning, the animals began
acting strangely. They lost control of their
movements and eventually died. Farmers watched
helplessly as this "mad cow disease" spread through
their cattle. In 1991, the disease affected more than
30,000 cattle.

Scientists studied the brains of cattle killed by mad cow
disease. They found that large areas of the animals' brains
had been destroyed. Under a microscope, holes in the
diseased tissue made the brain look like a sponge. Because
of this, the disease was given the name bovine spongiform
encephalopathy, or BSE.

Read for Mystery Clues What caused BSE? As you read this
chapter, look for clues that explain the cause of the disease.
Then, solve the mystery.

FOUNDATIONS
for Learning

Use a sheet of paper to make a z-fold similar to the one shown
below. Use one column of the z-fold for each lesson. Write down
what you learn as you read each lesson. At the end of the chapter
are two activities that will help you answer the question: Are all
microbes that make us sick made of living cells?

20.1 Viruses

20.2 Prokaryotes

20.3 Diseases
Caused by Bacteria
and Viruses

• Untamed Science Video   • Chapter Mystery

20.1 Viruses

MD CLG **3.2.1** Processes and Functions, **3.4.2** Relatedness Among Organisms, **3.5.1** Factors Influencing Ecosystems, **3.5.2** Interdependence of Organisms in the Biosphere. SPI **1.4.8** Use Models, **1.5.5** Create and Interpret Graphics, **1.5.7** Classification Systems, **1.5.8** Compare, **1.7.6** Science and Technology.

Key Questions

🔑 *How do viruses reproduce?*

🔑 *What happens after a virus infects a cell?*

BUILD Understanding

Venn Diagram Make a Venn diagram to compare viruses and cells. List similarities and differences between viruses and cells. Fill in the Venn diagram as you read the lesson.

In Your Workbook Go to your workbook to learn more about Venn diagrams. Complete the Venn diagram for Lesson 20.1.

The Discovery of Viruses

Imagine that you have to solve a mystery. Farmers have begun to lose their tobacco crop to tobacco mosaic disease. First, the leaves turn yellow. Eventually, the leaves fall off, killing the plant. You use a light microscope to search for the pathogen, or disease-causing agent. But it is too small, even for a microscope. Although you cannot see the pathogen, you are sure that it is there.

Discovery of Viruses In 1892, the Russian biologist Dmitri Ivanovski studied tobacco mosaic disease. He showed that liquid taken from infected plants could cause the disease. But he could not find the pathogen itself. In 1897, the Dutch scientist Martinus Beijerinck suggested that tiny particles caused the disease. He named these particles *viruses*, after the Latin word for "poison."

Then, in 1935, the American biochemist Wendell Stanley produced crystals of tobacco mosaic virus. Living organisms do not crystallize. So, Stanley concluded that viruses were not truly alive. Most biologists still think this today. A **virus** is a nonliving particle. It is made of proteins, nucleic acids, and sometimes lipids. Viruses can reproduce only by infecting living cells.

🔑 **Key Question** How do viruses reproduce?
Viruses can reproduce only by infecting living cells.

T4 Bacteriophage

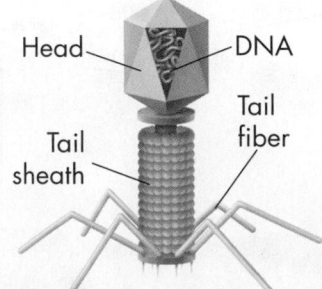

Head — DNA
Tail fiber
Tail sheath

Influenza Virus

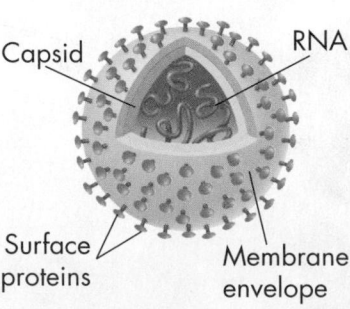

Capsid — RNA
Surface proteins
Membrane envelope

Tobacco Mosaic Virus

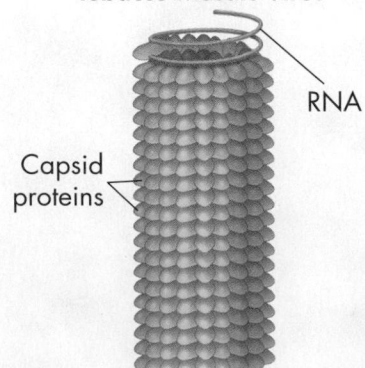

RNA
Capsid proteins

Viral Structure Most viruses are so small that they can be seen only with very powerful electron microscopes. The shapes of three kinds of viruses are shown here.

Viral Structure and Function Viruses come in many shapes and sizes. A protein coat called a **capsid** surrounds a virus particle. Some viruses also have a membrane around the capsid. The simplest viruses have only a few genes. Complex viruses may have hundreds of genes.

The structure of a virus allows it to infect living cells. Most viruses have proteins on their surface. These proteins bind to proteins on the surface of a host cell. Viral proteins "trick" the host cell into taking in the virus or its genetic material. Viruses must bind exactly to proteins on the host cell's surface. Therefore, most viruses infect only specific kinds of cells. Plant viruses infect plant cells. Most animal viruses infect only certain kinds of animals. Viruses that infect bacteria are called **bacteriophages** (bak TEER ee uh fayj uz). They infect only certain kinds of bacteria.

Viral Infections

What happens after a virus enters a host cell? The virus uses the host cell's genetic information to make copies of itself! Some viruses copy themselves immediately. This type of infection is called a lytic infection. Other viruses stay inactive for a period of time within the host cell. This type of infection is called a lysogenic infection.

First, the outlaw eliminates the town's existing authority.
Lytic Infection The host cell's DNA is chopped up.

Next, the outlaw demands to be outfitted with new equipment from the local townspeople.
Lytic Infection Viruses use the host cell to make viral DNA and viral proteins.

Finally, the outlaw forms a gang that leaves the town to attack new communities.
Lytic Infection The host cell bursts, releasing hundreds of virus particles.

Lytic Infection In a **lytic infection,** a virus enters a cell, makes copies of itself, then causes the cell to burst. For example, a bacteriophage injects its DNA into a bacterial cell. Then the bacterial cell makes messenger RNA (mRNA) from the viral genes. This mRNA is translated into viral proteins that chop up the cell's DNA. The host cell makes new virus particles. Before long, the cell bursts open. Copies of the bacteriophage are released to infect other cells.

Lysogenic Infection In a **lysogenic infection,** the host cell is not taken over right away. Instead, the virus inserts its nucleic acid into the host cell's DNA. The viral DNA is copied along with the cell's DNA. The cell is not damaged. Daughter cells are infected by the virus.

Bacteriophage DNA that becomes part of the bacterial host's DNA is called a prophage. A prophage may be a part of the host cell's DNA for many generations. Changes in the environment, such as heat or chemicals, can cause the prophage to become active. Then the lysogenic infection becomes a lytic infection.

🔑 **Key Question** What happens after a virus infects a cell?
Inside living cells, viruses use their host's genetic information to make many copies of themselves. Some viruses replicate right away. Other viruses stay inactive for a long period of time within the host cell.

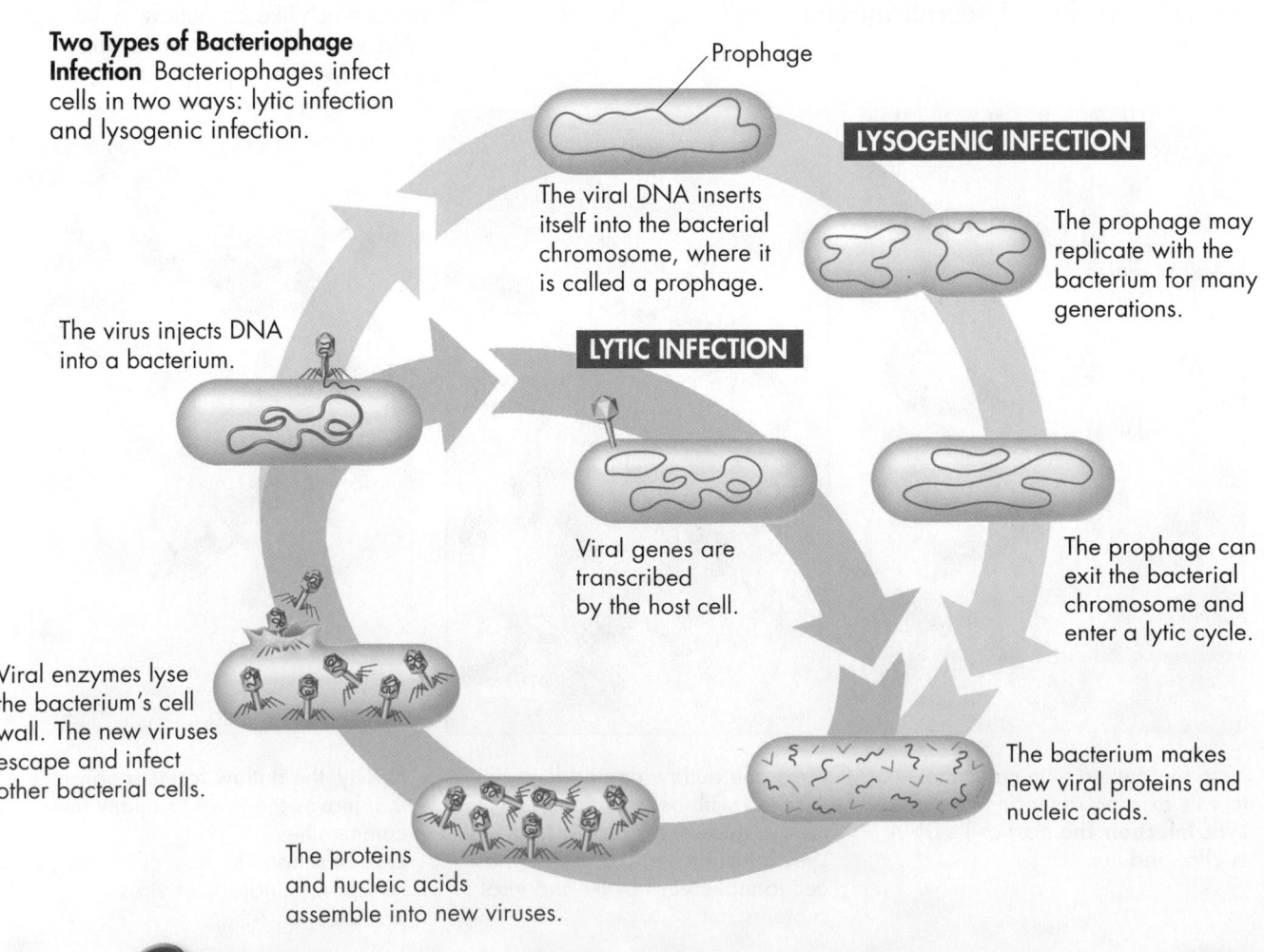

Two Types of Bacteriophage Infection Bacteriophages infect cells in two ways: lytic infection and lysogenic infection.

Prophage

The virus injects DNA into a bacterium.

Viral enzymes lyse the bacterium's cell wall. The new viruses escape and infect other bacterial cells.

The proteins and nucleic acids assemble into new viruses.

The viral DNA inserts itself into the bacterial chromosome, where it is called a prophage.

LYSOGENIC INFECTION

The prophage may replicate with the bacterium for many generations.

LYTIC INFECTION

Viral genes are transcribed by the host cell.

The prophage can exit the bacterial chromosome and enter a lytic cycle.

The bacterium makes new viral proteins and nucleic acids.

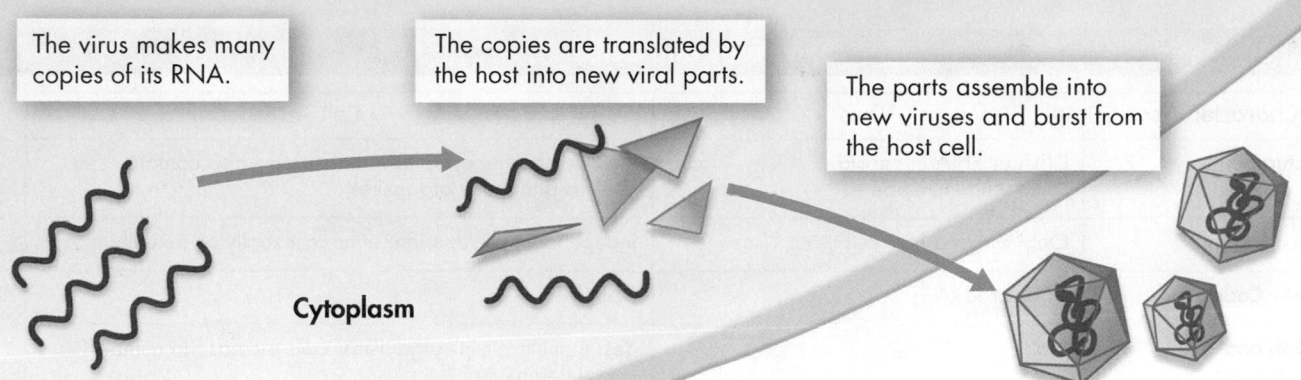

The virus makes many copies of its RNA.

The copies are translated by the host into new viral parts.

The parts assemble into new viruses and burst from the host cell.

Cytoplasm

Common Cold Infection Once a cold virus has entered the host cell, it uses the host cell to copy itself.

A Closer Look at Two RNA Viruses About 70 percent of viruses have RNA rather than DNA. In humans, RNA viruses cause a wide range of infections, from mild colds to AIDS.

▶ *The Common Cold* What happens when you get a cold? A capsid lands on a cell, often in your nose, and is brought inside a host cell. Inside the host cell, a viral protein makes many new copies of the viral RNA. The host cell's ribosomes mistake the viral RNA for the host's own mRNA. Viral RNA is translated into capsids and other viral proteins. New virus particles form. Within 8 hours, the host cell bursts. Hundreds of new virus particles then infect other cells.

▶ *HIV* The disease called acquired immune deficiency syndrome (AIDS) is caused by the human immunodeficiency virus (HIV). HIV belongs to a group of RNA viruses called **retroviruses.** The genetic information of a retrovirus is copied from RNA to DNA instead of from DNA to RNA.

Retroviral infections are similar to lysogenic infections. When a retrovirus infects a cell, it makes a DNA copy of its RNA. This DNA copy is inserted into the DNA of the host cell. Like a prophage, the viral DNA may remain inactive for many cell cycles. Eventually, it makes new virus particles. These new particles attack the cells of the host's immune system—the system that normally fights infection.

HIV Infection A retrovirus such as HIV makes a DNA copy of itself and inserts it into the host cell's DNA. The viral DNA may stay inactive for many cell cycles.

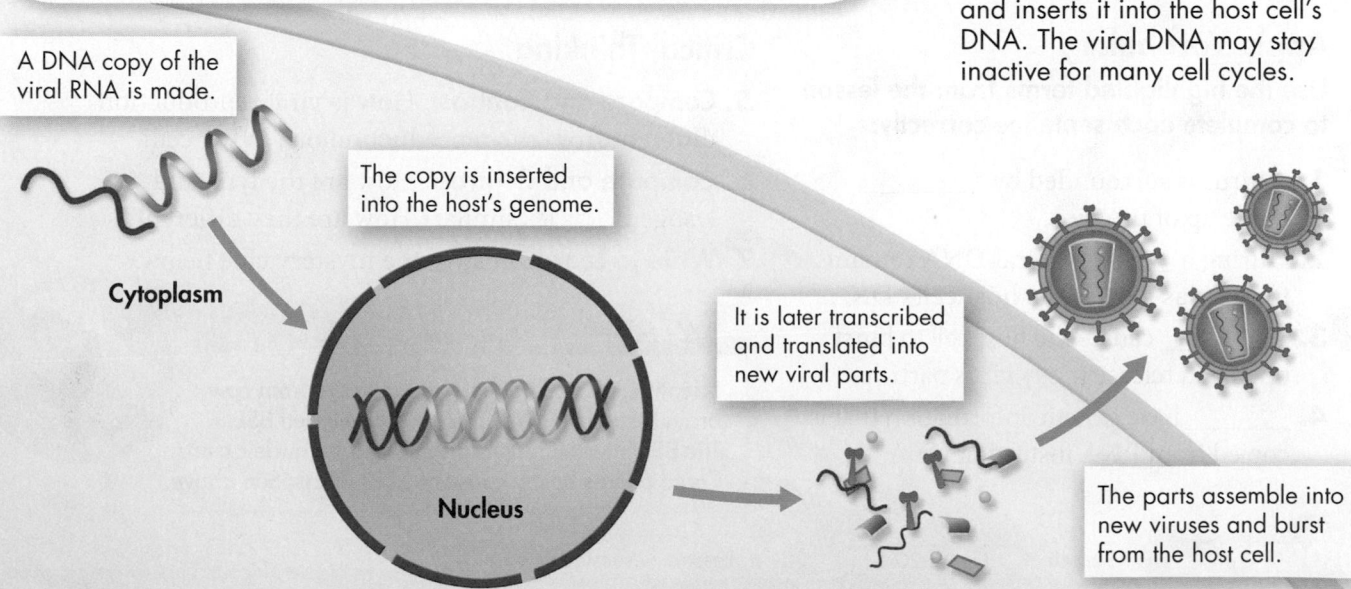

A DNA copy of the viral RNA is made.

The copy is inserted into the host's genome.

Cytoplasm

Nucleus

It is later transcribed and translated into new viral parts.

The parts assemble into new viruses and burst from the host cell.

Characteristic	Virus	Cell
Structure	DNA or RNA in capsid, some with envelope	Cell membrane, cytoplasm; eukaryotes also contain nucleus and many organelles
Reproduction	Only within a host cell	Independent cell division, either asexually or sexually
Genetic Code	DNA or RNA	DNA
Growth and Development	No	Yes; in multicellular organisms, cells increase in number and differentiate
Obtain and Use Energy	No	Yes
Response to Environment	No	Yes
Change Over Time	Yes	Yes

Comparing Viruses and Cells
The table above lists differences and similarities between viruses and living cells.

Viruses and Cells To grow and reproduce, viruses must infect living cells. Viruses rely on the nutrients and cellular machinery of their hosts. Therefore, viruses are parasites. Parasites rely on a host, harming it in the process.

Viruses are not alive. But they do have several characteristics of living things. After infecting living cells, viruses can reproduce. They have genetic material. They can evolve.

Although viruses are smaller and simpler than the smallest cells, it is unlikely that they appeared before living things. Because they depend on living organisms, viruses probably developed after living cells. Perhaps the first viruses evolved from the genetic material of living cells. Viruses, and the cells they infect, have been evolving for billions of years.

CHECK Understanding

Apply Vocabulary
Use the highlighted terms from the lesson to complete each sentence correctly.

1. A virus is surrounded by a _____ made up of proteins.

2. During a _____, viral DNA remains inactive as part of the host cell's DNA.

3. A _____ causes the host cell to burst open and release many virus particles.

4. _____ have genetic information that is copied from RNA instead of DNA.

Critical Thinking

5. **Compare and Contrast** How is viral reproduction different from the reproduction of a living cell?

6. **Compare and Contrast** How are the lytic and lysogenic cycles similar? How are they different?

7. **Write to Learn** Answer the mystery clue below.

MYSTERY CLUE

Scientists injected BSE-infected material from cow brain tissue into mice. The mice developed BSE. The BSE-infected material contained no nucleic acids. Could a virus be the cause of BSE? (Hint: See above.)

 BIOLOGY.com ▸ Search (Lesson 20.1) **GO** ● Lesson Assessment

20.2 Prokaryotes

MD CLG 3.1.3 Matter and Energy, 3.2.1 Processes and Functions, 3.3.1 Sexual Reproduction and Variation, 3.5.2 Interdependence of Organisms in the Biosphere. SPI 1.5.2 Communicate Information, 1.5.7 Classification Systems, 1.7.6 Science and Technology.

Classifying Prokaryotes

When the microscope was first invented, we humans discovered something amazing: We share every corner of our world with microorganisms! The smallest and most abundant of these microorganisms are **prokaryotes** (pro KAR ee ohts). Prokaryotes are single-celled organisms that lack a nucleus. The DNA of prokayotes is found in their cytoplasm. Biologists classify prokaryotes as either Bacteria or Archaea.

Key Question How are prokaryotes classified?
Prokaryotes are classified as Bacteria or Archaea, which are two of the three domains of life.

Bacteria Bacteria live almost everywhere—in fresh water, in salt water, and on land. They even live inside the bodies of humans and other eukaryotes. The art below shows the structure of a bacterium that lives in human intestines.

Most bacteria are surrounded by a cell wall that contains peptidoglycan. This molecule is made up of sugars and amino acids. Some bacteria are also protected by a membrane outside the cell wall. Bacteria may use flagella or pili (PY ly; singular: pilus) for movement. Pili also help them attach to surfaces or to other bacteria.

Key Questions

- How are prokaryotes classified?
- How do prokaryotes vary in their structure and function?
- What roles do prokaryotes play in the living world?

BUILD Understanding

Preview Visuals Look at the Prokaryotic Shapes figure on the next page. In your own words, describe the three shapes shown.

In Your Workbook Go to your workbook to complete the activity for Lesson 20.2.

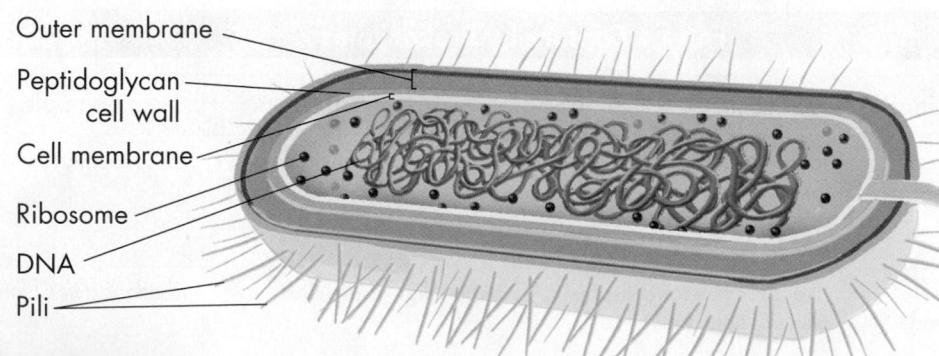

Outer membrane
Peptidoglycan cell wall
Cell membrane
Ribosome
DNA
Pili
Flagellum

TEM 9600×

Typical Bacterial Structure The bacterium *Escherichia coli* is shown here. It has a structure typical of most prokaryotes. *E. coli* has an outer membrane that is not found in all prokaryotes. The photograph shows *E. coli* reproducing by binary fission.

For more on the diversity of Bacteria and Archaea, go to the Visual Guide.
↻ **pp. DOL 6–9.**

Archaea Archaea look very much like bacteria. Both are tiny, lack nuclei, and have cell walls. However, the cell walls of archaea do not have peptidoglycan. Also, their cell membranes contain different lipids. The DNA of archaea is more like the DNA of eukaryotes than the DNA of bacteria. Many archaea live in harsh environments. Some live in places with little or no oxygen, such as mud and animal digestive tracts. Others live in very salty water or hot springs.

Structure and Function

Prokaryotes come in many sizes and shapes. They also get and use energy in a number of different ways.

Prokaryotic Shapes Prokaryotes usually come in one of three shapes: rod-shaped bacilli (left), spherical cocci (middle), and corkscrew-shaped spirilla (right).

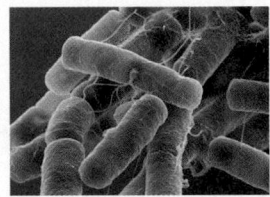 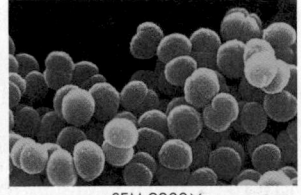 

SEM 8500×   SEM 9200×   SEM 2400×

Size, Shape, and Movement Prokaryotes are much smaller than most eukaryotic cells. They range in size from 1 to 5 micrometers. Rod-shaped prokaryotes are called bacilli (buh SIL eye; singular: bacillus). Sphere-shaped prokaryotes are called cocci (KAHK sy; singular: coccus). Spiral and corkscrew-shaped prokaryotes are called spirilla (spy RIL uh; singular: spirillum). Some prokaryotes use flagella to move. Others put down a layer of slime and slowly glide along it. And some prokaryotes do not move at all.

Energy Capture and Release in Prokaryotes Prokaryotes have different ways of getting food and releasing energy from food. Some bacteria can get food and release energy in more than one way.

Energy Capture by Prokaryotes			
Mode of Nutrition	**How Energy Is Captured**	**Habitat**	**Example**
Heterotroph "other feeder"	Take in organic molecules from environment or other organisms to use as both energy and carbon supply	Wide range of environments	*Clostridium*
Photoheterotroph "light and other feeder"	Like basic heterotrophs, but also use light energy	Where light is plentiful	*Rhodobacter, Chloroflexus*
Photoautotroph "light self-feeder"	Use light energy to convert CO_2 into carbon compounds	Where light is plentiful	*Anabaena*
Chemoautotroph "chemical self-feeder"	Use energy released by chemical reactions involving ammonia, hydrogen sulfide, etc.	In chemically harsh and/or dark environments: deep in the ocean, in thick mud, in digestive tracts of animals, in boiling hot springs	*Nitrosomonas*

Nutrition and Metabolism Like all organisms, prokaryotes need chemical energy, which they store in molecules such as sugars. Some prokaryotes make their own food. Others take in food for energy. Some can do both. Prokaryotes get energy from food by cellular respiration, fermentation, or both. Some can change the way they get or release energy depending on conditions in their environment.

🔑 **Key Question** How do prokaryotes vary in their structure and function? **Prokaryotes vary in their size and shape, in the way they move, and in the way they get and release energy.**

Growth, Reproduction, and Recombination When a prokaryote has nearly doubled in size, it can reproduce. First, it copies its DNA. Then, it divides in half, forming two identical cells. This kind of reproduction is known as **binary fission.** Binary fission is a form of asexual reproduction. When conditions are good, prokaryotes can divide quickly. Some can divide once every 20 minutes!

In organisms that reproduce sexually, genes are shuffled during meiosis. But prokaryotes reproduce asexually. How do their populations evolve? One way is through mutations. Mutations are random changes in DNA. These changes are passed on to daughter cells formed by binary fission.

Many prokaryotes exchange genetic information by **conjugation.** During conjugation, a hollow bridge forms between two bacterial cells. Genetic material moves from one cell to the other. This process makes populations more genetically diverse.

Formation of Endospores When conditions are not good, many prokaryotic cells can form an **endospore.** A thick internal wall forms around the DNA and part of the cytoplasm. Endospores can remain dormant for months or even years. By forming endospores, prokaryotes are able to live through very harsh conditions.

BUILD Vocabulary

prokaryote
a unicellular organism that lacks a nucleus

binary fission
a type of asexual reproduction in which an organism replicates its DNA and divides in half, producing two identical daughter cells

conjugation
the process in which paramecia and some prokaryotes exchange genetic information

endospore
a structure produced by prokaryotes in unfavorable conditions; a thick internal wall that encloses the DNA and a portion of the cytoplasm

PREFIXES

The prefix *endo-* comes from a Greek word that means "within." An endospore forms when a thick wall encloses DNA within a bacterial cell.

Energy Release by Prokaryotes			
Mode of Metabolism	**How Energy Is Released**	**Habitat**	**Example**
Obligate aerobe "requiring oxygen"	Cellular respiration; must have ready supply of O_2 to release fuel energy	Oxygen-rich environments, such as near water surface or in animal lungs	*Mycobacterium tuberculosis*: Sometimes found in human lungs
Obligate anaerobe "requiring a lack of oxygen"	Fermentation; die in presence of oxygen	◄ Environments lacking O_2, such as deep soil, animal intestines, or airtight containers	*Clostridium botulinum*: Sometimes found in improperly sterilized canned food, causing food poisoning
Facultative anaerobe "surviving without oxygen when necessary"	Can use either cellular respiration or fermentation as necessary	Oxygen-rich or oxygen-poor environments	*E. coli*: Lives aerobically in sewage and anaerobically in human large intestine

The Importance of Prokaryotes

Prokaryotes are necessary to the balance of the living world. How can such tiny organisms be so important?

Decomposers Prokaryotes break down, or decompose, dead organisms and wastes. This makes raw materials available to other organisms. If these materials were not recycled, life could not go on.

Producers Photosynthetic prokaryotes are some of the world's most important producers. They form the base of many food chains. For example, the tiny bacterium *Prochlorococcus* may be responsible for more than half of the primary production in the open ocean.

Nitrogen Fixers All organisms need nitrogen to make proteins, nucleic acids, and other molecules. Although nitrogen gas (N_2) makes up 80 percent of Earth's atmosphere, most organisms cannot use N_2 directly. Fortunately, a few prokaryotes can change N_2 into forms that can be used by other living things. This process is called nitrogen fixation. Nitrogen-fixing prokaryotes provide 90 percent of the nitrogen used by other organisms.

A few plants have symbiotic relationships with nitrogen-fixing bacteria. Nitrogen-fixing bacteria grow in nodules on the roots of plants such as clover and soybeans. The bacteria change nitrogen in the air into nitrogen that the plants need.

Human Use of Prokaryotes Bacteria are used to make many different foods and other products. For example, yogurt is made by the bacterium *Lactobacillus*. Some bacteria remove waste products from water. Others are used to make drugs in genetic engineering.

🔑 **Key Question** What roles do prokaryotes play in the living world? **Prokaryotes are decomposers, producers, and nitrogen fixers. In addition, some species are used in human industry.**

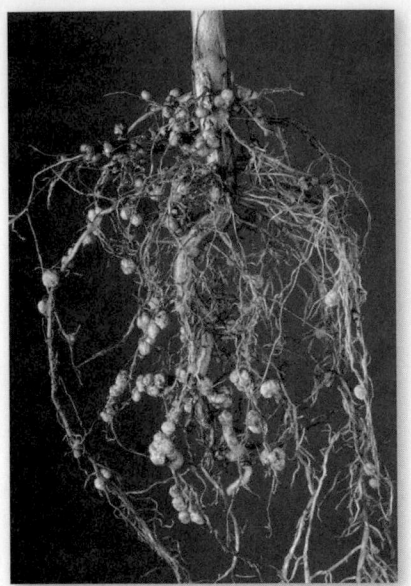

Rhizobium The root nodules of this soybean plant contain *Rhizobium* bacteria. These bacteria are nitrogen fixers.

CHECK Understanding

Apply Vocabulary
Use the highlighted terms from the lesson to complete each sentence correctly.

1. To survive long periods of harsh conditions, bacteria may form _____.
2. A bacterium undergoes _____, forming two identical daughter cells.
3. _____ increases the genetic diversity of prokaryote populations.

Critical Thinking

4. **Classify** Which two domains of life contain only prokaryotes?
5. **Apply Concepts** Many farmers practice crop rotation. They may plant a field with corn one year and plant soybeans the next year. Why might they do this?
6. **Write to Learn** Write a paragraph comparing and contrasting archaea and bacteria.

20.3 Diseases Caused by Bacteria and Viruses

MD | CLG 3.1.1 Chemical Substances and Macromolecules, 3.2.1 Processes and Functions, 3.2.2 Changes in Metabolic Activity, 3.6.2 Investigate a Biological Issue. SPI 1.4.1 Organize Data, 1.4.2 Analyze Data, 1.4.6 Determine Trends, 1.5.8 Compare, 1.6.1 Ratio and Proportion, 1.7.1 Apply Skills and Concepts, 1.7.2 Evaluate Ideas, 1.7.6 Science and Technology.

Bacterial Diseases

The first person to clearly show that bacteria cause disease was the French chemist Louis Pasteur. Pasteur helped establish the *germ theory of disease*. The germ theory states that viruses and prokaryotes cause many human and animal diseases. An agent that can cause sickness is a **pathogen.**

Disease Mechanisms Bacteria cause disease in two main ways. Some bacteria destroy living cells and tissues. Others release chemicals that upset the normal activities of the host. These chemicals are called toxins.

🔑 **Key Question** How do bacteria cause disease?
Bacteria cause disease by damaging host cells and tissues or by releasing chemicals that upset homeostasis.

Controlling Bacteria One of the most important things you can do to control bacteria is to wash your hands well and often. Also wash surfaces where bacteria might settle. Washing removes, but does not kill, bacteria. Disinfectants kill bacteria. Sterilization, or heating objects above 100°C, will also kill most bacteria. It is important to store and cook foods properly. The cold temperature in a refrigerator will slow the growth of bacteria.

Key Questions

🔑 **How do bacteria cause disease?**

🔑 **How do viruses cause disease?**

🔑 **Why are emerging diseases a threat to human health?**

BUILD Understanding

Two-Column Chart Make a two-column chart. In the left column, write the key questions from the lesson. In the right column, write answers to the questions.

In Your Workbook Go to your workbook for help completing this two-column chart. Complete the chart for Lesson 20.3.

Human Bacterial Diseases Some common bacterial diseases are described in the table.

Some Human Bacterial Diseases		
Disease	**Effect on Body**	**Transmission**
Lyme disease	"Bull's-eye" rash at site of tick bite, fever, fatigue, headache	Ticks transmit the bacterium *Borrelia burgdorferi*. ▶
Tetanus	Lockjaw, stiffness in neck and abdomen, difficulty swallowing, fever, elevated blood pressure, severe muscle spasms	Bacteria enter the body through a break in the skin.
Tuberculosis	Fatigue, weight loss, fever, night sweats, chills, appetite loss, bloody sputum from lungs	Bacteria particles are inhaled.
Strep throat	Fever, sore throat, headache, fatigue, nausea	Direct contact with mucus from an infected person or direct contact with infected wounds or breaks in the skin

SEM 7300x

pathogen
a disease-causing agent

vaccine
a preparation of weakened or killed pathogens used to produce immunity to a disease

antibiotic
a drug used to block the growth and reproduction of bacterial pathogens

✎ WORD ORIGINS

Pathogen comes from the Greek words *pathos*, which means "suffering," and *genes*, meaning "produced." Infection with a pathogen produces suffering in the form of illness.

Preventing Bacterial Disease Infections can sometimes be prevented by vaccines. A **vaccine** is a preparation of weakened or killed pathogens or inactivated toxins. A vaccine helps the body become immune to a specific disease. Immunity is the body's ability to fight off pathogens or to deal with toxins.

Treating Bacterial Diseases Many drugs can be used to treat a bacterial infection. These drugs include **antibiotics,** such as penicillin and tetracycline. Antibiotics keep bacteria from growing and reproducing by interfering with bacterial proteins or cell processes. Antibiotics affect proteins or cell processes that are found only in bacteria. For this reason, they do not harm the host's cells.

Viral Diseases

Like bacteria, viruses cause disease by upsetting the body's normal homeostasis. Several common diseases caused by viruses are listed below. Viruses also cause serious diseases in plants and animals.

Disease Mechanisms Some viruses cause disease by destroying living cells. They may also change processes in cells and upset homeostasis. Often, viruses attack only certain kinds of cells. For example, poliovirus destroys cells in the nervous system, causing paralysis. Other viruses change the way cells grow and develop. Such changes can lead to cancer.

🔑 **Key Question** How do viruses cause disease?
Viruses cause disease by destroying living cells or by affecting processes in cells in ways that upset homeostasis in the host.

Human Viral Diseases
This table describes some common viral diseases.

Some Human Viral Diseases

Disease	Effect on Body	Transmission
Common cold	Sneezing, sore throat, fever, headache, muscle aches	Contact with contaminated objects; droplet inhalation
Influenza	Body aches, fever, sore throat, headache, dry cough, fatigue, nasal congestion	Flu viruses spread in respiratory droplets caused by coughing and sneezing.
AIDS (HIV)	Helper T cells, which are needed for normal immune-system function, are destroyed.	Sexual contact; contact with contaminated blood or body fluids; can be passed to babies during delivery or during breastfeeding.
Chicken pox	Skin rash of blisterlike lesions	Virus particles are spread in respiratory droplets caused by coughing and sneezing; highly contagious
Hepatitis B	Jaundice, fatigue, abdominal pain, nausea, vomiting, joint pain	Contact with contaminated blood or bodily fluids
West Nile Virus	Fever, headache, body ache	Bite from an infected mosquito ▶
Human papillomavirus (HPV)	Genital or anal warts, also cancer of the cervix, penis, and anus	Sexual contact

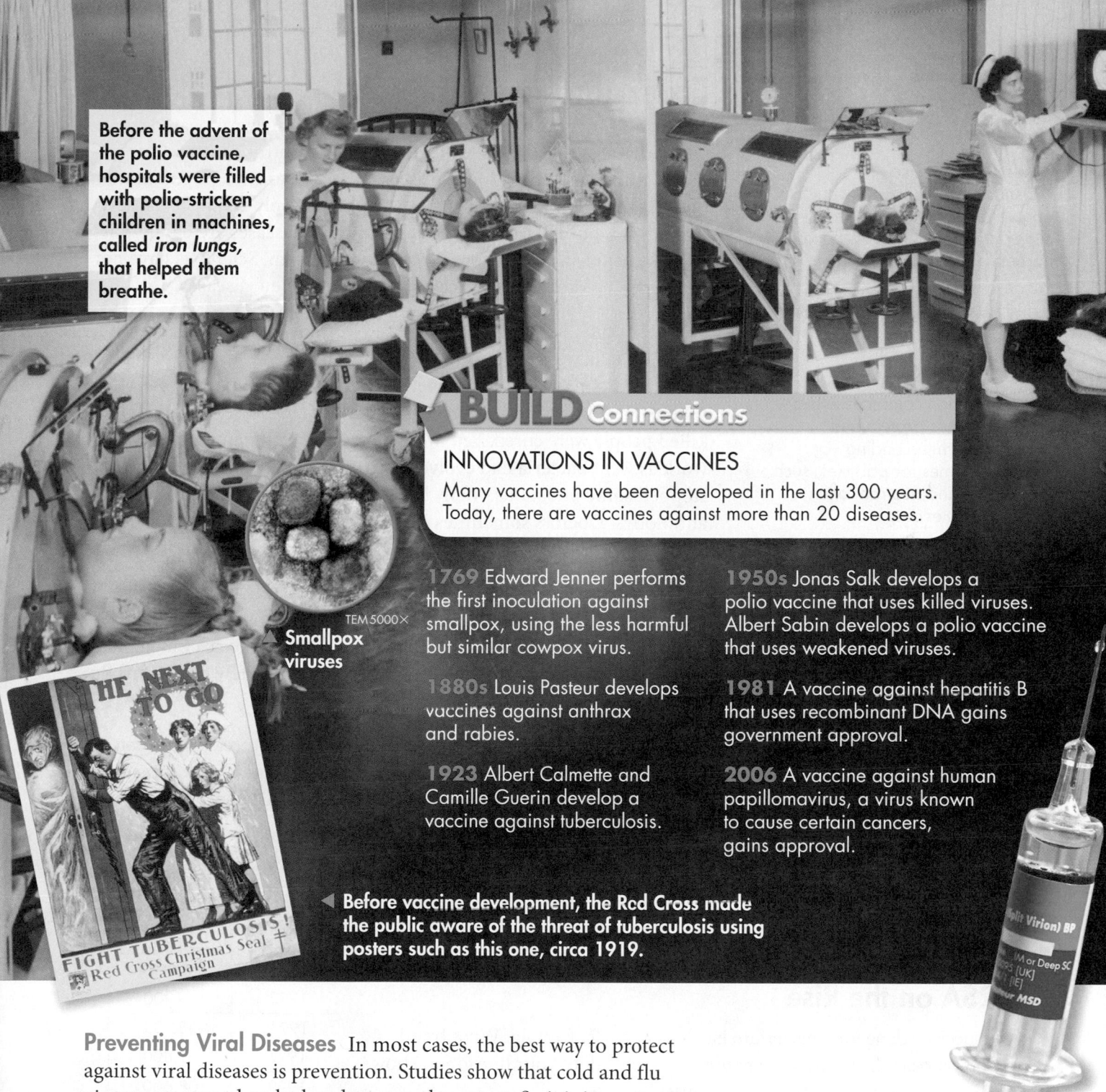

Before the advent of the polio vaccine, hospitals were filled with polio-stricken children in machines, called *iron lungs*, that helped them breathe.

TEM 5000×

Smallpox viruses

THE NEXT TO GO

FIGHT TUBERCULOSIS!
Red Cross Christmas Seal
Campaign

BUILD Connections

INNOVATIONS IN VACCINES

Many vaccines have been developed in the last 300 years. Today, there are vaccines against more than 20 diseases.

1769 Edward Jenner performs the first inoculation against smallpox, using the less harmful but similar cowpox virus.

1880s Louis Pasteur develops vaccines against anthrax and rabies.

1923 Albert Calmette and Camille Guerin develop a vaccine against tuberculosis.

1950s Jonas Salk develops a polio vaccine that uses killed viruses. Albert Sabin develops a polio vaccine that uses weakened viruses.

1981 A vaccine against hepatitis B that uses recombinant DNA gains government approval.

2006 A vaccine against human papillomavirus, a virus known to cause certain cancers, gains approval.

◀ Before vaccine development, the Red Cross made the public aware of the threat of tuberculosis using posters such as this one, circa 1919.

Preventing Viral Diseases In most cases, the best way to protect against viral diseases is prevention. Studies show that cold and flu viruses are passed on by hand-to-mouth contact. So it is important to wash your hands often. Cough or sneeze into a tissue rather than into your hands. Avoid contact with sick people.

Prevention of viral diseases often includes the use of vaccines. Some important events in the development of vaccines are shown above.

Treating Viral Diseases Viral diseases cannot be treated with antibiotics. Yet, there are some antiviral drugs. These drugs attack viral proteins that host cells do not have. Some antiviral drugs help people get over the flu more quickly. Other antiviral drugs help people who are infected with HIV live longer.

emerging disease
a disease that appears in the
population for the first time, or an
old disease that suddenly becomes
harder to control

prion
a misfolded protein that causes
disease

✦ WORD ORIGINS _____

The word *prion* combines letters
from the words *protein* and
infectious with the ending *–on*.
Scientific names for particles, such
as *electron* and *neutron,* often
have the *–on* ending.

Emerging Diseases

In the last thirty years, a number of new diseases have appeared. Other diseases that once seemed to be under control have become more dangerous. An unknown disease that appears in a population for the first time or a well-known disease that suddenly becomes harder to control is an **emerging disease.** Emerging diseases are dangerous because people have little or no resistance to them. Scientists have not developed medications or vaccinations to fight new diseases.

"Superbugs" Sometimes old diseases become harder to fight as the pathogens that cause them evolve. Pathogens often evolve in response to the medicines used against them. Penicillin was the first antibiotic used to treat infections. At first, it worked well. Diseases that had once killed people were cured. Yet, in just a few decades, penicillin did not work as well. Bacteria had evolved resistance to it. The drug no longer stopped some infections. Many bacteria are now resistant to many antibiotics. Doctors sometimes call these bacteria "superbugs."

New Viruses Sometimes, a virus evolves and jumps from one host species to another. Researchers have evidence that HIV did this. It likely moved from nonhuman primates into humans. Public health officials are worried about a new flu virus. A bird flu virus much like the most deadly human flu viruses has evolved. In a few cases, bird flu has infected humans. A major "jump" to humans may be possible.

Key Question Why are emerging diseases a threat to human health? **Humans have little or no resistance to emerging diseases. Scientists have not yet developed ways to control them.**

INQUIRY
into Scientific Thinking

MRSA on the Rise

An especially dangerous bacterium has recently appeared. *Staphylococcus aureus* (MRSA) is resistant to many drugs. It causes skin infections that can be spread by close contact. Infection by MRSA can spread very quickly among people in hospitals who have weakened immune systems.

Analyze and Conclude

1. Graph The table in the right-hand corner shows the number of MRSA infections in hospitals in the United States from 1993 through 2005. Use the table to make a line graph.

2. Explain What trend does your line graph show?

3. Calculate By what percentage did MRSA infections increase between 1995 and 2005?

Incidence of MRSA	
Year	Hospital Cases Reported
1993	1900
1995	38,100
1997	69,800
1999	108,600
2001	175,000
2003	248,300
2005	368,600

4. Relate Cause and Effect The average hospital stay in the United States lasts 4.6 days. That of the average MRSA-infected patient is 10.0 days. If the trend shown by the data above continues, how will MRSA infections affect hospital costs?

In Your Workbook Get more help for this activity in your workbook.

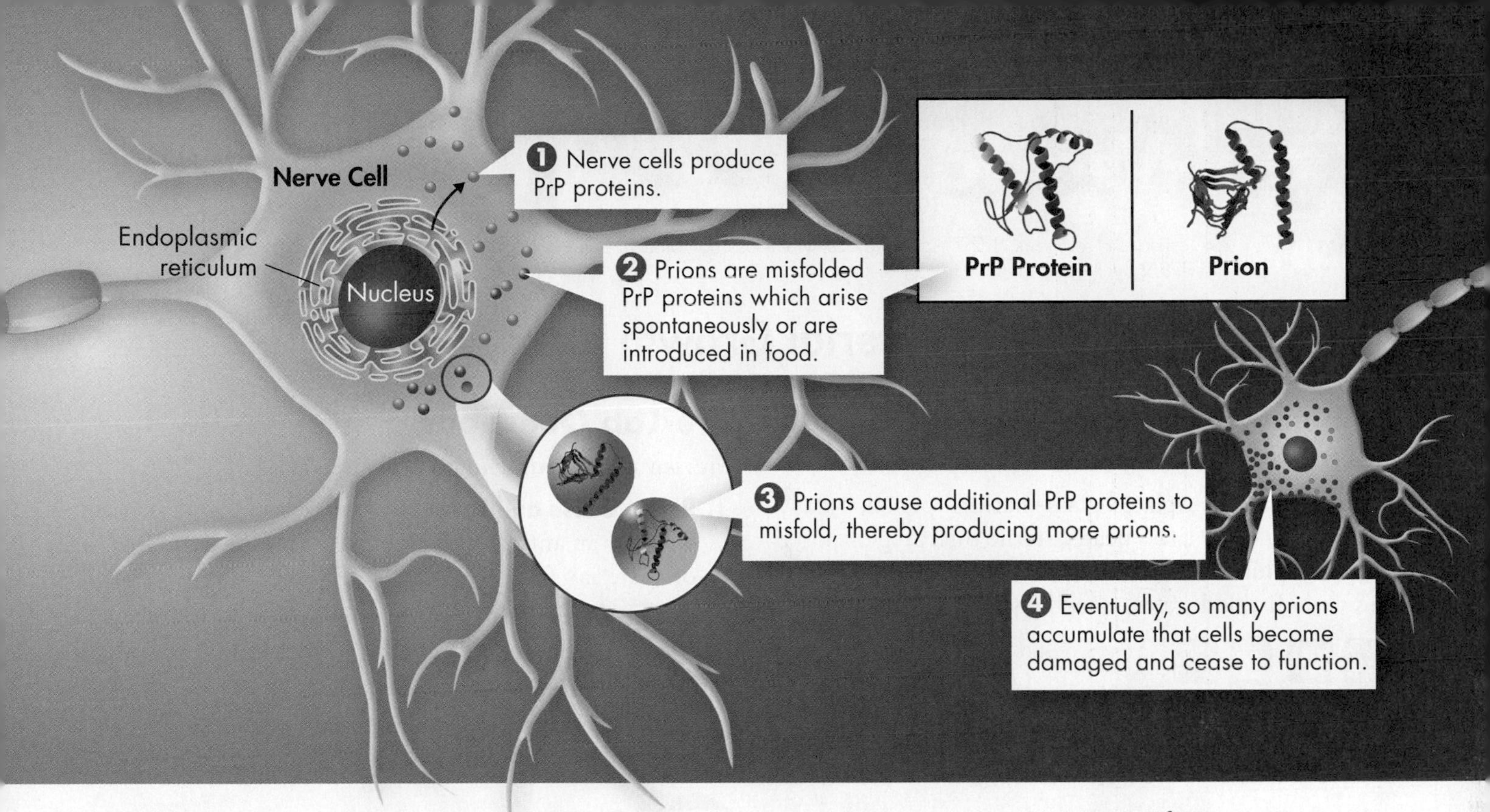
Nerve Cell
Endoplasmic reticulum
Nucleus
1 Nerve cells produce PrP proteins.
2 Prions are misfolded PrP proteins which arise spontaneously or are introduced in food.
PrP Protein
Prion
3 Prions cause additional PrP proteins to misfold, thereby producing more prions.
4 Eventually, so many prions accumulate that cells become damaged and cease to function.

Prion Infections Prions are PrP proteins that are folded incorrectly. Contact with prions can cause other PrP proteins to misfold, too. Prions can damage nerve cells in the brain.

Prions In 1972, the American scientist Stanley Prusiner began to study a disease that was making sheep sick. At first, Prusiner thought a virus caused the disease. Then clumps of misfolded proteins were discovered in the brains of infected sheep. Prusiner called these proteins **prions.** A prion forms when a certain type of protein, called PrP, folds incorrectly. As prions build up, they damage brain cells. Prion infections are spread when animals eat other animals that are infected. Prions can infect many animals, including humans.

CHECK Understanding

Apply Vocabulary

Use the highlighted terms from the lesson to complete each sentence correctly.

1. A(n)________ may contain dead or weakened pathogens.

2. ________ are medications that can be used to treat bacterial infections.

Critical Thinking

3. Compare and Contrast How does the treatment of viral diseases differ from the treatment of bacterial diseases?

4. Explain Why are "superbugs" hard to control?

5. Write to Learn Answer the third clue of the chapter mystery. Describe the structure and effect of prion infections in your answer.

MYSTERY CLUE

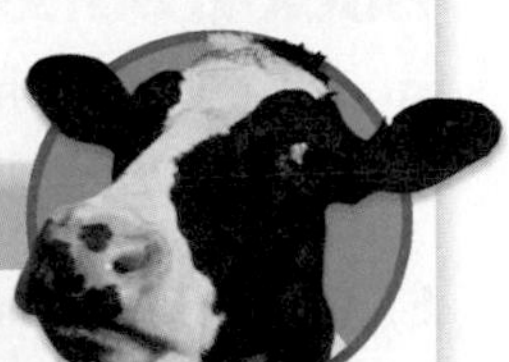

BSE virtually disappeared when the British government banned the use of ground-up cattle protein in feed. What does this indicate about how the pathogen was passed on? Could prions be the cause of BSE? Why or why not? (Hint: See above.)

BIOLOGY.com Search Lesson 20.3 GO • Lesson Assessment • Art in Motion

MD SPI **1.2.4** Testing a Hypothesis, **1.2.7** Apply Results, **1.3.1** Use Equipment, **1.3.3** Safe Handling of Materials, **1.5.9** Synthesize Ideas.

Pre-Lab: Controlling Bacterial Growth

Problem How can you determine the effectiveness of an antibiotic?

Materials agar plates, glass-marking pencil, bacterial cultures, glass beads, sterile micropipettes, disposal solution, forceps, paper disks with antibiotics and with distilled water, masking tape, metric ruler

Lab Manual Chapter 20 Lab

Skills Focus Observe, Measure, Draw Conclusions

Connect to the Big idea Bacteria can be found on and within the human body. Most of these bacteria are harmless and some are even beneficial to humans. But others can cause diseases. These pathogens need to be controlled. Physical removal of bacteria through hand washing is one of the most effective control methods. Proper food storage and preparation are also important, as are the vaccines that have been developed to help the body build up immunity to specific bacterial diseases.

What happens if a person does develop a bacterial infection? Then doctors use drugs, such as antibiotics, to fight the infection. These drugs are designed to kill bacteria but not to kill human cells. In this lab, you will compare the ability of two antibiotics to control the growth of two different types of bacteria.

Background Questions

a. Review What happens to a bacteria cell after it has grown to nearly double its size? What is this process called?

b. Explain How is genetic diversity increased in populations of bacteria?

c. Review What are the two general ways that bacteria can cause disease?

Pre-Lab Questions

Preview the procedure in the lab manual.

1. Relate Cause and Effect How will you know whether an antibiotic is able to control the growth of bacteria?

2. Design An Experiment Why is it important to leave space between the disks on the agar plates?

3. Control Variables Why must you avoid direct contact between your hands and the antibiotic disks?

BIOLOGY.com   Search   [Chapter 20]   GO

Visit Chapter 20 online to test yourself on chapter content and to find activities to help you learn.

Untamed Science Video Join the Untamed Science crew as they fire up the microscopes for a look at bacteria and all the ways they are good for us.

Art in Motion View a short animation of prion infection and see how misfolded proteins interact with normal proteins.

Art Review Review your understanding of the structure and classification of prokaryotes.

InterActive Art Build your understanding of lytic and lysogenic cycles.

Visual Analogy Compare an old west outlaw taking over a town to a lytic infection.

20.1 Viruses

- Viruses can reproduce only by infecting living cells.

- Inside living cells, viruses use their host's genetic information to make many copies of themselves. Some viruses replicate right away. Other viruses stay inactive for a long period of time within the host cell.

---

virus (p. 480)
capsid (p. 481)
bacteriophage (p. 481)
lytic infection (p. 482)
lysogenic infection (p. 482)
retrovirus (p. 483)

THE NEXT TO GO

FIGHT TUBERCULOSIS!
Red Cross Christmas Seal Campaign

20.2 Prokaryotes

- Prokaryotes are classified as Bacteria or Archaea, which are two of the three domains of life.

- Prokaryotes vary in their size and shape, in the way they move, and in the way they get and release energy.

- Prokaryotes are essential in maintaining the balance of the living world. They are decomposers, producers, and nitrogen fixers. In addition, some species are used in human industry.

---

prokaryote (p. 485)
binary fission (p. 487)
conjugation (p. 487)
endospore (p. 487)

20.3 Diseases Caused by Bacteria and Viruses

- Bacteria cause disease by damaging host cells and tissues or by releasing chemicals that upset homeostasis.

- Viruses cause disease by destroying living cells or by affecting processes in cells in ways that upset homeostasis in the host.

- Humans have little or no resistance to emerging diseases. Scientists have not yet developed vaccines or medicines to control them.

---

pathogen (p. 489)
vaccine (p. 490)
antibiotic (p. 490)
emerging disease (p. 492)
prion (p. 493)

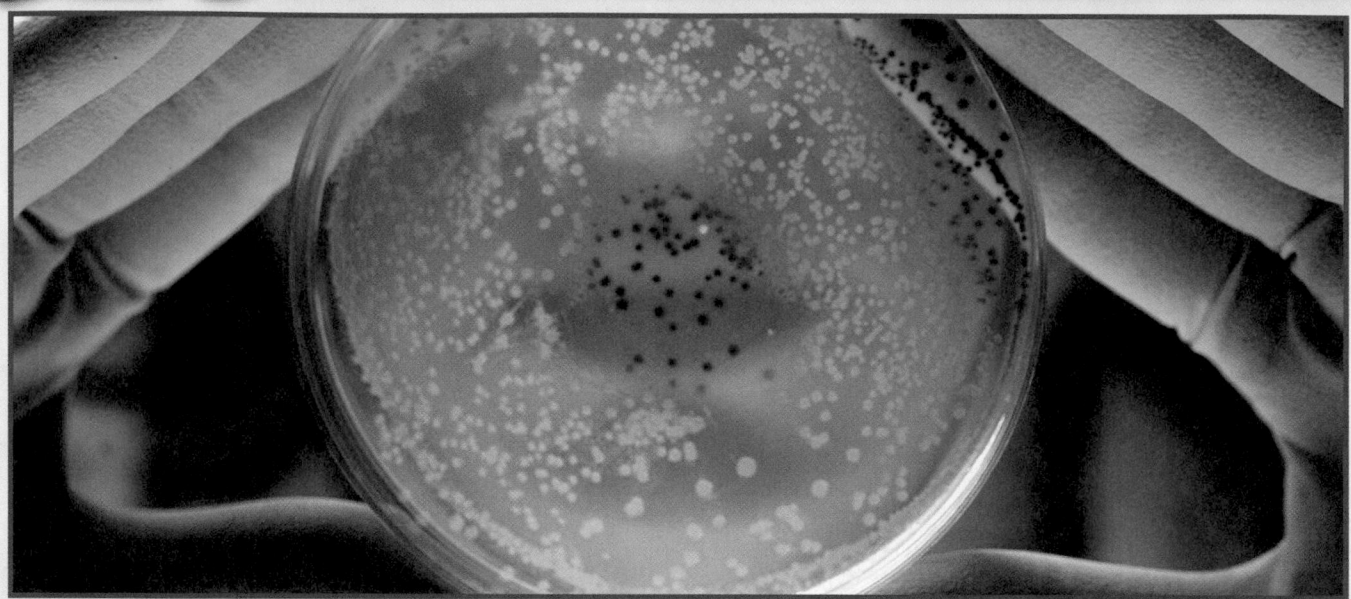

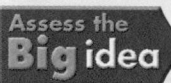 **Cellular Basis of Life**

Write an answer to the question below.

Q: Are all microbes that make us sick made of living cells?

Constructed Response

Write an answer to each of the questions below. The answer to each question should be one or two paragraphs long. To help you begin, read the **Hints** below each of the questions.

1. **Are viruses living organisms?**

   Hint Viruses form crystals.

   Hint Viruses are able to reproduce, and they have genetic material.

2. **How are prokaryotes classified, and how are they important?**

   Hint Prokaryotes are single celled and lack nuclei.

   Hint Prokaryotes are organized into two groups.

3. **How is the reproduction of viruses similar to that of prokaryotes? How is it different?**

   Hint Refer to the art comparing a virus to an outlaw on page 481.

Foundations for Learning Wrap-Up

Use the z-fold you made as you read the chapter to help organize your thoughts about viruses, bacteria, and disease.

Activity 1 Working in a small group, write questions for a crossword puzzle. Base your questions on the notes you took on your z-fold. Draw your puzzle and trade it with another team.

Activity 2 Working with a partner, use your z-folds to make an informative brochure about viruses, bacteria, and the risks they pose to human health. Your notes on the z-fold will be the facts you present about viruses, bacteria, and disease. Be sure to make an inviting cover for your pamphlet. Add pictures to describe viruses and bacteria.

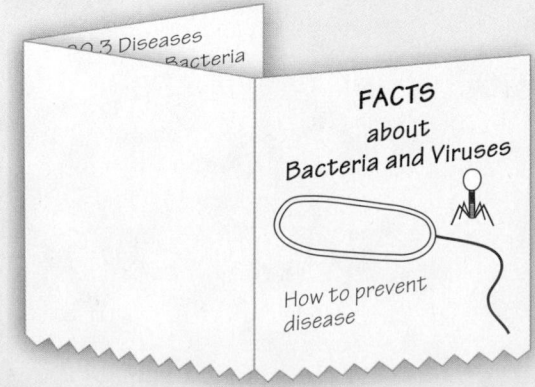

20.1 Viruses

Understand Key Concepts

1. Particles that are made up of proteins, nucleic acids, and sometimes lipids and that can only reproduce by infecting living cells are called
   a. bacteria.
   b. capsids.
   c. prokaryotes.
   d. viruses.

2. One group of viruses has RNA as their genetic information. These viruses are called
   a. bacteriophages.
   b. capsids.
   c. prophages.
   d. retroviruses.

Test-Taking Tip

Come Back to the Question Sometimes, you might be stumped by a question. If you can't figure out the answer, skip the question and continue the test. Come back to the question after you have completed the other test questions. Doing so can help you organize your thoughts and come up with an answer.

---

3. Describe the events that take place during a lytic infection.
4. What is a prophage?

Think Critically

5. **Apply Concepts** Explain how a virus can spread in a bacterial population during a lysogenic infection.

6. **Apply Concepts** How could a mutation in a bacterial cell help the bacterial population become resistant to a bacteriophage?

20.2 Prokaryotes

Understand Key Concepts

7. Prokaryotes differ from all other organisms in that their cells
   a. lack nuclei.
   b. have cell walls.
   c. have ribosomes.
   d. lack nucleic acids.

8. Prokaryotes reproduce asexually by
   a. binary fission.
   b. conjugation.
   c. endospores.
   d. mutation.

9. List and describe the three main cell shapes of prokaryotes.

10. Describe two ways by which prokaryotes move.

Think Critically

11. **Apply Concepts** A scientist finds a new organism. The organism is single celled and has a cell wall containing peptidoglycan. The cell lacks a nucleus. To what domain does the organism belong? Explain your reasoning.

12. **Infer** Imagine that nitrogen-fixing bacteria disappeared. How would this affect other organisms in the world?

20.3 Diseases Caused by Bacteria and Viruses

Understand Key Concepts

13. Viruses cause disease by
    a. releasing toxins.
    b. undergoing conjugation.
    c. infecting then destroying cells.
    d. causing mutations in the host's DNA.

14. Which of the following can be used to treat bacterial diseases but NOT viral diseases?
a. antibiotics
b. antiviral drugs
c. pathogens
d. vaccines

15. What is meant by the term *emerging disease*?

16. How do prions cause disease?

Think Critically

17. Infer Would antibiotics be effective in treating an outbreak of bird flu? Explain.

Connecting Concepts

Use Science Graphics

E. coli *bacteria can be grown on agar in a petri dish. The bacteria cloud the agar surface, forming a bacterial "lawn." This photograph shows a lawn over which a solution containing bacteriophage particles has been poured. Use the photograph to answer questions 18–19.*

18. Interpret Visuals What is the most reasonable explanation for the small, circular, clear areas on the bacterial lawn?

19. Form a Hypothesis Suppose you touched the tip of a glass rod to one of the clear areas and then touched it again to the surface of a petri dish with a fresh lawn of *E. coli*. What would happen to the new lawn of bacteria after several days?

solve the CHAPTER MYSTERY

THE MAD COWS

The mad cow disease that appeared in 1986 spread quickly among British cattle herds. People got a similar disease. This disease was called new variant Creutzfeld-Jacob disease (nvCJD). Many people died.

The British government made a law against feeding cattle using ground-up cattle. BSE and nvCJD almost disappeared. It now seems clear that "mad cow" and nvCJD were caused by prions. These prions were in the meat and brain tissue of infected cattle. When cattle ate the infected meat, the prions spread. People who ate meat from infected animals were also infected. Officials in Europe and the United States have made new laws about meat production to try to make sure there are no more outbreaks of BSE and nvCJD.

1. Infer The rapid rise of BSE between 1986 and 1991 ended when British authorities banned the use of meat and bone meal in cattle food. How does this support the hypothesis that BSE is caused by prions?

2. Apply Concepts Why did most scientists conclude that BSE was not caused by either viruses or bacteria?

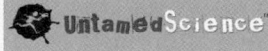 **Never Stop Exploring Your World.** Finding what caused this disease is only the beginning. Take a video field trip with the ecogeeks of Untamed Science to explore the other side of the story. You'll see that not all microbes are "bad."

Standardized Test Practice for Maryland

Multiple Choice

1. A type of virus that infects bacterial cells is called a
   A capsid.
   B prion.
   C bacteriophage.
   D retrovirus. CLG 3.5.1

2. Prokaryotic cells that have a spherical shape are called
   A cocci.
   B methanogens.
   C spirilli.
   D bacilli. SPI 1.5.7

3. What is a capsid?
   A viral DNA that inserts into a host's DNA
   B a protein coat surrounding a virus
   C a type of plant virus
   D a rod-shaped bacterium CLG 3.1.1

4. Which of the following is NOT used to identify specific prokaryotes?
   A type of nucleic acid
   B shape
   C movement
   D energy source SPI 1.5.7

5. Which method is NOT used to protect food against microorganisms?
   A heating
   B freezing
   C sterilization
   D vaccination SPI 1.7.2

6. Which illness is caused by a bacterium?
   A AIDS   C tuberculosis
   B polio   D common cold
   CLG 3.5.2

7. Which process is used for the exchange of genetic information between two bacterial cells?
   A endospore formation
   B lysogenic cycle
   C conjugation
   D binary fission CLG 3.2.1

8. All bacteria are classified as
   A eukaryotes.
   B protists.
   C archaea.
   D prokaryotes. SPI 1.5.7

Questions 9–10

Use the graph below to answer the questions.

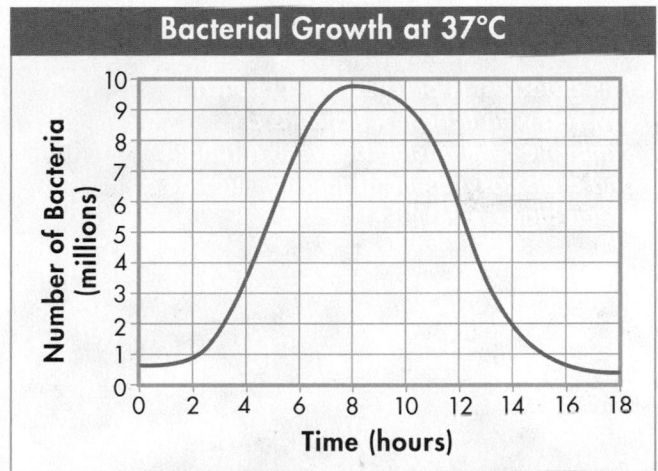

9. At which interval in the graph does the number of living bacteria increase at the greatest rate?
   A between hours 2 and 4
   B between hours 4 and 6
   C between hours 6 and 8
   D between hours 10 and 12 SPI 1.4.2

10. Which is the most likely reason for the decrease in bacteria shown?
    A The temperature of the bacterial culture was too high after 8 hours.
    B The bacteria stopped reproducing after 8 hours.
    C More nutrients were added to the culture at regular intervals.
    D Waste products from the bacteria accumulated in the nutrient solution. SPI 1.4.2

Open-Ended Response

11. Explain why antibiotics can be useful in treating bacterial diseases but not in treating viral diseases.
    CLG 3.5.2

If You Have Trouble With . . .

Question	1	2	3	4	5	6	7	8	9	10	11
See Lesson	20.1	20.2	20.1	20.2	20.3	20.3	20.2	20.2	20.2	20.2	20.3

21 Protists and Fungi

Interdependence in Nature

Q: How do protists and fungi affect the homeostasis of other organisms and ecosystems?

This goldcrest is perched on a branch covered with lichen. A lichen is a symbiotic relationship between a fungus and a photosynthetic organism, such as a green alga.

MARYLAND VOLUNTARY STATE CURRICULUM

Biology Indicators/Core Learning Goals (CLG) 3.1.1, 3.2.1, 3.2.2, 3.3.1, 3.4.2, 3.5.1, 3.5.2, 3.5.3, 3.5.4. **Skills and Processes Indicators (SPI)** 1.1.1, 1.1.2, 1.2.4, 1.2.6, 1.3.1, 1.3.3, 1.4.2, 1.4.9, 1.5.1, 1.5.2, 1.5.5, 1.5.7, 1.5.8, 1.5.9, 1.6.4. See lessons for details.

CHAPTER MYSTERY

"A BLIGHT OF UNUSUAL CHARACTER"

In the early 1800s, Irish farmers became heavily dependent on growing potatoes. Potatoes grew very well in the cool wet climate of Ireland. Soon potatoes became the main source of food for Irish families.

Then, during the summer of 1845, something strange began to happen. One magazine reported that "a blight of unusual character" was attacking the potatoes. Everywhere in Ireland, potatoes began to rot and turn black. Without their main food crop, many people starved. Others left Ireland to go to countries such as the United States. By the early 1900s, the population of Ireland was cut in half.

Read for Mystery Clues What caused this disaster? As you read this chapter, look for clues to help you find the cause of the potato blight. Then, solve the mystery.

FOUNDATIONS for Learning

If protists and fungi disappeared, our world would be a very different place. Make a double-door fold like the one shown below. Under Protists, write these headings: Autotrophs, Heterotrophs, Mutualists, Parasites. Under Fungi write Decomposers, Mutualists, Parasites. As you read the chapter, make notes under each of these headings. At the end of the chapter, you will find two activities that will help you answer the question: How do protists and fungi affect the homeostasis of other organisms and ecosystems?

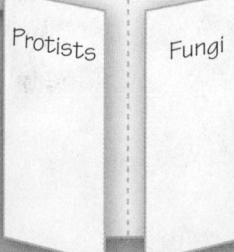

Protists   Fungi

• Untamed Science Video   • Chapter Mystery

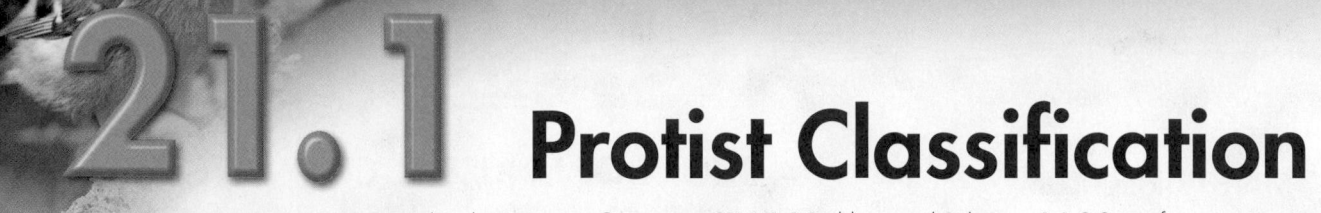

21.1 Protist Classification

MD CLG 3.4.2 Relatedness Among Organisms. SPI 1.1.1 Problems and Solutions, 1.1.2 Scientific Ideas, 1.3.1 Use Equipment, 1.3.3 Safe Handling of Materials, 1.5.1 Summarize Data, 1.5.2 Communicate Information, 1.5.5 Create and Interpret Graphics, 1.5.7 Classification Systems.

Key Questions

🔑 *What are protists?*

🔑 *How are protists related to other eukaryotes?*

BUILD Understanding

Preview Visuals Look at the photos in the cladogram about protist classification. Do you recognize any of these protists? Write down two questions that you have about the cladogram. As you read the lesson, try to answer the questions.

In Your Workbook Go to your workbook to learn more about previewing visuals. Complete the activity for Lesson 21.1.

Giant Kelp Otters wrap themselves in giant kelp, a multicellular protist, to keep from drifting out to sea while they sleep.

The First Eukaryotes

More than a billion years ago, a new kind of organism appeared. These organisms had one cell. Their fossils show they were the first eukaryotes. Eukaryotes have cells with nuclei. Single-celled eukaryotes are still with us today. They are often called *protists*, which means "first." Protists are eukaryotes that are not fungi, plants, or animals.

Most protists are single celled, but some have many cells. The largest protists—brown algae called kelp—have millions of cells. They also have tissues. Kelp is considered to be a protist because it is more closely related to certain single-celled protists than it is to members of any other kingdom.

🔑 **Key Question** What are protists? **Protists are eukaryotes that are not members of the fungi, plant, or animal kingdoms.**

Kingdom Protista Protists were once classified in kingdom Protista. But in recent years, biologists have discovered that kingdom Protista is far more diverse than any other eukaryotic kingdom. Many protists are more closely related to members of other kingdoms than to other protists. This causes a problem in classification. The members of a kingdom should be more like one another than they are like members of other kingdoms. This is not true of protists. As a result, biologists are still undecided as to the best way to classify protists.

Diatoms The shells of diatoms have beautiful patterns. Diatoms are a group of tiny protists that live in the ocean.

SEM 960×

What Are Protists?

Protists can be found in oceans, rivers, streams, lakes, and ponds. Many are too small to see without a microscope.

Procedure

❶ Place a drop of pond water on a microscope slide. Add a drop of methyl cellulose. Cover the sample with a coverslip. Look at the slide under the microscope at low and high magnifications.

❷ Write down your observations. Draw each kind of organism that you see. Label any structures, such as the nucleus, that you can identify.

Analyze and Conclude

1. Explain For any of the organisms that move, describe their motion. Describe any structures involved in producing the motion.

2. Evaluate Did you see any structures that you think are used to gather food? That are used for reproduction? Explain.

3. Apply Concepts Are any of the organisms you saw bacteria, plants, or animals? Explain your answer.

In Your Workbook
Get more help for this activity in your workbook.

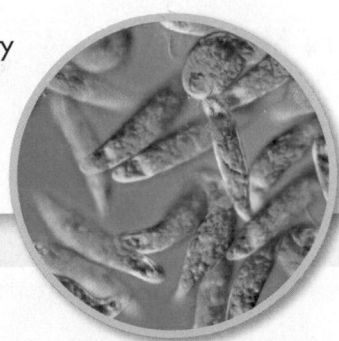

Euglena Photosynthetic *Euglena* are common freshwater protists that can move (LM 250×).

Multiple Kingdoms? The most recent studies of protists divide them into six major groups, or clades. Each could be considered a kingdom. The fungi, plant, and animal kingdoms fit among these six protist groups. In fact, animals and fungi likely evolved from the same protist ancestor.

The Name "Protist" Most biologists today agree that the protists should not be lumped together into a single kingdom. Even so, they continue to call these organisms "protists." So, in this book, we will use the word "protist" to refer to these organisms.

Ancestors and Descendants

Fossils of eukaryotic cells have been found in rocks as old as 1.5 billion years. Evidence from fossils and DNA shows that eukaryotes evolved from prokaryotes. Eukaryotes are more closely related to present-day Archaea than to Bacteria.

Protists were the first eukaryotes. How are they related to other eukaryotes? It may be tempting to look among living protists to find the ancestors of the first plants or fungi. But it would be a mistake to do so. Protists have evolved over time. Those alive today are very different from their ancestors.

Slime Molds At a certain stage of their life cycle, protists called slime molds come together into colonies like this one (SEM 15×).

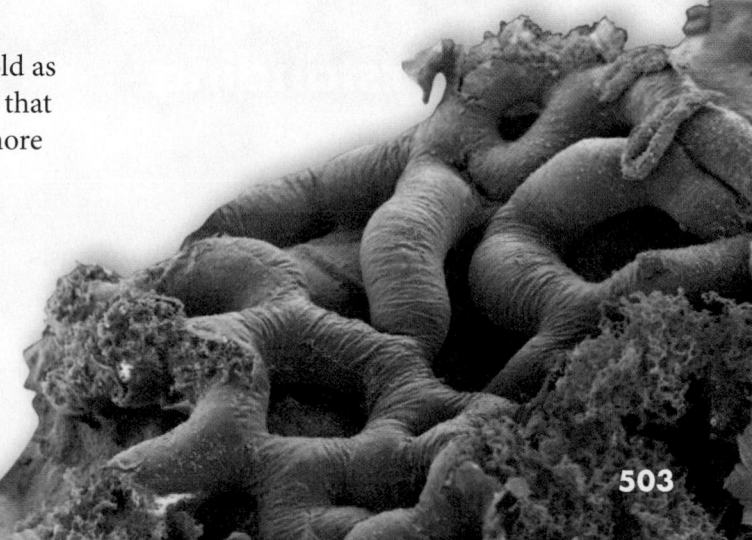

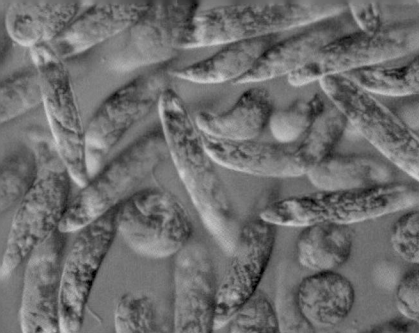
Euglena is classified as an excavate.

Brown algae, such as kelp (left), and diatoms (right) are examples of chromalveolates.

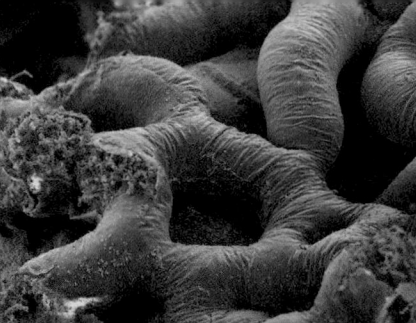
Slime molds are classified with the Amoebozoa.

Six Major Groups

Excavata

Chromalveolata

Cercozoa, Foraminifera, and Radiolaria

Rhodophyta (red algae)

Amoebozoa

Choanozoa

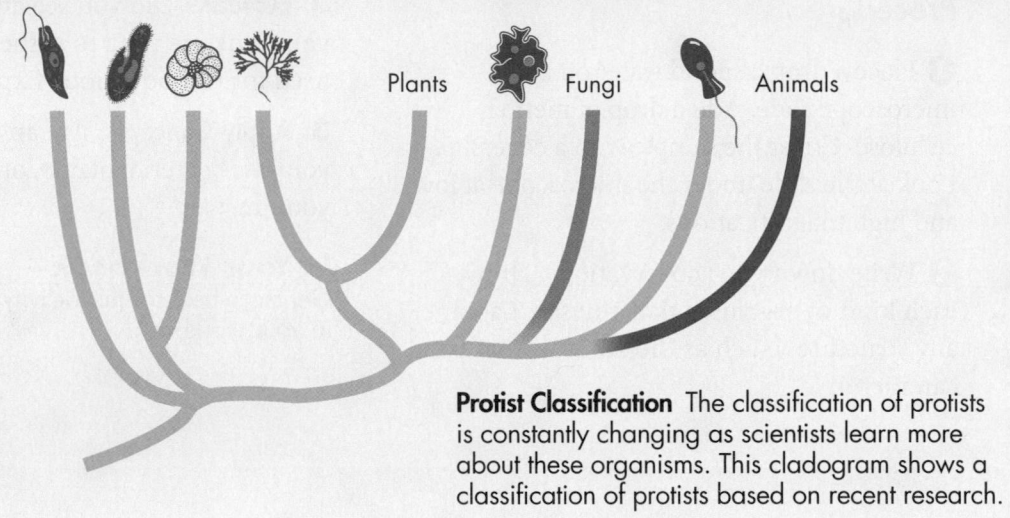

Plants   Fungi   Animals

Protist Classification The classification of protists is constantly changing as scientists learn more about these organisms. This cladogram shows a classification of protists based on recent research.

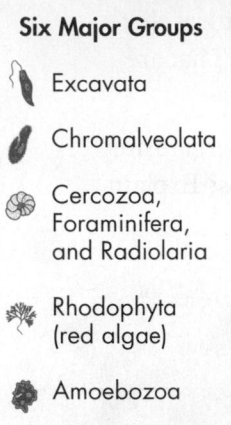
For more on the diversity of protists, go to the Visual Guide. ✆ **pp. DOL 10–15**

Today there are as many as 300,000 species of protists. Most are single celled. Some live in colonies. Two groups of protists—the red algae and the brown algae—include true multicellular organisms. Fungi, plants, and animals evolved from the ancestors of these two groups. Biologists continue to study protists closely. They know that clues about the beginnings of diversity in plants, animals, and fungi can be found among the protists.

🔑 **Key Question** How are protists related to other eukaryotes? **Today's protists include groups whose ancestors were among the last to split from the ancestors of plants, animals, and fungi.**

CHECK Understanding

Critical Thinking

1. **Explain** What is a protist?

2. **Compare and Contrast** Traditionally, protists were classified in kingdom Protista. How has the classification of protists changed?

3. **Relate Cause and Effect** What is a major reason why scientists need to reclassify protists?

4. **Apply Concepts** What three kingdoms arose from protist ancestors?

5. **Write to Learn** Scientists say that we should not look for the earliest ancestors of animals among modern-day protists. Write a short paragraph that explains why.

21.2 Protist Structure and Function

MD CLG 3.2.1 Processes and Functions, 3.3.1 Sexual Reproduction and Variation.
SPI 1.5.5 Create and Interpret Graphics, 1.5.8 Compare, 1.5.9 Synthesize Ideas.

How Protists Move

Your body is packed with specialized systems. Organ systems help you move, break down food, and sense your environment. Imagine having only one cell. How would you carry out these functions? Single-celled protists don't have organs or organ systems. They have to do it all within a single cell. Despite these challenges, protists are very successful organisms. They successfully carry out all the activities necessary for life.

Protists move in several different ways. Some move by changing their shape. Others have specialized organelles for movement. Many protists do not move actively. These protists are carried by wind, water, or other organisms.

Amoeboid Movement Many single-celled protists move by changing their cell shape. First, a projection, or bulge, forms on the side of the cell. This projection is called a **pseudopod** (soo doh pahd). The pseudopod fills with cytoplasm. As cytoplasm flows into the pseudopod, the rest of the cell follows. This causes the cell to move. Amoebas are the best-known group of protists that move this way. As a result, this type of motion is called amoeboid movement.

Amoeboid movement is powered by a protein called actin. Actin is also found in the muscles of animals. In animals, actin plays an important role in muscle contraction.

Key Questions

🔑 **How do protists move in the environment?**

🔑 **How do protists reproduce?**

BUILD Understanding

Compare/Contrast Table As you read the lesson, make a table that compares and contrasts the ways in which protists move.

In Your Workbook Go to your workbook to learn more about comparing and contrasting. Complete the table for Lesson 21.2.

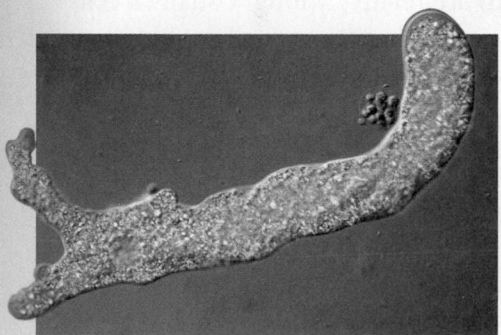
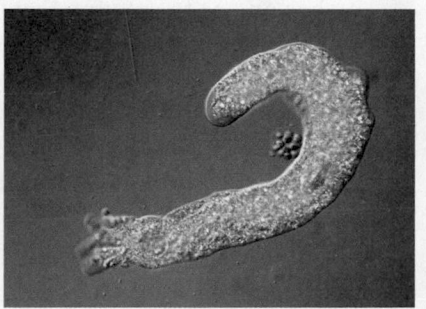
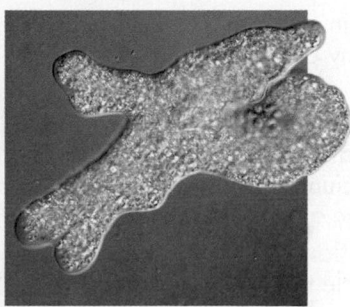

(LM 220×)

Amoeboid Movement An amoeba moves by extending a pseudopod away from its body. Cytoplasm streams into the pseudopod. Then the rest of the cell follows. Amoebas also use pseudopods to surround and take in food. In these photos, the amoeba is consuming algae.

HOW CELLS MOVE LIKE BOATS
Movement by cilia or some flagella is similar to two ways in which a boat is moved.

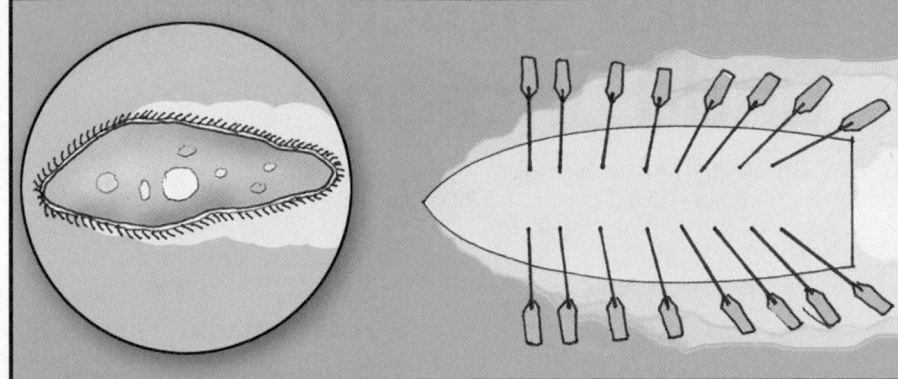

Motion by cilia is analogous to oars propelling a large rowboat forward through the water.

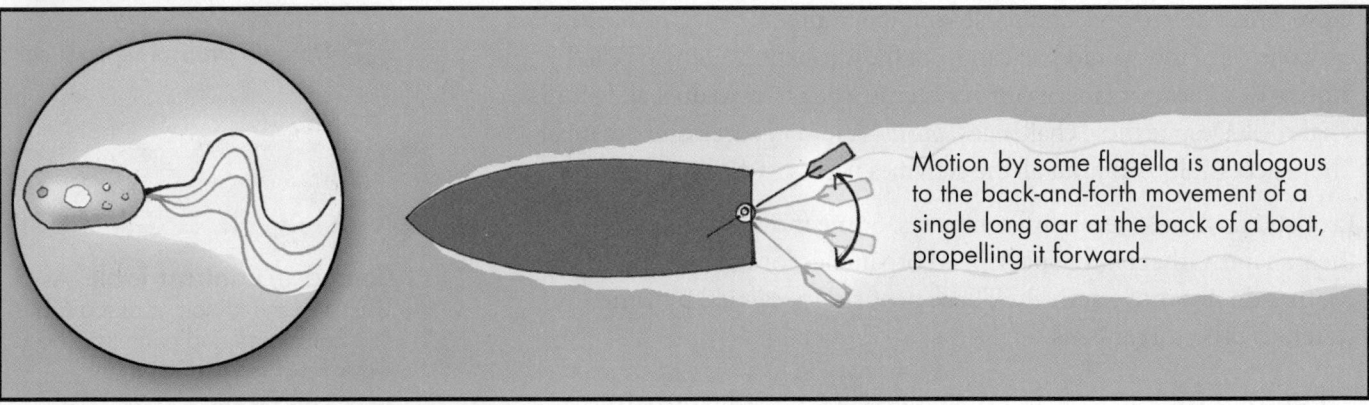

Motion by some flagella is analogous to the back-and-forth movement of a single long oar at the back of a boat, propelling it forward.

BUILD Vocabulary

pseudopod a temporary cytoplasmic projection used by some protists for movement

cilium a short, hairlike projection that produces movement

flagellum a structure used by protists for movement; produces movement in a wavelike motion

spore in prokaryotes, protists, and fungi, any of a variety of thick-walled life-cycle stages capable of surviving unfavorable conditions

conjugation a process in which paramecium and some prokaryotes exchange genetic information

alternation of generations a life cycle that has two alternating phases—a haploid (N) phase and a diploid (2N) phase

🔖 WORD ORIGINS

The word *pseudopod* comes from the Greek root *pseudo*, which means "false," and *pod*, which means "foot."

Cilia and Flagella Many protists move by means of cilia (SIL ee uh) and flagella (fluh JEL uh). These structures are supported by microtubules, which are part of a cell's cytoskeleton. Cilia and flagella have nearly identical internal structures. However, they produce motion in different ways.

Cilia (singular: cilium) are short and numerous. They move somewhat like oars on a boat. Protists that move with cilia are known as ciliates.

Flagella (singular: flagellum) are relatively long. Usually a cell has one or two. Some flagella spin like tiny propellers. But most flagella move like a wave from base to tip. Protists that move by flagella are called flagellates.

Passive Movement Many protists depend on air, water currents, or other organisms to carry them around. These protists form reproductive cells called **spores.** Some spores can enter other organisms and live as parasites. One spore-forming protist is *Plasmodium*. *Plasmodium* is carried by mosquitoes. It causes malaria. *Cryptosporidium* is spread through contaminated drinking water. It causes severe intestinal disease in humans.

🔑 Key Question How do protists move in the environment? **Some protists move by changing their cell shape. Some use cilia or flagella. Others do not move actively but are carried by wind, water, or other organisms.**

Protist Reproduction

Some protists reproduce asexually. A few protists exchange genetic material during conjugation. Other protists have a life cycle that combines both asexual and sexual reproduction.

Cell Division Amoebas and other protists reproduce asexually by mitosis. First, the protist copies its genetic material. Then, the parent cell divides into two identical daughter cells. Mitosis lets protists reproduce quickly. However, mitosis produces cells that are genetically identical to the parent. Identical cells limit genetic diversity.

Conjugation Paramecia and most other ciliates reproduce asexually by mitosis. But when conditions are unfavorable, paramecia undergo conjugation. **Conjugation** is a process in which two organisms exchange genetic material. After conjugating, the cells reproduce by mitosis.

Paramecia have two types of nuclei: a macronucleus and one or more smaller micronuclei. The macronucleus controls the daily activities of the cell. Micronuclei contain the cell's chromosomes. During conjugation, the cells exchange haploid micronuclei. These micronuclei fuse to form a diploid micronucleus. Conjugation produces new combinations of genes, which can aid in evolution.

Sexual Reproduction Many protists have sexual life cycles that are complex. They alternate between diploid and haploid phases, in a process that is called **alternation of generations.** Water molds are one group of protists that have alternation of generations. Water molds reproduce asexually by producing diploid spores in a structure called a sporangium (spoh RAN jee um). Water molds also reproduce sexually. They undergo meiosis, forming male and female structures. These structures produce haploid nuclei. The nuclei fuse during fertilization, forming a diploid zygote.

🔑 **Key Question** How do protists reproduce? **Some protists reproduce asexually by mitosis. Others have life cycles that combine sexual and asexual forms of reproduction.**

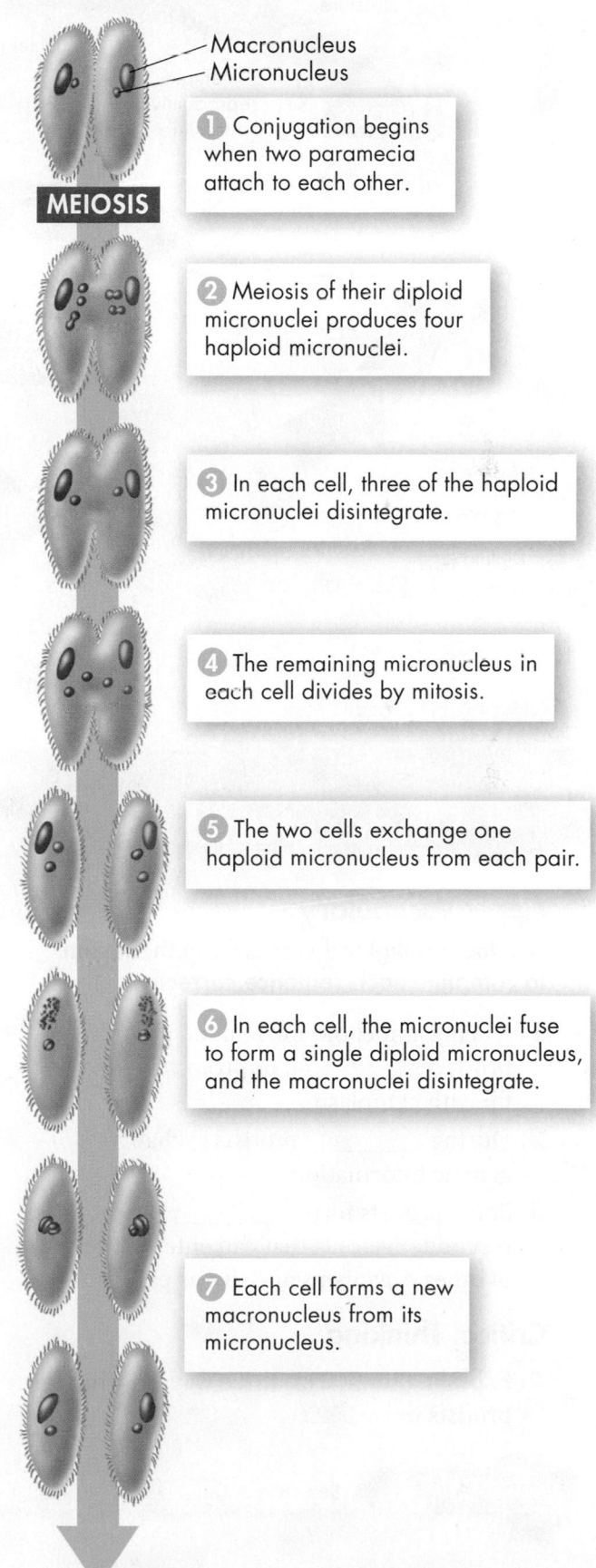

Conjugation During conjugation, two paramecia attach to each other and exchange genetic information.

— Macronucleus
— Micronucleus

MEIOSIS

1 Conjugation begins when two paramecia attach to each other.

2 Meiosis of their diploid micronuclei produces four haploid micronuclei.

3 In each cell, three of the haploid micronuclei disintegrate.

4 The remaining micronucleus in each cell divides by mitosis.

5 The two cells exchange one haploid micronucleus from each pair.

6 In each cell, the micronuclei fuse to form a single diploid micronucleus, and the macronuclei disintegrate.

7 Each cell forms a new macronucleus from its micronucleus.

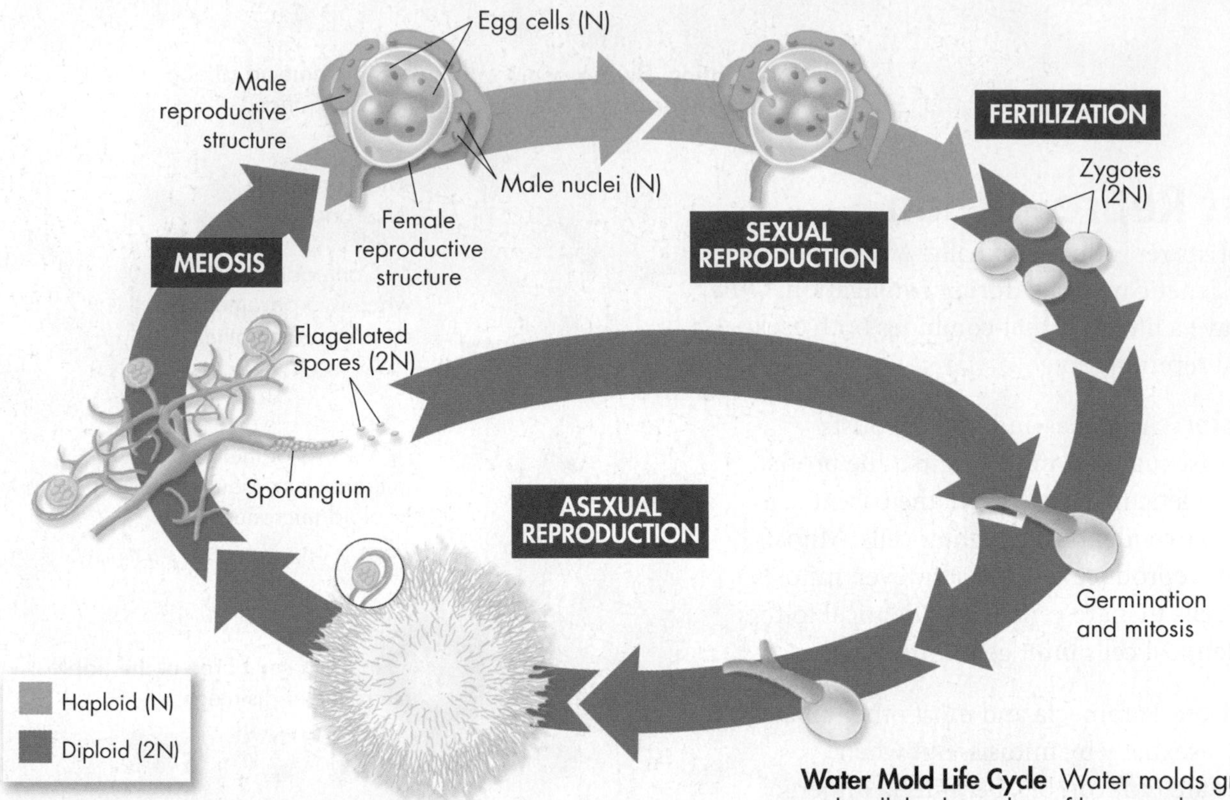

Egg cells (N)

Male reproductive structure

Male nuclei (N)

Female reproductive structure

MEIOSIS

FERTILIZATION

Zygotes (2N)

SEXUAL REPRODUCTION

Flagellated spores (2N)

Sporangium

ASEXUAL REPRODUCTION

Germination and mitosis

Haploid (N)

Diploid (2N)

Water Mold Life Cycle Water molds grow into multicellular branching filaments that produce sporangia for asexual reproduction or male and female structures for sexual reproduction.

CHECK Understanding

Apply Vocabulary

Use the highlighted words from the lesson to complete each sentence correctly.

1. During amoeboid movement, a protist produces _____, or projections that fill with cytoplasm.

2. During _____, protists exchange genetic information.

3. Some protists form _____, reproductive cells that can enter the cells of other organisms and live as parasites.

Critical Thinking

4. Explain Summarize three ways in which protists move.

5. Compare and Contrast How does movement by means of cilia differ from movement by means of flagella?

6. Review Describe how protists reproduce.

7. Write to Learn Answer the first mystery clue. Use the words *asexual reproduction* and *sexual reproduction* in your answer.

MYSTERY CLUE

To produce more potatoes, Irish farmers cut the eyes, or buds, from a crop and saved them for the next year. As a result, the potatoes grown were genetically identical. How might this practice have made the potato blight worse? (**Hint:** See p. 507.)

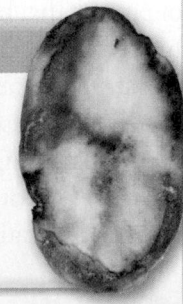

BIOLOGY.com   Search (Lesson 21.2) **GO** • Lesson Assessment

21.3 The Ecology of Protists

MD CLG **3.2.1** Processes and Functions, **3.2.2** Changes in Metabolic Activity, **3.5.1** Factors Influencing Ecosystems, **3.5.2** Interdependence of Organisms in the Biosphere, **3.5.3** Population Dynamics. SPI **1.5.5** Create and Interpret Graphics, **1.5.8** Compare, **1.5.9** Synthesize Ideas.

Autotrophic Protists

Seaweed in the ocean and the green scum on a pond are both commonly called *algae*. Many kinds of algae are protists.

Diversity of Algae Organisms called *algae* belong to several different groups. Some are prokaryotes. Others, such as green algae, are plants. Many are protists. All these organisms are autotrophs. They use energy from sunlight to make their own food by photosynthesis. Photosynthetic protists include many species of phytoplankton. Phytoplankton are small algae that float near the water's surface. Red and brown algae, euglenas, and dinoflagellates are also photosynthetic protists.

Ecological Roles Photosynthetic protists form the base of food chains in the ocean and in fresh water.

▶ *Feeding Fish and Other Animals* Phytoplankton carry out about half of the photosynthesis that takes place on Earth. Phytoplankton are eaten by organisms as diverse as shrimp and baleen whales. And when you eat fish such as tuna, you are indirectly getting energy from phytoplankton.

▶ *Supporting Coral Reefs* Algae play two key roles in coral reefs. They provide nutrients from photosynthesis to coral animals. They also provide the calcium carbonate that coral reefs need to grow.

Key Questions

🔑 How are photosynthetic protists important to ecosystems?

🔑 How do heterotrophic protists get food?

🔑 What types of symbiotic relationships involve protists?

BUILD Understanding

KWL Chart Before you read Lesson 21.3, make a chart with four columns. In the left column, write the titles and headings in the lesson. In the second column, write what you already know about each topic. In the third column, write what you expect to learn. After you read the lesson, write what you learned in the last column.

In Your Workbook Go to your workbook to learn more about making a KWL chart.

Baleen Whale

Coral Reef

Producers in the Food Chains Many ocean animals, including baleen whales, fishes, and coral animals, rely on photosynthetic protists for food.

algal bloom
an increase in the amount of algae and other producers that results from a large input of a limiting nutrient

food vacuole
a small cavity in the cytoplasm of a protist that temporarily stores food

gullet
a dent in one side of a ciliate that allows food to enter the cell

plasmodium
the amoeboid feeding stage in the life cycle of a plasmodial slime mold

🔖**MULTIPLE MEANINGS**

The name *Amoeba* refers to a genus of protists. Without italics or capitalization, the word *amoeba* can describe any protist that moves with pseudopods. In this sense, the adjective *amoeboid* describes the single-celled form of slime molds.

▶ *Providing Shelter* Giant kelp and *Sargassum* are multicellular brown algae. They provide shelter for marine species, such as sea otters and many kinds of fishes.

▶ *Recycling Wastes* Protists help break down and recycle nutrients in sewage and other waste materials. But if there is too much waste, populations of protists can quickly grow to huge numbers. This situation is called an **algal bloom.** An algal bloom can use up nutrients. As these protists die, their bodies decay. This decay removes oxygen from the water, killing fish and invertebrates. Blooms of protists called dinoflagellates cause red tides. Toxins from dinoflagellates can poison fish and shellfish.

🗝 **Key Question** How are photosynthetic protists important to ecosystems? **Photosynthetic protists form the base of food chains in the oceans and in freshwater environments.**

Heterotrophic Protists

Many protists are heterotrophs. They get food from other organisms. Some heterotrophic protists surround and digest their food. Others absorb nutrients from their surroundings.

Amoebas Amoebas feed by surrounding a cell or food particle. This food is held in a food vacuole. A **food vacuole** is a small cavity in the cytoplasm that temporarily stores food. The food is digested, and the nutrients are passed to the rest of the cell. The vacuole releases waste materials outside the cell.

Ciliates Ciliates sweep food into their **gullet,** a dent in one side of the organism. The particles are forced into food vacuoles at the base of the gullet. The food vacuoles fuse with lysosomes, which contain digestive enzymes. The vacuole releases waste materials through the anal pore.

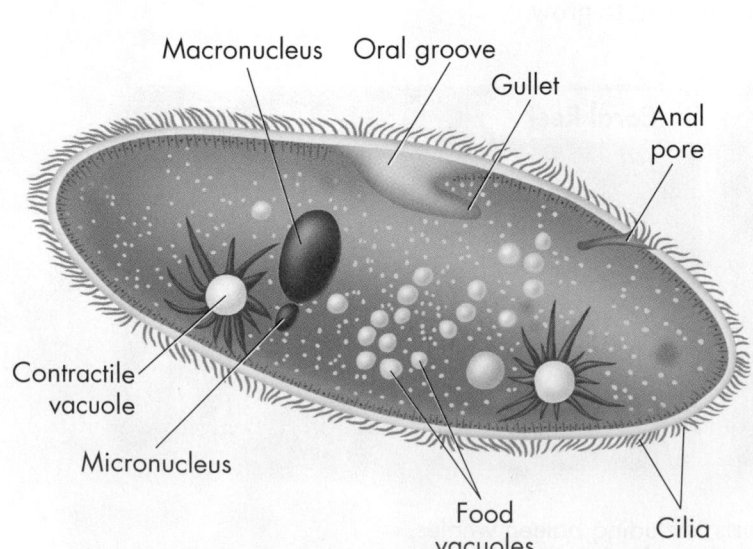

Macronucleus Oral groove Gullet Anal pore
Contractile vacuole
Micronucleus
Food vacuoles Cilia

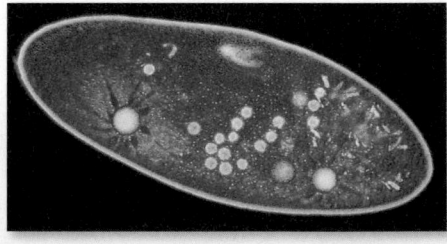

LM 230×

Feeding Structures of *Paramecium*
Cilia that line the oral groove and gullet move food into the cell. The food particles are surrounded, forming food vacuoles. Wastes are released through the anal pore.

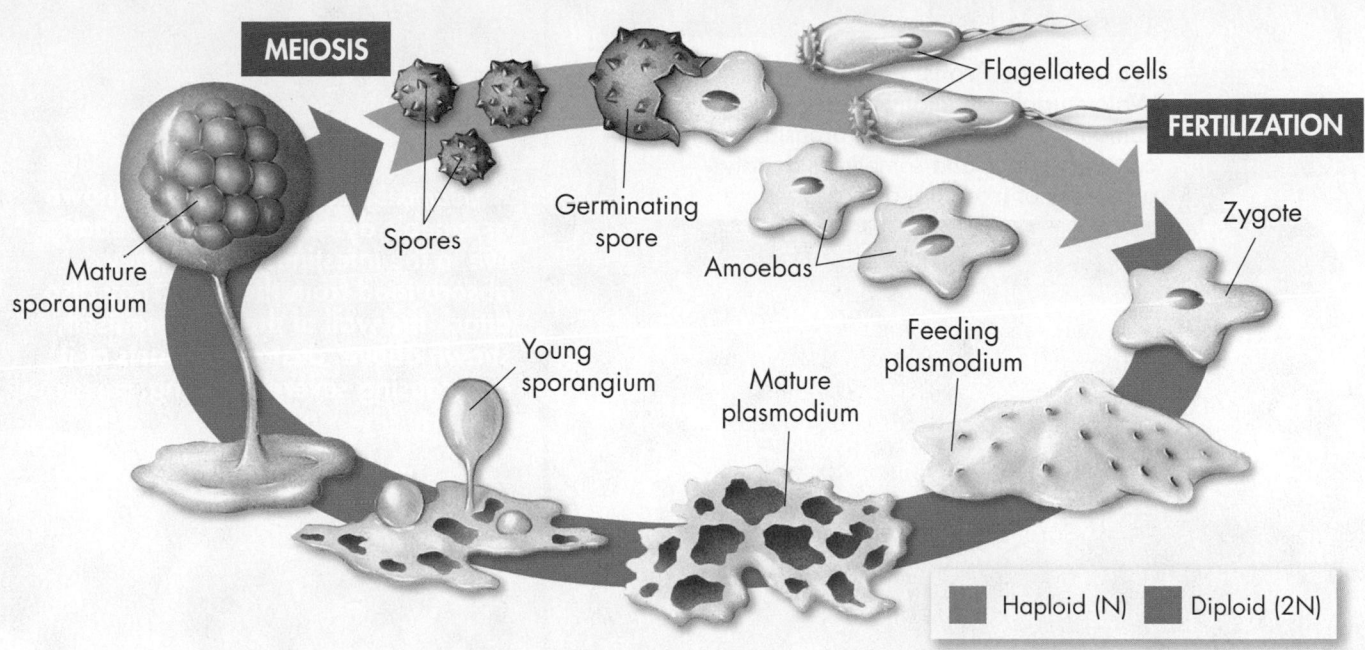

MEIOSIS

Flagellated cells

FERTILIZATION

Spores

Germinating spore

Zygote

Mature sporangium

Amoebas

Young sporangium

Mature plasmodium

Feeding plasmodium

■ Haploid (N)   ■ Diploid (2N)

Slime Molds Slime molds live in damp places that are rich in dead organic matter, such as a forest floor or a compost pile. Because they are decomposers, slime molds play key roles in recycling nutrients.

Slime molds have complex life cycles. In the haploid phase, slime molds are single-celled amoebas or flagellated cells. In the diploid phase, the amoebas form a multicellular structure called a **plasmodium.** The plasmodium develops sporangia, which produce haploid spores.

Protists That Absorb Food Some protists absorb nutrients that other organisms have released into the environment. For example, water molds absorb molecules from decaying plants and animals through their cell walls and cell membranes.

🔑 **Key Question** How do heterotrophic protists get food? **Some protists surround and digest their food. Other protists absorb food molecules from their surroundings.**

Slime Mold Life Cycle In the life cycle of a slime mold, the diploid feeding stage involves a collection of slime mold amoebas called a plasmodium. The plasmodium produces sporangia, which undergo meiosis and produce haploid spores. The spores grow into amoebalike or flagellated cells. Then the flagellated cells fuse to form diploid zygotes that repeat the cycle.

Symbiotic Protists

Many protists are involved in symbiotic relationships with other organisms. Recall that symbiosis is a relationship in which two species live closely together. Mutualism and parasitism are two kinds of symbiosis.

Mutualists Many protists are involved in mutualistic relationships. Both the protist and its host benefit. Termites and the protist *Trichonympha* are an example. Termites eat wood, but cannot break down the cellulose in wood. *Trichonympha* lives in the gut of the termite. It makes an enzyme called cellulase, which breaks down cellulose. This enzyme allows the termite to get energy from wood.

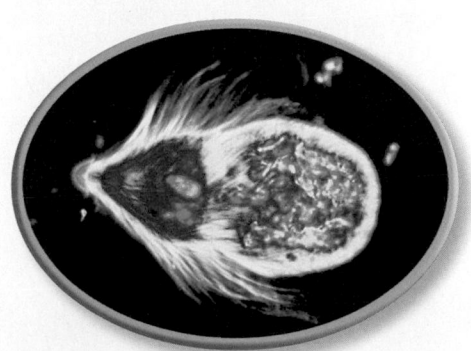

A Protist Mutualist *Trichonympha* lives in the gut of termites. This protist makes enzymes that break down the cellulose in wood (LM 250×).

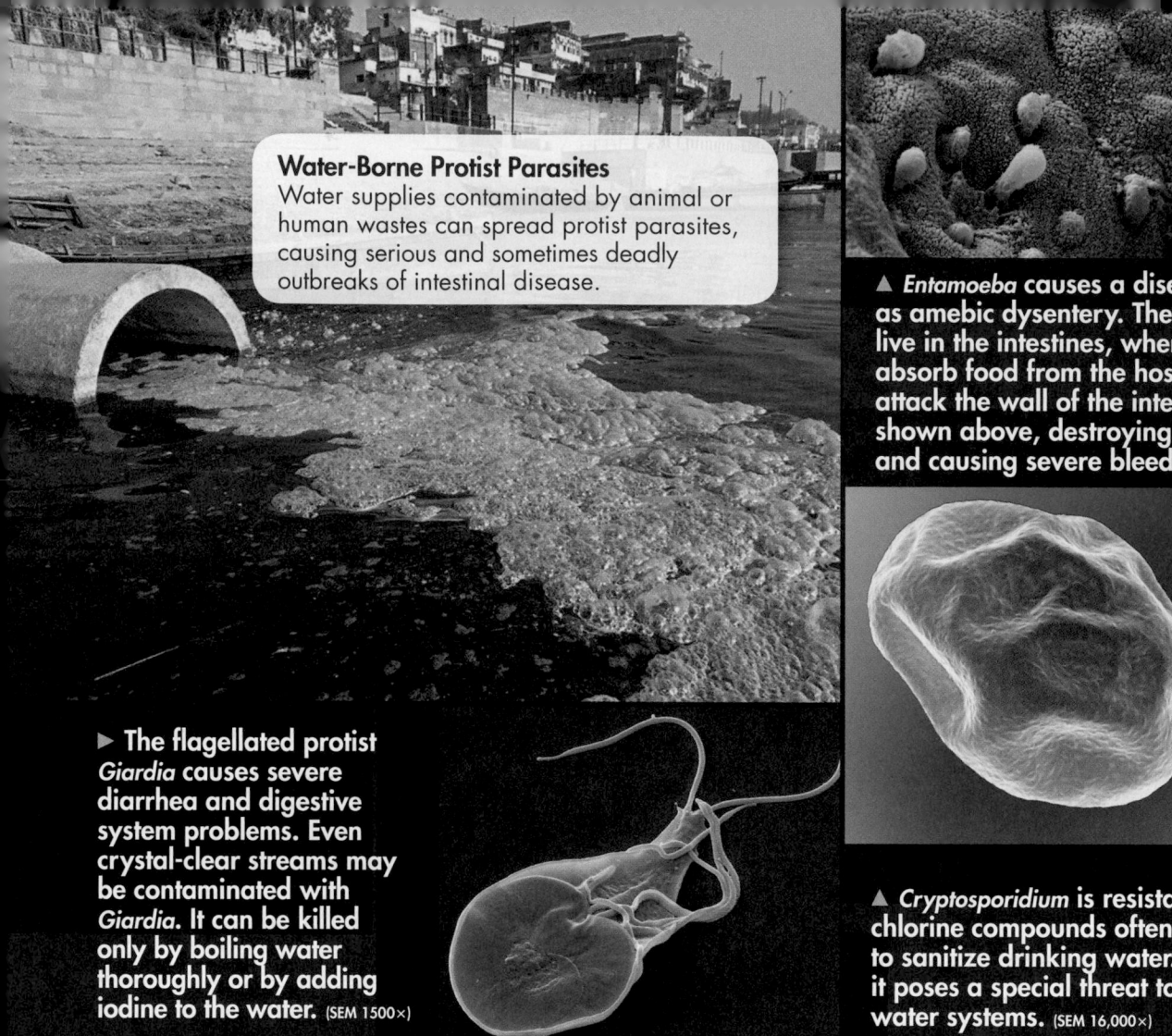

Water-Borne Protist Parasites
Water supplies contaminated by animal or human wastes can spread protist parasites, causing serious and sometimes deadly outbreaks of intestinal disease.

▲ *Entamoeba* causes a disease known as amebic dysentery. The amoebas live in the intestines, where they absorb food from the host. They also attack the wall of the intestine itself, shown above, destroying parts of it and causing severe bleeding. (SEM 2500×)

► The flagellated protist *Giardia* causes severe diarrhea and digestive system problems. Even crystal-clear streams may be contaminated with *Giardia*. It can be killed only by boiling water thoroughly or by adding iodine to the water. (SEM 1500×)

▲ *Cryptosporidium* is resistant to the chlorine compounds often used to sanitize drinking water. Therefore, it poses a special threat to public water systems. (SEM 16,000×)

Parasites and Disease Parasitic protists cause some of the world's deadliest diseases. In humans, they cause African sleeping sickness, malaria, and several intestinal diseases.

► *African Sleeping Sickness* Protists in the genus *Trypanosoma* cause African sleeping sickness. These protists destroy blood cells. They also infect other tissues, including nerve cells. Damage to the nervous system makes some people fall into a deep sleep, or even die. Trypanosomes are spread from person to person by the bite of the tsetse fly.

► *Malaria* Malaria is one of the world's most serious infectious diseases. More than 1 million people die from malaria every year. Malaria is caused by *Plasmodium*. This spore-forming protist is carried by the *Anopheles* mosquito. The art on the next page shows the life cycle of *Plasmodium*.

🔑 **Key Question** What types of symbiotic relationships involve protists? **Many protists are involved in mutualistic symbiosis, in which both they and their hosts benefit. Parasitic protists cause some of the world's deadliest diseases.**

***Plasmodium* Life Cycle** *Plasmodium*, which causes malaria, needs two hosts to complete its life cycle: an *Anopheles* mosquito and a human.

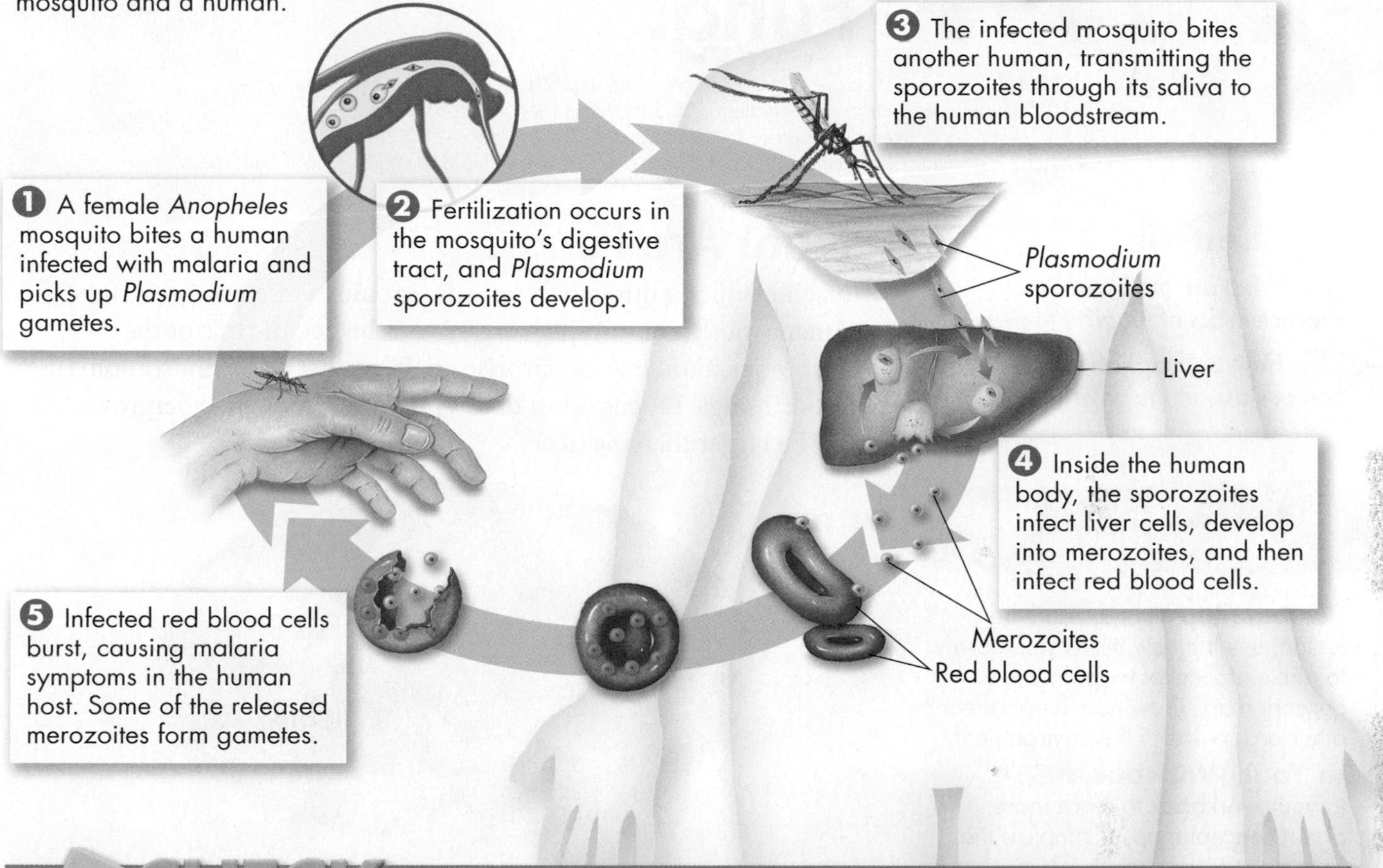

1 A female *Anopheles* mosquito bites a human infected with malaria and picks up *Plasmodium* gametes.
2 Fertilization occurs in the mosquito's digestive tract, and *Plasmodium* sporozoites develop.
3 The infected mosquito bites another human, transmitting the sporozoites through its saliva to the human bloodstream.
Plasmodium sporozoites
Liver
4 Inside the human body, the sporozoites infect liver cells, develop into merozoites, and then infect red blood cells.
Merozoites
Red blood cells
5 Infected red blood cells burst, causing malaria symptoms in the human host. Some of the released merozoites form gametes.

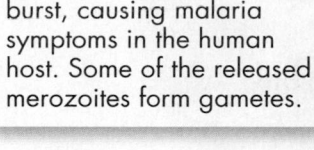

CHECK Understanding

Apply Vocabulary

Use the highlighted words from the lesson to complete each sentence correctly.

1. During the feeding stage, slime molds form a(n) ________.

2. During a(n) ________, the population of algae increases greatly.

3. A ciliate has a small dent on one side called a(n) ________, through which food enters the cell.

Critical Thinking

4. Explain What is the role of autotrophic protists in ocean ecosystems?

5. Compare and Contrast Compare how amoebas, ciliates, and water molds get food.

6. Explain Give one example of mutualism and one example of parasitism by protists.

7. Write to Learn Answer the second clue of the chapter mystery. Explain how the blight organism gets nutrients. Include the words *symbiosis* and *parasite*.

MYSTERY CLUE

The organism that caused the potato blight absorbs nutrients through its cell walls. What organism described in this lesson gets nutrients in a similar way? (Hint: See p. 511.)

BIOLOGY.com Search Lesson 21.3 GO • Lesson Assessment

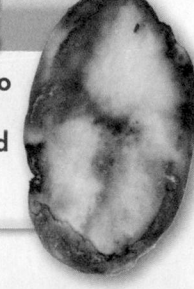

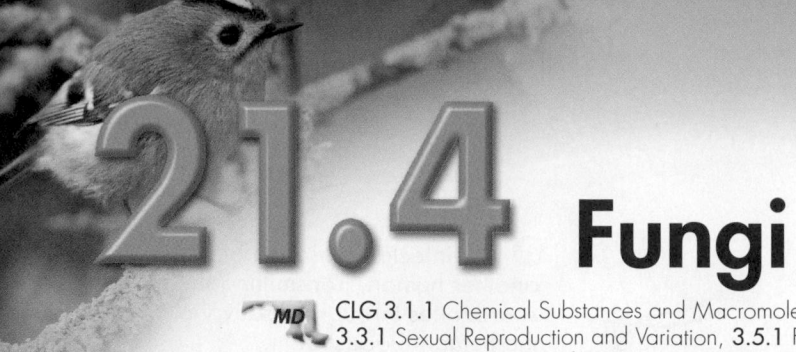

21.4 Fungi

MD CLG 3.1.1 Chemical Substances and Macromolecules, 3.2.1 Processes and Functions, 3.3.1 Sexual Reproduction and Variation, 3.5.1 Factors Influencing Ecosystems, 3.5.2 Interdependence of Organisms in the Biosphere, 3.5.4 Global Food Webs. SPI 1.5.2 Communicate Information, 1.5.7 Classification Systems, 1.5.8 Compare, 1.6.4 Equations.

Key Questions

🔑 **What are the basic characteristics of fungi?**

🔑 **How do fungi affect homeostasis in the environment?**

BUILD Understanding

Concept Map As you read the lesson, use the new terms you learn to make a concept map. In your concept map, show how fungi affect other organisms in the environment.

In Your Workbook Go to your workbook to learn more about concept maps. Complete the concept map for Lesson 21.4.

What Are Fungi?

Imagine walking through the woods. Around a tree, you see a ring of many mushrooms. Which organism is bigger, the tree or the mushrooms? You may be surprised to learn that all the mushrooms are part of a single fungus. Most of this fungus is growing underground. It may be bigger than the tree!

Because many fungi grow from the ground, scientists once classified them as plants. But instead of carrying out photosynthesis, fungi are heterotrophs. They produce enzymes that digest food outside their bodies. Then their bodies absorb the resulting nutrients. Many fungi absorb nutrients from decomposing matter in soil. Others live as parasites, absorbing nutrients from their hosts.

Fungi are eukaryotes. They have cells walls that contain chitin (KY tun). **Chitin** is a complex carbohydrate that is also found in the skeletons of insects. The presence of chitin shows that fungi are more closely related to animals than to plants. (The cell walls of plants contain cellulose, not chitin.)

🔑 **Key Question** What are the basic characteristics of fungi?
Fungi are heterotrophic eukaryotes. They have chitin in their cell walls.

Scarlet Cup Fungus

Structure and Function Fungi may have one cell or many. Yeasts are tiny fungi that live most of their lives as single cells.

Mushrooms and other fungi grow much larger. Their bodies are made up of cells that form long, slender branching filaments called **hyphae** (HY fee; singular: hypha). In most fungi, cross walls divide the hyphae into compartments resembling cells. Each compartment has one or two nuclei. Cytoplasm and organelles can move through openings in the cross walls.

What we call a mushroom is actually the **fruiting body,** or reproductive structure of the fungus. It grows from the **mycelium** (my SEE lee um; plural: mycelia), a mass of branching hyphae below the soil. The structure of a fungus is shown in the art below. The mycelia of some fungi live for many years and grow very large. Clusters and rings of mushrooms are often part of the same mycelium. That means they are all part of one organism.

BUILD
Vocabulary

chitin
a complex carbohydrate that makes up the cell walls of fungi; also found in the exoskeletons of insects

hypha (pl. hyphae)
one of the many long, slender filaments that make up the body of a fungus

fruiting body
the reproductive structure of a fungus that grows from the mycelium

mycelium
a densely branched network of the hyphae of a fungus

WORD ORIGINS

The word *hypha* comes from a Greek word that means "web." If you look closely at the hyphae in a mushroom, they will look much like a tangled web.

Structure of a Mushroom The fruiting body of a mushroom is used for reproduction. The main part of the organism is the mycelium, which grows underground. The mycelium is made up of hyphae.

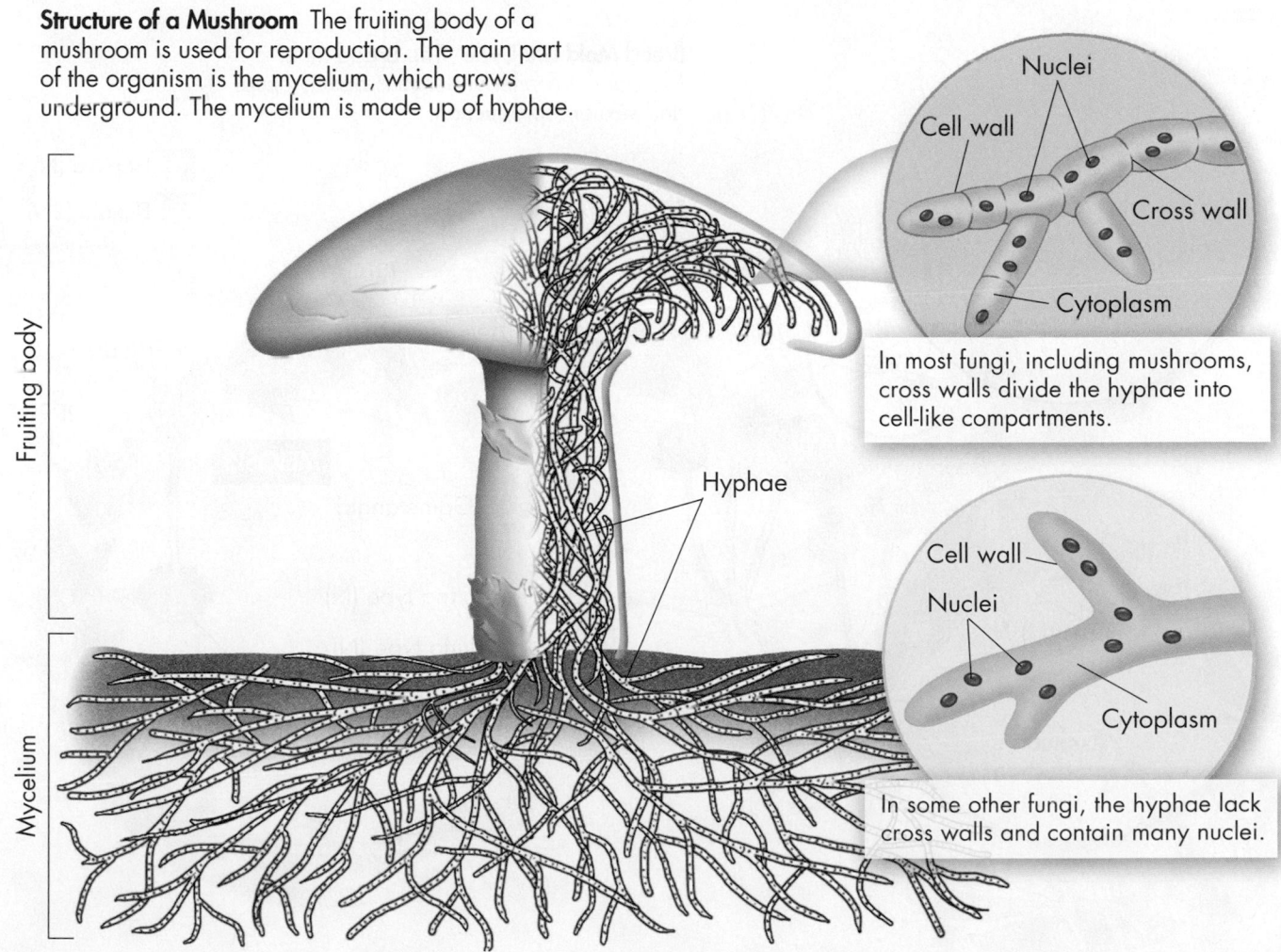

Fruiting body

Mycelium

Hyphae

Nuclei

Cell wall

Cross wall

Cytoplasm

In most fungi, including mushrooms, cross walls divide the hyphae into cell-like compartments.

Cell wall

Nuclei

Cytoplasm

In some other fungi, the hyphae lack cross walls and contain many nuclei.

Reproduction Fungi can reproduce asexually. They do so mainly by releasing spores that can travel through air and water. Other kinds of asexual reproduction include breaking off a hypha or budding off a cell.

Most fungi also reproduce sexually. Sexual reproduction often involves two mating types. They are not called male and female. Instead, they are called *plus* (+) and *minus* (−). When hyphae of opposite mating types meet, they fuse. The + and − nuclei are brought together in the same cell. The nuclei form pairs that divide together as the mycelium grows.

Many of the paired nuclei fuse to form diploid zygotes. Zygotes form within a structure called a zygospore. The zygospore germinates, producing a sporangium. The sporangium releases haploid spores that form by meiosis. Each spore has a different combination of parental genes. Each can grow into a new mycelium.

Diversity of Fungi More than 100,000 species of fungi have been identified. Biologists have used similarities and differences, along with DNA comparisons, to place the fungi into several groups. A major way in which these groups differ is their reproductive structures.

For more on the diversity of fungi, go to the Visual Guide. ♺ **DOL 16–19**

Bread Mold Life Cycle The bread mold *Rhizopus stolonifer* undergoes both asexual and sexual reproduction.

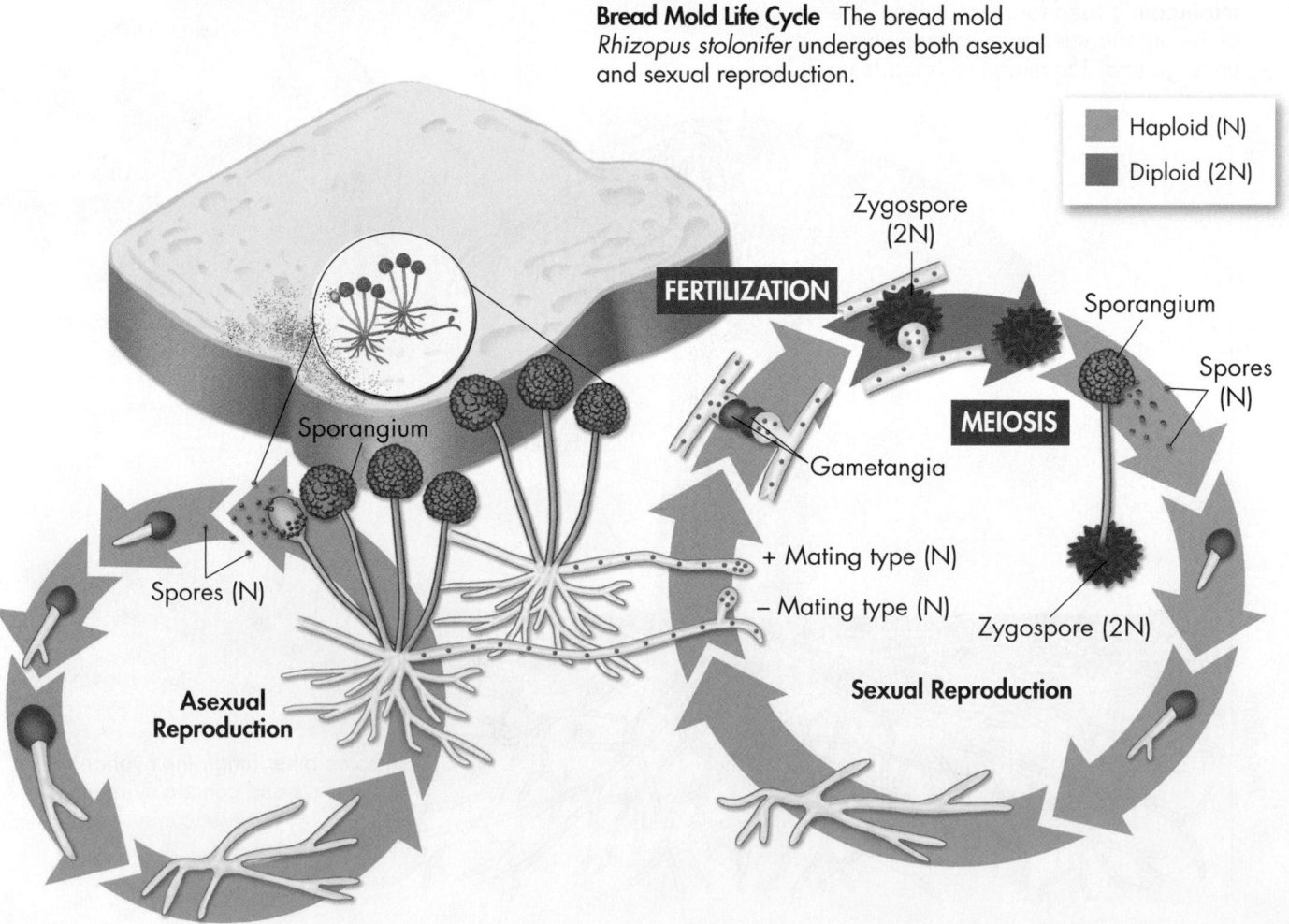

Haploid (N)
Diploid (2N)

FERTILIZATION

Zygospore (2N)

Sporangium

Spores (N)

MEIOSIS

Gametangia

+ Mating type (N)

− Mating type (N)

Zygospore (2N)

Sporangium

Spores (N)

Asexual Reproduction

Sexual Reproduction

The Major Phyla of Fungi

Phylum	Distinguishing Features	Examples
Basidiomycota (club fungi)	Sexual spores found in club-shaped cell called a basidium	Mushrooms, puffballs, earthstars, shelf fungi, jelly fungi, rusts
Ascomycota (sac fungi)	Sexual spores found in saclike structure called an ascus	Morels, truffles, *Penicillium* species, yeasts
Zygomycota (common molds)	Tough zygospore produced during sexual reproduction that can stay dormant for long periods	*Rhizopus stolonifer* (black bread mold), molds found on rotting strawberries and other soft fruits, mycorrhizae associated with plant roots
Chytridomycota (chytrids)	Only fungi with flagellated spores	Many species are decomposers found in lakes and moist soil.

The Ecology of Fungi

Fungi play a major role in nearly every ecosystem. Some fungi that are parasites cause diseases in plants and animals.

Decomposition Many fungi feed by releasing digestive enzymes. These enzymes break down leaves, fruit, and other organic material into simple molecules. The molecules then diffuse into the fungus. Enzymes from mycelia of mushrooms speed up the decomposition of wastes and dead organisms.

Fungi are champions of decomposition. Fungi help recycle essential elements and nutrients. Many plants remove important elements and nutrients from the soil. If these materials were not returned to the soil, other organisms could not use them. Without these nutrients, organisms would die. Eventually, Earth would become barren and lifeless.

Key Question How do fungi affect homeostasis in the environment? **Many fungi are decomposers that help ecosystems maintain homeostasis by breaking down dead organisms and recycling essential elements and nutrients.**

Parasitism Many fungi are helpful to other organisms. But parasitic fungi cause many serious diseases.

▶ *Plant Diseases* Several parasitic fungi cause diseases that threaten food crops. Corn smut, for example, destroys corn kernels. Wheat rust affects North American wheat crops. Some mildews, which infect many different plants, are also fungi. In temperate areas, fungi destroy about 15 percent of crops. In tropical areas, a greater percentage is lost to fungal diseases.

Phyla of Fungi This table summarizes the main differences among four phyla of fungi.

Parasitic Fungi Some fungi are parasites.

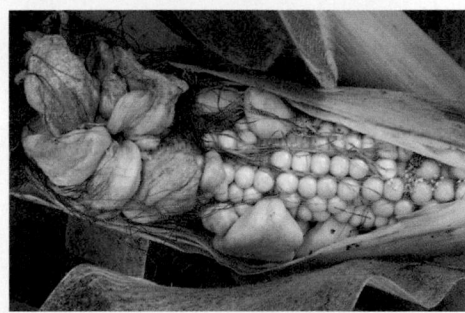

Corn smut infests the kernels of a corn plant, reducing the farmer's crop yield.

A moth is infected by a *Cordyceps* fungus.

Protists and Fungi **517**

lichen
a symbiotic relationship between a fungus and a photosynthetic organism

mycorrhiza
a symbiotic association of plant roots and fungi

RELATED WORD FORMS

Symbiosis is a noun that describes two unlike organisms living closely together. *Symbiotic* is an adjective referring to a symbiosis.

▶ *Animal Diseases* Fungal diseases also affect animals, including insects, frogs, and mammals. One deadly example is caused by a fungus in the genus *Cordyceps*. This fungus infects grasshoppers in rain forests in Costa Rica. Microscopic spores become lodged in the grasshopper. The spores germinate and produce enzymes. These enzymes slowly eat through the insect's tough outer skeleton. The spores multiply in the insect's body, digesting cells and tissues. Eventually, the insect dies. Hyphae develop, covering the insect skeleton. Reproductive structures emerge from the grasshopper's remains. They produce more spores and spread the infection.

Key Question How do parasitic fungi affect other organisms?
Parasitic fungi can cause serious diseases in plants and animals.

▶ *Human Diseases* Parasitic fungi also infect humans. For example, athlete's foot is caused by a fungus. Its mycelium grows in the outer layers of skin, causing sores. Spores from these sores can easily spread to other people.

The yeast *Candida albicans* also causes human diseases. It usually infects the mouth or vagina. *Candida* is usually kept in check by competition from bacteria and by the body's immune system. This balance can be upset by the use of antibiotics, which kill bacteria, or by damage to the immune system.

Lichens Some fungi form mutualistic relationships with photosynthetic organisms. Both partners benefit from these relationships. For example, a **lichen** (LY kun) is a mutualistic relationship between a fungus and a photosynthetic organism. The photosynthetic organism may be a green alga, or a photosynthetic bacterium called cyanobacteria. The green algae or cyanobacteria carry out photosynthesis. This provides the fungus with food. The fungus provides the green algae or cyanobacteria with water and minerals. The fungal hyphae protect the delicate green cells from bright sunlight.

Inside a Lichen The protective upper surface of a lichen is made up of densely packed fungal hyphae. Below this are layers of green algae or photosynthetic bacteria and loosely packed hyphae. The bottom layer attaches the lichen to a rock or tree.

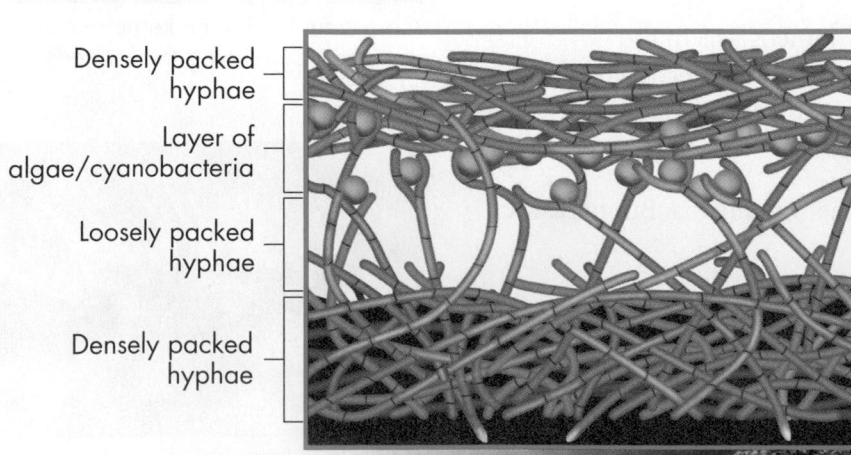

Densely packed hyphae

Layer of algae/cyanobacteria

Loosely packed hyphae

Densely packed hyphae

Lichens can grow in places where few other organisms can survive. For example, they grow on rocks in deserts and on the tops of mountains. They are often the first organisms to enter barren environments. They gradually break down the rocks on which they grow. In this way, lichens help in the early stages of soil formation.

Lichens are very sensitive to air pollution. They are among the first organisms affected when air quality gets worse.

Mycorrhizae Fungi also form mutualistic relationships with plant roots. These relationships are called **mycorrhizae** (my koh RY zee; singular: mycorrhiza). Hyphae of the fungi form a large web connecting the roots and the soil. The hyphae bring water and minerals to the roots. The fungi also make enzymes that free nutrients in the soil. The plants, in turn, give the fungi food from photosynthesis.

The partnership between plant and fungus does not end with a single plant. Mycorrhizae networks connect the roots of many plants. Some networks even connect plants of different species!

Many plants need mycorrhizae to grow. The seeds of orchids, for example, will not grow without mycorrhizal fungi. Many trees cannot live without mycorrhizae. Between 80 and 90 percent of all plant species may form mycorrhizae.

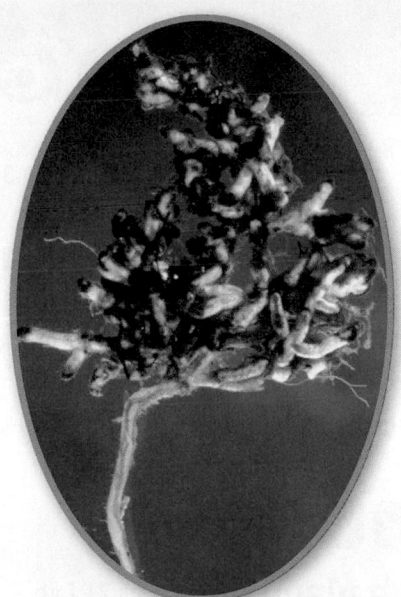

Mycorrhizae Research shows that mycorrhizae on Douglas fir roots help the trees get nutrients from other trees, including trees of other species.

🔑 **Key Question** How do fungi affect homeostasis in other organisms? **Some fungi form mutualistic relationships with photosynthetic organisms that help both partners.**

✓CHECK Understanding

Apply Vocabulary
Use the highlighted words from the lesson to complete each sentence correctly.

1. The _____ is the reproductive structure of a fungus.
2. Fungal cells that form long, slender filaments are called _____.
3. Fungal cell walls contain _____, a complex carbohydrate.
4. A _____ is the symbiotic association of plant roots and fungi.

Critical Thinking

5. **Apply Concepts** What characteristics do all fungi have in common?

6. **Infer** Tissue from several mushrooms found near the base of a tree were tested. They were found to be genetically identical. How would you explain this?
7. **Explain** Describe two kinds of symbiotic relationships that fungi form.
8. **Apply Concepts** Summarize two ways in which fungi maintain the homeostasis of a forest ecosystem.
9. **Write to Learn** Answer the third mystery clue. In your answer, use the words *chitin* and *hyphae*.

MYSTERY CLUE

Using a microscope, scientists found that the infected tissue from blighted potatoes had a network of hyphae. The hyphae cell walls did not contain chitin. Could the blight be caused by a fungus? (**Hint:** See p. 514.)

Design Your Own Lab

MD CLG 3.5.1 Factors Influencing Ecosystems. SPI 1.2.4 Testing a Hypothesis, 1.2.6 Investigative Methods, 1.3.3 Safe Handling of Materials, 1.4.9 Confirm Hypotheses.

Pre-Lab: Mushroom Farming

Problem How does the amount of available light affect mushroom growth?

Materials mushroom-growing kits, spray bottles with water, metric rulers

Lab Manual Chapter 21 Lab

Skills Focus Form a Hypothesis, Design an Experiment, Organize Data

Connect to the Big idea Fungi play an essential role in maintaining homeostasis in ecosystems. Many fungi speed up the decay of dead organisms and help recycle nutrients. Some fungi form symbiotic relationships with plants. These fungi deliver water and minerals to the plant roots. In turn, the plants supply the fungi with sugars. Do fungi grow better in some environments than in others? In this lab, you will investigate how the amount of light affects the growth and reproduction of a species of club fungi.

Background Questions

a. Review What are fungi?

b. Review Describe the general structure of a mushroom.

c. Explain How do fungi that are not in a symbiotic relationship obtain nutrients?

Pre-Lab Questions

Preview the procedure in the lab manual.

1. Infer Where will the mushrooms get the nutrients that they need to grow and develop?

2. Relate Cause and Effect Why will you have to wait about ten days to observe the mushrooms?

3. Apply Concepts The mushrooms you will grow are of a variety that is sold in food stores. Why do the instructions warn you not to eat the mushrooms?

BIOLOGY.com Search Chapter 21 GO

Visit Chapter 21 online to test yourself on chapter content and to find activities to help you learn.

Untamed Science Video Have a look at the fascinating world of mushrooms through the lenses of the Untamed Science crew.

Art in Motion View a short animation that shows the plasmodium life cycle and how malaria is transmitted by the *Anopheles* mosquito.

Art Review Review your understanding of the different structures of a mushroom.

InterActive Art Investigate the structures of an amoeba and paramecium.

Visual Analogy Compare the way boats move to the motion of flagella and cilia in a cell.

21.1 Protist Classification

- Protists are eukaryotes that are not members of the fungi, plant, or animal kingdoms.

- Today's protists include groups whose ancestors were among the very last to split from the ancestors of plants, animals, and fungi.

21.2 Protist Structure and Function

- Some protists move by changing their cell shape. Some use cilia or flagella. Others do not move actively but are carried by wind, water, or other organisms.

- Some protists reproduce asexually by mitosis. Others have life cycles that combine asexual and sexual forms of reproduction.

pseudopod (p. 505)
cilium (p. 506)
flagellum (p. 506)
spore (p. 506)
conjugation (p. 507)
alternation of generations (p. 507)

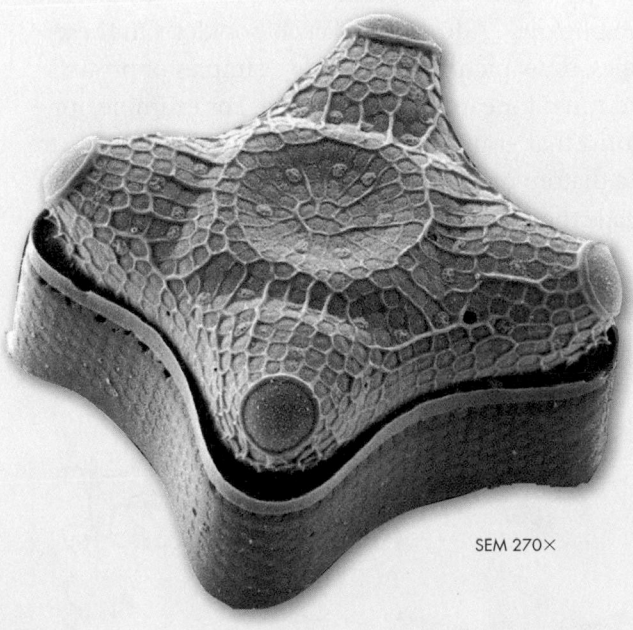

SEM 270×

21.3 The Ecology of Protists

- Photosynthetic protists form the base of food chains in the oceans and in freshwater environments.

- Some protists surround and digest their food. Other protists get food by absorbing molecules from their surroundings.

- Many protists are involved in mutualistic symbiosis, in which they and their hosts both benefit.

- These diseases include several kinds of intestinal disease, African sleeping sickness, and malaria. Parasitic protists cause some of the world's deadliest diseases.

algal bloom (p. 510)
food vacuole (p. 510)
gullet (p. 510)
plasmodium (p. 511)

21.4 Fungi

- Fungi are heterotrophic eukaryotes. They have chitin in their cell walls.

- Many fungi are decomposers that help ecosystems maintain homeostasis by breaking down dead organisms and recycling essential elements and nutrients.

- Parasitic fungi can cause serious diseases in plants and animals.

- Some fungi form mutualistic relationships with photosynthetic organisms that help both partners.

chitin (p. 514)
hypha (p. 515)
fruiting body (p. 515)
mycelium (p. 515)
lichen (p. 518)
mycorrhiza (p. 519)

Assess the Big idea ▷ Interdependence in Nature

Write an answer to the question below.

Q: How do protists and fungi affect the homeostasis of other organisms and ecosystems?

Constructed Response

Write an answer to each of the numbered questions below. The answer to each numbered question should be one or two paragraphs long. To help get ideas, read the bulleted **Hints** below the question.

1. **Why are photosynthetic protists some of the most important organisms in aquatic environments? Give examples of three ocean ecosystems where protists play a key role.**

   Hint Ocean ecosystems include coral reefs, kelp forests, and the open ocean.

2. **How do protists and fungi recycle materials in an ecosystem?**

   Hint Some protists and many fungi are decomposers.

   Hint Fungi release digestive enzymes.

3. **How do parasites affect humans? Include specific details about at least one protist and one fungal parasite.**

   Hint Study the photos of water-borne parasites on page 512.

   Hint When parasites attack food crops, they also affect humans.

Foundations for Learning Wrap-Up

Use the double-door fold you made while reading the chapter to help review how protists and fungi affect the world.

Activity 1 Work with a partner to review the roles of protists and fungi in ecosystems. One of you will quiz the other. The person who has the double-door fold will ask the questions. For example, you could ask: How do fungi that are decomposers affect an ecosystem?

After four questions, switch sides. Continue reviewing the chapter concepts until you can easily answer the questions.

Activity 2 Cut your double-door fold in half to make two booklets. Add pages to each booklet. On these pages, draw pictures that show examples of protists and fungi for each ecological role. For example, for a protist that is an autotroph, you could draw a picture of a diatom or a giant kelp. Write a caption for each image that explains the concept shown.

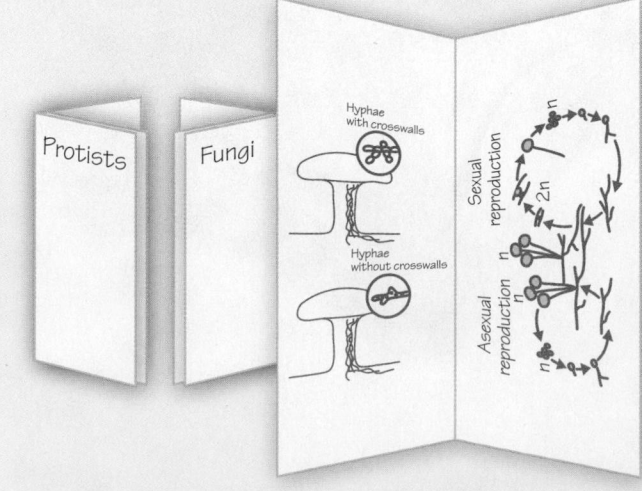

21.1 Protist Classification

Understand Key Concepts

1. Which of the following describes most protists?
   a. single-celled eukaryotes
   b. multicellular eukaryotes
   c. single-celled prokaryotes
   d. multicellular prokaryotes

> **Test-Taking Tip**
>
> **Visualization** Sometimes, it helps to picture a concept in your head or to draw it out on a scratch piece of paper. For example, in question 1, picture an organism for each answer. In this way, you can help eliminate incorrect answers and narrow your answer choices.

2. From what organisms did protists likely evolve?
3. Why is the word *protist* sometimes placed in quotation marks?

Think Critically

4. **Evaluate** Once, any organism that moved or that ate food was classified as an animal. Any organism that did not move or that made its own food was classified as a plant. Why can't this system be used to classify protists?

21.2 Protist Structure and Function

Understand Key Concepts

5. Which of the following is NOT true of amoebas?
   a. They have a rigid cell wall.
   b. They reproduce by mitosis.
   c. They move using pseudopods.
   d. The protein actin powers their movement.

6. Alternation of generations is the process of alternating between
   a. spores and eggs.
   b. diploid and haploid phases.
   c. male and female reproductive structures.
   d. positive and negative reproductive structures.

7. Compare the structure of a cilium and flagellum.
8. Is the process of conjugation in paramecia a form of reproduction? Why or why not?

Think Critically

9. **Apply Concepts** Some protists cannot move on their own. What generalization can you make about how these organisms survive?
10. **Infer** How do you think the ability to switch between asexual and sexual reproduction has aided the evolution of water molds and many other protists?

21.3 The Ecology of Protists

Understand Key Concepts

11. African sleeping sickness is caused by
    a. *Amoeba.*
    b. *Plasmodium.*
    c. *Trichonympha.*
    d. *Trypanosoma.*

12. Which of the following statements about photosynthetic protists is TRUE?
    a. Most photosynthetic protists are heterotrophs.
    b. All photosynthetic protists are closely related to plants.
    c. Giant kelp play an important role in the formation of coral reefs.
    d. Small photosynthetic organisms near the ocean's surface are called phytoplankton.

13. How do mosquitos spread malaria?
14. Describe the relationship between a termite and the protists that live in its gut.

Think Critically

15. **Apply Concepts** Holes in Earth's ozone layer may increase the amount of radiation that reaches the surface of the ocean. If this radiation affects the growth of phytoplankton, how do you think other organisms will be affected? Explain your answer.
16. **Infer** Study the diagram of the life cycle of *Plasmodium* on page 513. Do you think malaria could be transmitted by a blood transfusion? Why or why not?

21.4 Fungi

Understand Key Concepts

17. Which of these is a symbiotic relationship between a fungus and the roots of a plant?

a. fruiting body   **c.** mushroom

b. lichen   **d.** mycorrhiza

18. Distinguish between the terms *hypha* and *mycelium*.

19. How are the cell walls of fungi similar to the exoskeleton of insects?

Think Critically

20. Compare and Contrast Both fungi and humans are heterotrophs. Compare the way fungi get food with the way humans do.

Connecting Concepts

Use Science Graphics

This photograph shows a comparison of a corn plant grown without mycorrhizae (left) to a plant of the same age that was grown with mycorrhizae (right). Use the photograph to answer questions 21–22.

21. Compare and Contrast Which corn plant shows more growth?

22. Relate Cause and Effect What is the most likely explanation for the results shown?

solve the CHAPTER MYSTERY

"A BLIGHT OF UNUSUAL CHARACTER"

In Ireland in the 1840s, conditions were just right for the rapid spread of potato blight. The disease lasted from year to year because the new crop was grown from potato eyes saved from the previous year's crop. Genetically identical crops could not survive the blight.

What clues in the chapter point to the blight's cause? The blight organism had hyphae. It got food by absorbing molecules through its cell walls. These traits are shared by water molds and fungi. But the organism that caused the blight did not have chitin in its cells. So it could not be a fungus. The organism that caused the blight is a water mold—a protist called *Phytophthora*. This name means "plant eater."

Phytophthora hyphae invading a potato (SEM 100×)

1. Relate Cause and Effect The weather in 1845 was unusually wet and cool. How might these weather conditions have favored the blight organism's life cycle?

2. Infer Scientists think that *Phytophthora* came to Ireland with some potatoes from South America. Why hadn't the same organism caused such widespread destruction there?

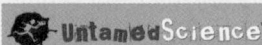 Finding the solution to this mystery is just the beginning. Take a video field trip with the ecogeeks of Untamed Science to see where this mystery leads.

Multiple Choice

1. All of the following are characteristics of some protists EXCEPT
   A peptidoglycan in the cell walls.
   B a membrane-bound nucleus.
   C flagella.
   D cilia.   SPI 1.5.7

2. The structures in *Amoeba* that help the organism move and feed are the
   A flagella.
   B cilia.
   C food vacuoles.
   D pseudopods.   CLG 3.2.1

3. In protists, the process of conjugation
   A is linked to photosynthesis.
   B results in an exchange of some genetic material.
   C produces offspring that are genetically identical to the parent.
   D decreases the genetic diversity of a population.
                                                     CLG 3.3.1

4. Which of the following statements about slime molds is FALSE?
   A Slime molds are eukaryotes.
   B Slime molds play an important part in recycling nutrients.
   C Slime molds are multicellular at some time during their life cycle.
   D Slime molds are photosynthetic protists.
                                                     CLG 3.4.2

5. Algal blooms can be made up of
   A paramecia.   C dinoflagellates.
   B lichens.   D *Trichonympha*.
                                                     CLG 3.5.1

6. Alternation of generations BEST describes sexual reproduction in
   A *Paramecium*.   C *Amoeba*.
   B water molds.   D yeast.   CLG 3.3.1

7. The primary carbohydrate found in the cell walls of fungi is
   A chitin.
   B actin.
   C cellulose.
   D starch.   CLG 3.2.1

Questions 8–10

Ripe grapes are covered with a grayish film, or bloom, that contains yeasts and other microorganisms. A group of students prepared three test tubes of fresh mashed grapes. They heated two of the test tubes to boiling and then cooled them. They inoculated one of those test tubes with live yeast, incubated all three test tubes at 30°C for 48 hours, and then examined the test tubes for signs of fermentation—an alcohol odor and bubbles. Their data are summarized in the table below.

Evidence of Fermentation		
Test-Tube Contents	Alcohol Odor (yes or no)	Bubbles (yes or no)
Unheated grape mash	yes	yes
Boiled grape mash	no	no
Boiled grape mash inoculated with yeast	yes	yes

8. What is the independent variable in the students' investigation?
   A the presence of live yeast   C bubbles
   B an odor of alcohol   D time   SPI 1.2.6

9. What is the dependent variable in the students' investigation?
   A time
   B boiling
   C the presence of alcohol
   D the presence of yeast   SPI 1.2.6

10. What can you conclude from the students' results?
    A Uninoculated, boiled grape mash does not seem to ferment over a 48-hour period.
    B Boiled grape mash that contains live yeast undergoes fermentation.
    C Grape mash does not ferment unless live yeast is added.
    D Both A and B are correct.   SPI 1.4.2

Open-Ended Response

11. How does each of the partners in the lichen symbiosis benefit from the relationship?
                                                     CLG 3.5.2

If You Have Trouble With . . .										
Question	1	2	3	4	5	6	7	8	9	10	11
See Lesson	21.2	21.2	21.2	21.3	21.3	21.2	21.4	21.4	21.4	21.4	21.4

22.4 Flowering Plants

MD CLG 3.2.1 Processes and Functions, 3.4.1 Evolutionary Change. SPI 1.3.1 Use Equipment, 1.3.3 Safe Handling of Materials, 1.4.1 Organize Data, 1.5.7 Classification Systems, 1.5.8 Compare, 1.5.9 Synthesize Ideas.

Key Questions

🔑 What are the key features of angiosperm reproduction?

🔑 How are angiosperms categorized?

BUILD Understanding

Compare/Contrast Table As you read, make a table to compare the three methods commonly used to put angiosperms into groups.

In Your Workbook Go to your workbook to learn more about using tables to compare and contrast characteristics. Complete the table for Lesson 22.4.

Flowers and Fruits

Flowering plants, or angiosperms, first appeared on land about 135 million years ago. They soon came to dominate the Earth. Today, angiosperms are the most abundant organisms in the plant kingdom. Why is this group of plants so successful?

Angiosperms have unique reproductive organs known as flowers. Flowers contain **ovaries,** which surround and protect seeds. The ovary gives angiosperms their name: *angiosperm* means "enclosed seed." After fertilization, ovaries develop into fruits. Fruits surround, protect, and help to spread the seeds.

Advantages of Flowers Most flowers attract animal pollinators, such as bees, moths, or hummingbirds. These animals are drawn by the color, scent, or shape of the flower. When they leave a flower, pollinators carry pollen with them. As they do this, the animals carry pollen to the next flower they visit. Pollination by animals is much more efficient than pollination by wind. Because they make pollination so efficient, flowers are a great evolutionary advantage to a plant.

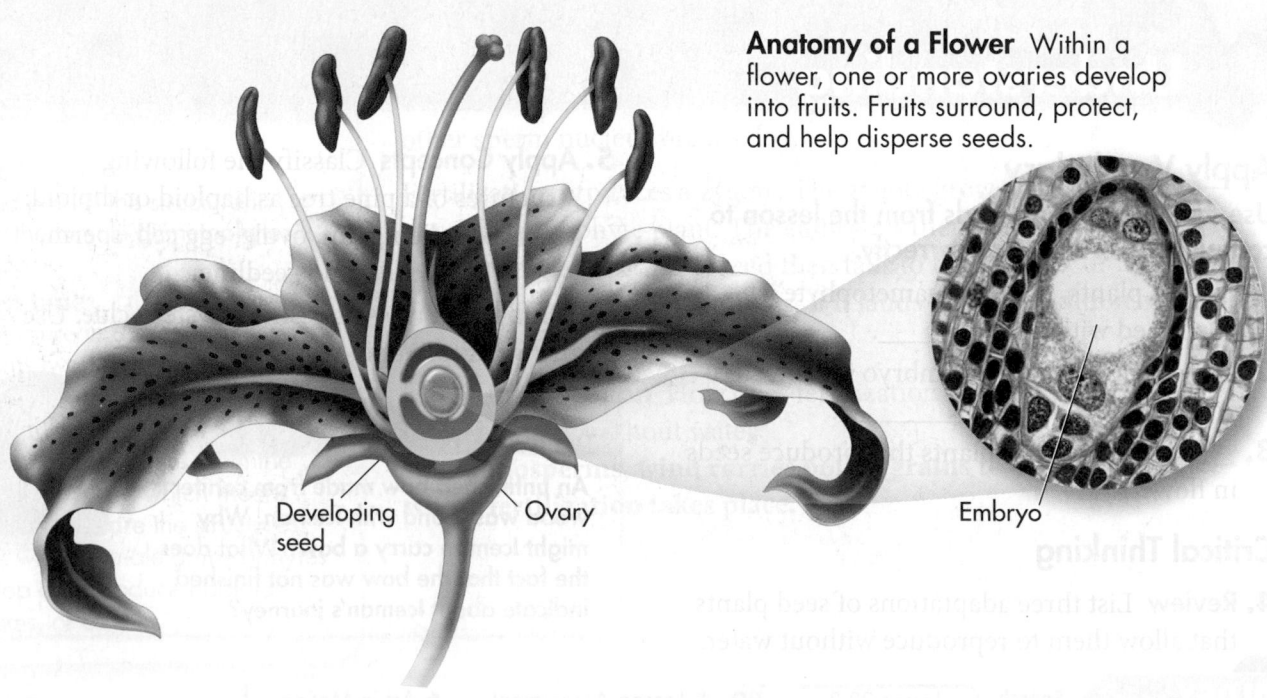

Anatomy of a Flower Within a flower, one or more ovaries develop into fruits. Fruits surround, protect, and help disperse seeds.

Developing seed Ovary Embryo

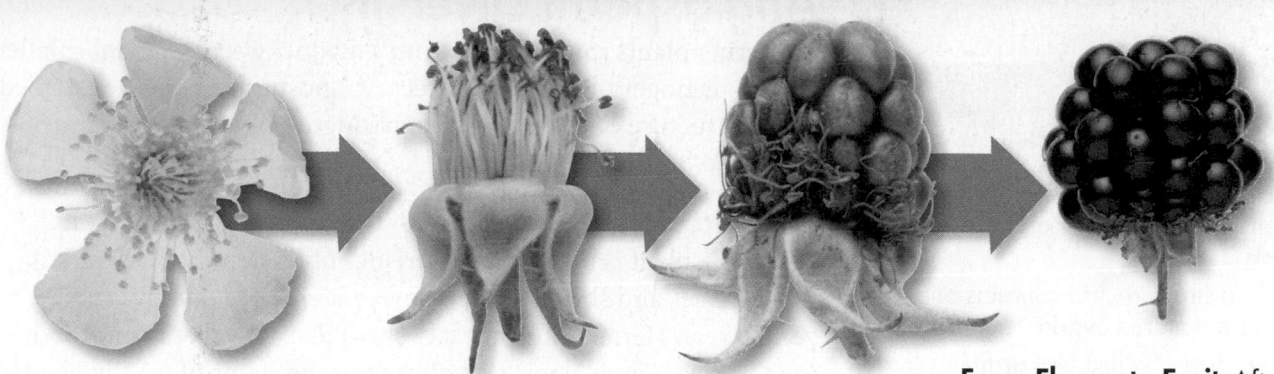

From Flower to Fruit After fertilization, the many ovaries of a blackberry flower develop into a cluster of individual fruits.

Advantages of Fruits After pollination, the ovary develops into a fruit. A **fruit** is a structure that contains one or more seeds. Fruits play an important role in spreading seeds. Consider what happens when a bird eats a fruit, such as a berry. Seeds from the berry enter the bird's digestive system. The bird may fly far from the parent plant before dropping the seeds. In this way, seeds can be spread over large areas of land. Thus, fruits are another reason why angiosperms are so successful.

Key Question What are the key features of angiosperm reproduction? **Angiosperms reproduce sexually by means of flowers. After fertilization, the ovaries develop into fruits. Fruits surround, protect, and help to spread the seeds.**

INQUIRY
into Scientific Thinking

What Forms Do Fruits Take?

Fruits vary widely. Some fruits, such as apples and pears, are fleshy. Other fruits, such as dandelion and maple fruits, have structures specialized for dispersal by wind. Some fruits, such as those of cockleburs, have structures that ensure the fruit is caught in the fur of a passing animal.

Procedure

1. Use a hand lens to examine different fruits. Write down your observations and make sketches of the fruits.

2. Place each fruit in a petri dish and use a scalpel to dissect it. **CAUTION:** Use care with sharp instruments.

3. Locate the seeds within each fruit. Write down your observations and make sketches of the dissected fruits.

Analyze and Conclude

1. Compare and Contrast Make a table that compares the characteristics of the fruits you observed.

2. Infer Fleshy fruits are often spread by animals. Dry fruits are often spread by the wind. For each of the fruits you examined, identify how the fruit is likely spread. Explain your answers.

In Your Workbook Get more help for this activity in your workbook.

ovary a structure in flowering plants that surrounds and protects seeds

fruit a structure that contains one or more matured ovaries

cotyledon the first leaf or first pair of leaves produced by the embryo of a seed plant

monocot an angiosperm with one seed leaf in its ovary

dicot an angiosperm with two seed leaves in its ovary

✦ PREFIXES

Mono- means "one," and *di-* means "two." Monocots have one seed leaf. Dicots have two seed leaves.

Angiosperm Diversity

Flowering plants range in size from tiny duckweed—a plant smaller than your fingernail—to giant trees. Angiosperms can be described by the structure of their stems, their length of life, or the number of their seed leaves.

Woody and Herbaceous Plants One of the easiest ways to describe a plant is by the characteristics of its stem. Woody plants, such as trees and shrubs, have stems that are hard and live from year to year. Herbaceous (hur BAY shus) plants do not form wood as they grow. Their stems are softer than the stems of woody plants. Dandelions, petunias, and sunflowers are herbaceous plants.

Annuals, Biennials, and Perennials Plants can also be described by their length of life. Flowering plants called annuals grow, flower, form seeds, and die in a single year. Cucumbers, pansies, and marigolds are annuals. Many other plants continue to grow from year to year. Biennials, such as foxgloves, grow for two years. Perennials, such as asparagus, can live for many years.

Monocots and Dicots Until recently, scientists classified flowering plants according to the number of seed leaves, or **cotyledons** (kaht uh LEED uns) in their embryos. Plants with one seed leaf were called **monocots.** Monocots included wheat, lilies, and palms. Plants with two seed leaves were called **dicots.** Dicots included roses, tomatoes, and oak trees. Monocots and dicots also differed in the structure of their leaves, stems, roots, and flowers.

🔑 Key Question How are angiosperms categorized? **Angiosperms are often grouped according to the characteristics of their stems, their life span, or the number of their seed leaves.**

Comparing Monocots and Dicots
This table compares the structure of monocots and dicots.

Characteristics of Monocots and Dicots					
	Seeds	**Leaves**	**Flowers**	**Stems**	**Roots**
Monocots	Single cotyledon	Parallel veins	Floral parts often in multiples of 3	Vascular bundles scattered throughout stem	Fibrous roots
Dicots	Two cotyledons	Branched veins	Floral parts often in multiples of 4 or 5	Vascular bundles arranged in a ring	Taproot

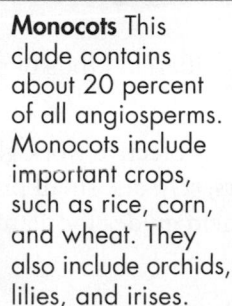
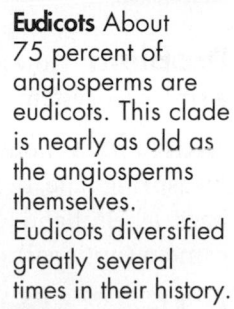

Amborella Clade Only one species still exists in this oldest branch of angiosperms. Its floral parts have a spiral arrangement.

Water Lily Clade The water lilies are another very old group. Early water lily flowers may have been no more than 1 cm across. Today water lilies are large and showy.

Magnoliids This clade contains a wide range of flowers, from species that have small, plain flowers to the dinner-plate sized *Magnolia* flower shown here.

Monocots This clade contains about 20 percent of all angiosperms. Monocots include important crops, such as rice, corn, and wheat. They also include orchids, lilies, and irises.

Eudicots About 75 percent of angiosperms are eudicots. This clade is nearly as old as the angiosperms themselves. Eudicots diversified greatly several times in their history.

Modern Classification Recall that biologists classify organisms according to their evolutionary relationships. Recent studies of fossils and plant genetics show that the history of angiosperms is very complicated. These discoveries are changing how biologists classify flowering plants. The art shows one modern view of how angiosperms could be classifed.

Biologists still classify the monocots in a single group. Dicots, however, have been divided into several different groups. Although it is no longer used in scientific classification, the term *dicot* is useful for describing plant structures. In the following chapters, the term is used for that purpose.

Angiosperm Clades Five major clades of angiosperms are shown here. Scientists are still working out how angiosperm clades are related.

CHECK Understanding

Apply Vocabulary
Use the highlighted words from the lesson to complete each sentence correctly.

1. A plant that has leaves with parallel veins and flowers with six petals is a _____.
2. After pollination and fertilization, the _____ of a flower develops into a fruit.
3. A _____ has two cotyledons.

Critical Thinking

4. **Review** What reproductive structures are found only in angiosperms? Briefly describe the function of each.

5. **Compare and Contrast** List three common ways of describing or grouping flowering plants. How are these three methods different from scientific classification?

6. **Write to Learn** Answer the next clue of the mystery. Use the words *monocot* and *seed leaf* in your answer.

MYSTERY CLUE
Scientists found fragments of wheat in Iceman's digestive tract. Scientists also discovered that the wheat was planted and grown by people. How did scientists determine that the seed fragments came from a monocot? (**Hint:** See p. 542.)

Real-World Lab

MD CLG 3.5.1 Factors Influencing Ecosystems. SPI 1.2.6 Investigative Methods, 1.2.7 Apply Results, 1.3.1 Use Equipment.

Pre-Lab: Exploring Plant Diversity

Problem How many different kinds of plants are in a small ecosystem?

Materials notebook, protective work gloves, measuring tape, tweezers, scissors, small plastic bags, labels, hand lens, field guides for plants, camera (optional)

Lab Manual Chapter 22 Lab

Skills Focus Observe, Measure, Classify, Infer

Connect to the Big idea There are more than 290,000 known species of plants that exist on Earth—from tiny green algae to large-leaved ferns to imposing redwood trees. What do these species have in common? They all need light, carbon dioxide, oxygen, water, and minerals to survive. But plant species vary in the way they obtain and retain resources.

Plants have adaptations that allow them to succeed in different habitats. Thus, you will not find 290,000 species of plants in your community. But you should be able to find a variety of plants. In this lab, you will survey a small ecosystem and identify as many plant species as possible.

Background Questions

a. Review What are the features that botanists use to divide the plant kingdom into five major groups?

b. Compare and Contrast Compare abiotic and biotic factors in an ecosystem.

c. Applying Concepts Suppose an ecosystem includes a stream or pond. Would you include that part of the ecosystem in your plant survey? Explain your answer.

Pre-Lab Questions

Preview the procedure in the lab manual.

1. Design an Experiment What are some ways that you can make sure that you survey all the plants in your ecosystem?

2. Classify What should you do if you are not sure that an organism is a plant?

3. Infer Why might you want to use a regional field guide rather than a national field guide when identifying plants?

BIOLOGY.com   Search   (Chapter 22)   GO

Visit Chapter 22 online to test yourself on chapter content and to find activities to help you learn.

Untamed Science Video The Untamed Science biologists interview plant experts to learn about healing chemicals manufactured by plants.

Tutor Tube Is this plant a girl? Compare animals and plants to understand plant reproduction.

Art Review See how well you can distinguish monocots and dicots.

InterActive Art Review and compare life cycles of vascular and nonvascular plants.

Art in Motion Follow the process of pollination and fertilization in a pine to see how a plant embryo is formed.

22.1 What Is a Plant?

- To survive, plants need sunlight, water, and minerals. They also need to exchange gases with the air.

- Over time, life on land favored the evolution of plants with adaptations that helped them survive the drying rays of the sun, prevented the loss of water, and allowed them to reproduce without water.

- Plants have alternation of generations, or life cycles with two phases. The two phases are a diploid (2N) sporophyte phase and a haploid (N) gametophyte phase.

alternation of generations (p. 530)
sporophyte (p. 530)
gametophyte (p. 530)

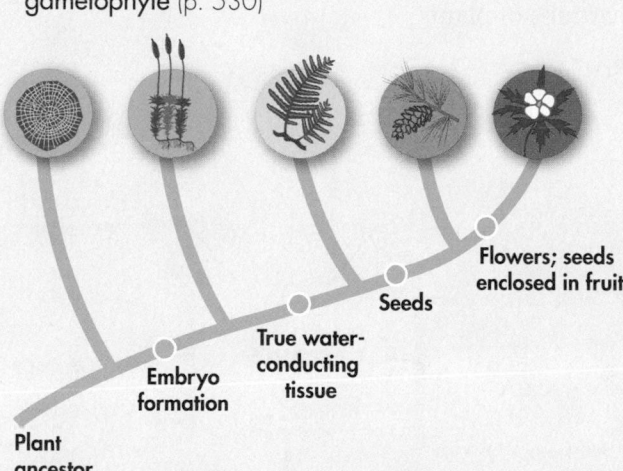

Flowers; seeds enclosed in fruit

Seeds

True water-conducting tissue

Embryo formation

Plant ancestor

22.2 Seedless Plants

- Green algae live mostly in fresh water or salt water; some live in moist areas on land. Some green algae are multicellular.

- Bryophytes are small because they lack vascular tissue.

- Vascular tissues—xylem and phloem—allow the movement of fluids through the body of a plant against the force of gravity.

bryophyte (p. 533)   xylem (p. 534)
vascular tissue (p. 533)   phloem (p. 534)

22.3 Seed Plants

- Adaptations that allow seed plants to reproduce without standing water include cones or flowers, the transfer of sperm by pollination, and the protection of embryos in seeds.

- Gymnosperms do not need water for reproduction, because wind carries pollen grains to female cones, where fertilization takes place.

seed (p. 536)
gymnosperm (p. 536)
angiosperm (p. 536)
pollen grain (p. 536)
pollination (p. 536)
seed coat (p. 537)
ovule (p. 538)
pollen tube (p. 538)

22.4 Flowering Plants

- Angiosperms reproduce sexually by means of flowers. After fertilization, ovaries within flowers develop into fruits. Fruits surround, protect, and help to spread the seeds.

- Angiosperms are often grouped according to the characteristics of their stems, their life span, or the number of seed leaves.

ovary (p. 540)
fruit (p. 541)
cotyledon (p. 542)
monocot (p. 542)
dicot (p. 542)

Assess the Big idea · Unity and Diversity of Life

Write an answer to the question below.

Q: What are the five main groups of plants, and how have four of these groups adapted to life on land?

Constructed Response

Write an answer to each of the numbered questions below. The answer to each question should be one or two paragraphs long. To help you begin, read the **Hints** below the questions.

1. **How did the evolution of vascular tissue affect the structure of land plants?**

   Hint Vascular tissue carries water and nutrients throughout the bodies of plants.

   Hint Mosses and other bryophytes do not have vascular tissue.

2. **Choose a group of seedless vascular plants and a group of seed plants. Then, compare the process of reproduction in these two groups.**

   Hint Ferns are seedless vascular plants. Conifers and flowering plants are seed plants.

   Hint Seeds have three parts: the embryo, the seed coat, and a supply of food. Each has an important role in protecting the young plant.

3. **Why are flowering plants the most numerous group of plants alive today?**

   Hint Angiosperms have two unique structures, flowers and fruits.

   Hint Animals play an important role in two parts of the plant life cycle.

Foundations for Learning Wrap-Up

Use the index cards you prepared when reading the chapter to help you organize your thoughts about the five types of plants.

Activity 1 Work with a partner to quiz each other on what you know about the five groups of plants. Shuffle your index cards and take turns sorting the cards based on whether each card describes green algae, bryophytes, seedless vascular plants, gymnosperms, or angiosperms.

Activity 2 Add one card to your deck and write Plants on it. Starting with the card labeled Plants, lay your cards on the table. Use pieces of yarn to create a cluster diagram that describes the five groups of plants.

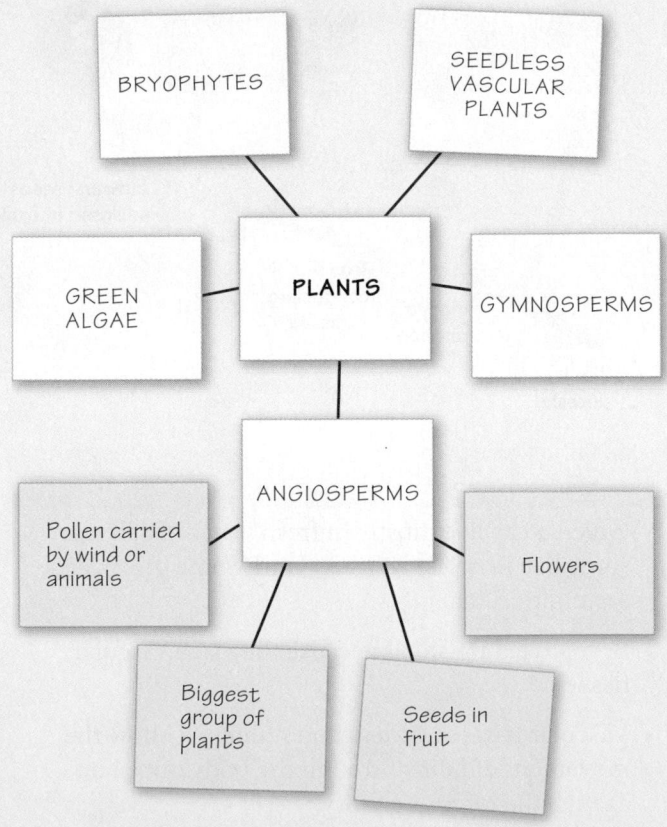

22.1 What Is a Plant?

Understand Key Concepts

1. Which of the following is NOT a characteristic of plants?
   a. eukaryotic cell
   b. multicellular structure
   c. cell walls containing chitin
   d. chlorophyll

> **Test-Taking Tip**
>
> **Process of Elimination** When answering multiple-choice questions, identify answers that you know are wrong. In question 1, you know that all plants are eukaryotes and have chlorophyll. You know that plants have many cells. Therefore, the answer must be **c,** cell walls containing chitin.

2. Two gases that plants must exchange with the air are
   a. oxygen and nitrogen.
   b. oxygen and carbon dioxide.
   c. carbon dioxide and nitrogen.
   d. carbon dioxide and carbon monoxide.

3. Land plants likely evolved from organisms that are similar to which modern group of plants?
   a. green algae
   b. angiosperms
   c. gymnosperms
   d. seedless plants

4. List the two phases of the plant life cycle.

Think Critically

5. **Sequence** Four characteristics that biologists use to distinguish the major groups of plants are flowers, embryos, seeds, and vascular tissue. List these characteristics in the order they arose.

22.2 Seedless Plants

Understand Key Concepts

6. In vascular plants, water is carried from the roots to the body of the plant by
   a. xylem.
   b. phloem.
   c. cell walls.
   d. chloroplasts.

7. In ferns, underground stems are called
   a. fronds.
   b. rhizoids.
   c. rhizomes.
   d. vascular tissues.

8. Why are green algae classified as plants and not as protists?

9. What do seedless plants need for fertilization to occur?

Think Critically

10. **Explain** How does the structure of cells in vascular tissue play a role in the function of vascular tissue?

22.3 Seed Plants

Understand Key Concepts

11. The male gametophyte of seed plants is found in
    a. sperm.
    b. ovules.
    c. ovaries.
    d. pollen grains.

12. Which of the following is NOT part of a seed?
    a. ovule
    b. seed coat
    c. stored food
    d. young plant

13. Describe pollination in gymnosperms such as conifers.

14. What is the function of the seed coat?

Think Critically

15. **Compare and Contrast** Describe how gymnosperms and angiosperms are similar. Then, describe how they differ.

22.4 Flowering Plants

Understand Key Concepts

16. In angiosperms, seeds are surrounded and protected by
  a. cones.
  c. flowers.
  b. fruits.
  d. seed leaves.

17. What kind of plants have life cycles that last several years?
  a. dicots
  b. annuals
  c. monocots
  d. perennials

18. How do woody plants differ from herbaceous plants?

19. How do fruits help spread seeds?

Think Critically

20. **Infer** Some fruits have adaptations that enable the seeds to be spread by wind. How might the structure of these fruits differ from the structure of fruits for seeds that are spread by animals?

21. **Compare and Contrast** Compare the size and function of the gametophyte in mosses, ferns, and seed plants.

Connecting Concepts

Use Science Graphics

Use the photograph to answer questions 22 and 23.

22. **Classify** Study the photograph of the flower above. Is this plant a monocot or dicot? Explain your answer.

23. **Infer** Would you expect the leaves of this plant to have parallel or branched veins? Would you expect the root system to have a taproot? Explain your reasoning.

solve the CHAPTER MYSTERY

STONE AGE STORYTELLERS

Scientists learn more about Iceman as they study the plant materials found with him. The large amount of chlorophyll in the maple leaves is common in spring and summer. Pollen is usually produced in spring. The leaves and the pollen found in Iceman's digestive tract suggest that he died in late spring.

The unfinished bow suggests that Iceman's trip into the mountains was not planned. He may have been running away from an enemy. Scientists later learned that a stone arrowhead was lodged beneath Iceman's left shoulder blade. The arrowhead cut a major blood vessel.

How did Iceman and his people live? The wheat in his digestive tract and other grains found on his clothes show that Iceman's society practiced an early form of farming.

1. **Apply Concepts** A clump of moss was also found with Iceman's possessions. Scientists hypothesize that Iceman used the moss the way that we use paper towels today. What property of moss makes this possible?

2. **Infer** Pollen and seeds are the most reliable plant-related evidence at archeological sites and at modern-day crime scenes because they are long lasting. Relate this quality to their structure and function.

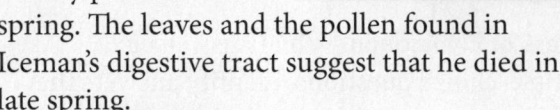 **Never Stop Exploring Your World.** Iceman used plants in ways that made sense for the time he lived in. Take a video field trip with the ecogeeks of Untamed Science to see how far humans have come in realizing what plants have to offer.

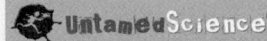

Standardized Test Practice for Maryland

Multiple Choice

1. Which of the following is a basic requirement of plants?
   A sunlight
   B carbon dioxide
   C water
   D all of the above   CLG 3.1.3

2. What stage in the alternation of generations is represented by fern fronds?
   A sporophyte
   B female gametophyte
   C male gametophyte
   D zygote   CLG 3.4.1

3. Which of the following is NOT a characteristic of dicots?
   A branched veins
   B taproot
   C parallel veins
   D two seed leaves   CLG 3.2.1

4. Which of the following is a structure associated with gymnosperms?
   A flower
   B cone
   C fruit
   D enclosed seed   CLG 3.2.1

5. In flowering plants, the mature plant ovary is also referred to as the
   A gymnosperm.
   B pollen grain.
   C fruit.
   D seed leaf.   CLG 3.2.1

6. Which is the largest group of plants?
   A gymnosperms
   B woody plants
   C angiosperms
   D bryophytes   SPI 1.5.7

Questions 7–9

A group of students placed a conifer sprig in a beaker of water. They measured the amount of oxygen given off during a set period of time to determine the rate of photosynthesis. They changed the temperature of the water in the beaker using an ice bucket and a hot plate. Their data are summarized in the graph below.

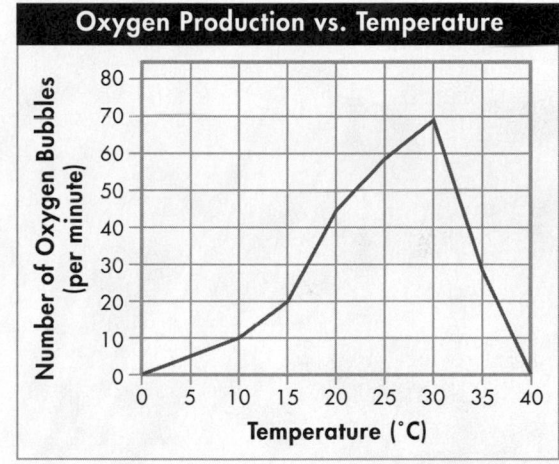

Oxygen Production vs. Temperature

7. What is the independent variable?
   A light intensity   C oxygen bubbles
   B temperature   D photosynthesis rate
                                                         SPI 1.2.6

8. Which variable(s) should the students have held constant?
   A plant type
   B temperature
   C light intensity
   D plant type and light intensity   SPI 1.2.6

9. What can you conclude based on the data?
   A The higher the temperature, the more oxygen bubbles are released.
   B There is an optimum temperature for photosynthesis in this species of conifer.
   C All plants are most efficient at 30°C.
   D The lower the temperature, the more oxygen bubbles are released.
                                                         SPI 1.4.2

Open-Ended Response

10. Explain why seeds were an important adaptation for the success of plants on Earth.   CLG 3.4.1

If You Have Trouble With . . .									
Question	1	2	3	4	5	6	7	8	9	10
See Lesson	22.1	22.2	22.4	22.3	22.4	22.4	22.3	22.3	22.3	22.3

23 Plant Structure and Function

Big idea **Structure and Function**

Q: How are cells, tissues, and organs organized into systems that carry out the basic functions of a seed plant?

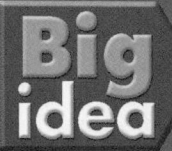

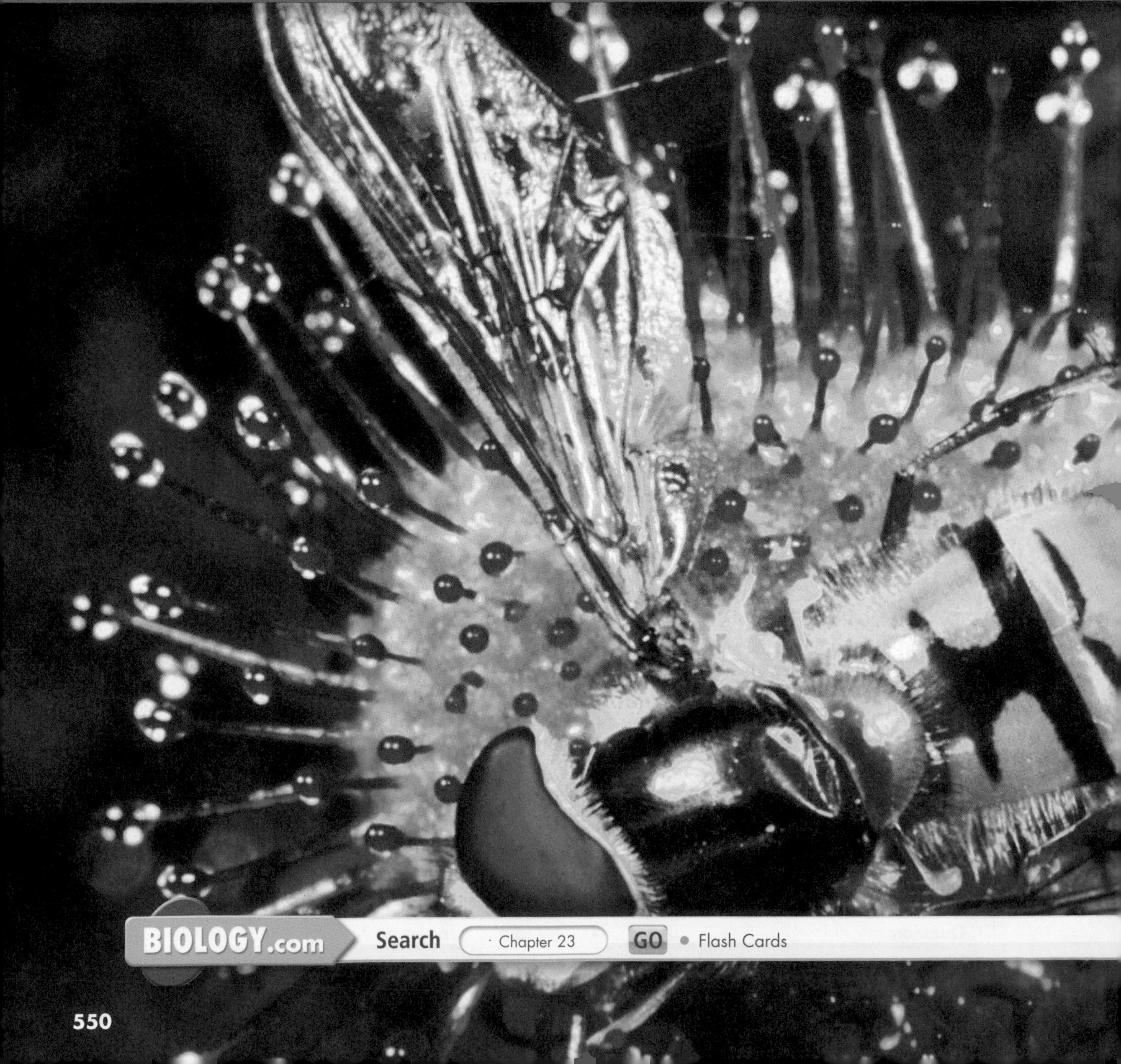

BIOLOGY.com Search Chapter 23 GO • Flash Cards

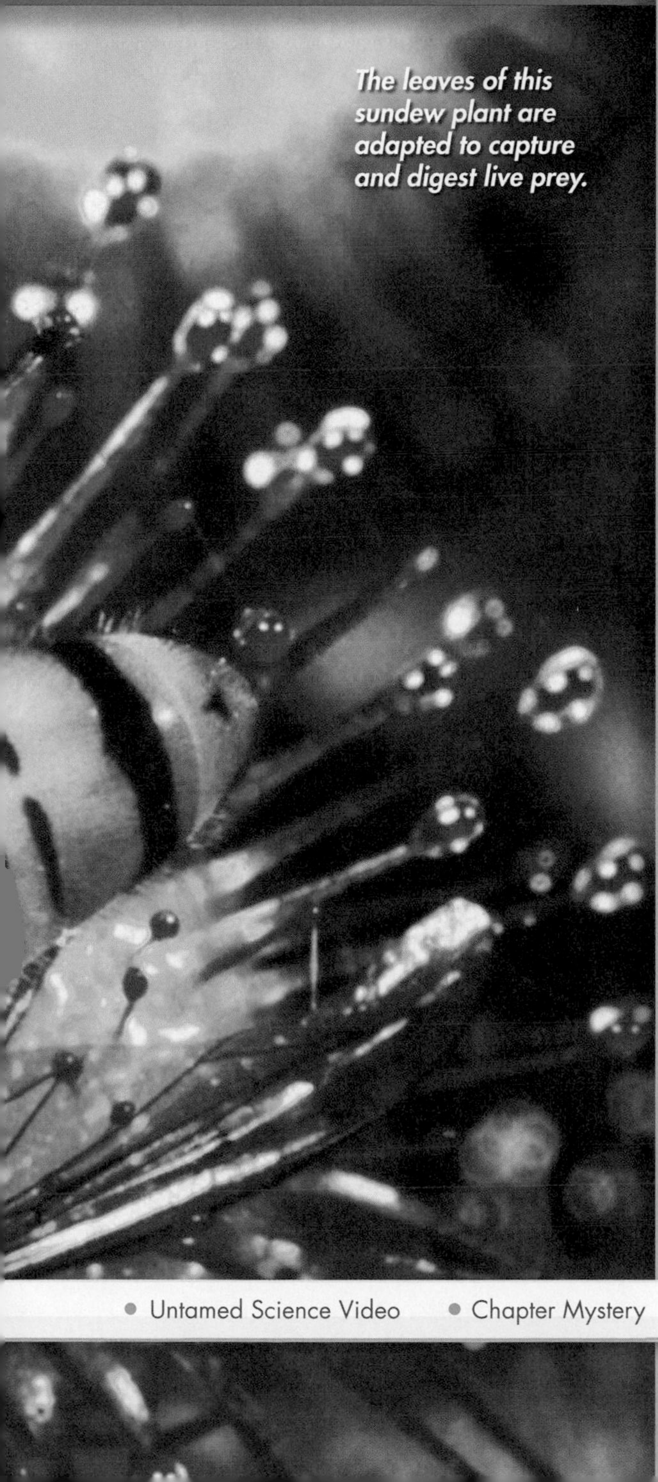

The leaves of this sundew plant are adapted to capture and digest live prey.

CHAPTER MYSTERY

THE HOLLOW TREE

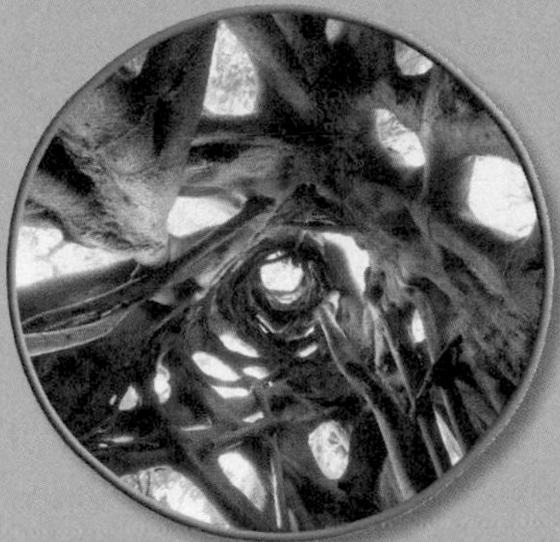

Imagine that you are hiking through a Central American rain forest on a hot afternoon. You see many unusual plants and animals. A monkey calls from a far-off tree, and a dense fog covers the landscape. Then, you stumble on a root and look up. You are standing in front of a huge tree. Its trunk seems to be made up of many tangled branches. Edging closer, you stick your head through a large opening between the branches. You look straight up. Inside, you find that the tree is hollow! This tree, a kind of fig, is indeed unusual.

Read for Mystery Clues What happened to the inside of the fig tree? And how did the tree grow so big if it has no center? As you read this chapter, look for clues that explain the structure of this strange plant.

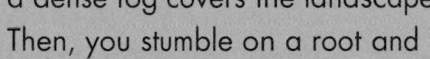

FOUNDATIONS for Learning

Like many living things, plants have cells, tissues, and organs. Fold a sheet of paper in half lengthwise. Then, use a pair of scissors to make five flaps as shown below. On the flaps, write Tissue, Stem, Root, Leaf, and Transport. As you read each lesson, write what you learn beneath the appropriate flap. At the end of the chapter are two activities that will help answer the question: How are cells, tissues, and organs organized into systems that carry out the basic functions of a seed plant?

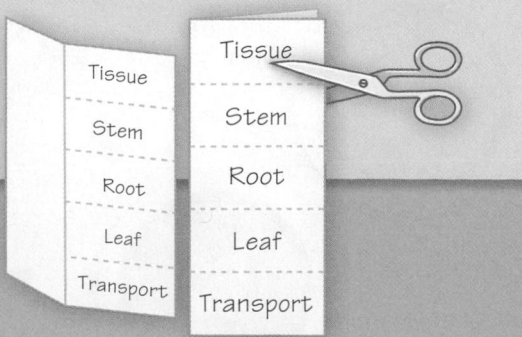

Tissue

Tissue

Stem

Stem

Root

Root

Leaf

Leaf

Transport

Transport

● Untamed Science Video ● Chapter Mystery

23.1 Specialized Tissues in Plants

Key Questions

🔑 **What are the three main organs of seed plants?**

🔑 **What are the functions of the main tissue systems of seed plants?**

🔑 **How do meristems differ from other plant tissues?**

BUILD Understanding

Concept Map As you read, make a concept map to organize the information in this lesson.

In Your Workbook Go to your workbook to learn more about concept maps. Complete the concept map for Lesson 23.1.

Structure of Seed Plants

Have you ever wondered if plants are really alive? Compared to animals, plants don't seem to do much. But if you could see inside a plant, this impression would disappear. Like animals, plants move materials, grow, repair themselves, and respond to their environment. Although their pace may seem slow, plants are, indeed, living organisms.

The cells of seed plants are organized into tissues, organs, and systems. The three main organs of seed plants are roots, stems, and leaves. Recall that an organ is a group of tissues that work together to carry out related functions.

Roots Roots hold plants in the ground and help hold the plant upright. Roots absorb water and nutrients from the soil. They then transport water and dissolved nutrients to the rest of the plant. Roots may also store food.

Stems Stems support the plant body. They contain vascular tissues that carry water and nutrients throughout the plant body. Stems help protect the plant against predators and disease. Stems also produce leaves and reproductive organs such as flowers.

Leaves Leaves are the plant's main photosynthetic organs. Oxygen and carbon dioxide move in and out of the leaf through tiny openings in the surface. Leaves also have adaptations that prevent water loss.

🔑 **Key Question** What are the three main organs of seed plants?
The three main organs of seed plants are roots, stems, and leaves.

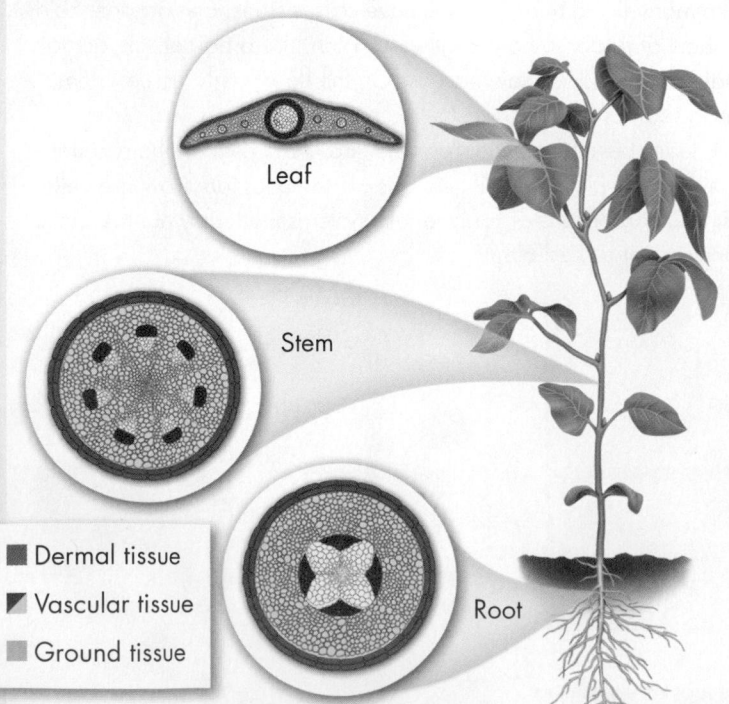

Leaf

Stem

Root

■ Dermal tissue
◪ Vascular tissue
■ Ground tissue

Main Organs of Plants These cross sections of the main organs of plants show that all three organs contain dermal tissue, vascular tissue, and ground tissue.

INQUIRY
into Scientific Thinking

What Parts of Plants Do We Eat?

When you eat your vegetables, you may be eating the leaves, stems, roots, or even flowers of a plant!

Procedure

❶ Examine the outside of an onion, a sweet potato, a cabbage, and an artichoke. Write down your observations of each vegetable. Include a sketch of each vegetable. Label the parts that you see. **CAUTION:** *Do not eat the vegetables.*

❷ Use a sharp knife or scalpel to cut each vegetable in half. Draw what you see inside. **CAUTION:** *Use care with sharp instruments.*

❸ Use your observations to classify each vegetable as a root, stem, leaf, or other plant part.

Analyze and Conclude

1. Classify How did you classify the onion? What characteristics did you use to make this decision?

2. Infer How did you classify the sweet potato? How is its structure related to its function?

3. Infer How did you classify the cabbage? What does its color tell you about its function?

4. Infer How did you classify the artichoke? What does its inner structure tell you about its function?

In Your Workbook Get more help for this activity in your workbook.

Tissue Systems in Plants

Roots, stems, and leaves are linked together by systems that run the length of the plant. These systems produce, store, and carry nutrients. They also provide support and protection for the plant. Plants have three main tissue systems: dermal, ground, and vascular.

Dermal Tissue Dermal tissue covers a plant the way that skin covers your body. In young plants, dermal tissue is made of a single layer of cells called the **epidermis** (ep uh DUR mis). The epidermis is often covered with a thick, waxy cuticle. The cuticle prevents water loss. In older plants, dermal tissue may have many layers of cells. It may be covered with bark.

Ground Tissue Ground tissue makes and stores food. Ground tissue also helps support the plant. The edible parts of plants such as potatoes and squash are mostly ground tissue.

Most ground tissue is made of **parenchyma** (puh RENG kih muh) cells. Parenchyma cells have a thin cell wall and a large central vacuole. In leaves, these cells contain many chloroplasts and carry out most of a plant's photosynthesis.

Ground tissue may also contain two types of cells with thicker cell walls. **Collenchyma** (kuh LENG kih muh) cells have strong cell walls that can bend. These flexible cells help support large plants. Chains of collenchyma make up the "strings" in a stalk of celery. **Sclerenchyma** (sklih RENG kih muh) cells have very thick, hard cell walls. These cells make some ground tissue, such as seed coats, tough and strong.

BUILD
Vocabulary

epidermis
the single layer of cells that makes up dermal tissue of plants

parenchyma
the main type of ground tissue; contains cells with thin cell walls and large central vacuoles.

collenchyma
a type of ground tissue that has strong, flexible cell walls; helps support larger plants

sclerenchyma
a type of ground tissue with extremely thick and rigid cell walls that make ground tissue tough and strong

🖋 WORD ORIGINS

The terms *epidermis* and *dermal* have a common word root: *derm*. This root comes from the Greek word *derma*, which means "skin." Both terms are used to describe an outer, protective covering.

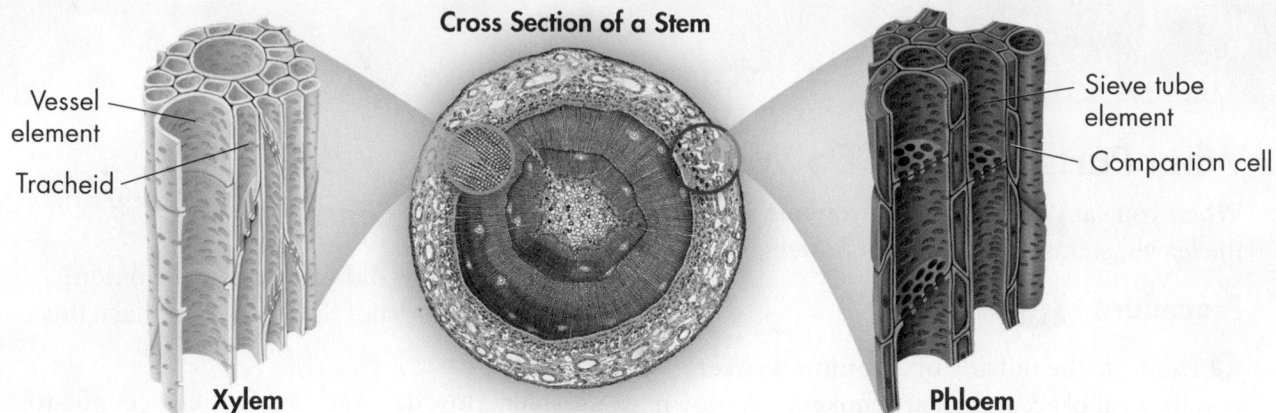

Cross Section of a Stem

Vessel element

Tracheid

Xylem

Sieve tube element

Companion cell

Phloem

Vascular Tissue Xylem and phloem move water and nutrients throughout a plant.

Vascular Tissue Vascular tissue supports the plant body. It transports water and nutrients throughout the plant. One kind of vascular tissue is xylem, which carries water. The other kind of vascular tissue is phloem, which carries dissolved nutrients. Both xylem and phloem cells are long and thin, almost like pipes.

▶ *Xylem* Seed plants have xylem cells called *tracheids*. Tracheids have tough cell walls that help support the plant. These cell walls contain the compound **lignin,** which makes them stiff and strong. As they mature, tracheids die, leaving only their cell walls. Openings in tracheid cell walls let water flow from cell to cell. Thinner areas of tracheid cell walls, known as pits, allow water to move into ground tissue.

Angiosperms have a second kind of xylem made up of cells known as *vessel elements*. Vessel elements are wider than tracheids. Like tracheids, vessel elements die as they mature.

▶ *Phloem* Unlike xylem cells, phloem cells are alive at maturity. The main phloem cells are *sieve tube elements*. These cells are arranged end to end. They form tubes through which dissolved nutrients move. *Companion cells* surround sieve tube elements. Companion cells support phloem cells. They aid in the movement of substances in and out of the phloem.

🔑 **Key Question** What are the functions of the main tissue systems of seed plants? **Dermal tissue protects the plant. Ground tissue makes and stores food and supports the plant body. Vascular tissue supports the plant body and transports water and nutrients.**

Plant Growth and Meristems

When most animals become adults, they stop growing larger. This is not true for most plants. Even the oldest trees produce new leaves and new reproductive organs every year. How do plants do it? How do plants stay "forever young"? The secret of plant growth is found in meristems. **Meristems** are areas of unspecialized cells that produce new cells. These new cells are produced by mitosis. Meristems are found in places where plants grow rapidly, such as the tips of stems and roots.

Apical Meristems Meristems in the tips of stems and roots are called **apical meristems.** Unspecialized cells produced in apical meristems divide rapidly, increasing the length of stems and roots. At first, the new, thin-walled cells look very much alike. Gradually, they develop into cells with specialized structures and functions. This development process is called differentiation. As cells differentiate, they produce dermal, vascular, and ground tissue.

Meristems and Flower Development The specialized cells of flowers and cones are also produced by meristems. The development of flowers and cones begins when genes cause changes in the apical meristem. In flowering plants, apical meristems are changed into floral meristems. Floral meristems then produce all the specialized tissues found in flowers.

🗝 **Key Question** How do meristems differ from other plant tissues?
Meristems are areas of undifferentiated cells that produce new cells by mitosis. These new cells can then differentiate into specialized cells.

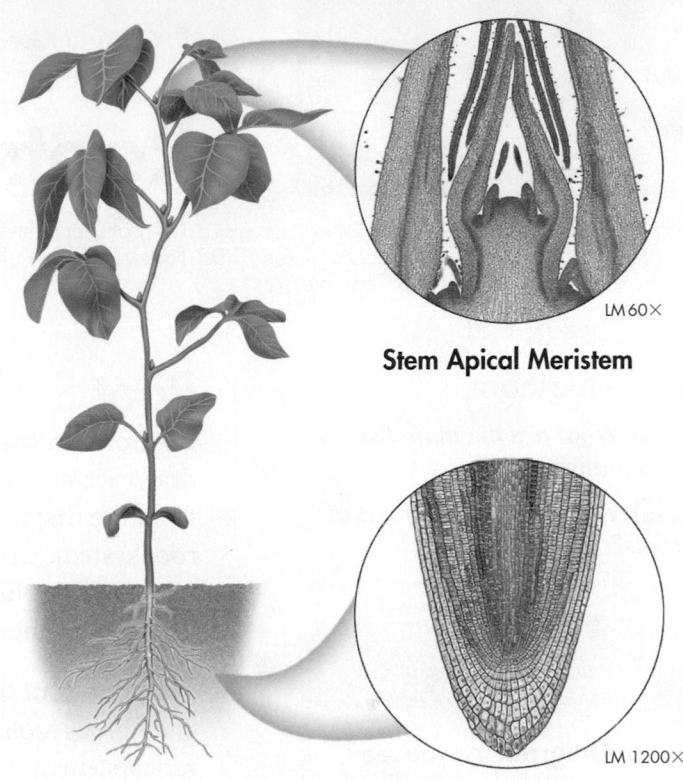
Stem Apical Meristem
LM 60×

LM 1200×
Root Apical Meristem

Apical Meristems Apical meristems are found in the growing tips of stems and roots. Within apical meristems, unspecialized cells are produced by mitosis.

✓CHECK Understanding

Apply Vocabulary
Use the highlighted words from the lesson to complete each sentence correctly.

1. The _____ is dermal tissue that is made up of a single layer of cells.

2. The compound that makes the cell walls of seed plants stronger is called _____.

3. The region that is made up of cells that divide to increase the length of stems and roots is called _____.

Critical Thinking

4. Review What are the three main organs of seed plants?

5. Interpret Diagrams Review the art of the main organs of a plant on page 552. How are the three main organs similar in structure?

6. Compare and Contrast Compare apical and floral meristems. How are they similar? How are they different?

7. Write to Learn Answer the first clue of the mystery.

MYSTERY CLUE

The tangled branches seen in the mature figs are not stems. The seeds of the fig species sprout high up in the branches of other forest trees. These trees are called hosts. What are the "branches" that make up the trunks of these figs? How do they grow? (**Hint:** See p. 552.)

Roots

MD CLG 3.1.2 Homeostasis, 3.1.3 Matter and Energy, 3.2.1 Processes and Functions, 3.2.2 Changes in Metabolic Activity, 3.5.1 Factors Influencing Ecosystems. SPI 1.5.7 Classification Systems, 1.5.8 Compare.

Key Questions

🔑 *What are the main tissues in a mature root?*

🔑 *What are the functions of roots?*

BUILD Vocabulary

root hairs small hairs on a root that produce a large surface area through which water and minerals can enter the root

cortex in plants, an area of ground tissue just inside the root through which water and minerals move

endodermis in plants, a layer of dermal tissue that completely surrounds the vascular cylinder

root cap the tough covering of the root tip that protects the meristem

🖋 PREFIXES

The prefix *endo-* means "inside." The endodermis is the inner layer of the cortex.

Root Structure and Growth

As soon as a seed begins to sprout, it puts out its first root. This root draws water and nutrients from the soil. Soon other roots branch out from the first root. These roots add length and surface area to the root system. Greater surface area lets the plant take in more water and nutrients. Rapid cell growth pushes the tips of the roots deeper into the soil. The new roots provide raw materials for the developing plant.

Types of Root Systems The two main types of root systems are taproots and fibrous roots. Taproot systems are found mainly in dicots. Fibrous root systems are found mainly in monocots. Recall from Chapter 22 that monocots and dicots are two groups of flowering plants.

▶ *Taproot System* In some plants, the main root grows long and thick. This root gives rise to much smaller branch roots. The main root is called a taproot. Taproots of oak and hickory trees grow so long that they can reach water several meters below the surface. Carrots, dandelions, radishes, and beets have short, thick taproots that store sugars and starches.

▶ *Fibrous Root System* In other plants, such as grasses, the root system begins with one root. This root is soon replaced by many other roots of about the same size. These roots grow separately from the base of the stem. They branch so much that no single root grows larger than the rest.

Two Root Systems Dandelions have a taproot system (left), while grasses have a fibrous root system (right).

Anatomy of a Root Roots contain the three tissue systems—dermal, ground, and vascular tissue. A mature root has an outside layer of dermal tissue, the epidermis. It also contains vascular tissue and a large area of ground tissue. The cells and tissues of a root are specialized to carry water and minerals.

▶ *Dermal Tissue* The epidermis protects the root. It also helps the root take in water and dissolved minerals. The cells of the epidermis project outward as long, thin **root hairs.** Root hairs reach into the spaces between soil particles. By increasing the surface area of the root that is in contact with the soil, root hairs help the root take in water and minerals.

▶ *Ground Tissue* Just inside the epidermis is an area of ground tissue called the **cortex.** After moving through the epidermis, water and minerals move through the cortex toward the center of the root. The cortex also stores the products of photosynthesis, such as starch.

A layer of ground tissue known as the **endodermis** completely surrounds the vascular tissue. The endodermis plays a key role in the movement of water and minerals into the center of the root.

▶ *Vascular Tissue* At the center of the root, xylem and phloem make up an area called the *vascular cylinder.* Dicot roots like the one shown at right have a central column of xylem.

▶ *Apical Meristem* Roots grow longer as apical meristems near the root tip produce new cells. The root tip is covered by a tough **root cap.** The root cap protects the meristem as the root tip forces its way through the soil. The root cap also releases a slippery substance that helps the root grow through the soil. Cells at the tip of the root cap are always being scraped away. New root cap cells are added by the meristem.

🔑 **Key Question** What are the main tissues in a mature root? **A mature root has an epidermis made up of dermal tissue. It contains ground tissue, which surrounds the vascular tissue.**

Anatomy of a Root A root has a central vascular cylinder that is surrounded by ground tissue and the epidermis.

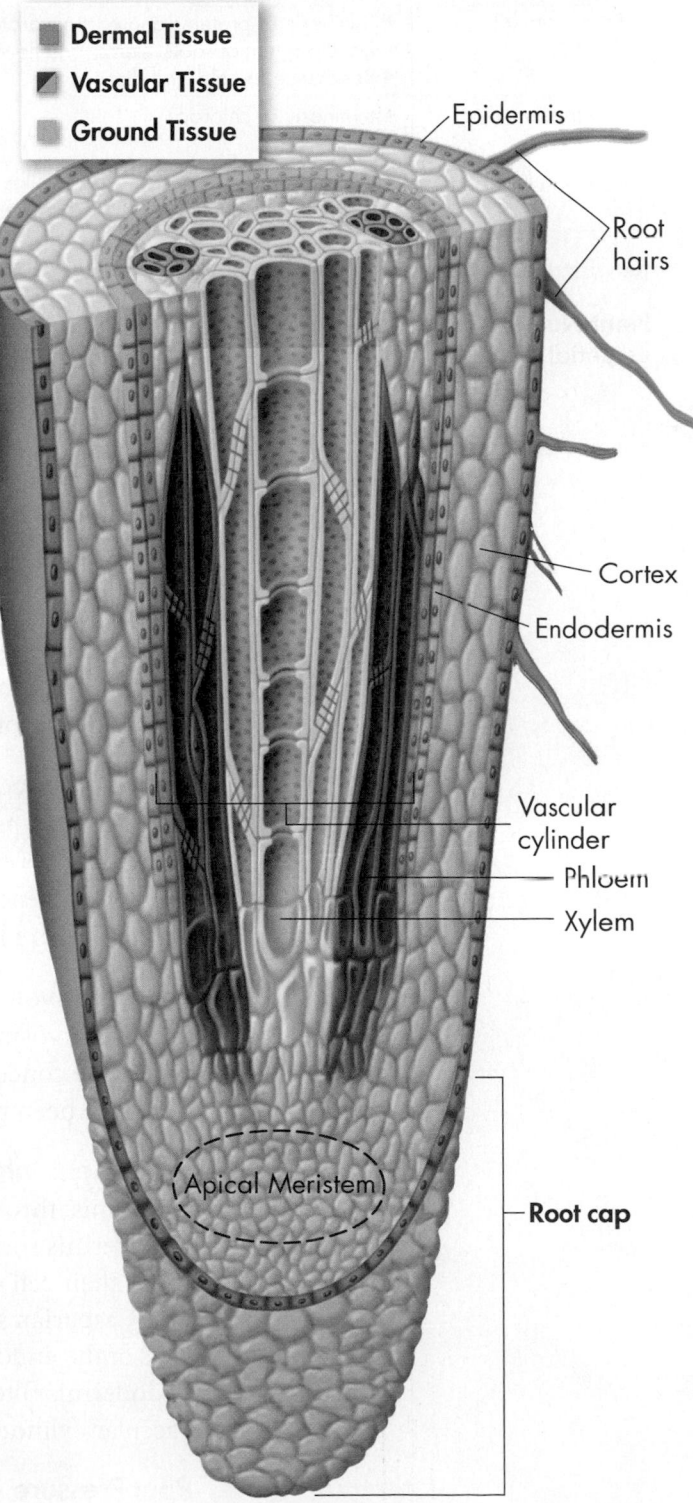

- ■ Dermal Tissue
- ▨ Vascular Tissue
- ▨ Ground Tissue

Epidermis

Root hairs

Cortex

Endodermis

Vascular cylinder

Phloem

Xylem

Apical Meristem

Root cap

Essential Plant Nutrients

Nutrient	Some Roles in Plant	Result of Deficiency
Nitrogen (N)	• Proper leaf growth and color • Synthesis of amino acids, proteins, nucleic acids, and chlorophyll	• Stunted plant growth • Pale yellow leaves ▶
Phosphorus (P)	• Synthesis of DNA • Development of roots, stems, flowers, and seeds	• Poor flowering • Stunted growth
Potassium (K)	• Synthesis of proteins and carbohydrates • Development of roots, stems, and flowers • Resistance to cold and disease	• Weak stems • Stunted roots • Edges of leaves turn brown ▶
Magnesium (Mg)	• Synthesis of chlorophyll	• Thin stems • Mottled, pale leaves
Calcium (Ca)	• Cell growth and division • Cellular transport • Cell wall structure • Enzyme action	• Stunted growth • Curled leaves ▶

Plant Nutrients Plants get many essential nutrients from soil.

Root Functions

Roots have several important functions. Roots support a plant and hold it in the ground. They store food. Roots take in water and nutrients from the soil. But materials do not just "soak" into the root. A plant must use energy to take in water and nutrients.

Uptake of Nutrients To grow, plants need several nutrients from the soil. Those needed in largest amounts are nitrogen, phosphorus, potassium, magnesium, and calcium. Plants also need small amounts of other nutrients, called trace elements. Trace elements include sulfur, iron, zinc, boron, copper, manganese, and chlorine.

Active Transport of Nutrients In the membranes of cells in the epidermis are proteins that can move ions by active transport. (Active transport uses energy to move materials across cell membranes.) These proteins use energy to move nutrients from the soil into the root. This action causes a high concentration of nutrient ions in the root cells.

Water Movement by Osmosis Water moves into the root by osmosis. In osmosis, water moves across a membrane to a place where the concentration of ions is higher. Water "follows" the ions that have been pumped into the root by active transport.

Movement Into the Vascular Cylinder Water moves from the epidermis, through the cortex, and into the vascular cylinder. The endodermis surrounds the vascular cylinder. Where these tissues meet, their cell walls form a waterproof zone called a *Casparian strip*. The Casparian strip forces water and nutrients to move through the cells of the endodermis. Water cannot pass between the cells. The endodermis filters and controls water and nutrients that enter the vascular cylinder.

Root Pressure The Casparian strip allows water and nutrients to move in only one direction—from the cortex into the vascular cylinder. Water and nutrients cannot move from the vascular cylinder back to the cortex.

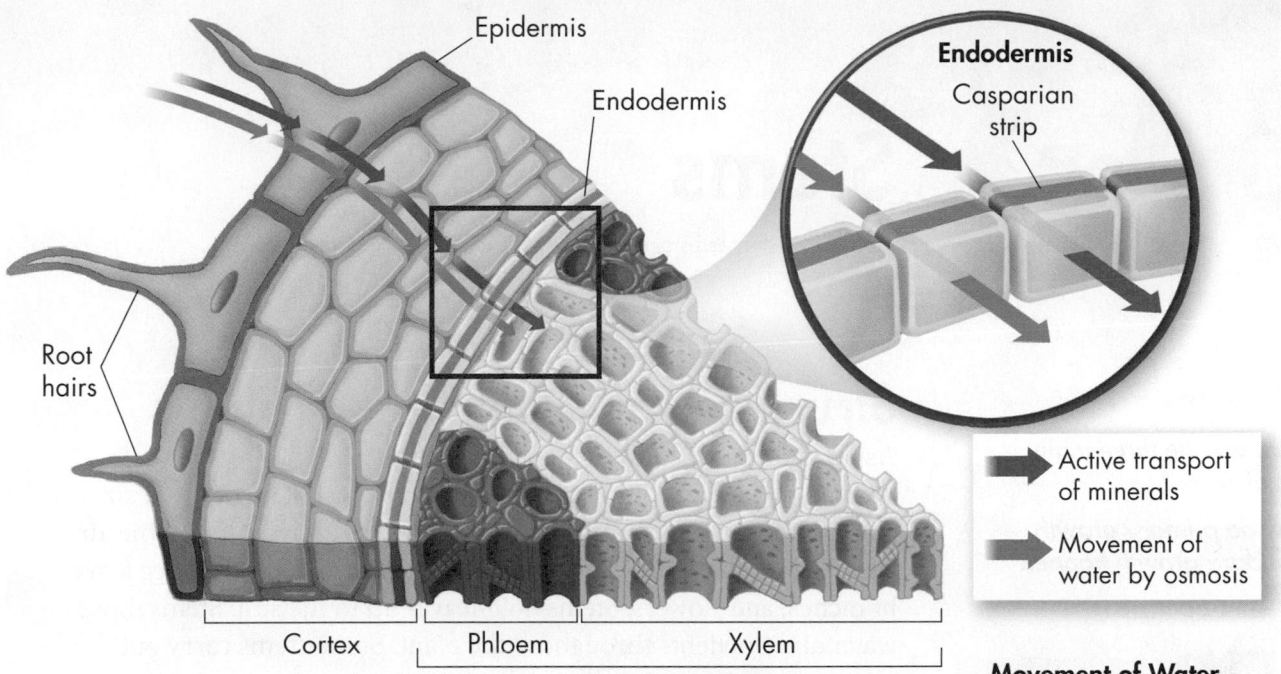

Epidermis

Endodermis

Endodermis
Casparian strip

Root hairs

Cortex   Phloem   Xylem

Vascular Cylinder

Active transport of minerals

Movement of water by osmosis

Movement of Water Into a Root
A root absorbs water and dissolved nutrients from soil.

Why is this one-way system important? As nutrients are pumped into the vascular cylinder, more water follows by osmosis. This movement of water causes strong pressure in the vascular cylinder. That water has just one place to go—up. Root pressure forces water through the vascular cylinder and into the xylem. As more water moves from the cortex into the vascular cylinder, water in the xylem is pushed upward. Root pressure starts the movement of water through the whole plant.

🔑 **Key Question** What are the functions of roots? **Roots support and anchor the plant, store food, and absorb water and nutrients.**

CHECK Understanding

Apply Vocabulary
Use the highlighted words from the lesson to complete each sentence correctly.

1. The tough cells of the _____ protect the apical meristem as the root grows through the soil.

2. The _____ surrounds the vascular cylinder.

3. Tiny projections from cells in the epidermis called _____ increase the surface area of a root.

Critical Thinking

4. Classify Roots contain dermal, vascular, and ground tissue. Name the tissue system to which each of these belongs: cortex, endodermis, epidermis, phloem, xylem.

5. Compare and Contrast Compare the role of active transport and the role of osmosis in taking in water and nutrients. How are these two processes connected?

6. Write to Learn Answer the mystery clue.

MYSTERY CLUE

The fig tree grows slowly until its roots reach the ground. Until its roots reach soil, how might the fig seedlings get nutrients?

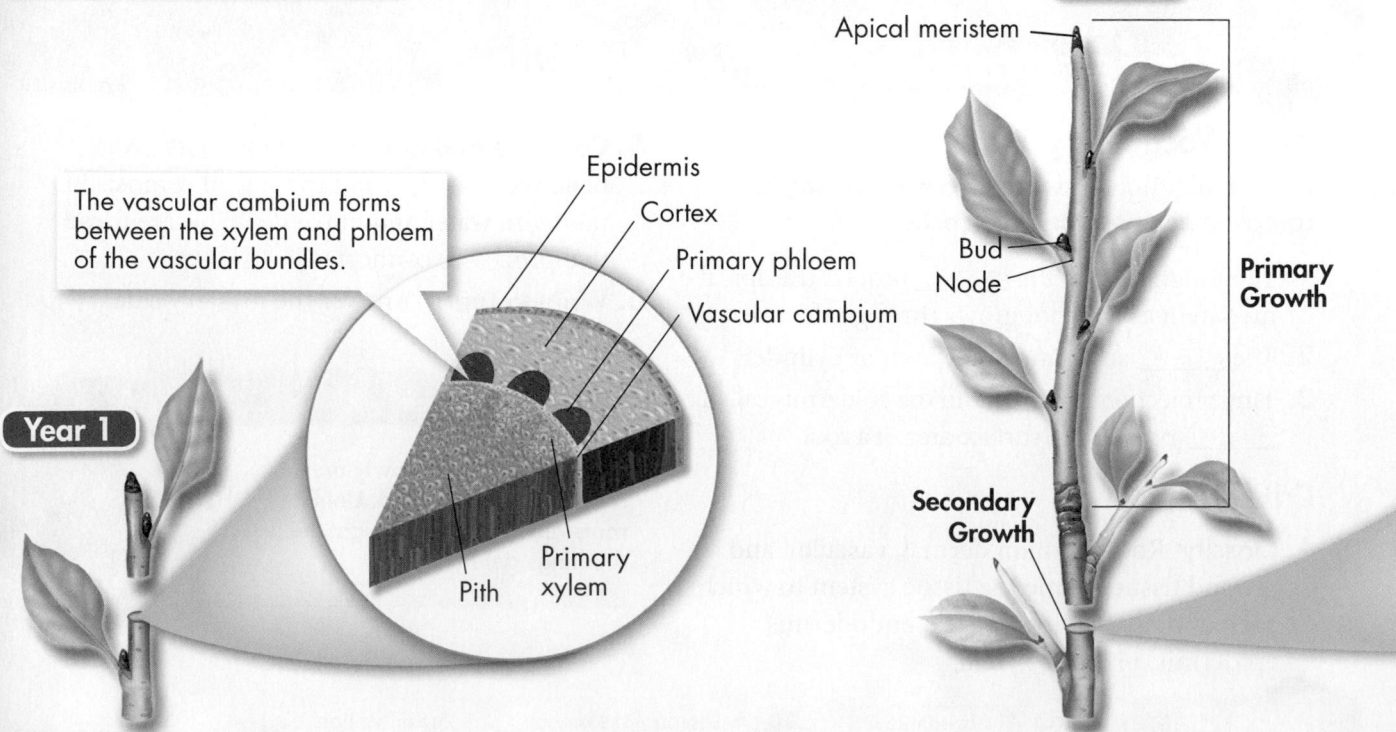

23.3 Stems

MD | CLG 3.1.3 Matter and Energy, 3.2.1 Processes and Functions. SPI 1.5.7 Classification Systems.

Key Questions

🔑 **What are the three main functions of stems?**

🔑 **How do primary growth and secondary growth happen in stems?**

BUILD Understanding

Preview Visuals Before you read, look at the figure that shows wood and bark formation. Define any familiar terms in your own words. List any terms you don't know. As you read, revise and add to your definitions.

In Your Workbook Go to your workbook to learn more about previewing visuals. Complete the table for Lesson 23.3.

Structures and Function of Stems

Asparagus, water chestnuts, onions, and potatoes. What do these vegetables have in common? They are all stems! Stems vary in size and shape. Some grow underground. Others reach high into the air. But all stems have several important functions. Stems produce leaves, branches, and flowers. Stems hold leaves up to the sun. Stems move water and nutrients throughout the plant. Some stems carry out photosynthesis or store materials.

Anatomy of a Stem Stems are surrounded by a layer of epidermal cells. These cells have thick cell walls and a waxy cuticle. The areas where leaves grow out of the stem are called **nodes.** Small buds are found where leaves attach to the nodes. **Buds** contain apical meristems that can produce new stems and leaves. In larger plants, stems develop woody tissue.

Primary and Secondary Growth
During primary growth, the apical meristem produces new cells. These cells cause the stem to get longer. During secondary growth, the stem grows wider.

The vascular cambium forms between the xylem and phloem of the vascular bundles.

Year 1

Year 2

Apical meristem

Epidermis
Cortex
Primary phloem
Vascular cambium

Bud
Node

Primary Growth

Secondary Growth

Pith

Primary xylem

Vascular Bundle Patterns The arrangement of tissues in a stem differs among seed plants. In monocots, clusters of xylem and phloem tissue, called **vascular bundles,** are scattered throughout the stem. In most dicots and gymnosperms, vascular bundles form a ring.

🔑 **Key Question** What are three main functions of stems? **Stems produce leaves, branches, and flowers; they hold leaves up to the sun; and they carry water and nutrients throughout the plant.**

Growth of Stems

Plants grow in ways that are very different from the ways that animals grow. When animals grow, they have set characteristics. For example, cows have four legs, ants have six legs, and spiders have eight. But roses, tomatoes, and other plants don't have a set number of branches, roots, or leaves. Even so, plant growth is carefully controlled. Each species has a typical size and shape.

Primary Growth Apical meristems produce new cells throughout the plant's lifetime. These cells add length to the roots and stems. This growth, which happens at the tips of shoots and roots, is called primary growth. **Primary growth** occurs when cells produced in the apical meristem become longer. Primary growth takes place in the stems of all seed plants.

BUILD Vocabulary

node the part on a growing stem where a leaf is attached

bud a plant structure containing apical meristem tissue that can produce new stems and leaves

vascular bundle clusters of xylem and phloem tissue in stems

primary growth a pattern of growth that takes place at the tips and shoots of a plant

secondary growth the type of growth in which stems increase in thickness

📖 ACADEMIC WORDS

Adjectives are words that describe nouns. Some describe order. *Primary* identifies something that comes first. *Secondary* identifies what happens next. Primary growth happens first. Secondary growth follows primary growth.

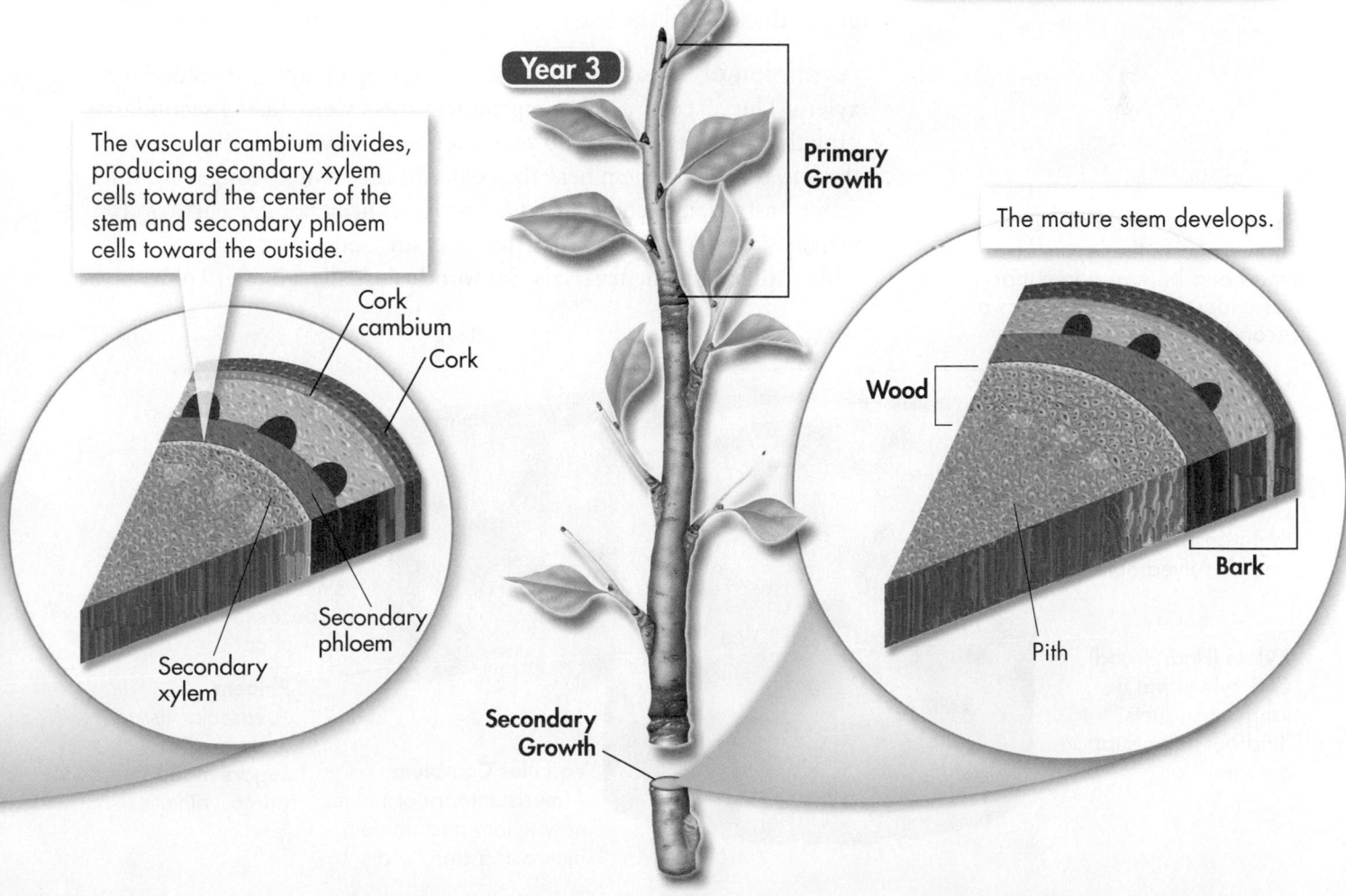

The vascular cambium divides, producing secondary xylem cells toward the center of the stem and secondary phloem cells toward the outside.

Cork cambium

Cork

Secondary phloem

Secondary xylem

Year 3

Primary Growth

Secondary Growth

The mature stem develops.

Wood

Pith

Bark

vascular cambium a meristem that produces vascular tissues and increases the thickness of stems

cork cambium a meristem that produces the outer covering of stems during secondary growth

🔹 WORD ORIGIN

The word *cambium* comes from a Latin word that means "exchange." Both the vascular cambium and the cork cambium produce vascular tissue cells that will be involved in the exchange of materials within the plant.

Secondary Growth As a plant grows larger, the older stems and roots have more weight to support. They also need to move greater amounts of fluid through their vascular tissues. As a result, stems must increase in thickness as well as in length. The increase in thickness is known as **secondary growth.**

Secondary growth is common among dicots and conifers. These plants have meristems in their stems and roots that can produce secondary growth. Secondary growth lets shrubs and trees grow tall. The increase in stem width supports the extra weight. Secondary growth is rare in monocots. As a result, monocots are often limited in size.

In stems, secondary growth takes place in two tissues—vascular cambium and cork cambium. **Vascular cambium** is a meristem that produces vascular tissues. Another meristem, **cork cambium,** produces the outer covering of stems. Similar kinds of cambium tissue play a role in root growth. The addition of cells in the cambium layers increases the thickness of stems and roots.

Growth From the Vascular Cambium In the stem of a young dicot, vascular bundles are arranged in a ring. A thin layer of vascular cambium forms between the xylem and phloem of each vascular bundle. As cells in the vascular cambium divide, new layers of xylem and phloem form. This growth makes the stem get wider. Each year, the cambium makes new layers of vascular tissue. Over time, the stem grows thicker and thicker.

Formation of Wood Most wood is made up of layers of secondary xylem. The vascular cambium produces this xylem during secondary growth. The xylem builds up year after year. As woody stems grow thicker, the older xylem near the center of the stem no longer conducts water. Instead, it becomes what is known as *heartwood.* Heartwood usually darkens with age. Heartwood is surrounded by *sapwood,* which still conducts materials. Sapwood is usually a lighter color.

Formation of Wood and Bark
This art shows the layers of wood and bark in a tree that has undergone several years of secondary growth.

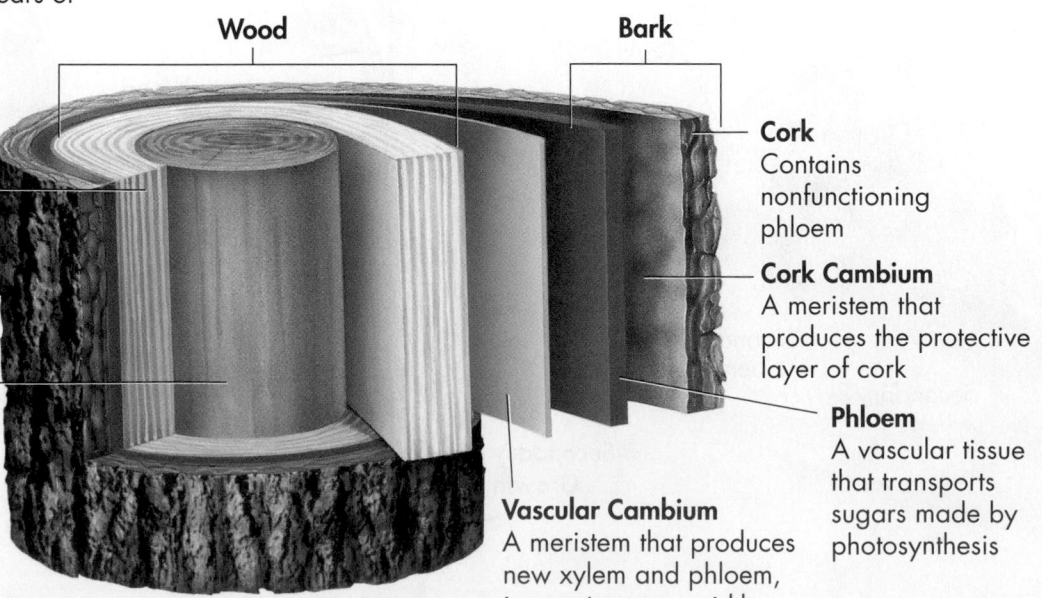

Wood

Bark

Xylem (Sapwood)
Contains active xylem that transports water and dissolved nutrients

Xylem (Heartwood)
Old xylem that no longer conducts fluid but helps support the tree

Cork
Contains nonfunctioning phloem

Cork Cambium
A meristem that produces the protective layer of cork

Phloem
A vascular tissue that transports sugars made by photosynthesis

Vascular Cambium
A meristem that produces new xylem and phloem, increasing stem width

Tree Rings In most of the temperate zone, tree growth is seasonal. When growth begins in the spring, the vascular cambium grows rapidly. Early growth produces large, light-colored xylem cells with thin cell walls. The result is a light-colored layer of wood. As the growing season continues, new cells become smaller and have thicker cell walls. As a result, a layer of darker wood forms. The alternation of light and dark wood produces tree rings. Little growth occurs during the winter or dry season, so there is usually a sharp boundary between rings.

Usually, each tree ring corresponds to a year of growth. By counting the rings in the cross section of a tree, you can estimate the tree's age. The size of the tree rings also provides information about weather conditions. For example, thick tree rings show that weather conditions were favorable for tree growth. There was plenty of rain. Thin rings show unfavorable conditions, such as a dry year.

Formation of Bark In a stem, all of the tissues found outside the vascular cambium make up the *bark*. Bark includes phloem, the cork cambium, and cork. During secondary growth, the vascular cambium adds secondary phloem to the bark.

🔑 **Key Question** How do primary growth and secondary growth happen in stems? **Primary growth is the result of the lengthening of cells produced in apical meristems. It takes place in all seed plants. Secondary growth increases the thickness of stems. It occurs in the vascular and cork cambiums of many dicots and conifers.**

Tree Rings A tree's age can be measured by counting its growth rings. The growing conditions for each year can be inferred by comparing the width and color of each ring.

CHECK Understanding

Apply Vocabulary
Use the highlighted words from the lesson to complete each sentence correctly.

1. The part of a stem where a leaf is attached is a _____.

2. A structure that holds apical meristem tissues that can produce new stems and leaves is a _____.

3. The clusters of xylem and phloem tissues found in stems are called _____.

Critical Thinking

4. **Apply Concepts** How do stems support the functions of leaves and roots?

5. **Explain** Which meristem is involved in primary growth? Which two meristems are involved in secondary growth? Briefly describe the role of each.

6. **Write to Learn** Answer the mystery clue question. Use the words *primary growth* and *secondary growth* in your answer.

MYSTERY CLUE

As the fig grows, the roots grow in both length and thickness. The roots wrap around the host tree's trunk. How might this growth affect the host? (**Hint:** See p. 561.)

23.4 Leaves

MD CLG 3.1.2 Homeostasis, 3.1.3 Matter and Energy, 3.2.1 Processes and Functions, 3.2.2 Changes in Metabolic Activity. SPI 1.5.2 Communicate Information, 1.5.5 Create and Interpret Graphics, 1.5.7 Classification Systems.

Key Questions

🔑 How is the structure of a leaf adapted to make photosynthesis more efficient?

🔑 What is the role of stomata in maintaining homeostasis?

BUILD Understanding

Preview Visuals Before you read, look at the figure of leaf anatomy. Find the three main tissue systems. After you read, identify which tissue system makes up leaf veins.

In Your Workbook Go to your workbook to learn more about previewing visuals.

Structure and Function of Leaves

Leaves are the world's most important factories. Using the energy captured in photosynthesis, plants make the sugars, starches, and oils that feed nearly all land animals. In photosynthesis, plants use carbon dioxide and water to produce sugars and oxygen.

Anatomy of a Leaf The structure of a leaf is ideal for carrying out photosynthesis. To collect as much light as possible, most leaves are thin and flat.

▶ *Epidermis* A tough epidermis covers the top and bottom of most leaves. The epidermis is coated with a waxy cuticle that limits the loss of water. Small openings in the epidermis called **stomata** (singular: stoma) let gases move in and out of the leaf.

▶ *Mesophyll* Photosynthesis takes place in specialized ground tissue called **mesophyll** (MES uh fil). Beneath the upper epidermis is *palisade mesophyll*. Palisade mesophyll is made of closely packed cells that absorb light. Beneath the palisade mesophyll is *spongy mesophyll*, which has many air spaces between cells.

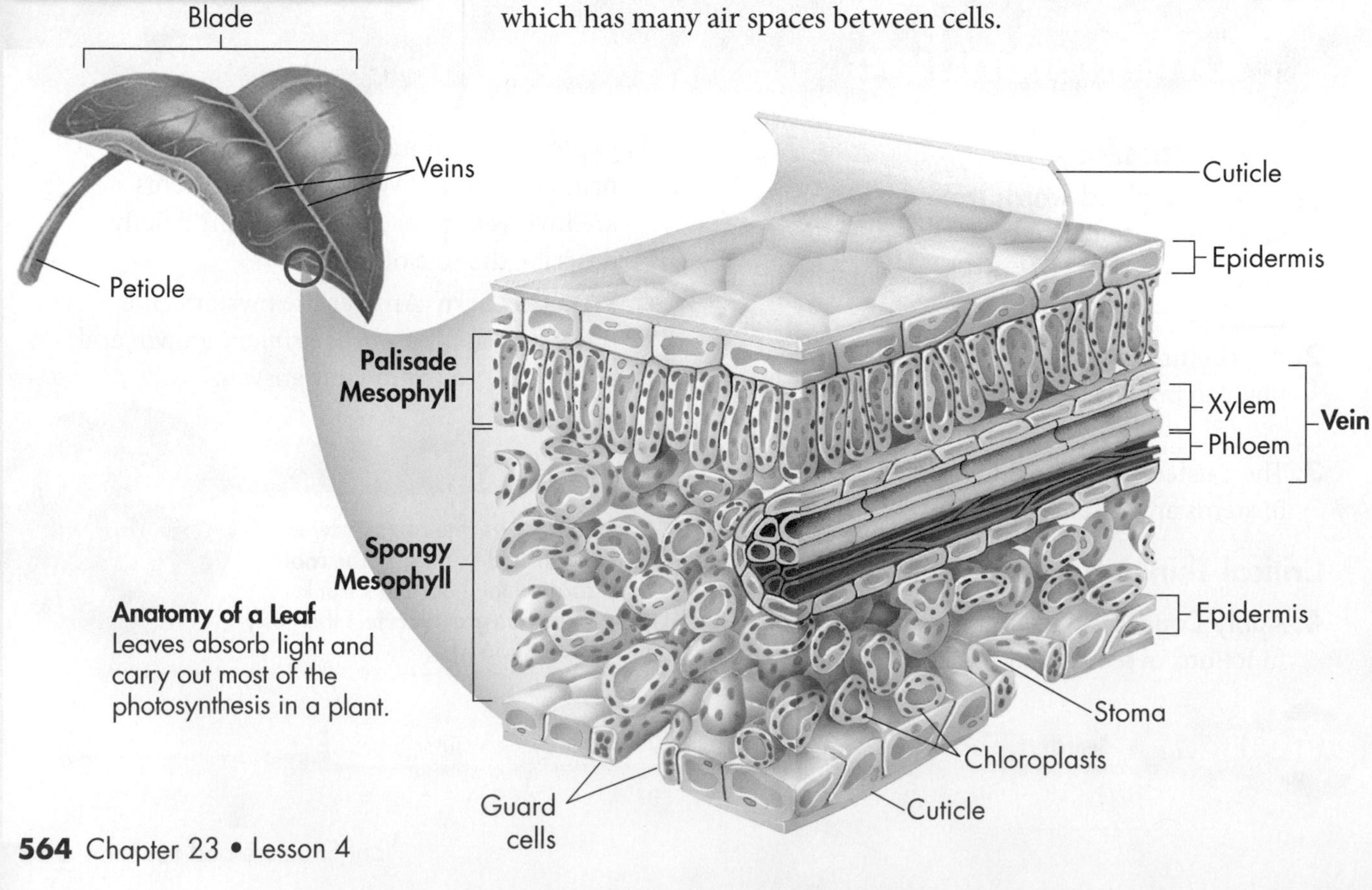

Blade

Veins

Petiole

Cuticle

Epidermis

Palisade Mesophyll

Xylem
Phloem — **Vein**

Spongy Mesophyll

Anatomy of a Leaf
Leaves absorb light and carry out most of the photosynthesis in a plant.

Epidermis

Stoma

Chloroplasts

Guard cells

Cuticle

▶ **Veins** Veins of xylem and phloem run throughout the leaf and connect it to the stem. Xylem carries water from the roots into the leaf. Sugars produced in the leaf are moved into the veins. Then, phloem carries these sugars to the rest of the plant.

🔑 **Key Question** How is the structure of a leaf adapted to make photosynthesis more efficient? **The structure of a leaf allows the plant to collect light and carry out photosynthesis.**

Gas Exchange and Homeostasis

Plants need to exchange gases with the atmosphere. During photosynthesis, leaves take in carbon dioxide and give off oxygen. In respiration, plants take in oxygen and give off carbon dioxide.

The Role of Stomata Gases move in and out of the leaf through stomata. If stomata were open all the time, the plant would lose too much water. So, stomata are open long enough for photosynthesis to take place but not so long that the plant loses too much water. **Guard cells** are specialized cells that surround the stomata and control their opening and closing.

Changes in water pressure within the guard cells cause the stomata to open and close. When water is abundant, it flows into the leaf. This increases pressure in the guard cells. The stomata open. When water is scarce, water pressure within the guard cells decreases. Stomata close, reducing water loss by transpiration. Usually, stomata are open during the day, when photosynthesis takes place. They are closed at night. But if conditions are hot and dry, stomata may also close during the day.

Transpiration and Wilting The walls of mesophyll cells are moist, which allows gases to move in and out of the cells easily. Water evaporates from these surfaces and is lost to the atmosphere. **Transpiration** is the loss of water through leaves. Lost water may be replaced by water drawn into the leaf through xylem. If it is very hot or windy, water may be lost to transpiration faster than it is replaced. The plant may wilt.

Wilting is caused by the loss of water—and pressure—in a plant's cells. Normally, pressure in a plant's cells makes its leaves stiff. But if there is not enough water, the cell walls bend inward, and the plant wilts. When a leaf wilts, its stomata close. Transpiration slows down. Thus, wilting helps a plant save water.

🔑 **Key Question** What is the role of stomata in maintaining homeostasis? **Stomata are kept open long enough for photosynthesis to take place, but not so long that plants lose too much water.**

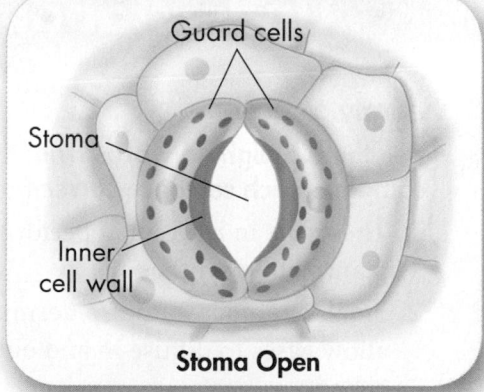

Stoma Open

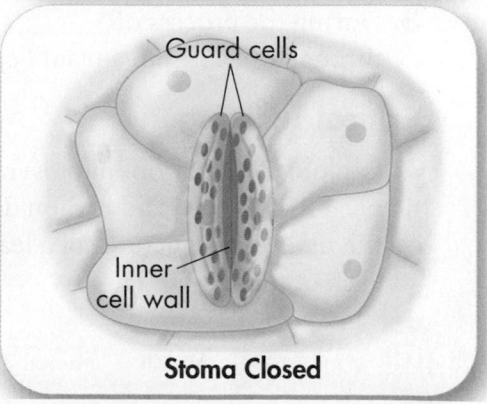

Stoma Closed

Guard Cell Function Stomata allow plants to balance the rate of photosynthesis and the loss of water.

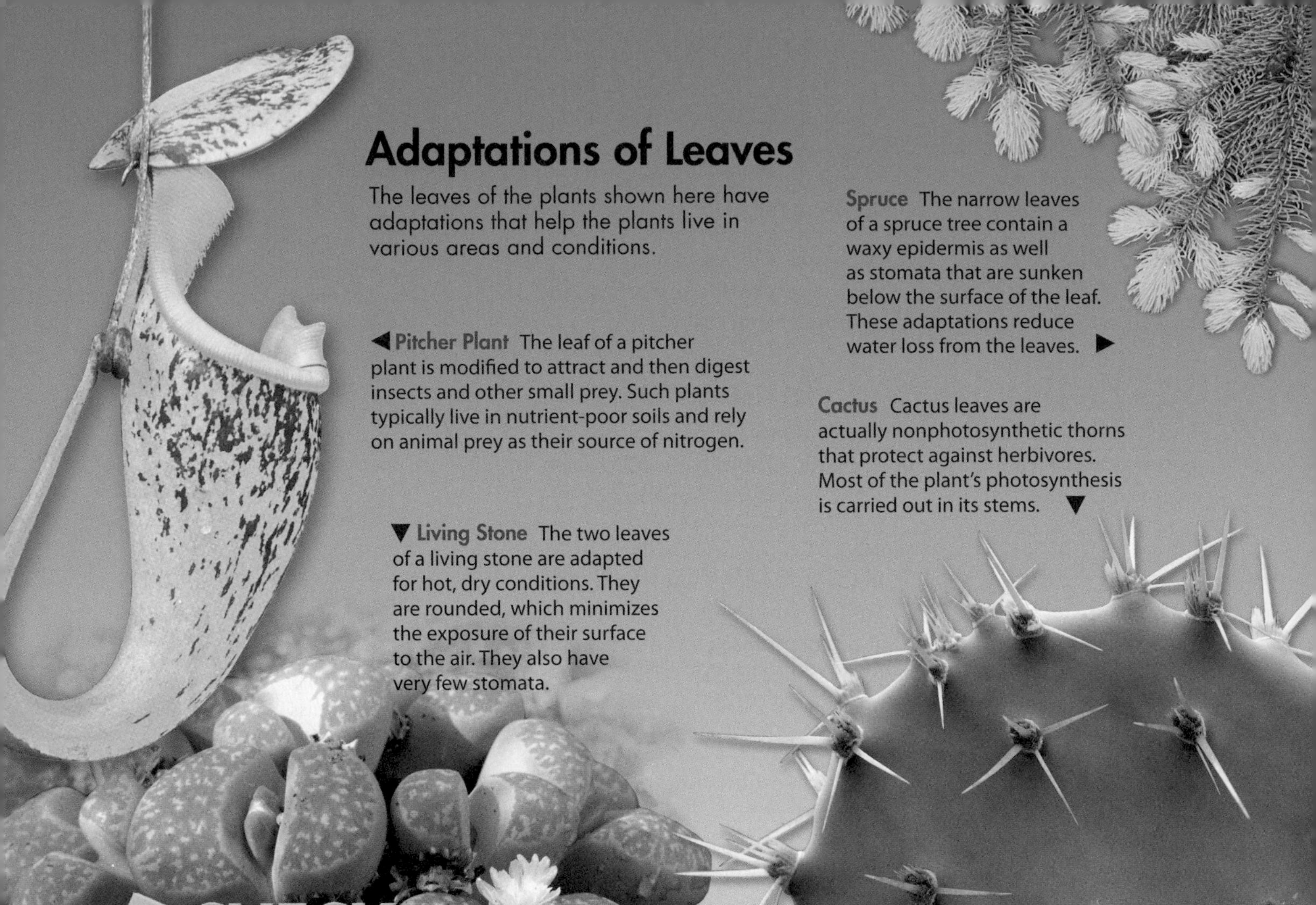

Adaptations of Leaves

The leaves of the plants shown here have adaptations that help the plants live in various areas and conditions.

◀ **Pitcher Plant** The leaf of a pitcher plant is modified to attract and then digest insects and other small prey. Such plants typically live in nutrient-poor soils and rely on animal prey as their source of nitrogen.

Spruce The narrow leaves of a spruce tree contain a waxy epidermis as well as stomata that are sunken below the surface of the leaf. These adaptations reduce water loss from the leaves. ▶

Cactus Cactus leaves are actually nonphotosynthetic thorns that protect against herbivores. Most of the plant's photosynthesis is carried out in its stems. ▼

▼ **Living Stone** The two leaves of a living stone are adapted for hot, dry conditions. They are rounded, which minimizes the exposure of their surface to the air. They also have very few stomata.

CHECK Understanding

Apply Vocabulary

Use the highlighted words from the lesson to complete each sentence correctly.

1. The tissue in leaves that performs most of a plant's photosynthesis is ______.

2. Small openings in the epidermis of a plant that allow gases to diffuse in and out of a leaf are called ______.

3. During the process of ______, water is lost through openings in a plant's epidermis.

Critical Thinking

4. Explain To carry out photosynthesis, leaves need light, water, and carbon dioxide. Identify the tissues or structures of a leaf that provide each of these materials.

5. Apply Concepts Imagine a field. The day is hot and it has not rained for a few weeks. Will the stomata of plants in the field be open or closed? Explain your reasoning.

6. Write to Learn Answer the mystery clue question. Write a paragraph that describes how leaf structure plays a role in photosynthesis and how the fig's growth affects this function in the host plant.

MYSTERY CLUE

The mature fig plant blocks sunlight from the host tree. How might this affect photosynthesis in the host? (Hint: See p. 564.)

BIOLOGY.com Search Lesson 23.4 GO • Lesson Assessment

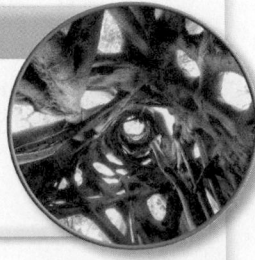

23.5 Transport in Plants

MD CIG 3.1.1 Chemical Substances and Macromolecules, 3.1.2 Homeostasis, 3.1.3 Matter and Energy, 3.2.1 Processes and Functions, 3.2.2 Changes in Metabolic Activity. SPI 1.4.8 Use Models, 1.5.8 Compare.

Water Transport

Look at a tall tree. Maybe there's a tree outside your school that is 15 meters tall or more. Imagine carrying a bucket of water to the top of that tree. You would have to do a lot of work! Now think of a giant redwood, 100 meters high. How does water reach the top?

Active transport and root pressure move water from the soil into a plant's roots. Water entering the vascular cylinder of the root creates pressure. This pressure pushes water upward into the stem. But root pressure does not produce nearly enough force to lift water up into trees. Other forces play a larger role.

Transpiration The major force in water transport is produced by the evaporation of water from leaves during transpiration. As water evaporates through open stomata, cell walls within the leaf begin to dry out. Plant cell walls contain cellulose, a complex carbohydrate. Paper is also made of cellulose. As you know, dry paper towels strongly attract water. Like a paper towel, the dry cell walls pull water from cells deeper inside the leaf. This pull is called transpirational pull. Transpirational pull also takes place in vascular tissue. It pulls water from the roots up through the xylem.

On a hot day, even a small tree may lose 100 liters of water to transpiration. The hotter and drier the air, the greater the amount of water lost. As a result of this loss, the plant draws up even more water from its roots.

Key Questions

🗝 **What are the major forces that transport water in a plant?**

🗝 **What drives the movement of fluid through phloem tissue in a plant?**

BUILD Connections

TRANSPIRATIONAL PULL

Imagine a chain of circus clowns. The clowns are tied together and climbing a tall ladder. When the first clown reaches the top, he falls off. He pulls the clowns behind him up and over the top of the ladder. Water molecules move through a plant this way. The chain of water molecules in a plant extends from the leaves down to the roots. As molecules exit the leaves through transpiration, they pull up the molecules behind them.

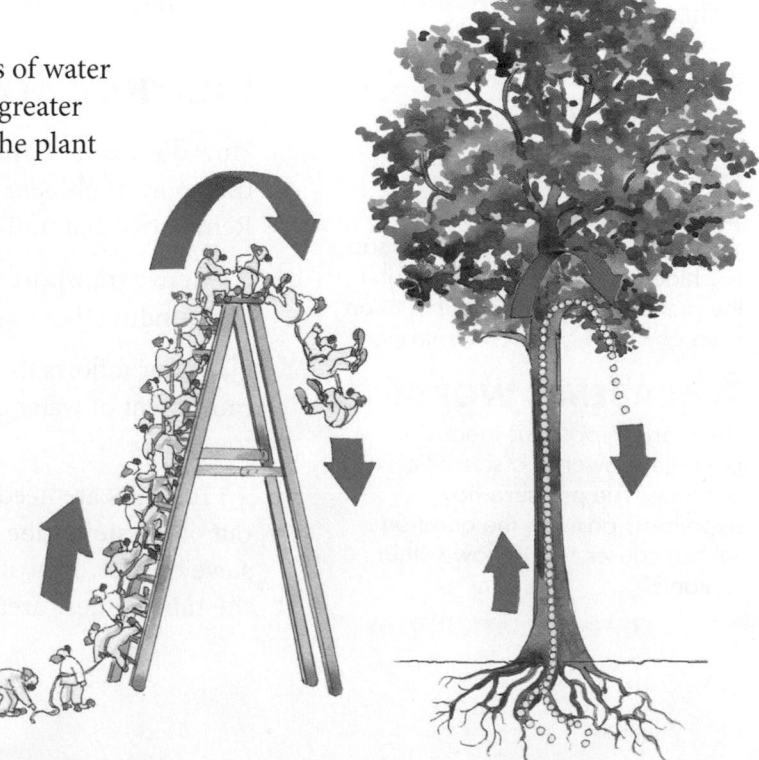

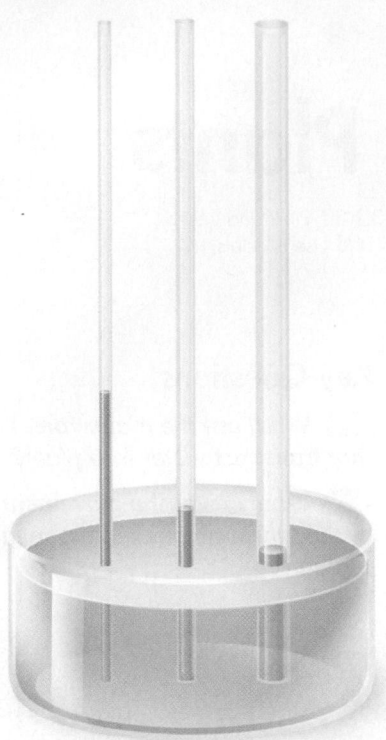

Capillary Action Capillary action causes water to move much higher in a narrow tube than in a wide tube.

Pulling Water Upward To pull water upward, plants make use of water's physical properties. One of these properties is cohesion. Cohesion is the attraction among molecules of the same substance. Water molecules are strongly attracted to one another. The cohesion of water is strong because water molecules form hydrogen bonds with each other. Water molecules also form hydrogen bonds with other substances. This results from the force of adhesion. **Adhesion** is the attraction between molecules that are unlike each other.

You can observe adhesion and cohesion at work. Here is how. Place a thin, empty glass tube in a dish of water. Water will move up into the tube. Why? Water is attracted to the walls of the tube. Water molecules are also attracted to one another. This tendency of water to rise in a thin tube is called **capillary action.**

Putting It All Together What do transpirational pull and capillary action have to do with the movement of water through xylem? Recall that xylem is made of tracheids and vessel elements. These cells connect to form long, hollow tubes. The walls of these hollow tubes are made of cellulose. Water adheres to cellulose. As water is lost by transpiration, adhesion pulls water from the wet inside of the leaf. This pull is so powerful that it reaches through the xylem down to the tips of the roots. It even reaches into the water in the soil. Together, transpiration and capillary action provide the major force that moves water upward through a plant.

🔑 **Key Question** What are the major forces that transport water in a plant?
Transpirational pull and capillary action are the major forces that move water from soil and through the xylem tissue to the rest of the plant.

Nutrient Transport

How do sugars move in phloem? The leading explanation for transport in phloem is known as the **pressure-flow hypothesis.** Remember that unlike xylem cells, phloem cells are alive.

❶ Active transport moves sugars into sieve tubes from the surrounding tissues.

❷ Water follows the sugars into the sieve tubes by osmosis. This movement of water creates pressure in the sieve tube at the source of the sugars.

❸ If sugars are needed in another area of the plant, they are pumped out of the sieve tube by active transport. Water then moves out of the sieve tube by osmosis. As the water leaves, it reduces the pressure in the tube at these areas.

Thus, pressure drives the flow of nutrient-rich fluid, or sap. Fluid moves from places where sugars are made to places where sugars are used or stored. Differences in nutrient concentration cause fluids to move in directions that meet the needs of the plant. The pressure-flow system helps plants respond to the seasons. During the growing season, sugars from the leaves are moved into ripening fruits or into roots for storage. As the growing season ends, the plant drops its fruits. Then nutrients are stored in the roots. As the growing season again approaches, chemical signals stimulate phloem cells in the roots. They pump sugars back into the phloem. Then, the pressure-flow system carries these sugars to the stems and leaves. This nutrient-rich fluid supports rapid growth.

Key Question What drives the movement of fluid through phloem tissue in a plant?
Changes in nutrient concentration cause the movement of fluid through phloem to meet the needs of the plant.

Pressure-Flow Hypothesis This diagram shows the movement of sugars as explained by the pressure-flow hypothesis. Fluid starts at places where sugars are made (source cells). The fluid moves to places where sugars are used or stored (sink cells).

CHECK Understanding

Apply Vocabulary
Use the highlighted words from the lesson to complete each sentence correctly.

1. Water is attracted to cellulose by the force of _____.

2. _____ is the tendency of water to rise in a thin tube.

3. The _____ explains the movement of fluids through phloem.

Critical Thinking

4. Relate Cause and Effect On a hot, dry day, the stomata of a plant close. How could this affect the plant's rate of photosynthesis? Explain.

5. Compare and Contrast Compare the role of active transport with that of osmosis in the movement of materials through phloem.

6. Write to Learn Answer the mystery clue question. In your answer, use the words *xylem* and *cohesion*.

MYSTERY CLUE

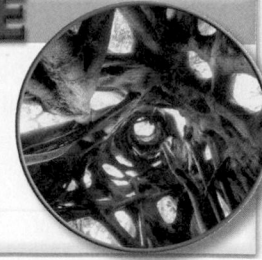

Fig vines can grow to the top of very tall trees. How do the leaves at the top of the vine get the water they need for photosynthesis?
(Hint: See p. 567.)

BIOLOGY.com > Search (Lesson 23.5) GO • Lesson Assessment

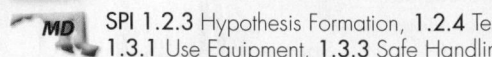# Design Your Own Lab

 SPI **1.2.3** Hypothesis Formation, **1.2.4** Testing a Hypothesis, **1.2.6** Investigative Methods,
1.3.1 Use Equipment, **1.3.3** Safe Handling of Materials, **1.4.9** Confirm Hypotheses.

Pre-Lab: Identifying Growth Zones in Roots

Problem Where does growth occur in plant roots?

Materials 150-mL beaker, paper towels, large bean seeds, petri dish, masking tape, metric ruler, fine-tip permanent marker

Lab Manual Chapter 23 Lab

Skills Focus Design an Experiment, Measure, Organize Data, Analyze Data

Connect to the  A plant's root system absorbs nutrients, stores food, and provides support for the rest of the plant. As a plant grows, the root system must be able to absorb more nutrients, store more food, and provide more support. Thus, growth in the root system must keep pace with growth in the other parts of a plant. Where in a root does the growth occur that increases the root's length? In this lab, you will design an experiment to answer this question.

Background Questions

a. Review What are the three principal organs of seed plants?

b. Compare and Contrast What are the main functions of dermal tissue, vascular tissue, and ground tissue?

c. Review What are meristems?

Pre-Lab Questions

Preview the procedure in the lab manual.

1. Predict A root is marked at two points along its length. What will happen to the distance between these marks if the root grows longer only near the tip? What will happen if growth occurs evenly along the entire length of the root?

2. Design an Experiment The procedure in Part A asks you to use four seeds. Why not use two seeds instead?

3. Design an Experiment How will you keep track of which seedling is which?

BIOLOGY.com   Search (Chapter 23)   GO

Visit Chapter 23 online to test yourself on chapter content and to find activities to help you learn.

Untamed Science Video The Untamed Science crew takes you to several exotic locations to see unique plant structures and adaptations.

Tutor Tube Tune in to Tutor Tube to see how new tissue growth makes plants taller.

Art Review Test your knowledge of leaf structures.

Art in Motion See how plant roots absorb nutrients and water molecules.

Visual Analogy Compare the motion of clowns climbing a ladder with water molecules being pulled up a tree.

23 CHAPTER Summary

23.1 Specialized Tissues in Plants

- The three main organs of seed plants are roots, stems, and leaves.

- Dermal tissue is the protective outer covering of a plant. Ground tissue produces and stores sugars and supports the plant. Vascular tissue supports the plant body and transports water and nutrients throughout the plant.

- Meristems are areas of unspecialized cells in which mitosis produces new cells that are ready for differentiation.

epidermis (p. 553)   lignin (p. 554)
parenchyma (p. 553)   meristem (p. 554)
collenchyma (p. 553)   apical meristem
sclerenchyma (p. 553)   (p. 554)

23.2 Roots

- A mature root has an outside layer called the epidermis. A mature root also contains vascular tissue and a large area of ground tissue.

- Roots support a plant, hold the plant in the ground, store food, and absorb water and dissolved nutrients from the soil.

root hair (p. 557)   endodermis (p. 557)
cortex (p. 557)   root cap (p. 557)

23.3 Stems

- Stems produce leaves, branches, and flowers. Stems hold leaves up to the sun. Stems transport substances throughout the plant.

- Primary growth of stems is the result of elongation of cells produced in the apical meristem. It takes place in all seed plants.

- In the stems of conifers and dicots, secondary growth takes place in meristems called the vascular cambium and cork cambium.

node (p. 560)
bud (p. 560)
vascular bundle (p. 561)
primary growth (p. 561)
secondary growth (p. 562)
vascular cambium (p. 562)
cork cambium (p. 562)

23.4 Leaves

- The structure of a leaf helps the plant collect light and carry out photosynthesis.

- Plants maintain homeostasis by keeping stomata open long enough for photosynthesis to take place, but not so long that plants lose too much water.

stoma (p. 564)   guard cell (p. 565)
mesophyll (p. 564)   transpiration (p. 565)

23.5 Transport in Plants

- Transpirational pull and capillary action provide most of the force needed to move water from soil through the xylem tissues of a plant.

- Changes in nutrient concentration drive the movement of fluid through phloem to meet the needs of the plant.

adhesion (p. 568)
capillary action (p. 568)
pressure-flow hypothesis (p. 568)

Assess the Big idea ▸ Structure and Function

Write an answer to the question below.

Q. How are cells, tissues, and organs organized into systems that carry out the basic functions of a seed plant?

Constructed Response

Write an answer to each of the numbered questions below. The answer to each numbered question should be one or two paragraphs long. To help you begin, read the **Hints** below the question.

1. **Explain how the cells in the vascular tissue of a plant are specialized for transport of water and minerals.**

   Hint Use the words *tracheids*, *vessel elements*, *sieve tube elements*, and *companion cells* in your answer.

   Hint Review the information on Water Transport and Nutrient Transport in Lesson 23.5.

2. **How do the cells and tissues in the trunk of a tree help it support the weight of all of its branches and leaves?**

   Hint Trunks are stems that have undergone secondary growth.

   Hint Xylem contains tracheids and vessel elements.

3. **How do several different types of tissues in a leaf work together in the functioning of the leaf?**

   Hint The primary function of a leaf is to carry out photosynthesis.

   Hint Leaves contain epidermis, mesophyll, and vascular tissue.

Foundations for Learning Wrap-Up

Use the folded page you prepared when reading the chapter to help you organize your thoughts about how cells, tissues, organs, and organ systems work together to help a plant survive.

Activity 1 Working with a partner or small group, discuss how each part of a plant works with another part of a plant. Use each tab of your folded paper to guide your discussion. For example, for the tabs labeled Leaf and Stem, identify how leaves work with stems to help the plant survive.

Activity 2 Complete each horizontal cut for each of the five topics to create five separate booklets. On the inside of each booklet, add a labeled sketch of the major structures in the lesson. Use the booklets to review the concepts from each lesson.

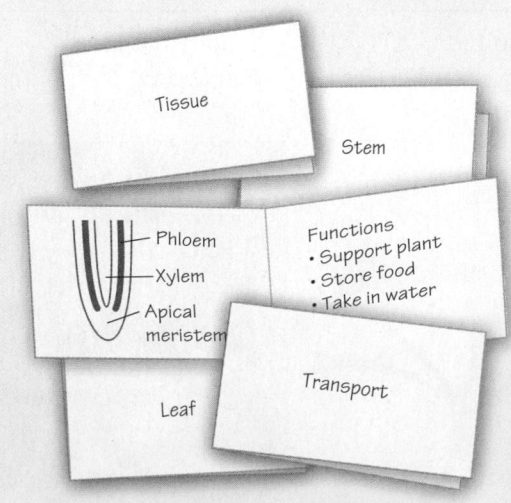

23.1 Specialized Tissues in Plants

Understand Key Concepts

1. The organ that supports the plant body and carries nutrients between different parts of the plant is the
   - **a.** root.
   - **b.** stem.
   - **c.** leaf.
   - **d.** flower.

2. Tracheids and vessel elements make up
   - **a.** meristem.
   - **b.** phloem.
   - **c.** xylem.
   - **d.** parenchyma.

3. What are the three main functions of ground tissue?

4. What is the main difference between mature xylem cells and mature phloem cells?

Think Critically

5. **Compare and Contrast** How are the epidermis of roots and leaves similar? How do they differ?

> **Test-Taking Tip**
>
> **Using Lists** It requires planning to answer an essay question. Before you start writing an answer, write a list of the points that you want to make. For a compare and contrast question, make two lists: one for similarities and one for differences.

23.2 Roots

Understand Key Concepts

6. Which of the following is a trace element that is absorbed by roots?
   - **a.** nitrogen
   - **b.** phosphorus
   - **c.** zinc
   - **d.** potassium

7. The waterproof barrier that separates the endodermis from the vascular cylinder is the
   - **a.** guard cell.
   - **b.** phloem.
   - **c.** Casparian strip.
   - **d.** cortex.

8. What are the two kinds of root systems?

9. How are root hairs important to plants?

Think Critically

10. **Explain** When you moved a plant to a large pot, you noticed that the plant's roots were very crowded in the old pot. After the plant was transplanted, it soon began to grow faster and looked healthier. Write a hypothesis that explains this observation.

23.3 Stems

Understand Key Concepts

11. A stem grows thicker when new tissue grows in
    - **a.** vascular cambium.
    - **b.** apical meristem.
    - **c.** nodes.
    - **d.** ground tissue.

12. Which of the following is part of the bark?
    - **a.** heartwood
    - **b.** sapwood
    - **c.** xylem
    - **d.** phloem

13. In stems, from what type of tissue does phloem develop?

14. What is the main difference between monocot and dicot stems?

Think Critically

15. **Infer** A plant undergoes only primary growth. Will it have a short life or a long life? Why?

23.4 Leaves

Understand Key Concepts

16. Most photosynthesis in a leaf takes place in the
    - **a.** leaf vein.
    - **b.** mesophyll.
    - **c.** epidermis.
    - **d.** cuticle.

17. Stomata open and close due to changes in the water pressure within
    - **a.** phloem.
    - **b.** xylem.
    - **c.** guard cells.
    - **d.** cell walls.

18. What is the function of the cuticle in a leaf?

Think Critically

19. **Infer** Cells in palisade mesophyll are closer together than cells in spongy mesophyll. How does this relate to the functions of these layers?

23.5 Transport in Plants

Understand Key Concepts

20. Water molecules are attracted to each other by the force of
  a. cohesion.
  b. adhesion.
  c. transpiration.
  d. capillary action.

21. As water evaporates from a plant's leaves, it causes water to move through the plant by the force of
  a. osmosis.
  b. active transport.
  c. capillary action.
  d. transpirational pull.

22. What explains the movement of sugars and nutrients through phloem?

23. What happens to water when active transport moves sugars into phloem cells?

Think Critically

24. Relate Cause and Effect Would transpirational pull be stronger on a cold, rainy day or on a hot, dry day? Explain your answer.

Connecting Concepts

Use Science Graphics

Use the graph to answer questions 25–26.

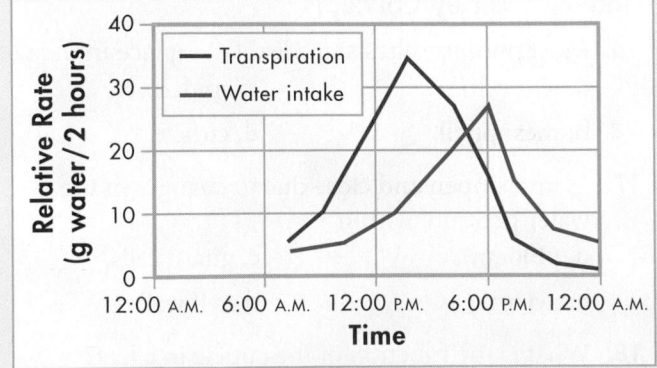

25. Analyze Data When is the greatest amount of water lost through transpiration?

26. Draw Conclusions What is the relationship between transpiration and water intake?

solve the CHAPTER MYSTERY

THE HOLLOW TREE

The life of a strangler fig starts with a sticky seed. This seed is dropped on a high tree branch by an animal such as a bird, bat, or monkey. At first, the plant grows slowly. This slow growth happens because the roots take in the few dissolved nutrients found in the rainwater and the leaf litter that collects in the host tree's branches. Eventually, the first roots grow down the host's trunk and enter the ground. Then, the fig's growth rate increases rapidly. The fig sends down many more roots. These roots become tangled together. They crush the host tree's bark, including the phloem. As a result, fewer nutrients can move through the phloem.

The fig's stems and leaves eventually grow taller than the host tree. This shades the host from the sun. The host performs less photosynthesis. The fig's roots compete with the host's roots for limited nutrients in the soil.

This triple punch—strangulation, competition for light, and competition for nutrients—usually kills the host. An impressive "hollow" fig tree is left behind.

1. Use Analogies One scientist has described the strangler fig as a "vegetable octopus." Explain how this analogy relates to the habits of the strangler fig.

2. Infer Plants that sprout and grow on top of other plants are called epiphytes. In what biome do you think epiphytes are most common? Explain your reasoning.

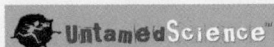 **Never Stop Exploring Your World.** Finding the solution to The Hollow Tree mystery is only the beginning. Take a video field trip with the ecogeeks of Untamed Science to see where the mystery leads.

Multiple Choice

1. Which of the following cell types is NOT found in a plant's vascular tissue?
   A tracheid
   B vessel element
   C guard cell
   D companion cell   CLG 3.2.1

2. Where in a plant does mitosis produce new cells?
   A meristems
   B chloroplasts
   C mesophyll
   D heartwood   CLG 3.2.1

3. Which tissues make up tree bark?
   A phloem
   B cork
   C cork cambium
   D all of the above   CLG 3.2.1

4. Which is NOT a factor in the movement of water through a plant's vascular tissues?
   A transpiration
   B capillary action
   C root pressure
   D meristems   CLG 3.1.2

5. All of the following conduct fluids in a plant EXCEPT
   A heartwood.   C phloem.
   B sapwood.   D xylem.   CLG 3.2.1

6. Where does most of the photosynthesis occur in a plant?
   A stomata
   B guard cells
   C vascular cambium
   D mesophyll tissue   CLG 3.2.1

7. Which of the following structures prevents the backflow of water into the root cortex?
   A palisade mesophyll
   B root cap
   C cambium
   D Casparian strip   CLG 3.2.1

8. Which of the following plants has a fibrous root system?
   A dandelion
   B beet
   C radish
   D grass   SPI 1.5.7

Questions 9–10

A student compared the average number of stomata on the top side and the underside of the leaves of different plants. Her data are summarized in the table below.

Average Number of Stomata (per square mm)		
Plant	Top Surfaces of Leaves	Bottom Surfaces of Leaves
Pumpkin	29	275
Tomato	12	122
Bean	40	288

9. What generalization can be made based on the data?
   A All plants have more stomata on the top side of their leaves than on the bottom side.
   B Plants have fewer stomata on the top side of their leaves than on the bottom side.
   C Some plants have more stomata on the top side of their leaves than on the bottom side.
   D The number of stomata is the same from plant to plant.   SPI 1.4.2

10. Pumpkins, tomatoes, and beans all grow in direct sunlight. Assuming the plants receive plenty of water, stomata on the lower surface of their leaves
    A are always closed.
    B are usually clogged with dust.
    C are unlikely to close at night.
    D stay open during daylight hours.   CLG 3.2.1

Open-Ended Response

11. Contrast the functions of xylem and phloem.
                                         CLG 3.2.1

If You Have Trouble With . . .										
Question	1	2	3	4	5	6	7	8	9	10	11
See Lesson	23.1	23.1	23.3	23.5	23.3	23.4	23.2	23.2	23.4	23.4	23.5

24.1 Reproduction in Flowering Plants

MD CLG 3.2.1 Processes and Functions, 3.3.1 Sexual Reproduction and Variation, 3.5.2 Interdependence of Organisms in the Biosphere. SPI 1.3.1 Use Equipment, 1.3.3 Safe Handling of Materials, 1.5.2 Communicate Information, 1.5.5 Create and Interpret Graphics, 1.5.7 Classification, 1.5.8 Compare, 1.7.1 Apply Skills and Concepts.

Key Questions

🔑 What are flowers?

🔑 How does fertilization in angiosperms differ from fertilization in other plants?

🔑 What is vegetative reproduction?

BUILD Understanding

Two-Column Table Make a two-column table. Write the heading Male Gametophyte at the top of one column. Write the heading Female Gametophyte at the top of the second column. As you read, take notes about each gametophyte.

In Your Workbook Complete the table for Lesson 24.1.

The Structure of Flowers

What makes a flower beautiful? Its color and shape? Of course, flowers vary greatly in color, size, and shape. But what is the point of a flower? To a plant, the whole point of a flower is sexual reproduction. Flowers help bring male and female gametes together and then protect the developing seeds.

Flowers are made up of four kinds of specialized leaves: sepals, petals, stamens, and carpels. The art below shows a typical flower with all of these structures.

Sepals and Petals The outermost flower parts are the sepals (SEE pulz). Often, sepals are green and look like leaves. Sepals surround and protect the flower bud as it develops. Inside the sepals are the petals. Petals, which are often brightly colored, attract pollinators to the flower.

Stamens and Carpels Within the petals are structures that produce gametophytes. Many flowering plants produce both male and female gametophytes. In other species, male and female gametophytes are produced on separate plants.

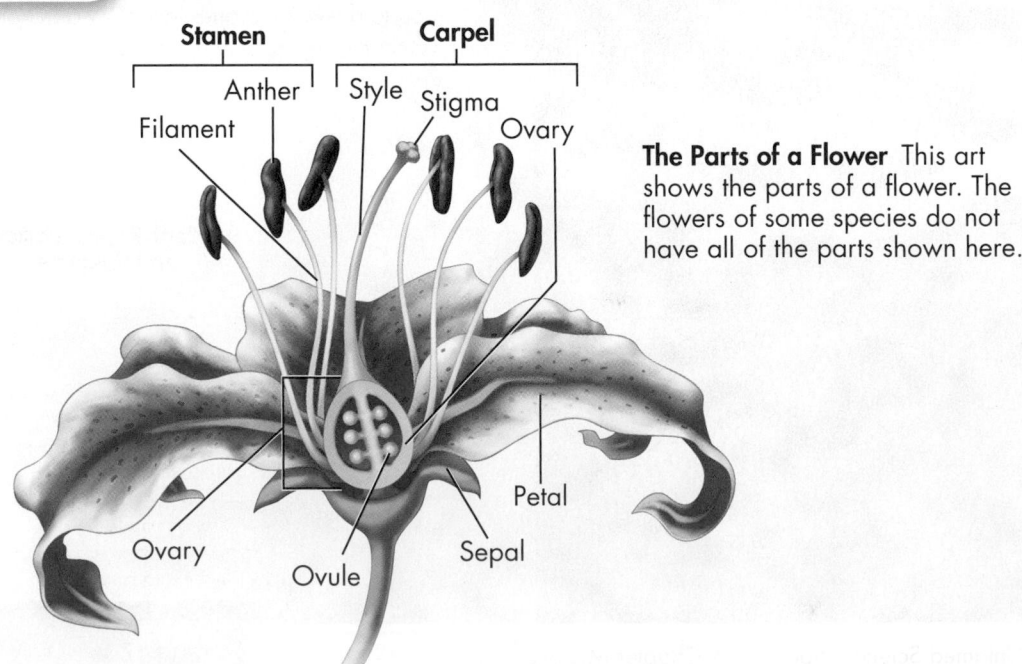

The Parts of a Flower This art shows the parts of a flower. The flowers of some species do not have all of the parts shown here.

What Is the Structure of a Flower?

Procedure

❶ Study a flower carefully. Use a hand lens if needed. Draw what you see, and label the parts of the flower.

❷ Use forceps to remove an anther. Place the anther on a slide. Use a scalpel to cut one or more thin slices of the anther. **CAUTION:** *Be careful with sharp tools and slides. Place the slide on a flat surface before cutting.*

❸ Lay the anther slices flat on the slide. Add a drop of water, and cover the anther slices with a coverslip. Use a microscope to look at the slices. Draw and label what you see.

Analyze and Conclude

1. Apply Concepts What structures did you find in the anthers? What is the function of these structures?

2. Apply Concepts What structures did you find in the ovaries? What is the function of these structures?

3. Infer Which parts of the flower will become seeds? Which parts will become fruit?

In Your Workbook Get more help for this activity in your workbook.

▶ *Stamens* **Stamens** are the male parts of a flower. Each stamen has a stalk called a filament. At the tips of filaments are **anthers.** Pollen grains, which are the male gametophytes, are produced in the anthers.

▶ *Carpels* The innermost parts of a flower are the carpels. **Carpels** produce and protect female gametophytes; later they produce seeds. Each carpel has a wide base called an ovary. The ovary contains one or more ovules. Female gametophytes grow inside the ovules. The carpel has a thin stalk called a style. At the top of the style is a sticky or feathery area known as the **stigma.** The stigma is specialized to capture pollen. Biologists sometimes call a single carpel or several carpels that are fused together a pistil.

🔑 **Key Question** What are flowers?
Flowers are reproductive organs that are made of four kinds of specialized leaves: sepals, petals, stamens, and carpels.

The Angiosperm Life Cycle

Like other plants, angiosperms have a life cycle with alternation of generations. The sporophyte phase is diploid (2N), and the gametophyte stage is haploid (1N). As with ferns and gymnosperms, the sporophyte of angiosperms is much larger than the gametophyte. In fact, the male and female gametophytes live within the tissues of the sporophyte.

BUILD Vocabulary

stamen the male part of the flower; includes an anther and a filament

anther a flower structure in which pollen grains are produced; part of the stamen

carpel the female part of the flower; the innermost part of a flower that produces and protects female gametophytes

stigma a sticky or feathery part of the carpel that is located at the top of a style; specialized to capture pollen

🖋 **WORD ORIGINS**

The word *carpel* comes from the Greek word *karpos*, which means "fruit." Carpels produce seeds and include the ovary, which develops into fruit.

Development of Male Gametophytes Male gametophytes develop inside anthers. First, meiosis produces four haploid cells called pollen spores. Then each pollen spore divides by mitosis. This division forms two haploid nuclei. A thick wall surrounds the two nuclei. Together, the nuclei and wall form the male gametophyte, or pollen grain. The art below shows this process.

Development of Female Gametophytes Female gametophytes form in ovules at the bottom of the carpel. Each ovule is a future seed. The ovary, which surrounds and protects the ovules, is the future fruit.

The process starts when a diploid cell in an ovule divides by meiosis. This division forms four haploid cells. Three of these cells break down. The fourth cell divides by mitosis, producing eight nuclei. These eight nuclei and the surrounding membrane make up the **embryo sac.** The embryo sac is the female gametophyte. The embryo sac is contained within the ovule.

Cell walls form around six of the eight nuclei. One of the eight nuclei is the nucleus of the egg, or female gamete. If fertilization takes place, the egg will fuse with a male gamete, forming a zygote. The zygote will grow into a new sporophyte.

The Development of Gametophytes
The male gametophyte develops inside an anther. The female gametophyte develops inside a single ovule.

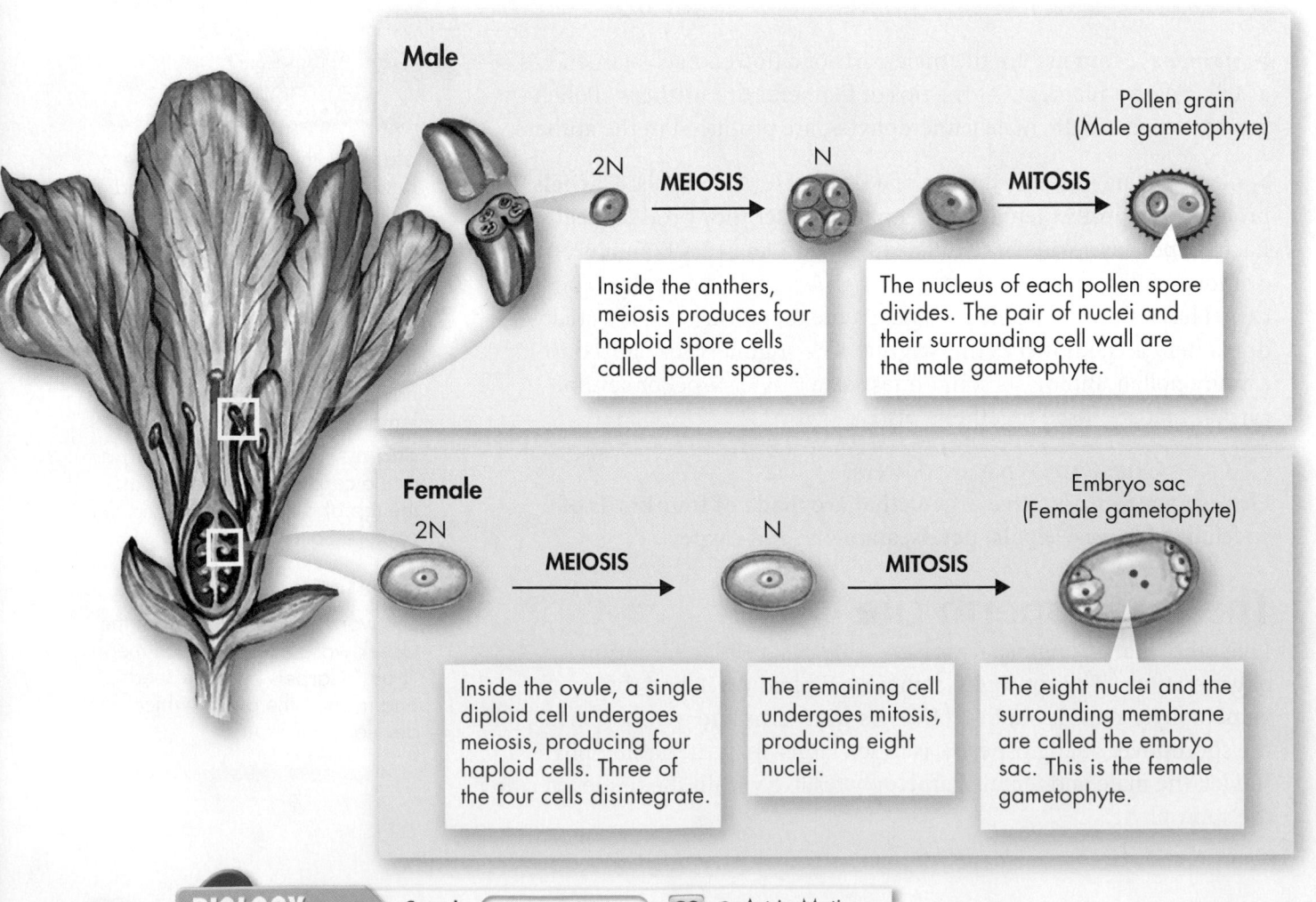

Male

Pollen grain (Male gametophyte)

2N   **MEIOSIS**   N   **MITOSIS**

Inside the anthers, meiosis produces four haploid spore cells called pollen spores.

The nucleus of each pollen spore divides. The pair of nuclei and their surrounding cell wall are the male gametophyte.

Female

Embryo sac (Female gametophyte)

2N   **MEIOSIS**   N   **MITOSIS**

Inside the ovule, a single diploid cell undergoes meiosis, producing four haploid cells. Three of the four cells disintegrate.

The remaining cell undergoes mitosis, producing eight nuclei.

The eight nuclei and the surrounding membrane are called the embryo sac. This is the female gametophyte.

Pollination The flowers of an oak tree (left) are pollinated by wind. They are small and not very showy. However, they produce large amounts of pollen. In contrast, flowers that are pollinated by animals (right) are often large and brightly colored.

Pollination Pollination is the transfer of pollen to the stigma of the flower. Most angiosperms are pollinated by animals, but some are pollinated by wind. Wind-pollinated flowers are usually small and not very colorful. Wind-pollinated plants rely on the production of huge numbers of pollen grains to carry pollen from one plant to another.

Animal pollinators, such as insects, birds, and bats, carry pollen from flower to flower. Flowers that are pollinated by animals have many adaptations that attract pollinators. These adaptations include bright colors, strong scents, and sweet nectar. Animal pollinators, in turn, have adaptations that help them get nectar from the flowers. Hummingbirds, for example, have long thin beaks that can reach the nectar deep inside tube-shaped flowers.

Flowering plants and their pollinators have a mutualistic relationship. The animals are rewarded by a source of food—pollen and nectar. The plants are helped because animals take pollen directly from flower to flower. The efficiency of animal pollination may be one of the main reasons why angiosperms have become the most successful group of plants.

Fertilization If a pollen grain lands on the stigma of a flower, the process of fertilization begins. One of the male gametophyte's nuclei forms a pollen tube. The pollen tube grows into the style. Eventually it reaches the ovary and enters an ovule. The other nucleus divides, forming two sperm cells. These sperm cells reach the egg through the pollen tube.

Inside the embryo sac, the two sperm fertilize different nuclei. This process is called **double fertilization.** First, one of the sperm nuclei fuses with the egg nucleus. A diploid (2N) zygote forms. The zygote will grow into the embryo. Next, the second sperm nucleus fuses with two other nuclei in the embryo sac to form a triploid (3N) cell. This 3N cell will grow into tissue known as **endosperm.** Endosperm contains a rich supply of food that will nourish the seedling as it grows.

Inside a Corn Seed The endosperm and embryo of a corn seed result from double fertilization.

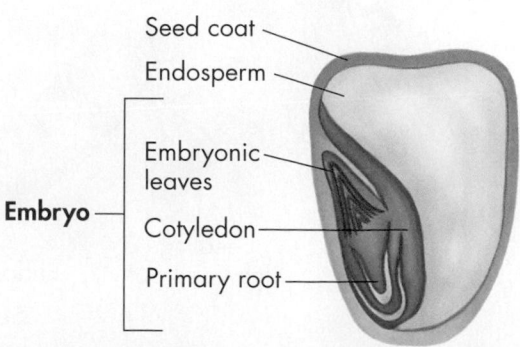

Seed coat
Endosperm
Embryonic leaves
Embryo
Cotyledon
Primary root

Double fertilization may be another reason why angiosperms are so successful. By using endosperm to store food, a plant spends very little energy on producing seeds from ovules until double fertilization has actually taken place. The energy saved can be used to make many more seeds.

🔑 **Key Question** How does fertilization in angiosperms differ from fertilization in other plants?

Angiosperms have two fertilization events. One produces a zygote. The other produces a tissue called endosperm.

Angiosperm Life Cycle In the life cycle of an angiosperm, the developing seeds are protected inside the ovary.

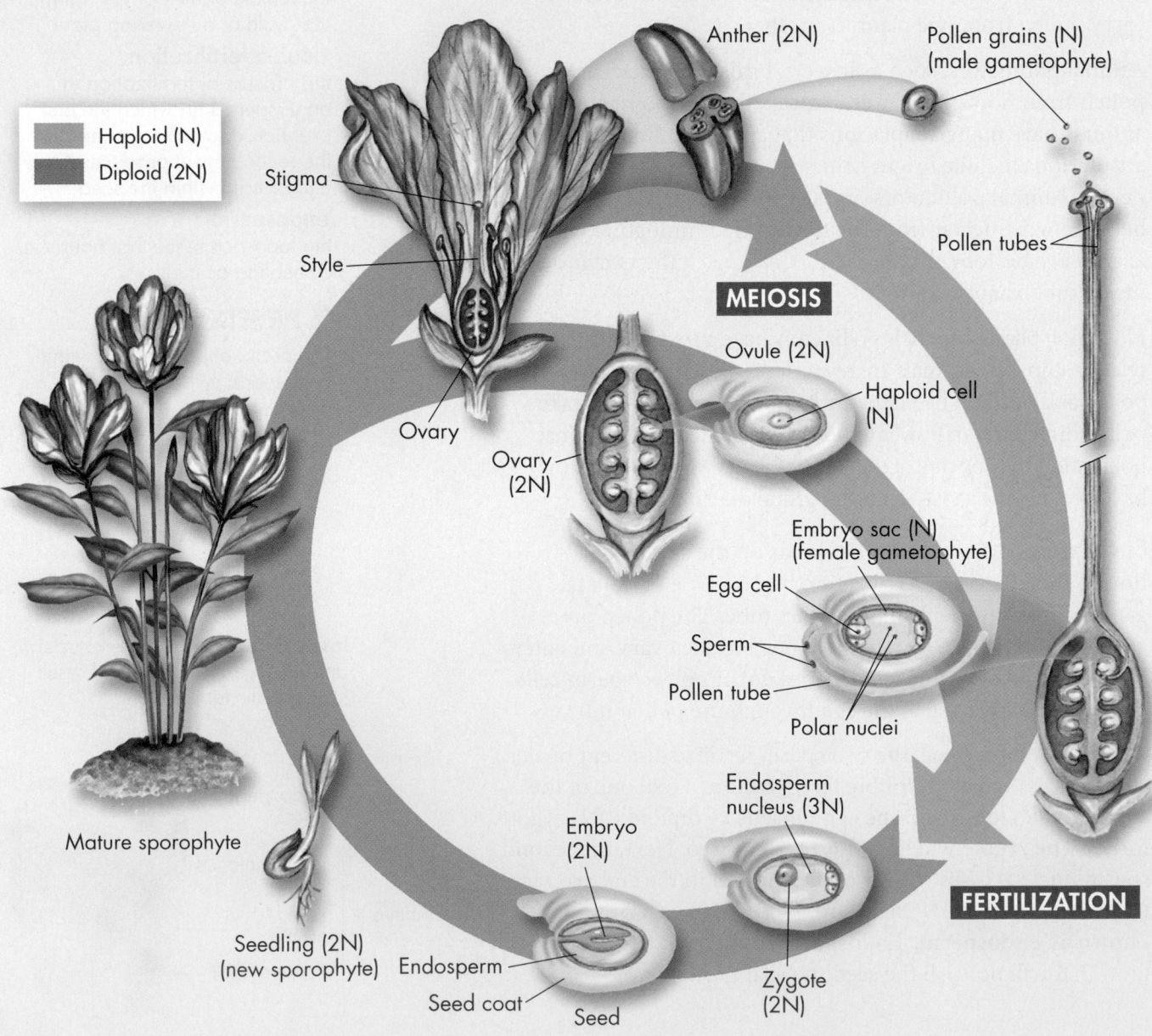

Haploid (N)
Diploid (2N)

Anther (2N)
Pollen grains (N) (male gametophyte)
Stigma
Style
Pollen tubes
MEIOSIS
Ovule (2N)
Ovary
Ovary (2N)
Haploid cell (N)
Embryo sac (N) (female gametophyte)
Egg cell
Sperm
Pollen tube
Polar nuclei
Endosperm nucleus (3N)
Embryo (2N)
FERTILIZATION
Mature sporophyte
Seedling (2N) (new sporophyte)
Endosperm
Seed coat
Seed
Zygote (2N)

Vegetative Reproduction

Many flowering plants can reproduce asexually by **vegetative reproduction.** In vegetative reproduction, a single plant produces offspring that are genetically identical to itself. New plants are formed by mitosis. Vegetative reproduction does not require flowers, gametes, or fertilization.

Key Question What is vegetative reproduction?
Vegetative reproduction is the formation of new individuals by mitosis.

Types of Vegetative Reproduction Vegetative reproduction takes place naturally in many plants. New plants may grow from roots, leaves, or stems. Some species form plantlets, which are small plants that fall off the parent plant.

Vegetative reproduction does not involve pollination or seed formation. So, a single plant can reproduce quickly. If the parent plant is well adapted to an environment, its offspring can spread quickly. All of these offspring have exactly the same genes as the parent. One of the drawbacks of asexual reproduction is that it does not produce new combinations of genes. Genetic diversity helps a species survive if the environment changes.

Examples of Vegetative Reproduction
Adaptations of the stem play a role in the vegetative reproduction of the plants shown here.

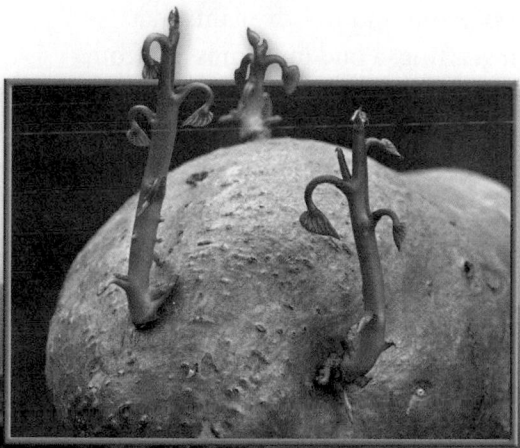

▲ A potato is an underground stem called a tuber that can grow whole new plants from buds called *eyes*.

▲ Strawberry plants send out long, trailing stems called stolons. Nodes that rest on the ground produce roots and upright stems and leaves.

Cholla and many other cactus species can reproduce by dropping sections of their stems. The small individuals growing at the base of the larger adults are, in fact, clones.

Grafting As it is just starting to bud, a branch from a lemon tree is grafted onto the branch of an established orange tree. Months later, the grafted branch bears lemons. This graft has formed a single plant bearing more than one species of fruit.

Plant Propagation People who grow, or propagate, plants often make use of vegetative reproduction. Two common ways of increasing the number of desirable plants are grafting and making cuttings.

To make a cutting, a grower cuts off a length of stem that has buds. (Remember that buds contain meristems.) The cut stem may then be partially buried in soil. Sometimes it is placed in a special mixture of nutrients that helps roots form.

Grafting is used to produce seedless plants and woody plants that cannot be grown from cuttings. In grafting, a bud or stem is cut from the parent plant. It is then attached to another plant. Grafting only works with plants that are closely related. A bud from a lemon tree can be grafted onto an orange tree, but not onto an oak tree.

✓CHECK Understanding

Apply Vocabulary
Use the highlighted words from the lesson to complete each sentence correctly.

1. In seeds, the _____ nourishes the seedling as it grows.

2. Pollen grains form inside the _____.

3. The _____ is the female part of a flower.

4. In the process of _____, a plant reproduces asexually by mitosis.

Critical Thinking

5. Explain List and describe the four kinds of specialized leaves that make up a flower.

6. Apply Concepts Describe a feature of fertilization that happens only in angiosperms.

7. Compare and Contrast Compare the advantages and disadvantages of sexual reproduction with those of asexual reproduction in flowering plants.

8. Write to Learn Answer the first clue of the mystery.

MYSTERY CLUE

Whether the lemons grew on a grafted branch did not affect their ripening. Something changed after the lemons were picked. This change kept the lemons from ripening. What was it? (**Hint:** See page 577.)

24.2 Fruits and Seeds

MD CLG 3.2.1 Processes and Functions, **3.5.1** Factors Influencing Ecosystems. SPI **1.5.2** Communicate Information, **1.5.7** Classification Systems, **1.5.8** Compare.

Seed and Fruit Development

What is a fruit? In everyday language, the word *fruit* describes sweet things, such as grapes or strawberries. But in biology, a fruit is a structure that surrounds and protects seeds. Therefore, many foods that we call vegetables, such as peas, corn, beans, cucumbers, and tomatoes, are also fruits.

Fruits develop from the ovary walls of a flower. After fertilization, nutrients from the plant flow into the flower tissues, feeding the developing seeds. As the seeds mature, the ovary walls around them thicken. A mature ovary wall may be fleshy, as in a tomato. Or it may be tough and dry, as in a peanut shell. (The peanuts themselves are seeds.)

Key Question How do fruits form?
As angiosperm seeds mature, the ovary walls thicken to form a fruit that surrounds the developing seeds.

Seed Dispersal

Fruits are rich in sugars and other nutrients. But fruits do not nourish seedlings. Seedlings get their food from endosperm. So why do angiosperms have seeds that are wrapped in another layer of nutrient-packed tissue? Think of wild blackberries. Each seed is enclosed in a sweet, juicy fruit. Blackberries are tasty treats for many animals that live in the forest. What good is a fruit if all it does is get eaten? Believe it or not, that's exactly the point! When an animal eats a fruit, it helps disperse, or scatter, the seeds.

Dispersal by Animals The seeds of many plants, especially those in fleshy fruits, are eaten by animals. These seeds have a tough coating that lets them pass through the animal's digestive system unharmed. Eventually, the seeds are deposited in the animal's droppings. Some dry fruits have burs that catch in an animal's fur. These fruits are then carried far away from the parent plant.

Key Questions

🔑 **How do fruits form?**

🔑 **How are seeds spread?**

🔑 **What factors influence the dormancy and germination of seeds?**

BUILD Understanding

Flowchart Make a flowchart that shows the process of germination. Include the factors that affect germination. Indicate differences between monocots and dicots.

In Your Workbook Go to your workbook to learn more about flowcharts. Complete the flowchart for Lesson 24.2.

Variety Among Fruits Like the flowers from which they develop, fruits vary greatly in structure.

Strawberries ▼

Rose Hips ▼

Peanut Shell ▼

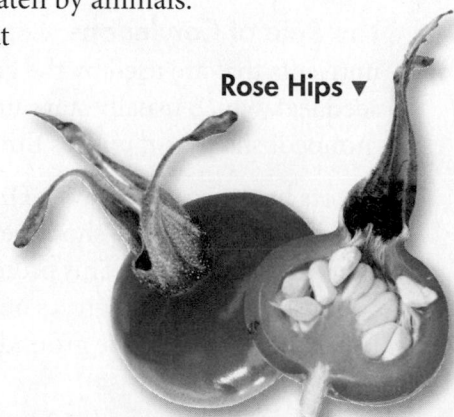

Dispersal of Seeds A bird called a Bohemian waxwing eats berries (left). Later, the bird will deposit the seeds in its droppings. Dandelion seeds (center) are spread by wind. The coconut fruit (right) can travel long distances by floating on water.

Dispersal by Wind and Water Some seeds are spread by wind. These seeds are usually contained in lightweight dry fruits. Consider a dandelion seed. It has a dry fruit that works like a parachute. Dandelion seeds can be blown far away from the parent plant. Other fruits travel by water. For example, coconut fruits can float long distances on seawater. That is why coconut trees can be found growing on islands that are far away from the mainland.

🔑 Key Question How are seeds spread?
Seeds in fleshy fruits are usually spread by animals. Seeds in dry fruits may be spread by animals, wind, or water.

Seed Dormancy and Germination
When they reach a good location, some seeds begin to grow right away. But many other seeds enter a period of **dormancy.** During dormancy, the embryo is alive, but it is not growing. The length of dormancy varies among species.

Germination Dormancy ends with **germination,** which is when the plant embryo grows again. Environmental factors such as temperature and moisture can cause germination. Before germinating, seeds absorb water. The seed swells, breaking open the seed coat. The root begins to grow. Then the shoot—the part of the plant that grows above ground—begins to sprout. The art on the next page compares the germination of a monocot with that of a dicot.

The Role of Cotyledons Cotyledons, or seed leaves, store nutrients that are used by the growing plant. Monocots have one seed leaf, which usually stays underground. A sheath protects the monocot shoot as it pushes through the soil.

Dicots have two seed leaves. Dicots do not have a sheath to protect the shoot. Instead, the shoot bends to form a hook that forces its way through the soil. This protects the delicate tip of the plant. The shoot straightens as it grows out of the soil. In some dicots, the seed leaves appear above the ground. In other dicots, the seed leaves stay underground.

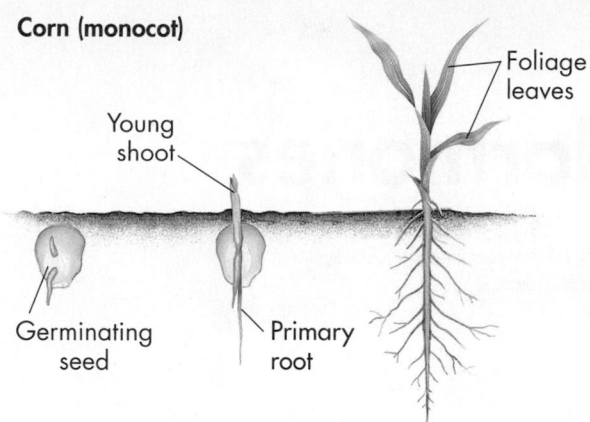

Corn (monocot)

Foliage leaves

Young shoot

Germinating seed

Primary root

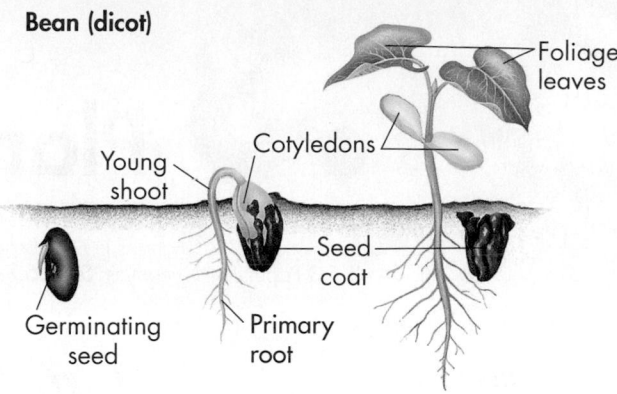

Bean (dicot)

Foliage leaves

Cotyledons

Young shoot

Seed coat

Germinating seed

Primary root

Advantages of Dormancy Dormancy makes it possible for seeds to be dispersed over long distances. It also lets seeds wait to germinate until conditions for growth are ideal. Plants that live in cold climates often have seeds that will not germinate until after a long period of cold. This dormancy stops their seeds from germinating until winter is over. Their seeds can survive freezing, but their seedlings cannot.

In some species, only extreme conditions will end dormancy. For example, the cones of some pine trees do not release their seeds until there is a forest fire. High temperatures cause the cones to open. Once the seeds are released, they germinate. This adaptation allows pine trees to quickly grow again after a fire.

🔑 **Key Question** What factors influence the dormancy and germination of seeds? **Temperature and moisture can cause a seed to end dormancy and germinate.**

Comparing Germination in Monocots and Dicots Corn is a monocot. A corn seedling (left) grows directly upward. It is protected by a sheath of tissue that surrounds the developing leaves. A bean is a dicot. A bean seedling (right) forms a hook in its stem. This hook gently pulls the new plant through the soil.

✓CHECK Understanding

Apply Vocabulary
Use the highlighted words from the lesson to complete each sentence correctly.

1. Some seeds undergo _____, so they do not grow right away.

2. The process in which the embryo in a seed starts to grow again is called _____.

Critical Thinking

3. Explain Describe how fruits form.

4. Classify Is a pumpkin a fruit? Why or why not?

5. Explain Describe two ways in which seeds are spread.

6. Compare and Contrast Compare the germination of a monocot with that of a dicot.

7. Write to Learn Answer the second clue of the mystery. Start a list of variables that affect seed development and fruit ripening. Add to your list as you continue reading the chapter.

MYSTERY CLUE

When the warehouse switched to electric heating, what might have changed in the lemons' environment? (**Hint:** See p. 586.)

Plant Hormones

MD CLG 3.1.1 Chemical Substances and Macromolecules, 3.1.2 Homeostasis, 3.2.1 Processes and Functions, 3.2.2 Changes in Metabolic Activity, 3.5.1 Factors Influencing Ecosystems, 3.5.3 Population Dynamics. SPI 1.5.7 Classification Systems.

Key Questions

🔑 **What roles do plant hormones play?**

🔑 **What are some examples of environmental stimuli to which plants respond?**

🔑 **How do plants respond to seasonal changes?**

BUILD Understanding

Concept Map As you read, make a concept map that shows the effects of various hormones on plant growth.

In Your Workbook Go to your workbook to learn more about concept maps. Complete the concept map for Lesson 24.3.

Hormones

Plants grow in response to factors such as light, temperature, and moisture. But how do plant tissues "know" when to grow or reproduce? The actions of plant tissues and organs are controlled by hormones. **Hormones** are chemical signals that affect a plant's growth, activity, and development. Hormones also coordinate the way that a plant responds to its environment.

Cells in an organism affected by a particular hormone are called **target cells.** To respond to a hormone, a cell must have receptors. **Receptors** are usually proteins to which hormones bind. The way that a target cell responds depends on the kind of receptor. One kind of receptor might speed growth. Another might slow growth. As a result, a given hormone can affect roots differently from stems.

Auxins Hormones called auxins control cell elongation and the growth of new roots. Auxins are produced in apical meristems, then travel to the rest of the plant. Recall that apical meristems are found at the tips of stems.

Auxins control cell division in meristems. Apical meristems produce auxins that inhibit, or slow down, the growth of other buds on the same stem. The closer a bud is to the stem's tip, the more it is inhibited. This inhibition is called apical dominance. If you cut off the bud at the tip of a stem, the growth of the other buds on the stem is no longer inhibited. The other buds grow more quickly. The plant becomes bushier because the source of the auxins has been removed.

Auxins also explain why plants grow toward the light. When light hits one side of a shoot, auxins collect in the shaded areas. These cells grow longer. This causes the shoot to bend toward the light.

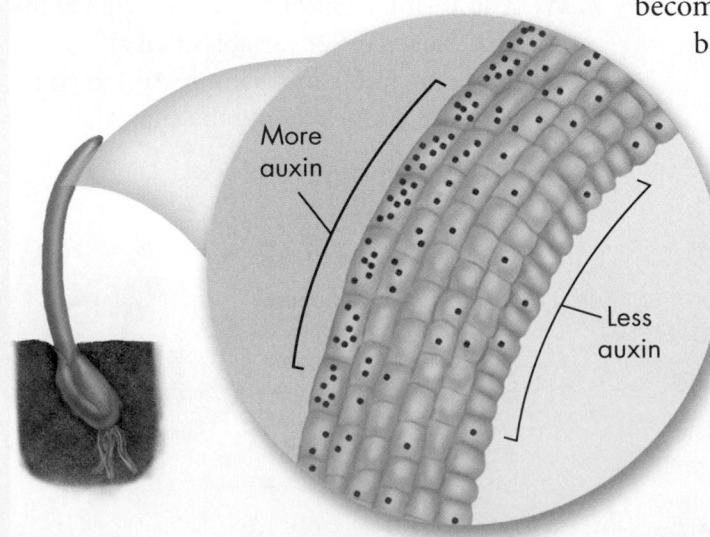

More auxin

Less auxin

Auxins and Cell Elongation Cells grow longer on the shaded side of the shoot. This area has a higher concentration of auxins.

Cytokinins Cytokinins are hormones that are produced in growing roots, fruits, and seeds. Cytokinins cause cell division. They interact with auxins to control the growth of new organs in injured plants and to balance root and shoot growth. The effects of cytokinins often oppose those of auxins. Auxins cause the growth of new roots and inhibit the growth of shoot tips. Cytokinins do the opposite.

Gibberellins Hormones called gibberellins promote growth. These hormones can produce great increases in size, particularly in stems and fruits. Gibberellins also stimulate germination.

Abscisic Acid The hormone abscisic acid keeps cells from dividing, thereby stopping growth. Abscisic acid and gibberellins work together to control seed dormancy. When a seed is fully grown, abscisic acid stops the growth of the embryo. The embryo becomes dormant. The embryo rests until environmental conditions change the balance of hormones. For example, a heavy spring rain may wash away the abscisic acid. (Gibberellins do not wash away as easily as abscisic acid.) Then, gibberellins in the seed can start germination.

Ethylene One plant hormone—ethylene—is a gas. Fruit tissues release small amounts of ethylene, which helps fruits ripen. Ethylene also causes plants to drop organs that are no longer needed. For example, leaves drop in autumn, and fruits drop after they ripen. In each case, ethylene signals cells at the base of the structure to seal it off from the rest of the plant.

Key Question What roles do plant hormones play?
Plant hormones serve as signals that control development of cells, tissues, and organs. They also control responses to the environment. The opposing effects of plant hormones balance each other, contributing to a plant's homeostasis.

A Summary of Plant Hormones		
Hormone	**Some of the Effects**	**Where Found**
Auxins	Promote cell elongation and apical dominance; stimulate growth of new roots	Produced in shoot apical meristem and transported elsewhere
Cytokinins	Stimulate cell division; affect root growth and differentiation; may work in opposition to auxins	Growing roots
Gibberellins	Stimulate growth; influence various developmental processes; promote germination	Meristems of shoot, root, and seed embryo
Abscisic acid	Inhibits cell division; promotes seed dormancy	Terminal buds; seeds
Ethylene	Stimulates fruits to ripen; causes plants to seal off and drop unnecessary organs, such as leaves in autumn	Fruit tissues; aging leaves and flowers

A Summary of Plant Hormones
This table lists some of the effects of plant hormones and where the hormones can be found within the plant.

Three Plant Tropisms
Plants respond to light (left), gravity (middle), and touch (right).

Phototropism   **Gravitropism**   **Thigmotropism**

Tropisms and Rapid Movements

Sometimes plants need to move in response to their environment. Many plant movements are slow. But some are so fast that even animals cannot keep up with them.

Tropisms Plants respond to environmental stimuli such as light, gravity, and touch. When plants sense these stimuli, they send signals to their roots and stems to change the direction of growth. These growth responses are called **tropisms.**

▶ *Light* The tendency of a plant to grow toward a light source is called **phototropism.** This response can be very quick. For example, young seedlings can bend toward a light source in just a few hours. Remember that changes in the concentration of auxin are responsible for phototropism. Experiments have shown that auxins move toward shaded tissue. This may be due to changes in membrane permeability caused by light.

▶ *Gravity* Auxins also affect **gravitropism,** the response of a plant to gravity. For reasons that are still not understood, auxins move to the lower sides of horizontal roots and stems. In stems, this movement causes the stem to bend upright. In roots, however, the movement of auxins causes roots to bend downward.

▶ *Touch* Some plants respond to touch, a process called **thigmotropism.** Vines and climbing plants show thigmotropism. When they encounter an object, they wrap around it. Other plants, such as grape vines, have tendrils. Tendrils grow from the base of the leaf and wrap tightly around any object they encounter.

Rapid Movements Some plant responses are surprisingly fast. One example of a plant that can respond rapidly is the carnivorous Venus' flytrap. When an insect lands on a flytrap's leaf, it triggers sensory cells on the leaf. Electrical signals are sent from cell to cell. Cell walls expand and osmotic pressure changes, causing the leaf to snap shut. The insect is trapped inside!

🔑 **Key Question** What are some examples of environmental stimuli to which plants respond?
Plants respond to environmental stimuli such as light, gravity, and touch.

Response to Seasons

Year after year, some plants flower in the spring. Other plants flower in summer. Still other plants flower in the fall. Plants such as chrysanthemums flower when nights are long and days are short. These plants are called short-day plants. Plants such as spinach and irises flower when nights are short and days are long. These are called long-day plants.

Photoperiod and Flowering In the early 1920s, scientists discovered that the flowering of tobacco plants depends on the amount of light they receive. Many plants respond to the relative lengths of darkness and light in a day, or the photoperiod. Their response is called **photoperiodism.**

Scientists have discovered that the pigment phytochrome (FYT oh krohm) plays a role in the way plants respond to photoperiod. Phytochrome absorbs red light. It also starts a number of signals within plant cells. These signals determine various plant responses, such as flowering and growth.

▣ **Key Question** How do plants respond to seasonal changes?
Photoperiodism is a major factor in the timing of seasonal activities such as flowering and growth.

BUILD Connections

EFFECTS OF PHOTOPERIOD

How much light a plant receives and when it receives the light can affect when the plant flowers.

In Your Workbook Go to your workbook to learn more about the effect of photoperiod. Complete the table for Response to Seasons.

Effect of Photoperiod on Flowering			
	Long Day Midnight ... Noon	**Short Day** Midnight ... Noon	**Interrupted Night** Midnight ... Noon
Short-Day Plant		Short-day plants flower only when exposed to an extended period of darkness.	
Long-Day Plant	Long-day plants flower when exposed to a short period of darkness.		Long-day plants also flower if a brief period of light interrupts the darkness—this essentially divides one long night into two short nights.

Adaptations for Winter In autumn, the leaves of deciduous trees stop photosynthesis and fall from the trees. The meristems at the tips of the branches produce thick, waxy scales. These scales cover and protect the new stem and leaf buds throughout the winter.

Winter Dormancy In winter, many plants become dormant. Phytochrome controls the many changes that prepare plants for winter dormancy. As cold weather approaches, deciduous plants move materials from leaves to roots. They stop photosynthesis and seal off leaves from the rest of the plant.

▶ *Leaf Loss* Many plants lose their leaves during the colder months. Because days are shorter in the fall, the phytochrome in leaves absorbs less light. The production of auxin drops, while the production of ethylene increases. The change in the relative amounts of these two hormones causes leaves to shut down. The pigment chlorophyll breaks down. Other pigments in the leaves, such as the bright yellow and orange carotenoids, can now be seen. Bright reds come from freshly made anthocyanins.

▶ *Changes to Meristems* Hormones also produce important changes in apical meristems. Meristems stop producing new leaves. Instead, they produce thick, waxy scales that protect leaf buds from the cold. Xylem and phloem tissues fill up with ions and organic compounds. This solution acts like antifreeze in a car: It keeps the tree's sap from freezing.

Key Question How do plants respond to cold winters? **As cold weather approaches, deciduous plants stop photosynthesis. They move materials from leaves to roots and seal off leaves from the rest of the plant.**

CHECK Understanding

Apply Vocabulary
Use the highlighted words from the lesson to complete each sentence correctly.

1. The relative lengths of light and darkness produce a stimulus known as _____.

2. The growth of a plant toward a light source is called _____.

Critical Thinking

3. **Explain** What are the main roles of plant hormones?

4. **Relate Cause and Effect** Explain why a person who trims bushes should understand the effect of auxins on the growth of stems.

5. **Apply Concepts** Describe three examples of plant responses to external stimuli.

6. **Write to Learn** Answer the third clue of the mystery. Use the words *hormone*, *stimulus*, and *respond* in your answer.

MYSTERY CLUE

Kerosene heaters give off carbon dioxide and ethylene as they burn kerosene. Electric heaters do not give off these gases. Could this difference explain why the lemons didn't ripen? (**Hint:** See p. 589.)

 **BIOLOGY**.com ⟩ Search (Lesson 24.3) **GO** • Lesson Assessment

24.4 Plants and Humans

MD CLG **3.2.2** Changes in Metabolic Activity, **3.3.1** Sexual Reproduction and Variation, **3.5.3** Population Dynamics, **3.5.4** Global Food Webs, **3.6.1** Analyze Consequences. SPI **1.1.1** Problems and Solutions, **1.5.2** Communicate Information, **1.7.2** Evaluate Ideas, **1.7.3** Role of Science.

Agriculture

Walk through a grocery store and you will see products made from hundreds of different plants. Which plants are most important? Are there plants that humans can't live without?

Origin of Agriculture Agriculture, or farming, is the foundation of human society. Evidence suggests that agriculture developed separately in many parts of the world about 10,000 to 12,000 years ago. Once people learned how to grow plants for food, they tended to stay in one place. This led to the development of governments and other social institutions. Even today, more humans focus on agriculture than on any other activity.

Worldwide Patterns Thousands of different plants are raised for food. But for the bulk of their food, most people in the world rely on the seeds of four angiosperms—rice, wheat, corn, and soybeans. Three of these crops are grasses. In the United States, about 80 percent of cropland is used to grow wheat, corn, soybeans, and hay. These four crops are used for both humans and livestock. Of these crops, wheat, corn, and hay are grasses.

🔑 **Key Question** Which crops are the major food supply for humans? **Worldwide, most people depend on a few crops, including rice, wheat, soybeans, and corn, for the major part of their food.**

Plants and Agriculture Rice is a major crop in China and much of Southeast Asia.

Key Questions

🔑 Which crops are the major food supply for humans?

🔑 In addition to food, what are some benefits that humans get from plants?

BUILD Understanding

Preview Visuals Look at the last picture in the lesson. Identify the plants that provided the raw materials for the products shown. Then, list other products that come from plants.

In Your Workbook Go to your workbook to learn more about previewing visuals. Complete the activity for Lesson 24.4.

green revolution
the development of highly productive crops and the use of modern agriculture to increase crop yields

🖋 ACADEMIC WORDS

The word *revolution* is used to describe a major change in society. During the Industrial Revolution, for example, improvements in technology changed the way goods were manufactured. The green revolution changed methods of farming in many parts of the world.

New Plants The introduction of new crop plants has often changed human history. Four hundred years ago, plants such as corn and peanuts were unknown in Europe. The introduction of these plants from the Americas changed European agriculture. We may think of potatoes as a German or Irish food. But, originally, potatoes came from South America.

Agriculture has been improved through selective breeding. Recall that humans use selective breeding to produce crops and animals that have desirable traits. The corn grown by Native Americans was selectively bred. It was developed thousands of years ago from teosinte (tee oh SIN tee), a grass from Mexico. Most crops grown today are the result of selective breeding. For example, cabbage, broccoli, and cauliflower were all developed from a single species of wild mustard.

Changes in Agriculture Between 1950 and 1970, people began a worldwide effort to fight hunger by improving methods of farming. This effort, called the **green revolution,** greatly increased the world's food supply. The green revolution used new varieties of seeds and fertilizers. Fertilizers provide plants with nutrients such as nitrogen, phosphorus, and potassium. These nutrients make plants grow larger and produce more food. For thousands of years, farmers have provided crops with nutrients from natural sources, such as animal remains and manure. Today, many farmers use artificial fertilizers.

Fertilizers and pesticides must be used with great care. Too much fertilizer can kill plants. Fertilizer that washes off fields can contaminate the water. Pesticides are chemicals that are used to kill pests such as insects. Because pesticides are poisons, they can harm wildlife and humans if not used correctly.

From Wild Grass to Crop The selective breeding of teosinte (left) began about 8000 years ago. It led to the development of modern corn (right). As you can see from the image of the quarter, modern corn has much larger kernels compared to its ancestor teosinte.

Teosinte

Modern Corn

Products From Plants Plants provide raw materials for many useful products.

◀ The succulent plant *Aloe vera* contains many chemicals that soothe and moisturize the skin. Extracts of this plant are used in many skin lotions as well as in burn and wound ointments.

Fiber, Wood, and Medicine

Some of the most important uses of plants have nothing to do with food. Plants produce materials that we use for homes and clothes. They also provide some of our most effective medicines. If you are reading this page in a printed book, you are looking at paper made from North American conifers. You may be sitting on a chair made from an oak tree. And you are probably wearing at least one piece of clothing made from the fibers of the cotton plant.

Key Question In addition to food, what are some benefits that humans get from plants? **Plants provide the raw materials for our homes and clothes, and some of our most effective medicines.**

The acoustical properties of Sitka spruce wood make it ideal for use in pianos, guitars, violins, and other musical instruments. ▼

Cotton is used in countless products including thread, fabrics, bandages, carpeting, and insulation. Cotton fibers are outgrowths of the seed coat epidermis. ▶

CHECK Understanding

Apply Vocabulary
Use the highlighted words from the lesson to complete each sentence correctly.

1. The _____ led to the production of much larger amounts of food.

Critical Thinking

2. Review What four crops form the base of the world's food supply?

3. Explain In addition to providing food, why are plants important to human society? Give three examples.

4. Write to Learn What would life be like if humans had never developed agriculture? Write a short story that describes such a world.

 BIOLOGY.com Search (Lesson 24.4) **GO** • Lesson Assessment

 **eal-World Lab**

 CLG **3.2.1** Processes and Functions. SPI **1.2.7** Apply Results, **1.3.1** Use Equipment, **1.3.3** Safe Handling of Materials, **1.4.1** Organize Data, **1.5.9** Synthesize Ideas.

Pre-Lab: Plant Hormones and Leaves

Problem How does a plant hormone affect leaf loss?

Materials leafy plant, masking tape, permanent marker, scissors, string, toothpick, auxin paste, plastic container or tray

Lab Manual Chapter 24 Lab

Skills Focus Observe, Draw Conclusions, Apply Concepts

Connect to the **Big idea** A plant may flower in response to a change in the hours of daylight, or a plant may stop growing in response to colder temperatures. These responses to changes in the environment are coordinated by plant hormones, which regulate plant development. A hormone may stimulate roots to grow, seeds to germinate, or fruits to ripen. A hormone may inhibit cell division or promote dormancy of seeds or plants. In this lab, you will investigate the effect of a plant hormone on leaf loss.

Background Questions

a. Explain Do all plant cells respond to every plant hormone? Why or why not?

b. Explain What is a photoperiod? What is dormancy? How are they related?

c. Review In the fall, what happens to the production of auxins and ethylene in the leaves of flowering plants?

Pre-Lab Questions

Preview the procedure in the lab manual.

1. Use Visuals Draw a simple leaf. Label the blade and the petiole.

2. Control Variables What is the control in this experiment?

3. Infer How will auxins move from the paste to the base of the petiole?

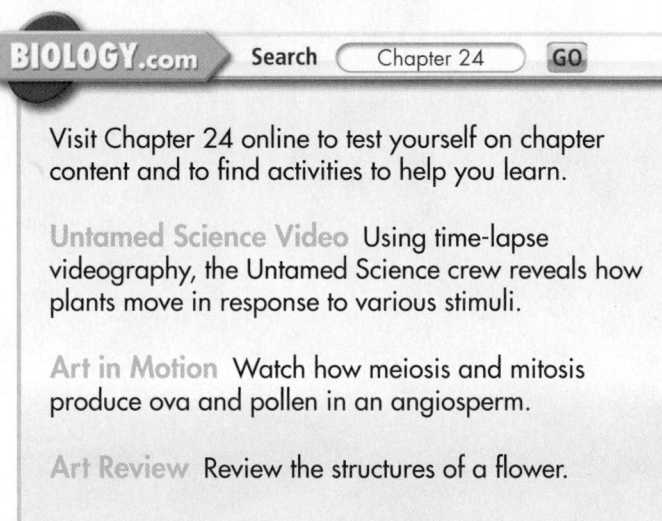

BIOLOGY.com ▸ Search (Chapter 24) GO

Visit Chapter 24 online to test yourself on chapter content and to find activities to help you learn.

Untamed Science Video Using time-lapse videography, the Untamed Science crew reveals how plants move in response to various stimuli.

Art in Motion Watch how meiosis and mitosis produce ova and pollen in an angiosperm.

Art Review Review the structures of a flower.

InterActive Art Change the length of day and see how it affects both short- and long-day plants.

24.1 Reproduction in Flowering Plants

- Flowers are reproductive organs that are made up of four kinds of specialized leaves: sepals, petals, stamens, and carpels.

- The process of fertilization in angiosperms differs from fertilization in other plants. In angiosperms, there are two fertilization events. One produces the zygote. The other produces a tissue called endosperm within the seed.

- Vegetative reproduction is the formation of new individuals by mitosis. Vegetative reproduction does not include gametes, flowers, or fertilization.

stamen (p. 579)
anther (p. 579)
carpel (p. 579)
stigma (p. 579)
embryo sac (p. 580)
double fertilization (p. 581)
endosperm (p. 581)
vegetative reproduction (p. 583)

24.2 Fruits and Seeds

- As angiosperm seeds mature, the ovary walls thicken to form a fruit. The fruit surrounds and protects the developing seeds.

- Seeds are spread by animals, wind, and water. Seeds in fleshy fruits are usually spread by animals. Seeds that are spread by wind or water usually have lightweight fruits that can be carried by wind or float on water.

- Environmental factors such as temperature and moisture can cause a seed to end dormancy and germinate.

dormancy (p. 586)
germination (p. 586)

24.3 Plant Hormones

- Plant hormones serve as signals that control the development of cells, tissues, and organs. They also coordinate a plant's responses to the environment.

- The opposing effects of plant hormones balance each other, contributing to a plant's homeostasis.

- Plants respond to environmental stimuli such as light, gravity, and touch.

- The relative length of darkness and light, or the photoperiod, affects seasonal activities such as flowering and growth.

- As cold weather approaches, deciduous plants stop photosynthesis. They move materials from leaves to roots and seal off leaves from the rest of the plant.

hormone (p. 588)
target cell (p. 588)
receptor (p. 588)
tropism (p. 590)
phototropism (p. 590)
gravitropism (p. 590)
thigmotropism (p. 590)
photoperiodism (p. 591)

24.4 Plants and Humans

- Worldwide, most people depend on a few crops, including rice, wheat, soybeans, and corn, for the major part of their food.

- Plants produce the raw materials for our homes and clothes. They also provide some of our most powerful and effective medicines.

green revolution (p. 594)

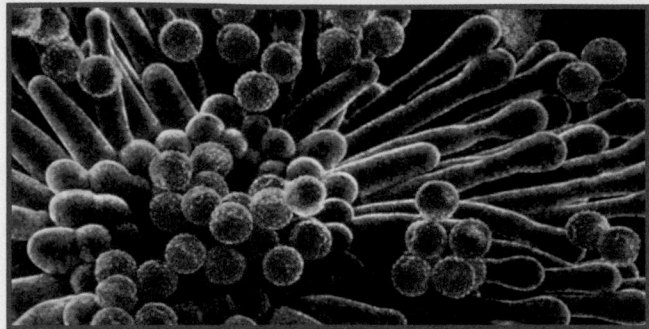

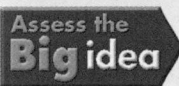 Assess the **Big** idea

Growth, Development, and Reproduction

Write an answer to the question below.

Q. How do changes in the environment affect the reproduction, development, and growth of plants?

Constructed Response

Write an answer to each of the numbered questions below. The answer to each numbered question should be one or two paragraphs long. To help get ideas, read the **Hints** below the question.

1. **How do animals in an ecosystem affect the reproduction of angiosperms?**

   Hint The key function of a flower is reproduction.

   Hint Fruits and seeds need to be dispersed.

2. **How do plants respond to light, gravity, and touch? Include the names of these three responses in your answer.**

   Hint Sometimes, a plant grows toward a stimulus. Sometimes, it grows away from a stimulus.

   Hint Sometimes, shoots and roots have different responses to the same stimulus.

3. **How does the interaction of hormones and the environment control the germination of seeds?**

   Hint Dormancy can ensure that a plant germinates under ideal conditions.

Foundations for Learning Wrap-Up

Use the layered book that you made while reading the chapter to help you review concepts related to how angiosperms reproduce and respond to the environment.

Activity 1 Work with a small group to make an illustrated book that describes how plants reproduce and how they respond to changes in their environment. You can add illustrations to your layered book, or you can make a new book.

Activity 2 The last page of your layered book is blank. Use this page to write review questions as shown below. Use these questions to help you learn the concepts in the chapter. When you are stumped, flip to the other pages in your layered book to find help.

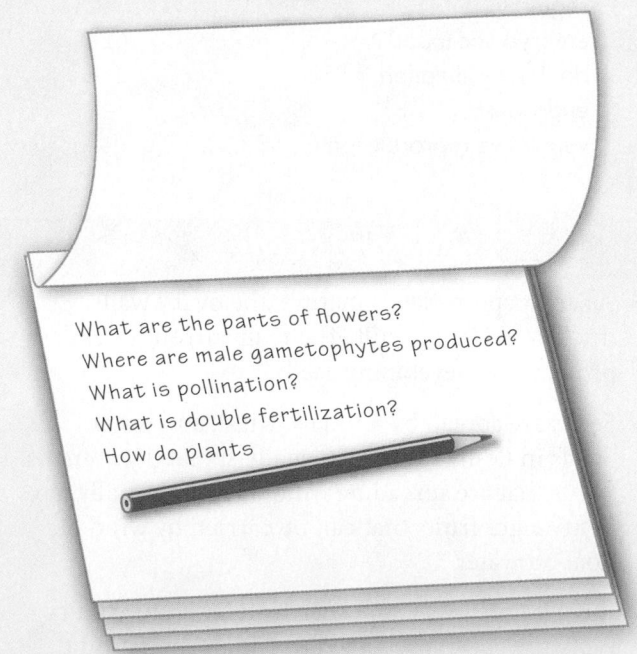

What are the parts of flowers?
Where are male gametophytes produced?
What is pollination?
What is double fertilization?
How do plants

24.1 Reproduction in Flowering Plants

Understand Key Concepts

Use this art to answer questions 1–3.

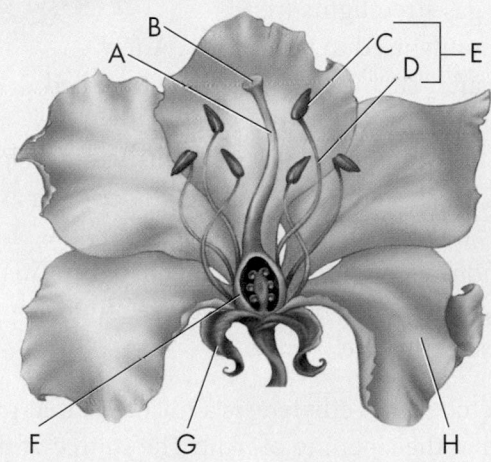

1. Which structure produces the male gametophytes?

a. A   **c.** C

b. B   **d.** D

2. Pollination takes place when a pollen grain lands on

a. B.   **c.** F.

b. C.   **d.** G.

Test-Taking Tip

Read All Letters Carefully Sometimes the answers are letters only. Don't get confused by the capital letter and the lowercase letter. As you read each answer choice, circle the corresponding letter in the diagram. Then write the name of the part next to the answer choice. So, in question 2, look at answer **a.** It is B, so circle B in the diagram. What is it? Write "stigma" next to B. This way, you can read the words, not just the letters.

---

3. What is the name for the entire female structure of a flower? Which three structures in the diagram make up the female part of a flower? Name each of these parts.

Think Critically

4. Infer Bees are important pollinators. Recently, scientists have discovered that bee populations are getting smaller, but they don't know why. What might happen to angiosperms if bees disappear?

24.2 Fruits and Seeds

Understand Key Concepts

5. A period during which an embryo is alive but not growing is called

a. dormancy.   **c.** germination.

b. fertilization.   **d.** pollination.

6. In the carpel, the thickened ovary wall will eventually become the

a. cotyledon.   **c.** female gametophyte.

b. endosperm.   **d.** fruit.

7. What is the function of seed dormancy? Give two examples of when it is helpful to a plant.

Think Critically

8. Infer Some flowers have stamens but lack carpels. Can these flowers produce fruits? Explain your reasoning.

24.3 Plant Hormones

Understand Key Concepts

9. The hormone that stimulates cell division and causes seeds to germinate is

a. auxin.   **c.** ethylene.

b. cytokinin.   **d.** gibberellin.

Think Critically

10. Form a Hypothesis Form a hypothesis that describes how plants such as vines benefit from thigmotropism.

11. Evaluate Spinach is a long-day plant. It grows best when night length is 10 hours or less. Will spinach grow well near the equator? Explain your reasoning.

24.4 Plants and Humans

Understand Key Concepts

12. Most human food comes from
   a. angiosperms.   **c.** gymnosperms.
   b. conifers.   **d.** trees.

Think Critically

13. Infer How is it possible that most of our food comes from seeds rather than the plant body?

Connecting Concepts

Use Science Graphics

Growth responses of plants to stimuli are called tropisms. *A tropism is positive if the affected plant part grows toward the stimulus. The response is negative if the plant part grows away from the stimulus. The experiment shown below tested the effect of gravitropism on plant growth. The conclusion drawn from the experiment was that the plant stems grow upward due to negative gravitropism. Use the diagram to answer questions 14–17.*

14. Interpret Visual Describe the three experimental setups and the result of each.

15. Form a Hypothesis What could be a probable hypothesis for this experiment?

16. Evaluate From the experimental setups shown, was the hypothesis successfully tested? Explain.

17. Evaluate What kinds of changes would you make to improve this experimental design?

solve the CHAPTER MYSTERY

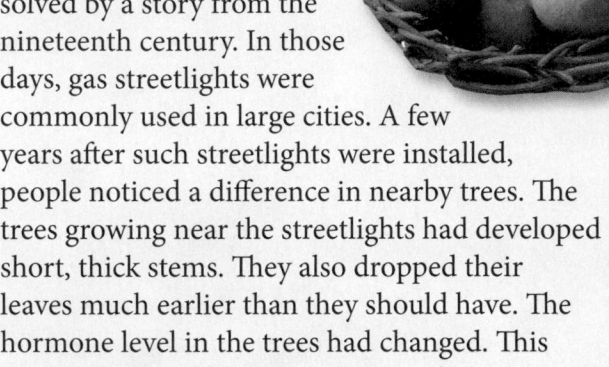

THE GREEN LEMONS

The mystery of why the lemons didn't ripen was solved by a story from the nineteenth century. In those days, gas streetlights were commonly used in large cities. A few years after such streetlights were installed, people noticed a difference in nearby trees. The trees growing near the streetlights had developed short, thick stems. They also dropped their leaves much earlier than they should have. The hormone level in the trees had changed. This change happened because the streetlights released ethylene.

Remember that ethylene is a hormone that plays a role in the ripening of fruit. The source of the ethylene does not matter. The ethylene made by a plant is the same as the ethylene released by a kerosene heater. Because ethylene is a gas, it can diffuse through the air, cell walls, and membranes of a plant and its fruit. Replacing the kerosene heaters with electric heaters removed the source of ethylene in the warehouse. As a result, the lemons stayed green and did not ripen.

1. Relate Cause and Effect Tomatoes that are put in a paper bag with apples ripen much more quickly than those placed in open air. What would this suggest about the effects of ripe apples on unripe tomatoes?

2. Propose a Solution How could farmers, shippers, and grocers use the effects of ethylene to their advantage?

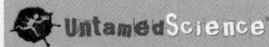 **Never Stop Exploring Your World.** Finding the solution to The Green Lemons mystery is only the beginning. Take a video field trip with the ecogeeks of Untamed Science to see where this mystery leads.

Multiple Choice

1. Where in a flower arc pollen grains produced?
A sepals   C anthers
B carpels   D ovary   CLG 3.2.1

2. Which part of the flower develops into a fruit?
A pollen tube   C stigma
B sepals   D ovary   CLG 3.2.1

3. Which flower structure includes all the others?
A style   C stigma
B carpel   D ovary   CLG 3.2.1

4. The trumpet honeysuckle has long, red, narrow tubular flowers. What is the most likely means of pollination?
A wind
B water
C bee
D hummingbird   CLG 3.5.1

5. All of the following are fruits EXCEPT
A tomato.
B corn.
C potato.
D cucumber.   CLG 3.2.1

6. Seeds that are contained in large, fleshy fruits are usually dispersed by
A animals.
B water.
C wind.
D rotting.   CLG 3.5.1

7. Which of the following causes fruit to ripen?
A auxin
B cytokinin
C ethylene
D gibberellin   CLG 3.2.1

8. Which is an example of thigmotropism?
A change in leaf color
B climbing vines
C blooming
D photoperiod   CLG 3.2.2

Questions 9–10

The results of an experiment are summarized in the art below.

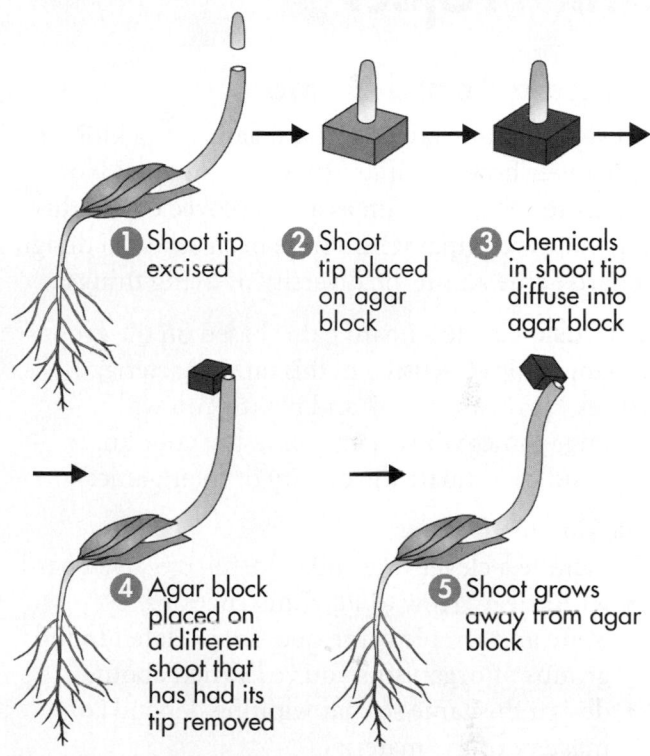

① Shoot tip excised
② Shoot tip placed on agar block
③ Chemicals in shoot tip diffuse into agar block
④ Agar block placed on a different shoot that has had its tip removed
⑤ Shoot grows away from agar block

9. Which of the following can be concluded from the results of this experiment alone?
A Hormones are produced in the growing tips of plant roots.
B Plants grow toward the sun due to compounds produced in their stems.
C Agar blocks contain a variety of plant compounds.
D Compounds produced in shoot tips can cause stems to bend.   SPI 1.4.2

10. Applying your knowledge of specific plant hormones, explain the results.   CLG 3.2.1

Open-Ended Response

11. Describe why seed dormancy is a valuable adaptation that has helped explain the evolutionary success of seed plants.   CLG 3.2.1

If You Have Trouble With . . .

Question	1	2	3	4	5	6	7	8	9	10	11
See Lesson	24.1	24.2	24.1	24.1	24.2	24.2	24.3	24.3	24.3	24.3	24.2

Unit Project

Create a Board Game

Did you have any favorite board games as a kid? Remember how much fun they were to play? Now you get to relive that fun as an employee of an educational toy company! You have been asked to design a board game about the diversity of living things.

Your Task Create a board game based on the groups of living things discussed in this unit—bacteria, viruses, "protists," fungi, and plants. You will exchange games with classmates to test your knowledge and to evaluate the quality of their game.

Be sure to
- include a clever title and colorful, creative board.
- write clear "How to Play" instructions.
- write answerable game questions related to the groups of organisms you've learned about.
- design the game so that winning depends on mastery of the material.

Reflection Questions

1. Score your game using the rubric below. What score did you give yourself?
2. What did you do well in this project?
3. What needs improvement?
4. What aspects of another group's game did you like? Why?
5. After playing the game, what topics did you do well with? What topics do you need to study more?

Assessment Rubric

Score	Scientific Content	Quality of Game
4	Game includes challenging, but answerable, questions about all of the groups discussed in the unit. Winning the game depends on how well a player knows the material.	Game is very well designed and creative. "How to Play" instructions are clear and easy to follow.
3	Game includes answerable questions on all of the groups discussed in the unit. Winning the game depends on how well a player knows the material.	Game is designed effectively. "How to Play" instructions can be followed.
2	Game includes some answerable questions, but others are unclear or impossible to answer. Winning the game does not necessarily depend on how well a player knows the material.	Game design could use improvement. "How to Play" instructions are difficult to follow.
1	Many questions are vague and/or unanswerable. Winning the game does not depend on how well a player knows the material.	Game design shows little evidence of planning. "How to Play" instructions are impossible to follow.

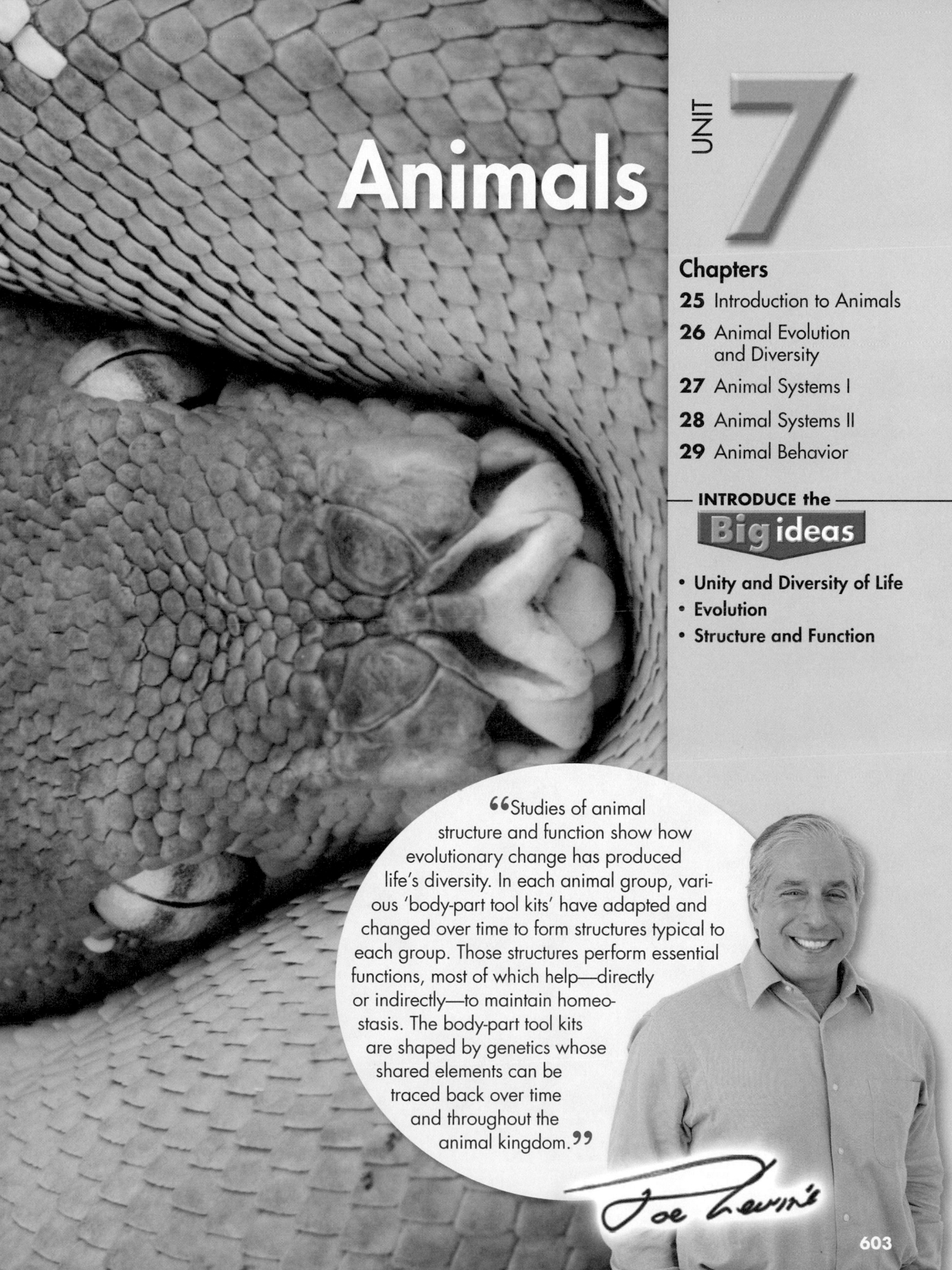

Animals

INTRODUCE the Big ideas

- **Unity and Diversity of Life**
- **Evolution**
- **Structure and Function**

"Studies of animal structure and function show how evolutionary change has produced life's diversity. In each animal group, various 'body-part tool kits' have adapted and changed over time to form structures typical to each group. Those structures perform essential functions, most of which help—directly or indirectly—to maintain homeostasis. The body-part tool kits are shaped by genetics whose shared elements can be traced back over time and throughout the animal kingdom."

Joe Levine

25 Introduction to Animals

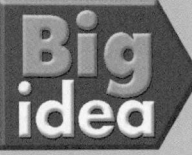

Big idea **Unity and Diversity of Life**

Q: What characteristics and traits define animals?

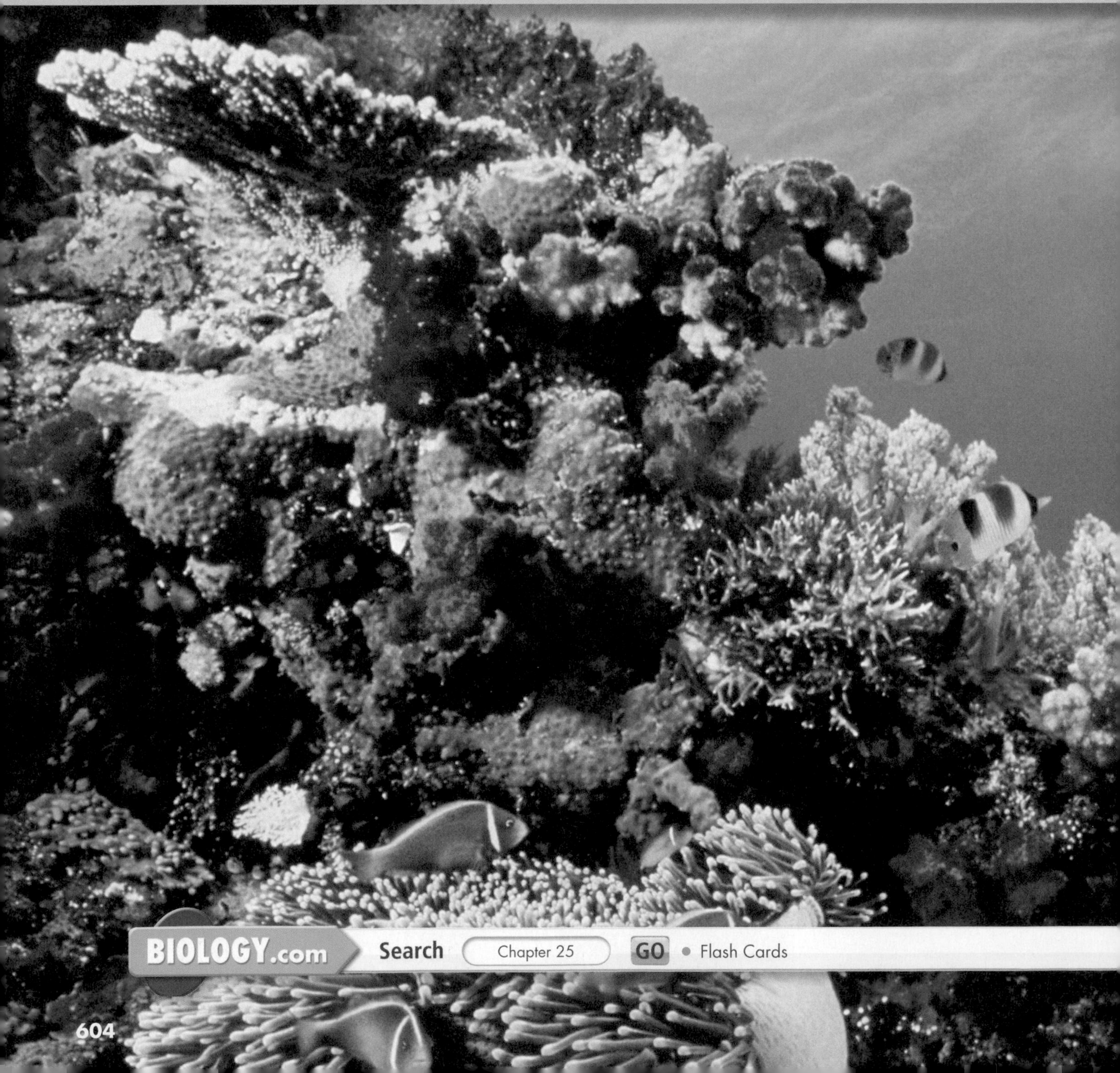

BIOLOGY.com Search Chapter 25 GO • Flash Cards

Though they look very different, the hundreds of animal species that make up or live near a coral reef share characteristics common to all animals.

CHAPTER
MYSTERY

SLIME DAY AT THE BEACH

It was a warm October day in Boston when people started calling beach offices, aquariums, and even 9-1-1. Beaches near Boston were coated with a layer of jellylike ooze. People were confused and worried. Some thought there had been an oil spill. However, police and firefighters found that the ooze was not oil.

More slimy masses kept washing up on the beach. When people looked more closely, they saw that the slime was made of small, individual creatures. Each creature was transparent and the size of a fingernail. What were they?

Read for Mystery Clues As you read this chapter, look for clues to help you find out what the slime was.

FOUNDATIONS for Learning

You can use a layered book to review the main ideas in this chapter. Make a layered book by stapling pieces of paper together. Your book should have visible tabs, as in the diagram below. Write the name of the first lesson on the front page of your book. Write the main topics from the lesson on the tabs that are showing. Write notes for each main topic on the part of each paper that is not showing. Use both words and pictures in your notes.

Make another layered book for Lesson 2. Make a third layered book using the key questions in the chapter, but do not write notes in this third book yet. At the end of the chapter are two activities that use your layered books to help answer the question: What characteristics and traits define animals?

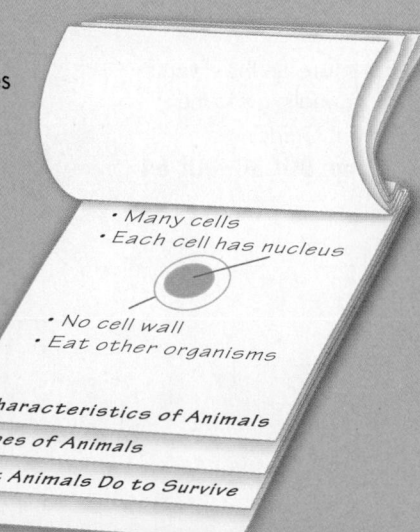

- Many cells
- Each cell has nucleus
- No cell wall
- Eat other organisms

Characteristics of Animals

Types of Animals

What Animals Do to Survive

25.1 What Is an Animal?

MD CLG **3.1.2** Homeostasis, **3.1.3** Matter and Energy, **3.2.1** Processes and Functions, **3.2.2** Changes in Metabolic Activity, **3.3.1** Sexual Reproduction and Variation. SPI **1.3.1** Use Equipment, **1.4.2** Analyze Data, **1.5.2** Communicate Information, **1.5.7** Classification Systems, **1.5.8** Compare.

Key Questions

🔑 *What characteristics do all animals share?*

🔑 *What characteristics distinguish invertebrates and chordates?*

🔑 *What essential functions must animals perform to survive?*

BUILD Understanding

Venn Diagram Use a Venn diagram to show the similarities and differences between invertebrates and chordates.

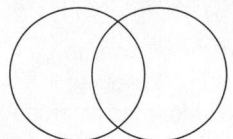

Invertebrates   Chordates

In Your Workbook Go to your workbook to learn more about making a Venn diagram. Complete the Venn diagram started for you.

For more on the diversity of animals, go to the Visual Guide.
↻ **pp. DOL 30–DOL 64**

Characteristics of Animals

A bald eagle circles a salt marsh looking for prey. Suddenly, it dives and captures a fish. At the bottom of the marsh, worms burrow beneath rocks. In the air above the marsh, mosquitoes buzz. The eagle, fish, worms, and mosquitoes are all animals. All members of the animal kingdom share certain characteristics. Animals are heterotrophs, organisms that get energy by eating other organisms. Animals are multicellular, or have bodies composed of many cells. Animal cells are eukaryotic—each cell has a nucleus. Animal cells do not have cell walls.

🔑 **Key Question** What characteristics do all animals share? **Animals are multicellular heterotrophs that get energy by eating other organisms. Animals have eukaryotic cells that do not have cell walls.**

Types of Animals

The animal kingdom is a large and diverse group. Animals can be classified into two main groups: invertebrates and chordates.

Invertebrates More than 95 percent of all animals can be lumped into a catch-all grouping called **invertebrates.** That term is used to describe animals that do not have a backbone. Invertebrates include sea stars, jellyfishes, worms, snails, and insects. They range in size from dust mites to giant squids that are more than 14 meters long. "Invertebrates" are not a proper clade according to evolutionary classification. Scientists classify invertebrates into 33 different phyla.

Chordates Fewer than 5 percent of animal species are **chordates** (KAWR dayts). Chordates are members of the phylum Chordata. All chordates have four characteristics that are present during at least one stage of life. Chordates have a hollow nerve cord that runs along the back (or dorsal) part of the body. They also have a **notochord** that is located below the nerve cord. A notochord is a long supporting rod that runs through the body just below the nerve cord. Most chordates only have a notochord when they are embryos.

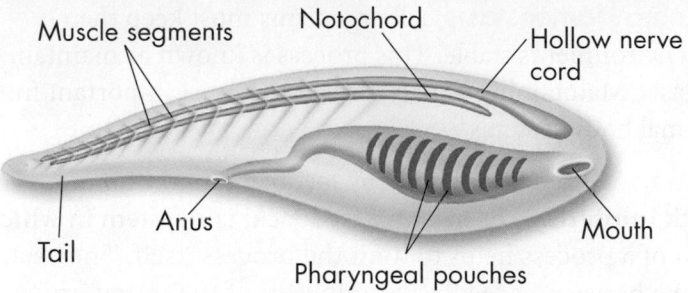

Muscle segments Notochord Hollow nerve cord

Anus

Tail

Pharyngeal pouches

Mouth

Characteristics of Chordates All chordates have a hollow nerve cord, a notochord, pharyngeal pouches, and a tail that extends past the anus. Some chordates have all these traits as adults. Other chordates only have some of these traits as embryos.

All chordates have a tail that extends past the anus. (The anus is the opening where wastes leave the body.) The tail disappears in some chordates as the embryo develops. All chordates also have **pharyngeal** (fuh RIN jee ul) **pouches.** Pharyngeal pouches are paired structures in the throat region. In some chordates, such as fishes, slits develop that connect pharyngeal pouches to the outside of the body. Pharyngeal pouches may develop into gills. Gills are structures that are used for gas exchange.

Phylum Chordata includes some odd aquatic animals known as nonvertebrate chordates. These chordates do not have a backbone. Most chordates develop a backbone, or vertebral column. Chordates with backbones are called **vertebrates.** Vertebrates include fishes, amphibians, reptiles, birds, and mammals.

Key Question What characteristics distinguish invertebrates and chordates?
Invertebrates lack a backbone. Chordates have all four of the following during at least one stage of life: a dorsal, hollow nerve cord; a notochord; a tail that extends past the anus; and pharyngeal pouches.

What Animals Do to Survive

Animals come in an amazing variety of body shapes, sizes, and colors. No matter what they look like, all animals must perform certain basic functions to stay alive. In addition, all animals must reproduce. Like all organisms, animals must keep their internal environments stable. They do this in three ways:
1. Animals gather and respond to information.
2. They take in and distribute oxygen and nutrients to cells.
3. They collect and get rid of carbon dioxide and other wastes.

Over time, members of different animal phyla have evolved very different body structures to perform the functions that keep them alive. You will study these structures in more detail in Chapters 27 and 28.

BUILD Vocabulary

invertebrate
an animal that lacks a backbone, or vertebral column

chordate
an animal that has, for at least one stage of its life, a dorsal, hollow nerve cord; a notochord; a tail that extends beyond the anus; and pharyngeal pouches

notochord
a long supporting rod that runs through a chordate's body just below the nerve cord

pharyngeal pouch
one of a pair of structures in the throat region of a chordate

vertebrate
an animal that has a backbone

PREFIXES

The prefix *in-* means "not." An invertebrate does *not* have a backbone. A vertebrate does have a backbone.

Maintaining Homeostasis All organisms must keep their internal environments stable. This process is known as maintaining homeostasis. Maintaining homeostasis is the most important function of all animal body systems.

Homeostasis is often maintained by feedback inhibition. **Feedback inhibition,** or negative feedback, is a system in which the result of a process helps to limit the process itself. The heating system in a house uses feedback inhibition. If the rooms are too cold, the thermostat turns on the heat. When the rooms get warm enough, the thermostat turns off the heat. Your body's thermostat works in a similar way. If you get too cold, you shiver. Shivering causes your muscles to generate heat. If you get too hot, you sweat. Sweating helps you to lose heat.

Gathering and Responding to Information Animals use many body systems to gather and respond to information in their environment. In many animals, the nervous system gathers information. Specialized cells called receptors sense light, sound, chemicals, and touch. Information from the receptors travels to other nerve cells, which determine how to respond. Some invertebrates have a loose network of nerve cells with no real center. Other invertebrates and most chordates have large numbers of nerve cells concentrated in a brain.

INQUIRY into Scientific Thinking

GUIDED INQUIRY

How Hydra Feed

The hydra is a small aquatic invertebrate that is related to jellyfish and sea anemones. The hydra has a tubelike body with long, thin tentacles at the top. *Daphnia* are also small aquatic invertebrates. They are related to shrimp and crabs. Each *Daphnia* has a round body and an eyespot. In this lab, you will investigate how hydra feed on *Daphnia*.

❶ Your teacher will provide you with hydra and *Daphnia*. Using a dropper pipette, gently place one hydra onto a well slide.

❷ Let the hydra adjust to its surroundings for 5 to 10 minutes.

❸ Using your dropper, add one *Daphnia* to the slide.

❹ Observe the hydra under the microscope.

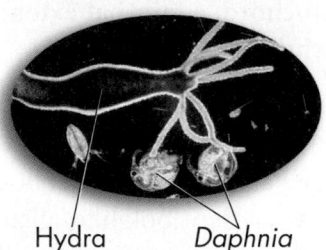

Hydra   *Daphnia*

Analyze and Conclude

1. Observe What happens when the *Daphnia* is added to the same slide as the hydra?

2. Draw Conclusions How do the hydra's tentacles help it to maintain homeostasis?

3. Quick Write What else would you like to learn about how the hydra survives in its environment? Write down two new questions.

In Your Workbook Get more help for this activity in your workbook.

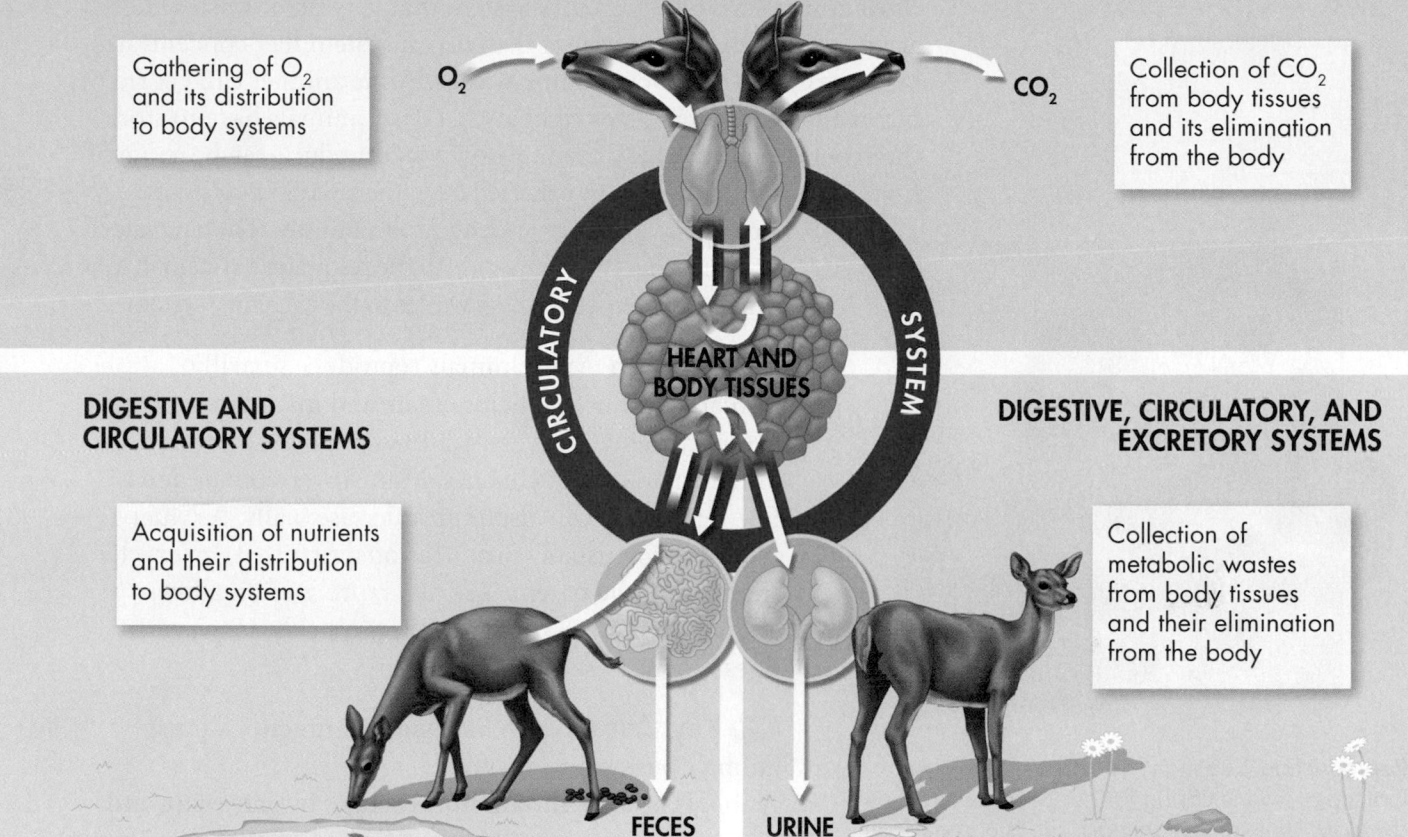

RESPIRATORY AND CIRCULATORY SYSTEMS

Gathering of O_2 and its distribution to body systems

O_2

CO_2

Collection of CO_2 from body tissues and its elimination from the body

CIRCULATORY SYSTEM

HEART AND BODY TISSUES

DIGESTIVE AND CIRCULATORY SYSTEMS

Acquisition of nutrients and their distribution to body systems

DIGESTIVE, CIRCULATORY, AND EXCRETORY SYSTEMS

Collection of metabolic wastes from body tissues and their elimination from the body

FECES

URINE

Animals often respond to the information they have processed by moving around. The nervous system causes muscles to become shorter. When muscles become shorter, they can move the animal's supporting structure, called a skeleton. Skeletons vary from phylum to phylum. Earthworms have fluid-filled, flexible skeletons. Insects and other invertebrates have skeletons outside their bodies. Vertebrates have skeletons inside their bodies that are made of bones.

Getting and Delivering Oxygen and Nutrients All animals must breathe to obtain oxygen. Small animals that live in wet places can "breathe" by allowing oxygen to diffuse across their skin. Larger animals use gills, lungs, or air passages to breathe.

All animals must eat to get nutrients. Many animals have digestive systems that break down food into nutrients. Then the body must deliver the oxygen and nutrients to its cells. Many animals use a circulatory system to carry oxygen and nutrients around the body. The circulatory system works together with the respiratory and digestive systems to keep an animal alive.

Collecting and Removing CO_2 and Other Wastes The activity of animal cells produces waste products. Some of these waste products contain nitrogen, often in the form of ammonia. Both carbon dioxide and ammonia are poisonous. In high concentrations, these substances can destroy cells. Therefore, the body must get rid of these wastes.

BUILD Connections

MOVING MATERIALS IN, AROUND, AND OUT OF THE BODY

The structures of an animal's respiratory, digestive, and excretory systems must work together with the structures of the animal's circulatory system.

Many animals use respiratory systems that get rid of carbon dioxide. Most animals have an excretory system that gets rid of wastes like ammonia. An excretory system is an organ system that concentrates or processes nitrogen-containing wastes. Some animals can get rid of nitrogen-containing wastes right away. Other animals have to store them before getting rid of them. Before waste products can be removed from the body, they have to be collected from the cells. Some sort of circulatory system is needed to collect wastes. The circulatory system brings carbon dioxide to the respiratory system. It also brings nitrogen-containing wastes to the excretory system.

Reproducing Most animals reproduce sexually. Sexual reproduction helps create and maintain genetic diversity. Genetic diversity allows a species to evolve as the environment changes. Many invertebrates and a few vertebrates can also reproduce asexually. Asexual reproduction usually produces offspring that are exactly the same as the parent. Asexual reproduction allows animals to increase their numbers quickly. However, it does not increase genetic diversity.

Reproduction Like many vertebrates, this pygmy marsupial frog is caring for her young while they develop. Unlike most animals, she is carrying her eggs on her back!

Key Question What essential functions must animals perform to survive?
Animals must maintain homeostasis by gathering and responding to information, getting and delivering oxygen and nutrients, and collecting and removing carbon dioxide and other wastes. They must also reproduce.

CHECK Understanding

Apply Vocabulary
Use the highlighted words from the lesson to complete each sentence correctly.

1. All _____ have a hollow nerve cord during at least one stage of life.

2. Fishes, amphibians, reptiles, birds, and mammals are all chordates that are also _____.

Critical Thinking

3. Compare and Contrast What is the defining characteristic of invertebrates? What are four characteristics of chordates?

4. Relate Name two waste products that are produced by an animal's cells. Why must these waste products be eliminated from an animal's body?

5. Write to Learn Answer the first clue of the mystery. Think about the characteristics of invertebrates and chordates. Which type of animal would have a stiff rod running along its tail?

MYSTERY CLUE

Scientists verified that the organisms were young animals that had a stiff rod running along the tail. What does this suggest about the slimy critters? (Hint: See p. 607.)

25.2 Animal Body Plans and Evolution

MD CLG 3.2.1 Processes and Functions, 3.3.1 Sexual Reproduction and Variation, 3.4.1 Evolutionary Change, 3.4.2 Relatedness Among Organisms. SPI 1.5.2 Communicate Information, 1.5.7 Classification Systems, 1.5.8 Compare.

Features of Body Plans

Why does a worm look so different from a fish? Why do butterflies have wings while dolphins have flippers? Body structures in animals that are alive today were shaped by millions of years of evolution. Each animal phylum has its own combination of body structures called a body plan. The eight main features of animal body plans are described below.

Levels of Organization As the first cells of most animals develop, they differentiate (or change) into specialized cells. These specialized cells are organized into tissues. Tissues combine during development to form organs. Organs work together to make up organ systems. Organ systems carry out complex functions for the body.

Body Symmetry The bodies of most animals show some kind of symmetry. Some animals have body parts that extend outward from the center. This type of symmetry is called **radial symmetry.** Radially symmetric animals can be sliced, like a pie, by imaginary planes beginning at the center. Some radially symmetric animals can be divided into an even number of "slices." Others, like sea stars, contain an odd number of radially symmetric parts.

Many animals have **bilateral symmetry.** In bilateral symmetry, a single imaginary plane divides the body into left and right sides that look the same. Animals with bilateral symmetry have a front (anterior) end and a back (posterior) end. Animals with bilateral symmetry also have an upper (dorsal) side and a lower (ventral) side. Your back is on your dorsal side. Your belly is on your ventral side.

Animals with radial symmetry have body parts that extend out from a central point. Animals with bilateral symmetry have distinct front (anterior) and back (posterior) ends and have right and left sides.

Key Questions

🔑 What are some features of animal body plans?

🔑 How are animal phyla defined?

BUILD Understanding

Concept Map You can use concept maps to show how ideas or concepts connect. As you read the lesson, draw a concept map showing the different features of animal body plans and the different types of each feature.

In Your Workbook Refer to your workbook to review the features of different body plans.

Radial Symmetry

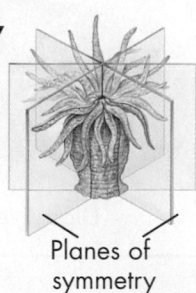

Planes of symmetry

Bilateral Symmetry

Posterior end

Dorsal side

Anterior end

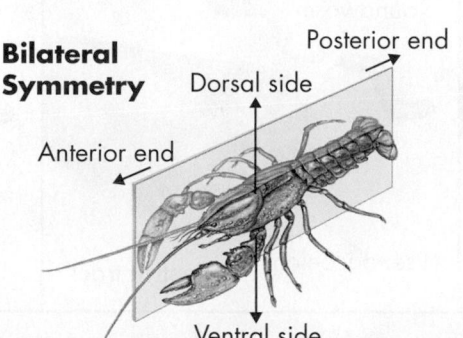

Ventral side

Body Symmetry Animals with radial symmetry have body parts that come out from a central point. Animals with bilateral symmetry have distinct front and back ends and left and right sides.

radial symmetry
a body plan in which body parts repeat around the center of the body

bilateral symmetry
a body plan in which a single imaginary line can divide the body into left and right sides that are mirror images of each other

endoderm
the innermost germ layer; develops into the linings of the digestive tract and much of the respiratory system

mesoderm
the middle germ layer; develops into muscles and much of the circulatory, reproductive, and excretory systems

ectoderm
the outermost germ layer; produces sense organs, nerves, and the outer layer of skin

coelom
a body cavity lined with mesoderm

pseudocoelom
a body cavity that is only partially lined with mesoderm

🖋 PREFIXES
You can use the prefixes for each word that describes a germ layer to remember where the germ layer is located in the embryo. The prefix *endo-* means "within." The prefix *meso-* means "middle." The prefix *ecto-* means "outside."

Differentiation of Germ Layers As fertilized eggs develop, the cells of most animals differentiate, or change, into three layers called germ layers. The **endoderm** is the inside germ layer. Its cells develop into the linings of the digestive system and most of the respiratory system. The **mesoderm** is the middle germ layer. Its cells develop into muscles and most of the circulatory, reproductive, and excretory systems. The **ectoderm** is the outer germ layer. Its cells develop into organs of the nervous system and the skin.

Formation of Body Cavity Most animals have some kind of body cavity. A body cavity is a space that is filled with fluid. A body cavity holds the organs and gives them space to grow. Your stomach and intestines are located in your body cavity. Many animals have a true **coelom** (SEE lum). A coelom is a body cavity that is completely lined with tissue that develops from the mesoderm. Some invertebrates have a **pseudocoelom** (soo doh SEE lum), which is only partly lined with tissue from the mesoderm. Other invertebrates, called acoelomates, do not have a body cavity at all.

Patterns of Embryo Development Every animal that reproduces sexually begins life as a fertilized egg, or **zygote** (ZY goht). As the zygote begins to develop, it develops into an embryo. As the embryo develops, it forms a hollow ball of cells called a **blastula** (BLAS tyoo luh). The blastula looks like an inflated balloon. As the blastula continues to develop, it folds in on itself. Imagine holding a partly inflated balloon in your hand and pushing your thumbs toward the center. This folding inward forms a tube down the middle of the blastula. This tube becomes a digestive tract. In a digestive tract, food enters through one opening, called the mouth. Wastes leave through another opening, called the anus.

The first opening that forms as the blastula folds is called a blastopore. This opening can become either the mouth or the anus, depending on the animal.

Body Cavities Acoelomates do not have a coelom between their body wall and digestive cavity. Pseudocoelomates have body cavities that are partly lined with tissue from the mesoderm.

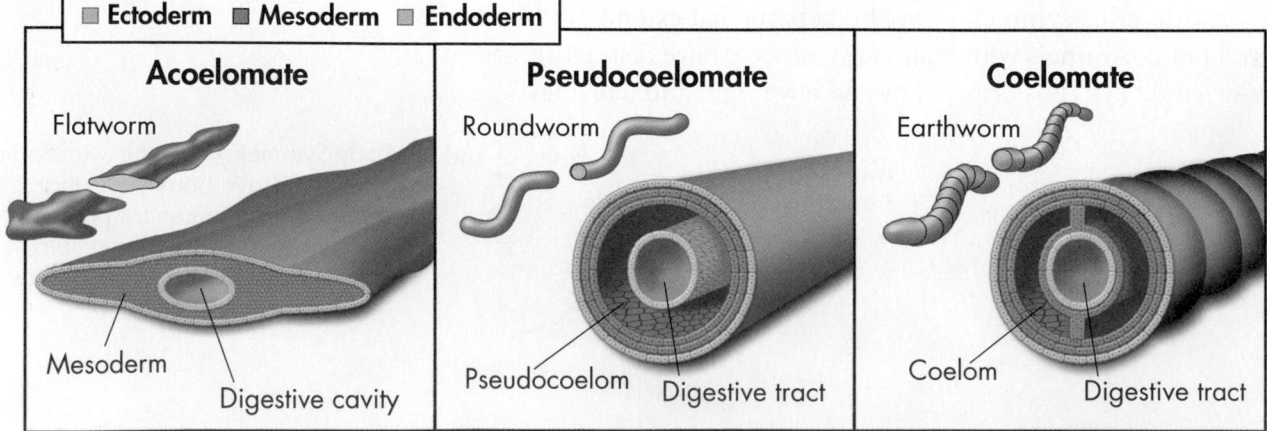

■ Ectoderm ■ Mesoderm ■ Endoderm

Acoelomate
Flatworm
Mesoderm
Digestive cavity

Pseudocoelomate
Roundworm
Pseudocoelom
Digestive tract

Coelomate
Earthworm
Coelom
Digestive tract

Blastopore Formation A hollow ball of cells called a blastula forms during the early development of an animal embryo. An opening called a blastopore forms in this ball. In deuterostomes, such as fishes, the blastopore forms an anus. In protostomes, such as grasshoppers, the blastopore forms a mouth.

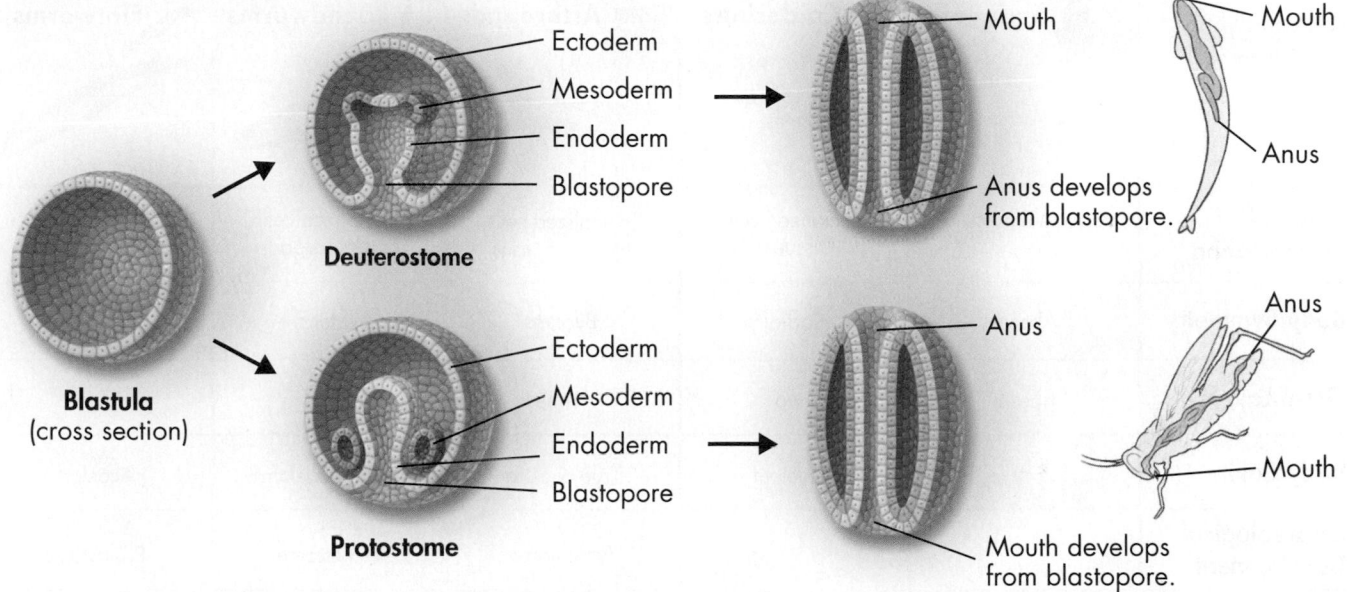

Blastula (cross section)

Deuterostome — Ectoderm, Mesoderm, Endoderm, Blastopore

Protostome — Ectoderm, Mesoderm, Endoderm, Blastopore

Mouth — Anus develops from blastopore. — Mouth — Anus

Anus — Mouth develops from blastopore. — Anus — Mouth

▶ *Protostomes* In phyla that are **protostomes** (PROH tuh stohms), the blastopore becomes the mouth. In protostomes, the anus forms from a second opening that develops at the opposite end of the tube. Most invertebrates are protostomes.

▶ *Deuterostomes* In **deuterostomes** (DOO tur uh stohms), the blastopore becomes the anus. The mouth is formed from the second opening that develops in the tube. Chordates and echinoderms are deuterostomes.

Segmentation: Repeating Parts As many animals that have bilateral symmetry develop, their bodies become divided into segments. Segments are body parts that are repeated. Worms, insects, and vertebrates usually have at least some parts that repeat on each side of the body. Bilateral symmetry and segmentation are often found together.

Cephalization: Getting a Head Animals with bilateral symmetry usually also have **cephalization** (sef uh lih ZAY shun). Cephalization is the concentration of sense organs and nerve cells at the front end of an animal. Cephalization often creates a head. Arthropods and vertebrates both show cephalization.

The heads of arthropods and vertebrates form when different body segments combine during embryo development. As the segments grow together, sense organs (such as eyes) and nerve cells become concentrated in the head. Animals with heads usually move in a "head-first" direction. Moving head first allows their sense organs to come into contact with new parts of their environment first.

Body Plans The different features of body plans are shown for nine animal phyla below. The body plans of modern animals suggest that invertebrates and chordates evolved from a common ancestor.

	Sponges 	Cnidarians 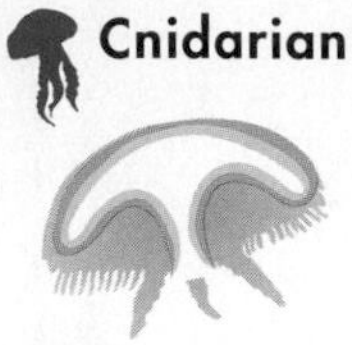	Arthropods 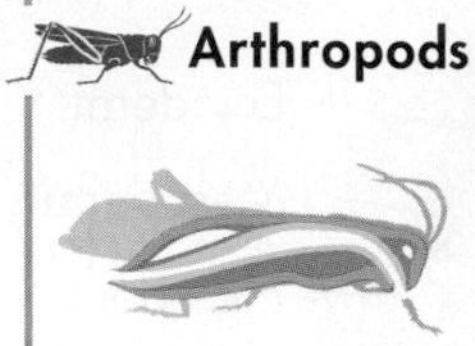	Roundworms 	Flatworms 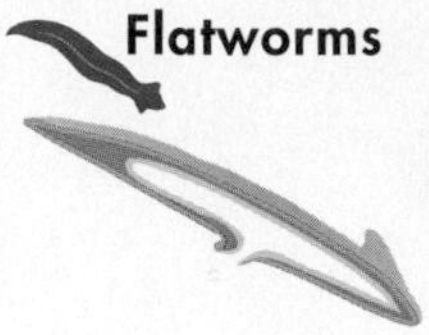
Ectoderm / Mesoderm / Endoderm					
Levels of Organization	Specialized cells	Specialized cells, tissues	Specialized cells, tissues, organs	Specialized cells, tissues, organs	Specialized cells, tissues, organs
Body Symmetry	Absent	Radial	Bilateral	Bilateral	Bilateral
Germ Layers	Absent	Two	Three	Three	Three
Body Cavity	–	Acoelom	True coelom	Pseudocoelom	Acoelom
Embryological Development	–	–	Protostome	Protostome	Protostome
Segmentation	Absent	Absent	Present	Absent	Absent
Cephalization	Absent	Absent	Present	Present	Present

	Annelids 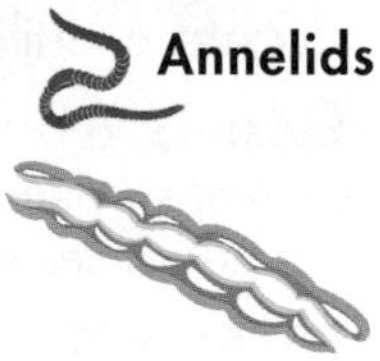	Mollusks 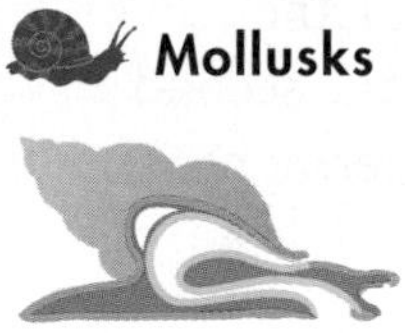	Echinoderms 	Chordates 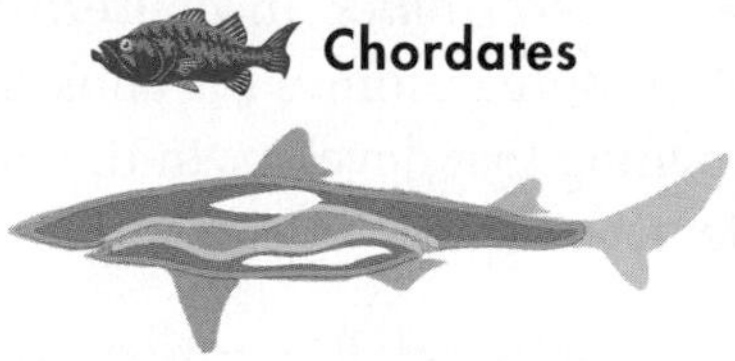
Ectoderm / Mesoderm / Endoderm				
Levels of Organization	Specialized cells, tissues, organs	Specialized cells, tissues, organs	Specialized cells, tissues, organs	Specialized cells, tissues, organs
Body Symmetry	Bilateral	Bilateral	Radial (as adults)	Bilateral
Germ Layers	Three	Three	Three	Three
Body Cavity	True coelom	True coelom	True coelom	True coelom
Embryological Development	Protostome	Protostome	Deuterostome	Deuterostome
Segmentation	Present	Absent	Absent	Present
Cephalization	Present	Present	Absent (as adults)	Present

Limb Formation: Legs, Flippers, and Wings Animals that have bilateral symmetry and segmentation usually have appendages on both sides of the body. Appendages can be bristles, legs, or other types of limbs. Dragonfly and bird wings, spider legs, dolphin flippers, and monkey arms are all appendages. Different kinds of appendages have evolved several times, and have been lost several times, in various animal groups.

🔑 **Key Question** What are some features of animal body plans? **Features of animal body plans include levels of organization, body symmetry, differentiation of germ layers, formation of body cavities, patterns of embryo development, segmentation, cephalization, and limb formation.**

The Cladogram of Animals

The features of animal body plans and other evidence provide information for building a cladogram, or phylogenetic tree, of animals. The cladogram below shows our current understanding of the relationships among animal phyla. Animal phyla are usually defined by their adult body plans and patterns of embryo development. For example, the phylum Arthropoda is defined by a body plan that includes bilateral symmetry, segmentation, cephalization, an external skeleton, and jointed legs. Every phylum has its own combination of ancient traits from ancestors and new traits that are found only in that phylum.

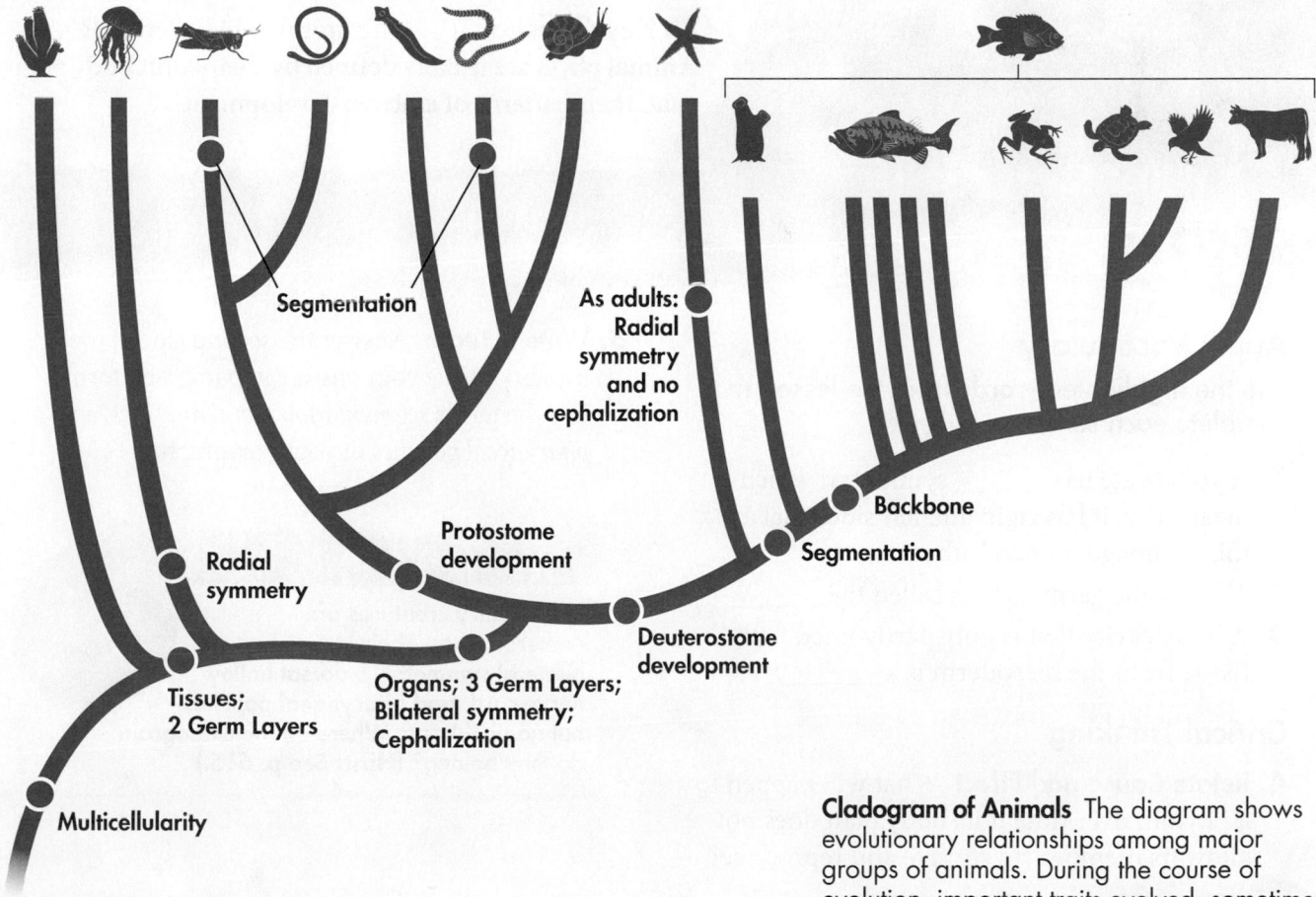

Segmentation

As adults:
Radial
symmetry
and no
cephalization

Protostome
development

Backbone

Segmentation

Radial
symmetry

Deuterostome
development

Tissues;
2 Germ Layers

Organs; 3 Germ Layers;
Bilateral symmetry;
Cephalization

Multicellularity

Single-celled animal ancestor

Cladogram of Animals The diagram shows evolutionary relationships among major groups of animals. During the course of evolution, important traits evolved, sometimes more than once, as shown by the circles.

Differences Between Phyla The cladogram shows the sequence in which important body plan features evolved. You may think that a cladogram shows "improvements" from one phylum to the next. This notion is not correct. The body systems of vertebrates are not better than the body systems of invertebrates. Any system found in a living animal is good enough to allow the animal to survive and reproduce.

Changes Within Phyla Different groups within each phylum show different variations on basic body plans. For example, land vertebrates usually have four limbs. Many of these animals, such as squirrels and frogs, walk or hop on four limbs that we call legs. In birds, the front limbs have evolved into wings. In monkeys, the front limbs have evolved into arms. And through evolution, snakes have lost all of their limbs!

Limb Variations Birds have evolved front limbs specialized as wings. Frogs have evolved four legs.

Evolutionary Experiments You can think of each phylum's body plan as an evolutionary "experiment." The first version of each major body plan appeared millions of years ago. Each body plan has changed as phylum members adapted to changing environments. If those changes enabled phylum members to survive and reproduce, the phylum still exists. If the body plan did not meet the changing challenges, groups in the phylum, or the entire phylum, have become extinct.

Key Question How are animal phyla defined?
Animal phyla are usually defined by their adult body plans and their patterns of embryo development.

CHECK
Understanding

Apply Vocabulary
Use the highlighted words from the lesson to complete each sentence correctly.

1. A vertebrate has _____ symmetry, which means that it has right and left sides that are mirror images of each other.
2. The middle germ layer is called the _____.
3. A body cavity that is only partly lined with tissue from the mesoderm is a _____.

Critical Thinking

4. **Relate Cause and Effect** What will happen to a phylum over time if its body plan does not allow its members to survive and reproduce?

5. **Write to Learn** Answer the second clue of the mystery. Write your answer in paragraph form. Use the terms *segmentation*, *deuterostomes*, and *pharyngeal pouches* in your paragraph.

MYSTERY CLUE

The mystery creatures are deuterostomes. Their larvae have bilateral symmetry, a dorsal hollow nerve cord, and pharyngeal pouches—but no backbone. Where on the cladogram do they belong? (**Hint:** See p. 615.)

BIOLOGY.com Search (Lesson 25.2) GO • Lesson Assessment

 SPI 1.3.1 Use Equipment, 1.5.1 Summarize Data, 1.5.7 Classification Systems.

Pre-Lab: Comparing Invertebrate Body Plans

Problem What characteristics can be used to classify invertebrates?

Materials compound microscope; prepared slides of cnidarian, roundworm, and earthworm cross sections; red, blue, and yellow colored pencils

Lab Manual Chapter 25 Lab

Skills Focus Observe, Classify, Compare and Contrast

Connect to the **Big idea** All members of Kingdom Animalia share a set of characteristics that define them as animals. However, the diversity within the kingdom is vast. For example, some animals have a backbone, but many do not. Some animals have radial symmetry, but many do not. In this lab, you will use preserved cross sections to compare the body plans of three invertebrates. You will pay particular attention to germ layers and body cavities.

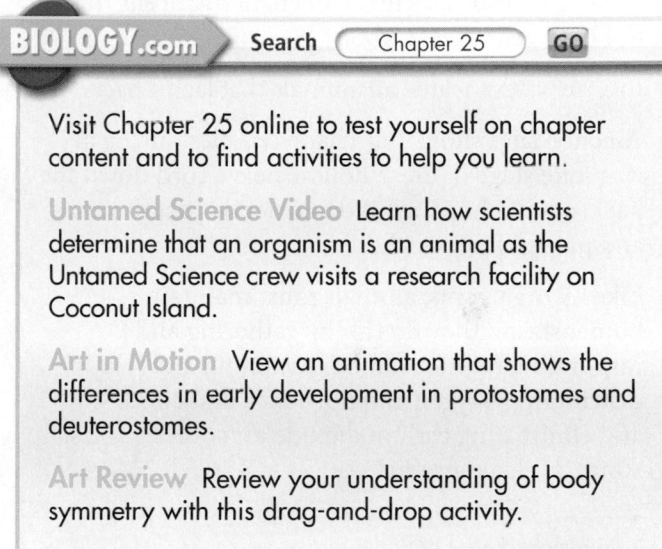

BIOLOGY.com   Search   Chapter 25   GO

Visit Chapter 25 online to test yourself on chapter content and to find activities to help you learn.

Untamed Science Video Learn how scientists determine that an organism is an animal as the Untamed Science crew visits a research facility on Coconut Island.

Art in Motion View an animation that shows the differences in early development in protostomes and deuterostomes.

Art Review Review your understanding of body symmetry with this drag-and-drop activity.

Background Questions

a. **Review** Describe three characteristics that all animals share.

b. **Review** What are the three germ layers, and what structures do they give rise to?

c. **Explain** What is the function of a body cavity?

Pre-Lab Questions

Preview the procedure in the lab manual.

1. **Compare and Contrast** Which two features of animal body plans will you be comparing in this lab?

2. **Apply Concepts** Where will you look for tissue that formed from the ectoderm layer?

3. **Infer** Is a hydra smaller than, larger than, or about the same size as an earthworm? Base your answer on the procedure in this lab.

25.1 What Is an Animal?

- Animals are members of the kingdom Animalia. Animals are heterotrophs that get nutrients and energy by eating other organisms. Animals have multicellular bodies made of eukaryotic cells that do not have cell walls.

- Invertebrates include all animals that lack a backbone.

- All chordates show four characteristics during at least one stage of life: a hollow nerve cord down the back, a notochord, a tail that extends past the anus, and pharyngeal pouches.

- Like all organisms, animals must maintain homeostasis. They do this by gathering and responding to information, obtaining and distributing oxygen and nutrients, and collecting and eliminating carbon dioxide and other wastes. Animals also reproduce.

invertebrate (p. 606)
chordate (p. 606)
notochord (p. 606)
pharyngeal pouch (p. 607)
vertebrate (p. 607)
feedback inhibition (p. 608)

25.2 Animal Body Plans and Evolution

- Features of animal body plans include levels of organization, body symmetry, differentiation of germ layers, formation of body cavities, patterns of embryo development, segmentation, cephalization, and limb formation.

- Animal phyla are usually defined according to adult body plans and patterns of embryo development.

radial symmetry (p. 611)	pseudocoelom (p. 612)
bilateral symmetry (p. 611)	zygote (p. 612)
endoderm (p. 612)	blastula (p. 612)
mesoderm (p. 612)	protostome (p. 613)
ectoderm (p. 612)	deuterostome (p. 613)
coelom (p. 612)	cephalization (p. 613)

Foundations for Learning Wrap-Up

Use the layered books you made when you started the chapter to help you to organize your thoughts about which characteristics define animals.

Activity 1 Get together in a group of three. Take out one of the layered books that summarizes the main topics in Lesson 1 or 2. Read aloud one of the main topics listed on the tabs of the book. Discuss the things that you should remember about that topic. Look inside the layered book to see if you have remembered all the important concepts.

Activity 2 Stay in your group of three. Take out all of the layered books that contain the key questions from the chapter. Work together to write notes and draw diagrams that answer each question. Do this without looking at your textbook.

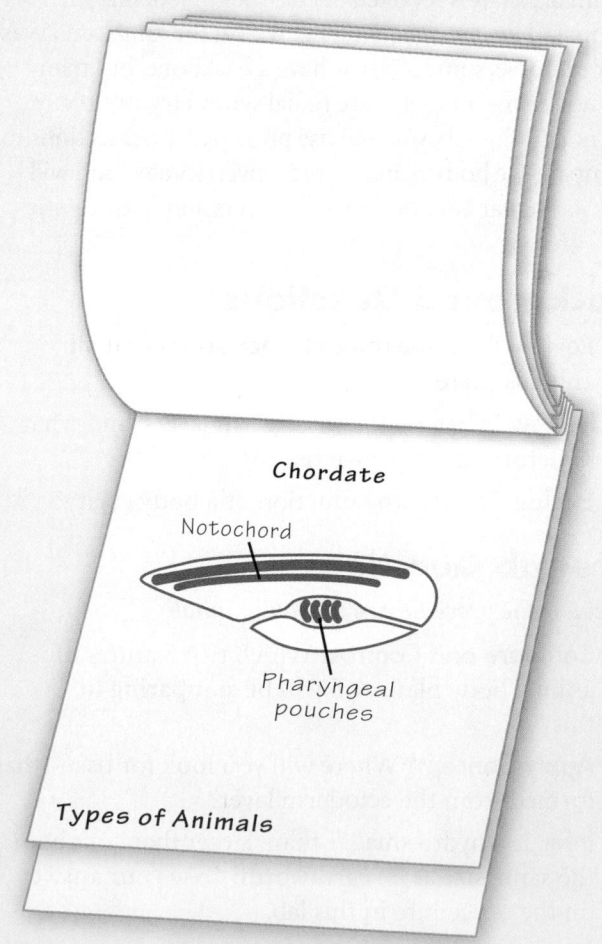

Assess the Big idea — Unity and Diversity of Life

Write an answer to the question below:

Q: What characteristics and traits define animals?

Constructed Response

Write an answer to each of the numbered questions below. The answer to each numbered question should be one or two paragraphs long. To help you begin, read the **Hints** below the questions.

1. **If you were presented with a small, living organism, how would you try to determine whether or not it was an animal?**

   Hint Remember the characteristics of organisms that belong to the animal kingdom.

2. **Animals need oxygen and nutrients in order to survive. How do animal systems work together to get oxygen and nutrients to the animal's cells?**

   Hint Review the Respiratory and Circulatory Systems diagram that shows how materials move in, around, and out of the body.

   Hint Think about which systems get oxygen and food into the body. Which system delivers oxygen and nutrients to cells?

3. **How have cephalization and segmentation led to the great diversity of animals?**

   Hint Remember how segmentation allowed the development of cephalization.

   Hint Refer to the chart of Body Plans and to the Cladogram of Animals to find examples of animals for your answer.

solve the CHAPTER MYSTERY

SLIME DAY AT THE BEACH

Although most people had never seen creatures like these before, biologists had no trouble identifying them. The slimy creatures were salps—descendants of the most ancient members of phylum Chordata. Salps belong to a group of chordates called tunicates. As adults, most tunicates live attached to rocks or the sea floor. Salps are different. The adults are free-swimming. They pump water in through their mouths and out the other end. This ability allows them to feed and move themselves through the water at the same time. Salps are usually found in tropical seas. They can be carried north by the Gulf Stream and are sometimes washed onto beaches by storms.

1. **Compare and Contrast** How are salps different from jellyfish?

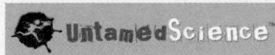 **Never Stop Exploring Your World.**

Discovering what the slime was is only the beginning. Take a video field trip with the ecogeeks of Untamed Science to see where the mystery leads.

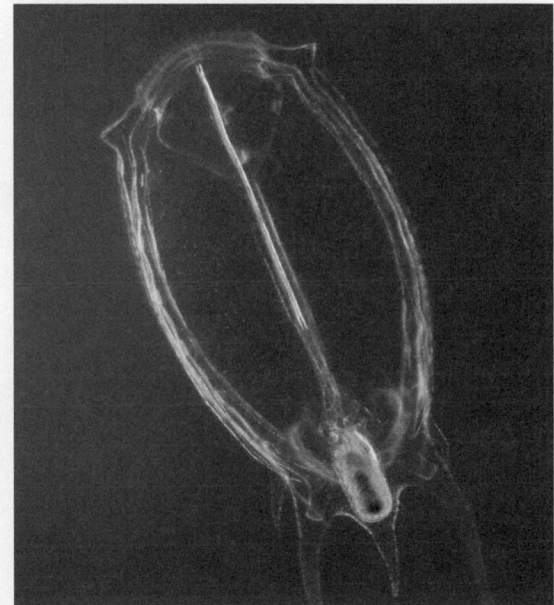

25.1 What Is an Animal?

Understand Key Concepts

1. Which of the following is a characteristic of all chordates but is not found in invertebrates?
   a. a notochord
   b. four legs
   c. a circulatory system
   d. a skeleton

2. Most animals reproduce
   a. sexually by producing diploid gametes.
   b. asexually by cloning.
   c. sexually by producing haploid gametes.
   d. asexually by fusion.

Think Critically

3. **Classify** What characteristic distinguishes vertebrates from nonvertebrate chordates?

4. **Compare and Contrast** How does the way vertebrates get rid of carbon dioxide differ from the way they get rid of ammonia?

25.2 Animal Body Plans and Evolution

Understand Key Concepts

5. Cnidarians and echinoderms have symmetry that extends from a central point. This type of symmetry is called
   a. radial.   c. circular.
   b. bilateral.   d. dorsal.

6. An animal whose mouth is formed from the blastopore is a(n)
   a. deuterostome.   c. protostome.
   b. endoderm.   d. mesoderm.

7. List the three germ layers.

8. Name two body plan characteristics that are shared by all arthropods and chordates.

Think Critically

9. **Sequence** List the following developments in the order of their appearance during evolution: tissues, deuterostome development, multicellularity, segmentation.

10. **Apply Concepts** Explain how bilateral symmetry was an important development in the evolution of animals.

11. **Infer** Why is it inaccurate to state that the cladogram of animals shows the improvements in body plans that have occurred over time?

Connecting Concepts

Use the graph to answer questions 12–14.

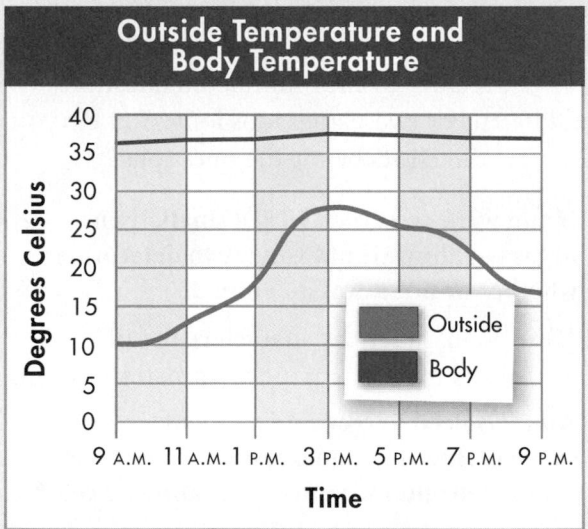

Outside Temperature and Body Temperature

12. **Interpret Graphs** At what time of day is the body temperature closest to that of the outside environment?

13. **Draw Conclusions** What is the relationship between human body temperature and the temperature of the environment?

14. **Infer** How do you explain the shape of the graph for human body temperature?

Standardized Test Practice for Maryland

Multiple Choice

1. Which of the following is a type of tissue that arises in MOST animals during development?
   - **A** endoderm
   - **B** mesoderm
   - **C** ectoderm
   - **D** all of the above

   CLG 3.2.1

2. Which of the following is NOT a characteristic of animals?
   - **A** the ability to make their own food
   - **B** the ability to move
   - **C** eukaryotic cells
   - **D** cells that lack cell walls

   SPI 1.5.7

3. A hollow ball of cells formed after the zygote undergoes division is called a
   - **A** coelom.
   - **B** protostome.
   - **C** deuterostome.
   - **D** blastula.

   CLG 3.2.1

4. Which trend did NOT occur during invertebrate evolution?
   - **A** specialization of cells
   - **B** development of a notochord
   - **C** bilateral symmetry
   - **D** cephalization

   CLG 3.4.1

5. What is a function of the excretory system?
   - **A** to supply cells with oxygen and nutrients
   - **B** to rid the body of metabolic wastes
   - **C** to gather information from the environment
   - **D** to break down food

   CLG 3.2.1

6. Animals often respond to information processed by their nervous system by moving around, using their
   - **A** circulatory system.
   - **B** excretory system.
   - **C** musculoskeletal system.
   - **D** digestive system.

   CLG 3.2.1

7. The concentration of nerve tissue and organs in one end of the body is called
   - **A** cephalization.
   - **B** segmentation.
   - **C** body symmetry.
   - **D** nerve nets.

   CLG 3.2.1

Questions 8 and 9

A biology student has two samples of earthworms in soil, as shown below. The student knows that, because the worms' body temperature changes with the environment, the worms in Sample A have a higher body temperature than those in Sample B. The student uses a stereomicroscope to count the number of heartbeats per minute for three worms from each sample.

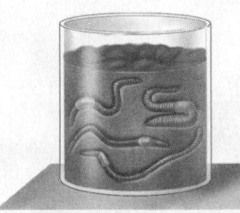 

Sample A:
At temperature of worms' soil environment

Sample B:
In ice water

8. Look at the student's two samples. What can you conclude?
   - **A** Sample A is the control.
   - **B** Sample B is the control.
   - **C** Either sample can serve as a control.
   - **D** This is not a controlled experiment.

   SPI 1.2.6

9. The student finds that the worms from Sample A have a faster heart rate than the worms from Sample B. What hypothesis might you form based on this observation?
   - **A** The worms in Sample A are healthier than the worms in Sample B.
   - **B** A decrease in body temperature corresponds to an increase in heart rate.
   - **C** There is no relationship between body temperature and heart rate.
   - **D** A decrease in body temperature corresponds to a decrease in heart rate.

   SPI 1.2.3

Open-Ended Response

10. What characteristics distinguish invertebrates from nonvertebrate chordates?

   SPI 1.5.7

If You Have Trouble With . . .

Question	1	2	3	4	5	6	7	8	9	10
See Lesson	25.2	25.1	25.2	25.2	25.1	25.1	25.2	25.1	25.1	25.1

26 Animal Evolution and Diversity

Big idea

Evolution

Q: How have animals descended from earlier forms through the process of evolution?

This skeleton of a gopher snake gives clues about how it is related to other vertebrates.

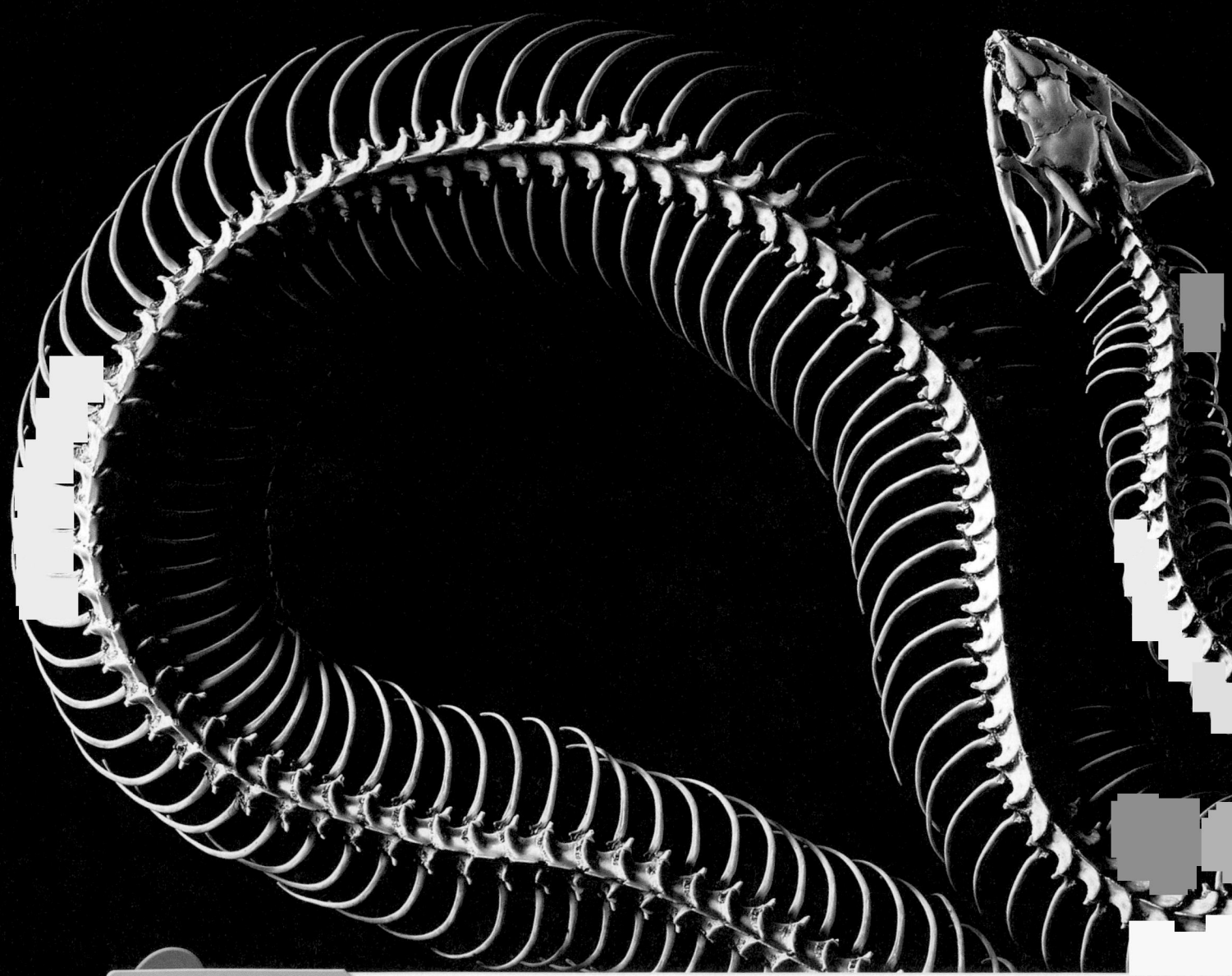

MARYLAND VOLUNTARY STATE CURRICULUM

Biology Indicators/Core Learning Goals (CLG) 3.2.1, 3.4.1, 3.4.2, 3.5.1, 3.5.3. **Skills and Processes Indicators (SPI)** 1.1.1, 1.1.2, 1.4.1, 1.4.2, 1.4.8, 1.5.2, 1.5.5, 1.5.7, 1.5.8, 1.5.9, 1.7.6. See lessons for details.

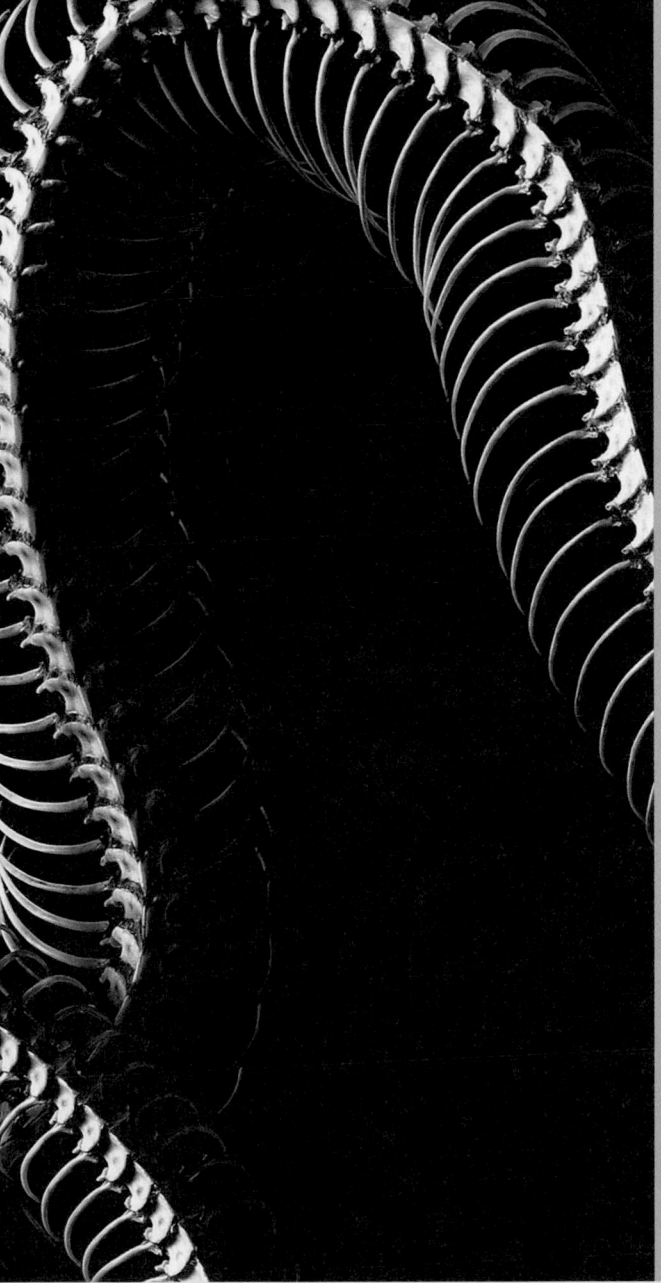

CHAPTER MYSTERY

FOSSIL QUEST

To Josh and Pedro, fossil hunting sounded like a great summer trip. But where should they go? Their parents said they must stay within the United States. Josh wanted to search for the very first animals. Pedro wanted to look for the ancestors of birds. Where could they find these fossils? Were any good sites close enough to keep their parents from worrying?

They realized that they needed to know when the animals they were searching for lived. Then, they needed to figure out where they could find rocks of the right ages. As you read this chapter, look for clues to the geologic time periods when the first animals and birds lived. Also look for clues about where the boys might find their fossils. Then, solve the mystery.

Read for Mystery Clues As you read this chapter, look for clues to help you discover where Josh and Pedro's "Fossil Quest" will take them. Then, solve the mystery at the end of the chapter.

FOUNDATIONS for Learning

Cladograms show the relationships among living things. Before you read the chapter, get three sheets of blank paper and three index cards. As you read each lesson, copy each cladogram from the book onto a sheet of paper. Then choose three animals mentioned in the chapter. Draw a picture of each animal and describe it. At the end of the chapter are two activities that use the cards and sheets of paper. They will help you answer the question: How have animals descended from earlier forms through the process of evolution?

26.1 Invertebrate Evolution and Diversity

MD CLG 3.2.1 Processes and Functions, 3.4.1 Evolutionary Change, 3.4.2 Relatedness Among Organisms. SPI 1.5.5 Create and Interpret Graphics, 1.5.7 Classification Systems.

Key Questions

🔑 When did the first animals evolve?

🔑 What does the cladogram of invertebrates illustrate?

Origins of the Invertebrates

The origins of the first animals are a great mystery. Fossils show that a huge number of animals first appeared between 530 and 515 million years ago. This period is called the "Cambrian Explosion." How did so many kinds of animals evolve so quickly? What simpler forms did they come from?

The first living things were single celled. For 3 billion years, all living things were single celled. Multicellular animals may have evolved from ancestors like choanoflagellates (koh AN uh FLAJ uh layts). These single-celled eukaryotes sometimes grow in groups. In many ways they are like sponges, the simplest animals.

Traces of Early Animals The first animals were tiny and had soft bodies. Soft bodies do not form fossils as well as hard body parts. Some early fossils come from sponges and animals like jellyfish. Scientists have also found trace fossils of tracks and burrows made by animals long ago. Such clues show that the first animals may have begun evolving 600 million years ago.

The Ediacaran Animals Some of the most exciting fossils of animals that lived before the Cambrian Period come from the Ediacara Hills of Australia. These strange fossils are about 565 to about 544 million years old. They show animals with body plans that are different from those of anything alive today. These animals had little cell or tissue specialization, and no organization into a front and back end. Some may have had algae living within their bodies. Others were segmented and had bilateral symmetry. Some seem to be related to jellyfishes and worms. Many were flat and lived on the bottom of shallow seas.

Fossil Clues Tiny fossils such as this 565-million-year-old embryo are rare and valuable finds (SEM 100×).

The Cambrian Explosion The Cambrian Period began about 542 million years ago. Many fossils of animals from this time can be found in China and Canada. These fossils show that over a period of 10 to 15 million years, animals evolved complex body plans. They had specialized cells, tissues, and organs. Many had body symmetry, segmentation, and a front end and a back end. Many had **appendages,** or parts such as legs or antennae that come out from the body. Some Cambrian animals had shells, skeletons, and other hard body parts. Animals with hard body parts are more likely to leave fossils than animals with soft bodies.

A number of Cambrian fossils are ancient members of modern invertebrate phyla. For example, *Marrella*, shown below, was an arthropod. Other Cambrian fossils come from strange groups that are now extinct. By the end of the Cambrian Period, all the basic animal body plans had evolved. Later evolutionary changes would form the structures of the animals we know today.

Modern Invertebrate Diversity Today, invertebrates are the most common animals on Earth. They live in nearly every ecosystem and are part of nearly every food web. There are far more invertebrates than so-called "higher animals," such as reptiles and mammals.

Key Question When did the first animals evolve?
Fossil evidence shows that the first animals began evolving long before the Cambrian Explosion.

Cladogram of Invertebrates

How are the groups of invertebrates related? On the top of the next page is a cladogram of invertebrates. It shows how scientists think that the major groups of living invertebrates are related to each other. It also shows the order in which some important features came about. Many of these features, such as tissues, first came about in the Cambrian animals.

Cambrian Animals The Burgess Shale in Canada contains fossils of animals from the Cambrian Period. This picture shows how some of those animals may have looked when they were alive.

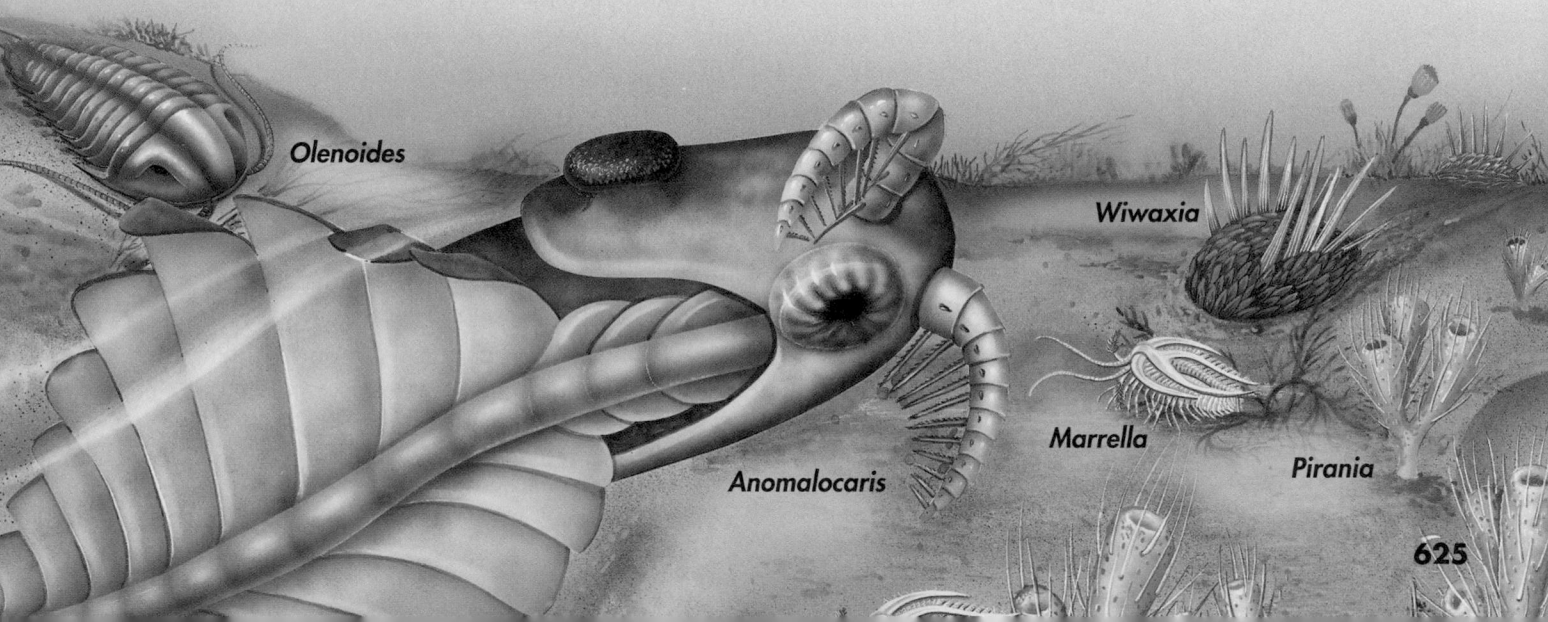

Olenoides

Wiwaxia

Anomalocaris

Marrella

Pirania

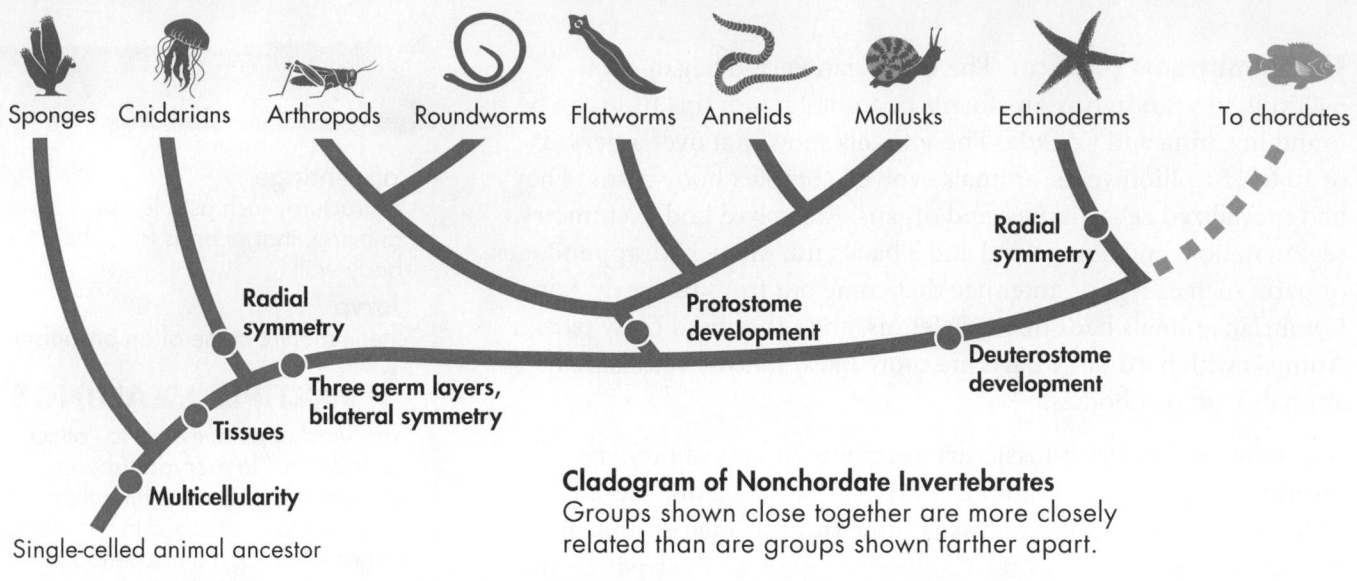

Radial symmetry

Protostome development

Radial symmetry

Deuterostome development

Sponges Cnidarians Arthropods Roundworms Flatworms Annelids Mollusks Echinoderms To chordates

Radial symmetry

Three germ layers, bilateral symmetry

Tissues

Multicellularity

Single-celled animal ancestor

Cladogram of Nonchordate Invertebrates
Groups shown close together are more closely related than are groups shown farther apart.

🔑 **Key Question** What does the cladogram of invertebrates illustrate? **The cladogram shows current hypotheses about the evolutionary relationships of major groups of modern invertebrates. It also shows the order in which some important features evolved.**

▶ *Sponges* Sponges are members of the phylum Porifera (por IHF er uh). These animals have pores, or tiny openings, all over their bodies. With few specialized cells, sponges are some of the simplest animals. But like all animals, sponges are multicellular heterotrophs that do not have cell walls. 🐚 **p. DOL 31**

▶ *Cnidarians* Jellyfishes, sea fans, sea anemones, hydras, and corals are in the phylum Cnidaria (ny DAYR ee uh). Cnidarians live in water. They have soft bodies, specialized tissues, and radial symmetry. They are carnivores that use rings of stinging tentacles around their mouths to capture prey. Some cnidarians live alone. Others live in groups called colonies. 🐚 **pp. DOL 32–33**

▶ *Arthropods* Spiders, centipedes, insects, and crabs are members of the phylum Arthropoda (ahr THRAHP oh duh). Arthropods have bodies that are divided into segments and covered in a hard outer skeleton, or exoskeleton. Their appendages have joints. They also have cephalization. They live in oceans, fresh water, on land, and in the air. More than a million species have been identified. That is more than three times the number of all other animal species on Earth! 🐚 **pp. DOL 34–37**

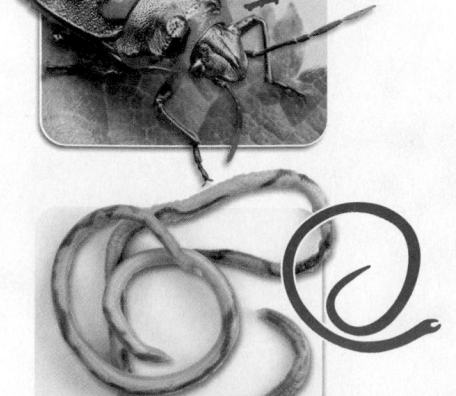

▶ *Nematodes (Roundworms)* Members of the phylum Nematoda are roundworms. They are unsegmented worms with bodies that have a pseudocoelom, a body space with tissue that loosely holds organs in place. Their digestive tracts have two openings—a mouth and an anus. Some live in soil or water. Others are parasites that live in plants or animals. 🐚 **p. DOL 38**

► **Flatworms** Flatworms are in the phylum Platyhelminthes (plat ih hel MIN theez). These soft, unsegmented worms have tissues and organ systems. They have bilateral symmetry and cephalization. They do not have coeloms. Most of these worms are only a few millimeters thick. ⟳ **p. DOL 39**

► **Annelids** Earthworms are members of the phylum Annelida (un NEL ih duh). So are leeches and some other worms that live in the ocean. Annelids have segmented bodies that look like stacks of little rings. They also have coeloms. ⟳ **pp. DOL 40–41**

► **Mollusks** Snails, slugs, clams, and octopi belong to the phylum Mollusca. Most mollusks have soft bodies with an inner or outer shell. They have coeloms and complex organ systems. The **larva** (plural: larvae), or young stage, of a mollusk is called a trochophore (TRAHK oh fawr). Trochophores can swim through the water. (Many annelids also have trochophore larvae. These similar larvae show that annelids and mollusks are closely related.) ⟳ **pp. DOL 42–43**

► **Echinoderms** Sea stars, sea urchins, and sand dollars are in the phylum Echinodermata (ee KY noh durm aht uh). Most adult echinoderms have five-part radial symmetry. Echinoderms have a spiny skin stretched over a hard inner skeleton. They also have a water vascular system—a group of water-filled tubes that end in tube feet. They use their tube feet for walking and for holding food. Like chordates, echinoderms are deuterostomes. ⟳ **pp. DOL 44–45**

CHECK Understanding

Apply Vocabulary
Use the highlighted words from the lesson to complete each sentence correctly.

1. The young stage of some animals is called a _____.

2. Legs, arms, and antennae are kinds of _____.

Critical Thinking

3. Describe What was the Cambrian Explosion?

4. Relate Cause and Effect Why is it rare to find fossils of animals from before the Cambrian Period? What about these animals makes it rare for them to form fossils?

5. Interpret Diagrams Look at the cladogram of invertebrates. Which group is more closely related to echinoderms: mollusks or chordates? How can you tell?

6. Sequence Which feature of echinoderm ancestors evolved first—radial symmetry or deuterostome development? (**Hint:** Study the cladogram.)

7. Write to Learn Answer the first clue of the mystery. In your answer, tell when the earliest known animals are thought to have lived.

MYSTERY CLUE
How old would rocks need to be in order to hold fossils of the earliest known animals? (**Hint:** See p. 624.)

BIOLOGY.com ▶ Search (Lesson 26.1) GO • Lesson Assessment

26.2 Chordate Evolution and Diversity

MD CLG 3.2.1 Processes and Functions, 3.4.1 Evolutionary Change, 3.4.2 Relatedness Among Organisms, 3.5.1 Factors Influencing Ecosystems, 3.5.3 Population Dynamics. SPI 1.4.1 Organize Data, 1.4.2 Analyze Data, 1.5.2 Communicate Information, 1.5.5 Create and Interpret Graphics, 1.5.7 Classification Systems, 1.5.8 Compare, 1.5.9 Synthesize Ideas.

Key Questions

🔑 **What are the most ancient chordates?**

🔑 **What can we learn by studying the cladogram of chordates?**

BUILD Understanding

Venn Diagram Create a Venn diagram that shows how nonvertebrate chordates and vertebrates are alike and different.

In Your Workbook Go to your workbook to learn more about making a Venn diagram. Complete the Venn diagram for Lesson 26.2.

Origins of the Chordates

Chordates are the animals we know best. Why? For one thing, they are large and easy to see. Some we keep as pets. Others we eat. Where did they all come from? What were the first chordates like?

The Earliest Chordates Studies of embryos suggest that the earliest chordates were related to the ancestors of echinoderms. The oldest known fossil of a chordate is *Pikaia* (pih KAY uh). When *Pikaia* was first found, scientists thought it was a worm. But it had a notochord and blocks of muscles that formed a pattern like that of simple modern chordates.

Another fossil called *Myllokunmingia* (MY loh kuhn min jee uh) is the earliest known vertebrate. It had muscles that form a pattern. It also had traces of fins and gills, and a head with sense organs. Its skull and skeleton were likely made of cartilage. **Cartilage** is a strong connective tissue that is softer than bone. It holds up many parts of a vertebrate's body. (Cartilage gives your ears their shape.)

Modern Chordate Diversity Today there are six groups of chordates. These are the nonvertebrate chordates and the five groups of vertebrates—fishes, amphibians, reptiles, birds, and mammals. Of these, fishes are the largest group. Today's chordate species are only a small part of the total number that have ever lived on Earth. 🔄 **pp. DOL 46–64**

🔑 **Key Question** What are the most ancient chordates? **Studies of embryos show that the most ancient chordates were related to the ancestors of echinoderms.**

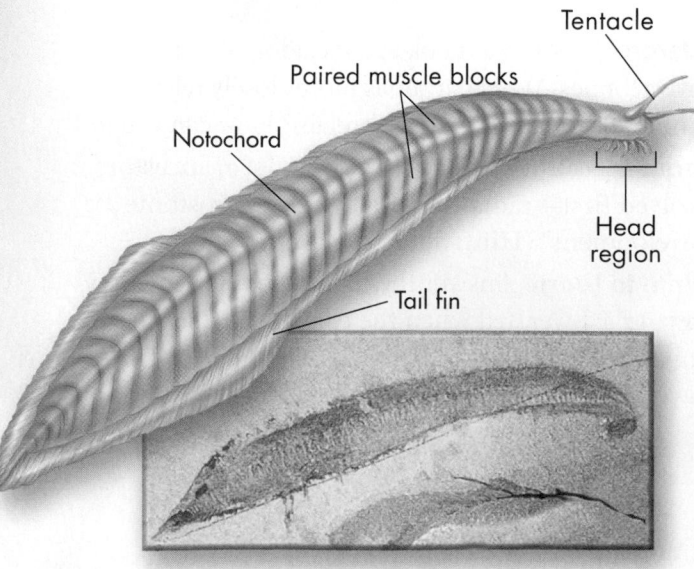

Notochord
Paired muscle blocks
Tentacle
Head region
Tail fin

Pikaia, an Early Chordate
Pikaia is the oldest known chordate.

Cladogram of Chordates Chordates include both vertebrates and nonvertebrates. All of the groups shown on the cladogram share a common invertebrate ancestor. The circles show the evolution of some important adaptations.

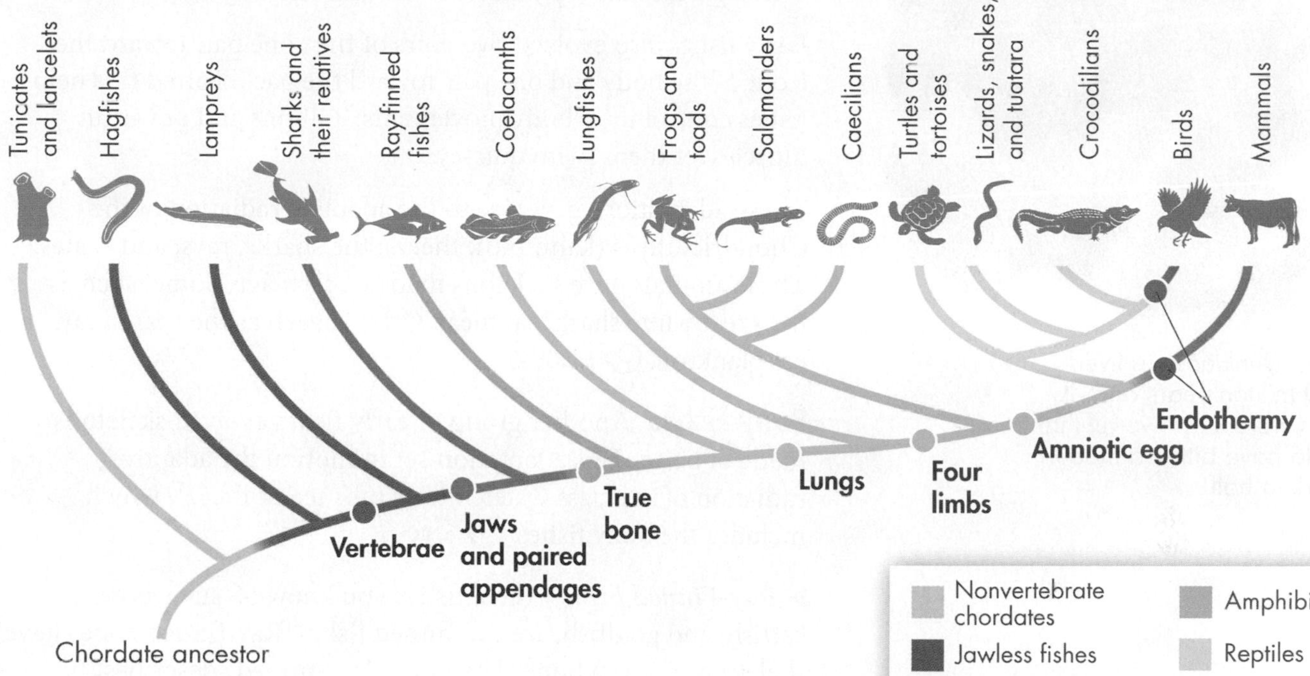

Tunicates and lancelets · Hagfishes · Lampreys · Sharks and their relatives · Ray-finned fishes · Coelacanths · Lungfishes · Frogs and toads · Salamanders · Caecilians · Turtles and tortoises · Lizards, snakes, and tuatara · Crocodilians · Birds · Mammals

Endothermy

Amniotic egg

Four limbs

Lungs

True bone

Jaws and paired appendages

Vertebrae

Chordate ancestor

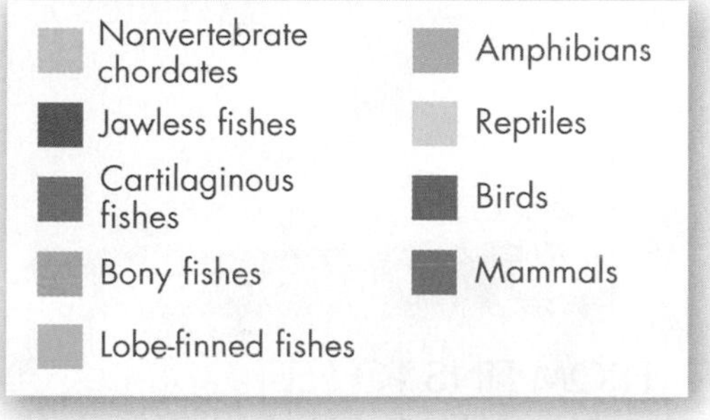

Legend:
- Nonvertebrate chordates
- Jawless fishes
- Cartilaginous fishes
- Bony fishes
- Lobe-finned fishes
- Amphibians
- Reptiles
- Birds
- Mammals

Cladogram of Chordates

The hard parts of many chordates form fossils easily. These fossils give a good record of their history. The cladogram of chordates above shows how scientists think the different groups are related. It also shows when features, such as jaws and limbs, came about.

Nonvertebrate Chordates Two groups of chordates do not have backbones. These nonvertebrate chordates are the tunicates and lancelets. Fossils show that their ancestors branched off from vertebrates more than 550 million years ago. Adult tunicates look more like sponges than humans. They do not have a notochord or a tail. But their larvae have all the key features of chordates. Lancelets look like small eels. They live on the sandy ocean bottom. ⏀ **pp. DOL 46–47**

Jawless Fishes The earliest fishes evolved during the late Cambrian Period, about 510 million years ago. These odd-looking animals did not have true jaws or teeth. Their skeletons were made of cartilage. In the Devonian Period, jawless fishes ruled the seas. For this reason, this time is called the Age of Fishes. Some armored jawless fishes, such as those shown at right, became extinct about 360 million years ago. Other kinds of jawless fishes gave rise to modern jawless fishes: lampreys and hagfishes. ⏀ **p. DOL 49**

Neither lampreys nor hagfishes have backbones. However, they do have notochords. As larvae, lampreys filter their food from water. As adults, they are parasites. Hagfishes look like big pink worms. They make slime, which helps them slip away from enemies. They can even tie their own bodies into knots!

Jawless Fishes of the Devonian These armored fishes did not have jaws. Their paired fins helped them swim.

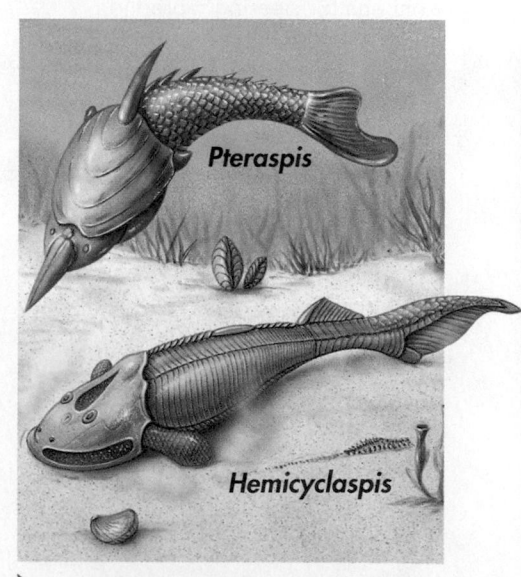

Pteraspis

Hemicyclaspis

Jaws *Dunkleosteus* lived 360 million years ago. Its jaws were so powerful that it could have bitten a modern shark in half!

Sharks and Their Relatives
Other early fishes evolved a very useful adaptation for feeding: jaws. Jaws hold teeth and muscles. These parts make it possible to bite and chew.

Early fishes also evolved two pairs of fins, one pair toward the front of the body and one pair toward the back. Paired fins help fishes control their body movements. Tail fins and powerful muscles let them swim quickly.

These adaptations gave rise to the adaptive radiation of the Chondrichthyes (kahn DRIK theez): the sharks, rays, and skates. These animals have skeletons made of cartilage. Some, such as the great white shark, eat meat. Others, such as the manta ray, eat plankton. p. DOL 50

Bony Fishes
Another group of early fishes evolved skeletons made of bone. This adaptation set in motion the adaptive radiation of the class Osteichthyes (ahs tee IK theez), which includes the bony fishes. p. DOL 51

▶ *Ray-Finned Fishes* Most fishes you know of, such as eels, catfish, and goldfish, are ray-finned fishes. Ray-finned fishes have skeletons made of bone. The name "ray-finned" describes the thin bones that hold up the skin in their fins. Most bony fishes also have fins, scales, and gills.

▶ *Lobe-Finned Fishes* Another group of bony fishes are the lobe-finned fishes. They evolved larger bones that support thick, fleshy fins. Modern lobe-finned fishes include lungfishes and coelacanths (SEE luh kanths). One ancient group of lobe-finned fishes gave rise to the four-limbed vertebrates, or **tetrapods.**

FROM FINS TO FEET
The feet of tetrapods evolved from the fins of ancient bony fish. This cladogram shows some animals in this line of evolution. All of the animals in the art are extinct.

Eusthenopteron was an early bony fish that used its muscular front fins for steering more than for swimming.

Panderichthys was a fish with sturdier, more mobile, and proportionately larger front fins than earlier fishes had.

Tiktaalik was not quite a fish and not quite a tetrapod. It had stout, stubby front fins with flexible wrists that likely enabled it to prop itself up on land, but it had no digits. It had gills and lungs.

To the Ancestors of Modern Fishes

Amphibians Frogs and toads are amphibians. The word *amphibian* means "double life." As larvae, these animals live in water. As adults, they can live on land. Most adults have lungs and can breathe air. But most amphibians need water to reproduce. Amphibians have moist skin. They do not have scales or claws. ↻ pp. DOL 52–53

▶ *The "Fishapod"* Adaptations for life on land evolved slowly, over millions of years. Some groups of lobe-finned fishes evolved sturdy fins. Over time, some of these appendages evolved features that looked like the limbs of tetrapods. Many fossils, discovered over many years, document these changes. Recently, scientists have discovered several fossils that show clearly how lobed fins evolved into front and hind limbs. One such fossil is *Tiktaalik*. This animal had a mix of fish and tetrapod features in many of its body parts. It had gills and could swim underwater. It also had lungs and could crawl on land. Many call it a "fishapod"—part fish, part tetrapod. It shows a clear middle stage between fishes and tetrapods.

▶ *Adaptations to Life on Land* To live on land, animals need more than legs. Early amphibians also evolved ways to breathe air and to protect themselves from drying out. With these adaptations, amphibians became the main vertebrates of the warm and wet Carboniferous Period, which lasted from 359 to 300 million years ago.

Their success did not last. Climate changes caused many swamps to dry up. Most amphibians became extinct by the end of the Permian Period, about 250 million years ago. Today, only three orders of amphibians survive—frogs and toads, salamanders, and caecilians (see SIL ee unz).

***Tiktaalik*, the Fishapod** This 375-million-year-old fossil of *Tiktaalik* was found in Canada. Like a fish, it had gills. Like a tetrapod, it had lungs and fins with wrist bones.

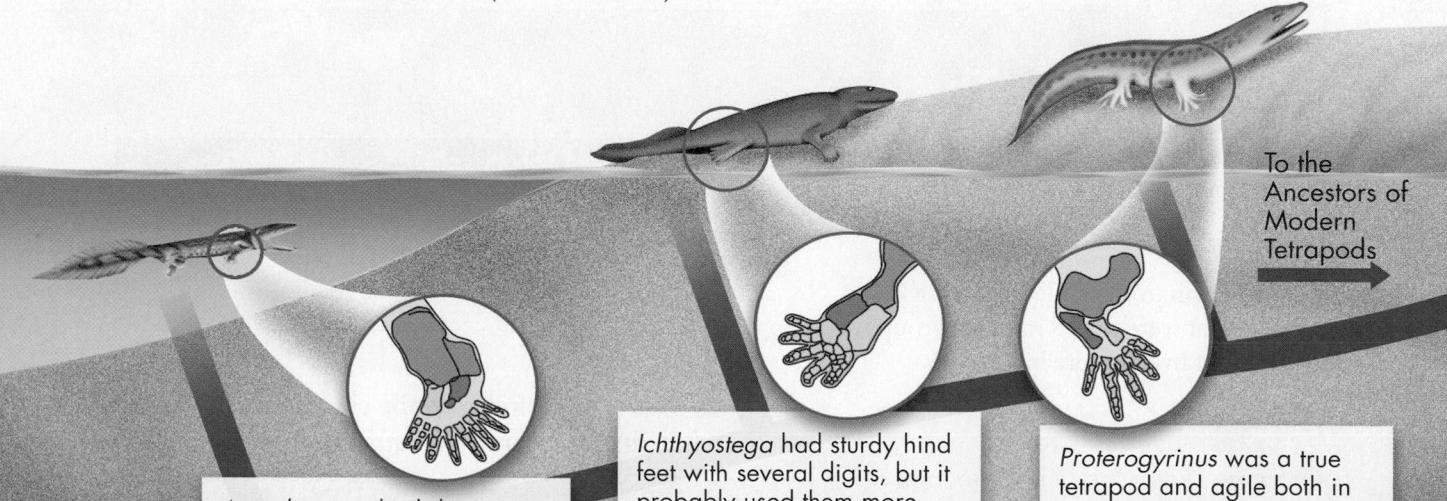

Acanthostega had digits on its front feet but spent most of its time in the water. Though it had gills, it may have used its limbs to prop itself out of oxygen-poor water so it could breathe air with its lungs.

Ichthyostega had sturdy hind feet with several digits, but it probably used them more often to paddle through the water than to walk on land. It may have moved like a seal on land.

Proterogyrinus was a true tetrapod and agile both in water and on land, much as today's alligators are.

To the Ancestors of Modern Tetrapods

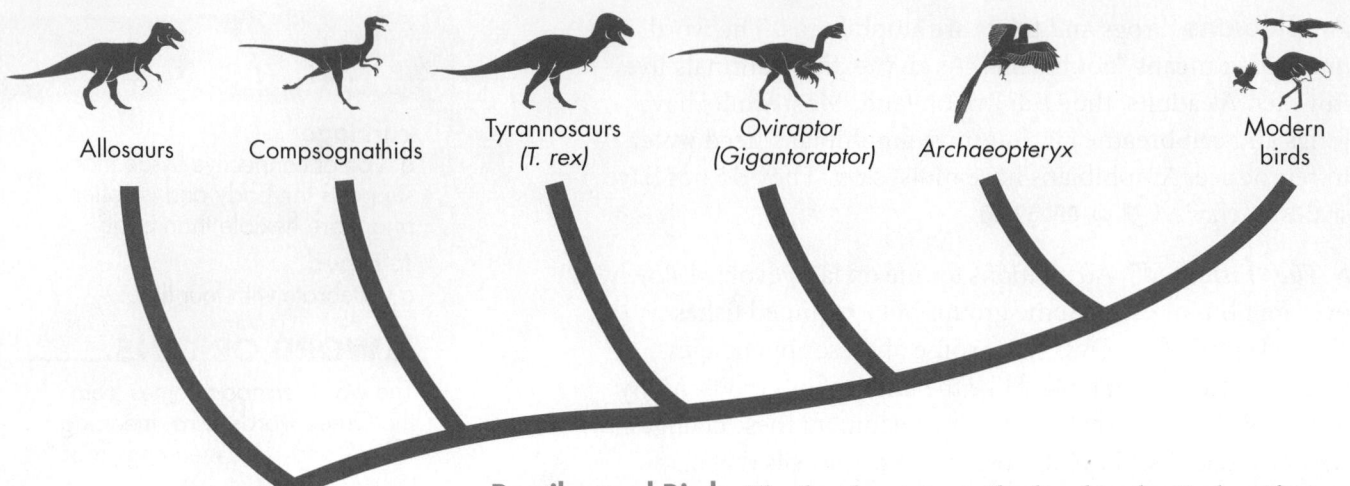

Allosaurs   Compsognathids   Tyrannosaurs
(T. rex)   Oviraptor
(Gigantoraptor)   Archaeopteryx   Modern
birds

Evolution of Birds and Reptiles
The cladogram shows current
hypotheses about the relationship
between living and extinct
reptiles. None of the groups
shown are direct ancestors of
modern reptiles or modern birds.

Reptiles and Birds The first known reptiles lived in the Carboniferous
Period, 350 million years ago. During this time, Earth's climate cooled
and many lakes and swamps dried up. In this cool, dry environment,
many kinds of reptiles evolved. Reptiles are adapted to living on dry
land. They have scaly skin, well-formed lungs, and strong legs. Their
eggs have shells and membranes that keep them from drying out.
There are four groups of reptiles living today: lizards and snakes,
crocodiles, turtles and tortoises, and the tuatara. ☙ **pp. DOL 54–55**

▶ *Dinosaurs* During the Triassic and Jurassic periods reptiles called
dinosaurs lived all over the world. Some were small. Others were
enormous. Some ate leafy plants. Others were carnivorous. Some
dinosaurs even had feathers. The first birdlike fossils to be discovered
came from the end of the Jurassic Period, about 150 million years
ago. Fossils show that one group of feathered dinosaurs included the
ancestors of modern birds.

INQUIRY
into Scientific Thinking

Feather Evolution

The information in the table shows the kinds
of feathers that were found in some groups of
dinosaurs that lived before birds.

Analyze and Conclude

1. Organize Data Copy the cladogram of
the Evolution of Reptiles and Birds into your
notebook. Then review the information about
drawing cladograms in Chapter 18.

Group (listed alphabetically)	Feather Status
Allosaurs	None
Archaeopteryx	Flight feathers
Compsognathids	Hairlike feathers
Oviraptors	True feathers
Tyrannosaurs	Branched feathers

2. Infer Draw circles on the cladogram to show
when different kinds of feathers evolved.

3. Draw Conclusions Which type of feathers would
you expect modern birds to have?

In Your Workbook Get more help for this activity
in your workbook.

▶ ***Mass Extinction*** At the end of the Cretaceous Period, about 66 million years ago, a mass extinction took place. Scientists hypothesize that it was caused by natural disasters, including volcanic eruptions and a fall in sea level. A huge asteroid smashing into Earth probably caused forest fires and dust clouds. After these events, dinosaurs and many other living things became extinct.

▶ ***Birds*** Modern birds make up the class Aves. Birds can keep their bodies warm when it is cold. Birds have feathers and strong, yet light bones. Their two legs are covered with scales and their front limbs are wings. pp. DOL 56–59

Mammals Members of the class Mammalia are mammals. They can be as small as mice or as large as whales. Mammals are covered in hair. They also breathe air, have four-chambered hearts, and are able to keep warm in cold weather. The mothers feed their young with milk from their mammary glands. Most mammals bear live young that have developed in the mother's body. pp. DOL 60–64

Mammals first evolved during the late Triassic Period, about 220 million years ago. They were very small and looked like tree shrews. While dinosaurs ruled, mammals were small. They were active mostly at night. After the great dinosaur extinction, about 65 million years ago, mammals began to get bigger and live in many different places. The Cenozoic Era is also called the Age of Mammals.

Key Question What can we learn by studying the cladogram of chordates? **The cladogram of chordates shows how chordate groups are related and the points at which different features evolved.**

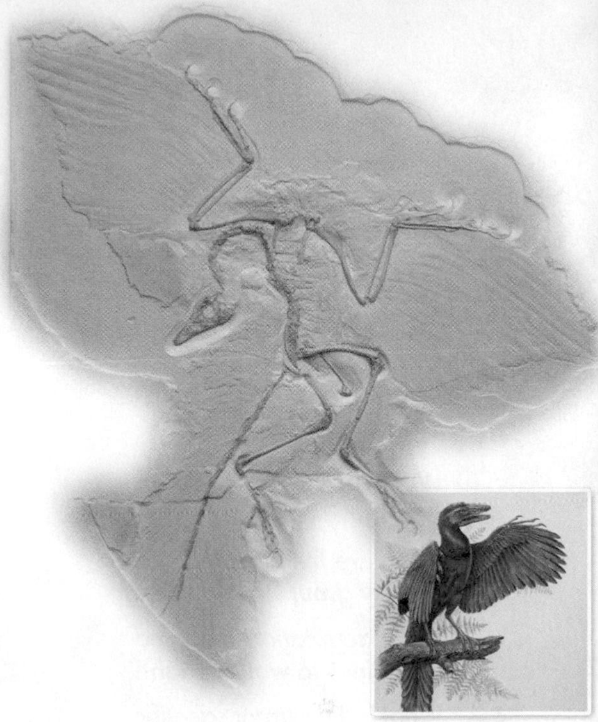

***Archaeopteryx*, an Early Bird** This fossil comes from the late Jurassic Period, about 150 million years ago. *Archaeopteryx* (ahr kee AHP tur iks) was a small, running dinosaur that had feathers. The drawing shows how *Archaeopteryx* may have looked.

CHECK Understanding

Apply Vocabulary

Use the highlighted words from the lesson to complete each sentence correctly.

1. _______ is a strong, flexible tissue that supports chordate muscles and body parts.
2. Animals that have four appendages are called _______.

Critical Thinking

3. **Review** Name the group of animals whose ancestors were related to the earliest chordates.
4. **Compare and Contrast** What are two ways that bony fishes differ from ancient jawless fishes?
5. **Compare and Contrast** How do nonvertebrate chordates differ from other chordates?
6. **Relate Cause and Effect** How could the climate changes of the Permian Period have caused many kinds of amphibians to become extinct?
7. **Write to Learn** Answer the second clue of the mystery.

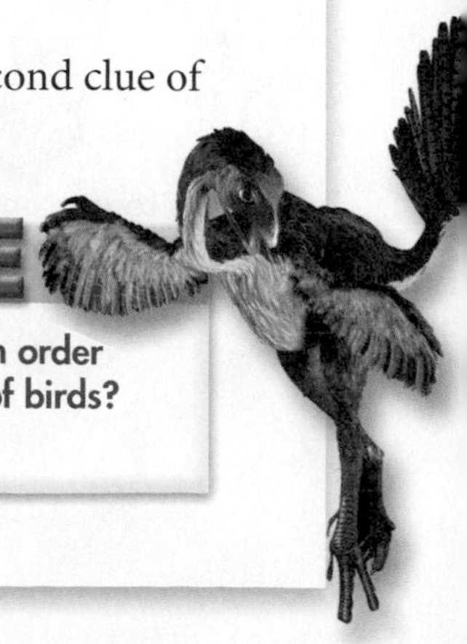

MYSTERY CLUE

How old would rocks need to be in order to contain fossils of the ancestors of birds? (Hint: See p. 632.)

BIOLOGY.com Search Lesson 26.2 GO • Lesson Assessment

26.3 Primate Evolution

MD CLG 3.4.1 Evolutionary Change, 3.4.2 Relatedness Among Organisms. SPI 1.1.1 Problems and Solutions, 1.1.2 Scientific Ideas, 1.5.5 Create and Interpret Graphics, 1.5.7 Classification Systems, 1.5.8 Compare, 1.5.9 Synthesize Ideas, 1.7.6 Science and Technology.

Key Questions

🔑 What characteristics do all primates share?

🔑 What are the major evolutionary groups of primates?

🔑 What adaptations enabled later hominines to walk upright?

🔑 What is the current scientific thinking about the genus Homo?

BUILD Understanding

T-Chart Before you read Lesson 3, make a T-chart that lists the main topics (green headings) in the left column. As you read, write details for each topic in the right column.

In Your Workbook Go to your workbook to learn more about making a T-chart.

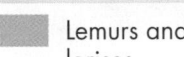 Lemurs and lorises

 Tarsiers

 Anthropoids

What Is a Primate?

Lemurs, monkeys, great apes, and humans are primates. All primates have evolved adaptations useful for life in trees. Primates have long fingers and toes that can curl around things and hold them tightly. Most primates have thumbs and big toes that can open and close against the other fingers like a hinge. All of us have nails instead of claws, and arms that can rotate at the shoulder. Primates also have a strong collar bone (clavicle) that helps tree-dwelling species to swing from branch to branch. Eyes on the front of our faces give us **binocular vision,** the ability to combine what we see with two eyes into one image that has depth. Finally, all primates have a well-developed cerebrum, or "thinking" part of the brain. ⟳ p. DOL 64

🔑 **Key Question** What characteristics do all primates share?
Primates have long fingers and toes, nails, arms that rotate at the shoulder, strong clavicles, binocular vision, and large cerebrums.

Evolution of Primates

The ancestors of modern primates lived more than 65 million years ago. Today there are three major groups of primates. One group includes lemurs and lorises. They are small and have large eyes that help them see in the dark. A second group is the tarsiers. They have broad faces and widely separated nostrils. The third group, **anthropoids** (AN thruh poydz), includes monkeys, great apes, and humans.

Hominoids

       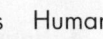

Lemurs · Lorises and bush babies · Tarsiers · New World monkeys · Old World monkeys · Gibbons · Orangutans · Gorillas · Chimpanzees · Humans

Common primate ancestor

Cladogram of Primates The cladogram shows how scientists think the modern primates are related.

When the continents separated 45 million years ago, anthropoids were split into two groups. New World monkeys live in Central and South America and they have prehensile tails. A **prehensile tail** can wrap around a branch and hold on like an extra hand.

The other group of anthropoids are the Old World monkeys and great apes. They live in Africa and Asia. Old World monkeys climb trees. But they do not have prehensile tails. Great apes include gibbons, orangutans, gorillas, chimpanzees, and humans. Great apes are also called hominoids.

Key Question What are the major evolutionary groups of primates? **The three major groups of primates are the lemurs and lorises, the tarsiers, and the anthropoids.**

Hominine Evolution

The study of human ancestors and other primates shows that chimpanzees are our closest living relatives. Recent fossil discoveries show that the evolutionary lines that led to humans split from the lines that led to chimpanzees around 6 or 7 million years ago. DNA studies agree with fossil evidence about the time these lines split.

All hominoids in the line that led to humans are called hominines. The fossils of early hominines show changes in the slope of the skull, neck, spine, hip bones, and leg bones. These changes in shape let later species walk upright. Animals that walk on two feet are said to be bipedal. Standing and walking upright left the hands free for using tools. Each hand had an **opposable thumb** that could touch the tips of the fingers. This thumb made it easier to use tools. Hominines also evolved much larger brains than other apes.

Time Line This time line shows hominine fossils and the time range during which each species probably lived. These time ranges may change as paleontologists gather new data. Right now, there are several different hypotheses about how these species are related. That's why we present these data as a time line, rather than as a cladogram.

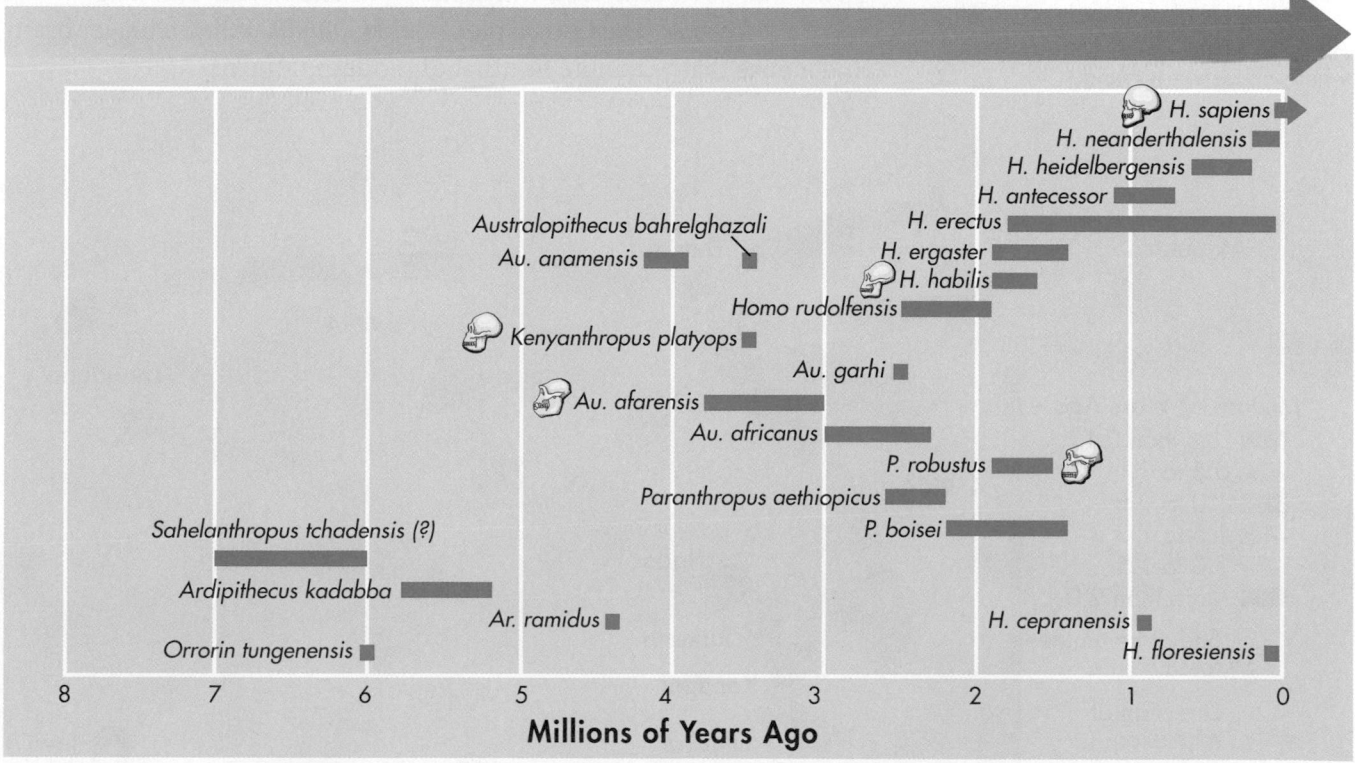

Australopithecus bahrelghazali
Au. anamensis
Kenyanthropus platyops
Au. afarensis
Au. africanus
Sahelanthropus tchadensis (?)
Ardipithecus kadabba
Ar. ramidus
Orrorin tungenensis
Au. garhi
P. robustus
Paranthropus aethiopicus
P. boisei
Homo rudolfensis
H. habilis
H. ergaster
H. erectus
H. antecessor
H. heidelbergensis
H. neanderthalensis
H. sapiens
H. cepranensis
H. floresiensis

Millions of Years Ago
8 7 6 5 4 3 2 1 0

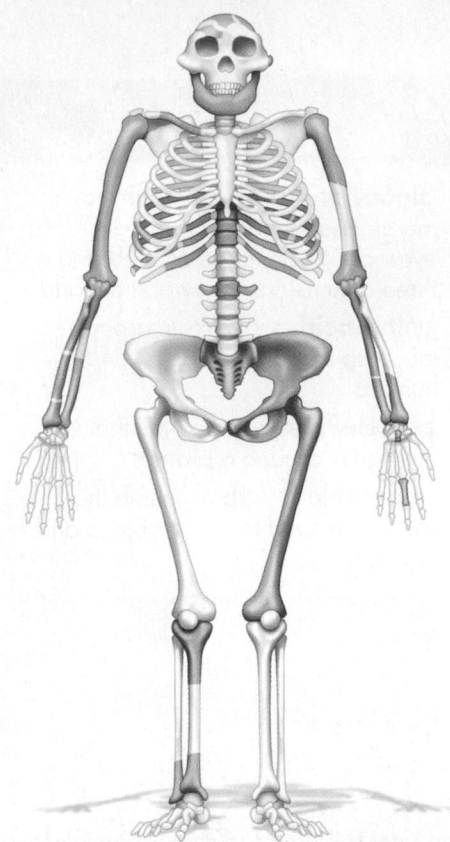

Lucy "Lucy" is the nickname of a fossil of *A. afarensis* that was discovered in Ethiopia. Lucy's skeleton was not complete. The bones that were found are dark blue.

Out of Africa Fossils show that relatives and ancestors of modern humans left Africa in waves. (Skull symbols show where bones were found.)

Hominine Relationships Researchers have found fossils of at least 20 species of hominines. All these species are relatives of modern humans. But not all of them are human ancestors. What's the difference? Think of your family. Your relatives may include aunts, uncles, cousins, parents, grandparents, and great grandparents. But only your parents, grandparents, and great grandparents are your ancestors.

It isn't easy to figure out which hominines are human ancestors and which are just distant relatives. It is now clear that there have been several hominine adaptive radiations. Each of these radiations produced several species. These species are shown in the time line on p. 635. From fossils alone, it is hard to tell how some of these species are related to each other and to humans.

Fossils of Hominines Fossils tell how early hominines looked and lived. *Australopithecus afarensis* lived from about 4 million to 2.5 million years ago. A skeleton of *A. afarensis* called "Lucy" stood about 1 meter tall. One set of trace fossils is thought to be of *Australopithecus* footprints. These footprints show that the ability to walk upright evolved long before large brains.

🔑 **Key Question** What adaptations enabled later hominine species to walk upright? **The skull, neck, spine, hip bones, and leg bones of early hominines changed shape in ways that let later species walk upright.**

The Road to Modern Humans

About 2 million years ago in Africa, a new group of hominines arose. Scientists classify these species in the genus *Homo*. One set of fossils was found with tools made of stone and bone. It was named *Homo habilis* (HAB ih lus), which means "handy man." Another species, *Homo ergaster*, was larger than *H. habilis*. It had a bigger brain and a nose that was more like that of modern humans.

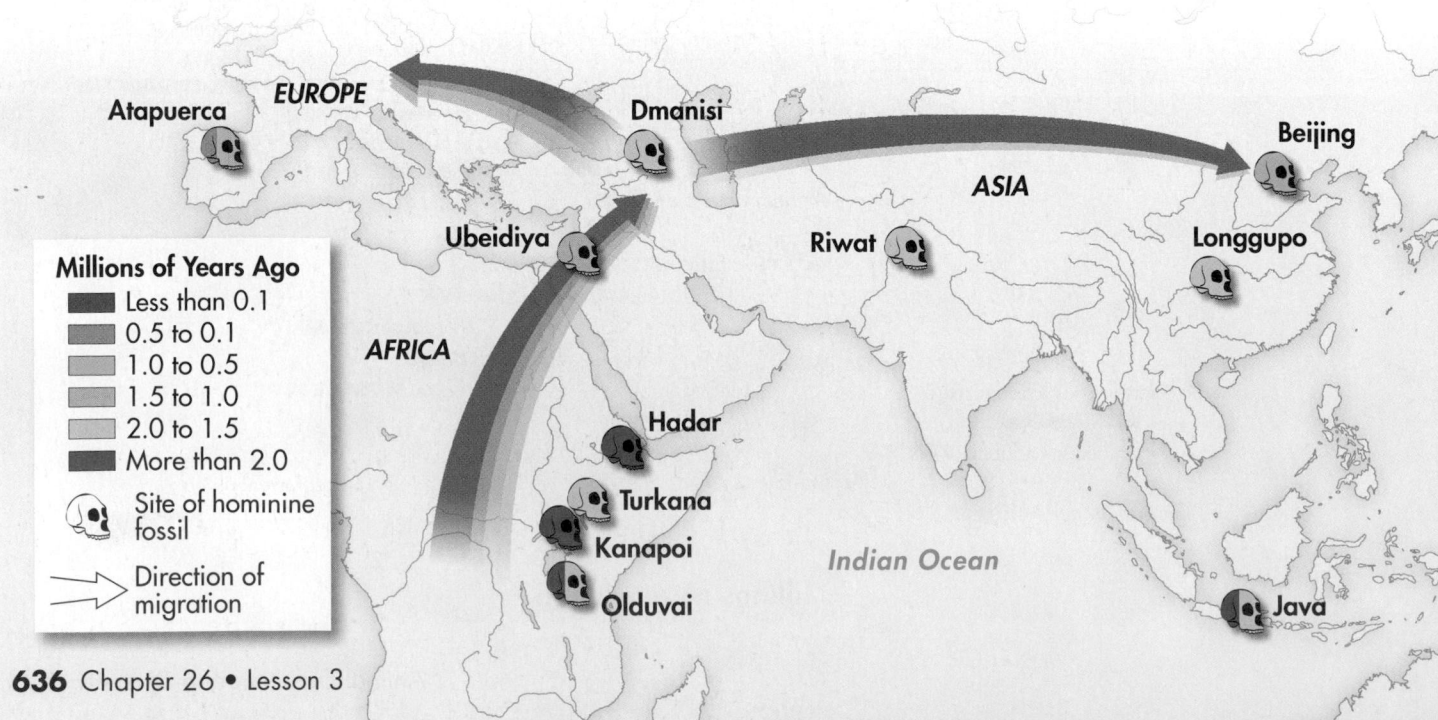

Millions of Years Ago	
■	Less than 0.1
■	0.5 to 0.1
■	1.0 to 0.5
■	1.5 to 1.0
■	2.0 to 1.5
■	More than 2.0
💀	Site of hominine fossil
➡	Direction of migration

Out of Africa—But When and Who? In time, some members of the genus *Homo* moved from Africa to other parts of the world. Where and when did our species, *Homo sapiens*, evolve? One hypothesis says that modern humans evolved in several different parts of the world at the same time. Another hypothesis says that modern humans evolved in Africa about 200,000 years ago. Then they moved out of Africa. Soon they took the place of other hominines that already lived elsewhere. DNA from living humans strongly supports the second hypothesis: *Homo sapiens* came out of Africa.

Modern Humans At least three other *Homo* species lived at the same time as early humans. The two most important were *Homo neanderthalensis* and *Homo sapiens*. Neanderthals began living in Europe and western Asia about 200,000 years ago. They lived in Europe until about 24,000 years ago. Neanderthals were very good hunters, made stone tools, and used fire. They lived in social groups and buried their dead with simple rituals.

Homo sapiens arrived in the Middle East from Africa about 100,000 years ago. About 50,000 years ago, they began making and using tools from stone and bones. They also painted on cave walls. They buried their dead with elaborate rituals.

Neanderthals and *Homo sapiens* lived side by side in the Middle East for about 50,000 years and in Europe for several thousand years. How and why did Neanderthals disappear? Did they inbreed with *Homo sapiens*? No one knows for sure. We do know this: For the last 24,000 years, *Homo sapiens* has been Earth's only hominine. Our species is the only surviving member of a clade that was once large and diverse.

🔑 **Key Question** What is the current scientific thinking about the genus *Homo*? **Many species of *Homo* lived before *Homo sapiens* appeared. At least three other *Homo* species lived at the same time as early humans.**

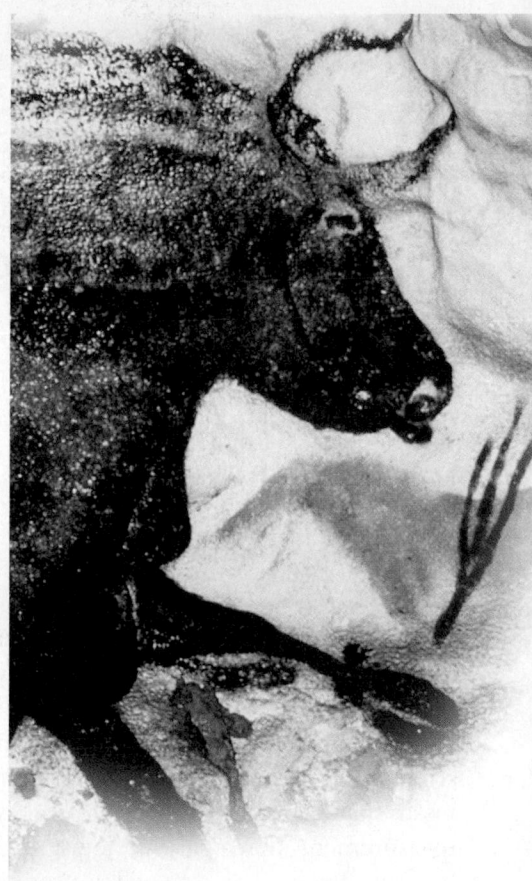

Cro-Magnon Art This ancient cave painting from France shows that Cro-Magnons were skilled artists.

CHECK Understanding

Apply Vocabulary
Use the highlighted words from the lesson to complete each sentence correctly.

1. _____ lets primates combine the images from two eyes into a single image.

2. A(n) _____ can wrap around a branch and hold on like a hand.

Critical Thinking
3. **Relate Cause and Effect** How was walking upright important to the evolution of hominines?

4. **Compare and Contrast** What is one way in which Neanderthals differed from *Homo sapiens*?

5. **Write to Learn** Describe the two hypotheses that explain how *Homo sapiens* spread throughout the world. How are these two hypotheses alike? How are they different?

BIOLOGY.com ⟩ Search (Lesson 26.3) GO • Lesson Assessment

# Forensics Lab

CLG 3.4.1 Evolutionary Change. SPI 1.4.2 Analyze Data, 1.4.8 Use Models, 1.5.8 Compare.

Pre-Lab: Investigating Hominoid Fossils

Problem What can a comparison of skulls and hands reveal about the evolution of humans?

Materials metric ruler

Lab Manual Chapter 26 Lab

Skills Focus Measure, Analyze Data, Compare and Contrast

Connect to the **Big idea** To learn about the evolution of humans, scientists study both close relatives and possible ancestors. Fossils of possible ancestors are rare, and complete skeletons are even rarer. Yet, scientists have gained valuable information from those fossils that have been found. In this lab, you will make measurements that a paleontologist might make after finding a fossil. Then, you will use your data to make inferences about human evolution.

Background Questions

a. Review What are hominoids, and what are hominines?

b. Explain Use the examples of chimpanzees and humans to explain the difference between evolutionary relatives and ancestors.

c. Compare and Contrast What is the difference between the locomotion of humans and the locomotion of chimpanzees?

Pre-Lab Questions

Preview the procedure in the lab manual.

1. Use Models What will you use instead of actual skulls and hands to make your measurements?

2. Interpret Visuals The bony cavities in a skull that protect the eyes are called orbits, or eye sockets. On the skulls, what does line AC measure? What does line BC measure?

3. Use Analogies Shoe sizes such as 9A and 11E (or 9 narrow and 11 extra-wide) are an example of an index. What two measurements are being compared in a shoe index?

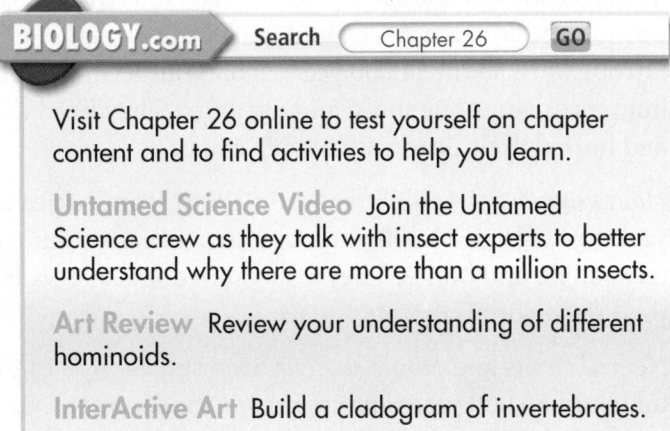

BIOLOGY.com Search [Chapter 26] GO

Visit Chapter 26 online to test yourself on chapter content and to find activities to help you learn.

Untamed Science Video Join the Untamed Science crew as they talk with insect experts to better understand why there are more than a million insects.

Art Review Review your understanding of different hominoids.

InterActive Art Build a cladogram of invertebrates.

26.1 Invertebrate Evolution and Diversity

- Fossil evidence shows that the first animals began evolving long before the Cambrian Explosion.

- The cladogram of invertebrates shows current hypotheses about the evolutionary relationships of major groups of modern invertebrates. It also shows the order in which some important features evolved.

appendage (p. 625)
larva (p. 627)

26.2 Chordate Evolution and Diversity

- Studies of embryos show that the most ancient chordates were related to the ancestors of echinoderms.

- The cladogram of chordates shows how chordate groups are related and the points at which different features evolved.

cartilage (p. 628)
tetrapod (p. 630)

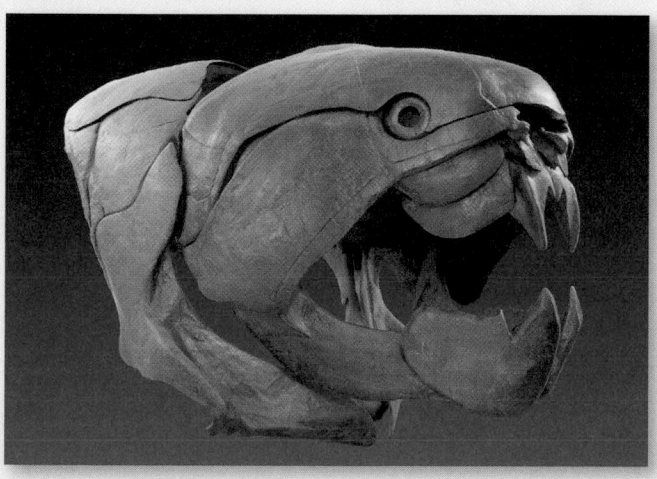

26.3 Primate Evolution

- Primates are mammals that have long fingers and toes, nails, arms that rotate at the shoulder, strong clavicles, binocular vision, and large cerebrums.

- The three major groups of primates are lemurs and lorises, tarsiers, and the anthropoids.

- The skull, neck, spine, hip bones, and leg bones of early hominines changed shape in ways that let later species walk upright.

- Many species of *Homo* lived before *Homo sapiens* appeared. At least three other *Homo* species lived at the same time as early humans.

binocular vision (p. 634)
anthropoid (p. 634)
prehensile tail (p. 635)
opposable thumb (p. 635)

Assess the Big idea ▶ Evolution

Write an answer to the question below.

Q: How have animals descended from earlier forms through the process of evolution?

Constructed Response

Write an answer to each of the questions below. The answer to each question should be one or two paragraphs. To help you begin, read the **Hints** below the questions.

1. **Analyze Concepts** What can you tell about the ancestors of different groups of animals by looking at a cladogram?

   Hint Cladograms show evolutionary relationships.

   Hint Cladograms show when features evolved.

2. **Relate Cause and Effect** Life on Earth began in water. What are some of the ways that animals evolved to live on land?

   Hint Tetrapods can move on land, while fish cannot.

   Hint Breathing air requires different body parts than breathing underwater.

3. **Infer** When scientists find hominine fossils, they measure their size and decide their age. Why is it important for scientists to know the age as well as the size of these hominine bones?

   Hint Bone size helps scientists know how animals walked.

Foundations for Learning Wrap-Up

Use the three cladograms and the animal index cards you prepared while you read the chapter to help review what you learned. They will help you understand how different groups of animals are related.

Activity 1 Compare your three cladograms. Find the places where they overlap with one another. For example, the right end of the cladogram of invertebrates has a symbol that represents all chordates. The cladogram of chordates starts with an invertebrate ancestor. Attach these two cladograms where they overlap.

Next, attach the cladogram of primates where it overlaps with the cladogram of chordates. Then draw lines to connect the three cladograms.

You have now made a much larger cladogram. It shows details for only one group of chordates. Imagine how big your cladogram would be if it showed all the animals!

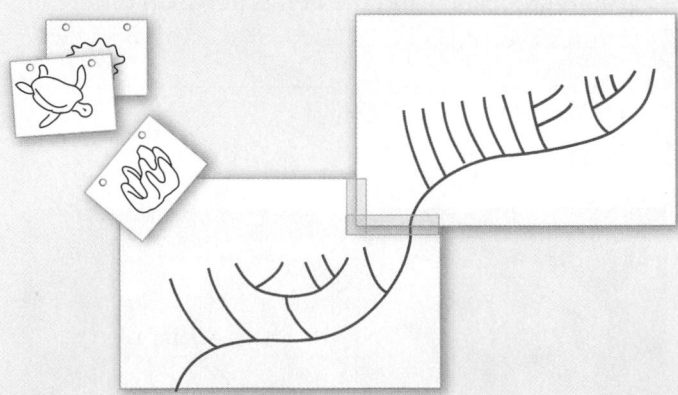

Activity 2 Study three index cards that each describe an animal in detail. Find where they belong in your large cladogram. Attach each one to the cladogram at the point where it belongs. Extend any lines that should connect with one another. Use the cladogram to find out how closely related your three animals are. Are they found within the same smaller cladogram? How closely related are they to humans? To a single-celled ancestor?

26.1 Invertebrate Evolution and Diversity

Understand Key Concepts

1. The ancestors of many modern animal phyla first appeared during the
   a. Burgess Period.
   c. Precambrian Era.
   b. Cambrian Period.
   d. Ediacaran Period.

2. Which of the following groups has species that live in water, on land, and in the air?
   a. arthropods
   c. mollusks
   b. annelids
   d. echinoderms

> **Test-Taking Tip**
>
> Think of examples to help you eliminate answer choices. For question 2, think of what adaptations are needed to survive in the different places. Then think of examples of each of the different groups of animals. Earthworms and other kinds of worms are annelids. Worms do not have wings, so they cannot live in the air.

3. What evidence indicates that annelids and mollusks are closely related?

Think Critically

4. **Infer** Most cnidarians do not swim. To catch prey, they let water currents carry the prey to them. How is this behavior related to special structures they have?

5. **Compare and Contrast** How is the structure of echinoderms different from that of arthropods?

26.2 Chordate Evolution and Diversity

Understand Key Concepts

6. Which adaptation is NOT characteristic of reptiles?
   a. scaly skin
   c. lungs
   b. shelled egg
   d. gills

7. What feature separates birds from other groups of living animals?
   a. feathers
   c. warm bodies
   b. two legs
   d. wings

8. Dinosaurs became extinct at the end of the
   a. Triassic Period.
   b. Cretaceous Period.
   c. Carboniferous Period.
   d. Permian Period.

9. What adaptation lets birds live in places that are colder than those in which most reptiles live?

10. Which two major groups of fishes that still survive today evolved from the early jawed fishes?

Think Critically

11. **Infer** What structures of nonvertebrate chordates make these animals seem more closely related to vertebrates than to other groups of animals?

26.3 Primate Evolution

Understand Key Concepts

12. Anthropoids include monkeys and
    a. lemurs.
    c. tarsiers.
    b. lorises.
    d. humans.

13. Which of the following is characteristic of primates, but not of other mammals?
    a. body hair
    b. rotation at the shoulder joint
    c. notochord
    d. ability to control body temperature

14. The first hominines evolved about
    a. 30,000 years ago.
    b. 100,000 years ago.
    c. 6 to 7 million years ago.
    d. 120 million years ago.

15. What features do hominines have? Give an example of a hominine.

Think Critically

16. Apply Concepts How are binocular vision and opposable thumbs useful to a primate?

Connecting the Concepts

Use Science Graphics

The chart below shows the relative number of species in four groups of vertebrates over time. The shapes are wide at times when there were many species. The shapes are narrow at times when there were few species. Use the chart to answer questions 17–19.

17. Interpret Visuals During which period did amphibians first evolve?

Era	Period	Number of Species
Cenozoic	Recent	
Cenozoic	Paleogene	
Mesozoic	Cretaceous	
Mesozoic	Jurassic	
Mesozoic	Triassic	
Paleozoic	Permian	
Paleozoic	Carboniferous	
Paleozoic	Devonian	
Paleozoic	Silurian	
Paleozoic	Ordovician	

Bony Fishes · Archosaurs · Birds · Mammals

— Vertebrates

18. Compare and Contrast How is this kind of diagram similar to a traditional cladogram? What additional information can be learned from it?

19. Interpret Visuals Which of the groups shown has the greatest number of species today?

solve the CHAPTER MYSTERY

FOSSIL QUEST?

Josh would have a hard time finding rocks old enough to show traces of the first animals. Such fossils would be about 600 million years old. Most of these rocks have been destroyed by geological activity. Most sites are in China and Australia. None are in the United States.

Pedro found better news. Reptiles related to bird ancestors lived during the Cretaceous Period. There are a number of places where fossils of that age have been found. One such place is the Green River area in Utah. Because both boys like dinosaurs, they joined a field trip for teens to the Green River to search for bird ancestors.

1. Infer The earliest known animals lived during the Proterozoic Eon, while the ancestors of birds lived during the Cretaceous Period. Why is it so much harder to find fossils of the earliest known animals than it is to find fossils of the ancestors of birds? (*Hint:* See the graph below.)

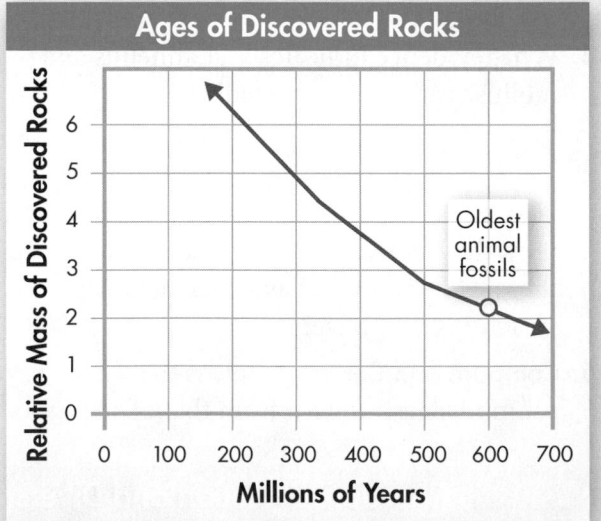

Ages of Discovered Rocks

Oldest animal fossils

Relative Mass of Discovered Rocks / Millions of Years

Untamed Science Finding the solution to the mystery is only the beginning. Take a video field trip with the ecogeeks of Untamed Science to see where the mystery leads.

Multiple Choice

1. Which of the following is NOT a mollusk?
A leech   C clam
B squid   D snail   SPI 1.5.7

2. Which of the following invertebrates have segmented bodies?
A flatworms   C cnidarians
B roundworms   D annelids   SPI 1.5.7

3. All animals have some form of body symmetry EXCEPT
A sponges.   C worms.
B jellyfishes.   D arthropods.   SPI 1.5.7

4. Which of the following groups can be classified as nonvertebrate chordates?
A sponges
B tunicates
C fishes
D all of the above   SPI 1.5.7

5. Many scientists think that birds evolved from
A mammal-like reptiles.
B amphibians.
C mammals.
D dinosaurs.   CLG 3.4.1

6. Which of the following is NOT a characteristic of reptiles?
A scaly skin   C lungs
B eggs with shells D mammary glands
                                 SPI 1.5.7

7. Which of the following are hominoids?
A all mammals   C humans only
B all primates   D all great apes
                                 CLG 3.4.1

8. When did the first true mammals appear?
A Cretaceous Period
B Triassic Period
C Cenozoic Era
D Carboniferous Period   SPI 1.5.7

Questions 9–11 Refer to the following cladogram.

Lamprey Trout Salamander Lizard Wallaby Human

Placenta
Mammary Glands
Amniotic Egg
Four Limbs
Backbone
Notochord

9. Which characteristic is shared by humans, wallabies, and trout?
A placenta   C four limbs
B notochord   D mammary glands
                                 SPI 1.5.5

10. Which animals have the closest evolutionary relationship, as shown by the cladogram?
A humans and wallabies
B humans and lizards
C humans and lampreys
D humans and trout   SPI 1.5.5

11. A valid conclusion from this cladogram is that
A salamanders, trout, and lampreys all have a backbone.
B four limbs appeared in vertebrate evolution before the notochord appeared.
C humans and lampreys share a common ancestor.
D mammary glands appeared in vertebrate evolution after the placenta appeared. SPI 1.4.2

Open-Ended Response

12. What is the difference between a hominoid and a hominine?   SPI 1.5.7

If You Have Trouble With . . .

Question	1	2	3	4	5	6	7	8	9	10	11	12
See Lesson	26.1	26.1	26.1	26.2	26.2	26.2	26.3	26.2	26.2	26.2	26.2	26.3

Structure and Function

Q: How do the structures of animals allow them to take in essential materials and get rid of wastes?

BIOLOGY.com | **Search** | Chapter 27 | **GO** • Flash Cards

*Red-billed oxpeckers are carnivores
that have a mutualistic relationship
with zebras. The birds eat ticks and
insects that are parasites on the
zebras. This action frees the zebras
of these parasites.*

CHAPTER
MYSTERY

(NEAR) DEATH BY
SALT WATER

It started as an adventure. Some college
buddies tried their own version of a "survivor" experience.
During summer vacation, the college friends were dropped
on a small, tropical island. They had few supplies. They would
be picked up in a few days.

The island was hot and dry. It had no fresh water. Some
members of the group drank coconut milk when they were
thirsty. One group member hated coconuts. He drank salt
water to get his fluids. At first, he was fine. Then, he became
sick and weak. He was dizzy, had headaches, and could not
concentrate. His friends began to panic. What was happening?
As you read the chapter, look for clues to explain why their
friend became so ill. Then, solve the mystery.

FOUNDATIONS
for Learning

Take a piece of paper and make a Z-fold, as shown below.
Write the key questions for the first lesson of the chapter on the
left panel of the fold. Predict the answers to these questions on
the middle panel of the fold. Leave the right panel blank for
now. Make three more Z-fold pages for the other three lessons
of the chapter. Write the key questions and predict the answers
for each of these lessons. At the end of the chapter are two
activities that use the Z-fold charts to help answer the question:
How do the structures of animals allow them to take in essential
materials and get rid of wastes?

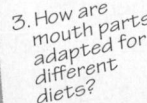

1. How do
animals
obtain food?

2. How does
digestion
occur in
animals?

3. How are
mouth parts
adapted for
different
diets?

1. Animals obtain
food by eating
plants or other
animals.

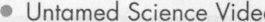

• Untamed Science Video   • Chapter Mystery

27.1 Feeding and Digestion

MD CLG **3.1.3** Matter and Energy, **3.2.1** Processes and Functions, **3.4.1** Evolutionary Change, **3.5.1** Factors Influencing Ecosystems, **3.5.2** Interdependence of Organisms in the Biosphere. SPI **1.5.2** Communicate Information, **1.5.7** Classification Systems, **1.5.8** Compare.

Key Questions

🔑 How do animals get food?

🔑 How does digestion occur in animals?

🔑 How are mouthparts adapted for different diets?

BUILD Understanding

Two-Column Table Before you read, look at the green headings in the lesson. As you read, make notes about the ideas developed in each heading.

In Your Workbook Refer to your workbook for suggestions about how to use a two-column chart to organize your notes.

Obtaining Food

All animals are heterotrophs that get their energy by eating food. Animals feed in many different ways. Tiny insects dine on blood. Bison feed on grasses. And giant blue whales feed on tiny plankton floating in the ocean. In fact, adaptations for feeding are a large part of what makes animals so interesting.

Filter Feeders Filter feeders eat by straining algae and tiny animals from water. Most filter feeders have gills or other structures that act like nets. Many invertebrate filter feeders, such as sponges, spend most of their lives in a single place. Vertebrate filter feeders, such as blue whales, usually feed while swimming.

Detritivores Detritivores eat bits of decaying plants and animals. They also eat bacteria and algae that live on decaying material. Many worms and crustaceans are detritivores.

Carnivores Carnivores eat other animals. Sharks and wolves are carnivores that use their sharp teeth to catch prey.

Herbivores Herbivores eat plants or parts of plants. Some herbivores can eat leaves. Others eat seeds or fruits.

Parasites Parasites live on or in another organism. They feed on the blood or tissues of their host. Many parasites cause disease.

Mutualists Some animals have mutualistic relationships that help both partners. For example, many coral animals have algae living in their tissues. The algae carry out photosynthesis, which is the corals' main source of energy. In addition, the algae recycle nutrients and help the corals make their calcium carbonate skeletons. The algae, in turn, get nutrients from the corals' wastes. The algae are also protected from algae eaters.

🔑 **Key Question** How do animals get food?
Some animals filter food out of water. Others feed on decaying material, other animals, or plants. Parasites feed on the tissues of living organisms.

Processing Food

Getting food is just the first step. Next, food must be broken down, or digested. Then food can be absorbed, giving energy and nutrients to cells throughout the body.

Intracellular Digestion Sponges and many other simple animals digest food inside specialized cells. Nutrients move from the specialized cells to other body cells by diffusion. This digestive process is called **intracellular digestion.**

Extracellular Digestion Most complex animals rely on extracellular digestion. In **extracellular digestion,** food is broken down outside of cells in a digestive system.

▶ *Gastrovascular Cavities* Some invertebrates have a space in their bodies that is surrounded by tissues that carry out digestion and circulation. This space is called a **gastrovascular cavity.** Gastrovascular cavities have a single opening. Animals that have a gastrovascular cavity obtain food and get rid of wastes through the same opening. Some cells lining the cavity secrete enzymes that digest food. Other cells surround food and digest it in vacuoles. Nutrients are then absorbed and carried to the rest of the body.

Obtaining Food The orca, sea slug, barnacles, and cleaner shrimp get their food in different ways.

Carnivore – Orca

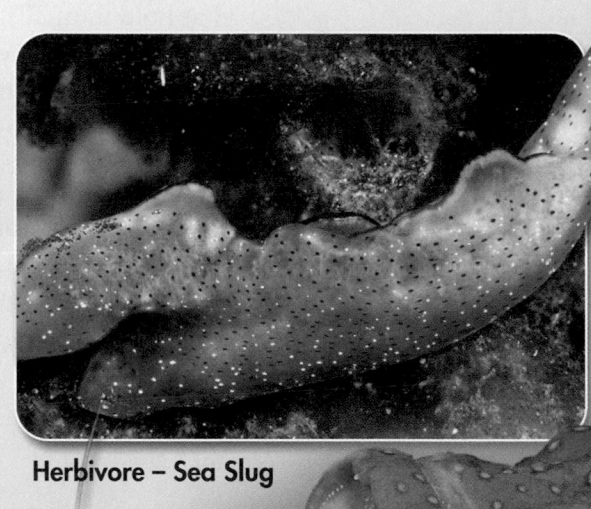

Herbivore – Sea Slug

Filter Feeders – Barnacles

Detritivore – Cleaner Shrimp

▶ *Digestive Tracts* Many invertebrates and all vertebrates digest food in a tube called a **digestive tract,** or gut. A digestive tract has two openings. Food moves through in one direction. Food enters through the mouth. Wastes leave through the anus.

Digestive tracts often have specialized structures that carry out different tasks as food passes through. Mouthparts such as teeth may cut or smash food into smaller pieces. Birds have a special organ called a gizzard that grinds food into smaller pieces. In many animals, the mouth secretes enzymes that start the process of chemical digestion. The stomach and intestines also secrete digestive enzymes. The intestines absorb nutrients that are released by digestion.

▶ *Solid Waste Disposal* Some materials in food cannot be digested. Organisms expel solid wastes called feces through either the single digestive opening or the anus.

Specialized Digestive Tracts Carnivorous invertebrates and vertebrates have short digestive tracts. These digestive tracts produce fast-acting enzymes. These enzymes are able to break down most animal tissues.

Plant tissues are more difficult to digest. No animal produces digestive enzymes that can break down the cellulose in plant tissue. Some herbivores have very long intestines that hold bacteria that are able to digest cellulose. Other herbivores have specialized pouches that hold mutualistic bacteria. For example, cows have a pouchlike extension of their esophagus called a **rumen.** Bacteria in the rumen digest cellulose. The food then moves back into the cow's mouth. The cow chews the food a second time, then swallows it again. This process is called "chewing the cud."

🔑 **Key Question** How does digestion occur in animals? **Some invertebrates, such as sponges, break down food using intracellular digestion. Most invertebrates and all vertebrates break down food using extracellular digestion.**

Digesting Food Animals have different digestive structures with different functions.

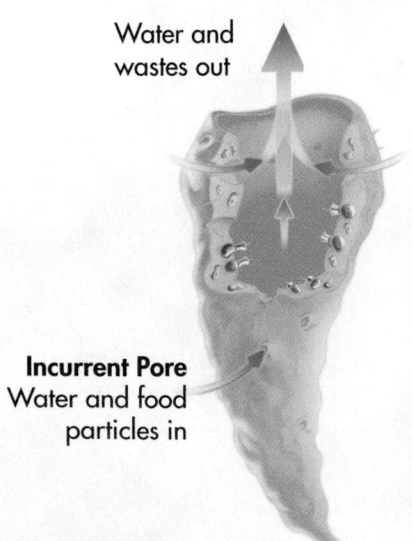

Water and wastes out

Incurrent Pore Water and food particles in

Sponge The sponge has one digestive opening and uses intracellular digestion.

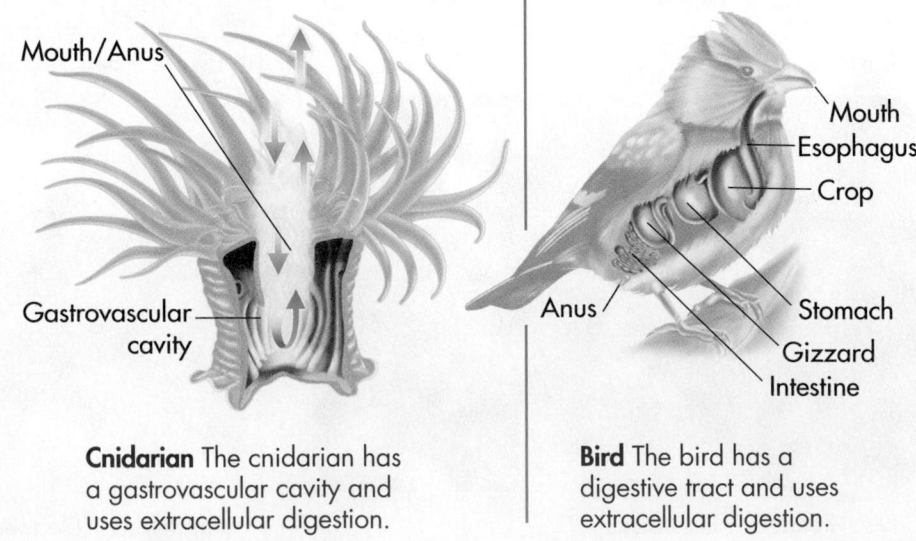

Mouth/Anus

Gastrovascular cavity

Cnidarian The cnidarian has a gastrovascular cavity and uses extracellular digestion.

Mouth
Esophagus
Crop
Anus
Stomach
Gizzard
Intestine

Bird The bird has a digestive tract and uses extracellular digestion.

Specializations for Diets

Animals with specialized diets have evolved specialized mouthparts that help them to grab and digest food.

For example, mammals that are carnivores have sharp teeth that help them grab and hold prey. These teeth can also slice meat. The jaws of these carnivores move up and down to chop meat into small pieces.

Herbivores have mouthparts that grind leaves. The front teeth and lips of mammalian herbivores can grab and tear. The jaws of these herbivores move from side to side to grind leaves.

🗝 **Key Question** How are mouthparts adapted for different diets? **Carnivores usually have sharp mouthparts that can capture food, hold it, and cut it into pieces. Herbivores usually have mouthparts that can grind plants.**

BUILD Connections

SPECIALIZED TEETH
The jaws and teeth of mammals are well adapted to their diets. How are mammal teeth like objects that you have around the house?

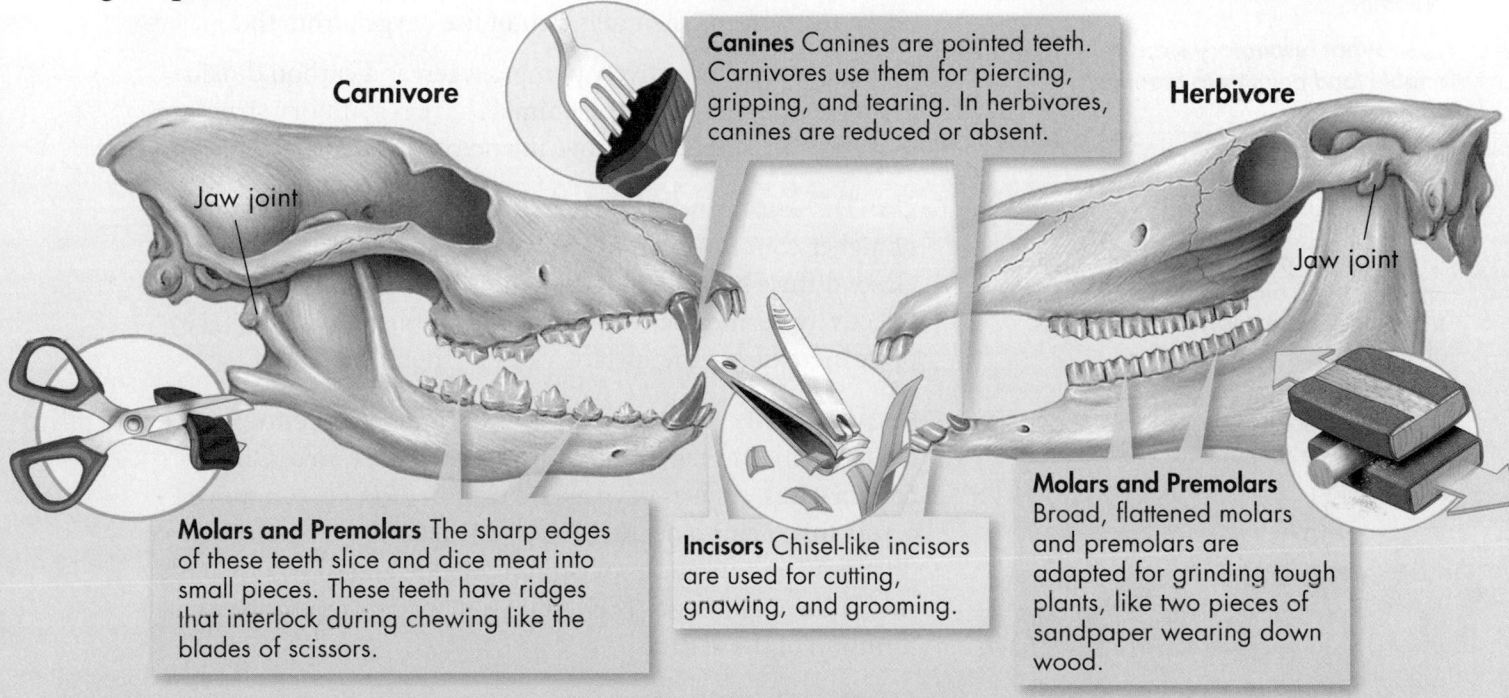

Carnivore

Jaw joint

Canines Canines are pointed teeth. Carnivores use them for piercing, gripping, and tearing. In herbivores, canines are reduced or absent.

Herbivore

Jaw joint

Molars and Premolars The sharp edges of these teeth slice and dice meat into small pieces. These teeth have ridges that interlock during chewing like the blades of scissors.

Incisors Chisel-like incisors are used for cutting, gnawing, and grooming.

Molars and Premolars Broad, flattened molars and premolars are adapted for grinding tough plants, like two pieces of sandpaper wearing down wood.

CHECK Understanding

Use the highlighted words from the lesson to complete each sentence correctly.

1. A digestive chamber that has a single opening is called a _____.
2. All vertebrates digest food in a tube called a _____.
3. The process by which food is broken down inside specialized cells is _____.

Critical Thinking

4. **Classify** Identify the following animals as a filter feeder, detritivore, parasite, or carnivore: a hawk that eats mice; a lobster that feeds on dead fish; a tick that feeds on a dog's blood; a blue whale that eats plankton.
5. **Compare and Contrast** How do the mouthparts of a leaf-eater differ from those of a meat-eater?
6. **Write to Learn** Describe how a cow digests food. Include the words *cellulose*, *rumen*, and *cud*.

BIOLOGY.com   Search   Lesson 27.1   **GO** • Lesson Assessment   • Visual Analogy

27.2 Respiration

MD CLG 3.2.1 Processes and Functions, 3.5.1 Factors Influencing Ecosystems. SPI 1.5.2 Communicate Information, 1.5.7 Classification Systems, 1.5.8 Compare.

Key Questions

🔑 What characteristics do the respiratory structures of all animals share?

🔑 How do aquatic animals breathe?

🔑 What respiratory structures enable land animals to breathe?

BUILD Understanding

Concept Map As you read the lesson, create a concept map that shows the characteristics of the lungs of vertebrates.

In Your Workbook Refer to your workbook for suggestions about how to use a concept map to organize your notes.

BUILD Vocabulary

gill a feathery structure specialized for the exchange of gases with water

lung an organ used for respiration; a place where gases are exchanged between the blood and inhaled air

⚡ MULTIPLE MEANINGS

The word *respiration* has two different meanings. At the level of an organism, respiration is the exchange of oxygen and carbon dioxide with the air. At the level of a cell, respiration is the process by which food molecules are broken down to release energy. Because cellular respiration requires oxygen, the two processes are related.

Gas Exchange

In respiration, all animal cells take in oxygen and give off carbon dioxide. Animals must get this oxygen from their environment. In other words, all animals need to "breathe." Humans can drown because our lungs cannot take oxygen from water. Fishes have the opposite problem. Their gills cannot use oxygen from the air.

Living cells cannot actively pump oxygen and carbon dioxide across membranes. Instead, animals have respiratory structures that allow these gases to move in and out by passive diffusion.

Gas Diffusion and Membranes Gases diffuse from an area of higher concentration to an area of lower concentration. Gases diffuse best across a thin, moist membrane that is selectively permeable. The amount of diffusion that can take place increases as the surface area of a membrane increases.

Requirements for Respiration Respiratory structures contain a moist membrane with a large surface area. Only certain gases, such as oxygen and carbon dioxide, can move across this membrane. Respiratory structures also maintain different concentrations of carbon dioxide and oxygen on either side of the membrane. These different concentrations promote diffusion of those gases.

🔑 **Key Question** What characteristics do the respiratory structures of all animals share?
Respiratory structures provide a large surface area of moist, selectively permeable membrane. The membrane keeps a difference in the relative concentrations of oxygen and carbon dioxide on either side of it. This difference in concentration helps diffusion take place.

Respiration in Aquatic Animals

Animals such as flatworms and amphibians have thin-walled bodies that are wet. Oxygen and carbon dioxide can diffuse through the body coverings of these animals. Larger, active animals cannot rely on respiration through the skin alone. Many aquatic invertebrates and most aquatic chordates exchange gases through gills.

Respiration With Gills Fish respire with gills. As water passes over the gills, oxygen enters the capillaries and carbon dioxide exits.

Operculum Water carrying carbon dioxide is pumped out behind the operculum, or gill cover.

Gill Filaments Water is pumped past thousands of threadlike gill filaments, which are rich with capillaries. Filaments absorb oxygen from water and release carbon dioxide.

Mouth A muscular pump pulls water in through the mouth and pushes it back across the gills.

Gills are feathery structures that expose a large surface area of membrane to water. Inside gills are many tiny blood vessels called capillaries. Animals pump water across their gills as blood flows inside. Pumping water over the gills helps to maintain differences between the oxygen and carbon dioxide concentrations in water and blood. When concentrations are different, diffusion can occur between the capillaries and water.

Reptiles that live in water and aquatic mammals such as whales, breathe with lungs. **Lungs** are organs that exchange oxygen and carbon dioxide between blood and air. Animals that breathe with lungs inhale air at the surface and hold their breath underwater.

Key Question How do aquatic animals breathe?
Most aquatic animals breathe through their skin or with gills. Aquatic reptiles and mammals breathe with lungs and must hold their breath underwater.

Respiration in Land Animals

Animals that live on land face a challenge that aquatic animals do not. Land animals must keep their respiratory membranes moist in dry conditions.

Respiration in Land Invertebrates Invertebrates that live on land have a wide variety of respiratory structures. Some land animals, such as earthworms, can respire across their skin as long as it stays moist. Land snails respire by using a mantle cavity, which is lined with moist tissue and blood vessels. Insects and spiders have very complex structures, as shown in the art.

Respiratory Structures of Land Invertebrates Invertebrates that live on land have a wide variety of respiratory structures that help their membranes stay moist, even in dry conditions.

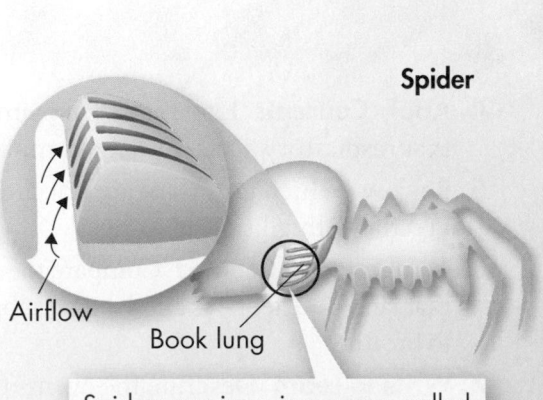

Insect

Tracheal tubes

Spiracles

Spider

Airflow

Book lung

Spiders respire using organs called book lungs, which are made of parallel, sheetlike layers of thin tissues that contain blood vessels.

In most insects, a system of tracheal tubes extends throughout the body. Air enters and leaves the system through openings in the body surface called spiracles. In some insects, oxygen and carbon dioxide diffuse through the tracheal system, and in and out of body fluids. In other insects, body movements help pump air in and out of the tracheal system.

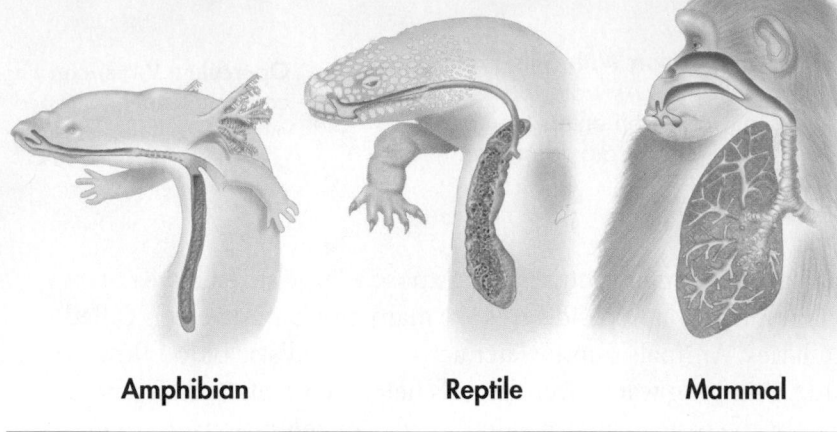

■ Nostrils, mouth, and throat
■ Trachea
■ Lung

Amphibian   **Reptile**   **Mammal**

Lungs Vertebrates that live on land breathe with lungs. Lungs with a larger surface area can take in more oxygen and release more carbon dioxide.

Lung Structure in Vertebrates All land vertebrates breathe with lungs. Inhaling brings oxygen-rich air into the lungs. Oxygen diffuses into the blood through capillaries in the lungs. Carbon dioxide diffuses out of the blood and is exhaled.

▶ *Amphibian, Reptilian, and Mammalian Lungs* The internal surface area of lungs increases from amphibians to reptiles to mammals. The lung of an amphibian is like a sac with ridges. The lung of a reptile is small but often divided into chambers. A mammalian lung is large with many branches. Bubblelike structures called **alveoli** (al VEE uh ly; singular: alveolus) fill the lungs of mammals. These structures provide a large surface area for gas exchange. In the lungs of mammals and most other vertebrates, air moves in and out through the same passage. For this reason, some stale air is trapped in the lungs.

▶ *Bird Lungs* Air flows through bird lungs in one direction. One-way air flow is more efficient than the in-and-out air flow of mammals. Stale air does not get trapped. One-way flow allows birds to get enough oxygen to power their flight muscles.

🔑 **Key Question** What respiratory structures enable land animals to breathe? **Land animals breathe by using structures such as the skin, mantle cavities, book lungs, tracheal tubes, and lungs.**

BUILD Vocabulary

alveolus
a tiny air sac at the end of the bronchiole in the lungs that provides surface area for gas exchange to occur

🖊 **WORD ORIGINS**

The Latin word *alveolus* means "small cavity." A cavity is a hollow space. The *alveoli* in the lungs are air sacs that are small and hollow.

CHECK Understanding

Use the highlighted words from the lesson to complete each sentence correctly.

1. The feathery structures that allow fish to obtain oxygen from water are _____.

2. The tiny air sacs in lungs where gas exchange occurs are called _____.

Critical Thinking

3. Explain How are the respiratory structures of all animals similar?

4. Apply Concepts Explain why it is important that respiratory surfaces remain moist.

5. Review Which groups of aquatic animals breathe with gills? With lungs?

6. Compare and Contrast Compare the structures that land invertebrates and land vertebrates use to breathe.

7. Write to Learn Describe the events that occur when a mammal breathes in and out. Include the path of air through its lungs.

27.3 Circulation

MD CLG 3.2.1 Processes and Functions, 3.4.1 Evolutionary Change. SPI 1.5.2 Communicate Information, 1.5.7 Classification Systems, 1.5.8 Compare.

Open and Closed Circulatory Systems

How do animals get oxygen and nutrients to their cells? How do their cells get rid of carbon dioxide and other wastes? In small aquatic animals that are only a few cells thick, materials move by diffusion. But most animals move these materials in blood. Usually one or more hearts pump blood through a circulatory system. A **heart** is a hollow, muscular organ that pumps blood.

Open Circulatory Systems Arthropods and most mollusks have **open circulatory systems.** In an open circulatory system, blood is only partly contained in blood vessels. The vessels empty into a system of sinuses, or spongy holes. There, blood is in direct contact with body tissues. Blood collects in another set of sinuses. Eventually it flows back to the heart.

Closed Circulatory Systems Larger invertebrates and all vertebrates have **closed circulatory systems.** In a closed circulatory system, blood moves entirely within blood vessels. Nutrients and oxygen reach body tissues by diffusing across the walls of tiny blood vessels called capillaries. Blood that is completely contained in vessels can be pumped under high pressure. Thus, a closed circulatory system is more efficient than an open circulatory system.

🔑 **Key Question** How do open and closed circulatory systems compare? **In an open circulatory system, blood is only partly contained within blood vessels. In a closed circulatory system, blood is completely contained in blood vessels.**

Key Questions

🔑 **How do open and closed circulatory systems compare?**

🔑 **How do the patterns of circulation in vertebrates compare?**

BUILD Understanding

Cycle Diagram As you read, draw a cycle diagram showing how blood moves through a closed, two-loop circulatory system. Use five steps in your diagram.

In Your Workbook Refer to your workbook to see how to make a cycle diagram.

Open and Closed Circulatory Systems
A grasshopper has an open circulatory system. Blood leaves vessels and moves through sinuses before returning to the heart. Earthworms have closed circulatory systems. Blood stays in the vessels of a closed circulatory system.

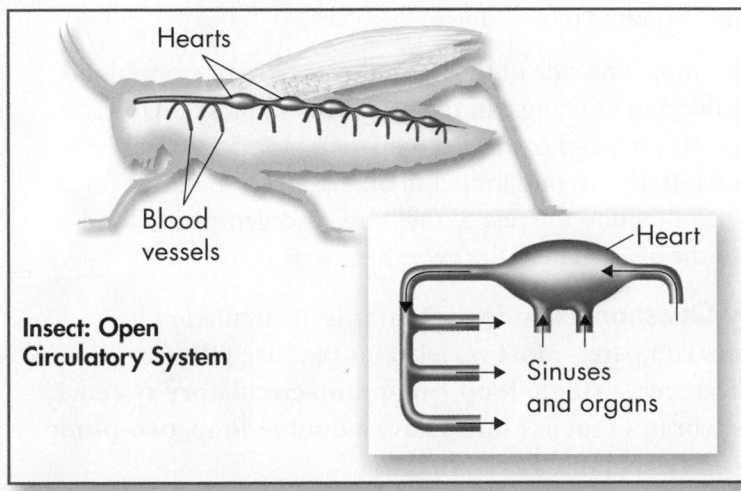

Insect: Open Circulatory System

Hearts

Blood vessels

Heart

Sinuses and organs

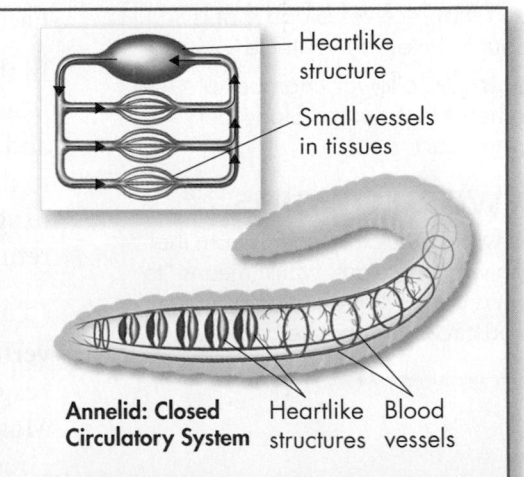

Heartlike structure

Small vessels in tissues

Annelid: Closed Circulatory System Heartlike structures Blood vessels

Single- and Double-Loop Circulation Most vertebrates that use gills for respiration have a single-loop circulatory system. Most vertebrates that use lungs have a double-loop circulatory system. (In diagrams of animals' circulatory systems, blood vessels carrying oxygen-rich blood are red. Blood vessels carrying oxygen-poor blood are blue.)

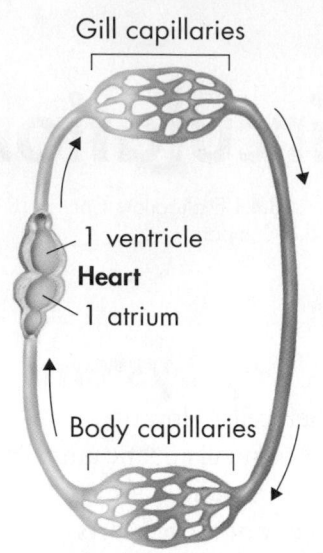

Gill capillaries

1 ventricle
Heart
1 atrium

Body capillaries

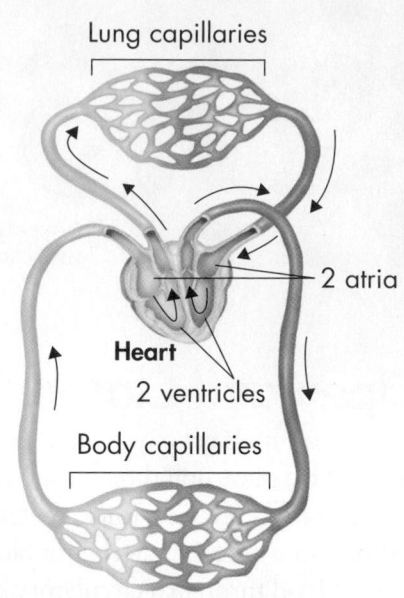

Lung capillaries

2 atria

Heart
2 ventricles

Body capillaries

BUILD Vocabulary

heart a hollow muscular organ that pumps blood throughout the body

open circulatory system a type of circulatory system in which blood is only partly contained within a system of blood vessels as it travels through the body

closed circulatory system a type of circulatory system in which blood circulates entirely within blood vessels that extend throughout the body

atrium an upper chamber of the heart that receives blood that is about to enter the ventricle

ventricle a lower chamber of the heart that pumps blood out of the heart

🍂 WORD ORIGINS

The word *circulatory* comes from the Latin word *circulare*, which means "to form a circle." In a circulatory system, blood circles around the body.

Single- and Double-Loop Circulation

As vertebrates evolved, they developed more complex circulatory systems. These systems move materials to and from body tissues very efficiently.

Single-Loop Circulation Most vertebrates with gills have a single-loop circulatory system. A single pump forces blood around the body in one direction. In fishes, the heart has two chambers. The **atrium** (plural: atria) is the chamber that receives blood that is about to enter the ventricle. The **ventricle** is the chamber that pumps blood out of the heart and to the gills. In the gills, blood picks up oxygen and releases carbon dioxide. It then travels to the rest of the body, delivering oxygen to the body's cells. By the time blood returns to the atrium, it has become oxygen-poor.

Double-Loop Circulation As larger and more active land vertebrates evolved, the capillary networks in both their lungs and body tissues became larger. A single pump would not have been strong enough to pump blood through these larger systems. In reptiles, birds, and mammals, a double-loop, two-pump circulatory system evolved. Each loop is powered by one side of the heart.

In the first loop, one side of the heart forces oxygen-poor blood from the heart to the lungs. In the lungs, blood picks up oxygen and drops off carbon dioxide. Oxygen-rich blood then returns to the heart. In the second loop, the other side of the heart forces oxygen-rich blood to the rest of the body. Oxygen-poor blood returns to the heart. Then, the cycle begins again.

🔑 **Key Question** How do the patterns of circulation in vertebrates compare? **Most vertebrates that use gills for respiration have a single-loop, one-pump circulatory system. Most vertebrates that use lungs have a double-loop, two-pump circulatory system.**

BIOLOGY.com ▶ Search | Lesson 27.3 | **GO** • InterActive Art

Evolution of the Four-Chambered Heart A four-chambered heart is actually two separate pumps working next to each other. Where did the second pump come from? During the evolution of vertebrates, partitions arose that divided the original two chambers into four chambers. This separated oxygen-rich blood from oxygen-poor blood. You can get an idea of how the four chambers evolved by looking at the hearts of modern vertebrates.

Amphibian hearts usually have three chambers: two atria and one ventricle. The left atrium gets oxygen-rich blood from the lungs. The right atrium gets oxygen-poor blood from the body. Blood from both atria flows into the ventricle. The shape of the ventricle helps direct the movement of blood. Most oxygen-poor blood goes to the lungs. Most oxygen-rich blood goes to the rest of the body. But there is some mixing of oxygen-rich and oxygen-poor blood.

Reptilian hearts usually have three chambers. Their ventricles are usually divided a little more than those of typical amphibians. This partial division allows less mixing of oxygen-rich and oxygen-poor blood.

Mammals have a four-chambered heart. The right atrium gets oxygen-poor blood from the body. The right ventricle pushes that blood to the lungs. The left atrium gets oxygen-rich blood from the lungs. The left ventricle pushes oxygen-rich blood out to the rest of the body. Oxygen-rich and oxygen-poor blood cannot mix.

Reptilian Heart Under the armor-like hide of this crocodile lies a heart with two atria and one ventricle.

CHECK
Understanding

Use the highlighted words from the lesson to complete each sentence correctly.

1. The upper chamber of the heart that receives blood that is about to enter the ventricle is called the _____.

2. In a(n) _____, blood empties into sinuses before returning to the heart.

3. The chamber of the heart that pumps blood out of the heart to the rest of the body is the _____.

Critical Thinking

4. **Compare and Contrast** Compare the structure of an open circulatory system to that of a closed circulatory system.

5. **Relate Cause and Effect** How does having a closed circulatory system benefit a large, active animal?

6. **Review** What are two different patterns of circulation found in vertebrates?

7. **Write to Learn** Answer the question in the mystery clue. What happens when you drink a thick liquid through a straw? Is it harder or easier than drinking water through a straw?

MYSTERY CLUE

Human blood is only about a third as salty as seawater. It needs to circulate through very small capillaries. What might happen if the water content of a person's blood were to drop too low? **(Hint: See p. 654.)**

BIOLOGY.com ▸ Search (Lesson 27.3) **GO** ● Lesson Assessment

27.4 Excretion

MD CLG 3.1.2 Homeostasis, 3.2.1 Processes and Functions, 3.2.2 Changes in Metabolic Activity, 3.4.1 Evolutionary Change, 3.5.1 Factors Influencing Ecosystems. SPI 1.3.1 Use Equipment, 1.3.3 Safe Handling of Materials, 1.5.1 Summarize Data, 1.5.8 Compare, 1.5.9 Synthesize Ideas.

Key Questions

🔑 How do animals manage toxic nitrogen-containing waste?

🔑 How do aquatic animals eliminate wastes?

🔑 How do land animals remove wastes while conserving water?

BUILD Understanding

Preview Visuals Write a question you have about the figure called Excretion in Aquatic Animals. As you read the lesson, try to answer your question.

In Your Workbook Refer to your workbook to see how previewing visuals can help you to understand the ideas in this lesson.

BUILD Vocabulary

excretion the process by which nitrogen-containing wastes are eliminated from the body

kidney an organ of excretion that separates wastes and extra water from the blood

🔖 **PREFIXES**

The prefix *ex-* means "out of, from." *Excretion* helps to get wastes "out" of the body.

The Ammonia Problem

So far in this chapter, you have learned how animals get rid of carbon dioxide. But cells also produce other wastes. What are those wastes? And how do animals get rid of them?

When cells break down proteins, they create a nitrogen-containing waste called ammonia. Ammonia is a problem, because it is poisonous! Animals get rid of ammonia by the process of **excretion**. Some small animals that live in water get rid of ammonia by allowing it to diffuse out of their body. Big animals and smaller ones that live in dry places have excretory systems that process and remove ammonia.

Storing Nitrogen-Containing Wastes Animals that cannot get rid of ammonia right away have evolved ways to store nitrogen-containing wastes. Ammonia is too toxic, or poisonous, to store. Many animals convert ammonia into compounds that are less toxic. Insects, reptiles, and birds change ammonia into a sticky white compound called uric acid. Uric acid is much less toxic than ammonia and does not dissolve easily in water. Mammals and some amphibians convert ammonia to urea. Like uric acid, urea is less toxic than ammonia. Unlike uric acid, urea easily dissolves in water.

Maintaining Water Balance Excretory systems help keep the correct balance of water in blood and body tissues. Some systems get rid of water when they get rid of nitrogen-containing wastes. Other systems get rid of nitrogen-containing wastes but conserve water.

Many animals use **kidneys** to separate wastes and extra water from blood. Kidney cells cannot actively pump water across their membranes. Yet they need to separate water from wastes. Kidneys solve this problem by pumping ions to create areas with higher osmotic concentrations. Water moves passively into these areas by osmosis. So this process saves water, but it cannot get rid of extra salt.

🔑 **Key Question** How do animals manage toxic nitrogen-containing waste? **Animals either get rid of ammonia quickly or convert it to other nitrogen-containing compounds that are less toxic.**

Excretion in Aquatic Animals

Most aquatic animals allow ammonia to diffuse out of their bodies. The surrounding water carries the ammonia away. But aquatic animals must still keep the right amount of water in their bodies. Animals have different challenges in fresh water and salt water.

Freshwater Animals Most freshwater animals have body fluids that are saltier than the water they live in. This higher concentration of salt causes water to move into their bodies and salts to diffuse out. Flatworms have cells called flame cells that remove extra water. Amphibians and freshwater fishes get rid of extra water by making lots of watery urine. Freshwater fishes also pump salt in through their gills.

Saltwater Animals Invertebrates that live in salt water usually have less of a problem with water balance than freshwater invertebrates. That is because the water concentration in their bodies is similar to that of the seawater around them. In contrast, the bodies of fishes are usually less salty than seawater. They tend to lose water to their surroundings. These fishes get rid of salt across their gills. Their kidneys conserve water by producing small amounts of concentrated urine.

🔑 **Key Question** How do aquatic animals eliminate wastes? **Aquatic animals generally allow ammonia to diffuse out of their bodies into the surrounding water.**

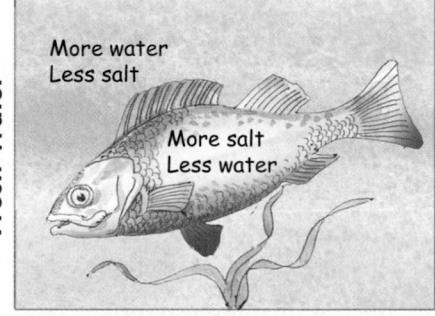

The bodies of freshwater animals, such as fishes, contain a higher concentration of salt than the water they live in.

So water moves into their bodies by osmosis, mostly across the gills. Salt diffuses out. If they didn't excrete water, they'd look like water balloons with eyes!

So they excrete water through kidneys that produce lots of watery urine. They don't drink, and they actively pump salt in across their gills.

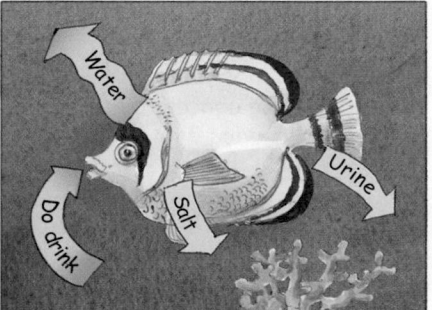

The bodies of saltwater animals, such as fishes, contain a lower concentration of salt than the water they live in.

So they lose water through osmosis, and salt diffuses in. If they didn't conserve water and eliminate salt, they'd shrivel up like dead leaves.

So they conserve water by producing very little concentrated urine. They drink, and they actively pump salt out across their gills.

INQUIRY
into Scientific Thinking

Water and Nitrogen Excretion

In this lab, you will investigate the differences between uric acid and urea.

1 Label one test tube Urea and the other Uric Acid. Place 2 grams of urea in the one labeled Urea. Place 2 grams of uric acid in the one labeled Uric Acid.

2 Add 15 mL of water to each test tube. Stopper and shake the test tubes for 3 minutes.

3 Observe each test tube. Record your observations.

Analyze and Conclude

1. Observe Which substance—urea or uric acid—is less soluble in water? Explain.

2. Infer Birds and reptiles excrete nitrogen-containing wastes in the form of uric acid. How does this adaptation help these animals to survive on land?

In Your Workbook Get more help for this activity in your workbook.

BUILD
Vocabulary

nephridium
an excretory structure of earthworms and other annelids that filters body fluid

Malpighian tubule
a structure in most terrestrial arthropods that concentrates uric acid and adds it to digestive wastes

✦ WORD ORIGINS

The word *nephridium* comes from the Greek word, *nephros*, which means "kidney." A nephridium is a structure in invertebrates that functions like a vertebrate kidney.

Excretion in Land Animals

Land animals also face challenges. In dry air, animals can lose large amounts of water through their respiratory membranes. And even though water may be scarce, they must use water to get rid of nitrogen-containing wastes. Land animals have evolved excretory systems that help conserve water.

Land Invertebrates Some invertebrates that live on land, such as earthworms and snails, produce urine in nephridia. **Nephridia** (singular: nephridium) are tubelike excretory structures that filter body fluid. Body fluid enters the nephridia through openings. The fluid becomes more concentrated as it moves along the tubes. Urine then leaves the body through excretory pores.

Insects and spiders convert ammonia into uric acid. Uric acid and other nitrogen-containing wastes are absorbed from body fluids by **Malpighian tubules.** These structures concentrate wastes and add them to digestive wastes moving through the gut. The uric acid and wastes form a thick paste that leaves the body through the anus. This paste does not contain much water, so this process reduces water loss.

Land Vertebrates In vertebrates, kidneys get rid of most nitrogen-containing wastes. Mammals and land-living amphibians convert ammonia to urea. Urea is excreted in urine. Most reptiles and birds convert ammonia to uric acid. This uric acid passes through ducts into a structure that also receives digestive wastes. The walls of this structure absorb most of the water from the wastes. The animal then excretes a thick, white paste that you would recognize as "bird droppings."

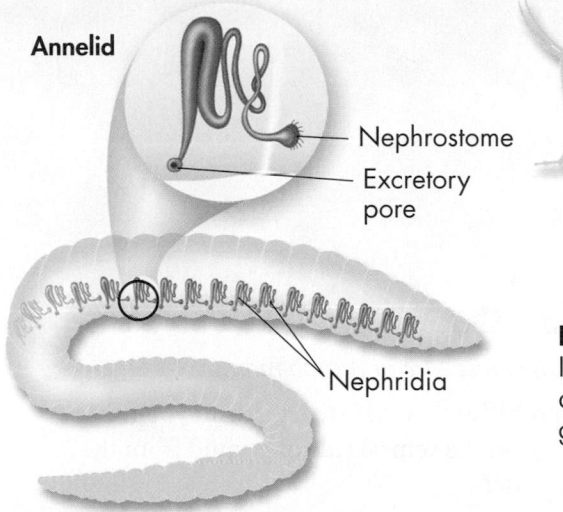

Annelid

Nephrostome

Excretory pore

Nephridia

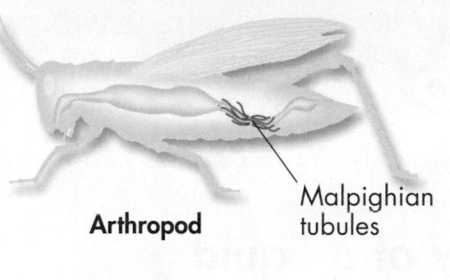

Arthropod

Malpighian tubules

Excretion in Land Animals
Invertebrates and vertebrates have different structures that allow them to get rid of nitrogen-containing wastes.

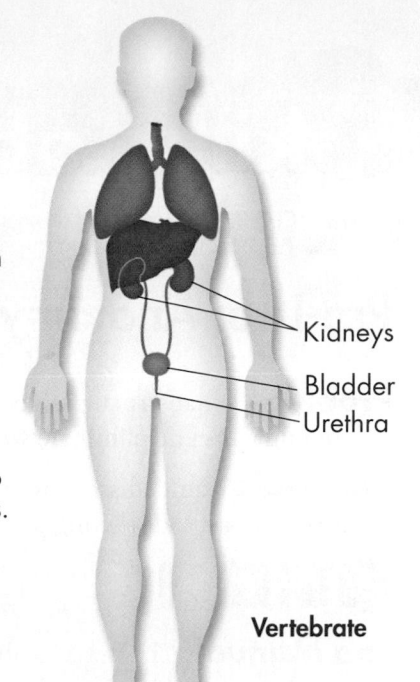

Kidneys

Bladder

Urethra

Vertebrate

Adaptations to Extreme Environments The kidneys of most land vertebrates cannot excrete concentrated salt. That is why most vertebrates cannot drink seawater. To get rid of the extra salt, the kidneys would have to excrete more water. This would make the blood even saltier. Eventually cells would become so dry that the animal would die.

Many animals that live where fresh water is not available have adaptations that conserve water and get rid of extra salt. Some marine reptiles and birds have glands in their heads that excrete salt solutions. Kangaroo rats that live in the American southwest have remarkably efficient kidneys. They produce urine that is 25 times more concentrated than their blood!

🔑 **Key Question** How do land animals remove wastes while conserving water? **Land animals have different specialized structures that allow them to get rid of nitrogen-containing compounds while also conserving water.**

CHECK Understanding

Use the highlighted words from the lesson to complete each sentence correctly.

1. In a spider, waste fluid becomes concentrated inside _____.

2. Land vertebrates have organs called _____ that separate wastes and extra water from the blood.

3. Excretory structures in earthworms that create urine are called _____.

Critical Thinking

4. Review Why does ammonia create a problem for all animals?

5. Compare and Contrast How do the different water-balance needs of freshwater animals and saltwater animals explain the different ways that they excrete nitrogen-containing waste?

6. Write to Learn Answer the question in the mystery clue below. Think about what happens when there is extra salt in the blood.

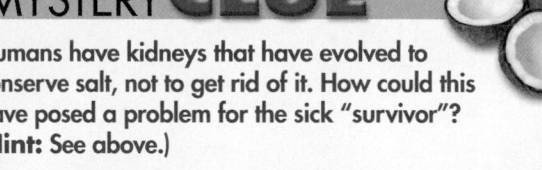

MYSTERY CLUE

Humans have kidneys that have evolved to conserve salt, not to get rid of it. How could this have posed a problem for the sick "survivor"? **(Hint:** See above.)

MD CLG 3.2.1 Processes and Functions. SPI 1.3.1 Use Equipment, 1.3.3 Safe Handling of Materials, 1.5.9 Synthesize Ideas.

Pre-Lab: Anatomy of a Squid

Problem What structures does a squid use to obtain nutrients and eliminate wastes?

Materials squid, dissecting tray, hand lens, forceps, dissecting scissors, dissecting pins, dissecting probe

Lab Manual Chapter 27 Lab

Skills Focus Observe, Infer, Sequence, Draw Conclusions

Connect to the **Big idea** All animals obtain their food by eating other organisms. All animals need a way to digest the food, and most animals need a way to circulate the absorbed nutrients to all the cells in the body. Animals also need to absorb oxygen from their environment for cellular respiration. Finally, animals need to rid their bodies of wastes.

The ways that animals meet these needs vary greatly. Often, different habitats require different structures. For example, an animal that must obtain its oxygen from air will not have the same respiratory structures as an animal that must obtain its oxygen from water. In this lab, you will dissect a squid and observe parts of several body systems.

Background Questions

a. Compare and Contrast How are a gastrovascular cavity and a digestive tract different?

b. Review What process takes place in all respiratory structures?

c. Compare and Contrast What is the difference between an open and a closed circulatory system?

Pre-Lab Questions

Preview the procedure in the lab manual.

1. Interpret Visuals What structure can you use to distinguish the ventral side of a squid from the dorsal side?

2. Infer Why is it important to lift the mantle while cutting it?

3. Predict What do you expect the gills to look like, and why?

BIOLOGY.com Search [Chapter 27] **GO**

Visit Chapter 27 online to test yourself on chapter content and to find activities to help you learn.

Untamed Science Video Trek carefully with the Untamed Science crew as they get up close and personal with bears to learn about their adaptations.

Art in Motion What happens when fresh- and saltwater fishes excrete water or salt? Find out by watching this animation.

Art Review Review your knowledge of the different types of respiratory systems with this activity.

InterActive Art See how single- and double-loop circulation systems compare.

Visual Analogy Compare the structure and function of the types of teeth with common objects.

27.1 Feeding and Digestion

- Most filter feeders have gills or other structures that strain algae and small animals from water. Detritivores eat decaying material. Carnivores eat other animals. Herbivores eat plants or parts of plants. Parasites feed on the blood or tissues of their host. Sometimes two types of animals have a relationship that helps both of them.

- Some invertebrates break down food through intracellular digestion. Most invertebrates and all vertebrates use extracellular digestion.

- Carnivores usually have sharp mouthparts that can capture food, hold it, and cut it into pieces. Herbivores usually have mouthparts that can grind plant material.

intracellular digestion (p. 647)
extracellular digestion (p. 647)
gastrovascular cavity (p. 647)
digestive tract (p. 648)
rumen (p. 648)

27.2 Respiration

- Respiratory structures provide a large surface area of moist, selectively permeable membrane. The membrane keeps a difference in the relative concentration of oxygen and carbon dioxide on either side of it. This difference in concentration allows diffusion to take place.

- Most aquatic animals breathe through their skin or with gills. Aquatic reptiles and mammals breathe with lungs and must hold their breath underwater.

- Invertebrates that live on land have a variety of different respiratory structures, including skin, mantle cavities, book lungs, and tracheal tubes. All vertebrates that live on land—reptiles, birds, mammals, and land-living amphibians—breathe with lungs.

gill (p. 651)
lung (p. 651)
alveolus (p. 652)

27.3 Circulation

- In an open circulatory system, blood is only partly contained within blood vessels. In a closed circulatory system, blood circulates entirely within blood vessels.

- Most vertebrates with gills have a single-loop circulatory system with a single pump. This pump forces blood through a single-loop circulatory system. Most vertebrates with lungs have a double-loop, two-pump circulatory system.

heart (p. 653)
open circulatory system (p. 653)
closed circulatory system (p. 653)
atrium (p. 654)
ventricle (p. 654)

27.4 Excretion

- Animals either get rid of ammonia quickly or convert it to other nitrogen-containing compounds that are less toxic.

- Aquatic animals generally allow ammonia to diffuse out of their bodies into the surrounding water.

- Some land invertebrates, including earthworms and snails, produce urine in nephridia. Insects and spiders convert ammonia to uric acid. Mammals and land amphibians convert ammonia to urea, which is excreted in urine. Most reptiles and birds convert ammonia into uric acid.

excretion (p. 656)
kidney (p. 656)
nephridium (p. 658)
Malpighian tubule (p. 658)

Assess the Big idea

Structure and Function

Write an answer to the question below:

Q: How do the structures of animals allow them to take in essential materials and get rid of wastes?

Constructed Response

Write an answer to each of the numbered questions below. The answer to each numbered question should be one or two paragraphs long. To help you begin, read the **Hints** below the questions.

1. **How is a digestive tract a more efficient structure for taking in and processing food than a gastrovascular cavity?**

   Hint A gastrovascular cavity has one opening. A digestive tract has two openings, and food moves in one direction.

   Hint A digestive tract may have specialized organs, such as a stomach and intestines.

2. **Do you think large, active vertebrates would have been likely to succeed without the evolution of closed circulatory systems? Explain your reasoning.**

   Hint Blood that is completely contained within blood vessels can be pumped under greater pressure. Therefore, it can travel a greater distance.

   Hint To move quickly, muscles need a large supply of oxygen.

3. **All animals need to control the amount of water within their bodies. They also need to get rid of nitrogen-containing wastes. Compare the way that earthworms and insects are able to control these functions.**

   Hint Excretion usually requires water. Earthworms and insects have different kinds of structures that help conserve water.

   Hint Review the art of excretory systems on page 659 as you plan your answer.

Foundations for Learning Wrap-Up

Use the Z-fold charts you made when you started the chapter to help you to organize your thoughts about how animals get food and get rid of wastes.

Activity 1 Get together in a group of three. Exchange the Z-fold charts for Lesson 1 with the members of your group. Look at the predicted answers for each key question. Discuss what is right about each answer and what might be missing. Do the same thing for the other lessons of the chapter.

Activity 2 Fold the Z-fold for Lesson 1 so that the predictions on the middle panel are hidden. Turn the Z-fold over. Write the answers for each of the key questions on the back of the Z-fold. Compare your predictions to the answers that you wrote after reading the chapter. Do the same thing for the other lessons of the chapter.

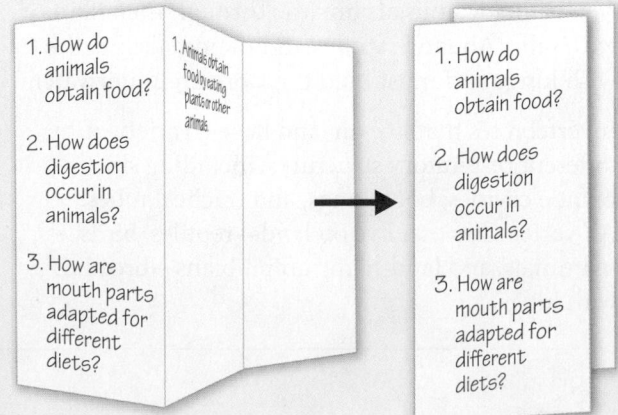

27.1 Feeding and Digestion

Understand Key Concepts

1. Animals that get food by eating decaying bits of plant and animal material are called
   a. herbivores.
   c. detritivores.
   b. carnivores.
   d. filter feeders.

Test-Taking Tip

When you are answering multiple-choice questions, be sure to read all the choices before you choose an answer. One choice may seem right. However, when you read the other choices, you may find that another choice is more correct. For example, consider question 1. Herbivores eat plants, so at first you might think that the answer is **a**. But the question asks about decaying bits of plants, so the correct answer is **c**.

2. Which animal below relies primarily on intracellular digestion?
   a. sponge
   c. dragonfly
   b. clam
   d. earthworm

3. Compare the processes of intracellular and extracellular digestion.

Think Critically

4. **Infer** The skull of a mammal has no sharp canine teeth. The large teeth toward the back of the jaw are very flat. What did this mammal eat?

27.2 Respiration

Understand Key Concepts

5. Most terrestrial insects breathe using a network of structures called
   a. gills.
   c. book gills.
   b. tracheal tubes.
   d. book lungs.

6. For the exchange of carbon dioxide and oxygen, an animal's respiratory surfaces must be
   a. cold.
   c. hot.
   b. dry.
   d. moist.

7. Most fishes exchange gases by pumping water
   a. over their gills.
   c. over their atria.
   b. through their lungs.
   d. through their alveoli.

8. With what respiratory structures do aquatic reptiles and mammals breathe? Why are these structures inconvenient when these animals swim underwater?

Think Critically

9. **Infer** Snails that live on land have a respiratory structure called a mantle cavity. The mantle cavity is often covered with mucus. What might the function of the mucus be?

27.3 Circulation

Understand Key Concepts

10. Most arthropods have
    a. no circulatory system.
    b. an open circulatory system.
    c. a closed circulatory system.
    d. skin gills.

11. In a closed circulatory system, blood
    a. comes in direct contact with tissues.
    b. empties into sinuses.
    c. does not transport oxygen.
    d. remains within blood vessels.

12. Most vertebrates that have gills have a(n)
    a. double-loop circulatory system.
    b. accessory lung.
    c. single-loop circulatory system.
    d. four-chambered heart.

13. Describe the circulatory system of a mammal. Is it open or closed? State the number of loops and the number of heart chambers in the system.

Think Critically

14. **Compare and Contrast** What is the major structural difference between vertebrates that have single-loop circulatory systems and those that have double-loop systems?

27.4 Excretion

Understand Key Concepts

15. The amount of salt and water in the body fluids of mammals is controlled by the

   a. lungs.   **c.** intestine.

   b. kidneys.   **d.** heart.

16. The elimination of nitrogen-containing wastes by the body is called

   a. excretion.   **c.** respiration.

   b. circulation.   **d.** digestion.

17. Why do most animals convert ammonia to urea or uric acid?

Think Critically

18. Apply Concepts Uric acid requires less water to excrete than urea does. How is the production of uric acid an advantage to animals that live on land?

Connecting Concepts

A student conducts an experiment to measure the effect of caffeine on the heart rate of a small pond-water animal called Daphnia. *The results are shown in the graph.*

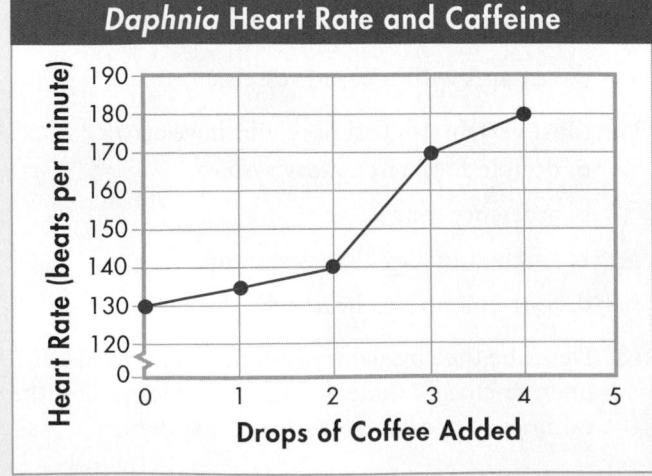

Daphnia Heart Rate and Caffeine

x-axis: Drops of Coffee Added
y-axis: Heart Rate (beats per minute)

19. Interpret Graphs Describe the effect that caffeine has on the heart rate of *Daphnia*.

20. Predict What would be the effect of five or more drops of coffee on the heart rate of *Daphnia*?

(NEAR) DEATH BY SALT WATER

Luckily, the group that was supposed to pick up the friends came earlier than planned. They took the sick man to the hospital. He was diagnosed with severe dehydration. The doctors gave him water and fluids through an intravenous drip. If he had gone much longer without treatment, he would have died. What had happened? Why didn't his friends have the same problem?

As sailors have known for centuries, humans cannot drink salt water. But why?

Seawater is saltier than human blood and body fluids. Drinking seawater loads the body with extra salt. Human kidneys cannot make urine with salt concentrations high enough to get rid of the salt. The kidneys are then forced to excrete too much water in urine, which lowers the amount of water in blood. The blood becomes thick and cannot pass through capillaries. Cells and tissues begin to dry out. This dehydration can cause fatal kidney failure and heat stroke.

1. Compare and Contrast The other group members who did not drink seawater experienced water stress as well. What was going on in their circulatory and excretory systems? Why wasn't their water stress as serious as the water stress experienced by their friend?

2. Propose a Solution If you were marooned on an island that had no fresh water, what would be your plan for getting some?

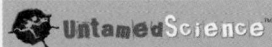 **Untamed Science** Finding out what happened to the college student who drank salt water is only the beginning. Take a video field trip with the ecogeeks of Untamed Science to see where the mystery leads.

Multiple Choice

1. Animals that live on an animal and feed on its body tissues are called
   A parasites.   C herbivores.
   B carnivores.   D detritivores.

   CLG 3.5.2

2. Examining the teeth of an animal can give information about whether it
   A practices intracellular or extracellular digestion.
   B is a filter feeder or a detritivore.
   C is a nutritional symbiont.
   D is a herbivore or a carnivore.   SPI 1.2.6

3. Movement of oxygen and carbon dioxide across a respiratory surface requires
   A that the respiratory surface be moist.
   B active transport by the cells of the respiratory surface.
   C alveoli.
   D an equal concentration of both gases on both sides of the membrane.   CLG 3.2.1

4. In an open circulatory system, blood
   A is confined to blood vessels at all times.
   B circulates around body tissues.
   C exchanges gases with lung alveoli.
   D is not required for exchanging gases with body cells.   CLG 3.2.1

5. In chordates with four-chambered hearts, there is
   A only one loop in the circulatory system.
   B mixing of oxygen rich and oxygen-poor blood.
   C partial partition of the ventricle.
   D no mixing of oxygen-rich and oxygen-poor blood.   CLG 3.2.1

6. Most reptiles excrete wastes in the form of
   A urea.   C uric acid.
   B ammonia.   D toxins.   CLG 3.2.1

7. What is a function of the excretory system?
   A to supply cells with oxygen and nutrients
   B to rid the body of metabolic wastes
   C to exchange oxygen and carbon dioxide with the environment
   D to break down food   CLG 3.2.1

Questions 8–9

A biology student is investigating the relationship between cricket chirping and air temperature. She catches a cricket and places it in a jar. She leaves the jar outside, and each day she counts the number of chirps during a 15-second period. At the same time, she records the outside temperature near the cricket. Her data for a 5-day period are shown below.

Temperature and Cricket Chirping		
Day	Number of Chirps in 15 Seconds	Outside Temperature (°C)
Monday	31	23
Tuesday	20	16
Wednesday	12	11
Thursday	29	21
Friday	25	19

8. At which of the following temperatures would a cricket be most likely to chirp 9 times in 15 seconds?
   A 10°C   C 0°C
   B 18°C   D 25°C   SPI 1.4.4

9. What can the student conclude from this experiment?
   A Crickets cannot chirp more than 31 times in 15 seconds.
   B The number of times a cricket chirps decreases when the temperature decreases.
   C The number of times a cricket chirps increases when the temperature decreases.
   D There is no relationship between the number of times a cricket chirps and temperature.

   SPI 1.4.2

Open-Ended Response

10. Which types of vertebrates have double-loop circulation and which types have single-loop circulation?   SPI 1.5.7

If You Have Trouble With . . .									
Question	1	2	3	4	5	6	7	8	9	10
See Lesson	27.1	27.1	27.2	27.3	27.3	27.4	27.4	27.3	27.3	27.3

28 Animal Systems II

Big idea **Structure and Function**

Q: How do the body systems of animals allow them to collect information about their environments and respond appropriately?

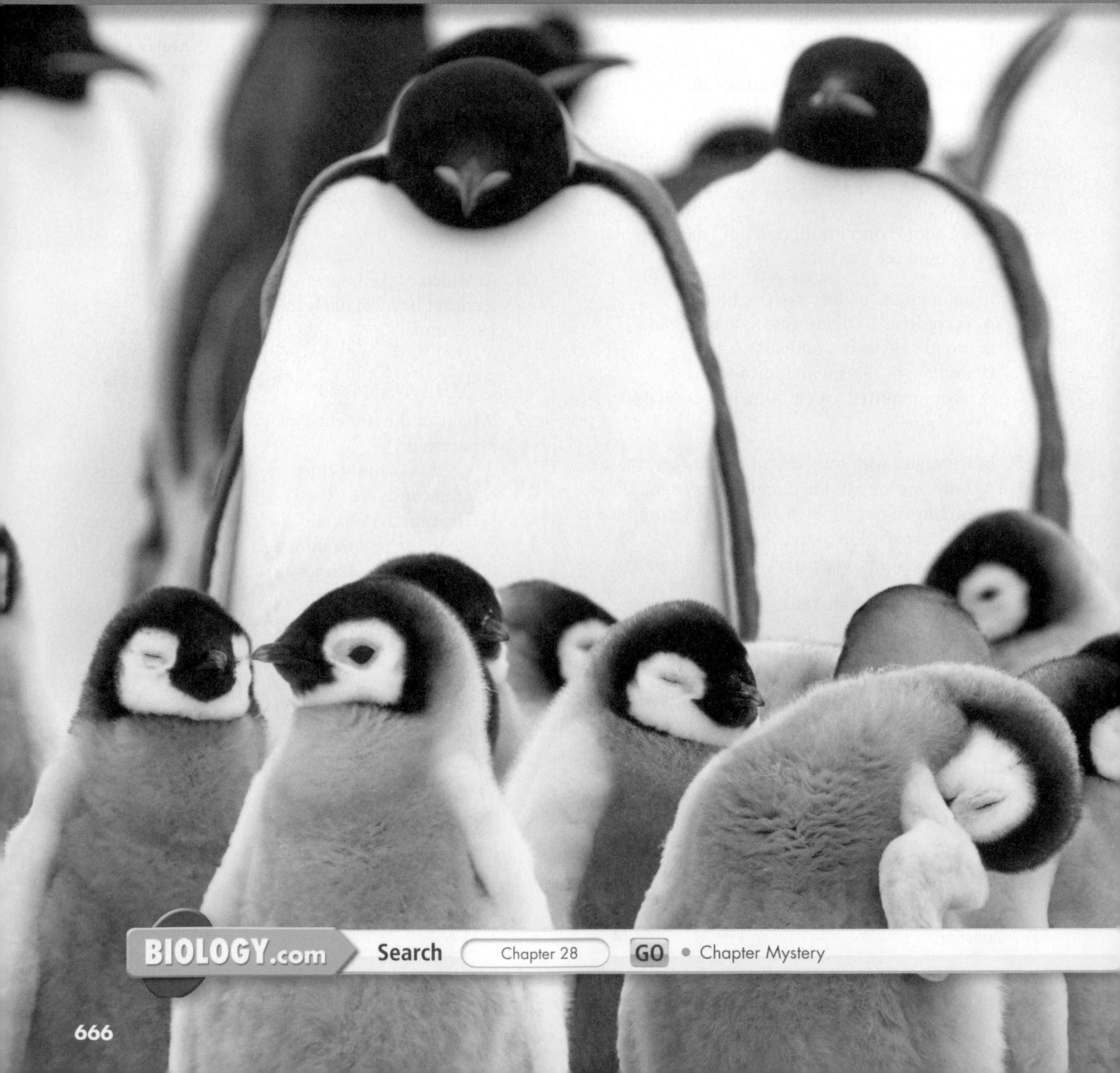

BIOLOGY.com Search Chapter 28 GO • Chapter Mystery

MARYLAND VOLUNTARY STATE CURRICULUM

Biology Indicators/Core Learning Goals (CLG) 3.1.2, 3.2.1, 3.2.2, 3.3.1. **Skills and Processes Indicators (SPI)** 1.2.3, 1.2.4, 1.2.7, 1.3.1, 1.3.3, 1.5.5, 1.5.7, 1.5.8, 1.5.9, 1.6.4. See lessons for details.

Thick down feathers keep these young penguins warm. They share their warmth by huddling close together.

CHAPTER
MYSTERY

SHE'S JUST LIKE HER MOTHER!

In 2001, a surprising thing happened at the Henry Doorly Zoo in Omaha, Nebraska. A bonnethead shark gave birth to a female baby bonnethead. Workers at the zoo were shocked. For three years, there had been only three bonnethead sharks in the tank where the baby was born. All of these sharks were female.

Some female sharks are able to store sperm for later fertilization. Does this explain how the shark got pregnant?

Read for Mystery Clues As you read the chapter, look for clues that help explain how the baby bonnethead's mother got pregnant. Also, think about how sharks usually reproduce. Think about how that process affects genetic material in the offspring. Then, solve the mystery.

FOUNDATIONS for Learning

Science uses many vocabulary words. These words can help you to understand basic science concepts. Before you read the chapter, write down the vocabulary words on index cards. As you read, write the definitions on the back of the cards. At the end of the chapter are two activities that use these cards to help you to answer the question: How do the body systems of animals allow the animals to collect information about their environments and respond appropriately?

Neuron	Endotherm	Viviparous
Response	Ectotherm	Cerebrum

• Untamed Science Video   • Flash Card

28.1 Response

MD CLG 3.2.1 Processes and Functions. SPI 1.5.7 Classification Systems, 1.5.8 Compare, 1.5.9 Synthesize Ideas.

Key Questions

🔑 How do animals respond to events around them?

🔑 What are the trends in nervous system evolution?

🔑 What are some types of sensory systems in animals?

BUILD Understanding

Preview Visuals Previewing visuals helps you prepare to read and understand the text. Before you read, preview the visual of neural circuits. Take note of any questions you have about it. As you read, try to answer your questions.

In Your Workbook Refer to your workbook for suggestions about how to use a T chart to organize your notes about the visuals in this lesson.

How Animals Respond

Imagine that you are at a favorite place, such as a beach. The sun feels warm on your face. You hear the waves crashing on the shore. You smell salt air. Now think about how your body experiences the place. Your senses gather information about how it looks, sounds, or smells. Your nervous system organizes this information. Your brain decides how to respond to it.

All animals experience and respond to their environments. Sometimes animals need to catch food. Other times, they need to escape from predators. Most animals have specialized nervous systems that allow them to respond to their environments. Nervous systems are made of specialized nerve cells, called **neurons.** Neurons work together to receive and organize information. Then, they "decide" how to respond.

Detecting Stimuli Information in the environment that causes an organism to react is called a **stimulus** (plural: stimuli). Chemicals, light, heat, and sounds can all be stimuli.

Specialized cells called **sensory neurons** are able to sense stimuli. Each type of sensory neuron responds to a particular stimulus. For example, sensory neurons in the ear sense sounds. Like humans, many other animals also respond to light, taste, sound, odor, temperature, gravity, and pressure. Some animals also have sensory cells that humans do not have. For example, some animals can sense weak electric currents or Earth's magnetic field.

Response Lions are predators that eat zebras and other animals. When a zebra or other prey senses the presence of a lion, it begins to run. The lion responds by running after the prey.

Neural Circuits In simple neural circuits, sensory neurons connect to motor neurons and allow fast but simple responses (left). In more complex neural circuits, interneurons and specialized sensory cells connect sensory neurons to motor neurons (right). Complex neural circuits allow a more complex response.

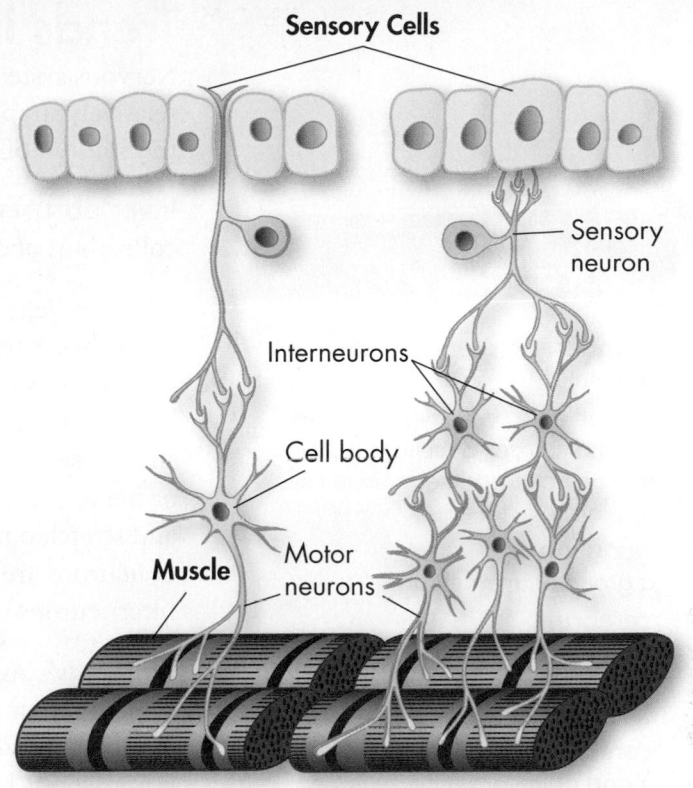

Sensory Cells

Sensory neuron

Interneurons

Cell body

Muscle

Motor neurons

Processing Information When sensory neurons sense a stimulus, they pass information about the stimulus to other nerve cells. **Interneurons** receive information from sensory neurons and usually pass the information to other neurons. Interneurons process information and determine how an animal responds to stimuli.

The number of interneurons an animal has can determine how flexible and complex an animal's behavior can be. Some invertebrates, such as cnidarians and worms, have very few interneurons. These animals only have simple responses to stimuli. They may swim toward light or toward a chemical stimulus that signals food. They may move away from a stimulus that signals danger.

Vertebrates have more complex nervous systems with larger numbers of interneurons. The vertebrate brain is made of many interneurons, which is why the behaviors of vertebrates can be more complex than the behaviors of most invertebrates.

Responding A specific reaction to a stimulus is called a **response.** Waking up when you hear an alarm is a response. So is licking your lips when you smell good food.

Many body systems work together to allow an animal to respond to a stimulus. The nervous system directs the response to a stimulus. However, the response is usually carried out by cells and tissues that are not nerve cells. A lion's decision to chase prey is carried out by muscle cells that produce movement. Nerve cells called **motor neurons** carry "directions" from interneurons to muscle cells. Other responses to environmental conditions may be carried out by other body systems, such as the respiratory or circulatory systems.

🔑 **Key Question** How do animals respond to events around them? **An animal's body systems—including the nervous system and the muscular system—work together to respond to a stimulus.**

Trends in Nervous System Evolution

Nervous systems vary greatly across the animal kingdom. Some are relatively simple. Others are complex. Nervous systems also differ in the amount of specialization and cephalization.

Invertebrates Invertebrate nervous systems range from simple collections of cells to complex systems with many interneurons.

▶ **Nerve Nets, Nerve Cords, and Ganglia** Cnidarians, such as jellyfishes, have simple nervous systems called nerve nets. In a nerve net, neurons are connected in a netlike arrangement. Neurons in a nerve net have few specializations. In radially symmetric invertebrates, such as sea stars, some interneurons are grouped together into nerves or nerve cords. These nerves form a ring around the animal's mouth and stretch out along its arms. In still other invertebrates, a number of neurons are grouped together into **ganglia** (singular: ganglion). Interneurons connect with each other in ganglia.

▶ **"Heads"** Animals that have bilateral symmetry often show cephalization. Cephalization (sef uh lih ZAY shun) is the concentration of sensory neurons and interneurons into a "head." Certain flatworms and roundworms have some cephalization. Cephalopod mollusks, such as octopi and squid, have more developed cephalization. So do many arthropods. In these animals, interneurons form ganglia throughout the body. The largest ganglia, called cerebral ganglia, are found in the head.

▶ **Brains** In some species of invertebrates, cerebral ganglia are organized into a brain. The brains of some cephalopods, such as octopi, allow complex behaviors and learning.

Invertebrate Nervous Systems Invertebrate nervous systems have different amounts of cephalization and specialization. Flatworms have centralized nervous systems with small ganglia in their heads. Cnidarians have a nerve net which allows them to be very successful predators. Arthropods and cephalopod mollusks have a brain and specialized sensory organs.

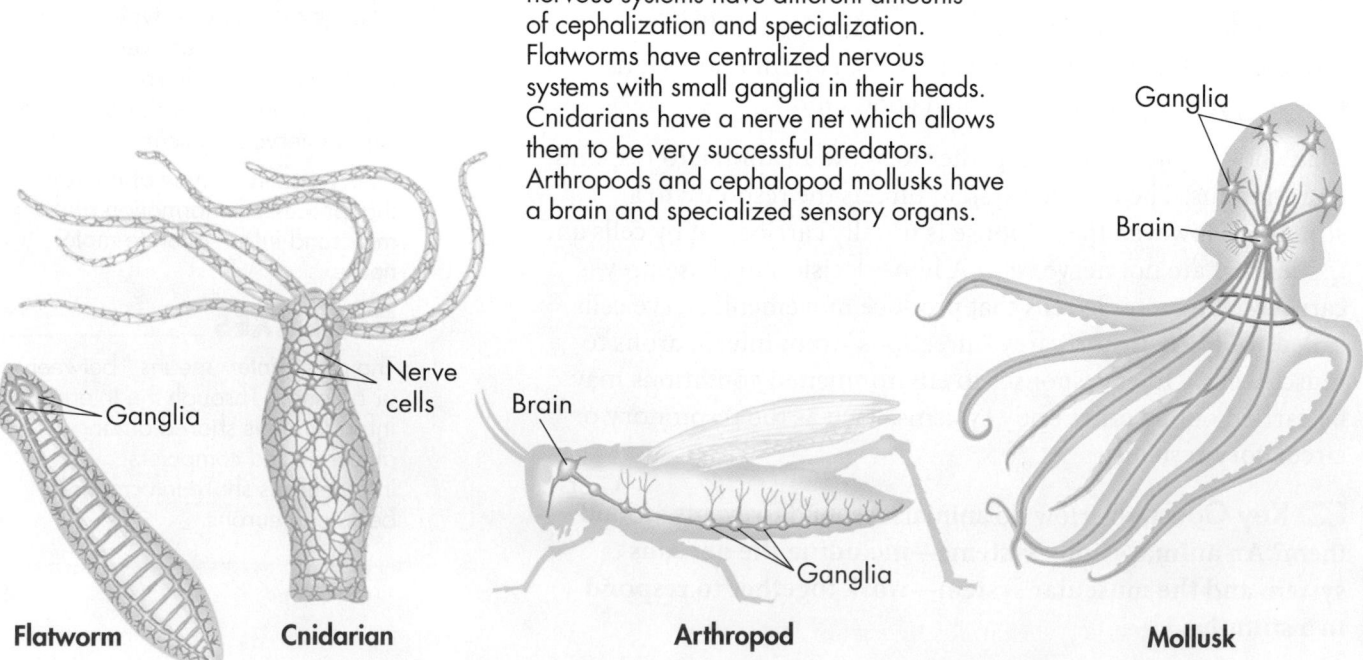

Ganglia

Nerve cells

Brain

Ganglia

Ganglia

Brain

Flatworm   Cnidarian   Arthropod   Mollusk

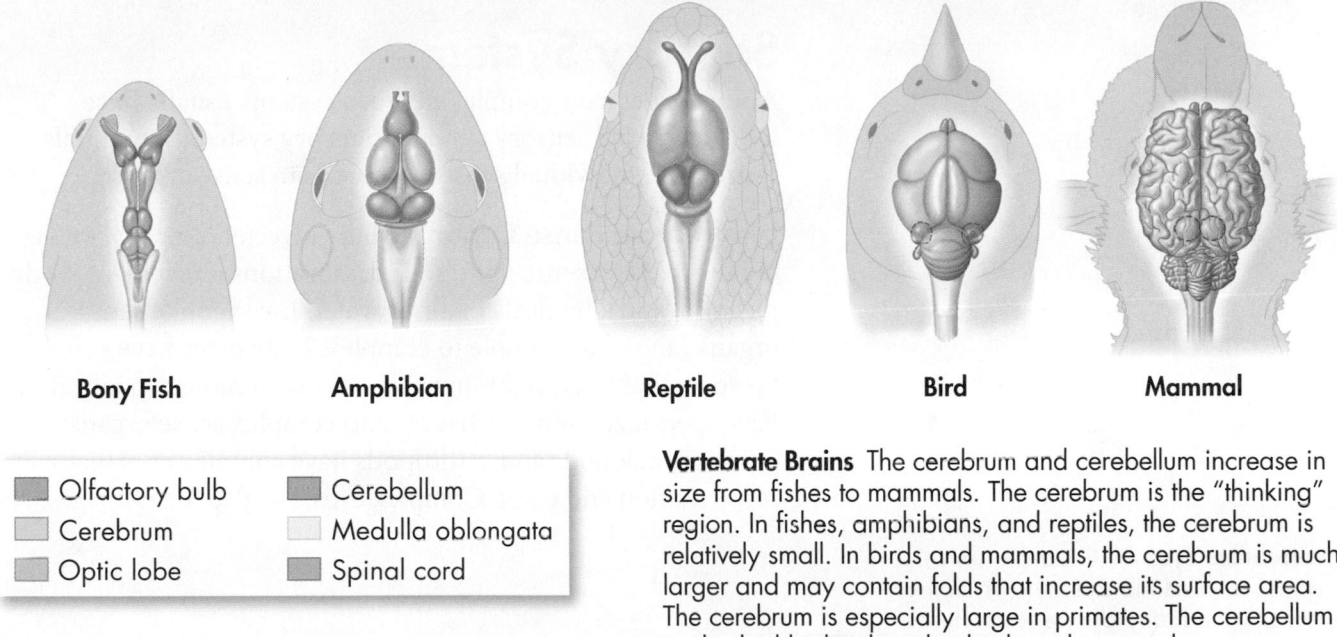

Bony Fish   Amphibian   Reptile   Bird   Mammal

◼ Olfactory bulb	◼ Cerebellum
◼ Cerebrum	◻ Medulla oblongata
◼ Optic lobe	◼ Spinal cord

Vertebrate Brains The cerebrum and cerebellum increase in size from fishes to mammals. The cerebrum is the "thinking" region. In fishes, amphibians, and reptiles, the cerebrum is relatively small. In birds and mammals, the cerebrum is much larger and may contain folds that increase its surface area. The cerebrum is especially large in primates. The cerebellum is also highly developed in birds and mammals.

Chordates Chordates have complex nervous systems. Nonvertebrate chordates have no heads as adults. However, they still have cerebral ganglia. All vertebrates, on the other hand, have brains. Vertebrate brains are formed from many interneurons that are connected to each other. These interneurons are also connected with sensory neurons and with motor neurons in the head and the rest of the body.

▶ *Parts of the Vertebrate Brain* The cerebrum, cerebellum, medulla oblongata, optic lobes, and olfactory bulbs are all parts of the vertebrate brain. The **cerebrum** (SEHR uh brum) is the "thinking" part of the brain. The cerebrum receives sensory information and signals the body to respond. The cerebrum is also involved in learning, memory, and conscious thought. The **cerebellum** (sehr uh BEL um) controls balance and helps to coordinate body movement. The medulla oblongata (mih DUH luh ahb lahn GAHT uh) controls the way that many organs work. Optic lobes help an animal to see. Olfactory bulbs help an animal to smell. Vertebrate brains are connected to the rest of the body by a spinal cord. The spinal cord is a thick collection of nerves that is surrounded by the spine.

▶ *Vertebrate Brain Evolution* As vertebrates evolved, their brains became larger and more complex. Vertebrate brains increase in size and complexity from fishes, through amphibians and reptiles, to birds and mammals.

🔑 **Key Question** What are the trends in nervous system evolution? **Invertebrate nervous systems range from simple collections of nerve cells to complex systems that include ganglia and brains. All vertebrate nervous systems include brains. As vertebrates evolved, their brains became larger and more complex.**

Not Such a Bird Brain The brains of chickadees are very complex. The part responsible for remembering locations gets bigger when the bird stores food in the fall. When winter comes, the tiny bird is able to find hundreds of storage places. In spring, the bird's brain returns to normal size.

Sensory Systems

Animals that have complex nervous systems usually have well-developed sensory systems. Sensory systems in animals range from individual sensory neurons to sense organs.

Invertebrate Sense Organs Many invertebrates have sense organs that can sense light, sound, vibrations, movement, body position, and chemicals in air or water. Invertebrate sense organs range from simple to complex. Flatworms have simple eyespots that sense light. Invertebrates with more cephalization have specialized sensory tissues and complex sense organs. Some cephalopods and arthropods have complex eyes that sense motion and color. Complex eyes can also form images.

Invertebrate Eyes Invertebrate sense organs, such as the eyes shown in these photos, have many different structures. Some invertebrate eyes are simple. Some are complex.

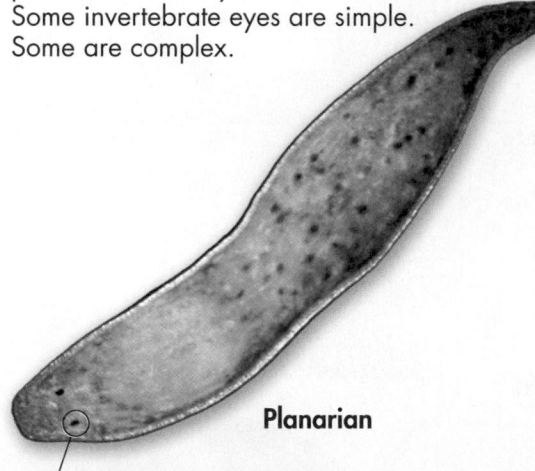

Planarian

Eyespot: Some animals have eyespots, which are groups of cells that can detect changes in the amount of light (LM 50×).

Scallop

Simple Eye: The 40–60 simple eyes of a scallop do not form images. They do, however, detect movement well enough to enable the scallop to escape its predators.

Mosquito

Compound Eye: The compound eyes of arthropods are made up of many lenses that detect minute changes in movement and color but produce less-detailed images than human eyes do.

Squid

Complex Eye: Octopi and squid have eyes as complex as fishes and humans, though their structures differ.

Chordate Sense Organs Nonvertebrate chordates do not have many specialized sense organs. For example, lancelets have a cerebral ganglion with a pair of eyespots that can see light.

Most vertebrates have highly specialized sense organs. Many vertebrates have very sensitive organs of taste, hearing, and smell. Sense organs in some sharks are so sensitive that they can detect 1 drop of blood in 100 liters of water! Many fishes, amphibians, reptiles, birds, and mammals have color vision that is as good as, or better than, the color vision of humans.

All mammal ears have the same basic parts. However, there are big differences in each animal's hearing range. Bats and dolphins can hear sounds at very high frequencies. Elephants can hear sounds at very low frequencies.

Certain fishes can sense weak electric currents in water. Sharks use their "electric sense" to find their way around the oceans. Other species use electric currents to find prey in dark water. Some fishes use electric pulses to communicate with one another. Earth has a magnetic field that some animals can sense. Many birds use this magnetic field to find their way during migration.

Key Question What are some types of sensory systems in animals? **Sensory systems in animals range from individual sensory neurons to sense organs such as eyes or ears. Many vertebrates also have specialized sense organs that are sensitive to tastes, odors, vibrations, or electrical currents.**

Animal	Hearing Range (Hz)
Tree frog	50–4000
Canary	250–8000
Dog	67–45,000
Bat	2000–110,000
Human	30–23,000
Elephant	16–12,000
Bottlenose dolphin	75–150,000

Vertebrate Hearing Many vertebrates can hear sounds that humans cannot hear. Would you expect to be able to hear the highest pitch that a dog can hear? Explain.

CHECK Understanding

Apply Vocabulary
Use the highlighted words from the lesson to complete each sentence correctly.

1. Information in the environment that causes an animal to react is called a _____.

2. Specialized cells called _____ help an animal to detect stimuli.

3. In invertebrates, interneurons are grouped together into structures called _____.

4. The _____ is the "thinking" region of the brain.

Critical Thinking

5. **Explain** What is the job of a motor neuron?

6. **Compare and Contrast** Describe the degree of cephalization shown by cnidarians, flatworms, octopi, and vertebrates.

7. **Infer** What is the general relationship between how complex an animal's nervous system is and how complex its sensory system is?

8. **Write to Learn** The compound eyes of insects sense movement better than they see details. How might sensing movement be more important to an insect than seeing details?

BIOLOGY.com Search (Lesson 28.1) GO • Lesson Assessment

28.2 Movement and Support

MD   CLG 3.2.1 Processes and Functions. SPI 1.5.7 Classification Systems, 1.5.8 Compare, 1.5.9 Synthesize Ideas.

Key Questions

🔑 *What are the three types of skeletons?*

🔑 *How do muscles allow movement?*

BUILD Understanding

Compare/Contrast Table As you read this lesson, create a table comparing and contrasting the three types of skeletons.

In Your Workbook Refer to your workbook to learn how to organize your ideas using a compare/contrast table.

Types of Skeletons

How does a salmon swim through the water and then leap into the air? How does a worm burrow into the ground? Animals move in many different ways. Yet, their body structures work in similar ways.

Skeletal Support To move efficiently, all animals must do two things. First, they must create a force. Then, they must use that force to push or pull themselves around. Stiff body parts help an animal move. Legs push against the ground. Wings push against the air. Body parts are made stiff and strong by skeletal systems.

▶ *Hydrostatic Skeletons* Some invertebrates, such as cnidarians and earthworms, have hydrostatic skeletons. **Hydrostatic skeletons** are fluid-filled body segments that work together with body cells that contract. A hydra has a hydrostatic skeleton. When a hydra closes its mouth, the cells that circle around its body tighten. This tightening allows the animal to get longer and reach out with its tentacles to grab prey. When the hydra opens its mouth, water flows out. Cells in its body wall contract, causing the hydra to become shorter.

Hydrostatic Skeleton Hydras have hydrostatic skeletons. When a hydra closes its mouth, water that is trapped in its body causes it to get longer. When it opens its mouth, water is released and the hydra becomes shorter.

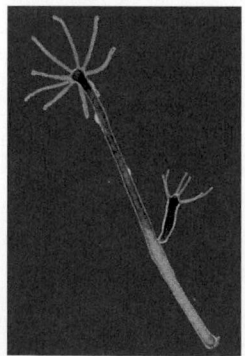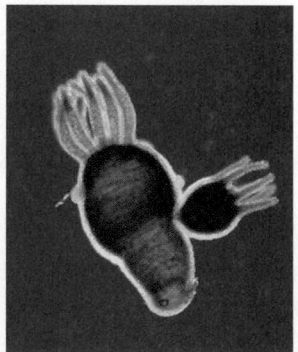

▶ *Exoskeletons* Many arthropods and mollusks have exoskeletons. An **exoskeleton** is a hard covering on the outside of an animal's body. Arthropods have exoskeletons made of a complex carbohydrate called chitin (KY tin). Most mollusks have exoskeletons that are shells made of calcium carbonate.

Exoskeletons have many advantages. Exoskeletons provide coverings that prevent the animals from drying out. They also provide protection from predators.

Exoskeletons also have disadvantages. When an arthropod needs to increase in size, it must break out of its old exoskeleton and grow a new one. This process is called **molting.** Exoskeletons are also relatively heavy. As an arthropod gets larger, its exoskeleton makes up a larger and larger portion of its body weight. This is one reason that some science fiction monsters could never exist. The legs of an elephant-size spider would break under the spider's weight!

▶ *Endoskeletons* Echinoderms and vertebrates have endoskeletons. An **endoskeleton** is a hard support system inside the body. Sea stars and other echinoderms have an endoskeleton composed of hard plates made of calcium. Sharks and some other fishes have endoskeletons made of cartilage. Other vertebrates have skeletons made of cartilage and bone.

Endoskeletons allow vertebrates to swim, fly, burrow, walk, crawl, or leap. All of these endoskeletons provide strong, lightweight support. Because endoskeletons are light in relation to the bodies that they support, vertebrates can grow very large.

Endoskeletons have some advantages and disadvantages over exoskeletons. Because an endoskeleton does not surround the body, it cannot protect the animal as an exoskeleton can. However, an endoskeleton can grow as an animal grows. Animals that have endoskeletons do not molt.

Joints Arthropods and vertebrates can move because their skeletons are divided into parts connected by joints. **Joints** are places where parts of a skeleton are held together in ways that allow the parts to move. In vertebrates, bones are connected to each other at joints by strong connective tissues called **ligaments.** Most joints are formed by a combination of ligaments, cartilage, and joint fluid. Joint fluid helps the bones to move without rubbing against each other.

🔑 **Key Question** What are the three types of skeletons? **The three main skeletal systems in animals are hydrostatic skeletons, exoskeletons, and endoskeletons.**

Endoskeleton Endoskeletons are structural support systems that are inside of the body. Some invertebrates, such as the sea star, have endoskeletons composed of hard plates made of calcium.

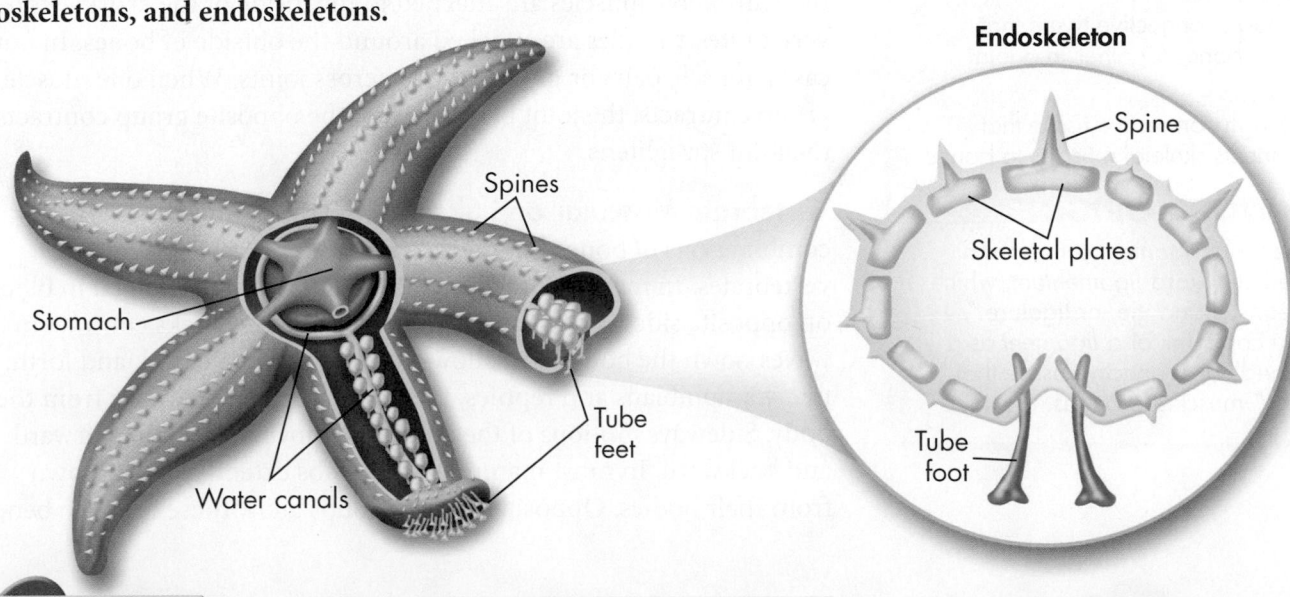

Endoskeleton

Spine

Skeletal plates

Tube foot

Spines

Stomach

Water canals

Tube feet

Muscles and Joints These diagrams show how muscles work with both a vertebrate endoskeleton and an invertebrate exoskeleton to bend and straighten joints.

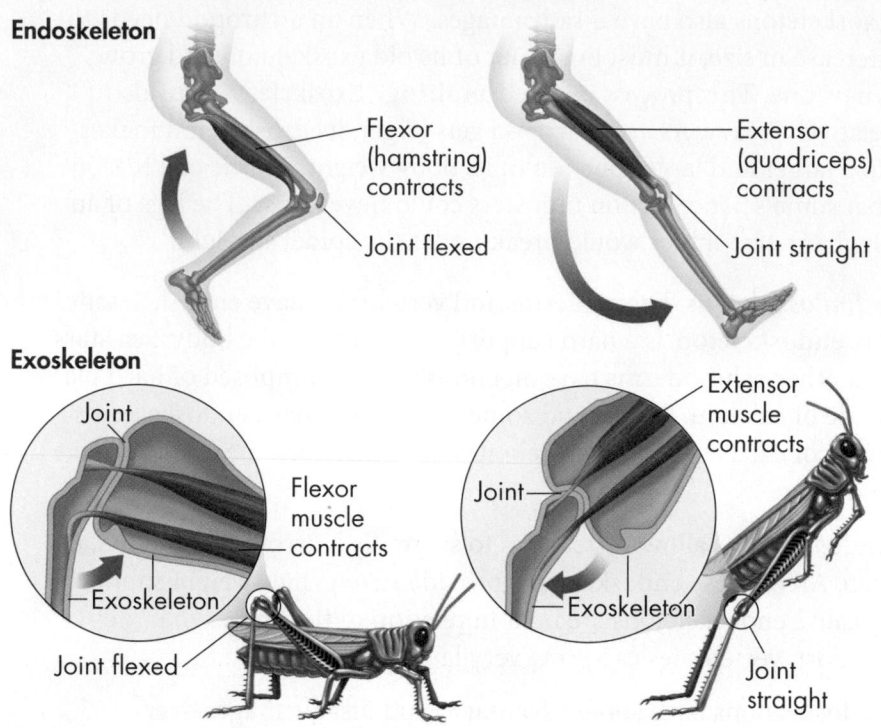

Endoskeleton

Flexor (hamstring) contracts

Joint flexed

Extensor (quadriceps) contracts

Joint straight

Exoskeleton

Joint

Flexor muscle contracts

Exoskeleton

Joint flexed

Extensor muscle contracts

Joint

Exoskeleton

Joint straight

Muscles and Movement

Muscles are tissues that provide the force for movement. Muscles produce force when they contract, or get shorter. Muscles are attached to bone around the joints by tough connective tissue called **tendons.** Tendons pull on bones when muscles contract.

Opposite Muscle Groups Muscles do not produce force as they relax, or get longer. Muscles can only pull; they cannot push. If muscles only pull in one direction, how do they allow animal bodies to move in many different directions? Usually, muscles work together in pairs or groups that pull parts of the skeleton in opposite directions.

In arthropods, muscles are attached to the inside of the exoskeleton. In vertebrates, muscles are attached around the outside of bones. In both cases, muscle pairs or groups attach across joints. When one muscle group contracts, the joint bends. When the opposite group contracts, the joint straightens.

Vertebrate Muscular and Skeletal Systems Amazing combinations of bones, muscle groups, and joints have evolved in vertebrates. In many fishes and snakes, muscles are arranged in blocks on opposite sides of the backbone. These muscle blocks contract in waves down the body. This allows the body to move back and forth. In many amphibians and reptiles, the limbs stick out sideways from the body. Sideways motions of the backbone move these limbs forward and backward. In most mammals, the limbs extend straight down from their bodies. Opposite muscle groups allow these limbs to bend.

Muscular and Skeletal Systems of Vertebrates A wide variety of bones, muscle groups, and joints have evolved in vertebrates. Differently shaped bones and muscles form limbs that are adapted for jumping (frog), flying through the air (hawk), and holding objects (raccoon).

The shapes and positions of bones, muscles, and joints in vertebrates relate to the functions that they perform. Limbs that allow animals to run or jump have very different shapes than limbs that allow animals to fly, swim, or hold objects. Scientists can understand how extinct vertebrates moved by studying the joints of fossil bones and the places where tendons and ligaments once attached to bones.

Key Question How do muscles allow movement? **Muscles work together in pairs or groups that are attached to different parts of a supporting skeleton.**

CHECK Understanding

Apply Vocabulary
Use the highlighted words from the lesson to complete each sentence correctly.

1. The hard covering on the outside of an arthropod is called a(n) _____.

2. The _____ of a sea star is composed of hard plates that are made of calcium.

3. Bands of connective tissue that connect bones at joints are called _____.

4. Bands of connective tissue that connect muscles to bones are called _____.

Critical Thinking

5. Review What is a hydrostatic skeleton?

6. Compare and Contrast How are exoskeletons and endoskeletons different from each other?

7. Review Which two body systems work together to allow animals to move?

8. Review What characteristics are common in the skeletons of all vertebrates?

9. Write to Learn Suppose that you found a vertebrate fossil and brought it to an expert. The expert showed you that the joint structure of the fossil was similar to the joint structure of a modern squirrel. Infer the kinds of movements for which the animal had been adapted. Explain your inferences in a paragraph.

BIOLOGY.com Search [Lesson 28.2] GO • Lesson Assessment

28.3 Reproduction

MD CLG 3.2.1 Processes and Functions, 3.3.1 Sexual Reproduction and Variation, 3.4.1 Evolutionary Change, 3.5.1 Factors Influencing Ecosystems. SPI 1.5.5 Create and Interpret Graphics, 1.5.7 Classification Systems, 1.5.8 Compare.

Key Questions

🔑 How do asexual and sexual reproduction in animals compare?

🔑 How do internal and external fertilization differ?

🔑 Where do embryos develop?

🔑 How are terrestrial vertebrates adapted to reproduction on land?

BUILD Understanding

Concept Map As you read lesson 28.3, use concept maps to show how ideas or concepts connect. Use circles to show the most important parts of the concept. Connect the circles with lines.

In Your Workbook Refer to your workbook for suggestions about how to use a concept map to organize the main ideas in this lesson.

Parthenogenesis Some whiptail lizard species reproduce only by parthenogenesis.

Asexual and Sexual Reproduction

Sexual reproduction can be dangerous. Just ask a male praying mantis, who may be eaten by his mate. Or ask a female deer, who carries young while trying to avoid predators. If sexual reproduction is dangerous, why do most animals engage in it? What are the advantages of sexual reproduction over asexual reproduction?

Asexual Reproduction Many invertebrates and a few chordates can reproduce asexually. Animals reproduce asexually in many ways. Some cnidarians divide in two. Some animals reproduce through budding, which produces new individuals from the parent's body wall. Females of some species produce eggs that develop without being fertilized, in a process called parthenogenesis (pahr thuh noh JEN uh sis). Parthenogenesis occurs in some invertebrates, but it is rare in vertebrates.

Asexual reproduction has advantages and disadvantages. Since it requires only one parent, individuals can reproduce quickly. However, since individuals carry DNA from only one parent, offspring have less genetic diversity than individuals that are produced sexually. A population with very little genetic diversity may not be able to adapt if the environment changes.

Sexual Reproduction Sexual reproduction involves meiosis, which produces reproductive cells called gametes. Gametes have half the number of chromosomes found in body cells. Male animals produce small gametes, called sperm, which swim. Females produce larger gametes, called eggs, which do not swim. When an egg and sperm join during fertilization, they produce a zygote that contains a full set of chromosomes.

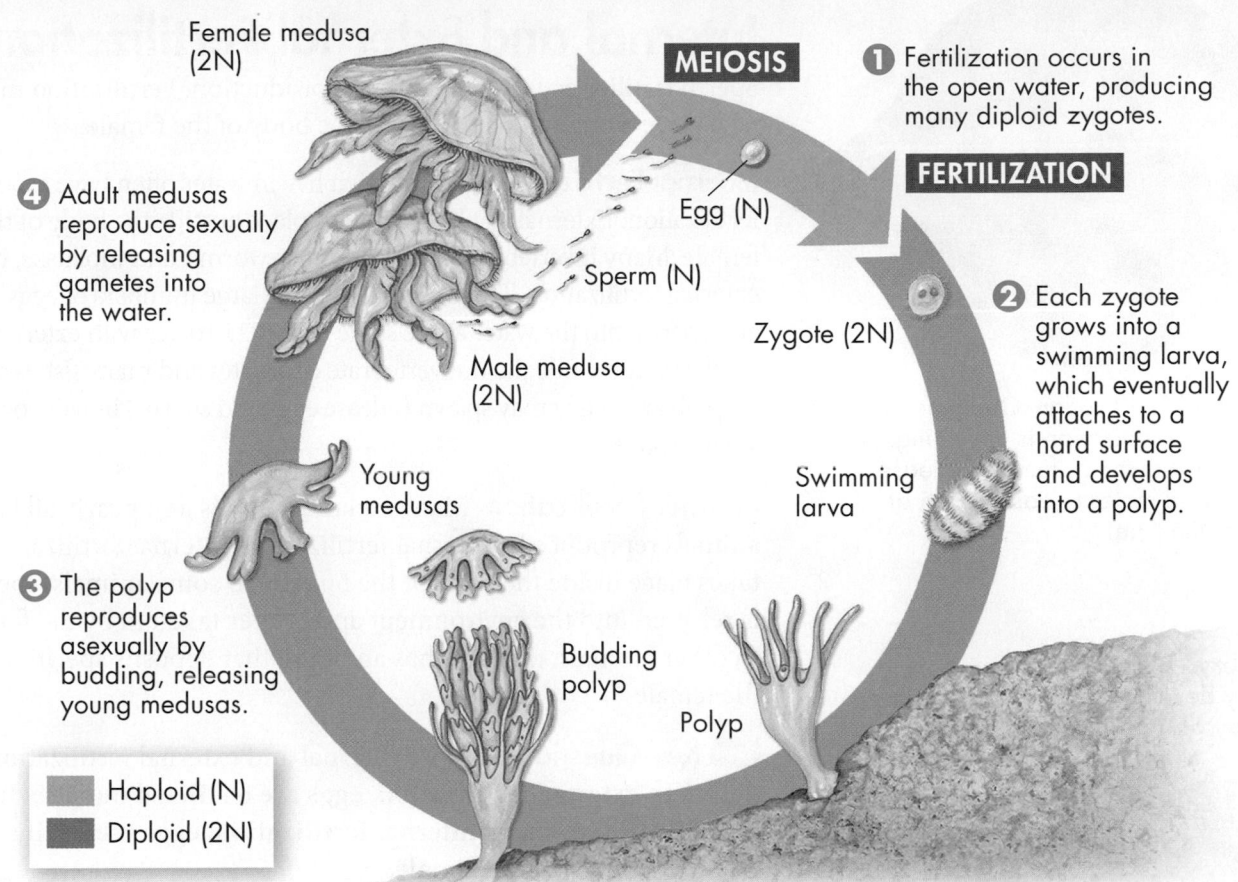

Female medusa (2N)

MEIOSIS

1 Fertilization occurs in the open water, producing many diploid zygotes.

FERTILIZATION

4 Adult medusas reproduce sexually by releasing gametes into the water.

Egg (N)

Sperm (N)

Male medusa (2N)

Zygote (2N)

Young medusas

Swimming larva

3 The polyp reproduces asexually by budding, releasing young medusas.

2 Each zygote grows into a swimming larva, which eventually attaches to a hard surface and develops into a polyp.

Budding polyp

Polyp

Haploid (N)
Diploid (2N)

Sexual reproduction increases genetic diversity in a population by creating individuals with new combinations of genes. Populations with greater genetic diversity are better able to adapt to changing environmental conditions.

In most animals that reproduce sexually, individuals are either male or female. But some species of worms, mollusks, and fishes are hermaphrodites (hur MAF roh dytes). Hermaphrodites can be both male and female at the same time, or they can change from one sex to the other.

Key Question How do asexual and sexual reproduction in animals compare?
In asexual reproduction, one parent produces offspring. In sexual reproduction, gametes from two parents combine to produce offspring. Sexual reproduction increases genetic diversity in a population.

Reproductive Cycles Many invertebrates have life cycles that alternate between sexual and asexual reproduction. For example, many cnidarians alternate between two body forms: polyps and medusas (muh DOO suhs). In jellyfish, polyps produce medusas asexually by budding. The medusas reproduce sexually by releasing eggs and sperm into the water. A fertilized egg grows into a larva that swims freely. The larva may attach to a hard surface and develop into a polyp.

BUILD Connections

ALTERNATING REPRODUCTIVE CYCLES

The reproductive cycle of this jellyfish alternates between sexual and asexual reproduction. Medusas can reproduce sexually when a female releases eggs and a male releases sperm. Fertilization forms a zygote that grows into a larva. The larva develops into a polyp. The polyp reproduces asexually by budding. This budding forms a new medusa.

External Fertilization One type of external fertilization is spawning. During spawning, females release eggs and males release sperm at the same time.

Embryo Development Embryos may develop inside or outside the body of a parent.

Robin - Oviparous

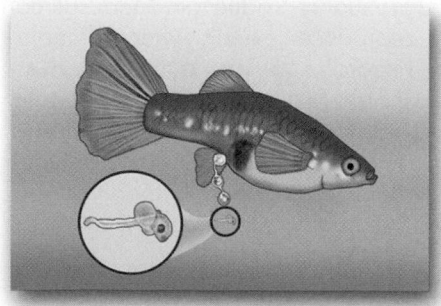

Guppy - Ovoviviparous

Horse - Viviparous

Internal and External Fertilization

Sperm fertilize eggs during sexual reproduction. Fertilization may take place either outside or inside the body of the female.

External Fertilization Animals that live in water often have external fertilization. External fertilization takes place outside the body of the female. Many invertebrates, such as corals, worms, and mollusks, have external fertilization. These animals release large numbers of eggs and sperm into the water at the same time. Chordates with external fertilization include the nonvertebrate chordates and many fishes and amphibians. They may spawn (release eggs and sperm) in pairs or in small groups.

Internal Fertilization Many aquatic animals and nearly all land animals reproduce by internal fertilization. Internal fertilization takes place inside the body of the female. In some animals, sperm is released into the environment and is later taken in by the female. In other animals, the male has an organ that deposits sperm inside the female.

🔑 **Key Question** How do internal and external fertilization differ? **In external fertilization, eggs are fertilized outside the body of the female. In internal fertilization, eggs are fertilized inside the body of the female.**

Development and Growth

When a fertilized egg starts to divide, it becomes an embryo. The care and protection given to developing embryos varies widely.

Where Embryos Develop Embryos develop either inside or outside the body of a parent.

▶ *Oviparous Species* In **oviparous** (oh VIP uh rus) species, embryos develop in eggs outside of the parents' bodies. Most invertebrates, many fishes and amphibians, most reptiles, all birds, and a few mammals are oviparous.

▶ *Ovoviviparous Species* In **ovoviviparous** (oh voh vy VIP uh rus) species, embryos develop in eggs inside their mother's body. The young rely on the yolk sac of their eggs for food. Young hatch inside the mother or outside right after the eggs leave her body. Some fishes, including some sharks, are ovoviviparous.

▶ *Viviparous Species* In **viviparous** (vy VIP uh rus) species, embryos get nutrients from their mother's body during development. Some insects, sharks, bony fishes, amphibians, and reptiles are viviparous. Most mammals are viviparous.

🔑 **Key Question** Where do embryos develop? **Embryos develop either inside or outside the mother's body.**

How Young Develop Most newborn mammals and newly hatched birds and reptiles look like small adults. In other groups of animals, young look very different from adults. As many animals develop, they go through metamorphosis. **Metamorphosis** is a process that causes many changes in the shape and form of a developing animal.

▶ *Aquatic Invertebrates* Many aquatic invertebrates have a larval stage that looks nothing like the adult animal. These larvae may float in open water before taking their adult form. Some groups, such as cnidarians, have a single larval stage. Other groups, such as crustaceans, go through several larval stages before becoming adults.

▶ *Terrestrial Invertebrates* Insects may go through incomplete or complete metamorphosis. Grasshoppers go through incomplete metamorphosis. In this process, immature forms called **nymphs** (nimfs) look like small adults. However, nymphs do not have adult structures such as wings or reproductive organs. These structures develop as the nymphs molt.

Butterflies go through complete metamorphosis. The larva eats, molts, and grows. After a final molt, it becomes a **pupa** (PYOO puh; plural: pupae). Body changes occur during the pupal stage. The adult that emerges is completely different from the larva.

Metamorphosis in arthropods is controlled by hormones. High levels of a juvenile hormone keep an insect in its larval stage during complete metamorphosis. When hormone levels decrease, the larva becomes a pupa. When hormone production stops, the pupa emerges as an adult.

▶ *Amphibians* Amphibians also go through metamorphosis that is controlled by hormones. This metamorphosis changes larvae that live in water into adults that live on land.

BUILD Vocabulary

oviparous
a species in which embryos develop in eggs outside the parent's body

ovoviviparous
a species in which the embryos develop within the mother's body but depend entirely on the yolk sac of their eggs

viviparous
animals that bear live young that are nourished directly by the mother as they develop

metamorphosis
a process of changes in shape and form of a larva into an adult

nymph
an immature form of an animal that looks like the adult form but does not have functional sexual organs

pupa
a stage of complete metamorphosis in which the larva develops into an adult

PREFIXES

The prefix *vivi-* comes from a Latin word meaning "alive." The prefix *ovi-* comes from a Latin word meaning "egg." A *viviparous* species is "born alive." An *oviparous* species hatches from an egg. An *ovoviviparous* species develops in an egg inside the mother but may hatch inside the mother to be "born alive."

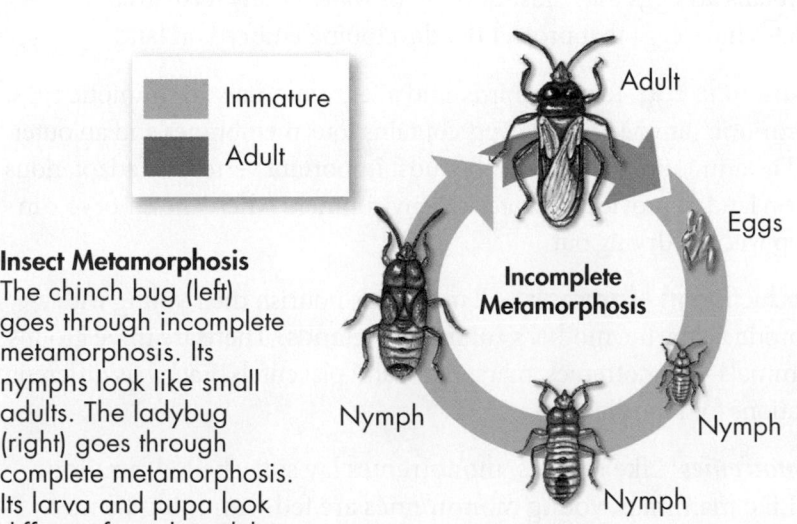

Immature

Adult

Adult

Incomplete Metamorphosis

Nymph

Nymph

Nymph

Eggs

Insect Metamorphosis
The chinch bug (left) goes through incomplete metamorphosis. Its nymphs look like small adults. The ladybug (right) goes through complete metamorphosis. Its larva and pupa look different from the adult.

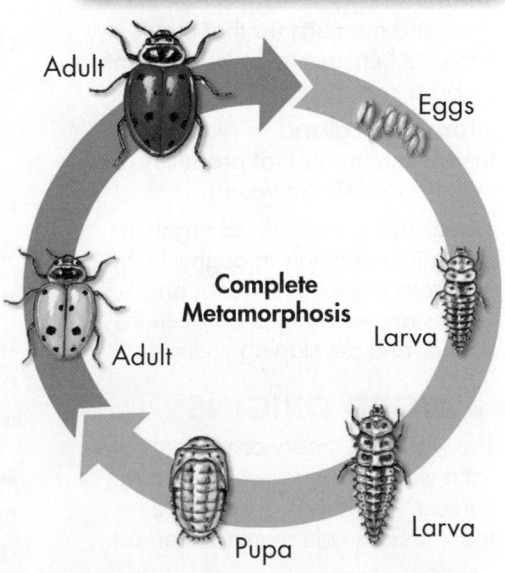

Adult

Eggs

Complete Metamorphosis

Adult

Pupa

Larva

Larva

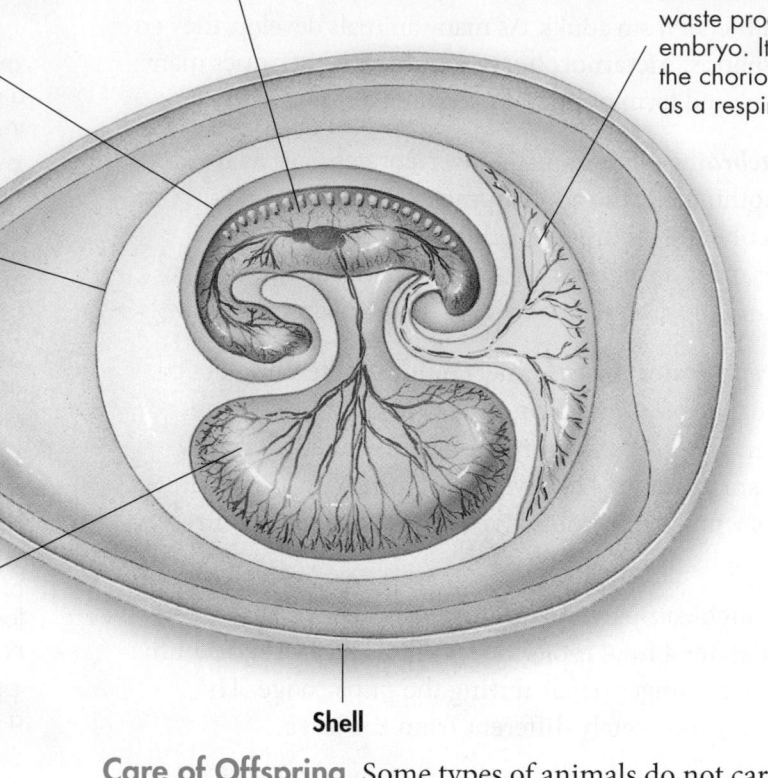

Amnion
The amnion is a fluid-filled sac that surrounds and cushions the developing embryo. It produces a protected, watery environment.

Chorion
The chorion regulates the transport of oxygen from the surface of the egg to the embryo and the transport of carbon dioxide, one product of respiration, in the opposite direction.

Yolk Sac
This baglike structure contains a yolk that serves as a nutrient-rich food supply for the embryo.

Embryo

Allantois
The allantois stores the waste produced by the embryo. It later fuses with the chorion and serves as a respiratory organ.

Shell

Amniotic Egg An amniotic egg contains four membranes and an outer shell. Although the egg is waterproof, it allows gases to pass through. The shell of a reptile egg is usually soft and leathery. The shell of a bird egg is usually hard and brittle.

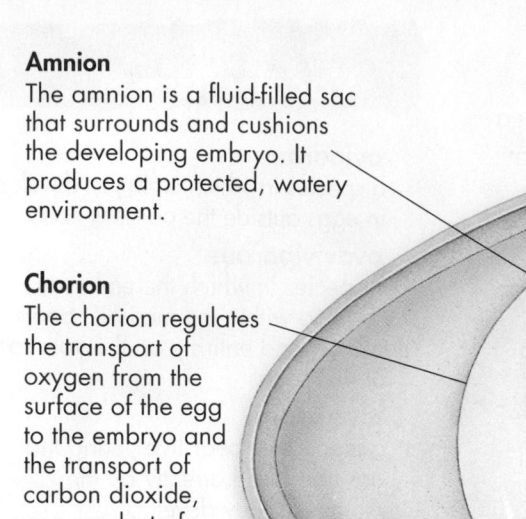

BUILD Vocabulary

amniotic egg an egg composed of shell and membranes that create a protected environment in which the embryo can develop out of water

mammary gland a gland in female mammals that produces milk to nourish the young

placenta a specialized organ in placental mammals through which respiratory gases, nutrients, and wastes are exchanged between the mother and developing young

✎ WORD ORIGINS

The word *mammary* comes from the Latin word *mamma*, which means "breast." Mammary glands are found in a female mammal's breast.

Care of Offspring Some types of animals do not care for their young. Many aquatic invertebrates, fishes, and amphibians release many eggs and then leave. Some young are likely to survive, even though adults do not protect them.

Many animals do care for their young. Some amphibians carry developing young in their mouths, backs, or stomachs. Birds and mammals usually provide parental care. Species that provide long-term parental care usually give birth to fewer young than do species that give no parental care.

Reproduction in Chordates

Chordate reproduction was first adapted for water. Most fishes and amphibians lay eggs that must develop in water. Many terrestrial chordates have eggs that protect the developing embryo on land.

The Amniotic Egg Reptiles, birds, and a few mammals lay amniotic eggs. An **amniotic** (am nee AH tik) **egg** contains four membranes and an outer shell. The amniotic egg is one of the most important vertebrate adaptations to life on land. It provides a protected environment where the embryo can develop without drying out.

Reproduction in Mammals All mammals nourish their young with milk produced by the mother's **mammary glands.** There are three groups of mammals—monotremes, marsupials, and placentals. Each has different adaptations for reproduction.

▶ *Monotremes* Like reptiles, monotremes lay soft-shelled, amniotic eggs. Like mammals, young monotremes are fed with milk. Female monotremes secrete milk through pores on the abdomen.

► *Marsupials* Marsupials are born at such an early stage of development that they are almost embryos. Young marsupials crawl across their mother's fur and attach to a nipple in her pouch, or marsupium (mahr soo pee um). The young remain in the marsupium until they can survive on their own.

► *Placentals* Placental mammals are named for the placenta. A **placenta** is a specialized organ that allows the exchange of nutrients, gases, and wastes between the young and the mother. The placenta allows the embryo to develop for a long time inside the mother. Placental mammals are born at an advanced stage of development.

🔑 **Key Question** How are terrestrial vertebrates adapted to reproduction on land? **Reptiles, birds, and some mammals have amniotic eggs in which an embryo can develop outside the mother without drying out. Most mammals bear live young and feed their young with mother's milk.**

Mammals Mammal groups include monotremes such as the echidna (top), marsupials such as the kangaroo (below), and placental mammals such as the harp seal (below left).

CHECK Understanding

Apply Vocabulary
Use the highlighted words from the lesson to complete each sentence correctly.

1. A species in which an embryo gets nutrients from the mother's body during development is called a(n) _____ species.
2. The process in which a developing animal changes in shape and form is _____ .
3. Female mammals have _____ that produce milk to nourish their young.

Critical Thinking

4. **Review** Which type of reproduction results in the most genetic diversity?
5. **Review** Define the two types of fertilization.

6. **Compare and Contrast** What is the difference between a nymph and a larva?
7. **Interpret Visuals** In your own words, describe the functions of two of the membranes shown in the art of the amniotic egg.
8. **Write to Learn** Answer the first clue of the mystery. What kind of reproduction in vertebrates can produce offspring from only one parent?

MYSTERY CLUE

The females in the tank had not had contact with a male for three years. And female bonnetheads do not store sperm for longer than five months. So what happened? (**Hint:** See p. 678.)

BIOLOGY.com ▸ Search (Lesson 28.3) **GO** • Lesson Assessment

28.4 Homeostasis

MD | CLG 3.1.2 Homeostasis, 3.2.1 Processes and Functions, 3.2.2 Changes in Metabolic Activity. SPI 1.2.3 Hypothesis Formation, 1.5.7 Classification Systems, 1.5.8 Compare, 1.5.9 Synthesize Ideas.

Key Questions

🔑 Why is the interdependence of body systems essential?

🔑 How do animals control their body temperature?

BUILD Understanding

Venn Diagram A Venn diagram is a useful tool for comparing two topics. Draw a Venn diagram to compare and contrast the ways that ectotherms and endotherms control body temperature.

In Your Workbook Refer to your workbook to learn how to fill in a Venn diagram.

Interrelationships of Body Systems

A herd of wildebeests moves across Africa's Serengeti Plain. The land is dusty and dry, so the herd is heading toward greener pastures. They move mechanically, so that their steps use as little energy as possible. Because they have not eaten in a long time, their bodies break down fat for energy. Their bodies also conserve water by producing very little urine. To survive the difficult journey, body systems work to keep internal conditions as constant as possible.

Recall that the word *homeostasis* is used to describe stable conditions inside the body. Homeostasis is necessary for an animal's survival. Animal cells must be supplied with glucose for energy. Cells must have enough water and be able to get rid of wastes. The cells of some animals must be kept at a constant temperature. Homeostasis must not fail, not even during dry conditions, extreme hunger, extreme heat, or extreme cold. If homeostasis fails, the animal could die.

All body systems work together to maintain homeostasis. Many body systems work closely with the circulatory system. After the respiratory system takes in oxygen, the circulatory system delivers the oxygen to cells. After the digestive system breaks food down into nutrients, the circulatory system delivers those nutrients to cells. The circulatory system collects wastes from body tissues. It then delivers these wastes to the lungs and kidneys of the excretory system.

The muscular and nervous systems work with other systems to maintain homeostasis. Muscles help to move food through the digestive system. The nervous system directs these muscle movements.

Interrelationships of Body Systems All body systems must work together to keep animals like these migrating wildebeests alive.

Fighting Disease The controlled environment inside an animal's body is a comfortable place for both body cells and unwanted invaders. Pathogens can use oxygen and nutrients in the body to grow and reproduce. If pathogens are not destroyed, they may cause disease by harming the function of one or more body systems. Most animals have an immune system that can recognize "self" and "other." Once the immune system identifies the "others" in the body, it can attack the invaders and restore homeostasis.

Chemical Controls All vertebrates and many invertebrates have an endocrine system that controls many body processes. **Endocrine glands** control body activities by releasing chemicals called hormones into the blood. Hormones are carried by the blood to the organs that they control. Some hormones control growth and development.

Mammals have hormones that control the way that the body stores energy. Other hormones control the amount of water in the body. Still others control the amount of calcium in bones.

Key Question Why is the interdependence of body systems essential? **All body systems work together to maintain homeostasis.**

Body Temperature Control

Control of body temperature is important for homeostasis. Many body functions are influenced by temperature. Muscles cannot work well if they are too cold or too hot. Cold muscles contract slowly, making an animal slow to react. Muscles that are too hot may get tired easily.

An animal must do three things to control body temperature. First, the animal must find a source of heat. Second, it must find a way to conserve heat when temperatures in the environment are too cold. Third, it must find a way to get rid of extra heat when temperatures in the environment are too hot. An animal is called an ectotherm or an endotherm, based on the way that it can control body temperature.

Ectotherms An **ectotherm** is an animal that usually depends on sources of heat outside of its body to control its body temperature. Invertebrates, fishes, and amphibians are ectotherms. So are most reptiles.

Ectotherms have low metabolic rates when resting, so their bodies do not create much heat. When these animals are active, their muscles can create heat. However, most ectotherms do not have much body insulation. Therefore, they quickly lose heat to the environment.

Most ectotherms control body temperature by absorbing heat from the environment or losing heat to the environment. For example, a lizard may lie in the sun on a cool morning to absorb heat. In the afternoon, the lizard may raise its body off of a hot surface—in a process called "stilting"—in order to lower its body temperature. Ectotherms often use underground burrows to escape from extreme temperatures. On hot, sunny days, they can use the burrow to cool off. On cold nights, they can use the same burrow to conserve their body heat.

Ectotherm The shovel-snouted lizard is an ectotherm that lives in the Namib Desert in Africa. This desert is one of the hottest places on Earth. The lizard controls its body temperature by stilting—raising its body off of the hot sand by performing a kind of push-up.

Comparing Ectotherms and Endotherms

An ectotherm is an animal that controls its body temperature mainly by using heat from outside its body. An endotherm is an animal that controls its body temperature mostly by using heat that is produced within its body. The graph shows the internal body temperatures maintained by several ectotherms and endotherms at different environmental temperatures.

1. Interpret Graphs Which animal has the highest body temperature when the environmental temperature is between 0°C and 10°C? Which has the lowest body temperature under these conditions?

2. Infer Which animals represented in the graph are ectotherms? Which are endotherms? Explain your answers.

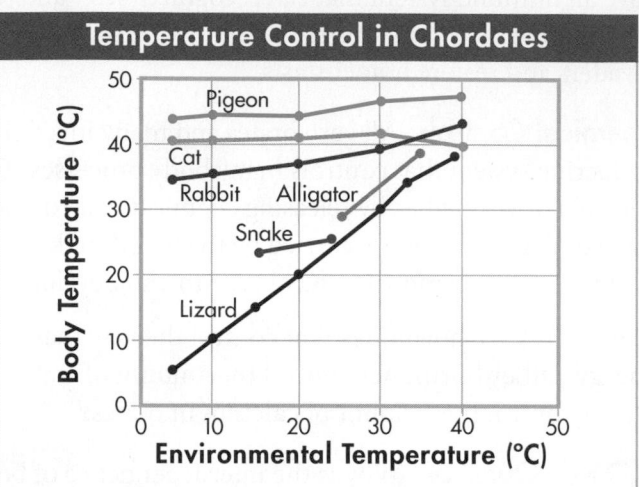

Temperature Control in Chordates

y-axis: Body Temperature (°C)
x-axis: Environmental Temperature (°C)

Labels on graph: Pigeon, Cat, Rabbit, Alligator, Snake, Lizard

3. Predict If these animals lived in your area, would you expect all of them to be equally active year-round? Why or why not?

In Your Workbook Get more help for this activity in your workbook.

Endotherm Many endotherms, such as this dingo, pant when they are very warm. Panting allows moisture in the mouth and respiratory tract to evaporate. This process helps to cool the blood.

Endotherms An **endotherm** is an animal whose body temperature is controlled, at least in part, by using heat that is produced by its own body. Endotherms have high metabolic rates that create heat, even when the animals are resting. All birds and mammals are endotherms.

Endotherms have different ways of conserving heat. Birds conserve body heat by fluffing out their feathers. Mammals use a combination of body fat and hair as insulation.

Endotherms have different ways of getting rid of extra heat. Some birds and most mammals get rid of heat by panting. When an animal pants, it breathes with its mouth open and its tongue sticking out. Heat flows out of the body as water evaporates from the mouth and tongue. Humans sweat to reduce their body temperature. As sweat evaporates, it removes heat from the skin. It also removes heat from the capillaries just below the surface of the skin. As warm blood flows into these cooled capillaries, the blood loses heat.

Comparing Ectotherms and Endotherms There are advantages and disadvantages to being an endotherm. Endotherms can move around on cool nights or in cold weather, because they create and conserve body heat. But it takes a lot of fuel to feed the high metabolic rate that makes heat. The amount of food that it takes to keep a single cow alive would be enough to feed ten cow-size lizards!

There are also advantages and disadvantages to being an ectotherm. It is more energy efficient to be an ectotherm in a warm environment. However, large ectotherms can get into trouble if it gets very cold at night or if the environment stays cold for long periods of time. It takes a long time for an animal to warm up in the sun after a cold night. That is one reason why most large lizards and amphibians can only live in tropical or subtropical areas.

Evolution of Temperature Control The first animals were ectotherms. When did endothermy evolve? Current evidence suggests that endothermy evolved at least twice in vertebrates. It evolved once in the line of ancient reptiles that led to birds. It evolved again in the line of ancient reptiles that led to mammals.

🔑 **Key Question** How do animals control their body temperature? **An ectotherm controls body temperature by exchanging heat with the environment. An endotherm controls body temperature by using heat made by its own body.**

Endotherm Insulation Birds such as this northern cardinal use feathers to stay warm. When a bird gets cold, its fluffy undercoat of down feathers stands up. Body heat becomes trapped in the air spaces between the feathers.

CHECK Understanding

Apply Vocabulary
Use the highlighted words from the lesson to complete each sentence correctly.

1. Structures that release hormones into the blood are called _____.
2. An animal that controls its body temperature mainly by absorbing heat from its surroundings is a(n) _____.
3. An animal that controls its body temperature mainly by producing its own heat is called a(n) _____.

Critical Thinking
4. **Explain** Give an example of how multiple body systems work together to maintain homeostasis.
5. **Compare and Contrast** Why must an endotherm eat more food than an ectotherm of the same size?
6. **Form a Hypothesis** Birds and mammals live in both warm and cold areas. Most reptiles and amphibians live in relatively warm areas. Form a hypothesis that would explain this difference.
7. **Write to Learn** Think about what you do during an average day. Write a paragraph describing how your body maintains homeostasis during some of your activities.

Real-World Lab

OPEN-ENDED INQUIRY

MD SPI **1.2.4** Testing a Hypothesis, **1.2.7** Apply Results, **1.3.1** Use Equipment, **1.3.3** Safe Handling of Materials, **1.6.4** Equations.

Pre-Lab: Comparing Bird and Mammal Bones

Problem Is the density of an animal's bones related to the way the animal moves?

Materials cross-sections of chicken, duck, and cow bones; hand lens; small chicken, duck, and cow bones; balance

Lab Manual Chapter 28 Lab

Skills Focus Form a Hypothesis, Design an Experiment, Measure

Connect to the Big idea In order to move, an animal must generate physical force and apply this force against the air, the water, or the ground. The force is generated by the contraction of muscles. In vertebrates, the muscles are attached to bones. The joints that connect bones bend or straighten when groups of muscles contract. There is a close link between the structure of an animal's skeletal and muscular systems and how the animal moves. In this lab, you will investigate whether there is a similar link between the density of bones and how an animal moves.

Background Questions

a. Review What type of skeleton do vertebrates have? List one advantage of this type of skeleton.

b. Explain Why are pairs of muscles or two different groups of muscles needed to bend and straighten a joint?

c. Apply Concepts Why do you think humans have only 4 bones in each arm and shoulder, but 27 bones in each wrist and hand? (**Hint:** Compare the movement of your arm and your hand when you button a shirt.)

Pre-Lab Questions

Preview the procedure in the lab manual.

1. Compare and Contrast Compare the type of data you will collect in Part A to the type of data you will collect in Part B.

2. Predict How might looking at cross sections of bones help you form a hypothesis about the relative density of the bones?

3. Design an Experiment Will you need to use samples with the same mass in Part B? Why or why not?

BIOLOGY.com   Search   Chapter 28   GO

Visit Chapter 28 online to test yourself on chapter content and to find activities to help you learn.

Untamed Science Video Join the Untamed Science crew as they interview experts to learn more about how the sex of offspring is determined in some animals.

Art in Motion Watch an animation that shows the motion of joints in both exoskeletons and endoskeletons.

Art Review Review your understanding of vertebrate brains.

InterActive Art Look at the structure and function of the water vascular system in a sea star.

28.1 Response

- When an animal responds to a stimulus, its body systems—including its nervous system and muscular system—work together to create a response.

- Animal nervous systems show different degrees of cephalization and specialization. Invertebrate nervous systems range from simple collections of nerve cells to complex systems that include ganglia and brains. All vertebrate nervous systems include brains. As vertebrates evolved, their brains became larger and more complex.

- Sensory systems in animals range from individual sensory neurons to sense organs, such as eyes and ears. Many vertebrates also have sense organs that are sensitive to tastes, odors, vibrations, or electrical currents.

neuron (p. 668)
stimulus (p. 668)
sensory neuron (p. 668)
interneuron (p. 669)
response (p. 669)
motor neuron (p. 669)
ganglion (p. 670)
cerebrum (p. 671)
cerebellum (p. 671)

28.2 Movement and Support

- Animals have three main kinds of skeletal systems: hydrostatic skeletons, exoskeletons, and endoskeletons.

- In many animals, muscles work together in pairs or groups that are attached to different parts of a supporting skeleton.

hydrostatic skeleton (p. 674)
exoskeleton (p. 674)
molting (p. 675)
endoskeleton (p. 675)
joint (p. 675)
ligament (p. 675)
tendon (p. 676)

28.3 Reproduction

- Asexual reproduction requires only one parent, so individuals may reproduce quickly. However, offspring that are produced asexually have less genetic diversity than do offspring that are produced sexually. Sexual reproduction increases genetic diversity in a population by creating individuals with new combinations of genes.

- In internal fertilization, eggs are fertilized inside the body of the egg-producing individual. In external fertilization, eggs are fertilized outside the body of the egg-producing individual.

- Animals may be oviparous, ovoviviparous, or viviparous.

- Reptiles, birds, and a few mammals have evolved amniotic eggs in which an embryo can develop without drying out. Different mammals reproduce and develop in different ways. However, all mammals feed their young with mother's milk.

oviparous (p. 680)
ovoviviparous (p. 680)
viviparous (p. 680)
metamorphosis (p. 681)
nymph (p. 681)
pupa (p. 681)
amniotic egg (p. 682)
mammary gland (p. 682)
placenta (p. 683)

28.4 Homeostasis

- All body systems work together to maintain homeostasis.

- Most reptiles, invertebrates, fishes, and amphibians are ectotherms. Most ectotherms control body temperature mainly by getting heat from the environment or losing heat to the environment. Birds and mammals are endotherms. Endotherms have high metabolic rates that create heat even when they are resting.

endocrine gland (p. 685)
ectotherm (p. 685)
endotherm (p. 686)

Assess the Big idea

Structure and Function

Write an answer to the question below:

Q: How do the body systems of animals allow them to collect information about their environments and respond appropriately?

Constructed Response

Write an answer to each of the numbered questions below. The answer to each numbered question should be one or two paragraphs long. To help you begin, read the **Hints** below the questions.

1. **How does a cat's nervous system sense and respond to a mouse?**

   Hint What kinds of sense organs do cats have that allow them to sense stimuli such as movements, sounds, and vibrations?

   Hint Think about how the neurons in a cat's nervous system work together to sense and respond to stimuli in the environment.

2. **The cat runs after the mouse to try to catch it. Describe how a cat is able to run.**

   Hint List the body systems that work together to allow an animal to move.

   Hint Look at the diagram that shows how muscles and joints work together.

3. **A cat can spend time outside on a warm summer day and a cool summer night. How does the cat control its body temperature?**

   Hint Cats are endotherms.

Foundations for Learning Wrap-Up

Use the index cards that you have made to help you review the vocabulary in this chapter.

Activity 1 Take a stack of blank index cards. Write the main topics from this chapter on these cards. (Green headings are main topics.) Write Not Sure on one of the cards. Put the topic cards on a table. Arrange the vocabulary cards in groups under each topic. Put any cards that you are not sure about in the Not Sure category. Get together with a classmate and talk about how each word fits into its category. Help each other to put the Not Sure cards under the right topics.

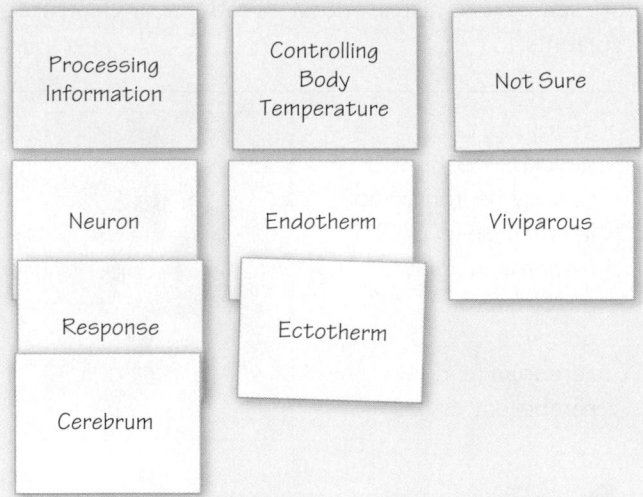

Activity 2 You can play a game to review the vocabulary words in this chapter. Get together with three of your classmates and divide yourselves into two teams. Shuffle all of the vocabulary cards and deal them out, face down, to both teams.

Set a timer for 2 minutes. When the timer starts, draw one of your vocabulary cards. Say words or sentences that relate to this vocabulary word to try to get your partner to say the word. If you accidentally say the vocabulary word, throw that card into a discard pile, so you won't get credit for it.

After 2 minutes, let the other team try. Play the game until one team is out of cards. At that point, the team with the most completed cards wins.

28.1 Response

Understand Key Concepts

1. An animal's reaction to a stimulus is called a
   a. response.
   b. ganglion.
   c. neuron.
   d. trigger.

2. The simplest nervous systems are called
   a. cephalopods.
   b. motor neurons.
   c. nerve nets.
   d. sensory neurons.

3. What kinds of environmental stimuli are some animals able to sense that humans cannot sense?

> **Test-Taking Tip**
>
> **Rephrase the Question** When you read a question that you do not understand, try to put the question in your own words. If it is written as a statement, make it into a question. Using simpler words and changing the way a question is written may help you to figure out how to answer a hard question.

Think Critically

4. **Compare and Contrast** List the three major types of neurons and compare their roles.

5. **Apply Concepts** Suppose a pet dog is having trouble coordinating its movements. Why might a veterinarian X-ray the dog's brain?

28.2 Movement and Support

Understand Key Concepts

6. Which of the following animals uses a hydrostatic skeleton to move?
   a. arthropod
   b. sponge
   c. fish
   d. earthworm

7. Muscles generate force
   a. only when they get longer.
   b. only when they get shorter.
   c. when they get longer or shorter.
   d. all the time.

8. How do a fish's muscles work when the fish swims?

Think Critically

9. **Compare and Contrast** List one advantage and one disadvantage of exoskeletons and endoskeletons.

10. **Infer** The largest land animals are vertebrates. Why are insects unable to grow as large as vertebrates?

28.3 Reproduction

Understanding Key Concepts

11. A species that has eggs that develop outside the mother's body is
    a. oviparous.
    b. viviparous.
    c. ovoviviparous.
    d. nonviparous.

12. What organ in many female mammals allows the exchange of gases, nutrients, and wastes between the mother and the developing young?
    a. marsupium
    b. amniotic egg
    c. mammary gland
    d. placenta

13. How did the evolution of the amniotic egg allow many animals to live on land?

Think Critically

14. **Compare and Contrast** Describe the differences between a newborn placental mammal and a newborn marsupial.

15. **Predict** Why would you expect most species that use external fertilization to reproduce in water?

28.4 Homeostasis

Understand Key Concepts

16. Stable conditions inside an animal's body are called
   a. homeostasis.
   b. ectothermy.
   c. endothermy.
   d. reactivity.

17. The main source of heat for an ectotherm is
   a. its high rate of metabolism.
   b. the environment.
   c. its own body.
   d. its food.

18. What does the immune system do?

Think Critically

19. **Apply Concepts** What two body systems work together to deliver hormones to the organs that they affect? Describe how this interaction takes place.

20. **Apply Concepts** Describe how the circulatory system helps maintain stable conditions inside the body.

21. **Relate Cause and Effect** Identify two ways in which endotherms conserve body heat.

Connecting Concepts

Use the diagram to answer questions 22 and 23.

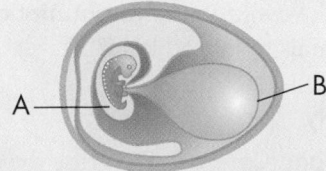

22. **Intrepret Visuals** What does the membrane labeled A do?

23. **Intrepret Visuals** What is membrane B? What does this membrane do?

solve the CHAPTER MYSTERY

SHE'S JUST LIKE HER MOTHER!

The baby bonnethead had been created by automictic parthenogenesis. In this process, the mother's unfertilized egg divided into two cells. These two cells came together to form a zygote with two sets of chromosomes that were exactly the same. (See below.) The identical nature of the chromosomes made the baby shark homozygous for every trait. She had two sets of alleles that were exactly the same.

Normal Fertilization

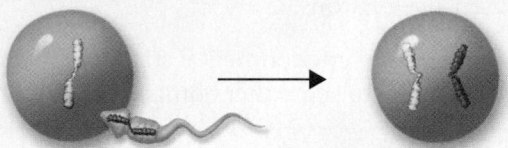

Egg is fertilized with sperm.

Baby shark has one set of chromosomes from each parent.

Automictic Parthenogenesis

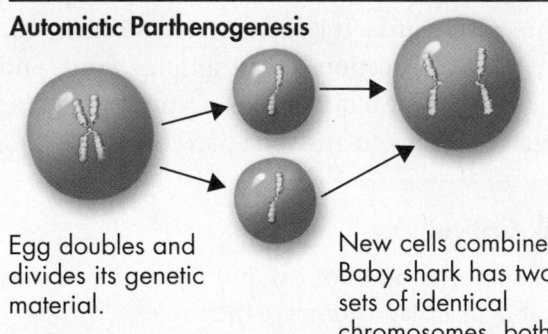

Egg doubles and divides its genetic material.

New cells combine. Baby shark has two sets of identical chromosomes, both from the mother.

1. **Apply Concepts** Explain why the baby shark was not a clone, or exact genetic copy, of its mother. (**Hint:** The mother was conceived by sexual reproduction.)

Untamed Science **Never Stop Exploring Your World.** Finding a solution to what happened in the shark tank is just the beginning. Take a video field trip with the ecogeeks of Untamed Science to see where the mystery leads.

Standardized Test Practice for Maryland

Multiple Choice

1. What part of a vertebrate's brain is the "thinking" region?
A olfactory bulb
B cerebellum
C cerebrum
D medulla oblongata CLG 3.2.1

2. Neurons that receive and send information from and to other neurons are called
A ganglia.
B motor neurons.
C sensory neurons.
D interneurons. CLG 3.2.1

3. The skeleton of a shark is composed primarily of
A bone.   C cartilage.
B vertebrae.   D tendons. CLG 3.2.1

4. Joints between bones of the human skeleton are held together mostly by
A tendons.   C ligaments.
B muscles.   D skin. CLG 3.2.1

5. In oviparous species, embryos
A develop internally.
B obtain nutrients directly from the mother's body.
C obtain nutrients from the external environment.
D develop outside of the body. SPI 1.5.7

6. Most animals reproduce sexually by producing
A buds.
B clones.
C haploid gametes.
D diploid gametes. CLG 3.3.1

7. Maintaining homeostasis in multicellular organisms requires
A a properly functioning heart.
B a nervous system.
C hormones.
D all body systems working together. CLG 3.1.2

8. Which of the following are endothermic?
A fish and amphibians
B mammals and birds
C reptiles and mammals
D all vertebrates SPI 1.5.7

Questions 9–10

Study the illustration of a reptile brain and answer questions 9 and 10.

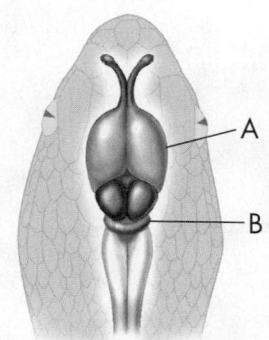

9. What is the name of the structure labeled A?
A cerebrum
B optic lobe
C cerebellum
D olfactory bulb CLG 3.2.1

10. What are some functions of the structure labeled B?
A vision
B control of internal organ functions
C connection of the brain to the rest of the body
D coordination of movement and control of balance CLG 3.2.1

Open-Ended Response

11. Why can't muscles function individually? CLG 3.2.1

If You Have Trouble With . . .										
Question	1	2	3	4	5	6	7	8	9	10	11
See Lesson	28.1	28.1	28.2	28.2	28.3	28.3	28.4	28.4	28.1	28.1	28.2

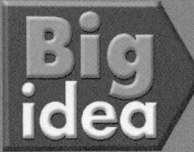

29 Animal Behavior

Big idea **Evolution**

Q: How do animals interact with one another and their environments?

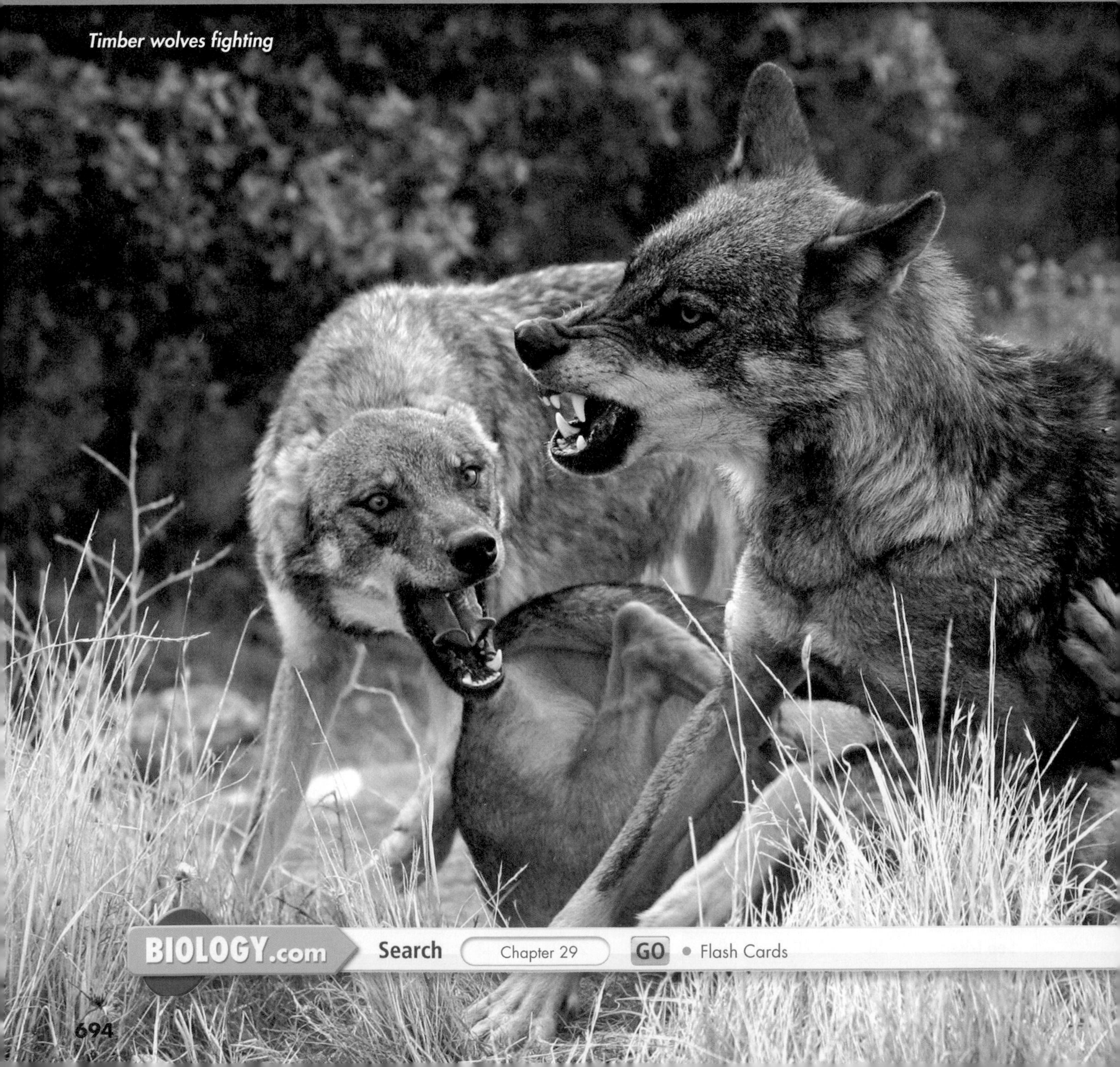

Timber wolves fighting

BIOLOGY.com Search Chapter 29 GO • Flash Cards

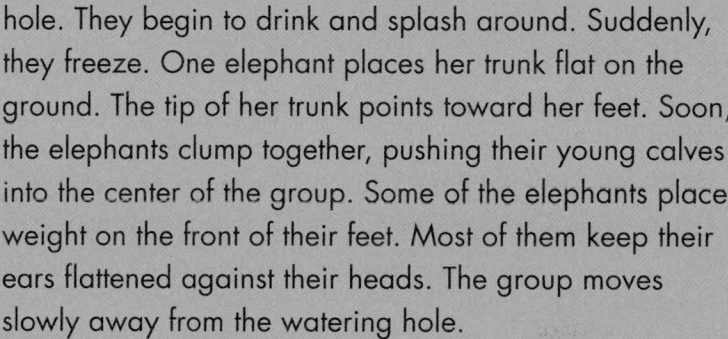

MD MARYLAND VOLUNTARY STATE CURRICULUM

Biology Indicators/Core Learning Goals (CLG) 3.4.1, 3.5.1, 3.5.2. **Skills and Processes Indicators (SPI)** 1.2.3, 1.2.4, 1.2.6, 1.3.1, 1.3.3, 1.4.2, 1.4.9, 1.5.8, 1.5.9. See lessons for details.

CHAPTER
MYSTERY

ELEPHANT CALLER ID?

It is a hot, dusty afternoon in Africa's Etosha National Park. A group of elephants walks toward a watering hole. They begin to drink and splash around. Suddenly, they freeze. One elephant places her trunk flat on the ground. The tip of her trunk points toward her feet. Soon, the elephants clump together, pushing their young calves into the center of the group. Some of the elephants place weight on the front of their feet. Most of them keep their ears flattened against their heads. The group moves slowly away from the watering hole.

Read for Mystery Clues People who are watching the elephants cannot see or hear anything that could have scared the group. What are these elephants doing and why? As you read this chapter, look for clues that explain the behavior of this elephant group. Then, solve the mystery.

FOUNDATIONS
for Learning

You can use table tents to help organize the ideas in this chapter. Fold a piece of construction paper into thirds. Color in the middle third of the paper. You will write notes on the other two thirds of the paper. Pick one of the main topics in Lesson 1. Use words and pictures to illustrate that topic, as shown in the diagram. Then, fold and tape the paper so that it makes a table tent. Make another table tent to illustrate one of the main topics from Lesson 2. At the end of the chapter are two activities that use table tents to help answer the question: How do animals interact with one another and their environments?

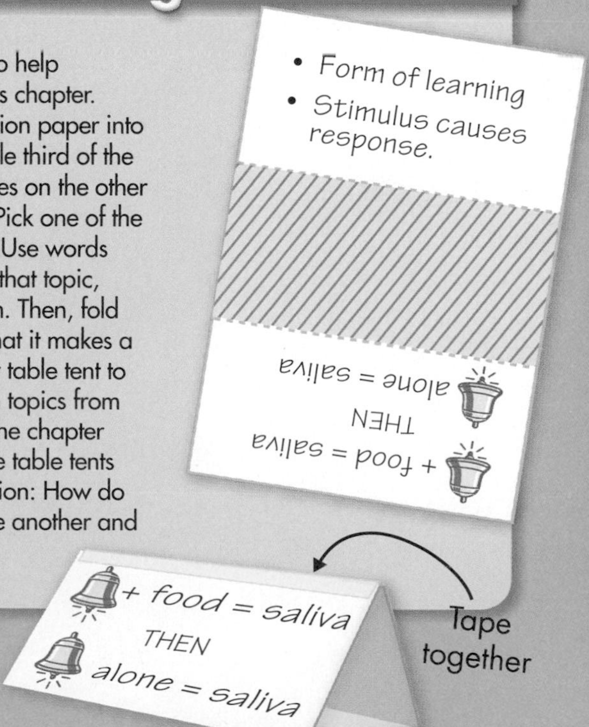

- Form of learning
- Stimulus causes response.

🔔 + food = saliva
THEN
🔔 alone = saliva

🔔 + food = saliva
THEN
🔔 alone = saliva

Tape together

29.1 Elements of Behavior

MD CLG **3.4.1** Evolutionary Change, **3.5.1** Factors Influencing Ecosystems. SPI **1.2.3** Hypothesis Formation, **1.4.2** Analyze Data, **1.5.8** Compare.

Key Questions

🗝 *How can behavior influence the evolution of animal species?*

🗝 *What is an innate behavior?*

🗝 *What are the major types of learning?*

🗝 *How do many complex behaviors arise?*

BUILD Understanding

Concept Map As you read, create a concept map to organize the information in this lesson.

In Your Workbook Go to your workbook to learn more about making a concept map.

Behavior and Evolution

A young boy eats lunch at a table outside of a Caribbean restaurant. In the bushes nearby, an iguana watches closely. The dangerous-looking iguana crawls closer. When the boy sees the lizard, he jumps out of his chair. But the iguana is not interested in the boy's toes. This lizard is a vegetarian. The iguana quickly eats the boy's French fries that have fallen to the ground.

What's so interesting about this scene? This species of iguana usually lives in trees. These iguanas are normally shy and do not come close to humans. However, this iguana has learned that getting close to humans can mean an easy meal!

The activity of the iguana is an example of behavior. **Behavior** is the way that an organism reacts to a stimulus in its environment. Recall that a stimulus is any information that causes an organism to react.

Some behaviors are simple. A dog turns its head when it hears a noise. Other behaviors are complex. For example, some animals wash their food before eating it. The way that an animal behaves often depends on an internal condition, such as hunger. If the iguana had not been hungry, he probably would have stayed away from the boy.

Most behaviors are necessary for survival. For example, animals must be able to find and catch food, choose a habitat, avoid predators, and find mates. Many behaviors are influenced by genes. If these behaviors help an animal survive and reproduce, they will be passed on to the next generation. Eventually helpful behaviors will spread throughout the population, or even the species. Thus, certain behaviors can evolve by natural selection, just like physical traits.

🗝 **Key Question** How can behavior influence the evolution of animal species? **If an inherited behavior allows an animal to survive and reproduce, the behavior can spread throughout the population.**

Innate Behavior

How does a spider know how to spin a web? How do chicks know how to beg for food? These animals are showing **innate behaviors,** or instincts. An animal performs an innate behavior even though it has no previous experience with the stimulus to which it is responding. Innate behaviors allow animals to survive without the need for experience. An animal's genes and its environment interact to cause innate behaviors.

One example of an innate behavior is a newborn mammal's ability to suck milk from its mother's body. This innate behavior is simple. Other innate behaviors, such as making a spider web, are complex.

🔑 **Key Question** What is an innate behavior? **An innate behavior is a behavior that an animal performs even though it has no previous experience with the stimulus to which it is responding.**

Learned Behavior

If all behaviors were innate, the behaviors would be hard or impossible for an animal to change during its lifetime. If that were the case, individual animals would have a hard time responding to changes in their environment. But when many animals experience something new, they are able to respond by changing their behavior. Making changes to behaviors based on experience is called **learning.**

Many animals have the ability to learn. Organisms with simple nervous systems, such as sea stars and most other invertebrates, learn only rarely. In a few invertebrates and many chordates, learning is common. Scientists have identified four main types of learning: habituation, classical conditioning, operant conditioning, and insight learning.

Habituation The simplest type of learning is habituation. **Habituation** happens when an animal stops responding to a repeating stimulus that does not harm or reward the animal. Imagine crows eating near a road. At first, passing cars cause the crows to fly away. Over time, they learn that the cars will not harm them. They stop flying away. The crows have become habituated to the cars. In other words, a stimulus (the cars) no longer causes a response (flight). An animal can save energy by ignoring a stimulus that does not affect its survival.

Habituation Crows by the side of a road fly away when a car passes. After many cars have passed without harming the crows, the birds become habituated to the cars. From then on, the crows do not fly away when cars pass them.

Operant Conditioning

1. A dog randomly brushes its tail against a bell hanging on a doorknob.

2. The owner responds by opening the door. The ring-the-bell, open-the-door sequence happens a few times.

3. The dog then learns to ring the bell when it wants to go out.

BUILD Vocabulary

classical conditioning
a type of learning that occurs when an animal makes a mental connection between a stimulus and some kind of reward or punishment

operant conditioning
a type of learning in which an animal learns to behave in a certain way through repeated practice, to receive a reward or avoid punishment

insight learning
a type of behavior in which an animal applies something it has already learned to a new situation, without a period of trial and error; also called reasoning

imprinting
a type of behavior based on early experience; once imprinting has occurred, the behavior cannot be changed

ACADEMIC VOCABULARY

The term *insight* means "a clear or deep understanding of a complex situation." In insight learning, an animal understands a new situation and then responds to it.

Classical Conditioning In **classical conditioning,** an animal responds to a stimulus that has become linked to a positive or negative experience. The Russian scientist Ivan Pavlov first described classical conditioning around 1900. Pavlov noticed that dogs have an innate response to food— they salivate, or drool. Pavlov rang a bell every time he offered his dogs food. After a while, his dogs would salivate when they heard the bell, even when there was no food. Pavlov's experiment caused the dogs to salivate (a response) in reaction to a bell (stimulus) associated with food.

Operant Conditioning **Operant conditioning** happens when an animal learns to behave in a certain way to get a reward or to avoid punishment. The American scientist B.F. Skinner first described operant conditioning in the 1940s. Skinner conducted experiments using a box that became known as a "Skinner box." A Skinner box has a lever inside. An animal that is put inside the box will accidentally push the lever at some point. When it pushes the lever, the animal receives food. After it is rewarded several times, the animal learns that it can get food by pushing the lever.

Operant conditioning is often called trial-and-error learning. After a random behavior produces a reward, the animal tries to get the reward again (a trial). Most trials result in errors (no reward). However, sometimes a trial will produce a reward.

Insight Learning In **insight learning,** an animal applies something it has already learned to a new situation. The animal does not go through a period of trial and error. Insight learning is also called reasoning. Humans use insight learning to solve new problems. Insight learning is also common in some nonhuman primates. In one experiment, a hungry chimpanzee used insight learning to stack boxes in order to reach bananas overhead.

🔑 **Key Question** What are the major types of learning?
The four major types of learning are habituation, classical conditioning, operant conditioning, and insight learning.

Imprinting in the Wild
This sandhill crane chick has imprinted on its mother. Because it has imprinted on its mother, it will follow her in flight during migration.

Complex Behaviors

Many complex behaviors combine innate behavior with learning. One example of complex behavior is imprinting. In **imprinting,** an animal has an innate urge to follow the first moving object that it sees. But the animal is not born knowing what that object will look like. It must learn from experience what to follow. Once imprinting has occurred, the behavior becomes fixed.

Usually young birds such as the sandhill crane shown above imprint on their mothers. Imprinting on their mothers improves their chance of survival. A young crane that stays close to its mother is protected from predators. It also learns where to get food.

INQUIRY
into Scientific Thinking

Caring for Young

Can experience help animals be better parents? The data in the table are from studies of a seabird, the short-tailed shearwater. Each pair produces only one egg a year. If that egg breaks or if the chick dies, the female bird does not lay another egg. The graph shows the percentage of eggs that develop into young birds, in relation to the age or breeding experience of the parents. This ratio is called reproductive success.

1. Interpret Tables What is the approximate success rate of a female shearwater with five years of breeding experience?

2. Compare and Contrast Are there obvious differences in reproductive success between male and female shearwaters?

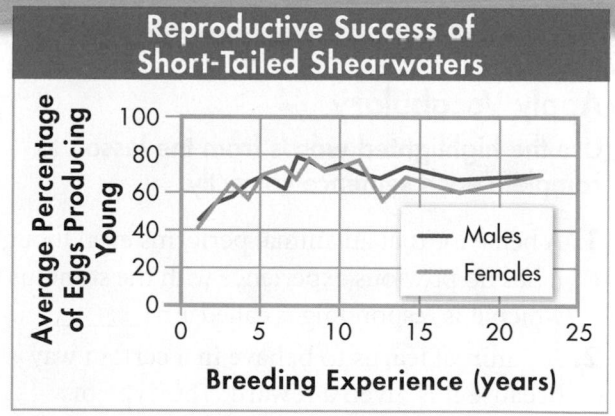

3. Draw Conclusions Do older shearwaters have better reproductive success than younger birds have? Explain your answer.

4. Form a Hypothesis Do you think these birds learn to raise young more successfully over time?

In Your Workbook Get more help for this activity in your workbook.

Imprinting in Captivity Recently hatched cranes that are raised in captivity imprint on a red-headed bird puppet worn on the hand of a researcher. Later, that puppet is used to help introduce these birds to the wild.

Researchers use imprinting to help raise endangered cranes in captivity. The researchers create hand puppets that look like adult cranes. When they show these puppets to baby cranes, the baby cranes imprint on the puppets. After the cranes have grown up, researchers use the puppets to train the cranes where to fly during migration.

Imprinting does not always involve vision. Animals can imprint on sights, sounds, odors, or other cues. Newly hatched salmon imprint on the odor of the stream in which they have hatched. When they are young, the salmon swim out to sea. Years later, adult salmon use that odor to help them return to their home stream to lay eggs.

Key Question How do many complex behaviors arise?
Many complex behaviors combine innate behavior with learning.

CHECK Understanding

Apply Vocabulary
Use the highlighted words from the lesson to complete each sentence correctly.

1. A behavior that an animal performs even though it has no previous experience with the stimulus to which it is responding is called a(n)_____.

2. An animal learns to behave in a certain way because it is given a reward. This type of learning is called _____.

3. An animal applies something that it has already learned to a new situation. This type of learning is called _____.

Critical Thinking

4. **Review** What is behavior?

5. **Review** Which aspect of imprinting is innate? Which aspect is learned?

6. **Write to Learn** Answer the first clue of the mystery.

MYSTERY CLUE

Elephants living elsewhere exhibit behaviors similar to those of the elephants at the watering hole. What does this suggest about the importance of these behaviors? (**Hint:** See p. 696.)

BIOLOGY.com Search Lesson 29.1 GO • Lesson Assessment

29.2 Animals in Their Environments

MD | CLG 3.5.1 Factors Influencing Ecosystems. 3.5.2 Interdependence of Organisms in the Biosphere, SPI 1.5.9 Synthesize Ideas.

Behavioral Cycles

As night falls on a coral reef, animals there act like city commuters during rush hour. Some species have "day jobs" feeding in bright light. They form "traffic jams" as they move into reef caves to rest for the night. Species that work the "night shift" come out to feed in the dark. At dawn, the cycle reverses.

Daily Cycles The behavior of animals in the coral reef is an example of a circadian rhythm. **Circadian** (sur KAY dee un) **rhythms** are behavioral cycles that happen daily. The human behavior of going to school during the day and sleeping at night is an example of a circadian rhythm.

Seasonal Cycles Other behavioral cycles are seasonal. In temperate and polar areas, many species are active during spring, summer, and fall. These species enter a sleeplike state, or dormancy, during winter. Some mammals enter a kind of dormancy called hibernation. Dormancy allows animals to survive periods when food and other resources are not available.

Migration is the seasonal movement of an animal from one environment to another. Many species of animals migrate, and many animals migrate over huge distances. Migration allows animals to take advantage of good environmental conditions. Many songbirds live in tropical regions when it is winter in temperate areas. When these birds fly north in the spring, they find lots of food. They also find space to raise young.

🔑 **Key Question** How do environmental changes affect animal behavior?
Many animals respond to the cycles in the environment with daily or seasonal cycles of behavior.

Key Questions

🔑 **How do environmental changes affect animal behavior?**

🔑 **How do social behaviors increase an animal's evolutionary fitness?**

🔑 **How do animals communicate with others in their environments?**

BUILD Understanding

KWL Chart Fill in a KWL chart as you read Lesson 29.2. In the first column, write down what you already know about the topic. In the second column, write what you want to find out. In the last column, write what you have learned after reading the lesson.

In Your Workbook Refer to your workbook for suggestions about how to use a KWL chart to organize your notes.

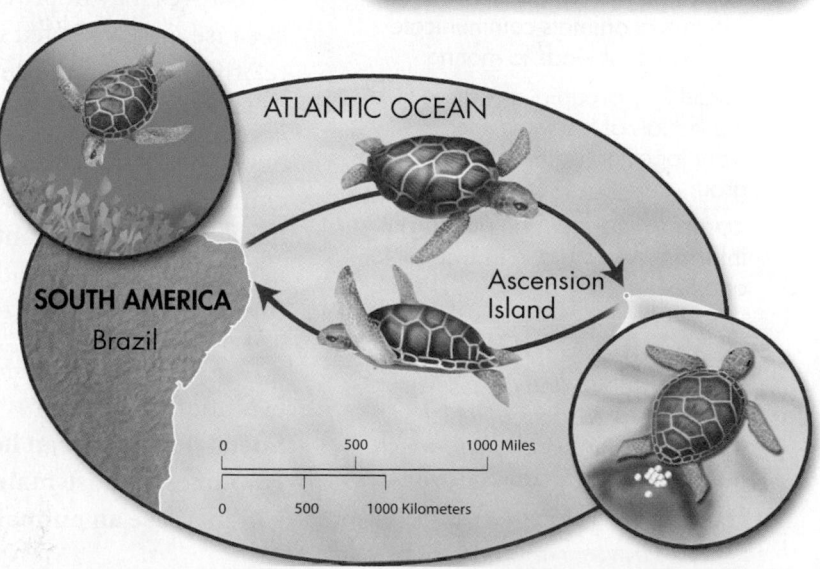

Seasonal Behavior of Green Sea Turtles
Each year, green sea turtles migrate back and forth between their feeding grounds on Brazil's coast and their nesting grounds on Ascension Island.

ATLANTIC OCEAN
SOUTH AMERICA
Brazil
Ascension Island

0   500   1000 Miles
0   500   1000 Kilometers

Territorial Behavior A bear marks its territory with its fur and scent.

BUILD Vocabulary

circadian rhythm a behavioral cycle that happens daily

migration seasonal behavior in which animals travel from one environment to another

territory a specific area occupied and protected by an animal or group of animals

aggression threatening behavior that one individual uses to show dominance over another individual

courtship a type of behavior in which two animals communicate in a way that leads to mating

society a group of closely related individuals of the same species that work together for the benefit of the group

communication the passing of information from one individual to another

🐾 WORD ORIGINS

The word *circadian* comes from two Latin words: *circa*, which means "about," and *diem*, which means "day." Circadian rhythms have a daily cycle.

Social Behavior

When animals interact with each other, they are performing social behaviors. Social behaviors help animals get food and other resources, compete for mates, and protect their offspring. Social behaviors include territoriality, aggression, courtship, and forming of societies.

Territoriality and Aggression Many animals behave in ways that keep other animals from using limited resources. Some animals live in a specific area, or **territory,** that they defend against competitors. Territories usually contain resources such as food, water, nesting sites, shelter, and potential mates. Animals often mark their territory with their fur or scent. If another animal comes into their territory, the "owner" chases it away. Animals may show aggression when defending their territories. **Aggression** is threatening behavior that is used to show the dominance, or greater power, of one animal over another.

Courtship An animal that reproduces sexually must find and mate with another member of its species. During **courtship** behavior, members of one sex (usually males) show that they are ready to mate. Members of the opposite sex (usually females) choose which individual they will accept. Animals may produce sounds, visual displays, or chemical signals to attract mates.

In some species, courtship involves rituals. Rituals are a series of behaviors that are always performed in the same way. Many rituals include signals and responses that continue until mating happens.

Animal Societies An animal **society** is a group of animals of the same species that live close to each other and work together. Societies can protect individuals from predators. They can also improve an animal's ability to find food, protect a territory, guard young, or fight off rivals. For example, African wild dogs hunt in packs. The females in the pack may take turns guarding all the pups, while other adults hunt for prey.

Members of a society are often closely related to one another. The help of relatives may improve the evolutionary fitness of an individual, because closely related individuals share many genes. Helping a relative increases the chance that the genes of an individual will be passed on to offspring.

Social insects, such as ants, bees, and wasps, have some of the most complex animal societies. In colonies of social insects each individual has a specific job. In ant colonies, all females except the queen are workers. The queen is the only female that reproduces. Male ants function only to fertilize the queen.

🔑 **Key Question** How do social behaviors increase an animal's evolutionary fitness?
Social behaviors can help animals claim or defend territories or resources, choose mates, and form social groups. These behaviors can increase an animal's evolutionary fitness.

Communication

Social behavior involves more than one individual, so it requires communication. **Communication** is the passing of information from one individual to another. Animals may communicate using chemical, visual, or sound signals. Some species also use their own kind of language. The kinds of signals a species uses depend on the sense organs it has and the environment in which it lives.

Chemical Signals Animals with good senses of smell, such as insects, fishes, and mammals, can communicate with chemicals. Some animals, such as bees, ants, and lampreys, release chemicals called pheromones (FEHR uh mohnz). Pheromones can mark a territory or signal that an animal is ready to mate. Pheromones affect the behavior of other individuals of the same species.

BUILD Connections

AN ANT SOCIETY

In a leaf-cutter ant society, only a single queen reproduces. Different groups of ants within the colony perform other tasks.

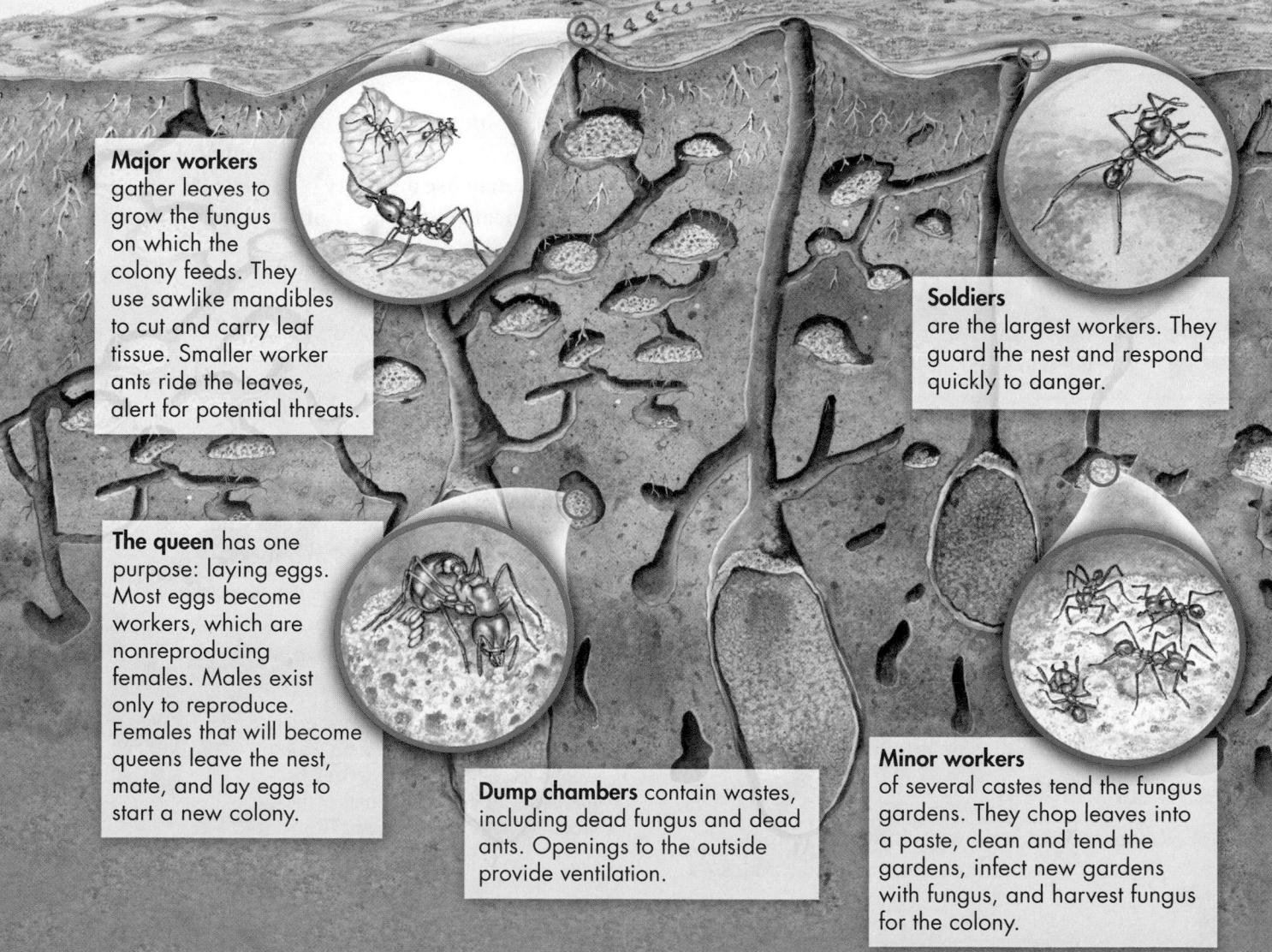

Major workers gather leaves to grow the fungus on which the colony feeds. They use sawlike mandibles to cut and carry leaf tissue. Smaller worker ants ride the leaves, alert for potential threats.

Soldiers are the largest workers. They guard the nest and respond quickly to danger.

The queen has one purpose: laying eggs. Most eggs become workers, which are nonreproducing females. Males exist only to reproduce. Females that will become queens leave the nest, mate, and lay eggs to start a new colony.

Dump chambers contain wastes, including dead fungus and dead ants. Openings to the outside provide ventilation.

Minor workers of several castes tend the fungus gardens. They chop leaves into a paste, clean and tend the gardens, infect new gardens with fungus, and harvest fungus for the colony.

language a system of communication that combines sounds, symbols, and movements according to a set of rules about sequence and meaning, such as grammar and syntax

Visual Signals Many animals have well-developed eyes that can sense shapes and colors. These animals often use visual signals to communicate. In many species, males use colorful displays to signal when they are ready to mate. Squids can change their color to send a variety of signals. Some animals, such as fireflies, even send signals using light that is made within their bodies.

Sound Signals Most animals with good senses of hearing and the ability to make noises can communicate using sound. Dolphins use sound signals to communicate in the ocean. Elephants make sounds with their feet and vocal cords that can be used to identify individuals. Elephants, and some other animals, can send messages that can be felt rather than heard.

Language **Language** is a complex system of communication that uses rules to combine sounds, symbols, and movements. Many animals, including elephants, primates, and dolphins, seem to have "words"—calls with specific meanings, such as "lions on the prowl." However, untrained animals do not seem to use a set of rules for communication like those in human language.

Key Question How do animals communicate with others in their environments? **Animals may use a variety of signals to communicate with one another. Some can also use language.**

CHECK
Understanding

Apply Vocabulary
Use the highlighted words from the lesson to complete each sentence correctly.

1. Behavioral cycles that happen daily are called _____.

2. _____ is seasonal movement from one environment to another.

3. Many animals defend a _____, which is an area that contains resources.

Critical Thinking

4. Review Name two ways in which animal behavior is related to environmental cycles.

5. Review List three types of social behavior.

6. Relate Cause and Effect How does membership in a society increase the evolutionary fitness of its members?

7. Write to Learn Answer the mystery clue.

MYSTERY CLUE

When threatened by predators, adult elephants form a circle around young elephants. What may have caused this behavior in the elephants at the watering hole? (**Hint:** See p. 703.)

Design Your Own Lab

 CLG 3.5.1 Factors Influencing Ecosystems. SPI 1.2.3 Hypothesis Formation, 1.2.4 Testing a Hypothesis, 1.2.6 Investigative Methods, 1.3.1 Use Equipment, *(continued below)*

Pre-Lab: Termite Tracks

Problem How can you determine the type of stimulus that triggers a particular response?

Materials petri dishes, paper, scissors, termites, small paintbrushes, forceps, ballpoint pens, rollerball pens, felt-tip pens

Lab Manual Chapter 29 Lab

Skills Focus Form a Hypothesis, Design an Experiment, Draw Conclusions

Connect to the Big idea Animals react to their environments as they search for food, avoid predators, and look for a mate. The survival of a species can depend on these behaviors. Some behaviors are inherited and evolve over time due to natural selection. Over many generations, behaviors that help animals survive spread through a population. Behaviors that are not adaptive become less common. In this lab, you will observe an inherited behavior of termites. Then you will design an experiment to determine the type of stimulus that triggers the behavior.

Background Questions

a. Review How is a behavior usually defined?

b. Explain How do innate behaviors, or instincts, help animals survive?

c. Infer You see an ant walk across the ground. A minute later, you see another ant walk in the same exact line. What type of communication do you think is taking place?

Pre-Lab Questions

Preview the procedure in the lab manual.

1. Control Variables Why do you think the instructions ask you to draw a figure eight rather than a straight line?

2. Draw Conclusions How will you decide whether a termite has a positive reaction, a negative reaction, or no reaction to a stimulus?

3. Predict Read pages 703–704 of your textbook. Which of the signals described could be a stimulus for the termite in this lab? Explain your answer.

 Search [Chapter 29] **GO**

Visit Chapter 29 online to test yourself on chapter content and to find activities to help you learn.

Untamed Science Video See how the latest technologies help the explorers from Untamed Science track the movements of different animals.

Tutor Tube Instinct? Sorting out everyday and scientific behavior terms.

Art Review Identify animal communication strategies.

Art in Motion Watch social behavior in a population.

 1.3.3 Safe Handling of Materials, 1.4.9 Confirm Hypotheses, 1.5.9 Synthesize Ideas.

29.1 Elements of Behavior

- If an inherited behavior allows an animal to survive and reproduce, the behavior can spread through the population.

- An innate behavior is a behavior that an animal performs even though it has no previous experience with the stimulus to which it is responding. Innate behaviors are also called instincts.

- The four major types of learning are habituation, classical conditioning, operant conditioning, and insight learning.

- Many complex behaviors combine innate behavior with learning.

behavior (p. 696)
innate behavior (p. 697)
learning (p. 697)
habituation (p. 697)
classical conditioning (p. 698)
operant conditioning (p. 698)
insight learning (p. 698)
imprinting (p. 699)

29.2 Animals in Their Environments

- Many animals respond to the cycles in the environment with daily or seasonal cycles of behavior.

- Social behaviors can help animals to find and protect food, guard young, avoid predators, and find mates. Since these behaviors can increase an animal's survival and reproduction, they can improve its evolutionary fitness.

- Animals may use a variety of signals to communicate with one another. Some animals can use language.

circadian rhythm (p. 701)
migration (p. 701)
territory (p. 702)
aggression (p. 702)
courtship (p. 702)
society (p. 702)
communication (p. 703)
language (p. 704)

Assess the Big idea ▶ Evolution

Write an answer to the question below:

Q: How do animals interact with one another and their environments?

Constructed Response

Write an answer to each of the numbered questions below. The answer to each numbered question should be one or two paragraphs long. To help you begin, read the **Hints** below the questions.

1. **You are studying the behavior of a chimpanzee. You observe that the chimpanzee has learned how to use a key to open a box that contains food. How do you know whether the chimpanzee has learned this behavior using operant conditioning or insight learning?**

   Hint Look at the steps that show how a dog learns using operant conditioning on p. 698. Could a chimpanzee learn how to unlock a box using similar steps?

2. **Describe how the behaviors of animals in the northern United States help them survive when seasons change from fall to winter.**

   Hint What is the difference between the behavior of songbirds and the behavior of mammals when winter arrives?

3. **Some animals live in societies. What are the benefits of living in a group? What are the costs?**

   Hint Would resources be more available to an animal that lived in a group or less available?

Foundations for Learning Wrap-Up

Use the table tents you made when you started the chapter to help you organize your thoughts about how animals interact with one another and with their environments.

Activity 1 Work together as a class. Write the seven main chapter topics on separate sheets of paper.

- Behavior and Evolution
- Innate Behavior
- Learned Behavior
- Complex Behaviors
- Behavioral Cycles
- Social Behavior
- Communication

Choose seven desks in the classroom. Put one of the sheets on each of the desks.

Have everyone place each of his or her table tents on the desk that matches its topic. Work together to make sure all the table tents are in the right place. Then, review each topic in small groups by looking at the table tents.

Activity 2 Divide up into pairs. Pick a topic from the chapter, but do not tell your partner what it is. Make a new table tent to illustrate that topic. Use mainly pictures on your table tent—just a few words. Be creative! Do not use the same pictures that are found in your textbook.

Tape the table tent together and give it to your partner. Have your partner guess what the table tent illustrates without looking at the textbook. Switch places and repeat the activity.

29.1 Elements of Behavior

Understand Key Concepts

1. The way an organism reacts to stimuli in its environment is called
   - **a.** behavior.
   - **c.** conditioning.
   - **b.** learning.
   - **d.** imprinting.

2. Animal behaviors can evolve through natural selection because
   - **a.** what an animal learns is added to its genes.
   - **b.** all behavior is completely the result of genes.
   - **c.** all behavior is completely the result of environmental influences.
   - **d.** genes that influence behaviors that increase fitness can increase in frequency from one generation to the next.

3. Which kind of behavior is shown below?

   - **a.** insight learning
   - **c.** classical conditioning
   - **b.** imprinting
   - **d.** operant conditioning

4. How can habituation contribute to an animal's survival?

Think Critically

5. **Infer** When a baby smiles, her mother picks her up and cuddles her. Over time, the baby smiles more and more often. Explain what type of learning the baby is showing.

> **Test-Taking Tip**
>
> **Use Time Wisely** When you are taking a test, answer all the questions you are sure about first. Put a mark next to the questions that you need to go back to. Skip any questions that you really cannot answer. Only go back to those questions if you have time.

29.2 Animals in Their Environments

6. Each year, a bird called the redstart travels from its winter home in South America to its nesting area in New York. This behavior is called
   a. imprinting.
   c. migration.
   b. competition.
   d. courtship.

7. Which of the following is NOT social behavior?
   a. courtship
   c. hunting in a pack
   b. territoriality
   d. operant conditioning

8. Describe two ways in which social behavior can benefit an animal.

9. Explain how aggression and territorial behavior are related.

Think Critically

10. **Apply Concepts** Because a highway has been constructed through a forest, many of the animals that once lived there have had to move to a different wooded area. Is this migration? Explain.

Connecting Concepts

In winter, some mammals enter into a state of dormancy. Dormancy is an energy-saving adaptation in which metabolism slows down, causing body temperature to become lower. The graph below tracks a ground squirrel's body temperature over the course of a year.

11. **Explain** Describe the pattern that you observe.

12. **Infer** What can you infer about the squirrel's behavior at different times of the year?

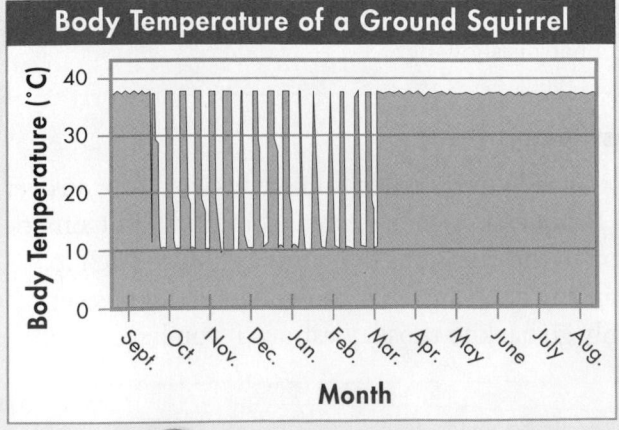

Body Temperature of a Ground Squirrel

Body Temperature (°C) vs. Month (Sept. through Aug.)

solve the CHAPTER MYSTERY

ELEPHANT CALLER ID?

Elephants can communicate with loud calls and vibrations that can travel long distances. Elephants send these vibrations by drumming on the ground with their feet. They also make low rumbling calls that contain very low-frequency vibrations. The air vibrations can travel up to 16 kilometers. The ground vibrations can travel up to 32 kilometers.

Elephants sense these vibrations with specialized pads of fat in their feet. They can also detect the vibrations with receptor cells in their feet and trunks. By standing still and pressing their feet and trunks to the ground, they can sense the vibrations better. Some patterns of vibrations can identify individuals—like caller ID for elephants!

The vibrations contain greetings, locations of food, and warnings of danger. The elephants at the watering hole had sensed a message from another herd of elephants: "Warning! Lions!"

1. **Compare and Contrast** How do vibrations in the ground compare with sounds in the air as a way to communicate over long distances?

2. **Form a Hypothesis** Sometimes researchers play sounds and vibrations from elephant groups that live far from Etosha. The elephants at Etosha do not always respond. Why might this be the case?

3. **Connect to the Big Idea** How do elephants' responses to low-frequency vibrations in their environment affect their survival?

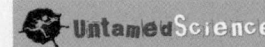 **Never Stop Exploring Your World.** Finding the solution to the Elephant Caller ID? mystery is only the beginning. Take a video field trip with the ecogeeks of Untamed Science to see where the mystery leads.

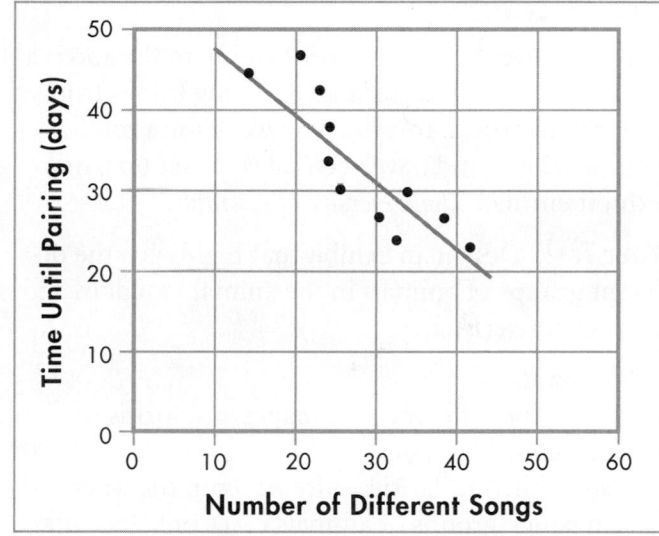
Multiple Choice

1. A rat that learns to press a button to get food is exhibiting
   A insight learning.   C classical conditioning.
   B operant conditioning.   D habituation.   CLG 3.5.1

2. A dog that always salivates at the ringing of a bell is exhibiting
   A insight learning.   C classical conditioning.
   B operant conditioning.   D habituation.   CLG 3.5.1

3. A chimpanzee that stacks boxes in order to reach a banana hanging from the ceiling is showing
   A insight learning.   C classical conditioning.
   B operant conditioning.   D habituation.   CLG 3.5.1

4. A bird that stops responding to a repeated warning call when the call is not followed by an attack is showing
   A insight learning.   C classical conditioning.
   B operant conditioning.   D habituation.   CLG 3.5.1

5. Which kind of behavior does NOT involve learning?
   A habituation   C imprinting
   B trial and error   D instinct   CLG 3.5.1

6. A male three-spined stickleback fish will attack male red-bellied sticklebacks and models of fishes that have a red underside. It will not attack males or models lacking a red underside. What can you conclude from the three-spined stickleback's behavior?
   A The stimulus for an attack is a red underside.
   B The stimulus for an attack is aggression.
   C The stimulus for an attack is the presence of a fish with red fins.
   D The stimulus for an attack is the presence of a fish model.   CLG 3.5.1

7. Which of the following is NOT an innate behavior?
   A a dog looking for its food dish
   B a baby mammal sucking milk
   C a worm moving away from bright light
   D a spider spinning a web   CLG 3.5.1

Questions 8–9

A researcher observed sedge warblers during breeding season. She charted the number of different songs a male bird sang compared to the time it took him to pair with a mate. The graph shows her data.

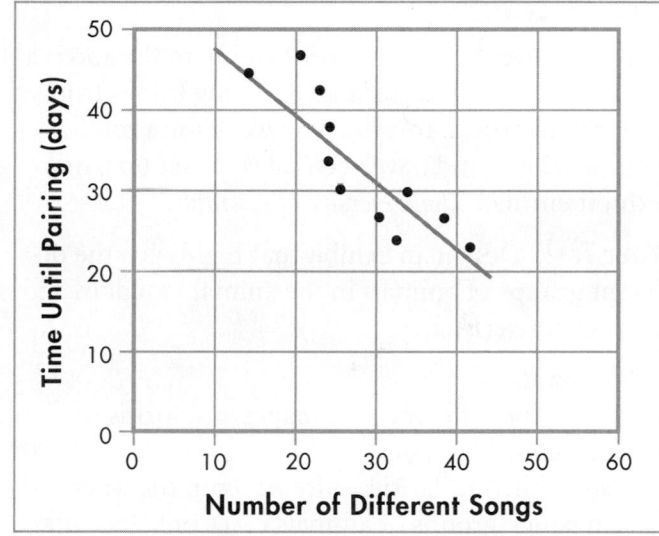

8. The researcher was trying to find out whether there is a correlation between
   A the number of a male bird's songs and the number of offspring.
   B the number of a male bird's songs and his attractiveness to females.
   C a male's age and when he mates.
   D a female's age and when she mates.   SPI 1.4.6

9. What can you conclude based on the graph?
   A Males prefer females that do not sing.
   B Females prefer males that do not sing.
   C Males prefer females with a larger number of songs.
   D Females prefer males with a larger number of songs.   SPI 1.4.2

Open-Ended Response

10. How does defending a specific territory benefit an animal?   CLG 3.5.1

If You Have Trouble With . . .

Question	1	2	3	4	5	6	7	8	9	10
See Lesson	29.1	29.1	29.1	29.1	29.1	29.1	29.1	29.2	29.2	29.2

Unit Project

Zoo Exhibit

Have you ever been to the zoo? Going to the zoo is a great way to see and learn about living things from around the world. Imagine you work for a zoo in your local city and have been asked to set up a new exhibit entitled *The Diversity of Animals.*

Your Task Design an exhibit that highlights the different groups of animals in the animal kingdom and their characteristics.

Be sure to
- show the differences in shapes and forms of animals.
- show the similarities/differences in the ways in which groups of animals carry out basic life processes (circulation, respiration, excretion, movement, response, feeding).
- design the exhibit so that it is clear and engaging.

Reflection Questions

1. Score your exhibit using the rubric below. What score did you give yourself?

2. What did you do well in this project?

3. What needs improvement?

4. What aspects of another group's exhibit did you like? Why?

Assessment Rubric

Score	Scientific Content	Quality of Exhibit
4	Exhibit reveals a thorough understanding of animals and the ways they carry out life processes.	Exhibit is very organized, educational, and engaging to visitors.
3	Exhibit reveals an adequate understanding of animals and the ways they carry out life processes.	Exhibit is organized and clear, but it could be more engaging to visitors.
2	Exhibit reveals a limited understanding of animals and the ways they carry out life processes.	Exhibit needs improvement in clarity and organization. It is somewhat engaging.
1	Exhibit reveals significant misunderstandings about animals and the ways they carry out life processes.	Exhibit is very unclear and disorganized. It is not engaging.

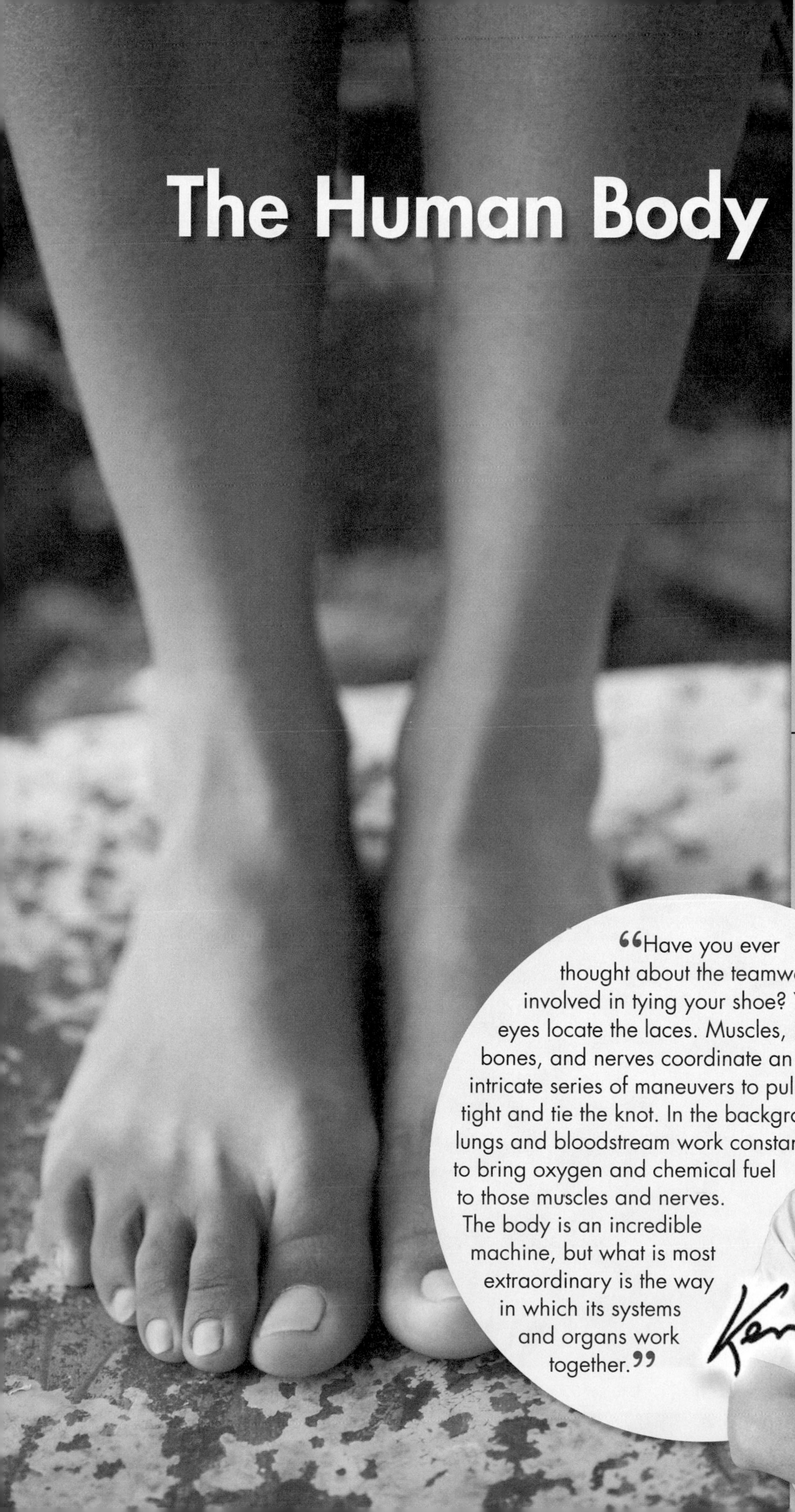

The Human Body

INTRODUCE the

Big ideas

- **Homeostasis**
- **Structure and Function**

"Have you ever thought about the teamwork involved in tying your shoe? Your eyes locate the laces. Muscles, bones, and nerves coordinate an intricate series of maneuvers to pull them tight and tie the knot. In the background, lungs and bloodstream work constantly to bring oxygen and chemical fuel to those muscles and nerves. The body is an incredible machine, but what is most extraordinary is the way in which its systems and organs work together."

Ken Miller

711

30 Digestive and Excretory Systems

Big idea

Homeostasis

Q: How are the materials that enter and leave your body related to the processes that maintain homeostasis?

Food sellers display their goods at a floating food market on Dal Lake in northern India.

MD MARYLAND VOLUNTARY STATE CURRICULUM

Biology Indicators/Core Learning Goals (CLG) 3.1.1, 3.1.2, 3.1.3, 3.2.1, 3.2.2. **Skills and Processes Indicators (SPI)** 1.2.7, 1.3.1, 1.3.3, 1.4.1, 1.4.2, 1.5.2, 1.5.5, 1.5.8, 1.5.9, 1.6.4, 1.7.1. See lessons for details.

CHAPTER
MYSTERY

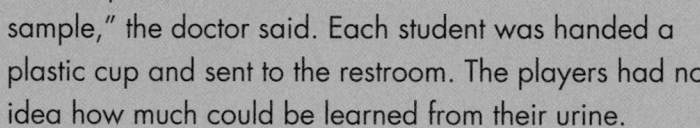

THE TELLTALE SAMPLE

All players had to get a physical on the first day of football practice. "Please provide me with a urine sample," the doctor said. Each student was handed a plastic cup and sent to the restroom. The players had no idea how much could be learned from their urine.

Philip and Seth handed in their samples. They were told right away to go home and drink plenty of water before practice the next day. The next day, Andrew was told he might have diabetes and should see his doctor. Several days later, another player was dropped from the team. He had violated the school's well-known antidrug policy. How was all this information learned from a urine sample?

Read for Mystery Clues As you read this chapter, look for clues to help you predict what can be learned by examining what leaves your body. Then, solve the chapter mystery.

FOUNDATIONS
for Learning

Think of organs as building blocks for an organ system. Before you read the chapter, make two layered pinwheels, one for the digestive system and one for the excretory system. Use two sheets of paper. Write the name of the system at the top of the first sheet. To make the tabs of the pinwheel, fold the second sheet in half twice. Then cut the paper diagonally and along each fold, as shown below. Tape the pinwheel to the first sheet of paper. As you read the chapter, write the name of an organ from the system on each tab. Then write the functions of the organ under the tab. At the end of the chapter are two activities that use the pinwheels to help answer the question: How are the materials that enter and leave your body related to the processes that maintain homeostasis?

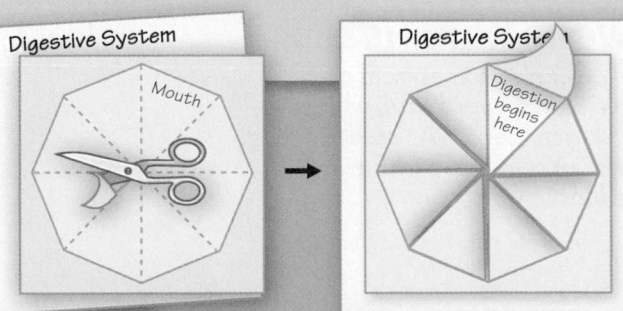

30.1 Organization of the Human Body

MD CLG 3.1.2 Homeostasis, 3.2.1 Processes and Functions, 3.2.2 Changes in Metabolic Activity.
SPI 1.5.2 Communicate Information.

Key Questions

🔑 How is the human body organized?

🔑 What is homeostasis?

BUILD Understanding

Previewing Visuals Study the Build Connections feature on p. 716. For each system, describe how it interacts with at least one other system.

In Your Workbook Go to your workbook for more about previewing visuals.

BUILD Vocabulary

epithelial tissue
a type of tissue that lines the interior and exterior body surfaces

connective tissue
a type of tissue that provides support for the body and connects its parts

nervous tissue
a type of tissue that transmits nerve impulses throughout the body

muscle tissue
a type of tissue that makes movements of the body possible

🖊 WORD ORIGINS

The word *tissue* comes from the Middle English word *tissu*, which means "rich fabric." A tissue is a "fabric" of cells that perform the same function.

Organization of the Body

How does a softball player field a ground ball? She uses her eyes and brain to figure out where to move. Her bones support her muscles as she moves. Her lungs absorb the oxygen her cells use during cellular respiration. Her brain monitors the ball and sends signals to guide her hand to catch it. An easy out, a routine play. How do all of these parts of the body work together to allow the softball player to field the ball?

Every cell in the human body works alone, yet also depends on the rest of the body. How can so many single cells and parts work together so efficiently? One way to answer this question is to study the organization of the human body.

Cells A cell is the basic unit of structure and function in living things. Remember that single cells in multicellular organisms are usually specialized. Bone cells, blood cells, muscle cells, and other types of cells each perform a specific function.

Tissues A group of cells that performs a single function is called a tissue. There are four basic types of tissue in the human body—epithelial, connective, nervous, and muscle.

▶ *Epithelial Tissue* The tissue that lines the interior and exterior surfaces of your body is **epithelial tissue.** Your skin and the lining of your stomach are examples of epithelial tissue.

▶ *Connective Tissue* The type of tissue that provides support for the body and connects its parts is called **connective tissue.** Fat cells, bone cells, and blood cells are types of connective tissue. Many connective tissues produce a protein called collagen. Collagen is a fiberlike protein that makes tissues strong and durable. Collagen helps the tissue keep its shape even when it is under pressure.

Types of Tissue The four major types of tissue are epithelial tissue, connective tissue, nervous tissue, and muscle tissue.

	Epithelial Tissue	Connective Tissue	Nervous Tissue	Muscle Tissue
FUNCTIONS	Protection, absorption, and excretion of materials	Binding of epithelial tissue to structures, support, and transport of substances	Receiving and transmitting nerve impulses	Voluntary and involuntary movements
LOCATIONS	Skin, lining of digestive system, certain glands	Under skin, surrounding organs, blood, bones	Brain, spinal cord, and nerves	Skeletal muscles, muscles surrounding digestive tract and blood vessels, the heart

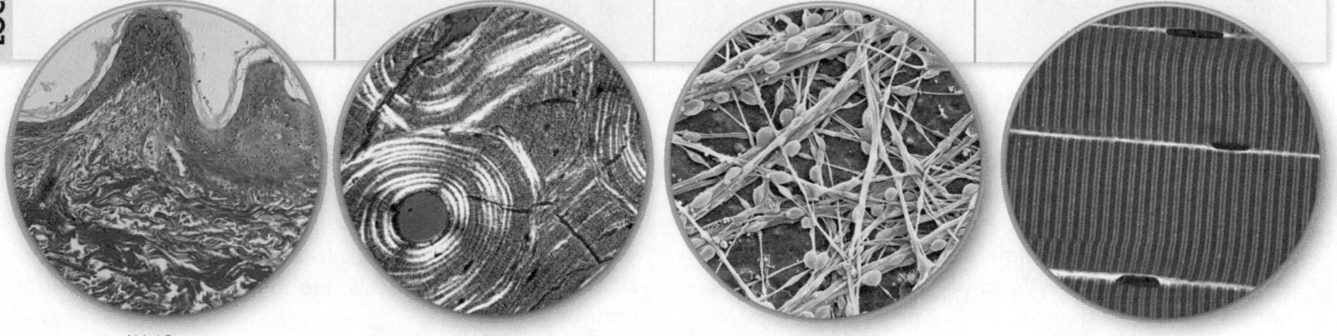

LM 65×   LM 280×   SEM 295×   LM 275×

▶ *Nervous Tissue* Nerve impulses are transmitted all over the body by **nervous tissue.** Neurons and glial cells are examples of nervous tissue. Neurons carry the nerve impulses, while glial cells surround and protect the neurons.

▶ *Muscle Tissue* Movements of the body are possible because of **muscle tissue.** Some muscles you can control, some you cannot control. For example, you can control the muscles in your arms and legs. But you cannot control the muscles in the pupils of your eyes.

Organs An organ is a group of different types of tissue that work together. An organ may perform a single function or a group of related functions. Your eye is an organ that has all four types of tissues. All four tissues work together to enable us to see.

Organ System A group of different organs that perform closely related functions is called an organ system. The brain and spinal cord are organs of the nervous system. The organ systems work together to keep the body stable. The organ systems are shown on the next page.

Key Question How is the human body organized?
The human body is organized into four levels: cells, tissues, organs, and organ systems.

HUMAN BODY SYSTEMS

Each organ system shown here has a different set of functions. However, they all work together to maintain homeostasis in the body.

In Your Workbook
Go to your workbook for an exercise about the functions of body systems.

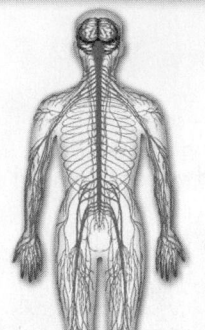 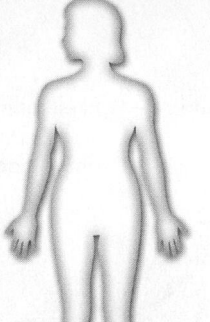 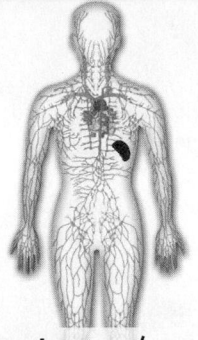 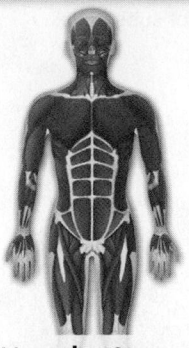 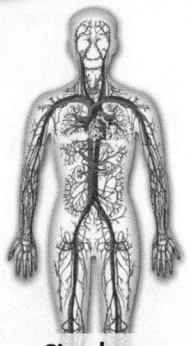 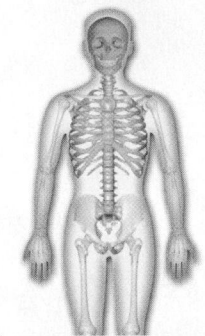

	Nervous System	Integumentary System	Immune/ Lymphatic Systems	Muscular System	Circulatory System	Skeletal System
STRUCTURES	Brain, spinal cord, nerves	Skin, hair, nails, sweat and oil glands	White blood cells, thymus, spleen, lymph nodes, lymph vessels	Skeletal muscle, smooth muscle, cardiac muscle	Heart, blood vessels, blood	Bones, cartilage, ligaments, tendons
FUNCTIONS	Recognizes and coordinates the body's response to changes in its internal and external environments	Guards against infection, injury, and ultraviolet radiation from the sun; helps to regulate body temperature	Helps protect the body from disease; collects fluid lost from blood vessels and returns it to the circulatory system	Works with skeletal system to produce voluntary movement; helps to circulate blood and move food through the digestive system	Transports oxygen, nutrients, and hormones to cells; fights infection; removes cell wastes; helps to regulate body temperature	Supports the body; protects internal organs; allows movement; stores mineral reserves; contains cells that produce blood cells

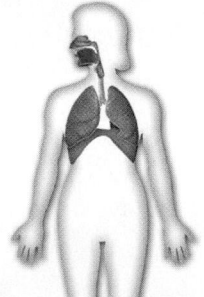 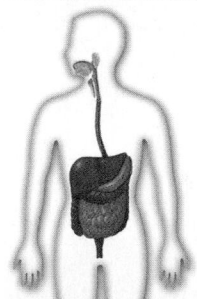 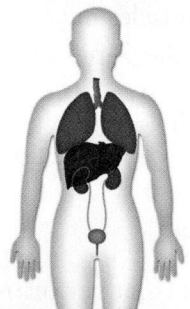 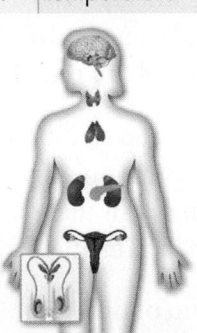 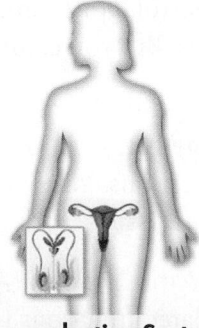

	Respiratory System	Digestive System	Excretory System	Endocrine System	Reproductive System
STRUCTURES	Nose, pharynx, larynx, trachea, bronchi, bronchioles, lungs	Mouth, pharynx, esophagus, stomach, small and large intestines, liver, pancreas, rectum	Skin, lungs, liver, kidneys, ureters, urinary bladder, urethra	Hypothalamus, pituitary, thyroid, parathyroids, adrenals, pancreas, ovaries (in females), testes (in males)	Testes, epididymis, vas deferens, urethra, and penis (in males); ovaries, Fallopian tubes, uterus, vagina (in females)
FUNCTIONS	Brings in oxygen needed for cellular respiration and removes excess carbon dioxide from the body	Breaks down food; absorbs nutrients; eliminates wastes	Eliminates waste products from the body	Controls growth, development, and metabolism; maintains homeostasis	Produces gametes; in females, nurtures and protects developing embryo

Homeostasis

Some things are easy to observe. When you run, swim, or even write, you can see your body at work. However, some things are not easy to see. Your body's systems work behind the scenes to keep your internal environment stable. This stable environment inside your body is called **homeostasis**. You cannot always see homeostasis, but to an organism it means life or death.

Feedback Inhibition Have you ever watched someone drive a car down a fairly straight road? Did you notice that the driver constantly moves the wheel left and right? Making small adjustments to the wheel helps keep the car in the middle of the road. Body systems also constantly make small adjustments. These adjustments keep your body's internal conditions within a certain range.

▶ *A Nonliving Example* One example of a system that automatically keeps conditions within a certain range is a home heating system. Many home heating systems use a furnace that burns oil or natural gas to provide heat. The system uses a device called a thermostat to monitor the home's air temperature. A sensor compares the air temperature to the one you set on the thermostat. When the air temperature is too cool, the thermostat turns the furnace on. Once the air temperature is warm enough, the thermostat turns the furnace off. The thermostat works to keep the air temperature within a narrow range.

The heating system is using a process called feedback inhibition to control the air temperature in the house. Your body uses **feedback inhibition** to stay in homeostasis. *Feedback* means "response." *Inhibit* means "to block." Feedback inhibition blocks the response to a stimulus. In the heating system, the warm air "feeds back" on the thermostat. The thermostat then "blocks" the release of more warm air by turning the furnace off.

▶ *The Body's Thermostat—A Living Example* One part of homeostasis is keeping your body temperature steady. Your body uses feedback inhibition to do this. The hypothalamus is the part of your brain that controls body temperature. The hypothalamus acts as your body's thermostat. Sensors in your body tell the hypothalamus when you are too cold or too hot.

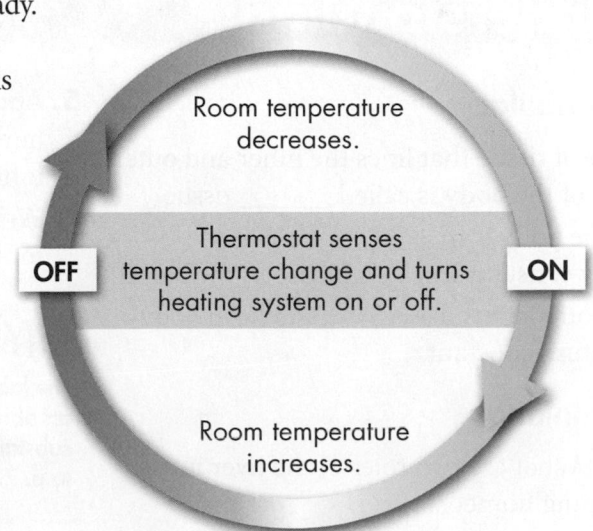

Feedback Inhibition
A home heating system uses feedback inhibition. This keeps the environment in the house stable and comfortable.

Room temperature decreases.

OFF

Thermostat senses temperature change and turns heating system on or off.

ON

Room temperature increases.

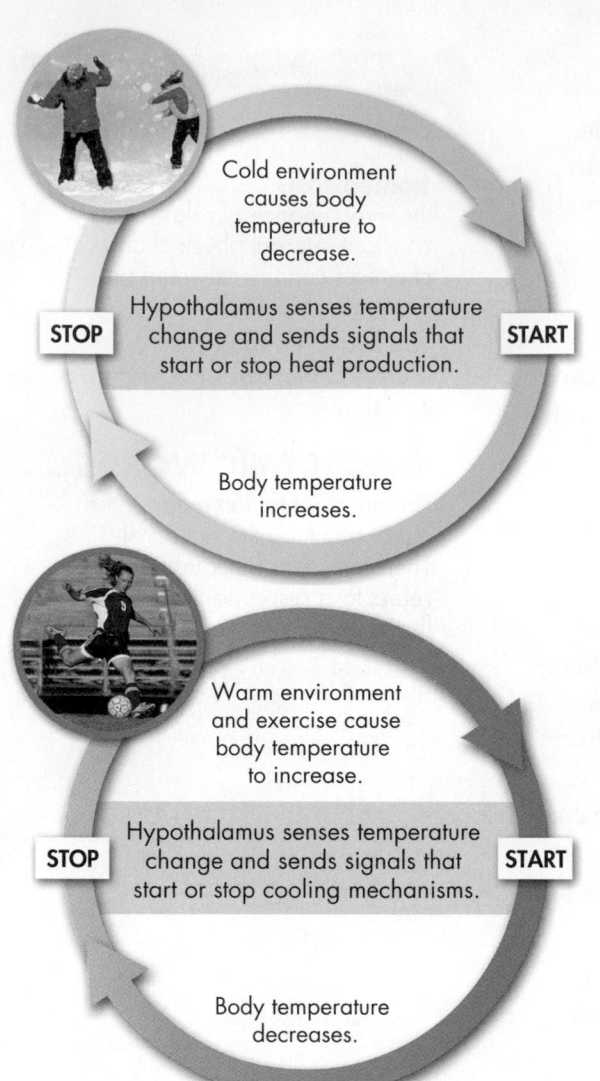

Cold environment causes body temperature to decrease.

Hypothalamus senses temperature change and sends signals that start or stop heat production.

STOP   **START**

Body temperature increases.

Warm environment and exercise cause body temperature to increase.

Hypothalamus senses temperature change and sends signals that start or stop cooling mechanisms.

STOP   **START**

Body temperature decreases.

Getting Warm and Staying Cool Your hypothalamus uses feedback inhibition to control your body's temperature.

If you are too cold, the hypothalamus tells cells to speed up their activities. The extra activity produces heat to warm your body. When you are warm enough, the hypothalamus tells the cells they can slow down again. If you are too hot, your hypothalamus tells your sweat glands to produce more sweat. The sweat evaporates, cooling your body surface. The hypothalamus also tells your cells to slow down to produce less heat. This is one reason you feel tired and slow on a hot day.

The Liver and Homeostasis The liver, a part of the digestive system, is important in homeostasis. The liver breaks down toxic chemicals in the blood such as ammonia and drugs. The liver converts ammonia to urea, which is less toxic.

Another function of the liver is to control the amount of glucose in the blood. When blood sugar rises, as it does after a meal, the liver removes extra glucose and stores it. High blood glucose levels can damage the eyes, kidneys, heart, and immune system. If levels in the blood fall too far, the nervous system slows down, and you may even pass out. The liver solves this problem by releasing stored sugar back into the blood. In this way, the liver keeps blood sugar from rising or falling beyond normal levels.

🔑 **Key Question** What is homeostasis?
Homeostasis is a state of relative balance in an organism's physical and chemical conditions. Homeostasis continues even when internal and external environments change.

CHECK Understanding

Apply Vocabulary

1. The type of tissue that lines the inner and outer surfaces of the body is called _____ tissue.

2. When the body is in _____, there is a relatively constant level of glucose in the blood.

3. The hypothalamus uses _____ to keep body temperature constant.

Critical Thinking

4. Explain What are two roles of the liver in maintaining homeostasis?

5. Apply Concepts Do you think that feelings of hunger and fullness are an example of feedback inhibition? Explain.

6. Write to Learn Answer the question in the clue to the mystery below.

MYSTERY CLUE

The lab test of Andrew's urine sample showed an abnormal amount of a certain substance. What substance do you think it was? (**Hint:** Look ahead to p. 731.)

BIOLOGY.com Search Lesson 30.1 GO • Lesson Assessment

30.2 Food and Nutrition

MD CLG 3.1.1 Chemical Substances and Macromolecules, 3.1.3 Matter and Energy, 3.2.2 Changes in Metabolic Activity. SPI 1.5.8 Compare, 1.5.9 Synthesize Ideas, 1.7.1 Apply Skills and Concepts.

Food and Energy

Have you ever wondered why you feel weak when you are hungry? Or, for that matter, why you need food in the first place? One answer is energy. You need energy to climb stairs, run, and even to think. Just as a car does, your body needs fuel, and it feels weak without it. Food is that fuel.

Energy The energy available in food can be measured in a laboratory. The way it is measured is surprisingly simple—the scientist burns it! When food is burned, most of the energy in the food is converted to heat. Heat is measured in calories. One calorie of heat raises the temperature of 1 gram of water by 1 degree Celsius. The "Calories" you have heard about in food are actually dietary Calories. Notice that a capital *C* is used. One dietary **Calorie** is equal to 1000 calories, or 1 kilocalorie (kcal). Remember that the energy stored in food molecules is released during cellular respiration. This energy is used to produce ATP molecules. ATP powers cellular activities.

Raw Materials Chemical pathways can get energy from almost any type of food. Why, then, does the type of food matter? Food supplies more than energy. It also supplies the raw materials used to build and repair body tissues. These raw materials are the building blocks needed to make molecules like enzymes and DNA. Food contains at least 45 substances that the body needs but cannot make. A healthy diet allows your body to get all of these required substances.

Key Question Why do we need to eat?
Molecules in food contain chemical energy. Cells use this energy to produce ATP. Food also supplies raw materials your body needs to build and repair tissues.

Food Supplies Raw Materials
Your body cannot make all of the raw materials it needs to build important molecules. Food contains at least 45 of the substances your body needs but cannot make.

Key Questions

- **Why do we need to eat?**
- **What nutrients does your body need?**
- **What is meant by the term "balanced diet"?**

BUILD Understanding

Two-Column Chart Use a two-column chart to take notes about main ideas and details. List the main ideas in the left column. In the right column, write details that explain the main ideas.

In Your Workbook Go to your workbook for help with using a two-column chart.

BUILD Vocabulary

Calorie
the measure of energy in food; 1 Calorie = 1000 calories, or 1 kilocalorie (kcal)

carbohydrate
A class of nutrients that are the main source of energy for the human body

ACADEMIC WORDS
The word *carbohydrate* means "carbon with water." Substances that are "hydrated" contain water. For each carbon atom, carbohydrates contain roughly one oxygen and two hydrogens, the same proportions found in water (H_2O).

fat
nutrient needed by the body for cell membranes, vitamin absorption, regulation, insulation, and energy

protein
a macromolecule that contains carbon, hydrogen, oxygen, and nitrogen; needed by the body for growth and repair

vitamin
an organic nutrient that the body needs in very small amounts

mineral
an inorganic nutrient the body needs in very small amounts

MULTIPLE MEANINGS
In biology, the word *minerals* refers only to inorganic elements like sodium and magnesium. In geology, minerals are the basic units of rocks, and can be elements or compounds.

Nutrients

Nutrients are substances in food that supply energy and raw materials. Your body needs the energy and raw materials for growth, repair, and maintenance. There are six main types of nutrients—water, carbohydrates, fats, proteins, vitamins, and minerals.

Water Every cell in the human body needs water, which is the most important nutrient. Body processes such as chemical reactions are carried out in water. Large amounts of water are found in blood, extracellular fluid, and other bodily fluids. Water is lost from the body in urine and in sweat. You also lose water with every breath you exhale.

Humans need to drink at least 1 liter of fluid each day. Dehydration can occur if the lost water is not replaced. Dehydration leads to problems with many body systems. Under extreme conditions it can be fatal.

Carbohydrates **Carbohydrates** are major sources of food energy for the body. Simple carbohydrates are either monosaccharides, like glucose, or disaccharides, like sucrose, ordinary table sugar. Complex carbohydrates are polysaccharides, like starch and glycogen. Your digestive system breaks down starches into simple sugars. Sugars are absorbed into the blood and carried to the body's cells. Excess blood sugar is converted into glycogen. Glycogen is stored in the liver and in skeletal muscles. Excess sugar can also be converted to fat and stored in the body.

Another complex carbohydrate is cellulose. Cellulose is often called fiber. Your digestive system cannot break down fiber, but you need it in your diet for bulk. Bulk helps muscles move food and waste through your digestive system. Fiber may also reduce the risk of heart disease and Type II diabetes.

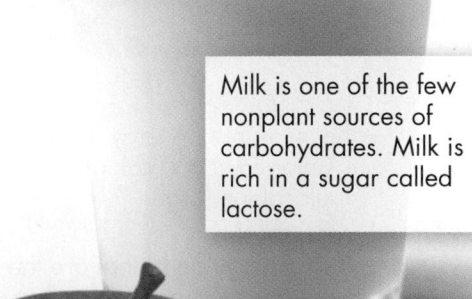

Milk is one of the few nonplant sources of carbohydrates. Milk is rich in a sugar called lactose.

Fruits, honey, and sugar cane contain sugars. Fruits are also rich in fiber.

Carbohydrates All of these foods are rich in carbohydrates. Pastas and cereals are also rich in carbohydrates. Simple carbohydrates do not have to be digested or broken down. Complex carbohydrates, like those found in whole grains, must be broken down before they can be used by the body.

Breads, grains, potatoes, and vegetables contain starch, a complex carbohydrate. Whole grains are also rich sources of fiber. Products made from whole grains have more fiber than products made from processed grains.

Fats Our bodies need fats, or lipids, as part of a healthy diet. **Fats** help the body absorb fat-soluble vitamins. Fats are found in cell membranes, nerve cells, and certain hormones. Body fat protects and insulates organs and stores energy.

Fats are made by combining glycerol molecules with fatty acids. Fats with only single bonds between carbons are called saturated. Unsaturated fats contain at least one double bond and fewer hydrogen atoms than saturated fats. Fats with more than one double bond are polyunsaturated. Trans fats are made by adding hydrogen atoms to unsaturated fats. Trans fats have been linked to health problems such as heart disease.

Proteins Proteins have many roles in the body. **Proteins** are used for growth and repair of tissues. Proteins called enzymes speed up chemical reactions in cells. Some proteins regulate different functions. Still others are transport molecules. Proteins can sometimes be used for energy.

Proteins are polymers of amino acids. The body is able to make 12 of the 20 amino acids used to make proteins. The other eight are essential amino acids. They must come from food. Animal sources usually provide all eight essential amino acids, but most plant foods do not.

Vitamins Organic molecules that the body needs in very small amounts are called **vitamins.** They help perform chemical reactions. Small amounts of the fat-soluble vitamins A, D, E, and K can be stored in body fat. The B vitamins and vitamin C are water-soluble. They dissolve in water and cannot be stored by the body. They must be included in the foods you eat each day.

A diet lacking in certain vitamins can cause serious health problems. Eating a variety of foods will meet the daily vitamin needs of most people.

Minerals **Minerals** are inorganic nutrients that the body needs, usually in small amounts. Calcium and iron are two examples of minerals needed by the body. Minerals are needed in the diet to replace those lost in sweat and bodily wastes.

🔑 **Key Question** What nutrients does your body need? **The body needs water, carbohydrates, fats, proteins, vitamins, and minerals.**

Essential Amino Acid Sources Meat, milk, eggs, and fish contain all eight essential amino acids. Most plant foods do not. However, eating a balanced variety of plant foods, such as corn, other grains, and beans, can provide each of the essential amino acids.

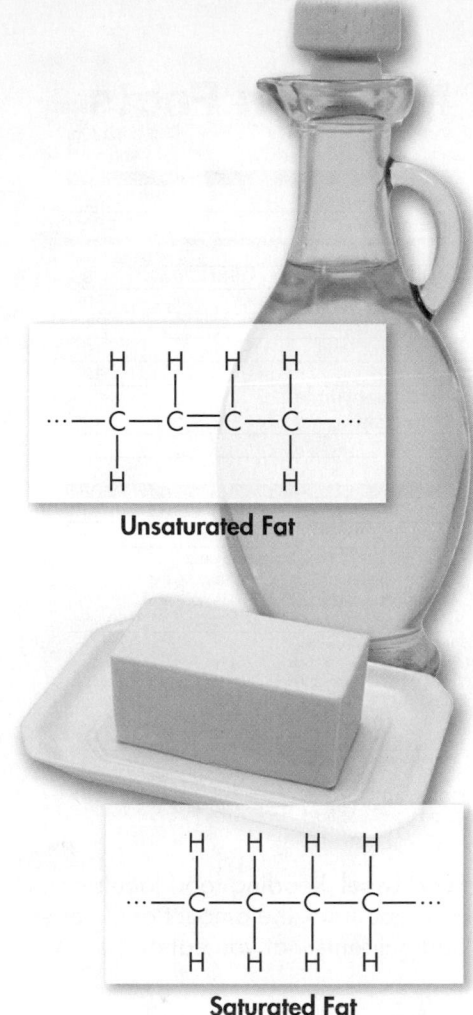

Unsaturated Fat

Saturated Fat

Fats Most saturated fats are solid at room temperature. Butter contains saturated fats. Most unsaturated fats are liquid at room temperature. Vegetable oils, like this olive oil, contain polyunsaturated fats.

Nutrition Facts

Serving Size	1 cup (30g)
Servings Per Container	About 10

Amount Per Serving

Calories 110	Calories from Fat 17

	% Daily Value*
Total Fat 2g	3%
Saturated Fat 0g	0%
Trans Fat 0.5g	
Cholesterol 0mg	0%
Sodium 280mg	12%
Total Carbohydrate 22g	7%
Dietary Fiber 3g	12%
Sugars 1g	
Protein 3g	

Vitamin A	10%	•	Vitamin C	20%
Calcium	4%	•	Iron	45%

* Percent Daily Values are based on a 2,000 Calorie diet. Your Daily Values may be higher or lower depending on your calorie needs:

		Calories	2,000	2,500
Total Fat	Less than		65g	80g
Sat. Fat	Less than		20g	25g
Cholesterol	Less than		300mg	300mg
Sodium	Less than		2,400mg	2,400mg
Total Carbohydrate			300g	375g
Fiber			25g	30g

Calories per gram:
Fat 9 • Carbohydrate 4 • Protein 4

Ingredients: Whole grain oats, sugar, salt, milled corn, oat fiber, dried whey, hon~~ey~~ almonds, ~~def~~

Food Label Reading food labels can help you track the amount of Calories and nutrients that you eat and drink.

Nutrition and a Balanced Diet

Nutrition is the study of food and its effects on the body. Nutrition tries to determine how food helps the body meet all its various needs. Nutritionists have developed many tools to help people plan healthful diets.

Balancing Your Diet How do you know which foods to eat for a balanced diet? Food labels can be used to choose healthful foods. You can use the labels to decide if you are consuming enough of some of the important vitamins and minerals. Nutrient needs are affected by age, gender, and lifestyle. People who are more active than average have greater energy needs. A person who stops growing or is less active has a lower need for energy.

Maintaining a Healthful Weight Exercising 30 minutes a day and eating a balanced diet helps maintain a healthful weight. Regular physical activity burns excess Calories and strengthens the heart, bones, and muscles.

Controlling fat intake is also important. Foods that contain high amounts of fat are high in Calories. Diets high in saturated and trans fats increase the risk of heart disease, Type II diabetes, or both.

Key Question What is meant by the term "balanced diet"? **A balanced diet provides the nutrients and energy needed for a person to maintain a healthful weight.**

CHECK Understanding

Apply Vocabulary
Use the highlighted words from the lesson to complete each sentence correctly.

1. The amount of energy in food is measured in _____.

2. _____ are the organic nutrients that are needed to help the body perform chemical reactions.

3. Monosaccharides, disaccharides, and cellulose are all types of _____.

Critical Thinking

4. **Infer** Foods that contain many Calories but few raw materials are said to contain empty Calories. What do you think the term *empty Calories* means?

5. **Compare and Contrast** Saturated and unsaturated fats both are made of glycerol and fatty acids. How is a saturated fat different from unsaturated fat?

6. **Write to Learn** Answer the second clue of the mystery. Why do you think the color of the urine led the doctor to his diagnosis?

MYSTERY CLUE

Philip's and Seth's samples were both a very dark yellow. Neither boy drank water before or during practice. Why do you think they were sent home from practice? **(Hint:** See p. 720.)

BIOLOGY.com › Search (Lesson 30.2) **GO** • Lesson Assessment

30.3 The Digestive System

MD CLG 3.1.3 Matter and Energy, 3.2.1 Processes and Functions, 3.2.2 Changes in Metabolic Activity.
SPI 1.5.8 Compare, 1.5.9 Synthesize Ideas.

Functions of the Digestive System

When you are hungry, your whole body needs food. But the only system in the body that food actually enters is the digestive system. How does food get to the rest of the body after you digest it? The digestive system's job is to convert the food into useful molecules. Digestion happens in four phases—ingestion, digestion, absorption, and elimination.

Ingestion The first phase in digestion is getting food into the system. Your mouth is the opening of the digestive tract. The process of putting food into your mouth is called *ingestion*.

Digestion As food passes through the digestive tract, it is broken down in two ways—by mechanical digestion and chemical digestion. Mechanical digestion is the physical breakdown of large pieces of food into smaller pieces. These smaller pieces can be swallowed and accessed by digestive enzymes. Chemical digestion is the chemical breakdown of food into smaller pieces. During chemical digestion, enzymes break down food into small molecules that the body can use.

Absorption Once food has been broken into small molecules, it can be absorbed by the small intestine. During absorption, molecules enter the circulatory system from the digestive tract. The circulatory system carries food molecules throughout the body.

Elimination The digestive system cannot digest and absorb all the food that enters your body. Substances that cannot be absorbed travel through the large intestine and are eliminated from the body as feces. Cellulose is one example of a material your body cannot digest.

Key Question What are the functions of the digestive system?
The digestive system breaks down food into molecules the body can use in its cells. Food is processed in four phases—ingestion, digestion, absorption, and elimination.

Key Questions

What are the functions of the digestive system?

What occurs during digestion?

How are nutrients absorbed and wastes eliminated?

BUILD Understanding

Flowchart Make a flowchart that shows the steps in the process of digestion.
In Your Workbook Refer to your workbook for suggestions about how to use a flowchart to organize your notes.

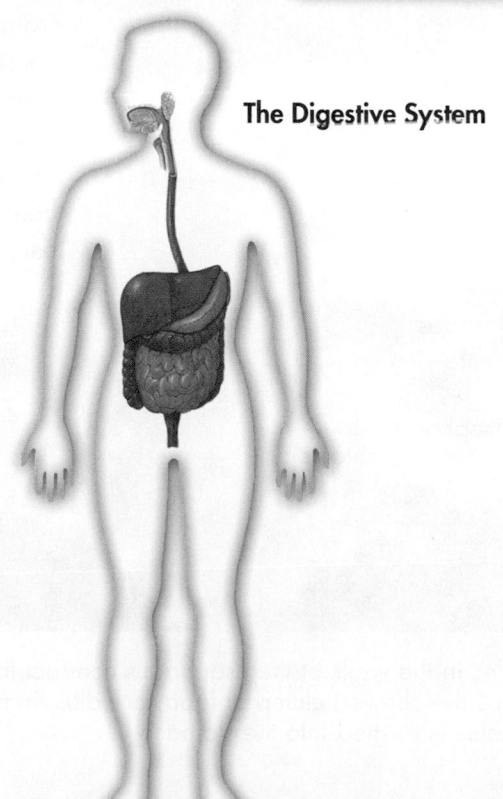

The Digestive System

The Mouth Digestion begins in the mouth. The tongue, teeth, and saliva form food into a moist lump that can be swallowed.

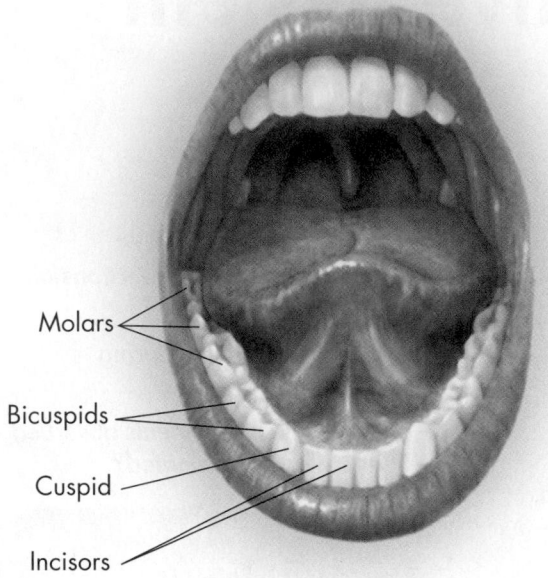

Molars

Bicuspids

Cuspid

Incisors

The Process of Digestion

The human digestive system is built around an alimentary canal. An alimentary canal is a one-way tube that passes all the way through the body. The entrance to this tube is the mouth.

Digestion Starts in the Mouth Once food enters your mouth, your teeth begin mechanical digestion. The incisors, cuspids, and bicuspids cut and tear the food. Then the molars grind the food into a paste that you can swallow. Your tongue moves the food around so that all of it can be chewed. While you are chewing, glands in your mouth release *saliva*. Saliva moistens the food and makes it easier to chew.

Saliva contains an enzyme called **amylase** that begins chemical digestion by breaking chemical bonds in starches to release sugars. Another enzyme, called lysozyme, fights infection. Lysozyme digests the cell walls of many bacteria that may enter the mouth with food.

Once food is chewed it moves into the pharynx, which is the back of the throat. As you swallow, a flap of tissue called the epiglottis closes over the opening to the trachea to keep food out. The trachea is the tube that leads from the pharynx to the lungs.

The Esophagus The food paste forms into a clump as it is swallowed. This clump, called a bolus, enters the **esophagus** from the pharynx. The esophagus is a muscular tube that connects the pharynx to the stomach. Muscle contractions push the bolus down the esophagus into the stomach. This process, called **peristalsis,** is shown below. A ring of muscle called the cardiac sphincter closes the esophagus after the bolus enters the stomach. This prevents food from moving back into the esophagus.

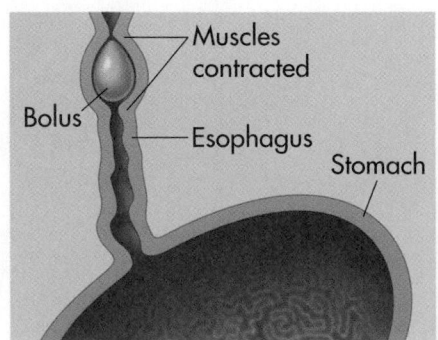
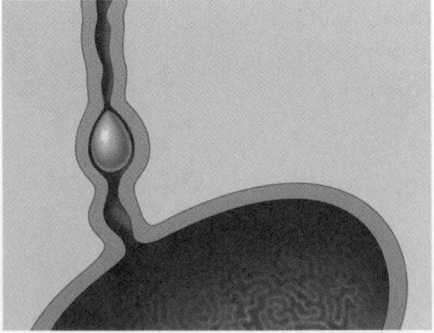
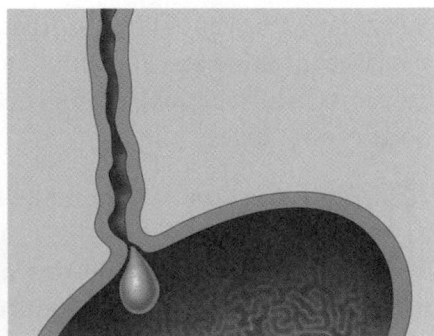

Muscles contracted

Bolus

Esophagus

Stomach

Peristalsis Muscles in the walls of the esophagus contract in waves. Each wave pushes the chewed clump of food, or bolus, in front of it. Eventually, the bolus is pushed into the stomach.

Digestion in the Stomach Chemical and mechanical digestion continues in the **stomach.** Tiny glands in the stomach lining release hydrochloric acid, **pepsin,** and mucus. Pepsin is an enzyme that breaks down proteins into smaller pieces, and works best in acidic conditions. Mucus is a fluid that protects the stomach lining from the acid and lubricates the food. Smooth muscle layers in the stomach contract to mix the food with the hydrochloric acid and pepsin. The mixture that leaves the stomach is called chyme.

Digestion in the Small Intestine Chyme enters the upper part of the **small intestine** through the pyloric valve. This area of the small intestine is called the duodenum (doo oh DEE num), and is where most of the digestion and absorption of food occurs. The chyme mixes with enzymes and digestive fluids from the pancreas, liver, and the lining of the duodenum.

▶ *Pancreas* The pancreas is a small gland located behind the stomach. The pancreas produces enzymes, sodium bicarbonate, and hormones. The enzymes break down carbohydrates, proteins, lipids, and nucleic acids in the small intestine. Sodium bicarbonate neutralizes the acid in the chyme, protecting the small intestine's lining. It also gives the enzymes the right conditions to work. The hormones, as part of the endocrine system, regulate blood sugar levels.

▶ *The Liver and Gallbladder* The liver helps the pancreatic enzymes with fat digestion. The liver produces bile, a fluid loaded with lipids and salts. Bile is stored in the gallbladder until fat enters the duodenum. Fats glob together, making it hard for enzymes to digest them. Bile breaks the fat globs into smaller droplets. This makes it easier for enzymes to digest the fat.

🔑 **Key Question** What occurs during digestion? **During digestion, food travels through the mouth, esophagus, stomach, and small intestine. Mechanical digestion and chemical digestion break food down into molecules that can be absorbed.**

Effects of Digestive Enzymes
Digestive enzymes speed up the breakdown of foods. This makes nutrients from the foods available to the body.

Effects of Digestive Enzymes

Active Site	Enzyme	Effect on Food
Mouth	Salivary amylase	Breaks down starches into disaccharides
Stomach	Pepsin	Breaks down proteins into large peptides
Small intestine (released from pancreas)	Pancreatic amylase	Continues the breakdown of starch
	Trypsin	Continues the breakdown of protein
	Lipase	Breaks down fat
Small intestine	Maltase, sucrase, lactase	Breaks down remaining disaccharides into monosaccharides
	Peptidase	Breaks down dipeptides into amino acids

THE DIGESTIVE SYSTEM

Food travels through many organs as it is broken down into nutrients your body can use. The time needed for each organ to perform its role varies based on the type of food consumed.

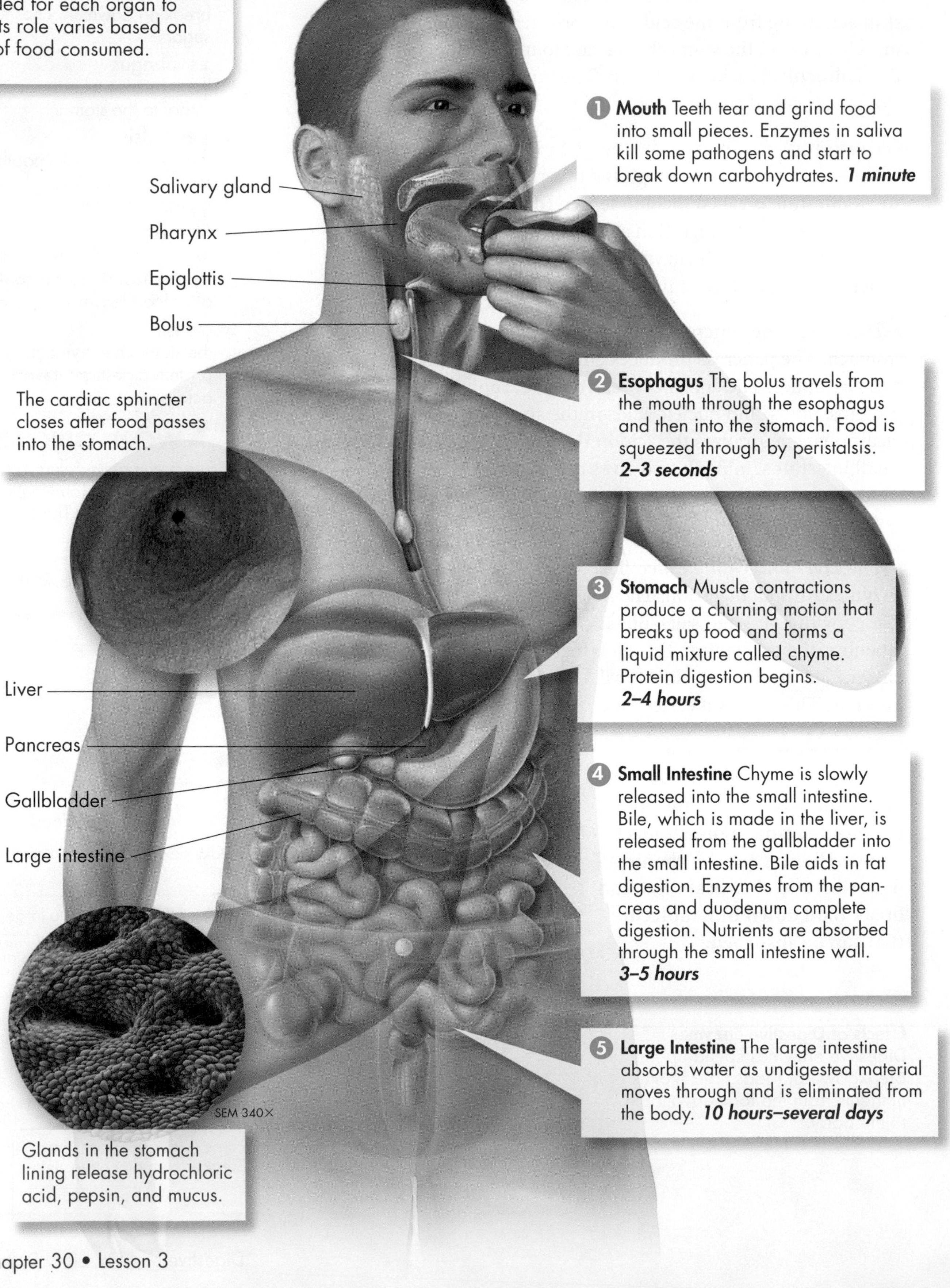

Salivary gland

Pharynx

Epiglottis

Bolus

The cardiac sphincter closes after food passes into the stomach.

Liver

Pancreas

Gallbladder

Large intestine

SEM 340×

Glands in the stomach lining release hydrochloric acid, pepsin, and mucus.

1 Mouth Teeth tear and grind food into small pieces. Enzymes in saliva kill some pathogens and start to break down carbohydrates. *1 minute*

2 Esophagus The bolus travels from the mouth through the esophagus and then into the stomach. Food is squeezed through by peristalsis. *2–3 seconds*

3 Stomach Muscle contractions produce a churning motion that breaks up food and forms a liquid mixture called chyme. Protein digestion begins. *2–4 hours*

4 Small Intestine Chyme is slowly released into the small intestine. Bile, which is made in the liver, is released from the gallbladder into the small intestine. Bile aids in fat digestion. Enzymes from the pancreas and duodenum complete digestion. Nutrients are absorbed through the small intestine wall. *3–5 hours*

5 Large Intestine The large intestine absorbs water as undigested material moves through and is eliminated from the body. *10 hours–several days*

Absorption and Elimination

Once digestion is finished in the small intestine, nutrients need to be absorbed from the alimentary canal. Absorption occurs in the intestines.

Absorption From the Small Intestine Muscles in the walls of the small intestine contract in waves. These contractions move the chyme down the intestine. By this time, most of the chemical digestion is complete. The chyme is now made of small and medium molecules that can be absorbed.

The structure of the small intestine is specialized for absorption of nutrients. The folded surface of the small intestine is covered in small structures called **villi** (singular *villus*). The villi are covered in tiny microvilli that absorb nutrients from the chyme. Most of the carbohydrates and proteins are absorbed into the capillaries in the villi. Most fats and fatty acids are absorbed by lymph vessels.

Chyme has almost no nutrients by the time it is ready to leave the small intestine. Complex food molecules have been digested and absorbed. The chyme now contains water, cellulose, and undigestable substances.

Absorption in the Small Intestine The lining of the small intestine consists of many folds. These folds are covered with tiny finger-like structures called villi. Each villus is covered in microvilli that absorb nutrients. Blood capillaries and lymph vessels in the villus carry the nutrients away from the villus.

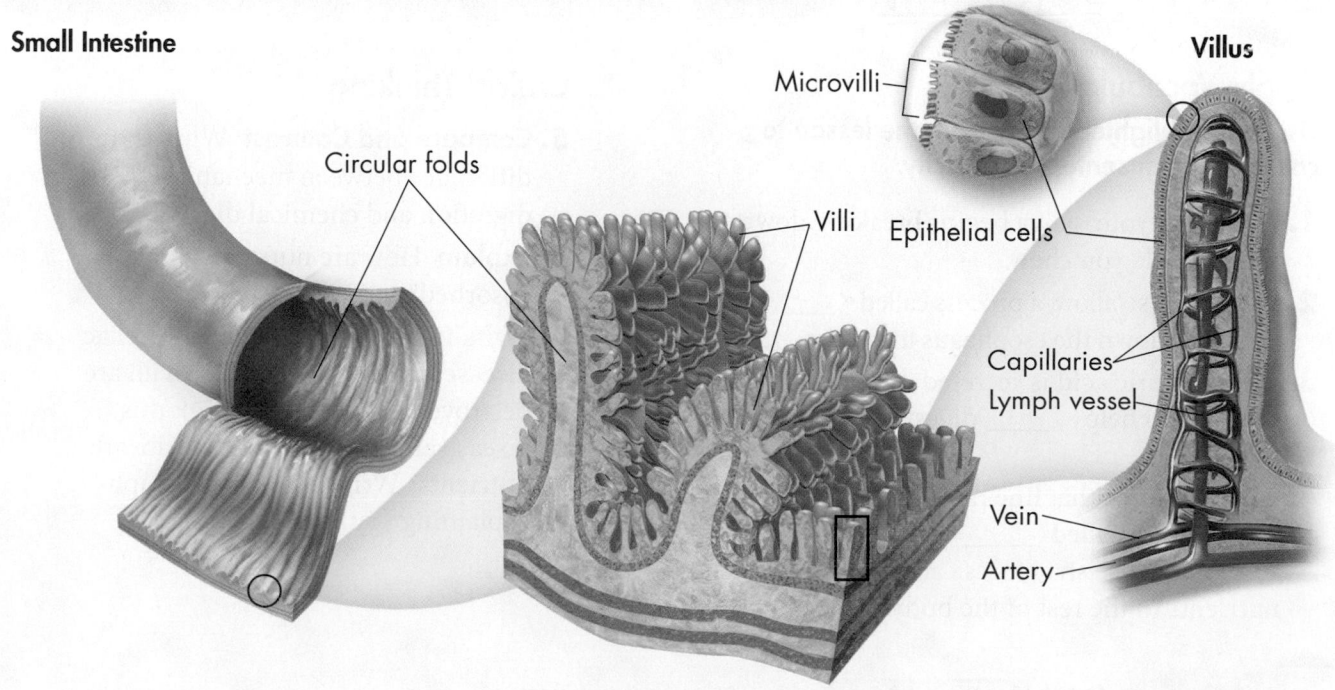

Small Intestine

Circular folds

Villi

Microvilli

Epithelial cells

Villus

Capillaries

Lymph vessel

Vein

Artery

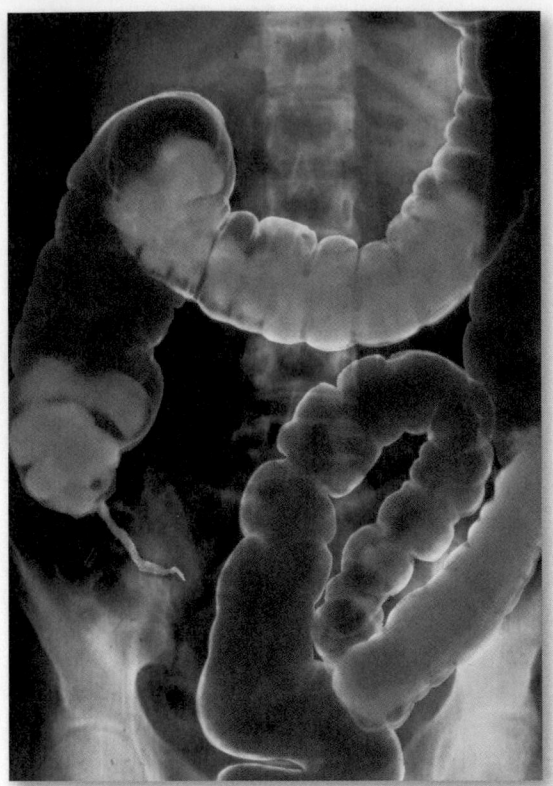

The Large Intestine This X-ray shows the large intestine and its contents.

Absorption from the Large Intestine Most nutrients have already been absorbed from the chyme before it enters the **large intestine.** The large intestine's job is to remove water from the chyme. The water is absorbed quickly, leaving the undigested material behind. Rich colonies of bacteria in the large intestine feed on this material. They produce compounds the body can use, such as vitamin K. Taking large doses of antibiotics for an infection can destroy these bacteria. When this happens, the body may not get enough vitamin K.

Elimination The waste material left after all of the water is absorbed is called feces. The feces move into the rectum and are eliminated from the body through the anus. If something happens to stop the large intestine from absorbing enough water, a condition called diarrhea occurs. If too much water is absorbed, a condition called constipation occurs.

Key Question How are nutrients absorbed and wastes eliminated?
Most nutrients are absorbed through the walls of the small intestine. The large intestine absorbs water and some vitamins, and prepares waste for elimination.

CHECK Understanding

Apply Vocabulary
Use the highlighted terms from the lesson to complete each sentence correctly.

1. _____ in your saliva begins breaking down starch while you chew.

2. When you swallow, a process called _____ moves the bolus down the esophagus to your stomach.

3. Hydrochloric acid is secreted into the stomach to help _____ digest proteins by lowering the pH.

4. The structures that line the folds in the small intestine are called _____. Blood and lymph vessels in these structures carry absorbed nutrients to the rest of the body.

Critical Thinking

5. Compare and Contrast What is the difference between mechanical digestion and chemical digestion?

6. Explain How are nutrients absorbed?

7. Write to Learn In people with celiac disease, many villi and microvilli are destroyed. How do you think this disease affects their ability to absorb nutrients? Write a short paragraph explaining your answer.

30.4 The Excretory System

MD CLG 3.1.1 Chemical Substances and Macromolecules, 3.1.2 Homeostasis, 3.2.1 Processes and Functions, 3.2.2 Changes in Metabolic Activity. SPI 1.4.2 Analyze Data, 1.5.5 Create and Interpret Graphics, 1.6.1 Ratio and Proportion, 1.7.1 Apply Skills and Concepts.

Structures of the Excretory System

Every living thing produces chemical waste products. Some waste products are so toxic that they will cause death unless they are eliminated. The process of removing wastes to maintain homeostasis is called **excretion.**

The Skin The skin excretes excess water, salts, and a small amount of urea in sweat. Your skin is always releasing very small amounts of sweat.

The Lungs Carbon dioxide is a waste product of cellular respiration. Your blood transports carbon dioxide from your cells to your lungs. When you exhale, you excrete carbon dioxide and small amounts of water vapor.

The Liver The liver's job in the excretory system is to convert toxic ammonia into urea. The ammonia is produced when protein is broken down in the cells. Blood transports the urea to the kidneys where it can be eliminated from the body.

The Kidneys The major organs of excretion are the kidneys. The kidneys are a pair of fist-sized organs located on either side of the spinal column. The kidneys filter excess water, urea, and other wastes from the blood. The kidneys excrete these wastes as urine.

🔑 **Key Question** What is the main role of the structures of the excretory system?
The excretory system includes the skin, lungs, liver, and kidneys. The system excretes wastes from chemical processes in the body.

Excretion and the Kidneys

Nearly a million individual units process the blood in each kidney. These units are called **nephrons.** Each nephron filters out impurities and collects wastes, then sends the clean blood back into circulation. Blood is purified through two processes—filtration and reabsorption.

Key Questions

🔑 **What is the main role of the structures of the excretory system?**

🔑 **How do the kidneys clean the blood?**

🔑 **How do the kidneys help maintain homeostasis?**

BUILD Understanding

Preview Visuals Examine the visuals in this lesson. Think of questions to ask about the visuals.

In Your Workbook Refer to your workbook to help answer your questions.

BUILD Vocabulary

excretion
the process by which metabolic wastes are eliminated from the body

nephron
an individual unit in the kidney that processes wastes

🔖 **WORD ORIGINS**

The word *glomerulus* comes from the Latin word *glomus*, which means "ball of yarn." The twisted capillaries of a glomerulus resemble a ball of yarn.

BUILD Connections

STRUCTURE AND FUNCTION OF THE KIDNEYS

Kidneys are made up of nephrons. Blood enters the nephrons, where impurities are filtered out and emptied into the collecting duct. Purified blood leaves nephrons through a vein.

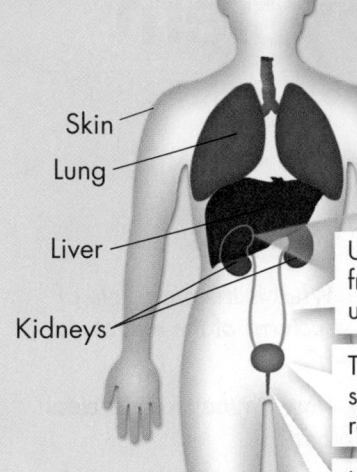

Skin
Lung
Liver
Kidneys

Ureters transport urine from each kidney to the urinary bladder.

The urinary bladder stores urine until it is released from the body.

Urine is released through a tube called the urethra.

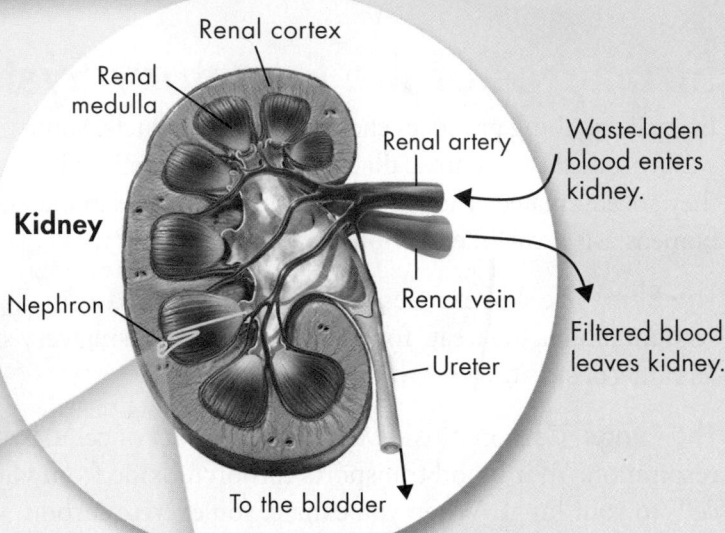

Kidney

Renal cortex
Renal medulla
Renal artery
Renal vein
Nephron
Ureter
Waste-laden blood enters kidney.
Filtered blood leaves kidney.
To the bladder

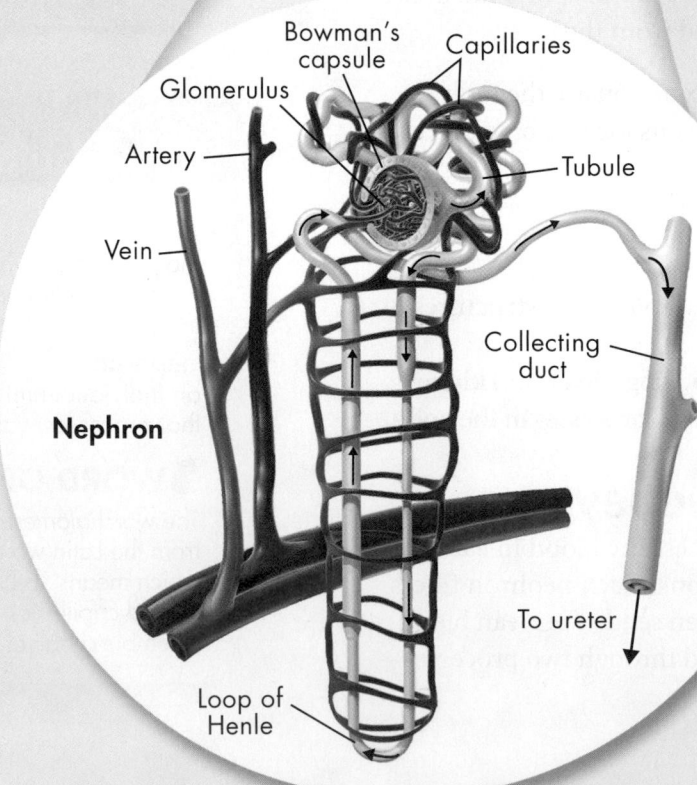

Nephron

Bowman's capsule
Capillaries
Glomerulus
Artery
Vein
Tubule
Collecting duct
Loop of Henle
To ureter

❶ Filtration Blood enters a nephron through a capillary. From the glomerulus, the filtrate flows into a tubule. Blood cells and large substances remain in the capillary.

❷ Reabsorption As the filtrate moves through the tubule, water and many other substances that are important to the body are reabsorbed through capillary walls into the blood.

❸ Urine Excretion Once water and other important substances are reclaimed by the blood, the filtrate is called urine. Collecting ducts gather urine and transport it to a ureter.

Filtration The process of passing a gas or liquid through a filter is called **filtration.** Blood filtration takes place mainly in the **glomerulus** (gloh MUR yoo lus). A glomerulus is a very small, dense network of capillaries. The glomerulus is enclosed in a hollow, cup-shaped structure called Bowman's capsule in the nephron.

Blood is under pressure. This pressure helps fluid from the blood move easily through the walls of the capillaries and into Bowman's capsule. This fluid in the Bowman's capsule, called the filtrate, contains water, urea, glucose, salts, amino acids, and some vitamins. Large substances like proteins and blood cells are too large to move through the capillary walls.

Reabsorption The filtrate contains some waste materials, but most of the filtrate is not waste and must be returned to the blood. Most of the filtrate is returned to the blood through **reabsorption.** Salts, vitamins, amino acids, fats, and glucose are removed from the filtrate by active transport. Water follows these substances into the blood through osmosis.

Almost 99 percent of the water that was filtered out of the blood is reabsorbed in the **loop of Henle.** The loop of Henle is responsible for conserving water and minimizing the amount of filtrate. The filtrate remaining in the tubule is called urine and empties into a collecting duct.

Urine Excretion Urine flows from collecting ducts to the **ureter** of each kidney. The ureters carry urine to the **urinary bladder** for storage. Urine leaves the body through the **urethra.**

🔑 **Key Question** How do the kidneys clean the blood?
The kidneys filter the blood to remove urea, excess water and minerals, and other wastes.

The Kidneys and Homeostasis

The kidneys play an important role in homeostasis. Besides removing wastes, they maintain blood pH and regulate water content.

Control of Kidney Function Kidney function is controlled mainly by the blood's composition. If you have too much salt in your blood, your kidneys will excrete the excess. They will also excrete excess glucose. Glucose in the urine is a sign of diabetes.

Hormones also control kidney function. Your pituitary gland releases antidiuretic hormone (ADH) into your blood when you lose too much water. ADH tells the kidneys to reabsorb more water and excrete less in the urine. When blood has too much water, ADH secretion stops.

Urine Testing Urine tells a lot about your health. The color tells how hydrated you are. If urine is pale yellow, you are well hydrated. Darker urine means that the blood has too little water and your kidneys are conserving water. Protein or glucose in urine can be a sign of high blood pressure or diabetes. Since drugs, including steroids and illegal drugs, usually are not reabsorbed by the kidneys, they end up in the urine.

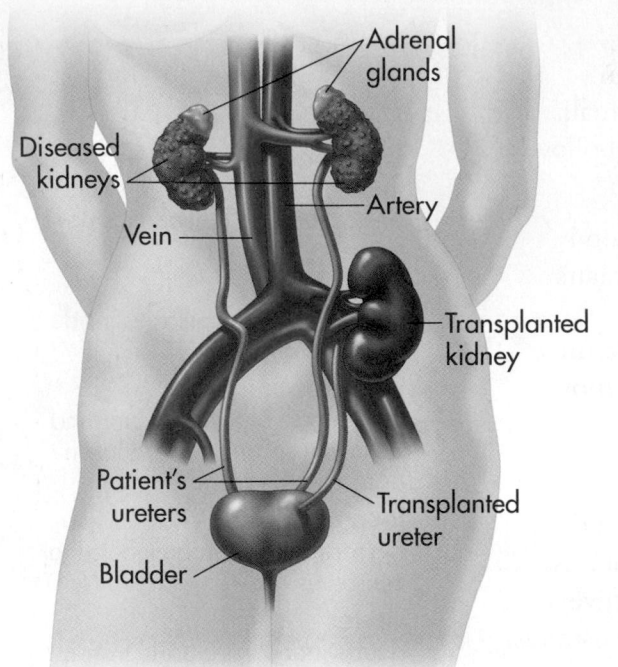

Diseased kidneys · Adrenal glands · Artery · Vein · Transplanted kidney · Patient's ureters · Transplanted ureter · Bladder

Kidney Transplantation A healthy kidney and ureter are transplanted from a donor. Diseased kidneys are left in place unless they are infected or causing high blood pressure.

Kidney Disorders If anything goes wrong with the kidneys, serious health problems will probably occur. Three of these problems are kidney stones, kidney damage, and kidney failure.

▶ **Kidney Stones** Sometimes minerals or uric acid salts in the urine form crystals. These crystals can grow into kidney stones. If the stones block a ureter, they cause great pain. Kidney stones can be broken into smaller pieces with sound waves. The pieces are then eliminated in the urine.

▶ **Kidney Damage** Many diseases, injuries, and dangerous substances can cause kidneys to function poorly. High blood pressure and diabetes are two of the leading causes of kidney damage in the United States.

▶ **Kidney Failure** Kidney failure occurs when the kidneys can no longer clean the blood and maintain homeostasis. Patients in kidney failure must have either dialysis or a kidney transplant. During dialysis, the blood is pumped through a machine that filters it. Dialysis is not painful. Dialysis patients must control their fluid intake and diet. In a kidney transplant, a person receives a kidney and ureter from a donor. The donor and the patient must have similar body chemistries. A person can survive with only one kidney.

Key Question How do the kidneys help maintain homeostasis?
The kidneys respond directly to blood composition and to hormones. Disruption of kidney function can lead to serious health problems.

CHECK Understanding

Apply Vocabulary

Use the highlighted terms from the lesson to complete each sentence correctly.

1. The individual unit in the kidney where filtration and reabsorption takes place is called the _____.

2. The _____ is a tightly wound network of blood vessels that filters the blood.

3. Water reabsorption takes place in the _____.

Critical Thinking

4. **Interpret Visual** Refer back to the figure on page 730. List in order the structures that blood flows through in a kidney.

5. **Apply Concepts** Why do you think protein in the urine is a sign of kidney damage?

6. **Write to Learn** Answer the third clue of the mystery. What characteristics of the urine samples led you to your conclusion about ADH levels?

MYSTERY CLUE

Would Seth's and Philip's blood contain a high level or low level of ADH? (Hint: See p. 731.)

The Composition of Urine

The kidneys are selective filters. They remove urea, other impurities, and excess salts as blood passes through them. However, important substances such as water, protein and glucose stay in the blood. The collected waste products are excreted in urine. The table shows how the amounts of several important substances differ between the blood and the urine.

Study the data in the table. Notice that only glucose is lower in urine than in blood. All other substances have a higher concentration in the urine than in the blood.

How can you determine how much greater the concentration of a substance is in the urine than in the blood? You can compare the two amounts for a substance by using a ratio. Look at the calculation for potassium:

We want to know how much greater the amount of potassium is in the urine, so we will write our ratio as

$$\frac{\text{Concentration of potassium in urine}}{\text{Concentration of potassium in blood}} = \frac{0.20}{0.02}$$

To find out how many times more concentrated the potassium is in urine than in the blood, simplify the fraction:

$$\frac{0.20}{0.02} = \frac{10}{1}$$

For potassium, the fraction simplifies to 10/1. This means that potassium is ten times more concentrated in the urine than in the blood.

Analyze and Conclude

1. Interpret Data

- Which substance has the highest concentration in the blood?

- Which substance has the lowest concentration in the blood?

- Which substance has the highest concentration in the urine?

- Which substance has the lowest concentration in the urine?

Concentrations of Selected Substances in Blood and Urine		
Substance	Average Concentration in Blood (g/mL)	Average Concentration in Urine (g/mL)
Calcium	0.01	0.02
Glucose	0.10	0.00
Potassium	0.02	0.20
Sodium	0.32	0.60
Urea	0.03	2.00

2. Calculate What is the ratio of urea in urine to urea in blood?

$$\frac{\text{Concentration of urea in urine}}{\text{Concentration of urea in blood}} = \frac{\quad}{\quad} = \frac{\quad}{1}$$

3. Predict Remember that urea is produced from ammonia, which is more toxic. Ammonia is produced when cells break down amino acids. Suppose someone eats a diet that is higher in protein than the person's usual diet. What do you think would happen to the urea concentrations in this person's blood and urine?

a. Urea increases in the blood and increases in the urine.

b. Urea increases in the blood and decreases in the urine.

c. Urea decreases in the blood and increases in the urine.

d. Urea decreases in the blood and decreases in the urine.

In Your Workbook Get help for this activity in your workbook.

Real-World Lab

MD CLG 3.1.1 Chemical Substances and Macromolecules. SPI 1.2.7 Apply Results, 1.3.1 Use Equipment, 1.3.3 Safe Handling of Materials, 1.4.1 Organize Data, 1.5.9 Synthesize Ideas.

Pre-Lab: Digestion of Dairy Products

Problem How can an enzyme deficiency affect digestion?

Materials spot plate, sheet of paper, glucose solution, milk, milk-digestion aid, toothpicks, glucose test strips, timer or clock

Lab Manual Chapter 30 Lab

Skills Focus Control Variables, Infer, Draw Conclusions

Connect to the **Big idea** Food is both a source of raw materials and a source of energy for your body. First the food must pass through your digestive system, where mechanical and chemical processes break the food down into smaller molecules. Enzymes play an essential role in chemical digestion. Different enzymes are needed to digest proteins, fats, and carbohydrates. In this lab, you will explore the role of enzymes in the digestion of milk and other dairy products.

Background Questions

a. Review What is an enzyme? Why are enzymes necessary for maintaining homeostasis?

b. Review Where do most digestive enzymes enter the digestive system?

c. Compare and Contrast Use glucose and sucrose to explain the difference between a monosaccharide and a disaccharide.

Pre-Lab Questions

Preview the procedure in the lab manual.

1. Design an Experiment What is the purpose of the glucose solution?

2. Control Variables What is the control in this lab?

3. Communicate Read the instructions on the package of glucose test strips. Then, briefly describe how you will test your samples for the presence of glucose.

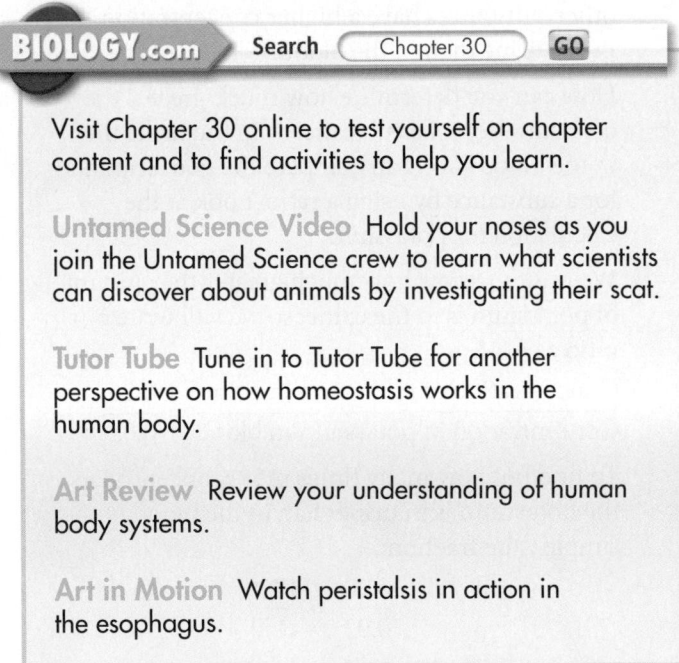

BIOLOGY.com Search ⟨ Chapter 30 ⟩ GO

Visit Chapter 30 online to test yourself on chapter content and to find activities to help you learn.

Untamed Science Video Hold your noses as you join the Untamed Science crew to learn what scientists can discover about animals by investigating their scat.

Tutor Tube Tune in to Tutor Tube for another perspective on how homeostasis works in the human body.

Art Review Review your understanding of human body systems.

Art in Motion Watch peristalsis in action in the esophagus.

30 CHAPTER Summary

30.1 Organization of the Human Body

- The human body is organized into four levels: cells, tissues, organs, and organ systems.

- Homeostasis is a state of relative balance in an organism's physical and chemical conditions. Homeostasis continues even when internal and external environments change.

epithelial tissue (p. 714)	homeostasis (p. 717)
connective tissue (p. 714)	feedback
nervous tissue (p. 715)	inhibition (p. 717)
muscle tissue (p. 715)	

30.2 Food and Nutrition

- Molecules in food contain chemical energy. Your cells use this chemical energy to produce ATP. Food also supplies raw materials your body needs to build and repair tissues.

- The body needs water, carbohydrates, fats, proteins, vitamins, and minerals.

- A balanced diet provides the nutrients a person needs to maintain a healthful weight.

Calorie (p. 719)	protein (p. 721)
carbohydrate (p. 720)	vitamin (p. 721)
fat (p. 721)	mineral (p. 721)

30.3 The Digestive System

- The digestive system breaks down food into molecules the body can use in its cells. Food is processed in four phases—ingestion, digestion, absorption, and elimination.

- During digestion, food travels through the esophagus, stomach, and small intestine. Mechanical digestion and chemical digestion break food down into molecules that can be absorbed.

- The small intestine absorbs most of the nutrients released during chemical digestion. The large intestine absorbs water and some vitamins, and prepares wastes for eliminaion.

amylase (p. 724)	pepsin (p. 725)
esophagus (p. 724)	small intestine (p. 725)
peristalsis (p. 724)	villus (p. 727)
stomach (p. 725)	large intestine (p. 728)

30.4 The Excretory System

- The excretory system includes the skin, lungs, liver, and kidneys. This system excretes the wastes from chemical processes in the body.

- The kidneys filter the blood to remove urea, excess water and minerals, and other wastes.

- The composition of the blood helps determine what the kidneys remove during filtration. Hormones also tell the kidneys what substances to remove or keep. If the kidneys do not function properly, serious health problems can occur.

excretion (p. 729)	loop of Henle (p. 731)
nephron (p. 729)	ureter (p. 731)
filtration (p. 731)	urinary bladder (p. 731)
glomerulus (p. 731)	urethra (p. 731)
reabsorption (p. 731)	

Assess the Big idea ▶ Homeostasis

Write an answer to the question below.

Q: How are the materials that enter and leave your body related to the processes that maintain homeostasis?

Constructed Response

Write an answer to each of the numbered questions below. The answer to each question should be one or two paragraphs. To help you begin, read the **Hints** below the questions.

1. **How do the digestive and excretory systems work together to help the body maintain homeostasis?**

   Hint The digestive system absorbs nutrients needed to keep the body's cells healthy.

   Hint The excretory system removes wastes and regulates the body's water levels.

2. **Why is mechanical digestion important?**

   Hint Mechanical digestion breaks food into smaller particles.

   Hint Mechanical digestion mixes food with digestive juices.

3. **How could a failure to respond to ADH be dangerous to an athlete?**

   Hint The glomerulus filters water from the blood and the tubules reabsorb what is needed.

   Hint The pituitary releases ADH when water levels in the body are too low.

Foundations for Learning Wrap-Up

The pinwheels you prepared when you started the chapter are tools you can use to arrange your thoughts about the organization of the human body.

Activity 1 Working with a partner, go through the organs on each pinwheel. Discuss how the organ on each tab relates to the other organs and to the body system to which it belongs.

Activity 2 Working in small groups, create a flowchart that shows, in order, the organs through which food passes as it moves through the digestive system.

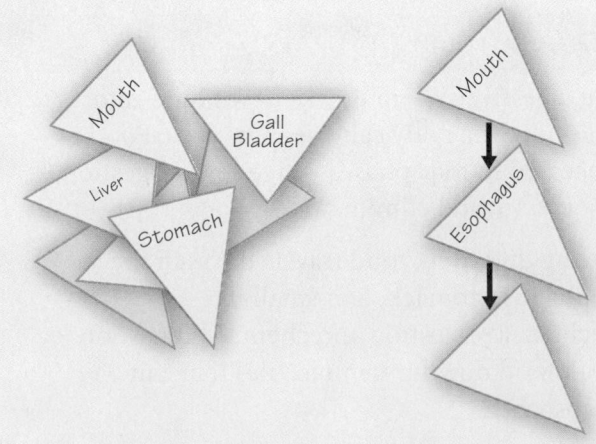

30.1 Organization of the Human Body

Understand Key Concepts

1. What do all types of tissue have in common?
   a. They are all made of connective tissue.
   b. They are all made of cells.
   c. They are all found in every organ.
   d. They are all made of organs.

2. Why is it important for an organism to maintain homeostasis?

3. Name the four types of tissues and describe one characteristic of each.

Think Critically

4. **Explain** Would you classify blood as a cell, tissue, or an organ? Explain.

30.2 Food and Nutrition

Understand Key Concepts

5. Inorganic nutrients that your body needs, usually in small amounts, are called
   a. vitamins.
   c. proteins.
   b. minerals.
   d. amino acids.

Test-Taking Tip

Watch for Qualifiers Sometimes questions have qualifiers that are clues to which answers are wrong. A qualifier gives you a limit, such as an amount. In question 5, you are told that the nutrients are usually needed in *small* amounts. Proteins and amino acids are needed in large amounts. So **c** and **d** are wrong answers. In this question you are also given the qualifier *inorganic*. So you can eliminate **a**, because vitamins are organic nutrients.

6. Energy in food is measured in
   a. ATP.
   c. Calories.
   b. fats.
   d. disaccharides.

7. Which nutrients provide the body with energy?

8. In what three ways are proteins important to the body?

Think Critically

9. **Infer** Many food manufacturers have replaced trans fats in their foods with other types of fats. The replacement fats have a lower level of heart disease risk. Some nutritionists fear that people will think foods such as French fries and doughnuts are healthful if they are not made with trans fats. Explain why these foods are still not healthful choices.

30.3 The Digestive System

Understand Key Concepts

10. Where does mechanical digestion begin?
    a. the esophagus
    c. the mouth
    b. the large intestine
    d. the small intestine

11. An enzyme in saliva that can break the chemical bonds in starch is
    a. pepsin.
    c. amylase.
    b. bile.
    d. chyme.

12. Explain why swallowed food does not normally enter the airway leading to the lungs.

13. Describe the functions of the pancreas.

Think Critically

14. **Relate Cause and Effect** Suppose that your doctor prescribed an antibiotic for an infection. The antibiotic killed all the bacteria in your body. What effect would this have on your digestive system?

30.4 The Excretory System

Understand Key Concepts

15. Urine is excreted from the body through the
    a. ureter.
    c. urethra.
    b. urinary bladder.
    d. renal vein.

16. Which of the following is the basic functional unit of the kidney?
    a. nephron
    c. Bowman's capsule
    b. glomerulus
    d. loop of Henle

17. What is the role of the skin in excretion?

18. What materials are filtered from the blood in the kidney? What materials are not filtered from the blood?

Think Critically

19. **Apply Concepts** Explain why kidney failure can be a fatal condition.

Connecting Concepts

Use Science Graphics

Pancreatic secretions contain sodium bicarbonate and enzymes. The graph shows the secretions of the pancreas in response to three different substances in chyme. Use the graph to answer questions 20 and 21.

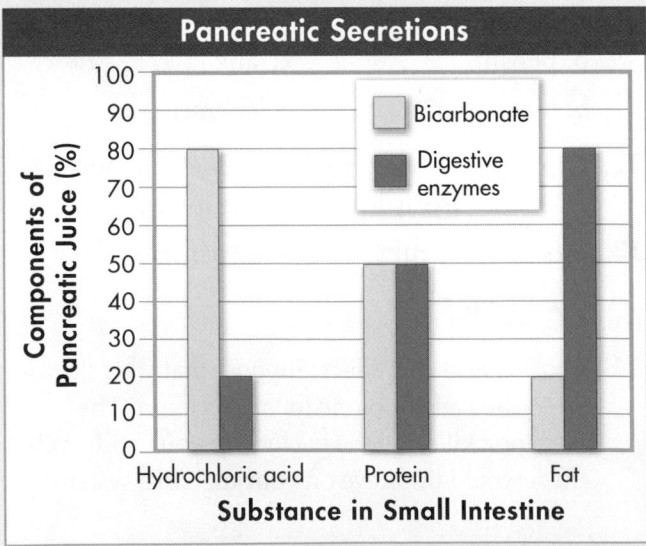

20. **Interpret Visuals** Each pair of bars represents the response of the pancreas to a different variable. What are the three variables?

21. **Compare and Contrast** Compare the composition of pancreatic secretions in the presence of hydrochloric acid and fat.

THE TELLTALE SAMPLE

For centuries, people have studied urine for clues to health and disease. For example, the Greeks knew that diabetics had too much sugar in their urine. They called this disease *diabetes mellitus. Mellitus* is the Greek word for "honey."

- **Physical Examination** First, doctors check the color of urine and look for cloudiness. The shade of yellow indicates the amount of water the kidneys are removing from the blood. Urine of a color other than yellow could indicate the presence of blood. Urine should be clear rather than cloudy.

- **Microscopic Examination** Mucus, white blood cells, or microorganisms in urine indicate a possible infection. Crystals may also cause cloudy urine. Crystals in the urine may indicate kidney stones or a problem with the chemical processes in the body.

- **Chemical Examination** Hundreds of chemical tests can be performed on urine. Chemical dipsticks that change color show that other chemicals are present. These tests can reveal a lot about kidney and liver function. They also reveal a lot about overall homeostasis in the body.

1. **Infer** How does urine reveal so much about the health of the human body?

2. **Form an Opinion** Most drug urine tests done for schools do not test for alcohol or tobacco. Why do you think this is the case? Do you agree or disagree? Explain.

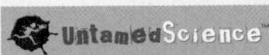 **Never Stop Exploring Your World.** Finding the solution to the Telltale Sample mystery is only the beginning. Take a video field trip with the ecogeeks of Untamed Science to see where this mystery leads.

Multiple Choice

1. Which of the following is NOT a kind of tissue in the human body?

A epithelial

B connective

C interstitial

D nervous   CLG 3.2.1

2. Each of the following aids in the process of digestion EXCEPT

A teeth   C stomach

B saliva   D kidney   CLG 3.2.1

3. In the human body, hydrochloric acid is responsible for the low pH of the contents of the

A kidney   C stomach

B gallbladder   D liver   CLG 3.1.1

4. Which is NOT a function of the kidneys?

A removal of waste products from the blood

B maintenance of blood pH

C regulation of water content of the blood

D excretion of carbon dioxide   CLG 3.2.1

5. The main function of the digestive system is to

A break down large molecules into smaller molecules.

B excrete oxygen and carbon dioxide.

C synthesize minerals and vitamins needed for a healthy body.

D remove waste products from the blood.

CLG 3.2.1

6. In the kidneys, both useful substances and wastes are removed from the blood by

A reabsorption.   C dialysis.

B excretion.   D filtration.   CLG 3.2.1

7. Which of the following is NOT a role of fats in the body?

A Deposits of fat act as insulation.

B They are components of cell membranes.

C They help with absorption of fat-soluble vitamins.

D They are enzymes.   CLG 3.1.1

Questions 8–9

A student is studying the effect of temperature on the action of an enzyme in stomach fluid. The enzyme digests protein. An investigation was set up using five identical test tubes. Each tube contained 40 mL of stomach fluid and 20 mm of glass tubing filled with gelatin. Each tube was subjected to a different temperature. After 48 hours, the amount of gelatin digested in each tube was measured in millimeters. The results for the five test tubes are shown in the table.

Effect of Temperature on Enzyme Action		
Test Tube	Temperature (°C)	Amount of Digestion After 48 Hours
1	2	0.0 mm
2	10	3.0 mm
3	22	4.5 mm
4	37	8.0 mm
5	100	0.0 mm

8. Which is the manipulated (independent) variable in this investigation?

A gastric fluid   C temperature

B length of glass tubing D time   SPI 1.2.6

9. Another test tube was set up that was identical to the other test tubes and placed at a temperature of 15°C for 48 hours. What amount of digestion would you expect to occur in this test tube?

A less than 3.0 mm

B between 3.0 mm and 4.5 mm

C between 4.5 mm and 8.0 mm

D more than 8.0 mm   SPI 1.4.2

Open-Ended Response

10. Fad diets that boast of rapid weight loss often become popular. Many of these diets involve eating only a limited variety of foods. Explain why these diets are an unhealthful way to lose weight.

SPI 1.7.1

If You Have Trouble With . . .

Question	1	2	3	4	5	6	7	8	9	10
See Lesson	30.1	30.3	30.3	30.4	30.3	30.4	30.2	30.3	30.3	30.2

31

The Nervous System

Big idea

Structure and Function

Q: How does the structure of the nervous system allow it to regulate functions in every part of the body?

The sights, sounds, and smells at a ball game provide a fan's nervous system with a lot of stimulation.

CHAPTER
MYSTERY

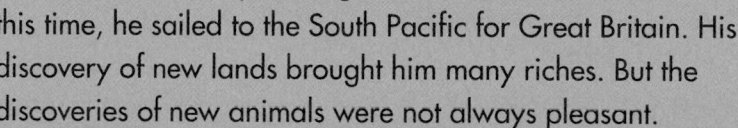

POISONING ON THE HIGH SEAS

From the middle to late 1700s, Captain James Cook commanded several voyages of discovery. During this time, he sailed to the South Pacific for Great Britain. His discovery of new lands brought him many riches. But the discoveries of new animals were not always pleasant.

September 7, 1774, was a remarkable day on the HMS *Resolution*. The ship's butcher died from a fall, and there was a solar eclipse. A clerk also traded some cloth for a freshly caught fish. Captain Cook ate only a few bites of the fish. But within a few hours, the captain felt an extraordinary weakness in his limbs. He also lost all sense of touch, and he could not sense the weight of objects. It took eleven days for the men who ate the fish to recover. A pig and dog that ate some of the fish's organs were dead by the next morning.

Read for Mystery Clues Look for clues as to how eating this fish could produce such deadly effects. Then, solve the mystery.

FOUNDATIONS for Learning

The nervous system is the control center for the body. Before you read the chapter, cut out about twenty 10 cm × 10 cm squares of paper. Punch small holes in each corner of the squares. As you read the chapter, write a structure or function of the nervous system on each square. Use the squares to keep track of important facts about each structure or function. At the end of the chapter are two activities that use these squares to help you answer the question: How does the structure of the nervous system allow it to regulate functions in every part of the body?

Brain

Vision

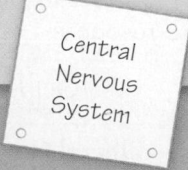

Central Nervous System

• Untamed Science Video • Chapter Mystery

31.1 The Neuron

MD CLG 3.1.1 Chemical Substances and Macromolecules, 3.2.1 Processes and Functions.
SPI 1.4.8 Use Models, 1.5.2 Communicate Information.

Key Questions

🔑 **What are the functions of the nervous system?**

🔑 **What is the function of neurons?**

🔑 **How does a nerve impulse begin?**

BUILD Understanding

Flowchart Create a flowchart to show information flow in the nervous system.

In Your Workbook Go to your workbook for help on creating the flowchart. Complete the flowchart in Lesson 31.1.

Information Flow in the Nervous System

Peripheral Nervous System
Gathers information and sends it to the central nervous system

⬇ Input

Central Nervous System
Processes the information and forms a response

⬇ Output

Peripheral Nervous System
Carries the response of the central nervous system to glands and muscles

Functions of the Nervous System

We are all aware of the world outside our bodies. But how do you know about that world? When you opened the book to this page, how did you make this happen? How did the words that you are reading right now get into your mind? The answers to these questions are found in the nervous system.

The nervous system is our window on the world. The nervous system collects information about the body's internal and external environment. The system then processes that information and responds to it. These functions are accomplished by the peripheral nervous system and the central nervous system. The **peripheral nervous system** consists of nerves and supporting cells. This system collects information about the body's external and internal environment. The **central nervous system** consists of the brain and spinal cord. This system processes the information collected by the peripheral nervous system and creates a response. The response is delivered to the appropriate body part through the peripheral nervous system.

Think about what happens when you search for a pencil in your backpack. Your fingertips send information to your central nervous system about the objects you are touching. Your brain processes the information. It determines that the first object you touch is too square to be a pencil. Then your brain sends messages via your peripheral nervous system to the muscles in your hand. The messages command them to keep searching.

Imagine the billions of messages that are sent throughout your body at any given moment. The messages may tell you to laugh at a funny joke. Or they may tell your brain that it's cold outside. These messages allow the different organs of the body to act together. They also allow the organs to react to conditions in the world around us. How does this communication occur?

🔑 **Key Question** What are the functions of the nervous system?
The nervous system collects information about the body's internal and external environment. The system then processes that information and responds to it.

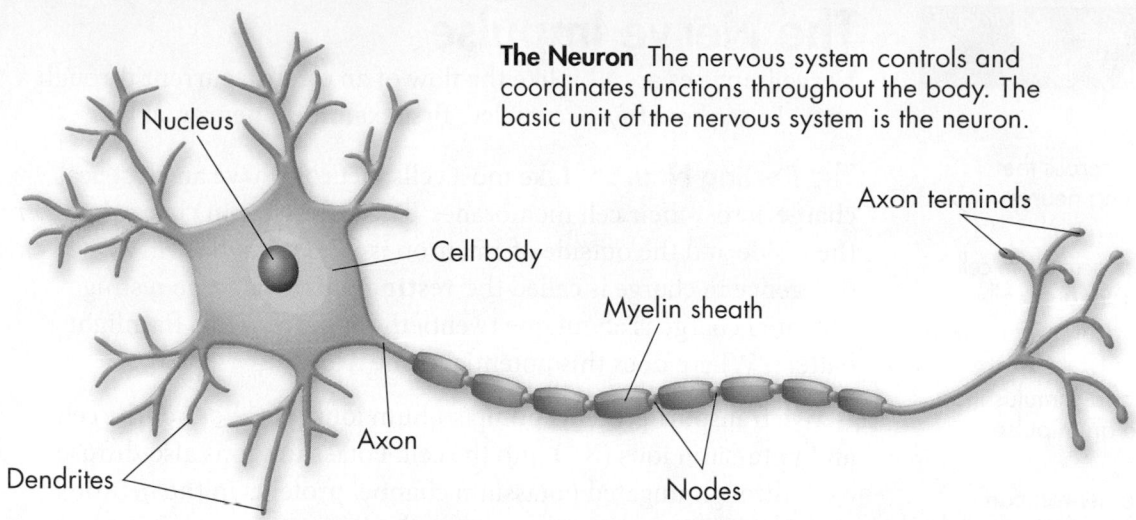

The Neuron The nervous system controls and coordinates functions throughout the body. The basic unit of the nervous system is the neuron.

Nucleus

Cell body

Axon terminals

Myelin sheath

Axon

Dendrites

Nodes

Neurons

The messages carried by the nervous system are electrical signals called impulses. Impulses are carried by cells called neurons.

Types of Neurons Neurons can be classified into three types based on the direction in which an impulse travels. Sensory neurons carry impulses from the sense organs to the spinal cord and brain. Motor neurons carry impulses from the brain and the spinal cord to muscles and glands. Interneurons do the high-level work. They process information from sensory neurons. Then they send commands to other interneurons or to motor neurons.

Structure of Neurons Neurons come in many shapes and sizes, but they all share certain features. The largest part of a typical neuron is its **cell body.** The cell body contains the nucleus and much of the cytoplasm.

Short, branched extensions called **dendrites** spread out from the cell body. They receive impulses from other neurons and carry impulses to the cell body. The long fiber that carries impulses away from the cell body is the **axon.** The axon ends in a series of small swellings called axon terminals. A neuron may have dozens of dendrites, but usually only one axon. Axons and dendrites of different neurons form bundles of fibers called nerves.

The axons of some neurons are insulated by a membrane known as the myelin (MY uh lin) sheath. The myelin sheath around a long axon has many gaps, called nodes. Impulses move along the axon by jumping from one node to the next. Impulses travel faster along these axons than along axons without myelin.

🔑 **Key Question** What is the function of neurons?
Nervous system impulses are carried by cells called neurons.

resting potential
an electrical charge across the membrane of a resting neuron

action potential
a reversal of charges across the cell membrane of a neuron; also called a nerve impulse

threshold
the minimum level of a stimulus that is required to cause an impulse

synapse
the point at which a neuron can transfer impulse to another cell

ACADEMIC WORDS

In science, the word *potential* refers to a difference in electrical charge. Another word for *potential* is "voltage." In cells, *potential* is measured in millivolts (mV). In contrast, the *potential* of a typical AA battery is 1.5 volts.

The Nerve Impulse

Nerve impulses are a bit like the flow of an electric current through a wire. To see how this occurs, let's first examine a neuron at rest.

The Resting Neuron Like most cells, neurons have an electrical charge across their cell membranes. The difference in charge between the inside and the outside of a neuron is -70 millivolts (mV). This difference in charge is called the **resting potential.** The resting potential charge is about one twentieth the voltage in a flashlight battery. Where does this potential come from?

Active transport proteins pump sodium ions (Na^+) out of the cell and potassium ions (K^+) into the cell. Potassium ions also diffuse back through ungated potassium channel proteins in the neuron's membrane. These potassium channels allow K^+ ions to diffuse across the membrane more easily than Na^+ ions. The concentration of K^+ ions is greater inside the cell because of active transport. This greater concentration causes positively charged K^+ ions to move out of the cell. Then, the inside of the cell becomes negatively charged compared to the outside, producing the resting potential.

The Moving Impulse A neuron stays in its resting state until it receives an impulse because of a stimulus. An impulse begins when a neuron is stimulated by another neuron or by the environment. Once it begins, the impulse travels quickly down the axon toward the axon terminals. Impulses in myelinated axons move even more rapidly because they skip from one node to the next.

The impulse is a sudden reversal of the resting potential. At the leading edge of an impulse, "gated" sodium channels open. Positively charged Na^+ ions flow into the cell. The inside of the membrane temporarily becomes more positive than the outside. This charge reversal is the nerve impulse, or **action potential.**

The Resting Neuron The sodium-potassium pump uses ATP to pump Na^+ ions out of the cell. At the same time, it pumps K^+ ions in. A small amount of K^+ diffuses out of the cell through ungated channels. But gated channels block Na^+ from flowing into the resting neuron.

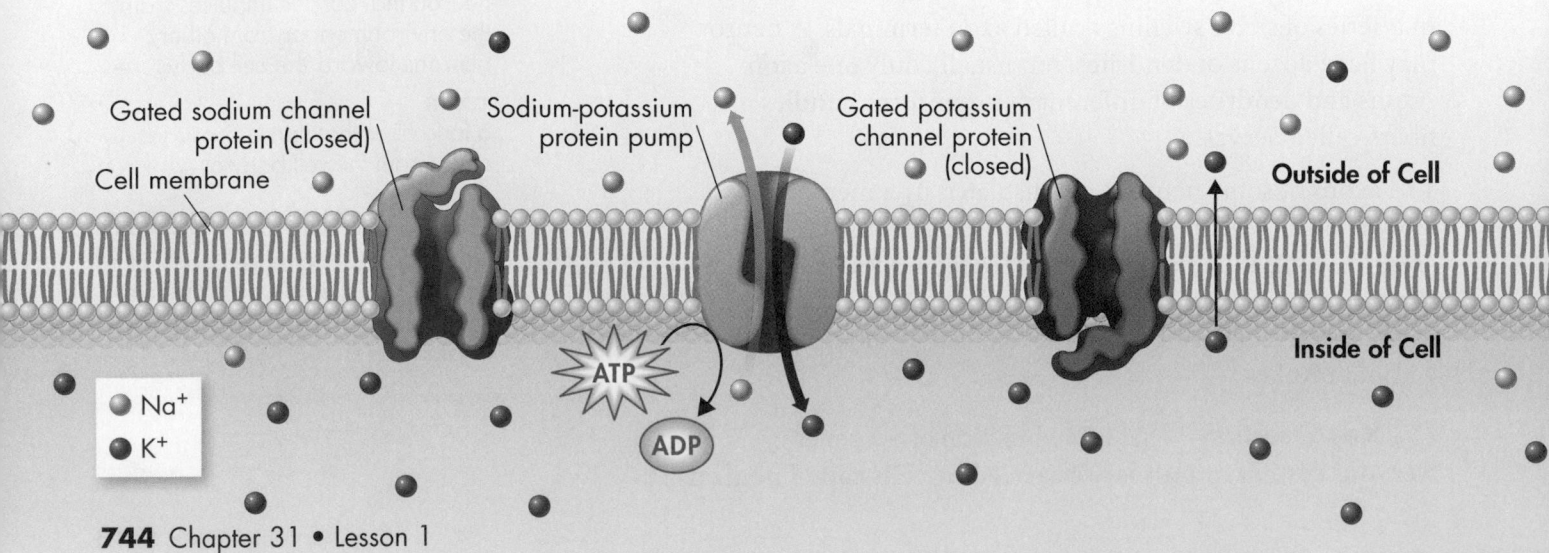

Gated sodium channel protein (closed)

Cell membrane

Sodium-potassium protein pump

Gated potassium channel protein (closed)

Outside of Cell

Inside of Cell

ATP

ADP

- Na^+
- K^+

BUILD Connections

A CHAIN REACTION

With a strong enough push, the fall of one domino leads to the fall of the next. An action potential moves along a neuron in a similar manner.

Once the impulse passes, sodium gates close and gated potassium channels open. The opening of these sodium channels allows K^+ ions to flow out, restoring the resting potential. The neuron is once again negatively charged on the inside. The sodium-potassium pump also keeps working, so the axon will be ready for more action potentials.

The flow of ions causes sodium channels just ahead of the point of impulse to open. The opening of these sodium channels allows the impulse to move rapidly along the axon. You could compare the flow of an impulse to the fall of a row of dominoes. As each domino falls, it causes the next domino to fall.

Threshold Not all stimuli can start an impulse in a neuron. The minimum level of a stimulus needed to cause an impulse is called the **threshold.** Any stimulus that is weaker than the threshold will not produce an impulse. A nerve impulse is an all-or-none response. Either the stimulus produces an impulse, or it does not produce an impulse.

The threshold principle can be illustrated by using a row of dominoes. If you were to gently press the first domino in a row, it might not move at all. A slightly harder push might make the domino wobble back and forth but not fall. A push may be strong enough to cause the first domino to fall into the second. If this push starts the whole row of dominoes falling, then the push is like a threshold stimulus.

All action potentials have the same strength. So how do we sense if a stimulus, like touch or pain, is strong or weak? The brain determines the strength of a stimulus from the frequency of action potentials. A weak stimulus might produce three or four action potentials per second, while a strong one might result in as many as 100 per second.

The Moving Impulse Once an impulse begins, it will continue down an axon until it reaches the end. In an axon with a myelin sheath, the impulse jumps from node to node.

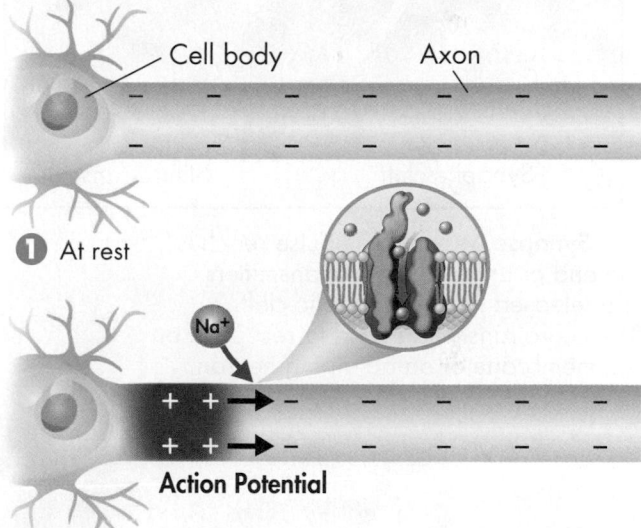

① At rest

Action Potential

② At the leading edge of the impulse, gated sodium channels open. Na⁺ ions flow into the cell, reversing the potential between the cell membrane and its surroundings. This rapidly moving reversal of charge is called an action potential.

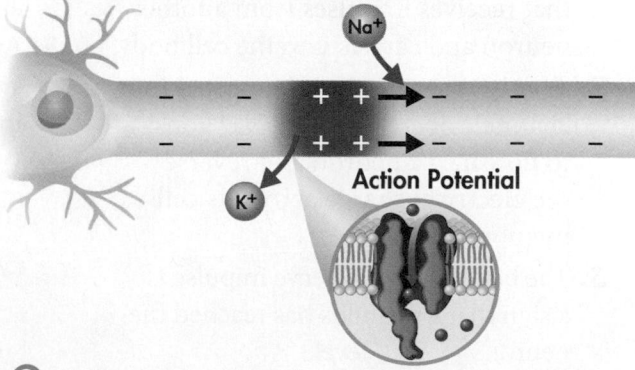

Action Potential

③ As the action potential passes, gated potassium channels open, allowing K⁺ ions to flow out and restoring the resting potential inside the axon.

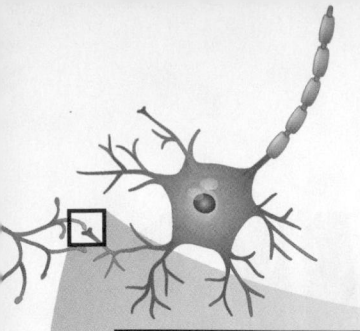

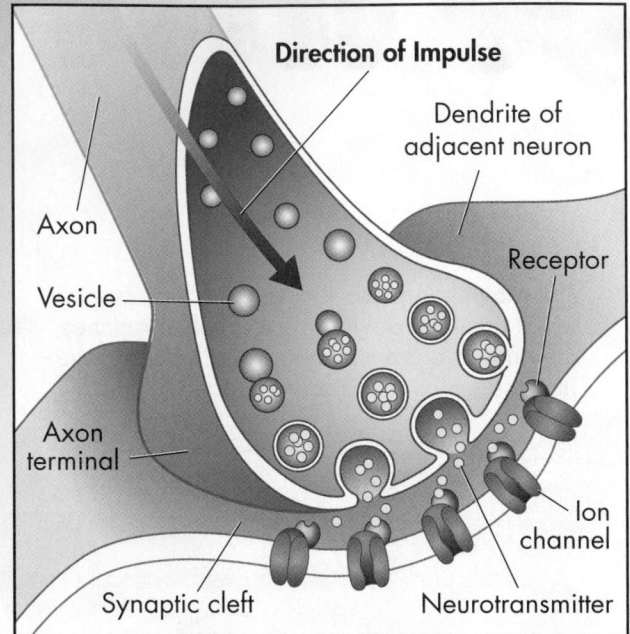

Direction of Impulse

Dendrite of
adjacent neuron

Axon

Vesicle

Receptor

Axon
terminal

Ion
channel

Synaptic cleft

Neurotransmitter

The Synapse When an impulse reaches
the end of an axon, neurotransmitters
are released into the synaptic cleft.
The neurotransmitters bind to receptors on
the membrane of an adjoining neuron.

The Synapse At the end of the neuron, the impulse
reaches an axon terminal. The axon terminal may pass
the impulse along to another cell. For example, a motor
neuron may pass impulses to a muscle cell. These
impulses cause the muscle cell to contract. The point
where a neuron transfers an impulse to another cell is
called a **synapse** (SIN aps). A space called the synaptic
cleft separates the axon terminal from the cell.

The axon terminal at a synapse contains tiny sacs
filled with neurotransmitters. Neurotransmitters are
chemicals that transmit an impulse across a synapse
to another cell. When an impulse arrives at the
synapse, the axon releases neurotransmitters. The
neurotransmitters diffuse across the synaptic cleft and
bind to receptors on the receiving cell's membrane.
These receptors then open ion channels in the
membrane of the receiving cell. If the stimulation
exceeds the cell's threshold, a new impulse begins.

Once their work is done, the neurotransmitters are
released from the receptors on the cell surface. Then
they are broken down by enzymes in the synaptic
cleft. Or they may be taken up and recycled by the
axon terminal.

Key Question How does a nerve impulse begin?
**An impulse begins when a neuron is stimulated
by another neuron or by the environment.**

CHECK Understanding

Apply Vocabulary

1. A(n) _____ is the part of a neuron
that receives impulses from another
neuron and carries it to the cell body.

2. A(n) _____ occurs when gated ion
channels open, allowing Na$^+$ ions
to flow into a neuron and reverse
the electrical charge across its cell
membrane.

3. The beginning of a nerve impulse is
a sign that a stimulus has reached the
neuron's _____ level.

Critical Thinking

4. Explain What happens when a neuron is stimulated by
another neuron?

5. Apply Concepts Describe how your peripheral nervous
system and your central nervous system were involved
in a simple activity you performed today.

6. Write to Learn Answer the first clue of the mystery.

MYSTERY CLUE

The toxin found in this fish binds to gated sodium
channels. This blocks the flow of Na$^+$ ions into a cell.
How do you think this might affect muscle movement?
(**Hint:** See p. 744.)

31.2 The Central Nervous System

MD CLG 3.1.1 Chemical Substances and Macromolecules, 3.1.2 Homeostasis, 3.2.1 Processes and Functions. SPI 1.5.2 Communicate Information, 1.7.1 Apply Skills and Concepts.

The Brain and the Spinal Cord

The nervous system contains billions of neurons, each capable of carrying impulses and sending messages. What keeps them from sending impulses everywhere and acting like an unruly mob? Is there a central place where information is processed, decisions are made, and order is enforced?

Brain The control point of the central nervous system is the brain. The major areas of the brain are the cerebrum, cerebellum, and brain stem. Each of these areas is responsible for processing and relaying information. Like the central processing unit of a computer, information processing is the brain's primary task.

Most organs in the body function to maintain homeostasis. But the brain itself is constantly changed by its interactions with the environment. Sensory experience changes many of the patterns of neuron connections in the brain. Stem cells in the brain also produce new neurons throughout life. Many of these new cells form in regions connected with learning and memory. These changes make the brain highly flexible.

Spinal Cord Most of the neurons that enter and exit the brain do so in the spinal cord. The spinal cord is a large cluster of neurons and other cells. The spinal cord is the main communication link between the brain and the rest of the body. It is a bit like a major telephone line. It carries thousands of signals at once between the central and peripheral nervous systems. Thirty-one pairs of spinal nerves branch out from the spinal cord. These pairs connect the brain to different parts of the body. Certain kinds of information, including many reflexes, are processed directly in the spinal cord. A reflex is a quick, automatic response to a stimulus. Pulling your hand back quickly when pricked by a pin is an example of a reflex.

Key Question Where does processing of information occur in the nervous system?
The major areas of the brain are the cerebrum, cerebellum, and brain stem. Each of these areas is responsible for processing and relaying information. The spinal cord is the main communication link between the brain and the rest of the body.

Key Questions

🔑 **Where does processing of information occur in the nervous system?**

🔑 **How do drugs change the brain and lead to addiction?**

BUILD Understanding

Concept Map As you read, make a concept map that shows how the structures of the central nervous system are related to each other.

In Your Workbook Go to your workbook for help making a concept map. Complete the concept map in Lesson 31.2.

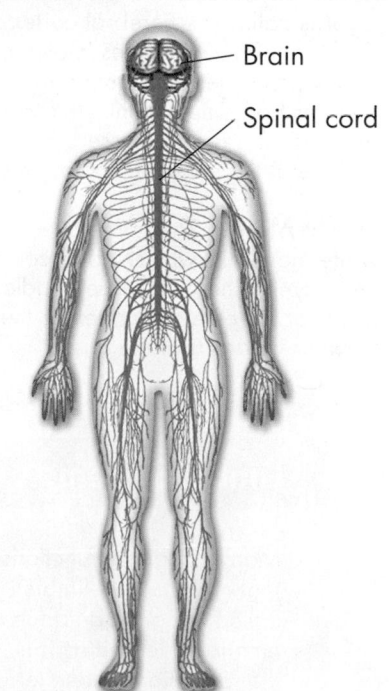

Brain

Spinal cord

The Central Nervous System The central nervous system consists of the brain and spinal cord.

BUILD Connections

THE BRAIN
The brain contains billions of neurons and other supporting tissue. The brain processes, relays, and forms responses to an unbelievable amount of information every moment.

In Your Workbook Explore the parts of the brain by completing the activity in Lesson 31.2.

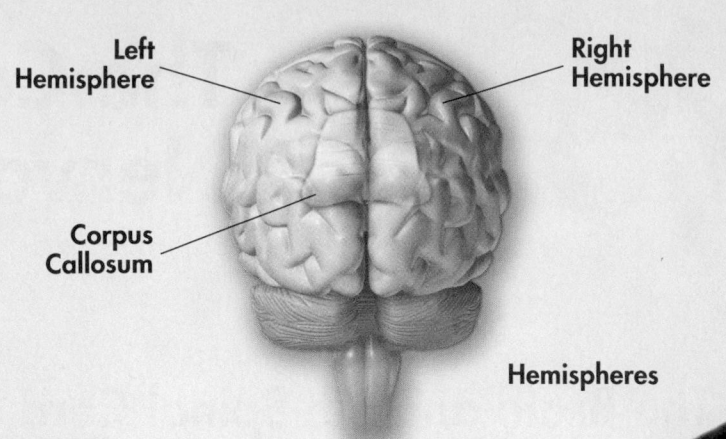

Left Hemisphere

Right Hemisphere

Corpus Callosum

Hemispheres

Cerebrum

The largest region of the human brain is the cerebrum. The **cerebrum** is responsible for the voluntary, or conscious, activities of the body. It is the site of intelligence, learning, and judgment.

Hemispheres A deep groove from front to back divides the cerebrum into right and left hemispheres. A band of tissue called the corpus callosum connects the hemispheres.

Remarkably, each hemisphere deals mainly with the opposite side of the body. Sensations from the left side of the body go to the right hemisphere. Sensations from the right side go to the left hemisphere. Commands to move muscles are generated in the same way.

Each hemisphere is divided into four regions called lobes. The lobes are named for the skull bones that cover them. Each lobe is associated with different functions.

Cerebral Cortex The cerebrum has two layers. The outer layer is called the cerebral cortex. It consists of densely packed nerve cell bodies known as gray matter. The cerebral cortex processes information from the sense organs and controls body movements. It is also where thoughts, plans, and learning are processed. Folds and grooves on the outer surface of the cerebral cortex greatly increase its surface area.

White Matter The inner layer of the cerebrum is known as white matter. Its whitish color comes from bundles of axons with myelin sheaths. These bundles may connect different areas of the cerebral cortex or they may connect the cerebrum to different areas of the brain.

Limbic System

Many important functions have been linked to the structures that make up the limbic system. A region deep within the brain called the amygdala (uh MIG duh luh), has been associated with emotional learning. This includes fear and anxiety, as well as the formation of long-term memories. The limbic system is also associated with the brain's pleasure center. This region produces feelings of satisfaction and well-being.

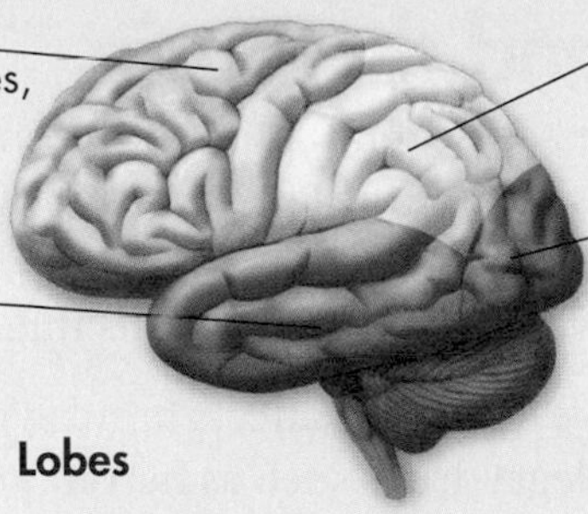

Frontal Lobe
Evaluating consequences, making judgments, forming plans

Temporal Lobe
Hearing and smell

Parietal Lobe
Reading and speech

Occipital Lobe
Vision

Lobes

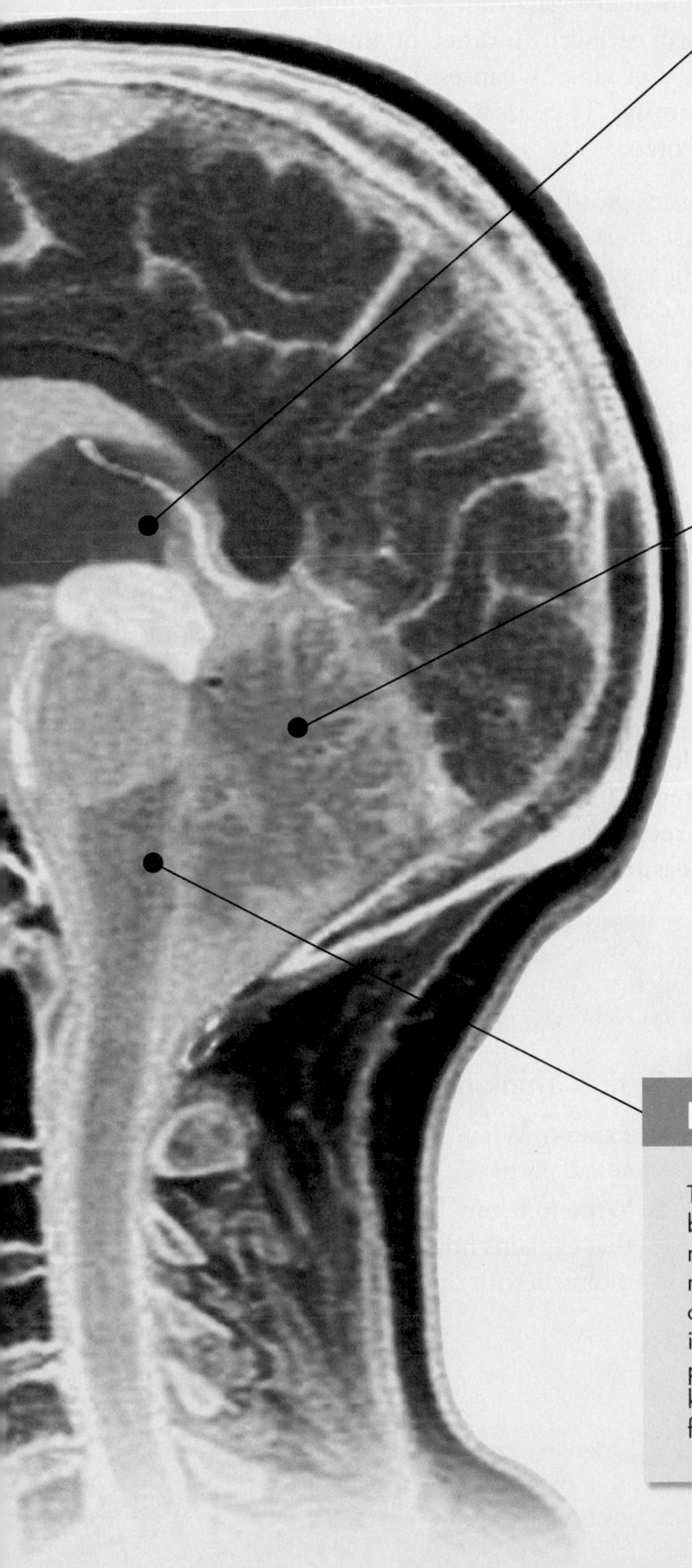

Thalamus and Hypothalamus

The thalamus and hypothalamus are found between the brain stem and the cerebrum. The thalamus receives messages from sensory receptors throughout the body. It then relays the information to the proper region of the cerebrum for further processing. Just below the thalamus is the hypothalamus. The **hypothalamus** recognizes and analyzes hunger, thirst, fatigue, anger, and body temperature. The hypothalamus also helps to coordinate the nervous and endocrine systems.

Cerebellum

The second largest region of the brain is the **cerebellum.** Information about muscle and joint position, and other sensory inputs, are sent to the cerebellum. The commands to move muscles come from the cerebral cortex. The sensory information allows the cerebellum to coordinate and balance the actions of these muscles. This ability to coordinate muscle actions allows the body to move gracefully and efficiently. When you begin any new activity involving muscle coordination, the cerebellum actually learns the movements. It then coordinates the actions of many individual muscles when the movement is repeated.

Brain Stem

The **brain stem,** located just below the cerebellum, connects the brain and spinal cord. The brain stem includes three regions—the midbrain, the pons, and the medulla oblongata. Each region regulates the flow of information between the brain and the rest of the body. The brain stem controls some of the body's most important functions. These functions include regulation of blood pressure, heart rate, breathing, and swallowing. The brain stem keeps the body functioning even when you lose consciousness from sleep or injury.

BUILD Vocabulary

cerebrum
the part of the brain responsible for voluntary activities of the body; the "thinking" region of the brain

hypothalamus
the portion of the brain that acts as a control center for recognition and analysis of hunger, thirst, fatigue, anger, and body temperature

cerebellum
the part of the brain that coordinates movement and controls balance

brain stem
a structure that connects the brain and spinal cord; includes the medulla oblongata and the pons

dopamine
a neurotransmitter that is associated with the brain's pleasure and reward centers

⬧ PREFIXES

The prefix *hypo-* means "under or below." The hypothalamus is located below the thalamus in the brain.

Addiction and the Brain

Synapses transfer messages from cell to cell, doing the conscious work of thinking. Synapses also do the less-conscious work of producing feelings and emotions. What would happen if a chemical changed the way those synapses worked? Such chemicals might change behavior.

Nearly every addictive substance affects brain synapses. These substances include illegal drugs such as heroin, methamphetamine, and cocaine. They also include legal drugs such as tobacco and alcohol. The chemistry of each drug is different. But they all produce changes in one particular group of synapses. These synapses use the neurotransmitter **dopamine.** They are associated with the brain's pleasure and reward centers.

When an activity brings us pleasure, neurons in the hypothalamus and the limbic system release dopamine. Dopamine molecules stimulate other neurons across these synapses. This stimulation produces the sensation of pleasure and a feeling of well-being.

Addictive drugs act on dopamine synapses in several ways. Methamphetamine releases a flood of dopamine, producing an instant "high." Cocaine keeps dopamine in the synaptic region longer, intensifying pleasure and suppressing pain. Nicotine and alcohol cause an increase in the release of dopamine.

The brain reacts to excessive dopamine levels by reducing the number of dopamine receptors. Normal activities no longer produce the sensations of pleasure they once did. Addicts feel depressed and sick without their drugs. It takes greater amounts of addictive chemicals to get the same high with fewer receptors. This addiction is hard to break.

🔑 **Key Question** How do drugs change the brain and lead to addiction? **The brain reacts to too much dopamine by reducing the number of dopamine receptors. As a result, normal activities no longer produce the pleasurable feelings they once did.**

CHECK Understanding

Apply Vocabulary

1. The part of the brain that processes information from the eyes, ears, and skin is the _____.

2. The _____ is the part of the brain that recognizes when you are tired and hungry.

3. The part of the brain that learns muscle movements needed for playing a musical instrument or playing a sport is the _____.

Critical Thinking

4. Explain What is the role of the spinal cord?

5. Write to Learn Write a paragraph that explains how the brain interacts with the environment.

BIOLOGY.com   Search ⟨ Lesson 31.2 ⟩ GO • Lesson Assessment

31.3 The Peripheral Nervous System

MD CLG 3.1.2 Homeostasis, 3.2.1 Processes and Functions. SPI 1.5.2 Communicate Information.

The Sensory Division

It's all about input and output. A computer isn't useful unless it can accept input from the world around it. And the result isn't meaningful unless there's a way to output it. The central nervous system faces the same issues. Can you guess what it uses for input and output devices?

The peripheral nervous system consists of all the nerves and associated cells that are not part of the brain or spinal cord, including cranial nerves and spinal nerves. Cranial nerves go through openings in the skull. They stimulate regions of the head and neck. Spinal nerves stimulate the rest of the body. The cell bodies of cranial and spinal nerves are arranged in clusters called ganglia.

The peripheral nervous system is our link with the outside world. It has two major divisions—the sensory division and the motor division. The sensory division transmits impulses from sense organs to the central nervous system. The motor division transmits impulses from the central nervous system to the muscles and glands.

Sensory receptors are cells that transmit information about changes in the internal and external environments. These changes are called stimuli. Sensory receptors are grouped by the type of stimuli to which they respond. When they are stimulated, sensory receptors transmit impulses to sensory neurons. Sensory neurons then transmit impulses to the central nervous system.

Key Question How does the central nervous system receive sensory information?
The peripheral nervous system's sensory division transmits impulses from sense organs to the central nervous system.

Sensory Receptors
Sensory receptors react to a specific stimulus such as light or sound by sending impulses to sensory neurons.

Key Questions

🔑 How does the central nervous system receive sensory information?

🔑 How do muscles and glands receive commands from the central nervous system?

BUILD Understanding

Venn Diagram As you read, make a Venn diagram that compares the somatic nervous system and the autonomic nervous system.

In Your Workbook Go to your workbook to complete the Venn diagram in Lesson 31.3.

Sensory Receptors		
Type	**Responds to**	**Some Locations**
Chemoreceptor	Chemicals	Mouth, nose, blood vessels
Photoreceptor	Light	Eyes
Mechanoreceptor	Touch, pressure, vibrations, and stretch	Skin, hair follicles, ears, ligaments, tendons
Thermoreceptor	Temperature changes	Skin, hypothalamus
Pain receptor	Tissue injury	Throughout the body

The Motor Division

The nervous system maintains homeostasis by gathering and processing information from other systems and organs. Then it sends commands to muscles or glands through the peripheral nervous system's motor division. This division has two parts—the somatic nervous system and the autonomic nervous system.

Somatic Nervous System The **somatic nervous system** regulates body activities that are under conscious control. These activities include movement of skeletal muscles. But when your body is in danger, the central nervous system may take over.

▶ *Voluntary Control* When you wiggle your toes, you use motor neurons of the somatic nervous system. Impulses from the brain are carried through the spinal cord, synapsing with motor neuron dendrites. Axons from these motor neurons extend from the spinal cord, carrying the impulses directly to muscles. These impulses cause muscle contractions that produce voluntary movements.

▶ *Reflex Arcs* The somatic nervous system is generally considered to be under conscious control. But some actions of the system occur automatically. Suppose you accidentally step on a tack with your bare foot. Your leg may pull back before you even notice the pain. This rapid response is a reflex. It is caused by impulses that travel a pathway called a **reflex arc.** ❶ Sensory receptors react to the feeling of the tack, sending an impulse to sensory neurons. ❷ Sensory neurons relay the information to the spinal cord. ❸ An interneuron in the spinal cord processes the information and forms a response. ❹ A motor neuron carries impulses that stimulate a muscle (its effector). ❺ The muscle contracts, moving your leg. At the same time, impulses carry information about the injury to your brain. But by the time your brain interprets the pain, your leg and foot have already moved.

The spinal cord does not control all reflexes. Many reflexes that involve structures in your head are controlled by the brain. For example, blinking and sneezing are controlled by the brain.

Reflex Arc When you step on a tack, sensory receptors stimulate a sensory neuron. The neuron relays the signal to an interneuron within the spinal cord. The signal is then sent to a motor neuron. This neuron stimulates a muscle that lifts your leg.

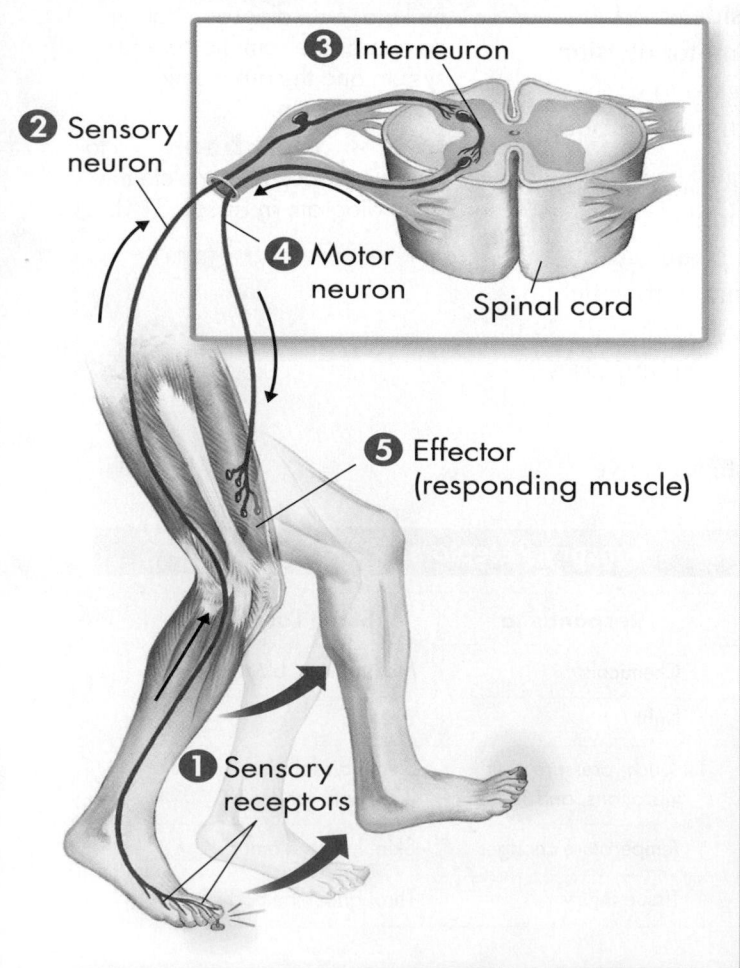

❸ Interneuron

❷ Sensory neuron

❹ Motor neuron

Spinal cord

❺ Effector (responding muscle)

❶ Sensory receptors

Autonomic Nervous System The **autonomic nervous system** regulates involuntary activities. These activities are not under conscious control. For instance, when you start to run, the autonomic nervous system speeds up your heart rate. It increases blood flow to the skeletal muscles and stimulates the sweat glands. It also slows down the contractions of smooth muscles in the digestive system. You may not be aware of some of these activities. But all of them help you run faster and farther.

The autonomic nervous system has two equally important parts, the sympathetic and parasympathetic nervous systems. In general, these systems have opposite effects on each organ they influence. The two systems produce a level of fine control that coordinates organs throughout the body.

For example, heart rate is increased by the sympathetic nervous system. But it is decreased by the parasympathetic nervous system. In general, the sympathetic system prepares the body for intense activity. When it is stimulated, blood pressure increases and energy-rich sugar is released into the blood. Activities not related to the body's "fight or flight" response to stress also shut down. But the parasympathetic system causes what might be called the "rest and digest" response. It lowers heart rate and blood pressure and activates digestion. It also activates pathways that store food molecules in the tissues of the body.

Key Question How do muscles and glands receive commands from the central nervous system? **The peripheral nervous system's motor division transmits impulses from the central nervous system to muscles or glands.**

CHECK Understanding

Apply Vocabulary
Use the highlighted words from the lesson to complete each sentence correctly.

1. The sensory receptors and effector are parts of a _____.

2. The heart, lungs, and muscles of the digestive tract are regulated by the _____.

3. When you reach for a glass of water, your hand and arm muscles are being controlled by the _____.

Critical Thinking

4. **Explain** Is a reflex a part of the central nervous system, the peripheral nervous system, or both?

5. **Apply Concepts** Give three examples of stimuli that your sensory division is responding to right now.

6. **Write to Learn** Answer the second clue to the mystery.

MYSTERY CLUE

Think about Captain Cook's symptoms of weakness. What part of his nervous system did consumption of the fish affect the most? (**Hint:** See p. 752.)

31.4 The Senses

MD CLG 3.1.2 Homeostasis, 3.2.1 Processes and Functions, 3.2.2 Changes in Metabolic Activity, 3.5.1 Factors Influencing Ecosystems. SPI 1.4.2 Analyze Data, 1.6.1 Ratio and Proportion, 1.6.3 Use Scientific Notation, 1.7.1 Apply Skills and Concepts.

Key Questions

🔑 How does the body sense touch, temperature, and pain?

🔑 How are the senses of smell and taste similar?

🔑 How do the ears and brain process sounds and maintain balance?

🔑 How do the eyes and brain produce vision?

BUILD Understanding

Preview Visuals Before reading, preview the figure The Eye. Write down at least two questions you have about the information in the figure.

In Your Workbook Go to your workbook for a chart for previewing visuals.

Taste Buds The surface of the tongue contains many tiny projections. Taste buds line the tops of some of these and line the sides of other projections (LM 80×).

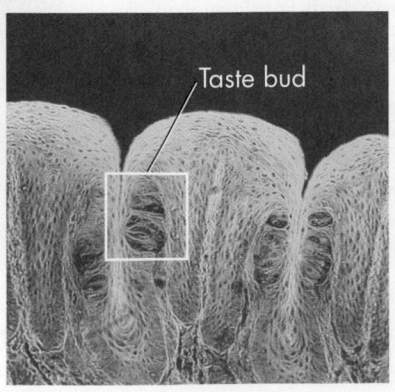

Taste bud

Touch and Related Senses

Different sensory receptors in the body respond to touch, temperature, and pain. Your skin has all three receptors, but some are also found in other areas. Nearly all regions of your skin are sensitive to touch.

Touch Human skin contains at least seven types of sensory receptors. Stimulation of these receptors creates the sensation of touch. But not all parts of the body are equally sensitive. For example, there is a higher density of touch receptors on your fingers than on your back.

Temperature Thermoreceptors are sensory cells that respond to heat and cold. They are found throughout the skin. They are also found in the hypothalamus, the part of the brain that senses blood temperature.

Pain Pain receptors are found throughout the body, but not in the brain. Many tissues also have pain receptors that respond to chemicals released during infection or inflammation.

🔑 **Key Question** How does the body sense touch, temperature, and pain? **Different sensory receptors in the body respond to touch, temperature, and pain.**

Smell and Taste

Your senses of smell and taste involve the ability of sensory cells that detect chemicals. These cells, called chemoreceptors, are located in the nose and mouth. They send impulses to the brain that are interpreted as sensations of smell and taste.

Smell Your sense of smell produces thousands of different sensations. Much of what we usually call the "taste" of food and drink is actually smell. Try eating a few bites of food while holding your nose. It seems to have little taste until you release your nose and breathe freely.

Taste The sense organs for taste are the taste buds. Most taste buds are on the tongue. Their sensory cells respond to salty, bitter, sweet, and sour foods. Scientists recently discovered that sensory cells also respond to the amino acid glutamate. This taste is called *umami* (Japanese for "savory").

🔑 **Key Question** How are the senses of smell and taste similar? **Sensations of smell and taste are both the result of impulses sent to the brain by chemoreceptors.**

Hearing and Balance

The human ear has two sensory functions—hearing and balance. Mechanoreceptors found in parts of the ear transmit impulses to the brain. The brain translates the impulses into sound and information about changes in position.

Hearing Sound is vibrations moving through the air around us. The ears can distinguish both the pitch and loudness of those vibrations.

Vibrations enter the ear through the auditory canal and cause the tympanum (TIM puh num), or eardrum, to vibrate. Three tiny bones (the hammer, anvil, and stirrup) transmit these vibrations to a membrane called the oval window. Its vibrations create pressure waves in the fluid-filled **cochlea** (KAHK lee uh) of the inner ear. The pressure waves push the cochlea's tiny hair cells back and forth. In response, the hair cells send nerve impulses to the brain, which processes them as sounds.

The Ear The structures in the ear transmit sound and allow a person to hear.

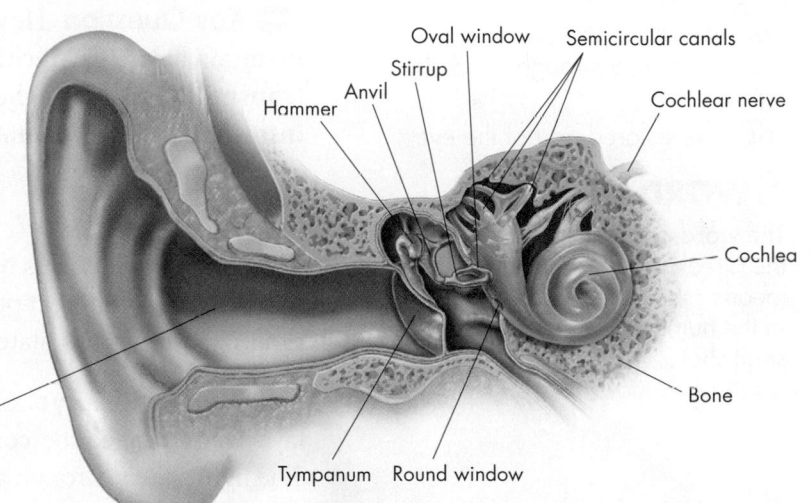

INQUIRY into Scientific Thinking

Sound Intensity

Sound intensity, or loudness, is measured in units called decibels (dB). The threshold of hearing for the human ear is 0 dB. For every 10 dB increase, the sound intensity increases ten times.

Based on the graph, how much more intense is a jet engine than a hair dryer?

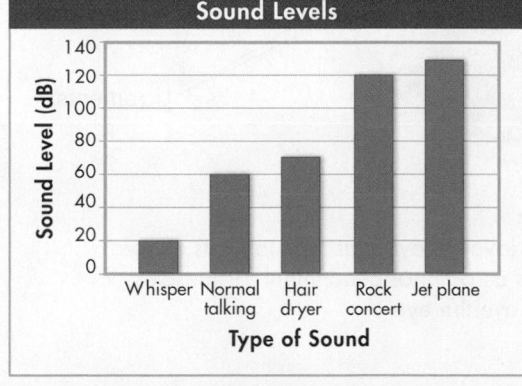

Sound Levels

(Graph: Sound Level (dB) vs. Type of Sound)
- Whisper: 20
- Normal talking: 60
- Hair dryer: 70
- Rock concert: 120
- Jet plane: 130

- The difference between the two sound intensities is

$$130 \text{ dB}_{jet} - 70 \text{ dB}_{hair\ dryer} = 60 \text{ dB}$$

- The jet engine is 60 dB louder than a hair dryer. This means it is 10^6 or 1,000,000 times louder than the hair dryer.

Loud noises can permanently damage the hair cells in the cochlea. These hair cells are the cells that sense vibrations. Exposure to sounds above 80 dB for several hours at a time can damage hearing. Exposure to sounds about 120 dB for even a few seconds can damage hearing.

Analyze and Conclude

1. Calculate How much more intense is normal talking than whispering?

2. Infer Repeated exposure to portable music devices set at high volume can cause hearing damage. Why do you think this damage might not reveal itself for many years?

In Your Workbook Get more help for this activity in your workbook.

BUILD Vocabulary

cochlea the fluid-filled part of the inner ear; contains nerve cells that detect sound

semicircular canal one of three structures in the inner ear that monitors the position of the body in relation to gravity

cornea a tough transparent layer of the eye through which light enters

iris the colored part of the eye

🗝 WORD ORIGINS

The word *cochlea* comes from the Greek word *kochlias*, which means "snail shell." The cochlea in the human ear is shaped like a snail shell.

Balance Your ears help your central nervous system maintain your balance. There are three tiny canals just above the cochlea called **semicircular canals.** These canals and two tiny sacs located behind them monitor your body's position.

The canals and sacs are filled with fluid that changes position as the head moves. These movements cause the hair on the hair cells lining the canals and sacs to bend. The brain uses the impulses created by this action to determine body motion and position.

🗝 Key Question How do the ears and brain process sounds and maintain balance? **Mechanoreceptors found in parts of the ear transmit impulses to the brain. The brain translates the impulses into sound and information about balance.**

Vision

The world around us is bathed in light that our eyes detect. Vision occurs when photoreceptors in the eyes transmit impulses to the brain. The brain translates these impulses into images.

Structures of the Eye Light enters the eye through a tough transparent layer of cells called the **cornea.** The cornea helps to focus the light. The light passes through a chamber filled with a fluid called aqueous (AY kwee uhs) humor. At the back of the chamber is a disk-shaped structure called the **iris.** The iris is the colored part of the eye.

The Eye The eye is a complicated sense organ. The sclera, choroid, and retina are three layers of tissues that form the inner wall of the eyeball.

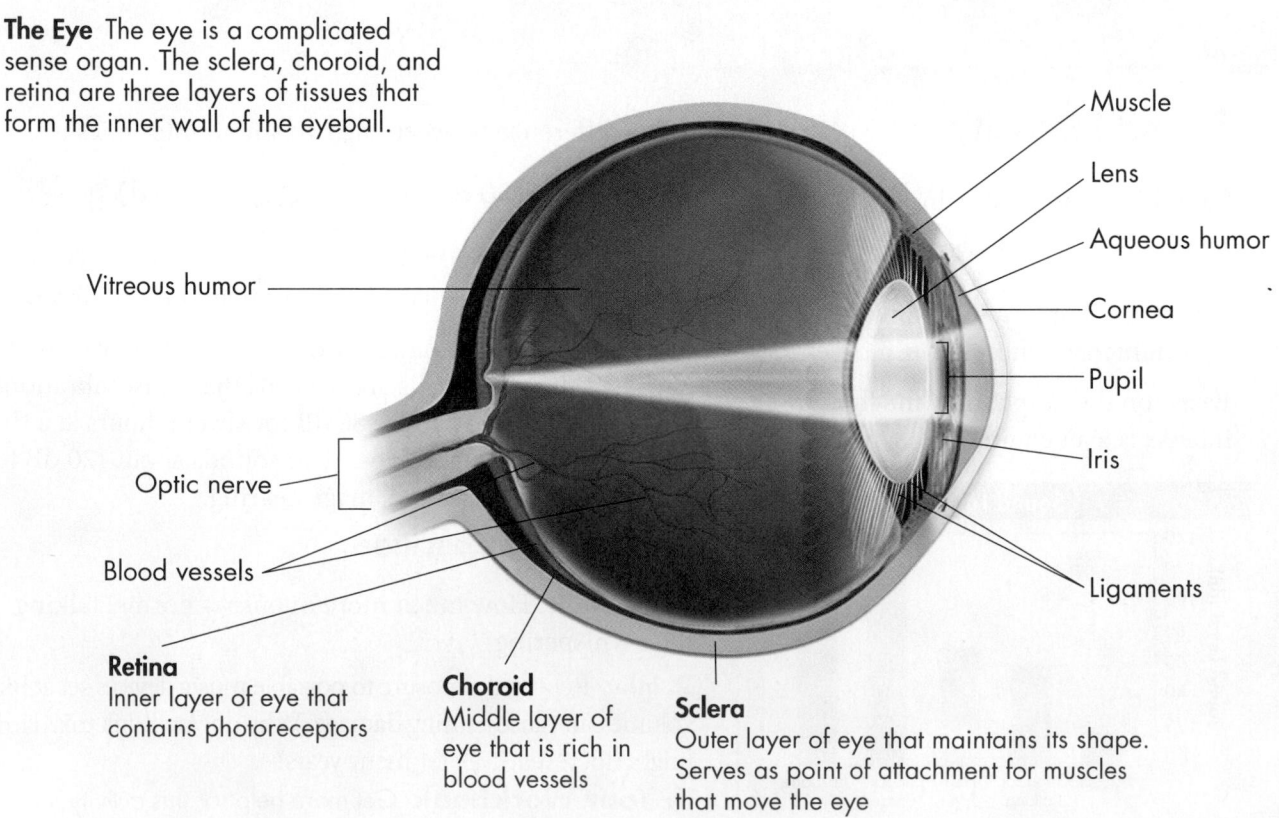

Muscle

Lens

Aqueous humor

Cornea

Pupil

Iris

Ligaments

Vitreous humor

Optic nerve

Blood vessels

Retina
Inner layer of eye that contains photoreceptors

Choroid
Middle layer of eye that is rich in blood vessels

Sclera
Outer layer of eye that maintains its shape. Serves as point of attachment for muscles that move the eye

The small opening in the middle of the iris is the **pupil.** Tiny muscles in the iris adjust the pupil's size. The pupil controls the amount of light that enters the eye. The pupil becomes smaller in bright light and larger in dim light.

Just behind the iris is the **lens.** Small muscles attached to the lens change its shape. This adjusts the eyes' focus to see near or distant objects clearly. The large chamber behind the lens is filled with a transparent, jellylike fluid called vitreous (VIH tree uhs) humor.

How You See The lens focuses light onto the **retina,** the inner layer of the eye. Photoreceptors in the retina convert light energy into nerve impulses. There are two types of photoreceptors: rods and cones. Rods are extremely sensitive to light, but they do not respond to colors. They only allow us to see black and white. Cones are less sensitive than rods. But they do respond to different colors, producing color vision. Cones are concentrated in the fovea, the site of sharpest vision.

The impulses gathered by this complicated layer of cells leave each eye through the optic nerve. This nerve carries the impulses to the appropriate regions of the brain. There are no photoreceptors where the optic nerve passes through the back of the eye. This lack of photoreceptors produces a blind spot in each image sent to the brain. The brain fills in the holes of the blind spot with information when it processes the impulses.

If the eye just took photographs, the images would be blurry and incomplete. The images we actually see are much more detailed. The reason is the complicated way in which the brain processes and interprets visual information.

Key Question How do the eyes and brain produce vision?
Vision occurs when photoreceptors in the eyes transmit impulses to the brain. The brain translates these impulses into images.

BUILD Vocabulary

pupil a small opening in the iris that admits light into the eye

lens a structure in the eye that focuses light rays on the retina

retina the innermost layer of the eye; contains photoreceptors

WORD ORIGINS

The word *retina* comes from the Middle English word *rethina*. *Rethina* is believed to come from the Latin word *rete*, which means "net."

CHECK Understanding

Apply Vocabulary
Use the highlighted words from the lesson to complete each sentence correctly.

1. Hair cells in the _____ send information about your body's position to the brain.

2. Muscles in the _____ control the amount of light that enters the eye.

3. Photoreceptors in the _____ convert light energy into nerve impulses.

4. The _____ is a fluid-filled structure with cells that detect sound.

Critical Thinking

5. **Infer** Some people suffer from night blindness. Which type of photoreceptor is likely not functioning correctly?

6. **Write to Learn** Answer the third clue of the mystery.

MYSTERY CLUE

Based on Cook's symptoms, which of his senses was greatly affected by the toxin? Explain. (**Hint:** See p. 754.)

BIOLOGY.com Search (Lesson 31.4) **GO** • Lesson Assessment

 MD CLG 3.2.1 Processes and Functions. SPI 1.27 Apply Results, 1.5.9 Synthesize Ideas.

Pre-Lab: Testing Sensory Receptors for Touch

Problem What factors affect a person's ability to sense gentle pressure on skin?

Materials bent paper clips, metric ruler

Lab Manual Chapter 31 Lab

Skills Focus Measure, Analyze Data, Draw Conclusions

Connect to the **Big idea** Your nervous system coordinates your response to stimuli from outside your body and inside your body. Sensory receptors react to stimuli by sending impulses to sensory neurons. Each receptor can detect only one type of stimulus. Receptors are classified by the type of stimuli to which they respond. Some respond to light, some to pain, some to chemicals, and so on. Mechanoreceptors are cells that respond to touch, pressure, vibrations, and stretch.

In this lab, you will investigate the mechanoreceptors in your skin that respond to gentle touch. You will compare the relative density of these receptors in three areas of your skin. You will also identify other factors that could affect a person's response to touch.

Background Questions

a. Review Which division of the peripheral nervous system transmits signals from receptors in your skin to your brain?

b. Relate Cause and Effect List two reasons why a touch might not produce a nerve impulse.

c. Infer People who are visually impaired use their fingertips to read books that are printed in Braille. In Braille, each letter of the alphabet is represented by a unique pattern of dots. What feature of the dots allows a reader to distinguish one set of dots from another?

Pre-Lab Questions

Preview the procedure in the lab manual.

1. Predict Which area will have the highest density of receptors for gentle pressure—your fingertips, the back of your hand, or your forearm?

2. Control Variables Why must you have your eyes closed while your partner touches your skin with the bent paper clip?

3. Predict Will you and your partner have the same density of touch receptors in a given area of skin? Give a reason for your prediction.

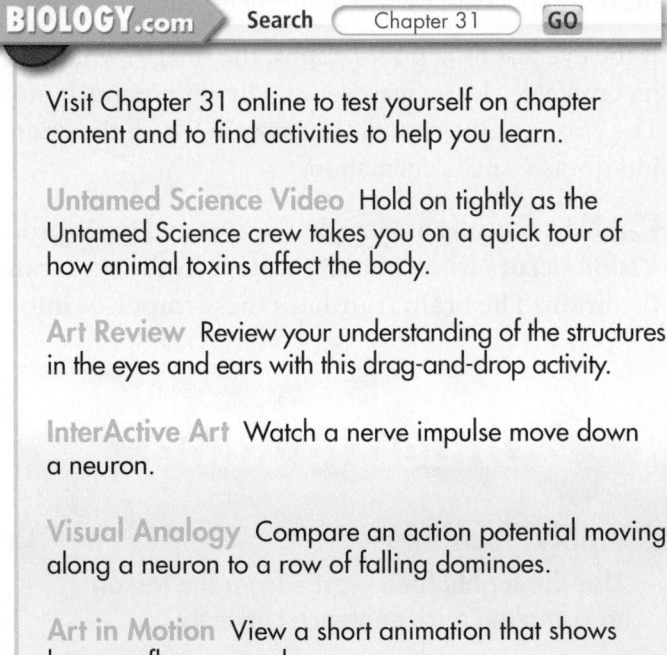

BIOLOGY.com   Search   (Chapter 31)   GO

Visit Chapter 31 online to test yourself on chapter content and to find activities to help you learn.

Untamed Science Video Hold on tightly as the Untamed Science crew takes you on a quick tour of how animal toxins affect the body.

Art Review Review your understanding of the structures in the eyes and ears with this drag-and-drop activity.

InterActive Art Watch a nerve impulse move down a neuron.

Visual Analogy Compare an action potential moving along a neuron to a row of falling dominoes.

Art in Motion View a short animation that shows how a reflex arc works.

31 CHAPTER Summary

31.1 The Neuron

- The nervous system collects information about the body's internal and external environment. The system then processes that information and responds to it.

- Nervous system impulses are transmitted by cells called neurons.

- An impulse begins when a neuron is stimulated by another neuron or by the environment.

peripheral nervous system (p. 742)
central nervous system (p. 742)
cell body (p. 743)
dendrite (p. 743)
axon (p. 743)
resting potential (p. 744)
action potential (p. 744)
threshold (p. 745)
synapse (p. 746)

31.2 The Central Nervous System

- The major areas of the brain are the cerebrum, cerebellum, and brain stem. Each of these areas is responsible for processing and relaying information. The spinal cord is the main communication link between the brain and the rest of the body.

- The brain reacts to too much dopamine by reducing the number of dopamine receptors. As a result, normal activities no longer produce the pleasurable feelings they once did.

cerebrum (p. 748)
hypothalamus (p. 749)
cerebellum (p. 749)
brain stem (p. 749)
dopamine (p. 750)

31.3 The Peripheral Nervous System

- The peripheral nervous system's sensory division transmits impulses from sense organs to the central nervous system.

- The peripheral nervous system's motor division transmits impulses from the central nervous system to muscles or glands.

somatic nervous system (p. 752)
reflex arc (p. 752)
autonomic nervous system (p. 753)

31.4 The Senses

- Different sensory receptors in the body respond to touch, temperature, and pain.

- Sensations of smell and taste are both the result of impulses sent to the brain by chemoreceptors.

- Mechanoreceptors found in parts of the ear transmit impulses to the brain. The brain translates the impulses into sound and information about balance.

- Vision occurs when photoreceptors in the eyes transmit impulses to the brain. The brain translates these impulses into images.

cochlea (p. 755)
semicircular canal (p. 756)
cornea (p. 756)
iris (p. 756)
pupil (p. 757)
lens (p. 757)
retina (p. 757)

Assess the Big idea ▸ Structure and Function

Write an answer to the question below.

Q: How does the structure of the nervous system allow it to regulate functions in every part of the body?

Constructed Response

Write an answer to each of the numbered questions below. The answer to each question should be one or two paragraphs. To help you begin, read the **Hints** below the questions.

1. What is the purpose of sodium-potassium pumps in a neuron?

   Hint The sodium-potassium pump moves sodium and potassium ions across the cell membrane.

   Hint Nerve impulses are reversals of resting potentials, which are electrical charges across the cell membrane.

2. Why must neurotransmitters be broken down or removed after a cell responds to a nerve impulse?

   Hint Axon terminals release neurotransmitters during a nerve impulse.

   Hint Neurotransmitters must bind to receptors on a cell to stimulate a response from the cell.

3. How do hair cells in the ear help transmit nerve impulses?

   Hint Hair cells are found in the cochlea, the semicircular canal, and the sacs associated with the semicircular canal.

   Hint Hair cells are mechanoreceptors.

Foundations for Learning Wrap-Up

Use the note squares you prepared when you started the chapter as tools to organize your thoughts about the nervous system.

Activity 1 Working with a partner, use your note squares to quiz each other about the structures and functions of the nervous system.

Activity 2 Working as a group, create idea "nervous systems" from your note squares by connecting the corners of the squares with brass fasteners. Use main ideas to create the "brain" and "spinal cord." Use details to create the "peripheral nerves." How do the "peripheral nerves" explain the main ideas in the "central nervous system"?

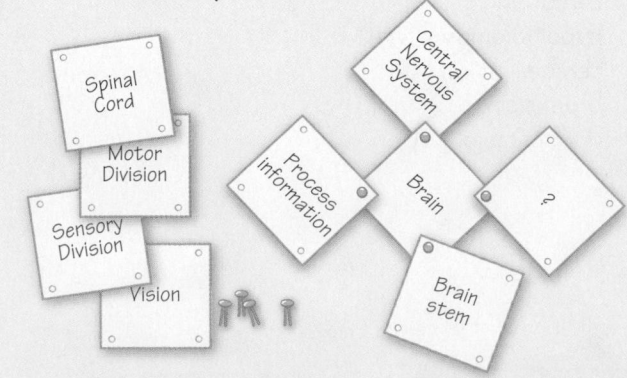

31.1 The Neuron

Understand Key Concepts

1. The basic units of structure and function in the nervous system are
   a. neurons. **c.** dendrites.
   b. axons. **d.** neurotransmitters.

2. In the diagram below, the letter A is pointing to a(n)
   a. myelin sheath. **c.** dendrite.
   b. axon. **d.** cell body.

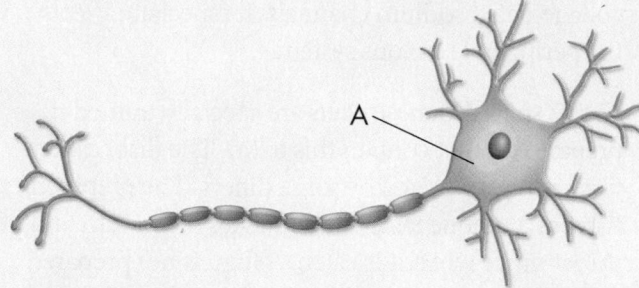

A

Test-Taking Tip

Interpret Graphics When you are asked to identify a structure in a figure, it is helpful to first review and label the figure. Question 2 includes the figure of a neuron. First, identify all the structures in the answer choices. The myelin sheath surrounds the axon. The axon is a long fiber that extends from the cell body. Dendrites are the short extensions of the cell body. The cell body contains the nucleus. So, **A** is pointing to the cell body.

3. The place where a neuron transfers an impulse to another cell is the
   a. synapse. **c.** myelin sheath.
   b. dendrite. **d.** receptor.

4. Why can an action potential be described as an all-or-none event?

Think Critically

5. **Infer** Suppose part of an axon is cut so that it does not connect to its cell body. How would that affect the transmission of impulses?

31.2 The Central Nervous System

Understand Key Concepts

6. The central nervous system consists of the
   a. sense organs.
   b. reflexes.
   c. brain and spinal cord.
   d. sensory and motor neurons.

7. Voluntary activities, or conscious activities of the body, are controlled primarily by the
   a. medulla oblongata. **c.** cerebellum.
   b. cerebrum. **d.** brain stem.

8. Describe the relationship between the brain stem and the spinal cord.

Think Critically

9. **Infer** Why might the folding of the cerebral cortex be important?

31.3 The Peripheral Nervous System

Understand Key Concepts

10. The sympathetic nervous system and parasympathetic nervous system are specific divisions of the
    a. peripheral nervous system.
    b. central nervous system.
    c. somatic nervous system.
    d. autonomic nervous system.

11. How do reflexes protect the body from injury?

12. What is the function of the sensory division of the peripheral nervous system?

Think Critically

13. **Apply Concepts** A routine examination by a doctor usually includes a knee-jerk reflex test. What is the purpose of this test?

31.4 The Senses

Understand Key Concepts

14. The senses of taste and smell involve sensory receptors called
- **a.** photoreceptors.
- **c.** thermoreceptors.
- **b.** chemoreceptors.
- **d.** mechanoreceptors.

15. What are the functions of the rods and cones?

16. What are the five basic tastes?

Think Critically

17. Sequence Trace the path of sound through the ear.

Connecting Concepts

Use Science Graphics

Use the illustration to answer questions 18 and 19.

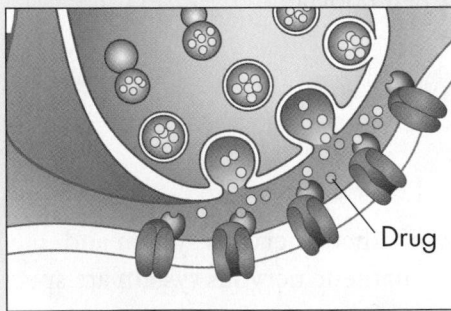

Drug

18. Interpret Visuals This illustration shows a drug
- **a.** interfering with enzymes that break down a neurotransmitter at a synapse.
- **b.** mimicking a neurotransmitter.
- **c.** stimulating an axon terminal.
- **d.** stimulating enzymes that break down a neurotransmitter at a synapse.

19. Apply Concepts Alcohol is called a depressant, because it depresses (slows) respiration and heart rate. Which part of the autonomic nervous system does alcohol most likely stimulate?

solve the CHAPTER MYSTERY

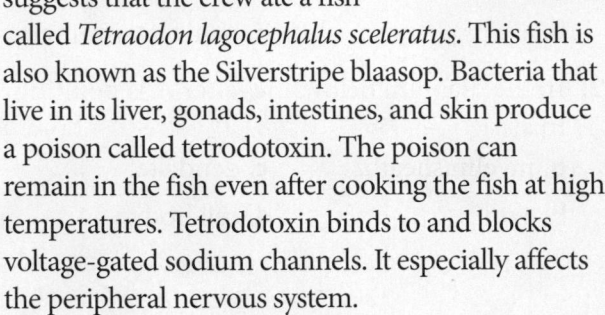

POISONING ON THE HIGH SEAS

A naturalist named Georg Forster traveled with Captain Cook. One of his sketches suggests that the crew ate a fish called *Tetraodon lagocephalus sceleratus*. This fish is also known as the Silverstripe blaasop. Bacteria that live in its liver, gonads, intestines, and skin produce a poison called tetrodotoxin. The poison can remain in the fish even after cooking the fish at high temperatures. Tetrodotoxin binds to and blocks voltage-gated sodium channels. It especially affects the peripheral nervous system.

Today, some Japanese chefs are specially trained to prepare fish that contain this toxin. The dish, called fugu, is highly prized by some diners. The prepared fish has a unique taste. It also makes the mouth and throat tingle when it is eaten. If fugu is not prepared correctly, it can lead to dangerous problems for the diner. Death is even possible.

Obviously, tetrodotoxin doesn't poison the fish that produce it. Studies of the fish's genome have revealed a mutation in an important gene. This gene codes for the structure of sodium channel proteins. The mutation changes the surface shape of the channel. This change prevents the toxin from binding to it.

1. Infer Some fish fillets are cooked and served with the skin left on. Would this be a safe way to prepare and serve fugu?

2. Apply Concepts Describe in your own words why the fish are not affected by their own toxin.

 **Never Stop Exploring Your World.** Finding the solution to this mystery is just the beginning. Take a video field trip with the ecogeeks of Untamed Science to see where this mystery leads.

MD Standardized Test Practice for Maryland

Multiple Choice

1. The largest and most prominent part of the human brain is the
A cerebrum.
B cerebellum.
C thalamus.
D brain stem. CLG 3.2.1

2. The point of connection between two neurons is called a
A threshold.
B synapse.
C neurotransmitter.
D dendrite. CLG 3.2.1

3. The part of a neuron that carries impulses away from the cell body is called a(n)
A axon.
B dendrite.
C vesicle.
D synapse. CLG 3.2.1

4. The minimum stimulus level that will cause a neuron to produce an action potential is called the
A resting potential.
B impulse.
C threshold.
D synapse. CLG 3.2.1

5. The part of the brain responsible for collecting sensory input from the body and relaying it to appropriate brain centers is the
A limbic system.
B thalamus.
C cerebellum.
D cerebrum. CLG 3.2.1

6. The major function of the spinal cord is
A emotional learning and memory storage.
B control of voluntary muscle movements.
C fine control of detailed muscle movement.
D a principal communication path between the brain and the rest of the body. CLG 3.2.1

7. Involuntary activities carried out throughout the body are the primary responsibility of the
A somatic nervous system.
B autonomic nervous system.
C spinal cord.
D limbic system. CLG 3.2.1

8. The part of the eye which contains photoreceptor cells is the
A cornea.
B iris.
C retina.
D optic nerve. CLG 3.2.1

Questions 9–10

Blood alcohol concentration (BAC) is a measure of the amount of alcohol in the blood per 100 mL of blood. In some states, if a driver has a BAC of 0.08 percent, he or she is considered legally drunk. The table below lists an average BAC as alcohol consumption increases. Use the information in the table to answer the questions.

Blood Alcohol Concentration (Percent)						
Drinks in One Hour	Body Mass					
	45 kg	54 kg	63 kg	72 kg	81 kg	90 kg
1	0.04	0.03	0.03	0.02	0.02	0.02
2	0.07	0.06	0.05	0.05	0.04	0.04
3	0.11	0.09	0.08	0.07	0.06	0.06
4	0.14	0.12	0.10	0.09	0.08	0.07
5	0.18	0.15	0.13	0.11	0.10	0.09
6	0.21	0.18	0.15	0.14	0.12	0.11
7	0.25	0.21	0.18	0.16	0.14	0.13
8	0.29	0.24	0.21	0.18	0.16	0.14

9. How many drinks in one hour would cause a 63 kg person to have a BAC of 0.08 percent?
A 1
B 3
C 5
D 7 SPI 1.5.5

10. If a 54 kg person had 3 drinks in one hour, what would his or her BAC percentage be?
A 0.06
B 0.08
C 0.09
D 0.11 SPI 1.5.5

Open-Ended Response

11. How do the parasympathetic and sympathetic nervous systems work together in the body?
CLG 3.2.1

If You Have Trouble With . . .										
Question	1	2	3	4	5	6	7	8	9	10	11
See Lesson	31.2	31.1	31.1	31.1	31.2	31.2	31.3	31.4	31.2	31.2	31.3

Big idea Structure...

Q: What sy...

Key ...

🔑 the sk...

🔑 typic...

B...
U...

T-Cha...
make...
colum...
rewrit...
quest...
answ...

In Y...
your ...
maki...
T-cha...

FU...

Supp...
supp...
huma...

Prote...
interr...
exam...
cage...

Move...
to pr...

Mine...
mine...
Mine...
body...
calci...
calci...

Bloo...
bloo...
in th...

The skeletal...
gymnast wo...

BUILD Vocabulary

axial skeleton
the skeleton that supports the central axis of the body; consists of the skull, vertebral column, and the rib cage

appendicular skeleton
the bones of the arms and legs along with the bones of the pelvis and shoulder area

cartilage
a type of connective tissue that is softer and more flexible than bone. In adults, cartilage supports both the nose and the ears.

joint
the place where one bone attaches to another bone

ligament
a tough connective tissue that holds bones together in a joint

🖋 WORD ORIGINS
The word *ligament* comes from the word *ligare*, a Latin word meaning "to tie." Ligaments "tie" two bones together.

Joints

A place where two or more bones meet is called a **joint.** Connective tissues hold the bones together. Joints let bones move without damaging each other.

Types of Joints Some joints, such as those of the shoulders, allow a lot of movement. Others, like the joints of the fully developed skull, allow no movement at all. There are three kinds of joints— immovable, slightly movable, and freely movable.

▶ *Immovable Joints* Immovable joints do not allow movement. The bones grow together until they are fused. The places where the bones in the skull meet are immovable joints.

▶ *Slightly Movable Joints* Slightly movable joints allow a small amount of movement. In immovable joints, the bones join and grow together. In slightly movable joints, the bones are separated from each other. The joints between the two bones of the lower leg are slightly movable joints. The joints between vertebrae are also slightly movable joints.

▶ *Freely Movable Joints* Freely movable joints allow movement in two or more directions. There are several kinds of freely movable joints. The types of joints are based on the amount of movement allowed by the joint.

Freely Movable Joints Freely movable joints make actions possible.

Ball-and-Socket Found in the shoulders and hips, these joints allow for movement in many directions. They are the most freely movable joints.

Hinge These joints permit back-and-forth motion, like the opening and closing of a door. They are found in the elbows, knees, and ankles.

Saddle These joints allow one bone to slide in two directions. Saddle joints allow a thumb to move across a palm.

Pivot These joints allow one bone to rotate or turn around another. Pivot joints allow you to turn your arm at your elbow and shake your head to say no.

Structure of Joints In freely movable joints, cartilage covers the surfaces where two bones come together. This protects the bones from damage as they move against each other. A joint capsule also surrounds the joint. The joint capsule helps hold the bones together while still allowing for movement.

The joint capsule has two layers. The outer layer forms strips of tough connective tissue called ligaments. The ligaments are connected to the membranes around the bones. **Ligaments** hold the bones in a joint together. The inner layer of the joint capsule is called the synovial (sih NOH vee uhl) cavity. This cavity holds cells that make synovial fluid. Small pockets of synovial fluid are called bursae (BUR see; singular: bursa). Synovial fluid allows the surfaces of the bones to slide over each other smoothly. Bursae also act as tiny shock absorbers.

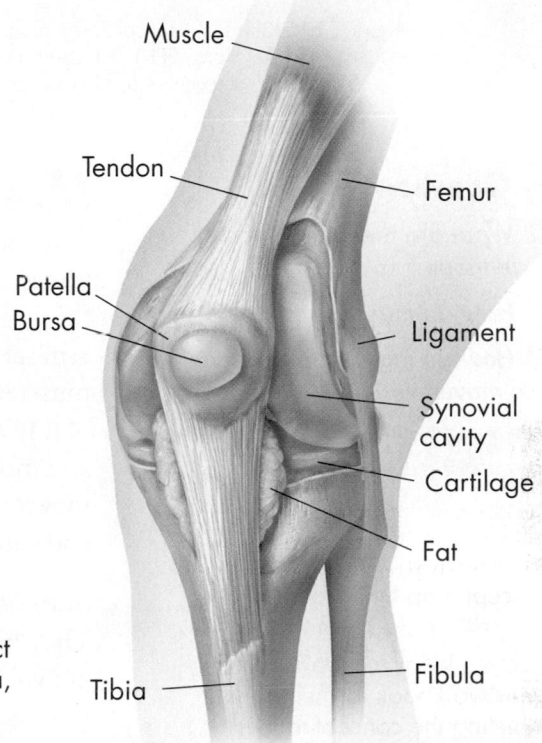

Muscle
Tendon
Patella
Bursa
Tibia
Femur
Ligament
Synovial cavity
Cartilage
Fat
Fibula

Key Question What is the role of joints?
Connective tissue in joints holds bones together. Joints allow bones to move without damaging each other.

The Knee Cartilage and bursae protect the knee joint. The tibia, femur, patella, and fibula make up the knee joint. Ligaments hold these bones together.

CHECK Understanding

Apply Vocabulary
Use the highlighted words from the lesson to complete each sentence correctly.

1. Connective tissues within a _____ hold two or more bones together.

2. The _____ forms the central axis of the skeleton.

3. _____ supports the body and is more flexible than bone.

Critical Thinking

4. **Compare and Contrast** Explain how a human knee joint is similar to a door hinge. How is it different from a door hinge?

5. **Relate Cause and Effect** Wear and tear over the years often leads to a condition called osteoarthritis. The cartilage in the joints of fingers, knees, and hips begins to break down. What is the likely effect on the bones?

6. **Write to Learn** Answer the first clue of the mystery.

MYSTERY CLUE

Children with rickets have soft, cartilagelike bones that may bend under their own weight. Why might their bones be so soft?
(**Hint:** See p. 767.)

BIOLOGY.com) Search (Lesson 32.1) **GO** • Lesson Assessment • InterActive Art

32.2 The Muscular System

MD CLG 3.1.1. Chemical Substances and Macromolecules, 3.1.3 Matter and Energy, 3.2.1 Processes and Functions. SPI 1.3.1 Use Equipment, 1.3.3 Safe Handling of Materials, 1.4.8 Use Models, 1.5.8 Compare, 1.5.9 Synthesize Ideas, 1.7.1 Apply Skills and Concepts.

Key Questions

🔑 **What are the main kinds of muscle tissue?**

🔑 **How do muscles contract?**

🔑 **How do muscle contractions cause movement?**

BUILD Understanding

Concept Map As you read, make a concept map that shows the relationship of ideas in this section.

In Your Workbook Go to your workbook for help in completing the concept map. Complete the concept map for Lesson 32.2.

Skeletal, Smooth, and Cardiac Muscle Skeletal muscle cells appear striped under the microscope. Smooth muscle cells appear to be smooth. Cardiac muscle cells, like skeletal muscle cells, look striped.

Muscle Tissue

You know that bones provide support, but it's muscles attached to your bones that make movements possible. Did you know that about one third of the mass of a person's body is muscle? Large muscles in your arms and legs help your body move. These large muscles are part of the muscular system. However, this system is also made up of thousands of tiny muscles. These tiny muscles help move blood through the body and move food through the digestive system. Muscles power every movement of the body. There are three kinds of muscle: skeletal, smooth, and cardiac. Each kind of muscle performs a different function.

Skeletal Muscles Skeletal muscles are often connected to bones. They help the body make voluntary movements. Dancing and waving are voluntary. You decide to dance or wave. When viewed under a microscope, skeletal muscle looks striped. The stripes in skeletal muscle are called striations.

Skeletal muscle cells are large and have many nuclei. The cells are not always the same length. However, they are often long and thin. Skeletal muscle cells are often called **muscle fibers.**

Smooth Muscles Smooth muscle cells do not have striations. They look smooth under the microscope. These cells usually have only one nucleus. Smooth-muscle movements are usually involuntary. This means that you can't control these muscles. Smooth muscles form part of the walls of hollow parts of your body such as the stomach, blood vessels, and intestines. Smooth muscles move food through your digestive tract. Smooth muscles control the way blood flows through your circulatory system. Smooth muscles even change the size of the pupils of your eyes in bright light.

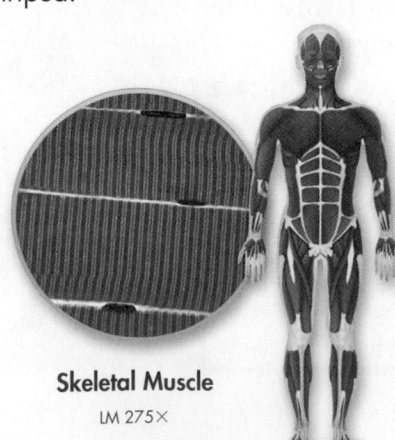

Skeletal Muscle
LM 275×

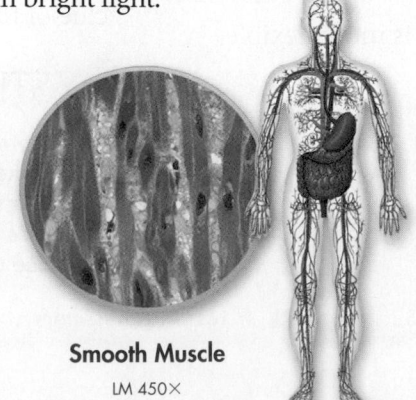

Smooth Muscle
LM 450×

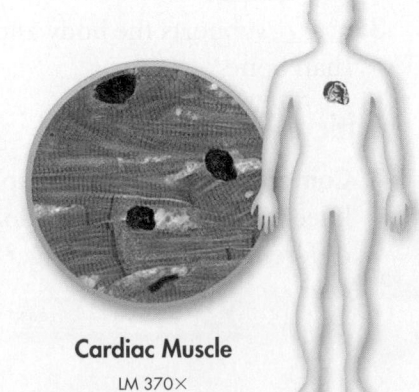

Cardiac Muscle
LM 370×

The cells in smooth muscles are connected to one another by gap junctions. Gap junctions allow the electrical impulses that trigger contractions to move from one muscle cell to the next.

Cardiac Muscle Cardiac muscle is found only in the heart. Cardiac muscle is striated like skeletal muscle, but its cells are smaller. Cardiac muscle cells almost always have only one or two nuclei. Cardiac muscle is not under voluntary control. Like smooth muscle cells, cardiac muscle cells are also connected by gap junctions.

🔑 **Key Question** What are the main kinds of muscle tissue? **The three kinds of muscle tissue are skeletal muscle, smooth muscle, and cardiac muscle.**

Muscle Contraction

Muscles cause parts of the body to move by getting shorter, or contracting, from end to end. Two kinds of filaments work together to cause contractions. These two filaments are called myosin and actin.

Muscle Fiber Structure Muscle fibers are filled with tightly packed filament bundles called **myofibrils** (MY uh FI bruhlz). Each myofibril is made up of two kinds of filaments. The thick protein filaments are called **myosin** (MY uh sin). The thin protein filaments are called **actin.** These filaments overlap within the myofibril. This pattern forms the striations that can be seen through a microscope. Actin filaments are bound together in areas called Z lines. Two Z lines and the filaments between them make up a unit called a sarcomere.

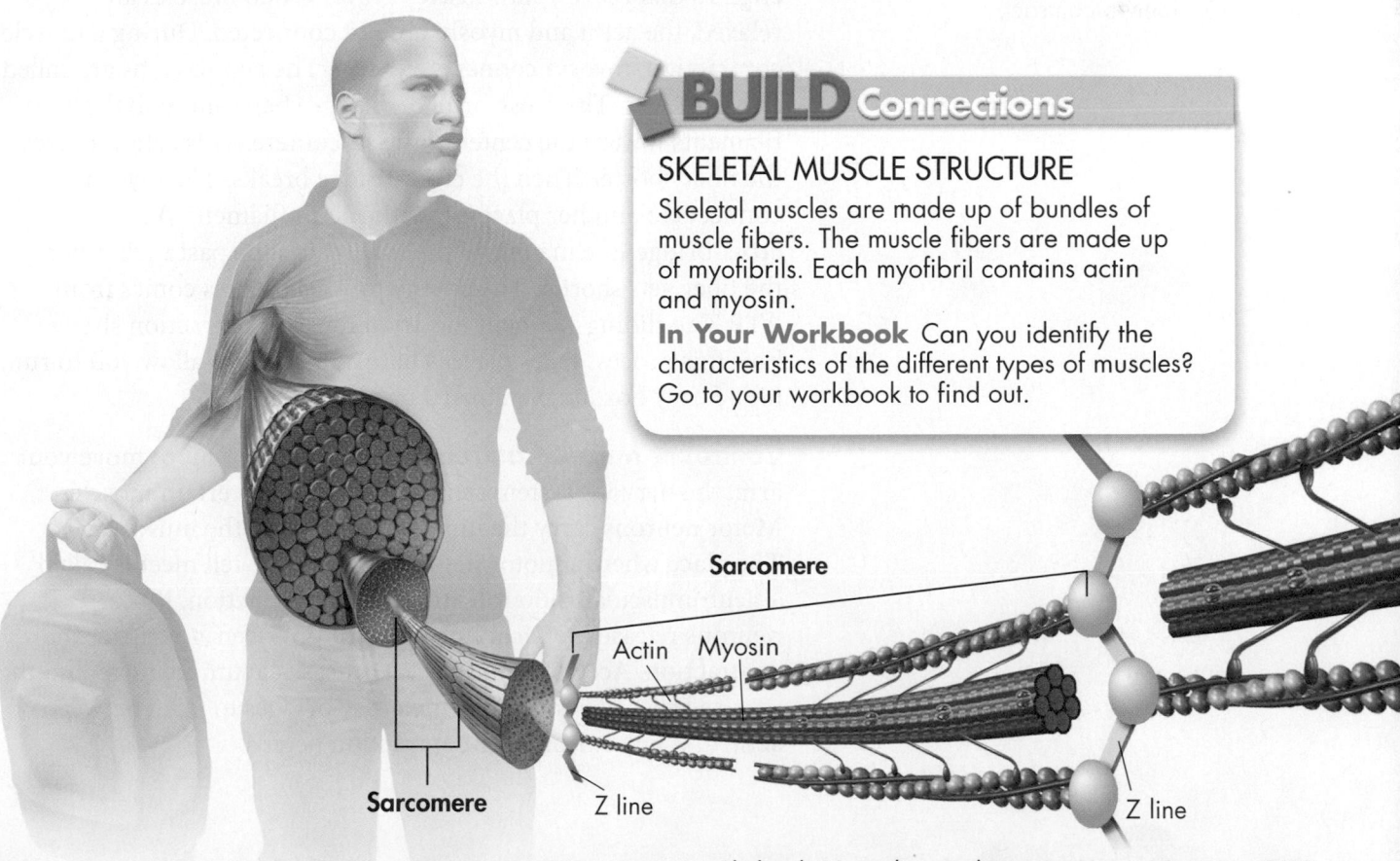

Sarcomere

Actin Myosin

Sarcomere   Z line   Z line

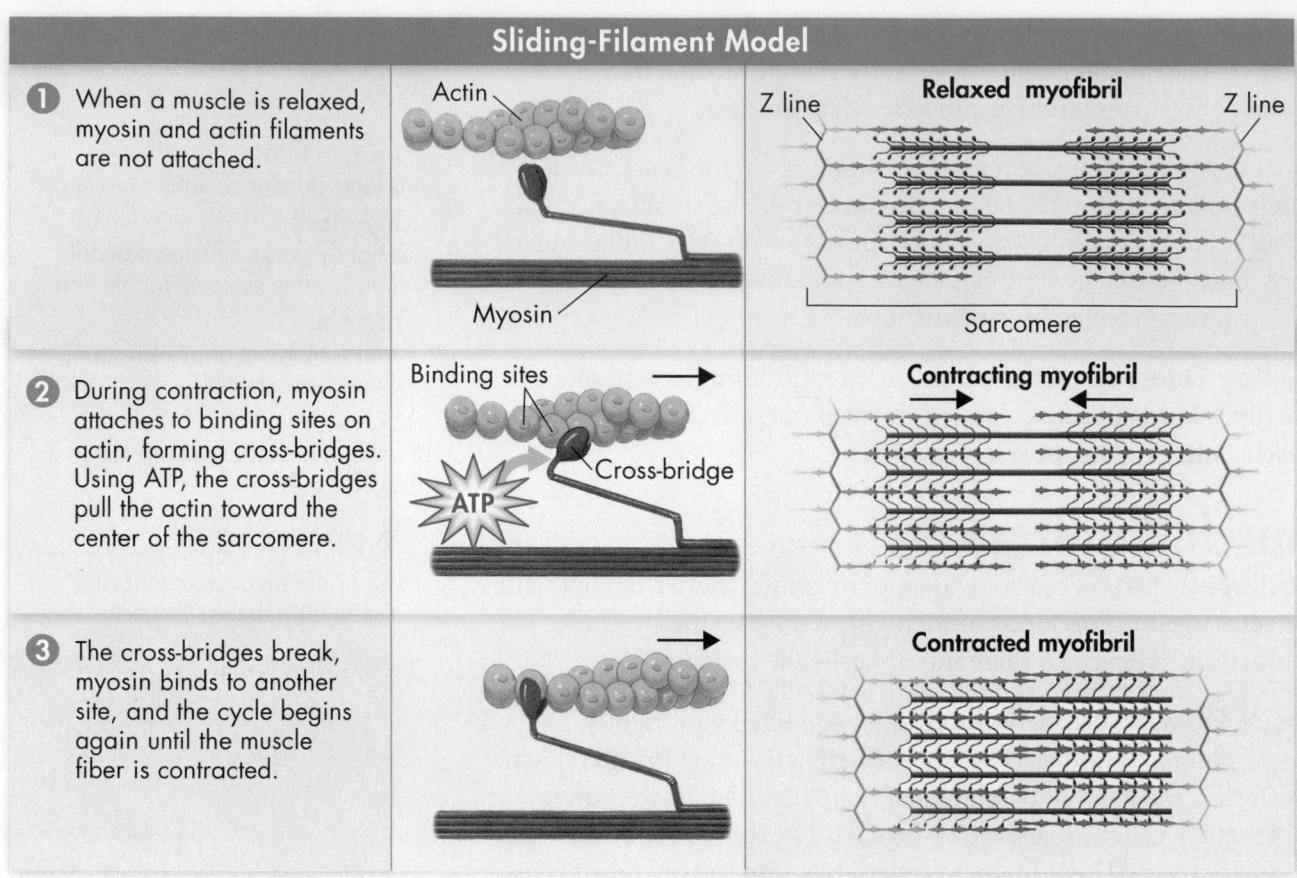

Sliding-Filament Model

1 When a muscle is relaxed, myosin and actin filaments are not attached.

Actin

Myosin

Z line

Relaxed myofibril

Z line

Sarcomere

2 During contraction, myosin attaches to binding sites on actin, forming cross-bridges. Using ATP, the cross-bridges pull the actin toward the center of the sarcomere.

Binding sites

Cross-bridge

ATP

Contracting myofibril

3 The cross-bridges break, myosin binds to another site, and the cycle begins again until the muscle fiber is contracted.

Contracted myofibril

Sliding-Filament Model During muscle contraction, interaction between myosin and actin causes a muscle fiber to contract.

The Sliding-Filament Model Myosin and actin are like tiny engines that make your muscles move. When muscles are relaxed, the actin and myosin are not connected. During a muscle contraction, myosin connects to actin. The connections are called cross-bridges. The cross-bridges change shape and pull the actin filaments toward the center of the sarcomere. This action makes the fiber shorter. Then the cross-bridge breaks. The myosin connects to another place along the actin filament. As cross-bridges are made and the filaments slide past each other, the fiber gets shorter. The energy for this process comes from ATP. The sliding-filament model of muscle contraction shows how this process takes place. These contractions allow you to run, lift a heavy box, or even turn a page in a book.

Control of Muscle Contraction When you want to move your arm, the nervous system sends an impulse to certain muscles. Motor neurons carry the impulses directly to the muscle cells. The place where a motor neuron and muscle cell meet is called a neuromuscular (noo roh MUS kyoo lur) junction. Motor neurons release acetylcholine (as ih til KOH leen) to trigger the contraction. Acetylcholine (ACh) causes calcium to move into the muscle cell. Calcium causes the cross-bridges to form between actin and myosin, and the contraction begins.

A muscle cell contracts until the motor neuron stops releasing ACh. Any remaining ACh is destroyed. The muscle cell pumps calcium back into storage. The cross-bridges stop forming, the contraction ends, and the muscle relaxes.

Key Question How do muscles contract?
During a muscle contraction, myosin filaments form cross-bridges with actin filaments. The cross-bridges change shape and pull the actin filaments toward the center of the sarcomere. This action shortens the fiber.

Muscles and Movement

Muscles can cause movement only by contracting in one direction. Yet, you know from experience that you can use your muscles in many directions. You can push and pull. How is this possible? Muscles work together to move your bones.

How Muscles and Bones Work Together Bones and joints act as levers. A lever is a machine that works around a fixed point. The fixed point is called the fulcrum. A seesaw is an example of one kind of lever. Skeletal muscles are connected to bones by tough tissue called **tendons.** By pulling on bones, tendons make bones work like levers.

The joint acts as the fixed point of the lever. Most of the time, several muscles pull in different directions around a joint to move the lever. When one muscle contracts, the other relaxes. In this way, muscles work in opposing pairs. Consider the muscles in your upper arm. When your biceps muscle contracts, it pulls the lower part of your arm. Your arm bends at the elbow joint. When the triceps muscle contracts, it opens the elbow joint. A controlled movement, such as holding a tennis racket, requires both muscles.

Exercise and Health Regular exercise is important for muscle strength and flexibility. Healthy muscles stay firm. Exercise increases the number of filaments in muscle cells. The large number of filaments increases the strength and size of the muscles.

Key Question How do muscle contractions cause movement? **Skeletal muscles cause movement by pulling on body parts as the muscles contract.**

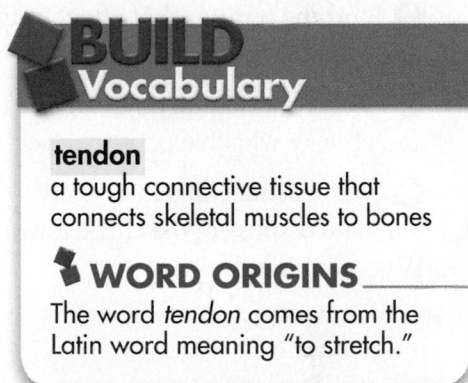

BUILD Vocabulary

tendon
a tough connective tissue that connects skeletal muscles to bones

WORD ORIGINS
The word *tendon* comes from the Latin word meaning "to stretch."

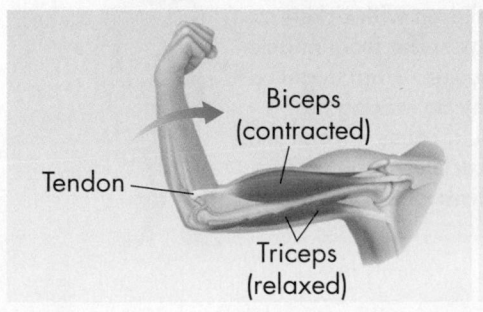

Biceps (contracted)

Tendon

Triceps (relaxed)

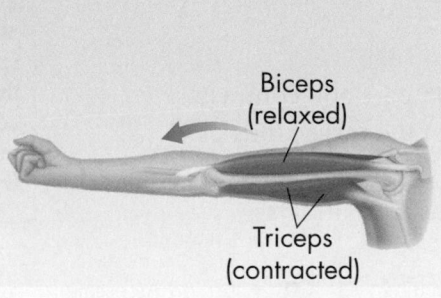

Biceps (relaxed)

Triceps (contracted)

Opposing Muscle Groups By contracting and relaxing, the biceps and triceps in the upper arm enable you to bend or straighten your elbow.

What Do Tendons Do?

In Lesson 32.2, you learned how the biceps and triceps work together to make your arm move. In this activity, you will explore how the biceps muscle and one of its tendons make a chicken wing move.

❶ Put on gloves and an apron. Place a chicken wing on a paper towel. Peel back or cut away the skin and fat of the largest wing segment to expose the biceps. **CAUTION:** *Do not touch your face with your hands during the lab.*

❷ Find the tendon that attaches the biceps to the bones of the middle segment of the wing.

❸ Use forceps to pull on the tendon of the biceps and observe what happens to the chicken wing.

❹ Your teacher will tell you how to clean your tools and dispose of the chicken wing and gloves. Wash your hands.

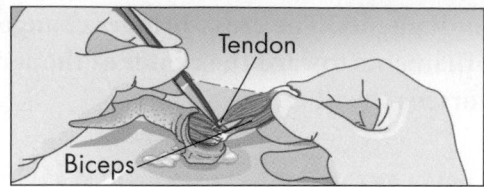

Analyze and Conclude

1. Observe What happened when you pulled on the tendon? In a live chicken, what structure would pull on the tendon to move the wing?

2. Compare and Contrast Observe the back of your hand as you move each of your fingers in turn. How is the way the wing moves similar to the way your fingers move?

In Your Workbook Go to your workbook for more help with this activity.

CHECK
Understanding

Apply Vocabulary
Use the highlighted words from the lesson to complete each sentence correctly.

1. A muscle is made up of groups of _____.

2. Skeletal muscles are joined to bones by tough tissue called _____.

3. Tightly packed bundles of actin and myosin filaments are called _____.

Critical Thinking

4. Compare and Contrast Compare and contrast the structure and function of the three kinds of muscle tissue.

5. Explain Describe how a muscle contracts.

6. Write to Learn Answer the second clue of the mystery. Write a paragraph that includes the terms *actin*, *myosin*, and *muscle fiber*.

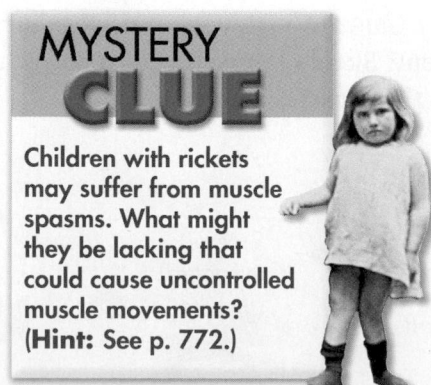

MYSTERY CLUE

Children with rickets may suffer from muscle spasms. What might they be lacking that could cause uncontrolled muscle movements? (**Hint:** See p. 772.)

32.3 Skin—The Integumentary System

MD CLG 3.1.1 Chemical Substances and Macromolecules, 3.1.2 Homeostasis, 3.2.1 Processes and Functions, 3.2.2 Changes in Metabolic Activity. SPI 1.5.2 Communicate Information.

Integumentary System Functions

What's the largest organ in your body? No, it's not your ears or stomach, or even your lungs or heart. Would you be surprised to learn that the largest organ is the skin? You may think of the skin only as the outside of your body. However, the skin has many functions besides just covering your body. Skin is part of the integumentary system. The integumentary system is made up of the skin, hair, nails, and several glands.

Protection The most important function of the skin is to protect the inside of your body. The skin keeps germs and dirt from entering the body. Hairs keep dirt and germs from entering the nose, ears, and eyes. The skin keeps the body from drying out and protects against the sun's rays. Nails, which are produced by the skin, protect the tips of fingers and toes.

Body Temperature Regulation Body cells generate heat. The skin releases the extra heat, keeping the body temperature stable. Hair helps stop heat loss from the head.

Excretion Your sweat glands are always releasing a little sweat. Sweat takes waste, such as urea and salts, out of the body.

Information Gathering The skin helps you sense what is happening in the outside environment. The skin receives information about pressure, heat, cold, and pain and sends the information to the nervous system.

Vitamin D Production The skin makes vitamin D. This is one of the skin's most important functions. The body uses vitamin D to absorb calcium and phosphorus from the small intestine. The skin needs sunlight in order to make vitamin D.

Key Question What are the main functions of the integumentary system?
The integumentary system protects the body from dirt and germs. It also protects the body from the sun's rays and keeps the body from drying out. The integumentary system works to maintain body temperature. It also removes wastes, gathers information, and produces vitamin D.

Key Questions

- What are the main functions of the integumentary system?
- What are the structures of the integumentary system?
- What are some problems that affect the skin?

BUILD Understanding

Preview Visuals Before you read, preview the figure Structure of the Skin on the next page. Make a two-column table. In the first column, list structures labeled in the figure. As you read, fill in the function of each structure in the second column.

In Your Workbook Go to your workbook for help in completing the table. Complete the table for Lesson 32.3.

epidermis
the outer layer of the skin

dermis
the layer of skin found beneath the epidermis

🔑 **WORD ORIGINS**

The prefix *epi-* in *epidermis* comes from the Greek word meaning "on" or "upon." *Dermis* comes from the Greek *derma*, meaning "skin."

Integumentary System Structures

The skin, hair, and nails work together to carry out the functions of the integumentary system. Skin has three layers—the epidermis, dermis, and hypodermis.

Epidermis The outer layer of the skin is the **epidermis.** The epidermis has two layers. Cells in the inner layer of epidermis divide quickly. The newer cells push older cells to the surface of the skin. These older cells produce a tough protein called keratin. As the cells fill up with keratin, they die, forming the outer layer of the skin.

The epidermis contains a dark brown pigment called melanin. Melanin protects the skin from the sun. Melanin is made by cells called melanocytes (MEL uh noh syts). These cells make more melanin in people with darker skin.

Dermis The **dermis** is the middle layer of skin, below the epidermis. The dermis helps keep the body temperature stable. On a cold day, the blood vessels in the dermis narrow. This keeps heat from escaping through the skin. On hot days, the blood vessels widen and sweat glands release sweat. Sweat takes heat away from your body as it evaporates.

Sebaceous (suh BAY shus) glands in the dermis make an oily substance called sebum. Sebum helps to keep the epidermis flexible and waterproof. It can also kill bacteria on the skin.

Hair and Nails Hair and nails are made mostly of keratin. Nails cover and protect the tips of the fingers and toes. Hair on the head protects the scalp from the sun's rays. It also keeps the head warm. Eyelashes and hairs in the nostrils and external ear canals keep dirt from entering the body. Hair is made by cells at the base of hair follicles. Hair follicles are pockets of epidermal cells that grow into the dermis.

🔑 **Key Question** What are the structures of the integumentary system? **The skin, hair, nails, and several glands make up the integumentary system.**

Structure of the Skin The skin has three layers. The outer layer is called the epidermis. The middle layer is called the dermis. The deepest layer is called the hypodermis.

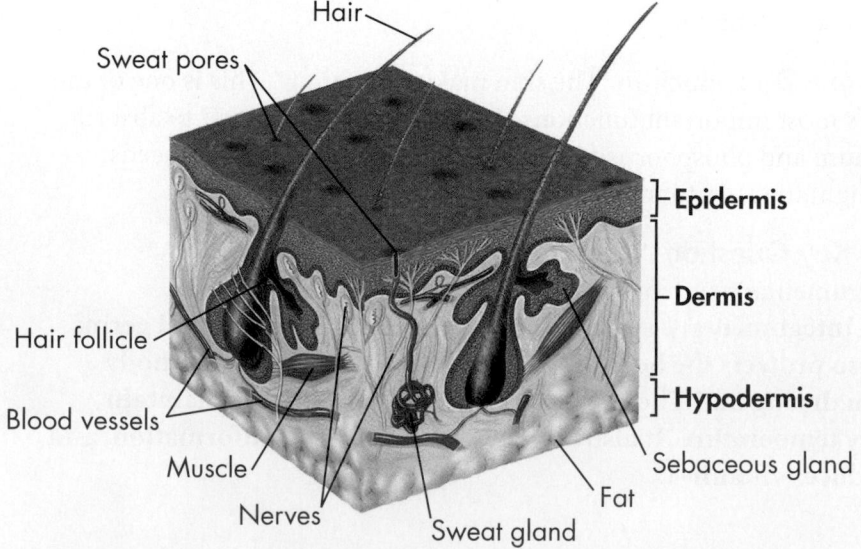

Skin Problems

The skin is always interacting with the environment. This interaction can cause many different problems. These problems can be as simple as a small scrape or as serious as skin cancer.

Acne Sometimes, sebum and dead skin cells form plugs in hair follicles. Trapped bacteria can then cause infection. Acne results from a bacterial infection of the sebaceous glands. Severe acne can leave scars on your skin for the rest of your life. A person with severe acne should see a dermatologist, a doctor who treats the skin.

Hives People with allergies sometimes get hives. During an allergic reaction, histamine causes small blood vessels to get bigger. Fluid can ooze from the vessels and move into the skin. This fluid causes swelling that leads to hives.

Skin Cancer Excessive tanning, outside or in a tanning bed, can cause skin cancer. Melanoma is the most dangerous form of skin cancer. Over 60,000 people are diagnosed with melanoma every year in the United States. As many as 8000 people die from it each year in the United States.

You can help protect yourself from skin cancer. Avoid tanning beds. Wear a hat and sunglasses whenever you plan to be outside for a long time. Always use a sunscreen that protects against UV-A and UV-B rays.

Key Question What are some problems that affect the skin?
Acne, hives, and skin cancer are some problems of the skin.

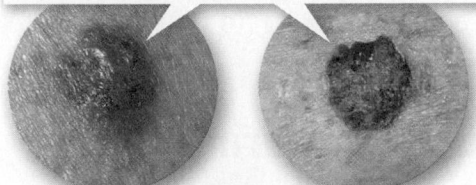

Basal cell carcinoma and squamous cell carcinoma are two of the most common types of skin cancer. Both types rarely spread to other parts of the body, but early treatment is important to prevent tissue damage.

Basal Cell Carcinoma

Squamous Cell Carcinoma

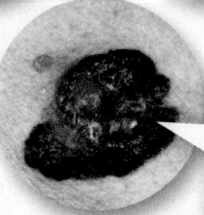

Melanomas are cancers that develop from melanocytes. Without early treatment, the cancer spreads to other organs in the body.

Melanoma

Skin Cancer Early detection is important in treating skin cancer. A sore that does not heal or a sudden change in a mole may be a sign of skin cancer. A mole that is larger than 6 mm or has irregular borders should be checked by a doctor. A mole that is an odd color should also be checked by a doctor.

CHECK Understanding

Apply Vocabulary
Use the highlighted words from the lesson to complete each sentence correctly.

1. New cells in the inner layer of the _____ push older cells out to the surface of the skin.

2. The middle layer of the skin is called the _____.

Critical Thinking

3. Apply Concepts Explain two ways that the skin can help remove excess heat from the body.

4. Sequence Explain the events that lead to acne.

5. Write to Learn Answer the third clue of the mystery. How is sunlight important to the skin's functions?

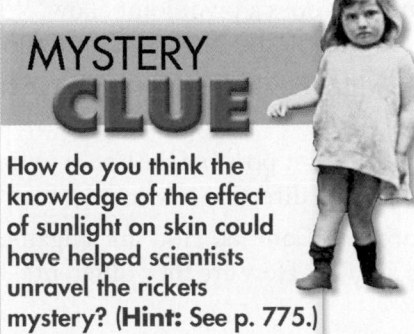

MYSTERY CLUE

How do you think the knowledge of the effect of sunlight on skin could have helped scientists unravel the rickets mystery? (**Hint:** See p. 775.)

 # Skills Lab

 MD SPI **1.3.1** Use Equipment, **1.3.3** Safe Handling of Materials, **1.7.1** Apply Skills and Concepts.

Pre-Lab: Comparing Limbs

Problem How is the structure of skeletal muscles and bones related to the functions of these body parts?

Materials disposable plastic gloves, chicken wing, disposable dissection tray, dissecting scissors, forceps, colored pencils or markers

Skills Focus Observe, Infer, Compare and Contrast

Connect to the **Big idea** The structure of your bones reflects the different functions of your skeleton. For example, your bones must be strong enough to support your body and protect internal organs. Your bones must also be rigid so that they provide a system of levers on which skeletal muscles can act.

Skeletal muscles have a structure that enables them to move bones around fixed points called joints. In skeletal muscles, the cells are long and narrow, which is why these cells are also called muscle fibers. When muscle fibers contract, they pull on the bone to which a muscle is attached. This force causes the bone to move in the direction of the contraction.

In this lab, you will observe and compare the structure and function of a human arm and leg. You will also compare the arm with a chicken wing.

Background Questions

a. Review What motion does a hinge joint allow? What motion does a pivot joint allow? Which of these joints are found in your elbows and knees?

b. Review What role does cartilage play in freely movable joints?

c. Explain How is it possible for bones to move in more than one direction around a joint?

d. Compare and Contrast How are a ligament and a tendon similar? How are they different?

Pre-Lab Questions

1. Observe How will you observe the structure and function of your elbow and knee joints?

2. Relate Cause and Effect Why is it important to wear goggles and disposable gloves while examining the chicken wing?

3. Predict Will the arrangement of bones and muscles in a chicken wing be similar to the arrangement in a human arm? Why or why not?

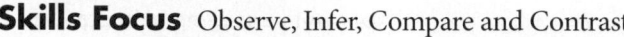 **BIOLOGY**.com Search Chapter 32 **GO**

Visit Chapter 32 online to test yourself on chapter content and to find activities to help you learn.

Untamed Science Video  Hold onto your seats as the Untamed Science crew whisks you to NASA to learn about the effect space travel has on an astronaut's bones.

Tutor Tube Watch an analogy to help you learn the sliding-filament model of muscle contraction.

Art Review Review your understanding of the structures of the skin.

InterActive Art Watch how the various joints in the body move.

Art in Motion Watch the process of muscle contraction.

Visual Analogy How is the skeleton like the framework of a house?

32 CHAPTER Summary

32.1 The Skeletal System

- The skeleton holds the body up and protects the internal organs. The skeleton helps the body move. It stores minerals and is the site of blood cell formation.

- Bones are made up of living cells and protein fibers. The fibers are surrounded by calcium salts.

- Connective tissue in joints holds bones together. Joints allow bones to move without damaging each other.

axial skeleton (p. 766)
appendicular skeleton (p. 766)
cartilage (p. 767)
joint (p. 768)
ligament (p. 769)

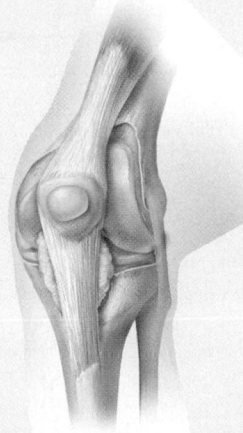

32.2 The Muscular System

- The three kinds of muscle tissue are skeletal muscle, smooth muscle, and cardiac muscle.

- During a muscle contraction, myosin filaments form cross-bridges with actin filaments. The cross-bridges change shape and pull the actin filaments toward the center of the sarcomere. This action shortens the fiber.

- Skeletal muscles cause movement by pulling on body parts as the muscles contract.

muscle fiber (p. 770)
myofibril (p. 771)
myosin (p. 771)
actin (p. 771)
tendon (p. 773)

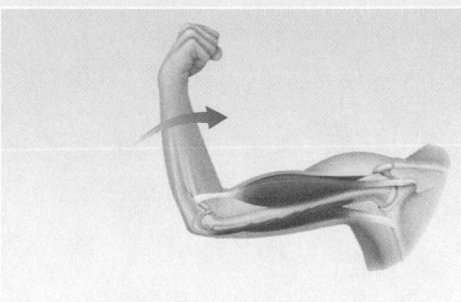

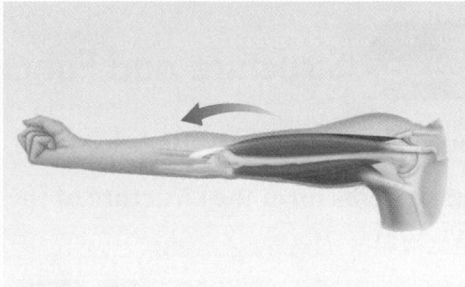

32.3 Skin—The Integumentary System

- The integumentary system protects the body from dirt and germs. It also protects the body from the sun's rays and keeps the body from drying out. The integumentary system works to maintain body temperature. It also removes wastes, gathers information, and produces vitamin D.

- The skin, hair, nails, and several glands make up the integumentary system.

- Acne, hives, and skin cancer are some problems of the skin.

epidermis (p. 776)   **dermis** (p. 776)

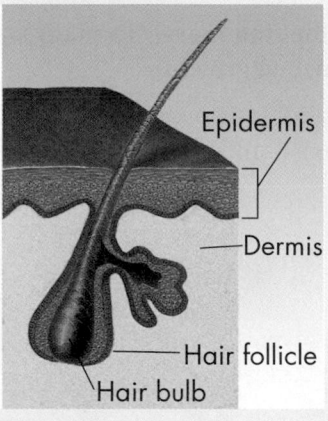

Epidermis

Dermis

Hair follicle

Hair bulb

Assess the Big idea ▶ Structure and Function

Write an answer to the question below.

Q: What systems form the structure of the human body?

Constructed Response

Write an answer to each of the numbered questions below. The answer to each numbered question should be one or two paragraphs long. To help you begin, read the **Hints** below each of the questions.

1. **How does the sliding-filament model explain how muscles contract?**

    Hint When muscles are relaxed, the actin and myosin filaments are not connected.

2. **How do opposing muscle groups make a joint act as a lever?**

    Hint The part of the lever that does not move is called the fulcrum.

    Hint When one muscle in the group contracts, the other relaxes.

3. **Explain the statement, "In many ways, a bone is never finished growing."**

    Hint Osteoclasts break down bone minerals. Osteoblasts build bone tissue.

Foundations for Learning Wrap-Up

Use the table you prepared at the start of the chapter as a tool to help you organize your thoughts about the structures and functions of body systems.

Activity 1 Working with a partner, fold your paper so that only the structures are visible. Take turns quizzing each other about the structures and functions listed.

Activity 2 Your lists are separated into structures and functions. In a small group, discuss how the structure of each organ or system relates to its functions. For example, how do different structures of the skeleton help it perform its many functions? You may want to add rows for this information.

STRUCTURES	FUNCTIONS	
Skeletal system	• Support, • Protection • Movement • Mineral storage • Blood cell formation	
Smooth muscle	• Involuntary movement • Form part of the wall of blood vessels, intestines, stomach	
Cardiac muscle	• Involuntary movement • Most of the heart	
Skeletal muscle	• Voluntary movement • Move bones around joints	
Integumentary system	• Protects the body from dirt and germs • Protects from the sun • Keeps the body from drying out • Maintains body temperature • Removes wastes • Gathers information • Produces vitamin D	

32.1 The Skeletal System

Understanding Key Concepts

1. The network of tubes that runs through compact bone is called the
   a. periosteum.   **c.** Haversian canals.
   b. joint.   **d.** marrow.

Test-Taking Tip

Eliminate Incorrect Answers If you are having trouble answering a multiple-choice question, eliminate answers you know are not correct. This will help you find the correct answer. In question 1, answer **a** is the thin outer layer of the bone. Answer **b** is the place where two or more bones meet. Answer **d** is the soft tissue inside some bones where fat is stored and blood cells are formed. Once you have eliminated these answers, you see that answer **c** is the correct answer. Nerves and blood vessels run through the Haversian canals.

2. Ossification begins up to seven months before birth. What happens during ossification?
   a. Bones lose minerals and mass.
   b. Cartilage is replaced by bone.
   c. Vitamin D is made.
   d. Bones fracture more easily.

3. Which connective tissue joins two bones at a joint?
   a. bursae
   b. ligaments
   c. tendons
   d. cartilage

4. Draw a diagram of a long bone and label the structures.

5. Which type of freely movable joint allows for the greatest range of motion?

6. **Infer** Disks of rubbery cartilage are found between the individual bones in the backbone. What function do you think these disks serve?

Think Critically

7. **Interpret Visuals** Look at the images below. One shows a healthy bone tissue. The other shows signs of osteoporosis. Which bone sample do you think shows signs of osteoporosis, choice *a* or choice *b*? Explain.

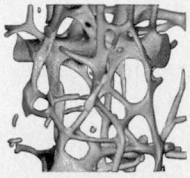 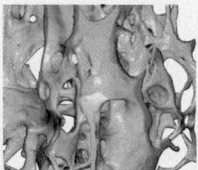

a.   **b.**

8. **Use Models** Imagine that you want to build a robotic arm that works the way the human elbow works. Describe or sketch the elbow that you could use in your model.

32.2 The Muscular System

Understand Key Concepts

9. Which kind of muscle tissue is striated and has cells that have only one or two nuclei?
   a. cardiac   **c.** smooth
   b. skeletal   **d.** voluntary

10. Which two protein filaments are involved in muscle contraction?
    a. sarcomere and myofibril
    b. actin and myosin
    c. periosteum and cartilage
    d. ATP and acetylcholine

11. Describe the primary function of each of the three types of muscle tissue.

12. Describe how acetylcholine affects a muscle cell.

13. Explain this statement: "Most skeletal muscles work in opposing pairs."

Think Critically

14. **Relate Cause and Effect** Certain bacteria make a toxin that affects motor neurons. The toxin prevents motor neurons from releasing acetylcholine. Explain what effect this toxin is likely to have on the body.

32.3 Skin—The Integumentary System

15. What is the outer layer of skin called?
  a. dermis   **c.** epidermis
  b. keratin   **d.** melanin

16. Which of the following is a function of the eyelashes and hairs in the ears and nose?
  a. They keep the body warm.
  b. The help in the production of vitamin D.
  c. They stop dirt and germs from entering the body.
  d. They produce keratin.

17. In what layer of the skin do newer cells push older cells to the surface of the body?
  a. the epidermis
  b. the hypodermis
  c. the dermis
  d. the sebum

18. Describe three ways the integumentary system protects the body.

19. Describe two ways the integumentary system helps regulate body temperature.

Connecting Concepts

Use Science Graphics

20. Infer Cartilage does not appear on X-ray film. Instead, it is seen as a clear area between the shaft and the ends of bones. Examine the X-rays shown below. Which hand belongs to the youngest person? Explain.

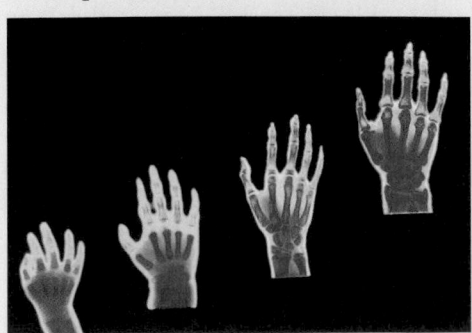

solve the CHAPTER MYSTERY

THE DEMISE OF A DISEASE

The research on the cause and a cure for rickets found two results. Both cod liver oil and exposure to ultraviolet light could prevent and cure rickets.

Cod liver oil has a nutrient involved in bone health. Starting in the 1930s, many parents in the United States gave their children a daily dose of cod liver oil.

The research also suggested that the sun influences bone health. This explained why children in colder climates were more likely to have rickets. They had little sun exposure during winter months.

But scientists still did not understand how such different treatments could have the same outcome.

Through the work of many scientists, we now know that both treatments provide vitamin D. Cod liver oil gives the body vitamin D. And, when exposed to the sun's rays, the skin helps the body make vitamin D. Vitamin D also helps the body absorb calcium and phosphorus from the digestive system.

Today, children are no longer given cod liver oil. Instead, vitamin D is added to milk. Rickets is now rare in the United States.

1. Explain Why were children in southern cities less likely to develop rickets?

2. Compare and Contrast Describe the structure of the bones of a healthy child in comparison to the bones of a child who developed rickets.

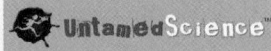 Solving the Demise of a Disease mystery is just the beginning. Take a video field trip with the ecogeeks of Untamed Science to see where the mystery leads.

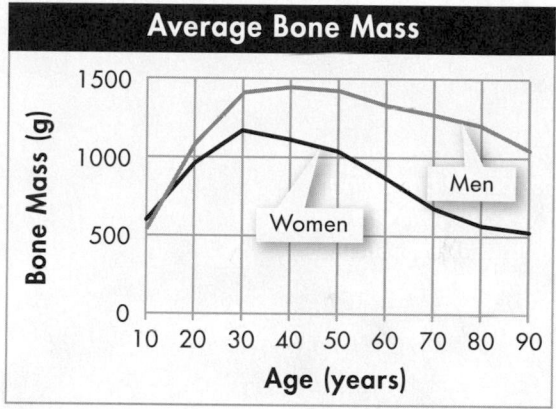 Standardized Test Practice for Maryland

Multiple Choice

1. What determines differences in skin color among individuals?
   A number of melanocytes
   B amount of melanin produced by each melanocyte
   C amount of keratin in the skin
   D amount of sebum produced   CLG 3.1.1

2. Smooth muscle is found in the
   A walls of blood vessels.
   B heart.
   C neuromuscular junctions.
   D joints.   CLG 3.2.1

3. All of the following are important roles of the skeletal system EXCEPT
   A protection of internal organs.
   B facilitation of movement.
   C storage of mineral reserves.
   D regulation of body temperature.   CLG 3.2.1

4. Which of the following supplies the energy required for muscle contractions?
   A myosin   C acetylcholine
   B ATP   D actin   CLG 3.1.1

5. The tough layer of connective tissue surrounding each bone is called
   A tendon.   C periosteum.
   B ligament.   D cartilage.   CLG 3.2.1

6. Joints that allow one bone to rotate around another are
   A gliding joints.
   B ball-and-socket joints.
   C hinge joints.
   D pivot joints.   CLG 3.2.1

7. Which of the following is NOT found in skin tissue?
   A keratin   C marrow
   B collagen   D melanin   CLG 3.1.1

8. What is a function of sebum?
   A It moistens the hair and skin.
   B It gives skin its color.
   C It insulates the body.
   D It makes nails and hair rigid.   CLG 3.2.1

Questions 9–10

As people age, the mineral content of their bone decreases. People who fail to build enough bone in adolescence and young adulthood or who lose bone at a faster than normal rate are at risk for developing osteoporosis. The graph below shows typical bone mass of men and women through most of the life span.

Average Bone Mass

(graph: Bone Mass (g) vs. Age (years), curves labeled Women and Men)

9. Between which ages do both men and women gain bone mass at the highest rate?
   A 10–20 years
   B 20–30 years
   C 30–40 years
   D 50–60 years   SPI 1.4.2

10. A valid conclusion that can be drawn from this graph is that, on average,
    A women lose more bone mass as they age than men do.
    B men lose more bone mass as they age than women do.
    C women and men lose the same bone mass as they age.
    D men continue to gain bone mass as they age.   SPI 1.4.2

Open-Ended Response

11. Doctors recommend that women eat calcium-rich foods and get plenty of exercise during adolescence and early adulthood. How could this help prevent osteoporosis later in life?   SPI 1.7.1

If You Have Trouble With . . .

Question	1	2	3	4	5	6	7	8	9	10	11
See Lesson	32.3	32.2	32.1	32.2	32.1	32.1	32.3	32.3	32.1	32.1	32.1

3

Big
idea

Usually, we a
conscious of b
but we can co
during activitie
as swimming.

784

33.1 The Circulatory System

MD CLG 3.1.2 Homeostasis, 3.2.1 Processes and Functions. SPI 1.4.8 Use Models,
1.5.2 Communicate Information, 1.5.7 Classification Systems, 1.7.1 Apply Skills and Concepts.

Key Questions

🔑 What are the functions of the circulatory system?

🔑 How does the heart pump blood through the body?

🔑 What are three types of blood vessels?

BUILD Understanding

Preview Visuals Before you read, look at the visual, The Heart. Draw a two-column chart. In the left column, write the structures listed in the image. In the right column, write down the functions of each structure.

In Your Workbook Go to your workbook for help completing the chart.

BUILD Connections

A CITY'S TRANSPORTATION SYSTEM

The human circulatory system is like the highways and streets of a large city.

In Your Workbook
Go to your workbook to compare the needs of a person living in a large city with the needs of a cell in the body.

Functions of the Circulatory System

More than 1 million Americans suffer a heart attack each year. Of those, more than one-third die. This sad fact shows how important the heart and circulatory systems are to life.

Some animals have only a few cells. These cells are in direct contact with the outside of the animal's body. These animals are able to get all of the oxygen and nutrients they need through active transport and diffusion. They also remove wastes through active transport and diffusion. The human body, on the other hand, has millions of cells that are not on the outside of the body. Because it has so many cells, the human body needs a circulatory system. This system carries oxygen, nutrients, and other things the body needs throughout the body. It also removes wastes.

You can think of the human body as a large city. The cells are like people who live in the city. The people need things that are made elsewhere in the city. They need food. They need to get rid of garbage, and they need to move around the city. Your cells need similar things. How are these needs met in a city? The needs are met by the city's streets, highways, and subway or train lines. In the human body, the circulatory system meets these needs. This system is made up of the heart, blood vessels, and blood.

🔑 **Key Question** What are the functions of the circulatory system?
The circulatory system carries oxygen, nutrients, and other substances throughout the body. It also removes wastes.

The Heart

Most of the time, you probably do not even notice your heart at work. But you notice it beating when you exercise.

Heart Structure An adult's heart beats about 72 times a minute. It beats more quickly during exercise. Your heart is about the size of your fist. It is almost all muscle. The muscles begin contracting before you are born. They stop only when you die. The layer of muscle in the walls of your heart is called the **myocardium.** Strong contractions of this muscle pump blood through the circulatory system.

The heart has four chambers. Each of the two upper chambers is called an **atrium** (plural: atria). Blood enters the heart through the atria. The lower chambers are called **ventricles.** They pump blood out of the heart.

Blood Flow Through the Heart Blood from the body enters the heart through the right atrium. Blood from the lungs enters the heart through the left atrium. Blood moves from the atria into the ventricles. Valves between the atria and ventricles keep the blood from flowing in the wrong direction. There are also valves at the exits of each ventricle. This system of valves keeps blood moving in one direction through the heart, similar to traffic on a one-way street.

The Heart The human heart has four chambers: the right atrium, the right ventricle, the left atrium, and the left ventricle. Valves prevent blood from flowing backward through the heart.

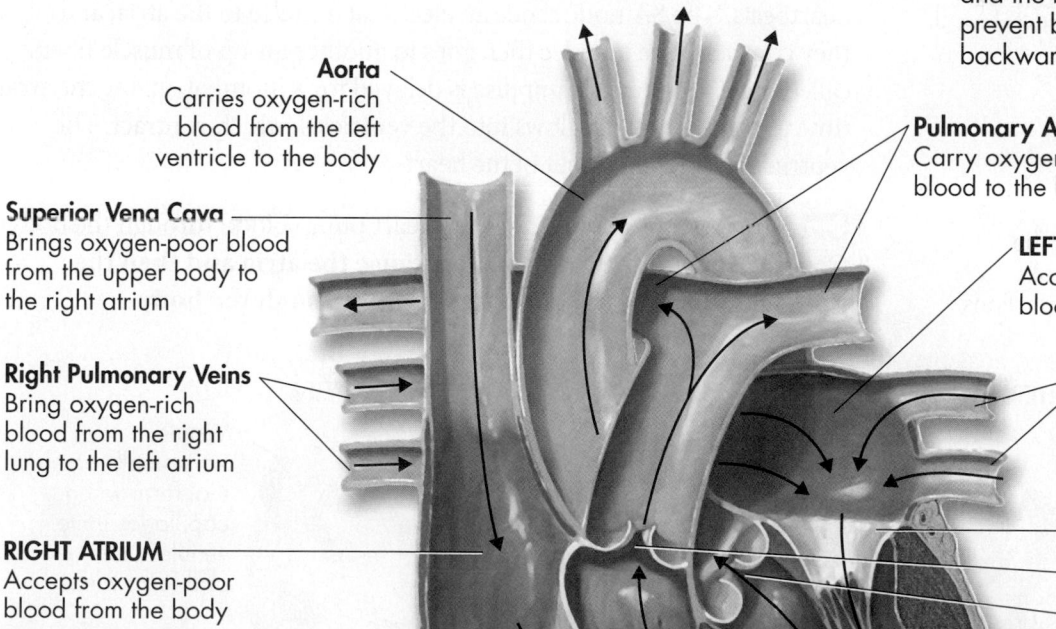

Aorta
Carries oxygen-rich blood from the left ventricle to the body

Superior Vena Cava
Brings oxygen-poor blood from the upper body to the right atrium

Right Pulmonary Veins
Bring oxygen-rich blood from the right lung to the left atrium

RIGHT ATRIUM
Accepts oxygen-poor blood from the body

RIGHT VENTRICLE
Pumps oxygen-poor blood to the lungs

Tricuspid Valve

Inferior Vena Cava
Brings oxygen-poor blood from the lower body to the right atrium

Pulmonary Arteries
Carry oxygen-poor blood to the lungs

LEFT ATRIUM
Accepts oxygen-rich blood from the lungs

Left Pulmonary Veins
Bring oxygen-rich blood from the left lung to the left atrium

Mitral Valve
Pulmonary Valve
Aortic Valve

LEFT VENTRICLE
Pumps oxygen-rich blood to the body

Septum

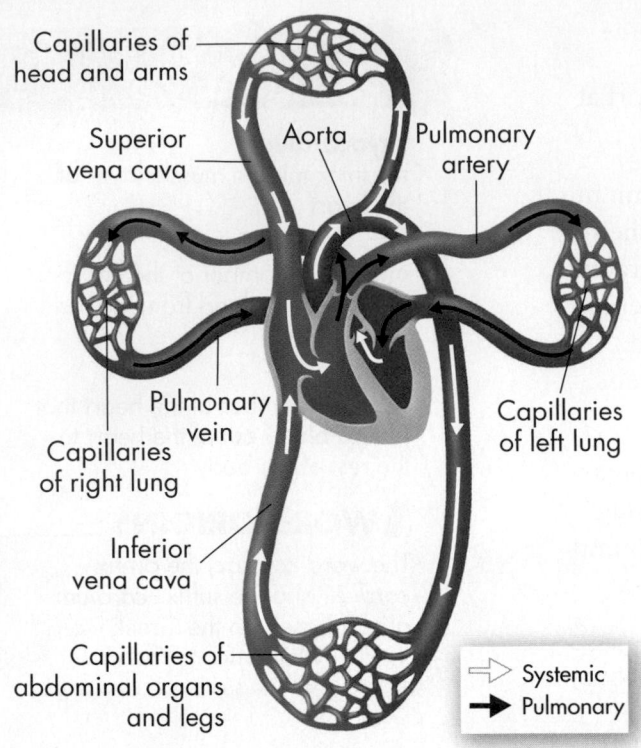

Capillaries of head and arms

Superior vena cava

Aorta

Pulmonary artery

Pulmonary vein

Capillaries of right lung

Capillaries of left lung

Inferior vena cava

Capillaries of abdominal organs and legs

⇨ Systemic
➡ Pulmonary

The Heart's Blood Supply The heart itself gets very little oxygen and nutrients from the blood it pumps through its chambers. Instead, a pair of vessels called *coronary arteries* run through the heart tissue. These provide blood to the heart muscle.

Circulation The heart acts as two pumps. One pump pushes blood to the lungs. The second pump pushes blood to the rest of the body.

▶ *Pulmonary Circulation* The first pump is the right side of the heart. It sends oxygen-poor blood from the heart to the lungs. This path is called pulmonary circulation. The blood picks up oxygen and gets rid of carbon dioxide in the lungs. Then the blood flows to the left side of the heart.

▶ *Systemic Circulation* The left side of the heart pumps oxygen-rich blood to the rest of the body. This path is called systemic circulation. The blood brings oxygen to the body's cells.

Circulation Pathways The circulatory system is divided into two pathways: pulmonary circulation and systemic circulation. Notice that the blue in this image represents oxygen-poor blood. The red represents oxygen-rich blood.

Heartbeat The heartbeat must be controlled. First the atria contract and then the ventricles contract. A small group of cardiac muscle fibers, called the SA node, is found in the right atrium. The SA node is sometimes called the pacemaker because it "sets the pace" of the heartbeats. The SA node sends an electrical impulse to the atria, and they contract. The impulse then goes to another group of muscle fibers called the AV node. The impulse is delayed for a moment, giving the atria time to contract. Blood flows into the ventricles, which contract. The ventricles pump blood out of the heart.

Structure of Blood Vessels The structure of blood vessel walls contributes to the vessels' functions.

🔑 **Key Question** How does the heart pump blood through the body? **Contractions of the myocardium cause the atria and then the ventricles to contract, pumping blood through the body.**

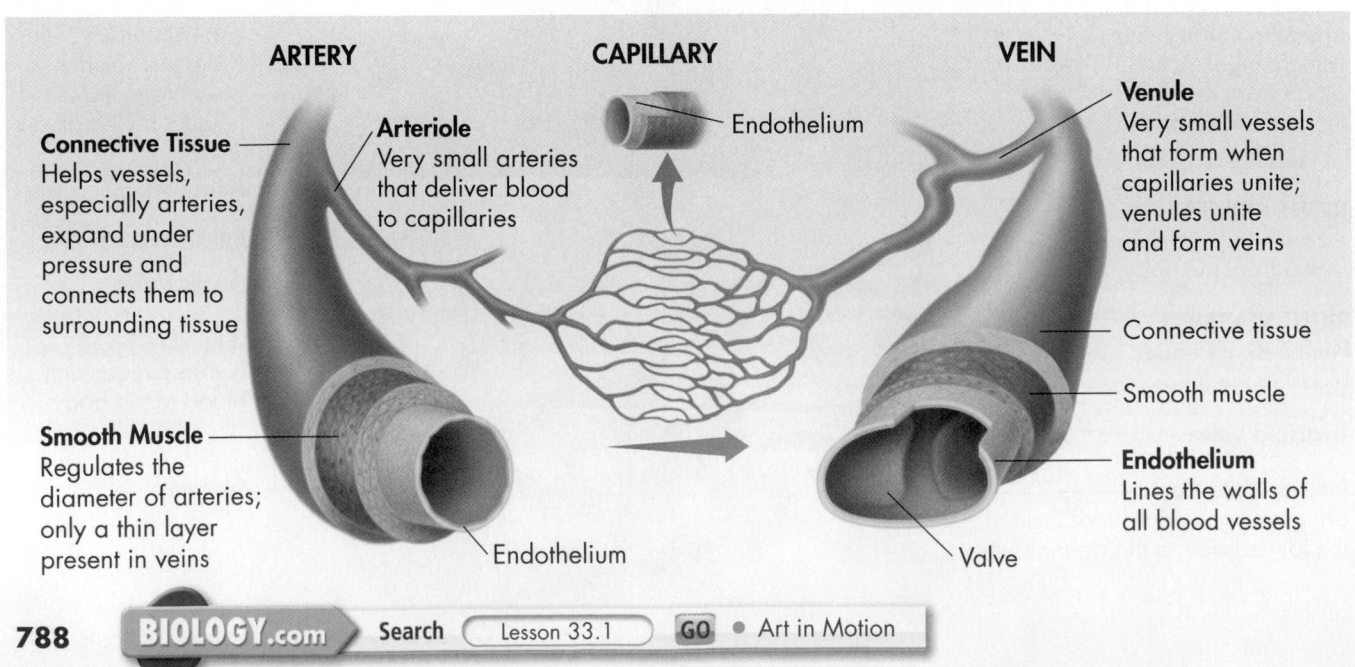

ARTERY

CAPILLARY

VEIN

Connective Tissue Helps vessels, especially arteries, expand under pressure and connects them to surrounding tissue

Arteriole Very small arteries that deliver blood to capillaries

Endothelium

Venule Very small vessels that form when capillaries unite; venules unite and form veins

Connective tissue

Smooth muscle

Smooth Muscle Regulates the diameter of arteries; only a thin layer present in veins

Endothelium

Endothelium Lines the walls of all blood vessels

Valve

Blood Vessels

Oxygen-rich blood leaving the left ventricle passes into the aorta. The aorta is the first of many vessels that carry blood through the body and back to the heart.

Arteries, Capillaries, and Veins As blood flows through the circulatory system, it moves through three kinds of blood vessels— arteries, capillaries, and veins. **Arteries** carry blood from the heart. Their thick walls can handle the pressure of the blood as it is pumped through them. **Capillaries** are tiny blood vessels. Many are so narrow that the blood cells pass through them in single file. Oxygen and nutrients diffuse through their thin walls into tissues. Carbon dioxide and other wastes move from tissues into capillaries. The blood returns to the heart through **veins.** When the skeletal muscles around many veins contract, they squeeze the veins. This squeezing action helps push the blood back toward the heart. Many veins also have valves to keep blood from flowing backward.

Blood Pressure Have you ever had your blood pressure taken at the doctor's office? Blood pressure that is too high or too low can cause big problems throughout the body. Skeletal muscles relax or contract if blood pressure is too high or too low. The kidneys help regulate blood pressure by controlling the amount of water in blood.

Key Question What are three types of blood vessels?
The three types of blood vessels are arteries, capillaries, and veins.

BUILD Vocabulary

artery
a large blood vessel that carries blood away from the heart to the tissues of the body

capillary
the smallest blood vessel; brings nutrients and oxygen to the tissues and absorbs carbon dioxide and waste products

vein
a blood vessel that carries blood from the body back to the heart

MULTIPLE MEANINGS

The word *artery* is often used to refer to major roads. This use of the term is making the same analogy between a city or town's transportation system and the body's circulatory system that was made at the beginning of this lesson.

CHECK Understanding

Apply Vocabulary
Use the highlighted words from the lesson to complete each sentence correctly.

1. Powerful contractions of the _____ pump blood through the circulatory system.

2. Oxygen-rich blood is pumped out of the heart to the body through the left _____.

Critical Thinking

3. Apply Concepts Why do humans need a circulatory system?

4. Relate Cause and Effect How would damage to the SA node affect the heart's function?

5. Sequence Through which blood vessels does blood flow on its path from the heart, to the rest of the body, and back to the heart?

6. Write to Learn Answer the first mystery clue. What is the function of the coronary arteries?

MYSTERY CLUE

The coronary arteries and vessels that branch from them are relatively narrow. Why is the heart especially susceptible to a disease that narrows blood vessels? (**Hint:** See p. 788.)

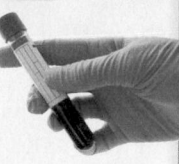

33.2 Blood and the Lymphatic System

MD CLG 3.1.1 Chemical Substances and Macromolecules, 3.2.1 Processes and Functions, 3.3.2 Inherited Traits. SPI 1.7.1 Apply Skills and Concepts, 1.7.6 Science and Technology.

Key Questions

🔑 What is the function of each component in blood?

🔑 What is the function of the lymphatic system?

🔑 What are three common circulatory diseases?

🔑 What is the connection between cholesterol and circulatory disease?

BUILD Understanding

Concept Map As you read, draw a concept map to organize the information in this lesson.

In Your Workbook Go to your workbook for help completing the concept map. Complete the concept map for Lesson 33.2.

Blood

Most likely, when you think about body tissues, you think of something with a definite shape, like muscle or skin. But blood is a tissue, too. It just happens to be in a liquid form. Blood has many important functions. It carries oxygen. It helps your body fight disease. It carries sources of energy such as sugars and fats. The different parts of blood also help keep body temperature stable and form clots to close wounds. How does this unusual tissue perform so many functions?

Plasma The human body contains 4 to 6 liters of blood. More than half of the body's blood is made up of a straw-colored fluid called **plasma.** Plasma is about 90 percent water. The other 10 percent is made up of dissolved gases, salts, nutrients, enzymes, hormones, waste products, plasma proteins, cholesterol, and other important compounds.

The water in plasma helps to control body temperature. Some proteins in plasma carry substances throughout the body. Others help the body fight infection or form blood clots.

Red Blood Cells The most numerous cells in blood are red blood cells. The main function of **red blood cells** is to carry oxygen through the body. They are red because of the iron in hemoglobin. Hemoglobin is a protein that binds to oxygen in the lungs. Hemoglobin releases the oxygen in capillary networks in other parts of the body. Red blood cells also carry carbon dioxide to the lungs.

Red blood cells are disks that are thinner in their center than along their edges. They are made in bone marrow. As they mature and fill with hemoglobin, they lose their nuclei and other organelles. Red blood cells stay in the blood for about 120 days. The cells are then destroyed in the liver and spleen.

Blood Cells The red disks in this micrograph are red blood cells. The gold spheres are white blood cells. The pink fragments are platelets.
(SEM 1866×)

White Blood Cells The main function of the **white blood cells** is to protect the body against infection, fight parasites, and attack bacteria. For example, B lymphocytes produce antibodies that provide immunity. When the body is fighting an infection, it makes more white blood cells. White blood cells do not always stay in blood vessels. Many white blood cells can move through capillary walls to fight pathogens. A pathogen is anything that can make you sick.

In a healthy person, there are many more red blood cells than white blood cells. Like red blood cells, white blood cells are made in bone marrow. Unlike red blood cells, white blood cells keep their nuclei and can live for years.

Platelets Losing too much blood can kill a person. Fortunately, a minor scrape or cut usually stops bleeding quickly. Why? Such minor wounds stop bleeding quickly because blood clots. The cytoplasm of some bone marrow cells divides into thousands of pieces. These pieces break away and enter the blood as **platelets.** Platelets are surrounded by cell membranes. Platelets and plasma proteins form blood clots. Platelets become sticky when they touch a broken blood vessel. They cluster around the wound, and the blood begins to clot.

🔑 **Key Question** What is the function of each component in blood?
Plasma controls body temperature, carries substances through the body, and fights infection. Red blood cells carry oxygen. White blood cells fight infection. Platelets form blood clots.

How Blood Clots Form When the clot is formed, filaments develop a net that prevents blood from leaving the damaged vessel.

plasma
the straw-colored liquid portion of the blood

red blood cell
a blood cell containing hemoglobin that carries oxygen

white blood cell
a type of blood cell that guards against infection, fights parasites, and attacks bacteria

platelet
a cell fragment released by bone marrow that helps in blood clotting

🔖 SUFFIXES

The suffix -*let* in *platelet* means "little." Under the microscope, platelets look like small, broken plates.

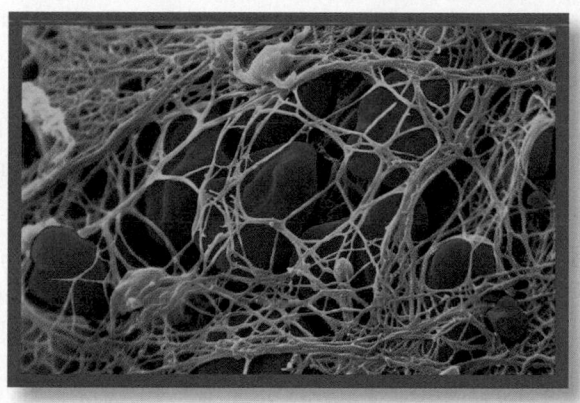

SEM 2200×

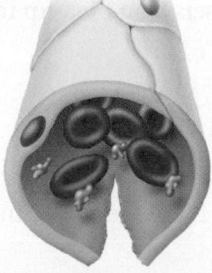

❶ **Capillary Wall Breaks**
A blood vessel is injured by a cut or scrape.

❷ **Platelets Take Action**
Platelets clump at the site, which triggers a series of reactions.

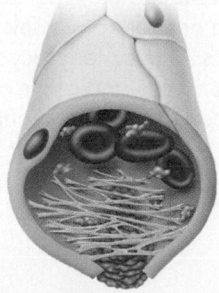

❸ **Clot Forms**
An enzyme called thrombin causes sticky fibrin filaments to form the clot. The clot seals the damaged area and prevents further loss of blood.

The Lymphatic System

As blood passes through the capillaries, some cells and parts of plasma leave the blood vessels. The cells and plasma form a fluid called **lymph.** Lymph carries nutrients, oxygen, and salts. Most of the lymph moves back into the capillaries. The rest becomes part of the lymphatic system. The lymphatic system collects the lymph, "screens" it for pathogens, and returns it to the circulatory system.

Role in Circulation Lymph collects in a system of lymphatic capillaries. It slowly moves into larger vessels. There is no pump in the lymphatic system. Instead, valves keep lymph from moving backwards. Skeletal muscles help move lymph through the system. Lymph is returned to the blood through openings in veins just below the shoulders.

Role in Nutrient Absorption The lymphatic system helps the body absorb nutrients. Lymph vessels running along the intestines pick up fats and fat-soluble vitamins. The vessels carry these nutrients into the blood.

Role in Immunity There are hundreds of lymph nodes throughout the body. These lymph nodes act as filters. They trap pathogens, damaged cells, and debris as lymph flows through them. White blood cells in the lymph nodes destroy the pathogens, damaged cells, and debris. When large numbers of pathogens are trapped in the lymph nodes, the lymph nodes may swell. When you are sick, you may notice "swollen glands" in your neck. You are really feeling swollen lymph nodes.

The thymus and spleen are organs of the lymphatic system. Certain white blood cells, called T lymphocytes, mature in the thymus. The spleen filters blood in much the same way that lymph nodes filter lymph. The spleen also removes old or damaged blood cells and stores platelets.

Key Question What is the function of the lymphatic system? **The lymphatic system collects lymph, filters it for pathogens, and returns it to the circulatory system. Lymph vessels also pick up fats and fat-soluble vitamins from the intestines.**

Circulatory System Diseases

Three common and serious diseases of the circulatory system are heart disease, stroke, and high blood pressure. Damage to the heart or brain can be fatal.

Heart Disease Heart disease is the leading cause of death in the United States. Heart muscle needs a constant supply of oxygen. Yet, the heart gets blood through only two coronary arteries and their smaller branches. Most forms of heart disease are caused when it becomes difficult for blood to flow through these vessels.

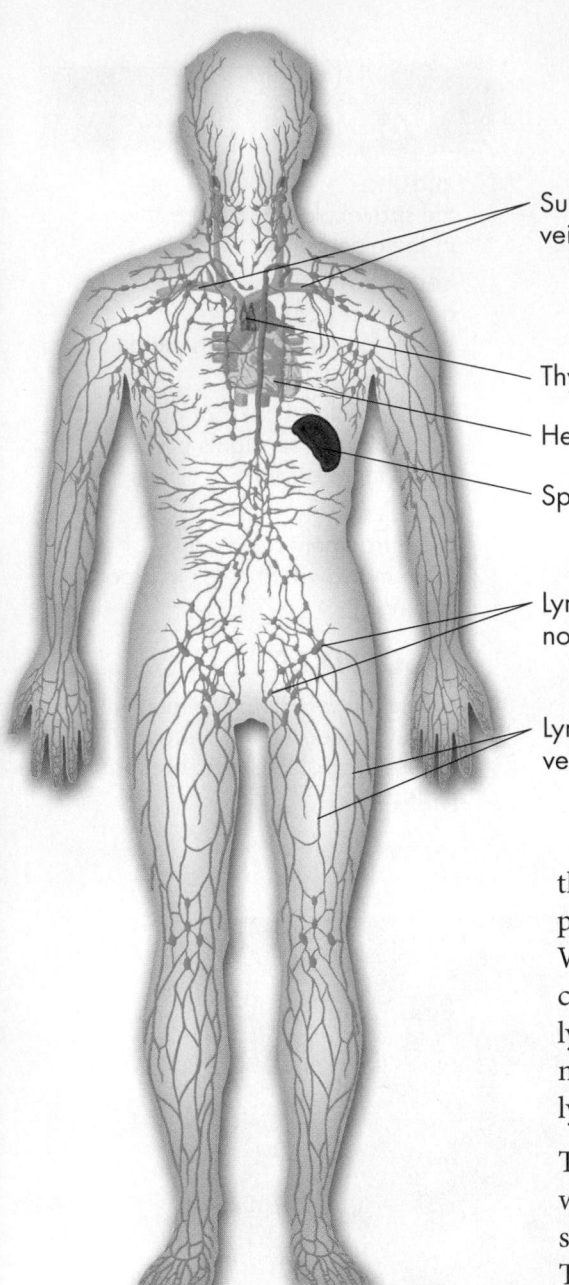

Subclavian veins

Thymus

Heart

Spleen

Lymph nodes

Lymph vessels

The Lymphatic System The lymphatic system is a network of vessels, nodes, and organs. This system recycles fluids from tissues and plays a role in nutrient absorption and immunity.

One type of heart disease is **atherosclerosis** (ath ur oh skluh ʀoʜ sis). Atherosclerosis is a condition in which fatty deposits called plaque build up in artery walls. The arteries become stiff. The plaque can make it difficult for blood to pass through the artery. The cap on a plaque can also rupture and cause a blood clot to form. The clot can block the artery. A heart attack happens as heart muscle cells are damaged and die from a lack of oxygen.

Symptoms of a heart attack include nausea, shortness of breath, and chest pain. People also often complain of pain in the neck, jaw, or left arm. These symptoms need *immediate* medical attention in order to save heart muscle.

Stroke When the blood supply to the brain is interrupted, some brain cells die. This event is called a stroke. Sometimes, a blood clot blocks a blood vessel in the brain and causes a stroke. A stroke may also be caused when a weak blood vessel breaks and causes bleeding in the brain. Symptoms include dizziness, severe headache, numbness, and trouble seeing or speaking. Some strokes cause death. Other strokes may cause paralysis or loss of speech.

High Blood Pressure A blood pressure reading above 140/90 is considered high. Doctors also call this condition hypertension. The heart is struggling to push blood through blood vessels. This pressure may damage the heart and the blood vessels. High blood pressure can lead to heart attack, stroke, and kidney damage.

🔑 **Key Question** What are three common circulatory diseases? **Three common circulatory diseases are heart disease, stroke, and high blood pressure.**

Atherosclerosis Most heart attacks happen when a plaque bursts in a coronary artery. A clot forms. The clot may block the artery. The clot could also break off and block a smaller artery.

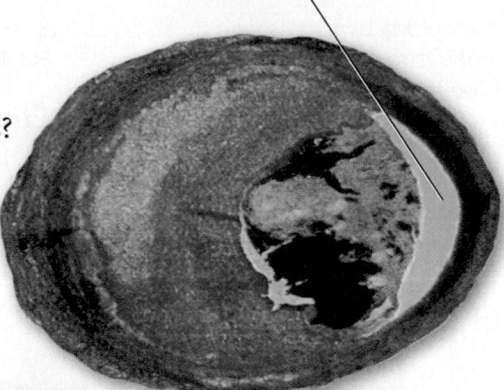

Artery narrowed by plaque buildup

TEM 25×

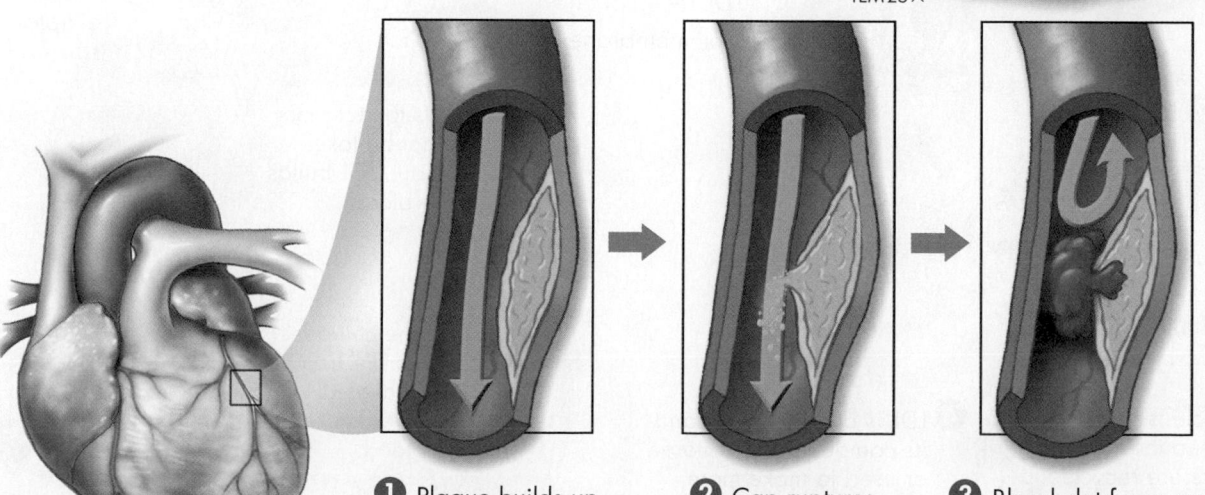

❶ Plaque builds up in wall.

❷ Cap ruptures.

❸ Blood clot forms and blocks the artery. Or, the clot dislodges and blocks a smaller artery.

Understanding Circulatory Disease

Many factors affect a person's risk for heart disease and stroke. Some risk factors can be controlled and others cannot. Risk factors that cannot be controlled include a person's age and family history. Sex is another uncontrollable risk factor. Men have more heart attacks than women. Some controllable risk factors include choosing a healthy diet, exercising regularly, and not smoking. High blood pressure and high cholesterol are risk factors that can sometimes be controlled by medications. Researchers have learned a lot about cholesterol and how it is related to heart disease.

What Is Cholesterol? Cholesterol is part of animal cell membranes. The body uses it to make bile, vitamin D, and some hormones. Two substances carry cholesterol in the blood—low-density lipoprotein (LDL) and high-density lipoprotein (HDL). LDL becomes part of plaque. HDL generally helps the body remove cholesterol.

The liver makes cholesterol, which then moves through the blood to other body tissues. People also get cholesterol when they eat meat, eggs, dairy foods, and most fried foods.

Cholesterol and Atherosclerosis High cholesterol levels can lead to atherosclerosis and a higher chance of heart attack. Researchers Michael Brown and Joseph Goldstein received a Nobel Prize in 1985 for their study about cholesterol.

Cholesterol and the LDL Receptor Brown and Goldstein found LDL receptors on liver cells. When blood cholesterol levels are high, liver cells take the LDL from the blood and do not make more cholesterol. When cholesterol levels are low, liver cells make more cholesterol.

LDL Receptors Liver cells with normal LDL receptors take up LDL and use it or store it. But liver cells with defective LDL receptors cannot remove cholesterol from the blood.

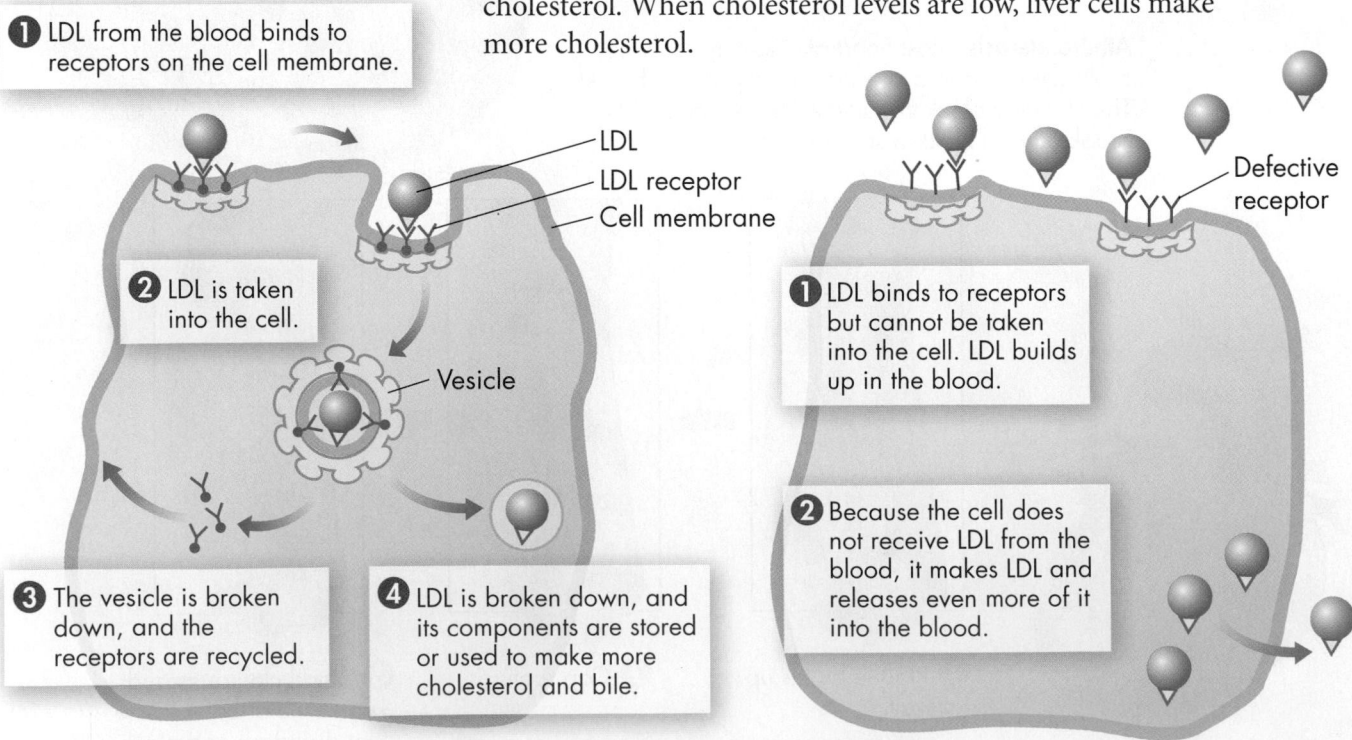

❶ LDL from the blood binds to receptors on the cell membrane.

❷ LDL is taken into the cell.

❸ The vesicle is broken down, and the receptors are recycled.

❹ LDL is broken down, and its components are stored or used to make more cholesterol and bile.

LDL
LDL receptor
Cell membrane
Vesicle

Defective receptor

❶ LDL binds to receptors but cannot be taken into the cell. LDL builds up in the blood.

❷ Because the cell does not receive LDL from the blood, it makes LDL and releases even more of it into the blood.

Cell With Normal LDL Receptors

Cell With Defective LDL Receptors

Brown and Goldstein also found that some people carry genes that make defective LDL receptors. In these people, the liver cells cannot remove cholesterol from the blood. Also, the liver cells do not receive the signal to stop making cholesterol.

From Genetic Disease to the Public The genetic disorder helps us understand high cholesterol in people who do not have the disorder. People who eat high-fat diets store cholesterol in their liver cells. The liver cells then stop making LDL receptors. The liver cells stop removing cholesterol from blood. All of the excess cholesterol remains in the blood vessels. Therefore, a high-fat diet can cause symptoms that are similar to a genetic disorder.

Brown and Goldstein's work led to the development of drugs that can help people with high cholesterol. Some of these drugs stop the liver cells from making cholesterol. This causes the liver to make more LDL receptors. The LDL receptors remove extra cholesterol from the blood.

Keeping Your Circulatory System Healthy It is much easier to prevent heart disease than to cure it. Healthy habits when you are young help protect your heart. By eating a healthy diet, exercising regularly, and not smoking, you can help keep your circulatory system healthy.

Key Question What is the connection between cholesterol and circulatory disease? **High cholesterol levels can lead to atherosclerosis and a higher chance of heart attack and stroke.**

CHECK Understanding

Apply Vocabulary
Use the highlighted words from the lesson to complete each sentence correctly.

1. The main function of _____ is to carry oxygen throughout the body.
2. Blood clotting is made possible by plasma proteins and cell fragments called _____.
3. The lymphatic system collects _____, removes pathogens from it, and returns it to the circulatory system.
4. When plaque builds up in artery walls and causes them to stiffen, the condition is called _____.

Critical Thinking

5. **Infer** Hemophilia is a genetic disorder. One of the proteins in the clotting pathway does not work properly. What do you think happens to a person with hemophilia who has a minor cut?

6. **Relate Cause and Effect** Why do you think atherosclerosis may lead to high blood pressure?
7. **Write to Learn** Answer the second clue of the mystery. Remember that you inherit genes from both of your parents. Look back at Chapter 14 to review inheritance patterns.

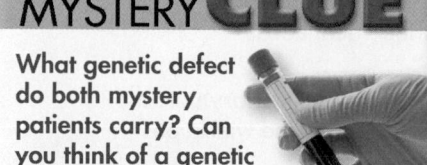

MYSTERY CLUE

What genetic defect do both mystery patients carry? Can you think of a genetic reason why Lila's symptoms are so much worse than John's? (**Hint:** See p. 794.)

BIOLOGY.com Search (Lesson 33.2) GO ● Lesson Assessment

33.3 The Respiratory System

MD CLG 3.1.2 Homeostasis, 3.1.3 Matter and Energy, 3.2.1 Processes and Functions, 3.2.2 Changes in Metabolic Activity. SPI 1.3.1 Use Equipment, 1.4.1 Organize Data, 1.4.2 Analyze Data, 1.7.1 Apply Skills and Concepts.

Key Questions

🔑 **What is the function of the respiratory system?**

🔑 **How are oxygen and carbon dioxide exchanged and transported throughout the body?**

🔑 **What mechanisms are involved in breathing?**

🔑 **How does smoking affect the respiratory system?**

BUILD Understanding

Flowchart As you read, make a flowchart that shows the path of air through the respiratory system.

In Your Workbook Go to your workbook to learn more about making a flowchart. Complete the flowchart for Lesson 33.3.

BUILD Vocabulary

pharynx
a tube at the back of the mouth that serves as a passageway for both air and food; also called the throat

larynx
a structure in the throat that contains the vocal cords

trachea
a tube that connects the larynx to the bronchi; also called the windpipe

🖋 WORD ORIGINS

The word *trachea* comes from the Greek phrase that means "rough artery." Rings of cartilage form the trachea and give it a rough surface.

Structures of the Respiratory System

Why do we need to breathe? All cells in our body, especially brain cells, need oxygen all of the time. Without oxygen, many cells die in minutes. The respiratory and circulatory systems work together to get oxygen to our cells.

For organisms, rather than single cells, *respiration* means the exchange of gases between a body and the environment. When you breathe in, your respiratory system picks up oxygen from the air. When you breathe out, your respiratory system lets carbon dioxide out into the air. The respiratory system is made up of the nose, pharynx, larynx, trachea, bronchi, and lungs.

Nose The lungs are made of some of the most delicate tissues in the body. Before entering the lungs, air must be filtered, moistened, and warmed. Hairs lining the inside of the nose trap large particles from the air. The air is warmed in the nasal cavity and sinuses. Mucus in these spaces moistens the air and catches even more dust particles.

Pharynx, Larynx, and Trachea Air moves from the nose to the throat, or **pharynx.** The pharynx is an area at the back of the mouth. Air and food move through the pharynx. When you swallow, a flap of tissue called the epiglottis at the back of the pharynx protects the airway. The epiglottis makes certain that the food moves into the esophagus.

Air moves from the pharynx to the larynx. The **larynx** contains the vocal cords. When muscles pull the vocal cords together, the air moving between them causes the cords to vibrate and produce sounds.

Air moves from the larynx to the **trachea,** or windpipe. Mucus in the trachea traps more particles from the air. Cilia push the particles and mucus away from the lungs toward the pharynx. From there, the mucus and particles can be swallowed or spit out.

Lungs Air moves from the trachea into two large tubes in the chest. These tubes are called **bronchi** (singular: bronchus). Each bronchus leads to a lung. Inside the lung, each bronchus divides into smaller and smaller passageways. These passageways are called bronchioles. These and the bronchi are surrounded by smooth muscles. These muscles are controlled by the autonomic nervous system. The contracting and relaxing of these muscles changes the size of the bronchi and bronchioles.

The bronchioles continue to divide until they reach a series of dead ends. The tiny air sacs at the end of the bronchioles are called **alveoli** (al VEE uh ly) (singular: alveolus). Alveoli are grouped in bunches, like grapes. Many capillaries surround each alveolus.

🔑 **Key Question** What is the function of the respiratory system? **The respiratory system picks up oxygen from the air we breathe in. It releases carbon dioxide back into the air when we breathe out.**

INQUIRY into Scientific Thinking

GUIDED INQUIRY

What's in the Air?

Your respiratory system has several structures that catch particles from the air before they can reach the lungs. For example, hairs in the nose trap large particles. In this activity, you will observe some of the particles in the air you breathe.

❶ Trace the outline of a microscope slide onto a piece of graph paper. Cut out the outline and tape it to the slide.

❷ Repeat step 1 to make four more slides.

❸ Choose five places to put your slides. Some of your spots should be inside. Some should be outside.

❹ On each piece of graph paper, write your initials, the date, and where you plan to place the slide.

❺ Cover the front of each slide with a thin coat of petroleum jelly.

❻ Leave your slides in your chosen spots for at least 24 hours.

❼ Collect the slides and look at them under a microscope. Count the number of particles in ten of the squares on each slide. Record your results.

Analyze and Conclude

1. Observe Where had you placed the slide that had the most particles? Where had you placed the slide with the fewest particles?

2. Draw Conclusions Were you surprised by the results? Why or why not?

3. Apply Concepts List the structures in your body that prevent most of these particles from entering your lungs.

In Your Workbook Get more help for this activity in your workbook.

BUILD Connections

THE RESPIRATORY SYSTEM

Air moves through the nose, pharynx, larynx, trachea, and bronchi into the lungs.

In Your Workbook Go to your workbook for more practice with the respiratory system.

1 Nose Air enters the body through the nose, where it is filtered, moistened, and warmed.

2 Pharynx, Larynx, and Trachea From the nose, air moves into the pharynx. Then, it passes through the larynx, which contains the vocal cords, and through the trachea.

3 Lungs From the trachea, air moves into the bronchi. Each bronchus leads to one lung. The bronchi divide into bronchioles, which eventually end at alveoli.

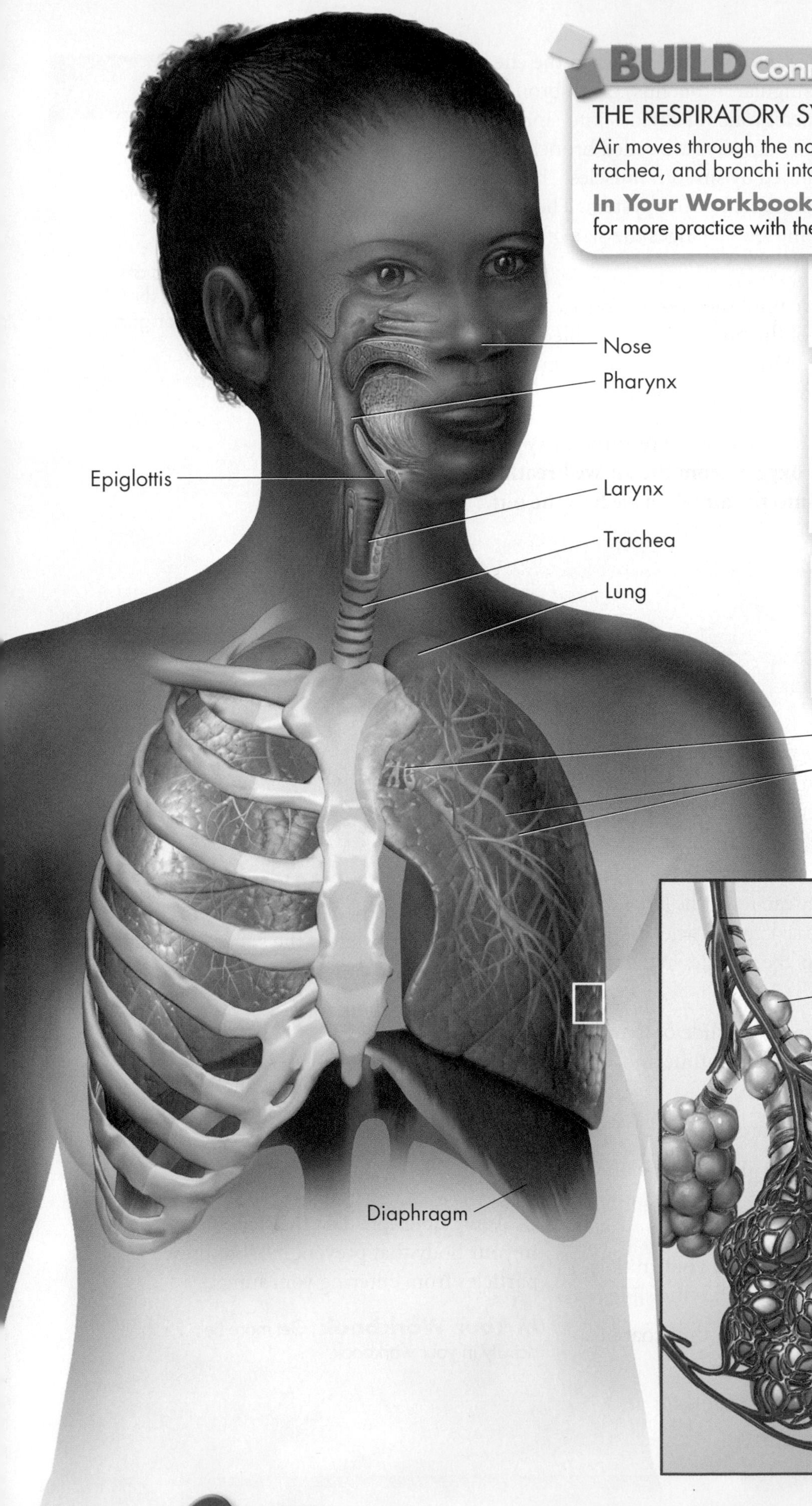

Nose
Pharynx
Epiglottis
Larynx
Trachea
Lung
Bronchus
Bronchioles
Diaphragm

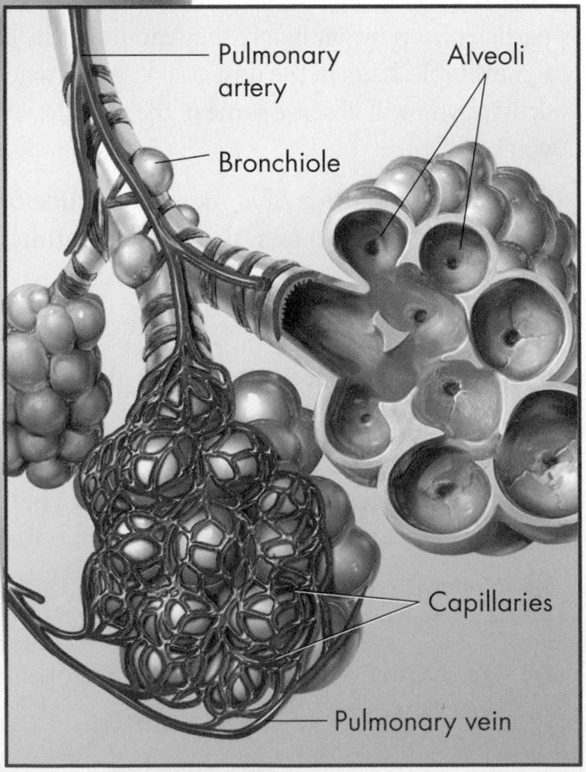

Pulmonary artery
Alveoli
Bronchiole
Capillaries
Pulmonary vein

Gas Exchange and Transport

Each healthy lung has about 150 million alveoli. The alveoli provide an enormous amount of surface area for gas exchange. Oxygen and carbon dioxide are exchanged across the alveoli and capillaries.

Gas Exchange The inner walls of alveoli are moist. When air enters the alveoli, oxygen dissolves in the moisture. There is more oxygen in the alveoli than in the blood inside the capillaries. So, the oxygen diffuses across thin capillary walls into the blood. At the same time, carbon dioxide diffuses into the alveoli.

Transport Oxygen diffuses passively from alveoli into capillaries. But diffusion stops if the oxygen concentration in the blood and the alveoli are the same. That's why hemoglobin in red blood cells is important. Hemoglobin binds to dissolved oxygen and removes it from the plasma. This helps to keep the concentration in the blood low.

Carbon dioxide diffuses from body tissues to capillaries in three ways. Most carbon dioxide combines with water in the blood. This combination forms carbonic acid. The rest dissolves in plasma or binds to proteins, including hemoglobin, in blood. When the blood reaches the lungs, the carbon dioxide is released into alveoli and exhaled.

🔑 **Key Question** How are oxygen and carbon dioxide exchanged and transported throughout the body?
Oxygen and carbon dioxide diffuse across the thin walls of alveoli and capillaries. Hemoglobin carries oxygen and some carbon dioxide. Carbon dioxide also dissolves in plasma or reacts with water to form carbonic acid.

Breathing

There are no muscles connected to our lungs. Breathing is driven by air pressure, the diaphragm, and muscles attached to the ribs.

Inhalation At the bottom of the chest cavity is a large muscle called the **diaphragm.** When you inhale, the diaphragm and muscles raise the rib cage. Because the lungs are sealed, this forms a small vacuum. Air rushes in to fill the space.

Exhalation Usually exhalation is passive. The diaphragm and rib cage relax. This relaxation causes air to be pushed out of the body. But to blow out a candle, sing, or yell, you need more force. The muscles between the ribs and the abdominal muscles can contract to push the air out.

This system works only because the chest cavity is sealed. If a wound punctures the chest, air may leak into the chest cavity. This leaking air makes breathing impossible.

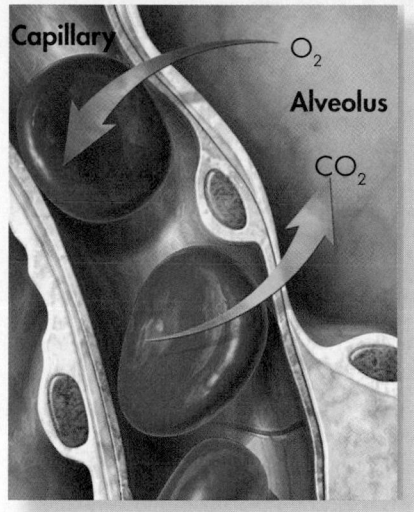

Gas Exchange Inside the lungs, the bronchi divide into bronchioles, which eventually end at alveoli. Carbon dioxide and oxygen diffuse across the walls of capillaries and alveoli.

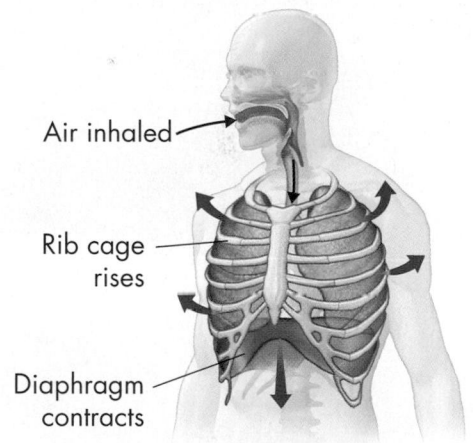

Inhalation

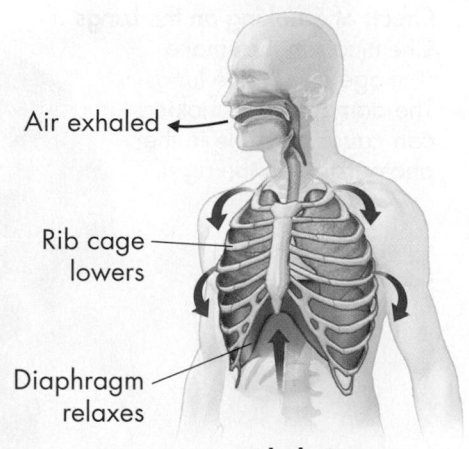

Exhalation

Breathing During inhalation, the rib cage rises and the diaphragm contracts. This increases the size of the chest cavity. During exhalation, the rib cage lowers and the diaphragm relaxes. This decreases the size of the chest cavity.

diaphragm
a large flat muscle at the bottom of the chest cavity that helps with breathing

MULTIPLE MEANINGS

In a camera, a diaphragm controls the amount of light that enters the camera. In the chest cavity, the diaphragm is a muscle that controls the amount of air that enters the body.

Breathing and Homeostasis You can control your breathing almost anytime you want. Yet, breathing is not purely voluntary, which is why people who drown have water in their lungs. When they lose consciousness, they "breathe" water into their lungs.

There is a breathing center in the brain that helps to control breathing and maintain homeostasis. The breathing center receives signals about the levels of carbon dioxide in the body. When carbon dioxide levels in the blood go up, the brain signals the diaphragm and chest muscles to contract. If carbon dioxide levels reach a certain point, you cannot keep yourself from breathing.

Key Question What mechanisms are involved in breathing? **Movements of the diaphragm and rib cage change the size of the chest cavity. Air rushes in during inhalation and is pushed out during exhalation.**

Smoking and the Respiratory System

The respiratory system filters out many particles that could damage the lungs. But some particles and chemicals can still reach the lungs. Chemicals in tobacco smoke damage structures throughout the respiratory system.

Effects on the Respiratory System Three of the most dangerous things in tobacco smoke are nicotine, carbon monoxide, and tar. Nicotine is addictive. It increases heart rate and blood pressure. Carbon monoxide blocks hemoglobin from binding with oxygen, which means that the blood cannot carry as much oxygen. Tar holds at least 60 compounds that cause cancer.

Tobacco smoke also damages cilia in the trachea. This damage allows more particles to enter the lungs. It also traps smoke-filled mucus along the passageways. Trapped particles and mucus lead to smoker's cough.

Effects of Smoking on the Lungs
Chemicals in the smoke damage cilia in the lungs. The damage that smoking can cause is visible in the photograph on the right.

Healthy Lung

Smoker's Lung

Diseases Caused by Smoking Smoking can cause permanent damage to the respiratory system. The damage from smoking can lead to chronic bronchitis, emphysema, and lung cancer. Smoking lowers life expectancy.

In chronic bronchitis, the bronchi become inflamed and clogged with mucus. Affected people often find simple activities, like climbing stairs, very hard. Emphysema (em fuh SEE muh) makes it hard to breathe because the lung tissue is damaged. People with this condition cannot get enough oxygen into the body. They cannot rid the body of extra carbon dioxide.

By the time lung cancer is found, it usually has spread to other parts of the body. Few people with lung cancer live more than five years after their diagnosis. About 87 percent of lung cancer deaths are due to smoking.

Other Effects of Smoking Smoking also hurts the circulatory system. It raises blood pressure, making the heart work harder to get oxygen to the body. Nonsmokers are also affected by secondhand smoke. Studies now show that children of smokers are twice as likely as children of nonsmokers to have asthma or other respiratory problems. Babies of women who smoked during pregnancy face many complications. Some of these can lead to lifelong problems.

Key Question How does smoking affect the respiratory system? **Chemicals in tobacco smoke damage structures throughout the respiratory system.**

CHECK Understanding

Apply Vocabulary
Use the highlighted words from the lesson to complete each sentence correctly.

1. The cavity at the back of the mouth called the _____ serves as a passageway for both air and food.

2. When you inhale, the _____ contracts and the rib cage rises.

Critical Thinking

3. **Explain** Describe the process of gas exchange in the lungs. What is hemoglobin's role in gas exchange?

4. **Relate Cause and Effect** Carbon monoxide gas binds to hemoglobin more easily than oxygen does. Based on this information, why do you think carbon monoxide alarms in homes have saved many lives?

5. **Apply Concepts** People with emphysema cannot exhale as much carbon dioxide as people with healthy lungs can. Why do you think this leaves them short of breath?

6. **Write to Learn** Answer the third clue of the mystery.

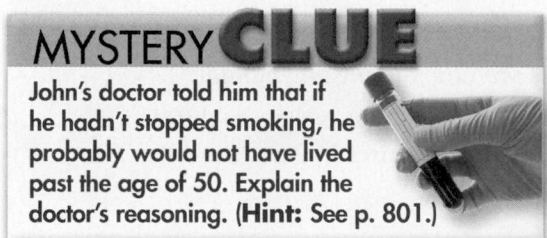

MYSTERY CLUE

John's doctor told him that if he hadn't stopped smoking, he probably would not have lived past the age of 50. Explain the doctor's reasoning. (**Hint:** See p. 801.)

BIOLOGY.com ⟩ Search (Lesson 33.3) **GO** • Lesson Assessment

Design Your Own Lab

 SPI 1.2.4 Testing a Hypothesis, **1.2.6** Investigative Methods, **1.3.3** Safe Handling of Materials, **1.4.9** Confirm Hypotheses, **1.6.4** Equations, **1.6.5** Judge Answers.

Pre-Lab: Tidal Volume and Lung Capacity

Problem What factors can affect lung capacity?

Materials round balloons, metric ruler, meterstick

⚠️

Lab Manual Chapter 33 Lab

Skills Focus Measure, Design an Experiment, Interpret Graphs

Connect to the Big idea Your lungs and circulatory system work together to provide the oxygen your cells need for cellular respiration. In your lungs, oxygen diffuses from the air you inhale into your blood. Carbon dioxide, a waste product of cellular respiration, diffuses from your blood into the inhaled air. Your lungs must have a large enough volume, or capacity, to supply all your cells with the oxygen they need.

Most of the time your lungs do not fill to capacity. But they can take in more air when you want to dive underwater or when you want to sing a long phrase without having to take another breath. In this lab, you will measure the volume of air you exhale when you are breathing normally and the volume of air you exhale after you take a deep breath.

Background Questions

a. Sequence List in order, from exterior to interior, the parts of the respiratory system that air passes through as you inhale.

b. Review Why does oxygen diffuse from inhaled air in the alveoli into the capillaries?

c. Compare and Contrast What is the difference between respiration and cellular respiration?

Pre-Lab Questions

Preview the procedure in the lab manual.

1. Control Variables What is the one difference between the procedures in Part A and Part B?

2. Design an Experiment Why must you use round balloons for this experiment?

3. Predict Which do you think will be greater—your estimated vital capacity or your measured vital capacity? Why?

 **Search** [Chapter 33] **GO**

Visit Chapter 33 online to test yourself on chapter content and to find activities to help you learn.

Untamed Science Video Bundle up as the Untamed Science crew journeys to cold climates to show us how some animals handle extreme environments.

Art in Motion View a short animation that shows the beating of the heart as well as the transmission of impulses from the SA and AV nodes.

Art Review Review your understanding of the different parts of the respiratory system.

InterActive Art Watch an animation that shows the process of breathing and the production of sound.

Visual Analogy Compare the structure and function of the circulatory system to a system of highways and secondary roads.

33.1 The Circulatory System

- The circulatory system carries oxygen, nutrients, and other substances throughout the body. It also removes wastes from body tissues.

- Heart action spreads through the myocardium, as first the atria and then the ventricles contract, pumping blood through the body.

- Arteries, capillaries, and veins are three kinds of blood vessels.

myocardium (p. 787)   artery (p. 789)
atrium (p. 787)   capillary (p. 789)
ventricle (p. 787)   vein (p. 789)

33.2 Blood and the Lymphatic System

- Plasma carries heat and a number of important substances through the body.

- Red blood cells carry oxygen. Hemoglobin in red blood cells binds to oxygen in the lungs and releases it in the capillaries.

- White blood cells fight infection.

- Platelets and plasma proteins form blood clots.

- The lymphatic system collects lymph, filters it for pathogens, and returns it to the circulatory system. It also picks up fat and fat-soluble nutrients from the intestines.

- Three common circulatory diseases are heart disease, stroke, and high blood pressure.

- High cholesterol levels can lead to atherosclerosis and a higher chance of heart attack and stroke.

plasma (p. 790)
red blood cell (p. 790)
white blood cell (p. 791)
platelet (p. 791)
lymph (p. 792)
atherosclerosis (p. 793)

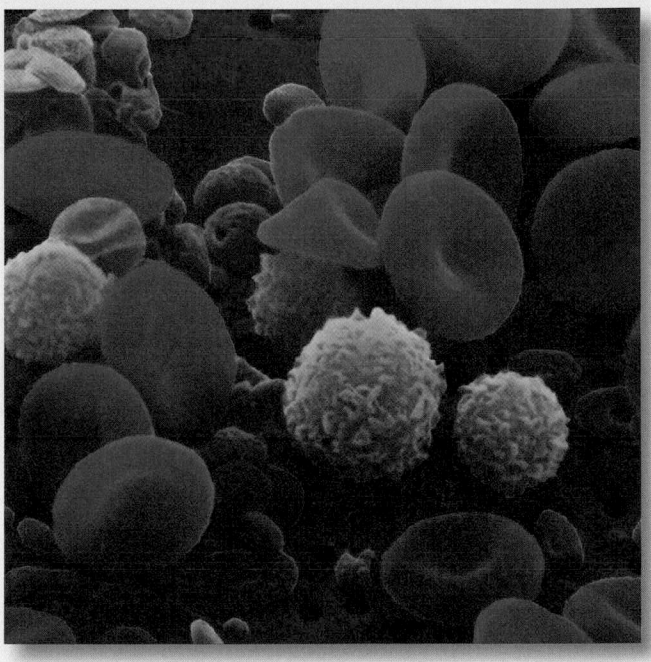

33.3 The Respiratory System

- The human respiratory system picks up oxygen from the air when you inhale. It releases carbon dioxide back into the air when you exhale.

- Oxygen and carbon dioxide diffuse across the thin walls of alveoli and capillaries. Hemoglobin carries oxygen and some carbon dioxide. Carbon dioxide also dissolves in plasma or reacts with water to form carbonic acid.

- Movements of the diaphragm and rib cage change the size of the chest cavity. Air rushes in during inhalation and is pushed out during exhalation.

- Chemicals in tobacco smoke damage structures throughout the respiratory and circulatory systems.

pharynx (p. 796)
larynx (p. 796)
trachea (p. 796)
bronchus (p. 797)
alveolus (p. 797)
diaphragm (p. 799)

Assess the Big Idea — Structure and Function

Write an answer to the question below.

Q: How do the structures of the circulatory and respiratory systems allow for their close functional relationship?

Constructed Response

Write an answer to each of the questions below. The answer to each question should be one or two paragraphs long. To help you begin, read the **Hints** below each of the questions.

1. **Explain how the structure of blood vessel walls contributes to the vessels' functions.**

   Hint As blood flows through the circulatory system, it moves through three kinds of blood vessels—arteries, capillaries, and veins.

   Hint Arteries carry blood away from the heart. Veins carry blood back to the heart.

   Hint Capillaries are the smallest blood vessels.

2. **Compare and contrast the functions of the lymphatic system and the rest of the circulatory system.**

   Hint The circulatory system includes the heart, blood vessels, and blood.

   Hint The lymphatic system is part of the circulatory system. The lymphatic system is a network of vessels, nodes, and organs including the spleen and thymus.

3. **Compare and contrast cellular respiration and respiration at the level of an organism.**

   Hint Cellular respiration is the process that releases energy from food, such as a sugar, when there is oxygen present. Review cellular respiration in Chapter 9.

   Hint For organisms, rather than single cells, *respiration* means gas exchange between a body and the environment.

Foundations for Learning Wrap-Up

Use the table tent you made while reading the chapter to help you organize your thoughts about the respiratory and circulatory systems.

Activity 1 Working with a partner, review the structures and functions of the respiratory, lymphatic, and circulatory systems. Add any structures and functions you may have missed. Then, quiz each other about the structures and functions of each system.

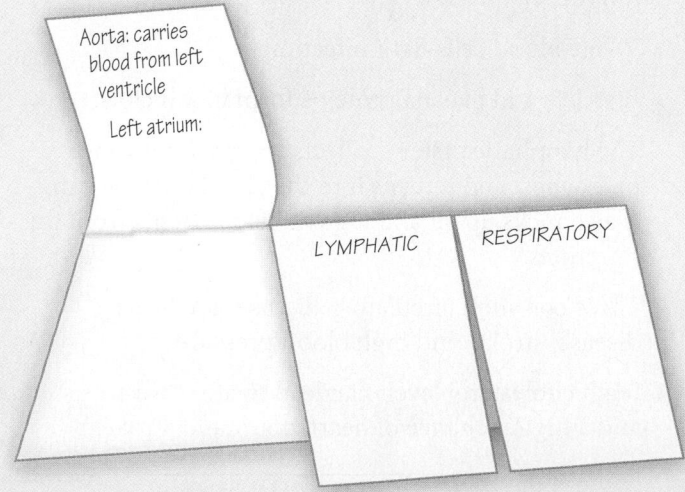

Activity 2 Work in a group. One person reads aloud any function in any system and anyone in the group can identify the structure. For every correct answer, add a tick mark to your table tent. Take turns. The person with the most tick marks at the end is the winner.

Extension: Working with a partner, read aloud the name of any structure in any system. Your partner has to spell the structure correctly. Take turns.

33.1 The Circulatory System

Understand Key Concepts

1. Which of the following is NOT a type of blood vessel?
   a. bronchus
   c. capillary
   b. artery
   d. vein

2. The circulatory system includes the
   a. lungs, heart, and brain.
   b. lungs, blood vessels, and heart.
   c. heart, blood, and blood vessels.
   d. heart, trachea, and alveoli.

> **Test-Taking Tip**
>
> **Choose Among Similar Answers** As you read each answer choice, notice what they have in common. In question 2, every answer choice includes *heart*. So, the heart must be part of the circulatory system. The heart pumps blood through the body, so the circulatory system includes "blood." Only answer **c** includes blood.

3. Which of the following describes the function of the circulatory system?
   a. It digests food.
   b. It carries oxygen and nutrients to the body's tissues and removes wastes from the tissues.
   c. It lets a person breathe.
   d. It responds to light and sound.

4. Compare the size and structure of arteries, capillaries, and veins.

5. Compare pulmonary circulation and systemic circulation.

Think Critically

6. **Apply Concepts** Some large veins have one-way valves, which keep blood flowing in only one direction. Why don't arteries need similar valves?

33.2 Blood and the Lymphatic System

Understand Key Concepts

7. Cells that protect the body by engulfing foreign cells or by producing antibodies are
   a. red blood cells.
   c. platelets.
   b. plasma.
   d. white blood cells.

8. The process shown below is made possible by plasma proteins and cell fragments called
   a. hemoglobins.
   c. platelets.
   b. thrombins.
   d. lymphocytes.

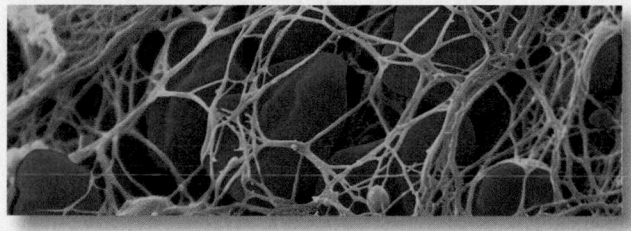

9. What are the primary functions of the lymphatic system?

10. List three common circulatory diseases.

Think Critically

11. **Apply Concepts** Why would a person with a low red blood cell count feel tired?

12. **Compare and Contrast** Explain how high blood cholesterol develops in a person with a genetic disorder versus someone who eats a high-fat diet.

33.3 The Respiratory System

Understand Key Concepts

13. The tiny hollow air sacs in the lungs where gas exchange takes place are called
   a. alveoli.
   c. capillaries.
   b. lymph nodes.
   d. bronchioles.

14. Which structure of the respiratory system contains the vocal cords?
   a. pharynx
   c. trachea
   b. diaphragm
   d. larynx

15. The large flat muscle that moves up and down and changes the volume of the chest cavity is the

   a. pharynx.
   c. trachea.
   b. diaphragm.
   d. larynx.

16. What is the function of the respiratory system?

Think Critically

17. Infer Tobacco smoke can kill white blood cells in the respiratory tract. The white blood cells help keep the respiratory system clean by consuming debris. How do you think this contributes to the development of smoker's cough?

Connecting Concepts

Use Science Graphics

The following graph is based on pulse rates taken each minute for two students doing the same exercises. The exercises begin at minute 1 and end at minute 8. Use the graph to answer questions 18–20.

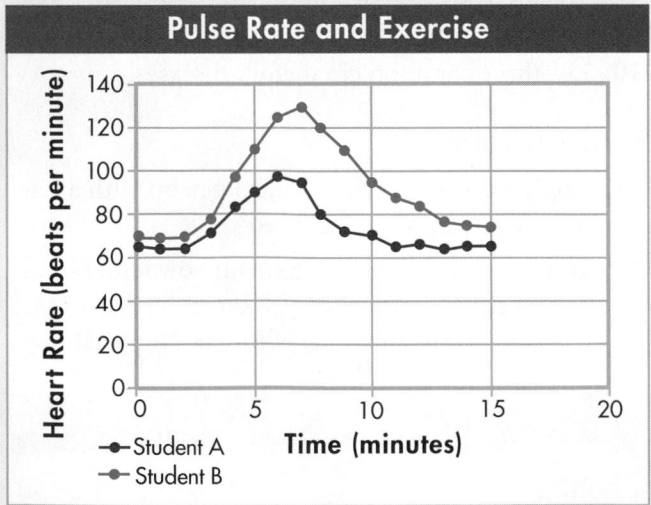

Pulse Rate and Exercise

Heart Rate (beats per minute) vs. *Time (minutes)*
— Student A
— Student B

18. Interpret Graphs At about which minute did each student reach his or her highest heart rate?

19. Draw Conclusions Which of the two students is most likely in better physical condition? What evidence from the graph supports your answer?

20. Predict What other changes in the circulatory and respiratory systems would you expect to take place in the time interval shown?

solve the CHAPTER MYSTERY

IN THE BLOOD

Both John and Lila have a genetic disease called familial hypercholesterolemia. This disease is caused by a gene defect on chromosome 19. John is heterozygous for the disorder. He inherited one functional copy of the gene and one defective copy. Although his liver cells make a mixture of normal and defective LDL receptors, his blood cholesterol levels were so high that he had serious atherosclerosis by age 35. Most people with this disease have had a heart attack by age 60.

Lila is homozygous for the defective allele—a very rare condition. Her liver cells do not produce any functional LDL receptors. Her atherosclerosis became apparent when she was only 4 years old. Fatty deposits can be seen in the corneas of her eyes and beneath the skin near her elbows and knees.

Research on this genetic defect helped uncover the role of liver cell LDL receptors in regulating blood cholesterol. Researchers then applied that information to cases of high cholesterol among the general public. The result was the development of several new classes of drugs that are helping many people live longer.

1. Predict If Lila were to have a child, what is the likelihood that she would pass on the allele for familial hypercholesterolemia? How likely is it that John passed on the allele to his son?

2. Infer Most patients with one defective allele can control their LDL levels with medication that keeps their liver from making cholesterol. But these medications generally do not lower the LDL levels of patients with two defective alleles. Why do you think that is so?

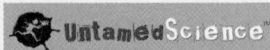 **Never Stop Exploring Your World.** Finding the solution to the In the Blood mystery is just the beginning. Take a video field trip with the ecogeeks of Untamed Science to see where the mysteries of the circulatory system lead.

Multiple Choice

1. In the human heart, oxygen-rich blood would be found in the
   A right atrium and the right ventricle.
   B right atrium and the left atrium.
   C left atrium and the left ventricle.
   D right ventricle and the left ventricle. CLG 3.2.1

2. Which statement BEST describes an interaction between the circulatory system and the respiratory system that helps maintain homeostasis?
   A Blood plasma transports salts, nutrients, and proteins through the body to keep it healthy.
   B The diaphragm and rib cage work together to move air into and out of the lungs.
   C Lymph nodes filter out bacteria that could cause disease.
   D Blood cells pick up and carry oxygen from the lungs to the body's cells. CLG 3.1.2

3. A heartbeat begins with an impulse from the
   A nervous system.
   B sinoatrial (SA) node.
   C atrioventricular node.
   D aorta. CLG 3.2.1

4. All of the following are components of human blood EXCEPT
   A plasma.   C phagocytes.
   B mucus.   D platelets. CLG 3.2.1

5. Nicotine in tobacco
   A is not addictive.
   B lowers blood pressure.
   C blocks the transport of oxygen.
   D increases heart rate. CLG 3.1.1

6. Antibodies are produced by
   A red blood cells.
   B platelets.
   C B lymphocytes.
   D hormones. CLG 3.2.1

Questions 7–10

Use the diagram below to answer the questions that follow.

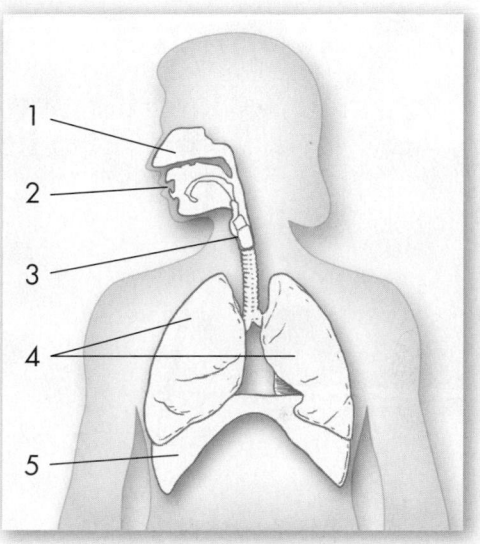

7. Which structure's primary function is to warm and moisten inhaled air?
   A 1   C 4
   B 3   D 5   SPI 1.5.5

8. Which structure contains the vocal cords?
   A 1   C 3
   B 2   D 4   SPI 1.5.5

9. Damage to which structure can lead to emphysema?
   A 2   C 4
   B 3   D 5   SPI 1.5.5

10. Which structure contains alveoli?
    A 2   C 4
    B 3   D 5   SPI 1.5.5

Open-Ended Response

11. Explain why the risk factors for heart disease and strokes are similar. SPI 1.7.1

If You Have Trouble With . . .

Question	1	2	3	4	5	6	7	8	9	10	11
See Lesson	33.1	33.3	33.1	33.2	33.3	33.2	33.3	33.3	33.3	33.3	33.2

34 Endocrine and Reproductive Systems

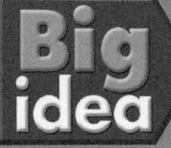

Big idea **Homeostasis**

Q: How does the body use chemical signals to maintain homeostasis?

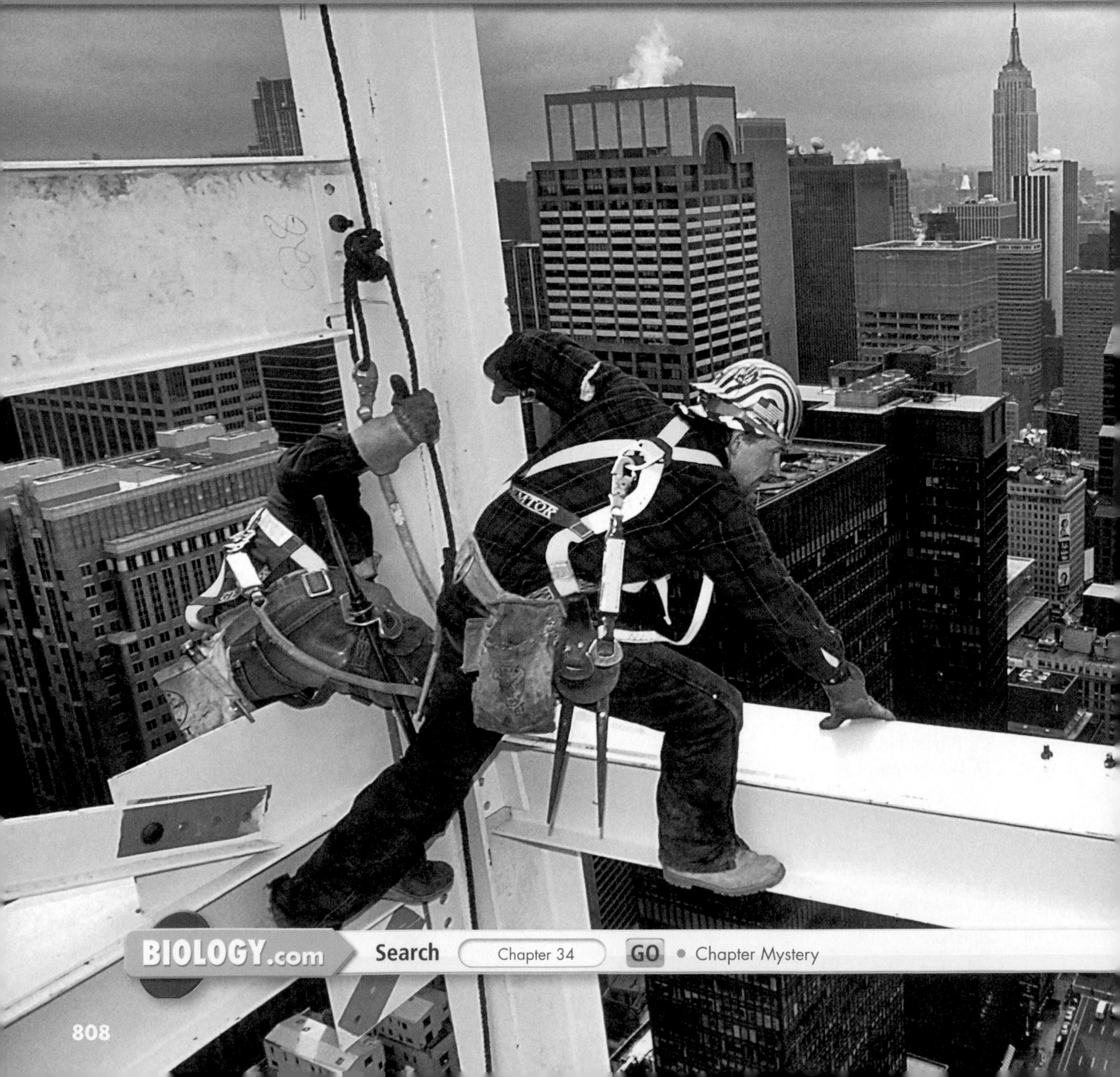

BIOLOGY.com Search Chapter 34 GO • Chapter Mystery

MD **MARYLAND VOLUNTARY STATE CURRICULUM**

Biology Indicators/Core Learning Goals (CLG) 3.1.1, 3.1.2, 3.2.1, 3.2.2, 3.3.1, 3.6.2. **Skills and Processes Indicators (SPI)** 1.3.1, 1.5.2, 1.5.5, 1.5.8, 1.5.9, 1.6.1, 1.7.1. See lessons for details.

This worker may have had sweaty palms and a racing heart his first day on the job. His endocrine system is partly responsible for these reactions.

CHAPTER
MYSTERY

OUT OF STRIDE

Lisa trained hard during spring track and over the summer. But as the new school year approached, she wasn't satisfied. She felt she needed to be faster for her team to win the state cross-country championship. A teammate suggested she lose a few pounds. Lisa had already lost weight over the summer, but she decided to lose some more.

Lisa continued her exhausting workouts. She also stopped snacking before practice and avoided high-calorie foods. She did lose weight. But she was always tired. She also noticed that she had not had a menstrual period in four months. The week before the championship meet, she collapsed in pain at practice. She had suffered a stress fracture to her lower leg. Her season was over.

Read for Mystery Clues Lisa's doctor told her that all of her symptoms were related to a single cause. As you read this chapter, look for clues to explain why too much exercise and dieting had these effects on Lisa. Then, solve the mystery.

FOUNDATIONS
for Learning

Think of the Big Idea as a collection of facts that are connected to each other. Before you read the chapter, make an envelope from the pattern below. Fold the flaps in order along the lines. Glue or tape flap 3 to flaps 1 and 2. As you read the chapter, write important facts about each lesson or draw a picture to help you remember important facts on a slip of paper. Put your slips of paper in your envelope. At the end of the chapter are two activities that use the facts to help answer the question: How does the body use chemical signals to maintain homeostasis?

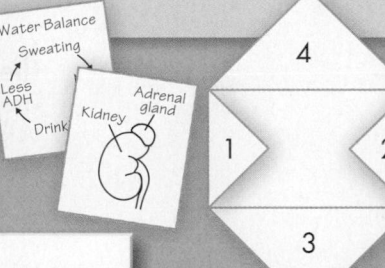

34.1

The Endocrine System

MD CLG **3.1.1** Chemical Substances and Macromolecules, **3.1.2** Homeostasis, **3.2.1** Processes and Functions, **3.2.2** Changes in Metabolic Activity. SPI **1.5.2** Communicate Information, **1.5.5** Create and Interpret Graphics, **1.5.8** Compare.

Key Questions

🔑 **What are the components of the endocrine system?**

🔑 **How do hormones affect cells?**

BUILD
Understanding

Compare/Contrast Table
As you read, make a table that compares and contrasts the two different types of hormones.

In Your Workbook
Refer to your workbook to learn how to make a compare/contrast table. Complete the compare/contrast table for Lesson 34.1.

Hormones and Glands

Your nervous system works like a telephone, with neurons acting as wires. Nerve impulses transmit messages directly from one cell to another cell. Your endocrine system works more like a radio station. It "broadcasts" chemical messages to all the cells in the body. The chemicals that carry these messages are called **hormones.** Hormones are released in one part of the body and travel through the blood to other parts of the body. Hormones can act on almost every cell in the body.

Hormones Hormones act by binding to specific chemical receptors on cell membranes or inside cells. Cells that have receptors for a particular hormone are called *target cells*. A cell must have receptors for a particular hormone for the hormone to affect it.

The body's responses to hormones are slower and last longer than its responses to nerve impulses. It may take several minutes, hours, or days for a hormone to have its full effect on its target cells. A nerve impulse may take only a fraction of a second to act on its target cells.

Glands A gland is an organ that produces and releases a secretion. **Exocrine glands** release their secretions through tube-like structures called ducts. Exocrine secretions are released either out of the body or directly into the digestive system. Exocrine glands include those that release sweat, tears, and digestive juices. **Endocrine glands** usually release their secretions (hormones) directly into the blood. Blood transports the secretions throughout the body. Bones, fat tissue, the heart, and the small intestine also produce and release hormones.

The Endocrine System
The endocrine system acts like a radio station. It broadcasts messages to the body's cells using hormones.

Prostaglandins Endocrine glands were once believed to be the only organs that produced hormones. However, nearly all cells produce small amounts of hormonelike substances called **prostaglandins** (prahs tuh GLAN dinz). Prostaglandins are modified fatty acids that are produced by a wide range of cells. They are sometimes called "local hormones" because they generally affect only nearby cells and tissues.

🔑 **Key Question** What are the components of the endocrine system?
The endocrine system is made up of glands that release hormones into the blood. Hormones deliver messages throughout the body.

Major Endocrine Glands
Endocrine glands produce hormones that affect many parts of the body.

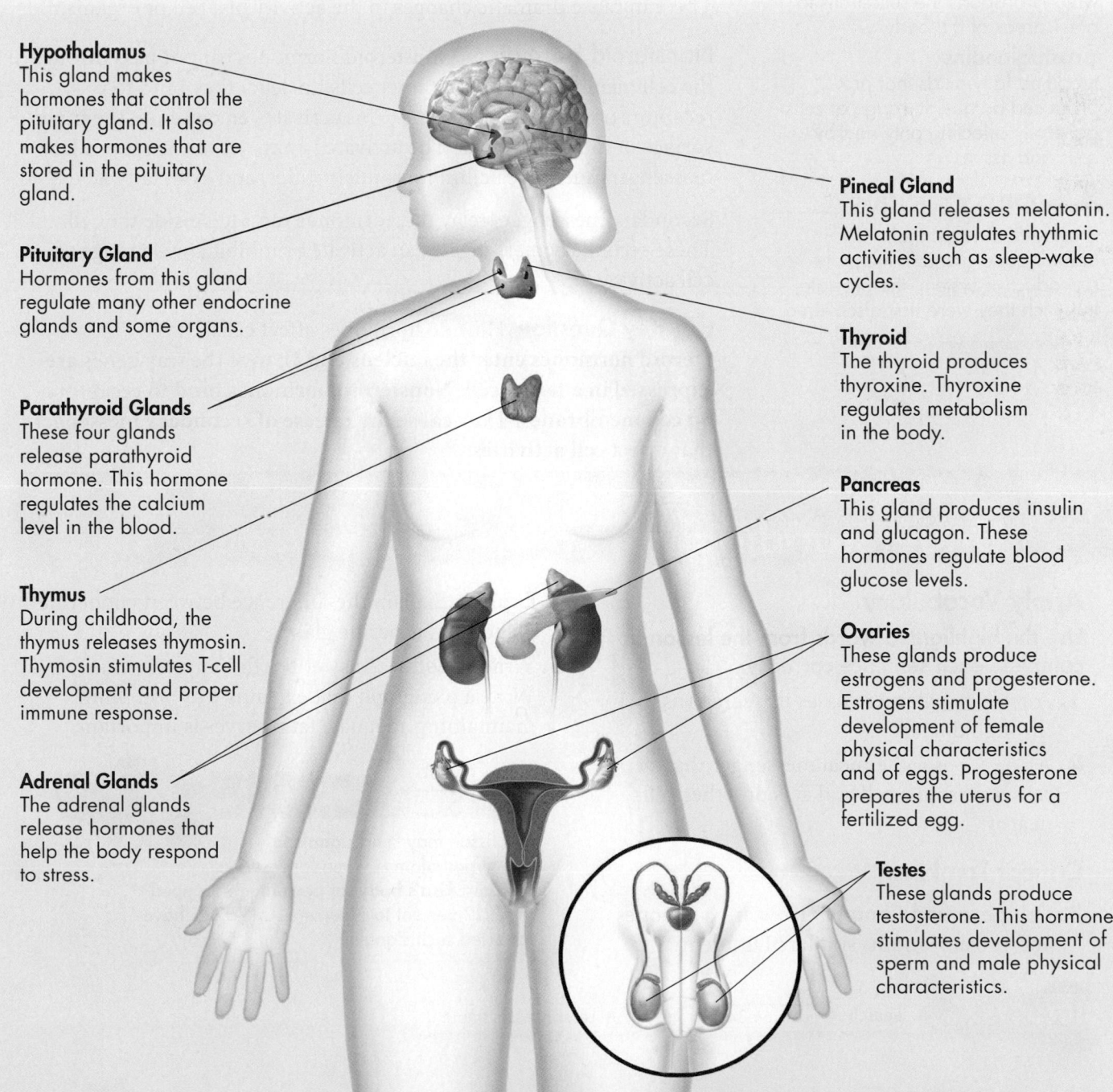

Hypothalamus
This gland makes hormones that control the pituitary gland. It also makes hormones that are stored in the pituitary gland.

Pituitary Gland
Hormones from this gland regulate many other endocrine glands and some organs.

Parathyroid Glands
These four glands release parathyroid hormone. This hormone regulates the calcium level in the blood.

Thymus
During childhood, the thymus releases thymosin. Thymosin stimulates T-cell development and proper immune response.

Adrenal Glands
The adrenal glands release hormones that help the body respond to stress.

Pineal Gland
This gland releases melatonin. Melatonin regulates rhythmic activities such as sleep-wake cycles.

Thyroid
The thyroid produces thyroxine. Thyroxine regulates metabolism in the body.

Pancreas
This gland produces insulin and glucagon. These hormones regulate blood glucose levels.

Ovaries
These glands produce estrogens and progesterone. Estrogens stimulate development of female physical characteristics and of eggs. Progesterone prepares the uterus for a fertilized egg.

Testes
These glands produce testosterone. This hormone stimulates development of sperm and male physical characteristics.

Endocrine and Reproductive Systems **811**

hormone
a chemical produced in one part of an organism that affects another part of the same organism

exocrine gland
a gland that releases its secretions, through tube-like structures called ducts, directly into an organ or out of the body

endocrine gland
a gland that releases its secretions (hormones) directly into the blood, which transports the secretions to other areas of the body

prostaglandins
modified fatty acids that are produced by a wide range of cells; generally affecting only nearby cells and tissues

⚑ WORD ORIGINS

Prostaglandins get their name from a gland in the male reproductive system, the prostate, in which they were first discovered.

Hormone Action

Hormones fall into two general groups—steroid hormones and nonsteroid hormones. Steroid hormones are produced from a lipid called cholesterol. Nonsteroid hormones include proteins, small peptides, and modified amino acids. Each type of hormone acts on a target cell in a different way.

Steroid Hormones Because steroid hormones are lipids, they can easily cross cell membranes. Inside the cell, a steroid hormone binds to a receptor found only in the hormone's target cells. The hormone and receptor form a hormone-receptor complex that enters the cell nucleus.

In the nucleus, the hormone-receptor complex regulates gene expression. Steroid hormones can turn whole sets of genes on or off. This can cause dramatic changes in the activity of a cell or organism.

Nonsteroid Hormones Nonsteroid hormones cannot pass through the cell membranes of their target cells. Instead, they bind to receptors on the cell membrane. This activates enzymes on the inner surface of the membranes. The activated enzymes release secondary messengers such as calcium ions, nucleotides, and even fatty acids.

Secondary messengers relay the hormone's message inside the cell. These secondary messengers can activate or inhibit a wide range of cell activities.

🔑 Key Question How do hormones affect cells?
Steroid hormones enter the nucleus and change the way genes are expressed in a target cell. Nonsteroid hormones bind to receptors on cell membranes. They cause the release of secondary messengers that affect cell activities.

✓CHECK Understanding

Apply Vocabulary
Use the highlighted words from the lesson to complete each sentence correctly.

1. An _____ gland releases its secretions through ducts.

2. A _____ is a chemical messenger that is released from a cell and acts on other cells nearby.

Critical Thinking

3. **Compare and Contrast** How are hormones and prostaglandins similar? Different?

4. **Explain** Explain the difference between endocrine glands and exocrine glands.

5. **Write to Learn** Answer the first mystery clue. Write a paragraph that explains why you think maintaining adequate fat reserves is important.

MYSTERY CLUE

Fat tissue may send signals to the hypothalamus when fat reserves are low. Lisa's body fat percentage dropped from 17 percent to 9 percent. Could this have affected such signals?

34.2 Glands of the Endocrine System

MD CLG **3.1.1** Chemical Substances and Macromolecules, **3.1.2** Homeostasis, **3.2.1** Processes and Functions, **3.2.2** Changes in Metabolic Activity. **SPI 1.5.8** Compare.

The Human Endocrine Glands

The endocrine system is different from other organ systems. Most of the glands in the endocrine system are scattered throughout the body. However, they still work as a single system, regulating a wide variety of activities.

Pituitary Gland The pituitary gland is a bean-sized gland that hangs under the base of the brain. A slender stalk of tissue attaches it to the brain. It is divided into two parts: the anterior pituitary and the posterior pituitary. The pituitary gland secretes some hormones that directly regulate many body functions. It secretes other hormones that control the actions of other endocrine glands.

Hypothalamus The hypothalamus links the central nervous system to the endocrine system. It directly and indirectly controls the secretions of the pituitary gland.

Neurons connect the posterior pituitary to the hypothalamus. The cell bodies in the hypothalamus produce two hormones, antidiuretic hormone (ADH) and oxytocin. These hormones are stored in the axons, which extend into the pituitary. When the cell bodies are stimulated, the axons release the hormones into the blood.

The hypothalamus indirectly controls the anterior pituitary with **releasing hormones.** These hormones are secreted into blood vessels that lead to the pituitary. Each releasing hormone controls a different pituitary hormone.

Key Questions

🔑 **What are the functions of the major endocrine glands?**

🔑 **How are endocrine glands controlled?**

BUILD
Understanding

Concept Map As you read, develop a concept map that shows the relationship between the human endocrine glands.

In Your Workbook Go to your workbook for help in completing your concept map for Lesson 34.2.

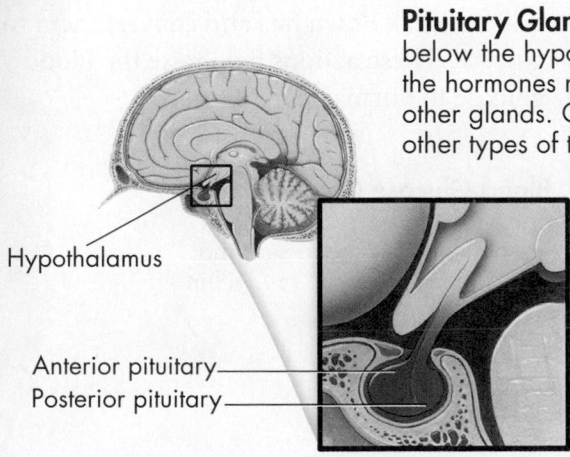

Pituitary Gland The pituitary gland is located below the hypothalamus in the brain. Some of the hormones released by the pituitary control other glands. Other hormones released affect other types of tissues.

Hypothalamus

Anterior pituitary
Posterior pituitary

releasing hormone
a hormone produced by the hypothalamus that makes the anterior pituitary secrete hormones

corticosteroid
a steroid hormone produced by the adrenal cortex

epinephrine
a hormone released by the adrenal glands that increases heart rate and blood pressure and prepares the body for intense physical activity; also called adrenaline

norepinephrine
a hormone released by the adrenal glands that increases heart rate and blood pressure and prepares the body for intense physical activity

PREFIXES
The prefix *nor-* means "parent of." Scientists use this prefix to indicate when one compound is made from another compound. This prefix tells us that the body makes epinephrine from norepinephrine.

Adrenal Glands The adrenal glands, which sit on top of the kidneys, have two layers. The outer layer is the adrenal cortex. It produces a group of steroid hormones called **corticosteroids** (kawr tih koh STEER oydz). Aldosterone (al DAHS tuh rohn) regulates blood volume and pressure. The adrenal cortex releases aldosterone when blood volume decreases. Cortisol helps control the metabolism of carbohydrates, fats, and proteins. The adrenal gland releases cortisol during physical stress, such as intense exercise.

The inner part is the adrenal medulla. It produces **epinephrine** and **norepinephrine.** When you are under stress, the sympathetic nervous system sends impulses to the adrenal medulla. The adrenal medulla releases large amounts of these hormones, causing heart rate and blood pressure to rise. Epinephrine and norepinephrine also widen air passageways in the lungs and cause the release of extra glucose.

Pancreas The pancreas is an exocrine gland that releases digestive enzymes to help break down food. The pancreas is also an endocrine gland. It has clusters of cells that release hormones into the blood. These clusters, called the "islets of Langerhans," contain both beta cells and alpha cells. Beta cells secrete the hormone insulin. Alpha cells secrete the hormone glucagon.

▶ *Blood Glucose Regulation* Insulin and glucagon work together to keep blood glucose levels stable. Blood glucose levels rise after you eat, which causes the pancreas to release insulin. Insulin causes cells to take glucose out of the blood. Liver cells, skeletal muscle cells, and fat tissue store the glucose. Storing glucose in these cells keeps blood glucose from rising too rapidly. Liver and muscle cells store the glucose as glycogen, while the glucose in fat is converted to lipids.

Blood glucose levels drop within one or two hours after a person has eaten. As a result, the pancreas releases glucagon. Glucagon stimulates the liver and skeletal muscle cells to break down glycogen and release glucose into the blood. Glucagon also causes fat cells to break down fats and convert them to glucose. These actions help raise the blood glucose to normal levels.

Blood Glucose Control Insulin and glucagon are opposing hormones. They make sure that blood glucose levels stay within a normal range.

Food intake increases blood glucose level.

GLUCAGON (promotes breakdown of glycogen)

Pancreas releases insulin or glucagon in response to blood glucose levels.

INSULIN (promotes glucose uptake)

Between meals, blood glucose level drops.

▶ **Diabetes Mellitus** Diabetes mellitus occurs when the body fails to produce or properly respond to insulin. Diabetes causes very high blood glucose levels. Very high blood glucose levels can damage almost every system and cell in the body.

There are two types of diabetes mellitus. Type I diabetes is an autoimmune disorder that destroys beta cells. Type I diabetes usually develops in people before age 15. People with Type I secrete little to no insulin. Type I diabetics must follow a strict diet and get a daily dose of insulin.

People with Type II diabetes produce insulin, but it does not bind to insulin receptors properly. Type II usually starts in people after age 40. However, it is increasing rapidly in young people due to childhood obesity. In its early stages, Type II diabetes can often be controlled through diet and exercise.

Thyroid and Parathyroid Glands

The thyroid gland is located in the neck and wraps around the upper part of the trachea. It plays a major role in regulating the body's metabolism and blood calcium levels. It produces two hormones: **thyroxine** and *calcitonin.* Thyroxine stimulates cells to become more active, use more energy, and produce more heat. Iodine is needed to make thyroxine. An iodine deficiency causes the thyroid to enlarge. This is called a goiter.

Calcitonin reduces blood calcium levels by signaling the kidneys to reabsorb less calcium from filtrate. It also inhibits calcium absorption from the small intestine and promotes absorption into bones. Its opposing hormone is parathyroid hormone (PTH), which is produced by the parathyroid glands. These glands are located on the back side of the thyroid. PTH increases the release of calcium from the bone. It also increases calcium reabsorption in the kidneys, and calcium uptake in the digestive system.

The Reproductive Glands

The gonads—ovaries and testes—are the body's reproductive glands. The gonads serve two important functions: the production of gametes and the secretion of sex hormones. You will learn more about the gonads and their hormones in the next lesson.

🔑 **Key Question** What are the functions of the major endocrine glands?
The pituitary gland secretes hormones that directly regulate many body functions or control other endocrine glands. The hypothalamus controls the secretions of the pituitary gland. The thyroid gland helps regulate the body's metabolic rate. The gonads produce gametes and secrete sex hormones.

Thyroid Gland The thyroid makes thyroxine, which speeds up metabolism and helps control growth and development.

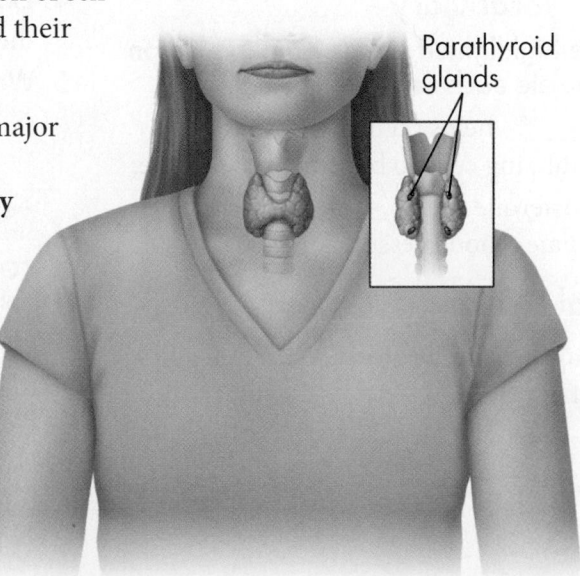
Parathyroid glands

Control of the Endocrine System

Like most other body systems, the endocrine system is regulated by feedback mechanisms, which help the body maintain homeostasis.

When you exercise heavily, you lose water as sweat. If water loss continued, you would become dehydrated. As you lose water, the blood becomes more concentrated. The hypothalamus responds by signaling the posterior pituitary to release antidiuretic hormone (ADH). ADH signals the kidneys to remove less water from the blood. Later, you experience a sensation of thirst. Thirst is a signal to replace lost water.

When you finally drink, you might take in a liter of water. Most of the water is absorbed by the blood. This rapid absorption could dilute the blood too quickly. Large amounts of water would diffuse out of the blood into body tissues. Body cells would swell with the excess water. The hypothalamus prevents this by signaling the pituitary to release less ADH when the blood becomes dilute. The kidneys respond by removing more water from the blood. So, the homeostatic system sets limits for water in the blood. When blood has too little water, ADH is released and the kidneys conserve water. An oversupply of water causes the kidneys to eliminate excess water in the urine.

Water Balance
The hypothalamus and posterior pituitary use a feedback mechanism to regulate water balance.

Sweating, reduced water intake, and urination reduce blood volume.

LESS ADH No thirst

Hypothalamus senses low or high concentration of water in blood and signals pituitary.

MORE ADH Thirst sensation

Drinking (response to thirst) and decreased kidney action increase blood volume.

Key Question How are endocrine glands controlled? **The endocrine system is regulated by feedback mechanisms that function to maintain homeostasis.**

CHECK Understanding

Apply Vocabulary

Use the highlighted words from the lesson to complete each sentence correctly.

1. _____ helps regulate metabolism by stimulating cells to become more active.

2. Aldosterone is a _____ that helps regulate blood pressure and volume.

Critical Thinking

3. Compare and Contrast Compare and contrast the two types of diabetes.

4. Explain Describe how the hypothalamus controls the secretions of the posterior pituitary gland.

5. Write to Learn Answer the second mystery clue.

MYSTERY CLUE

One effect of cortisol is the release of calcium from bones into the blood. This makes the calcium available for skeletal muscles. How could this effect of cortisol have contributed to Lisa's condition? (**Hint:** See p. 814.)

34.3 The Reproductive System

MD CLG 3.1.1 Chemical Substances and Macromolecules, 3.2.1 Processes and Functions, 3.3.1 Sexual Reproduction and Variation, 3.6.2 Investigate a Biological Issue. SPI 1.5.5 Create and Interpret Graphics, 1.5.8 Compare, 1.6.1 Ratio and Proportion, 1.7.1 Apply Skills and Concepts.

Sexual Development

The reproductive system may be the only system in the body that isn't necessary for the survival of an individual. But without the reproductive system, the human species itself would not survive. In some ways, this makes the reproductive system the most important system in the body.

Male and female human embryos look almost identical until they are about seven weeks old. Then male gonads begin secreting testosterone, causing the male reproductive system to develop. In females, the gonads produce estrogens instead of testosterone. Estrogens cause the female reproductive system to develop.

Testosterone and estrogens are steroid hormones that are primarily produced in the gonads. They control sexual development of the human embryo. They also act on other cells and tissues. Testosterone causes facial hair to grow and increases muscular development in males. It also causes the male voice to deepen. Estrogens stimulate breast development and widening of the hips in females.

The testes and the ovaries cannot produce active reproductive cells until puberty. Puberty is a period of rapid growth and sexual maturation. The reproductive system becomes fully functional during puberty, which usually occurs between ages 9 and 15. Puberty begins in the brain, when the hypothalamus signals the release of two hormones from the pituitary. These hormones are follicle-stimulating hormone (FSH) and luteinizing hormone (LH).

Key Question What effects do estrogens and testosterone have on females and males?
Estrogens stimulate breast development and widening of the hips in females. Testosterone stimulates the growth of facial hair, muscular development, and deepening of the voice in males.

The Male Reproductive System

The release of LH stimulates cells in the testes to produce increased amounts of testosterone. Testosterone causes the male physical changes associated with puberty. Testosterone also works with FSH to stimulate sperm development. When puberty is finished, the reproductive system can produce and release active sperm.

Key Questions

What effects do estrogens and testosterone have on females and males?

What are the main functions of the male reproductive system?

What are the main functions of the female reproductive system?

What are some of the most commonly reported sexually transmitted diseases?

BUILD Understanding

Preview Visuals Before you read, preview the diagram called Sperm. Think about how you would describe this diagram.

In Your Workbook Go to your workbook for help in previewing this visual.

BUILD Vocabulary

testis
the primary male reproductive organ; produces sperm

ovary
in animals, the primary female reproductive organ; produces eggs

⚡ MULTIPLE MEANINGS

In plants, an ovary is a structure that surrounds and protects seeds.

Testes The **testes** (singular: testis) are the primary male reproductive organs. Just before or just after birth, they descend from the abdomen into an external sac called a *scrotum*. This external sac is necessary because sperm must be cooler than body temperature (37° Celsius) to develop properly.

Sperm Development Inside each testis are clusters of hundreds of tiny tubules called seminiferous (sem uh NIF ur us) tubules. Sperm develop inside these tubules from specialized diploid cells. The diploid cells divide by meiosis to form the haploid nuclei found in mature sperm. A haploid cell contains only a single set of chromosomes.

Sperm move from the seminiferous tubules into the epididymis (ep uh DID ih mis) to mature and be stored. Some of the sperm move from the epididymis into another tube called the vas deferens. The vas deferens extends upward from the scrotum into the abdominal cavity. Here it merges with the urethra, which leads to the outside of the body through the penis.

Glands lining the reproductive tract produce seminal fluid. This fluid provides nutrients for the sperm. It also protects them from the acidity of the female reproductive tract. The combination of seminal fluid and sperm is called *semen*.

Sperm Release When the male is sexually aroused, the penis becomes erect. Contractions of smooth muscles in the reproductive tract then eject semen from the penis. This process is called ejaculation. Ejaculation is regulated by the autonomic nervous system, so it is not completely voluntary. If ejaculation takes place in or near the female reproductive tract, sperm may enter and successfully fertilize an egg.

Male Reproductive System The main structures of the male reproductive system produce and deliver sperm.

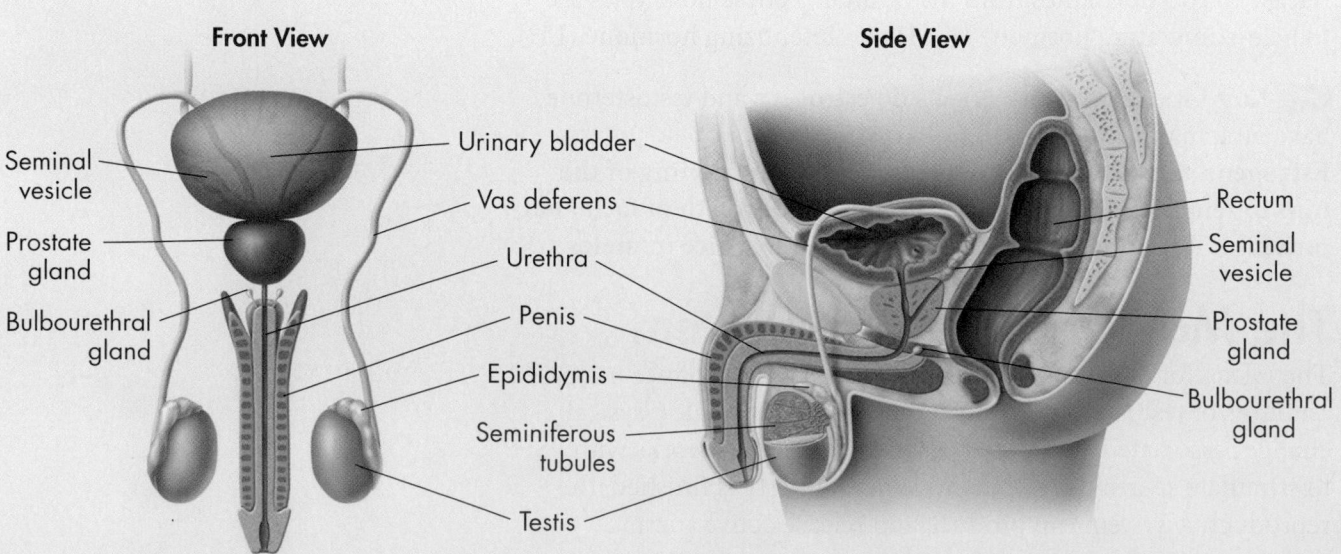

Front View

- Seminal vesicle
- Prostate gland
- Bulbourethral gland
- Urinary bladder
- Vas deferens
- Urethra
- Penis
- Epididymis
- Seminiferous tubules
- Testis

Side View

- Rectum
- Seminal vesicle
- Prostate gland
- Bulbourethral gland

Sperm Structure The head of a mature sperm cell contains a highly condensed nucleus. Its midpiece is packed with mitochondria that provide energy to the sperm. The tail (flagellum) moves the sperm forward. The tip of the head has a small cap that contains enzymes needed for fertilization.

🗝 Key Question What are the main functions of the male reproductive system?

When puberty is complete, the male reproductive system is fully functional, meaning that the male can produce and release active sperm.

The Female Reproductive System

The **ovaries** are a female's primary reproductive organs. When puberty starts, FSH stimulates cells inside the ovaries to produce more estrogens. FSH also signals the ovaries to start producing egg cells.

Female Reproductive Structures Each ovary contains up to 400,000 primary follicles. A follicle is a cluster of cells surrounding a single egg, or ovum. The follicle helps the egg mature. Then the egg is released into the reproductive tract, where it can be fertilized by a sperm. Only about 400 mature eggs are released in a female's lifetime.

Other structures in the female reproductive system include the Fallopian tubes, uterus, cervix, and the vagina.

Sperm Sperm have large numbers of mitochondria. The mitochondria provide power for a sperm cell's trip through the female reproductive tract. If a sperm reaches an egg, enzymes in its cap can break down the egg's outer layer.

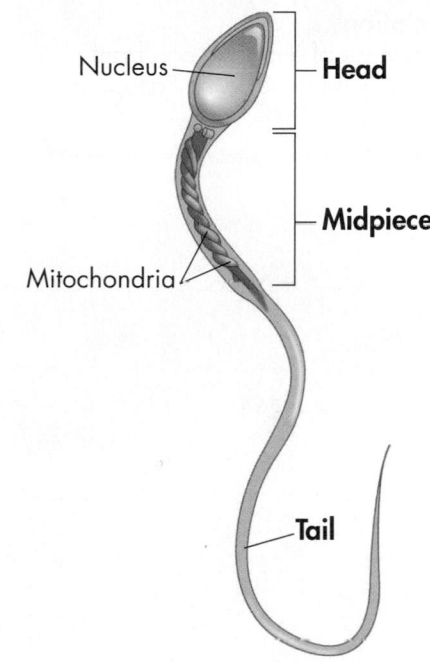

Female Reproductive System The main function of the female reproductive system is to produce eggs. The ovaries are the main organs of the female reproductive system.

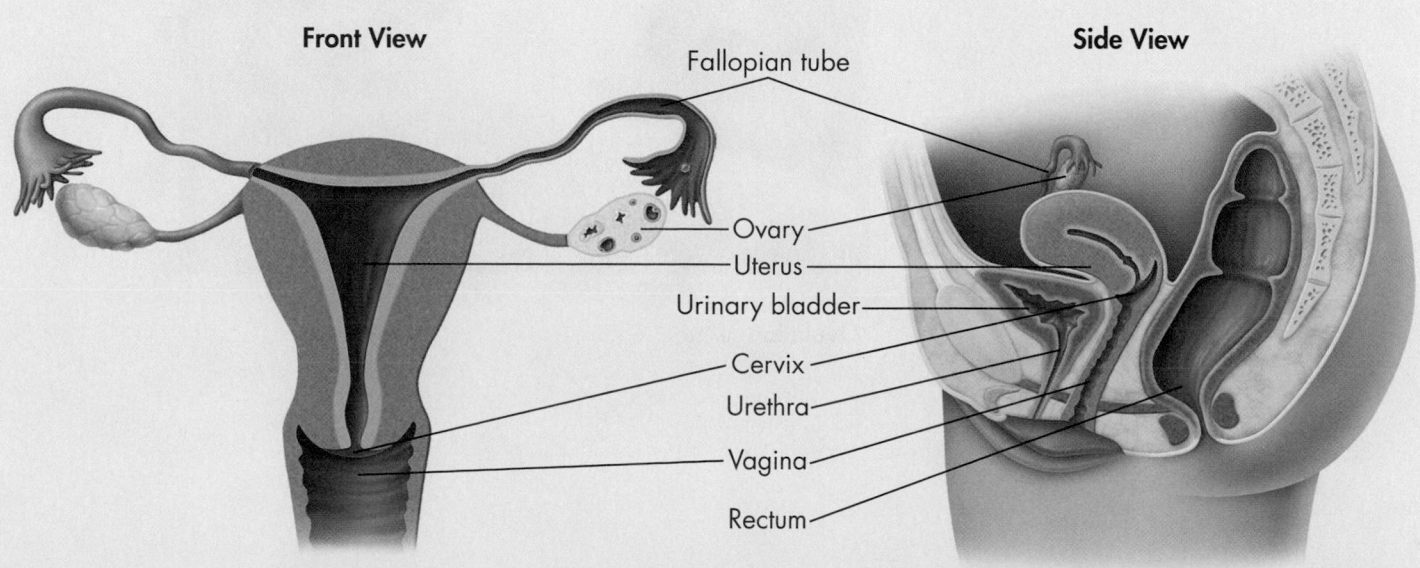

Front View

Side View

Fallopian tube
Ovary
Uterus
Urinary bladder
Cervix
Urethra
Vagina
Rectum

menstrual cycle
a regular sequence of events in which an egg develops and is released from the body

ovulation
the release of a mature egg from the ovary into one of the Fallopian tubes

The Menstrual Cycle One mature egg is usually produced and released from an ovary every 28 days or so. The process of egg production and release is part of the **menstrual cycle.** A menstrual cycle involves the ovaries, the lining of the uterus, and the endocrine system. Hormones from the hypothalamus, the pituitary, and the ovaries regulate this cycle.

During this cycle, an egg develops and is released from the ovary. If the egg is not fertilized, it leaves the body along with the lining of the uterus. If the egg is fertilized, then the menstrual cycle stops and embryonic development begins. The menstrual cycle includes the follicular phase, ovulation, the luteal phase, and menstruation.

▶ *Follicular Phase* Blood estrogen levels are low on day 1 of the menstrual cycle. The hypothalamus reacts to the low levels by producing a releasing hormone. The releasing hormone causes the anterior pituitary to release FSH and LH. These hormones stimulate the ovaries, causing a follicle to mature.

As the follicle develops, the cells surrounding the egg grow larger. The cells release more and more estrogens, causing FSH and LH levels to drop. The estrogens also cause the lining of the uterus to thicken so it can receive a fertilized egg. An egg matures in about 12 days.

▶ *Ovulation* The follicle releases more and more estrogens as it grows until the estrogens reach a certain level. This increased estrogen level triggers a burst of FSH and LH, causing the follicle to rupture. This rupture releases the egg into the Fallopian tube, a process called **ovulation.** Eggs are stalled in metaphase of meiosis II when they are released. Eggs remain in this phase of meiosis unless they are fertilized. Cilia push the egg down the Fallopian tube toward the uterus.

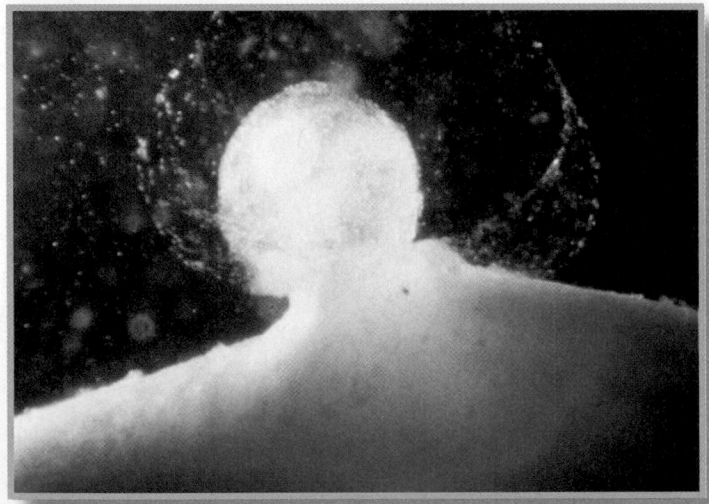

Ovulation (LM 160×)

▶ **Luteal Phase** Immediately after ovulation, the cells of the ruptured follicle change. The follicle turns yellow and is now called the *corpus luteum* (which means "yellow body"). The corpus luteum is still releasing estrogens, but it also begins releasing the steroid hormone, progesterone. Progesterone causes the uterine lining to develop. These hormones slow down the release of FSH and LH. This blocks the growth of more follicles during the cycle.

If the egg remains unfertilized, LH levels fall. This decrease in LH levels causes the corpus luteum to collapse. The collapse causes estrogen levels to decrease, and the follicular phase begins again.

▶ **Menstruation** When the new follicular phase starts, estrogen levels drop, causing the uterine lining to loosen. The tissue, blood, and the unfertilized egg are discharged through the vagina. This phase, called **menstruation,** lasts three to seven days. Estrogen production declines when a female is in her late forties to early fifties. This decrease in estrogen production stops ovulation and menstruation permanently. This phase is called menopause.

BUILD Connections

THE MENSTRUAL CYCLE
The menstrual cycle includes several phases. Notice the changes in hormone levels in the blood, follicle development, and the uterine lining.

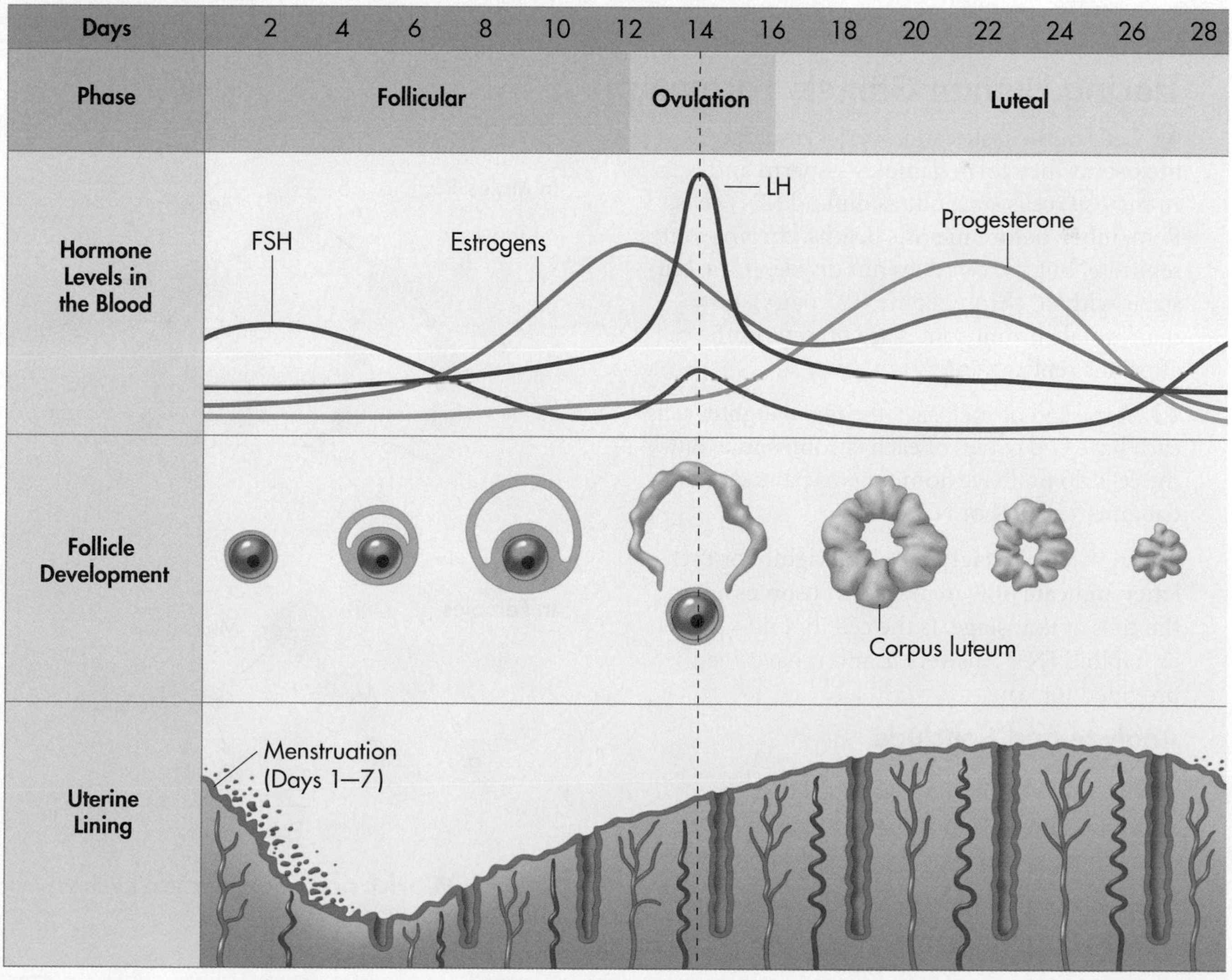

Days	2	4	6	8	10	12	14	16	18	20	22	24	26	28
Phase			Follicular				Ovulation				Luteal			

Hormone Levels in the Blood

FSH · Estrogens · LH · Progesterone

Follicle Development

Corpus luteum

Uterine Lining

Menstruation (Days 1—7)

Pregnancy The menstrual cycle stops if a woman becomes pregnant. An egg is most likely to be fertilized during the first two days after ovulation. A fertilized egg immediately completes meiosis and undergoes mitosis. It divides several times, forming a ball of cells that implants into the uterine lining. Soon, the uterus and embryo begin to release hormones that keep the corpus luteum functioning. This allows the uterine lining to nourish and protect the embryo for several weeks. It also blocks the menstrual cycle from starting again.

🔑 **Key Question** What are the main functions of the female reproductive system?
The main function of the female reproductive system is to produce eggs. It also prepares the female's body to nourish a developing embryo.

INQUIRY
into Scientific Thinking

Tracing Human Gamete Formation

❶ Cells in the testes and ovaries undergo meiosis as they form gametes—sperm and eggs. In meiosis, cells start out as diploid (2N) cells. Remember, before meiosis begins, chromosomes replicate, but the cell does not divide. If the cell starts with 46 chromosomes (23 pairs), how many total chromosomes are present in the cell after this replication?

❷ At the end of meiosis I, the two daughter cells each have two copies of each chromosome. But the cells do not have homologous pairs. Are the daughter cells 2N or N?

❸ Look at the diagrams to the right. For each letter, indicate how many chromosomes are in the cells at that stage. Is the cell diploid (2N) or haploid (N)? Answers *a.* and *e.* have been provided for you.

Analyze and Conclude

1. Interpret Visuals For every cell that undergoes meiosis in a male or female, how many more sperm than eggs are produced?

2. Infer What percentage of sperm cells will contain a Y chromosome?

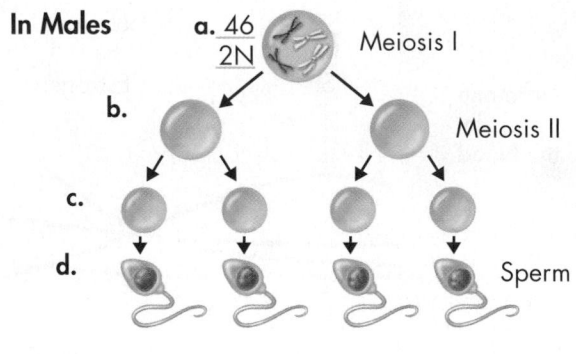

In Males

a. $\frac{46}{2N}$ Meiosis I

b.   Meiosis II

c.

d.   Sperm

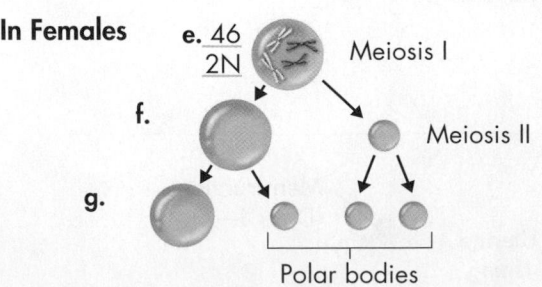

In Females

e. $\frac{46}{2N}$ Meiosis I

f.   Meiosis II

g.

Polar bodies

In Your Workbook Get more help for this activity in your workbook.

Sexually Transmitted Diseases

Some diseases are spread by sexual contact. These diseases are called **sexually transmitted diseases (STDs).** STDs can be caused by bacteria or by viruses. Bacterial STDs include chlamydia, gonorrhea, and syphilis. Viral STDs include hepatitis B, genital herpes, and genital warts. Unlike bacterial STDs, viral STDs cannot be treated with antibiotics. Some viral STDs can be fatal. Tens of thousands of people die from AIDS each year. Human papillomavirus (HPV), which causes genital warts, is a major cause of cervical cancer.

STDs can be avoided. The safest way is to abstain from sexual contact before marriage. The next safest way is to use a condom, but even condoms do not provide 100 percent protection.

🔑 **Key Question** What are some of the most commonly reported sexually transmitted diseases?
Some of the most common bacterial STDs are chlamydia, gonorrhea, and syphilis. Some of the most common viral STDs are hepatitis B, genital herpes, genital warts, and AIDS.

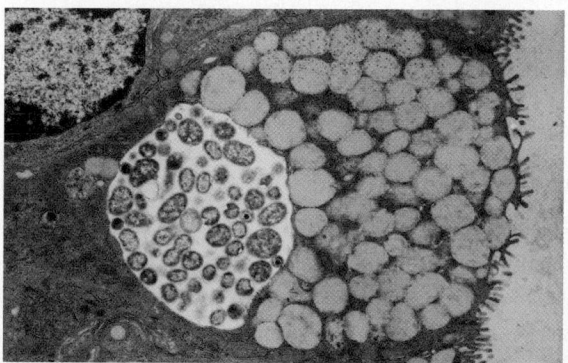

Infection This electron micrograph shows a group of *Chlamydia trachomatis* bacteria in green. The bacteria are growing inside a cell within the female reproductive tract. The bacteria will eventually cause the cell to burst, and the infection will spread.

BUILD Vocabulary

menstruation
the discharge of blood and the unfertilized egg from the body

sexually transmitted disease (STD)
a disease that is spread from person to person by sexual contact

🔑 WORD ORIGINS
The word *menstruation* comes from the Latin word *mensis,* meaning "month."

CHECK Understanding

Apply Vocabulary
Use the highlighted words from the lesson to complete each sentence correctly.

1. _____ are the primary male reproductive organs.

2. The _____ is characterized by a follicular phase, ovulation, and a luteal phase.

Critical Thinking

3. **Evaluate** Why do you think young people are especially at risk for STDs?

4. **Compare and Contrast** Compare and contrast the sexual development of male and female embryos.

5. **Sequence** Explain how sperm develop.

6. **Write to Learn** Answer the third clue of the mystery.

MYSTERY CLUE
Low fat reserves in women are related to low FSH and LH levels. Tests showed that Lisa's blood had very low levels of these hormones. How might this have affected her menstrual cycle? (**Hint:** See p. 820.)

Fertilization and Development

MD | CLG **3.2.1** Processes and Functions, **3.3.1** Sexual Reproduction and Variation.
SPI **1.5.9** Synthesize Ideas, **1.7.1** Apply Skills and Concepts.

Key Questions

🔑 **What takes place during fertilization and the early stages of human development?**

🔑 **What important events occur during the later stages of human development?**

BUILD Understanding

Flowchart As you read, draw a flowchart that shows the steps from fertilized egg to newborn baby.

In Your Workbook Go to your workbook to learn more about making a flowchart. Complete the flowchart for Lesson 34.4.

Fertilization and Early Development

Is anything more amazing than the formation of a new human from a single cell? The story of human development begins with the gametes. Gametes are sperm produced in the testes and egg cells produced in the ovaries. The process of development begins when a sperm and an egg cell fuse into a single cell.

Fertilization Hundreds of millions of sperm are released when semen is ejaculated into the vagina through the penis. Semen is generally released just below the cervix. The cervix is the opening that connects the vagina to the uterus. Sperm swim through the cervix and uterus into the Fallopian tubes. If an egg is in one of the Fallopian tubes, its chances of being fertilized are good.

The egg has a protective outer layer. A sperm can attach to binding sites on this layer. Its head then releases powerful enzymes that break down this protective layer. The sperm and egg are haploid (N). The sperm nucleus enters the egg, and their chromosomes are brought together. The two haploid nuclei fuse to form a single diploid (2N) nucleus. The nucleus contains a single set of chromosomes from each parent cell. The fertilized egg is called a **zygote,** or embryo.

The egg contains a layer of particles just inside its outer layer. It releases the contents of these particles when the sperm enters the egg. The material in the particles forms a barrier that prevents other sperm from attaching to, or entering, the egg.

🔑 **Key Question** What takes place during fertilization?
The fusion of a sperm and an egg is called fertilization.

Sperm Meet Egg Many sperm usually reach an egg. But only one sperm can successfully break through the egg's protective layer (SEM 650x).

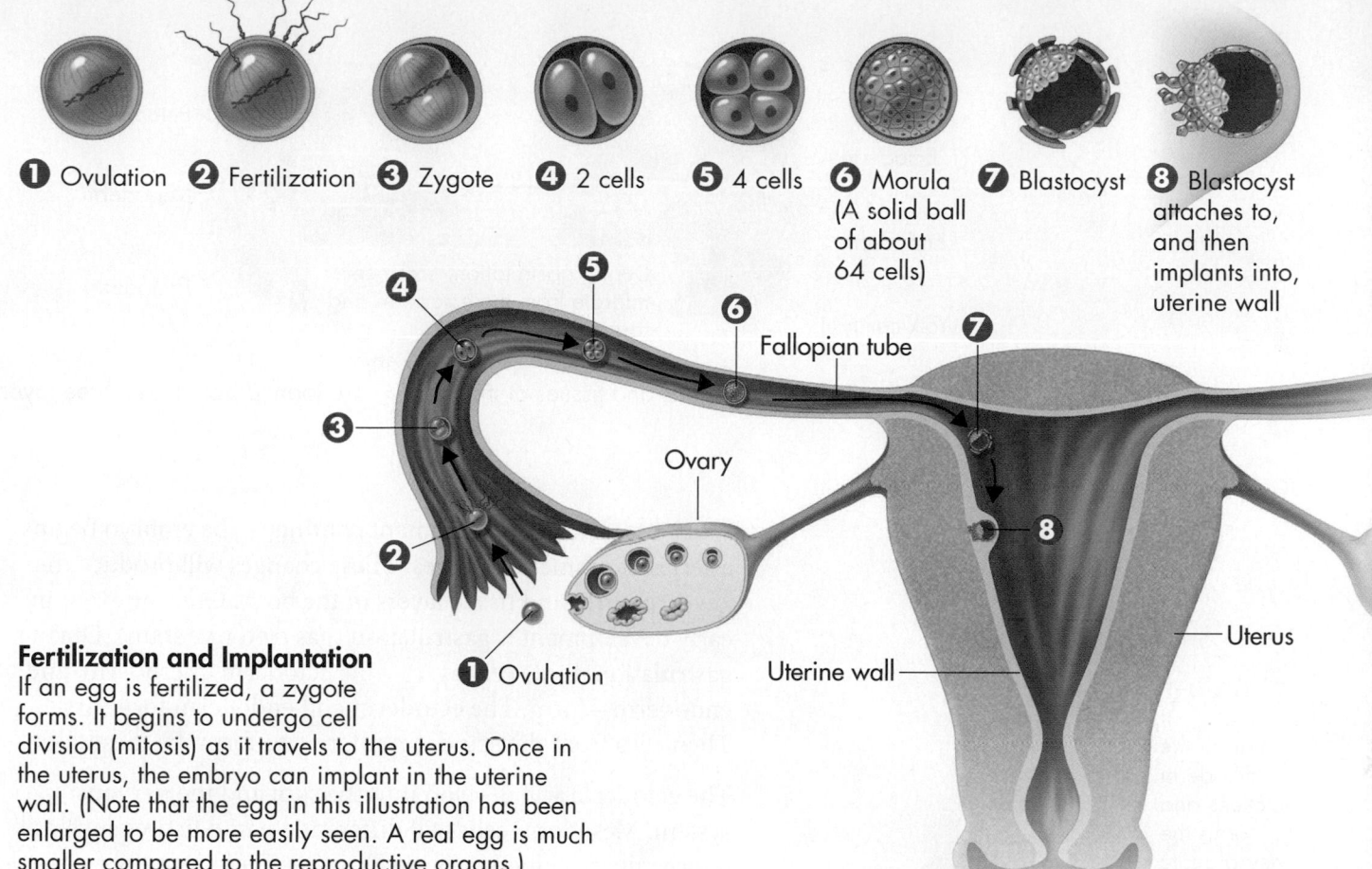

1 Ovulation **2** Fertilization **3** Zygote **4** 2 cells **5** 4 cells **6** Morula (A solid ball of about 64 cells) **7** Blastocyst **8** Blastocyst attaches to, and then implants into, uterine wall

Fallopian tube

Ovary

Uterus

Uterine wall

1 Ovulation

Fertilization and Implantation

If an egg is fertilized, a zygote forms. It begins to undergo cell division (mitosis) as it travels to the uterus. Once in the uterus, the embryo can implant in the uterine wall. (Note that the egg in this illustration has been enlarged to be more easily seen. A real egg is much smaller compared to the reproductive organs.)

Multiple Embryos Sometimes two eggs are released during the same menstrual cycle. If both are fertilized by different sperm, fraternal twins may result. Fraternal twins are not identical in appearance and may even be different sexes. If a single zygote splits apart, it produces two genetically identical embryos. These two identical embryos are called identical twins. Because they result from the same fertilized egg, identical twins are always the same sex.

Implantation The zygote begins to undergo mitosis inside the Fallopian tube. As the embryo grows, the ball of cells develops a cavity in the center. This hollow ball of cells is called the **blastocyst.** About six or seven days after fertilization, it attaches to the uterus wall. The blastocyst then grows into the tissues of the mother, a process called implantation.

At this point, cells in the blastocyst begin to specialize. This process is called differentiation. Differentiation causes the various types of body tissues to develop. A cluster of cells develops inside the inner cavity of the blastocyst. The body of the embryo will develop from this cluster. The remaining cells will differentiate into tissues that support and protect the embryo.

BUILD Vocabulary

zygote
a fertilized egg

blastocyst
a stage of early development in mammals that consists of a hollow ball of cells

placenta
a specialized organ in placental mammals through which respiratory gases, nutrients, and wastes are exchanged between the mother and her developing young

fetus
a human embryo after eight weeks of development

SUFFIXES

A *cyst* is a fluid-filled sac that forms in animal tissues. A structure in the body that has a fluid-filled cavity often has a name ending in -*cyst*. A blastocyst is a hollow ball of cells with a cavity in the center that contains fluid.

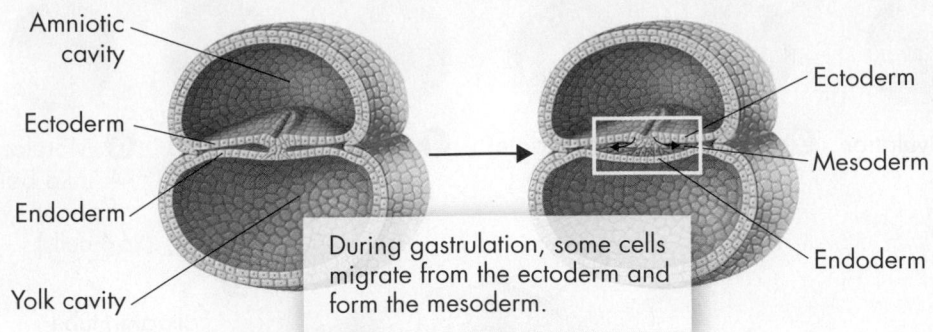

Amniotic cavity

Ectoderm

Endoderm

Yolk cavity

Ectoderm

Mesoderm

Endoderm

During gastrulation, some cells migrate from the ectoderm and form the mesoderm.

Gastrulation All of the organs and tissues of the embryo are formed from these three layers.

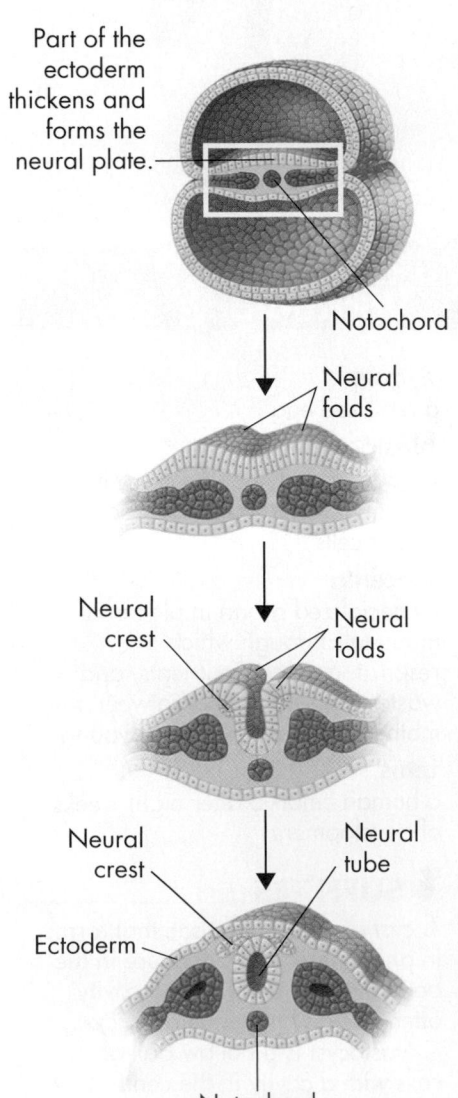

Part of the ectoderm thickens and forms the neural plate.

Notochord

Neural folds

Neural crest

Neural folds

Neural crest

Neural tube

Ectoderm

Notochord

Neurulation During neurulation, changes in the ectoderm lead to formation of the neural tube. The neural tube will develop into the brain and spinal cord. Cells from the neural crest will develop into many types of nerves.

Gastrulation As development continues, the embryo begins a series of dramatic changes. These changes will produce the key structures and tissue layers of the body. One key event in early development is gastrulation (gas troo LAY shun). During gastrulation, three cell layers—the ectoderm, mesoderm, and endoderm—form. The ectoderm and endoderm form first. Then cells from the ectoderm migrate to form the mesoderm.

The ectoderm will develop into the skin and the nervous system. Mesoderm cells will differentiate into tissues such as bones, muscle, blood cells, and gonads. Endoderm forms the linings of organs in the digestive system, respiratory system, and excretory system.

Neurulation Gastrulation is followed by neurulation (NUR uh lay shun), an important step in the development of the nervous system. First, mesodermal tissue differentiates into the notochord. Ectoderm near the notochord also thickens, forming the neural plate. The raised edges of the neural plate form the neural crest and the neural folds. The folds gradually move together to form the neural tube. This will become the brain and spinal cord. Neural crest cells migrate to other areas, becoming nerve cells, skin pigment cells, and other structures.

If the neural tube does not close completely, a serious birth defect can result. Most cases of this defect, called spina bifida, can be prevented by the vitamin folic acid. Neurulation usually occurs before a woman knows she's pregnant. So, folic acid is an important nutrient in any woman's diet.

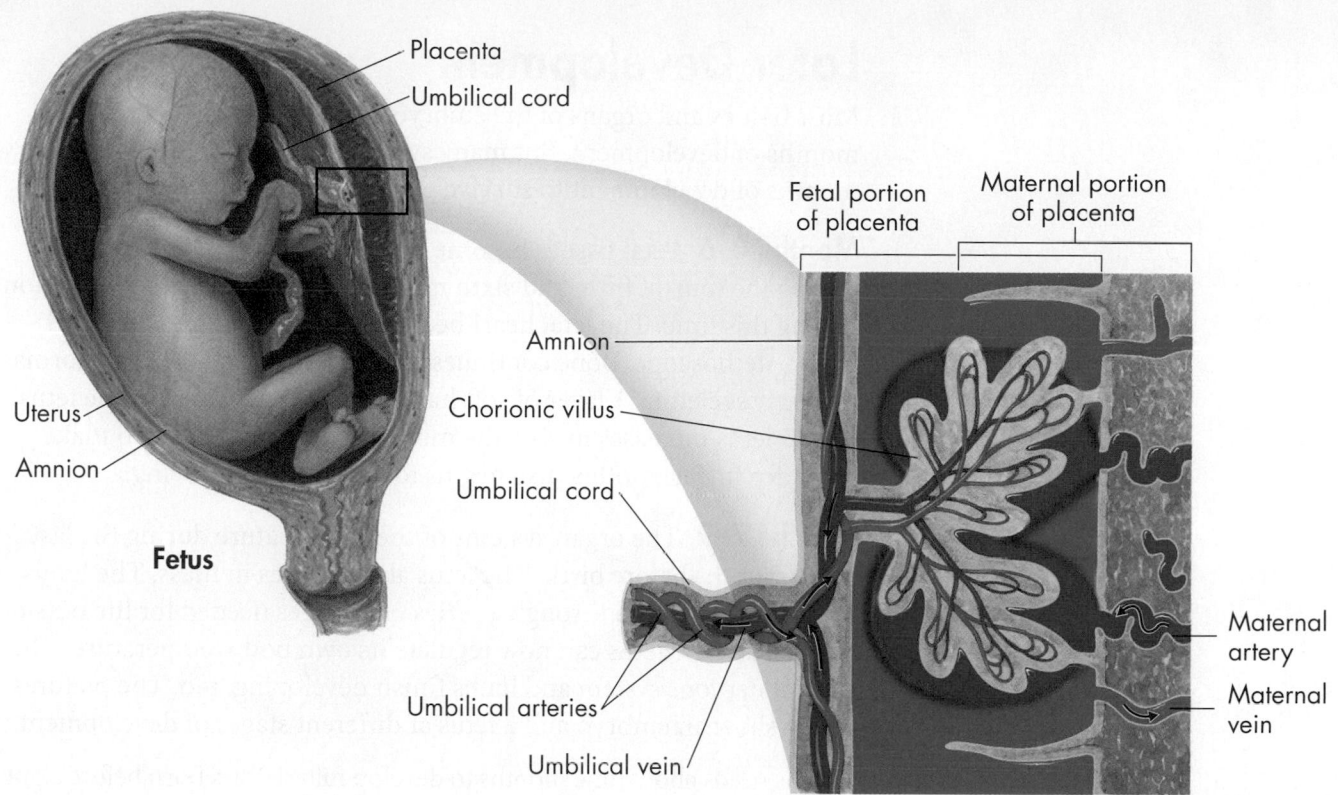

Placenta
Umbilical cord
Uterus
Amnion
Fetus

Fetal portion of placenta
Maternal portion of placenta
Amnion
Chorionic villus
Umbilical cord
Umbilical arteries
Umbilical vein
Maternal artery
Maternal vein

The Placenta The placenta is the connection between the mother and the embryo or fetus. The embryo gets oxygen and nutrients through the placenta. It sends wastes and carbon dioxide back to the mother through the placenta as well. The overlapping brackets show how the chorionic villi extend into the uterine lining.

The Placenta Specialized membranes form to protect and nourish the embryo as it develops. A sac called the amnion surrounds the embryo. It is filled with amniotic fluid, which cushions and protects the embryo. A sac called the chorion forms outside the amnion. Small, fingerlike projections called chorionic villi form on its outer surface.

The villi extend into the uterine lining, forming a vital organ called the **placenta.** The placenta connects the mother and embryo. The mother's blood and the embryo's blood flow past each other, separated by chorionic tissue. Gases, nutrients, and wastes diffuse across this tissue. Two arteries and a vein form the umbilical cord that connects the embryo to the placenta.

After eight weeks, the embryo is about 8 cm long and is called a **fetus.** Most major organs and tissues are fully formed by three months. The fetus may begin to move and show signs of reflexes.

Key Question What takes place during the early stages of human development?
Key events in early development are gastrulation and neurulation. Gastrulation produces the three cell layers of the embryo. Neurulation leads to the formation of the nervous system.

Later Development

Most tissues and organs of the embryo have been formed after three months of development. But many systems will need about six more months of development to survive outside the uterus.

Months 4–6 Fetal tissues become more complex and specialized during the fourth, fifth, and sixth months. They also begin to function during this time. The fetal heart becomes large enough to be heard with a stethoscope. Bone continues to replace the cartilage that forms the early skeleton. A layer of soft hair grows over the skin of the fetus. As the fetus increases in size, the mother's abdomen swells to make room for it. The mother also begins to feel the fetus moving.

Months 7–9 The organ systems of the fetus mature during the last three months before birth. The fetus also doubles in mass. The lungs and other organs go through a series of changes needed for life outside the uterus. The fetus can now regulate its own body temperature. The central nervous system and lungs finish developing, too. The pictures below show an embryo and a fetus at different stages of development.

A fetus needs about nine months to develop fully. Babies born before eight months of development are called premature babies. They often have severe breathing problems because their lungs are not fully developed.

Key Question What important events occur during the later stages of human development?
During the fourth, fifth, and sixth months, tissues become more complex and specialized. They also begin to function. During the last three months before birth, organ systems mature. The fetus grows in size and mass.

Human Development At 7 weeks, most organs have begun to form and the heart (large, dark, rounded structure) is beating. By 14 weeks, the hands, feet, and legs have reached their birth proportions. The eyes, ears, and nose are well developed. At 20 weeks, muscles are more developed, and eyebrows and nails have grown in. At full term, a fetus can live on its own.

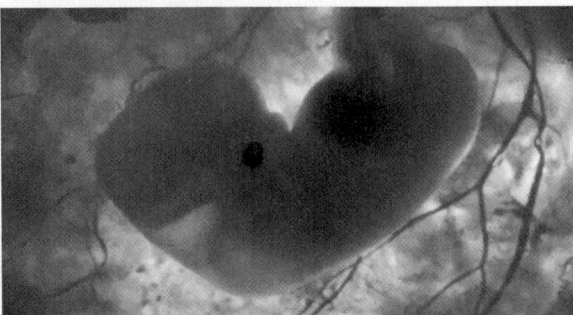

Embryo at 7 Weeks

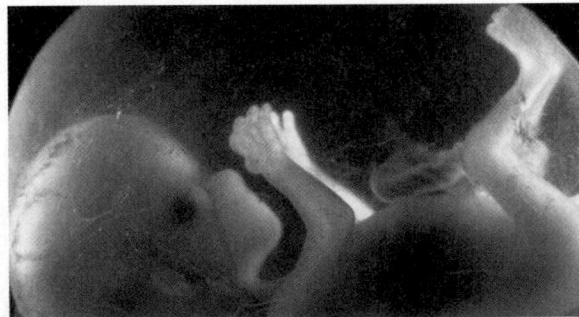

Fetus at 14 Weeks

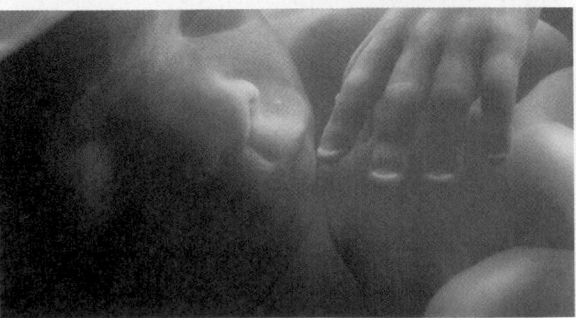

Fetus at 20 Weeks

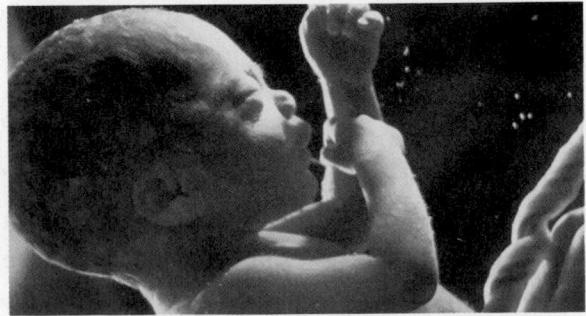

Fetus at Full Term

Childbirth Birth occurs about nine months after fertilization. Many factors trigger birth. One is the release of the hormone oxytocin from the mother's posterior pituitary gland. Oxytocin causes a series of rhythmic contractions, known as labor, to begin. During labor, the cervix expands until it is large enough for the head of the baby to pass through. The amniotic sac breaks, and the fluid it contains rushes out of the vagina. Soon, contractions force the baby out through the vagina. Most babies are delivered head first.

Babies often cough or cry when they emerge from the vagina. These actions help clear fluid from the baby's lungs, allowing the baby to start breathing almost immediately. The umbilical cord is clamped and cut. A small piece remains attached to the baby. This piece soon dries and falls off, leaving a scar called the navel. Now the newborn is independent. It can supply its own oxygen, excrete its own wastes, and maintain its body temperature.

A final series of uterine contractions expels the placenta and the empty amniotic sac. This is called the afterbirth. Within a few hours, the mother's pituitary releases the hormone prolactin. Prolactin signals the mother's breast tissues to produce milk. The mother's milk contains all the nutrients the baby needs for growth and development during the first few months of life.

Infant and Maternal Health The placenta acts as a barrier, but some diseases and chemicals can still cross it. Fetuses can be infected with AIDs. The virus that causes rubella (German measles) can cause birth defects. Alcohol, heroin, cocaine, and nicotine can also harm a fetus. A pregnant woman must behave responsibly and get proper medical care to protect the life inside her.

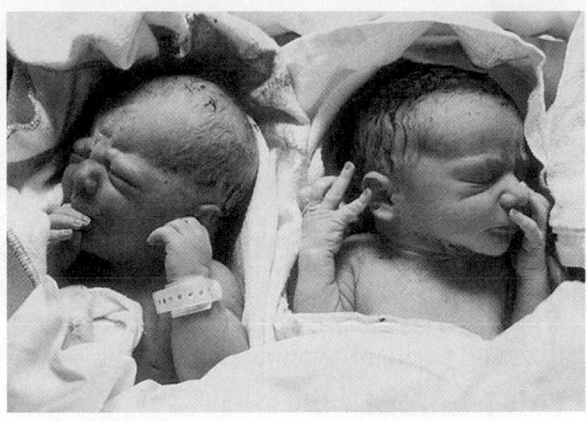

Newborns Twins, ten minutes after birth, adjusting to life outside the uterus

CHECK Understanding

Apply Vocabulary

Use the highlighted words from the lesson to complete each sentence correctly.

1. The hollow ball of cells that attaches to the uterine wall is the _____.
2. After eight weeks of development, an embryo is called a _____.

Critical Thinking

3. **Explain** What is the role of the placenta?
4. **Relate Cause and Effect** How do the results of gastrulation and neurulation contribute to human development?
5. **Quick Write** Doctors often recommend that pregnant women avoid many medications. Write one paragraph explaining why you think this is important.

BIOLOGY.com **Search** (Lesson 34.4) **GO** • Lesson Assessment

Forensics Lab

MD CLG 3.2.1 Processes and Functions. SPI 1.5.7 Classification Systems, 1.5.8 Compare, 1.5.9 Synthesize Ideas.

Pre-Lab: Diagnosing Endocrine Disorders

Problem Can you diagnose an endocrine disorder based on a patient's symptoms?

Lab Manual Chapter 34 Lab

Skills Focus Analyze Data, Draw Conclusions, Relate Cause and Effect

Connect to the `Big idea` Organs of the endocrine system secrete hormones into the blood. Each hormone triggers a response in specific cells. Almost every cell in the body is affected by at least one hormone. The endocrine system regulates important processes such as growth, metabolism, and water balance. If one part of the endocrine system is not working properly, the body will be thrown off balance. If the imbalance is severe, it could threaten the health, or even the life, of a person.

Endocrinologists are medical doctors who diagnose and treat disorders of the endocrine system. The clues these doctors use to solve their mysteries are a patient's symptoms and the results of lab tests. In this lab, you will model the process of diagnosing endocrine disorders.

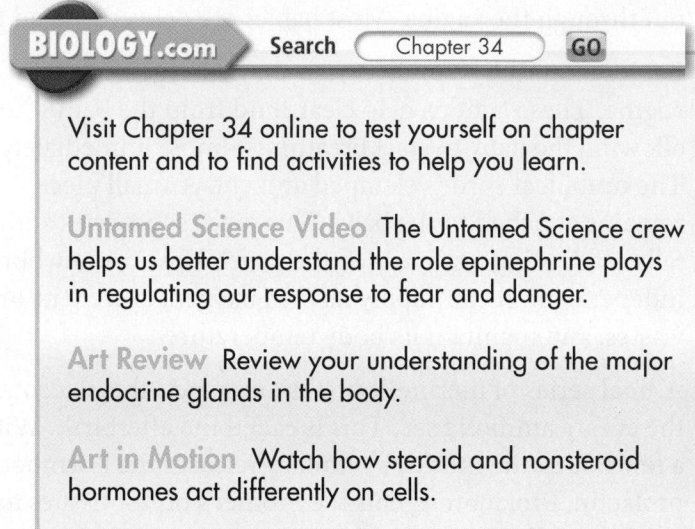

Visit Chapter 34 online to test yourself on chapter content and to find activities to help you learn.

Untamed Science Video The Untamed Science crew helps us better understand the role epinephrine plays in regulating our response to fear and danger.

Art Review Review your understanding of the major endocrine glands in the body.

Art in Motion Watch how steroid and nonsteroid hormones act differently on cells.

Background Questions

a. Review Why doesn't every hormone affect every cell in the body?

b. Review Use a flowchart to describe the feedback loop for regulating the metabolic rate.

c. Use Analogies How are the hormones that regulate the level of glucose in the blood similar to the muscles that bend and straighten an arm?

Pre-Lab Questions

Preview the procedure in the lab manual.

1. Interpret Tables When patients complain of fatigue they are usually referring to a lack of energy or motivation. Which conditions listed in the data table have fatigue as a symptom?

2. Apply Concepts Why do doctors typically use blood tests to diagnose endocrine disorders?

34.1 The Endocrine System

- The endocrine system is made up of glands that release hormones into the blood. Hormones deliver messages throughout the body.

- Steroid hormones can easily cross cell membranes. After they enter the nucleus, they change the way genes are expressed in target cells.

- Nonsteroid hormones bind to receptors on cell membranes. They cause the release of secondary messengers inside the cell. Secondary messengers then affect cell activities.

hormone (p. 810)   endocrine gland (p. 810)
exocrine gland (p. 810)   prostaglandin (p. 811)

34.2 Glands of the Endocrine System

- Hormones secreted by the pituitary gland directly regulate many body functions. Pituitary hormones also control the actions of other endocrine glands.

- The hypothalamus controls the secretions of the pituitary gland.

- The adrenal glands release hormones that help the body prepare for—and deal with—stress.

- Insulin and glucagon help to keep the blood glucose level stable.

- The thyroid gland has a major role in regulating the body's metabolism.

- The two functions of gonads are the production of gametes and the secretion of sex hormones.

- The endocrine system is regulated by feedback mechanisms that function to maintain homeostasis.

releasing hormone (p. 813)
corticosteroids (p. 814)
epinephrine (p. 814)
norepinephrine (p. 814)
thyroxine (p. 815)

34.3 The Reproductive System

- In females, the sex hormones cause breast development and a widening of the hips. In males, they cause the growth of facial hair and increased muscular development. They also cause deepening of the voice.

- The main functions of the male reproductive system are to produce and release active sperm.

- The main function of the female reproductive system is to produce egg cells. The system also prepares the female's body to nourish an embryo.

- Common bacterial STDs include chlamydia, gonorrhea, and syphilis. Common viral STDs include hepatitis B, genital herpes, genital warts, and AIDS.

testis (p. 818)
ovary (p. 819)
menstrual cycle (p. 820)
ovulation (p. 820)
menstruation (p. 821)
sexually transmitted disease (STD) (p. 823)

34.4 Fertilization and Development

- Fertilization occurs when a sperm and an egg cell fuse to form one cell.

- Gastrulation produces the three cell layers of the embryo. Neurulation leads to the formation of the nervous system.

- Fetal tissues become more complex and specialized during the fourth, fifth, and sixth months.

- The organ systems of the fetus mature during the last three months before birth. The fetus also doubles in mass.

zygote (p. 824)
blastocyst (p. 825)
placenta (p. 827)
fetus (p. 827)

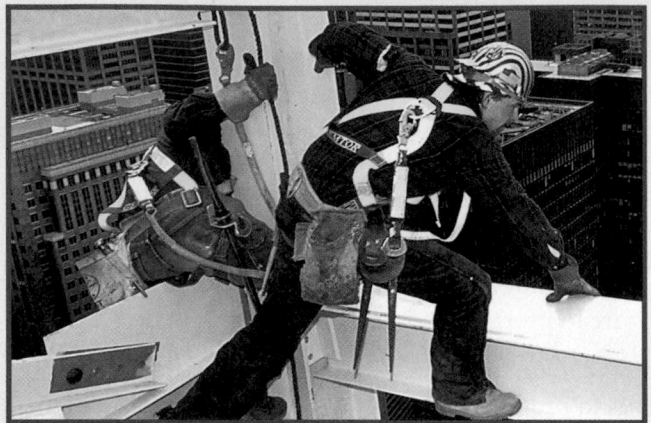

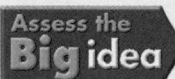 **Homeostasis**

Write an answer to the question below.

Q: How does the body use chemical signals to maintain homeostasis?

Constructed Response

Write an answer to each of the numbered questions below. The answer to each question should be one or two paragraphs. To help you begin, read the **Hints** below the questions.

1. **How do the hypothalamus and pituitary gland work together to help the body maintain homeostasis?**

   Hint The hypothalamus has direct and indirect control over the pituitary.

   Hint Pituitary hormones regulate other endocrine glands as well as other tissues and organs.

2. **Why is it important for the menstrual cycle to stop during pregnancy?**

   Hint The uterine lining becomes part of the placenta during pregnancy.

   Hint Estrogen levels fall at the end of the luteal phase.

3. **Why is it important that the egg cell prevents more than one sperm from fertilizing it?**

   Hint A sperm and egg cell each contain a haploid (N) nucleus.

Foundations for Learning Wrap-Up

The facts you collected as you read the chapter are tools you can use to arrange your thoughts about the endocrine and reproductive systems.

Activity 1 Work with a partner. On a separate sheet of paper, draw and label a chart with the following categories: Hormones, Endocrine glands, and Processes. Invite your partner to choose one card from your envelope and place it in the correct category on the chart. You then have to tell your partner everything you remember about the fact. Take turns. As you sort your facts, you may need to make up your own categories.

Activity 2 Working in small groups, create chains of related facts by pulling facts from each of the categories you created with your partners in Activity 1. Identify how the body uses chemical signals to maintain homeostasis in each chain of facts.

Endocrine Glands	Processes	Hormones
Kidney — Adrenal gland	Water Balance: Sweating, Less ADH, More ADH, Drinking	Testosterone - Male hormone - Produced in testes - Facial hair - Deep voice
	Neurulation: The first step in the development of the nervous system.	

34.1 The Endocrine System

Understand Key Concepts

1. Which is a chemical messenger that can directly influence gene expression?
   - **a.** nonsteroid hormone
   - **b.** steroid hormone
   - **c.** ATP
   - **d.** receptor

Test-Taking Tip

Find Key Words in the Question As you read the question, look for key words that can help you answer it. In question 1, the key words are *chemical messenger*. A chemical messenger is a hormone, so you know that answer **a** or **b** is correct. Read the question again. Another key word is *directly*. Only a steroid hormone can cross cell membranes and enter the nucleus. It affects the cell directly. The correct answer is **b**.

2. A modified fatty acid that is released by a cell and affects local cells and tissues is probably a(n)
   - **a.** nonsteroid hormone.
   - **b.** steroid hormone.
   - **c.** prostaglandin.
   - **d.** exocrine secretion.

3. Many body functions are influenced by the action of two hormones with opposing effects. Why are such pairs of hormones useful?

Think Critically

4. **Infer** After a hormone is secreted by a gland, the circulatory system transports it throughout the body. Why doesn't every cell respond to the hormone?

34.2 Glands of the Endocrine System

Understand Key Concepts

5. A hormone that helps regulate blood calcium levels is produced by the
   - **a.** posterior pituitary.
   - **b.** thymus.
   - **c.** thyroid.
   - **d.** pancreas.

6. Which hormone influences a person's rate of metabolism?
   - **a.** PTH
   - **b.** aldosterone
   - **c.** thyroxine
   - **d.** calcitonin

7. How does the secretion of epinephrine prepare the body to handle emergencies?

8. What happens if blood glucose levels are not properly regulated?

Think Critically

9. **Apply Concepts** The heartbeat of a swimmer was found to increase significantly both before and during a swim meet. Explain why this could happen.

34.3 The Reproductive System

Understand Key Concepts

10. The diagram shows the female reproductive system. Which structure is located at the X?
    - **a.** uterus
    - **b.** Fallopian tube
    - **c.** ovary
    - **d.** cervix

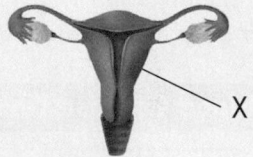

11. Which male reproductive structure releases sperm into the urethra?
    - **a.** epididymis
    - **b.** vas deferens
    - **c.** prostate gland
    - **d.** testis

12. Which two hormones stimulate the gonads to produce their hormones?

Think Critically

13. **Apply Concepts** Sperm cells contain many mitochondria. Explain how mitochondria might influence sperm activity.

34.4 Fertilization and Development

Understanding Key Concepts

14. Another name for a fertilized egg is a
    - **a.** gastrula.
    - **b.** placenta.
    - **c.** zygote.
    - **d.** blastocyst.

15. Fertilization usually occurs in the
- **a.** uterus.
- **c.** Fallopian tube.
- **b.** vagina.
- **d.** ovary.

16. Explain the importance of the three layers that form during gastrulation.

17. What is the function of the placenta?

Think Critically

18. Infer Occasionally, a zygote does not move into the uterus. Instead, it attaches to the wall of a Fallopian tube. Why might this be a very dangerous situation for the mother?

Connecting Concepts

Use Science Graphics

The graph shows the levels of glucose in the blood of two people during a five-hour period immediately following the ingestion of a typical meal. Use the graph to answer questions 19 and 20.

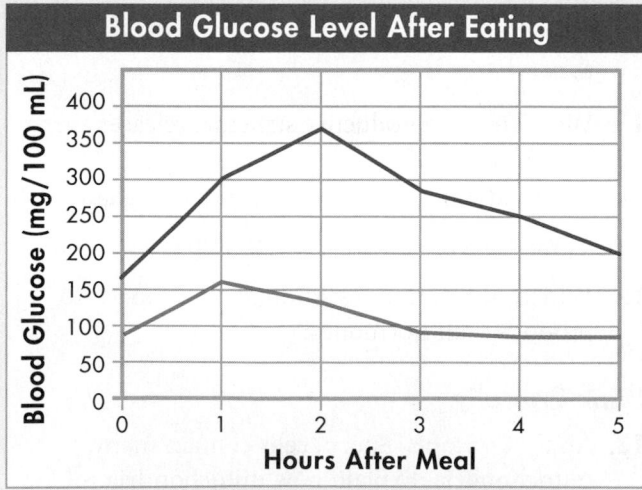

Blood Glucose Level After Eating

19. Interpret Graphs How long does it take the blood glucose level of the person represented by the blue line to return to a homeostatic value?

20. Draw Conclusions Which line represents a person who may have diabetes? Which line represents a person who does not have diabetes? Explain your answer.

solve the CHAPTER MYSTERY

OUT OF STRIDE

A healthful diet and exercise contribute to maintaining a healthy body. But a balance between the two is important. Lisa lost this balance. The reactions from her endocrine system led to a disorder known as the female athlete triad. The triad consists of three factors:

- **Disordered Eating** Lisa did not provide her body with enough nutrients and energy to support all of its functions.

- **Amenorrhea** Lack of menstrual cycles for three or more months is called amenorrhea. Lisa's hypothalamus detected her low energy levels. As a result, it did not signal the pituitary to release FSH and LH. This caused her menstrual cycle to stop and her estrogen levels to drop.

- **Weakened Bones** Lisa's bones lost more calcium than normal because of high cortisol and low estrogen levels. She also did not consume enough calcium because of her poor diet. This made her bones weak. Weak bones are at risk for stress fractures.

The problems associated with the female athlete triad are related to poor nutrition. Lisa used more energy and nutrients than she took in. The reaction of her endocrine system was normal, but it had negative effects on her health.

1. Relate Cause and Effect Explain why the menstrual cycle cannot continue without FSH and LH.

2. In your own words, explain what led to Lisa's stress fracture. What are some ways that Lisa can prevent this from happening again?

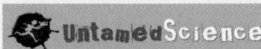 **Never Stop Exploring Your World.** Finding the solution to the Out of Stride mystery is only the beginning. Take a video field trip with the ecogeeks of Untamed Science to see where this mystery leads.

Multiple Choice

1. Which sequence correctly describes the route sperm take through the human male reproductive system?
   A vas deferens, urethra, epididymis
   B epididymis, vas deferens, urethra
   C vas deferens, epididymis, urethra
   D urethra, epididymis, vas deferens CLG 3.2.1

2. Each of these terms refers to a stage in the human menstrual cycle EXCEPT
   A ovulation.   C corpus phase.
   B luteal phase.   D follicular phase.
                                        CLG 3.1.2

3. Which of the following is NOT an endocrine gland?
   A pituitary gland   C sweat gland
   B parathyroid gland   D adrenal gland
                                        CLG 3.2.1

4. During which stage of embryonic development does the neural tube form?
   A implantation   C neurulation
   B gastrulation   D fertilization CLG 3.2.1

5. Which of the following is a cluster of cells that surround a developing egg?
   A follicle   C ovary
   B blastocyst   D ovum   CLG 3.1.1

6. The structure(s) in the male reproductive system that stores mature sperm until they are released by the male reproductive system is (are) the
   A vas deferens.   C seminiferous tubules.
   B penis.   D epididymis. CLG 3.2.1

7. Which statement best describes the relationship between the hypothalamus and the pituitary gland?
   A The anterior pituitary gland makes hormones that are released by the hypothalamus.
   B The hypothalamus produces releasing hormones that promote the release of particular hormones from the anterior pituitary.
   C The hypothalamus produces releasing hormones that promote the release of particular hormones from the posterior pituitary.
   D The posterior pituitary sends nervous signals to the hypothalamus to prompt the release of hormones. CLG 3.2.1

Questions 8–11

The diagram below shows the female endocrine system. Use the diagram to answer the questions.

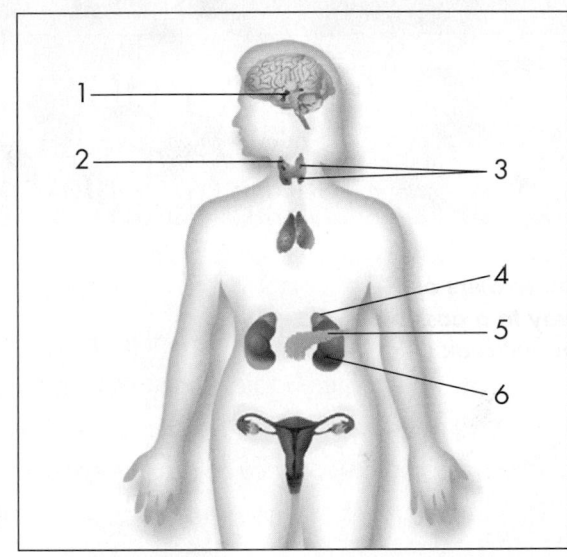

8. Which gland helps the body prepare for and deal with stress?
   A 1   C 4
   B 2   D 6   SPI 1.5.5

9. Which gland is both an endocrine and an exocrine gland?
   A 2   C 4
   B 3   D 5   SPI 1.5.5

10. Which gland secretes ADH?
    A 1   C 3
    B 2   D 5   SPI 1.5.5

11. Which gland secretes thyroxine?
    A 1   C 3
    B 2   D 4   SPI 1.5.5

Open-Ended Response

12. In a paragraph, describe the difference between the origins of fraternal and identical twins.
                                        CLG 3.2.1

If You Have Trouble With . . .

Question	1	2	3	4	5	6	7	8	9	10	11	12
See Lesson	34.3	34.3	34.1	34.4	34.3	34.3	34.2	34.2	34.2	34.2	34.2	34.4

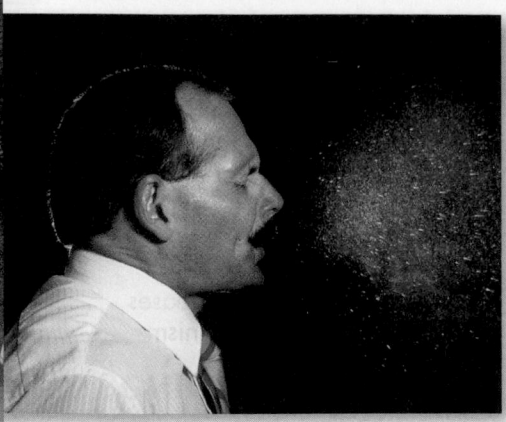

Sneezing Some infectious diseases are spread from person to person by sneezing. Thousands of pathogen particles can be released in a sneeze.

BUILD
Vocabulary

vector
an animal that transports a pathogen to a human

🖊 WORD ORIGINS

Vector comes from the Latin word for "bearer" or "carrier." A vector carries the pathogen or parasite to the host.

Coughing, Sneezing, and Physical Contact Coughing and sneezing send thousands of tiny droplets flying into the air. Other people can breathe these into their bodies. Some droplets may land on things other people touch. Some pathogens can be spread through almost any body-to-body contact and through towels and some sports equipment. The best way to slow the spread of these pathogens is by washing your hands well and often. If you are ill, cover your mouth when you cough or sneeze.

Exchange of Body Fluids Some pathogens are spread only through specific kinds of direct contact. Sexually transmitted diseases, including chlamydia and AIDS, are spread through sexual contact. Some, including AIDS, may also be spread when drug users share needles. Diseases that are transmitted through blood and body fluids can be completely prevented only by avoiding sexual activity and drug use.

Contaminated Water or Food Many pathogens are spread through water contaminated with feces from infected people or other animals. People may drink the water. The water may also carry pathogens onto fruits or vegetables. Pathogens may also be present in seafood and uncooked meat. These foods must be stored and cooked properly.

Animals Diseases that can be spread from other animals to people are called zoonoses. Mad cow disease, Lyme disease, and Ebola are all zoonoses. An animal that carries one of these diseases from an animal host to a human host is called a **vector.** Vectors do not usually get sick themselves. A person can also pick up pathogens from an animal if the person is bitten or comes in close contact with a sick animal.

🔑 **Key Question** How are infectious diseases spread? **Infectious diseases can be spread through coughing, sneezing, or physical contact. Others spread through body fluids, contaminated food or water, or through bites or contact with other animals.**

CHECK
Understanding

Apply Vocabulary
Use the highlighted words from the lesson to complete each sentence correctly.

1. The _____ states that any infectious disease is caused by microorganisms.
2. West Nile virus is transferred from birds to humans by mosquitos. Mosquitos are _____.

Critical Thinking

3. **Explain** What are some ways that pathogens can cause disease in their hosts?

4. **Apply Concepts** Many pathogens make their hosts very sick without killing the host. Why do you think this is a beneficial adaptation? (**Hint:** Think about how viruses replicate.)
5. **Write to Learn** Answer the first clue of the mystery. Write a paragraph that uses the term *vector*.

MYSTERY CLUE

Many of the sick children remembered getting strange insect bites that summer. The bites developed into rashes. What clue did this give Steere? (Hint: See above.)

35.2 Defenses Against Infection

MD CLG **3.2.1** Processes and Functions, **3.2.2** Changes in Metabolic Activity. SPI **1.4.2** Analyze Data, **1.5.7** Classification Systems, **1.7.1** Apply Skills and Concepts.

Nonspecific Defenses

There are pathogens all around us. Yet we are not usually sick. How do we stay healthy? How do we get better when we are sick? Our bodies have several amazing lines of defense.

First Line of Defense The skin blocks pathogens from entering the body. Cilia in the respiratory tract push pathogens away before they enter the body. Tears, saliva, and mucus have chemicals that break down bacterial cell walls.

Second Line of Defense If a pathogen gets past the skin, the body's second line of defense swings into action.

▶ *The Inflammatory Response* When a pathogen enters the body, the **inflammatory response** causes the infected area to become red and painful. Cells called mast cells release histamines. Histamines are chemicals that increase the flow of blood and other fluids to the area around the wound. This fluid can cause swelling. White blood cells, or phagocytes, move from the blood vessels into the tissue. Some of the white blood cells surround and destroy bacteria.

Key Questions

🔑 What are the body's nonspecific defenses against pathogens?

🔑 What are the functions of the immune system's specific defenses?

🔑 What are the body's specific defenses against pathogens?

BUILD Understanding

Concept Map Use the headings in this lesson to make a concept map. Add details to your map as you read.

In Your Workbook Go to your workbook for a partially completed concept map for Lesson 35.2.

Inflammatory Response The inflammatory response is a nonspecific defense against pathogens. When pathogens enter the body, white blood cells move into the area and destroy the pathogens.

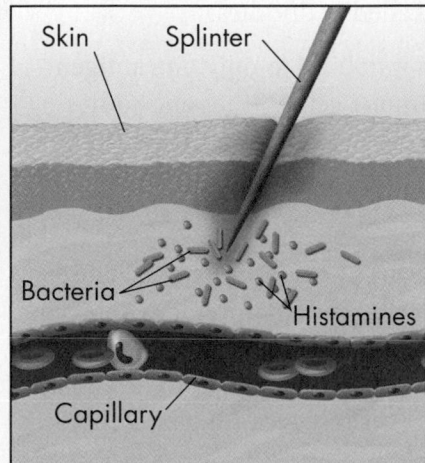

❶ In response to the wound and invading pathogens, histamines increase blood flow to the area.

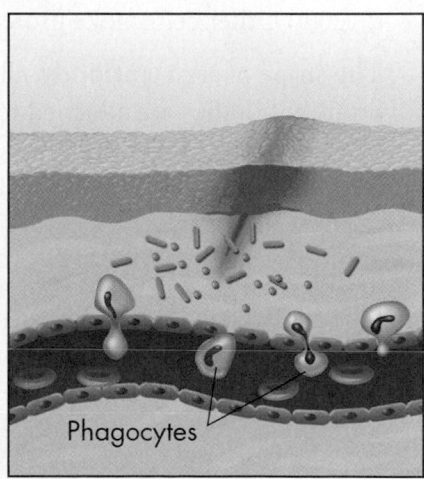

❷ Local blood vessels open. Fluid leaves the capillaries and causes swelling. White blood cells move into the tissue.

❸ White blood cells called phagocytes destroy the bacteria and damaged cells.

Immune System and Disease **841**

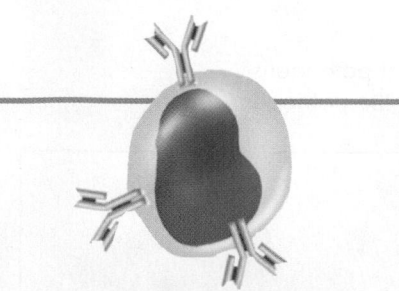

B Lymphocytes The antibodies on the surface of a B lymphocyte recognize one specific antigen.

T Lymphocytes T lymphocytes recognize infected body cells. Each T lymphocyte recognizes only one antigen.

▶ *Interferons* When a virus enters the body, the body makes interferons. These proteins make it harder for viruses to make their own proteins. In this way, interferons slow down the infection.

▶ *Fever* Body temperature may rise during an infection. Fever may slow down or stop the growth of some pathogens. It also speeds up several parts of the immune response.

🗝 **Key Question** What are the body's nonspecific defenses against pathogens? **Nonspecific defenses include skin, hair, tears, the inflammatory response, interferons, and fever.**

Specific Defenses: The Immune System

The body's specific defenses attack particular pathogens with powerful weapons.

Recognizing "Self" A healthy immune system recognizes cells and proteins that belong in the body as "self." Your body's cells and proteins carry chemical markers that act like a secret password. That password tells the immune system "Don't attack me! I belong here!"

Recognizing "Nonself" The immune system's main job is to recognize anything that does not belong in the body. When the system notices something that is "nonself," it attacks. This reaction to specific pathogens is the **immune response.** If the same pathogen enters the body again, the body "recognizes" and attacks it even more quickly.

Antigens The immune response is triggered by certain molecules on the outer surfaces of bacteria, viruses, and parasites. These molecules are called **antigens.** The immune system responds to antigens in two ways. Certain body cells may attack the pathogen directly. Other cells make proteins called antibodies.

The shape of each **antibody** allows it to bind to only one antigen. Some antibodies are attached to immune cells. Other antibodies float around in plasma. Antibodies that bind to antigens act like signal flags. Those signal flags tell the immune system to destroy pathogens.

Lymphocytes The main cells in the immune response are white blood cells called B lymphocytes (B cells) and T lymphocytes (T cells). B cells are made in red bone marrow. T cells are also made in red bone marrow, but mature in the thymus. Each B cell and T cell is able to respond to *one* specific antigen. B cells discover antigens in body fluids. T cells discover infected cells.

🗝 **Key Question** What are the functions of the immune system's specific defenses? **The specific defenses distinguish between "self" and "nonself" and respond to specific pathogens.**

The Immune System in Action

There are two major parts of the specific immune response. They are humoral immunity and cell-mediated immunity.

Humoral Immunity Sometimes antibodies on B cells bind directly to the antigens on the surface of a pathogen. This part of the immune response is called humoral immunity. An antibody is shaped like the letter Y. It has two antigen-binding sites. Both sites recognize the same specific antigen. When the antigen and antibody on the B cell bind, T cells stimulate the B cell to grow and divide quickly. Two kinds of B cells are formed: plasma cells and memory B cells.

▶ *Plasma Cells* Plasma cells make antibodies and put them into the bloodstream. Antibodies bind to antigens that are free-floating or attached to pathogens. Then many immune system cells and proteins respond and attack the pathogen.

▶ *Memory B Cells* Once the pathogen has been "beaten," the plasma cells die. But memory B cells remain. If the same pathogen enters the body again, the memory B cells make plasma cells quickly. This secondary response happens very quickly and gives us long-term immunity to certain diseases.

Cell-Mediated Immunity Some pathogens infect the body's cells. This kind of infection is fought by T cells and macrophages. The response is called cell-mediated immunity. T cells also fight the body's own cells if they become cancerous.

Macrophages are B cells that engulf pathogens. When this happens or when a cell has been infected by a pathogen, the cell displays part of the antigen on its surface. This signals the helper T cells to divide and make more helper T cells. These activate B cells and cytotoxic T cells. Helper T cells also make memory T cells. Cytotoxic T cells kill infected body cells. Memory T cells help the immune system respond quickly if the same pathogen enters the body again.

Key Question What are the body's specific defenses against pathogens?
The body's specific defenses are humoral and cell-mediated immunity.

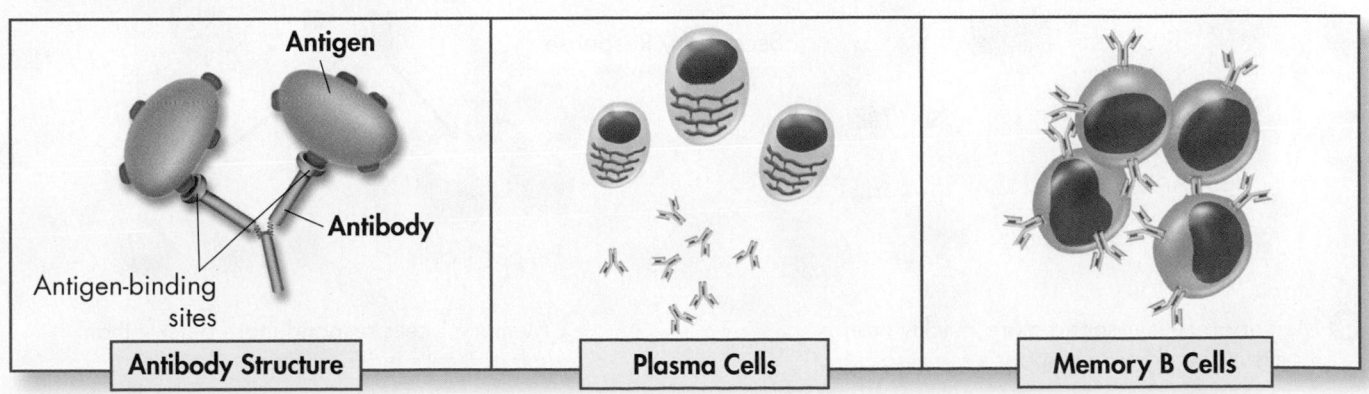

| Antibody Structure | Plasma Cells | Memory B Cells |

SPECIFIC IMMUNE RESPONSE

In humoral immunity, antibodies bind to antigens in body fluids and tag them for destruction by other parts of the immune system. In cell-mediated immunity, body cells that contain antigens are destroyed.

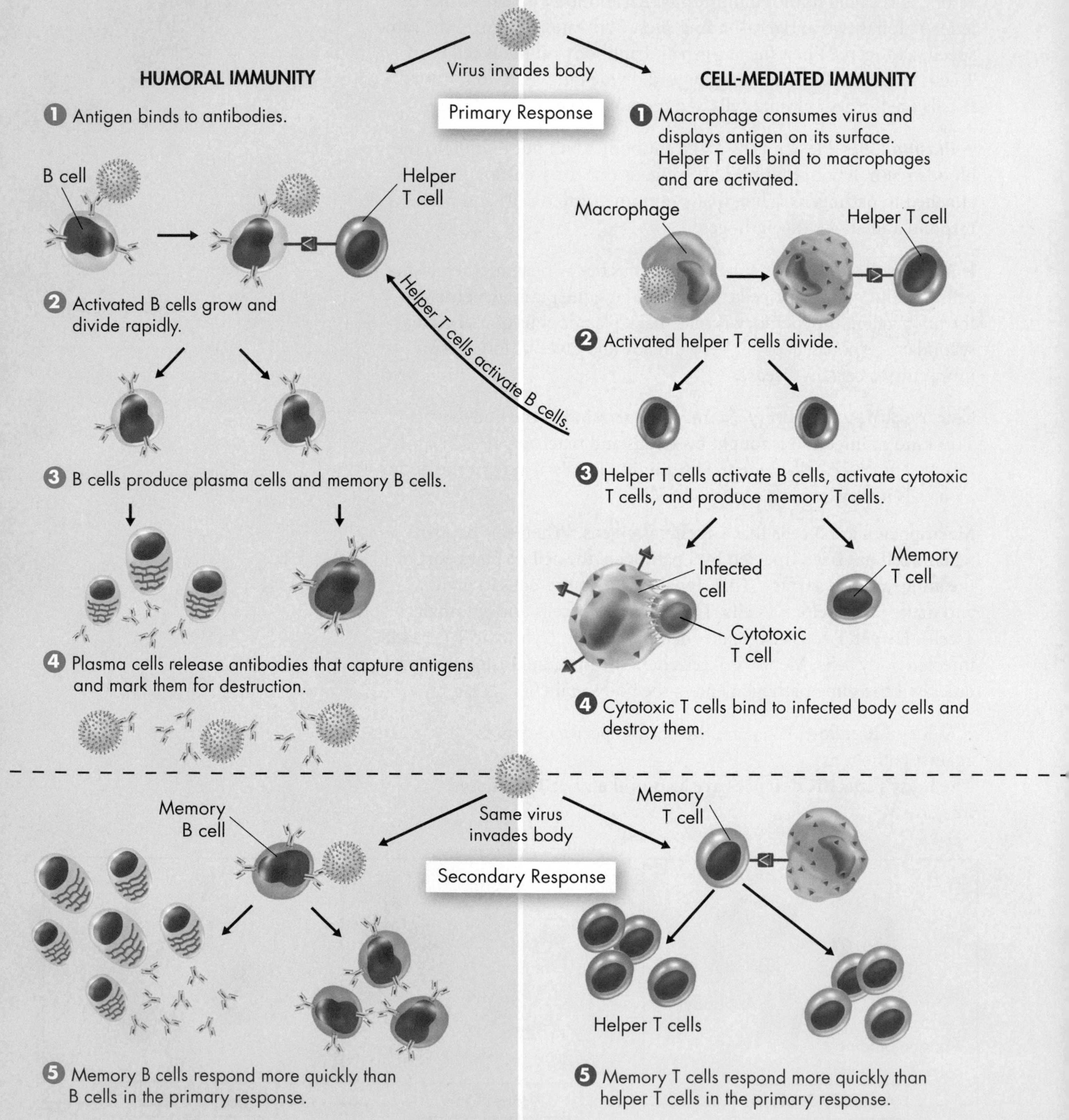

Virus invades body

Primary Response

HUMORAL IMMUNITY

❶ Antigen binds to antibodies.

B cell

Helper T cell

❷ Activated B cells grow and divide rapidly.

❸ B cells produce plasma cells and memory B cells.

❹ Plasma cells release antibodies that capture antigens and mark them for destruction.

Helper T cells activate B cells.

CELL-MEDIATED IMMUNITY

❶ Macrophage consumes virus and displays antigen on its surface. Helper T cells bind to macrophages and are activated.

Macrophage

Helper T cell

❷ Activated helper T cells divide.

❸ Helper T cells activate B cells, activate cytotoxic T cells, and produce memory T cells.

Infected cell

Memory T cell

Cytotoxic T cell

❹ Cytotoxic T cells bind to infected body cells and destroy them.

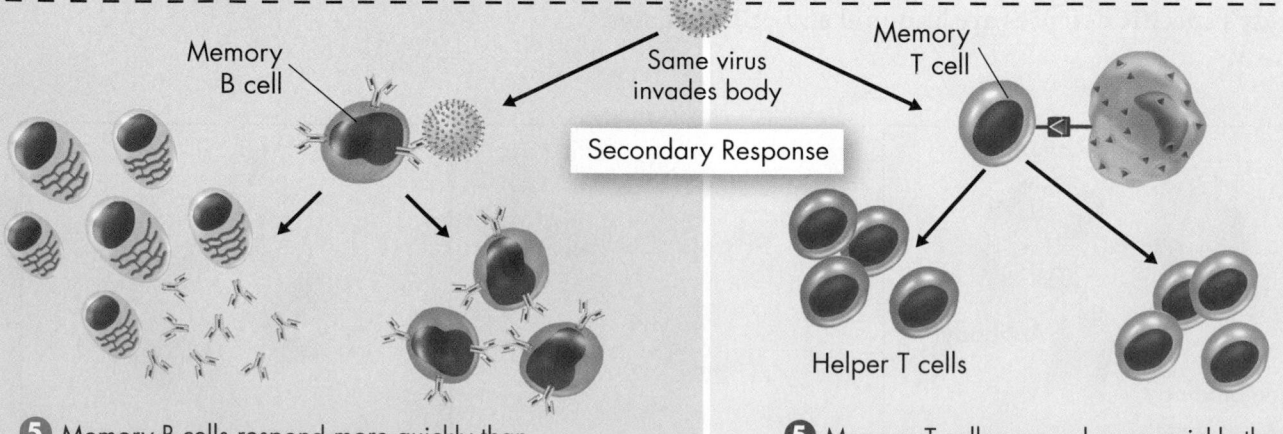

Memory B cell

Same virus invades body

Memory T cell

Secondary Response

Helper T cells

❺ Memory B cells respond more quickly than B cells in the primary response.

❺ Memory T cells respond more quickly than helper T cells in the primary response.

Immune System "Memory"

Your body is able to recognize pathogens and parasites as "nonself." Cells in your immune system recognize and try to destroy pathogens. During the initial infection, your body makes memory B cells. These cells allow your body to respond even more quickly if you are infected by the same pathogen again. Memory B cells make new plasma cells very quickly. Plasma cells then make and release antibodies to respond to the antigens on the surfaces of the pathogen.

The number of antibodies in a person's blood reveals the difference between the first and second immune response. Look at the graph. Assume the person was first exposed to Antigen A on Day 1. On Day 28, the person was exposed to Antigen A again and to Antigen B for the first time. The red line shows the levels of antibodies to Antigen A. The blue line shows the levels of antibodies to Antigen B. Use the graph to answer the questions that follow.

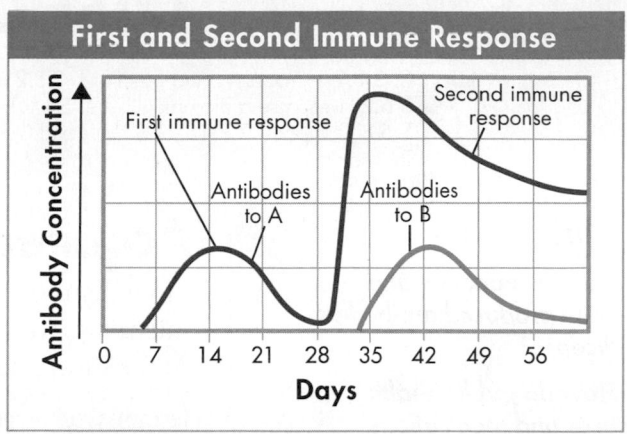

First and Second Immune Response

Analyze and Conclude

1. Interpret Graphs About how long does it take for your body to make antibodies after the first exposure to an antigen? About how long does it take for antibody levels to increase after the second exposure to an antigen?

2. Infer What could explain the significant increase in antibodies to Antigen A seen after Day 30?

In Your Workbook Get more help for this activity in your workbook.

CHECK
Understanding

Apply Vocabulary
Use the highlighted words from the lesson to complete each sentence correctly.

1. Histamines are released during a(n) _____.

2. Pathogens have specific _____ that cause an immune response.

3. The body's specific recognition of, response to, and memory of a pathogen is called the _____.

Critical Thinking

4. Sequence Describe the steps of the inflammatory response.

5. Apply Concepts Although cytotoxic T cells are helpful in the immune system, they also make organ transplantation more difficult. How do you think cytotoxic T cells affect organ transplantation?

6. Write to Learn These two T cells are attached to a cancer cell. What kind of immune response are these cells a part of?

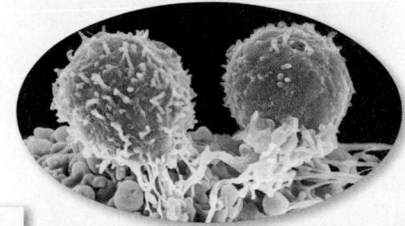

 BIOLOGY.com Search (Lesson 35.2) GO • Lesson Assessment

35.3 Fighting Infectious Disease

MD CLG 3.2.1 Processes and Functions, 3.5.2 Interdependence of Organisms in the Biosphere, 3.6.2 Investigate a Biological Issue. SPI 1.1.1 Problems and Solutions, 1.2.4 Testing a Hypothesis, 1.5.8 Compare, 1.7.1 Apply Skills and Concepts, 1.7.2 Evaluate Ideas, 1.7.6 Science and Technology.

Key Questions

🔑 How do vaccines and externally produced antibodies fight disease?

🔑 How do public health measures and medications fight disease?

🔑 Why have patterns of infectious diseases changed?

BUILD Understanding

Venn Diagram Make a Venn diagram that compares and contrasts active and passive immunity.

In Your Workbook Go to your workbook to learn more about making a Venn diagram. Complete the Venn diagram for Lesson 35.3.

Acquired Immunity

More than 200 years ago, English physician Edward Jenner noticed that milkmaids who got a mild disease called cowpox did not get smallpox. At the time, smallpox killed many people.

Jenner wondered if people could be protected from smallpox by infecting them with cowpox. Jenner tested his hypothesis on a young boy named James Phipps. His experiment is outlined below:

❶ Jenner put fluid from a cowpox sore into a small cut he made on James Phipps's arm.

❷ Phipps got cowpox.

❸ Two months later, Jenner injected Phipps with fluid from a smallpox infection.

❹ Phipps did not get smallpox.

Ever since that time, doctors have used **vaccinations** to produce immunity. Doctors inject patients with a weakened form of a pathogen or a similar but less dangerous pathogen.

Active Immunity Today, we understand how vaccination works. The immune system makes memory B cells and memory T cells in response to antigens carried by the pathogen. This kind of immunity is called **active immunity.** People may develop active immunity after they are vaccinated. People may also develop active immunity after they fight an infection.

Passive Immunity Disease can be prevented in another way. Antibodies made against a pathogen by other individuals or animals can be used to give temporary immunity. If these antibodies are introduced into a person's blood, the result is **passive immunity.** Passive immunity lasts only a short time, because the immune system will destroy the foreign antibodies.

The First Vaccination Edward Jenner used the cowpox virus to vaccinate James Phipps against smallpox.

Passive immunity can also happen naturally. A pregnant woman passes antibodies to her fetus. An infant gets antibodies through breast milk. In some cases, people can be given antibodies like a vaccination. For example, people who have been bitten by a rabid animal are injected with antibodies for the rabies virus.

Key Question How do vaccines and externally produced antibodies fight disease?
The immune system makes memory B cells and memory T cells in response to the antigen in the vaccination. Externally produced antibodies can be used to give temporary immunity.

Public Health and Medications

In 1900, more than 30 percent of deaths in the United States were caused by infectious disease. In 2005, less than 5 percent of deaths were caused by infectious disease. Public health measures and the development of medications helped to make this happen.

Public Health Measures When people live in large groups, behavior, cleanliness of food and water supplies, and sanitation all influence the spread of disease. The field of public health offers services and advice that help keep living conditions healthy. Public health measures help keep the food and water supplies clean. Encouraging vaccinations and recommending ways to avoid getting sick are also public health measures. Rules that make parents get vaccinations for their children, and education about hand washing, have greatly reduced the spread of many diseases.

Medications It is not possible to prevent every infectious disease. Medications are other weapons that can fight pathogens. Antibiotics can kill bacteria. Some antiviral medications can slow down viral activity.

The term *antibiotic* means something that kills bacteria without harming the host. In 1928, Alexander Fleming was the first scientist to discover an antibiotic. Fleming noticed that the mold *Penicillium notatum* seemed to make something that slowed bacterial growth. Research showed that this "something" was a compound Fleming named penicillin. Researchers learned to make large amounts of penicillin just in time to save the lives of thousands of World War II soldiers. Since then, dozens of antibiotics have saved millions of people.

Antibiotics have no effect on viruses. However, antiviral drugs have been made that fight certain viral infections. These drugs generally make it more difficult for viruses to get into the body's cells or to multiply once inside cells.

Key Question How do public health measures and medications fight disease?
Public health measures help keep living conditions healthy. Medications can be used to fight pathogens after someone is sick.

Broad Street Pump In 1854, Dr. John Snow interviewed residents and mapped cases to determine the source of a London cholera epidemic. He discovered that a water pump like this replica was the source. This is a major event in the history of public health.

New and Re-Emerging Diseases

By 1980, many people thought that medicine had won the fight against infectious disease. Vaccination and other public health measures had wiped out polio in the United States. Smallpox had been wiped out around the world. Antibiotics seemed to have bacterial diseases under control. Researchers thought that epidemics would soon be history. They were wrong.

Recently, several new diseases have started making people sick. These include AIDS, SARS, hantavirus, monkeypox, West Nile virus, Ebola, and avian influenza ("bird flu"). Other diseases that people thought were gone are coming back, or re-emerging, and spreading to new places. What's going on?

Changing Interactions With Animals As people clear new land and as environments change, people come in contact with different animals and pathogens. Exotic animal trade, for pets and food, has also given pathogens new chances to jump from animals to humans. Both monkeypox and SARS are thought to have started this way.

Misuse of Medications Misuse of medications has led to the re-emergence of diseases that many people thought were under control. For example, many strains of the pathogens that cause tuberculosis and malaria are becoming resistant to many antibiotics and other medications. In addition, diseases such as measles are coming back because some people are not getting vaccinations.

🔑 **Key Question** Why have patterns of infectious diseases changed?
Through development and the exotic animal trade, people are coming into contact with new animals and pathogens. The misuse of medications has led to the re-emergence of certain diseases.

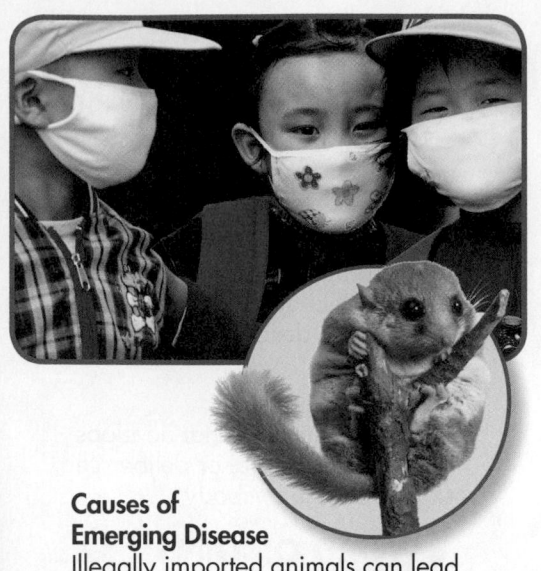

Causes of Emerging Disease
Illegally imported animals can lead to the spread of emerging disease. In 2003, dormice and other rodents from Africa spread monkeypox to prairie dogs in the United States. Humans were soon infected. The spread of SARS also has been associated with the wild animal trade.

CHECK Understanding

Apply Vocabulary
Use the highlighted words from the lesson to complete each sentence correctly.

1. The injection of a weakened form, or of a similar but less dangerous form, of a pathogen to give the patient immunity is called a(n) _____.

2. Vaccination provides _____ by exposing a person to an antigen.

Critical Thinking

3. **Compare and Contrast** Describe the difference between active and passive immunity.

4. **Infer** In the past few decades, it has become much easier to travel around the world. How do you think this has affected the spread of emerging diseases? Explain.

5. **Write to Learn** Answer the second clue of the mystery. Think about what the term *antibiotic* means.

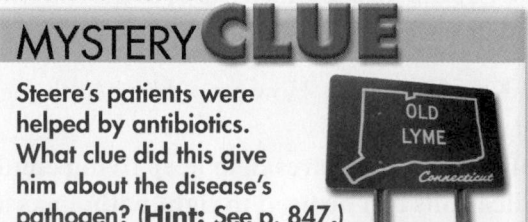

MYSTERY CLUE

Steere's patients were helped by antibiotics. What clue did this give him about the disease's pathogen? (**Hint:** See p. 847.)

OLD LYME
Connecticut

35.4 Immune System Disorders

MD CLG **3.2.1** Processes and Functions, **3.5.1** Factors Influencing Ecosystems, **3.6.2** Investigate a Biological Issue. SPI **1.4.2** Analyze Data, **1.7.1** Apply Skills and Concepts, **1.7.2** Evaluate Ideas, **1.7.6** Science and Technology.

When the Immune System Overreacts

Sometimes, the immune system fights the body's own cells. Other times, the immune system itself is weakened by sickness. Then what happens? A strong immune response to harmless antigens can cause allergies, asthma, and autoimmune disease.

Allergies Antigens on things like pollen, dust mites, and mold can cause allergic reactions. The overreaction of the immune system to these harmless antigens is called an **allergy.** Allergies cause mast cells to release histamines.

Asthma Allergic reactions in the respiratory system can cause asthma. **Asthma** is a disease that causes air passages to narrow. This causes wheezing and coughing. It also makes it difficult for the person to breathe. Asthma attacks can be triggered by infections, exercise, stress, and some medications. Cold or dry air, smoke, pollen, and dust can also cause an attack.

Asthma can be life-threatening. Patients need to take their medication properly. If they do not, an attack can cause long-term harm to the lungs. There is no cure, but some medications can relax the muscles around the airways and relieve symptoms.

Autoimmune Diseases Sometimes the immune system does not properly recognize "self." When this happens, it may attack cells or compounds in the body as if they were pathogens. This kind of illness is called an autoimmune disease. Type I diabetes and lupus are autoimmune diseases. Some autoimmune diseases can be treated with medications that lessen the symptoms. Others are treated by lowering the immune response. These also lower the normal immune response. The patient must be watched carefully.

🔑 Key Question How can misguided immune responses cause problems?
A strong immune response to harmless antigens can cause allergies, asthma, and autoimmune disease.

Pet Dander Pet dander is dead skin shed from cats and dogs. It often causes allergies.

Key Questions

🔑 *How can misguided immune responses cause problems?*

🔑 *What causes AIDS and how is it spread?*

BUILD Understanding

Anticipation/Reaction Guide
Before you read this lesson, try to answer the two key questions in your own words. As you read, modify your answers.

In Your Workbook Go to your workbook to complete the Anticipation/Reaction guide for Lesson 35.4.

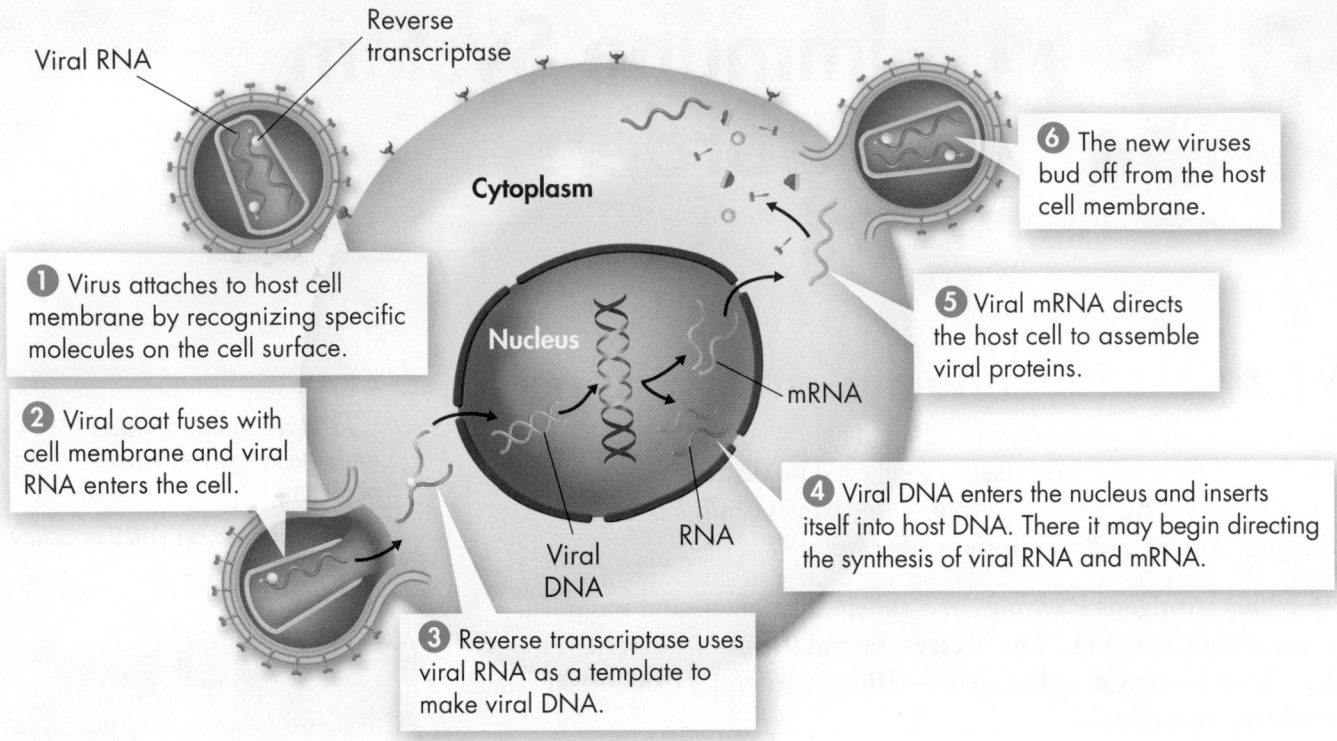

Reverse transcriptase

Viral RNA

Cytoplasm

❶ Virus attaches to host cell membrane by recognizing specific molecules on the cell surface.

❷ Viral coat fuses with cell membrane and viral RNA enters the cell.

Nucleus

Viral DNA

❸ Reverse transcriptase uses viral RNA as a template to make viral DNA.

RNA

mRNA

❻ The new viruses bud off from the host cell membrane.

❺ Viral mRNA directs the host cell to assemble viral proteins.

❹ Viral DNA enters the nucleus and inserts itself into host DNA. There it may begin directing the synthesis of viral RNA and mRNA.

BUILD Connections

HIV INFECTION

HIV travels through the blood, where it binds to receptors on helper T cells. Inside the cell, the viral DNA directs the cell to make many new viruses. These new viruses are quickly released back into the blood, where they infect more cells.

In Your Workbook Do you know all of the steps of HIV infection? Go to your workbook to find out.

BUILD Vocabulary

allergy an overreaction of the immune system to an antigen

asthma a chronic respiratory disease in which air passages narrow, causing wheezing, coughing, and difficulty breathing

🗡 WORD ORIGINS

Allergy comes from the Greek words that mean "different or strange activity." An allergy is a strange or unusual reaction to something that should be harmless to the immune system.

HIV and AIDS

During the late 1970s, doctors began to report that some people were getting very sick from microorganisms that did not usually make people sick. Doctors concluded that these people must have weakened immune systems. Diseases that attack a person with a weakened immune system are called opportunistic diseases. Researchers concluded that these people all had the same disorder. They called it acquired immunodeficiency syndrome (AIDS). Eventually, it was discovered that this "syndrome" was caused by a pathogen new to science.

HIV Researchers discovered the pathogen that causes AIDS in 1983. They called it the human immunodeficiency virus (HIV). HIV is deadly for two reasons. It can hide from the immune system, and it can attack key cells in the immune system. This leaves the body with little protection from other pathogens.

Target: T Cells One of HIV's main targets is helper T cells. Helper T cells are important to the specific immune response. HIV destroys T cells. Eventually, the immune system is unable to fight HIV and other pathogens. When the patient's T cell count drops to about one sixth the normal level, he or she is said to have AIDS.

HIV Transmission HIV is deadly. But it does not pass from one person to the next easily. It cannot be passed through coughing, sharing clothes, or any casual contact. HIV can be spread only through contact with infected blood, semen, vaginal secretions, or breast milk.

Preventing HIV Infection You can choose behaviors that reduce your risk of becoming infected with HIV. The only way to be safe from HIV infection is to avoid sexual activity and intravenous drug use. Before 1985, HIV was transmitted to some patients through transfusions of infected blood or blood products. Now that doctors know the cause of HIV, such cases have been virtually eliminated. The blood supply is screened for HIV antibodies. Also, people who engage in certain activities are discouraged from donating blood.

Can AIDS Be Cured? Right now, there is no cure for AIDS. New drugs make it possible to survive HIV infection for years. However, HIV mutates and evolves rapidly. There are many strains that are resistant to most drugs.

The only way to control the virus is to use several expensive drugs. These drugs interfere with some of the virus' enzymes. These drugs are allowing more people in the United States to live with HIV rather than to die from it. However, these drugs are not available in many parts of Africa and Asia. Because HIV can now be treated (but not cured), some people have the dangerous misconception that HIV infection is not serious.

Key Question What causes AIDS and how is it spread? **AIDS is caused by HIV, a virus that attacks the immune system. It is spread though contact with infected blood, semen, vaginal secretions, or breast milk.**

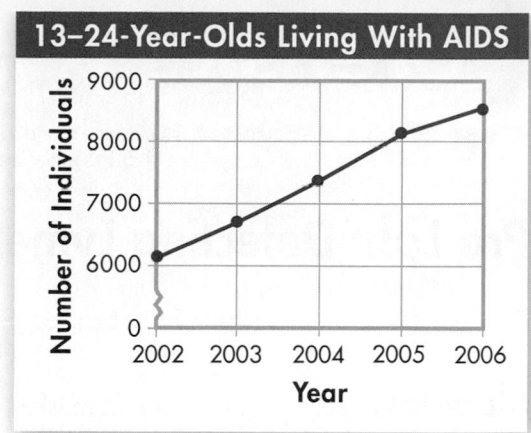

13–24-Year-Olds Living With AIDS

13–24-Year-Olds Living With AIDS The number of adolescents and young adults infected with HIV in the United States has been rising steadily since 2002.

CHECK Understanding

Apply Vocabulary

Use the highlighted words from the lesson to complete each sentence correctly.

1. An unusually strong immune response to an antigen is called a(n) _____.

2. A chronic respiratory illness that involves wheezing and narrowed air passages is called _____.

Critical Thinking

3. **Apply Concepts** When a person first visits a doctor about asthma symptoms, the doctor is likely to ask the patient to list times and places his or her asthma attacks tend to happen. Why do you think doctors do this?

4. **Infer** Why is it hard for a person with HIV to fight off other infections?

5. **Draw Conclusions** Look again at the graph at the top of this page. What are two conclusions that you can draw regarding the increasing number of adolescents living with AIDS?

6. **Write to Learn** Answer the third clue in the mystery. Consider what the pathogen might do to the immune system.

MYSTERY CLUE

As with HIV, blood tests of patients with the mystery disease showed that patients were making antibodies to a pathogen. What could be a reason the immune system cannot overcome the disease? (**Hint:** See p. 850.)

 BIOLOGY.com Search (Lesson 35.4) **GO** • Lesson Assessment

GUIDED INQUIRY

SPI 1.3.1 Use Equipment, 1.3.3 Safe Handling of Materials, 1.4.8 Use Models,
1.5.7 Classification Systems, 1.5.9 Synthesize Ideas.

Pre-Lab: Detecting Lyme Disease

Problem How can a blood test be used to detect Lyme disease?

Materials well plate, permanent marker, white paper, 400-mL beaker, 100-mL beaker, distilled water, micropipettes, test solutions

Lab Manual Chapter 35 Lab

Skills Focus Control Variables, Analyze Data, Draw Conclusions

Connect to the **Big idea** To maintain homeostasis, your immune system must defend against invasions by harmful pathogens. Some invaders enter the body through bites from insects. For example, a tiny deer tick can infect you with the bacterium that causes Lyme disease. As a precaution, you should avoid areas where deer ticks are active. If you visit a location where ticks are active, wear clothing that covers the skin and check for ticks.

Symptoms for Lyme disease can vary widely, but many people develop a bull's-eye rash at the location of the bite. People who suspect that they have been exposed to the bacteria that cause Lyme disease should consult a medical professional. Blood tests are used to diagnose Lyme disease. In this lab, you will model one of these tests.

Pre-Lab Questions

Preview the procedure in the lab manual.

1. **Sequence** Use a flowchart to show the order in which the solutions will be added to the well plate.

2. **Infer** What is the advantage of having a control for a positive test and a control for a negative test?

3. **Control Variables** Why must you rinse the micropipette with distilled water before adding a different solution to the well plate?

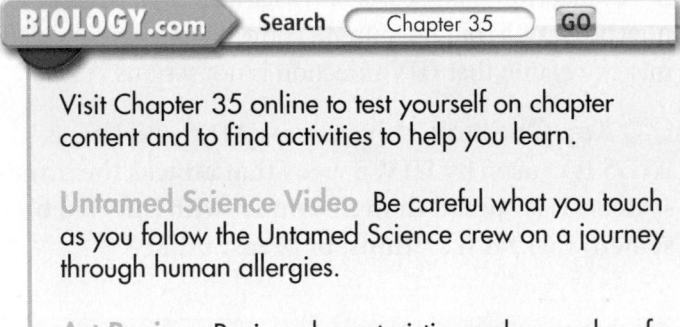

BIOLOGY.com Search Chapter 35 GO

Visit Chapter 35 online to test yourself on chapter content and to find activities to help you learn.

Untamed Science Video Be careful what you touch as you follow the Untamed Science crew on a journey through human allergies.

Art Review Review characteristics and examples of the different types of pathogens and parasites with this drag-and-drop activity.

Art in Motion View an animation of HIV infecting a cell.

Background Questions

a. **Review** What is an antigen?

b. **Review** How does the immune system respond to antigens?

c. **Explain** Why does the presence of antibodies in blood suggest that a person was exposed to an antigen?

35 CHAPTER Summary

35.1 Infectious Disease

- Infectious diseases are caused by microorganisms. Diseases can be caused by viruses, bacteria, fungi, "protists," and parasites.

- Infectious diseases can be spread through coughing, sneezing, or physical contact. Others spread through body fluids, contaminated food or water. Some diseases can be spread to humans from other animals.

infectious disease (p. 838)
germ theory of disease (p. 838)
vector (p. 840)

35.2 Defenses Against Infection

- Nonspecific defenses against pathogens include skin, hair, tears, and the inflammatory response. Interferons and fever play an important role in the inflammatory response.

- The immune system's specific defenses distinguish between "self" and "nonself" and respond to specific pathogens.

- The body's specific defenses against pathogens are humoral and cell-mediated immunity.

inflammatory response (p. 841)
immune response (p. 842)
antigen (p. 842)
antibody (p. 842)

35.3 Fighting Infectious Disease

- The immune system makes memory B cells and memory T cells in response to the antigen in the vaccination. Vaccination provides active immunity.

- Antibodies produced against a pathogen by other individuals or animals can be used to give temporary passive immunity.

- Public health measures help keep living conditions healthy. Medications can be used to fight pathogens after someone is sick. Antibiotics kill bacteria. Some antiviral medications can slow down viral activity.

- Through human development and the exotic animal trade, people are coming into contact with new animals and pathogens. The misuse of medications has led to the re-emergence of certain diseases.

vaccination (p. 846)   passive immunity (p. 846)
active immunity (p. 846)

35.4 Immune System Disorders

- A strong immune response to harmless antigens can cause allergies, asthma, and autoimmune disease.

- AIDS is caused by HIV, a virus that attacks the immune system. It is spread though contact with infected blood, semen, vaginal secretions, or breast milk.

allergy (p. 849)   asthma (p. 849)

OLD LYME
Connecticut

Assess the Big idea ▶ Homeostasis

Write an answer to the question below.

Q: How does the body fight against invading organisms that may disrupt homeostasis?

Constructed Response

Write an answer to each of the questions below. The answer to each question should be one or two paragraphs long. To help you begin, read the **Hints** below each of the questions.

1. **Animals infected with the virus that causes rabies often salivate a lot and are more likely than healthy animals to bite other animals. Explain how these symptoms may be beneficial to the virus.**

   Hint Some pathogens are transferred by the exchange of bodily fluids.

   Hint Many viruses cannot live outside a host's body.

2. **Describe several ways that infectious diseases may be spread.**

   Hint Infectious diseases are caused by microorganisms, including bacteria, viruses, and fungi. These microorganisms are called pathogens.

   Hint Pathogens are often spread by symptoms of the disease they cause.

3. **Describe the steps in HIV infection.**

   Hint HIV targets helper T cells.

   Hint HIV uses an enzyme called reverse transcriptase to change the functioning of the cell.

Foundations for Learning Wrap-Up

Use the undercover vocabulary study guide you prepared before reading the chapter as a tool to help you organize your thoughts about homeostasis and the immune system.

Activity 1 Working with a partner, review the definitions you wrote on your undercover vocabulary study guide. If necessary, fill in any missing information and correct any errors. Then, quiz each other about each of the definitions.

Activity 2 Cut apart the vocabulary words and definitions to form two piles of "cards." Then shuffle the cards together. Working with a partner, try to match vocabulary words with their definitions.

Extension: Working with a partner, use the "cards" to make a flowchart describing how the body responds to infection. Challenge yourselves to use as many of the cards as possible.

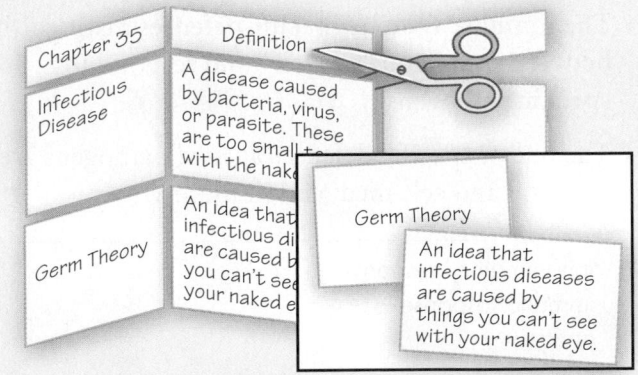

35.1 Infectious Disease

Understand Key Concepts

1. Anything, including bacteria, viruses, and fungi, that can cause disease is called a(n)
   a. antibody.
   c. pathogen.
   b. antigen.
   d. vector.

2. Which of the following describes a zoonosis?
   a. any disease that can be transmitted through the exchange of bodily fluids
   b. any disease that is caused by microorganisms
   c. any disease that can be transmitted from animals to humans
   d. any disease that disrupts the body's normal functions

> **Test-Taking Tip**
>
> **Rephrase the Question** You might understand a question better if you rephrase it in your own words. Question 2 asks you to describe *zoonosis*. Rephrase the question to: "Define *zoonosis*." Zoonosis is a disease that can be spread from animals to humans. Answer **c** is the correct choice.

3. What are some things that can prevent the spread of disease?

Think Critically

4. **Compare and Contrast** Compare and contrast harmless microorganisms that live in or on the human body to pathogens.

35.2 Defenses Against Infection

Understand Key Concepts

5. Which of the following structures is NOT involved in the body's first line of defense against infectious disease?
   a. skin
   c. T cells
   b. hair
   d. tears

6. A nonspecific defense reaction to tissue damage caused by injury or infection is known as
   a. the inflammatory response.
   b. the immune response.
   c. active immunity.
   d. passive immunity.

7. Distinguish between humoral immunity and cell-mediated immunity.

Think Critically

8. **Compare and Contrast** How does the secondary response to an antigen differ from the primary response to an antigen?

35.3 Fighting Infectious Disease

Understand Key Concepts

9. Antibodies made by animals are sometimes injected into a human to provide temporary immunity. This kind of immunity is called
   a. active immunity.
   c. vaccination.
   b. passive immunity.
   d. zoonosis.

10. Who discovered the first antibiotic and how did he discover it?

11. List two public health measures that have reduced the spread of infectious disease.

Think Critically

12. **Apply Concepts** How are human activities such as land-clearing related to the spread of new and re-emerging diseases?

35.4 Immune System Disorders

Understand Key Concepts

13. The main target cells of HIV are
    a. mast cells.
    c. B cells.
    b. T cells.
    d. red blood cells.

14. A strong response by a person's immune system to a harmless antigen is called

a. cell-mediated immunity.

b. an allergy.

c. an antibiotic.

d. an autoimmune disease.

15. Describe how HIV makes an infected person unable to fight off other infections.

Think Critically

16. Apply Concepts Why is a second bee sting more dangerous than the first for a person who is allergic to bee stings?

Connecting Concepts

Use Science Graphics

John Snow made a map similar to the one below to help him determine the source of the cholera outbreak in London in 1854. The dots represent the locations of people who died of cholera. The Xs represent pumps. Use the map to answer questions 17 and 18.

17. Infer Which pump do you think Snow determined was most likely the source of the cholera outbreak? Explain.

18. Apply Concepts Do you think a map such as this one could be used to discover the source of a food poisoning outbreak? Explain.

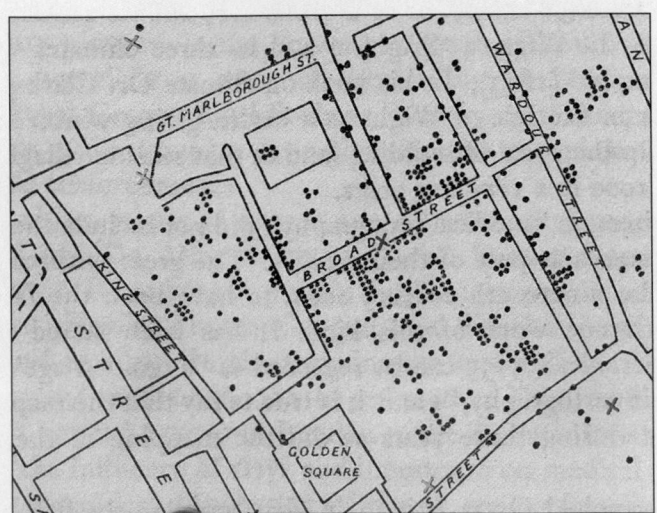

THE SEARCH FOR A CAUSE

Many of the patients suffering from this new disease lived in Lyme, Connecticut. The new disease was named Lyme disease, after the town. A researcher found a bacterium called *Borrelia burgdorferi* in deer ticks. These ticks had been captured in wooded areas near the patients' homes. Steere also found this bacterium in the patients. Could this bacterium be the cause of Lyme disease?

Steere infected healthy mice with the bacterium in his laboratory. The infected mice showed signs of the disease. Steere took bacteria from the sick mice and injected them into healthy mice. This second set of mice also became sick.

Now researchers know that a bite from a deer tick carrying *B. burgdorferi* can spread Lyme disease. The bacteria "swim" through tissues around the tick bites, causing the spreading rash. The bacteria can infect many types of cells. Some of the proteins made by the bacteria look like proteins around human nerve cells. This may cause an autoimmune response that leads to arthritis and other problems.

1. Explain What set of rules did Steere use to determine if *B. bergdorferi* was the pathogen responsible for Lyme disease?

2. Infer Deer and deer ticks thrive in wooded areas that grow back after the areas have been cleared and at the edges of woodlands. How might suburban development contribute to an increase in Lyme disease?

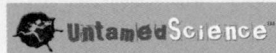 **Never Stop Exploring Your World.** Finding the solution to this medical mystery is only the beginning. Take a video field trip with the ecogeeks of Untamed Science to see where this mystery leads.

Multiple Choice

1. All of the following prevent pathogens from entering the human body EXCEPT
   A red blood cells.   C mucus.
   B tears.   D skin.   CLG 3.2.1

2. Which of the following is NOT part of the inflammatory response?
   A White blood cells rush to infected tissues.
   B Blood vessels near the wound shrink.
   C Phagocytes engulf and destroy pathogens.
   D The wound becomes red.   CLG 3.2.1

3. What is the role of a vector in the spread of disease?
   A A vector is an inanimate object, such as a doorknob, where pathogens may collect.
   B A vector must infect a host for its life cycle to continue.
   C Vectors usually do not suffer from the infection, they just spread it from host to host.
   D A vector is a pathogen.   CLG 3.5.1

4. Which type of lymphocyte produces antibodies that are released into the bloodstream?
   A cytotoxic T cells   C phagocytes
   B helper T cells   D plasma cells CLG 3.2.1

5. Which of the following is NOT a white blood cell?
   A interferon   C cytotoxic T cell
   B macrophage   D lymphocyte CLG 3.2.1

6. Which is an example of naturally occurring passive immunity?
   A vaccination
   B exposure to a disease
   C an infant consuming antibodies in breast milk
   D antibodies injected from another person
   CLG 3.2.1

7. How do medications help a person with asthma?
   A They counteract the effects of histamines.
   B They suppress the immune system.
   C They increase mucus production in the lungs.
   D They relax smooth muscles around airways.
   CLG 3.2.1

Questions 8–9

A researcher measured the concentrations of HIV and T cells in 120 HIV-infected patients over a period of 10 years. Her data are summarized in the graph.

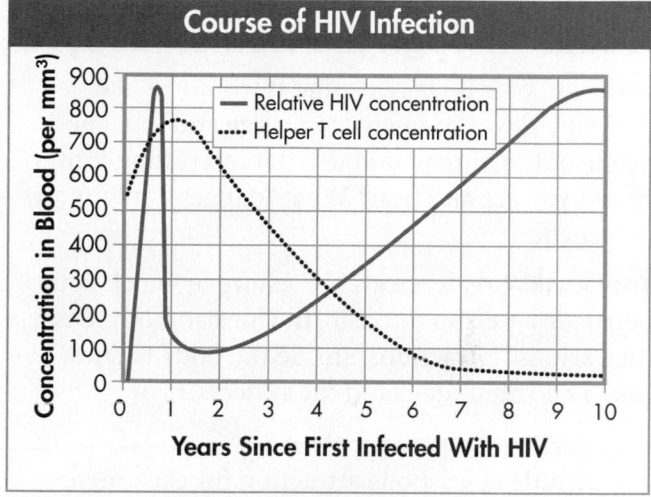

8. What happened to the HIV concentration over years 2 through 9?
   A It stayed about the same, then suddenly increased.
   B It stayed about the same, then suddenly decreased.
   C It steadily increased.
   D It steadily decreased.   SPI 1.4.2

9. What is probably responsible for the change in HIV concentration during the first year?
   A immune response
   B inflammatory response
   C passive immunity
   D HIV stopped replicating   SPI 1.4.2

Open-Ended Response

10. Explain why some symptoms of disease such as coughing and sneezing are advantageous to the pathogen that causes the disease.   CLG 3.2.1

If You Have Trouble With . . .

Question	1	2	3	4	5	6	7	8	9	10
See Lesson	35.2	35.2	35.1	35.2	35.2	35.3	35.4	35.4	35.4	35.1

Unit Project

A Tour Through the Human Body

Have you ever imagined what it would be like to shrink down to microscopic size and tour the inside of the human body? What interesting things would you see and hear? What "dangers" might you encounter?

Your Task Create a travel brochure in which you persuade a person to "visit" the human body. Discuss the various "attractions" inside the body to show how well you understand the systems.

Be sure to
- include at least one attraction for each organ system covered in this unit.
- design the brochure so that it is clear and easy to follow.
- be creative!

Reflection Questions

1. Score your brochure using the rubric below. What score did you give yourself?
2. What did you do well in this project?
3. What needs improvement?
4. What "attractions" would you choose to visit? Why?
5. Exchange travel brochures with a partner. What attractions did he/she include?

Assessment Rubric

Score	Scientific Content	Quality of Brochure
4	Brochure reveals an exceptionally thorough understanding of the human organ systems.	Brochure is clear, informative, and creative.
3	Brochure reveals a solid understanding of the human organ systems.	Brochure effectively conveys information about various attractions.
2	Brochure reveals a limited understanding of the human organ systems.	Brochure could be more clear and creative. It needs some editing.
1	Brochure reveals significant misunderstandings about the human organ systems.	Brochure is unclear and needs significant editing.

A Visual Guide to
The Diversity of Life

▲ The Chambered Nautilus, found today in the Pacific Ocean, is one of the few living representatives of a group that once flourished in ancient seas 265 million years before the dinosaurs evolved. This Visual Guide will give you a glimpse of life's great variety and evolutionary history.

A Visual Guide to
The Diversity of Life

CONTENTS

HOW TO USE THIS GUIDE

Use this visual reference tool to explore the classification and characteristics of organisms, including their habitats, ecology, behavior, and other important facts. This guide reflects the latest understandings about phylogenetic relationships within the three domains of life. Divided into six color-coded sections, the Visual Guide begins with a brief survey through the Bacteria and Archaea domains. It next discusses the major groups of protists, fungi, and plants. The final section provides information on nine animal phyla.

1 See how the group of organisms relates to others on the tree of life.

2 Learn about the general characteristics that all members of the group share.

3 Discover the members of the group and learn about their traits.

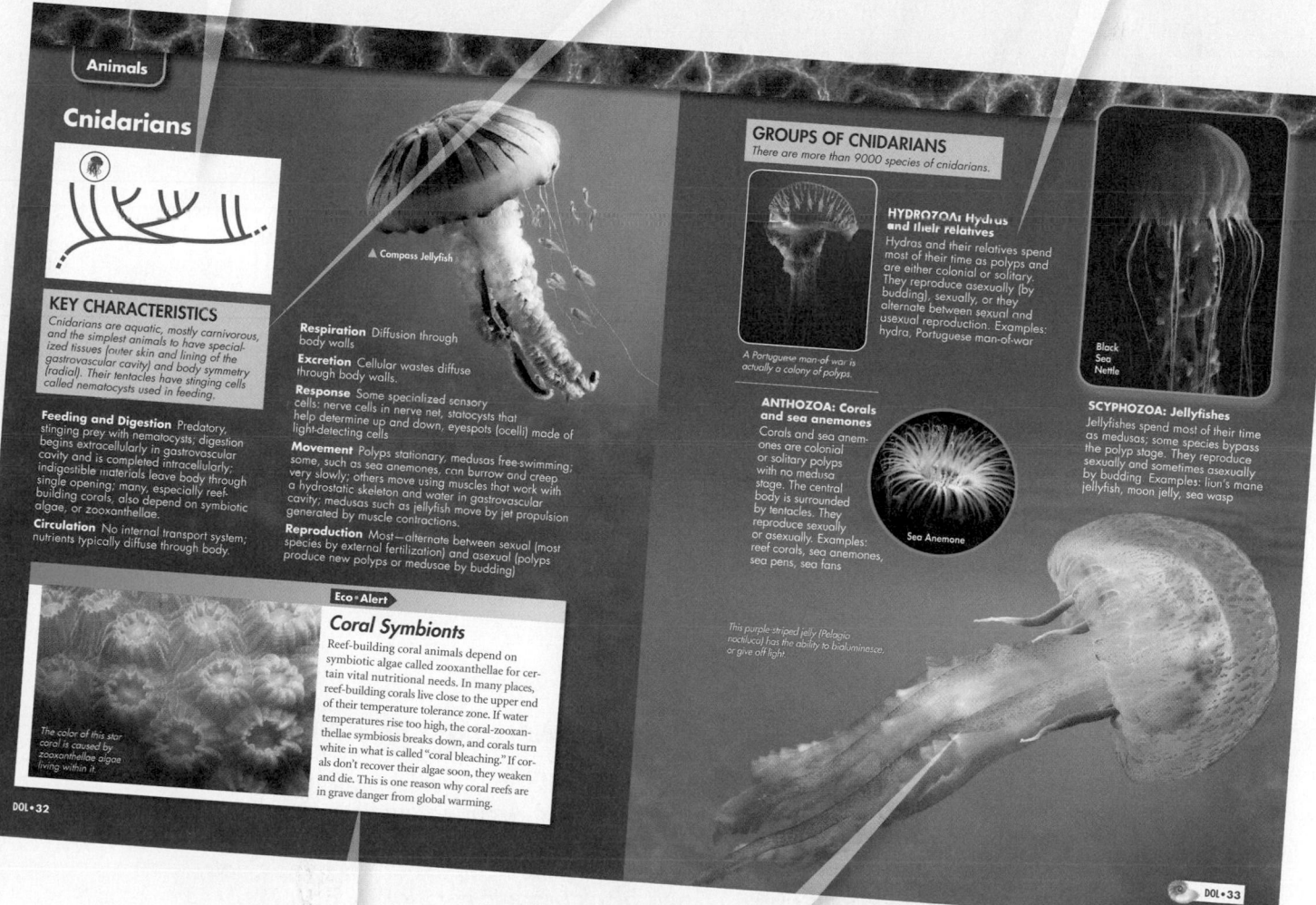

4 Investigate current news and interesting facts about the group.

5 See photographs of representative animals within each group.

Animals

Cnidarians

KEY CHARACTERISTICS

Cnidarians are aquatic, mostly carnivorous, and the simplest animals to have specialized tissues (outer skin and lining of the gastrovascular cavity) and body symmetry (radial). Their tentacles have stinging cells called nematocysts used in feeding.

Feeding and Digestion Predatory, stinging prey with nematocysts; digestion begins extracellularly in gastrovascular cavity and is completed intracellularly; indigestible materials leave body through single opening; many, especially reef-building corals, also depend on symbiotic algae, or zooxanthellae.

Circulation No internal transport system; nutrients typically diffuse through body.

Respiration Diffusion through body walls.

Excretion Cellular wastes diffuse through body walls.

Response Some specialized sensory cells; nerve cells in nerve net, statocysts that help determine up and down, eyespots (ocelli) made of light-detecting cells

Movement Polyps stationary, medusas free-swimming; some, such as sea anemones, can burrow and creep very slowly; others move using muscles that work with a hydrostatic skeleton and water in gastrovascular cavity; medusas such as jellyfish move by jet propulsion generated by muscle contractions.

Reproduction Most—alternate between sexual (most species by external fertilization) and asexual (polyps produce new polyps or medusae by budding)

▲ Compass Jellyfish

Eco•Alert

Coral Symbionts

Reef-building coral animals depend on symbiotic algae called zooxanthellae for certain vital nutritional needs. In many places, reef-building corals live close to the upper end of their temperature tolerance zone. If water temperatures rise too high, the coral-zooxanthellae symbiosis breaks down, and corals turn white in what is called "coral bleaching." If corals don't recover their algae soon, they weaken and die. This is one reason why coral reefs are in grave danger from global warming.

The color of this star coral is caused by zooxanthellae algae living within it.

GROUPS OF CNIDARIANS

There are more than 9000 species of cnidarians.

HYDROZOA: Hydras and their relatives
Hydras and their relatives spend most of their time as polyps and are either colonial or solitary. They reproduce asexually (by budding), sexually, or they alternate between sexual and asexual reproduction. Examples: hydra, Portuguese man-of-war

A Portuguese man-of war is actually a colony of polyps.

ANTHOZOA: Corals and sea anemones
Corals and sea anemones are colonial or solitary polyps with no medusa stage. The central body is surrounded by tentacles. They reproduce sexually or asexually. Examples: reef corals, sea anemones, sea pens, sea fans

Sea Anemone

This purple-striped jelly (Pelagia noctiluca) has the ability to bioluminesce, or give off light.

Black Sea Nettle

SCYPHOZOA: Jellyfishes
Jellyfishes spend most of their time as medusas; some species bypass the polyp stage. They reproduce sexually and sometimes asexually by budding. Examples: lion's mane jellyfish, moon jelly, sea wasp

THE TREE OF LIFE

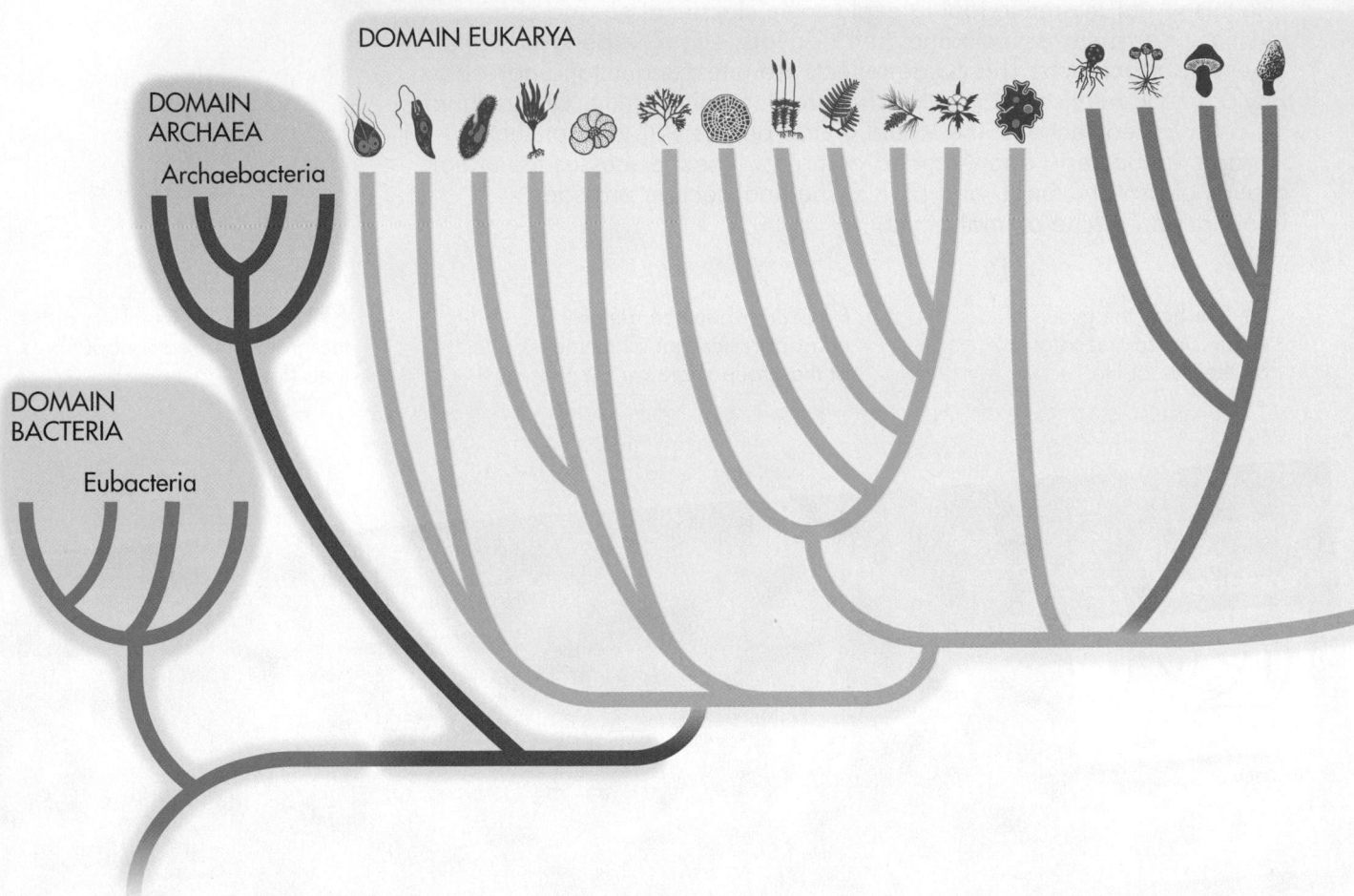

DOMAIN EUKARYA

DOMAIN ARCHAEA

Archaebacteria

DOMAIN BACTERIA

Eubacteria

Before you begin your tour through the kingdoms of life, review this big picture from Chapter 18. The pages that follow will give you a glimpse of the incredible diversity found within each of the "branches" shown here.

DOMAIN BACTERIA

Members of the domain Bacteria are unicellular and prokaryotic. The bacteria are ecologically diverse, ranging from free-living soil organisms to deadly parasites. This domain corresponds to the kingdom Eubacteria.

DOMAIN ARCHAEA

Also unicellular and prokaryotic, members of the domain Archaea live in some of the most extreme environments you can imagine, including volcanic hot springs, brine pools, and black organic mud totally devoid of oxygen. The domain Archaea corresponds to the kingdom Archaebacteria.

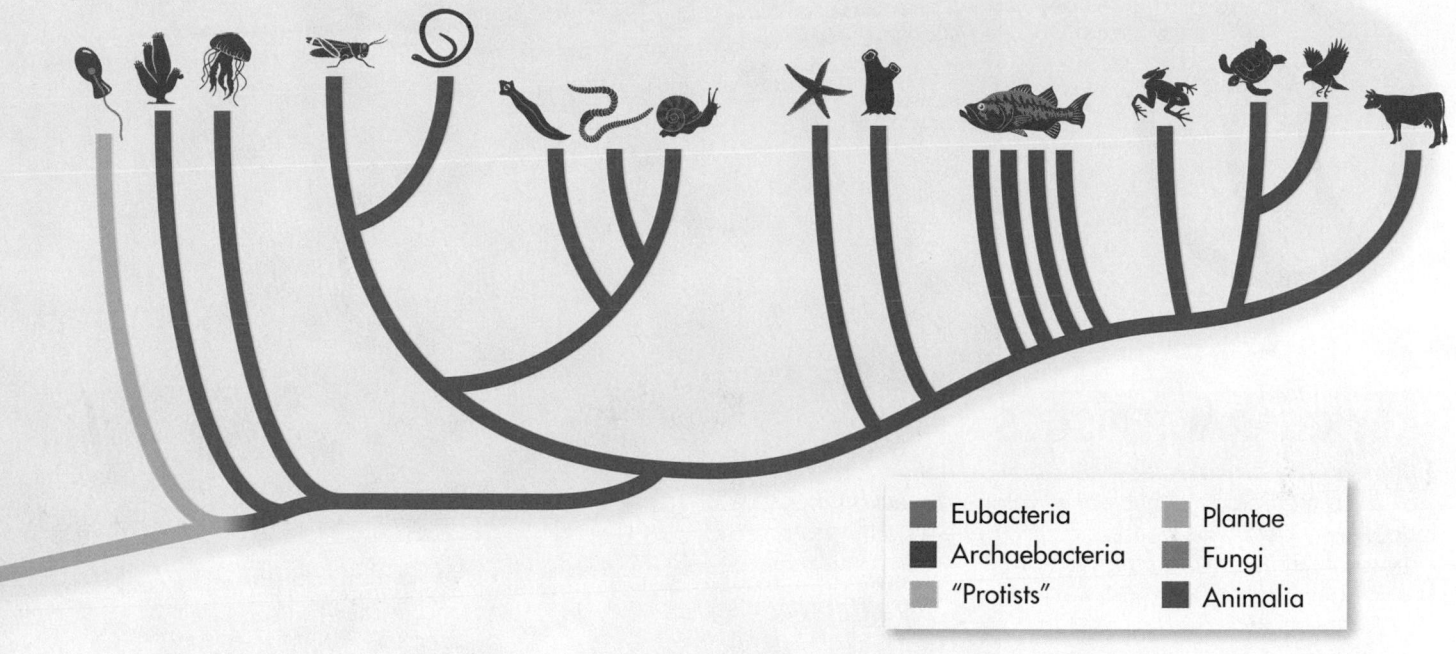

■ Eubacteria	■ Plantae
■ Archaebacteria	■ Fungi
■ "Protists"	■ Animalia

DOMAIN EUKARYA

The domain Eukarya consists of all organisms that have cells with nuclei. It is organized into the four remaining kingdoms of the six-kingdom system: Protista, Fungi, Plantae, and Animalia.

THE "PROTISTS"

Notice that the branches for the kingdom Protista are not together in one area, as is the case with the other kingdoms. In fact, recent molecular studies and cladistic analyses have shown that "eukaryotes formerly known as Protista" do not form a single clade. Current cladistic analysis divides these organisms into at least six clades. They cannot, therefore, be properly placed into a single taxon.

FUNGI

Members of the kingdom Fungi are heterotrophs. Most feed on dead or decaying organic matter. The most recognizable fungi, including mushrooms, are multicellular. Some fungi, such as yeasts, are unicellular.

PLANTS

Members of the kingdom Plantae are autotrophs that carry out photosynthesis. Plants have cell walls that contain cellulose. Plants are nonmotile—they cannot move from place to place.

ANIMALS

Members of the kingdom Animalia are multicellular and heterotrophic. Animal cells do not have cell walls. Most animals can move about, at least for some part of their life cycle.

Bacteria

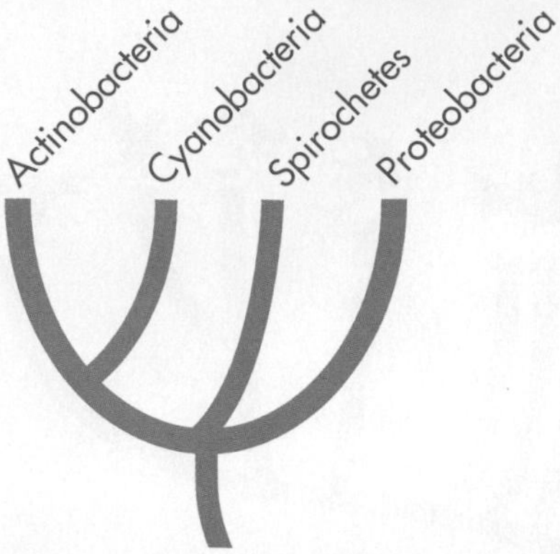

Actinobacteria Cyanobacteria Spirochetes Proteobacteria

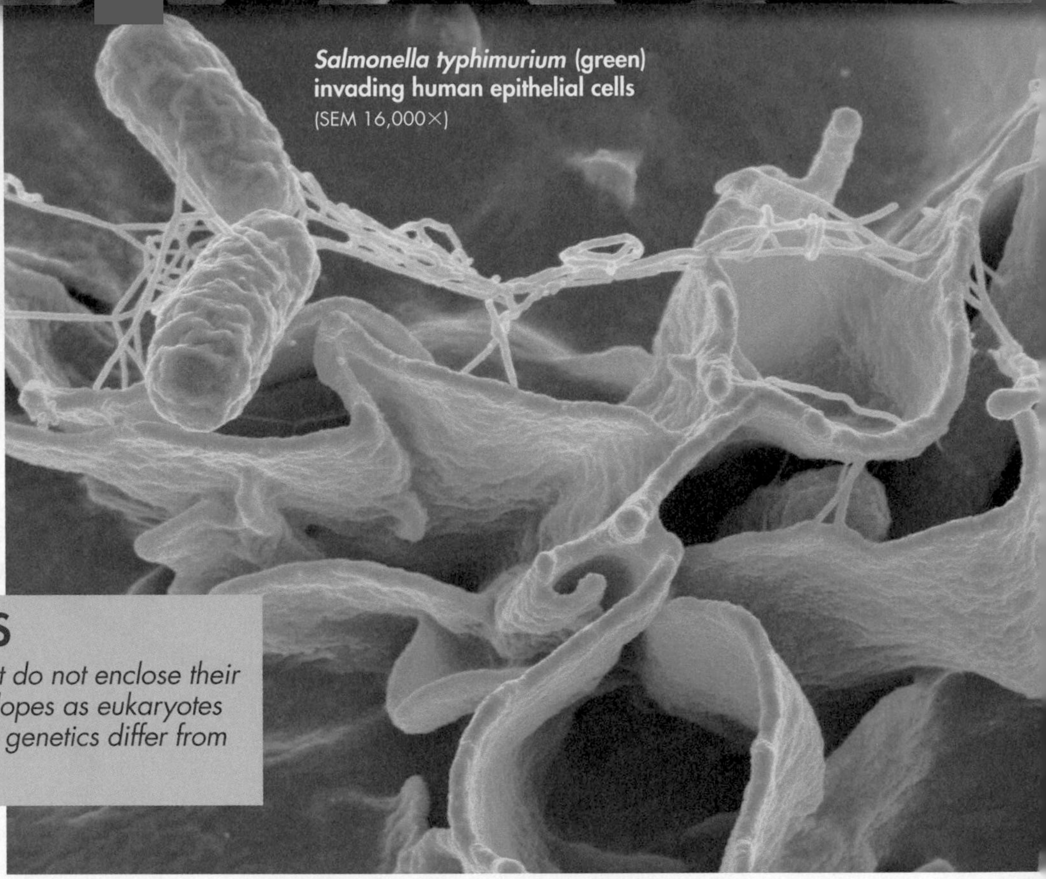

Salmonella typhimurium (green) invading human epithelial cells
(SEM 16,000×)

KEY CHARACTERISTICS

Bacteria are prokaryotes—cells that do not enclose their DNA in membranous nuclear envelopes as eukaryotes do. Many details of their molecular genetics differ from those of Archaea and Eukarya.

Cell Structure Variety of cell shapes, including spherical, rodlike, and spiral; most have cell walls containing peptidoglycan. Few if any have internal organelles. Some have external flagella for cell movement.

Genetic Organization All essential genes are in one large DNA double helix that has its ends joined to form a closed loop. Smaller loops of DNA (plasmids) may carry nonessential genes. Simultaneous transcription and translation; introns generally not present; histone proteins absent

Reproduction By binary fission; no true sexual reproduction; some achieve recombination by conjugation.

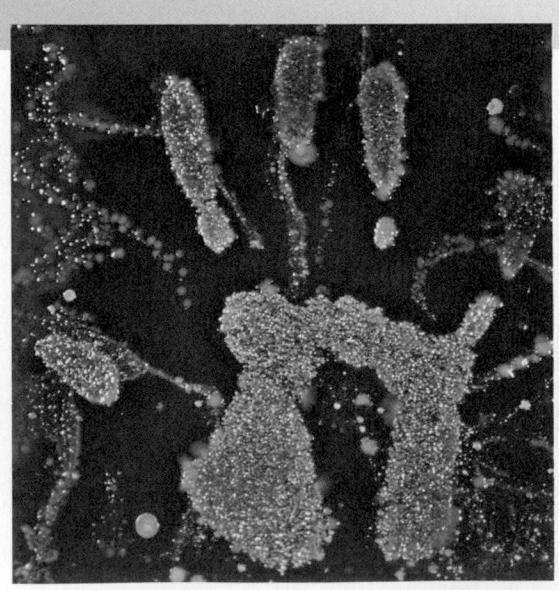

● Did You Know?

A World of Bacteria

Putting Bacteria in Proper Perspective

"Planet of the Bacteria" was the title of an essay by the late Stephen Jay Gould. He pointed out that the dominant life forms on planet Earth aren't humans, or animals, or plants. They are bacteria. They were here first, and they inhabit more places on the planet than any other form of life. In fact, bacteria make up roughly 10 percent of our own dry body weight! In terms of biomass and importance to the planet, bacteria truly do rule this planet. They, not we, are number one.

◀ *The bacterial colonies shown here are growing in the print of a human hand on agar gel.*

GROUPS OF BACTERIA

There is no generally agreed phylogeny for the bacteria. Included here are some of the major groups within the domain.

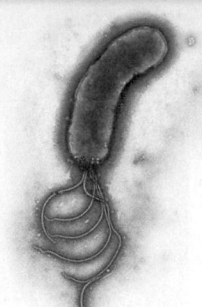

◄ *Helicobacter pylori is rod-shaped and has several flagella used for movement. This bacterium infects the stomach lining and causes ulcers in some people.* (TEM 7100×)

PROTEOBACTERIA

This large and diverse clade of bacteria includes *Escherichia* (*E. coli*), *Salmonella*, *Helicobacter*, and the nitrogen-fixing soil bacterium *Rhizobium*.

The spiral-shaped bacterium that causes syphilis is Treponema pallidum. (SEM 10,000×) ▼

SPIROCHAETES

The spirochaetes (SPY roh keets) are named for their distinctive spiral shape. They move in a corkscrew-like fashion, twisting along as they are propelled by flagella on both ends of the cell. Most are free-living, but a few cause serious diseases, including syphilis, Lyme disease, and leptospirosis.

ACTINOBACTERIA

A large number of soil bacteria belong to this group. Some form long filaments. Members include the *Streptomyces* and *Actinomyces*, which are natural producers of many antibiotics, including streptomycin. A related group is the *Firmicutes*. The *Firmicutes* include *Bacillus anthracis* (anthrax), *Clostridia* (tetanus and botulism), and *Bacillus thuringensis*, which produces a powerful insecticide used for genetic engineering in plants.

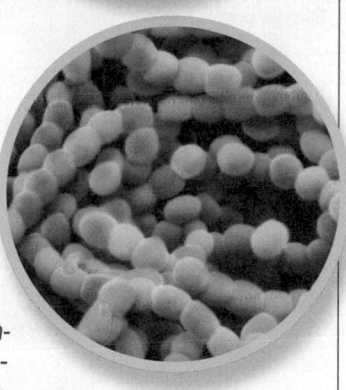

▲ *Chains of spores of soil bacteria, genus* Streptomyces (SEM 3400×)

CYANOBACTERIA

The cyanobacteria are photosynthetic prokaryotes that were once called "blue-green algae." They are among the oldest organisms on Earth, having been identified in rocks dating to more than 3 billion years ago. They are found in salt water and fresh water, in the soil, and even on the surfaces of damp rocks. They are the only organisms on Earth that are able to fix carbon and nitrogen under aerobic conditions, and this enables them to play critical roles in the global ecosystem, where they serve as key sources of carbon and nitrogen.

▼ *Many cyanobacteria form long filaments of attached cells, like those shown here (genus* Lyngbya, SEM 540×*).*

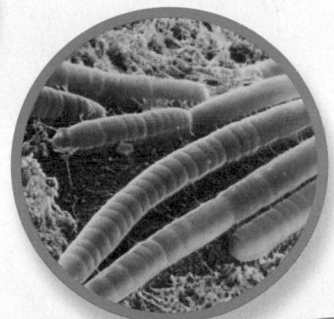

● **A Closer Look** ▶

The Gram Stain

A Microbiologist's Quick Diagnostic

Gram-positive bacteria appear purple after staining, while gram-negative bacteria appear pink. (LM 1000×) ▶

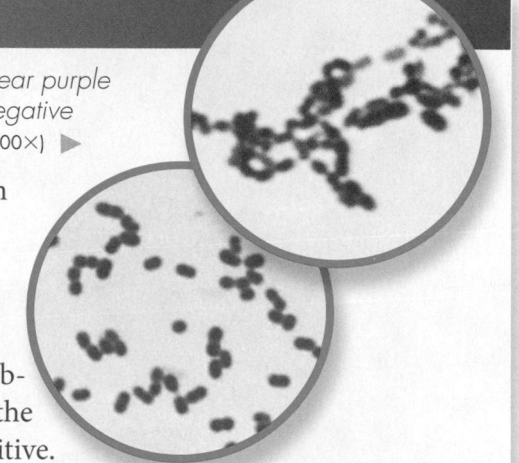

The Gram stain, developed by the nineteenth-century Danish physician Hans Christian Gram, allows microbiologists to categorize bacteria quickly into one of two groups based on their cell wall composition. Gram-positive bacteria lack a membrane outside the cell wall and take up the stain easily. Gram-negative bacteria, on the other hand, have an outer membrane of lipids and carbohydrates that prevents them from absorbing the gram stain. Many gram-negative bacteria are found among the proteobacteria. On the other hand, actinobacteria are mostly gram-positive.

Protists

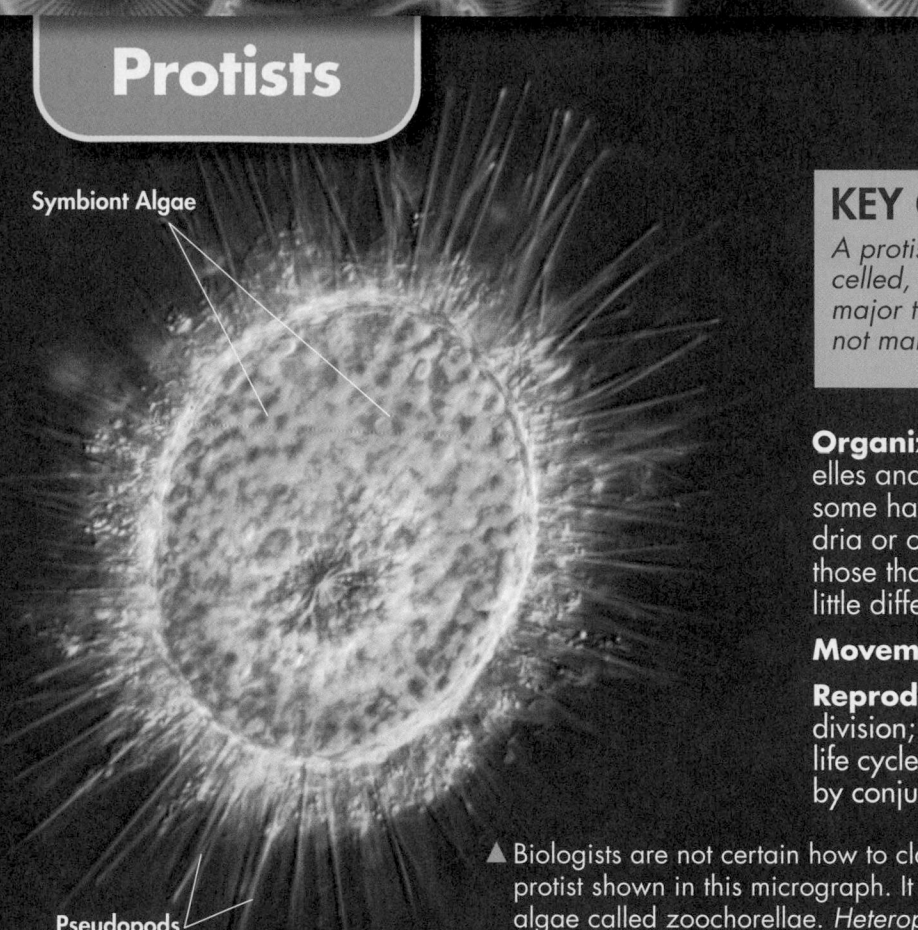

Symbiont Algae

Pseudopods

KEY CHARACTERISTICS

A protist is a eukaryote, generally single-celled, that does not fit into any of the other major taxonomic groups. The protists do not make up a true kingdom.

Organization Great diversity of cell organelles and organization: some have cell walls, some have chloroplasts, most have mitochondria or organelles related to mitochondria; those that are multicellular have relatively little differentiation into tissues.

Movement Some move by cilia or flagella.

Reproduction Most reproduce by cell division; many have sexual phases to their life cycle; some exchange genetic material by conjugation.

▲ Biologists are not certain how to classify *Heterophrys*, the freshwater protist shown in this micrograph. It harbors symbiotic photosynthetic algae called zoochorellae. *Heterophrys* is one of many protists called "heliozoans" (literally, "sun animals") because of the thin pseudopods extending from its surface, giving it a sun-like appearance.

● Did You Know?

The Kingdom That Isn't
The Challenges of Classifying Protists

Biologists traditionally classified protists by splitting them into funguslike, plantlike, and animal-like groups. This seemed to work for a while, but when they studied protists more carefully with new research tools, including genome-level molecular analysis, this traditional system simply fell apart.

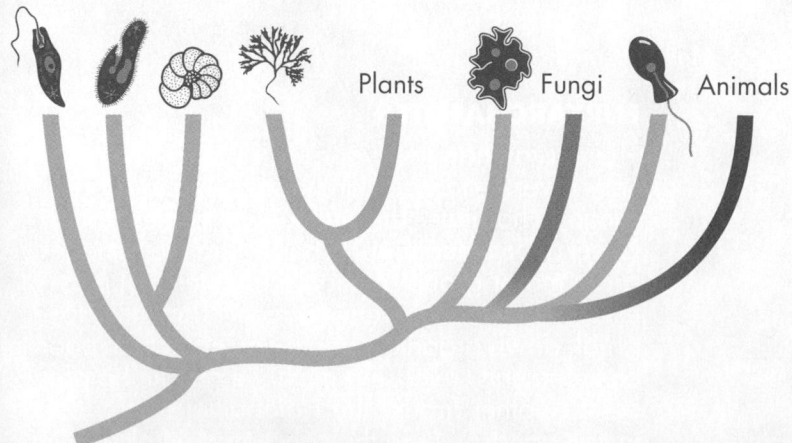

Plants   Fungi   Animals

Biologists now think that protists shouldn't be classified as a kingdom at all. In fact, when scientists look for the deepest and most fundamental divisions among eukaryotes, they find that all of those divisions are within the protists themselves, not between protists and other eukaryotes. Starting over, biologists could simply use those divisions to define newer, more accurate "kingdoms," but that might cause new problems. For one thing, it would lump two of the traditional kingdoms (animals and fungi) together, and it would leave a handful of kingdoms that contain only unicellular organisms. There is no perfect solution to this problem. Here, "protists" are considered a kingdom for the sake of convenience, but keep in mind that their differences are really too great for any single kingdom to contain.

Excavates

KEY CHARACTERISTICS

Excavates (EKS kuh vayts) have a characteristic feeding groove, usually supported by microtubules. Most have flagella. A few lack mitochondria and are unable to carry out oxidative phosphorylation, although they do possess remnants of the organelle.

GROUPS OF EXCAVATES

The excavates include a wide diversity of protists, from free-living photosynthesizers to some of humankind's most notorious pathogens.

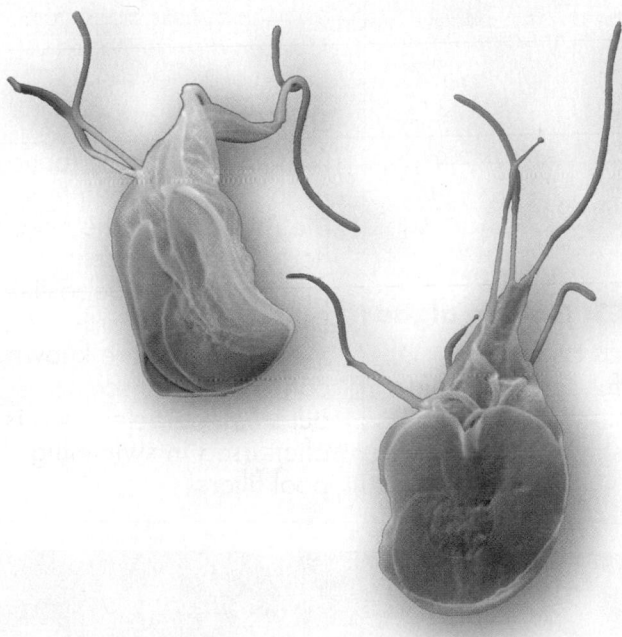

▲ The diplomonad Giardia is a dangerous intestinal parasite that frequently contaminates freshwater streams. Giardia infections are common in wildlife and pet dogs and cats. (SEM 1800×)

DIPLOMONADS

These organisms get their name from the fact that they possess two distinct and different nuclei (from Greek, diplo = double). The double nuclei probably derived from an ancient symbiotic event in which one species was engulfed by another. Cells contain multiple flagella, usually arranged around the body of the cell. Most species of diplomonads are parasitic.

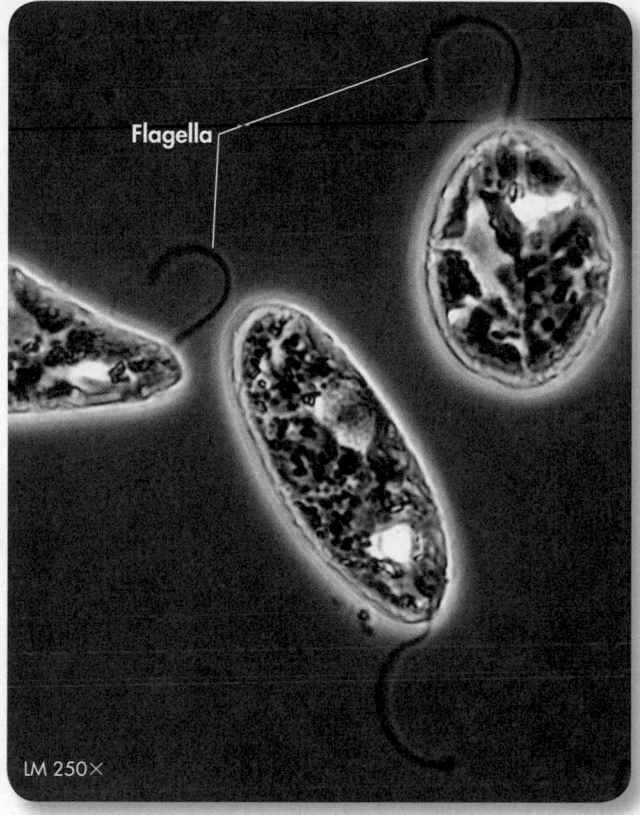

Flagella

LM 250×

▲ *Photosynthetic Euglena gracilis is commonly found in lakes and ponds.*

DISCICRISTATES

Discicristates (disk ee KRIS tayts) are named for the disc-shaped cristae present in their mitochondria. Some species are photosynthetic and free-living, such as *Euglena*, while others are dangerous parasites.

▼ *The ribbonlike cells of Trypanosoma brucei cause African sleeping sickness. The parasitic protist is transmitted by tsetse flies to humans, where it infects the blood, lymph, and spinal fluid. Severe nervous system damage and death are the usual result.* (SEM 6700×)

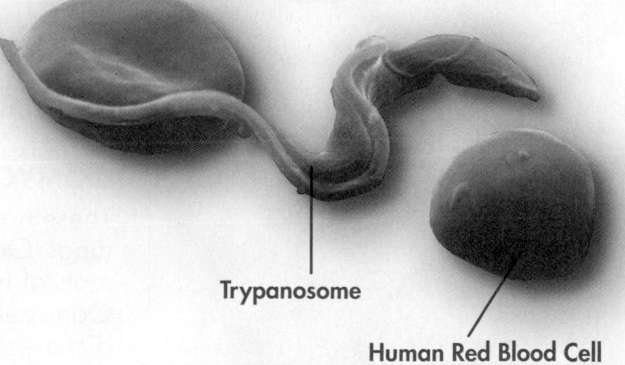

Trypanosome

Human Red Blood Cell

Chromalveolates

SEM 280×

KEY CHARACTERISTICS

Chromalveolates (krohm AL vee uh layts) get their name from alveoli, flattened vesicles that line the cell membrane. The prefix chromo-, meaning "pigment," reflects evidence that members of this clade share a common ancestor that had accessory pigments used in photosynthesis.

GROUPS OF CHROMALVEOLATES

The chromalveolates are one of the largest and most diverse groups of eukaryotes.

PHAEOPHYTES: Brown algae

Phaeophytes (FAY uh fyts) are mostly found in salt water. They are some of the most abundant and visible of the algae. Most species contain fucoxanthin, a greenish-brown pigment from which the group gets its common name. The multicellular brown alga known as giant kelp can grow as large as 60 meters in length.

▼ Brown algae in genus Fucus are commonly found in tidepools and on rocky shorelines of the United States.

LM 200×

▲ This species, in genus Synura, is a colonial alga.

CHRYSOPHYTES: Golden algae

Chrysophytes (KRIS oh fyts) are known for colorful accessory pigments in their chloroplasts. Most are found in fresh water and are photosynthetic.

SEM 1000×

▲ Diatoms often produce intricate shells made from silicon dioxide that persist long after they die.

DIATOMS

Diatoms are mostly found in salt water. When they die, they sink to the ocean floor, and their shells pile up in large deposits. Diatomaceous earth, as these deposits are known, can be used to screen out small particles, and is often used in swimming pool filters.

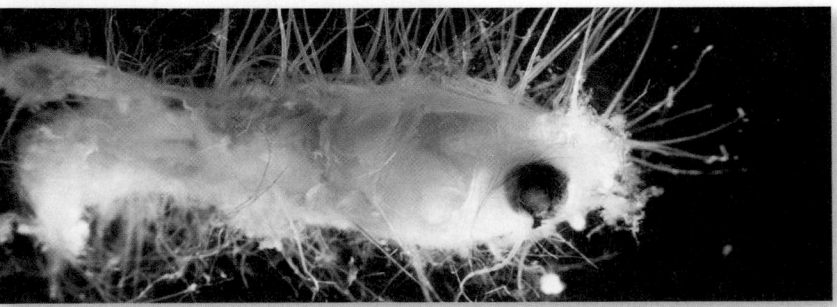

▲ Water molds growing on a dead goldfish

OOMYCETES: Water molds

These nonphotosynthetic organisms are often confused with fungi. Oomycetes (oh uh MY seed eez) typically produce fuzzy mats of material on dead or decaying animals and plants. Oomycetes are also responsible for a number of serious plant diseases, including potato blight, sudden oak death, and ink disease, which infects the American chestnut tree.

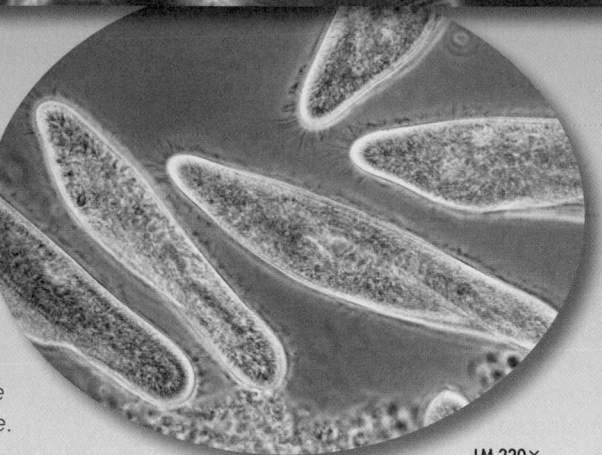

▶ Paramecium multimicronucleatum *is the largest paramecium, with cells that are visible to the naked eye.*

LM 220×

CILIATES

These common organisms may contain hundreds or even thousands of short cilia extending from the surface of the cell. The cilia propel the ciliate through the water, and may sweep food particles into a gullet. Ciliates are large compared to other protists, with some cells exceeding 1 mm in length.

DINOFLAGELLATES

Dinoflagellates are photosynthetic protists found in both fresh and salt water. Their name comes from their two distinct flagella, usually oriented at right angles to each other. Roughly half of dinoflagellate species are photosynthetic; the other half live as heterotrophs. Many dinoflagellate species are luminescent, and when agitated by sudden movement in the water, give off light.

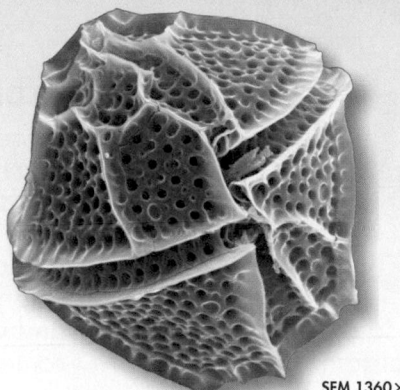

SEM 1360×

▲ *The two flagella of dinoflagellates originate in grooves within thick plates of cellulose that resemble a cross shape, as shown here* (genus Protoperidinium).

Human Red Blood Cell SEM 5000×

▲ *Apicomplexans in genus Plasmodium are mosquito-borne parasites. Shown in green are the remnants of a red blood cell that burst when plasmodia reproduced inside.*

APICOMPLEXANS

The apicomplexans (AYP ih kum plek sunz) are named for a unique organelle near one end of the cell known as the apical complex. This structure contains vesicles with enzymes that allow apicomplexans to enter other cells and take up residence as parasites.

Eco•Alert ▶

Toxic Blooms
Dangerous Dinoflagellates

Great blooms of the dinoflagellates *Gonyaulax* and *Karenia* have occurred in recent years on the East Coast of the United States, although scientists are not sure of the reason. These blooms are known as "red tides." *Gonyaulax* and *Karenia* produce a toxin that can become amplified in the food chain when filter-feeding shellfish such as oysters contentrate it in their tissues. Eating shellfish from water affected by red tide can cause serious illness, paralysis, and even death.

▲ *A red tide containing toxic dinoflagellates*

Cercozoa, Foraminiferans, and Radiolarians

There is no single morphological characteristic that unites this diverse trio, but many have extensions of cytoplasm called pseudopods and many produce protective shells. The grouping together of Cercozoa, Foraminifera, and Radiolaria is based almost entirely on molecular analyses and not on morphology.

FORAMINIFERANS

Foraminifera (fawr uh min IF uh ra) produce intricate and beautiful shells that differ from species to species. Slender pseudopods that emerge through tiny holes in the shell enable them to capture food, including bacteria. As many as 4000 species exist.

▼ *Peneroplis pertusus has a spiral-shaped shell.*

LM 100×

SEM 175×

▲ *Radiolarian shells are composed of silica or strontium sulfate.*

CERCOZOA

Members of this clade are common in soil, where they feed on bacteria as well as decaying organic matter. Many have flagella, and some produce scales made of silica that protect their surfaces.

RADIOLARIANS

These organisms have an intricate structure in which the nucleus is found in an inner region of the cell known as the endoplasm. The outer portion of the cell, known as the ectoplasm, contains lipid droplets and vacuoles. These organisms sometimes form symbiotic relationships with photosynthetic algae, from which they obtain food.

• A Look Back in Time

Foraminiferan Fossils

Ancient Climates Revealed

Abundant fossils of foraminiferans have been found in sediments dating to the Cambrian period (560 million years ago). For decades, oil companies have taken advantage of these ancient fossils to locate the sediments most likely to contain oil, but now there is another use for them—measuring the sea temperature of ancient Earth. Foraminiferans take dissolved oxygen from seawater to make the calcium carbonate ($CaCO_3$) in their shells, and when they do so, they take up two isotopes of oxygen, ^{16}O and ^{18}O. Because water made from ^{16}O is less dense, more of it evaporates into the atmosphere when the seas are warm—increasing the amount of ^{18}O in

the remaining seawater, and in the fossil shells. The ratio between ^{16}O and ^{18}O in these fossils allows scientists to study the history of seawater temperature, as shown in the graph above.

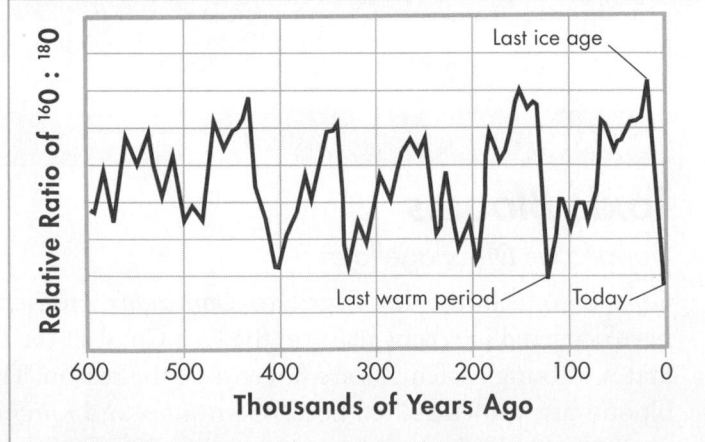

Foraminiferan Isotope Ratios and Climate Change

Relative Ratio of ^{16}O : ^{18}O

Last ice age

Last warm period — Today

Thousands of Years Ago

Rhodophytes

▼ Some things that we call seaweeds, such as this rhodophyte, are actually protists

Also known as the red algae, these organisms get their name (from Greek, *rhodo* = red and *phyte* = plant) from reddish accessory pigments called phycobilins (fy koh BIL inz). These highly efficient pigments enable red algae to grow anywhere from the ocean's surface to depths as great as 268 meters. Most species are multicellular. Rhodophytes are the sister group to kingdom Plantae.

Amoebozoa

Members of the Amoebozoa (uh MEE boh zoh ah) are amoebalike organisms that move by means of cytoplasmic streaming, also called amoeboid movement, using pseudopods.

▼ Slime molds live as single microscopic amoebas in the soil, but aggregate into a colony when conditions are right, forming a multicellular fruiting body. In this image, some of the fruiting bodies have burst, releasing spores.

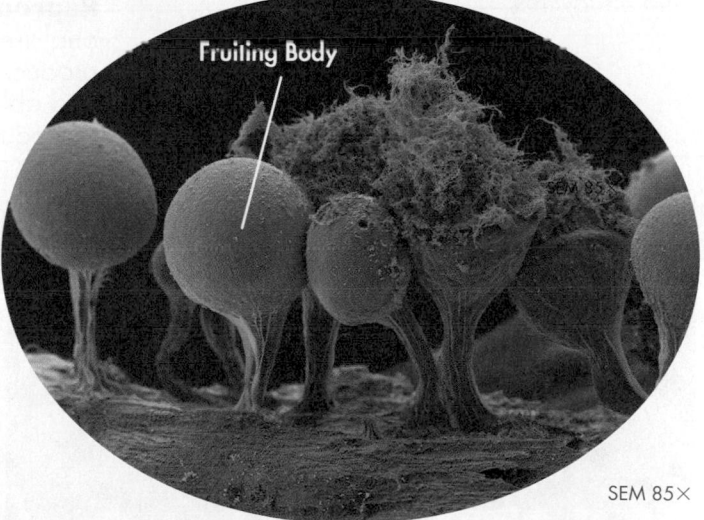

Fruiting Body

SEM 85×

▼ This solitary amoeba, Penardia mutabilis, has very slender pseudopods.

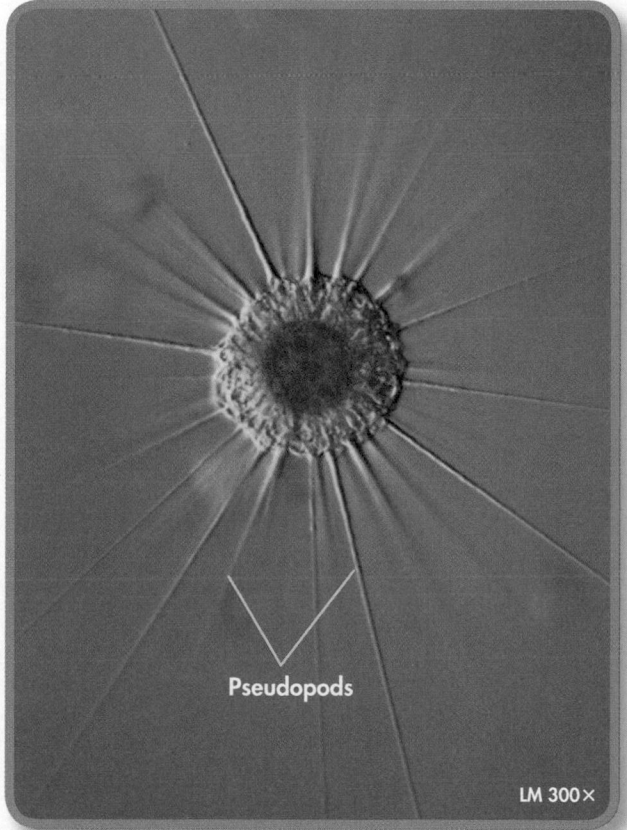

Pseudopods

LM 300×

Choanozoa

Members of the clade Choanozoa (koh AN uh zoh uh) can be solitary or colonial and are found in aquatic environments around the world. This clade is the sister group to kingdom Animalia.

Choanoflagellates are a major group in the clade Choanozoa. They get their name from a collar of cytoplasm that surrounds their single flagellum (form Greek, *choano* = collar.) Many species trap food within the collar and ingest it.

Fungi

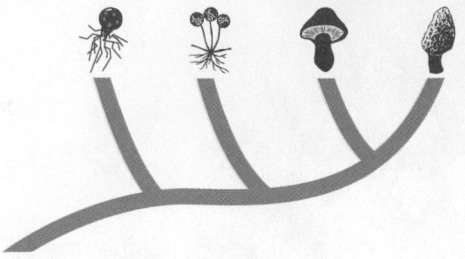

KEY CHARACTERISTICS

Fungi are heterotrophic eukaryotes with cell walls that contain chitin. Fungi were once thought to be plants that had lost their chloroplasts. It is now clear, however, that they are much more closely related to animals than to plants. More than 100,000 species of fungi are known. Distinctions among the phyla are made on the basis of DNA comparisons, cell structure, reproductive structures, and life cycles.

▲ *Stinkhorn fungus (genus* Dictyophora)

Organization Some are unicellular yeasts, but most have a multicellular body called a mycelium that consists of one or more slender, branching cells called hyphae.

Feeding and Digestion Obtain food by extracellular digestion and absorption

Reproduction Most have sexual phases to their life cycle and are haploid at most points during the cycle. Most produce tough, asexual spores, which are easily dispersed and able to endure harsh environmental conditions. Asexual reproduction by budding and splitting is also common.

▲ *Fly agaric (Amanita muscaria) is poisonous to humans.*

●**A Closer Look**

Consumers Beware!
Edible and Inedible Mushrooms

Many types of fungi have long been considered delicacies, and several different species of mushrooms are cultivated for food. You may have already tasted sliced mushrooms on pizza, feasted on delicious sautéed portobello mushrooms, or eaten shiitake mushrooms. When properly cooked and prepared, domestic mushrooms are tasty and nutritious.

Wild mushrooms are a different story: Although some are edible, many are poisonous. Because many species of poisonous mushrooms look almost identical to edible mushrooms, you should never pick or eat any mushrooms found in the wild. Instead, mushroom gathering should be left to experts who can positively identify each mushroom they collect. The result of eating a poisonous mushroom can be severe illness, or even death.

Basidiomycetes

The basidiomycetes, or club fungi, are named for the basidium (buh SID ee um; plural: basidia). The basidium is a reproductive cell that resembles a club.

Life Cycle Basidiomycetes undergo what is probably the most elaborate life cycle of all the fungi, shown below.

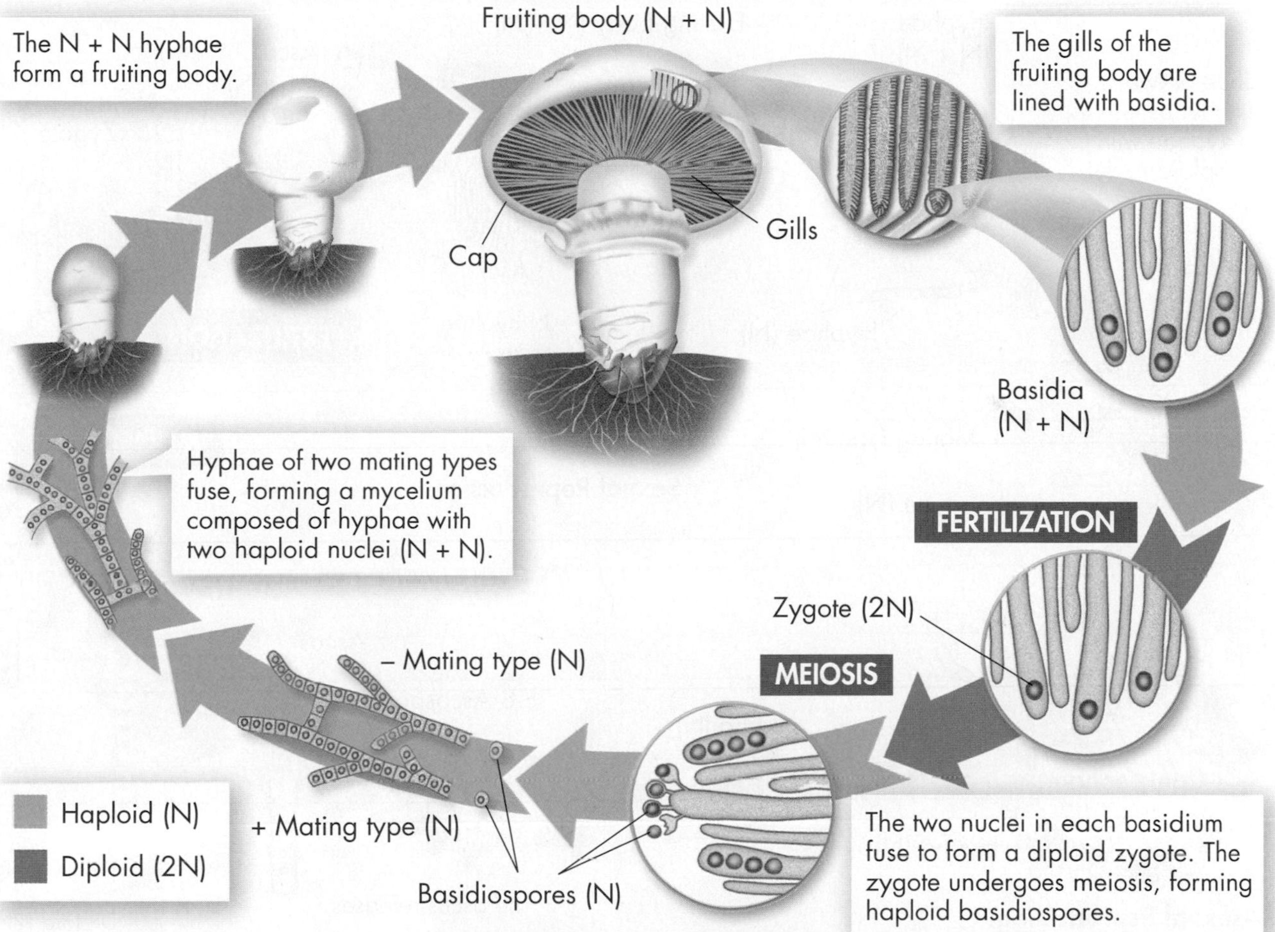

The N + N hyphae form a fruiting body.

Fruiting body (N + N)

The gills of the fruiting body are lined with basidia.

Cap

Gills

Basidia (N + N)

Hyphae of two mating types fuse, forming a mycelium composed of hyphae with two haploid nuclei (N + N).

FERTILIZATION

Zygote (2N)

MEIOSIS

– Mating type (N)

Haploid (N)

Diploid (2N)

+ Mating type (N)

Basidiospores (N)

The two nuclei in each basidium fuse to form a diploid zygote. The zygote undergoes meiosis, forming haploid basidiospores.

Diversity More than 26,000 species of basidiomycetes have been described, roughly a quarter of all known fungal species. Examples include the stinkhorn and fly agaric mushrooms shown on the previous page, and the shelf fungus and puffball at right.

▶ Shelf fungi (Polypore family) often grow on the sides of dead or dying trees.

▼ A puffball releases its spores.

Ascomycetes

The ascomycetes, or sac fungi, are named for the ascus (AS kus), a saclike reproductive structure that contains spores.

Life Cycle The ascomycete life cycle includes an asexual phase, in which haploid spores are released from structures called conidiophores, and a sexual phase.

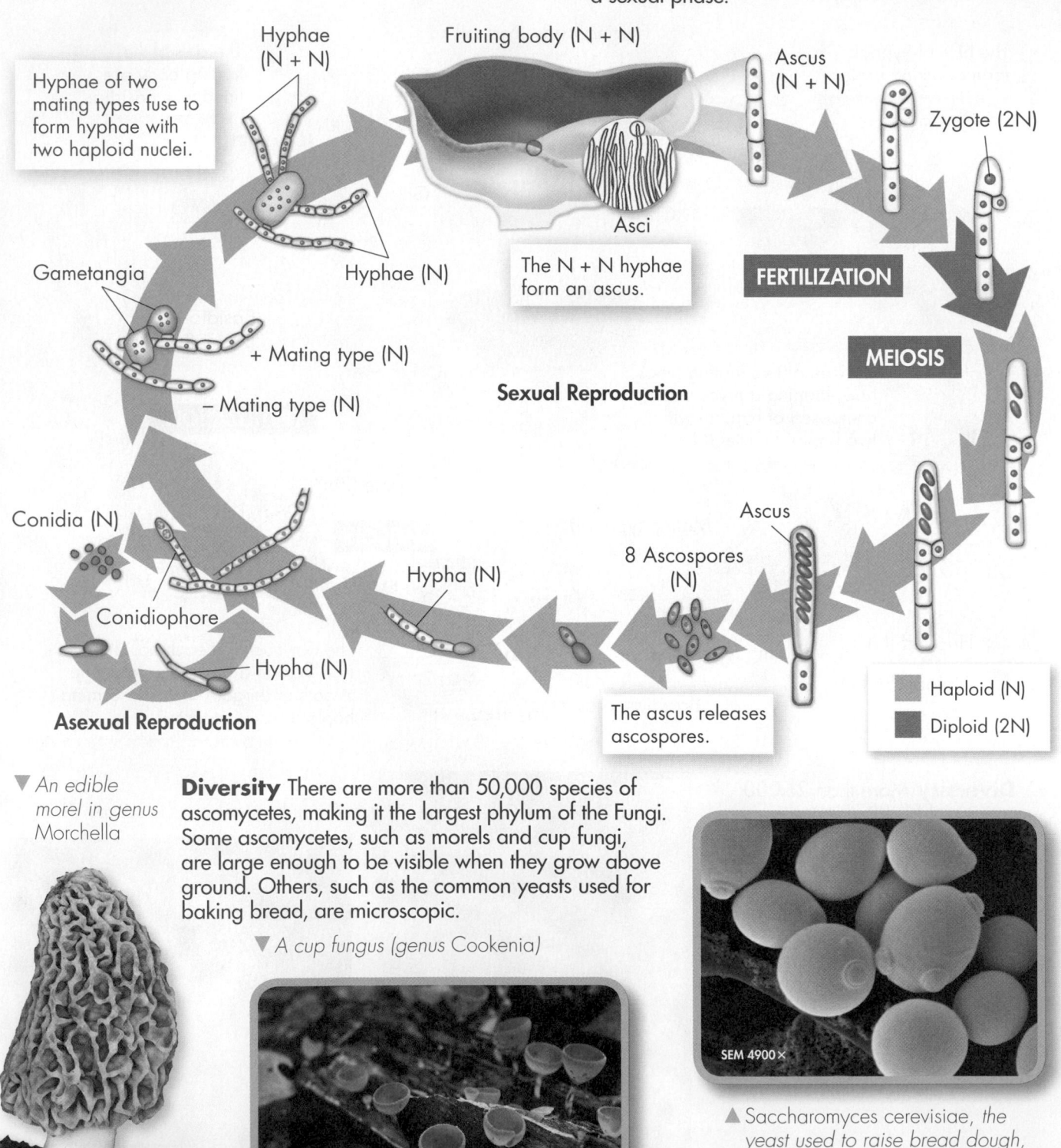

Hyphae (N + N)

Hyphae of two mating types fuse to form hyphae with two haploid nuclei.

Fruiting body (N + N)

Ascus (N + N)

Zygote (2N)

Hyphae (N)

The N + N hyphae form an ascus.

Asci

FERTILIZATION

MEIOSIS

Gametangia

+ Mating type (N)

– Mating type (N)

Sexual Reproduction

Conidia (N)

Conidiophore

Hypha (N)

Hypha (N)

Ascus

8 Ascospores (N)

The ascus releases ascospores.

Asexual Reproduction

Haploid (N)

Diploid (2N)

▼ *An edible morel in genus* Morchella

Diversity There are more than 50,000 species of ascomycetes, making it the largest phylum of the Fungi. Some ascomycetes, such as morels and cup fungi, are large enough to be visible when they grow above ground. Others, such as the common yeasts used for baking bread, are microscopic.

▼ *A cup fungus (genus* Cookenia*)*

SEM 4900×

▲ Saccharomyces cerevisiae, *the yeast used to raise bread dough, is a unicellular ascomycete that reproduces asexually by budding.*

Zygomycetes

The hyphae of zygomycetes generally lack cross walls between cells. Zygomycetes get their name from the sexual phase of their reproductive cycle, which involves a structure called a zygosporangium that forms between the hyphae of two different mating types. One group within the zygomycetes, the Glomales, form symbiotic mycorrhizae (my koh RY zee) with plant roots.

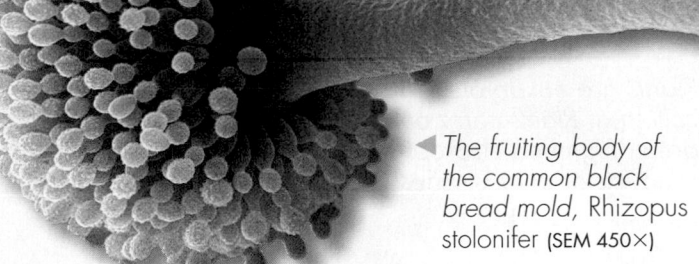

◀ The fruiting body of the common black bread mold, Rhizopus stolonifer (SEM 450×)

◀ This micrograph shows mycorrhizal fungi in symbiosis with soybean roots. The soybean plant provides nutrient sugars to the fungus, while the fungus provides water and essential minerals to the plant. (SEM 200×)

Chytrids

▶ Spores of Synchytrium endobioticum in potato cells (LM 500×)

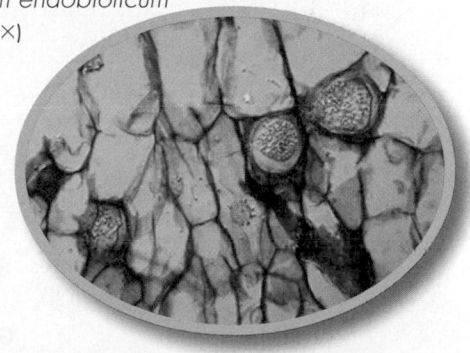

Members of this phylum live in water or moist soil. Their reproductive cells have flagella, making them the only fungi known to have a motile stage to their life cycle. Chytrids are especially good at digesting cellulose, the material of plant cell walls—some live in the digestive systems of cows and deer, helping them to digest plant matter. Others are pathogens—certain chytrids have recently been associated with the decline of frog populations around the world. About 1000 species are known, many of them recently discovered.

▲ Lichen-covered Japanese beech

Eco•Alert

Look to the Lichens
Lichens as Bio-Indicators

Lichens are mutualistic associations between a fungus, usually an ascomycete, and a photosynthetic organism, usually an alga. They are incredibly durable, and have even been reported to survive in the vacuum of space. However, they are also incredibly sensitive indicators of the state of the atmosphere. In particular, when sulfur dioxide is released into the atmosphere, it often reacts with water to form acids (including sulfuric acid) that pollute rainfall. Lichens can be severely damaged by acidic rainfall, although the degree of damage depends on the substrate upon which they grow. Lichens disappear first from the bark of pine and fir trees, which are themselves somewhat acidic. Lichens on elms, which have alkaline bark, are the last to go. By carefully monitoring the health of lichen populations of various trees, scientists can use these remarkable organisms as low-tech monitors for the health of the environment.

Plants

KEY CHARACTERISTICS

Plants are eukaryotes with cell walls composed of cellulose. Plants carry out photosynthesis using the green pigments chlorophyll a and b, and they store the products of photosynthesis as starch.

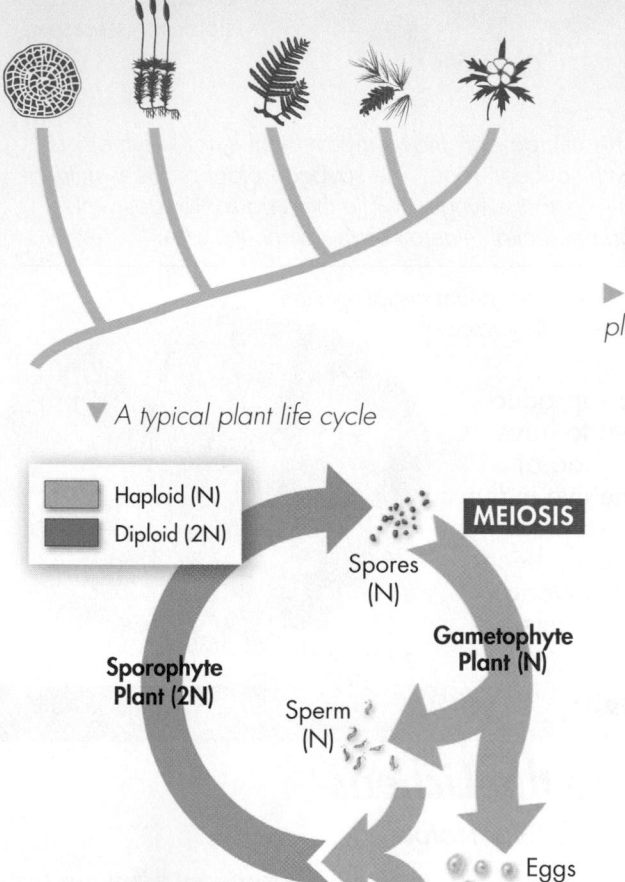

▶ *A banana plant in bloom*

▼ *A typical plant life cycle*

	Haploid (N)
	Diploid (2N)

MEIOSIS

Spores (N)

Gametophyte Plant (N)

Sporophyte Plant (2N)

Sperm (N)

Eggs (N)

FERTILIZATION

● A Closer Look

Prokaryotes Within
The Origins of Chloroplasts

Chloroplasts, which contain their own DNA, are found in all green plants, but where did they come from? In 1905, the Russian botanist Konstantin Mereschkowsky, noticing the similarities between chloroplasts and cyanobacteria, proposed that these organelles originated from a symbiotic relationship formed with the ancestors of today's plants.

This hypothesis still holds up very well today. New DNA studies suggest that all chloroplasts are descended from a single photosynthetic prokaryote, closely related to today's cyanobacteria.

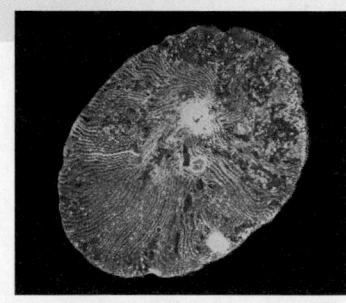

The photosynthetic membranes (shown in green) visible in this thin section of a cyanobacterium resemble the thylakoid membranes of plant cell chloroplasts. (TEM 14,000×)

Green Algae

KEY CHARACTERISTICS

The green algae are plants that do not make embryos. All other plants form embryos as part of their life cycle. The green algae include both unicellular and multicellular species, and they are primarily aquatic.

Organization Single cells, colonies, and a few truly multicellular species

Movement Many swim using whiplike flagella.

Water Transport Water diffuses in from the environment.

Reproduction Asexual and sexual, with gametes and spores; some species show alternation of generations.

GROUPS OF GREEN ALGAE

The three most diverse groups of green algae are profiled below.

▲ *Clumps of Spirogyra, a filamentous green alga, are commonly called water silk or mermaid's tresses.*

CHLOROPHYTES: Classic green algae

These algae usually live as single cells, like *Chlamydomonas*, or in colonies, like *Volvox*. They are found in both fresh and salt water, and some species are even known to live in arctic snowbanks.

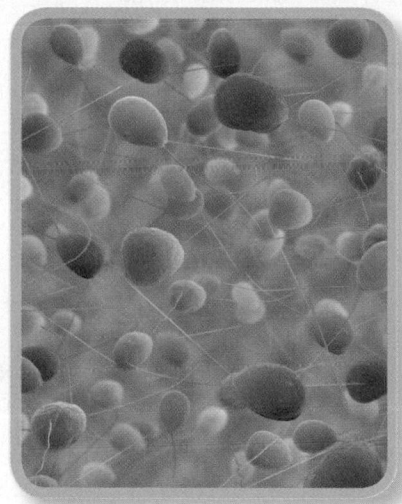

▶ *Chlamydomonas is a unicellular green alga. Each cell has two flagella, which are used in movement.* (SEM 3000×)

CHAROPHYTES: Stoneworts

Among the green algae, the charophytes (KAHR uh fyts) are the closest relatives of more complicated plants. They are mostly freshwater species. Their branching filaments may be anchored to the substrate by thin rhizoids.

Antheridia

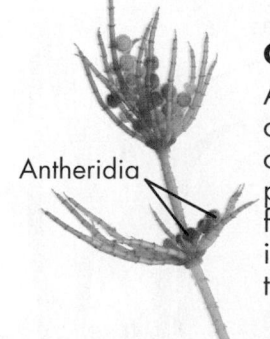

◀ *Chara with antheridia (sperm-producing structures) visible*

ULVOPHYTES: Sea lettuces

The ulvophytes are large organisms composed of hundreds or thousands of cells. Most form large, flattened green sheets and are often simply called seaweed. They show both haploid and diploid phases in their life cycle, but in many species, such as the common sea lettuce, *Ulva*, it is difficult to tell the two phases apart.

▼ *Ulva lactuca*

Bryophytes

KEY CHARACTERISTICS

Bryophytes (BRY oh fyts), found mostly on land, are multicellular plants that lack true vascular tissue. This lack of vascular tissue limits their height to just a few centimeters and restricts them to moist soils.

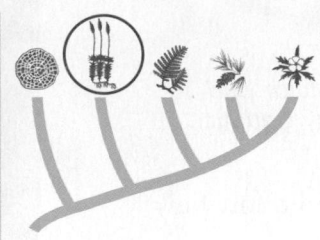

Organization Complex and specialized tissues, including protective external layers and rhizoids

Movement Adults stationary; male gametes swim to egg cells using flagella.

Water Transport Diffusion from cell to cell; in some mosses, water flows through specialized tissue.

Reproduction All reproduce sexually with alternation of generations, producing gametes and spores. Most reproduce asexually, too. The gametophyte stage is dominant, with the sporophyte stage dependent on the gametophyte.

▲ *Mosses thrive in shady, damp locations, such as along the banks of this Oregon creek.*

GROUPS OF BRYOPHYTES

Although they are listed together here, the three major groups of bryophytes are now considered to have evolved independently from each other.

MOSSES:
Classic bryophytes

Mosses are found on damp, well-shaded soil, and occasionally along the sides of tree trunks.

Sporophyte

Mat of gametophytes

LIVERWORTS

Liverworts are flat, almost leaf-like plants that grow on the damp forest floor. Sporophytes are small and grow on the underside of female gametophytes.

Gametophyte

HORNWORTS

Hornworts get their name from their sporophytes, tiny green structures resembling horns. Like other bryophytes, hornworts are found mostly in damp, well-shaded areas. Only about 100 species are known.

Sporophytes

Gametophyte

Seedless Vascular Plants

KEY CHARACTERISTICS

This informal grouping lumps together all the plants that have true vascular tissue but lack seeds. Vascular tissue is a key adaptation to life on land. By carrying water and food throughout plant structures, vascular tissue permitted the evolution of roots and tree-size plants, and it allowed plants to spread into dry areas of land.

Organization Complex and specialized tissues, including true roots, stems, and leaves

Movement Adults stationary; male gametes swim to egg cells using flagella.

Water Transport Through vascular tissue

Reproduction Alternation of generations, producing spores, eggs, and swimming sperm; the sporophyte stage is dominant, but the sporophyte is not dependent on the gametophyte as it is in bryophytes.

GROUPS OF SEEDLESS VASCULAR PLANTS

Besides the flowering plants, these organisms make up the most diverse collection of land plants, with more than 10,000 known species.

FERNS

Ferns are common and abundant. Because they need standing water to reproduce, ferns are generally found in areas that are damp at least part of the year. The sporophyte phase of the life cycle is dominant. Spores are produced in prominent clusters known as sori (SOH ry) on the undersides of leaves.

▼ *Polypodium vulgare*

Sori

CLUB MOSSES

Not really mosses, these vascular plants are also called lycopods (LY koh pahdz). These plants were especially abundant during the Carboniferous Period 360 to 290 million years ago, when they grew as large as trees. Today, their remains make up a large part of coal deposits mined for fuel.

▼ *The small club moss known as* Lycopodium *can be found growing on the forest floor throughout the temperate regions of North America. They look like tiny pine trees at first glance, but they are, in fact, small, seedless plants.*

HORSETAILS

Only a single living genus of horsetails is known, *Equisetum* (ek wi SEET um). They get their name due to their resemblance to horses' tails. Today, only 25 species are known, confined to wet areas of soil. But horsetails were once much more diverse, larger in size, and abundant. Abrasive silica, found in many horsetails, was used in colonial times as a scouring powder to help clean pots and pans.

▼ *Equisetum*

Gymnosperms

KEY CHARACTERISTICS

Gymnosperms are seed-bearing vascular plants whose seeds are exposed to the environment, rather than being enclosed in a fruit. The seeds are usually located on the scales of cones.

Organization True roots, stems, and leaves

Movement Adults stationary; within pollen grains, male gametophytes drift in air or are carried by animals to female structures, where they release sperm that move to eggs.

Water Transport Through vascular tissue

Reproduction Sexual; alternation of generations; the sporophyte stage is dominant. Female gametophytes live within the parent sporophyte. Because pollen grains carry sperm to eggs, open water is not needed for fertilization.

▶ *Some bristlecone pines are thousands of years old, such as this one growing in Nevada.*

● Did You Know?

Rising From the Ashes
Fire's Role in Seed Germination

We generally think of forest fires as being natural disasters, and that's typically true. Some gymnosperm species, however, are so well adapted to the arid conditions of the American West that they actually depend upon such fires to spread their seeds.

The best-known example is the Jack pine, *Pinus banksiana*. Its seed cones are thick and heat resistant. When engulfed in a fire, its seeds escape damage. The fire's high heat helps to open the outer coat of the cone, enabling the seeds to pop out afterward. As a result, Jack pines are among the very first plants to repopulate a forest that has been damaged by fire.

▲ *The high heat of a forest fire opens the cones of the Jack pines, releasing their seeds. In this photograph, Jack pine seedlings are growing among the charred remnants of mature trees that burned in a forest fire.*

GROUPS OF GYMNOSPERMS

There are four groups of gymnosperms, representing about 800 species in total.

CONIFERS

Conifers are by far the most diverse group of living gymnosperms, represented by nearly 700 species worldwide. They include the common pine, spruce, fir, and redwood trees that make up a large share of the forests in the temperate regions of the world. Conifers have enormous economic importance. Their wood is used for residential building, to manufacture paper, and as a source of heat. Compounds from their resins are used for a variety of industrial purposes.

▲ *Most conifers retain their leaves year-round.*

CYCADS

Cycads (SY kads) are beautiful palmlike plants that have large cones. Cycads first appeared in the fossil record during the Triassic Period, 225 million years ago. Huge forests of cycads thrived when dinosaurs roamed Earth. Today, only nine genera of cycads exist. Cycads can be found growing naturally in tropical and subtropical places such as Mexico, the West Indies, Florida, and parts of Asia, Africa, and Australia.

▶ *A Sago Palm, Cycas revoluta*

▲ *Ginkgoes are often planted in urban settings, where their toughness and resistance to air pollution make them popular shade trees.*

GINKGOES

Ginkgoes (GING kohs) were common when dinosaurs were alive, but today the group contains only one species, *Ginkgo biloba*. The living *Ginkgo* species looks similar to its fossil ancestors—in fact, *G. biloba* may be one of the oldest seed plant species alive today.

GNETOPHYTES

About 70 present-day species of gnetophytes (NET oh fyts) are known, placed in just three genera. The reproductive scales of these plants are clustered in cones.

▶ *Welwitschia mirabilis, an inhabitant of the Namibian desert in southwestern Africa, is one of the most remarkable gnetophytes. Its huge leathery leaves grow continuously and spread across the ground.*

Cones

Angios

KEY CHARA

Angiosperms are
in a closed ovary
of a reproductive
flower. Seeds are
fertilization event
embryo and a tri
As seeds mature,
fruits that help to

Organization

Movement Ad
grains, male ga
are carried by c
where they rele

Water Transp

Reproduction
of generations;
stage is domina
within the parer
sperm to eggs,
for fertilization.

GROUPS OF ANGIOSPERMS CONTINUED...

MONOCOTS

The monocots include an estimated 65,000 species, roughly 20 percent of all flowering plants. They get their name from the single seed leaf found in monocot embryos, and they include some of the plants that are most important to human cultures. Monocots grown as crops account for a majority of the food produced by agriculture. These crops include wheat, rice, barley, corn, and sugar cane. Common grasses are monocots, as are onions, bananas, orchids, coconut palms, tulips, and irises.

Aerial
roots

▲ Onions are just one of many examples of monocot crop species.

▲ This African hillside is dotted with clumps of Wild Pampas Grass.

▲ Many orchid species are grown by enthusiasts for their rare beauty. Notice the aerial roots on this specimen, which grows as an epiphyte in its natural environment.

◄ After harvest, sugar cane regrows without being planted again for several cycles.

Whatever
to Monoc

Traditionally, fl
just two groups
number of seed
ever, molecular
aren't really one
flowering plant
some of the mc
monocots fall r
indeed a single
informal, thoug

Eco•Alert

Coevolution: Losing the Pollinators

The successes of flowering plants are clearly due to coevolution with their insect pollinators. Common honey bees are among the most important of these, because they gather nectar from the flowers of hundreds of plant species and spread pollen from plant to plant as they go.

Unfortunately, beekeepers around the world, including the United States, are facing a serious crisis. "Colony collapse disorder," as beekeepers describe it, causes bees to fly away from the hive and either never return, or return only to weaken and die. The disease threatens to affect scores of important crops, which depend upon bees to produce fruit and seeds. Suspicion has centered on a fungus or a virus that might spread from colony to colony, but at this point there is no definitive cause or cure.

EUDICOTS: "TRUE DICOTS"

Eudicots (YOO dy kahts) account for about 75 percent of all angiosperm species. The name means "true dicots," and these plants are the ones usually given as examples of dicot stem, leaf, and flower structure. Eudicots have distinctive pollen grains with three grooves on their surfaces, and DNA studies strongly support their classification in a single group. They include a number of important subgroups, five of which are described here.

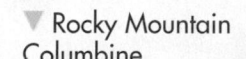

Ranunculales

The ranunculales subgroup (ruh NUNH kyu lay les) includes, and is named after, buttercups (genus *Ranunculus*). Also included in this subgroup are a number of well-known flowers such as columbines, poppies, barberries, and moonseed.

▼ Rocky Mountain Columbine

▲ Clusterhead Pinks

Caryophyllales

Cacti are probably the most well-known plants in the caryophyllales subgroup (KAR ee oh fy lay les). Pinks and carnations, spinach, rhubarb, and insect-eating plants, such as sundews and pitcher plants, are also members.

Saxifragales

Plants in the saxifragales (SAK suh frij ay les) subgroup include peonies, witch hazel, gooseberries, and coral bells.

Rosids

The rosids include, as you might expect, the roses. However, this subgroup also includes many popular fruits, such as oranges, raspberries, strawberries, and apples. Some of the best-known trees, including poplars, willows, and maples, are also members.

▲ Orange

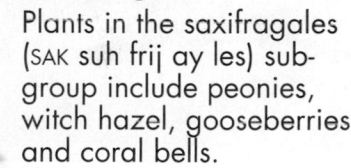
◄ Peony

Asterids

The nearly 80,000 asterid species include sunflowers, azaleas, snapdragons, blueberries, tomatoes, and potatoes.

▼ *The flower heads in a field of sunflowers all track the sun as it moves across the sky; thus, they all face the same direction.*

Animals

Snow Leopard

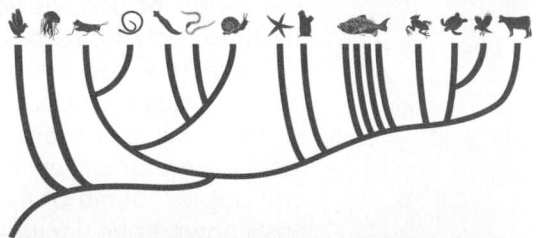

KEY CHARACTERISTICS

Animals are multicellular, heterotrophic, eukaryotic organisms whose cells lack cell walls.

● A Closer Look

A Common Ancestor

Recent molecular studies and cladistic analyses recognize the clade Choanozoa to be the true sister group to all Metazoa—multicellular animals. Choanozoa is one group of organisms formerly called "protists" and is named for choanoflagellates (art and photo right), single-celled, colonial organisms that look like certain cells of sponges and flatworms. Evidence suggests that the choanoflagellates alive today are the best living examples of what the last common ancestor of metazoans looked like.

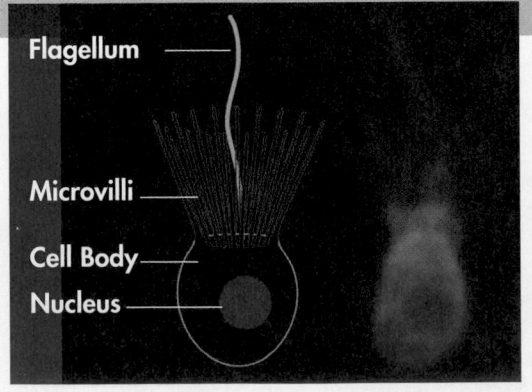

Flagellum

Microvilli

Cell Body

Nucleus

Porifera (Sponges)

Feeding and Digestion Filter feeders; intracellular digestion.

Circulation Via flow of water through body

Respiration Oxygen diffuses from water into cells as water flows through body.

Excretion Wastes diffuse from cells into water as water flows through body.

Response No nervous system; little capacity to respond to environmental changes.

Movement Juveniles drift or swim freely; adults are stationary.

Reproduction Most—sexual with internal fertilization; water flowing out of sponge disperses sperm, which fertilizes eggs inside sponge(s); may reproduce asexually by budding or producing gemmules.

KEY CHARACTERISTICS

Sponges are the simplest animals. They are classified as animals because they are multicellular, heterotrophic, lack cell walls, and have some specialized cells. They are aquatic, lack true tissues and organs, and have internal skeletons of spongin and/or spicules of calcium carbonate or silica. Sponges have no body symmetry.

GROUPS OF SPONGES

There are more than 5000 species of sponges; most are marine. Three major groups are described below.

DEMOSPONGIAE: Typical sponges

More than 90 percent of all living sponge species are in this group, including the few freshwater species. They have skeletons made of spongin, a flexible protein. Some species have silica spicules. Examples: Yellow Sponge, bath sponges, Carnivorous Mediterranean Sponge, tube sponges

▼ **Orange Elephant Ear Sponge**

HEXACTINELLIDA: Glass sponges

Glass sponges live in the deep ocean and are especially abundant in the Antarctic. They are called "glass" sponges because their skeletons are made of glasslike silica spicules. Examples: Venus's Flower Basket, Cloud Sponge

◄ **Glass Sponge**

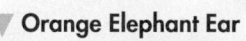

CALCAREA: Calcareous sponges

Calcareous sponges live in shallow, tropical marine waters and are the only sponges with calcium carbonate spicules. Example: *Clathrina*

Yellow Tubular Sponge ▶

Cnidarians

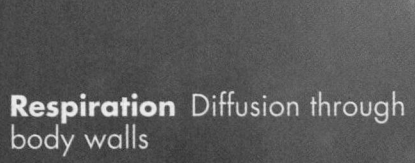

▲ Compass Jellyfish

KEY CHARACTERISTICS

Cnidarians are aquatic, mostly carnivorous, and the simplest animals to have specialized tissues (outer skin and lining of the gastrovascular cavity) and body symmetry (radial). Their tentacles have stinging cells called nematocysts used in feeding.

Feeding and Digestion Predatory, stinging prey with nematocysts; digestion begins extracellularly in gastrovascular cavity and is completed intracellularly; indigestible materials leave body through single opening; many, especially reef-building corals, also depend on symbiotic algae, or zooxanthellae.

Circulation No internal transport system; nutrients typically diffuse through body.

Respiration Diffusion through body walls

Excretion Cellular wastes diffuse through body walls.

Response Some specialized sensory cells: nerve cells in nerve net, statocysts that help determine up and down, eyespots (ocelli) made of light-detecting cells

Movement Polyps stationary, medusas free-swimming; some, such as sea anemones, can burrow and creep very slowly; others move using muscles that work with a hydrostatic skeleton and water in gastrovascular cavity; medusas such as jellyfish move by jet propulsion generated by muscle contractions.

Reproduction Most—alternate between sexual (most species by external fertilization) and asexual (polyps produce new polyps or medusae by budding)

The color of this star coral is caused by zooxanthellae algae living within it.

Eco•Alert

Coral Symbionts

Reef-building coral animals depend on symbiotic algae called zooxanthellae for certain vital nutritional needs. In many places, reef-building corals live close to the upper end of their temperature tolerance zone. If water temperatures rise too high, the coral-zooxanthellae symbiosis breaks down, and corals turn white in what is called "coral bleaching." If corals don't recover their algae soon, they weaken and die. This is one reason why coral reefs are in grave danger from global warming.

GROUPS OF CNIDARIANS

There are more than 9000 species of cnidarians.

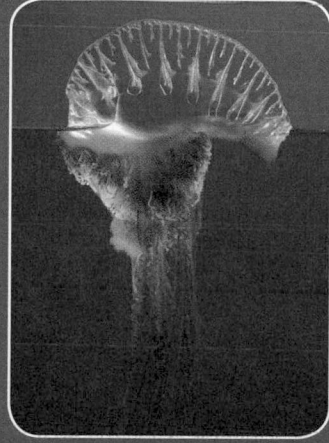

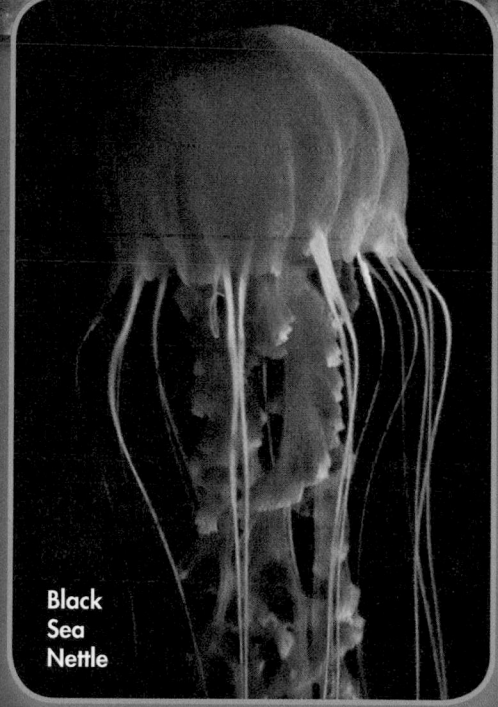

Black
Sea
Nettle

HYDROZOA: Hydras and their relatives

Hydras and their relatives spend most of their time as polyps and are either colonial or solitary. They reproduce asexually (by budding), sexually, or they alternate between sexual and asexual reproduction. Examples: hydra, Portuguese man-of-war

A Portuguese man-of-war is actually a colony of polyps.

ANTHOZOA: Corals and sea anemones

Corals and sea anemones are colonial or solitary polyps with no medusa stage. The central body is surrounded by tentacles. They reproduce sexually or asexually. Examples: reef corals, sea anemones, sea pens, sea fans

Sea Anemone

SCYPHOZOA: Jellyfishes

Jellyfishes spend most of their time as medusas; some species bypass the polyp stage. They reproduce sexually and sometimes asexually by budding. Examples: lion's mane jellyfish, moon jelly, sea wasp

This purple-striped jelly (Pelagia noctiluca) has the ability to bioluminesce, or give off light.

Arthropods

KEY CHARACTERISTICS

Arthropods are the most diverse of all multicellular organisms. They have segmented bodies and jointed appendages. They are supported by tough exoskeletons made of chitin, which they periodically shed as they grow. Arthropods are coelomate protostomes with bilateral symmetry.

Eco•Alert

Beetle Damage

You probably know that some insects can seriously damage crop plants. But insects affect plants in natural habitats, too. One example is the mountain pine beetle, which is dramatically extending its range. Global warming appears to be enabling the beetle to survive farther north, and at higher altitudes, than it used to. The new beetle infestation is causing extensive damage to northern and high-altitude forests in North America. The death of millions of acres of trees has resulted in the release of large amounts of carbon dioxide, a greenhouse gas, into the atmosphere. You can see the sort of damage the beetles cause in the photo at right.

▲ Mountain pine beetle damage to pine trees in White River National Forest, Colorado

Feeding and Digestion Extremely diverse: herbivores, carnivores, detritivores, parasites, bloodsuckers, scavengers, filter feeders; digestive system with two openings; many feeding specializations in different groups

Circulation Open circulatory system with heart and arteries

Respiration Terrestrial—tracheal tubes or book lungs; aquatic—gills or book gills (horseshoe crabs)

Excretion Terrestrial—Malpighian tubules; aquatic—diffusion into water

Response Well-developed nervous system with brain; sophisticated sense organs

Movement Muscles attached internally to jointed exoskeletons

Reproduction Usually sexual, although some species may reproduce asexually under certain circumstances; many undergo metamorphosis during development

Most animals, including this land crab, are arthropods.

GROUPS OF ARTHROPODS

Phylum Arthropoda contains more known species than any other phylum. Scientists have identified more than 1,000,000 arthropod species, and some scientists expect there are millions yet to be identified. Arthropods are classified based on the number and structure of body segments and appendages.

▲ Lobster

CRUSTACEA: Crustaceans

There are crustacean species in almost every habitat, but most are aquatic, and most of these are marine. They have two or three body sections, two pairs of antennae, and chewing mouthparts called mandibles. Many have a carapace, or "shell," that covers part or all of the body. Examples: crabs, lobsters, crayfish, pill bugs, water fleas, barnacles

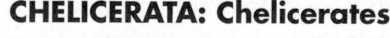

CHELICERATA: Chelicerates

Living chelicerates include horseshoe crabs and arachnids. (Their extinct relatives include trilobites and giant "sea-scorpions.") Most living chelicerates are terrestrial. The body is composed of two parts— the cephalothorax and abdomen. The first pair of appendages are specialized feeding structures called chelicerae. Chelicerates have no antennae.

Horseshoe crabs are actually more closely related to spiders than to crabs!

Merostomata: Horseshoe crabs

The class Merostomata once included many species, but only four species of horseshoe crab survive today. All are marine. They have five pairs of walking legs and a long, spinelike tail.

Arachnida: Arachnids

The vast majority of arachnids are terrestrial. They have four pairs of walking legs and no tail. Examples: spiders, ticks, mites, scorpions, daddy longlegs

▲ Mexican Fireleg Tarantula

UNIRAMIA: Uniramians

Most uniramians are terrestrial, although some are aquatic for all or part of their lives. They have one pair of antennae, mandibles, and unbranched appendages. Uniramians include at least three fourths of all known animal species!

Uniramians include centipedes, millipedes, and insects—more than three fourths of all known animal species, including this green snaketail dragonfly.

Praying Mantis

Insecta: Insects

There are more than 1,000,000 insect species in more than 25 orders. An insect body is divided into three parts—head, thorax, and abdomen. Insects have three pairs of legs and usually one or two pairs of wings attached to the thorax. Some insects undergo complete metamorphosis.
Examples: termites, ants, beetles, dragonflies, flies, moths, grasshoppers

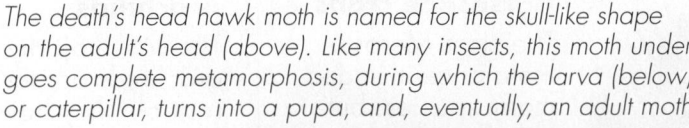

The death's head hawk moth is named for the skull-like shape on the adult's head (above). Like many insects, this moth undergoes complete metamorphosis, during which the larva (below), or caterpillar, turns into a pupa, and, eventually, an adult moth.

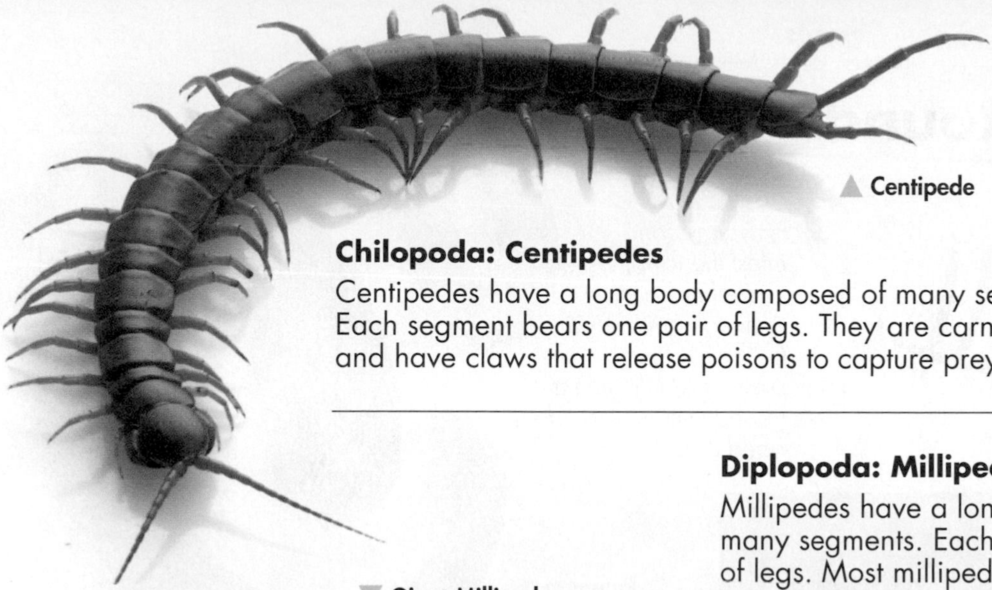

▲ Centipede

Chilopoda: Centipedes

Centipedes have a long body composed of many segments. Each segment bears one pair of legs. They are carnivorous and have claws that release poisons to capture prey.

Diplopoda: Millipedes

Millipedes have a long body composed of many segments. Each segment bears two pairs of legs. Most millipedes are herbivorous.

▼ Giant Millipede

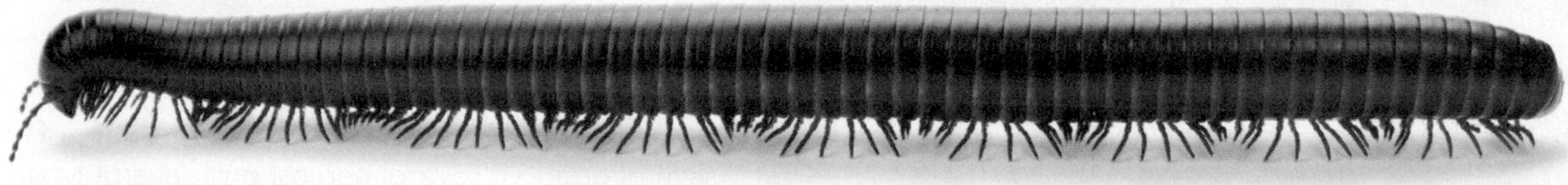

Insecta (continued)

▼ Leaf Beetle

Many "bugs" benefit humans. For example, ladybugs (which are not all "ladies") eat garden pests and bees pollinate plants. Insects such as praying mantises, katydids, flies, moths, beetles, and ants also have important roles in ecosystems.

Flower Beetle ▲

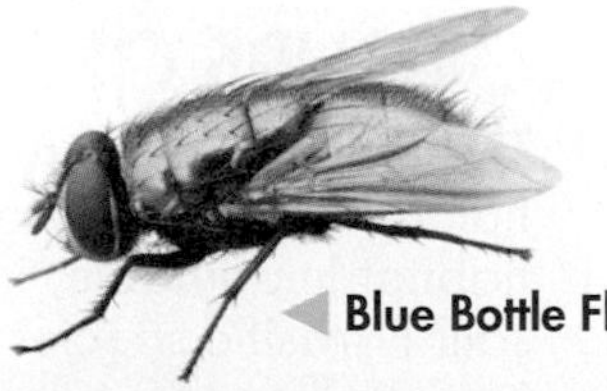

Blue Bottle Fly ◄

Honeybee ▲

Ladybug ▲

▼ Horn Katydid

Forest Ant ▲

Nematodes (Roundworms)

Pinworms can infest the intestinal tract of humans. Although anyone can become infected with pinworms, infection is most common in children aged 5 to 10.

Pinworm ▶
(colorized SEM)

KEY CHARACTERISTICS

Nematodes, or roundworms, are unsegmented worms with a tough outer cuticle, which they shed as they grow. This "molting" is one reason that nematodes are now considered more closely related to arthropods than to other wormlike animals. Nematodes are the simplest animals to have a "one-way" digestive system through which food passes from mouth to anus. They are protostomes and have a pseudocoelom.

Feeding and Digestion Some predators, some parasites, and some decomposers; one-way digestive tract with mouth and anus

Circulation By diffusion

Respiration Gas exchange through body walls

Excretion Through body walls

Response Simple nervous system consisting of several ganglia, several nerves, and several types of sense organs

Movement Muscles work with hydrostatic skeleton, enabling aquatic species to move like water snakes and soil-dwelling species to move by thrashing around.

Reproduction Sexual with internal fertilization; separate sexes; parasitic species may lay eggs in several hosts or host organs.

GROUPS OF ROUNDWORMS

There are more than 15,000 known species of roundworms, and there may be half a million species yet to be described. Free-living species live in almost every habitat imaginable, including fresh water, salt water, hot springs, ice, and soil. Parasitic species live on or inside a wide range of organisms, including insects, humans, and many domesticated animals and plants. Examples: *Ascaris lumbricoides*, hookworms, pinworms, *Trichinella, C. elegans*

● A Closer Look ▶

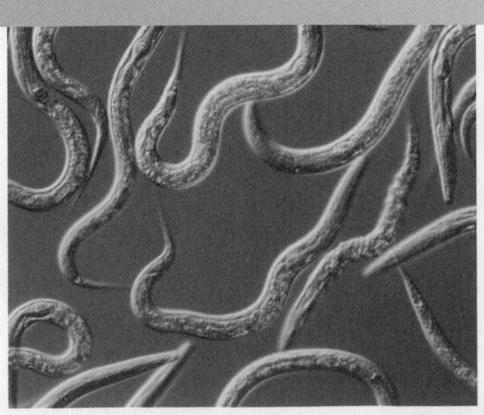

A Model Organism?

Caenorhabditis elegans is a small soil nematode. Fifty years ago, this species was selected as a "model organism" for the study of genetics and development. We can now chart the growth and development of *C. elegans*, cell by cell, from fertilization to adult. This information is invaluable in understanding the development of other species—including many other nematodes that cause serious disease.

◀ **C. elegans** (LM 64×)

Platyhelminthes (Flatworms)

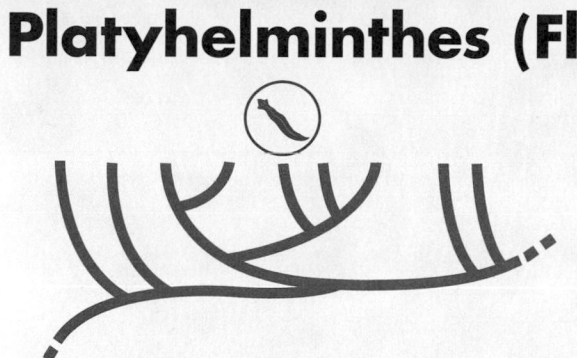

Some marine flatworms have astonishing colors and patterns!

▲ **Blue Pseudoceros Flatworm**

KEY CHARACTERISTICS

Flatworms are soft worms with tissues and internal organ systems. They are the simplest animals to have three embryonic germ layers, bilateral symmetry, and cephalization. They are acoelomates.

Feeding and Digestion Free-living—predators or scavengers that suck food in through a pharynx and digest it in a system that has one opening. Parasitic—feed on blood, tissue fluids, or cell pieces of the host, using simpler digestive systems than free-living species have. Tapeworms, which absorb nutrients from food that the host has already digested, have no digestive system.

Circulation By diffusion

Respiration Gas exchange by diffusion

Excretion Some—flame cells remove excess water and may remove metabolic wastes such as ammonia and urea. Many flame cells are connected to tubules that release substances through pores in the skin.

Response Free-living—several ganglia connected by nerve cords that run through the body, along with eye-spots and other specialized sensory cells; parasitic—simpler nervous system than free-living forms have

Movement Free-living—using cilia and muscle cells.

Reproduction Free-living—most are hermaphrodites that reproduce sexually with internal fertilization; parasitic—commonly reproduce asexually by fission but also often reproduce sexually

GROUPS OF FLATWORMS

Flatworms are an amazingly diverse group of worms that include more than 20,000 species. They have historically been placed into three classes, but these taxa now appear not to be true clades, and will probably change.

TREMATODA: Flukes

Most flukes are parasites that infect internal organs of their hosts, but some infect external parts such as skin or gills. The life cycle typically involves more than one host or organ. Examples: *Schistosoma*, liver fluke

TURBELLARIA: Turbellarians

Turbellarians are free-living aquatic and terrestrial predators and scavengers. Many are colorful marine species. Examples: planarians, polyclad flatworm

CESTODA: Tapeworms

Tapeworms are very long intestinal parasites that lack a digestive system and absorb nutrients directly through their body walls. The tapeworm body is composed of many repeated sections (proglottids) that contain both male and female reproductive organs.

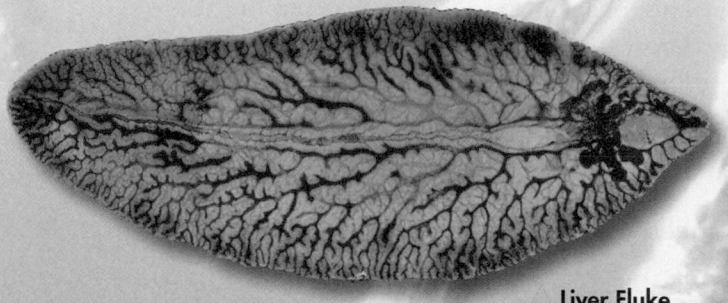

Liver Fluke

Annelids (Segmented Worms)

KEY CHARACTERISTICS

Annelids are coelomate protostome worms whose bodies are composed of segments separated by internal partitions. The annelid digestive system has two openings.

Peacock worms, whose feather-shaped gills look somewhat like peacock feathers, are marine annelids, or polychaetes.

Feeding and Digestion Filter feeders, carnivores, or parasites; many obtain food using a muscular pharynx, often equipped with "teeth"; widely varied digestive systems—some, such as earthworms, have complex digestive tracts.

Circulation Closed circulatory system with dorsal and ventral blood vessels; dorsal vessel pumps blood like a heart.

Respiration Aquatic—gills; terrestrial—skin

Excretion Digestive waste exits through anus; nitrogenous wastes eliminated by nephridia

Response Nervous system includes a rudimentary brain and several nerve cords; sense organs best-developed in free-living saltwater species

Movement Hydrostatic skeleton based on sealed body segments surrounded by longitudinal and circular muscles; many annelids have appendages that enable movement.

Reproduction Most—sexual, some through external fertilization with separate sexes, but others are simultaneous hermaphrodites that exchange sperm; most have a trochophore larval stage

● **Did You Know?**

Not-So-Modern Medicine

You may have heard that medieval healers used leeches to remove "excess" blood from patients and to clean wounds after surgery. But did you know that leeches—or at least compounds from leech saliva—have a place in modern medicine? Leech saliva contains the protein hirudin, which prevents blood from clotting. Some surgeons use leeches to relieve pressure caused by blood that pools in tissues after plastic surgery. Hirudin is also used to prevent unwanted blood clots.

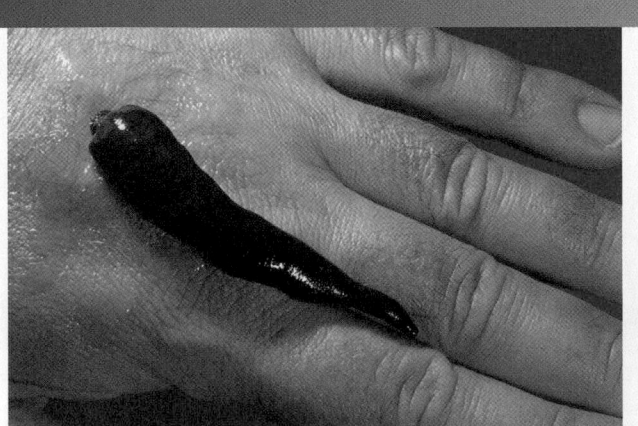

▲ *Leech* (Hirudo medicinalis) *drawing blood from a hand*

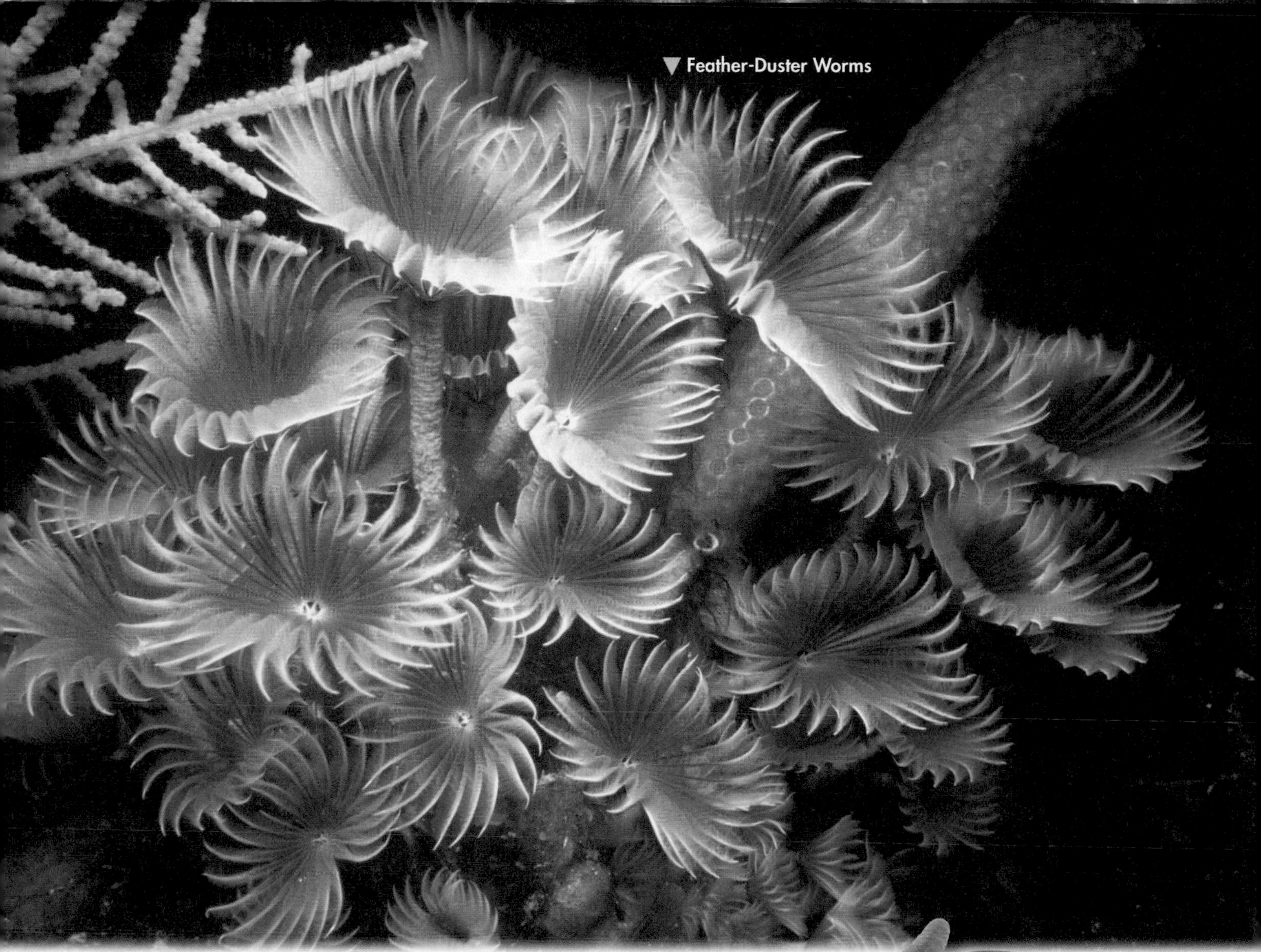

▼ Feather-Duster Worms

GROUPS OF ANNELIDS

There are more than 15,000 species of annelids.

HIRUDINEA: Leeches

Most leeches live in fresh water. They lack appendages. Leeches may be carnivores or blood-sucking external parasites. Example: medicinal leech *(Hirudo medicinalis)*

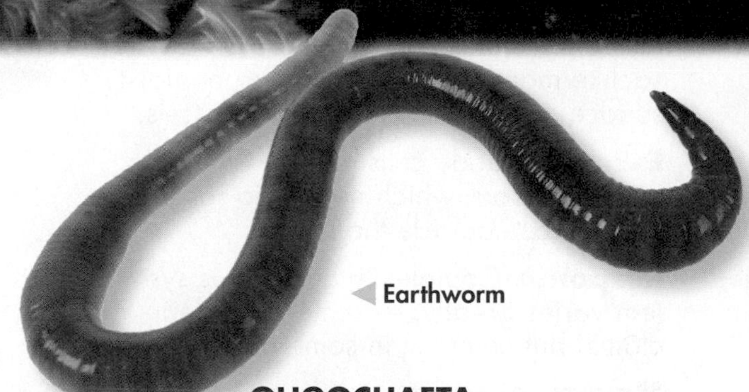

◀ Earthworm

POLYCHAETA: Polychaetes

Polychaetes live in salt water; many move with paddle-like appendages called parapodia tipped with bristle-like setae. Examples: sandworms, bloodworms, fanworms, feather-duster worms

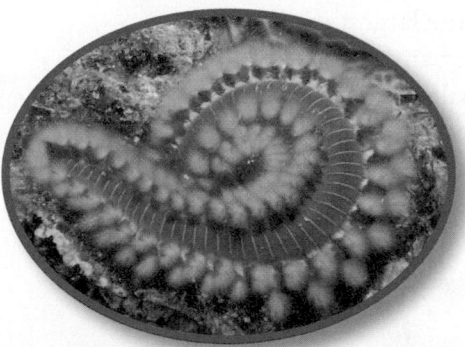

The white, bristle-like structures on the sides of this bearded fireworm are setae.

OLIGOCHAETA: Oligochaetes

Oligochaetes live in soil or fresh water. They lack appendages. Some use setae for movement but have fewer than polychaetes.
Examples: *Tubifex*, earthworms

Mollusks

Colossal Squid

KEY CHARACTERISTICS

Mollusks have soft bodies that typically include a muscular foot. Body forms vary greatly. Many mollusks possess a hard shell secreted by the mantle, but in some, the only hard structure is internal. Mollusks are coelomate protostomes with bilateral symmetry.

Feeding and Digestion Digestive system with two openings; diverse feeding styles—mollusks can be herbivores, carnivores, filter feeders, detritivores, or parasites

Circulation Snails and clams—open circulatory system; octopi and squid—closed circulatory system

Respiration Aquatic mollusks—gills inside the mantle cavity; land mollusks—a saclike mantle cavity whose large, moist surface area is lined with blood vessels.

Excretion Body cells release ammonia into the blood, which nephridia remove and release outside the body.

Response Complexity of nervous system varies greatly; extremely simple in clams, but complex in some octopi.

Movement Varies greatly, by group. Some never move as adults, while others are very fast swimmers.

Reproduction Sexual; many aquatic species have a free-swimming trochophore larval stage.

•Did You Know?

The Colossal Squid

The colossal squid, the largest of all mollusks, has the largest eyes of any known animal. One 8-meter-long, 450-kilogram specimen of the species *Mesonychoteuthis hamiltoni* had eyes 28 centimeters across—larger than most dinner plates! The lens of this huge eye was the size of an orange.

GROUPS OF MOLLUSKS

Mollusks are traditionally divided into several classes based on characteristics of the foot and the shell; specialists estimate that there are between 50,000 and 200,000 species of mollusks alive today.

▲ Chambered Nautilus

▲ Giant Clam

BIVALVIA: Bivalves

Bivalves are aquatic. They have a two-part hinged shell and a wedge-shaped foot. They are mostly stationary as adults. Some burrow in mud or sand; others attach to rocks. Most are filter feeders that use gill siphons to take in water that carries food. Clams have open circulatory systems. Bivalves have the simplest nervous systems among mollusks. Examples: clams, oysters, scallops, mussels

Garden Snail ▲

GASTROPODA: Gastropods

There are both terrestrial and aquatic gastropods. Most have a single spiral, chambered shell. Gastropods use a broad, muscular foot to move and have a distinct head region. Snails and slugs feed with a structure called a radula that usually works like sandpaper. Some species are predators whose harpoon-shaped radula carries deadly venom. They have open circulatory systems. Many gastropod species are cross-fertilizing hermaphrodites. Examples: snails, slugs, nudibranchs, sea hares

CEPHALOPODA: Cephalopods

Cephalopods live in salt water. The cephalopod has a highly developed brain and sense organs. The head is attached to a single foot, which is divided into tentacles. They have closed circulatory systems. Octopi use beaklike jaws for feeding; a few are venomous. Cephalopods have the most complex nervous systems among mollusks; octopi have complex behavior and have shown the ability to learn in laboratory settings. Examples: octopi, squids, nautilus, cuttlefish

Nudibranchs, such as this Hypseiodoris species, are marine gastropods without shells. They breathe through gills (the orange structures) on their backs.

Echinoderms

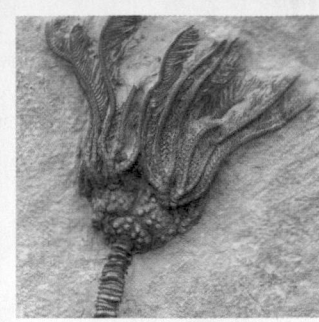

Crinoid fossil, about 400 million years old

Living modern crinoid (feather star)

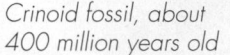
• **A Look Back in Time**

Crinoids Then and Now

Echinoderms have a long fossil record that dates all the way back to the Cambrian Period. Although these animals have been evolving for millions of years, some fossil crinoids look a great deal like living crinoids.

KEY CHARACTERISTICS

Echinoderms are marine animals that have spiny skin surrounding an endoskeleton. Their unique water vascular system includes tube feet with suction-cuplike ends used in moving and feeding. The water vascular system also plays a role in respiration, circulation, and excretion. Echinoderms are coelomate deuterostomes. Adults exhibit 5-part radial symmetry.

Feeding and Digestion Method varies by group—echinoderms can be filter feeders, detritivores, herbivores, or carnivores.

Circulation Via fluid in the coelom, a rudimentary system of vessels, and the water vascular system

Respiration Gas exchange is carried out by surfaces of tube feet, and, in many species, by skin gills.

Excretion Digestive wastes released through anus; nitrogenous cellular wastes excreted as ammonia through tube feet and skin gills.

Response Minimal nervous system; nerve ring is connected to body sections by radial nerves; most have scattered sensory cells that detect light, gravity, and chemicals secreted by prey.

Movement In most, tube feet work with endoskeleton to enable locomotion.

Reproduction Sexual, with external fertilization; larvae have bilateral symmetry, unlike adults.

You can't miss the 5-part radial symmetry of this red mesh sea star moving across a coral reef.

GROUPS OF ECHINODERMS

There are more than 7000 species of echinoderms.

◀ Sea Star

CRINOIDEA: Crinoids

Crinoids are filter feeders; some use tube feet along feathery arms to capture plankton. The mouth and anus are on the upper surface of the body disk. Some are stationary as adults while others can "walk" using short "arms" on the lower body surface. Examples: sea lily, feather star

▶ Feeding Crinoid

ASTEROIDEA: Sea stars

Sea stars are bottom dwellers whose star-shaped bodies have flexible joints. They are carnivorous—the stomach pushes through the mouth onto the body tissues of prey and pours out digestive enzymes. The stomach then retracts with the partially digested prey; digestion is completed inside the body. Examples: crown-of-thorns sea star, sunstar

▼ Basket Star

ECHINOIDEA: Echinoids

Echinoids lack arms. Their endoskeletons are rigid and boxlike and covered with movable spines. Most echinoids are herbivores or detritivores that use five-part jawlike structures to scrape algae from rocks. Examples: sea urchin, sand dollar, sea biscuit

▼ *Sea urchins grazing on kelp*

OPHIUROIDEA: Ophiuroids

Ophiuroids have small body disks, long, armored arms, and flexible joints. Most are filter feeders or detritivores. Examples: brittle star, basket star

▼ Sea cucumber

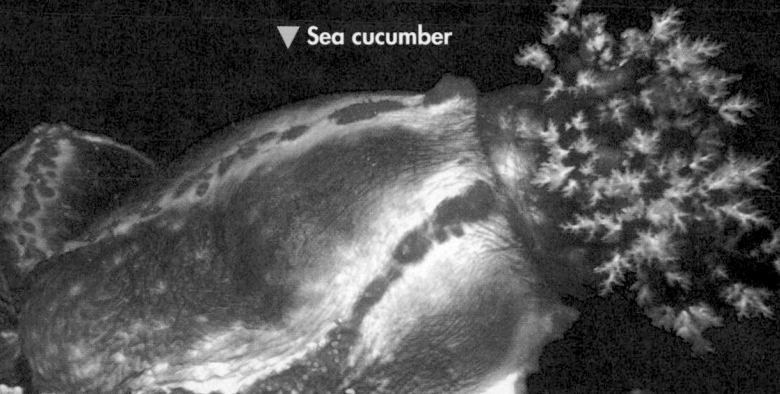

HOLOTHUROIDEA: Sea cucumbers

Sea cucumbers have a cylindrical, rubbery body with a reduced endoskeleton and no arms. They typically lie on their side and move along the ocean floor by the combined action of tube feet and body-wall muscles. These filter feeders or detritivores use a set of retractable feeding tentacles on one end to take in sand and detritus, from which they glean food.

Nonvertebrate Chordates

Tunicates are chordates named for the colorful tunic-like covering the adults have. As larvae, tunicates have all the characteristics of chordates, as well as bilateral symmetry, but as adults, they look very, very different.

KEY CHARACTERISTICS

The nonvertebrate chordates are the only chordates that lack a backbone. Like other chordates, they have a nerve cord, notochord, pharyngeal pouches, and a tail at some point during development. They are coelomate deuterostomes. The two subphyla, tunicates and lancelets, differ significantly.

Feeding and Digestion Filter feeders; tunicates—in most, water carrying food particles enters through an incurrent siphon; food is strained out in the pharynx and passed to the digestive system; lancelets—mucus in the pharynx catches food particles carried in by water, which are then carried into digestive tract

Circulation Closed; tunicates—heart pumps blood by "wringing out," and flow periodically reverses direction; lancelets—no heart, but blood vessels pump blood through body in one direction

Respiration Tunicates—gas exchange occurs in the gills and across other body surfaces; lancelets—through pharynx and body surfaces

Excretion Tunicates—most through excurrent siphon; lancelets—flame cells in nephridia release water and nitrogenous wastes into the atrium and out through an opening called an atriopore

Response Cerebral ganglion, few specialized sensory organs; tunicates—sensory cells in and on the siphons and other internal surfaces help control the amount of water passing through the pharynx; lancelets—a pair of eyespots detect light

Movement Tunicates—free-swimming larvae, but most are stationary as adults; lancelets—no appendages: they move by contracting muscles paired on either side of the body

Reproduction Tunicates—most sexual and hermaphroditic with external fertilization, but some reproduce by budding; most have free-swimming tadpole-like larvae that metamorphose into adults; lancelets—sexual with external fertilization

Eco Alert

Asian Stalked Tunicate

Out-of-Control Tunicates

You've never heard of them, but Asian stalked tunicates are disrupting marine ecosystems in Washington State; Prince Edward Island, Canada; and elsewhere. Tunicate larvae are carried in the ballast water of freight ships and discharged wherever the ships make port. There, away from their usual predators, the tunicates grow out of control, smothering shellfish beds and covering boats, docks, and underwater equipment. Researchers are still trying to figure out how to control them.

GROUPS OF NONVERTEBRATE CHORDATES

There are two major groups of nonvertebrate chordates: tunicates and lancelets (sometimes called amphioxus).

Two lancelets, Branchiostoma lanceolatum, poking out of sand.

CEPHALOCHORDATA: Lancelets

Lancelets are fishlike animals that have bilateral symmetry and live in salt water. They are filter feeders and have no internal skeleton. Example: *Branchiostoma*

▼ **Pastel Sea Squirt**

UROCHORDATA: Tunicates

Tunicates are filter feeders that live in salt water. Most adults have a tough outer covering ("tunic") and no body symmetry; most display chordate features and bilateral symmetry only during larval stages. Many adults are stationary; some are free-swimming. Examples: sea squirts, sea peaches, salps

Sea Squirts

Fishes

KEY CHARACTERISTICS

The word fish *is used informally to describe aquatic vertebrates that look similar even though they belong to several different clades, because all are adapted to life in water. Most vertebrates we call fishes have paired fins, scales, and gills.*

Feeding and Digestion Varies widely, both within and between groups: herbivores, carnivores, parasites, filter feeders, detritivores; digestive organs often include specialized teeth and jaws, crop, esophagus, stomach, liver, pancreas

Circulation Closed, single-loop circulatory system; two-chambered heart

Respiration Gills; some have specialized lungs or other adaptations that enable them to obtain oxygen from air.

Excretion Diffusion across gill membranes; kidneys

Response Brain with many parts; highly developed sense organs, including lateral line system

Movement Paired muscles on either side of backbone; many have highly maneuverable fins; the largest groups have two sets of paired fins; some have a gas-filled swim bladder that regulates buoyancy.

Reproduction Methods vary within and between groups: external or internal fertilization; oviparous, ovoviviparous, or viviparous

---

● **A Look Back in Time** ▶

Live Birth in Devonian Seas

You might think that live birth is a recent addition to chordate diversity. Guess again. Recent fossil finds of fishes from the Devonian Period show that at least one group of fishes was already bearing live young 380 million years ago. Two incredibly well preserved fossils, including that of the fish *Materpiscis*, show the remains of young with umbilical cords still attached to their mother's bodies. This is the earliest fossil evidence of viviparity in vertebrates.

▲ *Artist's conception of Materpiscis giving birth*

GROUPS OF FISHES

Fishes are the largest group of vertebrates, including more than 30,000 species. Evolutionary classification of these animals is still a work in progress; many traditional groups are not clades. "Fishes" actually represent several ancient clades, one of which includes tetrapods, or four-limbed vertebrates. Fishes, as we treat them here, include two groups of jawless fishes (hagfishes and lampreys), cartilaginous fishes, and bony fishes.

Sweetlips are, despite their funny faces, easily recognizable as fish.

"JAWLESS FISHES"

Hagfishes and lampreys make up separate clades, but their bodies share common features that distinguish them from other fishes. They have no jaws, lack vertebrae, and their skeletons are made of fiber and cartilage.

PETROMYZONTIDA: Lampreys

Lampreys are mostly filter feeders as larvae and parasites as adults. The head of an adult lamprey is taken up almost completely by a circular, tooth-bearing, sucking disk with a round mouth. Adult lampreys typically attach themselves to fishes. They hold on to their hosts using the teeth in their sucking disk and then scrape away at the skin with a rasping tongue. Lampreys then suck up their host's tissues and body fluids. Because lampreys feed mostly on blood, they are called "vampires of the sea."

▲ Lamprey mouth

▲ Lamprey

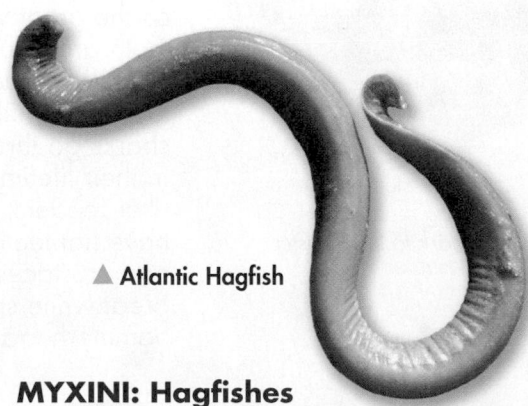

▲ Atlantic Hagfish

MYXINI: Hagfishes

Hagfishes have pinkish gray wormlike bodies and four or six short tentacles around their mouths. They retain notochords as adults. Hagfishes lack image-forming eyes, but have light-detecting sensors scattered around their bodies. They feed on dead and dying animals using a rasping tongue that scrapes away layers of flesh.

Tiger Shark

CHONDRICHTHYES: Cartilaginous Fishes

Members of this clade are considered "cartilaginous" because they lack true bone; their skeletons are built entirely of cartilage. Most cartilaginous fishes also have tough scales, which make their skin as rough as sandpaper.

Holocephalans: Chimaeras

Chimaeras have smooth skin that lacks scales. Most have just a few platelike, grinding teeth and a venomous spine located in front of the dorsal fin. Examples: ghostfish, ratfish, rabbitfish

Elephant Fish

Elasmobranchii: Sharks, skates, and rays

Sharks, skates, and rays are very diverse, but all have skin covered with toothlike scales known as dermal denticles. Elasmobranchii make up the vast majority of living cartilaginous fish species.

Galeomorphi: Sharks

Most of the 350 or so shark species have large, curved asymmetrical tails, torpedo-shaped bodies, and pointed snouts with a mouth underneath. Predatory sharks, such as the great white, have many teeth arranged in rows. As teeth in the front rows are worn out or lost, new teeth replace them. Some sharks go through 20,000 teeth in their lifetime! Other sharks are filter feeders, and some species have flat teeth for crushing mollusk and crustacean shells. Examples: great white shark, whale shark, hammerhead shark

Squalomorphi: Skates and rays

Skates and rays have diverse feeding habits. Some feed on bottom-dwelling invertebrates by using their mouths as powerful vacuums. Others filter-feed on plankton. When not feeding or swimming, many skates and rays cover themselves with a thin layer of sand and rest on the ocean floor. Example: stingray

Dermal denticles on shark skin reduce drag, helping the shark to swim faster. (SEM 40×)

Blue-Spotted Stingray

Hammerhead Shark

OSTEICHTHYES: BONY FISHES

The skeletons of these vertebrates are made of true bone. This clade includes the ancestors and living members of all "higher" vertebrate groups—including tetrapods.

Rainbow Trout

Actinopterygii: Ray-finned fishes

Almost all living bony fishes, such as these rainbow trout, belong to a huge group called ray-finned fishes. The name *ray-finned* refers to the slender bony rays that are connected to one another by a layer of skin to form fins.

Coelacanth

Sarcopterygii: Lobe-finned fishes

Seven living species of bony fishes, including lungfishes and coelacanths, are classified as lobe-finned fishes. Lungfishes live in fresh water; coelacanths live in salt water. The fleshy fins of lobe-finned fishes are supported by strong bones rather than rays. Some of these bones are homologous to the limb bones of land vertebrates. Examples: lungfish, coelacanths

This clade includes the ancestors of tetrapods, which means, that all living tetrapods (including us!) are Sarcopterygians. As a result, the bony-fish clade includes almost half of all chordate species.

Amphibians

Marsupial Frog

KEY CHARACTERISTICS

The word amphibian means "double life," an apt name for these vertebrates, most of which live in water as larvae and on land as adults. Most adult amphibians breathe with lungs, lack scales and claws, and have moist skin that contains mucous glands.

Feeding and Digestion Tadpoles—usually filter feeders or herbivores with long, coiled intestines to digest plant material; adults—carnivores with shorter intestines for processing meat

Circulation Double-loop system with three-chambered heart

Respiration Larvae breathe through skin and gills; most adult species have lungs, though a few use gills; lungless salamanders breathe through their mouth-cavity lining and skin.

Excretion Kidneys produce urine.

Response Well-developed nervous and sensory systems; organs include protective nictitating membrane over moveable eyes, tympanic membranes, lateral line system

Movement Larvae have tails; adults have limbs (except caecilians); some have specialized toes for climbing.

Reproduction Most lay eggs without shells that are fertilized externally; most undergo metamorphosis from aquatic tadpole larvae that breathe with gills to land-dwelling adults, which usually have lungs and limbs.

Eco•Alert

The Frogs Are Disappearing!

Red-Eyed Treefrog

For several decades, scientists have noticed that amphibian populations worldwide have been decreasing, and a number of species have become extinct. Scientists have not yet pinpointed a single cause for this problem. It is, however, becoming clear that amphibians are susceptible to a variety of environmental threats, including habitat loss, ozone depletion, acid rain, water pollution, fungal infections, and introduced aquatic predators.

To better understand this decline, biologists worldwide have been focusing their efforts and sharing data about amphibian populations. One amphibian-monitoring program covers all of North America.

GROUPS OF AMPHIBIANS

The three orders of amphibians include more than 6000 species, roughly 5000 of which are frogs and toads.

Fire Salamander

URODELA: Salamanders and newts

Salamanders and newts have long bodies and tails. Most also have four legs. All are carnivores. Adults usually live in moist woods, where they tunnel under rocks and rotting logs. Some salamanders, such as the mud puppy, keep their gills as adults and live in water all their lives. Examples: barred tiger salamander, red eft

American Toad

ANURA: Frogs and toads

Adult frogs and toads are amphibians without tails that can jump. Frogs tend to have long legs and make long jumps, whereas toads have shorter legs that limit them to shorter hops. Frogs are generally more dependent on bodies of fresh water than toads, which may live in moist woods or even deserts. Examples: treefrogs, leopard frog, American toad, spadefoot toad

APODA: Caecilians

The least-known and most unusual amphibians are the legless caecilians. They have tentacles, and many have fishlike scales embedded in their skin—which shows that not all amphibians fit the general definition. Caecilians live in water or burrow in moist soil or sediment, feeding on small invertebrates such as termites. Examples: ringed caecilian, yellow-striped caecilian

Ringed Caecilian

▶ Because amphibian eggs must develop in water, most amphibians live in moist climates. Some, such as this alpine newt, live on cool, rainy mountain slopes.

Reptiles

Saltwater crocodiles, such as this young one, are the largest living reptiles and sometimes reach 6 meters long. This is about the same length as a giraffe!

KEY CHARACTERISTICS OF REPTILES

Living reptiles, traditionally classified in the class Reptilia, are ectothermic vertebrates with dry, scaly skin; lungs; and amniotic eggs. Modern evolutionary classification now recognizes a larger clade Reptilia that includes living reptiles, extinct dinosaurs, and birds—the living descendants of one dinosaur group.

Feeding and Digestion Feeding methods vary by group; digestive systems—herbivores have long digestive systems to break down plant materials; carnivores may swallow prey whole

Circulation Two loops; heart with two atria and one or two ventricles

Respiration Spongy lungs provide large surface area for gas exchange; lungs operated by muscles and moveable ribs

Excretion Kidneys; urine contains ammonia or uric acid

Response Brain; well-developed senses including, in some species, infrared detectors that can spot warm-bodied prey in the dark

Movement Strong limbs (except snakes)

Reproduction Internal fertilization via cloaca; amniotic egg with leathery shell

Eco•Alert

Calling Doctor 'Gator!

You might think of alligators mostly as killing machines, but their blood may soon provide medicines that can save lives. An alligator's immune system works quite differently from our own. Proteins in their white blood cells can kill multidrug resistant bacteria, disease-causing yeasts, and even HIV. Remarkably, these proteins work against pathogens to which the animals have never been exposed. Researchers are currently sequencing the genes for these proteins and hope to develop them into human medicines in the near future.

GROUPS OF REPTILES

There are nearly 9000 species of reptiles (not including birds).

SPHENODONTA: Tuataras

The tuatara, found only on a few small islands off the coast of New Zealand, is the only living member of this group. Tuataras resemble lizards in some ways, but they lack external ears and retain primitive scales.

Tuatara

SQUAMATA: Lizards, snakes, and relatives

There are more than 8000 species of lizards and snakes. Most lizards have legs, clawed toes, and external ears. Some lizards have evolved highly specialized structures, such as glands in the lower jaw that produce venom. Snakes are legless; they have lost both pairs of legs through evolution. Examples: iguanas, milk snake, coral snake

ARCHOSAURS: Crocodilians; pterosaurs and dinosaurs (extinct); and birds

This clade includes some of the most spectacular animals that have ever lived. The extinct dinosaurs and pterosaurs (flying reptiles), whose adaptive radiations produced some of the largest animals ever to walk Earth or fly above it, are the closest relatives of birds. Living crocodilians are short-legged and have long and typically broad snouts. They are fierce carnivorous predators, but the females are attentive mothers. Crocodilians live only in regions where the climate remains warm year-round. We discuss birds separately. Examples: extinct types: *Tyrannosaurus*, *Pteranodon*; living types: alligators, crocodiles, caimans, and birds (see following pages)

Leopard Gecko

Leopard Tortoise

TESTUDINE: Turtles and tortoises

Turtles and tortoises have a shell built into their skeleton. Most can pull their heads and legs into the shell for protection. Instead of teeth, these reptiles have hornlike ridges covering their jaws equipped with sharp beaklike tips. Strong limbs can lift their body off the ground when walking or, in the case of sea turtles, can drag their body across a sandy shore to lay eggs. Examples: snapping turtles, green sea turtles, Galápagos tortoise

Spectacled Caiman

Birds

Today, only birds have feathers. These delicate, intricately interlocking and beautiful structures keep birds warm and cool and enable most to fly.

Common Kingfisher

KEY CHARACTERISTICS OF BIRDS

Birds, once placed in a class of their own, are now recognized as endothermic reptiles with feathers and hard-shelled, amniotic eggs that are descended from dinosaurs. Birds have two scaly legs and front limbs modified into wings, which enable most species to fly.

Feeding and Digestion No teeth; bills adapted to widely varied foods, including insects, seeds, fruits, nectar, fish, meat; organs of the digestive system include crop, gizzard, cloaca

Circulation Two loops with four-chambered heart; separation of oxygen-rich and oxygen-poor blood

Respiration Constant, one-way flow of air through lungs and air sacs increases the efficiency of gas exchange and supports high metabolic rate

Excretion Kidneys remove nitrogenous wastes from blood, converting them to uric acid, which is excreted through cloaca

Response Brain with large optic lobes and enlarged cerebellum; highly evolved sense organs including, in some species, eyes that can see ultraviolet light

Movement Skeleton made up of lightweight, hollow bones with internal struts for strength; powerful muscles; most fly

Reproduction Internal fertilization via cloaca; amniotic egg with hard, brittle shell; depending on species, newly hatched young may be precocial—downy-feathered chicks able to move around and feed themselves, or altricial—bare-skinned and totally dependent on their parents

● A Look Back in Time ▶

Birds of a Feather

Fossils recently discovered in lake beds in China have greatly expanded our understanding of bird evolution. One exciting discovery was that of a four-winged dinosaur named *Microraptor gui* from about 125 million years ago. *Microraptor gui*, which was related to *Tyrannosaurus rex*, had feathers on both its wings *and* its legs, so some researchers hypothesize that it flew like a biplane! This and other fossils show that several lineages of dinosaurs and ancient birds evolved various kinds of feathers over millions of years.

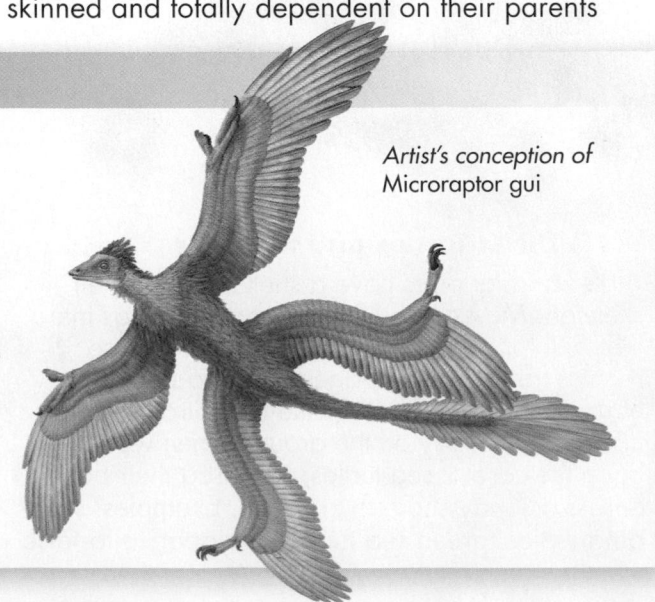

Artist's conception of Microraptor gui

GROUPS OF BIRDS

Evolutionary classification of living birds is still a work in progress, as different techniques and analyses produce different results. There are about 10,000 species. The groups described below illustrate some of the diversity of birds.

Ostrich

PALEOGNATHAE: Ostriches, emus, kiwis, and relatives

This group represents an early branch of the bird family tree that is separate from all other living birds. This clade includes the largest birds alive today. Ostriches can be 2.5 meters tall and weigh 130 kilograms! Kiwis, however, are only about the size of chickens. Roughly a dozen living species are scattered throughout the Southern Hemisphere. All are flightless, but the larger species can run very fast. They generally eat a variety of plant material, insects, and other small invertebrates. Examples: ostrich, emus, brown kiwi, greater rhea, dwarf cassowary

SPHENISCIDAE: Penguins

These flightless birds of the Southern Hemisphere are adapted to extreme cold and hunting in water. Though they cannot fly, they use their wings as flippers when they swim. Penguins have more feathers per square centimeter than any other bird; this density allows them to repel water and conserve heat effectively. Some species form large colonies. Examples: emperor penguin, chinstrap penguin, king penguin

King Penguins

Redhead

ANATIDAE: Ducks, geese, and swans

These birds spend much of their time feeding in bodies of water. Webbed feet enable them to paddle efficiently across the surface of the water. Most fly well, however, and many species migrate thousands of kilometers between breeding and resting locations. Examples: redhead, Ross's goose, trumpeter swan

Ferruginous Hawk

FALCONIDAE AND ACCIPITRIDAE:
Falcons, eagles, and hawks

These fierce predators, often called raptors, typically have powerful hooked bills, large wingspans, and sharp talons. Raptors have powerful flight muscles and keen eyesight, enabling them to see prey at a distance. Examples: Eurasian kestrel, golden eagle, Galápagos hawk

PICIDAE AND RAMPHASTIDAE:
Woodpeckers and toucans

Woodpeckers are tree-dwelling birds with two toes in front and two in back. (Most birds have three in front and one in back; the two-and-two arrangement makes moving up and down tree trunks easier.) Woodpeckers are typically carnivores that eat insects and their larvae. Toucans usually use their huge, often colorful bills to eat fruit. Examples: black woodpecker, keel-billed toucan

Great-Spotted Woodpecker

Keel-Billed Toucan

PASSERIFORMES: Passerines

Also called perching birds, this is by far the largest and most diverse group of birds, with about 5000 species. Most are songbirds. Examples: flycatchers, mockingbirds, cardinals, crows, chickadees, and finches.

Hooded Warbler

Scarlet Tanager

Blue Grosbeak

Lark Sparrow

Great Crested Flycatcher

Mammals

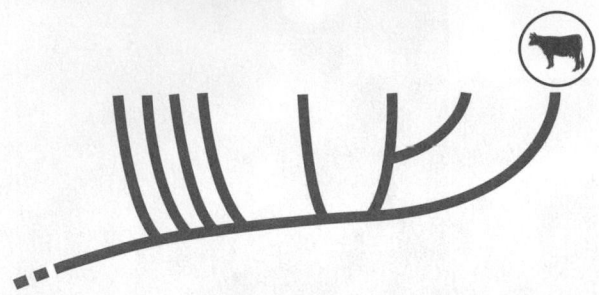

KEY CHARACTERISTICS

Mammals are endothermic vertebrates with hair and mammary glands that produce milk to nourish their young.

Feeding and Digestion Diet varies with group; foods range from seeds, fruits, and leaves to insects, fish, meat, and even blood; teeth, jaws, and digestive organs are adapted to diet

Circulation Two loops; four-chambered heart; separation of oxygen-rich and oxygen-poor blood

Respiration Lungs controlled by two sets of muscles.

Excretion Highly evolved kidneys filter urea from blood and produce urine.

Response Most highly evolved brain of all animals; keen senses

Movement Flexible backbone; variations in limb bones and muscles enable wide range of movement across groups: from burrowing and crawling to walking, running, hopping, and flying

Reproduction Internal fertilization; developmental process varies with group (monotreme, marsupial, placental)

●**Did You Know?**

Platypus: Mix-and-Match Genome

The duckbill platypus has such an odd mix of reptile and mammal features that some scientists thought the first specimens were hoaxes produced by sticking parts of different animals together! Recent genome studies have revealed an equally odd mix of reptilian and mammalian genes. Genes for reptile-like vision, the production of egg yolk, and the production of venom link the platypus to reptiles. Genes for the production of milk link it to other mammals. The evidence provides confirmation that this monotreme represents a truly ancient lineage, one from the time close to that at which mammals branched off from reptiles.

GROUPS OF MAMMALS

The three living groups of mammals are the monotremes, the marsupials, and the placentals. There are about 5000 species of mammals, usually divided into about 26 orders, most of which are placentals. There is only one order of monotremes.

This young moose is enjoying a moment of independence from its mother. Mammals provide intensive parental care to their young.

Short-Beaked Echidna

MONOTREMATA: Monotremes

Monotremes—egg-laying mammals—share two important characteristics with reptiles. First, the digestive, reproductive, and urinary systems of monotremes all open into a cloaca similar to that of reptiles. Second, monotreme development is similar to that of reptiles. Like a reptile, a female monotreme lays soft-shelled eggs incubated outside her body. The eggs hatch in about ten days. Unlike reptiles, however, young monotremes are nourished by mother's milk, which they lick from pores on the surface of her abdomen. Only five monotreme species exist today, all in Australia and New Guinea. Examples: duckbill platypus, echidnas

MARSUPIALIA: Marsupials

Marsupials bear live young at an extremely early stage of development. A fertilized egg develops into an embryo inside the mother's reproductive tract. The embryo is then "born" in what would be an embryonic stage for most other mammals. It crawls across its mother's fur and attaches to a nipple that, in most species, is located in a pouch called the marsupium. The embryo spends several months attached to the nipple. It continues to nurse until it can survive on its own. Examples: kangaroos, wallabies, wombats, opossums

Wombat

PLACENTALIA: Placental Mammals

Placental mammals are the mammals with which you are most familiar. This group gets its name from a structure called the placenta, which is formed when the embryo's tissues join with tissues within the mother's body. Nutrients, gases, and wastes are exchanged between embryo and mother through the placenta. Development may take as little as a few weeks (mice), to as long as two years (elephants). After birth, most placental mammals care for their young and provide them with nourishment by nursing. Examples: mice, cats, dogs, seals, whales, elephants, humans

Chiroptera: Bats

These are the only mammals capable of true flight. There are more than 900 species of bats! They eat mostly insects or fruit and nectar, although a few species feed on the blood of other vertebrates. Examples: fruit bats, little brown myotis, vampire bat

Lioness attacking Greater Kudu

Epauletted Bat, roosting

Carnivora: Carnivores

Many members of this group, such as tigers and hyenas, chase or stalk prey by running or pouncing, then kill with sharp teeth and claws. Dogs, bears, and other members of this group may eat plants as well as meat. Examples: dogs, cats, skunks, seals, bears

Sirenia: Sirenians

Sirenians are herbivores that live in rivers, bays, and warm coastal waters scattered throughout the world. These large, slow-moving mammals lead fully aquatic lives. Examples: manatees, dugongs

Four-Toed Hedgehog mother and baby

Manatee mother and nursing calf

Insectivora: Insectivores

These insect eaters have long, narrow snouts and sharp claws that are well suited for digging. Examples: shrews, moles, hedgehogs

Perissodactyla: Hoofed, odd-toed mammals

Tapir hoof

This group is made up of hoofed animals with an odd number of toes on each foot. Like artiodactyls, this group contains mostly large, grazing animals. Examples: horses, zebras, rhinoceroses

Central American Tapir

Artiodactyla: Hoofed, even-toed mammals

These large, grazing, hoofed mammals have an even number of toes on each foot. Examples: cattle, sheep, pigs, hippopotami

Giraffe Hoof

Angolan Giraffes

Rodentia: Rodents

Marmot

Rodents have a single pair of long, curved incisor teeth in both their upper and lower jaws, used for gnawing wood and other tough plant material. Examples: rats, squirrels, porcupines

Cetacea: Cetaceans

Atlantic Spotted Dolphin

Like sirenians, cetaceans—the group that includes whales and dolphins— are adapted to underwater life, yet must come to the surface to breathe. Most cetaceans live and breed in the ocean. Examples: whales, dolphins

European Hare

Tamandua

Xenarthra: Edentates

The word *edentate* means "toothless," which refers to the fact that some members of this group (sloths and anteaters) have simple teeth without enamel or no teeth at all. Armadillos, however, have more teeth than most other mammals! Examples: sloths, anteaters, armadillos

Lagomorpha: Rabbit, hares, and pikas

Lagomorphs are entirely herbivorous. They differ from rodents by having two pairs of incisors in the upper jaw. Most lagomorphs have hind legs that are adapted for leaping.

Proboscidea: Elephants

These are the mammals with trunks. Some time ago, this group went through an extensive adaptive radiation that produced many species, including mastodons and mammoths, which are now extinct. Only two species, the Asian Elephant and the African elephant, survive today.

Asian Elephant and calf

Primates: Lemurs, monkeys, apes, humans, and relatives

Members of this group are closely related to ancient insectivores but have a highly developed cerebrum and complex behaviors.

Sifaka

Tarsier

Langur

Baboon and baby

Orangutan

Gorilla

Chimpanzee

Data Tables and Graphs

How can you make sense of the data from a science experiment? The first step is to organize the data. You can organize data in data tables and graphs to help you interpret them.

Data Tables

You have gathered your materials and set up your experiment. But before you start, you need to plan a way to record what happens during the experiment. By creating a data table, you can record your observations and measurements in an orderly way.

Suppose, for example, that a scientist conducted an experiment to find out how many kilocalories people of different body masses burned while performing various activities for 30 minutes. The data table below shows the results.

Notice in this data table that the independent variable (body mass) is the heading of the first column. The dependent variable (for Experiment 1, the number of kilocalories burned while bicycling for 30 minutes) is the heading of the next column. Additional columns were added for related experiments.

Calories Burned in 30 Minutes			
Body Mass	Experiment 1: Bicycling	Experiment 2: Playing Basketball	Experiment 3: Watching Television
30 kg	60 Calories	120 Calories	21 Calories
40 kg	77 Calories	164 Calories	27 Calories
50 kg	95 Calories	206 Calories	33 Calories
60 kg	114 Calories	248 Calories	38 Calories

Bar Graphs

A bar graph is useful for comparing data from two or more distinct categories. In this example, pancreatic secretions in the small intestine are shown.
To create a bar graph, follow these steps.

1. On graph paper, draw a horizontal, or x-axis, and a vertical, or y-axis.

2. Write the names of the categories (the independent variable) along one axis, usually the horizontal axis. You may put the categories on the vertical axis if that graph shape better fits on your page. Label the axis.

3. Label the other axis with the name of the dependent variable and the unit of measurement. Then, create a scale along that axis by marking off equally spaced numbers that cover the range of the data values.

4. For each category, draw a solid bar at the appropriate value. Then, fill in the space from the bar to the axis representing the independent variable. Make all the bars the same width.

5. Add a title that describes the graph.

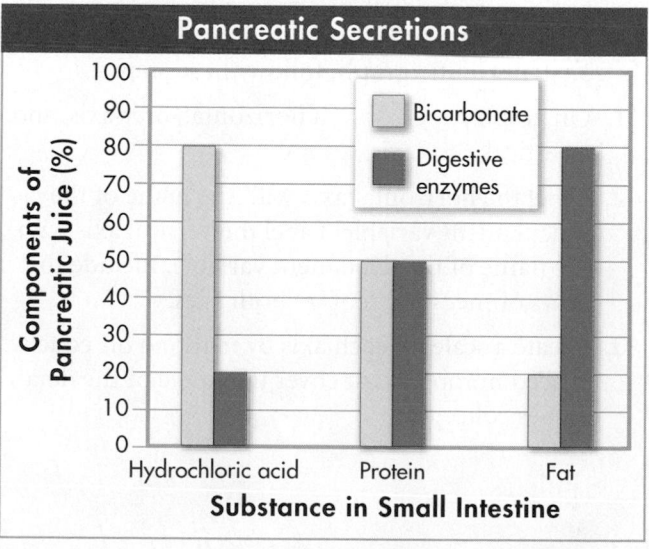

Line Graphs

A line graph is used to display data that show how the dependent variable changes in response to manipulations of the independent variable. You can use a line graph when your independent variable is continuous, that is, when there are other points between the ones that you tested. For example, the graph below shows how the growth of a bacterial population is related to time. The graph shows that the number of bacteria approximately doubles every 20 minutes. Line graphs are powerful tools because they also allow you to estimate values for conditions that you did not test in the experiment.

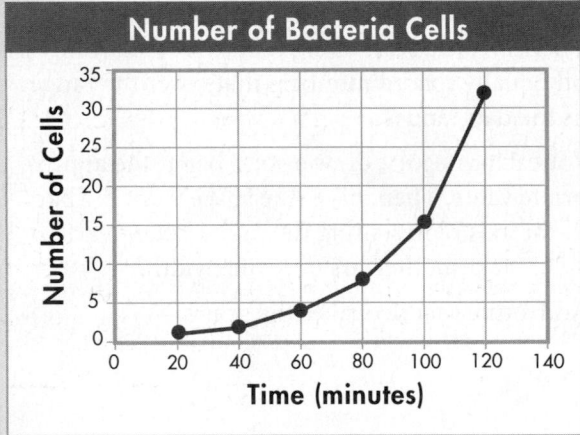

To construct a line graph, follow these steps.

1. On graph paper, draw a horizontal, or *x*-axis, and a vertical, or *y*-axis.

2. Label the horizontal axis with the name of the independent variable. Label the vertical axis with the name of the dependent variable. Include the units of measurement on both axes.

3. Create a scale on each axis by marking off equally spaced numbers that cover the range of the data values collected.

4. Plot a point on the graph for each data value. To do this, follow an imaginary vertical line extending up from the horizontal axis for an independent variable value. Then, follow an imaginary horizontal line extending across from the vertical axis at the value of the associated dependent variable. Plot a point where the two lines intersect. Repeat until all your data values are plotted.

5. Connect the plotted points with a solid line. Not all graphs are linear, so you may discover that it is more appropriate to draw a curve to connect the points.

The data in the graph at the left fit neatly on a smooth curve. But if you were to connect each data point on the graph below, you would have a mess that yielded little useful information. In some cases, it may be most useful to draw a line that shows the general trend of the plotted points. This type of line is often called a line of best fit. Such a line runs as closely as possible to all the points and allows you to make generalizations or predictions based on the data. Some points will fall above or below a line of best fit.

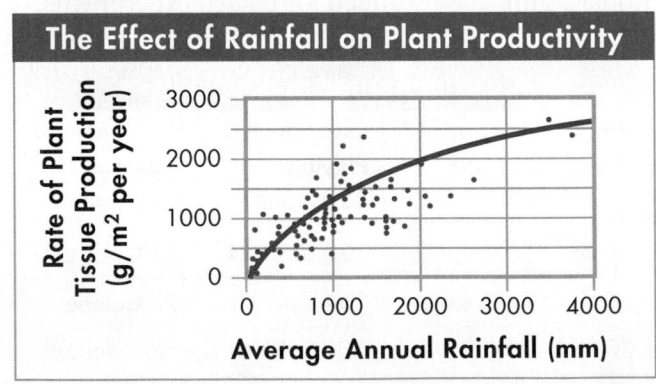

Circle Graphs

Circle graphs, or pie charts, display data as parts of a whole. Like bar graphs, circle graphs can be used to display data that fall into separate categories. Unlike bar graphs, however, circle graphs can only be used when you have data for all the categories that make up a given group. The circle, or "pie," represents 100 percent of a group, while the sectors, or slices, represent the percentages of each category that make up that group. The example below compares the different blood groups found in the U.S. population.

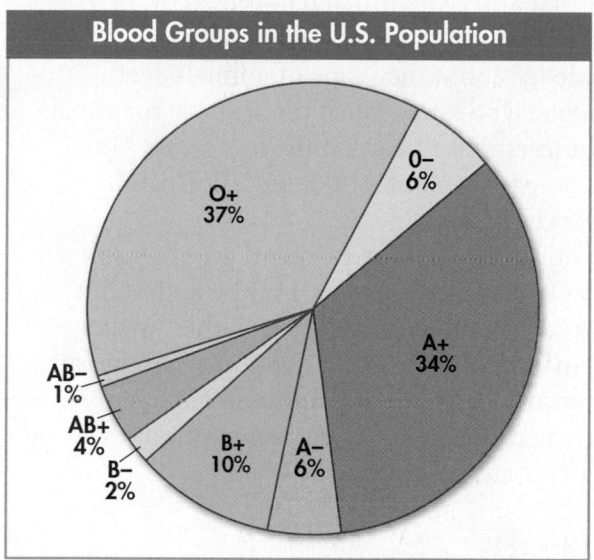

Blood Groups in the U.S. Population

O+ 37%
O– 6%
A+ 34%
A– 6%
B+ 10%
B– 2%
AB+ 4%
AB– 1%

To construct a circle graph, follow these steps.

1. Draw a circle and mark the center. Then, draw a radius line from the center to the circle's edge.

2. Determine the size of a sector of the graph by calculating the number of degrees that correspond to a percentage you wish to represent. For example, in the graph shown, B^+ makes up 10 percent of all blood groups; 360 degrees × 0.10 = 36 degrees.

3. With a protractor fixed at the center of the circle, measure the angle—in this example, 36 degrees—from the existing radius, and draw a second radius at that point. Label the sector with its category and the percentage of the whole it represents. Repeat for each of the other categories, measuring each sector from the previous radius so the sectors don't overlap.

4. For easier reading, shade each sector differently.

5. Add a title that describes the graph.

Reading Diagrams

In scientific figures showing a cut-away of a structure, the diagram or photograph is showing the structure from a particular angle. Look for clues throughout this book that will help you interpret the view being shown.

Cross Sections

A cross section shows a horizontal cut through the middle of a structure. This icon will help you locate cross sections.

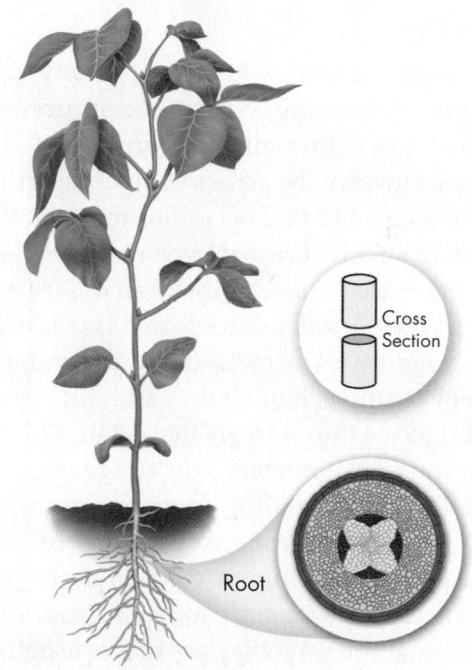

Cross Section

Root

Longitudinal Sections

A longitudinal section shows a vertical cut through the middle of a structure. This icon will help you locate longitudinal sections.

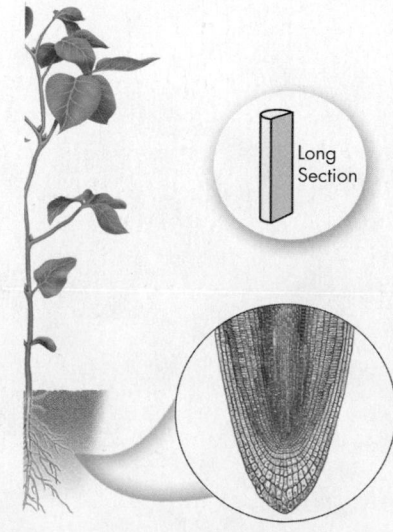

Long Section

Basic Process Skills

During a biology course, you often carry out short lab activities as well as lengthier experiments. Here are some skills that you will use.

Observing

In every science activity, you make a variety of observations. Observing is using one or more of the five senses to gather information. Many observations involve the senses of sight, hearing, touch, and smell. On rare occasions in a lab—but only when explicitly directed by your teacher—you may use the sense of taste to make an observation.

Sometimes you will use tools that increase the power of your senses or make observations more precise. For example, hand lenses and microscopes enable you to see things in greater detail. Rulers, balances, and thermometers help you measure key variables. Besides expanding the senses or making observations more accurate, tools may help eliminate personal opinions or preferences.

In science, it is customary to record your observations at the time they are made, usually by writing or drawing in a notebook. You may also make records by using computers, cameras, videotapes, and other tools. As a rule, scientists keep complete accounts of their observations, often using tables to organize their observations.

Inferring

In science, as in daily life, observations are usually followed by inferences. Inferring is interpreting an observation or statement based on prior knowledge.

For example, suppose you're on a mountain hike and you see footprints like the ones illustrated below. Based on their size and shape, you might infer that a large mammal had passed by. In making that inference, you would use your knowledge about the shape of animals' feet. Someone who knew much more about mammals might infer that a bear left the footprints. You can compare examples of observations and inferences in the table.

Notice that an inference is an act of reasoning, not a fact. An inference may be logical but not true. It is often necessary to gather further information before you can be confident that an inference is correct. For scientists, that information may come from further observations or from research done by others.

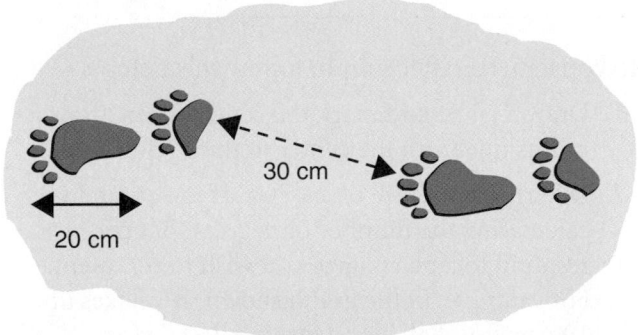

Comparing Observations and Inferences	
Sample Observations	**Sample Inferences**
The footprints in the soil each have five toes.	An animal made the footprints.
The larger footprints are about 20 cm long.	A bear made the footprints.
The space between each pair of footprints is about 30 cm.	The animal was walking, not running.

As you study biology, you may make different types of inferences. For example, you may generalize about all cases based on information about some cases: *All the plant roots I've observed grow downward, so I infer that all roots grow downward.* You may determine that one factor or event was caused by another factor or event: *The bacteria died after I applied bleach, so I infer that bleach kills bacteria.* Predictions may be another type of inference.

Predicting

People often make predictions, but their statements about the future could be either guesses or inferences. In science, a prediction is an inference about a future event based on evidence, experience, or knowledge. For example, you can say, *On the first day of next month, it will be sunny.* If your statement is based on evidence of weather patterns in the area, then the prediction is scientific. If the statement was made without considering any evidence, it's just a guess.

Predictions play a major role in science because they provide a way to test ideas. If scientists understand an event or the properties of a particular object, they should be able to make accurate predictions about that event or object. Some predictions can be tested simply by making observations. At other times, carefully designed experiments are needed.

Classifying

If you have ever heard people debate whether a tomato is a fruit or a vegetable, you've heard an argument about classification. Classifying is the process of grouping items that are alike according to some organizing idea or system. Classifying occurs in every branch of science, but it is especially important in biology because living things are so numerous and diverse.

You may have the chance to practice classifying in different ways. Sometimes you will place objects into groups using an established system. At other times, you may create a system of your own by examining a variety of objects and identifying their properties.

Classification can have different purposes. Sometimes it's done just to keep things organized, to make lab supplies easy to find, for example.

More often, though, classification helps scientists understand living things better and discover relationships among them. For example, one way biologists determine how groups of vertebrates are related is to compare their bones. Biologists classify certain animal parts as bone or muscle and then investigate how they work together.

Using Models

Some cities refuse to approve any new buildings that could cast shadows on a popular park. As architects plan buildings in such locations, they use models that can show where a proposed building's shadow will fall at any time of day in any season of the year. A model is a mental or physical representation of an object, process, or event. In science, models are usually made to help people understand natural objects and processes.

Models can be varied. Mental models, such as mathematical equations, can represent some kinds of ideas or processes. For example, the equation for the surface area of a sphere can model the surface of Earth, enabling scientists to determine its size. Physical models can be made of a huge variety of materials; they can be two dimensional (flat) or three dimensional (having depth). In biology, a drawing of a molecule or a cell is a typical two-dimensional model. Common three-dimensional models include a representation of a DNA molecule and a plastic skeleton of an animal.

Physical models can also be made "to scale," which means they are in proportion to the actual object. Something very large, such as an area of land being studied, can be shown at 1/100 of its actual size. A tiny organism can be shown at 100 times its size.

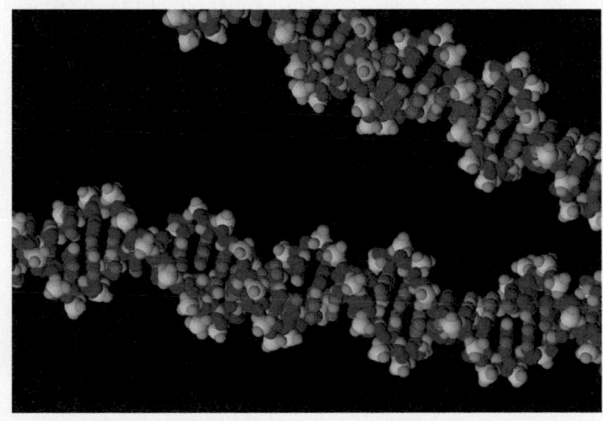

Organizing Information

When you study or want to communicate facts and ideas, you may find it helpful to organize information visually. Here are some common graphic organizers you can use. Notice that each type of organizer is useful for specific types of information.

Flowcharts

A flowchart can help you represent the order in which a set of events has occurred or should occur. Flowcharts are useful for outlining the steps in a procedure or stages in a process with a definite beginning and end.

To make a flowchart, list the steps in the process you want to represent and count the steps. Then, create the appropriate number of boxes, starting at the top of a page or on the left. Write a brief description of the first event in the first box, and then fill in the other steps, box by box. Link each box to the next event in the process with an arrow.

Concept Maps

Concept maps can help you organize a topic that has many subtopics. A concept map begins with a main idea and shows how it can be broken down into specific topics. It makes the ideas easier to understand by presenting their relationships visually.

You construct a concept map by placing the concept words (usually nouns) in ovals and connecting the ovals with linking words. The most general concept usually is placed at the top of the map or in the center. The content of the other ovals becomes more specific as you move away from the main concept. The linking words, which describe the relationship between the linked concepts, are written on a line between two ovals. If you follow any string of concepts and linking words down through a map, they should sound almost like a sentence.

Some concept maps may also include linking words that connect a concept in one branch to another branch. Such connections, called cross-linkages, show more complex interrelationships.

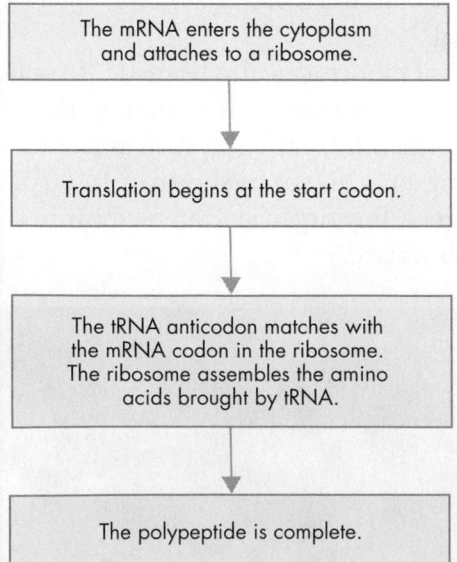

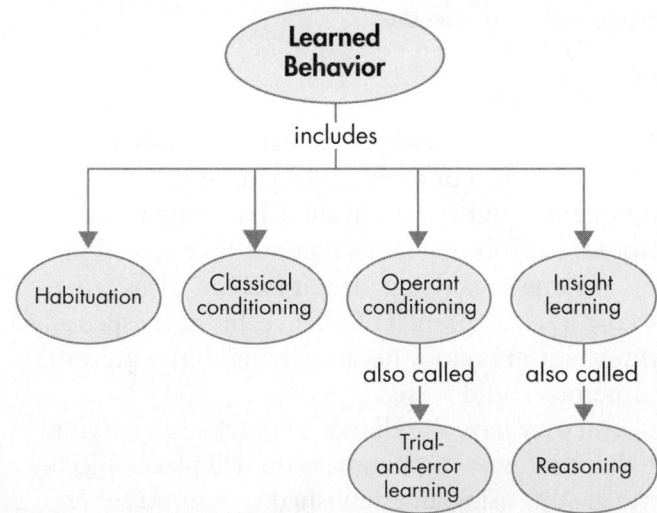

Compare/Contrast Tables

Compare/contrast tables are useful for showing the similarities and differences between two or more objects or processes. The table provides an organized framework for making comparisons based on specific characteristics.

To create a compare/contrast table, list the items to be compared across the top of the table. List the characteristics that will form the basis of your comparison in the column on the left. Complete the table by filling in information for each item.

Comparing Fermentation and Cellular Respiration		
Characteristic	Fermentation	Cellular Respiration
Starting reactants	Glucose	Glucose, oxygen
Pathways involved	Glycolysis, several others	Glycolysis, Krebs cycle, electron transport
End products	CO_2 and alcohol or CO_2 and lactic acid	CO_2, H_2O
Number of ATP molecules produced	2	36

Venn Diagrams

Another way to show similarities and differences between items is with a Venn diagram. A Venn diagram consists of two or more ovals that partially overlap. Each oval represents a particular object or idea. Characteristics that the objects share are written in the area of overlap. Differences or unique characteristics are written in the areas that do not overlap.

To create a Venn diagram, draw two overlapping ovals. Label them with the names of the objects or the ideas they represent. Write the unique characteristics in the part of each oval that does not overlap. Write the shared characteristics within the area of overlap.

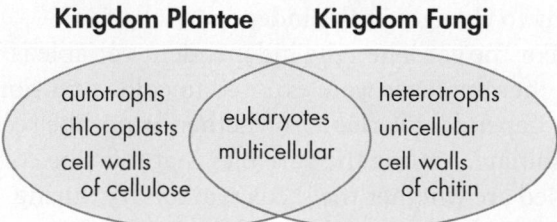

Cycle Diagrams

A cycle diagram shows a sequence of events that is continuous, or cyclical. A continuous sequence does not have a beginning or an end; instead, each event in the process leads to another event. The diagram shows the order of the events.

To create a cycle diagram, list the events in the process and count them. Draw one box for each event, placing the boxes around an imaginary circle. Write one of the events in an oval, and then draw an arrow to the next oval, moving clockwise. Continue to fill in the boxes and link them with arrows until the descriptions form a continuous circle.

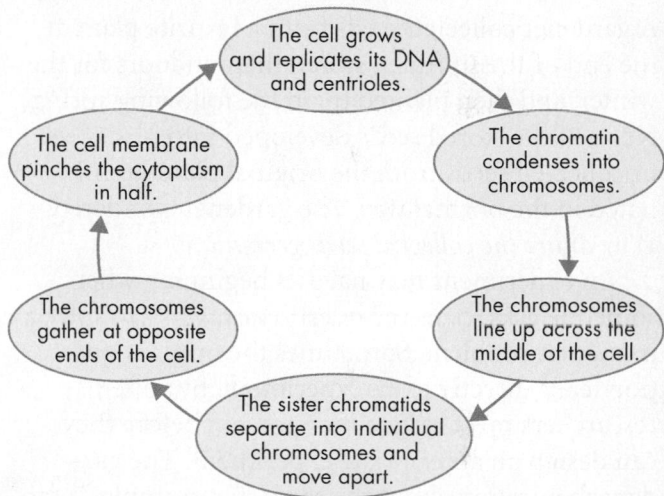

Conducting an Experiment

A science experiment is a procedure designed to test a prediction. Some types of experiments are fairly simple to design. Others may require ingenious problem solving.

Starting With Questions or Problems

A gardener collected seeds from a favorite plant at the end of the summer, stored them indoors for the winter, and then planted them the following spring. None of the stored seeds developed into plants, yet uncollected seeds from the original plant germinated in the normal way. The gardener wondered: *Why didn't the collected seeds germinate?*

An experiment may have its beginning when someone asks a specific question or wants to solve a particular problem. Sometimes the original question leads directly to an experiment, but often researchers must restate the problem before they can design an appropriate experiment. The gardener's question about the seeds, for example, is too broad to be tested by an experiment, because there are so many possible answers. To narrow the topic, the gardener might think about related questions: *Were the seeds I collected different from the uncollected seeds? Did I try to germinate them in poor soil or with insufficient light or water? Did storing the seeds indoors ruin them in some way?*

Developing a Hypothesis

In science, a question about an object or event is answered by developing a possible explanation called a hypothesis. The hypothesis may be developed after long thought and research, or it may come to a scientist "in a flash." How a hypothesis is formed doesn't matter; it can be useful as long as it leads to predictions that can be tested.

The gardener decided to focus on the fact that the nongerminating seeds were stored in the warm conditions of a heated house. That premise led the person to propose this hypothesis: *Seeds require a period of low temperatures in order to germinate.*

The next step is to make a prediction based on the hypothesis, for example: *If seeds are stored indoors in cold conditions, they will germinate in the same way as seeds left outdoors during the winter.* Notice that the prediction suggests the basic idea for an experiment.

Designing an Experiment

A carefully designed experiment can test a prediction in a reliable way, ruling out other possible explanations. As scientists plan their experimental procedures, they pay particular attention to the factors that must be controlled.

The gardener decided to study three groups of seeds: (1) some that would be left outdoors throughout the winter, (2) some that would be brought indoors and kept at room temperature, and (3) some that would be brought indoors and kept cold.

Controlling Variables

As researchers design an experiment, they identify the variables, factors that can change. Some common variables include mass, volume, time, temperature, light, and the presence or absence of specific materials. An experiment involves three categories of variables. The factor that scientists purposely change is called the independent variable. An independent variable is also known as a manipulated variable. The factor that may change because of the independent variable and that scientists want to observe is called the dependent variable. A dependent variable is also known as a responding variable. Factors that scientists purposely keep the same are called controlled variables. Controlling variables enables researchers to conclude that the changes in the dependent variable are due exclusively to changes in the independent variable.

For the gardener, the independent variable is whether the seeds were exposed to cold conditions. The dependent variable is whether or not the seeds germinate. Among the variables that must be controlled are whether the seeds remain dry during storage, when the seeds are planted, the amount of water the seeds receive, and the type of soil used.

Interpreting Data

The observations and measurements that are made in an experiment are called data. Scientists usually record data in an orderly way. When an experiment is finished, the researcher analyzes the data for trends or patterns, often by doing calculations or making graphs, to determine whether the results support the hypothesis.

For example, after planting the seeds in the spring, the gardener counted the seeds that germinated and found these results: None of the seeds kept at room temperature germinated, 80 percent of the seeds kept in the freezer germinated, and 85 percent of the seeds left outdoors during the winter germinated. The trend was clear: The gardener's prediction appeared to be correct.

To be sure that the results of an experiment are correct, scientists review their data critically, looking for possible sources of error. Here, *error* refers to differences between the observed results and the true values. Experimental error can result from human mistakes or problems with equipment. It can also occur when the small group of objects studied does not accurately represent the whole group. For example, if some of the gardener's seeds had been exposed to an herbicide, the data might not reflect the true seed germination pattern.

Drawing Conclusions

If researchers are confident that their data are reliable, they make a final statement summarizing their results. That statement, called the conclusion, indicates whether the data support or refute the hypothesis. The gardener's conclusion was this: *Some seeds must undergo a period of freezing in order to germinate.* A conclusion is considered valid if it is a logical interpretation of reliable data.

Following Up an Experiment

When an experiment has been completed, one or more events often follow. Researchers may repeat the experiment to verify the results. They may publish the experiment so that others can evaluate and replicate their procedures. They may compare their conclusion with the discoveries made by other scientists. And they may raise new questions that lead to new experiments. For example, *Are the spores of fungi affected by temperature as these seeds were*?

Researching other discoveries about seeds would show that some other types of plants in temperate zones require periods of freezing before they germinate. Biologists infer that this pattern makes it less likely the seeds will germinate before winter, thus increasing the chances that the young plants will survive.

The Metric System

The standard system of measurement used by scientists throughout the world is known as the International System of Units, abbreviated as SI (Système International d'Unités, in French). It is based on units of 10. Each unit is 10 times larger or 10 times smaller than the next unit. The table lists the prefixes used to name the most common SI units.

Common SI Prefixes		
Prefix	Symbol	Meaning
kilo-	k	1000
hecto-	h	100
deka-	da	10
deci-	d	0.1 (one tenth)
centi-	c	0.01 (one hundredth)
milli-	m	0.001 (one thousandth)

Commonly Used Metric Units

Length To measure length, or distance from one point to another, the unit of measure is a meter (m). A meter is slightly longer than a yard.

Useful equivalents:

1 meter = 1000 millimeters (mm)
1 meter = 100 centimeters (cm)
1000 meters = 1 kilometer (km)

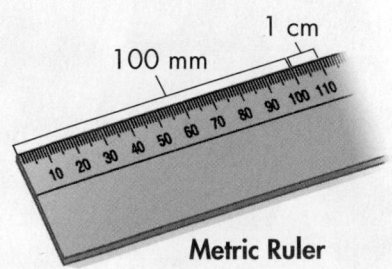

Metric Ruler

Volume To measure the volume of a liquid, or the amount of space an object takes up, the unit of measure is a liter (L). A liter is slightly more than a quart.

Useful equivalents:

1 liter = 1000 milliliters (mL)

Mass To measure the mass, or the amount of matter in an object, the unit of measure is the gram (g). A paper clip has a mass equal to about one gram.

Useful equivalents:

1000 grams = 1 kilogram (kg)

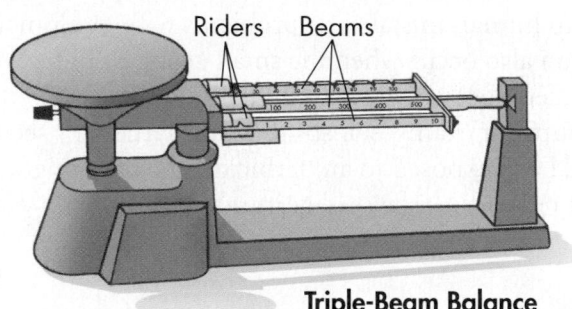

Triple-Beam Balance

Temperature To measure the hotness or coldness of an item, or its temperature, you use the unit degrees. The freezing point of water is 0°C (Celsius). The boiling point of water is 100°C.

Metric-English Equivalents

2.54 centimeters (cm) = 1 inch (in.)
1 meter (m) = 39.37 inches (in.)
1 kilometer (km) = 0.62 miles (mi)
1 liter (L) = 1.06 quarts (qt)
236 milliliters (mL) = 1 cup (c)
1 kilogram (kg) = 2.2 pounds (lb)
28.3 grams (g) = 1 ounce (oz)
°C = 5/9 × (°F − 32)

Safety Symbols

These symbols appear in laboratory activities to alert you to possible dangers and to remind you to work carefully.

Safety Goggles Always wear safety goggles to protect your eyes during any activity involving chemicals, flames or heating, or the possibility of flying objects, particles, or substances.

Lab Apron Wear a laboratory apron to protect your skin and clothing from injury.

Plastic Gloves Wear disposable plastic gloves to protect yourself from contact with chemicals or organisms that could be harmful. Keep your hands away from your face, and dispose of the gloves according to your teacher's instructions at the end of the activity.

Breakage Handle breakable materials such as thermometers and glassware with care. Do not touch broken glass.

Heat-Resistant Gloves Use an oven mitt or other hand protection when handling hot materials. Hot plates, hot water, and glassware can cause burns. Never touch hot objects with your bare hands.

Heating Use a clamp or tongs to hold hot objects. Do not touch hot objects with your bare hands.

Sharp Object Scissors, scalpels, pins, and knives are sharp. They can cut or puncture your skin. Always direct sharp edges and points away from yourself and others. Use sharp instruments only as directed.

Electric Shock Avoid the possibility of electric shock. Never use electrical equipment around water or when the equipment or your hands are wet. Be sure cords are untangled and cannot trip anyone. Disconnect equipment when it is not in use.

Corrosive Chemical This symbol indicates the presence of an acid or other corrosive chemical. Avoid getting the chemical on your skin or clothing, or in your eyes. Do not inhale the vapors. Wash your hands when you are finished with the activity.

Poison Do not let any poisonous chemical get on your skin, and do not inhale its vapor. Wash your hands when you are finished with the activity.

Flames Tie back loose hair and clothing, and put on safety goggles before working with fire. Follow instructions from your teacher about lighting and extinguishing flames.

No Flames Flammable materials may be present. Make sure there are no flames, sparks, or exposed sources of heat present.

Fumes Poisonous or unpleasant vapors may be produced. Work in a ventilated area or, if available, in a fume hood. Avoid inhaling a vapor directly. Test an odor only when directed to do so by your teacher, using a wafting motion to direct the vapor toward your nose.

Physical Safety This activity involves physical movement. Use caution to avoid injuring yourself or others. Follow instructions from your teacher. Alert your teacher if there is any reason that you should not participate in the activity.

Animal Safety Treat live animals with care to avoid injuring the animals or yourself. Working with animal parts or preserved animals may also require caution. Wash your hands when you are finished with the activity.

Plant Safety Handle plants only as your teacher directs. If you are allergic to any plants used in an activity, tell your teacher before the activity begins. Avoid touching poisonous plants and plants with thorns.

Disposal Chemicals and other materials used in the activity must be disposed of safely. Follow the instructions from your teacher.

Hand Washing Wash your hands thoroughly when finished with the activity. Use soap and warm water. Lather both sides of your hands and between your fingers. Rinse well.

General Safety Awareness You may see this symbol when none of the symbols described earlier applies. In this case, follow the specific instructions provided. You may also see this symbol when you are asked to design your own experiment. Do not start your experiment until your teacher has approved your plan.

Science Safety Rules

Working in the laboratory can be an exciting experience, but it can also be dangerous if proper safety rules are not followed at all times. To prepare yourself for a safe year in the laboratory, read the following safety rules. Make sure that you understand each rule. Ask your teacher to explain any rules you don't understand.

Dress Code

1. Many materials in the laboratory can cause eye injury. To protect yourself from possible injury, wear safety goggles whenever you are working with chemicals, burners, or any substance that might get into your eyes. Avoid wearing contact lenses in the laboratory. Tell your teacher if you need to wear contact lenses to see clearly, and ask if there are any safety precautions you should observe.

2. Wear a laboratory apron or coat whenever you are working with chemicals or heated substances.

3. Tie back long hair to keep it away from any chemicals, burners, candles, or other laboratory equipment.

4. Before working in the laboratory, remove or tie back any article of clothing or jewelry that can hang down and touch chemicals and flames.

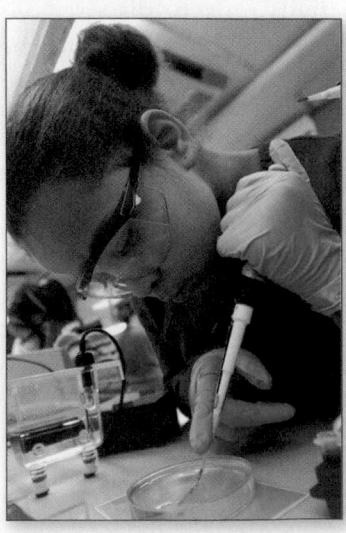

General Safety Rules and First Aid

5. Read all directions for an experiment several times. Follow the directions exactly as they are written. If you are in doubt about any part of the experiment, ask your teacher for assistance.

6. Never perform investigations your teacher has not authorized. Do not use any equipment unless your teacher is in the lab.

7. Never handle equipment unless you have specific permission.

8. Take care not to spill any material in the laboratory. If spills occur, ask your teacher immediately about the proper cleanup procedure. Never pour chemicals or other substances into the sink or trash container.

9. Never eat or drink in, or bring food into, the laboratory.

10. Immediately report all accidents, no matter how minor, to your teacher.

11. Learn what to do in case of specific accidents, such as getting acid in your eyes or on your skin. (Rinse acids off your body with lots of water.)

12. Be aware of the location of the first-aid kit. Your teacher should administer any required first aid due to injury. Your teacher may send you to the school nurse or call a physician.

13. Know where and how to report an accident or fire. Find out the location of the fire extinguisher, fire alarm, and phone. Report any fires to your teacher at once.

Heating and Fire Safety

14. Never use a heat source such as a candle or burner without wearing safety goggles.

15. Never heat a chemical you are not instructed to heat. A chemical that is harmless when cool can be dangerous when heated.

16. Maintain a clean work area and keep all materials away from flames. Be sure that there are no open containers of flammable liquids in the laboratory when flames are being used.

17. Never reach across a flame.

18. Make sure you know how to light a Bunsen burner. (Your teacher will demonstrate the proper procedure for lighting a burner.) If the flame leaps out of a burner toward you, turn the gas off immediately. Do not touch the burner. It may be hot. Never leave a lighted burner unattended!

19. When you are heating a test tube or bottle, point the opening away from yourself and others. Chemicals can splash or boil out of a heated test tube.

20. Never heat a closed container. The expanding hot air, vapors, or other gases inside may blow the container apart, causing it to injure you or others.

21. Never pick up a container that has been heated without first holding the back of your hand near it. If you can feel the heat on the back of your hand, the container may be too hot to handle. Use a clamp or tongs when handling hot containers or wear heat-resistant gloves if appropriate.

Using Chemicals Safely

22. Never mix chemicals for "the fun of it." You might produce a dangerous, possibly explosive substance.

23. Many chemicals are poisonous. Never touch, taste, or smell a chemical that you do not know for certain is harmless. If you are instructed to smell fumes in an experiment, gently wave your hand over the opening of the container and direct the fumes toward your nose. Do not inhale the fumes directly from the container.

24. Use only those chemicals needed in the investigation. Keep all container lids closed when a chemical is not being used. Notify your teacher whenever chemicals are spilled.

25. Dispose of all chemicals as instructed by your teacher. To avoid contamination, never return chemicals to their original containers.

26. Be extra careful when working with acids or bases. Pour such chemicals from one container to another over the sink, not over your work area.

27. When diluting an acid, pour the acid into water. Never pour water into the acid.

28. If any acids or bases get on your skin or clothing, rinse them with water. Immediately notify your teacher of any acid or base spill.

Using Glassware Safely

29. Never heat glassware that is not thoroughly dry. Use a wire screen to protect glassware from any flame.

30. Keep in mind that hot glassware will not appear hot. Never pick up glassware without first checking to see if it is hot.

31. Never use broken or chipped glassware. If glassware breaks, notify your teacher and dispose of the glassware in the proper trash container.

32. Never eat or drink from laboratory glassware. Thoroughly clean glassware before putting it away.

Using Sharp Instruments

33. Handle scalpels or razor blades with extreme care. Never cut material toward you; cut away from you.

34. Notify your teacher immediately if you cut yourself when in the laboratory.

Working With Live Organisms

35. No experiments that will cause pain, discomfort, or harm to animals should be done in the classroom or at home.

36. Your teacher will instruct you how to handle each species that is brought into the classroom. Animals should be handled only if necessary. Special handling is required if an animal is excited or frightened, pregnant, feeding, or with its young.

37. Clean your hands thoroughly after handling any organisms or materials, including animals or cages containing animals.

End-of-Experiment Rules

38. When an experiment is completed, clean up your work area and return all equipment to its proper place.

39. Wash your hands with soap and warm water before and after every experiment.

40. Turn off all burners before leaving the laboratory. Check that the gas line leading to the burner is off as well.

Use of the Microscope

The microscope used in most biology classes, the compound microscope, contains a combination of lenses. The eyepiece lens is located in the top portion of the microscope. This lens usually has a magnification of 10×. Other lenses, called objective lenses, are at the bottom of the body tube on the revolving nosepiece. By rotating the nosepiece, you can select the objective through which you will view your specimen.

The shortest objective is a low-power magnifier, usually 10×. The longer ones are of high power, usually up to 40× or 43×. The magnification is marked on the objective. To determine the total magnification, multiply the magnifying power of the eyepiece by the magnifying power of the objective. For example, with a 10× eyepiece and a 40× objective, the total magnification is 10 × 40 = 400×.

Learning the name, function, and location of each of the microscope's parts is necessary for proper use. Use the following procedures when working with the microscope.

1. Carry the microscope by placing one hand beneath the base and grasping the arm of the microscope with the other hand.

2. Gently place the microscope on the lab table with the arm facing you. The microscope's base should be resting evenly on the table, approximately 10 cm from the table's edge.

3. Raise the body tube by turning the coarse adjustment knob until the objective lens is about 2 cm above the opening of the stage.

4. Rotate the nosepiece so that the low-power objective (10×) is directly in line with the body tube. A click indicates that the lens is in line with the opening of the stage.

5. Look through the eyepiece and switch on the lamp or adjust the mirror so that a circle of light can be seen. This is the field of view. Moving the lever of the diaphragm permits a greater or smaller amount of light to come through the opening of the stage.

6. Place a prepared slide on the stage so that the specimen is over the center of the opening. Use the stage clips to hold the slide in place.

7. Look at the microscope from the side. Carefully turn the coarse adjustment knob to lower the body tube until the low-power objective almost touches the slide or until the body tube can no longer be moved. Do not allow the objective to touch the slide.

8. Look through the eyepiece and observe the specimen. If the field of view is out of focus, use the coarse adjustment knob to raise the body tube while looking through the eyepiece. **CAUTION:** *To prevent damage to the slide and the objective, do not lower the body tube using the coarse adjustment while looking through the eyepiece.* Focus the image as best you can with the coarse adjustment knob. Then, use the fine adjustment knob to focus the image more sharply. Keep both eyes open when viewing a specimen. This helps prevent eyestrain.

1. **Eyepiece:** Contains a magnifying lens.
2. **Arm:** Supports the body tube.
3. **Low-power objective:** Provides a magnification of 10x.
4. **Stage:** Supports the slide being observed.
5. **Opening of the stage:** Permits light to pass up to the eyepiece.
6. **Fine adjustment knob:** Moves the body tube slightly to adjust the image.
7. **Coarse adjustment knob:** Moves the body tube to focus the image.
8. **Base:** Supports the microscope.
9. **Illuminator:** Produces light or reflects light up toward the eyepiece.
10. **Diaphragm:** Regulates the amount of light passing up toward the eyepiece.
11. **Stageclips:** Hold the slide in place.
12. **High-power objective:** Provides a magnification of 40x.
13. **Nosepiece:** Holds the objectives and can be rotated to change the magnification.
14. **Body tube:** Maintains the proper distance between the eyepiece and the objectives.

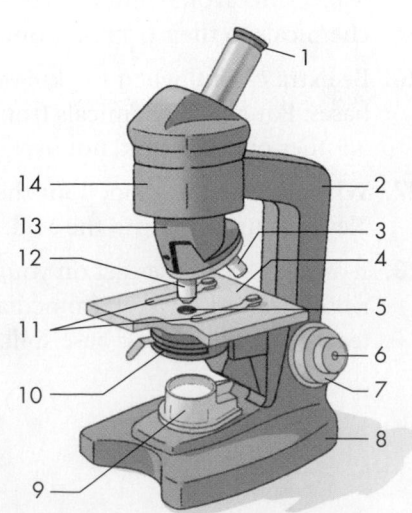

9. Adjust the lever of the diaphragm to allow the right amount of light to enter.

10. To change the magnification, rotate the nosepiece until the desired objective is in line with the body tube and clicks into place.

11. Look through the eyepiece and use the fine adjustment knob to bring the image into focus.

12. After every use, remove the slide. Return the low-power objective into place in line with the body tube. Clean the stage of the microscope and the lenses with lens paper. Do not use other types of paper to clean the lenses; they may scratch the lenses.

Preparing a Wet-Mount Slide

1. Obtain a clean microscope slide and a coverslip. A coverslip is very thin, permitting the objective lens to be lowered very close to the specimen.

2. Place the specimen in the middle of the microscope slide. The specimen must be thin enough for light to pass through it.

3. Using a dropper pipette, place a drop of water on the specimen.

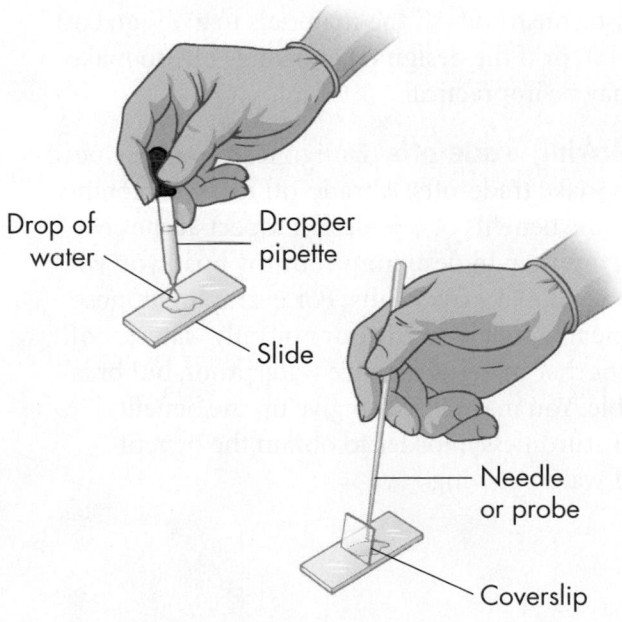

Drop of water

Dropper pipette

Slide

Needle or probe

Coverslip

4. Lower one edge of the coverslip so that it touches the side of the drop of water at about a 45° angle. The water will spread evenly along the edge of the coverslip. Using a dissecting needle or probe, slowly lower the coverslip over the specimen and water as shown in the drawing. Try not to trap any air bubbles under the coverslip. If air bubbles are present, gently tap the surface of the coverslip over the air bubble with a pencil eraser.

5. Remove any excess water around the edge of the coverslip with a paper towel. If the specimen begins to dry out, add a drop of water at the edge of the coverslip.

Staining Techniques

1. Obtain a clean microscope slide and coverslip.

2. Place the specimen in the middle of the microscope slide.

3. Using a dropper pipette, place a drop of water on the specimen. Place the coverslip so that its edge touches the drop of water at a 45° angle. After the water spreads along the edge of the coverslip, use a dissecting needle or probe to lower the coverslip over the specimen.

4. Add a drop of stain at the edge of the coverslip. Using forceps, touch a small piece of lens paper or paper towel to the opposite edge of the coverslip, as shown in the drawing. The paper causes the stain to be drawn under the coverslip and to stain the cells in the specimen.

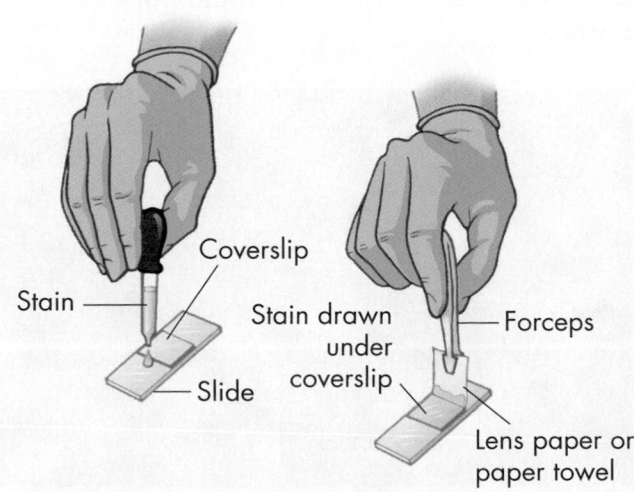

Stain

Coverslip

Stain drawn under coverslip

Slide

Forceps

Lens paper or paper towel

Engineers are people who use scientific and technological knowledge to solve practical problems. To design new products, engineers usually follow the process described here, even though they may not follow these steps in the exact order.

Identify a Need

Before engineers begin designing a new product, they must first identify the need they are trying to meet. For example, suppose you are a member of a design team in a company that makes toys. Your team has identified a need: a toy boat that is inexpensive and easy to assemble.

Research the Problem

Engineers often begin by gathering information that will help them with their new design. This research may include finding articles in books, in magazines, or on the Internet. It may also include talking to other engineers who have solved similar problems. Engineers also often perform experiments related to the product they want to design.

For your toy boat, you could look at toys that are similar to the one you want to design. You might do research on the Internet. You could also test some materials to see whether they would work well in a toy boat.

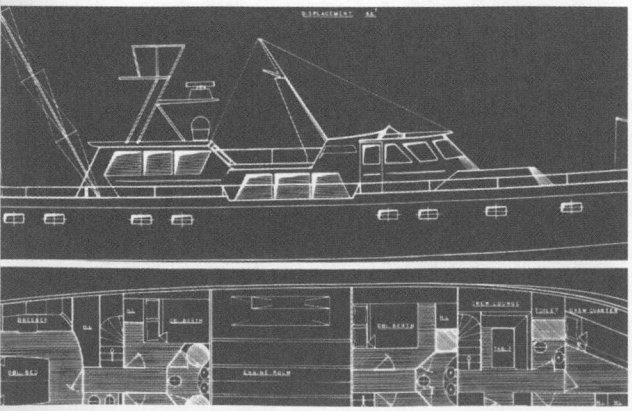

Design a Solution

Research gives engineers information that helps them design a product. When engineers design new products, they usually work in teams.

Generating Ideas Often, design teams hold brainstorming meetings in which any team member can contribute ideas. Brainstorming is a creative process in which one team member's suggestions can spark ideas in other group members. Brainstorming can lead to new approaches to solving a design problem.

Evaluating Constraints During brainstorming, a design team will often come up with several possible designs. The team must then evaluate each one.

As part of their evaluation, engineers consider constraints. Constraints are factors that limit or restrict a product design. Physical characteristics, such as the properties of materials used to make your toy boat, are constraints. Cost and time are also constraints. If the materials in a design cost a lot, or if the design takes a long time to make, it may be impractical.

Making Trade-offs Design teams usually need to make trade-offs. A trade-off is the acceptance of the benefits of one design aspect at the cost of another. In designing your toy boat, you will have to make trade-offs. For example, suppose one material is sturdy but not fully waterproof. Another material is more waterproof, but breakable. You may decide to give up the benefit of sturdiness in order to obtain the benefit of waterproofing.

Build and Evaluate a Prototype

Once the team has chosen a design plan, the engineers build a prototype of the product. A prototype is a working model used to test a design. Engineers evaluate the prototype to see whether it works well, is easy to operate, is safe to use, and holds up to repeated use.

Think of your toy boat. What would the prototype be like? Of what materials would it be made? How would you test it?

Troubleshoot and Redesign

Few prototypes work perfectly, which is why they need to be tested. Once a design team has tested a prototype, the members analyze the results and identify any problems. The team then tries to troubleshoot, or fix the weaknesses in the design. For example, if your toy boat leaks or wobbles, the boat should be redesigned to eliminate those problems.

Communicate the Solution

A team needs to communicate the final design to the people who will manufacture the product. To do this, teams may use sketches, detailed drawings, computer simulations, and written descriptions.

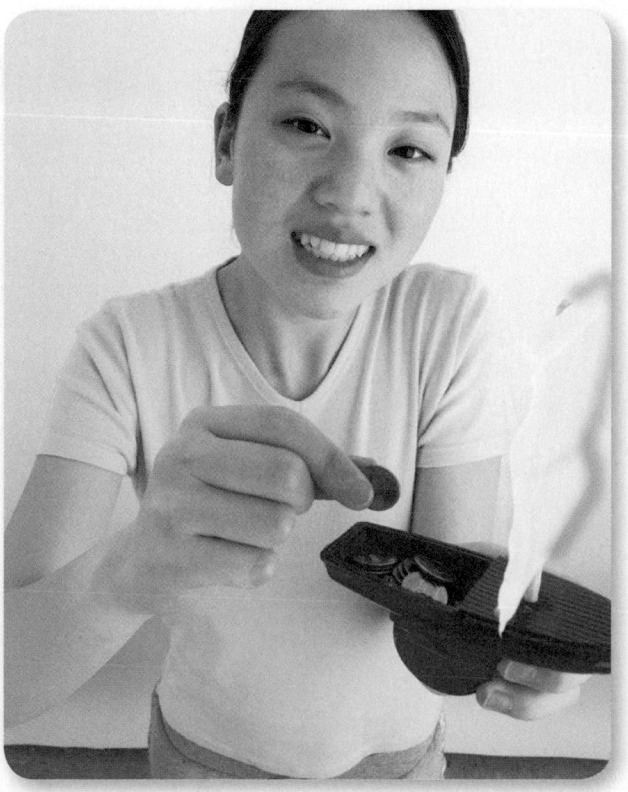

Activity

You can use the technology design process to design and build a toy boat.

Research and Investigate

1. Visit the library or go online to research toy boats.

2. Investigate how a toy boat can be powered, including wind, rubber bands, or baking soda and vinegar.

3. Brainstorm materials, shapes, and steering methods for your boat.

Design and Build

4. Based on your research, design a toy boat that
   • is made of readily available materials
   • is no larger than 15 cm long and 10 cm wide
   • includes a power system, a rudder, and a cargo area
   • travels 2 meters in a straight line while carrying a load of 20 pennies

5. Sketch your design and write a step-by-step plan for building your boat. After your teacher approves your plan, build your boat.

Evaluate and Redesign

6. Test your boat, evaluate the results, and identify any technological design problems in your boat.

7. Based on your evaluation, redesign your toy boat so it performs better.

8. As a class, compare the test results for each boat. Choose the model which best meets the needs of the toy company.

Appendix D Math Skills

Scientists use math to organize, analyze, and present data. This appendix will help you review some basic math skills.

Formulas and Equations

Formulas and equations are used in many areas of science. Both formulas and equations show the relationships between quantities. Any numerical sentence that contains at least one variable and at least one mathematical operator is called an equation. A formula is a type of equation that states the relationship between unknown quantities represented by variables.

For example, Speed = Distance ÷ Time is a formula, because no matter what values are inserted, speed is always equal to distance divided by time. The relationship between the variables does not change.

Example

Follow these steps to convert a temperature measurement of 50°F to Celsius.

1. Determine the formula that shows the relationship between these quantities.
   °F = (9/5 × °C) + 32°F

2. Insert values you know into the formula.
   50°F = (9/5 × °C) + 32°F

3. Solve the resulting equation.
   50°F − 32°F = (9/5 × °C)
   18°F = 9/5 × °C
   18°F × 5/9 = 10°C

Applying Formulas and Equations

There are many applications of formulas in science. The example described below uses a formula to calculate density.

Example

Follow these steps to calculate the density of an object that has a mass of 45 g and a volume of 30 cm^3.

1. Determine the formula that shows the relationship between these quantities.
   Density = Mass/Volume

2. Insert values you know into the formula.
   Density = 45 g/30 cm^3

3. Solve the resulting equation.
   Density = 1.5 g/cm^3

Mean, Median, and Mode

The mean is the average, or the sum of the data divided by the number of data items. The middle number in a set of ordered data is called the median. The mode is the number that appears most often in a set of data.

Example
A scientist counted the number of distinct songs sung by seven different male birds and collected the data shown below.

Male Bird Songs							
Bird	A	B	C	D	E	F	G
Number of Songs	36	29	40	35	28	36	27

To determine the mean number of songs, find the sum of the songs sung by all the male birds and divide by the number of male birds.

$$\text{Mean} = 231/7 = 33 \text{ songs}$$

To find the median number of songs, arrange the data items in numerical order and identify the number in the middle.

$$27 \quad 28 \quad 29 \quad 35 \quad 36 \quad 36 \quad 40$$

The number in the middle is 35, so the median number of songs is 35.

The mode is the value that appears most frequently. In the data, 36 appears twice, while every other item appears only once. Therefore, 36 is the mode.

Estimation

An estimate is a reasonable approximation of a numerical value. Estimates are made based on careful assumptions and known information.

Scientists use estimates in biology for two primary reasons: when an exact count or calculation cannot be made or is impractical to make, and to make reasonable approximations of answers that will be calculated or measured later.

One method for estimation used in biology is sampling. In sampling, the number of organisms in a small area (a sample) is multiplied to estimate the number of organisms in a larger area.

Example
Follow these steps to use sampling to estimate the total number of birds in the photo.

1. Count the birds in the highlighted area of the photo. In the highlighted area of the photo, there are 36 birds.

2. Determine the portion of the entire photo represented by the highlighted area. In this case, the highlighted area is 1/6 of the total area.

3. Calculate your estimate by multiplying the number of birds in the sample area by 6 (because the entire photo is 6 times as large as the sample area). A reasonable estimate of the total number of birds is 36 × 6, or 216 birds.

HINT: Estimates and calculated answers are rarely exactly the same. However, a large difference between an estimated answer and a calculated answer indicates there may be a problem with the estimate or calculation.

Using Measurements in Calculations

Density is an example of a value that is calculated using two measurements. Density represents the amount of mass in a particular volume of a substance. The units used for density are grams per milliliter (g/mL) or grams per cubic centimeter (g/cm^3). Density is calculated by dividing an object's mass by its volume.

Example
Follow these steps to calculate the density of an object.

1. Measure and record the mass of an object in grams.

2. Measure and record the volume of an object in mL or cm^3.

3. Use the following formula to calculate density:

$$Density = Mass/Volume$$

Effects of Measurement Errors

Density is calculated using two measured values. An error in the measurement of either mass or volume will result in the calculation of an incorrect density.

Example
A student measured the mass of an object as 2.5 g and its volume as 2.0 cm^3. The actual mass of the object is 3.5 g; the actual volume is 2.0 cm^3. What is the effect of the measurement error on the calculation of density?

Follow these steps to determine the effect of a measurement error on calculation.

1. Determine the density using the student's measurements.
   Density = Mass/Volume
   Density = 2.5 g/2.0 cm^3
   Density = 1.25 g/cm^3

2. Determine the density using the actual values.
   Density = Mass/Volume
   Density = 3.5 g/2.0 cm^3
   Density = 1.75 g/cm^3

3. Compare the calculated and the actual values.

In this case, a measurement of mass that was less than the actual value resulted in a calculated value for the density that was less than the actual density.

Accuracy

The accuracy of a measurement is its closeness to the actual value. Measurements that are accurate are close to the actual value.

Both clocks on this page show a time of 3:00. Suppose, though, that these clocks had not been changed to reflect daylight savings time. The time shown on the clocks would be inaccurate. On the other hand, if the actual time is 3:00, these clocks would be accurate.

Precision

Precision describes the exactness of a measurement. The clocks shown on this page differ in precision. The analog clock measures time to the nearest minute. The digital clock measures time to the nearest second. Time is measured more precisely by the digital clock than by the analog clock.

Comparing Accuracy and Precision

There is a difference between accuracy and precision. Measurements can be accurate (close to the actual value) but not precise. Measurements can also be precise but not accurate. When making scientific measurements, both accuracy and precision are important. Accurate and precise measurements result from the careful use of high-quality measuring tools.

Significant Figures

Significant figures are all of the digits that are known in a measurement, plus one additional digit, which is an estimate. In the figure below, the length of a turtle's shell is being measured using a centimeter ruler. The ruler has unnumbered divisions representing millimeters. In this case, two numbers can be determined exactly: the number of centimeters and the number of millimeters. One additional digit can be estimated. So, the measurement of this turtle's shell can be recorded with three significant figures as 8.80 centimeters.

Rules for Significant Digits
Follow these rules to determine the number of significant figures in a number.
<u>All nonzero numbers are significant.</u>
    Example: 3217 has four significant digits.
<u>Zeros are significant if</u>
• They are between nonzero digits. Example: 509
• They follow a decimal point and a nonzero digit.
    Example: 7.00
<u>Zeros are not significant if</u>
• They follow nonzero digits in a number without a decimal. Example: 7000
• They precede nonzero digits in a number with a decimal. Example: 0.0098

Calculating With Significant Figures

When measurements are added or subtracted, the precision of the result is determined by the precision of the least-precise measurement. The result may need to be rounded so the number of digits after the decimal is the same as the least-precise measurement.

Example
Follow these steps to determine the correct number of significant figures when adding 4.51 g, 3.27 g, and 6.0 g.

1. Determine which measurement is reported with the least degree of precision. In this case, the least-precise measurement, 6.0 g, has one digit after the decimal point.

2. The result must be rounded so that it also has one digit after the decimal point. After rounding, the result of this calculation is 13.8 g.

When measurements are multiplied or divided, the answer must have the same number of significant figures as the measurement with the fewest number of significant figures.

Example
Follow these steps to determine the correct number of significant figures when multiplying 120 m by 6.32 m.

1. Determine the number of significant figures in each of the measurements. In this case, the measurement 120 m has two significant figures; the measurement 6.32 m has three significant figures.

2. The result must be rounded to have only two significant figures. After rounding, the result of this calculation is 760 m^2.

Scientific Notation

In science, measurements are often very large or very small. Using scientific notation makes these large and small numbers easier to work with.

Using scientific notation requires an understanding of exponents and bases. When a number is expressed as a base and an exponent, the base is the number that is used as a factor. The exponent tells how many times the base is multiplied by itself. For example, the number 25 can be expressed as a base and an exponent in the following way:

$$25 = 5 \times 5 = 5^2$$

In the example above, 5 is the base and 2 is the exponent. In scientific notation, the base is always the number 10. The exponent tells how many times the number 10 is multiplied by itself.

A number written in scientific notation is expressed as the product of two factors, a number between 1 and 10 and the number 10 with an exponent. For example, the number 51,000 can be expressed in scientific notation. To find the first factor, move the decimal to obtain a number between 1 and 10. In this case, the number is 5.1. The exponent can be determined by counting the number of places the decimal point was moved. The decimal point was moved four places to the left. So, 51,000 expressed in scientific notation is 5.1×10^4.

Numbers that are less than one can also be expressed in scientific notation. In the case of numbers less than one, the decimal point must be moved to the right to obtain a number between 1 and 10. For example, in the number 0.000098, the decimal point must move five places to the right to obtain the number 9.8. When the decimal point is moved to the right, the exponent is negative. So, 0.000098 expressed in scientific notation is 9.8×10^{-5}.

Calculating With Scientific Notation

Numbers expressed in scientific notation can be used in calculations. When adding or subtracting numbers expressed in scientific notation, the first factors must be rewritten so the exponents are the same.

Example
Follow these steps to add $(4.30 \times 10^4) + (2.1 \times 10^3)$.

1. Move the decimal point in one of the expressions so the exponents are the same.
$(43.0 \times 10^3) + (2.1 \times 10^3)$

2. Add the first factors, keeping the value of the exponents the same.
$(43.0 \times 10^3) + (2.1 \times 10^3) = 45.1 \times 10^3$

3. Move the decimal point so the first factor is expressed as the product of a number between and 1 and 10 and an exponent with base 10.
$45.1 \times 10^3 = 4.51 \times 10^4$

When numbers expressed in scientific notation are multiplied, the exponents are added. When numbers expressed in scientific notation are divided, the exponents are subtracted.

Example
Use the following steps to determine the area of a rectangular field that has a length of 1.5×10^3 meters and a width of 3.2×10^2 meters.

1. Write down the expressions to be multiplied.
$(1.5 \times 10^3 \text{ m})(3.2 \times 10^2 \text{ m})$

2. Multiply the first factors, add the exponents, and multiply any units.
$= (1.5 \times 3.2)(10^{3+2}) \text{ m} \times \text{m}$
$= 4.8 \times 10^5 \text{ m}^2$

Dimensional Analysis

Scientific problems and calculations often involve unit conversions, or changes from one unit to another. Dimensional analysis is a method of unit conversion.

Suppose you were counting a pile of pennies. If there were 197 pennies in the pile, how many dollars would the pennies be worth? To determine the answer, you need to know the conversion factor between pennies and dollars. A conversion factor simply shows how two units are related. In this case, the conversion factor is 100 pennies = 1 dollar. Determining that 197 pennies is equal to $1.97 is an example of a unit conversion.

In dimensional analysis, the conversion factor is usually expressed as a fraction. Remember that the two values in any conversion factor are equal to one another. So, the two values form a fraction with the value of 1. Look at the example below to see how dimensional analysis can be applied to an everyday problem.

Example
A student walked 1.5 kilometers as part of a school fitness program. How many meters did the student walk?

1. 1.5 km = _?_ m

2. 1 km = 1000 m

3. 1000 m/1 km

4. 1.5 km × 1000 m/1 km = 1500 m (cross out "km" in two places); 1.5 km = 1500 m

Applying Dimensional Analysis

There are many applications of dimensional analysis in science. The example below demonstrates the use of dimensional analysis to convert units.

Example
The average teenage girl needs about 2200 kilocalories of energy from food each day. How many calories is this equivalent to?

Use the following steps to convert kilocalories to calories.

1. Determine the conversion factor that relates the two units.
   1 kilocalorie = 1000 calories

2. Write the conversion factor in the form of a fraction.
   1000 calories/1 kilocalorie

3. Multiply the measurement by the conversion factor.
   2200 kilocalories × 1000 calories/1 kilocalorie = 2,200,000 calories

Appendix E — Periodic Table

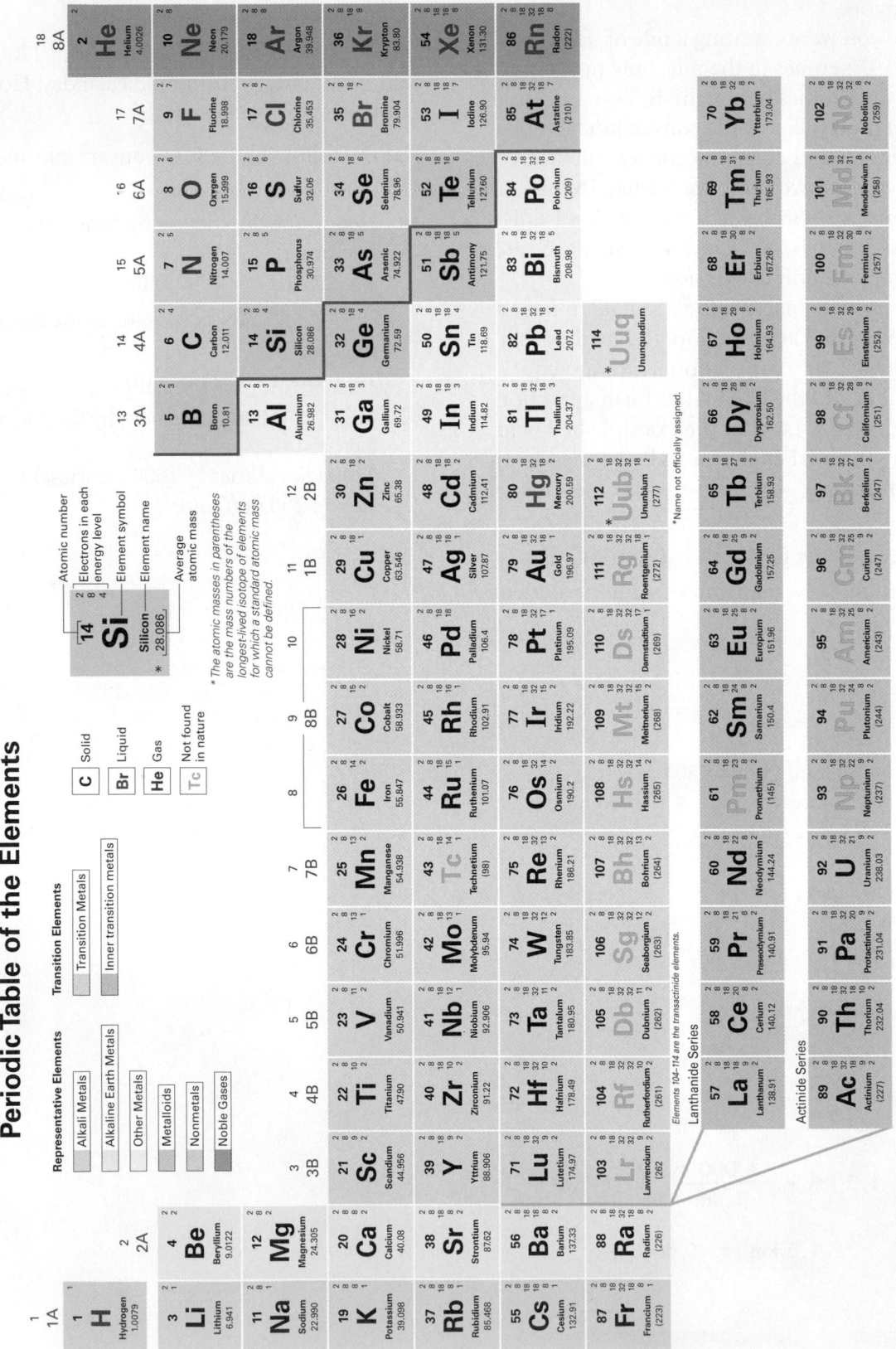

Periodic Table of the Elements

*Name not officially assigned.

*The atomic masses in parentheses are the mass numbers of the longest-lived isotope of elements for which a standard atomic mass cannot be defined.

Elements 104–114 are the transactinide elements.

Glossary

A

abiotic factor: physical, or nonliving, factor that shapes an ecosystem (58)
factor abiótico: factor físico, o inanimado, que da forma a un ecosistema

abscisic acid: plant hormone that inhibits cell division and, therefore, growth (589)
ácido abscísico: hormona vegetal que inhibe la división celular y, por ende, el crecimiento

acetylcholine: neurotransmitter that produces an impulse in a muscle cell (772)
acetilcolina: neurotransmisor que produce un impulso en una célula muscular

acid: compound that forms hydrogen ions (H^+) in solution; a solution with a pH of less than 7 (36)
ácido: compuesto que en una solución produce iones hidrógeno (H^+); una solución con un pH inferior a 7

acid rain: rain containing nitric and sulfuric acids (136)
lluvia ácida: lluvia que contiene ácido nítrico y ácido sulfúrico

actin: thin filament of protein found in muscles (771)
actina: microfilamento de proteína que se halla en los músculos

action potential: reversal of charges across the cell membrane of a neuron; also called a nerve impulse (744)
potencial de acción: inversión de las cargas a través de la membrana de una neurona; también llamado impulso nervioso

activation energy: energy that is needed to get a reaction started (43)
energía de activación: energía necesaria para que comience una reacción

active immunity: immunity that develops as a result of natural or deliberate exposure to an antigen (846)
inmunidad activa: inmunidad que se desarrolla a consecuencia de la exposición natural o deliberada a un antígeno

adaptation: heritable characteristic that increases an organism's ability to survive and reproduce in an environment (388)
adaptación: característica heredable que aumenta la capacidad de un organismo de sobrevivir y reproducirse en un medio ambiente

adaptive radiation: process by which a single species or a small group of species evolves into several different forms that live in different ways (459)
radiación adaptativa: proceso mediante el cual una sola especie o un grupo pequeño de especies evoluciona y da lugar a diferentes seres que viven de diversas maneras

adenosine triphosphate (ATP): compound used by cells to store and release energy (192)
trifosfato de adenosina (ATP): compuesto utilizado por las células para almacenar y liberar energía

adhesion: force of attraction between different kinds of molecules (34, 568)
adhesión: fuerza de atracción entre diferentes tipos de moléculas

aerobic: process that requires oxygen (214)
aeróbico: proceso que requiere oxígeno

age structure: number of males and females of each age in a population (109)
estructura etaria: número de machos y de hembras de cada edad en una población

aggression: threatening behavior that one animal uses to exert dominance over another animal (702)
agresión: comportamiento amenazador que emplea un animal para ejercer control sobre otro animal

algal bloom: increase in the amount of algae and other producers that results from a large input of a limiting nutrient (510)
florecimiento de algas: aumento de la cantidad de algas y otros productores debido a una gran entrada de un nutriente limitante

allele: one of a number of different forms of a gene (263)
alelo: cada una de las diversas formas de un gen

allele frequency: number of times that an allele occurs in a gene pool compared with the number of alleles in that pool for the same gene (406)
frecuencia alélica: número de veces que aparece un alelo en un caudal genético, comparado con la cantidad de alelos en ese caudal para el mismo gen

allergy: overreaction of the immune system to an antigen (849)
alergia: reacción exagerada del sistema inmune ante un antígeno

alternation of generations: life cycle that has two alternating phases—a haploid (N) phase and diploid (2N) phase (507, 530)
alternancia de generaciones: ciclo vital con dos fases que se alternan, una fase haploide (N) y una fase diploide (2N)

alveolus (pl. alveoli): one of many tiny air sacs at the end of a bronchiole in the lungs that provides surface area for gas exchange to occur (652, 797)
alvéolos: pequeños sacos, ubicados en las terminaciones de los bronquiolos pulmonares, que proporcionan una superficie en la que tiene lugar el intercambio gaseoso

amino acid: compound with an amino group on one end and a carboxyl group on the other end (40)
aminoácido: compuesto que contiene un grupo amino en un extremo y un grupo carboxilo en el otro extremo

amniotic egg: egg composed of shell and membranes that creates a protected environment in which the embryo can develop out of water (682)

huevo amniota: huevo formado por una cáscara y membranas que crea un ambiente protegido en el cual el embrión puede desarrollarse en un medio seco

amylase: enzyme in saliva that breaks the chemical bonds in starches (724)

amilasa: enzima de la saliva que fragmenta los enlaces químicos de los almidones

anaerobic: process that does not require oxygen (214)

anaeróbico: proceso que no requiere oxígeno

analogous structures: body parts that share a common function, but not structure (393)

estructuras análogas: partes del cuerpo que tienen la misma función, mas no la misma estructura

anaphase: phase of mitosis in which the chromosomes separate and move to opposite ends of the cell (242)

anafase: fase de la mitosis en la cual los cromosomas se separan y se desplazan hacia los extremos opuestos de la célula

angiosperm: group of seed plants that bear their seeds within a layer of tissue that protects the seed; also called flowering plant (536)

angiospermas: grupo de plantas con semillas, que están protegidas con una capa de tejido. Se conocen también como plantas que florecen.

anther: flower structure in which pollen grains are produced (579)

antera: estructura de la flor en la cual se generan los granos de polen

anthropoid: primate group made up of monkeys, apes, and humans (634)

antropoide: grupo de primates constituido por monos, simios y humanos

antibiotic: group of drugs used to block the growth and reproduction of bacterial pathogens (490)

antibiótico: grupo de drogas utilizadas para bloquear el desarrollo y la reproducción de organismos patógenos bacterianos

antibody: protein that either attacks antigens directly or produces antigen-binding proteins (842)

anticuerpo: proteína que ataca directamente a los antígenos o produce proteínas que se unen a los antígenos

anticodon: group of three bases on a tRNA molecule that are complementary to the three bases of a codon of mRNA (313)

anticodón: grupo de tres bases en una molécula de ARN de transferencia que son complementarias a las tres bases de un codón de ARN mensajero

antigen: any substance that triggers an immune response (842)

antígeno: cualquier sustancia que provoca una respuesta inmune

aphotic zone: dark layer of the oceans below the photic zone where sunlight does not penetrate (96)

zona afótica: sección oscura de los océanos donde no penetra la luz solar, situada debajo de la zona fótica

apical dominance: phenomenon in which the closer a bud is to the stem's tip, the more its growth is inhibited (588)

dominancia apical: fenómeno por el cual cuanto más cerca de la punta del tallo está un brote, más se inhibe su crecimiento

apical meristem: group of unspecialized cells that divide to produce increased length of stems and roots (555)

meristemo apical: grupo de células no especializadas que se dividen para producir un aumento en la longitud de tallos y raíces

apoptosis: process of programmed cell death (246)

apoptosis: proceso de muerte celular programada

appendage: structure, such as a leg or antenna, that extends from the body wall (625)

apéndice: estructura, como una pierna o una antena, que se proyecta desde la superficie corporal

appendicular skeleton: the bones of the arms and legs along with the bones of the pelvis and shoulder area (766)

esqueleto apendicular: los huesos de los brazos y de las piernas junto con los huesos de la pelvis y del área de los hombros

aquaculture: raising of aquatic organisms for human consumption (146)

acuicultura: cría de organismos acuáticos para el consumo humano

aquaporin: water channel protein in a cell (177)

acuaporina: proteína que canaliza el agua en una célula

Archaea: domain consisting of unicellular prokaryotes that have cell walls that do not contain peptidoglycan; corresponds to the kingdom Archaebacteria (439)

Arqueas: dominio formado por procariotas unicelulares cuyas paredes celulares no contienen peptidoglicano; corresponden al reino de las Arqueabacterias

artery: large blood vessel that carries blood away from the heart to the tissues of the body (789)

    arteria: vaso sanguíneo grande que transporta la sangre desde el corazón a los tejidos del cuerpo

artificial selection: selective breeding of plants and animals to promote the occurrence of desirable traits in offspring (387)

    selección artificial: cría selectiva de plantas y animales para fomentar la ocurrencia de rasgos deseados en la progenie

asexual reproduction: process of reproduction involving a single parent that results in offspring that are genetically identical to the parent (15, 236)

    reproducción asexual: proceso de reproducción que involucra a un único progenitor y da por resultado descendencia genéticamente idéntica a ese progenitor

asthma: chronic respiratory disease in which air passages narrow, causing wheezing, coughing, and difficulty breathing (849)

    asma: enfermedad respiratoria crónica en la cual las vías respiratorias se estrechan, provocando jadeos, tos y dificultad para respirar

atherosclerosis: condition in which fatty deposits called plaque build up inside artery walls and eventually cause the arteries to stiffen (793)

    arteriosclerosis o ateroesclerosis: enfermedad en la cual se acumulan depósitos de grasa llamados placas en el interior de las paredes arteriales que, con el tiempo, causan un endurecimiento de las arterias

atom: the basic unit of matter (28)
    átomo: unidad básica de la materia

ATP synthase: cluster of proteins that span the cell membrane and allow hydrogen ions (H^+) to pass through it (199)

    ATP sintasa: complejo de proteínas unidas a la membrana celular que permiten el paso de los iones de hidrógeno (H^+) a través de ella

atrium (pl. atria): upper chamber of the heart that receives blood from the rest of the body (654, 787)

    aurícula: cavidad superior del corazón que recibe sangre del resto del cuerpo

autonomic nervous system: part of the peripheral nervous system that regulates activities that are involuntary, or not under conscious control; made up of the sympathetic and parasympathetic subdivisions (753)

    sistema nervioso autónomo: parte del sistema nervioso periférico que regula las actividades involuntarias, o que son independientes de la conciencia; está compuesto por las subdivisiones simpática y parasimpática

autosome: chromosome that is not a sex chromosome; also called autosomal chromosome (335)

    autosoma: cromosoma que no es un cromosoma sexual; también llamado cromosoma autosómico

autotroph: organism that is able to capture energy from sunlight or chemicals and use it to produce its own food from inorganic compounds; also called a producer (60, 194)

    autótrofo: organismo capaz de atrapar la energía de la luz solar o de las sustancias químicas y utilizarla para producir su propio alimento a partir de compuestos inorgánicos; también llamado productor

auxin: regulatory substance produced in the tip of a growing plant that stimulates cell elongation and the growth of new roots (588)

    auxina: sustancia reguladora producida en la punta de una planta en crecimiento que estimula el alargamiento celular y el crecimiento de raíces nuevas

axial skeleton: skeleton that supports the central axis of the body; consists of the skull, vertebral column, and the rib cage (766)

    esqueleto axial: esqueleto que sostiene al eje central del cuerpo; consiste en el cráneo, la columna vertebral y la caja torácica

axon: long fiber that carries impulses away from the cell body of a neuron (743)

    axón: fibra larga que lleva los impulsos desde el cuerpo celular de una neurona

B

bacillus (pl. bacilli): rod-shaped prokaryote (486)
    bacilo: procariota con forma de bastón

background extinction: extinction caused by slow and steady process of natural selection (457)

    extinción de fondo: extinción causada por un proceso lento y continuo de selección natural

Bacteria: domain of unicellular prokaryotes that have cell walls containing peptidoglycan; corresponds to the kingdom eubacteria (439)

    Bacteria: pertenece al dominio de los unicelulares procariota cuyas paredes celulares contienen peptidoglicano; corresponde al reino de las Eubacterias

bacteriophage: kind of virus that infects bacteria (289, 481)
    bacteriófago: clase de virus que infecta a las bacterias

bark: tissues that are found outside the vascular cambium, including the phloem, cork cambium, and cork (563)

    corteza: tejidos que se hallan fuera del cámbium vascular, incluidos el floema, el cámbium suberoso y el corcho

base: compound that produces hydroxide ions (OH^-) in solution; solution with a pH of more than 7 (36)

    base: compuesto que en una solución produce iones hidróxido (OH^-); una solución con un pH superior a 7

base pairing: principle that bonds in DNA can form only between adenine and thymine and between guanine and cytosine (295)

apareamiento de bases: principio que establece que los enlaces en el ADN sólo pueden formarse entre adenina y timina y entre guanina y citocina

behavior: manner in which an organism reacts to changes in its internal condition or external environment (696)

comportamiento: manera en que un organismo reacciona a los cambios que ocurren en su condición interna o en el medio ambiente externo

behavioral isolation: form of reproductive isolation in which two populations develop differences in courtship rituals or other behaviors that prevent them from breeding (415)

aislamiento conductual: forma de aislamiento reproductivo en la cual dos poblaciones desarrollan diferencias en sus rituales de cortejo o en otros comportamientos que evitan que se apareen

benthos: organisms that live attached to or near the bottom of lakes, streams, or oceans (96)

bentos: organismos que viven adheridos al fondo, o cerca del fondo, de lagos, arroyos u océanos

bias: particular preference or point of view that is personal, rather than scientific (12)

parcialidad: preferencia especial o punto de vista que es personal en lugar de ser científico

bilateral symmetry: body plan in which a single imaginary line can divide the body into left and right sides that are mirror images of each other (611)

simetría bilateral: diseño corporal en el cual una línea imaginaria divide al cuerpo en dos lados, izquierdo y derecho, que son imágenes reflejas una del otra

binary fission: type of asexual reproduction in which an organism replicates its DNA and divides in half, producing two identical daughter cells (487)

fisión binaria: tipo de reproducción asexual en la cual un organismo replica su ADN, se divide por la mitad y produce dos células hijas idénticas

binocular vision: ability to merge visual images from both eyes, providing depth perception and a three-dimensional view of the world (634)

visión binocular: capacidad de fusionar las imágenes visuales provenientes de ambos ojos, lo cual proporciona una percepción profunda y una visión tridimensional del mundo

binomial nomenclature: classification system in which each species is assigned a two-part scientific name (428)

nomenclatura binaria: sistema de clasificación en el cual a cada especie se le asigna un nombre científico que consta de dos partes

biodiversity: total of the variety of organisms in the biosphere; also called biological diversity (138)

biodiversidad: totalidad de los distintos organismos que se hallan en la biósfera; también denominada diversidad biológica

biogeochemical cycle: process in which elements, chemical compounds, and other forms of matter are passed from one organism to another and from one part of the biosphere to another (68)

ciclo biogeoquímico: proceso en el cual los elementos, los compuestos químicos y otras formas de materia pasan de un organismo a otro y de una parte de la biósfera a otra

biogeography: study of past and present distribution of organisms (392)

biogeografía: estudio de la distribución pasada y presente de los organismos

bioinformatics: application of mathematics and computer science to store, retrieve, and analyze biological data (344)

bioinformática: aplicación de las matemáticas y de la informática para almacenar, recuperar y analizar información biológica

biological magnification: increasing concentration of a harmful substance in organisms at higher trophic levels in a food chain or food web (134)

bioacumulación: concentración creciente de sustancias perjudiciales en los organismos de los niveles tróficos más elevados de una cadena o red alimentaria

biology: scientific study of life (13)

biología: estudio científico de la vida

biomass: total amount of living tissue within a given trophic level (67)

biomasa: cantidad total de tejido vivo dentro de un nivel trófico dado

biome: a group of ecosystems that share similar climates and typical organisms (57)

bioma: un grupo de ecosistemas que comparten climas similares y organismos típicos

biosphere: part of Earth in which life exists including land, water, and air or atmosphere (17, 56)

biósfera: parte de la Tierra en la cual existe vida, y que incluye el suelo, el agua y el aire o atmósfera

biotechnology: process of manipulating organisms, cells, or molecules, to produce specific products (355)

biotecnología: proceso de manipular organismos, células o moléculas con el fin de obtener productos específicos

biotic factor: any living part of the environment with which an organism might interact (57)

factor biótico: cualquier parte viva del medio ambiente con la cual un organismo podría interaccionar

bipedal: term used to refer to two-foot locomotion (635)

bípedo: término utilizado para referirse a la locomoción sobre dos pies

blastocyst: stage of early development in mammals that consists of a hollow ball of cells (249, 825)

blastocisto: etapa temprana del desarrollo de los mamíferos que consiste en una bola hueca formada por una capa de células

blastula: hollow ball of cells that develops when a zygote undergoes a series of cell divisions (612)

blástula: esfera hueca de células que se desarrolla cuando un cigoto atraviesa una serie de divisiones celulares

bone marrow: soft tissue found in bone cavities (767)

médula ósea: tejido blando que se halla en las cavidades de los huesos

bottleneck effect: a change in allele frequency following a dramatic reduction in the size of a population (411)

efecto cuello de botella: un cambio en la frecuencia alélica que resulta cuando el tamaño de una población reduce drásticamente

Bowman's capsule: cuplike structure that encases the glomerulus; collects filtrate from the blood (731)

cápsula de Bowman: estructura en forma de taza que encierra al glomérulo; recoge los filtrados provenientes de la sangre

brain stem: structure that connects the brain and spinal cord; includes the medulla oblongata and the pons (749)

tronco cerebral: estructura que conecta al cerebro con la médula espinal; incluye el bulbo raquídeo y el puente de Varolio

bronchus (pl. bronchi): one of two large tubes in the chest cavity that leads from the trachea to the lungs (797)

bronquio: cada uno de los dos conductos largos ubicados en la cavidad torácica que parten desde la tráquea y llegan a los pulmones

bryophyte: group of plants that have specialized reproductive organs but lack vascular tissue; includes mosses and their relatives (533)

briofitas: grupo de plantas que tienen órganos reproductores especializados pero carecen de tejido vascular; incluyen a los musgos y sus congéneres

bud: plant structure containing apical meristem tissue that can produce new stems and leaves (560)

yema o gema: estructura de las plantas que contiene tejido del meristemo apical y puede producir nuevos tallos y hojas

buffer: compound that prevents sharp, sudden changes in pH (36)

solución amortiguadora: compuesto que evita cambios bruscos y repentinos en el pH

C

calcitonin: hormone produced by the thyroid that reduces blood calcium levels (815)

calcitonina: hormona producida por la tiroides que reduce los niveles de calcio en la sangre

Calorie: measure of heat energy in food; equivalent to 1000 calories (719)

Caloría: medida de la energía térmica de los alimentos, equivalente a 1000 calorías

calorie: amount of energy needed to raise the temperature of 1 gram of water by 1 degree Celsius (212)

caloría: cantidad de energía necesaria para elevar la temperatura de 1 gramo de agua en 1 grado Celsius

Calvin cycle: light-independent reactions of photosynthesis in which energy from ATP and NADPH is used to build high-energy compounds such as sugar (201)

ciclo de Calvin: reacciones de la fotosíntesis independientes de la luz en las cuales se utiliza la energía del ATP y del NADPH para elaborar compuestos con alto contenido energético, como el azúcar

cancer: disorder in which some of the body's cells lose the ability to control growth (247)

cáncer: enfermedad en la cual algunas de las células del cuerpo pierden la capacidad de controlar su crecimiento

canopy: dense covering formed by the leafy tops of tall rain-forest trees (92)

dosel forestal: cubierta densa formada por las copas de los árboles altos del bosque tropical

capillary: smallest blood vessel; brings nutrients and oxygen to the tissues and absorbs carbon dioxide and waste products (789)

capilar: más pequeño de los vaso sanguíneo más pequeño; lleva nutrientes y oxígeno a los tejidos y absorbe dióxido de carbono y productos de desecho

capillary action: tendency of water to rise in a thin tube (568)

capilaridad: tendencia del agua a ascender en un tubo delgado

capsid: protein coat surrounding a virus (481)

cápsida: cobertura de proteínas que rodea a un virus

carbohydrate: compound made up of carbon, hydrogen, and oxygen atoms; type of nutrient that is the major source of energy for the body (38, 720)

hidrato de carbono: compuesto formado por átomos de carbono, hidrógeno y oxígeno; tipo de nutriente que es la fuente principal de energía para el cuerpo

carnivore: organism that obtains energy by eating animals (62)

carnívoro: organismo que obtiene energía al comer otros animales

carpel: innermost part of a flower that produces and shelters the female gametophytes (579)

carpelo: parte interna de una flor que produce y alberga los gametofitos femeninos

carrying capacity: largest number of individuals of a particular species that a particular environment can support (111)

capacidad de carga: mayor cantidad de individuos de una especie en particular que un medio ambiente específico puede mantener

cartilage: type of connective tissue that supports the body and is softer and more flexible than bone (628, 767)

cartílago: tipo de tejido conectivo que sostiene al cuerpo y es más blando y flexible que el hueso

Casparian strip: waterproof strip that surrounds plant endodermal cells and is involved in the one-way passage of materials into the vascular cylinder in plant roots (558)

banda de Caspary: banda impermeable que rodea a las células endodérmicas de las plantas y participa en el transporte unidireccional de las sustancias hacia el interior del cilindro vascular de las raíces de las plantas

catalyst: substance that speeds up the rate of a chemical reaction (44)

catalizador: sustancia que acelera la velocidad de una reacción química

cell: basic unit of all forms of life (160)

célula: unidad básica de todas las formas de vida

cell body: largest part of a typical neuron; contains the nucleus and much of the cytoplasm (743)

cuerpo celular: parte más grande de una neurona típica; que contiene el núcleo y gran parte del citoplasma

cell cycle: series of events in which a cell grows, prepares for division, and divides to form two daughter cells (240)

ciclo celular: serie de sucesos en los cuales una célula crece, se prepara para dividirse y se divide para formar dos células hijas

cell division: process by which a cell divides into two new daughter cells (236)

división celular: proceso por el cual una célula se divide en dos células hijas nuevas

cell membrane: thin, flexible barrier that surrounds all cells; regulates what enters and leaves the cell (162)

membrana celular: barrera flexible y delgada que rodea a todas las células; regula lo que entra y sale de la célula

cell theory: fundamental concept of biology that states that all living things are composed of cells; that cells are the basic units of structure and function in living things; and that new cells are produced from existing cells (160)

teoría celular: concepto fundamental de la Biología que establece que todos los seres vivos están compuestos por células; que las células son las unidades básicas estructurales y funcionales de los seres vivos; y que las células nuevas se producen a partir de células existentes

cell wall: strong, supporting layer around the cell membrane in some cells (171)

pared celular: capa resistente que sirve de sostén y está situada alrededor de la membrana celular de algunas células

cell-mediated immunity: immune response that defends the body against viruses, fungi, and abnormal cancer cells inside living cells (843)

inmunidad celular: respuesta inmune que desde las células defiende al cuerpo contra virus, hongos y células anormales cancerígenas

cellular respiration: process that releases energy by breaking down glucose and other food molecules in the presence of oxygen (213)

respiración celular: proceso que libera energía al descomponer la glucosa y otras moléculas de los alimentos en presencia de oxígeno

central nervous system: includes the brain and spinal cord; processes information and creates a response that it delivers to the body (742)

sistema nervioso central: incluye el cerebro y la médula espinal; procesa información y genera una respuesta que es enviada al cuerpo

centriole: structure in an animal cell that helps to organize cell division (167, 242)

centríolo: estructura de una célula animal que contribuye a organizar la división celular

centromere: region of a chromosome where the two sister chromatids attach (242)

centrómero: región de un cromosoma donde se unen las dos cromátidas hermanas

cephalization: concentration of sense organs and nerve cells at the anterior end of an animal (613)

cefalización: concentración de órganos sensoriales y células nerviosas en el extremo anterior de un animal

cerebellum: part of the brain that coordinates movement and controls balance (671, 749)

cerebelo: parte del encéfalo que coordina el movimiento y controla el equilibrio

cerebral cortex: outer layer of the cerebrum of a mammal's brain; center of thinking and other complex behaviors (748)

corteza cerebral: capa externa del cerebro de un mamífero; centro del raciocinio y otros comportamientos complejos

cerebrum: part of the brain responsible for voluntary activities of the body; "thinking" region of the brain (671, 748)
  cerebro: parte del encéfalo responsable de las actividades voluntarias del cuerpo; región "pensante" del encéfalo

chemical digestion: process by which enzymes break down food into small molecules that the body can use (723)
  digestión química: proceso por el cual las enzimas descomponen los alimentos en moléculas pequeñas que el cuerpo puede utilizar

chemical reaction: process that changes, or transforms, one set of chemicals into another set of chemicals (42)
  reacción química: proceso que cambia, o transforma, un grupo de sustancias químicas en otro grupo de sustancias químicas

chemosynthesis: process in which chemical energy is used to produce carbohydrates (61)
  quimiosíntesis: proceso en el cual la energía química se utiliza para producir hidratos de carbono

chitin: complex carbohydrate that makes up the cell walls of fungi; also found in the external skeletons of arthropods (514)
  quitina: hidrato de carbono complejo que forma las paredes celulares de los hongos; también se halla en los esqueletos externos de los artrópodos

chlorophyll: principal pigment of plants and other photosynthetic organisms (195)
  clorofila: pigmento fundamental de las plantas y de otros organismos fotosintéticos

chloroplast: organelle found in cells of plants and some other organisms that captures the energy from sunlight and converts it into chemical energy (170)
  cloroplasto: orgánulo de las células de las plantas y de otros organismos que captura la energía de la luz solar y la convierte en energía química

chordate: animal that has, for at least one stage of its life, a dorsal, hollow nerve cord, a notochord, a tail that extends beyond the anus, and pharyngeal pouches (606)
  cordado: animal que, al menos durante una etapa de su vida, tiene un cordón nervioso hueco y dorsal, un notocordio, una cola que se prolonga más allá del ano y bolsas faríngeas

chromatid: one of two identical "sister" parts of a duplicated chromosome (242)
  cromátida: una de las dos partes "hermanas" idénticas de un cromosoma duplicado

chromatin: substance found in eukaryotic chromosomes that consists of DNA tightly coiled around histones (239)
  cromatina: sustancia que se halla en los cromosomas eucarióticos y que consiste en ADN enrollado apretadamente alrededor de las histonas

chromosome: threadlike structure of DNA and protein that contains genetic information; in eukaryotes, chromosomes are found in the nucleus; in prokaryotes, they are found in the cytoplasm (239)
  cromosoma: estructura larga de ADN y proteina, con foma de hilo, que posee información genética; en los eucariotas, los cromosomas están dentro del núcleo; en los procariotas, los cromosomas están en el citoplasma

chyme: mixture of enzymes and partially digested food (725)
  quimo: mezcla de enzimas y alimentos parcialmente digeridos

cilium (pl. cilia): short hairlike projection that produces movement (506)
  cilio: pequeña prolongación parecida a un pelo que produce movimiento

circadian rhythm: behavioral cycles that occur daily (701)
  ritmo circadiano: ciclos conductuales que ocurren diariamente

clade: evolutionary branch of a cladogram that includes a single ancestor and all its descendants (433)
  clado: rama evolutiva de un cladograma que incluye a un único ancestro y a todos sus descendientes

cladogram: diagram depicting patterns of shared characteristics among species (433)
  cladograma: diagrama que representa patrones de características compartidas entre especies

class: in classification, a group of closely related orders (430)
  clase: en la clasificación, un grupo de varios órdenes relacionados estrechamente

classical conditioning: type of learning that occurs when an animal makes a mental connection between a stimulus and some kind of reward or punishment (698)
  condicionamiento clásico: tipo de aprendizaje que ocurre cuando un animal realiza una conexión mental entre un estímulo y algún tipo de recompensa o castigo

climate: average year-to-year conditions of temperature and precipitation in an area over a long period of time (82)
  clima: promedio anual de las condiciones de temperatura y precipitación en un área durante un largo período de tiempo

clone: member of a population of genetically identical cells produced from a single cell (361)
  clon: miembro de una población de células genéticamente idénticas producidas a partir de una célula única

closed circulatory system: type of circulatory system in which blood circulates entirely within blood vessels that extend throughout the body (653)
  sistema circulatorio cerrado: tipo de sistema circulatorio en el cual la sangre circula completamente dentro de los vasos sanguíneos que se extienden por todo el cuerpo

coccus (pl. cocci): spherical prokaryote (486)
  coco: procariota de forma esférica

cochlea: fluid-filled part of inner ear; contains nerve cells that detect sound (755)
  cóclea: parte del oído interno llena de fluidos; contiene las células nerviosas que detectan el sonido

codominance: situation in which the phenotypes produced by both alleles are completely expressed (271)

codominancia: situación en la cual los fenotipos producidos por ambos alelos están expresados completamente

codon: group of three nucleotide bases in mRNA that specify a particular amino acid to be incorporated into a protein (311)

codón: grupo de tres bases de nucleótidos en el RNA mensajero que especifican la incorporación de un aminoácido en particular en una proteína

coelom: body cavity lined with mesoderm (612)

celoma: cavidad corporal revestida de mesodermo

coevolution: process by which two species evolve in response to changes in each other over time (460)

coevolución: proceso por el cual dos especies evolucionan en respuesta a cambios mutuos en el transcurso del tiempo

cohesion: attraction between molecules of the same substance (34)

cohesión: atracción entre moléculas de la misma sustancia

collenchyma: in plants, type of ground tissue that has strong, flexible cell walls; helps support larger plants (553)

colénquima: en las plantas, tipo de tejido fundamental que tiene paredes celulares fuertes y flexibles; contribuye a sostener las plantas más grandes

commensalism: symbiotic relationship in which one organism benefits and the other is neither helped nor harmed (87)

comensalismo: relación simbiótica en la cual un organismo se beneficia y el otro ni se beneficia ni sufre daño

communication: passing of information from one organism to another (703)

comunicación: traspaso de información desde un organismo a otro

community: assemblage of different populations that live together in a defined area (56)

comunidad: conjunto de varias poblaciones que viven juntas en un área definida

companion cell: in plants, phloem cell that surrounds sieve tube elements (554)

célula anexa: en las plantas, célula del floema que rodea a los vasos cribosos

competitive exclusion principle: principle that states that no two species can occupy the same niche in the same habitat at the same time (86)

principio de exclusión competitiva: principio que afirma que dos especies no pueden ocupar el mismo nicho en el mismo hábitat al mismo tiempo

compound: substance formed by the chemical combination of two or more elements in definite proportions (30)

compuesto: sustancia formada por la combinación química de dos o más elementos en proporciones definidas

cone: in the eye, photoreceptor that responds to light of different colors, producing color vision (757)

cono: en el ojo, receptor de luz que responde a la luz de diferentes colores, produciendo la visión a color

coniferous: term used to refer to trees that produce seed-bearing cones and have thin leaves shaped like needles (93)

coníferas: término utilizado para referirse a los árboles que producen conos portadores de semillas y que tienen hojas delgadas con forma de aguja

conjugation: process in which paramecia and some prokaryotes exchange genetic information (487, 507)

conjugación: proceso mediante el cual los paramecios y algunos procariotas intercambian información genética

connective tissue: type of tissue that provides support for the body and connects its parts (714)

tejido conectivo: tipo de tejido que proporciona sostén al cuerpo y conecta sus partes

consumer: organism that relies on other organisms for its energy and food supply; also called a heterotroph (61)

consumidor: organismo que depende de otros organismos para obtener su energía y su provisión de alimentos; también llamado heterótrofo

control group: group in an experiment that is exposed to the same conditions as the experimental group except for one independent variable (6)

grupo de control: en un experimento, grupo que está expuesto a las mismas condiciones que el grupo experimental, excepto por una variable independiente

controlled experiment: experiment in which only one variable is changed (6)

experimento controlado: experimento en el cual sólo se cambia una variable

convergent evolution: process by which unrelated organisms independently evolve similarities when adapting to similar environments (460)

evolución convergente: proceso mediante el cual organismos no relacionados evolucionan independientemente hacia caracteres similares cuando se adaptan a ambientes parecidos

cork cambium: meristematic tissue that produces the outer covering of stems during secondary growth of a plant (562)

cámbium suberoso: tejido del meristemo que produce la cubierta exterior de los tallos durante el crecimiento secundario de una planta

cornea: tough transparent layer of the eye through which light enters (756)

córnea: membrana dura y transparente del ojo a través de la cual entra la luz

corpus luteum: name given to a follicle after ovulation because of its yellow color (821)

cuerpo lúteo: nombre dado a un folículo después de la ovulación debido a su color amarillo

cortex: in plants, region of ground tissue just inside the root through which water and minerals move (557)

    corteza radicular: en las plantas, región de tejido fundamental situada en el interior de la raíz a través de la cual pasan el agua y los minerales

corticosteroid: steroid hormone produced by the adrenal cortex (814)

    corticosteroide o corticoide: hormona esteroídica producida por la corteza de las glándulas adrenales

cotyledon: first leaf or first pair of leaves produced by the embryo of a seed plant (542)

    cotiledón: primera hoja o primer par de hojas producidas por el embrión de una planta fanerógama

courtship: type of behavior in which an animal sends out stimuli in order to attract a member of the opposite sex (702)

    cortejo: tipo de comportamiento en el cual un animal emite estímulos para atraer a un miembro del sexo opuesto

covalent bond: type of bond between atoms in which the electrons are shared (31)

    enlace covalente: tipo de enlace entre átomos en el cual se comparten los electrones

crossing-over: process in which homologous chromosomes exchange portions of their chromatids during meiosis (276)

    entrecruzamiento: proceso por el cual los cromosomas homólogos intercambian partes de sus cromátidas durante la meiosis

cyclin: one of a family of proteins that regulates the cell cycle in eukaryotic cells (246)

    ciclina: un componente de la familia de proteínas que regulan el ciclo celular de las células eucariotas

cytokinesis: division of the cytoplasm to form two separate daughter cells (241)

    citocinesis: división del citoplasma para formar dos células hijas separadas

cytokinin: plant hormone produced in growing roots and in developing fruits and seeds (589)

    citoquinina: hormona vegetal que se genera en las raíces en crecimiento y en los frutos y semillas en desarrollo

cytoplasm: in eukaryotic cells, all cellular contents outside the nucleus, in prokaryotic cells, all of the cells' contents (164)

    citoplasma: en una célula eucariota, todo el contenido celular fuera del núcleo; en las células procariotas, todo el contenido de las células

cytoskeleton: network of protein filaments in a eukaryotic cell that gives the cell its shape and internal organization and is involved in movement (167)

    citoesqueleto: en una célula eucariota, red de filamentos proteínicos que otorga a la célula su forma y su organización interna y participa en el movimiento

D

data: evidence; information gathered from observations (6)

    datos: evidencia; información reunida a partir de observaciones

deciduous: term used to refer to a type of tree that sheds its leaves during a particular season each year (92)

    caduco: término utilizado para referirse a un tipo de árbol que pierde sus hojas cada año durante una estación en particular

decomposer: organism that breaks down and obtains energy from dead organic matter (62)

    descomponedor: organismo que descompone y obtiene energía de la materia orgánica muerta

deforestation: destruction of forests (133)

    deforestación: destrucción de los bosques

demographic transition: change in a population from high birth and death rates to low birth and death rates (118)

    transición demográfica: en una población, cambio de índices de nacimiento y mortalidad altos a índices de nacimiento y mortalidad bajos

demography: scientific study of human populations (118)

    demografía: estudio científico de las poblaciones humanas

dendrite: extension of the cell body of a neuron that carries impulses from the environment or from other neurons toward the cell body (743)

    dendrita: prolongación del cuerpo celular de una neurona que transporta impulsos desde el medio ambiente o desde otras neuronas hacia el cuerpo celular

denitrification: process by which bacteria convert nitrates into nitrogen gas (71)

    desnitrificación: proceso por el cual las bacterias del suelo convierten los nitratos en gas nitrógeno

density-dependent limiting factor: limiting factor that depends on population density (112)

    factor limitante dependiente de la densidad: factor limitante que depende de la densidad de la población

density-independent limiting factor: limiting factor that affects all populations in similar ways, regardless of the population density (114)

    factor limitante independiente de la densidad: factor limitante que afecta a todas las poblaciones de manera similar, sin importar la densidad de la población

deoxyribonucleic acid (DNA): genetic material that organisms inherit from their parents (14)

    ácido desoxirribonucleico (ADN): material genético que los organismos heredan de sus padres

dependent variable: variable that is observed and that changes in response to the independent variable; also called the responding variable (6)

    variable dependiente: variable que está siendo observada y cambia en respuesta a la variable independiente; también llamada variable de respuesta

derived character: trait that appears in recent parts of a lineage, but not in its older members (434)
   carácter derivado: rasgo que aparece en los descendientes recientes de un linaje, pero no en sus miembros más viejos

dermis: layer of skin found beneath the epidermis (778)
   dermis: capa de la piel situada debajo de la epidermis

desertification: lower land productivity caused by over-farming, overgrazing, seasonal drought, and climate change (132)
   desertificación: disminución de la productividad de la tierra debido al cultivo y al pastoreo excesivo, a la sequía estacional y al cambio climático

detritivore: organism that feeds on plant and animal remains and other dead matter (62)
   detritívoro: organismo que se alimenta de restos animales y vegetales y demás materia orgánica muerta

deuterostome: group of animals in which the blastopore becomes an anus, and the mouth is formed from the second opening that develops (613)
   deuteróstomos: grupo de animales en los cuales el blastoporo se convierte en ano y la boca se forma a partir del desarrollo de una segunda abertura

diaphragm: large flat muscle at the bottom of the chest cavity that helps with breathing (799)
   diafragma: músculo plano y grande ubicado en la parte inferior de la cavidad torácica que participa en la respiración

dicot: angiosperm with two seed leaves in its ovary (542)
   dicotiledónea: angiosperma con dos cotiledones (hojas embrionarias) en su ovario

differentiation: process in which cells become specialized in structure and function (248, 323)
   diferenciación: proceso en el cual las células se especializan en estructura y función

diffusion: process by which particles tend to move from an area where they are more concentrated to an area where they are less concentrated (176)
   difusión: proceso por el cual las partículas tienden a desplazarse desde un área donde están más concentradas hacia un área donde están menos concentradas

digestive tract: tube that begins at the mouth and ends at the anus (648)
   tracto digestivo: tubo que comienza en la boca y termina en el ano

diploid: term used to refer to a cell that contains two sets of homologous chromosomes (275)
   diploide: término utilizado para referirse a una célula que contiene dos series de cromosomas homólogos

directional selection: form of natural selection in which individuals at one end of a distribution curve have higher fitness than individuals in the middle or at the other end of the curve (410)
   selección direccional: forma de selección natural en la cual los individuos que se hallan en un extremo de la curva de distribución poseen una mayor capacidad de adaptación que los individuos que se hallan en el centro o en el otro extremo de la curva

disruptive selection: natural selection in which individuals at the upper and lower ends of the curve have higher fitness than individuals near the middle of the curve (410)
   selección disruptiva: forma de selección natural en la cual los individuos que se hallan en los extremos superior e inferior de la curva poseen una mayor capacidad de adaptación que los individuos que se hallan cerca del centro de la curva

DNA fingerprinting: tool used by biologists that analyzes an individual's unique collection of DNA restriction fragments; used to determine whether two samples of genetic material are from the same person (365)
   prueba de ADN: herramienta utilizada por los biólogos mediante la cual se analiza el conjunto de los fragmentos de restricción de ADN exclusivo de cada individuo; utilizada para determinar si dos muestras de material genético pertenecen a la misma persona; también llamada huella genética o análisis de ADN

DNA microarray: glass slide or silicon chip that carries thousands of different kinds of single-stranded DNA fragments arranged in a grid. A DNA microarray is used to detect and measure the expression of thousands of genes at one time (364)
   chip de ADN: superficie de vidrio o chip de silicona que contiene miles de diferentes tipos de fragmentos de ADN de una sola cadena dispuestos en una cuadrícula. Un chip de ADN se utiliza para detectar y medir la expresión de miles de genes a la vez

DNA polymerase: principal enzyme involved in DNA replication (297)
   ADN polimerasa: enzima fundamental involucrada en la replicación del ADN

domain: larger, more inclusive taxonomic category than a kingdom (438)
   dominio: categoría taxonómica más amplia e inclusiva que un reino

dopamine: neurotransmitter that is associated with the brain's pleasure and reward centers (750)
   dopamina: neurotransmisor que está asociado con los centros de placer y de recompensa del cerebro

dormancy: period of time during which a plant embryo is alive but not growing (586)
   latencia: período de tiempo durante el cual un embrión vegetal está vivo pero no crece

double fertilization: process of fertilization in angiosperms in which the first event produces the zygote, and the second, the endosperm within the seed (581)

   doble fertilización: proceso de fecundación de las angiospermas en el cual se produce, en el primer suceso el cigoto y en el segundo, el endospermo dentro de la semilla

E

ecological footprint: total amount of functioning ecosystem needed both to provide the resources a human population uses and to absorb the wastes that population generates (143)

   huella ecológica: cantidad total de ecosistema en funcionamiento necesaria para proporcionar los recursos que utiliza una población humana y para absorber los residuos que genera esa población

ecological hot spot: small geographic area where significant numbers of habitats and species are in immediate danger of extinction (142)

   zona de conflicto ecológico: área geográfica pequeña donde cantidades importantes de hábitats y especies se hallan en peligro de extinción inmediato

ecological pyramid: illustration of the relative amounts of energy or matter contained within each trophic level in a given food chain or food web (66)

   pirámide ecológica: ilustración de las cantidades relativas de energía o materia contenidas dentro de cada nivel trófico en una cadena o red alimenticia dada

ecological succession: series of gradual changes that occur in a community following a disturbance (88)

   sucesión ecológica: serie de cambios graduales que ocurren en una comunidad después de una alteración

ecology: scientific study of interactions among organisms and between organisms and their environment (56)

   ecología: estudio científico de las interacciones entre organismos y entre los organismos y su medio ambiente

ecosystem: all the organisms that live in a place, together with their nonliving environment (57)

   ecosistema: todos los organismos que viven en un lugar, junto con su medio ambiente inanimado

ecosystem diversity: variety of habitats, communities, and ecological processes in the biosphere (138)

   diversidad de ecosistemas: variedad de hábitats, comunidades y procesos ecológicos que existen en la biósfera

ectoderm: outermost germ layer; produces sense organs, nerves, and outer layer of skin (612)

   ectodermo: capa embrionaria más externa; desarrolla órganos sensoriales, nervios y la capa exterior de la piel

ectotherm: animal whose body temperature is determined by the temperature of its environment (685)

   animal de sangre fría: animal cuya temperatura corporal está determinada por la temperatura de su medio ambiente

electron: negatively charged particle; located in the space surrounding the nucleus (28)

   electrón: partícula con carga negativa; ubicada en el espacio que rodea al núcleo

electron transport chain: series of electron carrier proteins that shuttle high-energy electrons during ATP-generating reactions (199)

   cadena de transporte de electrones: serie de proteínas transportadoras que llevan electrones de alta energía, durante las reacciones generadoras de ATP

element: pure substance that consists entirely of one type of atom (29)

   elemento: sustancia pura que consiste íntegramente en un tipo de átomo

embryo: developing stage of a multicellular organism (248)

   embrión: una de las etapas de desarrollo de un organismo multicelular

embryo sac: female gametophyte within the ovule of a flowering plant (580)

   saco embrionario: gametofito femenino dentro del óvulo de una planta que produce flores

emerging disease: disease that appears in the population for the first time, or an old disease that suddenly becomes harder to control (492)

   enfermedad emergente: enfermedad que aparece en una población por primera vez o una enfermedad antigua que de pronto se vuelve más difícil de controlar

emigration: movement of individuals out of an area (109)

   emigración: desplazamiento de individuos fuera de un área

endocrine gland: gland that releases its secretions (hormones) directly into the blood, which transports the secretions to other areas of the body (685, 810)

   glándula endocrina: glándula que vierte sus secreciones (hormonas) directamente en la sangre, para ser transportadas a otras áreas del cuerpo

endoderm: innermost germ layer; develops into the linings of the digestive tract and much of the respiratory system (612)

   endodermo: capa embrionaria más interna, a partir de la cual se desarrollan los revestimientos del tracto digestivo y gran parte del sistema respiratorio

endodermis: in plants, layer of ground tissue that completely encloses the vascular cylinder (557)

   endodermis: en las plantas, un capa de tejido fundamental que envuelve completamente al cilindro vascular

endoplasmic reticulum: internal membrane system found in eukaryotic cells; place where lipid components of the cell membrane are assembled (168)

   retículo endoplasmático: sistema de membranas internas de las células eucariotas; lugar donde se reúnen los componentes lipídicos de la membrana celular

endoskeleton: internal skeleton; structural support system within the body of an animal (675)

   endoesqueleto: esqueleto interno; sistema estructural de sostén dentro del cuerpo de un animal

endosperm: food-rich tissue that nourishes a seedling as it grows (581)

endospermo: tejido nutritivo que alimenta a una plántula a medida que crece

endospore: structure produced by prokaryotes in unfavorable conditions; a thick internal wall that encloses the DNA and a portion of the cytoplasm (487)

endospora: estructura producida por los procariotas en condiciones desfavorables; una gruesa pared interna que encierra al ADN y a una parte del citoplasma

endosymbiotic theory: theory that proposes that eukaryotic cells formed from a symbiotic relationship among several different prokaryotic cells (464)

teoría endosimbiótica: teoría que propone que las células eucariotas se formaron a partir de una relación simbiótica entre varias células procariotas distintas

endotherm: animal whose body temperature is regulated, at least in part, using heat generated within its body (686)

endotermo: animal cuya temperatura corporal se regula, al menos en parte, utilizando el calor generado dentro de su cuerpo

enzyme: protein catalyst that speeds up the rate of specific biological reactions (44)

enzima: proteína catalizadora que acelera la velocidad de reacciones biológicas específicas

epidermis: in plants, single layer of cells that makes up dermal tissue (553); in humans, the outer layer of the skin (778)

epidermis: en las plantas, única capa de células que forma el tejido dérmico; en los seres humanos, la capa exterior de la piel

epididymis: organ in the male reproductive system in which sperm mature and are stored (818)

epidídimo: órgano del sistema reproductor masculino en el cual el esperma madura y se almacena

epinephrine: hormone released by the adrenal glands that increases heart rate and blood pressure and prepares the body for intense physical activity; also called adrenaline (814)

epinefrina: hormona liberada por las glándulas adrenales que aumenta la frecuencia cardíaca y la presión sanguínea y prepara al cuerpo para una actividad física intensa; también llamada adrenalina

epithelial tissue: type of tissue that lines the interior and exterior body surfaces (714)

tejido epitelial: tipo de tejido que reviste el interior y el exterior de las superficies del cuerpo

era: major division of geologic time; usually divided into two or more periods (454)

era: división principal del tiempo geológico; usualmente dividida en dos o más períodos

esophagus: tube connecting the mouth to the stomach (724)

esófago: tubo que conecta la boca con el estómago

estuary: kind of wetland formed where a river meets the ocean (98)

estuario: tipo de humedal que se forma donde un río se une al océano

ethylene: plant hormone that stimulates fruits to ripen (589)

etileno: hormona vegetal que estimula la maduración de los frutos

Eukarya: domain consisting of all organisms that have a nucleus; includes protists, plants, fungi, and animals (440)

Eukarya **(eucariontes):** dominio compuesto por todos los organismos que tienen un núcleo; incluye a los protistas, las plantas, los hongos y los animales

eukaryote: organism whose cells contain a nucleus (162)

eucariota: organismo cuyas células contienen un núcleo

evolution: change over time; the process by which modern organisms have descended from ancient organisms (380)

evolución: cambio en el transcurso del tiempo; el proceso por el cual los organismos actuales se derivaron de los organismos antiguos

excretion: process by which metabolic wastes are eliminated from the body (656, 729)

excreción: proceso por el cual se eliminan del cuerpo los residuos metabólicos

exocrine gland: gland that releases its secretions, through tubelike structures called ducts, directly into an organ or out of the body (810)

glándula exocrina: glándula que vierte sus secreciones directamente a un órgano o al exterior del cuerpo a través de estructuras tubulares denominadas conductos

exon: expressed sequence of DNA; codes for a protein (310)

exón: secuencia expresada de ADN; codifica una porción específica de una proteína

exoskeleton: external skeleton; tough external covering that protects and supports the body of many invertebrates (674)

exoesqueleto: esqueleto externo; cubierta externa dura que protege y sostiene el cuerpo de muchos invertebrados

exponential growth: growth pattern in which the individuals in a population reproduce at a constant rate (109)

crecimiento exponencial: patrón de crecimiento en el cual los individuos de una población se reproducen a una tasa constante

extinct: term used to refer to a species that has died out and has no living members (450)

    extinto: término utilizado para referirse a una especie que ha desaparecido y de la que ninguno de sus miembros está vivo

extracellular digestion: type of digestion in which food is broken down outside the cells in a digestive system and then absorbed (647)

    digestión extracelular: tipo de digestión en la cual el alimento es degradado fuera de las células dentro de un sistema digestivo y luego se absorbe

F

facilitated diffusion: process of diffusion in which molecules pass across the membrane through cell membrane channels (177)

    difusión facilitada: proceso de difusión en el cual las moléculas atraviesan la membrana a través de los canales de la membrana celular

family: in classification, group of similar genera (430)

    familia: en la clasificación, grupo de géneros similares

fat: lipid; made up of fatty acids and glycerol; type of nutrient that protects body organs, insulates the body, and stores energy (721)

    grasa: lípido; compuesto de ácidos grasos y glicerina; tipo de nutriente que protege a los órganos del cuerpo, actúa como aislante térmico y almacena energía

feedback inhibition: process in which a stimulus produces a response that opposes the original stimulus; also called negative feedback (608, 717)

    inhibición de la retroalimentación: proceso en el cual un estímulo produce una respuesta que se opone al estímulo original; también llamada retroalimentación negativa

fermentation: process by which cells release energy in the absence of oxygen (223)

    fermentación: proceso por el cual las células liberan energía en ausencia de oxígeno

fertilization: process in sexual reproduction in which male and female reproductive cells join to form a new cell (262)

    fecundación: proceso de la reproducción sexual en el cual las células reproductoras masculinas y femeninas se unen para formar una célula nueva

fetus: a human embryo after eight weeks of development (827)

    feto: un embrión humano después de ocho semanas de desarrollo

fever: increased body temperature that occurs in response to infection (842)

    fiebre: temperatura corporal elevada que se produce como respuesta a una infección

filtration: process of passing a liquid or gas through a filter to remove wastes (731)

    filtración: proceso de hacer pasar un líquido o un gas a través de un filtro para quitar los residuos

fitness: how well an organism can survive and reproduce in its environment (388)

    aptitud: capacidad de un organismo para sobrevivir y reproducirse en su medio ambiente

flagellum (pl. flagella): structure used by protists for movement; produces movement in a wavelike motion (506)

    flagelo: estructura utilizada por los protistas para desplazarse; produce un desplazamiento con un movimiento semejante al de una onda

food chain: series of steps in an ecosystem in which organisms transfer energy by eating and being eaten (63)

    cadena alimenticia: serie de pasos en un ecosistema, en que los organismos transfieren energía al alimentarse y al servir de alimento

food vacuole: small cavity in the cytoplasm of a protist that temporarily stores food (510)

    vacuola alimenticia: pequeña cavidad situada en el citoplasma de los protistas que almacena alimentos por algún tiempo

food web: network of complex interactions formed by the feeding relationships among the various organisms in an ecosystem (63)

    red alimenticia: red de interacciones complejas constituida por las relaciones alimenticias entre los varios organismos de un ecosistema

forensics: scientific study of crime scene evidence (365)

    ciencias forenses: estudio científico de las pruebas en la escena del crimen

fossil: preserved remains or traces of ancient organisms (382)

    fósil: restos conservados o vestigios de organismos antiguos

founder effect: change in allele frequencies as a result of the migration of a small subgroup of a population (411)

    efecto fundador: cambio en las frecuencias alélicas como consecuencia de la migración de un subgrupo pequeño de una población

frameshift mutation: mutation that shifts the "reading frame" of the genetic message by inserting or deleting a nucleotide (317)

    mutación de corrimiento de estructura: mutación que cambia el "marco de lectura" del mensaje genético insertando o eliminando un nucleótido

fruit: structure in angiosperms that contains one or more matured ovaries (541)

    fruto: estructura de las Angiospermas que contiene uno o más ovarios maduros

fruiting body: reproductive structure of a fungus that grows from the mycelium (515)

    cuerpo fructífero: estructura reproductora de los hongos que se desarrolla a partir del micelio

G

gamete: sex cell (264)
  gameto: célula sexual

gametophyte: gamete-producing plant; multicellular haploid phase of a plant life cycle (530)
  gametofito: planta que produce gametos; fase haploide multicelular del ciclo vital de una planta

ganglion (pl. ganglia): group of interneurons (670)
  ganglio nervioso: grupo de interneuronas

gastrovascular cavity: digestive chamber with a single opening (647)
  cavidad gastrovascular: cámara digestiva con una sola apertura

gastrulation: process of cell migration that results in the formation of the three cell layers—the ectoderm, the mesoderm, and the endoderm (826)
  gastrulación: proceso de migración celular que da por resultado la formación de las tres capas celulares—el ectodermo, el mesodermo y el endodermo

gel electrophoresis: procedure used to separate and analyze DNA fragments by placing a mixture of DNA fragments at one end of a porous gel and applying an electrical voltage to the gel (342)
  electroforesis en gel: procedimiento utilizado para separar y analizar fragmentos de ADN colocando una mezcla de fragmentos de ADN en un extremo de un gel poroso y aplicando al gel un voltaje eléctrico

gene: sequence of DNA that codes for a protein and thus determines a trait; factor that is passed from parent to offspring (263)
  gen: secuencia de ADN que contiene el código de una proteína y por lo tanto determina un rasgo; factor que se transmite de un progenitor a su descendencia

gene expression: process by which a gene produces its product and the product carries out its function (314)
  expresión génica: proceso por el cual un gen produce su producto y el producto lleva a cabo su función

gene pool: all the genes, including all the different alleles for each gene, that are present in a population at any one time (406)
  caudal de genes: todos los genes, incluidos todos los alelos diferentes para cada gen, que están presentes en una población en un momento dado

gene therapy: process of changing a gene to treat a medical disease or disorder. An absent or faulty gene is replaced by a normal working gene. (364)
  terapia genética o génica: proceso en el cual se cambia un gen para tratar una enfermedad o una afección médica. Se reemplaza un gen ausente o defectuoso con un gen de funcionamiento normal.

genetic code: collection of codons of mRNA, each of which directs the incorporation of a particular amino acid into a protein during protein synthesis (311)
  código genético: conjunto de codones del ARN mensajero, cada uno de los cuales dirige la incorporación de un aminoácido en particular a una proteína durante la síntesis proteica

genetic diversity: sum total of all the different forms of genetic information carried by a particular species, or by all organisms on Earth (138)
  diversidad genética: suma de todas las distintas formas de información genética portadas por una especie en particular, o por todos los organismos de la Tierra

genetic drift: random change in allele frequency caused by a series of chance occurrences that cause an allele to become more or less common in a population (411)
  tendencia genética: alteración al azar de la frecuencia alélica causada por una serie de acontecimientos aleatorios que hacen que un alelo se vuelva más o menos común en una población

genetic equilibrium: situation in which allele frequencies in a population remain the same (412)
  equilibrio genético: situación en la cual las frecuencias alélicas de una población se mantienen iguales

genetic marker: alleles that produce detectable phenotypic differences useful in genetic analysis (360)
  marcador genético: alelos que producen diferencias fenotípicas detectables, útiles en el análisis genético

genetics: scientific study of heredity (262)
  genética: estudio científico de la herencia

genome: entire set of genetic information that an organism carries in its DNA (334)
  genoma: todo el conjunto de información genética que un organismo transporta en su ADN

genomics: study of whole genomes, including genes and their functions (344)
  genómica: estudio integral de los genomas, incluyendo los genes y sus funciones

genotype: genetic makeup of an organism (267)
  genotipo: composición genética de un organismo

genus: group of closely related species; the first part of the scientific name in binomial nomenclature (428)
  género: grupo de especies relacionadas estrechamente; la primera parte del nombre científico en la nomenclatura binaria

geographic isolation: form of reproductive isolation in which two populations are separated by geographic barriers such as rivers, mountains, or bodies of water, leading to the formation of two separate subspecies (414)

aislamiento geográfico: forma de aislamiento reproductivo en el cual dos poblaciones están separadas por barreras geográficas como ríos, montañas o masas de agua, dando lugar a la formación de dos subspecies distintas

geologic time scale: time line used to represent Earth's history (453)

escala de tiempo geológico: línea cronológica utilizada para representar la historia de la Tierra

germ theory of disease: idea that infectious diseases are caused by microorganisms (838)

teoría microbiana de la enfermedad: idea de que las enfermedades infecciosas son causadas por microorganismos

germination: resumption of growth of the plant embryo following dormancy (586)

germinación: reanudación del crecimiento del embrión de la planta después de la latencia

gibberellin: plant hormone that stimulates growth and may cause dramatic increases in size (589)

giberelina: hormona de las plantas que estimula el crecimiento y puede causar aumentos significativos de tamaño

gill: feathery structure specialized for the exchange of gases with water (651)

branquia: estructura tegumentaria especializada en el intercambio de los gases con el agua

global warming: increase in the average temperatures on Earth (147)

calentamiento global: aumento del promedio de temperatura en la tierra

glomerulus: small network of capillaries encased in the upper end of the nephron; where filtration of the blood takes place (731)

glomérulo: pequeña red de capilares encerrados en el extremo superior del nefrón; donde tiene lugar la filtración de la sangre

glycolysis: first set of reactions in cellular respiration in which a molecule of glucose is broken into two molecules of pyruvic acid (216)

glicólisis: primer conjunto de reacciones en la respiración celular, en las cuales una molécula de glucosa se descompone en dos moléculas de ácido pirúvico

Golgi apparatus: organelle in cells that modifies, sorts, and packages proteins and other materials from the endoplasmic reticulum for storage in the cell or release outside the cell (169)

aparato de Golgi: orgánulo de las células que modifica, clasifica y agrupa las proteínas y otras sustancias provenientes del retículo endoplasmático para almacenarlas en la célula o enviarlas fuera de la célula

gradualism: the evolution of a species by gradual accumulation of small genetic changes over long periods of time (458)

gradualismo: evolución de una especie por la acumulación gradual de pequeños cambios genéticos ocurridos en el transcurso de largos períodos de tiempo

grafting: method of propagation used to reproduce seedless plants and varieties of woody plants that cannot be propagated from cuttings (584)

injerto: método de propagación utilizado para reproducir plantas sin semillas y algunas variedades de plantas leñosas que no pueden propagarse a partir de esquejes

gravitropism: response of a plant to the force of gravity (590)

geotropismo: respuesta de una planta a la fuerza de la gravedad

green revolution: development of highly productive crop strains and use of modern agriculture techniques to increase yields of food crops (594)

revolución verde: el desarrollo de variedades de cultivos altamente productivos y el uso de técnicas agrícolas modernas para aumentar el rendimiento de los cultivos

greenhouse effect: process in which certain gases (carbon dioxide, methane, and water vapor) trap sunlight energy in Earth's atmosphere as heat (83)

efecto invernadero: proceso mediante el cual ciertos gases (dióxido de carbono, metano y vapor de agua) atrapan la energía de la luz solar en la atmósfera terrestre en forma de calor

growth factor: one of a group of external regulatory proteins that stimulate the growth and division of cells (246)

factor de crecimiento: una de las proteínas del grupo de proteínas reguladoras externas que estimulan el crecimiento y la división de las células

guard cell: specialized cell in the epidermis of plants that controls the opening and closing of stomata (565)

célula de guarda (o célula oclusiva): célula especializada de la epidermis vegetal que controla la apertura y el cierre de los estomas

gullet: indentation in one side of a ciliate that allows food to enter the cell (510)

citofaringe: hendidura a un costado de un ciliado que permite que los alimentos entren a la célula

gymnosperm: group of seed plants that bear their seeds directly on the scales of cones (536)

Gimnospermas: grupo de plantas fanerógamas que tienen sus semillas directamente sobre las escamas de los conos

H

habitat: area where an organism lives, including the biotic and abiotic factors that affect it (85)

hábitat: área donde vive un organismo, incluidos los factores bióticos y abióticos que lo afectan

habitat fragmentation: splitting of ecosystems into pieces (140)

fragmentación del hábitat: la ruptura, o separación en partes, de los ecosistemas

habituation: type of learning in which an animal decreases or stops its response to a repetitive stimulus that neither rewards nor harms the animal (697)

habituación: tipo de aprendizaje en el cual un animal disminuye o cancela su respuesta ante un estímulo repetido que no recompensa ni castiga al animal

hair follicle: tubelike pockets of epidermal cells that extend into the dermis; cells at the base of hair follicles produce hair (776)

folículo piloso: sacos tubulares de las células epidérmicas que se prolongan hacia el interior de la dermis; las células situadas en la base de los folículos pilosos, producen pelo

half-life: length of time required for half of the radioactive atoms in a sample to decay (452)

vida media: período de tiempo requerido para que se desintegre la mitad de los átomos radiactivos de una muestra

haploid: term used to refer to a cell that contains only a single set of genes (275)

haploide: tipo de célula que posee un solo juego de cromosomas

Hardy-Weinberg principle: principle that states that allele frequencies in a population remain constant unless one or more factors cause those frequencies to change (412)

principio de Hardy-Weinberg: el principio que afirma que las frecuencias alélicas de una población permanecen constantes a menos que uno o más factores ocasionen que esas frecuencias cambien

Haversian canal: one of a network of tubes running through compact bone that contains blood vessels and nerves (767)

conducto de Havers: uno de los tubos de una red que recorre longitudinalmente el hueso compacto y contiene vasos sanguíneos y nervios

heart: hollow muscular organ that pumps blood throughout the body (653)

corazón: órgano muscular hueco que bombea la sangre a todo el cuerpo

heartwood: in a woody stem, the older xylem near the center of the stem that no longer conducts water (562)

duramen: en un tallo leñoso, el xilema más viejo situado cerca del centro del tallo que ya no conduce agua

hemoglobin: iron-containing protein in red blood cells that binds oxygen and transports it to the body (790)

hemoglobina: proteína de los glóbulos rojos que contiene hierro, fija el oxígeno y lo transporta al organismo

herbaceous plant: type of plant that has smooth and non-woody stems; includes dandelions, zinnias, petunias, and sunflowers (542)

planta herbácea: tipo de planta que tiene tallos blandos y no leñosos; incluye dientes de león, cinias, petunias y girasoles

herbivore: organism that obtains energy by eating only plants (62)

herbívoro: organismo que obtiene energía alimentándose solo de plantas

herbivory: interaction in which one animal (the herbivore) feeds on producers (such as plants) (86)

herbivorismo: interacción en la cual un animal (el herbívoro) se alimenta de productores (como las plantas)

heterotroph: organism that obtains food by consuming other living things; also called a consumer (61, 194)

heterótrofo: organismo que obtiene su alimento consumiendo otros seres vivos; también llamado consumidor

heterozygous: having two different alleles for a particular gene (267)

heterocigota: que tiene dos alelos diferentes para un gen dado

histamine: chemical released by mast cells that increases the flow of blood and fluids to the infected area during an inflammatory response (841)

histamina: sustancia química liberada por los mastocitos que aumenta el flujo de la sangre y los fluidos hacia el área infectada durante una respuesta inflamatoria

homeobox gene: The homeobox is a DNA sequence of approximately 130 base pairs, found in many homeotic genes that regulate development. Genes containing this sequence are known as homeobox genes, and they code for transcription factors, proteins that bind to DNA, and they also regulate the expression of other genes. (324)

gen homeobox: el homeobox es una secuencia de ADN de aproximadamente 130 pares de bases, presente en muchos genes homeóticos que regulan el desarrollo. Los genes que contienen esta secuencia se denominan genes homeobox y codifican los factores de transcripción, las proteínas que se adhieren al ADN y regulan la expresión de otros genes

homeostasis: relatively constant internal physical and chemical conditions that organisms maintain (15, 181, 717)

homeostasis: las condiciones internas, químicas y físicas, que los organismos mantienen relativamente constantes

homeotic gene: a class of regulatory genes that determine the identity of body parts and regions in an animal embryo. Mutations in these genes can transform one body part into another (324)

   gen homeótico: tipo de genes reguladores que determinan la identidad de las partes y regiones del cuerpo en un embrión animal. Las mutaciones de estos genes pueden transformar una parte del cuerpo en otra

hominine: hominoid lineage that led to humans (635)

   homínino: linaje hominoide que dio lugar a los seres humanos

hominoid: group of anthropoids that includes gibbons, orangutans, gorillas, chimpanzees, and humans (635)

   homínido: grupo de antropoides que incluye a los gibones, orangutanes, gorilas, chimpacés y seres humanos

homologous: term used to refer to chromosomes in which one set comes from the male parent and one set comes from the female parent (275)

   homólogos: término utilizado para referirse a los cromosomas en los que un juego proviene del progenitor masculino y un juego proviene del progenitor femenino

homologous structures: structures that are similar in different species of common ancestry (393)

   estructuras homólogas: estructuras que son similares en distintas especies que tienen un ancestro común

homozygous: having two identical alleles for a particular gene (267)

   homocigota: que tiene dos alelos idénticos para un gen dado

hormone: chemical produced in one part of an organism that affects another part of the same organism (588, 810)

   hormona: sustancia química producida en una parte de un organismo que afecta a otra parte del mismo organismo

Hox gene: a group of homeotic genes clustered together that determine the head to tail identity of body parts in animals. All hox genes contain the homeobox DNA sequence. (324)

   gen Hox: grupo de genes homeóticos agrupados en un conjunto que determinan la identidad posicional de las partes del cuerpo de los animales. Todos los genes Hox contienen la secuencia de ADN homeobox

humoral immunity: immunity against antigens in body fluids, such as blood and lymph (843)

   inmunidad humoral: inmunidad contra los antígenos presentes en los fluidos corporales, como la sangre y la linfa

humus: material formed from decaying leaves and other organic matter (93)

   humus: material formado a partir de hojas en descomposición y otros materiales orgánicos

hybrid: offspring of crosses between parents with different traits (263)

   híbrido: descendencia del cruce entre progenitores que tienen rasgos diferentes

hybridization: breeding technique that involves crossing dissimilar individuals to bring together the best traits of both organisms (355)

   hibridación: técnica de cría que consiste en cruzar individuos diferentes para reunir los mejores rasgos de ambos organismos

hydrogen bond: weak attraction between a hydrogen atom and another atom (33)

   enlace de hidrógeno: atracción débil entre un átomo de hidrógeno y otro átomo

hydrostatic skeleton: skeleton made of fluid-filled body segments that work with muscles to allow the animal to move (674)

   esqueleto hidrostático: esqueleto constituido por segmentos corporales llenos de fluido que trabajan con los músculos para permitir el movimiento del animal

hypertonic: when comparing two solutions, the solution with the greater concentration of solutes (178)

   hipertónica: al comparar dos soluciones, la solución que tiene la mayor concentración de solutos

hypha (pl. hyphae): one of many long, slender filaments that makes up the body of a fungus (515)

   hifa: uno de muchos filamentos largos y delgados que componen el cuerpo de un hongo

hypothalamus: structure of the brain that acts as a control center for recognition and analysis of hunger, thirst, fatigue, anger, and body temperature (749)

   hipotálamo: estructura del cerebro que funciona como un centro de control para el reconocimiento y el análisis del hambre, la sed, la fatiga, el enojo y la temperatura corporal

hypothesis: possible explanation for a set of observations or possible answer to a scientific question (5)

   hipótesis: explicación posible para un conjunto de observaciones o respuesta posible a una pregunta científica

hypotonic: when comparing two solutions, the solution with the lesser concentration of solutes (178)

   hipotónica: al comparar dos soluciones, la solución que tiene la menor concentración de solutos

I

immigration: movement of individuals into an area occupied by an existing population (109)

   inmigración: desplazamiento de individuos a un área ocupada por una población ya existente

immune response: the body's specific recognition, response, and memory to a pathogen attack (842)

   respuesta inmune: reconocimiento, respuesta y memoria específicos que tiene el cuerpo respecto al ataque de un organismo patógeno

implantation: process in which the blastocyst attaches to the wall of the uterus (825)

   implantación: proceso en el cual la blástula se adhiere a la pared del útero

imprinting: type of behavior based on early experience; once imprinting has occurred, the behavior cannot be changed (699)

impronta: tipo de comportamiento basado en las primeras experiencias; una vez que ocurre la impronta, el comportamiento no puede cambiarse

inbreeding: continued breeding of individuals with similar characteristics to maintain the derived characteristics of a kind of organism (355)

endogamia: la cría continua de individuos con características semejantes para mantener las características derivadas de un tipo de organismo

incomplete dominance: situation in which one allele is not completely dominant over another allele (271)

dominancia incompleta: situación en la cual un alelo no es completamente dominante sobre otro alelo

independent assortment: one of Mendel's principles that states that genes for different traits can segregate independently during the formation of gametes (269)

distribución independiente: uno de los principios de Mendel que establece que los genes para rasgos diferentes pueden segregarse independientemente durante la formación de los gametos

independent variable: factor in a controlled experiment that is deliberately changed; also called manipulated variable (6)

variable independiente: en un experimento controlado, el factor que se modifica a propósito; también llamada variable manipulada

index fossil: distinctive fossil that is used to compare the relative ages of fossils (451)

fósil guía: fósil distintivo usado para comparar las edades relativas de los fósiles

infectious disease: disease caused by microorganism that disrupts normal body functions (838)

enfermedad infecciosa: enfermedad causada por un microorganismo que altera las funciones normales del cuerpo

inference: a logical interpretation based on prior knowledge and experience (5)

inferencia: interpretación lógica basada en la experiencia y en conocimientos previos

inflammatory response: nonspecific defense reaction to tissue damage caused by injury or infection (841)

respuesta inflamatoria: reacción defensiva no específica al daño causado a los tejidos por una herida o una infección

innate behavior: type of behavior in which the behavior appears in fully functional form the first time it is performed even though the animal has had no previous experience with the stimuli to which it responds; also called instinct (697)

comportamiento innato: tipo de comportamiento en el cual la conducta aparece en forma completamente funcional la primera vez que se lleva a cabo, aunque el animal no tenga ninguna experiencia previa con los estímulos a los que responde; también llamado instinto

insight learning: type of behavior in which an animal applies something it has already learned to a new situation, without a period of trial and error; also called reasoning (698)

aprendizaje por discernimiento: tipo de comportamiento en el cual un animal aplica algo que ya ha aprendido a una situación nueva, sin un período de ensayo y error; también llamado razonamiento

interferon: one of a group of proteins that help cells resist viral infection (842)

interferón: un tipo de proteína que ayuda a las células a combatir las infecciones virales

interneuron: type of neuron that processes information and may relay information to motor neurons (669)

interneurona: tipo de neurona que procesa información y la puede transmitir para estimular las neuronas

interphase: period of the cell cycle between cell divisions (241)

interfase: período del ciclo celular entre las divisiones celulares

intracellular digestion: type of digestion in which food is digested inside specialized cells that pass nutrients to other cells by diffusion (647)

digestión intracelular: tipo de digestión en la cual los alimentos se digieren dentro de células especializadas que pasan los nutrientes a otras células mediante difusión

intron: sequence of DNA that is not involved in coding for a protein (310)

intrón: secuencia de ADN que no participa en la codificación de una proteína

invertebrate: animal that lacks a backbone, or vertebral column (606)

invertebrado: animal que carece de columna vertebral

ion: atom that has a positive or negative charge (30)

ion: átomo que tiene una carga positiva o negativa

ionic bond: chemical bond formed when one or more electrons are transferred from one atom to another (30)

enlace iónico: enlace químico que se forma cuando uno o más electrones se transfieren de un átomo a otro

iris: colored part of the eye (756)

iris: parte coloreada del ojo

isotonic: when the concentration of two solutions is the same (178)

isotónica: cuando la concentración de dos soluciones es la misma

isotope: one of several forms of a single element that contains the same number of protons but different numbers of neutrons (29)

    isótopo: cada una de las diferentes formas de un único elemento, que contiene la misma cantidad de protones pero cantidades distintas de neutrones

J

joint: place where one bone attaches to another bone (675, 768)

    articulación: sitio donde un hueso se une a otro hueso

K

karyotype: micrograph of the complete diploid set of chromosomes grouped together in pairs, arranged in order of decreasing size (334)

    cariotipo: micrografía de la totalidad del conjunto diploide de cromosomas agrupados en pares, ordenados por tamaño decreciente

keratin: tough fibrous protein found in skin (776)

    queratina: proteína fibrosa y resistente que se halla en la piel

keystone species: single species that is not usually abundant in a community yet exerts strong control on the structure of a community (86)

    especie clave: especie que habitualmente no es abundante en una comunidad y sin embargo ejerce un fuerte control sobre la estructura de esa comunidad

kidney: an organ of excretion that separates wastes and excess water from the blood (656)

    riñón: órgano excretor que separa los residuos y el exceso de agua de la sangre

kingdom: largest and most inclusive group in Linnaean classification (431)

    reino: grupo más grande e inclusivo del systema de clasificación inventado por Linneo

Koch's postulates: set of guidelines developed by Koch that help identify the microorganism that causes a specific disease (839)

    postulados de Koch: conjunto de pautas desarrollado por Koch que ayuda a identificar al microorganismo que causa una enfermedad específica

Krebs cycle: second stage of cellular respiration in which pyruvic acid is broken down into carbon dioxide in a series of energy-extracting reactions (218)

    ciclo de Krebs: segunda fase de la respiración celular en la cual el ácido pirúvico se descompone en dióxido de carbono en una serie de reacciones que liberan energía

L

language: system of communication that combines sounds, symbols, and gestures according to a set of rules about sequence and meaning, such as grammar and syntax (704)

    lenguaje: sistema de comunicación que combina sonidos, símbolos y gestos según un conjunto de reglas sobre la secuencia y el significado, como la gramática y la sintaxis

large intestine: organ in the digestive system that removes water from the undigested material that passes through it; also called the colon (728)

    intestino grueso: órgano del sistema digestivo que extrae el agua del material no digerido que pasa por él; también llamado colon

larva: (pl. larvae): immature stage of some organisms (627)

    larva: etapa inmadura de algunos organismos

larynx: structure in the throat that contains the vocal cords (796)

    laringe: órgano situado en la garganta que contiene las cuerdas vocales

learning: changes in behavior as a result of experience (697)

    aprendizaje: cambios en el comportamiento a consecuencia de la experiencia

lens: structure in the eye that focuses light rays on the retina (757)

    cristalino: estructura del ojo que enfoca los rayos luminosos en la retina

lichen: symbiotic association between a fungus and a photosynthetic organism (518)

    liquen: asociación simbiótica entre un hongo y un organismo fotosintético

ligament: tough connective tissue that holds bones together in a joint (675, 769)

    ligamento: tejido conectivo resistente que mantiene unidos a los huesos en una articulación

light-dependent reactions: set of reactions in photosynthesis that use energy from light to produce ATP and NADPH (197)

    reacciones dependientes de la luz: en la fotosíntesis, conjunto de reacciones que emplean la energía proveniente de la luz para producir ATP y NADPH

light-independent reactions: set of reactions in photosynthesis that do not require light; energy from ATP and NADPH is used to build high-energy compounds such as sugar; also called the Calvin cycle (197)

reacciones independientes de la luz: en la fotosíntesis, conjunto de reacciones que no necesitan luz; la energía proveniente del ATP y del NADPH se emplea para construir compuestos con gran contenido energético, como el azúcar; también llamado ciclo de Calvin

lignin: substance in vascular plants that makes cell walls rigid (554)

lignina: sustancia de las plantas vasculares que hace rígidas a las paredes celulares

limiting factor: factor that causes population growth to decrease (112)

factor limitante: un factor que hace disminuir el crecimiento de la población

limiting nutrient: single essential nutrient that limits productivity in an ecosystem (72)

nutriente limitante: un solo nutriente esencial que limita la productividad de un ecosistema

lipid: macromolecule made mostly from carbon and hydrogen atoms; includes fats, oils, and waxes (39)

lípido: macromolécula compuesta principalmente por átomos de carbono e hidrógeno; incluye las grasas, los aceites y las ceras

lipid bilayer: flexible double-layered sheet that makes up the cell membrane and forms a barrier between the cell and its surroundings (171)

bicapa lipídica: lámina flexible de dos capas que constituye la membrana celular y forma una barrera entre la célula y su entorno

logistic growth: growth pattern in which a population's growth slows and then stops following a period of exponential growth (111)

crecimiento logístico: patrón de crecimiento en el cual el desarrollo de una población se reduce y luego se detiene después de un período de crecimiento exponencial

loop of Henle: section of the nephron tubule that is responsible for conserving water and minimizing the volume of the filtrate (731)

asa de Henle: una sección del túbulo de nefrón responsable de conservar el agua y minimizar el volumen del material filtrado

lung: respiratory organ; place where gases are exchanged between the blood and inhaled air (651)

pulmón: órgano respiratorio; lugar donde se intercambian los gases entre la sangre y el aire inhalado

lymph: fluid that is filtered out of the blood (792)

linfa: fluido procedente de la sangre

lysogenic infection: type of infection in which a virus embeds its DNA into the DNA of the host cell and is replicated along with the host cell's DNA (482)

infección lisogénica: tipo de infección en la cual un virus inserta su ADN en el ADN de la célula huésped y se replica junto con el ADN de dicha célula huésped

lysosome: cell organelle that breaks down lipids, carbohydrates, and proteins into small molecules that can be used by the rest of the cell (166)

lisosoma: orgánulo celular que descompone los lípidos, los hidratos de carbono y las proteínas en moléculas pequeñas que pueden ser utilizadas por el resto de la célula

lytic infection: type of infection in which a virus enters a cell, makes copies of itself, and causes the cell to burst (482)

infección lítica: tipo de infección en la cual un virus penetra una célula, hace copias de sí mismo y provoca la ruptura o muerte celular

M

macroevolutionary patterns: changes in anatomy, phylogeny, ecology, and behavior that take place in clades larger than a single species (456)

patrones de macroevolución: cambios que ocurren en la anatomía, filogenia, ecología y comportamiento de clados que abarcan a más de una especie

Malpighian tubule: structure in most terrestrial arthropods that concentrates the uric acid and adds it to digestive wastes (658)

túbulo de Malpighi: estructura de la mayoría de los artrópodos terrestres que concentra el ácido úrico y lo incorpora a los residuos digestivos

mammary gland: gland in female mammals that produces milk to nourish the young (682)

glándula mamaria: glándula de las hembras de los mamíferos que produce leche para alimentar a las crías

mass extinction: event during which many species become extinct during a relatively short period of time (457)

extinción masiva: suceso durante el cual se extinguen muchas especies durante un período de tiempo relativamente corto

matrix: innermost compartment of the mitochondrion (218)

matriz: compartimento más interno de la mitocondria

mechanical digestion: physical breakdown of large pieces of food into smaller pieces (723)

digestión mecánica: descomposición física de grandes pedazos de comida en pedazos más pequeños

meiosis: process in which the number of chromosomes per cell is cut in half through the separation of homologous chromosomes in a diploid cell (276)

meiosis: proceso por el cual el número de cromosomas por célula se reduce a la mitad mediante la separación de los cromosomas homólogos de una célula diploide

melanin: dark brown pigment in the skin that helps protect the skin by absorbing ultraviolet rays (776)

melanina: pigmento marrón oscuro de la piel que contribuye a protegerla al absorber los rayos ultravioletas

melanocyte: cell in the skin that produces a dark brown pigment called melanin (776)

melanocito: célula de la piel que produce un pigmento marrón oscuro llamado melanina

menstrual cycle: regular sequence of events in which an egg develops and is released from the body (820)

ciclo menstrual: secuencia regular de sucesos en la cual un huevo se desarrolla y se elimina del cuerpo

menstruation: discharge of blood and the unfertilized egg from the body (821)

menstruación: descarga de sangre y del huevo no fertilizado del cuerpo

meristem: regions of unspecialized cells responsible for continuing growth throughout a plant's lifetime (554)

meristemos: regiones de células no especializadas responsables del crecimiento continuo de una planta durante su vida

mesoderm: middle germ layer; develops into muscles, and much of the circulatory, reproductive, and excretory systems (612)

mesodermo: capa embrionaria media; se desarrolla para dar lugar a los músculos y gran parte de los sistemas circulatorio, reproductor y excretor

mesophyll: specialized ground tissue found in leaves; performs most of a plant's photosynthesis (564)

mesófilo: tejido fundamental especializado que se halla en las hojas; realiza la mayor parte de la fotosíntesis de una planta

messenger RNA (mRNA): type of RNA that carries copies of instructions for the assembly of amino acids into proteins from DNA to the rest of the cell (309)

ARN mensajero: tipo de ARN que transporta copias de las instrucciones para el ensamblaje de los aminoácidos en proteínas, desde el ADN al resto de la célula

metabolism: the combination of chemical reactions through which an organism builds up or breaks down materials (15)

metabolismo: la combinación de reacciones químicas a través de las cuales un organismo acumula o desintegra materiales

metamorphosis: process of changes in shape and form of a larva into an adult (681)

metamorfosis: proceso de cambios en la estructura y forma de una larva hasta que se convierte en adulto

metaphase: phase of mitosis in which the chromosomes line up across the center of the cell (242)

metafase: fase de la mitosis en la cual los cromosomas se alinean a través del centro de la célula

microclimate: environmental conditions within a small area that differs significantly from the climate of the surrounding area (82)

microclima: condiciones medioambientales de un área pequeña que difieren significativamente del clima del área circundante

migration: seasonal behavior resulting in the movement from one environment to another (701)

migración: comportamiento estacional que da por resultado el desplazamiento desde un medio ambiente a otro

mineral: inorganic nutrient the body needs, usually in small amounts (721)

mineral: nutriente inorgánico que el cuerpo necesita, usualmente en pequeñas cantidades

mitochondrion: cell organelle that converts the chemical energy stored in food into compounds that are more convenient for the cell to use (170)

mitocondria: orgánulo celular que convierte la energía química almacenada en los alimentos en compuestos más apropiados para que la célula los use

mitosis: part of eukaryotic cell division during which the cell nucleus divides (241)

mitosis: fase de la división de las células eucariotas durante la cual se divide el núcleo celular

mixture: material composed of two or more elements or compounds that are physically mixed together but not chemically combined (34)

mezcla: material compuesto por dos o más elementos o compuestos que están mezclados físicamente pero no están combinados químicamente

molecular clock: method used by researchers that uses mutation rates in DNA to estimate the length of time that two species have been evolving independently (417)

reloj molecular: método de investigación que emplea las tasas de mutación del ADN para estimar el lapso de tiempo en que dos especies han evolucionado independientemente

molecule: smallest unit of most compounds that displays all the properties of that compound (31)

molécula: la unidad más pequeña de la mayoría de los compuestos que exhibe todas las propiedades de ese compuesto

molting: process of shedding an exoskeleton and growing a new one (675)

muda: proceso de desprendimiento de un exoesqueleto y el crecimiento de uno nuevo

monocot: angiosperm with one seed leaf in its ovary (542)

monocotiledónea: angiosperma con un cotiledón (hoja embrionaria) en su ovario

monoculture: farming strategy of planting a single, highly productive crop year after year (129)

    monocultivo: estrategia agrícola que consiste en plantar año tras año un único cultivo altamente productivo

monomer: small chemical unit that makes up a polymer (38)

    monómero: pequeña unidad química que forma un polímero

monophyletic group: group that consists of a single ancestral species and all its descendants and excludes any organisms that are not descended from that common ancestor (433)

    grupo monofilético: grupo que consiste en una especie con un único ancestro y todos sus descendientes y excluye a todos los organismos que no descienden de ese ancestro común

monosaccharide: simple sugar molecule (38)

    monosacárido: molécula de azúcar simple

motor neuron: type of nerve cell that carries directions from interneurons to either muscle cells or glands (669)

    neurona motora: tipo de célula nerviosa que lleva las instrucciones provenientes de las interneuronas a las células musculares o las glándulas

multiple alleles: a gene that has more than two alleles (272)

    alelos múltiples: un gen que tiene más de dos alelos

multipotent: cell with limited potential to develop into many types of differentiated cells (250)

    multipotentes: células con potencial limitado para generar muchos tipos de células diferenciadas

muscle fiber: long slender skeletal muscle cells (770)

    fibra muscular: células largas y delgadas de los músculos esqueléticos

muscle tissue: type of tissue that makes movements of the body possible (715)

    tejido muscular: tipo de tejido que hace posibles los movimientos del cuerpo

mutagen: chemical or physical agents in the environment that interact with DNA and may cause a mutation (318)

    mutágeno: agentes físicos o químicos del medioambiente que interaccionan con el ADN y pueden causar una mutación

mutation: change in the genetic material of a cell (316)

    mutación: cambio en el material genético de una célula

mutualism: symbiotic relationship in which both species benefit from the relationship (87)

    mutualismo: relación simbiótica en la cual ambas especies se benefician

mycelium (pl. mycelia): densely branched network of the hyphae of a fungus (515)

    micelio: la red de filamentos muy ramificados de las hifas de un hongo

mycorrhiza (pl. mycorrhizae): symbiotic association of plant roots and fungi (519)

    micorriza: asociación simbiótica entre las raíces de las plantas y los hongos

myelin sheath: insulating membrane surrounding the axon in some neurons (743)

    vaina de mielina: membrana aislante que rodea al axón de algunas neuronas

myocardium: thick middle muscle layer of the heart (787)

    miocardio: capa media, gruesa y musculosa del corazón

myofibril: tightly packed filament bundles found within skeletal muscle fibers (771)

    miofibrilla: manojos de filamentos muy apretados que se hallan dentro de las fibras de los músculos esqueléticos

myosin: thick filament of protein found in skeletal muscle cells (771)

    miosina: filamento grueso de proteína que se halla en las células de los músculos esqueléticos

N

NAD$^+$ (nicotinamide adenine dinucleotide): electron carrier involved in glycolysis (216)

    NAD$^+$ (dinucleótido de nicotinamida adenina): transportador de electrones que participa en la glucólisis

NADP$^+$ (nicotinamide adenine dinucleotide phosphate): carrier molecule that transfers high-energy electrons from chlorophyll to other molecules (196)

    NADP$^+$ (fosfato de dinucleótido de nicotinamida adenina): molécula transportadora de electrones que transfiere electrones de alta energía desde la clorofila a otras moléculas

natural selection: process by which organisms that are most suited to their environment survive and reproduce most successfully; also called survival of the fittest (389)

    selección natural: proceso por el cual los organismos más adaptados a su medioambiente sobreviven y se reproducen más exitosamente; también llamada supervivencia del más apto

nephridium (pl. nephridia): excretory structure of an annelid that filters body fluid (658)

    nefridio: estructura excretora de los anélidos que filtra el fluido corporal

nephron: blood-filtering structure in the kidneys in which impurities are filtered out, wastes are collected, and purified blood is returned to the circulation (729)

    nefrón: estructura filtradora de la sangre en los riñones, en la cual se filtran las impurezas, se recogen los desechos y la sangre purificada se devuelve a la circulación

nervous tissue: type of tissue that transmits nerve impulses throughout the body (715)

tejido nervioso: tipo de tejido que transmite los impulsos nerviosos por el cuerpo

neuromuscular junction: the point of contact between a motor neuron and a skeletal muscle cell (772)

unión neuromuscular: el punto de contacto entre una neurona motora y una célula de un músculo esquelético

neuron: nerve cell; specialized for carrying messages throughout the nervous system (668)

neurona: célula nerviosa; especializada en conducir mensajes a través del sistema nervioso

neurotransmitter: chemical used by a neuron to transmit an impulse across a synapse to another cell (746)

neurotransmisor: sustancia química utilizada por una neurona para transmitir un impulso a otra célula a través de una sinapsis

neurulation: the first step in the development of the nervous system (826)

neurulación: primer paso en el desarrollo del sistema nervioso

niche: full range of physical and biological conditions in which an organism lives and the way in which the organism uses those conditions (85)

nicho: toda la variedad de condiciones biológicas y físicas en las que vive un organismo y la manera en la que dicho organismo utiliza esas condiciones

nitrogen fixation: process of converting nitrogen gas into nitrogen compounds that plants can absorb and use (71)

fijación de nitrógeno: el proceso por el cual el gas nitrógeno se convierte en los compuestos nitrogenados que las plantas pueden absorber y utilizar

node: part on a growing stem where a leaf is attached (560)

nudo: parte de un tallo en crecimiento donde está adherida una hoja

nondisjunction: error in meiosis in which the homologous chromosomes fail to separate properly (341)

no disyunción: error que ocurre durante la meiosis, en el que cromosomas homólogos no logran separarse adecuadamente

nonrenewable resource: resource that cannot be replenished by a natural process within a reasonable amount of time (131)

recurso no renovable: recurso que no se puede reponer mediante un proceso natural dentro de un período de tiempo razonable

norepinephrine: hormone released by the adrenal glands that increases heart rate and blood pressure and prepares the body for intense physical activity (814)

norepinefrina o noradrenalina: hormona liberada por las glándulas adrenales que aumenta la frecuencia cardíaca y la presión sanguínea y prepara al cuerpo para realizar actividad física intensa

notochord: long supporting rod that runs through a chordate's body just below the nerve cord (606)

notocordio: extenso bastón de apoyo que se extiende a lo largo del cuerpo de los cordados, justo por debajo del cordón nervioso

nucleic acid: macromolecules containing hydrogen, oxygen, nitrogen, carbon, and phosphorus (40)

ácido nucleico: macromoléculas que contienen hidrógeno, oxígeno, nitrógeno, carbono y fósforo

nucleotide: subunit of which nucleic acids are composed; made up of a 5-carbon sugar, a phosphate group, and a nitrogenous base (40)

nucleótido: subunidad que constituye los ácidos nucleicos; compuesta de un azúcar de 5 carbonos, un grupo fosfato y una base nitrogenada

nucleus: the center of an atom, which contains the protons and neutrons (28); in cells, structure that contains the cell's genetic material in the form of DNA (162)

núcleo: el centro de un átomo, contiene los protones y los neutrones; en las células, la estructura que contiene el material genético de la célula en forma de ADN

nutrient: chemical substance that an organism needs to sustain life (70)

nutriente: sustancia química que un organismo necesita para continuar con vida

nymph: immature form of an animal that resembles the adult form but lacks functional sexual organs (681)

ninfa: forma inmadura de un animal que se parece a la forma adulta, pero carece de órganos sexuales funcionales

observation: process of noticing and describing events or processes in a careful, orderly way (5)

observación: el método de percibir y describir sucesos o procesos de manera atenta y ordenada

omnivore: organism that obtains energy by eating both plants and animals (62)

omnívoro: organismo que obtiene energía alimentándose de plantas y animales

open circulatory system: type of circulatory system in which blood is only partially contained within a system of blood vessels as it travels through the body (653)

sistema circulatorio abierto: tipo de sistema circulatorio en el cual la sangre, cuando fluye por el cuerpo, está solo parcialmente contenida dentro de un sistema de vasos sanguíneos

operant conditioning: type of learning in which an animal learns to behave in a certain way through repeated practice, to receive a reward or avoid punishment (698)

acondicionamiento operante: tipo de aprendizaje en el cual un animal aprende a comportarse de cierta manera mediante una práctica repetida, para recibir una recompensa o evitar un castigo

operator: short DNA region, adjacent to the promoter of a prokaryotic operon, that binds repressor proteins responsible for controlling the rate of transcription of the operon (321)

  operador: pequeña región de ADN, adyacente al promotor del operón de una procariota, que une las proteínas represoras responsables de controlar la tasa de transcripción del operón

operon: in prokaryotes, a group of adjacent genes that share a common operator and promoter and are transcribed into a single mRNA (320)

  operón: en las procariotas, grupo de genes adyacentes que comparten un operador y un promotor en común y que son transcritas a un solo ARN mensajero

opposable thumb: thumb that enables grasping objects and using tools (635)

  pulgar oponible o prensible: un pulgar que permite aferrar objetos y utilizar herramientas

order: in classification, a group of closely related families (430)

  orden: en la clasificación, un grupo de familias relacionadas estrechamente

organ: group of tissues that work together to perform closely related functions (182)

  órgano: grupo de tejidos que trabajan juntos para realizar funciones estrechamente relacionadas

organ system: group of organs that work together to perform a specific function (182)

  sistema de órganos: grupo de órganos que trabajan juntos para realizar una función específica

organelle: specialized structure that performs important cellular functions within a cell (164)

  orgánulo: estructura especializada que realiza funciones celulares importantes dentro de una célula

osmosis: diffusion of water through a selectively permeable membrane (177)

  ósmosis: la difusión de agua a través de una membrana de permeabilidad selectiva

osmotic pressure: pressure that must be applied to prevent osmotic movement across a selectively permeable membrane (178)

  presión osmótica: la presión que debe aplicarse para evitar el movimiento osmótico a través de una membrana de permeabilidad selectiva

ossification: process of bone formation during which cartilage is replaced by bone (767)

  osificación: el proceso de formación de hueso durante el cual el cartílago es reemplazado por hueso

osteoblast: bone cell that secretes mineral deposits that replace the cartilage in developing bones (767)

  osteoblasto: célula ósea que secreta depósitos minerales que reemplazan al cartílago de los huesos en desarrollo

osteoclast: bone cell that breaks down bone minerals (767)

  osteoclasto: célula ósea que degrada los minerales óseos

osteocyte: bone cell that helps maintain the minerals in bone tissue and continue to strengthen the growing bone (767)

  osteocito: célula ósea que ayuda a conservar los minerales en el tejido óseo y continúa fortaleciendo al hueso en crecimiento

ovary: in plants, the structure that surrounds and protects seeds (540); in animals, the primary female reproductive organ; produces eggs (819)

  ovario: en las plantas, la estructura que rodea a las semillas y las protege; órgano reproductor femenino fundamental en los animales; produce huevos

oviparous: species in which embryos develop in eggs outside a parent's body (680)

  ovíparo: especie animal en la cual los embriones se desarrollan en huevos fuera del cuerpo del progenitor

ovoviviparous: species in which the embryos develop within the mother's body but depend entirely on the yolk sac of their eggs (680)

  ovovíparo: especie animal en la cual los embriones se desarrollan dentro del cuerpo de la madre, pero dependen completamente del saco vitelino de sus huevos

ovulation: the release of a mature egg from the ovary into one of the Fallopian tubes (820)

  ovulación: liberación de un huevo maduro desde el ovario a una de las trompas de Falopio

ovule: structure in seed cones in which the female gametophytes develop (538)

  óvulo: estructura de las semillas coníferas donde se desarrollan los gametos femeninos

ozone layer: atmospheric layer in which ozone gas is relatively concentrated; protects life on Earth from harmful ultraviolet rays in sunlight (145)

  capa de ozono: capa atmosférica en la cual el gas ozono se encuentra relativamente concentrado; protege a los seres vivos de la Tierra de los perjudiciales rayos ultravioletas de la luz solar

P

pacemaker: small group of cardiac muscle fibers that maintains the heart's pumping rhythm by setting the rate at which the heart contracts; the sinoatrial (SA) node (788)

  marcapasos: grupo pequeño de fibras musculares cardíacas que mantiene el ritmo de bombeo del corazón estableciendo la frecuencia a la que se contrae el corazón; el nodo sinusal

paleontologist: scientist who studies fossils (450)

  paleontólogo: científico que estudia los fósiles

palisade mesophyll: layer of cells under the upper epidermis of a leaf (564)

    mesófilo en empalizada: capa de células situada bajo la epidermis superior de una hoja

parasitism: symbiotic relationship in which one organism lives on or inside another organism and harms it (87)

    parasitismo: relación simbiótica en la cual un organismo vive sobre otro organismo o en su interior y lo perjudica

parathyroid hormone (PTH): hormone produced by parathyroid gland that increases calcium levels in the blood (815)

    hormona de la paratiroides: hormona producida por la glándula paratiroides que aumenta los niveles de calcio en la sangre

parenchyma: main type of ground tissue in plants that contains cells with thin cell walls and large central vacuoles (553)

    parénquima: tipo principal de tejido fundamental de las plantas que contiene células con paredes celulares delgadas y vacuolas centrales grandes

passive immunity: temporary immunity that develops as a result of natural or deliberate exposure to an antibody (846)

    inmunidad pasiva: inmunidad transitoria que se desarrolla a consecuencia de una exposición natural o deliberada a un anticuerpo

pathogen: disease-causing agent (489)

    patógeno: agente que causa una enfermedad

pedigree: chart that shows the presence or absence of a trait according to the relationships within a family across several generations (336)

    árbol genealógico: diagrama que muestra la presencia o ausencia de un rasgo de acuerdo con las relaciones intrafamiliares a través de varias generaciones

pepsin: enzyme that breaks down proteins into smaller polypeptide fragments (725)

    pepsina: enzima que descompone las proteínas en fragmentos de polipéptidos más pequeños

period: division of geologic time into which eras are subdivided (454)

    período: división del tiempo geológico en la que se subdividen las eras

peripheral nervous system: network of nerves and supporting cells that carries signals into and out of the central nervous system (742)

    sistema nervioso periférico: red de nervios y células de apoyo que transporta señales hacia y desde el sistema nervioso central

peristalsis: contractions of smooth muscles that provide the force that moves food through the esophagus toward the stomach (724)

    peristalsis: contracciones de los músculos lisos que proporcionan la fuerza que hace avanzar los alimentos a través del esófago hacia el estómago

permafrost: layer of permanently frozen subsoil found in the tundra (94)

    permacongelamiento: capa de subsuelo congelado en forma permanente que se halla en la tundra

pH scale: scale with values from 0 to 14, used to measure the concentration of H^+ ions in a solution; a pH of 0 to 7 is acidic, a pH of 7 is neutral, and a pH of 7 to 14 is basic (35)

    escala del pH: escala con valores de 0 a 14, utilizada para medir la concentración de iones H^+ en una solución; un pH de 0 a 7 es ácido, un pH de 7 es neutro y un pH de 7 a 14 es básico

pharyngeal pouch: one of a pair of structures in the throat region of a chordate (607)

    bolsa faríngea: cada una de las dos estructuras situadas en la región de la garganta de los cordados

pharynx: tube at the back of the mouth that serves as a passageway for both air and food; also called the throat (796)

    faringe: tubo situado a continuación de la boca que sirve de conducto para que pasen el aire y los alimentos; también llamada garganta

phenotype: physical characteristics of an organism (267)

    fenotipo: características físicas de un organismo

phloem: vascular tissue that transports solutions of nutrients and carbohydrates produced by photosynthesis through the plant (534)

    floema: tejido vascular que transporta por toda la planta las soluciones de nutrientes e hidratos de carbono producidos en la fotosíntesis

photic zone: sunlight region near the surface of water (96)

    zona fótica: región cerca de la superficie del mar en la que penetra la luz solar

photoperiodism: plant response to the relative lengths of light and darkness (591)

    fotoperíodismo: la respuesta de una planta a los tiempos relativos de luz y oscuridad

photosynthesis: process used by plants and other autotrophs to capture light energy and use it to power chemical reactions that convert carbon dioxide and water into oxygen and energy-rich carbohydrates such as sugars and starches (60, 194)

    fotosíntesis: proceso empleado por las plantas y otros organismos autótrofos para atrapar la energía luminosa y utilizarla para impulsar reacciones químicas que convierten el dióxido de carbono y el agua en oxígeno e hidratos de carbono de gran contenido energético, como azúcares y almidones

photosystem: cluster of chlorophyll and proteins found in thylakoids (199)

    fotosistema: conjunto de clorofila y proteínas que se hallan en los tilacoides

phototropism: tendency of a plant to grow toward a light source (590)

    fototropismo: la tendencia de una planta a crecer hacia una fuente de luz

phylogeny: the evolutionary history of a lineage (433)
  filogenia: historia evolutiva del linaje

phylum (pl. phyla): in classification, a group of closely related classes (431)
  filo: en la clasificación, un grupo de clases estrechamente relacionadas

phytoplankton: photosynthetic algae found near the surface of the ocean (63)
  fitoplancton: algas fotosintéticas que se hallan cerca de la superficie del océano

pigment: light-absorbing molecule used by plants to gather the sun's energy (195)
  pigmento: moléculas que absorben la luz, empleadas por las plantas para recolectar la energía solar

pioneer species: first species to populate an area during succession (88)
  especies pioneras: las primeras especies en poblar un área durante la sucesión ecológica

pistil: single carpel or several fused carpels; contains the ovary, style, and stigma (579)
  pistilo: un único carpelo o varios carpelos unidos; contiene el ovario, el estilo y el estigma

pituitary gland: small gland found near the base of the skull that secretes hormones that directly regulate many body functions and controls the actions of several other endocrine glands (813)
  glándula pituitaria: pequeña glándula situada cerca de la base del cráneo que secreta hormonas que regulan directamente muchas funciones corporales y controla las acciones de varias otras glándulas endocrinas

placenta: specialized organ in placental mammals through which respiratory gases, nutrients, and wastes are exchanged between the mother and her developing young (683, 827)
  placenta: órgano especializado de los mamíferos placentarios a través del cual se intercambian los gases respiratorios, los nutrientes y los residuos entre la madre y su cría en desarrollo

plankton: microscopic organisms that live in aquatic environments; includes both phytoplankton and zooplankton (97)
  plancton: organismos microscópicos que viven en medios ambientes acuáticos; incluye el fitoplancton y el zooplancton

plasma: straw-colored liquid portion of the blood (790)
  plasma: parte líquida de la sangre de color amarillento

plasmid: small, circular piece of DNA located in the cytoplasm of many bacteria (359)
  plásmido: pequeña porción circular de ADN ubicada en el citoplasma de muchas bacterias

plasmodium: amoeboid feeding stage in the life cycle of a plasmodial slime mold (511)
  plasmodio: etapa de alimentación ameboide del ciclo vital de los mohos mucilaginosos

plate tectonics: geologic processes, such as continental drift, volcanoes, and earthquakes, resulting from plate movement (454)
  tectónica de placas: procesos geológicos, como la deriva continental, los volcanes y los terremotos, que son consecuencia de los movimientos de las placas

platelet: cell fragment released by bone marrow that helps in blood clotting (791)
  plaqueta: fragmento celular liberado por la médula espinal que interviene en la coagulación de la sangre

pluripotent: cells that are capable of developing into most, but not all, of the body's cell types (249)
  pluripotentes: células capaces de convertirse en la mayoría de células del cuerpo, pero no en todas

point mutation: gene mutation in which a single base pair in DNA has been changed (317)
  mutación puntual: mutación genética en la cual se ha modificado un único par de bases en el ADN

pollen grain: structure that contains the entire male gametophyte in seed plants (536)
  grano de polen: la estructura que contiene a todo el gametofito masculino en las plantas fanerógamas

pollen tube: structure in a plant that contains two haploid sperm nuclei (538)
  tubo polínico: en una planta, estructura que contiene dos núcleos espermáticos haploides

pollination: transfer of pollen from the male reproductive structure to the female reproductive structure (536)
  polinización: transferencia de polen desde la estructura reproductora masculina hacia la estructura reproductora femenina

pollutant: harmful material that can enter the biosphere through the land, air, or water (134)
  contaminante: material nocivo que puede ingresar en la biósfera a través de la tierra, el aire o el agua

polygenic trait: trait controlled by two or more genes (272, 408)
  rasgo poligénico: rasgo controlado por dos o más genes

polymer: molecules composed of many monomers; makes up macromolecules (38)
  polímero: molécula compuesta por muchos monómeros; forma macromoléculas

polymerase chain reaction (PCR): the technique used by biologists to make many copies of a particular gene (358)

reacción en cadena de la polímerasa (PCR): técnica usada por los biólogos para hacer muchas copias de un gen específico

polypeptide: long chain of amino acids that makes proteins (311)

polipéptido: cadena larga de aminoácidos que constituye las proteínas

polyploidy: condition in which an organism has extra sets of chromosomes (319)

poliploidía: condición en la cual un organismo tiene grupos adicionales de cromosomas

population: group of individuals of the same species that live in the same area (56)

población: grupo de individuos de la misma especie que viven en la misma área

population density: number of individuals per unit area (108)

densidad de población: número de individuos que viven por unidad de superficie

predation: interaction in which one organism (the predator) captures and feeds on another organism (the prey) (86)

depredación: interacción en la cual un organismo (el predador) captura y come a otro organismo (la presa)

prehensile tail: long tail that can coil tightly enough around a branch (635)

cola prensil: cola larga que puede enrollarse apretadamente alrededor de una rama

pressure-flow hypothesis: hypothesis that explains the method by which phloem sap is transported through the plant from a sugar "source" to a sugar "sink" (568)

teoría de flujo por presión: teoría que explica el método por el cual la savia del floema recorre la planta desde una "fuente" de azúcar hacia un "vertedero" de azúcar

primary growth: pattern of growth that takes place at the tips and shoots of a plant (561)

crecimiento primario: patrón de crecimiento que tiene lugar en las puntas y en los brotes de una planta

primary producer: first producer of energy-rich compounds that are later used by other organisms (60)

productor primario: los primeros productores de compuestos ricos en energía que luego son utilizados por otros organismos

primary succession: succession that occurs in an area in which no trace of a previous community is present (88)

sucesión primaria: sucesión que ocurre en un área en la cual no hay rastros de la presencia de una comunidad anterior

principle of dominance: Mendel's second conclusion, which states that some alleles are dominant and others are recessive (263)

principio de dominancia: segunda conclusión de Mendel, que establece que algunos alelos son dominantes y otros son recesivos

prion: protein particles that cause disease (493)

prión: partículas de proteína que causan enfermedades

probability: likelihood that a particular event will occur (266)

probabilidad: la posibilidad de que ocurra un suceso dado

product: elements or compounds produced by a chemical reaction (42)

producto: elemento o compuesto producido por una reacción química

prokaryote: unicellular organism that lacks a nucleus (162, 485)

procariota: organismo unicelular que carece de núcleo

promoter: specific region of a gene where RNA polymerase can bind and begin transcription (310)

promotor: región específica de un gen en donde la ARN polimerasa puede unirse e iniciar la transcripción

prophage: bacteriophage DNA that is embedded in the bacterial host's DNA (482)

profago: ADN del bacteriófago que está alojado en el interior del ADN del huésped bacteriano

prophase: first and longest phase of mitosis in which the genetic material inside the nucleus condenses and the chromosomes become visible (242)

profase: primera y más prolongada fase de la mitosis, en la cual el material genético dentro del interior del núcleo se condensa y los cromosomas se hacen visibles

prostaglandin: modified fatty acids that are produced by a wide range of cells; generally affect only nearby cells and tissues (811)

prostaglandina: ácidos grasos modificados que son producidos por una amplia gama de células; generalmente afectan solo a las células y tejidos cercanos

protein: macromolecule that contains carbon, hydrogen, oxygen, and nitrogen; needed by the body for growth and repair (40, 721)

proteína: macromolécula que contiene carbono, hidrógeno, oxígeno y nitrógeno; necesaria para el crecimiento y reparación del cuerpo

protostome: animal whose mouth is formed from the blastopore (613)

protóstomo: animal cuya boca se desarrolla a partir del blastoporo

pseudocoelom: body cavity that is only partially lined with mesoderm (612)

pseudoceloma o falso celoma: cavidad corporal que está revestida sólo parcialmente con mesodermo

pseudopod: temporary cytoplasmic projection used by some protists for movement (505)

   seudópodo: prolongación citoplasmática transitoria utilizada por algunos protistas para moverse

puberty: period of rapid growth and sexual maturation during which the reproductive system becomes fully functional (817)

   pubertad: período de crecimiento rápido y de maduración sexual durante el cual el sistema reproductor se vuelve completamente funcional

pulmonary circulation: path of circulation between the heart and lungs (788)

   circulación pulmonar: recorrido de la circulación entre el corazón y los pulmones

punctuated equilibrium: pattern of evolution in which long stable periods are interrupted by brief periods of more rapid change (458)

   equilibrio interrumpido: patrón de evolución en el cual los largos períodos de estabilidad se ven interrumpidos por breves períodos de cambio más rápido

Punnett square: diagram that can be used to predict the genotype and phenotype combinations of a genetic cross (267)

   cuadro de Punnett: un diagrama que puede utilizarse para predecir las combinaciones de genotipos y fenotipos en un cruce genético

pupa: stage in complete metamorphosis in which the larva develops into an adult (681)

   pupa: etapa de la metamorfosis completa en la cual la larva se convierte en un adulto

pupil: small opening in the iris that admits light into the eye (757)

   pupila: pequeña abertura en el iris que deja pasar la luz al ojo

Q, R

radial symmetry: body plan in which any number of imaginary planes drawn through the center of the body could divide it into equal halves (611)

   simetría radial: diseño corporal en el cual cualquier número de ejes imaginarios dibujados a través del centro del cuerpo lo dividirá en mitades iguales

radiometric dating: method for determining the age of a sample from the amount of a radioactive isotope to the nonradioactive isotope of the same element in a sample (452)

   datación radiométrica: método para determinar la edad de una muestra a partir de la cantidad de isótopo radioactivo en relación a la de isótopo no radiactivo del mismo elemento en dicha muestra

reabsorption: process by which water and dissolved substances are taken back into the blood (731)

   reabsorción: proceso por el cual el agua y las sustancias disueltas regresan a la sangre

reactant: elements or compounds that enter into a chemical reaction (42)

   reactante: elemento o compuesto que participa en una reacción química

receptor: on or in a cell, a specific protein to whose shape fits that of a specific molecular messenger, such as a hormone (183, 588)

   receptor: proteína específica que puede encontrarse en la membrana celular o dentro de la célula, cuya forma se corresponde con la de un mensajero molecular específico, por ejemplo una hormona

recombinant DNA: DNA produced by combining DNA from different sources (359)

   ADN recombinante: ADN producido por la combinación de ADN de orígenes diferentes

red blood cell: blood cell containing hemoglobin that carries oxygen (790)

   glóbulo rojo: célula sanguínea que contiene hemoglobina y transporta oxígeno

reflex: quick, automatic response to a stimulus (747)

   reflejo: respuesta rápida y automática a un estímulo

reflex arc: the sensory receptor, sensory neuron, motor neuron, and effector that are involved in a quick response to a stimulus (752)

   arco reflejo: el receptor sensorial, la neurona sensorial, la neurona motora y el efector que participan en una respuesta rápida a un estímulo

relative dating: method of determining the age of a fossil by comparing its placement with that of fossils in other rock layers (451)

   datación relativa: método para determinar la edad de un fósil comparando su ubicación con la de los fósiles hallados en otras capas de roca

releasing hormone: hormone produced by the hypothalamus that makes the anterior pituitary secrete hormones (813)

   hormona liberadora: hormona producida por el hipotálamo que hace que la glándula pituitaria anterior secrete hormonas

renewable resource: resource that can be produced or replaced by healthy ecosystem functions (131)

   recurso renovable: recurso que se puede producir o reemplazar mediante el funcionamiento saludable del ecosistema

replication: process of copying DNA prior to cell division (296)

   replicación: proceso de copia de ADN previo a la división celular

reproductive isolation: separation of a species or population so that they no longer interbreed and evolve into two separate species (414)

    aislamiento reproductor: separación de una especie o de una población de tal manera que ya no pueden aparearse y evolucionan hasta formar dos especies separadas

resource: any necessity of life, such as water, nutrients, light, food, or space (85)

    recurso: todo lo necesario para la vida, como agua, nutrientes, luz, alimento o espacio

response: specific reaction to a stimulus (669)

    respuesta: reacción específica a un estímulo

resting potential: electrical charge across the cell membrane of a resting neuron (744)

    potencial de reposo: carga eléctrica que pasa a través de la membrana celular de una neurona en reposo

restriction enzyme: enzyme that cuts DNA at a sequence of nucleotides (342)

    enzima restrictiva: enzima que corta el ADN en una secuencia de nucleótidos

retina: innermost layer of the eye; contains photoreceptors (757)

    retina: membrana más interna del ojo; contiene receptores susceptibles a la luz

retrovirus: RNA virus that contains RNA as its genetic information (483)

    retrovirus: ARN viral cuya información genética está contenida en el ARN

ribonucleic acid (RNA): single-stranded nucleic acid that contains the sugar ribose (308)

    ácido ribonucleico (ARN): hebra única de ácido nucleico que contiene el azúcar ribose

ribosomal RNA (rRNA): type of RNA that combines with proteins to form ribosomes (309)

    ARN ribosomal: tipo de ARN que se combina con proteínas para formar los ribosomas

ribosome: cell organelle consisting of RNA and protein found throughout the cytoplasm in a cell; the site of protein synthesis (168)

    ribosoma: orgánulo celular formado por ARN y proteína que se halla en el citoplasma de una célula; lugar donde se sintetizan las proteínas

RNA interference (RNAi): introduction of double-stranded RNA into a cell to inhibit gene expression (323)

    ARN de interferencia: introducción de un ARN de doble hebra en una célula para inhibir la expresión de genes específicos

RNA polymerase: enzyme that links together the growing chain of RNA nucleotides during transcription using a DNA strand as a template (309)

    ARN polimerasa: enzima que enlaza los nucleótidos de la cadena de ARN en crecimiento durante la transcripción, usando una secuencia de ADN como patrón o molde

rod: photoreceptor in the eyes that is sensitive to light but can't distinguish color (757)

    bastoncillo: receptor ubicado en los ojos que es susceptible a la luz, pero que no puede distinguir el color

root cap: tough covering of the root tip that protects the meristem (557)

    cofia: cubierta dura de la punta de las raíces que protege al meristemo

root hair: small hairs on a root that produce a large surface area through which water and minerals can enter (557)

    pelo radicular: pelos pequeños sobre una raíz que producen una superficie extensa a través de la cual pueden penetrar el agua y los minerales

rumen: stomach chamber in cows and related animals in which symbiotic bacteria digest cellulose (648)

    panza: cavidad del estómago de las vacas y otros rumiantes en la cual las bacterias simbióticas digieren la celulosa

S

sapwood: in a woody stem, the layer of secondary phloem that surrounds the heartwood; usually active in fluid transport (562)

    albura: en un tallo leñoso, la capa de floema secundario que rodea al duramen; participa usualmente en el transporte de fluidos

sarcomere: unit of muscle contraction; composed of two z-lines and the filaments between them (771)

    sarcómero: unidad de contracción muscular; compuesto por dos líneas "z" y los filamentos que hay entre ellas

scavenger: animal that consumes the carcasses of other animals (62)

    carroñero: animal que consume los cadáveres de otros animales

science: organized way of gathering and analyzing evidence about the natural world (4)

    ciencia: manera organizada de reunir y analizar la información sobre el mundo natural

sclerenchyma: type of ground tissue with extremely thick, rigid cell walls that make ground tissue tough and strong (553)

    esclerénquima: tipo de tejido fundamental con células extremadamente rígidas y gruesas que lo hacen fuerte y resistente

scrotum: external sac that houses the testes (818)

    escroto: bolsa externa que contiene a los testículos

sebaceous gland: gland in the skin that secretes sebum (oily secretion) (776)

    glándula sebácea: glándula de la piel que secreta sebo (secreción oleosa)

secondary growth: type of growth in dicots in which the stems increase in thickness (562)

    crecimiento secundario: tipo de crecimiento de las dicotiledóneas en el cual los tallos aumentan su grosor

secondary succession: type of succession that occurs in an area that was only partially destroyed by disturbances (88)

    sucesión secundaria: tipo de sucesión que ocurre en un área destruida sólo parcialmente por alteraciones

seed: plant embryo and a food supply encased in a protective covering (536)

    semilla: embrión vegetal y fuente de alimento encerrada en una cubierta protectora

seed coat: tough covering that surrounds and protects the plant embryo and keeps the contents of the seed from drying out (537)

    envoltura de la semilla: cubierta dura que rodea y protege al embrión de la planta y evita que el contenido de la semilla se seque

segregation: separation of alleles during gamete formation (264)

    segregación: separación de los alelos durante la formación de gametos

selective breeding: method of breeding that allows only those organisms with desired characteristics to produce the next generation (354)

    reproducción selectiva o selección artificial: método de reproducción que sólo permite la producción de una nueva generación a aquellos organismos con características deseadas

selectively permeable: property of biological membranes that allows some substances to pass across while others cannot; also called semipermeable membrane (173)

    permeabilidad selectiva: propiedad de las membranas biológicas que permite que algunas sustancias pasen a través de ellas mientras que otras no pueden hacerlo; también llamada membrana semipermeable

semen: the combination of sperm and seminal fluid (818)

    semen: combinación de esperma y de fluido seminal

semicircular canal: one of three structures in the inner ear that monitor the position of the body in relation to gravity (756)

    canal semicircular: una de las tres estructuras ubicadas en el oído interno que controlan la posición del cuerpo en relación con la fuerza de la gravedad

seminiferous tubule: one of hundreds of tubules in each testis in which sperm develop (818)

    túbulo seminífero: uno de los cientos de túbulos situados en cada testículo, en los cuales se produce el esperma

sensory neuron: type of nerve cell that receives information from sensory receptors and conveys signals to central nervous system (668)

    neurona sensorial: tipo de célula nerviosa que recibe información de los receptores sensoriales y transmite señales al sistema nervioso central

sex chromosome: one of two chromosomes that determines an individual's sex (334)

    cromosoma sexual: uno de los pares de cromosomas que determina el sexo de un individuo

sex-linked gene: gene located on a sex chromosome (336)

    gen ligado al sexo: gen situado en un cromosoma sexual

sexual reproduction: type of reproduction in which cells from two parents unite to form the first cell of a new organism (15, 236)

    reproducción sexual: tipo de reproducción en la cual las células de dos progenitores se unen para formar la primera célula de un nuevo organismo

sexual selection: when individuals select mates based on heritable traits (412)

    selección sexual: cuando un individuo elige a su pareja sexual atraído por sus rasgos heredables

sexually transmitted disease (STD): disease that is spread from person to person by sexual contact (823)

    enfermedad de transmisión sexual (ETS): enfermedad que se transmite de una persona a otra por contacto sexual

sieve tube element: continuous tube through the plant phloem cells, which are arranged end to end (554)

    tubo crivoso: tubo continuo que atraviesa las células del floema vegetal, que están puestas una junto a otra

single-gene trait: trait controlled by one gene that has two alleles (408)

    rasgo de un único gen (monogénico): rasgo controlado por un gen que tiene dos alelos

small intestine: digestive organ in which most chemical digestion and absorption of food takes place (725)

    intestino delgado: órgano digestivo en el cual tiene lugar la mayor parte de la digestión química y la absorción de los alimentos

smog: gray-brown haze formed by a mixture of chemicals (136)

    esmog: neblina marrón grisácea formada por una mezcla de compuestos químicos

society: group of closely related animals of the same species that work together for the benefit of the group (702)

    sociedad: grupo de animales de la misma especie, estrechamente relacionados, que trabajan juntos para el beneficio del grupo

solute: substance that is dissolved in a solution (34)

    soluto: sustancia que está disuelta en una solución

solution: type of mixture in which all the components are evenly distributed (34)

    solución: tipo de mezcla en la cual todos los compuestos están distribuidos de forma homogénea

solvent: dissolving substance in a solution (34)

disolvente: sustancia que disuelve una solución

somatic nervous system: part of the peripheral nervous system that carries signals to and from skeletal muscles (752)

sistema nervioso somático: parte del sistema nervioso periférico que conduce señales hacia y desde los músculos esqueléticos

speciation: formation of a new species (414)

especiación: formación de una nueva especie

species: a group of similar organisms that can breed and produce fertile offspring (414)

especie: un grupo de organismos similares que pueden reproducirse y producir una descendencia fértil

species diversity: number of different species that make up a particular area (138)

diversidad de especies: número de especies diferentes que forman un área determinada

spirillum (pl. spirilla): spiral or corkscrew-shaped prokaryote (486)

espirilo: procariota con forma helicoidal o espiral

spongy mesophyll: layer of loose tissue found beneath the palisade mesophyll in a leaf (564)

mesófilo esponjoso: capa de tejido suelto situado debajo del mesófilo en empalizada de una hoja

sporangium (pl. sporangia): spore capsule in which haploid spores are produced by meiosis (507)

esporangio: cápsula en la cual se producen las esporas haploides mediante meiosis

spore: in prokaryotes, protists, and fungi, any of a variety of thick-walled life cycle stages capable of surviving unfavorable conditions (506)

espora: en los procariotas, los protistas y los hongos, cada una de las células que, en un momento de su ciclo de vida, produce una membrana gruesa y resistente capaz de sobrevivir en condiciones desfavorables

sporophyte: spore-producing plant; the multicellular diploid phase of a plant life cycle (530)

esporofito: planta productora de esporas; la fase diploide multicelular del ciclo vital de una planta

stabilizing selection: form of natural selection in which individuals near the center of a distribution curve have higher fitness than individuals at either end of the curve (410)

selección estabilizadora: forma de selección natural en la cual los individuos situados cerca del centro de una curva de distribución tienen mayor aptitud que los individuos que se hallan en cualquiera de los extremos de la curva

stamen: male part of a flower; contains the anther and filament (579)

estambre: parte masculina de una flor; contiene la antera y el filamento

stem cell: unspecialized cell that can give rise to one or more types of specialized cells (249)

célula troncal: célula no especializada que puede originar uno o más tipos de células especializadas

stigma: sticky part at the top of style; specialized to capture pollen (579)

estigma: parte pegajosa situada en la parte superior del estilo; especializado en atrapar el polen

stimulus (pl. stimuli): signal to which an organism responds (14, 668)

estímulo: señal a la cual responde un organismo

stoma (pl. stomata): small opening in the epidermis of a plant that allows carbon dioxide, water, and oxygen to diffuse into and out of the leaf (564)

estoma: pequeña abertura en la epidermis de una planta que permite que el dióxido de carbono, el agua y el oxígeno entren y salgan de la hoja

stomach: large muscular sac that continues the mechanical and chemical digestion of food (725)

estómago: gran bolsa muscular que continúa la digestión mecánica y química de los alimentos

stroma: fluid portion of the chloroplast; outside of the thylakoids (195)

estroma: parte fluida del cloroplasto; en el exterior de los tilacoides

substrate: reactant of an enzyme-catalyzed reaction (44)

sustrato: reactante de una reacción catalizada por enzimas

suspension: mixture of water and nondissolved material (35)

suspensión: mezcla de agua y material no disuelto

sustainable development: strategy for using natural resources without depleting them and for providing human needs without causing long-term environmental harm (131)

desarrollo sostenible: estrategia para utilizar los recursos naturales sin agotarlos y para satisfacer las necesidades humanas sin causar daños ambientales a largo plazo

symbiosis: relationship in which two species live close together (87)

simbiosis: relación en la cual dos especies viven en estrecha asociación

synapse: point at which a neuron can transfer an impulse to another cell (746)

sinapsis: punto en el cual una neurona puede transferir un impulso a otra célula

systematics: study of the diversity of life and the evolutionary relationships between organisms (430)

sistemática: estudio de la diversidad de la vida y de las relaciones evolutivas entre los organismos

systemic circulation: path of circulation between the heart and the rest of the body (788)

circulación sistémica: recorrido de la circulación entre el corazón y el resto del cuerpo

T

taiga: biome with long cold winters and a few months of warm weather; dominated by coniferous evergreens; also called boreal forest (94)

    taiga: bioma con inviernos largos y fríos y pocos meses de tiempo cálido; dominado por coníferas de hojas perennes; también llamada bosque boreal

target cell: cell that has a receptor for a particular hormone (588, 810)

    célula diana o célula blanco: célula que posee un receptor para una hormona determinada

taste bud: sense organs that detect taste (754)

    papila gustativa: órgano sensorial que percibe los sabores

taxon (pl. taxa): group or level of organization into which organisms are classified (430)

    taxón: grupo o nivel de organización en que se clasifican los organismos

telomere: repetitive DNA at the end of a eukaryotic chromosome (297)

    telómero: ADN repetitivo situado en el extremo de un cromosoma eucariota

telophase: phase of mitosis in which the distinct individual chromosomes begin to spread out into a tangle of chromatin (242)

    telofase: fase de la mitosis en la cual los distintos cromosomas individuales comienzan a separarse y a formar hebras de cromatina

temporal isolation: form of reproductive isolation in which two or more species reproduces at different times (415)

    aislamiento temporal: forma de aislamiento reproductivo en la cual dos o más especies se reproducen en épocas diferentes

tendon: tough connective tissue that connects skeletal muscles to bones (676, 773)

    tendón: tejido conectivo resistente que une los músculos esqueléticos a los huesos

territory: a specific area occupied and protected by an animal or group of animals (702)

    territorio: área específica ocupada y protegida por un animal o un grupo de animales

testis (pl. testes): primary male reproductive organ; produces sperm (818)

    testículo: órgano reproductor masculino fundamental; produce esperma

tetrad: structure containing four chromatids that forms during meiosis (276)

    tétrada: estructura con cuatro cromátidas que se forma durante la meiosis

tetrapod: vertebrate with four limbs (630)

    tetrápode: vertebrado con quatro membros

thalamus: brain structure that receives messages from the sense organs and relays the information to the proper region of the cerebrum for further processing (749)

    tálamo: estructura cerebral que recibe mensajes de los órganos sensoriales y transmite la información a la región adecuada del cerebro para su procesamiento ulterior

theory: well-tested explanation that unifies a broad range of observations and hypotheses, and enables scientists to make accurate predictions about new situations (11)

    teoría: explicación basada en pruebas que unifica una amplia gama de observaciones e hipótesis; permite que los científicos hagan predicciones exactas ante situaciones nuevas

thigmotropism: response of a plant to touch (590)

    tigmotropismo: respuesta de una planta al tacto

threshold: minimum level of a stimulus that is required to cause an impulse (745)

    umbral: nivel mínimo que debe tener un estímulo para causar un impulso

thylakoid: saclike photosynthetic membranes found in chloroplasts (195)

    tilacoide: membranas fotosintéticas con forma de bolsa situadas en los cloroplastos

thyroxine: hormone produced by the thyroid gland, which increases the metabolic rate of cells throughout the body (815)

    tiroxina: hormona producida por la glándula tiroides que aumenta el metabolismo de las células de todo el cuerpo

tissue: group of similar cells that perform a particular function (182)

    tejido: grupo de células similares que realizan una función en particular

tolerance: ability of an organism to survive and reproduce under circumstances that differ from their optimal conditions (85)

    tolerancia: capacidad de un organismo de sobrevivir y reproducirse en circunstancias que difieren de sus condiciones óptimas

totipotent: cells that are able to develop into any type of cell found in the body (including the cells that make up the extraembryonic membranes and placenta) (249)

    totipotentes: células capaces de convertirse en cualquier tipo de célula del cuerpo (incluidas las células que forman las membranas situadas fuera del embrión y la placenta)

trachea: tube that connects the larynx to the bronchi; also called the windpipe (796)

    tráquea: tubo que conecta a la laringe con los bronquios

tracheid: hollow plant cell in xylem with thick cell walls strengthened by lignin (534)

    traqueida: célula vegetal ahuecada del xilema con paredes celulares gruesas, fortalecida por la lignina

trait: specific characteristic of an individual (262)
   rasgo: característica específica de un individuo

transcription: synthesis of an RNA molecule from a DNA template (309)
   transcripción: síntesis de una molécula de ARN a partir de una secuencia de ADN

transfer RNA (tRNA): type of RNA that carries each amino acid to a ribosome during protein synthesis (309)
   ARN de transferencia: tipo de ARN que transporta a cada aminoácido hasta un ribosoma durante la síntesis de proteínas

transformation: process in which one strain of bacteria is changed by a gene or genes from another strain of bacteria (288)
   transformación: proceso en el cual una cepa de bacterias es transformada por uno o más genes provenientes de otra cepa de bacterias

transgenic: term used to refer to an organism that contains genes from other organisms (360)
   transgénico: término utilizado para referirse a un organismo que contiene genes provenientes de otros organismos

translation: process by which the sequence of bases of an mRNA is converted into the sequence of amino acids of a protein (312)
   traducción (genética): proceso por el cual la secuencia de bases de un ARN mensajero se convierte en la secuencia de aminoácidos de una proteína

transpiration: loss of water from a plant through its leaves (565)
   transpiración: pérdida del agua de una planta a través de sus hojas

trochophore: free-swimming larval stage of an aquatic mollusk (627)
   trocófora: estado larvario de un molusco acuático durante el cual puede nadar libremente

trophic level: each step in a food chain or food web (66)
   nivel trófico: cada paso en una cadena o red alimenticia

tropism: movement of a plant toward or away from stimuli (590)
   tropismo: movimiento de una planta hacia los estímulos o en dirección opuesta a ellos

tumor: mass of rapidly dividing cells that can damage surrounding tissue (247)
   tumor: masa de células que se dividen rápidamente y pueden dañar al tejido circundante

U

understory: layer in a rain forest found underneath the canopy formed by shorter trees and vines (92)
   sotobosque: en un bosque tropical, la capa de vegetación que se halla bajo el dosel forestal, formada por árboles más bajos y enredaderas

ureter: tube that carries urine from a kidney to the urinary bladder (731)
   uréter: conducto que transporta la orina del riñón a la vejiga urinaria

urethra: tube through which urine leaves the body (731)
   uretra: conducto por donde la orina sale del cuerpo

urinary bladder: saclike organ in which urine is stored before being excreted (731)
   vejiga urinaria: órgano en forma de bolsa en el cual se almacena la orina antes de ser excretada

V

vaccination: injection of a weakened, or a similar but less dangerous, pathogen to produce immunity (846)
   vacunación: inyección de un patógeno debilitado o similar al original, pero menos peligroso, para producir inmunidad

vaccine: preparation of weakened or killed pathogens used to produce immunity to a disease (490)
   vacuna: preparación hecha con organismos patógenos debilitados o muertos que se utiliza para producir inmunidad a una enfermedad

vacuole: cell organelle that stores materials such as water, salts, proteins, and carbohydrates (166)
   vacuola: orgánulo celular que almacena sustancias como agua, sales, proteínas e hidratos de carbono

valve: flap of connective tissue located between an atrium and a ventricle, or in a vein, that prevents backflow of blood (787)
   válvula: pliegue de tejido conectivo ubicado entre una aurícula y un ventrículo, o en una vena, que impide el retroceso de la sangre

vas deferens: tube that carries sperm from the epididymis to the urethra (818)
   conducto deferente: tubo que transporta el esperma desde el epidídimo a la uretra

vascular bundle: clusters of xylem and phloem tissue in stems (561)
   hacecillo vascular: manojo de tejidos del xilema y del floema en los tallos

vascular cambium: meristem that produces vascular tissues and increases the thickness of stems (562)
   cámbium vascular: meristemo que produce tejidos vasculares y aumenta el grosor de los tallos

vascular cylinder: central region of a root that includes the vascular tissues—xylem and phloem (557)

  cilindro vascular: región central de una raíz que incluye a los tejidos vasculares xilema y floema

vascular tissue: specialized tissue in plants that carries water and nutrients (533)

  tejido vascular: tejido especializado de las plantas que transporta agua y nutrientes

vector: animal that transports a pathogen to a human (840)

  vector: animal que transmite un patógeno a un ser humano

vegetative reproduction: method of asexual reproduction in plants, which enables a single plant to produce offspring that are genetically identical to itself (583)

  reproducción vegetativa: método de reproducción asexual de las plantas que permite que una única planta produzca descendencia genéticamente idéntica a sí misma

vein: blood vessel that carries blood from the body back to the heart (789)

  vena: vaso sanguíneo que transporta la sangre del cuerpo de regreso al corazón

ventricle: lower chamber of the heart that pumps blood out of heart to the rest of the body (654, 787)

  ventrículo: cavidad inferior del corazón que bombea la sangre fuera del corazón hacia el resto del cuerpo

vertebrate: animal that has a backbone (607)

  vertebrado: animal que posee una columna vertebral

vessel element: type of xylem cell that forms part of a continuous tube through which water can move (554)

  elemento vascular (o vaso): tipo de célula del xilema que forma parte de un tubo continuo a través del cual el agua puede desplazarse

vestigial structure: structure that is inherited from ancestors but has lost much or all of its original function (393)

  estructura vestigial: estructura heredada de los ancestros que ha perdido su función original en gran parte o por completo

villus (pl. villi): fingerlike projection in the small intestine that aids in the absorption of nutrient molecules (727)

  vellosidad: proyección en forma de dedo en el intestino delgado que contribuye a la absorción de las moléculas nutrientes

virus: particle made of proteins, nucleic acids, and sometimes lipids that can replicate only by infecting living cells (480)

  virus: partícula compuesta por proteínas, ácidos nucleicos y, a veces, lípidos, que puede replicarse sólo infectando células vivas

vitamin: organic molecule that helps regulate body processes (721)

  vitamina: molécula orgánica que ayuda a regular los procesos corporales

viviparous: animals that bear live young that are nourished directly by the mother's body as they develop (680)

  vivíparo: animal que da a luz crías vivas que se nutren directamente dentro del cuerpo de la madre mientras se desarrollan

W

weather: day-to-day conditions of the atmosphere, including temperature, precipitation, and other factors (82)

  tiempo: condiciones diarias de la atmósfera, entre las que se incluyen la temperatura, la precipitación y otros factores

wetland: ecosystem in which water either covers the soil or is present at or near the surface for at least part of the year (97)

  humedal: ecosistema en el cual el agua cubre el suelo o está presente en la superficie durante al menos una parte del año

white blood cell: type of blood cell that guards against infection, fights parasites, and attacks bacteria (791)

  glóbulo blanco: tipo de célula sanguínea que protege de las infecciones, combate a los parásitos y ataca a las bacterias

woody plant: type of plant made primarily of cells with thick cell walls that support the plant body; includes trees, shrubs, and vines (542)

  planta leñosa: tipo de planta constituida fundamentalmente por células con paredes celulares gruesas que sostienen el cuerpo de la planta; en este tipo se incluyen los árboles, arbustos y vides

X, Y, Z

xylem: vascular tissue that carries water upward from the roots to every part of a plant (534)

  xilema: tejido vascular que transporta el agua hacia arriba, desde las raíces a cada parte de una planta

zoonosis (pl. zoonoses): disease transmitted from animal to human (840)

  zoonosis: enfermedad transmitida por un animal a un ser humano

zygote: fertilized egg (277, 612, 824)

  cigoto: huevo fertilizado

Index

Page numbers for vocabulary terms are printed in **boldface** type.

A

Abiotic factors, **58,** 92, 100
Abscisic acid, 589
Absorption, 723
Acanthostega, 631
Acetylcholine, 772–773
Acid rain, 136, 150
Acids, **36**
  amino, **40**–41, 71, 311, 398, 721
  fatty, 39
  nucleic, 40, 292
Acne, 777
Acoelomates, 612
Acquired characteristics, 385
Acquired immune deficiency syndrome (AIDS), 483, 490, 823, 848, 850–851
Acquired immunity, 846
Actin, 167, 505, **771**–772
Action potential, **744**–745
Activation energy, **43**–44
Active immunity, **846**
Active site, 45
Active transport, 179–180, 193
  in plants, 529, 533, 554, 558–559, 567–569
Adaptations, **388**
  to biomes, 92–94
  in chordates, 629–631, 682–683
  excretory, 659
  of leaves, 566
  of mouthparts, 649
  and natural selection, 388–391
  in pathogens, 840
  and reproduction, 237
  seasonal, 591–592
  of seed plants, 536
Adaptive radiation, **459**
Addiction, 750
Adenine, 292–293, 295, 311
Adenosine diphosphate (ADP), 193, 199
Adenosine triphosphate (ATP), 40, **192**–193
  ATP synthase, 220–221
  and cellular respiration, 214, 216–222
  and exercise, 225

  and fermentation, 223–224
  and photosynthesis, 199–203
Adhesion, **34, 568**
Adrenal glands, 811, 814
Adult stem cells, 250
Aerobic respiration, **214**
African sleeping sickness, 512
Age of Fishes, 629
Age of Mammals, 633
Age structure of populations, **109,** 118
Aggression, **702**
Agriculture, 129, 139, 593–594
Agrobacterium, 360
AIDS, 483, 490, 823, 840, 848, 850–851
Air pollution, 136–137
Alcohol, 750
Alcoholic fermentation, 223
Aldosterone, 814
Algae, 74, 509
  brown, 502–504, 510
  in food chains and webs, 63
  green, 441, 509, 518, 530, 532
  and photosynthesis, 60
  phytoplankton, 63, 96
  red, 509
  single-celled, 158–159, 181
Algal bloom, **510**
Allantois, 682
Alleles, **263,** 406. *See also* Genetics
  allele frequencies, **407,** 411–412
  dominant and recessive, 263–265, 270, 335
  multiple and codominant, **272,** 335
  and phenotypes, 409
  segregation of, **264**–267, 270
  and traits, 337, 408
Allergies, **849**
Aloe vera, 595
Alpine meadow, 526–527
Alternation of generations, **507, 530**
Alveoli, **652, 797,** 799
Amborella, 543
Ambulocetus, 394
Amebic dysentery, 512
Amenorrhea, 834
Amino acids, **40**–41, 721
  and evolution, 398
  and genetic code, 311
  in nitrogen cycle, 71
Ammonia, 656, 718
Amnion, 682, 826
Amniota, 434–435
Amniotic egg, **682**
Amoebas, 180, 505, 507, 510
Amoeboid movement, 505

Amphibians, 631, 652, 655, 657
  brains of, 671
  fertilization in, 680
  metamorphosis in, 681
Amygdala, 748
Amylase, **724**
Anabaena, 486
Anaerobic respiration, **214,** 223
Anaphase of meiosis, 276–277
Anaphase of mitosis, 242
Angina, 793
Angiosperms, **536,** 540–543
  classification of, 542–543
  double fertilization in, **581**–582
  fruit development in, 585
  life cycle of, 579–582
  vessel elements in, 554
Animal behavior, 696–699
  and climate change, 148
  communication, **703**–704
  complex, 699–700
  cycles of, 701
  and evolution, 696, 702
  innate, **697,** 699–700
  learned, 697–698
  social, 702–704
Animalia, 431, 438–439, 441
Animals, 606–617. *See also* Chordates; Invertebrates; Vertebrates
  animal society, **702**–704
  animal starch, 39
  asexual reproduction in, 236, 610, 678
  body plans of, 611–615
  cells of, 171, 174–175, 178
  characteristics of, 606
  cladogram of, 615–616
  cloned, 361
  cytokinesis, 243
  development of young, 681
  differentiation stages in, 613–615
  diseases of, 518
  embryo development in, 612–613, 680
  and emerging diseases, 848
  genetically modified, 362
  homeostasis in, 608, 684–687
  and language, 704
  parental care in, 682
  and pollination, 581
  response to stimuli, 608–609, 668–669
  and seed dispersal, 585
  sexual reproduction in, 610, 678–680
  transgenic, 360–361, 362
  types of, 606–607
Animal systems
  circulation, 609, 653–655

Birds
  behavioral isolation in, 415–416
  bones of, 688
  brains of, 671
  digestion in, 648
  evolution of, 393, 436, 457, 632
  excretion in, 658
  imprinting in, 699–700
  learned behavior in, 697
  lungs of, 652
  and migration, 673, **701**
  and natural selection, 396–397, 410, 416–417
  and resource sharing, 86
  temperature control in, 686–687
Birthrate, 109, 117–118
Blackberry, 541, 585
Blastocyst, 249, **825**
Blastopore, 612
Blastula, **612**
Blood, 35, 790–791. *See also*
    Circulatory system, human
  carbon dioxide removal from, 42
  cell formation, 766
  clotting, 791
  groups, 335
  and kidneys, 729–732
  pH of, 36
  pressure, 731–732, 789, 793–794
  red blood cells, **790**
  types, 274
  vessels, 789
  white blood cells, **791**
B lymphocytes, 791, 842–844
Body cavity, 612
Body plans of animals, 611–615
Body temperature, 685–687, 717–718, 775
Bolus, 724
Bonds, chemical, 30–31, 192
  carbon, 37
  covalent, **31**, 292
  hydrogen, 33–34, 294–295
  ionic, **30**
Bone marrow, 767
Bones, 767
Bony fishes, 630
Boreal forests, 94
Borrelia burgdorferi, 489, 856
Bottleneck effect, **411**
Bovine spongiform encephalopathy (BSE), 479
Bowman's capsule, 731
Brain, human, 747–750
Brains, 670–671
Brain stem, **749**
Bread mold, 516
Breathing, 799–800

Breeding
  artificial selection, **387**
  inbreeding, **355**
  selective, **354**–355, 594
Bronchi, **797**–798
Bronchioles, 797–798
Bronchitis, 801
Brown, Michael, 794–795
Brown algae, 502–504, 510
Brown bears, 427, 428, 446
Bryophytes, **533**
Bt toxin, 362
Buds of plant, **560**
Buffers, **36**
Bulbourethral gland, 818
Burbank, Luther, 355
Bursae, 769
Butterflies, 273, 404–405, 681

C

C4 plants, 203
Cacti, 566, 583
Caecilians, 631
Calcitonin, 815
Calcium, 70, 721, 767, 772, 815
Calmette, Albert, 491
Calorie, 212, **719**
Calvin, Melvin, 201
Calvin cycle, 201
Cambium, 562–563
Cambrian Explosion, 625, 629
Cambrian Period, 454, 466
Camelidae, 430
Camelus bactrianus, 430–431
Camelus dromedarius, 430
Camouflage, 93
CAM plants, 203
Canadian pondweed, 190–191
Cancer, 247
  lung, 801
  skin, 287, 304, 777
  viral, 490–491
Candida albicans, 518
Canines, 649
Canopy, **92**
Capillaries, 651, 654, **789**, 797
Capillary action, 34, **568**
Capsid, **481**
Carbohydrates, **38**–39, 213, 720
Carbon, 29, 37–41
Carbon credits, 142
Carbon cycle, 70–71
Carbon dating, 452
Carbon dioxide
  atmospheric, 136, 141, 148
  and breathing, 799–800

  and cellular respiration, 215
  and climate, 455
  and nutrient cycles, 70–71
  and photosynthesis, 201, 203, 215
  removal from bloodstream, 42
Carboniferous Period, 467, 631–632
Carbon monoxide, 800
Carboxyl group, 40
Cardiac muscle, 770–771
Carnivora, 435
Carnivores, 61–62, 646, 649
Carp, 115
Carpels, **579**
Carrying capacity
  of Earth, 128
  of species, **111**
Cartilage, **628, 767**
Casparian strip, 558–559
Catalysts, **44**
Catfish, 630
Cats, 336, 352–353, 434–435
C. elegans, 325
Cell, 15–16, **160**–183
  active transport, 179–180, 193
  animal, 171, 174–175, 178
  B and T, 842–844
  beta, 815
  Casparian strip, 558
  cell membranes, 162, 171–173, 177–188
  cell plate, 243
  cell stains, 161
  cell theory, **160**
  companion, 554
  daughter, 236, 240, 277
  diploid and haploid, **275**–279
  discovery of, 160
  flame, 657
  and food molecules, 212
  glial, 715
  in ground tissue of plants, 553
  guard, **565**
  helper T, 850
  and homeostasis, **181**–183
  human, 334–335, 714
  in meristems, 554
  and microscopes, 160–161
  multipotent, **250**
  mutations of, 318
  organelles, **164,** 166–170
  passive transport, 176–178
  plant, 171, 174–175, 178, 528
  plasma, 843, 845
  pluripotent, **249**
  red blood, **790**
  RNA synthesis in, 309–310
  size of, 162, 234–235, 238
  in skin, 776

Classification (cont'd)
  of prokaryotes, 485–486
  of protists, 502–504
  systematics, **430**
  three-domain system, 438–441
Climate, **82**–84
  and biomes, **57,** 91–95
  change, 141, 147
  evolution of, 455
  regional, 91
  and temperature, 95
Climax communities, 89–90
Clone, 361
Closed circulatory systems, **653**
Clostridium, 486–487
Clotting, blood, 791, 793
Clownfish, 87
Club mosses, 534
Cnidarians, 626, 648, 670, 674, 679
Coastal ocean, 98
Cocaine, 750
Cocci, 486
Cochlea, **755**
Coconut, 586
Cod, 108, 113, 146
Codominance, **271,** 335
Codons, **311**
Coelacanths, 630
Coelom, **612**
Coevolution, **460**–461
Cohesion, **34,** 568
Collagen, 714
Collenchyma, **553**
Colorblindness, 336, 338
Commensalism, **87**
Common ancestors, 391–393,
  433–437, 456
Common cold, 483, 490
Common descent, 391
Communication, **703**–704
Communities, **56,** 85–86, 89–90
Companion cells, 554
Competition, ecological
  and communities, 85–86
  and natural selection, 396, 416
  and population density, 114, 116
  and speciation, 420
Competitive exclusion principle, 86
Complex carbohydrates, 39
Compounds, chemical, **30**–31,
  37–41
Conditioning. *See also* Animal
    behavior
  classical, **698**
  operant, **698**
Cones, 536–537, 555
Cones (of eye), 757
Coniferous forests, 93

Conifers, 93, 538, 562
Conjugation, **487, 507**
Connective tissue, **714**
Conservation, 135, 141–142, 146.
    See also Resources, natural
Constipation, 728
Consumers, **61**–62
Continental shelf, 98
Contour plowing, 133
Contractile vacuole, 166
Control group, **6**–7
Controlled experiment, **6**
Convergent evolution, **460**
Cook, James, 741, 762
Coral reefs, 98, 509, 604–605, 701
Corals, 13, 626
Cordyceps, 517
Cork, 160
Cork cambium, **562**–563
Corn, 355, 581, 594
Cornea, **756**
Corn smut, 517
Coronary arteries, 788, 793
Corpus callosum, 748
Corpus luteum, 821
Cortex, **557**
Corticosteroids, **814**
Cortisol, 814
Cotton, 595
Cotyledons, 542, 586
Coughing, 840
Courtship behavior, **702**
Covalent bonds, **31,** 292
Cow, 648
Cowpox, 846
Cowpox virus, 491
Crabs, 106–107, 432, 458
Cranes, 389, 699–700
Creativity, 9
Cretaceous Period, 454, 457, 468, 632
Creutzfeld-Jacob Disease, 498
Crick, Francis, 293–296
Crocodiles, 632
Crop plants, 362–363, 368, 517,
  593–594
Crop rotation, 133
Crossing-over, **276,** 279, 407
Cross-pollination, 263
Cryptosporidium, 506, 512
Curiosity, 9
Currents, ocean, 84, 96
Cutting, plant, 584
Cyanobacteria, 518
Cycads, 538
Cycles
  carbon, 70–71
  cell, **240**–247
  matter, 68–73

nitrogen, 71
nutrients, 70–72
phosphorous, 72
water, 69
Cyclins, 246
Cystic fibrosis (CF), 340, 364
Cytochrome *c,* 395
Cytokinesis, **241,** 243, 276
Cytokinins, 589
Cytoplasm, **164,** 485
Cytosine, 292–293, 295, 311
Cytoskeleton, **167,** 766

D

Dandelion, 586
Daphnia, 608
Darwin, Charles, 11, 380–397, 406,
  433, 458–461
Data, **6**–7
Dating techniques, 394, 451–452
Daughter cells, 236, 240, 277
Dead zones, 135
Death rate, 109, 117–118
Decibels (dB), 755
Deciduous plants, 92, 592
Decomposers, 62, 64, 488
Decomposition, 517
Deep time, 384
Deer, 86
Deforestation, **133**
Dehydration, 159, 720
Democritus, 28
Demographic transition, **118**
Demography, **118.** *See also* Population
    growth
Dendrites, **743**
Denitrification, **71**
Density-dependent limiting factors,
  112–116
Density-independent limiting factors,
  114–115
Deoxyribonucleic acid. *See* DNA
Deoxyribose, 292, 308
Dependent variable, **6**
Derived characters, **434,** 436
Dermal tissue, 553, 557
Dermis, **776**
Descent with modification, 391
Desertification, **132**
Deserts, 93
Detritivores, 62, 64, 646
Deuterostomes, **613**
Devonian Period, 467, 629
Diabetes mellitus, 718, 731, 815, 849
Dialysis, 732
Diaphragm, 798, **799**
Diarrhea, 728

Insulin, 814–815
Integumentary system, 716, 775–777
Interdependence, 17, 63–65
Interferons, 842
Intergovernmental Panel on Climate Change (IPCC), 147
International System of Units (SI), 18
Interneurons, **669,** 743
Interphase, **241,** 276
Intertidal zone, 98
Intestinal diseases, 512
Intestine
  large, **728**
  small, **725,** 727
Intracellular digestion, **647**
Introduced species, 141
Introns, 310
Invertebrates, **606.** *See also* Chordates; Vertebrates
  body cavities of, 612
  body plans of, 617
  cladogram of, 626–627
  development of young, 681
  evolution of, 624–625
  fertilization in, 680
  nervous systems of, 670
  respiratory systems of, 650–651
  response to stimuli in, 669
  sense organs of, 672
  skeletons of, 674
Iodine, 815
Ionic bonds, **30**
Ions, **30,** 35–36
Iris (of eye), **756**
Irish Potato Famine, 501, 524
Iron oxide, 42
Islets of Langerhans, 814
Isolation, reproductive, **414**–415
Isotonic solutions, 178
Isotopes, **29**
Ivanovski, Dmitri, 480

J

Jawless fishes, 629
Jaws, 629–630
Jellyfish, 357, 626, 679
Jenner, Edward, 491, 846
Joints, 675, **768**–769
Jurassic Period, 468, 632

K

Kangaroo rats, 659
Kangaroos, 633
Karyotypes, **334**–335
Kelp, 86, 98, 502, 510
Keratin, 776

Keystone species, 86, 139
Kidneys, **656,** 729–732, 816
  and blood pressure, 731–732
  and salt, 659
Kilocalorie, 212
Kingdoms, **431,** 438–439
Klinefelter's syndrome, 341
Knee, 769
Koalas, 633
Koch, Robert, 838–839
Koch's postulates, **839**
Krakatau, 88, 90
Krebs cycle, 214, **218**–219

L

Lac operon, 320–321, 324
Lac repressor, 321
Lactic acid fermentation, 224–225
Lactobacillus, 488
Lactose, 321, 324
Lakes, 97
Lama, 430
Lamarck, Jean-Baptiste, 385, 388
Lampreys, 629
Lancelets, 629, 673
Land plants, 530
Language, **704**
Large intestine, **728**
Larvae, **627,** 681
Larynx, **796,** 798
Lateral gene transfer, 407
Leaf-cutter ants, 703
Leaf loss, 592, 596
Learning, **698**–700. *See also* Animal behavior
Leaves of plants, 429, 552, 564–566
Leeches, 627
Lemons, 577, 600
Lens, **757**
Leucine, 311
Levels of organization
  animals, 611
  ecological, 57
  human body, 714–716
  multicellular organisms, 182
  proteins, 41
Lichens, 89, **518**–519
Life cycle of plants, 530–531
  angiosperms, 579–582
  ferns, 534–535
  green algae, 532
  gymnosperms, 538–539
  mosses, 533
Ligaments, **675, 769**
Light. *See also* Sunlight
  absorption, 195
  and energy, 196

  and photosynthesis, 202
  plant response to, 588, 590–591
Light dependent reactions, **197,** 199–200, 203
Light independent reactions, **197,** 201–202
Light microscopes, 161
Lignin, 534, **554**
Limb formation, 393, 615
Limbic system, 748
Limes, 319
Limiting factors, **112**–116
Limiting nutrient, 72–73
Limpets, 432
Linnaean classification system, 430–432
Linnaeus, Carolus, 430, 432–433
Lipid bilayer, **171**–173
Lipids, **39,** 172, 721
Lipoproteins, 794
Liver, 169, 718, **725,** 729, 794–795
Living stone, 566
Living things, **13**–15
Lizards, 632, 685
Lobe-finned fishes, 630
Lobes, 748
Local hormones, 811
Logistic growth, **110**–111
Long day plants, 591
Loop of Henle, **731**
Loudness, 755
Low-density lipoprotein (LDL), 794–795
"Lucy," 636
Lung cancer, 801
Lungfishes, 630
Lungs, **651**–652, 729, 788, 796, 798–802
Lupus, 849
Luteal phase, 821
Luteinizing hormone (LH), 817
Lye, 36
Lyell, Charles, 384–385
Lyme disease, 489, 840, 852, 856
Lymph, **792**
Lymphatic system, 716, **792**
Lymph nodes, 792
Lymphocytes, 842–844
Lysogenic infections, 481–**482**
Lysosomes, **166**
Lysozyme, 724
Lytic infections, 481–**482**

M

Macroevolution, **456**–457
Macromolecules, 38–41
Macrophages, 843

Mycelium, **515**
Mycobacterium tuberculosis, 487, 838
Mycorrhizae, **519**
Myelin sheath, 743
Myllokunmingia, 628
Myocardium, **787**
Myofibrils, **771**
Myosin, **771**–772

N

NAD⁺, **216,** 223–224
NADH, 216–217, 223–224
NADP⁺, **196,** 200
NADPH, 196–197, 200–202
Nails, human, 776
Natural resources. *See* Resources, natural
Natural selection, **389.** *See also* Evolution
  and adaptations, 388–391
  and beak size, 396–397, 416–417
  and competition, 396, 416
  directional, **410**
  disruptive, **410**
  and extinction, 457
  and genetic diversity, 679
  and phenotypes, 406, 409
  on polygenic traits, 410
  sexual, **412**
  on single-gene traits, 409
  stabilizing, **410**
  and viruses, 424
Navigation, 673
Neanderthals, 637
Negative feedback, 608
Nematodes, 627
Neogene Period, 469
Nephridia, **658**
Nephrons, **729**–731
Nerve impulses, 743–746
Nerve nets, 670
Nerves, 743
Nervous system, human, 716, 742–753
  autonomic, **753**
  central, **742,** 747–750
  peripheral, **742,** 751–753
  sensory receptors, 751
  somatic, **752**
  sympathetic/parasympathetic, 753
Nervous systems, animal, 608–609, 668–671
Nervous tissue, **715**
Neuromuscular junction, 772
Neurons, **668**–669, 715, 743–744, 772–773

Neurotransmitters, 746
Neurulation, 826
Neutral mutations, 407, 417
Neutrons, **28**–29
New World monkeys, 635
Niches, **85**
Nicotinamide adenine dinucleotide (NAD⁺), **216**
Nicotinamide adenine dinucleotide phosphate (NADP⁺), **196,** 200
Nicotine, 750, 800
Nitrogen-containing waste, 656
Nitrogen cycle, 71
Nitrogen fixation, **71,** 488
Nitrogenous bases, 292
Nitrosomonas, 486
Nodes of plant stem, **560**
Nondisjunction, **341**
Nonpoint source pollution, 134
Nonrenewable resources, **131**
Nonsteroid hormones, 812
Nonvertebrate chordates, 607, 629–629, 671, 673, 680
Norepinephrine, **814**
North Atlantic Fisheries, 146
Northwestern coniferous forests, 93
Nose, 796, 798
Notochord, **606**
Nucleic acids, **40,** 292
Nucleolus, 165
Nucleotides, 40, 292, 304
Nucleus, **28,** 162–163, 165
Nutrient cycles, 70–72
  carbon, 70–71
  limitations of, 72–73
  nitrogen, 71
  phosphorous, 72
Nutrients, 70–73
  absorption of, 792
  and human body, 720–722, 727
  limiting, 72–73
  and plant growth, 133, 558, 568–569
Nymphs, **681**

O

Observation
  ecological, 59
  scientific, **5,** 8
Occipital lobe, 749
Ocean currents, 84, 96
Oceans, 98–99. *See also* Aquatic ecosystems
Octopi, 627, 669

Old World monkeys, 635
Olive oil, 39
Omnivores, 62
1000 Genomes Project, 345
On the Origin of Species, 388
Open circulatory systems, **653**
Open-mindedness, 9
Open ocean, 98
Operant conditioning, **698**
Operator (O), **321**
Operons, **320**–321
Opposable thumb, 635
Optic lobes, 671
Optic nerve, 757
Orangutans, 635
Orca, 647
Order, **430**
Ordovician Period, 466
Organelles, **164,** 166–170
Organic chemistry. *See* Chemistry of life
Organic molecules, 462
Organisms, interactions of, **57**
Organs
  cellular, **182**
  human, 715–716
Organ systems
  cellular, **182**
  human, 715–716
Osmosis, **177**–178, 184
  and kidneys, 656
  in plants, 558
Osmotic pressure, **178**
Ossification, 767
Osteichthyes, 630
Osteoblasts, 767
Osteoclasts, 767
Osteocytes, 767
Osteoporosis, 767
Ostrich, 381
Ova, 819–821, 824–825
Ovaries
  of flowers, **540,** 579
  human, 811, **819**
Overfishing, 146
Oviparous species, **680**
Ovoviviparous species, **680**
Ovulation, **820**
Ovules, **538,** 579
Oxpecker, 644–645
Oxygen
  accumulation of, 464
  in glycolysis, 216
  molecules of, 31
  and photosynthesis, 199, 215
  and respiration, 211, 213–215, 230, 799–800
Oxytocin, 813, 829

Credits

Staff Credits
Jennifer Angel, Amy C. Austin, Laura Baselice, Neil Benjamin, Peggy Bliss, Diane Braff, Daniel Clem, Glen Dixon, Alicia Franke, Julia Gecha, Ellen Granter, Katherine Immel, Anne Jones, Stephanie Keep, Beth Kun, Kimberly Fekany Lee, Ranida Touranont McKneally, Anne McLaughlin, Rich McMahon, Laura Morgenthau, Debbie Munson, Deborah Nicholls, Michelle Reyes, Rashid Ross, Laurel Smith, Lisa Smith-Ruvalcaba, Ted Smykal, Amanda M. Watters, Merce Wilczek, Berkley Wilson

Additional Credits
Bryan Cholfin, Lisa Furtado Clark, Sharon Donahue, Amy Hamel, Courtenay Kelley, Hilary L. Maybaum, Anakin S. Michele, Julia Osborne, Lisa Redmond, Kelly Rizk, Jan Van Aarsen, Rachel Youdelman

Front Cover, Spine, and Title Page: © Ralph A. Clevenger/Corbis.
Back Cover: hotshotsworldwide/Fotolia.

Photographs
Every effort has been made to secure permission and provide appropriate credit for photographic material. The publisher deeply regrets any omission and pledges to correct errors called to its attention in subsequent editions. Unless otherwise acknowledged, all photographs are the property of Pearson Education, Inc. Photo locators denoted as follows Top (T), Center (C), Bottom (B), Left (L), Right (R), Background (Bkgd)

iii (T, B) Stew Milne; **iv** (L) Ralph A. Clevenger/Corbis; **v** (R) Ralph A. Clevenger/Corbis; **ix** (CR) PhotoLibrary Group, Inc., (TL) Ralph A. Clevenger/Corbis; **x** (B) Ed Reschke/Peter Arnold/PhotoLibrary Group, Inc.; **xi** (TC) Photo Researchers, Inc.; **xii** (BL) Colin Keates/Courtesy of the Natural History Museum, London/©DK Images, (TC) Colin Keates/Natural History Museum, London/©DK Images; **xiii** (B) Getty Images, (CL) Peter Chapwick/©DK Images, (TR) Southhampton General Hospital/Science Photo Library/Photo Researchers, Inc.; **xiv** (B) Alamy Images, (TR) iStockphoto; **xv** (TR) Corbis, (TL) Ocean/Corbis; **xix** (BR) Stew Milne; **xx** (BR) Stew Milne. **1** (BR) Stew Milne; (L) Keren Su/Corbis; **2** ClassicStock/Alamy Inc.; **3** (T) Comstock/Jupiter Images; **4** (B) Suzanne Long/Alamy Inc.; (T) ClassicStock/Alamy Inc.; **7** Michael Melford/Getty Images, Inc.; **8** Comstock/Jupiter Images; **9** ClassicStock/Alamy Inc.; **12** Comstock/Jupiter Images; **13** (B) Masa Ushioda/Image Quest 3-D; (T) ClassicStock/Alamy Inc.; **14** (Bkgd) Martin Rugner/Age Fotostock/AGE Fotostock; (BL) Nigel Cattlin/Alamy Inc.; (BR) Cathy Keifer/Shutterstock; **15** (BR) G. Thomas Bishop/Custom Medical Stock/Custom Medical Stock Photo; (CR) Ilyashenko Oleksiy/Shutterstock; (TR) John Marshall/Corbis; **16** (B) Klein/Peter Arnold, Inc./Photolibrary Group; **17** Joseph Nettis/Photo Researchers, Inc.; **18** (B) Tek Image/Photo Researchers, Inc.; (T) Michael Nichols/National Geographic/Getty Images, Inc.; **19** (B) Comstock/Jupiter Images; (T) Chinafotopres-US/Sipa/NewsCom; **21** Brand X Pictures/Jupiter Images; **22** ClassicStock/Alamy Inc.; **24** Comstock/Jupiter Images; **26** Image by Hans Strand/Corbis; **27** Julian Gutt/AFP/Getty Images/NewsCom; **28** Image by Hans Strand/Corbis; **31** Julian Gutt/AFP/Getty Images/NewsCom; **33** Image by Hans Strand/Corbis; **34** Richard Megna/Fundamental Photographs; **35** (B) Noam Armonn/istockphoto.com; (BC) fanelie rosier/istockphoto.com; (T) Nancy Louie/istockphoto.com; (TC) Milos Luzanin/istockphoto.com; **36** Julian Gutt/AFP/Getty Images/NewsCom; **37** Image by Hans Strand/Corbis; **42** Image by Hans Strand/Corbis; **45** (B) Julian Gutt/AFP/Getty Images/NewsCom; (T) Thomas Steitz/Howard Hughes Medical Institute Yale University; **48** Image by Hans Strand/Corbis; **50** Julian Gutt/AFP/Getty Images/NewsCom; **52** (T) Keren Su/Corbis; **53** (L) konmesa/Shutterstock; Stew Milne/Stew Milne; **54** Stan Osolinski/Jupiter Images; **55** Jeff Rotman/Jeff Rotman Photography; **56** (BC) Anup Shah/WILDLIFE/Peter Arnold, Inc.; (BL) Tim Graham/Getty Images, Inc.; (BR) nik wheeler/Alamy Inc.; (TL) Stan Osolinski/Jupiter Images; **57** (BC) Planetary Visions Ltd./Photo Researchers, Inc.; (BL) Dmitri Kessel/Time Life Pictures/Getty Images, Inc.; (BR) NASA/NASA; **59** (T) Jeff Rotman/Jeff Rotman Photography; (B) Benjamin Alblach Galan/Shutterstock; **60** (B) Cathy Keifer/Shutterstock; (T) Stan Osolinski/Jupiter Images; **61** Vincenzo Lombardo/Getty Images, Inc.; **62** (B) Jeff Rotman/Jeff Rotman Photography; (Bkgd) Will & Deni McIntyre/Stone/Getty Images, Inc.; (BL) MJ Prototype/Shutterstock; (BR) Devon Graham/Project Amazonas, Inc.; (M) Roy Toft/Getty Images, Inc.; (ML) Carol Farneti/Photolibrary New York; (TL) Kevin Schafer/Peter Arnold, Inc.; (TR) Anna Yu/Alamy Inc.; **63** Stan Osolinski/Jupiter Images; **67** Jeff Rotman/Jeff Rotman Photography; **68** Stan Osolinski/Jupiter Images; **73** Jeff Rotman/Jeff Rotman Photography; **75** Cathy Keifer/Shutterstock; **76** Stan Osolinski/Jupiter Images; **78** Jeff Rotman/Jeff Rotman Photography; **80** Bryan Busovicki/Shutterstock; **81** George McCarthy/Nature Picture Library; **82** Bryan Busovicki/Shutterstock; **85** Bryan Busovicki/Shutterstock; **87** George McCarthy/Nature Picture Library; **88** Bryan Busovicki/Shutterstock; **90** (B) Hallmark Institute/Photolibrary Group/Photolibrary New York; (Bkgd) Gary Braasch/Corbis; (ML) Macduff Everton/Corbis; (MR) Reuters/Corbis; **91** Bryan Busovicki/Shutterstock; **92** (B) Michele Burgess/SuperStock, Inc.; (M) Staffan Widstrand/Nature Picture Library; (T) Juan Carlos Muñoz/AGE Fotostock; **93** (B) Radius Images/Alamy Royalty Free; (BC) Natural Selection Jerry Whaley/Design Pics/Corbis; (C) Debra Behr/Alamy Inc.; (T) Danita Delimont/Alamy Inc.; (TC) JLImages/Alamy Royalty Free; **94** (B) ImageState/Alamy Inc.; (T) age fotostock/SuperStock, Inc.; **95** George McCarthy/Nature Picture Library; **96** (B) Corbis/SuperStock, Inc.; (T) Bryan Busovicki/Shutterstock; **97** (C) irishman/Shutterstock; (CL) Mark Hodnett/Fotolia, LLC; (CR) cappi thompson/Shutterstock; (L) Philippe Clement/Nature Picture Library; (R) David Noton/Nature Picture Library; **98** (B) Dante Fenolio/Photo Researchers, Inc.; (TL) Cindy Ruggieri; (TR) age fotostock/SuperStock, Inc.; **99** George McCarthy/Nature Picture Library; **102** Bryan Busovicki/Shutterstock; **103** Anthony Bannister; Gallo Images/Corbis; **104** George McCarthy/Nature Picture Library; **106** FLPA/Alamy Inc.; **107** Geoff Dann/Dorling Kindersley Ltd; **108** (B) U.S. Department of Agriculture, Agricultural Research Center; (T) FLPA/Alamy Inc.; **109** SciMAT/Photo Researchers, Inc./Photo Researchers, Inc.; **110** Digital Vision/Thinkstock; **111** Geoff Dann/Dorling Kindersley Ltd; **112** FLPA/Alamy Inc.; **113** D. Robert & Lorri Franz/Corbis; **114** Les Stocker/Photolibrary Group/Photolibrary New York; **115** (B) Geoff Dann/Dorling Kindersley Ltd; (T) Xinhua Photo, Jiang Yi/AP Images; **117** FLPA/Alamy Inc.; **119** image100/Photolibrary/Photolibrary New York; **121** (L) Digital Vision/Thinkstock; (R) Xinhua Photo, Jiang Yi/AP Images; **122** FLPA/Alamy Inc.; **124** Geoff Dann/Dorling Kindersley Ltd; **126** NASA/NSSDC/NASA; **127** SIME s.a.s/eStock Photo/eStock Photo; **128** (BL) Douglas Peebles/eStock Photo; (BR) Douglas Peebles/eStock Photo; (T) NASA/NSSDC/NASA; **129** Elena Elisseeva/Shutterstock; **130** (Bkgd) By Gary Sullivan, /Wetlands Initiative, The; (Inset) The Wetlands Initiative archives/Wetlands Initiative, The; **131** SIME s.a.s/eStock Photo/eStock Photo; **132** (B) AP Images; (T) NASA/NSSDC/NASA; **135** Maxphotos/Newscom/Newscom; **136** Jason Lee/Reuters Pictures/Reuters Pictures; **137** SIME s.a.s/eStock Photo/eStock Photo; **138** (B) Penn State University, S. Blair Hedges/AP Images; (T) NASA/NSSDC/NASA; **139** (C) Noel Hendrickson/Getty Images, Inc.; (L) Paolo Aguilar/epa/Corbis; (R) Marcos G. Meider/Superstock/SuperStock, Inc.; **140** Creatas/Photolibrary New York; **141** ZUMA Press/Newscom; **142** (B) SIME s.a.s/eStock Photo/eStock Photo; (T) Barbara Walton/epa/Corbis; **143** NASA/NSSDC/NASA; **145** (B) Jerry Mason/Photo Researchers, Inc./Photo Researchers, Inc.; (T) Images by Greg Shirah, NASA Goddard Space Flight Center Scientific Visualization Studio/NASA; **146** (B) BRIAN J. SKERRY/National Geographic Society; (T) Jeffrey L. Rotman/Corbis; **147** Armin Rose/Shutterstock, Inc.; **148** Laura Romin & Larry Dalton/Alamy Inc.; **149** (B) Charmagne Leung/California Academy of Sciences; (T) UPPA/Photoshot/Newscom; (TC) Realimage/Alamy Inc.; **151** Elena Elisseeva/Shutterstock; **152** (T) NASA/NSSDC/NASA; **154** SIME s.a.s/eStock Photo/eStock Photo; **156** Konmesa/Shutterstock; **157** (L) Clouds Hill Imaging Ltd./CORBIS; (B) Stew Milne/Stew Milne; **158** Robert Berdan/Dr. Robert Berdan; **159** simple stock shots/AGE Fotostock; **160** (B) Biophoto Associates/Photo Researchers, Inc.; (BC) Grafissimo/istockphoto.com; (T) Robert Berdan/Dr. Robert Berdan; **161** (L) Michael Abbey/Photo Researchers, Inc.; (M) Dr. Gopal Murti/Photo Researchers, Inc.; (R) SciMAT/Photo Researchers, Inc.; **163** simple stock shots/Age Fotostock/PhotoLibrary Group Ltd; **164** Robert Berdan/Dr. Robert Berdan; **166** (L) Biophoto Associates/Photo Researchers, Inc.; (R) Eric Grave/Photo Researchers, Inc.; **167** Torsten Wittmann/Photo Researchers, Inc.; **168** SIME s.a.s/eStock Photo; **170** Eric Grave/Biophoto Associates/Photo Researchers, Inc.; **171** Ed Reschke/Peter Arnold, Inc.; **172** Science Photo Library/Custom Medical Stock Photo; **176** Robert Berdan/Dr. Robert Berdan; **180** (B) simple stock shots/Age Fotostock/PhotoLibrary Group Ltd; (T) NIBSC/Photo Researchers, Inc./Photo Researchers, Inc.; **181** (B) Volker Steger/Christian Bardele/SPL/Photo Researchers, Inc.; (T) Robert Berdan/Dr. Robert Berdan; **183** Don W. Fawcett/Photo Researchers, Inc.; **185** Volker Steger/Christian Bardele/SPL/Photo Researchers, Inc.; **186** Robert Berdan/Dr. Robert Berdan; **190** Perennou Nuridsany/Photo Researchers, Inc.; **191** Watering can (earthenware), English School, (16th century)/Museum of London, UK, /The Bridgeman Art Library International/Bridgeman Art Library International Ltd.; **192** Perennou Nuridsany/Photo Researchers, Inc.; **194** (B) Watering can (earthenware), English School, (16th century)/Museum of London, UK, /The Bridgeman Art Library International/Bridgeman Art Library International Ltd.; (T) Michael Lohmann/Glow Images; **195** (B) GAP Photos/Getty Images, Inc.; (T) Perennou Nuridsany/Photo Researchers, Inc.; **197** Watering can (earthenware), English School, (16th century)/Museum of London, UK, /The Bridgeman Art Library International/Bridgeman Art Library International Ltd.; **199** Perennou Nuridsany/Photo Researchers, Inc.; **201** Imagewerks/Getty Images, Inc.; **203** (B) Watering can (earthenware), English School, (16th century)/Museum of London, UK, /The Bridgeman Art Library International/Bridgeman Art Library International Ltd.; (T) Dorn1530/Shutterstock; **205** Michael Lohmann/Glow Images; **208** Watering can (earthenware), English School, (16th century)/Museum of London, UK, /The Bridgeman Art Library International/Bridgeman Art Library International Ltd.; **210** (M) Professor Pietro M. Motta/Photo Researchers, Inc./Photo Researchers, Inc.; **211** Kike Calvo/V&W/Image Quest Marine; **212** (B) Stock Food Creative/Getty Images, Inc.; (T) Professor Pietro M. Motta/Photo Researchers, Inc./Photo Researchers, Inc.; **215** Kike Calvo/V&W/Image Quest Marine; **216** (B) Shutterstock; (T) Professor Pietro M. Motta/Photo Researchers, Inc./Photo Researchers, Inc.; **220** Jim McIsaac/Getty Images, Inc.; **222** Kike Calvo/V&W/Image Quest Marine; **223** Professor Pietro M. Motta/Photo Researchers, Inc.; **225** (B) Kike Calvo/V&W/Image Quest Marine; (T) Brand X Pictures/PhotoLibrary Group Ltd; **227** Brand X Pictures/PhotoLibrary Group Ltd; **228** Professor Pietro M. Motta/Photo Researchers, Inc.; **230** Michael Nolan/Peter Arnold, Inc.; **232** Michael Abbey/Photo Researchers, Inc.; **233** Joe McDonald/Corbis; **234** Michael Abbey/Photo Researchers, Inc.; **236** (C) Oxford Scientific/PhotoLibrary Group Ltd; (L) CNRI/Photo Researchers, Inc.; (R) Art Wolfe/Photo Researchers, Inc.; **237** Joe McDonald/Corbis; **239** Michael Abbey/Photo Researchers, Inc.; **243** (B) Joe McDonald/Corbis; (C) Wood/Custom Medical Stock Photo; (T) DR GOPAL MURTI/SCIENCE PHOTO LIBRARY/Photo/Photo Researchers, Inc.; **244** (BC, BL, BR, TC, TL, TR) Ed Reschke/Peter Arnold, Inc.; **245** (BL) Paul Aresu/Getty Images, Inc.; (BR) Scott Camazine/Photo Researchers, Inc.; (TL) Michael Abbey/Photo Researchers, Inc.; **246** (L) National Institutes of Health; (R) Paul Martin/Wellcome Images; **247** Joe McDonald/Corbis; **248** (BCL) Jim Haseloff/The Wellcome Trust/Medical Photographic Library; (BL) Professor Ray F. Evert/University of Wisconsin - Madison; (BR) Neil Fletcher/Dorling Kindersley; (BCR) John Durham/Photo Researchers, Inc.; (T) Michael Abbey/Photo Researchers, Inc.; **251** Joe McDonald/Corbis; **253** (L) Art Wolfe/Photo Researchers, Inc.; (R) DR GOPAL MURTI/SCIENCE PHOTO LIBRARY/Photo/Photo Researchers, Inc.; **254** Michael Abbey/Photo Researchers, Inc.; **256** Joe McDonald/Corbis; **259** (B) Stew Milne/Stew Milne; (Bkgd) Science Photo Library/BSI/Photo Researchers, Inc.; **260** Biosphoto/Labat J.-M. & Rouquette F./Peter Arnold, Inc.; **261** blickwinkel/Alamy Inc.; **265** blickwinkel/Alamy Inc.; **266** (B) Brand X/Jupiter Images; (T) Biosphoto/Labat J.-M. & Rouquette F./Peter Arnold, Inc.; **270** Maximilian Weinzierl/Alamy Inc.; **271** (BL, BR, inset) Christopher Burrows/Alamy Inc.; (T) Biosphoto/Labat J.-M. & Rouquette F./Peter Arnold, Inc.; **273** (B) blickwinkel/Alamy Inc.; (TL) Alvin E. Staffan/Photo Researchers, Inc.; (TR) Robert Shantz/Alamy Inc.; **275** Biosphoto/Labat J.-M. & Rouquette F./Peter Arnold, Inc.; **279** blickwinkel/Alamy Inc.; **281** Biosphoto/Labat J.-M. & Rouquette F./Peter Arnold, Inc.; **283** Ryerson Clark/iStock International, Inc.; **284** (R) blickwinkel/Alamy Inc.; **286** Charles Benton/Charles C. Benton; **287** (BR) aliciahh/istockphoto.com; **288** Charles Benton/Charles C. Benton; **292** Charles Benton/Charles C. Benton; **293** (C) With permission of the University Archives, Columbia University in the City of New York/Columbia University Archives; (R) Courtesy Ava Helen & Linus Pauling Papers/Special Collections/Oregon State University/Oregon State University Libraries; (T) by Courtesy of the National Portrait Gallery, London/National Portrait Gallery, London; **294** (B) Wellcome Library/The Wellcome Trust/Medical Photographic Library; (Bkgd) A. Barrington Brown/Photo Researchers, Inc.; **295** (BR) aliciahh/istockphoto.com; **296** (B) Dr. Gopal Murti/Science Photo Library/Photo Researchers, Inc.; (T) Charles Benton/Charles C. Benton; **299** (BR) aliciahh/istockphoto.com; **301** Courtesy Ava Helen & Linus Pauling Papers/Special Collections/Oregon State University/Oregon State University Libraries; **302** Charles Benton/Charles C. Benton; **304** (BR) aliciahh/istockphoto.com; **306** Jan Daly/Shutterstock; **307** EYE OF SCIENCE/SPL/Photo Researchers, Inc.; **308** Jan Daly/Shutterstock; **311** Jan Daly/Shutterstock; **315** (B) EYE OF SCIENCE/SPL/Photo Researchers, Inc.; **316** (BL) Bob Gibbons/Photo Researchers, Inc.; (BR) Tony Camacho/Photo Researchers, Inc.; (T) Jan Daly/Shutterstock; **318** Eye of Science/Photo Researchers, Inc.; **319** travismanley/istockphoto.com; **320** (B) Dr. Gopal Murti/Science Photo Library/Photo Researchers, Inc.; (T) Jan Daly/Shutterstock; **325** EYE OF SCIENCE/SPL/Photo Researchers, Inc.; **327** Bob Gibbons/Photo Researchers, Inc.; **328** Jan Daly/Shutterstock; **330** EYE OF SCIENCE/SPL/Photo Researchers, Inc.; **332** Digital Vision/PhotoLibrary Group Ltd; **333** Sebastian Kaulitzki/Fotolia, LLC; **334** (B) CNRI/Photo Researchers, Inc.; (T) Digital Vision/PhotoLibrary Group Ltd; **336** Dave King/Dorling Kindersley; **337** Sebastian Kaulitzki/Fotolia, LLC; **339** Digital Vision/PhotoLibrary Group Ltd; **341** Sebastian Kaulitzki/Fotolia, LLC; **342** Digital Vision/PhotoLibrary Group Ltd; **345** (B) Sebastian Kaulitzki/Fotolia, LLC; (T) Reprinted by permission from Macmillan Publishers Ltd Nature, February 15, 2001, Volume 409, Number 6822. Copyright © 2001/Nature Magazine; **346** AP/AP Images; **347** Dave King/Dorling Kindersley; **348** Digital Vision/PhotoLibrary Group Ltd; **349** CNRI/Photo Researchers, Inc.; **350** Sebastian Kaulitzki/Fotolia, LLC; **352** Yonhap News/YNA/NewsCom; **353** David Parker/Photo Researchers, Inc.; **354** (B) Corbis Royalty Free/Jupiter Images; (TL) Yonhap News/YNA/NewsCom; (TR) Thinkstock/Jupiter Images; **356** (TL) Jose Poblete/Corbis; **357** (B) Wernher Krutein/PhotoVault; (T) Yonhap News/YNA/NewsCom; **359** Torunn Berge/Photo Researchers, Inc.; **361** David Parker/Photo Researchers, Inc.; **362** (B) Katrina Brown/istockphoto.com; (B) Jan L. Carson/University of California- Davis, Animal Sciences; (T) Yonhap News/YNA/NewsCom; **363** MIKE ALQUINTO/EPA/NewsCom; **366** (B) David Parker/Photo Researchers, Inc.; (T) Index Stock/SuperStock, Inc.; **367** (B) Susan Walsh/Corbis; (T) Yonhap News/YNA/NewsCom; **369** (B) David Parker/Photo Researchers, Inc.; (T) www.glofish.com/GloFish, LLC; **372** Yonhap News/YNA/NewsCom; **374** David Parker/Photo Researchers, Inc.; **377** (L) Frans Lanting Studio/Alamy Inc.; (B) Stew Milne/Stew Milne; **378** Chip Clark/Chip Clark; **379** Chris Johns/National Geographic Stock; **380** (L) Chip Clark/Chip Clark; (R) AKG/Photo Researchers, Inc.; **381** DK IMAGES/Dorling Kindersley; **382** (B) CarolineTolsma/Shutterstock; (T) Pete Oxford Danita Delimont Photography/NewsCom; **383** (B) Chris Johns/National Geographic Stock; (T) Courtesy The Field Museum/The Field Museum; **384** (B) Momatiuk - Eastcott/Corbis; (T) Chip Clark/Chip Clark; **385** David Acosta Allely/Shutterstock; **386** Snark/Art Resource; **387** (C) Portrait of Pouter Pigeon (coloured engraving), Wolsenholme, D. (fl.1862)/Down House, Kent, UK, /The Bridgeman Art Library International/Bridgeman Art Library International Ltd.; (L) Portrait of a Carrier Pigeon (coloured engraving), Wolsenholme, D. (fl.1862)/Down House, Kent, UK, /The Bridgeman Art Library International/Bridgeman Art Library International Ltd.; (R) Portrait of a Beard Pigeon (coloured engraving), Wolsenholme, D. (fl.1862)/Down House, Kent, UK, /The Bridgeman Art Library International/Bridgeman Art Library International Ltd.; **388** Chip Clark/Chip Clark; **389** (BL) Steve Kaufman/Peter Arnold, Inc.; (BR) Barry Mansell/Nature Picture Library; (TL) Hal Beral/The Image Works; (TR) Markus Varesvuo/Nature Picture Library; **391** (B) Chris Johns/National Geographic Stock; (T) Cambridge University Library/Cambridge University Library; **392** Chip Clark/Chip Clark; **397** Chris Johns/National Geographic Stock; **400** Chip Clark/Chip Clark; **402** Chris Johns/National Geographic Stock; **404** R.Hoelzl/Peter Arnold, Inc.; **406** R.Hoelzl/Peter Arnold, Inc.; **407** (T) Brand X/SuperStock, Inc.; **409** (B) Charlie Ott/Photo Researchers, Inc.; (T) R.Hoelzl/Peter Arnold, Inc.; **412** (TL) Ashley Cooper/Corbis; **414** (B) Thomas & Pat Leeson/Photo Researchers, Inc.; (C) Rick & Nora Bowers/Alamy Inc.; (T) R.Hoelzl/Peter Arnold, Inc.; **417** R.Hoelzl/Peter Arnold, Inc.; **422** R.Hoelzl/Peter Arnold, Inc.; **424** (B) James Cavallini/Custom Medical Stock Photo; **426** (C) Chip Clark/Chip Clark; **427** (BR) Mark Hamblin/AGE Fotostock; (TR) Kevin Schafer/AGE Fotostock; **428** (B) Hans Strand/AGE Fotostock; (T) Chip Clark/Chip Clark; **429** (BL, BR, T) Matthew Ward/Dorling Kindersley; (Chart, Lower CR, T, Upper CL) Matthew Ward/Dorling Kindersley; (Chart, Upper CR) Peter Chadwick/Dorling Kindersley; **430** Portrait of Carl von Linnaeus (1707–78) (oil on canvas), Roslin, Alexander (1718–93)/Chateau de Versailles, France, Lauros/Giraudon//Bridgeman Art Library International Ltd.; **431** W. Perry Conway/Corbis; **432** (B) Mark Hamblin/AGE Fotostock; (CL) age fotostock/SuperStock, Inc.; (CR) Richard Waters/iStock International, Inc.; (TL) 2006 Kåre Telnes/Image Quest 3-D; **433** (T) Chip Clark/Chip Clark; **436** (B) Chris Zwaenepoel/istockphoto.com; (C) B.K. Wheeler/VIREO; (T) AfriPics.com/Alamy Inc.; **437** (B) Mark Hamblin/AGE Fotostock; (CL) Corbis/SuperStock, Inc.; (CR) Josep Pena Llorens/iStock International, Inc.; (TL) Raven Regan/Robertstock; (TR) Frank Leung/iStock International, Inc.; **438** Chip Clark/Chip Clark; **439** Eye of Science/Photo Researchers, Inc.; **443** (B) Science Source/Photo Researchers, Inc.; (T) Portrait of Carl von Linnaeus (1707–78) (oil on canvas), Roslin, Alexander (1718–93)/Chateau de Versailles, France, Lauros/Giraudon/Bridgeman Art Library International Ltd.; **444** Chip Clark/Chip Clark; **446** (B) Mark Hamblin/AGE Fotostock; (T) Kevin Schafer/AGE Fotostock; **448** The Natural History Museum, London; **449** Marvin